TRUST AND FEAR NOT

RETURN TO
LETCHWORTH
LIBRARY
TEL: 5646
REFERENCE STOCK
FOR USE IN THE LIBRARY
ONLY

D0269167

WHO'S WHO IN ART

AN APPEAL

TO

ARTISTS

AND

AGENTS

WHO'S WHO IN ART

EIGHTEENTH EDITION

Biographies of leading Men and Women in the World of Art today—Artists, Designers, Craftsmen, Critics, Writers, Teachers and Curators, with an Appendix of Signatures

THE ART TRADE PRESS LTD
HAVANT HANTS

9 BROCKHAMPTON ROAD, HAVANT, HANTS

First Published *1927*
Second Edition *1929*
Third Edition *1934*
Fourth Edition *1948*
Fifth Edition *1950*
Sixth Edition (Reset) *1952*
Seventh Edition *1954*
Eighth Edition *1956*
Ninth Edition *1958*
Tenth Edition *1960*
Eleventh Edition *1962*
Twelfth Edition *1964*
Thirteenth Edition *1966*
Fourteenth Edition *1968*
Fifteenth Edition *1970*
Sixteenth Edition *1972*
Seventeenth Edition *1974*
Eighteenth Edition *1977*

ISBN 0 900083 07 7

Printed in Great Britain by
Page Bros (Norwich) Ltd, Norwich

CONTENTS

PUBLISHER'S NOTES

IN COMPILING *Who's Who in Art* it is our aim to produce a truly comprehensive list of biographical details of living artists in Britain today.

This is a tremendous task when one thinks of the number of art forms and mediums which now exist, and indeed it is often very difficult to decide whether a subject is art at all. How does one define art? There are, of course, many art forms, but we are concerned only with the visual arts. This narrows the field, perhaps, slightly, but it is none the less still very wide.

We have concluded that *Who's Who in Art* should embrace exponents of all forms of painting and drawing, graphic art and sculpture in their widest forms and in any mediums.

One of the criticisms always levied at "Who's Who"-type publications is that many famous names are excluded. The omission of well-known names is most regrettable, but we are limited to those artists who wish their names to appear.

A former Editor of early editions of *Who's Who in Art* was personally acquainted with a prominent contemporary painter, but he had the utmost difficulty in persuading him to include his particulars. If by any chance there are any artists of repute in Britain today who have never been approached by us, we can only apologize for the oversight and hope that if they should read these Publisher's Notes they will inform us of the omission so that they may appear in the next edition of *Who's Who in Art*, which will be published in 1979.

Who's Who in Art is principally concerned with British artists, and so far as overseas artists are concerned we include only a representative selection of the most outstanding contemporaries.

All the entries in the last edition have been submitted to the individuals concerned and any corrections or additions sent in by them have been incorporated in the *Eighteenth Edition*. We have approached numerous additional artists, and many new names appear for the first time. We always welcome applicants and names of artists recommended by others.

Exactly the same procedure has been followed as in the compilation of former editions. We gratefully acknowledge the kind assistance of all who have contributed information, including the various societies, art galleries and numerous individuals who have helped us in this edition.

Production difficulties always frustrate the publisher's aim to ensure that a publication is absolutely up to date, and the readers' indulgence is asked if some of the latest dates and changes have evaded this issue. Unfortunately, several months must elapse between the closing dates for accepting revision of entries and final publication.

AIMS AND ACTIVITIES OF ACADEMIES, GROUPS, SOCIETIES, ETC.

Art Registration Committee

(Intellectual Property in Works of Art)

The registration of the disposal of works of art by sale or gift.

Chairman: John Alexander-Sinclair, S.M.O.M., F.R.S.A., A.R.M.S. *Vice-Chairman:* Richard Carline. *Hon. Secretary:* Mrs. Griselda Bear. *Address:* 5 Aysgarth Rd., London SE21 7JR.

Chelsea Art Society

Exhibition held annually at the Chenil Galleries, King's Rd., London SW3.

President: A. Egerton Cooper, R.B.A. *Vice-President:* Terence Cuneo, R.G.I., P.I.P.G. *Hon. Treasurer:* Maria Zollinger. *Hon. Secretary:* Pamela Mellor. *Council:* Irene Egerton Cooper, G. M. O. Davy, C.B., C.B.E., D.S.O., Mary Lomax, S.W.A., Trevor Chamberlain, N.S., R.S.M.A., Clifford Hall, R.O.I., Deirdre Henty-Creer, F.R.S.A.

European Group

The Group was founded in 1974. Members are elected from European countries and exhibitions are arranged in a different country each year. The first group exhibition was held at the Mall Galleries, London and later toured Britain, Luxembourg, 1975, Belgium, 1976. All the members are realist painters.

Director: Charles White, Old Castle House, Malmesbury, Wilts.

Federation of British Artists

The Federation of British Artists was incorporated on 13 Feb., 1961, with the following objects: (1) To provide adequate and modern facilities for art exhibitions, concerts, conferences, lectures, etc., at a reasonable cost. (2) By using the accommodation to the utmost extent, to reduce the costs to the art societies, thus enabling each society to retain its individual character and raise the standard of its exhibitions by being more selective. (3) To provide a central source of information on all contemporary art matters. (4) To provide a central forum for the arts and to establish a representative body which will speak with authority. (5) To reduce administration costs by co-operation in the use of the Secretariat. The Federation is a charity and incorporates the majority of the London art societies, including the Royal Society of British Artists, the Royal Society of Portrait Painters, the Royal Institute of Painters in Watercolours, the Royal Institute of Oil Painters, the Royal Society of Marine Artists, the Royal Society of Miniature Painters, Sculptors and Gravers, the Royal British Colonial Society of Artists (temporarily known as the Commonwealth Society of Artists), the Royal Drawing Society, the New English Art Club, the National Society, the Society of Portrait Sculptors, the Society of Aviation Artists, the Pastel Society, the United Society of Artists, the Senefelder

Group, the Society of Mural Painters, the Society of Wildlife Artists and the Art Exhibitions Bureau. The present Governors are: William Bowyer, A.R.A., R.W.S., R.P., N.E.A.C., Patrick de Laszlo, Edward I. Halliday, C.B.E., P.P.R.B.A., P.R.P. (*Chairman*), Peter Greenham, R.A., Norman Hepple, R.A., Rowland Hilder, P.P.R.I., Adrian Hill, P.P.R.O.I., R.B.A., Sir Gilbert Inglefield, G.B.E., A.R.I.B.A., Hon. R.B.A., Raymond Lister, P.R.M.S., Michael Noakes, P.R.O.I., Michael Rizzello, P.P.S.P.S., Aubrey Sykes, P.R.I. *Secretary General:* Maurice Bradshaw. *Deputy Secretary General:* Carl de Winter. *Address:* 17 Carlton House Terr., London SW1Y 5BD.

Free Painters and Sculptors (F.P.S.)

This Society was founded in 1952 by a group of artists interested in contemporary painting and sculpture, with the object of providing increased opportunities for the general public to view representative exhibitions of art of a high standard. Many of its founder members belonged to the Institute of Contemporary Arts. The term "Free" indicates that a wide variety of styles and of differing artistic allegiances can be accepted, providing the standard is sufficiently high.

An annual exhibition is held in London, and includes the work of non-members. A special feature is the organization of provincial or travelling exhibitions which reach all parts of the British Isles, the object of these being to bring before the public a balanced cross-section of the international art scene.

Membership (£4 annually) may be applied for by anyone interested in the visual arts, and after election by the Executive Committee painters and sculptors may submit examples of their work with a view to qualifying for Full Membership. A limited proportion of Members can also be raised to the status of Fellow.

F.P.S. is an incorporated body and is registered under the Charities Act. It is a member of L'Association Internationale des Arts Plastiques (affiliated to U.N.E.S.C.O.), and is also represented on the City of Westminster Arts Council.

Chairman: John Newson. *Address:* 15 Buckingham Gate, London SW1.

Glasgow Art Club

This Club was formed in 1867 to advance the cause of and stimulate interest in art in all its branches by means of exhibitions of works of art, life classes, the acquisition of publications on art, lectures on art subjects, and by such other means as the Council may decide from time to time. Consequently, the Club's membership comprises painters, sculptors, architects and artist craftsmen as Artist Members and gentlemen interested in art as Lay Members. To be admitted to Artist Membership, candidates must submit examples of their work for the approval of the Artist Members. Painters, sculptors and members pay on admission an entry fee of £5.

Industrial Painters' Group

With the object of attracting further patronage of the arts by industry, the Society of Aviation Artists decided to expand its scope to include in the annual exhibition painters of industrial subjects, and adopting the title "Industrial Painters' Group." The Group has permanent headquarters and a staff available to advise industrialists and introduce them to painters capable of meeting their requirements.

President: Terence Cuneo, R.G.I. *Hon. Secretary:* Roy Nockolds. *Hon. Treasurer:* David Shepherd. *Secretary:* Maurice Bradshaw. *Address:* 17 Carlton House Terr., London SW1Y 5BD.

National Society of Painters, Sculptors and Printmakers

The formation of the National Society was the natural fruition of a growing desire among artists of every creed and outlook for an annual exhibition which would represent all aspects under one roof, without prejudice or favour to anyone.

President: Krome Barratt, V.P., R.O.I. *Hon. Secretary:* M. J. Boenisch. *Hon. Treasurer:* Albert Garrett. *Secretary:* Carl de Winter. *Address:* 17 Carlton House Terr., London SW1Y 5BD.

New English Art Club

The New English Art Club was founded in 1886. Its origin was a wave of foreign influence in the person of a number of students who had worked in the Parisian schools. The New English Art Club came into existence as a protest against a false concept of tradition, and it stands today against an equally false rejection of tradition. The annual exhibitions are held in the galleries of the Federation of British Artists, Mall Galleries, The Mall, SW1, during November, when the work of non-members is exhibited.

Hon. Secretary: William Bowyer, A.R.A., R.W.S., R.P. *Hon. Treasurer:* Frederick Dubery. *Secretary:* Carl de Winter. *Address:* 17 Carlton House Terr., London SW1Y 5BD.

The Passmore Edwards Art Gallery

The Passmore Edwards Art Gallery was built in 1895 for the artists of Cornwall. It played an important part in showing the work of the "Newlyn School," which included Stanhope Forbes, R.A., Frank Bramley, Walter Langley, T. C. Gotch, and many others. Today the Gallery shows contemporary painting, pottery and sculpture by members of the Newlyn Society of Artists, and is open throughout the spring and the summer to the public. The exhibitions also include works by non-members living in Cornwall.

Curator: Alister McLeod. *Address:* Newlyn, Penzance, Cornwall.

Royal Academy of Arts

The Royal Academy was founded by King George III in 1768 as "a Society for promoting the arts of design". Since that date over 6,600 students have received free training in the Royal Academy Schools. The Summer Exhibitions, promoting the work of living artists, have been held annually since 1769. The Academy takes no commission on the sale of these works. Other Exhibitions, frequently of Old Masters, date from 1870. The Royal Academy has never received any subsidy from the State. It is an independent, self-supporting institution, under the patronage of the Crown, and its activities are directed by its Members (Painters, Engravers, Sculptors and Architects) who serve in rotation on the Council. The President is elected annually.

Address: Burlington House, Piccadilly, London W1V 0DS.

Royal Birmingham Society of Artists

The Royal Birmingham Society of Artists is a non-profit-making society, unique in the Midlands for possessing its own spacious exhibition galleries. Specially designed for art exhibitions and opening on to Birmingham's busiest central street, these galleries are well illuminated by day or night. Except when the Society's own functions are being held, the galleries are available for hire. Schedules for the two open Spring Exhibitions—oil and sculpture, water-colour and craft—may be obtained by including a stamped addressed 9 by 3 inch envelope in a letter to the Secretary during January. There is also a flourishing Friends of the R.B.S.A., for details apply Hon. Sec.

President: James Priddey. *Vice-Presidents:* Peter B. Gross, Alex. Jackson. *Hon. Treasurer:* Joan Woollard. *Hon. Secretary:* Graham Benham. *Address:* 69A New St., Birmingham, 2.

Royal Cambrian Academy of Art

The Royal Cambrian Academy of Art was founded in 1881, and was granted a Royal Charter in 1882. The headquarters are established in the Elizabethan building in Conwy known as Plas Mawr, where exhibitions are held throughout the year, the main one being the Annual Exhibition of Paintings and Sculpture by Members. Non-members' works may be admitted to these exhibitions if the judging panel consider such works merit exhibition. Sending-in forms for the Annual Summer Exhibition may be obtained from the Secretary on 1 Mar. of any year.

President: Kyffin Williams, R.A., M.A., R.C.A. *Vice-President:* Mrs. M. della R. Whitehead, S.W.A. *Hon. Treasurer:* Roy Ostle. *Hon. Secretary:* John R. Webster. *Curator and Secretary:* Leonard H. S. Mercer. *Address:* Plas Mawr, Conwy.

Royal Glasgow Institute of the Fine Arts

This Institute was founded in 1862, and has now over 1,000 Members. Its object is "to promote a taste for art generally, and more especially to encourage contemporary art; to further the diffusion of artistic and aesthetic knowledge, and to aid the study, advancement and development of art in its applications." Towards the attainment of this object, the Institute holds annual exhibitions in the McLellan Galleries, Glasgow, and shows approximately 400 works in all mediums. The Membership fee is a single payment of £5·25, but if under twenty-six years of age, £1·05.

President: Alan D. Cuthbert. *Secretary:* John G. Barclay, C.A., 12 Sandyford Pl., Glasgow G3 7NE.

Royal Hibernian Academy

The Academy was incorporated by Charter in 1823 with the intention of encouraging the fine arts in Ireland by giving Irish artists the opportunity of exhibiting their works annually. It was reorganized under a new Charter in 1861 and enlarged to thirty Constituent Members, and up to the present time has consistently fulfilled its original aims.

In 1824 Francis Johnston, P.R.H.A., endowed the Academy with a house and exhibition gallery in Lower Abbey St. This was later enlarged by his widow, and again by Sir Thomas Jones, P.R.H.A., who erected a school for the study of the antique and living model, where many of the future artists received their training. The Academy House and Exhibition Galleries were destroyed by fire during Easter Week, 1916, and the Academy was without premises until 1939, when it acquired the house and garden of 15 Ely Place with the intention of erecting an exhibition hall and school when it had the funds to do so.

The Academy has encouraged and developed art in Ireland since its foundation.

It has given the Irish artist his status; and the present position of Irish Art can be said to be the outcome of the encouragement it has afforded to Irish men and women of talent and the part it has taken in art affairs generally in the country. There is hardly an Irish artist of note living or dead who has not been a member of the Academy or who has not benefited in one way or another by its activities.

President: Maurice MacGonigal. *Treasurer:* Henry Healy. *Secretary:* Desmond Carrick. *Keeper:* John F. Kelly. *Address:* 15 Ely Place, Dublin.

Royal Institute of Oil Painters

Founded in 1883 as the Institute of Painters in Oil Colours. The exhibitions, which are open to all artists, subject to selection, are held in the Galleries of the Federation of British Artists in October/November.

President: Michael Noakes, R.P. *Vice-President:* Krome Barratt. *Hon. Treasurer:* Ken Howard, N.E.A.C. *Hon. Secretary:* Clifford Charman. *Secretary:* Carl de Winter. *Address:* 17 Carlton House Terr., London SW1Y 5BD.

The Royal Institute of Painters in Water-colours

Formed in 1831 as the "New Society of Painters in Water-colours," a title which was afterwards changed to the "Institute of Painters in Water-colours." Shortly after the opening of the 1884 Exhibition the command of Queen Victoria was received that the Society should henceforth be called "The Royal Institute of Water-colours."

The honour of a diploma under the Royal Sign Manual was given to the members on August 29, 1884, by virtue of which they rank as *Esquires.*

Members are limited to 100. Annual Open Exhibition.

President: Aubrey Sykes. *Vice-President:* Charles Bone. *Hon. Exhibitions Secretary:* Ronald Maddox. *Hon. Treasurer:* Edward Wesson. *Secretary:* Maurice Bradshaw. *Address:* 17 Carlton House Terr., London SW1Y 5BD.

Royal Scottish Academy

The Academy is an independent body incorporated by Royal Charter for the furtherance of art and for educational purposes. Annual exhibitions of contemporary art: Mid-April to August; special Festival exhibitions: August to mid-September.

President: Robin Philipson, P.R.S.A., H.R.A., A.R.A. *Secretary:* Esme Gordon, R.S.A., F.R.I.B.A., F.R.I.A.S. *Treasurer:* James Cumming, R.S.A. *Librarian:* John Houston, R.S.A. *Assistant Secretary:* J. J. Marshall, M.B.E. *Address:* The Mound, Edinburgh EH2 2EL.

Royal Scottish Society of Painters in Water-colours

This Society was founded in 1878, and in 1888 Queen Victoria conferred on it the title "Royal". In its first Exhibition twenty-five artists showed their works; today there are seventy exhibiting Members. The object of the Society is to encourage and develop the art of painting in water-colours and the appreciation of this art, and toward the attainment of that object exhibitions of water-colour painting are held annually. While these are normally held in Edinburgh, they have on occasion been held in Glasgow, Aberdeen, Dundee and Perth. Candidates for Membership must be sponsored by Members of the Society, and must submit works for the consideration of the Members at an election meeting. The entrance fee is £10·50 and the annual subscription £6·00.

Secretary: John G. Barclay, C.A. *Address:* 12 Sandyford Pl., Glasgow G3 7NE.

Royal Society of British Artists

This Society was founded in 1823, incorporated by Royal Charter in 1847 and constituted a Royal Society in 1887. Membership is limited to 200. Associate Membership is by invitation. Annual exhibition held each year, during June, when the work of non-members is admitted.

President: Peter Greenham, R.A. *Vice-President:* David Winfield. *Hon. Treasurer:* Alex Koolman, R.P. *Hon. Secretary:* Charlotte Halliday. *Keeper:* Carl de Winter. *Address:* 17 Carlton House Terr., London SW1Y 5BD.

Royal Society of British Sculptors

Activities: Meetings, lectures, social occasions; award of medals; administration of Feodora Gleichen Memorial Fund (to assist women sculptors); publication of Annual Report and Supplement; Copyright Pamphlet; forms of contract; "Notes on Business Guidance for Sculptors"; Certificate of Authenticity certifying number of casts to rank as original work. Photograph files of members' work may be seen at the office by appointment. There is also a permanent display screen at the London Building Centre, Store St., W.C.1. Administers also Otto Beit Medal and Gold and Silver Medals.

President: Michael Clark. *Vice-President:* John Skelton. *Hon. Treasurer:* Darsie Rawlins. *Secretary:* M/S Fionnuala McGregor Eadie. *Address:* 8 Chesham Place, London SW1X 8HN.

Royal Society of Marine Artists

This Society was formed in 1939 with the object of promoting and encouraging marine art in any form, and of obtaining its recognition as an important element in the artistic life of a maritime nation. Membership is in two categories: Artist Members, whose work is exhibited in the Society's exhibition, and Lay Members, who, not themselves painters, are interested in marine painting and wish to foster it. The Diploma Collection is housed at the National Maritime Museum. The Annual Exhibition is held at the London Guildhall during October and November, when the work of non-members is admissible.

President: Keith Shackleton. *Vice-President:* David Cobb, R.O.I. *Hon. Secretary:* John Worsley. *Hon. Treasurer:* Josiah Sturgeon, F.R.B.A., R.I. *Secretary:* Carl de Winter. *Address:* 17 Carlton House Terr., London SW1Y 5BD.

Royal Society of Miniature Painters, Sculptors and Gravers

This Society was established to promote the fine art of miniature painting or any allied craft, and the annual exhibition is held during November/December, when paintings in miniature style are displayed. Works in illuminating, engraving, sculpture, modelling, carving and gem-work are admissible as well as paintings, and the work of non-members is shown.

President: Raymond Lister, F.R.S.A. *Hon. Treasurer:* H. E. Hervey. *Hon. Secretary:* Suzanne Lucas. *Secretary:* Carl de Winter. *Address:* 17 Carlton House Terr., London SW1Y 5BD.

Royal Society of Painter-Etchers and Engravers

The Royal Society of Painter-Etchers and Engravers was founded in 1880. The Society was granted a Royal Charter in 1911. Eminent Past-Presidents have been Sir F. Seymour Haden, Sir Frank Short, Malcolm Osborne and Robert Austin. All the well-known etchers and engravers have exhibited with the Society, whose annual exhibition caters for engraving in all its forms. The exhibition is open to non-members, who may submit work for the consideration of the Council. An election of Associates is held annually in January.

An important associated body is the Print-collectors' Club, which is open to those interested in etching and engraving. Members receive a presentation print annually.

President: H. N. Eccleston, R.W.S. *Secretary:* Malcolm Fry. *Address:* 26 Conduit St., London W1R 9TA.

Royal Society of Painters in Water-colours

The Royal Society of Painters in Water-colours, which is next in seniority to the Royal Academy, was founded in 1804. It has numbered amongst its distinguished Members John Varley, Peter de Wint, David Cox, John Sell Cotman, Samuel Prout, Samuel Palmer, Ambrose McEvoy and D. Y. Cameron to mention but a few. Two exhibitions are held annually—in the spring and autumn. These exhibitions are confined to the works of Members. There is an annual election of Associates.

The Old Water-colour Society's Club for connoisseurs and those interested in water-colour painting is run in conjunction with the main Society. Members receive a privately printed volume on water-colour painting and painters annually.

President: Andrew Freeth, R.A., R.E. *Secretary and Curator:* Malcolm Fry. *Address:* 26 Conduit St., London W1R 9TA.

Royal Society of Portrait Painters

This Society was founded in 1891 and has for its object the promotion of the fine arts—in particular the fine art of portrait painting. Exhibitions include the work of non-members, and are held annually during May in the Mall Galleries, The Mall, SW1.

President: Edward Halliday, C.B.E., P.P.R.B.A. *Vice-President:* Norman Hepple, R.A. *Hon. Treasurer:* Patrick Phillips. *Hon. Secretary:* George Bruce. *Secretary:* Maurice Bradshaw. *Address:* 17 Carlton House Terr., London SW1Y 5BD.

Royal Ulster Academy of Painting, Sculpture and Architecture

President: Miss Mercy Hunter, M.B.E., A.R.C.A., R.U.A., U.W.A. *Chairman:* George C. Morrison, M.A., R.U.A. *Hon. Secretary-Administrator:* Mrs. Lee Stewart, 10 Coolsara Pk., Lisburn, Co. Antrim BT28 3BG. *Hon. Treasurer:* Francis J. Neill. All communications to *Secretary.*

Royal West of England Academy

The Academy was founded in 1844. Election to Associateship (A.R.W.A.) and full Membership (R.W.A.) is by postal ballot. An "Open" exhibition is held every autumn. Application for forms should be made in August and September to the Organizing Secretary. Other art exhibitions are held during the year.

President: Donald Milner, O.B.E., Hon. M.A., R.W.A., A.R.C.A. *Organizing Secretary:* Miss Jean McKinney. *Address:* Queen's Rd., Clifton, Bristol BS8 1PX.

St. Ives Society of Artists

President: Rodney J. Burn, R.A. *Secretary and Curator:* Mrs. M. E. Leddra. *Address:* Old Mariners Church, Norway Sq., St. Ives, Cornwall.

Scottish Artists' Benevolent Association

This Association was formed in 1889, and gives assistance to distressed deserving artists, their widows and dependents. Each year it disburses over £3,000 in sums ranging from £10 to £350. Membership is open to anyone and the fees payable are £5·25 (Life) or 52½p (Annual).

Scottish Society of Women Artists

The Society, which was founded about forty years ago, exists to promote interest in art, both traditional and contemporary, and particularly in the work of women artists, fostering this interest by the holding of exhibitions and other functions periodically. An Annual Exhibition, with a formal opening and a reception during the month, is held every year in the Royal Scottish Academy, The Mound, Edinburgh, from mid-November to mid-December; it has sections for painting, design and craft, black and white, and sculpture, and also shows loan works of interest, from both home and abroad. The entry fee is £2 and the subscription £4·00 for Professional Members, £1·50 for Lay and £1·00 for Associate Members.

Honorary President: H.R.H. Princess Alice, the Duchess of Gloucester. *President:* Mrs. Nan Fergusson. *Secretary and Treasurer:* Mrs. Lynne Arnott, East Redford House, Redford Rd., Edinburgh EH13 0AS. *Exhibition Organiser:* Mrs. Elsa L. A. Hendry, Netherlea, Old Mill Lane, Edinburgh 16.

Senefelder Group of Artist Lithographers

Engraving, etching and lithography are the three main types of graphic reproduction now used by the creative artist, and lithography, invented by Alois Senefelder in 1798, is the most recent of them. The Group was formed in 1913, and holds an Annual Exhibition at which the work of non-members is shown.

Chairman: Henry Trivick, R.B.A. *Hon. Treasurer:* Helena Markson. *Secretary:* Maurice Bradshaw. *Address:* 17 Carlton House Terr., London SW1Y 5BD.

Society of Designer-Craftsmen

The Society was founded in 1888 as The Arts and Crafts Exhibition Society by William Morris and others, with the object of raising the standards and status of craftsmen and bringing their work before the public. Its main concern is still the organizing of exhibitions, an annual lecture and conferences. But in addition it has assumed the responsibilities of a national professional body representing designer-craftsmen in Britain in all their aspects, including art education. To this end it has established a qualification, Licentiate of the Society of Designer-Craftsmen (L.S.D.-C.) available on assessment to students at the end of their training. It has also inaugurated an annual silver medal awarded for excellence in design and craftsmanship.

Applications for Membership (M.S.D.-C.) supported by examples of work are considered three times a year by a sub-committee of the Council of the Society. The Fellowship of the Society (F.S.D.-C.) is awarded by the unanimous vote of the Council. Subscriptions: Fellows, £10; Members, £8; Licentiates and Associate Members, £4; Student Members, £2 p.a.

Chairman: Jeanne Werge-Hartley, F.S.D.-C. *Address:* 6 Queen Sq., London WC1.

Society of Industrial Artists and Designers

The Society of Industrial Artists and Designers, the first society of industrial designers in the world, came into being in 1930 and in 1976 received formal recognition—the award of a Royal Charter. It unites in a single organisation those who are concerned with design in engineering, consumer products, textiles, graphic design, visual communications and interiors.

In private practice or salaried employment its members are working in industry and commerce, for local and national government and in the fields of entertainment. They are united in their concern for the visual aspects of design, in applying their creative faculties to the solution of design problems and in their attention to the details involved in translating conception into actuality. Members are concerned not only with designing but also with design administration and education.

The Society is concerned with standards of competence, professional conduct and integrity. It makes a significant contribution to the establishment of high standards of education in the field of design. The Society represents the interests and views of professional designers on other bodies and with government and promotes the cause of high standards of design for the benefit of public, industry and commerce.

The Society promotes the understanding and use of good design through its journal "The Designer" as well as more specialised literature, and the Society's Design Medal is awarded every year to an individual designer for outstanding achievement in industrial design and focusing attention on a particular achievement which can stand for the aspirations of the whole profession.

The Society is a founder member of the International Council of Societies of Industrial Design (ICSID) and the International Council of Graphic Design Associations (ICOGRADA) and in the field of international design affairs works closely with the Council of Industrial Design.

Chief Executive Officer: Geoffrey Adams. *Address:* 12 Carlton House Terr., London SW1 5AH.

Society of Mural Painters

This Society was founded to increase public interest in mural paintings, and to stimulate the use of mural paintings by public authorities, industrial undertakings, architects and all others who might be potential users. It endeavours to promote a close relationship between architects and mural painters, and provides information of a technical nature which may be useful in assisting its Members to obtain the most suitable materials.

Chairman: Robert Lyon, R.B.A., R.P. *Hon. Secretary:* Rupert Shephard. *Secretary:* Maurice Bradshaw. *Address:* 17 Carlton House Terr., London SW1Y 5BD.

Society of Scottish Artists

The Society, founded in 1891, has a professional membership drawn mainly from all over Scotland, and divided into painting, sculpture, architecture and applied art sections. There is also an ordinary membership. The Annual Exhibition is normally held in the Royal Scottish Academy Galleries, Edinburgh, in September to November each year. Non-members may submit works which are subject to selection and hanging under exactly the same conditions as Members' works. For particulars of membership and exhibitions, write to the Secretary. For submitting for the Exhibition and applying for professional membership, write before the middle of August in each year.

Secretary: H. J. S. Henderson, W.S. *Address:* 19 York Pl., Edinburgh EH1 3EL.

Society of Women Artists

This Society was founded in 1855 for the encouragement of women artists, sculptresses and craftswomen in all media and holds an exhibition in London in the late summer of each year. (There are no Fellows or Associates.)

President: Lady Muriel Wheeler, F.R.B.S. *Vice-President:* Miss A. R. Kendall. *Hon. Treasurer:* Miss Gladys Dawson. *Hon. Secretary:* Mrs. Winifred Pickford. *Secretary:* Maurice Bradshaw. *Address:* 17 Carlton House Terr., London SW1Y 5BD.

United Society of Artists

This Society was founded in 1921 under the title "New Society of Artists," and its function is to hold Annual Exhibitions during the month of July in the Federation of British Artists Galleries, Mall Galleries, The Mall, SW1. It is particularly intended for the display of work of artists resident in the country and abroad who wish to submit their work to be shown in London. Non-members' work is admissible.

Hon. Secretary: Constance Nash. *Secretary:* Carl de Winter. *Address:* 17 Carlton House Terr., London SW1Y 5BD.

WHO'S WHO IN ART

A

ABELL, Roy, A.R.C.A., Silver Medal, Painting (1957); artist in oils, drawing media, etching and teacher; Head of School of Painting, Birmingham Polytechnic; *b* Birmingham, 21 Jan., 1931; *s* of Alfred Abell, engineer; *m* Mary Patricia; two *s*, one *d*. *Educ.:* Waverley Grammar School, Birmingham; *studied art* at Birmingham College of Art, 1947-52 (Harold Smith, Fleetwood-Walker); Royal College of Art, 1954-57 (Carel Weight, Ruskin Spear, John Minton). *Exhib.:* Young Contemporaries, R.A., John Moore's; one-man exhbns.: R.B.S.A. Gallery, Ikon Gallery. *Work in permanent collections:* Bradford, Lichfield, Birmingham. *Address:* 204 Birmingham Rd., Sutton Coldfield, Birmingham. *Signs work:* "Roy Abell."

ABLETT, Dorothy, F.S.D-C. (1958), A.T.D.; designer-craftsman in weaving, spinning and dyeing in cotton, wool, silk, linen, fleece, vegetable and chemical dyes; *b* Egypt, 1 July, 1918; *d* of Norman Lloyd Ablett, B.Sc., M.I.M.E. *Educ.:* Wimbledon High School, G.P.D.S.T.; *studied art* at Kingston, Central and Chelsea Art Schools under Graham Sutherland and John Farleigh in book production. *Exhib.:* one-man shows, Grange, Rottingdean and Worthing A.G., Building Centre and Design Centre, London, Brighton A.G., Commonwealth Institute, London. *Work in permanent collection:* Stoke-on-Trent Educ. Com. (contemporary crafts). *Publications:* articles in quarterly Journal of Weavers, Newsletter of S.D-C. *Address:* 76 Dean Ct. Rd., Rottingdean, Brighton BN2 7DJ. *Clubs:* British Crafts Centre, S.D-C., Guild of Sussex Craftsmen. *Signs work:* "Dorothy Ablett."

ACHESON, Joseph, B.A. Lond., Dip. F.A., Lond., M.S.I.A.; artist in oil, gouache, line; Head of History of Art, West Surrey College of Art and Design; Lecturer and Tutor, University of London and the Open University; Capt., R.A. (1942-46); *b* Marylebone, London, 30 Dec., 1918; *s* of Capt. Joseph Acheson, M.C.; *m* Eileen Veronica Adie; two *d*. *Educ.:* U.S.A.; Canada; Royal Grammar School, Guildford; *studied art* at Slade School and Courtauld Institute, London (1946-50), and subs. France, Italy, Greece, U.S.A. *Exhib.:* R.A., R.P.S., Arts Council, Leicester Galleries. *Official purchases:* Min. of Works, Army, Football Assoc. and public bodies, and for leading publishers and industrial concerns (1954-75). *Address:* Littleworth Cross Lodge, Seale, nr. Farnham, Surrey. *Signs work:* "Joseph Acheson."

ADAIR: see PAVEY, Donald Adair.

ADAM-TESSIER, Maxime; sculptor; *b* Rouen, France, 2 June, 1920. *Work in permanent collections:* Waddington Galleries, museums of Modern Art, Paris, São Paulo, Le Havre and Rouen. Steel Relief, Metro Station, La Defense. *Address:* 3 rue Schoelcher, Paris, 14. *Signs work:* see appendix.

ADAMS, Danton F., F.I.A.L.; abstract painter; *b* Eastbourne, 1904; *m*; one *s*. *Educ.:* St. Saviours, Eastbourne; *studied art* at Putney School of Art, Chelsea School of Art. *Exhib.:* R.A., Paris Salon, R.P., R.O.I., R.W.S., R.B.A., United Artists Soc., Imperial War Museum, Author and lecturer of the textbook Musical Colour (Douglass & Gilson Ltd.). *Address:* Westview Studios, 13 Westbury Rd., New Malden, Surrey. *Club:* President and Founder of Wimbledon Art Group. *Signs work:* "DANTON ADAMS."

ADAMS, Hervey, R.B.A. (1932); art master and portraitist, Berkhamsted School, 1937-40, Tonbridge School, 1940-63 (Lecturer on Painting); landscape painter in oils and water-colour; *b* 15 Feb., 1903; *s* of C. E. Adams, company director; *m* Iris Gabrielle Bruce. *Educ.:* Charterhouse, and *studied art* with Bernard Adams, 1928-30. *Exhib.:* R.A., R.B.A., Leicester Galleries. *Publications:* The Student's Approach to Landscape Painting (Pitman), Art and Everyman (Batsford), 18-19th Century Painting in Europe (Medici), The Adventure of Looking (Bell). *Address:* Pummel, Houndscroft, nr. Stroud, Glos. *Signs work:* "Hervey Adams."

ADAMS, James Frederick; painter in water-colour and publicity art consultant; *b* Stoke-on-Trent, 24 July, 1914; *s* of James Adams, accountant; *m* Vera Hall Capey; one *s*. *Educ.:* Penkhull Snr. School, and Balliol, Oxford; Burslem College of Art, Stoke-on-Trent, 1930-34 (Gordon M. Forsyth, R.I., and H. Tittensor, R.I.). *Exhib.:* R.A., R.I., R.W.S., R.W.E.A., R.B.A., United Soc. of Artists, Somerset Soc. of Artists, Bristol, Taunton, Brighton and Bath, and Staff Artists Soc. *Work in permanent collections:* Newcastle-u.-Lyme and Canada. *Work repro.:* in Studio and Art du Moderne (Paris); calendars, Staffordshire Life, etc. *Publications:* articles in Studio; and How to Draw Churches and Cathedrals. *Address:* Dymboro, Porthill Bk., Port-Hill, Newcastle, Staffs. *Signs work:* see appendix.

ADAMS, Norman, A.R.C.A., R.A.; painter; *b* London, 9 Feb., 1927; *s* of A. Adams; *m* Anna; two *s*; *studied art* at Harrow Art School, and R.C.A. *Exhib.:* R.A., Tate Gallery, City Art Galleries of Bradford, Leeds, York; also Rome, Paris, Brussels, Pittsburgh. *Official purchases:* C.A.S., Arts Council, National Gallery, N.Z., Tate Gallery, most provincial galleries, various education committees. Murals in public buildings. Décor for Sadler's Wells and Covent Garden. *Work repro.:* magazines, etc. *Addresses:* Butts, Horton-in-Ribblesdale, Settle, Yorks.; Scarp, Outer Hebrides, Scotland. *Signs work:* "Norman Adams," "N.A."

ADAMS, Robert; sculptor and designer; *b* Northampton, 5 Oct., 1917; *s* of Arthur Adams; *m* Patricia Adams. *Educ.:* Hardingstone School; *studied art* at Northampton School of Art. *Exhib.:* London, Paris, New York, Venice, Brazil, Rome, Milan, Antwerp, London Group; International Biennales, Brazil (1951-57), Antwerp (1951, 1953), Venice (1952); Tate Gallery, Holland Park (1955-57), Dublin, Chicago. *Work in permanent collections:* Arts Council, British Council, Museum of Modern Art, New York, New York Public Library, Brit. Council, Mus. of Modern Art (Turin), São Paulo Museum, University of Michigan, Tate Gallery. *Address:* Rangers Hall, Gt. Maplestead, Halstead, Essex. *Signs work:* "ADAMS."

ADAMSON, Arthur Cecil, N.R.D. (1940), L.S.I.A. (1946); R.S.A. Competitions 1st Prize metalwork (1933), 2nd Prize metalwork (1934); designer of architectural metalwork and lighting fittings; *b* London, 14 July, 1907; *s* of Horace Adamson; *m* Dorothy E. E. (*née* Clarke); one *s*. *Educ.:* Chiswick Polytechnic; *studied art* at the Sir John Cass Inst. under Harold Stabler, Hammersmith School of Art under Enison Goodison. *Exhib.:* Lighting at St. Botolph's Church, Bishopsgate, Watford Town Hall, Bromley Town Hall, Cambridge Guild Hall, Public Rooms of Charing Cross Hotel, Entrance Hall, etc., of Masonic Temple, Gt. Queen St., London. *Address:* 5 Ruislip Gdns., Aldwick, Bognor Regis, W. Sussex.

ADAMSON, Edward James; artist, lecturer, art-psychotherapist, author, art director; Curator, Adamson Collection of Schizophrenic Art; Consultant-therapist, Netherne and Fairdene Psychiatric Hospital, Coulsdon, Surrey; Council mem., Société International de Psychopathologie de l'Expression, Paris; Consultant in remedial art, Roehampton Institute of Higher Education, London; Senior Tutor and Consultant art-therapist, Herts. College of Art and Design, St. Albans; Founder Chairman, British Assoc. of Art Therapist. Lectures internationally at major universities, medical centres, art schools and teachers' colleges. Work featured widely in press, films, radio and television. *Exhib.:* mainly in London and Paris. *Publications:* Art for Mental Health in The Social Context of Art (Tavistock). *Address:* (Home, studio and private practice): The Studio, 16 Hollywood Rd., Chelsea, London SW10 9HY. *Signs work:* "Adamson."

ADAMSON, George Worsley, M.S.I.A.; illustration, humorous drawing; *b* New York City, 7 Feb., 1913; *s* of George William Adamson, engineer; *m* Peggy Diamond; two *s*. *Studied art* at Wigan and Liverpool City Schools of Art. *Exhib.:* Walker Gallery, Liverpool; R.A.; Arts Council Exhbn. of Book Illus.: American Institute of Graphic Arts (N.Y.), covering Punch Exhbn. *Work in permanent collections:* War Artists Coll. *Official purchases:* seven drawings by War Artists' Advisory Com. *Work repro.:* magazines, Designers in Britain, book illustrations, advertising, Faber Book of Nursery Verse, A Finding Alphabet, Finding 1 to 10, Rome Done Lightly. *Address:* 46 Bridge Rd., Countess Weir, Exeter, Devon.

ADDISON, Byron Kent; sculptor, painter and teacher; Professor, Chairman, Art Dept., Maryville College; *b* St. Louis, Mo., 12 July, 1937; *s* of M. F. Addison; *m* Sharon Lee; one *s*, one *d*. *Educ.:* Grade and High School, Springfield, Ill.; *studied art* at Washington Univ. (1955-59), Univ. of Notre Dame with Ivan Mestrovic (1959-60). *Work in permanent collections:* Metropolitan Church Federation, St. Justin the Martyr Church, Sunray D.X. Oil Co., Continental Telephone Corp., Packless Metal Hose Co., Maryville College. *Address:* 616 Spring Meadows Dr., Ballwin, Mo. 63011. *Signs work:* see appendix.

ADDISON, David, B.A., Dip.Ed., A.M.A.; Director, Cheltenham Art Gallery and Museum (1972-); formerly schoolmaster (1960-64); W.E.A. and Extra Mural tutor (1960-72); Open University tutor (1971-72); Chairman, Extension Services Panel Yorkshire Area Museum Service (1969-72); Keeper, Museums Education Service, Bradford (1967-72). Mem., Arts Council Art Exhbns. Panel, Visual Arts Panel S.W. Arts; hon. mem., Cheltenham Art Club, Cheltenham Ceramic Circle; examiner, Welsh G.C.E.; Museums Assoc.; *b* Nottingham, 2 May, 1937; *s* of Frank Addison; *m* Joyce Hudd; two *s*, one *d*. *Educ.:* Kings College, Durham, and Wells Theological College. *Exhib.:* Young Contemporaries (1960) and provincial galleries. *Publications:* articles on art, museums and education. *Address:* Stonecroft, Bisley, Stroud, Glos.

ADHÉMAR, Jean, Officier de la Légion d'Honneur, Commandeur du Mérite; Conservateur en chef du Cabinet des Estampes, Bibliothèque nationale, Paris; *b* Paris, 1908; *s* of Pierre Adhémar, avocat au conseil d'état; *m* Hélène, Conservateur en chef des Musées du Jen de Paume et de l'Orangerie; two *s*, one *d*. *Address:* 56 rue Raynouard, Paris.

ADLER, Lee; Amer. Acad. of Arts & Letters Purch. Award (1969); Burndy Corp. Award (1969); Grumbacher Award (1968); painter, serigrapher; *b* New York, 22 May, 1934; one *s*. *Educ.:* N.Y.U., Syracuse U., Sorbonne; *studied art* at

Pratt Graphics Center (1969), Bklyn. Mus. Art School (1964-65); Art Students League (1962-64). *Exhib.:* 18 one-man shows: Instituto de Cultura Hispanica, Madrid (1976); New Bertha Schaefer Gall., N.Y. (1975); Mickelson Gall., Wash., D.C. (1974); Hagley Mus. (1974); Fairleigh Dickinson Univ. (1975); N.Y.U. (1972). *Work in permanent collections:* Metro. Mus., N.Y.; B.M.; Whitney Mus., N.Y.; Bklyn. Mus.; Art Inst. of Chicago; Corcoran Gall. of Art, Wash., D.C.; Harvard Univ., Cambridge, Mass. and many others. *Address:* 168 Clinton St., Bklyn., N.Y. *Signs work:* "LEE ADLER."

AERON, Idris: see WILLIAMS, Idris Elgina.

AGAR, Eileen; painter in oil, gouache, collage; *b* Buenos Aires (of British parents), 1904; *d* of James Agar; *m* Dr. Joseph Bard, F.R.S.L., author. *Educ.:* Heathfield, Ascot; *studied art* at the Slade under Henry Tonks; Paris. *Exhib.:* Hanover Gallery, Redfern, Obelisk, Brook St., Il Bilico, Rome, Retrospective Commonwealth Art Gallery, Kensington (1971). *Work in permanent collections:* Tate, Arts Council, Contemporary Art Soc., V. & A., National Gallery of N.Z. *Work repro.:* Herbert Read's Surrealism, The Museum of Modern Arts, Fantastic Art, Dada, Surrealism; London Bulletin, Minotaure, etc. *Address:* West House, 1 Melbury Rd., Kensington, London W14.

AINLEY, John Anthony; Headmaster of St. Philip's Special School, Chessington; *b* Sheffield, 1931; *m*; two children. M.Sc., Diploma in the Visual Arts; Diploma in Child Development. Secretary of Leatherhead Art Club, Secretary of Kingston Teachers Art Group. *Address:* Bridleside, Yarm Ct. Rd., Leatherhead, Surrey.

AINSLIE, Peter; potter; lecturer, Chester College of Education; *b* Kingston-upon-Hull, 26 June, 1925; *s* of George Henry Ainslie, shipbuilding draughtsman; *m* Margaret Wilkinson; one *s,* one *d. Educ.:* Bede Grammar School, Sunderland; *studied art* at Sunderland School of Art, Loughborough College School of Art. *Address:* 21 Sandon Rd., Newton Pk., Chester. *Signs work:* Impressed monogram "PA."

AITCHISON. Craigie Ronald John; painter in oil; Edwin Austin Abbey Premier Scholarship for Painting (1970), represented modern British painters, Tokyo (1970); *b* 13 Jan., 1926; *s* of The Rt. Hon. Lord Aitchison, P.C., K.C., LL.D., and Lady Aitchison. *Educ.:* Scotland; *studied art* at Slade School of Fine Art (1952-54). *Exhib.:* 23rd Salon Actualité de L'Esprit Paris (1975); one-man exhbn.:Rutland Gallery (1975), Scottish Arts Council (1975), Marlborough Fine Art (1968); Gimpel Fils, Gallery One, Beaux Arts Gallery. *Official purchases:* Arts Council of Great Britain, C.A.S., Tate Gallery, National Gallery of Scotland. *Work repro.:* Architectural Review, "X" Quarterly Review, Listener, Apollo Magazine, Connoisseur, Vogue. Represented Calouste Gulbenkian International Exhbn. (1964), 2nd International Biennial, Bologna (1967). *Address:* c/o Royal Bank of Scotland, Burlington Gardens, London W1. Awarded Lorne Scholarship (1974-75), Arts Council Bursary (1975-76), Italian Government Scholarship for painting, 1955, through British Council. *Signs work:* all unsigned.

ALDRIDGE, Eileen, artist in oil, water-colour, etc.; writer; *d* of Edward William Aldridge, company director and explorer; *m* William Ware; one *s. Educ.:* privately; *studied art* at Kingston School of Art (Principal, Reginald Brill, 1933-38). *Exhib.:* R.A., N.E.A.C., W.I.A.C., R.B.A., Leger Gallery, Leicester Gallery, William Ware Gallery, Gallery 2, various provincial and Continental galleries. *Work repro.:* La Revue Moderne (Paris), Chelsea News, R.A.; illustrated catalogue (1969). *Work purchased:* Brighton Corporation. *Publications:* Children's books written and illustrated for the Medici Soc. book on porcelain written for Paul Hamlyn. *Address:* 226 Fulham Rd., London SW10. *Signs work:* "E. Aldridge."

ALDRIDGE, John Arthur Malcolm, M.A., R.A. (1963); painter; Assistant at Slade School (1949-70); *b* 26 July, 1905; *s* of Major J. B. Aldridge, D.S.O., R.H.A. *Educ.:* Uppingham School, C.C.C. Oxford. *Exhib.:* R.A. and provincial galleries. *Official purchases:* Tate Gallery, National Portrait Gallery, V. & A.; Contemporary Art Society; Ministry of Works; Arts Council; British Council; Aberdeen, Leamington, Leeds, Lincoln, Manchester, Newport (Mon.), Northampton and Whitworth Art Galleries; L.C.C. (Educ. Dept.) and Italian Ministry of Education. *Work repro.:* The Life of the Dead (Laura Riding) and Adam was a Ploughman (C. Henry Warren). *Address:* The Place House, Gt. Bardfield, Essex. *Signs work:* "John Aldridge."

ALEXANDER-SINCLAIR, John, F.R.S.A., S.M.O.M., A.R.M.S.; Diplomatist and U.N.O. (Rtd); Chairman, Art Registration Committee; Chairman, Human Rights Trust; Vice-Chairman, Brit. Institute of Human Rights; Vice-Chairman, The Anti-Slavery and Aborigines Protection Soc.; jewellery designer in gold, silver, precious stones and wood carving; *b* Simla, India, 22 Feb., 1906; *m* Maureen, painter; one *s,* two *d. Educ.:* Charterhouse and Munich University; *studied art* direct from the antique, China, France, Italy, etc. *Address:* 5 Aysgarth Rd., London SE21 7JR. *Clubs:* various Polo clubs, R.A.C., Athenaeum. *Signs work:* see appendix.

ALEXANDRI, Sara; Dip. of Royal Academy of Fine Arts in Painting (Florence. Italy); art teacher; landscape, flower and figure painter in oil and water-colour; etcher; *b* Kherson, Russia, 22 Oct., 1913; *d* of Schneior Alexandri, teacher; *m* Michael Perkins; one *s. Educ.:* High School, Palestine, and privately in Italy and Switzerland; *studied art* at Royal Inst. d'Arte, Florence, and Royal Academy of Fine Arts, Florence (1936-40, 1946-47). *Exhib.:* R.A., R.B.A., W.I.A.C., R.W.E.A., Paris Salon, foreign and main provincial galleries. *Address:* 28 Gensing Rd., St. Leonards-on-Sea, Sussex. *Signs work:* "S. ALEXANDRI" or "S. Alexandri."

ALI, AlHaj Sheikh Nur, F.W.A.S.C.E. (1976), A.R.D.S.(Lond.) (1961-62), M.F.P.S. (1972); artist in oil, water-colour and tempera; Chairman, World Art Science and Cultural Exchanges; P.R.O. International Cultural Exchange; resident artist, International Art Centre; *b* Nairobi, 23 Apr., 1928; *s* of Sheikh Mohamed Hussein; *m* Ijaz Fatima; two *s,* three *d. Educ.:* Royal College, University College E.A., Nairobi; Garnett and Holborn Colleges, London; *studied art* (1956-59) under John and Una Baines, A.R.C.A. *Exhib.:* various local and abroad. *Work in permanent collections:* I.L.E.A., Ministry of Public Buildings and Works, Philadelphia, U.S.A. *Address:* 34 Selsdon Rd., W. Norwood, London SE27 0PG. *Clubs:* City of Westminster Arts Council, Art Society of Paddington. *Signs work:* see appendix.

ALLAN, Rosemary; painter in oil and water-colour; *b* Bromley, Kent, Oct., 1911; *d* of H. P. Allan; *m* Allan Gwynne-Jones, D.S.O., A.R.A., painter; one *d. Educ.:* Kinnaird Park School; *studied art* at Slade School. *Exhib.:* R.A., N.E.A.C., London Group, Wildenstein's. Leicester Galleries, Redfern Gallery; one-man shows, Upper Grosvenor Gallery, Bath, Swindon. *Official purchases:* Contemp. Arts Soc., Nuffield Trust, War Artists. *Work repro.:* History for Schools (O.U.P.). *Address:* Eastleach, Cirencester, Glos., and 15 Gardner House, Albany St., London NW1. *Signs work:* "Rosemary Allan."

ALLARD, Reginald Geoffrey, Dip.A.D., John Moores Scholarship (1969); artist in acrylic and water-colour; *b* Chester, 16 Nov., 1947; *s* of R. F. Allard.

Educ.: Ellesmere Port Grammar School; *studied art* at Chester School of Art (1964-66) under Jack Shore, Liverpool Regional College of Art (1966-69) under John Roberts, A.R.C.A. *Exhib.:* one-man show Fine Art Soc. *Work in permanent collections:* Duchess of Westminster, Ralli International, First National City Bank of New York. *Address:* 16 Flag La. South, Upton-by-Chester, Ches. *Signs work:* "R. G. Allard."

ALLEN, Daphne; artist in water-colour, pastel, oil and black and white; *b* London, 6 Jan., 1899; *d* of Hugh Allen, pupil of John Ruskin. *Studied art* under artist parents. *Exhib.:* from the age of 13; later, one-man exhbns., London, Bath, Birmingham, and exhbns. at Gloucester and Stroud. *Work in permanent collections:* Drawings done as a child in V. & A., reredos, St. Christopher's Chapel, Newcastle Cathedral, Australia, High Altar and Lady Chapel, Streatham Parish Church, window, Scotby Church, Cumberland, pictures, "Music" in Temple of Music, Philadelphia, "The Kingdom," exhib. Elgar Cen. Exhbn., Royal Festival Hall, London (1957), "Son et Lumiere, Gloucester, 1958," purchased for Church House, Gloucester, "Iona shall be as it was" given to the Iona Community, Scotland (1960). *Work repro.:* Pictures of imaginative and religious subjects, legend, folklore and landscape. Illustrated London News, Medici Soc., and others. *Publications:* At age of 12 and 13 two books of drawings, A Child's Visions and The Birth of the Opal. *Address:* Green Court, Chalford, nr. Stroud, Glos. *Clubs:* R.W.S. Art Club, Glos. Soc. of Artists. *Signs work:* "Daphne Allen."

ALLEN, Frank Humphrey; painter in oil, acrylic, tempera; *b* London, 22 March, 1896; *s* of James Allen; *m* Florence Annie Findlay. *Educ.:* Kings College, London; *studied art* at Chelsea School of Art under H. S. Williamson, Graham Sutherland. *Exhib.:* Leicester Galleries, London, London Group, A.I.A., Cooling Gallery, William Ware Gallery, London, Paris, Bradford City Art Gallery, Oxford University, Oxford Gallery, Walberswick Gallery, Norwich Twenty Group, Ashgate Gallery, Surrey. *Work in permanent collections:* City of B'ham A.G. and private collections. *Address:* 1 St. Giles Terr., Norwich, Norfolk NR2 1NS. *Signs work:* "F. H. Allen."

ALLEY, Ronald Edgar, B.A. (1950); art historian; Keeper of the Modern Collection, Tate Gallery (since 1965), Assistant Keeper (1951-54), Deputy Keeper (1954); *b* Bristol, 12 Mar., 1926; *s* of Edgar Thomas Alley; *m* Anthea Alley (*née* Oswell), painter and sculptor; two *d. Educ.:* Bristol Grammar School, London University; *studied history of art* at The Courtauld Institute of Art. *Publications:* Tate Gallery; Foreign Paintings, Drawings and Sculpture (1959), Gaugin (1961), William Scott (1963), Ben Nicholson (1963), Francis Bacon (1964), British Painting since 1945 (1966), Picasso's "Three Dancers" (1967), Recent American Art (1969). *Club:* I.C.A. *Address:* 61 Deodar Rd., London SW15. *Signs work:* "Ronald Alley."

ALLOWAY, Lawrence; art critic; Curator, Guggenheim Museum (1962-66); Professor of Art History, State University of New York at Stony Brook; *b* 17 Sept., 1926; *s* of Francis Lawrence Alloway; *m* Sylvia Margaret. *Publications:* The Venice Biennale, 1895-1968 (New York, 1968), Violent America, The Movies 1946-1964 (New York, 1971), American Pop Art (New York, 1974). *Address:* 330 West 20th St., New York, 11.

ALLSOPP, Bruce, B.Arch. 1st Class Hons. (1933), Dip. C.D. (1935), A.R.I.B.A. (1935), A.M.T.P.I. (1938), F.R.I.B.A. (1955), F.S.A. (1968); author, university teacher, painter and designer; Chairman of Oriel Press, Ltd. since 1962; Chairman of the Society of Architectural Historians (1960); Master of the Art Workers Guild (1970); Chairman of the Independent Publishers Guild (1971); *b*

Oxford, 4 July, 1912; *s* of Henry Allsopp, B.A.; *m* Florence Cyrilla Woodroffe, A.R.C.A.; two *s*. *Educ.:* Manchester Grammar School; *studied art* at Liverpool University. *Address:* Stocksfield Studio, Branch End, Stocksfield, Northumberland NE43 7NA. *Signs work:* "Bruce Allsopp" or "B.A.," the "A" lower than the "B."

ALSOP, Will, A.A.dip. (1973), S.A.D.G. (1973), William Van Allen Medal (1972), Bernard Webb Rome Scholarship (1973); architect, artist, lecturer in photography, video, steel; Cedric Pruce, architects; tutor, Architectural Assoc.; tutor, St. Martin's School of Art (Sculpture Dept.); *b* Northampton, 12 Dec., 1947; *s* of Francis John Alsop; *m* Sheila Bean. *Educ.:* Eaglehurst College, Northampton; *studied art* at Northampton School of Art (1967) under Malcom Pollard. *Exhib.:* Fruit Market Gallery, Edinburgh (1976), R.C.A. (1975), Padua, Italy (1975), 5 Young Architects, Art Net (1974), Alexandra Palace (1971), Compendium Gallery, Birmingham (1969). *Publications:* Bit Book of Visions (1973). *Address:* 72 Pembroke Rd., London W8. *Club:* London Architecture. *Signs work:* "Will Alsop."

AMBRUS, Victor Gyozo Laszio, A.R.C.A. (1960), F.R.E. (1973); Library Assoc., Kate Greenaway Gold Medal (1966); book illustrator, graphic designer; assistant lecturer, West Surrey College of Art (dept. Graphic Design); *b* Budapest, 19 Aug., 1935; *s* of Gyozo Ambrus, Dipl. Eng. of Chemistry; *m* Glenys Rosemary, A.R.C.A., one *s*. *Educ.:* St. Imre Grammar School, Budapest; *studied art* at Hungarian Academy of Fine Art, Budapest; R.C.A., London. *Exhib.:* R.A., R.E., Biennale: Bratislava; Bologna, Italy, Belgium. *Work in permanent collections:* University of Southern Mississippi, U.S.A.; Library of Congress, U.S.A.; O.U.P., London. *Publications:* The Royal Navy, British Army, Royal Air Force, Merchant Navy, Three Poor Tailors, Brave Soldier Janos, The Little Cockerell, The Sultan's Bath, Hot Water for Boris, Country Wedding. *Address:* 52 Crooksbury Rd., Farnham, Surrey. *Signs work:* "V. G. Ambrus."

ANDERSON, Douglas Hardinge, R.P.; portrait painter in oils; *b* 8 Aug., 1934; *studied art* under Pietro Annigoni in Florence. *Exhib.:* R.P., R.A. *Address:* c/o Douglas Anderson Ltd., 2 King's House Studios, King's Rd., London SW3. *Clubs:* Chelsea Arts, Arts, Turf. *Signs work:* "Douglas Anderson."

ANDERSON, John Colin, N.D.D., F.Inst.D. (1949); artist in oil, water-colour, and designer; Young Contemporaries Com. (1949); Man. Director, Anderson Art Studios Ltd.; *b* Borrowash, nr. Derby, 2 Feb., 1926; *s* of John Darley Anderson; *m* Hazel June Beryl Anderson; three *s*, one *d*. *Educ.:* St. James, Derby; Harrow Weald; *studied art* at Harrow School of Art under J. Platt, C. Sanders, R.A., De Saumarez, etc. (1939-43 and 1947-49). *Exhib.:* R.A., R.B.A., Young Contemporaries, N.E.A.C., etc. *Official purchases:* Bucks C.C. (1949), Oliver Trust (1971). *Work repro.:* advertising materials. *Address:* 14 The Fairway, Northwood, Middx. *Signs work:* "Anderson."

ANDERSON, Madeleine Elizabeth, A.R.C.A. (1934); awarded scholarship (1931, 1932), painting prize and other awards (1934, 1964, 1970); artist in oil, water-colour and print (semi-retd.); *b* Belvedere, Kent, 18 Sept., 1910; *d* of Harry Percival Harvey Anderson, inventor, consultant, M.Inst., P.I.C.M.E.; ex husband G. H. Holtom; two *s*, two *d*. *Educ.:* Airdrie Academy, Lanarkshire; *studied art* at Kingston-upon-Thames (1931-32) under Prof. Anthony Betts and J. Platt; R.C.A. (1932-34) under Sir W. Rothenstein and Prof. Spencer. *Work in permanent collections:* Friendship House, Moscow; Queen's College, Oxford; Cuming Museum and Art Gallery; Fawcett House, London; Cheltenham Art Gallery; M. of W. *Work repro.:* Signature (1936-37). *Address:* St. John's Coachhouse, Lechlade, Glos. GL7 3AT. *Clubs:* B.F.U.W., Fawcett Soc., London Bach Choir. *Signs work:* "M. E. Anderson."

ANDERTON, Eileen, A.R.M.S. (1950), F.R.S.A. (1970); freelance artist in body-colour, water-colour, mixed media; *b* Bradford, Yorks., 26 April, 1924; *d* of Sam Anderton, schoolmaster (art), M.R.S.T. *Educ.:* Bradford Girls' Grammar School; *studied art* at Bradford Art School (1939-44) under John Greenwood and Vincent Lines. *Exhib.:* Cartwright Hall, Bradford, Wakefield, Halifax, S.W.A., Royal Water-colour Soc. Gallery; one-man show at Bradford Library Gallery. *Work in permanent collections:* Bradford University. *Address:* 43 Spring Gardens Rd., Heaton, Bradford. *Club:* Bradford Arts. *Signs work:* "E. Anderton."

ANDRESEN, Margaret Kirkwood, D.A. post. Dip. (H.Comm.); freelance illustrator in pencil, water-colour, pen and ink; *b* Dunfermline, Fife, 10 July, 1951; *d* of George Hutchison, journalist and editor; *m* Trycvepeton Andresen, B.Sc., B.Arch. *Educ.:* Beath Senior High School, Cowdenbeath, Fife; *studied art* at Duncan of Jordanstone College of Art, Dundee (1969-75) under Ronald Stenberg, Myer Lacomb. *Exhib.:* one-man shows, Kynd Kyttocks Gallery, Falkland, Stirling Gallery, Stirling. *Address:* 8 Stirling Rd., Drymen, Glasgow G63 0BN. *Signs work:* "Margaret Andresen."

ANDREWS, Arthur H., A.R.C.A. (1929), F.R.S.A. (1935), N.R.D. (1936); portrait, landscape and flower painter, industrial designer, using oil, tempera, and wood-engraving; principal, Poole College for Further Education; art adviser, Dorset County Education Committee since 1947; *b* Birmingham, 23 Jan., 1906; *s* of the late Henry Burgum Andrews; *m* Sushila Singh, A.R.C.A. *Educ.:* Latymer School, Middx.; *studied art* at Hornsey School of Art, R.C.A. *Exhib.:* R.A., London and provincial galleries; one-man show at Foyle's Gallery. *Work in permanent collections:* Leeds and Bournemouth Art Gall., V. & A. *Address:* 35 Branksome Hill Rd., Bournemouth, Dorset. *Signs work:* "A. H. Andrews."

ANDREWS, Dorothy Eileen (Mrs.), A.R.C.A., A.T.D.; craft worker and artist in oil and water-colour; *b* West Bridgeford, Nottingham, 14 May, 1897; *d* of Arthur James Alderton; *m* L. Gordon Andrews, A.M.C., A.S.A.M. *Educ.:* Northampton; R.C.A. under Prof. Rothenstein (1921-23). *Exhib.:* S.M.A., N.S., R.O.I., R.I., Flower Painting, summer and winter salons, Russell Cotes Art Gall., Bournemouth, Britain in Water-colours, Northampton Town and County Art Soc. *Address:* 115 Monkhams La., Woodford Green, Essex. *Signs work:* "EILEEN ANDREWS."

ANDREWS, Edith Lovell; M. St. Ives Soc. of Artists; landscape painter in water-colour and poster-designer; *b* Newport, Mon., 7 Nov., 1886; *studied art* at Glasgow School of Art under Fra. H. Newbery and Anne Macbeth (1908-10), and Heatherley's under Gerald Massey (1911-14). *Exhib.:* Glasgow (1911), Toronto (1912), Canadian National Exhbns. (1913, 1914), Helsingfors and Stockholm (1912), Turin (1913), Kensington (1918), St. Ives, Cornwall (1949-74), Winnipeg (1953); one-man show, St. Ives (1957), Britain in Water-colours (1963). *Work in permanent collections:* B.M. and Australia. *Work repro.:* in Studio Year Book (1913), Christian Science Monitor (1920-25), The Spinning Wheel (U.S.A.). *Publications:* by Studio (1912, 1913). *Address:* 2 Bellair Terr., St. Ives, Cornwall. *Club:* St. Ives Arts. *Signs work:* "ANDREWS" or "E. L. ANDREWS" (works for reproduction).

ANDREWS, Marcia, M.F.P.S.; W.I. Gold Star; painter in oil; British Council Staff; *b* London; *d* of Walter James Tricker; *m* Edward Andrews; one *s*, one *d*. *Educ.:* St. Andrews, London; New City, London; *studied art* at Medway College of Art, Rochester (1960-64) under Eric Frankland. *Exhib.:* Brangwyn; Mall;

Loggia; Culham College; Rochester Cathedral; Tunbridge Wells A.G.; Bentlif Gallery; Corn Exchange, Chesterfield; Portland Place; R.C.A.; Westminster Art Workshop; Cockpit Theatre; Medway Little Theatre; Turret Gallery; nine one-man shows in London and provinces. *Work in permanent collections:* Medway Council Library Loan and *private collections* in England, France, India, Australia. *Work repro.:* Slough Observer. *Address:* 40 Robin Hood La., Walderslade, Chatham, Kent. *Clubs:* I.A.A., F.P.S., I.C.A., A.I.R., Medway Little Theatre. *Signs work:* "M. ANDREWS" or "M.A."

ANGADI, Patricia; artist in oil; Chairman, Hampstead Artists' Council; *b* Hampstead, 23 Sept., 1914; *d* of Robert Fell-Clark, decd.; *m* Ayana Angadi, Indian author and lecturer; three *s*, one *d*. *Educ.:* Prior's Field, Godalming, Surrey; *studied art* at Heatherleys under Frederick Whiting, Bernard Adams (1933-37). *Exhib.:* R.P., W.I.A.C., S.W.A., R.B.A., R.O.I., Goupil Galleries, Paris Salon, N.E.A.C., Utd. Artists. *Official purchases:* Portraits of James Maxton, M.P., by Glasgow People's Gallery, C. E. M. Joad by Birkbeck College, Baron Reuter by Reuter's Press Museum, Aachen. *Address:* 48 Flask Walk, London NW3. *Signs work:* "Angadi" in red.

ANGEL, Marie, A.R.C.A. (1948); calligraphist, illustrator; *b* 1923; *d* of Cyril Angel. *Educ.:* Coloma Convent; *studied art* at Croydon School of Art (1940-45), R.C.A. Design School (1945-48). *Exhib.:* R.A., Society of Scribes and Illuminators, Society of Designer Craftsmen, and widely in U.S.A.; one-man shows at San Francisco (1967), Casa del Libro (1975). *Work in permanent collections:* Harvard College Library, Hunt Botanical Library, Casa del Libro, Puerto Rico, U.S.A. and V. & A. *Publications:* books of miniature drawings, A Bestiary, A New Bestiary, Two Poems by Emily Dickinson, An Animated Alphabet (Harvard College Library, U.S.A.); illustrated: We Went Looking, The Twentythird Psalm, My Cat has Eyes of Sapphire Blue (Thomas Y. Crowell, N.Y.); The Tale of The Faithful Dove and The Tale of Tuppenny by Beatrix Potter (Frederick Warne and Co., London and New York); The Ark (Harper and Row, N.Y.); Two by Two (Follet Publishing Co., Chicago); Beasts in Heraldry (The Stephen Greene Press, Vermont). *Address:* Silver Ley, Oakley Rd., Warlingham, Surrey CR3 9BE. *Signs work:* "Marie Angel" or "Angel."

ANGERER, Mea, N.R.D. (1938), M.S.I.A. (1949); textile designer, decorative and commercial designer, artist in gouache, pen and ink, scraper-board; *b* Vienna, 28 June, 1905; *d* of Dr. Franz Angerer. *Educ.:* Vienna; *studied art* at Academy of Applied Art, Vienna. *Exhib.:* Cotton Board, Manchester, Rayon and Synthetic Fibres Assoc., London, Festival of Britain. *Work in permanent collection:* V. & A. *Work repro.:* in Woman and Mother (Odhams Press). *Publications:* British Textile Designers Today; Exhibition Design. *Address:* 260 Randolph Ave., London W9. *Signs work:* "MEA" with the centre stroke of the E joined to the M and A.

ANGULO-IÑIGUEZ, Diego; M. of the Real Academia de la Historia, Real Academia de Bellas Artes, and Hispanic Soc. of New York; catedrático emeritus (full prof.) of History of Art, University of Madrid; director emeritus, Museo del Prado; director emeritus, Instituto de Arte Diego Velazquez, of Consejo Sup. de Inves, Cients.; *b* Valverde (Huelva), Spain, 18 July, 1901; *s* of Diego Angulo and Angela Iñiguez. *Educ.:* Sevilla and Madrid; *studied art* at Universities of Sevilla, Madrid, Berlin. *Publications:* Historia del Arte Hispano-americano (1945-56), Historia del Arte (2 vols., 1953), Pintura del Renacimiento (1954), Pintura del Siglo XVII (1971). *Address:* Instituto Diego Velazquez, Medinaceli, 4, Madrid.

ANHALT, H. Highness Anastasia Prinzess of; painter in oil, mainly of flowers;

b 25 July, 1901; *m* in 1935, H.H. Eugen Prince of Anhalt, Duke of Saxony; one *d*. *Educ.:* University of Munich (Dr. of Nationalökonomie, 1925); *studied art* at Munich under Jules Fehr and Prof. Heymann, Fellow of Franklin Institute, corresp. mem. of Fine Arts Academy "San Telmo" Malaga, la grande Medaille de "San Telmo." *Exhib.:* Gallery Bernheim, Paris, 1934. *Works repro.:* L'art de la peinture des fleurs (Academy of Sciences, Letters and Arts, Modena, Italy, 1956), La peinture de la fleur vivante et l'œuvre d'Anastasia Jung, by Prof. E. Schaub-Koch (1956). *Address:* La Tour de Peilz, Vaud, Suisse, 102 avenue de Sully.

ANNAN, Dorothy, S.M.P.; painter, mosaicist, potter, mural painter; teacher Bath College of Art (1949). *Exhib.:* R.A., N.E.A.C., London Group, etc.; one-man show, Leicester Gallery (1947). *Work in permanent collections:* Manchester, Brighton, Stoke-on-Trent, Leicester, Bodmin, Loughborough, New Zealand. *Official purchases:* Mosaic panels Durham University Library; represented Berlin Building Exhbn. (1957), tiled mural Bank of England Returned Note Building (1960), 9 tiled murals P.O. Building, Farringdon St. (1961), ceramic fountain Oadby Junior School, Leics. (1961), 5 mosaic panels for Lloyds Bank, SW1 (1962-63), glass mural L.C.C. Caley Primary School (1966). *Work repro.:* R.A. catalogue, R.I.B.A. Journal, Studio, Hutchinson's Encyclopedia, French publications. *Address:* 14B Downshire Hill, London NW3. *Club:* W.I.A.C.

ANNIGONI, Pietro, Accademia, S. Luca, Roma, and Cherubini Firenze, Accademia Arti del Disegno, Firenze, Royal Soc. of Portrait Painters; artist in oil, tempera, fresco; *b* Milan, 7 June, 1910; *s* of Ricciardo Annigoni, engineer; *m* Anna Maggini; one *s*, one *d*. *Educ.:* Accademia Belle Arti, Firenze. *Exhib.:* at Rome, Turin, R.A., Paris, Milan, London, New York, San Francisco. *Work in permanent collections:* Galleria Arte Moderna, Milan, Print Room, Uffizi, Firenze, Metropolitan Museum, New York. *Address:* Borgo Albizi 8, Florence, Italy. *Signs work:* see appendix.

ANSELL, Norah; sculptor in wood and ivory; *b* 6 July, 1906; *d* of W. H. G. Ansell; *studied art* at Birmingham College of Arts and Crafts (evenings, under William Bloye). *Exhib.:* R.A., Carlebach Gallery, New York, seven pieces in collection of Dr. S. A. Schneidman, New York. *Address:* Flat 9, 47 York Rd., Edgbaston, Birmingham. *Signs work:* "Norah Ansell," on sculpture "N.A."

ANSON, Peter Frederick, R.S.M.A. (founder-member, 1938); artist in water-colour, black-and-white; author; *b* Portsmouth, 22 Aug., 1889; *s* of Admiral Charles E. Anson, R.N. *Educ.:* Wixenford, Wokingham, Berks.; *studied art* at Architectural Assoc. School (1908-10) and under F. L. Griggs, R.A. (1919). *Exhib.:* R.A., R.S.A., N.E.A.C., R.H.A., G.I., R.S.M.A., etc. *Work in permanent collections:* Aberdeen Art Gallery (Macduff Harbour); Nat. Maritime Museum, Greenwich (200 drawings and water-colours of British fishing vessels and ports); National Buildings Records (100 drawings of churches); Maritime Museum, Buckie, Banffshire (450 water-colours composing a panorama of the Scottish fishing industry). *Work repro.:* in 14 books by himself. *Address:* Caldey Island, off Tenby, Dyfed, S. Wales. *Signs work:* "Peter F. Anson" or "P.F.A."

ANTRIM, Angela Christina, the Countess of, R.U.A.; sculptor, stone carving, bronze, terra-cotta; *b* Sledmere, Malton, Yorks, 6 Sept., 1911; *d* of the late Sir Mark Sykes, Bt., M.P.; *m* the Earl of Antrim; two *s*, one *d*. *Educ.:* privately; *studied art* at Brussels, studio of M. d'Haveloose (1927-32), British School in Rome. *Exhib.:* R.A., R.U.A., R.H.A., Whitechapel A.G., Living Art Exhbn., Dublin, one-man show, Beaux Arts Gallery, London (1937), Belfast (1949) and Hamet Gallery—cartoons (1972). *Work in permanent collections:* Northern Ireland Hospitals Authority, R.U.A. *Work repro.:* Tatler, Sketch, Country Life, La Revue

Moderne, etc. *Address:* Glenarm Castle, Co. Antrim, N. Ireland. *Signs work:* "A.A."

APPEL, Karel; painter in oil; First Prize for Painting in Pittsburgh International (1958); *b* Amsterdam, 1921. *Studied art* at Royal Academy of Fine Arts, Amsterdam. *Exhib.:* Holland (19 46), Paris and New York (1954), Paris, Holland (1955), Germany, Switzerland, London. *Work in permanent collections:* Stedelijk Museum, Amsterdam, Tate Gallery. *Address:* c/o Arthur Tooth & Sons Ltd., Bruton St., London W1. *Signs work:* "K. Appel."

APPLETON, Richard William, M.I.E.D., A.I.A.L.; artist in oil, water-colour; chief draughtsman, Merseyside and N. Wales Electricity Board, No. 4 Sub-area; Chairman E. Denbighshire Art Soc. (Sept., 1953-58); *b* Norwich, 10 Sept., 1909; *s* of Cubitt Walter Appleton, electrical engineer; *m* Kathleen Mary Roberts; two *s*. *Educ.:* City of Norwich School; *studied art* in life-class, Denbighshire Technical College (figure drawing only). *Exhib.:* R.Cam.A., R.O.I., R.W.E.A., Royal National Eisteddfod of Wales, N. Wales Group, Federation of Art Societies Exhbns., local exhbns. (N. Wales), Atkinson Art Gallery, Southport. *Address:* 73 Mold Rd., Wrexham, Clwyd. *Club:* Wrexham Art Group. *Signs work:* "Richard Appleton."

ARCHAMBAULT, Louis, B.A., University of Montreal (1936), R.A.I.C. Allied Arts Medal (1958), Officer, Order of Canada (1968), R.C.A. Academician (1968); fellowships: Canadian Government (1953), Canada Council (1959, 1962, 1969); sculptor in metal; professor, University of Quebec; *b* Montreal, 4 Apr., 1915; *s* of A. S. Archambault, lawyer; *m* Mariette Provost; three *s*. *Educ.:* Jesuit educated; *studied art:* ceramic at École des Beaux-Arts of Montreal; self-taught in sculpture. *Exhib.:* festivals: Britain (1951), 10th and 11th Milan (1954, 1957), XXVIIIth Venice (1956), Brussels Universal (1958), Pittsburgh International (1958), Montreal Expo 67, 300 Years of Canadian Art, National Gallery, Ottawa (1967). *Work in permanent collections:* Montreal: Place des Arts, Canadian Imperial Bank of Commerce, Fraser-Hickson Library; Ottawa: National Gallery, Airport, City Hall, Canadian Exhibition Commission; Quebec: Musée de la Province; Toronto: Art Gallery, Airport, Sun Life Building, Queen's Park, Scarborough College; Faenza: Museo Internazionale della Ceramica. *Address:* 278 Sanford Ave., St. Lambert, Quebec, Canada J4P 2X6. *Signs work:* "Archambault."

ARCHER, Patricia Margaret Alice, Slade Diploma (1947), A.T.D. (1948), M.M.A.A. (1951), F.M.A.A. (1969), A.I.M.B.I. (1969); Hon. Sec. of the Medical Artists' Assoc. of Gt. Britain (1964-68), artist in oil, water-colour, ross-board, pen and ink; medical artist, all types of medical illustration and displays, including models; assistant artist at Moorfields Eye Hospital (1948-49), artist to London Hospital Medical College (1949-57), artist to the Plastic Burns and Oral Surgery Centre, Rooksdown House, Basingstoke, Hants (1957-59); transferred to Queen Mary's Hospital, Roehampton (Westminster Hospital Teaching Group) (1959-64); appointed Head of the Department of Medical Illustration, Guy's Hospital, London, in April, 1964; *b* Westminster; *d* of Henry P. Archer. *Educ.:* Convent of Sacred Heart of Mary, Chilton, Bucks; *studied art* at Slade School of Fine Art. *Exhib.:* Walker's Galleries (1947), M.A.A. exhbns., London and Manchester (1952), London (1955); one-man show at London Hospital (1955). *Work repro.:* Numerous medical books and in all medical, dental and scientific journals. *Address:* Rangemore, Park Ave., Caterham, Surrey. *Signs work:* "Archer."

ARCHER, William, A.R.C.A. (1955); draughtsman and artist in oil and sculptor; lecturer, Leeds College of Art; *b* Thornley (Co. Durham), 12 Sept.,

1928; *s* of Thomas R. Archer. *Educ.:* Durham School; *studied art* at Sunderland College of Art (1946, 1949-52) and R.C.A. (1952-55). *Exhib.:* R.A. (1954-57) and Northern Artists, R.S.A. (1957), S.E.A. *Official purchases:* Art Introduction Scheme, Northumberland Educ. Authority. *Address:* 3 The Gables, Thornley, Durham. *Signs work:* "William Archer."

ARCHIBALD, John, A.T.D. (1952), F.R.S.A. (1952), Mem. of Textile Inst. (1952), M.S.I.A. (1954), L.R.A.M. (1954); free-lance textile designer; *b* Stretton-on-Fosse, 19 Dec., 1930. *Educ.:* Chipping Campden Grammar School; *studied art* at Birmingham College of Art under Mr. Smith, Miss Mackay, Mr. J. Frith, Mr. Rossetti, Mrs. Burroughs (1947-52). *Exhib.:* Rayon Industry Design Centre, London, Cotton Board, Manchester, Birmingham Art Gallery. *Address:* Dalry, 8 Beauchamp Rd., Chedgrave, Loddon, Norwich, Norfolk.

ARDIZZONE, Edward, C.B.E., R.A., R.D.I., (Hon.) A.R.C.A.; water-colour painter, lithographer, official war artist (1940-45); *b* 10 Oct., 1900; *s* of Auguste Ardizzone; *m*; two *s*, one *d*. *Educ.:* Clayesmore School; Westminster School of Art (Bernard Meninsky, 1921-26). *Official purchases:* Tate Gallery, provincial galleries. *Work repro.:* illustrations to more than 150 books. *Publications:* Tim and the Brave Sea Captain, and many books for children. *Address:* No. 5 Vine Cottages, Rodmersham Green, Sittingbourne, Kent. *Signs work:* "E.A." or "Edward Ardizzone" or "DIZ."

ARGAN, Giulio Carlo, C.I.A.M.; professor of History of Art. University of Rome; *b* Turin, 17 May, 1909. *Educ.:* University of Turin. *Publications:* about ancient and modern art, Roman and Gothic architecture in Italy (1936-37), Borromini (1952), Brunelleschi (1955), Angelico (1955), Botticelli (1957), Modern Art and Architecture (W. Gropius, 1951), Marcel Breuer (1957), sculpture (H. Moore, 1948). Studi e Note (1955), Salvezza e caduta nell'arte moderna (1964), L'Europa delle capitali (1964), Progetto e destino (1965), The Renaissance City (1969), Storia dell'arte italiano (1968-70), Dal Bramante al Canova (1969), L'arte moderna 1770-1970 (1971). *Address:* via Gaetano Sacchi 20, Roma, Italy. *Signs work:* "Giulio Carlo Argan."

ARMAN, Frederic Marcus, F.F.P.S. (1965), F.R.S.A.; former curator, National Postal Museum, London; sculptor in wood and cast metal; *b* Ipswich, 1908; *s* of Henry Marcus Arman; *m* Kitt Fookes; one *s*, one *d*. *Educ.:* Monmouth School. *Exhib.:* F.P.S. Trends, Stockwell College, Bromley, British Week, Pittsburg, U.S.A., Bexley Old Hall, New Metropole Gallery, Folkestone, Lincoln Cathedral, etc. *Publication:* The R. M. Phillips Collection of 19th Century British Postage Stamps. *Address:* 28 Rodway Rd., Bromley, Kent. *Club:* R.S.A. *Signs work:* "Arman."

ARMFIELD, Diana M. (Mrs. Bernard Dunstan), M.S.I.A., N.E.A.C., R.W.A.; painter, textile and wallpaper designer, freelance designs for leading wallpaper manufacturers; taught at Central School, tutor at Byam Shaw School of Art; *b* Ringwood, Hants, 1920; *d* of Harold Armfield; three *s*. *Educ.:* Bedales, Slade School, Central School. *Exhib.:* Festival of Britain; one-man shows, paintings at R.A., R.W.A., N.E.A.C., New Grafton, Royal Cambrian Academy, Tegfryn Gall., Bruton Gall., etc. *Work in permanent collections:* V. & A., R.W.A. *Work repro.:* designs in House & Garden, Design, paintings in The Artist, Studio Vista and Watson-Guptill publications. *Address:* 10 High Park Rd., Kew, Surrey. *Signs work:* "D.M.A."

ARMFIELD, Stuart Maxwell; artist in egg tempera; Assistant Art Director, Ealing Film Studios (1935-40); *b* Sanderstead, Surrey, 24 May, 1916; *s* of Leonard Armfield. *Educ.:* Sidcot School, Somerset; *studied art* at W. of England

College of Art. *Exhib.:* R.A., Plymouth Municipal Galleries, St. Ives Soc., R.W.S., also in New York, Newlyn Soc., R.I., Arthur Jeffries Gallery. *Work repro.:* in Studio, Artist, Medici Publications, etc. *Publication:* Tempera Painting (Artist Publishing Co.) *Address:* 1666 House Studio, Fore St., Looe, Cornwall. *Clubs:* E. Cornwall Soc. of Artists, St. Ives Soc., Plymouth Soc. *Signs work:* "Stuart Armfield."

ARMITAGE, Joshua Charles; freelance artist in black and white and colour; *b* Hoylake, Cheshire, 26 Sept., 1913; *s* of Joshua Armitage; *m* Catherine Mary Buckle; two *d*. *Studied* at Liverpool School of Art (1929-36). *Work repro.:* Punch, Amateur Gardening, Financial Times, etc. *Publications:* 100th Open Championship at Royal Birkdale and illustrations for many books for adults and for children. Many water-colour drawings with golf as the subject. *Address:* 34 Avondale Rd., Hoylake, Cheshire. *Clubs:* Deeside Art Group (President) and Royal Liverpool Golf. *Signs work:* "Ionicus."

ARMITAGE, Kenneth; sculptor; *b* 18 July, 1916. *Address:* 22A Avonmore Rd., London W14.

ARMOUR, Mary, A.R.S.A. (1941), R.S.W. (1956), R.S.A. (1958); artist in oil, water-colour; *b* Blantyre, Lanarkshire, 27 Mar., 1902; *d* of William Steel, iron-dresser; *m* William Armour. *Educ.:* Low Blantyre Public School; Hamilton Academy; *studied art* at Glasgow School of Art under D. Forrester Wilson, R.S.A., Maurice Grieffenhagen, R.A. (1920-25). *Exhib.:* R.A., R.S.A., S.S.A., Royal Glasgow Institute. *Work in permanent collections:* Glasgow Municipal Gallery, Greenock A.G., Victoria (Australia), Paisley A.G., Aberdeen A.G., Perth A.G., Edinburgh A.G. *Work repro.:* The Studio. *Address:* 2 Gateside, Kilbarchan, Renfrewshire. *Signs work:* "Mary Armour."

ARMOUR, William, R.S.A. (1966), R.S.W. (1941); artist in oil, water-colour, pastel, wood-engraving; *b* Paisley, Renfrewshire, 20 Aug., 1903; *s* of Hugh Armour, designer; *m* Mary Armour. *Educ.:* Paisley; *studied art* at Glasgow School of Art (1918-23) under Maurice Greiffenhagen. *Work in permanent collections:* R.S.A., Belfast, Aberdeen, Perth, Paisley, Glasgow, Greenock, Milngavie art galleries, Arts Council (Scotland). *Address:* 2 Gateside Pl., Kilbarchan, Renfrewshire. *Club:* Glasgow Art. *Signs work:* "Wm. Armour."

ARMSTRONG, Arthur Charlton; artist in oil, water-colour, etchings, etc.; *b* Carrickfergus, Co. Antrim, 12 Jan., 1924; *studied art:* self-taught. *Work in permanent collections:* Arts Council, (N. of Ireland); Arts Council (Irish Republic); Belfast Museum and Art Gallery; Waterford Art Gallery; Cork Museum; many Irish public and private collections, also in England, U.S.A., Spain, France, Canada. *Address:* 28 Chelmsford Ave., Ranelagh, Dublin 6, Ireland. *Clubs:* Arts Club, Dublin and Belfast. *Signs work:* "Armstrong."

ARMSTRONG, Shearer; painter; *b* London; *d* of D. F. Shearer, F.R.C.S.; *m* Henry Armstrong, M.C. *Studied art:* Karlsruhe and Slade School. Fellow of the Royal Society of Arts; founder member of the Penwith Society of Arts in Cornwall. *One-man exhbns.:* Edinburgh (1959, 1963), London (1961, 1963). *Mixed exhbns.:* R.A., R.S.A., Cornish Artists, Plymouth; Arts Council Travelling Exhibitions; John Moores Liverpool Exhibition; C.E.M.A. Open Exhibitions, Belfast; Provence Festival of Arts (Château de Blauvac); British Columbia (Kootenay School); Toronto; many municipal galleries England, Scotland. *Paintings bought* by H.R.H. Prince Philip, Duke of Edinburgh; Scottish Education Committee, Edinburgh; Kingston-upon-Hull Education Committee; Cornwall Education Authority; private collectors. *Address:* 9 Porthmeor Studios, St. Ives, Cornwall. *Signs work:* "Shearer Armstrong."

ARMSTRONG, Tim, B.A. (1975), London University Postgraduate Diploma in Fine Art (1969); lecturer, Glasgow School of Art; *b* Cambridge, 27 July, 1945; *s* of Edward A. Armstrong. *Educ.:* St. Mark's Vicarage, Newnham, Cambridge; Walberswick, Suffolk; *studied art* at Cambridgeshire College of Arts and Technology (1962-64); Nottingham College of Art and Design (1964-67); Slade School of Fine Art (1967-69). *Exhib.:* in England, Scotland, Wales, Republic of Ireland, Germany, France and U.S.A. *Work in permanent collections:* Doncaster Museum and A.G.; Australian National University; Glasgow Corp.; Scottish Arts Council; Biochemical Laboratory, Cambridge University; Sidhartha Films, Edinburgh; Strathclyde Regional Council. *Work repro.:* illustrated Physiology of Mammals and other Vertebrates by P. T. Marshall and G. M. Hughes (C.U.P., 1965). *Address:* 32 Bankhead Rd., Waterside, Kirkintilloch, Dunbartonshire. *Memberships:* Art Information Registry; Scottish Artists' Registry; Glasgow League of Artists; Edinburgh Printmakers' Workshop; British Printmakers' Council; Friends of the Earth; Conservation Society. *Signs work:* "Tim Armstrong."

ARNOLD, Charles Geoffrey, Dip. Fine Art, Slade School (1950), R.W.A. (1952); artist in oil and water-colour; teacher; studio artist with Marshall Hardy Ltd., advertising agents (1935-40); *b* Clayton, Yorks, 28 March, 1915; *s* of Will Arnold. *Educ.:* Bradford Grammar School (1927-31); *studied art* at Bradford College of Art under Henry Butler (1931-34), Camberwell School of Art (1946-47), Slade School under Professors Schwabe and Coldstream (1947-50). *Exhib.:* R. A., London Group, R.W.A. *Address:* The Cottage, 2 Town-end Rd., Clayton, Bradford, Yorks. *Signs work:* "C. G. Arnold."

ARNOLD, William Arthur, Committee member Armed Forces Art Society, A.W.G., Bucks. Art Society; commercial artist in water-colour and scraperboard; *b* Leytonstone, 4 Dec., 1909; *s* of W. A. Arnold; *m* Lena Ethel; one *s*. *Educ.:* Leyton School of Art. *Exhib.:* R.A., Army Art Soc., Britain in Water-colour Exhbn. regularly each year, one-man show at Towner Art Gallery, Eastbourne (1947). *Official purchase:* Pakistan Government (water-colour). *Address:* 7 White Close, St. Andrew's Green, Bridport, Dorset. *Signs work:* "WILLIAM A. ARNOLD" (with horizontal stroke from base of last letter).

ARROBUS, Sydney; water-colourist, collagist and commercial artist; *b* 17 June, 1901. *Studied art* at Heatherleys. *Exhib.:* R.B.A., R.I., N.S., R.W.E.A., S.G.A., City of London Art Exhbn., Armed Forces Art Soc., Bradford City Art Gallery, Hampstead Artists Council, Ben Uri Art Gallery; one-man shows, Walker's Galleries (Nov., 1953), Woodstock Gallery (1958), John Whibley Gallery (1960), Gallery Vincitore, (1965, 1968), Cooling Gallery (1966, 1968, 1969), Assembly House, Norwich (1967, 1968), Fairfield Halls, Croydon (1968, 1969), Fitzhamon Art Centre, Tewkesbury (1970), Everyman Foyer Gallery (1967, 1970, 1973, 1974, 1975). *Official purchases:* New College and Lincoln College, Oxford, London Borough Camden, London Borough Islington, City of Westminster. *Address:* Studio A, 119 Haverstock Hill, London NW3. *Signs work:* see appendix.

ARTHUR, Herbert Henry Gascoign, F.L.A. (1948), F.R.S.A. (1949), M.B.I.M. (1974), Mem., Museums Assoc. (1949); Chief Librarian and Arts Officer, Wirral, Curator of Art Galleries and Museums; formerly held library and museum posts at Bristol and Blackpool, and as Borough Librarian and Curator, Buxton (1949-50), Director of Libraries and Arts, Wigan (1950-68), Borough Librarian and Director, Williamson A.G. and Museum, Birkenhead (1968-1974); *b* Bristol, 30 June, 1920; *s* of H. J. M. Arthur of Liverpool; *m* Kathleen Joan Fuge; one *s*, one *d*. *Educ.:* Bristol Cathedral School; *studied art* at West of England

College of Art. *Publications:* History of Haigh Hall; Guide to the Williamson A.G. and Museum; Guide to the Wirral Maritime Museum; Lee Tapestry Room. *Address:* 20 Christchurch Rd., Oxton, Birkenhead.

ASCHAN, Marit Guinness; enamellist and painter; *d* of H. S. H. Guinness; formerly *m* to C. W. Aschan; one *s*, one *d*. *Exhib.:* R.A., Leicester Galleries, etc.; one-man shows, Beaux Arts, International Faculty of Arts, The Leicester Galleries, London; The Minories, Colchester; Lilienfeld Gallery and Van Diemen-Lilienfeld Galleries, New York; Parrish Art Museum, Southampton, New York; Oslo Kunstforening, Norway; Inter Art Gallery, Caracas, Venezuela; Waldhorn Gallery, New Orleans, Louisiana; Bodley Gallery, New York; Galleri Galtung, Oslo, Norway. *Work in permanent collections:* Central enamel on Louis Osman Cross, Exeter Cathedral; J. R. Abbey Coll.; Worshipful Company of Goldsmiths, London; Brooklyn Museum; New York University Art Coll.; Finch College Art Coll.; Fordham University Art Coll.; Lincoln Center; Rochester Art Gallery, N.Y.; Parrish Art Museum, Southampton, N.Y.; Yale University Art Gallery; Nelson Gallery and Atkins Museum, Kansas City, Missouri; University of Kansas Museum of Art, Lawrence, Kansas; North Carolina State Museum, Raleigh; Weatherspoon Art Gallery, University of North Carolina, Greensboro; New Orleans Museum of Art, Louisiana; Kunstindustrimuseet. Oslo; Royal Norwegian Foreign Office, Norway.*Addresses:* (residence) 25 Chelsea Park Gdns., London SW3; (studio) Moravian Close, 381 King's Rd., London SW3.

ASHBY, Derek Joseph, D.A. (Edin.); artist in steel and aluminium; lecturer in drawing and painting, Gray's School of Art, Aberdeen; *b* 24 June, 1926; *s* of Oswald Roy Ashby; *m* Mairi Catriona; one *s*, one *d*. *Educ.:* Oldham High School; *studied art* at Edinburgh College of Art (1948-51) under Gillies, Henderson, Blyth; R.A. Schools (1953-55) under Rushbury. *Exhib.:* R.S.A., Aberdeen Artists, S.S.A. *Work in permanent collection:* Scottish Arts Council. *Address:* Old Invery, Auchattie, Banchory, Kincardineshire. *Clubs:* A.A.S., S.S.A. *Signs work:* "D. Ashby."

ASHE, Faith: see WINTER, Faith.

ASHER, Florence May, F.R.S.A., R.B.A.; painter in oils; *b* 2 May, 1888; *d* of J. W. Asher. *Educ.:* Nottingham; *studied art* at Royal Academy Schools, 1913-18. *Exhib.:* All leading galleries. *Address:* 2 Yorke Gdns., Reigate, Surrey. *Signs work:* "F. M. Asher."

ASHTON-BOSTOCK, David A., F.I.A.L. (1960), N.D. (1950), intermed. (1949); artist in oil and interior decorator; member of I.D.D.A. Ltd.; *b* London, 17 Feb., 1932; *s* of Cdr. J. Bostock, D.S.C., R.N. (retd.) (additional surname Ashton assumed by deed poll); *m* Victoria Rosamont White; one *d*. *Educ.:* Wellington College; *studied art* at Maidstone College of Art (1947-50) under A. G. Cary and W. Eade, Byam Shaw School of Art (1953-54) under P. E. Philips. *Exhib.:* United Artists, Nat. Soc., R.B.A., N.E.A.C., R.O.I., Paris Salon, Summer Salon, Chelsea Artists, City of London Artists, Ridley Art Club, Hambledon Galleries (Blandford). *Work repro.:* La Revue Moderne, Queen, Country Life, Times, Sunday Express, Christmas cards, posters. *Addresses:* Wormshill House, nr. Sittingbourne, Kent; 11 Westmoreland Pl., London SW1. *Club:* Ridley Art. *Signs work:* "Ashtock."

ASKEW, Victor, Council R.O.I., F.I.A.L., P.S., medal, Paris Salon (1969), Chantrey Bequest (R.A.); artist in oil (palette knife specialist), water-colour, acrylic, pastel; *b* Rotherham, 1 Feb., 1909; *m* Margaret Mitchell Askew, artist. *Educ.:* Sheffield; *studied art* at Sheffield College of Arts. *Work in permanent collections:* Chantrey Bequest (R.A.), Municipal Galleries Preston, Toronto,

Winnipeg, Ottawa. *Publications:* Painting for Everyone (George Rowneys), articles in The Artist. *Address:* East Cottage Studio, Ashendene, Bayford, Herts. *Club:* Cricketers. *Signs work:* see appendix.

ASPDEN, Ruth Spencer, A.R.E., A.R.C.A.; *d* of W. E. Aspden, timber merchant; *m* Robert Rutter; one *d. Studied art* at Blackburn School of Art and Royal College of Art. *Exhib.:* R.A., R.E., principal provincial cities in Britain, Canada and U.S.A. *Official purchases:* Blackburn Art Gallery. *Works repro.:* The Artist, photographic works in Encyclopedia of Gardening, Mind Alive, Discovering English Gardens, Evening Standard. *Address:* Flat 4, 181/3 Warwick Rd., Kensington, London W14. *Signs work:* "Ruth Aspden" and "Ruth Rutter."

ASPLUND, Karl, M.A. (1915), Professor's title (1964); author, formerly Managing Director of A.-B. H. Bukowskis Konsthandel, Stockholm, and P. Bellman Soc., Stockholm; *b* 1890, Jäder, Södermanland, Sweden; *s* of Conrad Asplund, merchant; *m* Elvira Sjödin; one *d. Educ.:* Stockholm High School and Uppsala University. *Publications:* Anders Zorn, His Life and Work (Studio, 1920), Zorn's Engraved Work (1920), Hj. Wicander's Collection of Portrait Miniatures (1920, 1929), P. A. Hall's Correspondence de Famille (1955), and many others. *Address:* Rådmansgatan 17, Stockholm. *Club:* Sällskapet, Stockholm.

ASSCHER, Sofy, certified teacher, Amsterdam; oil painter of portraits, flowers and miniatures; *b* 29 Sept., 1901; *d* of the late Benjamin Asscher; *m* Ronald J. Horton. *Educ.:* Zaandam High School; *studied art* at Girls' Art School, Amsterdam. *Exhib.:* Leger Galleries, Tooth's, R.A., United Soc. of Artists, one-man show at Foyle's; Middlesbrough, Brighouse, Worcester, Stretford (Longford Hall Art Gallery), Cooling Galleries. *Work in permanent collection:* Preparatory School, Alcester, Warwicks. *Work repro.:* Auto Sport Italiana, Autosport, Sketch, John Bull and privately. *Address:* 11 Bainbridge Cl., Heathfield Rd., Seaford, Sussex. *Clubs:* New Arts, New Century. *Signs work:* "S. Asscher," "Sofy Asscher."

ASTON, Evelin Winifred, F.R.S.A.; sculptor and painter, artist in oils and wood; *d* of Walter E. Aston. *Educ.:* Privately; *studied art* at Birmingham College of Art and under B. Fleetwood-Walker, A.R.A. *Exhib.:* London, R.S.A., Paris Salon. *Work repro.:* Paris Salon illustrated catalogue. *Address:* 176 Shortheath Rd., Erdington, Birmingham. *Club:* Art Circle and Soroptimist Club. *Signs work:* "Evelin W. Aston."

ATKIN, Ron, R.A.S. (1961), F.R.S.A. (1962); artist in water-colour, oil and acrylic; tutor, Beaford Centre, N. Devon; *b* Leicestershire, 1938; *s* of O. R. Atkin, signwriter, glass guilder; *m* Ann Fawssett; two *s. Educ.:* Limehurst Boys' School; *studied art* at Loughborough College of Art (1954-57); Royal Academy Schools (1957-61). *Exhib.:* Roland, Browse & Delbanco, R.A., Beaford Centre, Plymouth City Museum and A.G. *Work in permanent collections:* Dartington Trust, Dartington Hall, Devon; Devon C.C. Museum Service; Roman Catholic School, Leics.; Lincoln College, Oxford; Plymouth City Museum and A.G. *Work repro.:* Apollo. *Address:* The Old Rectory, West Putford, Devon EX22 7XE. *Signs work:* "Ron Atkin."

ATKINSON, Anthony Claude, A.R.C.A. (1954); painter in oil; Head, Colchester School of Art (1964), Senior Examiner, Cambridge Institute for Education; *b* London, 20 July, 1929; *s* of Claude Atkinson, publicity executive and artist; *m* Joan Irving Dawson; one *s*, David, one *step-d*, Juanita. *Educ.:* Wimbledon College; *studied art* at Royal College of Art, 4th Year Scholarship. *Exhib.:* R.A., Leicester Galleries; one-man exhbns., Minories Museum, Colchester (1962, 1967 and 1970), Hitchin Museum (1971), Leighton House, London (1965), Gainsborough's House, Sudbury (1973), Mercury Theatre, Colchester (1974). *Work repro.:* Shell Co., London Transport posters, G.P.O. *Address:* Coach House, Great Horkesley, Colchester, Essex. *Signs work:* "ATKINSON."

ATKINSON, Edward, D.F.A. (Lond., 1952), A.R.B.S. (1957), F.R.S.A. (1957), Slade Prize Winner (1952); sculptor; Head of Sculpture School, Coventry College of Art; *b* Liverpool, 21 Mar., 1929; *s* of Edward Atkinson, musician. *Educ.:* Oulton School, Liverpool; *studied art* at Liverpool College of Art (under Karel Vogel), Slade School, Univ. of London (under Butler, Moore), Slade Post-graduate Scholar (1952-53). *Work in permanent collections:* Arts Council, London, Dallas Art Museum, Keele Univ., Kunst Academie, Dresden, Manchester Art Gallery, Museum of Modern Art, N.Y., Seattle Art Museum, Tate Gallery, Univ. of Exeter, etc.; civic sculptures in Coventry (Precinct), Dusseldorf and Exeter. *Address:* c/o College of Art, Gosford St., Coventry. *Signs work:* see appendix.

ATKINSON, Eric Newton; Mem. N.E.A.C. (1955); painter in oils and collage; Dean, Applied Arts, Fanshawe College, London, Ontario; Nat. Dipl. (1st hons., painting), R.A. Drawing Medal, Silver Medal for Painting; *b* West Hartlepool, 23 July, 1928; *s* of James Atkinson; *m* Muriel H. Ross; one *s*, one *d*. *Educ.:* Dyke House, W. Hartlepool; *studied art* at W. Hartlepool College of Art and R.A. Schools. *Exhib.:* Redfern Gallery, Tate Gallery, Austin Hayes, York, Leeds Univ., Wakefield and Middlesbrough city galleries, Zwemmer Gallery, Corcoran Gallery, Washington, D.C., Rothman Gallery, Ontario, Kingpitcher Gallery, Pittsburgh, Morse, Capponi Gallery, Detroit. *Work in permanent collections:* Contemporary Art Soc., Ministry of Works, Leeds, Leicester, Wakefield, Hereford and Kendal A.G., Leeds City Art Library Collection, U.W.O., Ontario, San Antonio Arts Inst., Texas, Ford Foundation, U.S.A. *Address:* 69 Paddock Green Cres., London 64, Ontario, Canada. *Signs work:* "Eric Atkinson."

ATKINSON, Marshall Forster, F.R.S.A. (1944), President's award for painting (1952-53), R.G.I. (1954), A.M.S. (1956), C.I.A.L., Mem. Free Painters Group, cert. of merit, S.E.F.A.S. (1962); artist in oil, water-colour, pastel, gouache, pen and ink, carbon pencils, etc.; *b* Gateshead, 18 Aug., 1913; *m* E. R. Harlund; one *s*, one *d*. *Educ.:* Redheugh School; *studied art* at King's College, Newcastle. *Exhib.:* Manchester A.G. Arts Exhbn. Bureau, Municipal Galleries, Britain at Play, N.E.A.C., R.W.E.A., P.S., R.I., S.G.A., N.S., U.A., R.G.I., R.B.A., R.W.S., B.W.C., R.C.A., R. Cam.A., S.E.F.A.S., Paris Salon, Laing A.G., Westgate A.G., Univision Gallery, Newcastle, Sunderland and Middlesbrough Galleries, one-man exhbn. Shipley A.G. (1952). Chairman 10 years (one-man exhbns.). *Work in permanent collections:* Shipley A.G. *Official purchases:* Picture Lending Libraries, Extra Murals: Newcastle University, private collections, etc. *Work repro.:* Art News and Review, FPG News, Univision Modern Art, Durham and Gateshead, The Sign, La Revue Moderne, Evening Chronicle, Northern Echo Journal, Gateshead Post. *Address:* 62 Bensham Ct., Rectory Rd., Gateshead, Tyne & Wear NE8 1XX. *Clubs:* Gateshead Art Soc. (founder member), Park Road Group, Univision Group, Avant Club. *Signs work:* "M.F.A."

AUERBACH, Arnold; sculptor, painter and etcher; former Lecturer, Polytechnic Art School, Regent St., and Chelsea Polytechnic; *b* Liverpool, 11 Apr., 1898; *s* of Jonas Auerbach; *m* Jean M. Campbell. *Educ.:* Liverpool Institute; *studied art* at Liverpool City School of Arts, Paris, etc. *Exhib.:* R.A., Goupil, W.A.G., Newcastle, Brighton, etc. *Work repro.:* Modern Architectural Sculpture by William Aumonier, British Sculpture 1944-46, by Eric Newton, Encyclopædia Britannica (Sculpture, Technique). *Publications:* Sculpture (Paul Elek), Modelled Sculpture and Plastercasting (Elek Books, London, and Thos. Yoseloff, U.S.A.), 1961.

Address: 152 Holland Rd., Kensington, London W14. *Signs work:* "ARNOLD AUERBACH," or "A. Auerbach" (sculpture and paintings). Written signature (drawings and etchings).

AUERBACH, Erna, Dr.Phil. (Frankf.), Ph.D. (Lond.); Art Historian, Lecturer City of London Polytechnic and other centres of adult education; *b* Frankfort/Main; *d* of the late Dr. Ernst Auerbach, Mem. of the Bar of Frankfort, Pres. Frankfort Bar Assoc., Mem. Bar Council of Frankfort. *Studied history of art* at Universities of Frankfort, Bonn, Munich and Courtauld Institute; *studied painting* under Baumeister, Cissarz, etc. *Exhib.:* W.I.A.C., etc. *Publications:* Tudor Artists (Athlone Press, 1954), Nicholas Hilliard (Routledge & Kegan Paul, 1961), Paintings and Sculptures of Hatfield House (jointly with C. Kingsley Adams, Constable, 1972); articles in Burlington Magazine, Connoisseur, Apollo, Archives, etc. *Address:* 15 Gale Hill Ct., London W11. *Clubs:* W.I.A.C., B.F.U.W.

AUERBACH, Frank Helmuth; painter; *b* Berlin, 29 Apr., 1931; *s* of Max Auerbach, lawyer, and Charlotte Norah Auerbach. *Educ.:* privately; St. Martin's School of Art; R.C.A. *Exhib.:* one-man shows: Beaux-Arts Gallery (1956, 1959, 1961, 1962, 1963); Marlborough Fine Art (1965, 1967, 1971, 1974); Marlborough-Gerson, N.Y. (1969); Villiers, Sydney, Australia (1972); Galleria Bergamini, Milan (1973); University of Essex, Colchester (1973); group exhbns.: Carnegie International, Pittsburgh (1958, 1962); Dunn International, Fredericton (1963); Gulbenkian International, Tate Gallery (1964); Palazzo Reale, Genoa (1972); Basle Fair (1975); Los Angeles County Museum (1975), etc. *Work in permanent collections:* Tate Gallery, London; National Gallery of Victoria, Melbourne; Chrysler Museum, Provincetown; Univ. of Cincinnati; Bedford, Hull, Leeds, Manchester, Nottingham, Oldham Galleries; Arts Council, Contemporary Art Society, etc. *Address:* c/o Marlborough Fine Art Ltd., 6 Albemarle St., London W1X 3HF.

AULD, John Leslie M., D.A. Belfast, A.R.C.A., N.R.D., F.I.A.L.; art teacher, designer-craftsman in goldsmiths' work; head, Art Dept., Municipal Tech. College, Londonderry (1940-46); Senior Lecturer, Glasgow School of Art since 1946; *b* Belfast, 21 Jan., 1914; *s* of Joseph Auld; *m* Doreen M. W. Auld (*née* Sproul). *Educ.:* Methodist College, Belfast; *studied art* at Belfast Coll. of Art (1931-35); Royal Coll. of Art (1935-39). *Exhib.:* London, Brussels, Paris, New York, Stockholm, Arts Council, etc. *Work in permanent collections:* Goldsmiths' Company, London, New York City Corpn. *Publication:* Your Jewellery. *Address:* Braehead Rd., Thorntonhall, Glasgow. *Signs work:* "J. L. AULD," but see appendix.

AUSTIN, Frank, F.S.I.A.; industrial designer, furniture and interiors; Chairman, B.O.T. Design Panel (1947-48); Council, Soc. of Industrial Artists (1948-52); Chairman, Furniture and Interior Design Group (1951-53), Head of Department of Furniture and Interior Design, L.C.C. Central School of Arts and Crafts (1953-58); partner, Ward and Austin; *b* Letchworth, Herts; *s* of accountant, Civil Service; *m* Sigrid Christina Adams; three *s*, one *d*. *Educ.:* St. Christopher's; studied art in Germany (1930-33) and in travelling, Europe, America, China and Japan. *Addresses:* 68 Grafton Way, London W1; Springfield House, Linton, Cambs.

AVERMAETE, Roger, Grand Officier Ordre Leopold (Belgium), Officier Ordre Couronne (Belgium), Chevalier Légion d'Honneur (France), Croix Civique (1st Class), Médaille Centenaire, Médaille Croix Rouge, Prix Renaissance d'Occident, Prix Halphen (Academic Française), Prix Charles Blanc (Académie

Française), Officer of Merit (Germany), Prix Michot (Académie Royale de Langue et de Littérature françaises de Belgique), Prix de Borchgrave d'Altena; novelist, art critic, playwright; hon. prof. of art history, Institut National Superieur des Beaux Arts, honorary director, Instituut voor Kunstambachten, Member, Royal Flemish Academy of Sciences, Letters and Fine Arts of Belgium; *b* Antwerp, 27 Oct., 1893; *m* Lucienne de Kinder; one *s*. *Address:* 32 Lange Lozanastraat, Antwerp. *Signs work:* see appendix.

AYERS, Eric, A.R.C.A., M.S.I.A.; designer; *b* 12 Aug., 1921; *s* of Vivian Ayers; *m* Betty Rothenstein (*née* Fitzgerald). *Educ.:* Balgowan Grammar School; *studied art* at Beckenham School of Art, R.C.A. *Exhib.:* Design in Business Printing Exhibition, Festival of Britain (Dome of Discovery); Milwaukee Library, Wisconsin (U.S.A.); C. of I.D. "100 Good Catalogues." *Work repro.:* Graphis, Graphis Annual, Visiting Fellow, Fine Art Dept., University of Newcastle. *Address:* 4 Regent Sq., London WC1. *Signs work:* "ERIC AYERS."

AYLING, Joan, V.P., R.M.S., Paris Salon Silver Medal (1952), Gold Medal (1957); artist in tempera and water-colour on ivory; *b* Edinburgh, 16 Sept., 1907; *d* of the late John Ayling, publisher and printer; *m* Evan Robert Rees, M.D., F.R.C.O.G. *Educ.:* Convent of Our Lady of Sion and St. Mary's Abbey, Mill Hill; *studied art* at Kilburn Polytechnic, School of Arts and Crafts, Birmingham, Slade and under F. L. Griggs, R.A., etcher. *Exhib.:* Walker Art Gallery, Paris Salon, R.A. *Address:* 5 Sunnydene Lodge, Bridgewater Rd., Wembley, Middx. HA0 1AT. *Signs work:* "J. Ayling."

AYRES, Arthur James John, Prix de Rome (1931); Teacher of Carving, R.A. Schools; *b* June, 1902; *s* of James Ayres; *m* Elsa Gronvold, painter; one *s*, one *d*. *Studied art* R.A. Schools, Carlo Rossi, Paris, British School at Rome. *Exhib.:* R.A., Rome and provincial galleries. *Official purchases and commissions:* Bolton Art Gallery. Civil Defence medal for United Kingdom; medals for various dominions and protectorates. *Works to be seen* at Mitchell Engineering, Peterborough, Tyburn Convent, Marble Arch, Lagos University and Churchill Memorial, Fulton, Missouri, U.S.A. *Address:* 32 Gunter Grove, London SW10. *Club:* Chelsea Arts. *Signs work:* "Arthur J. J. Ayres."

AYRES, Gillian; painter; teacher at Bath Academy, St. Martin's since 1966; *b* Barnes, London, 3 Feb., 1930; two children. *Educ.:* St. Paul's Girls' School; *studied art* at Camberwell School of Art. *Exhib.:* group shows: Musée d'Art Moderne; Bienale de Paris, Paris (1959); Situation, London (1960-61); one-man shows, Gallery One (1956), Kasmin Gallery (1965-66, 1969), Hayward Gallery (1972). Awarded Japan International Art Promotion Association Award (1963). *Work in permanent collections:* Tate Gallery, Museum of Modern Art, N.Y. *Address:* 14 Beverley Rd., London SW13. *Signs work:* "Gillian Ayres."

AYRTON, Michael; painter, sculptor, theatre designer, book illustrator etc.; author; *b* London, 20 Feb., 1921. *Educ.:* London, Paris, Vienna, Italy. *Exhib.:* London and provinces, Dublin, Milan, Rome, Zürich, Paris, Chicago, Johannesburg, Toronto, Buffalo and N.Y. *Work in permanent collections:* Wadsworth Atheneum, Philadelphia Museum, Tel Aviv Museum, Ottawa and Montreal Art Galleries, Tate Gallery, War Artists Advisory Com., Arts Council, British Council, V. & A., National Portrait Gallery and British provincial galleries. *Publications:* Tittivulus, Sculpture and Drawings, The Testament of Daedalus, Golden Sections, The Maze-Maker, Berlioz, a Singular Obsession, Giovanni Pisano, Sculptor, The Rudiments of Paradise, Fabrications, The Midas Consequence, etc. *Address:* Bradfields, Toppesfield, Essex. *Club:* Savile. *Signs work:* see appendix.

AYRTON, Millicent E. (Mrs.), M.B.E., R.C.A. (1950); painter in oil and water-colour; teacher of private school; Chairman, Deeside Art Group; Member, Liverpool Academy of Art; *b* Hoylake, Cheshire, 23 Nov., 1913; *d* of Frederick Pollock; *m* Col. B. Ayrton (deceased); one *s*. *Educ.:* Westlands, Acton Reynold, Salop.; *studied art* at Liverpool College of Art (1930-35) under William Penn, R.O.I., R.I. *Work in permanent collections:* Keele and Liverpool Universities, Williamson Gallery, Birkenhead. *Address:* The Anchorage, Queen's Rd., Hoylake, Ches. *Signs work:* "M. E. Ayrton."

AZIZ, Philip, B.F.A. (Yale, 1947), M.F.A. (Yale, 1949), F.I.A.L. (1957); artist in egg-tempera, oil, water-colour, graphic media, stained glass, fresco; lecturer in art, University of Western Ontario, London, Canada, 1950-55; Member, University Club of Toronto, Yale Club of N.Y.C.; *b* St. Thomas, Ont., 15 Apr., 1923; *s* of Charles Aziz, deceased, born in Lebanon. *Educ.:* in secondary schools, London, Ontario; Yale and Harvard Universities; *studied art* at Yale and Harvard Universities. *Exhib.:* in Canada, U.S.A., Europe, R.S.P.P., Gallery of Modern Art, N.Y. (1969). *Work in permanent collections:* Montreal Museum of Fine Arts, the Vatican, Detroit Institute of Arts, Univ. of Toronto Art Gallery, Lincoln Centre Plaza, N.Y., public buildings in Canada and U.S.A. *Work in private collections:* in Europe, Canada and U.S.A.; Cathedrals, chapels and monasteries in Canada. *Address:* London, Canada. *Signs work:* "AZIZ," with date.

B

BAARD, Henricus Petrus; Keeper of the Frans Halsmuseum, Haarlem, Holland (1946-72); Scient. Assoc., Rijksmuseum, Amsterdam (1928-46); *b* 26 Oct., 1906; *s* of C. W. H. Baard, sometime director of Municipal Galleries, Amsterdam; *m* W. de Groot; one *s*, two *d*. *Educ.:* Amsterdam; *studied art* at Amsterdam. *Publications:* The Sea-Painters Willem van de Velde the Elder and the Younger ("Paletserie," Becht, Amsterdam); Anton Mauve ("Paletserie," Becht, Amsterdam); Kunst in Schuilkelders; N. V. Daamen, Den Haag; Hals' Schuttersmaaltijd van 1616 (Staflew, Leiden), Frans Hals Schuttersstukken; The Civic Guard Portrait Groups (Elsevier); Frans Hals Museum (The Little Art Book, edited by B. Fricke). *Address:* Pieter Keylaan, 40 Bloemendaal, Holland. *Signs work:* see appendix.

BACKHOUSE, David John, A.R.W.A.; sculptor in bronze, steel, polyester and ciment fondu; *b* Corsham, Wilts., 5 May, 1941; *s* of J. H. Backhouse; *m* Sarah Barber. *Educ.:* Lord Weymouth School, Warminster; *studied art* at West of England College of Art. *Work in collections:* R.W.A., British Steel Corp., and private collections in U.S.A. England, Belgium, France, Germany, Italy, Spain, Luxembourg. *Addresses:* 31 Pinckney Green, Farleigh Wick, Bradford-on-Avon, Wilts.; *studio:* Old Baptist Chapel, Lower Westwood, Bradford-on-Avon. *Signs work:* see appendix.

BACON, Cecil Walter, M.S.I.A.; illustrator and designer; specialist M.O.I., 1942-46; *b* 24 Aug., 1905; *s* of Walter Bacon; *m* Irene Maude Procter; two *s*. *Educ.:* Sutton Valence; St. Lawrence College, Ramsgate; Hastings Art School. *Work repro.:* in Radio Times, current publications, etc. *Publications:* Scraperboard Drawing ("How to Do It" Series, Studio Ltd.). *Address:* The Lawn, Chick Hill, Pett, nr. Hastings, Sussex TN35 4JG. *Signs work:* "C.W.B." or "C. W. Bacon."

BACZKOWSKA, Pamela; sculptor in cast bronze and aluminium, cement, carved wood and stone; *b* Bradford, Yorks., 8 Jan., 1938; *d* of Maurice Lacy Wright; *m* Henry Baczkowski, painter; one *d. Educ.:* Bradford Girls' Grammar School, Hubbard College of Scientology, E. Grinstead; *studied art* at Regional College of Art, Bradford (pottery under Bruce Adams). *Exhib.:* Centrum Gallery, Bern; mixed shows: Woodstock Gallery, London, Sackville Gallery, E. Grinstead. *Work in permanent collections:* mainly private in Switzerland. *Address:* Rozel, Coombe Hill, E. Grinstead, Sussex. *Club:* F.P.S. *Signs work:* circle within a square.

BADMIN, S. R., A.R.C.A. (1928), R.E. (Hon., retired; 1935), R.W.S. (1935), F.S.I.A. (1957); artist in water-colour, lithography, engraving; lecturer; *b* London, 18 Apr., 1906; *s* of C. J. Badmin; *m* Rosaline Flew; one *s,* two *d. Studied art* at Camberwell School of Art, R.C.A. *Exhib.:* R.A., R.W.S., R.E., Leicester Gallery, Fine Art Society, Worthing Municipal Gallery, New York. *Work in permanent collections:* V. & A., B.M., South London, Chicago, Huddersfield, Boston, U.S.A., Newport, Mon., Liverpool and Birmingham A.G. *Work repro.:* Country Bouquet, British Countryside in Colour, Famous Trees, The Seasons, The Trees of Britain, Shell Guide to Trees and Shrubs, Reader's Digest publications. *Address:* Streamfield, Bignor, Pulborough, Sussex. *Signs work:* "S. R. Badmin."

BAILEY, Arthur, O.B.E., F.R.I.B.A.; artist in water-colour; architect, articled to Riley and Glanfield (1919-23), asst. to E. Vincent Harris, R.A. (1924-36), partner to W. H. Ansell, M.C., C.B.E., P.P.R.I.B.A. (1936-50), proprietor of practice styled Ansell and Bailey (1950), consultant (1971); *b* Alsager, Ches., 1903; *s* of C. H. Bailey; *m* Phyllis Bailey; one *s. Educ.:* Orme School, Newcastle-under-Lyme, and privately; *studied art* at Central School of Arts and Crafts (articled pupil), Councillor to Artists General Benevolent Institution. *Exhib.:* R.A. *Work repro.:* in national and technical press. *Publications:* articles in technical press. *Address:* 12 Gray's Inn Sq., London WC 1. *Clubs:* Athenæum and Reform. *Signs work:* "A. Bailey."

BAILEY, Keith, F.S.D.C., A.T.D.; sculptor in slate, stone, wood, metals; letterer; visiting tutor, West Dean College; *b* St. Helens, 25 Sept., 1929. *Educ.:* Cowley School, St. Helens; *studied art* at Liverpool College of Art (1946-48), Manchester College of Art (1948-51), City and Guilds School of Art (1953-54). *Exhib.:* one-man show Cambridge Building Centre (1967). *Work in permanent collections:* Portland Mother and Child Collection, Melbourn Village College, architectural panels in many church and college buildings around this country and abroad. *Address:* 10 Meldreth Rd., Shepreth, Royston, Herts. *Signs work:* "Keith Bailey."

BAIN, Donald; painter; *b* Kilmacolm, Scotland, 1904; *s* of Donald Bain, physiotherapist; *m* Eunice Taylor; three *s. Educ.:* in Scotland; *studied art* with W. Y. Macgregor, founder of the Glasgow School (1880-95); studied in Paris. *Exhib.:* 1st Retrospective, MacLellan Galleries, Glasgow (1952); exhibited Europe from 1946, N. America, S. America and Canada from 1950, Scotland from 1943, Retrospective Exhbn. Tour, Dundee, Aberdeen, Perth, Stirling, Edinburgh, Inverness, Glasgow, Art Galleries (1973). *Official purchases:* Glasgow Art Gallery, Perth Art Gallery, Arts Council (Scottish Committee), Glasgow University Collection, Musée d'Art Contemporain, Skopje, Yugoslavia, Dundee Art Gallery, Calouste Gulbenkian Foundation Collection. *Awards:* Scottish Arts Council Bursary (1966), Medal, Diploma of honour, Annuale International Italiana d'Arts Grafica, Ancona (1968), Medal, Diploma honourable mention, La Biennale delle Regioni, Ancona (1968-69), Grand Prix De New-York 1969, Diplôme De Medaille D'or. *Work repro. and reviewed:* in British and international publications. *Publication:* Donald Bain, a Modern Scottish Painter (Glasgow, 1950).

Intro. by Wm. Montgomerie. Founder member New Art Club, Glasgow, 1940, New Scottish Group, 1942. *Address:* 28 Barmulloch Rd., Glasgow G21 4YF. *Signs work:* "D. BAIN" on front, signed and dated also back of canvas.

BAIN, Peter; painter in oil; *b* London, 15 December, 1927; *m* Jennifer; four *s.* *Studied art* at Bath Academy of Art. *Address:* Tiled Cottage, Old Bosham, Sussex. *Signs work:* "Bain."

BAINBRIDGE, Kenneth, A.R.C.A. (1937), F.R.S.A. (1952); artist in lettering, illuminating, lithography, bookbinding, jewellery; art master; *b* Colne, Lancs., 13 June, 1908; *s* of Thomas Albert Bainbridge; *m* Grace Mary Walsh; one *d.* *Educ.:* Elementary School and Grammar School, Colne; *studied art* at Burnley Municipal School of Art (1929-34), Free studentship R.C.A. under Prof. E. W. Tristram and Edward Johnston (1934-38), L.C.C. Central School of Arts and Crafts under W. Matthews and R. A. Massey (1934-38). *Exhib.:* London, Preston, Burnley. *Work repro.:* Lancs. C.C., Burnley Town Council. *Address:* Gracken, 11 Essex Ave., Burnley, Lancs. *Signs work:* "K. Bainbridge."

BAINES, John Manwaring, B.Sc., F.S.A., F.R.S.A., F.Z.S., F.M.A., past-president, South Eastern Federation of Museums and Art Galleries; curator, Public Museum and Art Gallery, Hastings (1935-73); assistant curator, Leeds City Museums (1931-35); *b* Headingley, Leeds, 6 Oct., 1910; *s* of Fred T. Baines; *m*; one *s.* *Educ.:* Marlborough and Leeds University. *Publications:* Historic Hastings, Burtons St. Leonards, Sussex Pottery, Wealden Firebacks, Rushlights and Candles, Hastings and its Harbours, etc. *Address:* 138 St. Helen's Rd., Hastings. *Club:* hon. mem., East Sussex Arts.

BAINES, Richard John Manwaring, R.O.I., N.D., A.T.D., F.R.S.A., N.S.; painter and etcher; lecturer, Design Dept., London College of Fashion, W1; *b* Hastings, 12 Feb., 1940; *s* of John Manwaring Baines, B.Sc., F.S.A., F.R.S.A., F.Z.A., F.M.A. *Educ.:* Eastbourne College; *studied art* Regent Street Polytechnic (Norman Blamey, Clifford Hall); Goldsmiths' College. President, East Sussex Arts Club. *Exhib.:* R.O.I., R.B.A., N.S., Painter/Etchers, one-man show Hastings Borough A.G., and provinces. *Work in permanent collections:* Leigh Court Coll., Donovan Coll., County Borough of Hastings. *Official purchases:* as above. Royal Arms and mural restorations, All Saints Church, Hastings. *Address:* Studio Two, 32 Fletcher Rd., Chiswick, London W4 5AS. *Clubs:* East Sussex Arts, Musical Box. *Signs work:* "Dick Baines"; and see appendix.

BALDWIN, Arthur Mervyn, N.D.D. (1955), Rome Scholarship, Sculpture, 1960; sculptor in metals and synthetics; Principal Lecturer in Fine Art, Newport College of Art; *b* Immingham, Lincs., 1 Feb., 1934; *s* of William Henry Baldwin; *m* Patricia Mary; two *s.* *Educ.:* Humberstone Foundation School, Old Clee, Lincs.; *studied art* at Grimsby School of Art, Leicester College of Art. *Work in permanent collections:* National Museum of Wales, Arts Council (Wales); Städtischen Kunstammlungen, Ludwigshafen. *Address:* 18 The Walk, Cardiff. *Signs work:* sculpture unsigned; drawings etc. signed "MERVYN BALDWIN."

BALFOUR, Maria, Associated Mem. Paris Salon, M.F.P.S., F.R.S.A.; painter in oil; *b* London, 27 June, 1934; *d* of Morogh Bernard, interior decorator; *m* Hon. Ian Balfour; one *d.* *Educ.:* America and British Isles; *studied art* privately. *Exhib.:* Loggia Gallery (1975), Paris Salon, Galerie Internationale, N.Y., Chelsea Art Soc., F.P.S., N.S., S.W.A., Kensington & Chelsea Artists; R.I. Galleries, Medici Galleries. *Commission:* crest for Bridal Kneeler to celebrate 250th year of founding of Guy's Hospital (1976). *Address:* 10 Limerston St., London SW10. *Signs work:* initials "MB" joined.

BALL, Bernard Raymond, M.F.P.S.; sculptor in wood, stone, fibreglass, steel, copper, silver and slate; *b* Brisbane, Australia, 21 May, 1921; *s* of John Irwin Ball; *m* (divorced); one *s*. *Educ.:* Institution Ste. Marie, La Seyne, France; *studied art* at Sir John Cass College (1946) under Bainbridge Copnall, Academie Julian (1951). *Exhib.:* Argonaut Gallery, Loggia Gallery, R.A., Circle Artists, Art Colony, N.S., Birmingham University, Berkeley Sq. *Address:* 4 Middle Wall, Whitstable, Kent. *Signs work:* "Ball" and see appendix.

BALL, Robert, A.R.C.A. (1942), A.R.E. (1943), A.R.B.S.A. (1943), R.B.S.A. (1949), F.R.S.A. (1950), British Inst. Scholarship for Engraving (1937); teacher of painting, drawing and anatomy, Birmingham College of Art (1942); Princ. Stroud School of Arts and Crafts (Jan., 1953); teacher of painting, Glos. College of Art (1959); artist in oil, drawing, etching, line-engraving, mezzotint, aquatint, drypoint and wood-engraving and litho; *b* Birmingham, 11 July, 1918; *s* of John William Ball, silversmith; *m* Barbara Minchin; one *s*, two *d*. *Studied art* at Birmingham Junior School of Art (1930-33), Birmingham College of Art (1933-40); R.C.A. (1940-42). *Exhib.:* R.A., N.E.A.C., R.E., R.B.S.A. *Address:* 22 Folly La., Stroud, Glos. *Signs work:* "Robert Ball."

BALLANTYNE, David, A.T.D., F.S.D-C.; potter, fine domestic wares and arch. commissions in ceramics, wood, concrete; teacher, Bournemouth College of Art; Hon. Co-ordinating Sec. S.D-C. since 1967; Consult. Des. for potter's equipment; *b* Oct., 1913; *s* of Rev. John and Muriel Ballantyne; *m* Katharine Harris; one *s*, three *d*. *Studied art* at Liverpool, London Central School, University Inst. of Educ. *Exhib.:* four one-man, many mixed exhbns., Design and Building Centres, Commonwealth Inst., Smithsonian, Stoke, Lincoln Cathedral. *Work in permanent collections:* V. & A. *Address:* 2 Chewton Farm Rd, Christchurch, Dorset. *Trades* as "Saviac Prototypes."

BALLARD, Arthur; artist in oil; teacher; Head of Dept., Foundation Studies, Liverpool Polytechnic; *b* Liverpool, 2 Apr., 1915; *m* Carolyn Anne Taylor; two *s*, two *d*. *Educ.;* St. Margaret's, Liverpool; *studied art* at Liverpool College of Art (1932-35); Paris, Ac. Grand Chaumier (1935-36); Paris (Fellowship) (1957-58). *Exhib.:* Roland, Browse & Delbanco, Arts Council of Gt. Britain, I.C.A. Gallery, London, Galerie de Chaudin, Paris, John Moores, Liverpool. *Work in permanent collections:* W.A.G., Atkinson Gallery, Southport, Liverpool University, Lancs., Cheshire and Herts. Educ. Committees, Henry Roland, Alfred Holt. *Address:* 11 Airlie Rd., Hoylake, Wirral, Merseyside, L47 4AB. *Club:* Liverpool Academy of Arts (President, 1964-68).

BALMER, Barbara, A.R.S.A. (1973), R.S.W. (1966), D.A. (1951); artist in oil, water-colour; visiting lecturer, Gray's School of Art; *b* Birmingham, 23 Sept., 1929; *d* of Arnold Balmer, N.R.D.; *m* George Mackie; two *d*. *Educ.:* Solihull High School for Girls; *studied art* at Coventry School of Art (1947-48), Edinburgh Coll. of Art (1949-52) under William Gillies, Robin Philipson, Leonard Rosoman, Robert Henderson Blyth. *Work in permanent collections:* Scottish Arts Council, G.L.C., Aberdeen Art Gallery, Glasgow Art Gallery. *Addresses:* 7 Park Rd., Cults, Aberdeen, and 37 Queensferry St., Edinburgh. *Signs work:* "Barbara Balmer."

BANKS, Brian; painter in acrylic, oil, mixed media on canvas and board; *b* London, 21 Oct., 1939; *s* of William John Ralph; *m* Christine, divorced 1974; two *s*, one *d*. *Educ.:* Sir Walter St. John's Grammar School, London; *studied art* at St. Martin's (1956-57), Peter de Francia, Edward Middleditch, James Dring; privately with John Flavin, A.R.C.A. (1958). *Exhib.:* one-man shows: Colin Jellicoe Gallery, Manchester; Ansdell Gallery, London; Zaydler Gallery, London;

Fermoy Art Gallery, King's Lynn. *Work in private collections:* Britain, Australia, France, U.S.A., Denmark. *Address:* 61A Albert Bridge Rd., London SW11. *Signs work:* "BANKS" (year).

BANKS, Robert Louis, M.C., Mentioned in Dispatches; A.A.Dip. Stanhope Forbes Prizewinner (1932), formerly F.R.I.B.A., M.T.P.I.; artist in water-colour; architect and town planner until 1957; *b* Cheltenham, 1911. *Address:* 31A Belsize Pk., London NW3. *Signs work:* "BANKS" (all works numbered).

BANNER, Delmar Harmood; painter in oils and water and portrait draughtsman; *m* Josephina de Vasconcellos, F.R.B.S. *Educ.:* Cheltenham, Oxford, Regent St. Polytechnic. *Exhib.:* R.A., R.I., R.P.S.; two one-man shows with wife. *Represented:* City Art Gallery, Nottingham, Glasgow, Hull, Sheffield, Aberdeen, Ashmolean, Fitzwilliam, V. & A., National Portrait Gallery, etc.; Norwich, Khartoum and Johannesburg cathedrals, Cambridge, Polytechnic, Queen's and Magdalen Colleges, Oxford. *Address:* Bield, Little Langdale, Ambleside, Cumbria. *Signs work:* "Delmar Banner."

BANNERMAN, Afrakuma, B.A.Hons.; artist in oil, enamel on steel and copper; freelance painter; *b* Accra, Ghana, 28 July, 1950. *Studied art* at Kingston Polytechnic (1969-73); London University (1973-74). *Exhib.:* Woodstock Gallery, Ibis Gallery, Commonwealth Society, Geneva. *Publication:* Dualistic Monism. *Address:* 27 Madrid Rd., Barnes, London SW13. *Signs work:* see appendix.

BANNISTER, Geoffrey Ernest John; served Royal Navy Minesweepers (1942-46); E.V.T. instructor in Commercial Art (Royal Navy, 1945-46); artist/designer, figure, scraper-board, water-colour, retouching, 15 years; Sales Director of colour printers, 6 years; *b* Birmingham, 15 Jan., 1924; *s* of Henry J. Bannister; *m* Beryl Parr Robinson, 1949 (deceased, 1966); one *s,* one *d.*; remarried, 1967, Susan Jennefer Peters; two *s. Educ.:* St. Philip's Grammar School. Present position, Sales Manager with King's Norton Press Group Ltd., Birmingham. *Address:* Crossways, 811 Sutton Rd., Aldridge, Walsall, Staffs. WS9 0QJ. *Clubs:* Birmingham Publicity Association, Great Barr Golf, The Gables. *Signs work:* "Ban."

BARANOWSKA, Janina; artist in oil; *b* Poland, 28 Oct., 1925; *d* of Josef Zbaraszewski, officer in Polish Army; *m* Maksymilian Baranowski; one *s. Educ.:* In Poland, Middle East and Scotland; *studied art* at Borough Polytechnic under Prof. Bomberg (1947-50), School of Art at the Polish University of Stefan Batory in London (1951-54). *Exhib.:* One-man shows: Drian Gallery (1958), Grabowski Gallery (1960, 1962, 1965, 1971, 1973, 1975), Raymond Duncan Galleries (1960, 1966), Alwin Gallery (1969), Grand Prix Rencontre Lyon, France (1970). Mixed exhib.: Royal Academy, Burlington Gallery, Cassel Gallery, R.B.A. Galleries, New Vision Centre, Walker's Galleries, Whitechapel Art Gallery, Edinburgh. *Clubs:* W.I.A.C., Group 49, International Institute of Art and Letters, International Assoc. of Art—U.K. National Committee. *Address:* 20 Strathmore Rd., London SW19. *Signs work:* "Baranowska."

BARBARIGO, Ida; artist in oil and etching; *b* Venice, 1925; *d* of Guido Cadorin, painter, Professore Accademia Belle Arti, Venice. *Educ.:* Marco Polo H.S., Venice; *studied art* at Accademia Belle Arti, Venice. *Exhib.:* one-man shows at Museo di Vicenza, Italy, Museo d'Arte Moderna of Llubljana, Zagreb, Rijeka, Yugoslavia, Wolfsbourg, Germany, Handschin Gallery, Basle. *Work in permanent collections:* Grosvenor Gallery, London, Kunsthalle, Nürnberg, Bergamini Gallery, Milan, Paul Facchetti Gallery, Paris. *Work repro.:* XX Siecle, Paris, Quandrum, Brussels, Art International, Lugano, Le Arti, Milan, Kunstwerk, Baden-Baden, and newspapers. *Publications:* I Cadorin (Marchiori); monograph: Chairs and Voyeurs (De Sölier ed. Alfieri). *Addresses:* 21 Rue du Bac, Paris, VII, and Carmini 2534, Venice. *Signs work:* "BARBARIGO."

BARBER, Raymond, A.B.S.I., A.M.B.I.M., City and Guilds, London Inst. (1943), E.M.E.U. (1937), S.S.I.A. (1945); full-time teacher at Boot and Shoe Technical College, Rushden; *b* 30 Sept., 1921. *Educ.:* Kettering Rd. Inst., Northampton, College of Technology, Northampton, Leicester College of Technology. *Exhib.:* Walsall, London, in conjunction with "Leather, Footwear and Allied Industries" Export Corp., Ltd.; Quality Footwear Exhib., Seymour Hall, London. *Address:* 10 Wantage Cl., Moulton, Northampton. *Club:* N.C.T.S.A. *Signs work:* "Renny."

BARCLAY, Sir Colville, Bart., M.A.; painter in oil and water-colour; *b* London, 7 May, 1913; *s* of Sir Colville Barclay, K.C.M.G.; *m* Rosamond Elliott; three *s*. *Educ.:* Eton and Oxford; *studied art* at Ruskin School, Oxford. *Exhib.:* R.B.A., R.A., London Group, Brighton and Bradford A.G. *Official purchases:* L.C.C. Schools, Arts Council, Bradford City Art Gallery. *Address:* Pitshill, nr. Petworth, Sussex. *Club:* St. James. *Signs work:* "Barclay."

BARCLAY, John George, C.A. (1952); Secretary of: R.G.I., R.S.W., Scottish Artists Benevolent Assoc., Glasgow Civic Art Assoc., Paisley Art Institute, Incorporated Glasgow Renfrewshire Soc.; chartered accountant; *b* Glasgow, 26 June, 1926. *Educ.:* Queen's Park. *Address:* 12 Sandyford Pl., Glasgow. G3 7NE. *Club:* Glasgow Art.

BARGERY, Geoffrey Maxwell; painter and illustrator in various media; *b* Cardiff, 1938; *s* of R. G. Bargery; *m;* two *s*. *Studied art* at Kingston School of Art (1953-58), Royal Academy Schools (1958-61). Works on a wide range of illustration and mural commissions and has produced work for Shell, Institute of Directors, Charterhouse Group, Chatto & Windus, B.B.C., Canterbury Cathedral (The Story of a Cathedral), etc. *Address:* 4 St. Andrew's Sq., Surbiton, Surrey. *Signs work:* "Bargery."

BARKER, Allen, artist; *b* Australia, 1937; *s* of Keith David, F.C.A.; *m* Marilyn Morton; two *s*. *Educ.:* Lismore High School; *studied art* at National Art School, Sydney (1955-60). *Exhib.:* one-man shows: Universities of Kent and Essex, Galerie Junge Generation, Vienna, Lucy Milton Gallery, London, Galerie Van Hulsen, Amsterdam, Ikon Gallery, Birmingham, Park Square Gallery, Leeds, Kinsman Morrison Gallery, London, Structured Theatre, I.C.A., London, Ferens A.G., Hull, City A.G., Manchester, Laing A.G., Newcastle-upon-Tyne, Museum and City A.G., Leicester, City Museum and A.G., Portsmouth. *Work in permanent collections:* museums in England: Sheffield, Leicester, Manchester; A.T. & T., New York, Museum Boymans, Van Beuningen, Rotterdam. *Address:* 12 Bassett Rd., London W10 6JJ. *Signs work:* "Barker."

BARKER, Cicely Mary; author, artist in oil, water-colour, pastel; *b* Croydon, 28 June, 1895; *d* of Walter Thomas Barker. *Educ.:* privately; *studied art:* mainly self-taught. *Exhib.:* P.S., S.G.A., R.I.: Pictures of Children by Living Artists Exhibition, Bournemouth (1944 and 1952). *Work in permanent collections:* at St. George's Church, Waddon; St. Andrew's Church, Croydon; Methodist Church, Norbury. *Publications:* author and illustrator of Flower Fairy Books, etc. *Address:* 4 Manor Cl., Church St., Storrington, Sussex. *Club:* Croydon Art Soc. *Signs work:* see appendix.

BARKER, Clive; sculptor in bronze and chrome; lecturer, Croydon College of Art; *b* Luton, Beds., 29 Aug., 1940; *s* of F. Barker; *m* Rose Bruen; two *s*. *Educ.:* Beech Hill Secondary Modern; *studied art* at Luton College of Technology and Art (1957-59) under Clifford Barry, A.R.C.A. *Exhib.:* Robert Fraser Gallery.

London, Hanover Gallery, London, Musee d'Art Moderne, Paris, Museum of Modern Art, N.Y., Palais des Beaux-Arts, Brussels, Palazzo Strozzi, Florence, Staatlichen Kunsthalle, Baden-Baden, Galerie Bischofberger, Zurich. *Work in public collections:* Arts Council of Great Britain, British Council, V. & A. Museum, Tate Gallery, Joseph H. Hirshhorn, N.Y., McCrory Corporation, N.Y. *Work repro.:* Pop Art Re-defined (Thames & Hudson), Image as Language (Penguin), Pop Art (Studio Vista), Art in Britain 1969-70 (Dent), Objekt Kunst (Dumont). *Address:* 6 The Clocktower, Heath St., Hampstead, London NW3. *Signs work:* "Clive Barker."

BARKER, Kit; painter in oil; *b* London, 6 Feb., 1916; *s* of George Barker; *m* Ilse Barker, novelist (pen-name Kathrine Talbot); one *s. Educ.:* Westbourne Grammar School. *Work in permanent collections:* South London Art Gallery, Camberwell; Olsen Foundation, New Haven, Connecticut; Nuffield, Magdalen, New, Pembroke colleges, Oxford; Memorial Museum, Rochester, N.Y.: Towner A.G., Eastbourne; Municipal A.G., Aberdeen; West Riding, Yorkshire, Education Committee; Bradford City A.G. *Work repro.:* Contemporary British Painting, by Sir Herbert Read (Penguin Books). *Address:* The Old Cottage, Bexley Hill, Lodsworth, Petworth, Sussex. *Signs work:* "Barker" (on back of canvas).

BARKER-MILL, Peter; illustrator, mural painter. *Publications:* Bligh's Voyage in the *Resource* (1937), The First Fleet (1939), A Voyage Round the World (1944), Topiary (1955). *Murals:* Red Lion, Wells (1959); Selwood School, Frome (1960); Nursling School, Hants (1961); Cockade Ltd., London (1962); James Robertson, Bristol (1962); Clarks Ltd. (1963); Yeovil Technical College (two) (1963); Standard Life Co., Edinburgh (1964); R.A.C., Bovington Camp (1965); Foxhills School, Colbury (1966), hotel, Bridgwater (1967), Nursling Hall, Southampton (1967), R.A.C. Memorial Sculpture, Bovington (1969). *Address:* Wookey Hole, Somerset. *Signs work:* "Peter Barker-Mill."

BARKLAM, Harold, A.R.C.A. (1936); artist in oil, water-colour; art lecturer, Derby College of Art; art teacher, Lowestoft School of Art (1946-50); *b* Tipton, Staffs., 14 Jan., 1912; *s* of George R. Barklam; *m* Marjorie Hale; one *d. Educ.:* Ryland Memorial School of Art, W. Bromwich, R.C.A. and College of Art, Birmingham. *Exhib.:* Birmingham A.G., Derby A.G., Norwich Castle, Nottingham Castle. *Work repro.:* oil paintings of Dunster Castle, Hardwicke Hall, Serlby Hall, Berkeley Castle, Blithfield Hall, Ingestre Hall; mural paintings entitled "Children's Games" painted for Lady Bagot of Blithfield Hall. *Address:* 9 Eastwood Drive, Littleover, Derby. *Signs work:* "H. BARKLAM."

BARNARD, Gwen, painter; *b* 1912; *d* of the late T. H. Barnard, banker. *Educ.:* privately; *studied art* at Chelsea School of Art. *Exhib.:* W.I.A.C., A.I.A.; one-man shows: A.I.A., London (1954), Paris (1956), Drian Gallery, London (1959), New End Gallery, Hampstead (1963), New Gallery, Belfast (1964), Florence (1966), Rome (1966), Oxford Gallery (1968, 1970), A.I.A. (1971), Upper Street Gallery (1972). *Publications:* Shapes of the River (Gaberbocchus, 1955). *Address:* 1 Mall Studios, Tasker Rd., London NW3.

BARNARD, Osbert Howard; senior partner Craddock and Barnard; specialist in old engravings, etchings, woodcuts, fine drawings; *b* Headley, 28 Mar., 1903; *s* of Rev. P. Mordaunt Barnard, B.D. *Educ.:* Rossall; *studied art* at British Museum, Paris, Berlin, Amsterdam, etc. *Publications:* Rembrandt's Etchings True and False (in collaboration with G. Biörklund), contributions to Print Collector's Quarterly, etc. *Address:* 12 Aberdeen Pk., Highbury, London N5.

BARNARD, Thomas Henslow, A.T.D. (.938), A.R.W.A. (1961), R.W.A. (1972); artist in oil, wood-engraving; art teacher, 1938-59; Army officer (1917-

37 and 1939-45); *b* 25 Aug., 1898; *s* of Henslow Barnard, civil engineer; *m* Ruth Anderson; one *s*, one *d*. *Educ.:* Malvern College; R.M.C., Sandhurst; *studied art* at W. of England College of Art, Bristol, under D. E. Milner. *Exhib.:* R.A., N.E.A.C., R.W.A. *Address:* Giffards, Church Rd., Leckhampton, Cheltenham, Glos. *Club:* Cheltenham Group of Artists. *Signs work:* "T. H. Barnard."

BARNDT, Helen Grace; artist in sepia ink, oil, tempera; instructor of life drawing, Academy of Art, S.F., basic art, University of San Francisco; *b* Santa Rosa, Calif. *Educ.:* Santa Rosa High School (Grad. 1947); *studied art* Chicago Art Institute, Calif. Art League, Graziotti Studio of Fine Arts, Anna Lee Stacey Scholarship (1959). *Exhib.:* De Young Museum, Palace of the Legion of Honor, San Francisco, Art Assoc. *Commissioned by:* Metaphysical Research Society of Denver (1968—) for series of religious oil paintings, ceiling murals and interior designs. *Address:* 1001 E. 7th Ave., Denver, Colorado. *Signs work:* "H. G. Barndt."

BARNETT, Doreen Elaine: see BURFORD, Doreen Elaine.

BARNETT, Olaf Blayney, N.S.P.S.; landscape, seascape and portrait artist; art consultant, valuer and critic; Director, Collectors' Gallery; Art Adviser, Drusillas Collectors' Gallery, Alfriston; teaches privately; mural and ballet designer, N.Y. Museum of Modern Art (1937); Lieut. R.N.V.R. (1940-45); *b* London, 1917; *s* of Rider von Danneborg; *m* Pamela; three *s*, two *d*. *Educ.:* Wadham College and Ruskin, Oxford; Slade School (prize winner 1934). *Exhib.:* War Artists, R.A., N.E.A.C., R.B.A., N.S.P.S., Paris, Milan, Washington. *Work in permanent collections:* American galleries, Eastbourne, Bradford, etc. *Publications:* critiques of Brangwyn, Stevens, Annigoni, Hockney, etc. *Studio:* Channel View, Cliff Rd., Seaford, Sussex. *Club:* R.N.V.R. *Signs work:* "Olaf Barnett."

BARNETT, Richard David, C.B.E., M.A., D.Litt., F.B.A., F.S.A.; Keeper, Dept. of Western Asiatic Antiquities, British Museum (1955-1975) retd.; *b* Acton, London, 23 Jan., 1909; *s* of L. D. Barnett, C.B., M.A., D.Litt.; *m* Barbara J. Pinto; two *s*, one *d*. *Educ.:* St. Paul's School, London, Corpus Christi College, Cambridge, and British School of Archaeology, Athens. *Publications:* dealing with archaeology of the ancient Near East and Judaica. *Address:* 14 Eldon Grove, Hampstead, London NW3.

BARR, Alfred Hamilton, Jr., Princeton B.A. (1922), Harvard Ph.D. (1946), honorary degrees, Princeton (1949), Bonn (1960), Yale (1967), Columbia (1969); museum official and art historian; Instructor Art, Princeton (1925-26); Assoc. Prof. Art, Wellesley College (1926-29); Director Museum of Modern Art, New York City (1929-43); Director Research (1944-46); Director Collections (1947-67); Trustee since 1939; *b* Detroit, 28 Jan., 1902; *s* of Alfred Hamilton Barr, D.D.; *m* Margaret Scolari-Fitzmaurice; one *d*. *Educ.:* Yale. *Publications:* Cubism and Abstract Art (1936); Picasso, 50 years of His Art (1946); Matisse, His Art and His Public (1951). *Addresses:* 49 E. 96 St., N.Y., 28, and 11 W. 53 St., N.Y., 19.

BARRATT, Krome, V.P.R.O.I., R.B.A., P.N.S., F.W.S.O.M., N.D.D., H.N.C. (Civil Engineering), F.R.S.A.; abstract painter, lecturer and writer in the theory and history of design, mural designer. Served in Fleet Air Arm (1942-46). Travelled Far East, studied comparative religions and social function of the arts. Since 1964 works listed and numbered as "Lights", derived from Yoga concept of "prana". A keen sailor, has produced a few seascapes in the English tradition. However, major works are experiments in "kinetic colour."Analogous pigments are juxtaposed to create a "vibrato," with second and third order harmonies controlling the drawing; *b* London, 18 Apr., 1924; *s* of Archibald William Barratt;

g-g-s of Sir Rowland Hill (Penny Post). *Educ.:* East Ham Grammar School, West Ham College of Technology; *studied art* at Sir John Cass College, London (1947-51). *One-man shows:* Drian Galleries, London, A.I.A., New Gallery, Belfast, Richmond Hill Gallery, Gordon Gallery, Old Bakehouse Gallery, Mall Galleries, London. *Works in collections* in University of Gainesville, University of Windsor, University of Surrey, Oxford University, Towner Gallery, Old Bakehouse Gallery, also Australia, New Zealand, Rhodesia, Norway and many in U.S.A. "Submarine cables" commissioned by I.T.T. Corporation (New York) 1971. Lecturer in School of Architecture, Polytechnic of North London. *Publications:* Readers Digest 1965, The Artist Vol. 72/2-4, Vol. 79/1-6, Vol. 184/3-6, FBA Quarterly Apr. 1973. *Address:* The Studio, 1 Marylands Ave., Hockley, Essex. *Signs work:* "Krome"; early work: "KB."

BARRETT, Elsie May, Dip.d'onore Roma (1974), Diplome International de Peinture de Deauville (1973), Diploma International Arts Guild (1974), F.R.S.A. (1968), R.G.I. (1968-69); freelance artist in oil and water-colour; *b* Stoke-on-Trent, 8 Aug., 1913; *d* of F. E. Burrows; *m* L. R. Barrett, M.A., M.Sc.; one *d. Educ.:* Longton, Stoke-on-Trent; *studied art* at St. Martin's under Harold Workman, R.B.A.; City & Guilds under Middleton Todd, R.A., Barnard Adans. *Work in permanent collections:* Halford House and U.S.A. *Address:* 18 Park Ave., Harpenden, Herts. AL5 2EA. *Clubs:* Contemporary Portrait Society, F.P.S., Harpenden Arts, St. Albans, etc. *Signs work:* "Elsie M. Barrett."

BARRETT, Franklin Allen; chartered accountant (retd.); mem. English Ceramic Circle; *b* Edgbaston, Birmingham, 4 Apr., 1906; *s* of Frank Bernard Barrett, B.Sc.; *m* Winifred Mary Webb; one *s. Educ.:* King Edward's Grammar School, Five Ways, Birmingham. *Publications:* Caughley and Coalport Porcelain (F. Lewis); Worcester Porcelain (Faber and Faber); Lund's Bristol & Worcester Porcelain (Faber and Faber); papers in English Ceramic Circle Transactions; co-author (with A. L. Thorpe), Derby Porcelain (Faber and Faber); contributor to English Porcelain, 1745-1850 (Ernest Benn Ltd., 1965); Joint Editor (with A. L. Thorpe), Pinxton China Factory, Exley (Cook-Steel, Derby). *Address:* Mallards Keep, Alison Rd., Church Stretton, Salop.

BARRETT, Roderic; artist in oil; visiting lecturer, Central School of Art and Design (1947-68); invited to P.E.A., Exeter, U.S.A. (1957-58); tutor, Royal Academy Schools (1968—); *m* Lorna Blackmore; two *s,* one *d. Educ.:* St. Christopher's School, Letchworth; *studied art* at the Central (1936-40). *Exhib.:* One-man shows: London (1954, 1956, 1964, 1966, 1970), Cambridge (1947, 1963, 1966), Exeter, N.H., U.S.A. (1957), Boston, U.S.A. (1958), Oxford Gallery (1971, 1975), The Minories Colchester (1962, 1974), Chilham (1969, 1972), Harlow (1974), University of Essex (1966), University of Southampton (1975), University of Warwick (1975), Norwich Museum (1974); London Group, Wildensteins, Beaux Arts, Manchester, Nottingham, Cardiff, Aldeburgh Festival, Hintlesham Festival, Bath Festival, Bristol City Art Gallery, Brussels, Zürich, Nice, Holland, Boston Arts Festival, U.S.A. Princetown U.S.A., Worcester Museum, U.S.A., Chicago, U.S.A., New York, etc. *Work in permanent collections:* V. & A., Lamont Gallery, U.S.A., University of Essex, University of Southampton; in private collections in France, England, Belgium, Italy, Eire, U.S.A. *Address:* Rooks End, Church Lane, Stanway, Colchester, Essex CO3 5LR. *Signs work:* "R.B."

BARRON, Howard, F.I.A.L.; portrait and landscape artist in oil; Yeoman Mem. Ironmongers' Livery Co. London, and a Freeman; *b* Sidcup, Kent, 7 June, 1900; *s* of Charles Harrison Barron, draughtsman and engineer; *m* Sylvia Chudleigh, decd.; one *d; m* Peggy Olivey, Sydney. *Educ.:* Christ's Hospital, Horsham;

studied art in Sydney, Australia, under late Sir Will Ashton, O.B.E., R.O.I. (1925-49), Kennington City and Guilds' School. *Exhib.:* Paris Salon (Silver Medal), R.A., R.P., R.O.I., National Soc., Soc. Marine Artists. *Work in permanent collections:* Imperial War Museum, Canberra, Teachers' College, Armidale, N.S.W., Australia House, London, National Galleries of Sydney, Brisbane, Albany, Parliament House, Canberra. Has held one-man shows in Australian capitals and Qantas Gallery, London. *Official commissions:* H.M. Queen Elizabeth II for R.A.F., Germany (1968), the 50th anniversary R.A.F. Royal Banquet at Lancaster House (1968), H.M. Queen Elizabeth II for United Services Club, Germany (1971). *Address:* 1 Huntingdon Pl., Berowra, N.S.W. 2081, Australia. *Signs work:* "HOWARD BARRON."

BARRON, Paul, A.R.C.A., F.S.D-C.; potter in reduced stoneware; Senior Lecturer Ceramics, W. Surrey College of Art; *b* Wantage, 14 June, 1917; *s* of W. A. Barron, M.A.; *m* Penny Barron, A.R.C.A.; one *s,* two *d. Educ.:* Brighton Grammar School; *studied art* at Brighton School of Art (1936-39) under Norah Braden. *Work in permanent collections:* V. & A. Loan etc. *Workshop:* Thornfield, Bentley, Farnham, Surrey. *Signs work:* see appendix.

BARTLETT: see ROBINSON, Margaret Nancy.

BARTLETT, Charles, R.W.S., R.E., A.R.C.A.; artist in oil and water-colour, printmaker; *b* Grimsby, 23 Sept., 1921; *s* of Charles Henry Bartlett; *m* Olwen Jones; one *s. Educ.:* Eastbourne Grammar School;*studied art* at Eastbourne School of Art, R.C.A. *Exhib.:* two one-man shows in London. *Work in permanent collections:* V. & A. Museum, National Gallery of S. Australia, Arts Council of Great Britain, numerous public and private collections in Britain and abroad. *Address:* St. Andrew's, Fingringhoe, nr. Colchester, Essex CO5 7BG. *Signs work:* "Charles Bartlett."

BARTLETT-MERRIMAN, Horace, B.Sc., C.Eng., F.I.C.E., F.I.Mech.E., M.A.S.M.E., F.Inst.W., F.Inst.F., M.I.Prod.E., F.I.PlantE., F.R.S.A.; Engineering Consultant, Mobil Oil Co.; mechanical engineer and industrial designer; *b* Birmingham, 19 Feb., 1914; *s* of Percival Cecil Bartlett-Merriman; *m* Mary Eileen Walters; one *d. Educ.:* Birmingham Central School of Arts and Crafts and Birmingham Central Technical College; *studied art* at Birmingham Central School of Art. *Exhib.:* Bombay, Calcutta, Delhi, Cairo. *Address:* "Kingfishers," Coronation Rd., Ascot, Berks. *Signs work:* "HB-M."

BARTOLOME, Jaime; painter; 1958 Press Assoc., Barcelona, 1st Prix; 1970 Grand Prix New York, Nice (France), 2nd Prix; 1971 Grand Prix Paques, Nice, 2nd Prix; *b* Santander, Spain, 4 Apr., 1927. *Educ.:* Barcelona. *Exhib.:* Individual show in Barcelona, 1958-62-64-65 and 1969. Bilbao, 1966. Madrid, Palma, Mallorca, 1967; group shows in Barcelona, Madrid, Alicante, München, Italy, Sweden, Hong Kong, France. *Work in permanent collections:* Museum of Modern Art, Barcelona. *Address:* Studio, Diputación, 321, Barcelona, Spain. *Clubs:* Circulo Artistico "Saint Lluc," Instituto Estudios Hispanicos, Barcelona. *Signs work:* "Bartolomé."

BARTON, Patricia: see MYNOTT, Patricia.

BASE, Irene, F.R.S.A., N.R.D., Mem. Soc. of Scribes and Illuminators; Art Workers' Guild; calligrapher and illuminator of MSS. on vellum; Lecturer in calligraphy and illuminating, W. of England College of Art, Bristol (1945-71); *d* of George William Base. *Educ.:* Private schools; *studied art* at Norwich School of Art under C. W. Hobbis, Chelsea Polytechnic under M. C. Oliver. *Exhib.:* Arts and Crafts Exhbn. Soc., Soc. of Scribes and Illuminators, Crafts Centre, A.I.G.A.,

R.M.S., S.W.A., W.I.A.C., Rome, Vienna, Amsterdam, N.Z., U.S.A. *Work in permanent collections:* V. & A., L.C.C. *Official purchases* include Somerset Roll of Honour, Martock Roll of Honour, Beccles Book of Remembrance, Bristol Grammar School Roll of Honour, Volume IX of the Book of the Royal Air Force. *Publication:* the chapter on gilding in The Calligrapher's Handbook. *Work repro.:* Modern Lettering, Studio, Crafts, Svensk Typograftidnung, La Revue Moderne, Calligraphy Today. *Address:* Ivanhoe, 23 Station Rd., Shirehampton, Bristol BS11 9TU. *Signs work:* "Irene Base" in a formal hand.

BASKO, Maurice P. Duviella, Dip. Salon Automne, France; Figuratif Chateau of Senaud, France; painter in oil and water-colour, art researcher; *b* Biarritz, 30 Sept., 1921; *s* of J. L. Duviella, contractor and art dealer. *Educ.:* Jules Ferry College, Biarritz; *studied art* at Academy Frochot, Paris. *Exhib.:* Museum of Modern Art, Paris, Salon Automne, Salon Bosio, Grand Prix, Pont Aven, Salon Art Libre, Paris, Salon Versailles, France, Paris Gallery, N.Y., Galerie Colise, Paris, Fontainebleu Gallery, N.Y.; one-man shows: Paris, N.Y., Lyon, Mallorca, Vichy, etc. *Work in permanent collections:* Guggenheim Museum, N.Y., Albertina Museum, Vienna, Museum of Modern Art, Miami, Public Library, N.Y.; and more than 400 works in private collections. *Address:* Bielle, Pyrénées Atlantique 64, France. *Signs work:* "BASKO" and sometimes "Duviella."

BASSINGTHWAIGHTE, Lewin, A.R.C.A. (1953); painter; *b* Southminster, Essex, 17 June, 1928; *m*; two *s*. *Studied art* at S.W. Essex Technical College, St. Martin's School of Art, Royal College of Art. *Exhib.:* one-man: Leicester Galleries (1957), Arthur Jeffries Galleries (1959, 1961), Lane Galleries, Los Angeles (1963), Piccadilly Gallery (1964, 1965, 1967, 1968, 1970, 1972), Galleria Cavana, Venice (1966), Bear Lane Gallery, Oxford (prints, 1968), Kunsthaus Bühler, Stuttgart (1973). *Work in permanent collections:* V. & A., Arts Council, Eastbourne Art Gallery, Glasgow University, Nuffield Foundation, Essex Education Authority, Redland College, Surrey Education Authority, Galleria Milano, Chantry Bequest (1971). *Address:* 24 Winscombe St., London N19. *Signs work:* see appendix.

BASU, Hella; senior lecturer, Regional College of Art, Hull; creative lettering; *b* Kassel, Germany, 25 Nov., 1924; *d* of Hans Schwiefert. *Studied art* at Art College, Kassel, Germany. *Exhib.:* V. & A., Herbert A.G. and Museum, Coventry, Crafts Advisory Com.; one-man shows: British Council, West Berlin; German Cultural Institute, Calcutta; Fine Arts Gallery, Leicester; North West Arts Assoc., Manchester; Kulturamt, Kassel; University of Santiniketan; Klingspor Museum, Offenbach; County Museum, Warwick; University of Leicester; National Library, Ottawa; Worcester College of Educ.; Goethe Institute, Toronto, etc. *Address:* 4 Muirfield Pk., Hull. *Signs work:* "Hella Basu."

BATCHELOR, Bernard Philip, R.W.S.; painter in water-colour and oil; *b* Teddington, May, 1924. *Trained* at St. Martin's School of Art (R. Kirkland Jamieson) and City and Guilds (A. R. Middleton Todd, R.A.); Company of Fanmakers Design Award (1950); David Murray Scholarship (1952). *Exhib.:* R.A., R.W.S. *Official purchases:* M.O.W. (1953) and work in private collections. *Address:* 31 The Avenue, St. Margaret's-on-Thames, Middx. *Signs work:* "B. P. Batchelor" or "B.P.B."

BATCHELOR, Bernard William Roland, R.W.S.; painter in oils and water-colours; *b* Chelsea, 16 Oct., 1889; *s* of Bernard Batchelor; *m*; one *s*. *Studied art* at Putney (George Morrow) Polytechnic, Regent St. (Harry Watson, R.W.S.), Central School of Arts and Crafts (W. P. Robins, R.W.S., R.E.), City and Guilds (A. R. Middleton Todd, R.A., R.W.S., R.E.). *Work in permanent collections:*

Huddersfield, and in private collections all over the world. *Publication:* The Dunstable Book. *Address:* 31 The Avenue, St. Margaret's-on-Thames, Middx. *Signs work:* "ROLAND BATCHELOR."

BATES, Ken, A.T.D. (1949); portrait and figure painter in oil, pastel, charcoal, pencil and graphic media; executive committee mem., Sutton Arts Council; *b* London, 20 Mar., 1927; *s* of Thomas Bates; *m* Sheilah Bates; one *s*, one *d*. *Educ.:* Christ's College, Finchley, London; *studied art* at Willesden Art School (1943-45) under Maurice De Sausmarez; Guildford School of Art (1946-49) under Maurice Wheatley. *Exhib.:* N.S., R.B.A., P.S., S.G.A. *Address:* 1 Norman Rd., Cheam, Surrey. *Signs work:* "Ken Bates."

BATTEN, Mark, Associate of the Société des Artistes Français (1970), past pres. R.B.S., Pres. R.B.S. (1956-61), F.R.B.S. (1953), R.B.A. (1962), F.R.S.A. (1936), Hon. Mem. National Sculpture Society of the U.S.A. (1956); Silver Medal Paris (1952); sculptor, direct carver in stone; *b* Kirkcaldy, 21 July, 1905; *s* of Edward Batten, M.I.Mech.E.; *m* Elsie Thorneloe; one *d*. *Exhib.:* Paris Salon, R.A., R.S.A., R.G.I., N.E.A.C. *Official purchases:* Trinity College and Bodleian Library, Oxford, St. Saviour's, Eastbourne, L.C.C. Golders Hill Park. *Work repro.:* in Studio, Apollo, The Artist, Arts Review. *Publications:* Stone Sculpture by Direct Carving (1957), Direct Carving in Stone (1966). *Address:* Christian's River, Dallington, Heathfield, Sussex. *Club:* Chelsea Arts. *Signs work:* "Mark Batten" (for drawings).

BAXANDALL, David, C.B.E. (1959), B.A.; director, National Galleries of Scotland (1952-70); asst. keeper (1928-39) and keeper (1939-41), Dept. of Art, National Museum of Wales; director of Manchester City Art Galleries (1945-52); *b* London, 11 Oct., 1905; *s* of David Baxandall, deceased; *m* Isobel Thomas; one *s*, two (twin) *d*. *Educ.:* King's College School, Wimbledon; University of London, King's College. *Publications:* Ben Nicholson, 1962; gallery handbooks and catalogues, numerous articles and broadcast talks. *Address:* 12 Darnaway St., Edinburgh EH3 6BG.

BAXTER, Denis Charles Trevor, F.R.S.A.; artist in oil, printmaker, and teacher; *b* Portsmouth, 1 Mar., 1936; *s* of P. E. Baxter. *Educ.:* Southbourne Preparatory School; Ryde School, I.o.W.; *studied art* at Bournemouth and Poole College of Art (1964-65) under L. Randall; Stockwell College, Bromley, Kent (1965-68) under P. Smale. *Exhib.:* group shows: N.S., Rotunda Gallery, London, Bakehouse Gallery, Sevenoaks. *Address:* 20 Church Rd., Southbourne, Bournemouth, Dorset BH6 4AT. *Signs work:* "Denis."

BAXTER, Douglas Gordon, D.A. (Edin.), R.S.W., post-graduate student of Edinburgh College of Art, travelling scholarship awards to Spain, France and Scandinavia; Director of Art, Loretto Public School; Tutor/Lecturer, Edinburgh College of Art; elected to membership, S.S.A., 1961. *Official purchases:* Arts Council, Edinburgh Corporation, Usher's Brewery, Thos. Menzies & Co. *Address:* Millhill Ct., Musselburgh.

BAYNES, Keith Stuart; artist in oil and water-colour; *b* Reigate, 11 Nov., 1887. *Educ.:* Harrow; Trinity College, Cambridge; Slade School. *Exhib.:* London Group, London Artists' Association, Independent, Lefevre, Agnew and Adams Galleries, New York, Paris, Hamburg, Venice, Copenhagen, Oslo, Canada, Australia. *Official purchases:* British Council, Arts Council, Glasgow, Manchester, South Africa. *Work repro.:* Studio and Burlington magazines, Modern Movement in Art by R. H. Wilenski. *Address:* The Athenæum, Pall Mall, London SW1. *Signs work:* "Keith Baynes."

BAYNES, Pauline Diana, W.I.A.C. (1938; resigned 1946); designer and illustrator, M.S.I.A. (1952); *b* 1922; *studied art* at Farnham School of Art and Slade. *Books illustrated* include: A Treasury of French Tales, Farmer Giles of Ham and Tom Bombadil (Allen and Unwin), Arabian Nights and Fairy Tales of the British Isles (Blackie), seven Narnia Books by C. S. Lewis (Bles and Bodley Head), Sister Clare, Miracle Plays, St. George and the Dragon (Houghton Mifflin, U.S.A.), Dictionary of Chivalry (Longmans), Kate Greenaway Medal (1968). *Address:* Rock Barn Cottage, Dockenfield, nr. Farnham, Surrey. *Signs work:* "PAULINE BAYNES"—occasionally with a small bird—see appendix.

BAZAINE, Jean; *b* Paris, 1904. *Educ.:* L. ès L. *Awards:* Prix National des Arts (1964). Executed stained-glass windows for the church of Assy (1946), ceramic mural and windows at Audincourt (1951-54), ceramic mural at U.N.E.S.C.O. (1960), ceramic mural Maison de l'O.R.T.F., Paris (1963), windows Saint Séverin, Paris (1966). *Exhib.:* Galerie Carré and Maeght, Paris, Retr. exhbn., Berne (1958), Eindhoven (1959), Hanover, Zürich, Oslo (1963), Paris (1965); repr. Biennele de Venice, São Paulo and Carnegie (member of the jury, 1952). *Publications:* Notes sur la peinture d'aujourd'hui (ed. Seuil, Paris, 1948), Exercice de la peinture (ed. Seuil, 1973).

BEALE, Elizabeth Helen; artist in water-colour, pencil, ink, oil pastel and oils; *b* Yorks., 19 July, 1946; *d* of Peter Dunlop Green; *m* Stephen D. N. Beale; one *d. Educ.:* Wycombe Abbey School, Bucks.; *studied art* at Harrogate School of Art (1962-63); Brighton College of Art (1963-64); Liverpool College of Art (1964-67); Isle of Mull (1972) under Julie Wroughton, A.R.C.A. *Exhib.:* one-man shows: Rookery A.G., Yorks., Victoria A.G., Harrogate. *Work in permanent collections:* Berlitz School of Languages, Leeds, Yorks. *Address:* Winston House, Gillingham, nr. Beccles, Suffolk. *Clubs:* F.P.S., Cotswold Art. *Signs work:* "Helen Beale"; early works "E. Helen Green."

BEAMISS, Frederick Harold; artist in indian ink and scraper-board; *b* Hornsey, Middx., 29 July, 1898. *Studied art* at Cologne School of Art (1919-20), Tottenham Polytechnic, etc. *Exhib.:* Exeter Art Soc. *Work repro.:* in various publications; specializes in Devon churches and landscape. *Address:* Dieu Donné, Castle View, Longdown, Exeter, Devon. *Signs work:* "Frederick H. Beamiss" or "Calbeam."

BEANLAND, Frank Charles, N.D.D. (1956), Slade Diploma (1961), Boise Travelling Scholarship (1961); painter in oils; *b* Bridlington, 15 Apr., 1936; *s* of Ernest Beanland. *Educ.:* Bridlington School; *studied art* at Hull College of Art & Crafts under D. Booth, A.R.C.A., Slade School of Fine Art under Claude Rogers. *Exhib.:* Young Contemporaries, London Group, Drian Galleries, Grabowski Gallery, Tooth's, Galerie Alphonse Chave, Vence, France. *Address:* Poplar Hall, Frostenden, nr. Wangford, East Suffolk. *Signs work:* "Frank Beanland."

BEARD, Mark Leo; designer and decorator of ceramic pieces, mainly musical and figure subjects; *s* of John Albert Beard, musician; *m* Lavender Groves (*q.v.*). *Address:* Upton Pottery, 17 High St., Upton-upon-Severn, Worcs. *Club:* B.B.C. (Life Member).

BEATON, Sir Cecil, Kt. (1972); stage-designer, illustrator, writer, photographer; *b* 1904; *s* of Ernest Beaton. *Educ.:* Harrow; Cambridge. *Exhib.:* Cooling, Redfern and Lefevre Galleries, National Portrait Gallery, London, Museum of the City of New York. *Publications:* Book of Beauty; C.B.'s New York; My Royal Past; Chinese Album; Indian Album; Near East; Far East; Photobiography; Ballet; Persona Grata, The Glass of Fashion, It Gives Me Great Pleasure, The Face of the World, Japanese; Cecil Beaton's Diaries: The Wandering Years, The Years

Between, The Happy Years, The Strenuous Years, etc. *Addresses:* 8 Pelham Pl., London SW7; Reddish House, Broadchalke, Wilts. *Signs work:* "Cecil Beaton."

BEAVER, Robert Atwood, M.A., B.M., B.Ch., F.F.A.R.C.S., F.R.S.A. (1950); doctor of medicine; anaesthetist, London Chest Hospital, King's College Group; artist in oil; *b* Poole, 5 Dec., 1906; *s* of Arnold Atwood Beaver (decd.); *m* Gabrielle Seagrim; two *d. Educ.:* Winchester, New College, Oxford, St. Thomas'; *studied art* in Brussels. *Exhib.:* R.A., R.I., R.O.I., N.E.A.C., N.S., International Salon des Medecins, St. Mawes Group of Artists, Medical Art Soc. *Work in permanent collections:* two in collection of late Lord Doverdale. *Work repro.:* in L'Art Illustrée (Paris, 1949). *Address:* 61 Ward Ave., Cowes, I.O.W. *Clubs:* Royal Thames, British Racing Drivers, R.C.S. *Signs work:* "R. Beaver" or "R.B."

BEDDINGTON, Roy, landscape painter; illustrator (especially water-colour); *b* 16 June, 1910; *s* of Reginald Beddington, C.B.E.; *m* Diana Dobson. *Educ.:* Rugby; Corpus Christi College, Oxford; *studied art* at Slade School (Prof. Schwabe) and Florence. *Exhib.:* R.A., New English Art Club, Brighton, Huddersfield, Eastbourne and Ackermann's (Bond St.), Walker Galleries. *Work repro.:* illustrations to numerous books, etc., and contributions to Country Life, Field, etc. *Publications:* The Adventures of Thomas Trout (Methuen), To be a Fisherman (Geoffrey Bles), The Pigeon and the Boy (Geoffrey Bles), Pindar—a dog to remember (Michael Joseph, 1975). *Address:* Home Farm, Chute Cadley, nr. Andover, Hants. *Clubs:* F.R.S.A., Arts Club. *Signs work:* "Roy Beddington."

BEDELLS, Sheila, N.S.; artist in oil; *b* Duston, Northampton, 21 Mar., 1916; *d* of John Faulkner Stops, solicitor. *Educ.:* Hamilton House, Tunbridge Wells, Kent, and Miss Spaldings, Queen's Gate, S.W.7; *studied art* at Epsom School of Art under David Birch, R.O.I., Karl Hagedorn, R.B.A., R.I., Leslie Worth, Peter Oliver. *Work repro.:* greetings and Christmas cards designed and printed. *Address:* Old Orchard, Betchworth, Surrey.

BEESON, Jane; Arnolfini Open Competition 2nd prize, 1963; painter in P.V.A., oil and enamel; *b* Weybridge, Surrey, 10 Apr., 1930; *d* of Sir Noel Bowater, Bt.; *m* Christopher Beeson; three *s,* one *d. Educ.:* various schools, including Benenden, Kent; *studied art* at Kingston School of Art, Surrey (1949-51) (Principals, R. Brill and W. Fairclough); Atelier Julien (1951) (Principal, Sabourand); Beaux Arts, Paris (1951-52), under Brianchon; Slade, London (1953). *Exhib.:* John Moore's (1961); London exhib., Rowan Gallery and New Art Centre. *Work in permanent collections:* "Mauve and Yellow" bought by Director, Ferens Art Gallery, Hull. *Address:* Ford Farm, Manaton, S. Devon. *Signs work:* "J. Beeson."

BEGGS, Thomas Montague, B.F.A. (Yale, 1924), 1st and 2nd medals B.A.I.D. (1922-24); artist in oil, water-colour, fresco and tempera; Director National Collection of Fine Arts (1948-64), Spec. Asst. to the Secretary, Smithsonian Inst. (1964-65); Fine Arts Consultant (1966—); *b* Brooklyn, N.Y., 22 Apr., 1899; *s* of Thomas P. Beggs; *m* Alice E. Powers; two *s,* one *d. Educ.:* Manual Training High School, Brooklyn (1913-17); *studied art* at Pratt Inst., Art Students' League, Yale School of Fine Arts, Fontainebleau, France, Harvard University. *Publications:* Artists-in-Residence, Weather in Art. *Address:* 6540 Hitt Ave., McLean, Va. *Club:* Cosmos. *Signs work:* "THOMAS MONTAGUE BEGGS."

BEILBY, Pauline Margaret, N.D.D. (1950); textile designer, freelance; *b* Bramcote, Notts., 21 June, 1927; *d* of Percy Goold Beilby; *m* Keith David Barnes, lace manufacturer; two *s. Educ.:* Nottingham Girls' High School; *studied art* at Nottingham College of Arts and Crafts under A. H. Rodway, A.R.C.A., F.R.S.A., principal. *Address:* Burleigh House, 15 Albemarle Rd., Woodthorpe, Notts. *Signs work:* see appendix.

BELL FOSTER, Arthur, R.B.S.A.; professional painter in oil, water-colour; designer and illustrator; *b* Northallerton, Yorks. *Educ.:* Northallerton Grammar School; *studied art* at Sheffield School of Art. *Exhib.:* R.A., R.B.A., R.I., R.C.A., R.S.A., N.E.A.C., Royal Scottish Soc. of Painters in Water-colour, Glasgow Institute of Fine Arts, Paris Salon, British Arts Council (Scotland) Touring Exhbn., Britain in Watercolour Exhbn., Touring exhbns., Art Exhbns. Bureau. *Official purchases:* Darlington A.G., Worcester A.G., Bilston A.G. *Work repro.:* In Water-colour, a truly English Art, by Percy V. Bradshaw (Studio Publication). The Dalesman. *Address:* 3 Springfield Rd., Kings Heath, B'ham. *Clubs:* B'ham Art Circle. *Signs work:* "BELL FOSTER."

BELSKY, Franta, A.R.C.A., F.R.B.S.; P.Pres. Soc. of Portrait Sculptors; *b* Brno, 1921; *m* Margaret C. Owen. *Studied sculpture* at Prague Academy, R.C.A. (Hons. Dip.). *Work in permanent collections:* The Queen, Queen Mother, Europe and U.S.A., c. councils, ind. and pte. companies, e.g., "Joy-ride," Stevenage; "Triga," Tattersalls, Knightsbridge; "Lessou," Bethnal Green; "Astronomer Herschell," Slough; "Oracle," Temple Way, Bristol; Q.E. Hospital, Birmingham; Admiral Cunningham, Trafalgar Square; Winston Churchill statue, Fulton, Missouri; fountains: Shell Centre, London; Yate New Town. *Work repro.:* Times, Studio, Domus, Habitat, etc. *Address:* 12 Pembroke Studios, Kensington, London W8. *Signs work:* see appendix.

BENENSON, Leslie Charlotte, A.R.E. (1974), N.D.D. (1962), S.S.I. (1964); sculptor, painter, engraver and calligrapher in resin casting, ceramic sculpture, wood, water-colour, wood engraving, calligraphy on vellum; *b* London, 13 Jan., 1941; *d* of Marcel Benenson, L.S.C. (Antwerp University). *Educ.:* La Sagesse Convent High School, London; *studied art* at Regent St. Polytechnic (1958-63) under Geoffrey H. Deeley, A.R.C.A., James Osborne, R.E.; privately (calligraphy) with Anthony Wood, F.R.S.A. (1963-64). *Exhib.:* one-man shows: John Gage Gallery, Eastbourne (1975), Michelham Priory (1971, 1976), Rye A.G. (1971); group shows: R.A. (1966, 1967, 1969-72), R.E. (from 1968); V. & A. (The Decorated Page) (1971), etc. *Work in permanent collection:* Towner Gallery, Eastbourne. ***Publication:*** illustrated, Hare Coursing (The Standfast Press, 1976). *Address:* 25 Upperton Gdns., Eastbourne, Sussex. *Signs work:* see appendix.

BENESCH, Otto, Ph.D.; em. director of the Albertina, Vienna; prof., University of Vienna, Légion d'Honneur; *b* Ebenfurth, 29 June, 1896; *m* Eva Steiner. *Educ.:* Vienna; *studied art* at University of Vienna under Max Dvorak. *Publications:* Rembrandt Werk und Forschung, Rembrandt's Drawings (Complete Edition) (1954-57), Enlarged ed. 1973, Albrecht Altdorfer, The Art of the Renaissance in Northern Europe, Oesterreichische Handzeichnungen des 15 und 16 Jahrhunderts, Venetian Drawings of the 18th Century in America, Critical Catalogue of the Drawings in the Albertina, Rembrandt (Genève, 1957), Rembrandt as a Draughtsman, Edvard Munch, Great Drawings of All Time, Vol. II (New York, 1962), Meisterzeichnungen der Albertina (1964), Die Deutsche Malerei/Von Dürer bis Holbein (1966), Collected Writings, Vols. I-IV (London 1970-73). *Address:* Vienna I, Spiegelgasse 8, Austria. *Signs work:* "Otto Benesch."

BENISON, John; advertising designer; artist in wood carving, water-colour, chalk and pastel, flowmaster, pencil, pen and ink; Export Advertising Service, Robert Brandon & Partners, Garland Advertising Service, Kemsley Newspapers; teacher of advertising design; *b* London, 3 Sept., 1918; *s* of Steven Spurrier, artist; *m* Lydia Whitby; two *s,* one *d. Educ.:* Felstead School, Essex; *studied art* at

Central School of Arts and Crafts under Meninsky, John Farleigh, John Skeaping, Cecil Wade, and at St. John's Wood School under Ernest Perry and P. F. Millard. *Exhib.:* R.B.A., R.A. *Address:* 86 Park Rd., Loughborough LE11 2HH. *Signs work:* "BENISON."

BENNETT, June, N.D.D., A.T.D.; artist/jeweller in silver and gold; *b* Grange over Sands, 1935; *d* of E. B. Steer; *m* Michael Bennet; two *s. Educ.:* Ulverston Grammar School; *studied art* at Lancaster and Leicester Colleges of Art. *Exhib.:* Goldsmiths Hall (1975, 1976), Midland Group Gallery, Nottingham, Park Square Gallery, Leeds, Mignon Gallery, Bath, Ashgate Gallery, Farnham, Bluecoat Crafts Centre, Liverpool, Guild of Lakeland Craftsmen. *Work in permanent collection:* Abbot Hall Gallery, Kendal. *Address:* Hill Garth, Seascale, Cumbria. *Signs work:* "June Bennett" and Sheffield Assay Office hallmark.

BENNETT, Michael, N.D.D., A.T.D.: painter in oils and water-colours; *b* Windermere, 1934; *s* of T. W. Bennett; *m* June Steer; two *s. Educ.:* Windermere Grammar School; *studied art* at Lancaster and Leicester Colleges of Art. *Exhib.:* one-man shows: Park Square Gallery, Leeds, Mignon Gallery, Bath, Bluecoat Gallery, Liverpool, Ashgate Gallery, Farnham, Abbot Hall, Kendal, A.I.A. Gallery, London; Leeds, Birmingham, Hull and Lancaster Universities. *Work in permanent collections:* Abbot Hall Gallery, Wakefield City A.G., Lincolnshire Arts Assoc., John Player Collection, Leeds Educ. Authority. *Address:* Hill Garth, Seascale, Cumbria. *Signs work:* "Bennett" and date.

BENNEY, Prof. Adrian Gerald Sallis, R.D.I. (1971), Hon. M.A. (Leics., 1963), Des. R.C.A. (1954); goldsmith and silversmith; appointed Professor of Silversmithing and Jewellery at Royal College of Art (1974); *b* Hull, 21 Apr., 1930; *s* of Ernest Alfred Sallis Benney, A.R.C.A.; *m* Janet Edwards; three *s*, one *d. Educ.:* Brighton Grammar School; *studied art* at Brighton College of Art (1946-50); Royal College of Art (1951-54) under Prof. Robert Gooden, R.D.I. Royal Warrants of Appointment to H.M. The Queen (1974) and H.R.H. The Duke of Edinburgh (1975). *Address:* Beenham House, Beenham, nr. Reading, Berks. RG7 5LJ. *Signs work:* "Gerald Benney."

BENNEY, Derek Ward Sallis, A.R.C.A. (1950), Soc. Scribes and Illuminators (1953); Lecturer, Guildford School of Art, 1950-61; Head of Flintshire School of Art 1962-66; Head of Ipswich School of Art (Civic College) since 1966; *b* Salisbury, 1924; *s* of E. A. Sallis Benney, R.B.A., A.R.C.A., former Principal, Brighton College of Art and Crafts; *m* Elizabeth Weston, 1956; two *d. Educ.:* Brighton, Hove and Sussex Grammar School; *studied art* at Brighton College of Art and Royal College of Art. *Exhib.:* R.A. *Official purchases include:* Addresses to visiting royalty for the L.C.C. and Books of Remembrance for Brighton and the R.A.F. Church of St. Clement Danes. *Address:* 30 Kingsfield Ave., Ipswich, Suffolk IP1 3TA.

BENSUSAN-BUTT, John Gordon; landscape painter in water-colour; *b* Colchester, 6 June, 1911; *s* of Geoffrey Crawford Bensusan-Butt, F.C.A. *Educ.:* Gresham's School, Holt; Magdalen College, Oxford; *studied art* as pupil of Lucien Pissarro (1935-39), and at R.C.A., etching (1935), Central School of Art and Crafts, lithography (1939). *Exhib.:* R.A., N.E.A.C., R.B.A., Leicester Galleries, Redfern, etc. One-man shows at French Gallery (1937), Kensington A.G. (1949), Leicester Galleries (1957), Minories, Colchester (1962, 1964, 1975). *Address:* 31B Lexden Rd., Colchester CO3 3PX. *Signs work:* see appendix.

BENT, Medora Heather, F.I.A.L.; painter in oil, water-colour; from 1965 has taken up pottery; *b* North Kilworth, family home and chief influence, Connemara; *m* Roger Bent; one *s. Educ.:* The Laurels, Rugby, and Upper Chine, I.O.W.;

studied art at Slade School (1930-33), Diploma under Professor Schwabe; Central School of Arts and Crafts: stained glass, pottery and modelling; worked in Ireland, France, Hungary, Sark and Belgium. *Exhib.:* N.E.A.C., London Group, S.G.A., S.W.A., Nat. Soc. *Publication:* Paintings of Historical Houses of Purbeck (1958). *Address:* 10 East St., Wareham, Dorset. *Signs work:* "M. H. Bent."

BENTLEY, Nicolas, F.S.I.A. (1946); black and white artist; *b* 14 June, 1907; *s* of E. C. Bentley, author. *Educ.:* University College School, London; Heatherley's School of Art. *Address:* 7 Hobury St., Chelsea, London SW10. *Club:* Garrick. *Signs work:* see appendix.

BENYON, Margaret, Slade Diploma (1965); painter; holographer, screen-printing; part-time lecturer; Fellow in Fine Art, Nottingham University; *b* Birmingham, 29 Apr., 1940; *d* of John Benyon. *Educ.:* Kenya High School, Nairobi; *studied art* at Birmingham College of Art (1959-61), Slade School (1961-63, 1964-66). *Work in permanent collections:* Castle Museum, Nottingham, Ministry of Public Buildings and Works, Ministry of Aviation Supply; private collections. *Address:* 14 Queen's Mansions, West End La., London NW6. *Signs work:* "Margaret Benyon."

BERESFORD-WILLIAMS, Mary E., B.A.Hons. Fine Art Reading (1953 Class 1); Cert. Educ. (1954); print-maker and artist; screen-printer and painter in most media; *b* London, 30 Apr., 1931; *d* of F. N. Elliott; *m* David Beresford-Williams; one *s*. *Educ.:* Watford Grammar School; *studied art* at Reading University under Prof. J. A. Betts. *Exhib.:* Chagford, Devon (1976), Samian, Torquay (1976), Hambledon, Blandford Forum (1976), Llandrindod Wells (1970). *Work in permanent collection:* Swansea University. *Address:* 11 Langdon Lane, Galmpton, nr. Brixham, S. Devon. *Signs work:* "M. Beresford-Williams" or "M. B. Williams."

BERG, Adrian; painter; *b* London, 1929; *s* of Charles Berg, M.D., psychoanalyst and author. *Educ.:* Charterhouse, Borlands (Tutors) Ltd., Gonville and Caius College, Cambridge (M.A.), Trinity College, Dublin (H.Dip.Ed.); *studied art* at St. Martin's, Chelsea, R.C.A. *Exhib.:* Tooth's (1964, 1967, 1969, 1972). *Work in permanent collections:* Arts Council, Ministry of Works. *Address:* 8 Gloucester Gate, London NW1. *Signs work:* "Adrian Berg."

BERGER, René; Dir.-curator, Cant. Fine Arts Museum, Lausanne, President, A.I.C.A.; *b* Brussels, 29 Apr., 1915; *m* Rose-Marie Quartier-La-Tente. *Educ.:* Univs. Lausanne, Paris. Prof. Univ. and School of Fine Arts; founder, cultural movement, "Pour l'Art"; curator of Fine Arts Museum; lecturer, writer. *Publications:* Découverte de la peinture (ed. Guilde du Livre and des Fauconnières, Lausanne); Discovery of Painting (ed. Viking Press, New York); The Language of Art (ed. Thames and Hudson, London), trans. Germ., Engl., It., Sp.; Connaissance de la peinture, 12 vols. (ed. Club français du Livre Paris); Art et Communication, Editions Casterman La Mutation des signes, Editions Denoël. *Address:* Musée cant. des beaux-arts, Palais de Rumine, Lausanne T. (021) 22 83 33.

BERLIN, Sven; sculptor in stone and bronze, painter and writer; *b* 14 Sept., 1911; *s* of Karl Berlin, Swedish; mother English; two *s*, one *d*. *Educ.:* St. Winifred's, Kenley; *studied art* at Redruth, Cornwall, under A. C. Hambly. *Exhib.:* Lefevre, Tooth's, Houston, Texas, New York, etc. *Work in permanent collections:* Musee d'Art, Ovar, Portugal, Imperial War Museum, I.S.R., Fawley, Poole Technical College, etc. *Publications:* Alfred Wallis; Primitive (Nicholson & Watson, 1948), I Am Lazarus (Dent, 1961), Dark Monarch (Dent, 1962), Jonah's Dream (Dent, 1964), Dromengro (Collins, 1971), Pride of the Peacock

(Collins, 1972). *Address:* Higher Gaunts, Stanbridge, Wimborne, Dorset. *Signs work:* see appendix.

BERRISFORD, Peter, N.D.D., A.T.D.; painter, lithographer, illustrator, lecturer in History of Art (especially Italian), Guest Lecturer; Swan's Hellenic; oils, lithography, water-colour; *b* Northampton, 11 Feb., 1932; *s* of Ernest Berrisford; *m* Jackie Elizabeth; one *s*. *Studied art* at Northampton Art School (Travelling Scholarship to Italy, 1953); Chelsea Art School under Ceri Richards; Bournemouth College of Art. *Work in permanent collections:* Leicestershire, Hertfordshire and Surrey Educ. Committees, Hull and Northampton Art Galleries, East Midlands Electricity Board. Lithographs for Book of the Month Club, N.Y. *Address:* East Sussex College of Higher Education, Darley Rd., Eastbourne.

BERRY, June, D.F.A. (Lond.) (1949), N.D.D. (1954); painter in oil, acrylic, and printmaker; *b* Melbourne, Derbyshire, 1924; *m* John Berry; one *s*, two *d*. *Studied art* at Slade School, University College, London (1946-49). *Address:* 81 Kent House Rd., Sydenham, London SE26. *Signs work:* "June Berry."

BERRY-HART, David James, N.D.D., A.T.D., A.T.C.; sculptor in steel, perspex and stone; lecturer in sculpture; *b* Trinidad, 13 May, 1940; *s* of Ralph Alexander Berry-Hart. *Studied art* at St. Martin's School of Art (1959-61) under Frederick Gore and Joe Tilson. *Exhib.:* one-man shows: A.I.A. Gallery, London (1969), Herbert A.G., Coventry (1970), Camden Arts Centre (1975); group shows; Art in Steel (1972), Gawthorpe Festival (1974), Spectrum Central (1971). *Work repro.:* Midlands Art Magazine (1971), I.C.I. Taking Shape (1976). *Address:* 13A Manor Court Rd., Nuneaton, Warwicks. *Signs work:* "D. J. Berry-Hart."

BERTRAM, Anthony, M.A. (Oxon.), Legion d'Honneur, Croix de Guerre (1946); lecturer and writer on art; lecturer, Oxford University Extramural Delegacy (1927-66); editor, Design for Today (1934); deputy-representative, British Council, Paris (1945-46); visiting professor, Elmira College, N.Y., U.S.A. (1958-60); *b* 19 Nov., 1897; *s* of Ernest Bertram; *m* Barbara Randolph; two *s*. *Educ.:* Douai Abbey; Pembroke College, Oxford. *Publications:* Life of Rubens (1928); The House (1935); Paul Nash (1955); Michelangelo (1964); 1,000 Years of Drawing (1966); Florentine Sculpture (1969), etc.; nine novels; two travel books, etc. *Address:* 2 Coates Castle, Fittleworth, Sussex. *Club:* Savile.

BESTALL, Alfred Edmeades; illustrator and painter in oil, water-colour, line and wash; *b* Mandalay, 1892; *s* of Rev. Arthur H. Bestall, K-i-H. *Educ.:* Rydal School; *studied art* at Birmingham C. under Catterson Smith (1912-14) and L.C.C., Central, F. V. Burridge, A. S. Hartrick, and Noel Rooke (1919-22). *Exhib.:* R.A., R.B.A., etc. *Work repro.:* illustrations to Myths and Legends of Many Lands, The Play's the Thing. The Spanish Goldfish, Folk Tales of Wales, Salute to the Village, and about fifty other books; Tatler, Punch, etc. *Publications:* all the Rupert stories (Daily Express), 1935-65, and other children's books. *Address:* 8/44 Ewell Rd., Surbiton. *Signs work:* "A. E. BESTALL" (initials frequently omitted).

BETHEL, David, A.R.W.A., F.R.S.A., N.D.D., A.T.D., F.S.A.E., A.S.I.A.; graphic and typographic designer; Director, Leicester Polytechnic; Chairman, CNAA Committee for Art and Design; *b* Bath, 7 Dec., 1923; *s* of Wm. Geo. Bethell; *m* Margaret; one *s*, one *d*. *Educ.:* King Edward's School, Bath; *studied art* at Gloucester College of Art (1946-48), West of England College of Art (1948-51). *Work in permanent collections:* Gloucester and Stafford Art Galleries, R.W.A., and private collections in U.S.A. and Israel. *Address:* 48 Holmfield Rd., Stoneygate, Leicester LE2 1SA. *Signs work:* "David Bethel."

BETHEL, Marion Ross; illuminator and letterer in water-colour, gold leaf, ink, parchment in illuminated books; *b* Wiesbaden, Germany, 19 Mar., 1929; *d* of Herbert H. Bethel, D.D.S. (U.S.A.). *Educ.:* P.N.E.U. correspondence course; *studied art* with Gladys Best, R.W.A., and Daisy Alcock, A.R.C.A., F.R.S.A. *Exhib.:* Salon de Soc. des Artistes Français. *Work repro.:* in Revue Moderne. *Address:* 17 Strand, Topsham, Devon. *Signs work:* "M.R.B." or "Marion Ross Bethel."

BETHERS, Ray; artist in oil, gouache and wood engraving; author; Lecturer on Art, University of London (Dept. of Extra Mural Studies); *b* Corvallis, Oreg., 25 Apr., 1902; *m* Peggy Bethers. *Educ.:* University of Oregon; *studied art* at California School of Fine Arts, Art Students League (N.Y.), Académie André Lhote (Paris). *Exhib.:* San Francisco Legion of Honour, Salon de Mai (Paris). *Publications:* Pictures, Painters and You (1948), Composition in Pictures (1949), From Eye to Camera (1951), How Paintings Happen (1951), Photo-Vision (1957), Art Always Changes (1958), Language of Paintings (1964). *Address:* c/o Macmillan, Little Essex St., London WC2. *Signs work:* "Ray Bethers."

BETTS, J. Anthony, A.R.C.A., Lond.; Emeritus Professor of Fine Art, Reading University; *b* 1897; *m* N. S. Flexen; one *s*; *studied art* at Bradford College of Art, R.C.A. and abroad. *Exhib.:* London, Paris, New York. *Address:* c/o The University, Reading, Berks. *Club:* Athenæum. *Signs work:* "Anthony Betts."

BEVAN, Daniel Vaughan Gwillim, R.I.; technical publicity consultant; self taught artist in water-colour; *b* Cardiff, 8 June, 1921; *s* of Daniel Thomas Bevan; *m* Betty Eileen, divorced; two *d. Educ.:* Willesden and Hendon Technical Colleges. *Address:* 110 Francklyn Gdns., Edgware, Middx. HA8 8SA. *Signs work:* "Vaughan Bevan."

BHATT, Janardan T.; artist in oil; *b* Nairobi, Kenya, 21 Dec., 1941; *s* of T. A. Bhatt; *m* Shuchismita Bhatt; one *s*, one *d. Educ.:* Regent St. Polytechnic; Westminster College; Duke of Gloucester School; *studied art* at Regent St. Polytechnic (1959-61). *Address:* 37 Blenheim Gdns., London NW2. *Clubs:* Friends of the Tate Gallery, Institute of Contemporary Arts, Life Friend of the Federation of British Artists, Hampstead Theatre. *Signs work:* "Janardan."

BICAT, Andre, O.B.E.; painter, sculptor, printmaker, ceramist; tutor, R.C.A.; *b* 1909. *Work in permanent collections:* B.M., V. & A., Arts Council, Ministry of the Environment, South London Art Gallery, Greenwich Library, National Gallery of Wales, City of Portsmouth, City of Leeds, Nottingham College of Art, West of England College of Art, Reading Art Gallery, Oxford University, Dublin University, National Gallery, South Australia, Toledo Museum, Ohio, Brooklyn Museum, Oregon, Dallas Museum, Cleveland Museum. *Exhib.:* one-man shows: London, Leicester Galleries (1949, 1958, 1959, 1960, 1961, 1966, 1968, 1970); Milan (1972); Paris, Galerie de l'Institut (1962); Dublin (1963); Reading (1964-66); Newcastle (1966); Oxford (1969, 1973). *Address:* Crays Pond House, nr. Pangbourne, Berks. *Club:* London Group. *Signs work:* see appendix.

BICE, Clare, O.S.A. (1939), R.C.A. (1966), LL.D. (Univ. of West Ontario, 1962), C.M. (1973, Order of Canada); artist in oil; curator, London, Ont., Museum and Art Gallery (1940-72); Fellowship, Canadian Government Overseas Award for study in France (1953-54); Canada Council Senior Arts Fellowship (1962-63); President, Canadian Art Museum Directors (1966-68); President, Royal Canadian Academy (1967-70); *b* Durham, Ont., 24 Jan., 1909; *s* of Albert A. Bice, Archdeacon of London, Ont.; *m* Marion Agnes Bice; one *s*, one *d. Educ.:* University of W. Ontario (B.A., 1928); *studied art* at N.Y. Art Students League. *Exhib.:* R.C.A. (1937-70), O.S.A. (1937-62), N.Y. World's Fair (1940). *Publica-*

tions: Jory's Cove (Macmillan, N.Y., 1941), Across Canada (Macmillan, N.Y., 1949), The Great Island (Macmillan, N.Y., 1953), A Dog for Davie's Hill (Macmillan, N.Y., 1957), Hurricane Treasure (Viking, N.Y., 1965). *Address:* 1010 Wellington St., London, Ont. *Signs work:* "Clare Bice."

BICKERTON, Leonard Marshall, F.L.A. (1938), F.M.A. (1958); librarian and curator, Hereford City Library Museum and Art Gallery (1945-49); chief librarian and curator, Worthing Library, Museum and Art Gallery (1949-74); Art Consultant to the Edward James Foundation since 1970; *b* 15 July, 1914; *m*; two *s*. *Educ.:* Rivington Grammar School. *Publication:* Eighteenth Century English Drinking Glasses (Barrie & Jenkins, 1972). *Address:* 63 First Ave., Worthing.

BIÉLER, André, LL.D., R.C.A., O.S.A., C.S.P.W.C.; Resident Artist and Professor of Art, Queen's University, Kingston, Ontario (1936-61), now Professor Emeritus; Banff School Fine Arts (1940-47-49-52); Vice-Pres. C.G.P. (1943); painter and sculptor; *b* Lausanne, 8 Oct., 1896; *s* of Prof. Charles Biéler; *m* Jeannette Meunier; two *s*, two *d*. *Educ.:* Lycée Carnot, Paris, Stanstead College, Quebec, Art Students League in New York and Woodstock, N.Y., Ecole du Louvre in Paris. *Work in permanent collections:* National Gallery, Ottawa; Art Gallery of Ontario; Musée de la Province de Quebec; Winnipeg, and Edmonton-Windsor, London, Ont., and in numerous other public galleries and private collections. *Address:* Glenburnie, Ontario, Canada. *Signs work:* see appendix.

BIGGS, John R., A.T.D., M.S.I.A.; designer, engraver on wood, typographer; head of Graphic Design School, Brighton College of Art; *b* Derby, 25 July, 1909; *m*; five *s*. *Educ.:* Derby, London University; *studied art* at Derby, Central School of Arts and Crafts. *Exhib.:* R.A., R.Cam.A., Redfern Gallery, Brussels, San Francisco, etc. *Work in permanent collections:* B.M. *Work repro.:* in Studio, London Mercury, Monotype Recorder, etc. *Publications:* Basic Typography, An Approach to Type, Woodcuts, Story of the Alphabet, The Craft of Lettering, The Craft of the Pen, The Craft of Woodcuts, Sinfin Songs; illustrator of Robinson Crusoe, Green Grows the City. *Address:* 68 Stanford Ave., Brighton, Sussex. *Signs work:* "John R. Biggs."

BILL, John Gordon, A.R.W.A. (1971); artist in oil, landscape painter and teacher; *b* London, 6 Nov., 1915; *s* of Lieut.-Col. James G. Bill; *m* Coral Nerelle, portrait painter. *Educ.:* Radley College; *studied art* at Byam Shaw School, under Charles Mahoney, A.R.A., and Bernard Dunstan, R.A. *Exhib.:* N.E.A.C., R.W.A., and Cheltenham Group; one-man shows: Oxford, Cheltenham. *Work in permanent collections:* Cheltenham Art Gallery, Royal West of England Academy. *Address:* Salperton Pk., nr. Cheltenham, Glos. *Signs work:* see appendix.

BILL, Max, M. of B.S.A., D.W.B., G.S.M.B.A., Hon. F.A.I.A., Berlin Art Academy, Flamish Academy; architect, painter, sculptor, writer; Director Hochschule für Gestaltung, Ulm, Germany (1951-1956); professor for Environmental Design, Hochschule für bildende Künste, Hamburg, Germany (1967-1974); Member of Swiss National Parliament; architect, Cultural Section, Swiss National Exhibition, Lausanne (1964); Grand Prix Biennale São Paulo (1951), Grand Prix Triennale di Milan (1936 and 1951), Zürich Art Prize (1968); *b* Winterthur, Switzerland, 22 Dec., 1908. *Studied at:* "Bauhaus" (College of Design), Dessau. *Work repro.:* Monographs by Margit Staber (1963 and 1971), Wood (1974). *Address:* Albulastrasse 39, 8048, Zürich, Switzerland. *Signs work:* see appendix.

BILLIN, Edward S.; free-lance commercial artist in water-colour, wood engraving; *b* Sheffield, 19 June, 1911; *s* of H. M. Billin; *m* Dorothy Mount; one *d*. *Educ.:* Western Rd. Secondary School, Sheffield; *studied art* at Sheffield College of Art under Eric Jones, R.S., A.R.C.A., in engraving, Noel Spencer, A.R.C.A., in design. *Exhib.:* Soc. of Wood Engravers, R.A., R.S.A., R.B.A., Britain in Water-colour, R.W.S., Art Institute of Chicago, On tour with Arts Council and Art exhbns. Bureau. *Work in permanent collections:* Graves A.G., Sheffield, Derby Educ. Com. *Work repro.:* The Studio (1951), Woman's Journal, Coronation Issue. *Publications:* Drawing on scraper board (Pitman). *Address:* 36 Botanical Rd., Sheffield S11 8RP.

BILLINGS, Kathleen Wyatt, R.I., S.M.; *b* Christchurch, N.Z.; *m* F. J. W. Billings; one *s*, one *d*. *Studied* at Canterbury College School of Art (1928-31). *Exhib.:* R.I., S.M., N.Z. Academy of Fine Arts; abstract collages with Group 60 (1967); one-man show, Osborne Galleries, Auckland (1973). *Work repro.:* La Revue Moderne. *Publication:* folio of prints entitled Flowers of the South Pacific. Spent 1964-66 in Cook Islands; painted flowers there, sixteen of which were printed for Cook Islands' first definitive issue of stamps. Commissioned to design set of flower paintings to form first definitive issue of stamps for Niue (1969). At present engaged on imaginative collages, and making hand-made paper. *Address:* 5 Kotare St., Waikanae, N.Z. *Signs work:* "Kay W. Billings" or "K.W.B."

BILLYARD, Kenneth Harry, B.A. (Hons.) Fine Art (1966); professional painter in acrylics on prepared hardboard, lecturer in fine art; *b* Sale, Ches., 18 Dec., 1943; *s* of H. A. Billyard, chief jig and tool draughtsman. *Educ.:* Lymm Grammar School; *studied art* at Newcastle University (1962-66) under Kenneth Rowntree, Richard Hamilton, Matt Rugg. *Exhib.:* one-man show: Bolton Octagon Theatre (1975); two-man shows: Chester Arts and Recreation Trust, Chester (1975), "Contrasts", Wythenshawe Forum, Manchester (1974), "Northern Images '74", Manchester (1974); four-man show: Portico Gallery, Manchester (1975). *Work in permanent collection:* Portland Gallery, Manchester. *Publication:* Degree thesis on 'Vorticism' and the English Abstract Painters 1912–15. *Address:* 13 Mauldeth Rd., Withington, Manchester, M20 9NE. *Signs work:* "K. Billyard."

BINDER, Joseph Frederick; advertising artist, painter, industrial designer at every stage from trade-mark to poster; *b* Ludwigshafenrhein. *Studied art* at Bernhard, Klinger, Deffke, Schule, and self-taught. *Work in permanent collections:* Brooklyn Museum, Chicago, Europäische Hauptstädte, Ludwigshafen/Rhine Museum of Arts, Binder Saal. *Work repro.:* International Advertising Art, Die Reklame, Commercial Art, Vendre, Die Anzeige, Europäische Werbung, Gebrauchsgraphik, Graphis, Graphik. *Publications:* Binder: A Survey of his Work, Binder Trade Marks, The Artist Satisfies the Engineer, Binder-Monographie 1960, In Grossen und Internationalen Wettbewerben an Erster Stelle Preisgekrönt. *Address:* 13 Mauldeth Rd., Withington, Manchester M20 9NE. *Signs work:* "K. Billyard."

BINNING, Bertram Charles, R.C.A. (1955), Diploma Graduate, Vancouver School of Art (1935); painter in oil and teacher; Prof., Fine Arts Dept., University of British Columbia, since 1948; *b* Medicine Hat, Alberta, Canada, 10 Feb., 1909; *s* of Arthur Franklin Binning; *m* Jessie Isobel. *Educ.:* Vancouver, and University of Oregon; *studied art* at Vancouver, New York, London. *Work in permanent collections:* Toronto Art Gallery, Hart House (University of Toronto), University of Manitoba, Vancouver Art Gallery. *Official purchases:* National Gallery of Canada. *Address:* 2968 Mathers Cres., West Vancouver, British Columbia, Canada. *Clubs:* Canadian Group of Painters, Canadian Graphic Arts Soc. *Signs work:* see appendix.

BINNS, Lorna, A.R.C.A. (1938), A.R.W.S. (1973); painter in water-colour; *b*

Sheffield, 23 Oct., 1914; *d* of Harold John Harrison; *m* John Dawson Binns; two *d*. *Educ.:* Abbeydale Girls' Grammar School, Sheffield; *studied art* at Sheffield College of Art (1930-35) under Maurice Wheatley, R.C.A. (1935-39) under Prof. Tristram. *Exhib.:* R.A., F.B.A. Gallery, The Guildhall, R.W.S. Gallery. *Address:* 71 Fairfield Rd., Kingston-upon-Thames, Surrey. *Signs work:* "Lorna Binns."

BINYON, Helen, A.R.C.A.; book-illustrator, puppeteer, water-colour painter; lecturer at Bath Academy of Art (1950-65); *b* London, 9 Dec., 1904; *d* of the poet Laurence Binyon. *Studied art* at Royal College of Art (1922-26). Ran a travelling marionette theatre with Margaret Binyon up to 1938. Short puppet-show seasons in London at Poetry Bookshop, a Chelsea studio and the Mercury Theatre. *Publications:* Puppetry To-day (Studio Vista, 1965); boocs illustrated include The Street of Queer Houses, by Vernon Knowles, Brief Candles, by Laurence Binyon (Golden Cockerel Press), Pride and Prejudice (Penguin IVLLUSTRATED Classics), the Binyon Books, a series for little children made with Margaret Binyon (Oxford University Press), The Children Next Door (Aladdin Books, New York), An Everyday Alphabet (Oxford University Press). *Address:* 7 Market Ave., Chichester, Sussex. *Signs work:* "Helen Binyon."

BIRBECK, Thomas Towning; artist in water-colour; *b* Sunderland, 7 July, 1902; *s* of Thomas Wilkinson Birbeck, schoolmaster. *Exhib.:* Cardiff Museum and Art Gallery, Newport Corpn. and Swansea Glyn Vivian Art Galleries. *Publications:* Illustrator of publications of the Chepstow Soc. *Address:* Vauxhall Crest, Chepstow. *Club:* Wye Valley Art Club. *Signs work:* "Thos. T. Birbeck" and date.

BIRCH, John Anthony, B.A. (Fine Art); audio-visual aids specialist; artist in acrylic on canvas and multi-screen slide projection; *b* Clevedon, Som., 1946; *m* Jane Tapley; one *s*, one *d*. *Studied art* at West of England College of Art (1964-67). *Exhib.:* group show: Arnolfini (1975); one-man show: Bristol Arts Centre (1973). *Work in permanent collection:* Arnolfini Trust. *Address:* 61 Dongola Rd., Horfield, Bristol. *Club:* A.I.R. *Signs work:* signature stencilled on back of canvas in letters 3″ high.

BIRD, Henry Richard, A.R.C.A. (1933), F.R.S.A. (1951), F.I.A.L. (1957), Soc. of Mural Painters (1939), M. Tempera Soc., A.W.G.; painter, mural decorator; *b* Northampton, 1909; *s* of William Bird; *m* Freda Jackson, actress; one *s*. *Educ.:* Northampton; *studied art* at Northampton, R.C.A. *Exhib.:* Tate, V. & A., Lambeth Palace; one-man shows include Bristol City Art Gallery; Arts Unlimited, London; Northampton Art Gallery Centenary; Greco, Chelsea; University Church, Cambridge; Peterborough Cathedral. *Work in permanent collections:* National Library of Wales; Drottingholm, Sweden; Carlisle; Northampton; Brighton; Earls Barton Church; Inst. of Commonwealth Studies, University of London; complete schemes of decoration, St. Crispin Hospital Chapel, Daventry Hospital Chapel, Denton Church, Northants. *Address:* Hardingstone House, Northants. *Signs work:* "H. Bird."

BIRD, Mary Holden; landscape artist in water-colour; *d* of the late William Hay Caldwell; *m* Kenneth Bird (Fougasse, deceased); *studied art* at Heatherleys'. *Exhib.:* R.A., R.I., R.S.W., R.B.A., Paris Salon, etc. *Work repro.:* several by the Medici Soc. *Address:* 123 Swan Ct., London SW3. *Signs work:* see appendix.

BIRD, Peter, M.A. (Cantab.), F.M.A.; Assistant Art Director, the Arts Council of Great Britain; *b* London, 16 Nov., 1924. *Educ.:* Latymer Upper School, London; King's College, Cambridge. *Address:* 5 Westmoreland Pl., London SW1.

BIRO, B. S. (Val), F.S.I.A.; free-lance designer, illustrator, painter; assistant production manager, Sylvan Press (1945-46), production manager and art director, C. & J. Temple (1946-48), John Lehmann, Ltd. (1948-53); *b* Budapest,

Hungary, 6 Oct., 1921; *s* of Dr. B. Biro, solicitor; *m* (1) Vivien Woolley; one *d*; (2) Marie-Louise Ellaway; one *step-s*, one *step-d*. *Educ.:* School of the Cistercian Monks, Budapest; *studied art* at Central School of Arts and Crafts, London. *Publications:* Author of the Gumdrop Series and other books for children. *Work in permanent collections:* V. & A. Museum. *Address:* 95 High St., Amersham, Bucks. *Signs work:* "Biro."

BISHOP, Edward, R.B.A. (1950), N.E.A.C. (1960); artist in oil, pastel, lithography, pencil, and graphic designer; *b* 11 Nov., 1902; *s* of Jacob Bishop and Eliza Harriet Metcalfe. *Educ.:* Elementary School; *studied art* at Central School of Arts and Crafts under A. S. Hartrick, F. W. Jackson, A.R.A., Bernard Meninsky, Noël Rooke (1920-26). *Exhib.:* R.A., Leicester Galleries, Wildenstein Gallery, N.E.A.C., R.B.A., Arts Council, etc. *Work in permanent collections:* National Gallery, Sydney, Australia, Nottingham Art Gallery and private collections. *Work repro.:* various newspapers and magazines. *Address:* 6 East Heath Rd., Hampstead, London NW3. *Club:* Past President, Chelsea Arts. *Signs work:* see appendix.

BLACK, Ian, Art Teaching Diploma, Bristol University (1956), A.R.W.A. (1970); art teacher and artist in oil, acrylic, pen and ink; Head of Art, Bristol Cathedral School, pottery tutor, Clifton College; *b* Bury St. Edmunds, 31 May, 1929; *s* of Frederick Black, chemist; *m* Judith Rhiannon; three *d*. *Educ.:* Culford School, Bury St. Edmunds; *studied art* at Southampton College of Art (1949), Merton College, Oxford (1950), Bath Academy of Art (1952-56) under William Scott, Martin Froy, Jack Smith, Terry Frost, Peter Lanyon. *Exhib.:* five one-man shows, R.W.A., R.A., travelling exhibs. *Work in permanent collections:* R.W.A., Walsall Educ. Centre, Bath University, N.Z. Government, St. Catherine's College, Oxford, Wadham College, Oxford, Oxford Corp., Clifton High School, Redland School, Dorset House, Oxford. *Address:* 64 Pembroke Rd., Clifton, Bristol BS8 3DX. *Signs work:* "IB" or "Ian Black."

BLACK, Sir Misha, Kt. (1972), O.B.E., R.D.I., F.S.I.A., F.F.A.S.; industrial designer; *b* 26 Oct., 1910; senior partner Design Research Unit; Prof. in Industrial Design at R.C.A. (since 1959), Emeritus 1975; exhbns. designed in Gt. Britain, U.S.A., France, Spain, Italy, Belgium, Ceylon, Mexico, Southern Rhodesia, Canada and Israel; principal exhbn. architect to M.O.I. (1940-45); co-ordinating architect, South Bank Exhbn. (1951); design consultant to British Railways (1957-61) and London Transport since 1964; Pres. S.I.A.D. (1953-56); Pres. I.C.S.I.D. (1956-61); mem. Council of C. of I.D. (1955-64); mem. Advisory Council of Science Museum (since 1967); Trustee, British Museum (since 1968). *Address:* 32 Aybrook St., London W1M 4BB. *Club:* Reform. *Signs work:* "Misha Black."

BLACK, Noël, D.L.C.A. (1953), A.T.D. (1954); sculptor in metal, polyester, acrylic and ceramic; senior lecturer in sculpture, Kesteven College of Education and The University of Evansville; *b* Prescot, 25 Dec., 1931; *m* Pamela Black; one *d*. *Educ.:* Nelson, Lancs.; *studied art* at Loughborough College of Art (1949-53); Leicester College of Art (1953-54). *Exhib.:* Upstairs Gallery, Stamford. *Work in private and public collections* includes commissioned work for schools and churches. *Address:* The Old Vicarage, Skillington, Grantham, Lincs. *Signs work:* "Noël Black."

BLACKBURN, Clarence E.; designer and draughtsman, etching, water-colour and oils; mural painter, church work, commercial art work; manufactured small pottery fancy goods during career from 1944 to 1959; commenced artistic career 1943; *b* 5 Sept., 1914. *Educ.:* St. Peter's School, Stoke-on-Trent; *studied art* at

Burslem College of Art. *Exhib.:* R.E. and R.A.; Contemporary European Painters, Waldorf-Astoria, New York. Subject of notice in Volume IV, Dictionary of International Biography, 1968, and subject of commendation in Volume, 1969, The Two Thousand Men of Achievement for Distinguished Service to Art. *Address:* 30 Cedars Rd., Hampton Wick, Kingston, Surrey. *Signs work:* "C. E. Blackburn."

BLACKBURN, David, Des. R.C.A. (1962); painter in pastel; visiting lecturer, University of Melbourne (1971-72, 1973-74); *b* Huddersfield, 1939; *s* of Wilfrid Blackburn. *Educ.:* Huddersfield College; *studied art* at Huddersfield School of Art (1955-59), R.C.A. (1959-62). *Work in permanent collections:* Leeds City Art Gallery, Sheffield Art Gallery, National Gallery of Victoria, Oldham Art Gallery, Hatton Gallery, Newcastle. *Work repro.:* in Apollo, Studio International, Art in Australia, Art International. *Address:* 45 May St., Crosland Moor, Huddersfield, Yorks. *Signs work:* "David Blackburn."

BLACKMAN, Audrey, F.S.D-C.; painter and sculptor in ceramics and bronze; *b* London, 1907; *d* of Dr. Richard Seligman; *m* Prof. G. E. Blackman, F.R.S. *Educ.:* Wimbledon High School, Kunstgewerbeschule, Graz, Goldsmiths' College and Reading University. *Exhib.:* widely at home and abroad. *Work in permanent collections:* Fitzwilliam Museum, Cambridge, City of Stoke-on-Trent Museum, Paisley Museum, Cecil Higgins Museum, Bedford, Melbourne University, Magdalen College, Oxford, Czechoslovak Ceramics Museum, Bechyne, Oxfordshire County Museum. *Publication:* Making Rolled Pottery Figures (Mills & Boon, 1976). Chairman, Society of Designer-Craftsmen (1967-70); Instigated Federation of British Craft Societies (1970); Mem. Crafts Advisory Com. (1971-73). *Address:* Wood Croft, Foxcombe La., Boars Hill, Oxford OX1 5DH. *Signs work:* "A. Blackman."

BLAIN, Iris, N.D.D., painting (1951); potter, painter in oil, gouache, and stage designer (ballet décor, etc.); *b* London; *d* of E. Snowman; *m* John Blain; one *s*, one *d*. *Educ.:* Camden School for Girls; *studied art* at Regent St. Polytechnic, R.A. Schools, Anglo-French Art Centre. *Exhib.:* R.A., R.B.A., W.I.A.C., London Group, R.W.E.A., Arts Council Tours, one-man exhbn., Manchester (1959); second one-man exhbn., Manchester Central Library (1963). *Official purchases:* Hertford C.C. and Liverpool University. *Work repro.:* some stage and ballet designs, also commercial art. *Address:* Oakfield, Langham Rd., Bowdon, Altrincham, Ches. *Signs work:* see appendix.

BLAKE, Frederick Donald, R.I. (1952); artist and industrial designer in oil, water-colour, etching, pen and ink; *b* 7 June, 1908; *s* of F. H. Blake. *Educ.:* Camberwell School of Arts and Crafts; Goldsmiths' College; Brixton School of Building. *Exhib.:* R.A., R.O.I., R.I., R.B.A. *Work repro.:* newspaper maps, war illustrations, railway posters, advertising drawings. *Address:* Flat 2, Hereford House, Lauriston Rd., London SW19. *Clubs:* London Sketch, Chelsea Arts. *Signs work:* "F. Donald Blake."

BLAKELY, Zelma, R.E.; Slade Diploma in Fine Art (1947), F.R.E., Wilson Steer Gold Medal (1946); illustrator in woodcut and wood engraving; teacher, Heatherley School of Art; *b* London; *d* of James Francis Blakely; *m* Keith Mackenzie; three *s*. *Educ.:* in the U.S.A. and England; *studied art* at Kingston-upon-Thames (1939-42) under Reginald Brill and Wilfred Fairclough; Slade School (1945-48) under Prof. Schwabe and William Coldstream. *Work repro.:* illustrations for English Fare and French Wines (André Simon); Kippers to Caviar (Helen Burke); El Zarco, the Bandit (Folio Society); Geordies Mermaid (Methuen); Nuki and the Sea Serpent (Longmans); and others. *Address:* Rose

Cottage, Pin Mill, Ipswich, Suffolk. *Clubs:* R.E., Pin Mill Sailing. *Signs work:* "Zelma Blakely."

BLAKER, Michael, N.D.D. (1949), A.R.E. (1957), R.E. (1975); figurative painter in oil and water-colour, etcher, modeller, and writer on art; *b* Hove, 19 Jan., 1928; *s* of John Blaker. *Educ.:* Brighton Grammar School, Heversham School, Westmorland; *studied art* at Brighton College of Art. *Exhib.:* R.A., R.E., Leicester Gall., Suffolk St. Galls., New Grafton Gall., Artist Enamellers; one-man shows: London and provinces, U.S.A. *Work in permanent collections:* V. & A., South London Gall., Brighton Art Gall., Hove Art Gall. *Work repro.:* Studio, Artist, Pictures and Prints, and periodicals. *Address:* 20 Hova Villas, Hove, Sussex. *Signs work:* see appendix.

BLAKESTON, Oswell. *One-man shows include:* Gallery 273 (1974), Perrin's (1973), Bruce Castle (1972), Everyman (1971), B.H. Corner Gallery (1970, 1969), Hampton Court (1968), Drian Gallery (1967, 1966), Nicholas Treadwell Gallery, Croydon (1966), New Vision Centre (1964, 1962), Municipal Gallery, Great Yarmouth (1964), Gallery 60, Colchester (1962), Grabowski Gallery (1962), etc. *Shared and group shows include:* Leicester Gallery, Mercury Gallery, etc. *Overseas:* The International Exhibition of Abstract Water-colourists, Bodensee Museum, British Artists, Toronto, etc. *Address:* c/o Drian Gallery, 5-7 Porchester Pl., London W2. *Signs work:* "O.B."

BLAMEY, Norman Charles, R.O.I. (1952), A.R.A. (1970), R.A. (1975); painter in oil and teacher of painting; *b* London, 16 Dec., 1914; *s* of Charles Henry Blamey; *m* Margaret Kelly; one *s*. *Educ.:* Holloway School, London; *studied art* at The Polytechnic School of Art, Regent St. (1931-37). *Exhib.:* R.A., R.H.A., R.O.I., R.B.A., N.E.A.C. and provincial galleries. Work in permanent and private collections. *Address:* 39 Lyncroft Gdns., London NW6.

BLASZKOWSKI, Martin, 2nd Prize Sculpture, Mardel Plata (1958), Bronze Medal, Brussels (1958), Mencion Honorifica, Salon Nacional Bellas Artes, Argentina (1959); painter in oil, sculptor in wood; *b* Berlin, 1920 (Argentine citizenship since 1958). *Studied art* at Lodz, Poland. *Exhib.:* Brussels, Biennale Venecia, Argentine, Chile, Tate Gallery, London, Bienale de São Paulo, Brazil. *Work repro.:* in Artistas Abstractos Buenos Aires, Arte Nuevo, Leonardo, 2.223 (1969) Oxford, Sculpture International 2.26 (1968) Oxford, Sculpture International 3.28 (1970) London, Sculpture of this Century, Editions du Griffon, Neuchatel, Switzerland (1959), Dictionnaire de la Sculpture Moderne, Fernand Hazan, Paris (1970). *Address:* Santa Fé 3786-11-A, Buenos Aires, Argentine. *Signs work:* "BLASZKO."

BLENSDORF, Ernst M.; Professor of Art; Gold Medal for Sculpture (1968) at the Grand Salon International de Charleroi; Diplôme d'Honneur Hors Concours (1969); founder mem. and Commandeur of International Arts Guild, Monte Carlo; Centro Studi e Scambi Internazionali Diploma di Benemerenza, Roma; R.W.A.; sculptor in wood, cement, clay; *b* Denmark, 25 Sept., 1896; *m* Rosemary Jane Lawson; three *s*, three *d*. *Studied art* at several art academies in Europe. *Exhib.:* United Artists, Royal British Artists, Royal Scottish Academy, Cambrian Academy, Leicester Galleries, Festival Ballet Exhib., London (1959), Wadham College, Oxford; one-man shows: All Hallows-on-the-Wall Church, London, Cambridge Building Centre. *Magazine articles:* Press, TV, and radio coverage, La Revue Moderne, Paris (1948, 1955, 1968). *Address:* Gladen, Brewham Rd., Bruton, Som. *Signs work:* see appendix.

BLESKY, Witold John; sculptor, painter, teacher in stainless steel, resin, ceramic, mixed media, oil and acrylic paints; *b* Poland, 26 July, 1934 (U.S.A.

Nationality); *s* of Dr. C. Blesky; *m* (divorced); two *s*. *Educ.:* Poland; Christ Church College, Canterbury; San Francisco State College, California. *Exhib.:* Le Salon, Paris, Majorie Parr Galleries, London, London Hilton Galleries, Loggia Gallery, London, Mall Galleries, London; other London and provincial galleries and Open Air Exhbns. *Address:* 113 Central Parade, Herne Bay, Kent. *Clubs:* Association Internationale des Arts Plastiques—UNESCO, I.C.A., F.P.S. *Signs work:* "W. John Blesky."

BLOCH, Gunther, F.R.A.I.; 1st prize winner of First National Crafts Competition (1948); art master of L.C.C. schools since 1948; sculptor in wood, stone, clay and ivory; *b* Dt. Krone, Germany, 24 Aug., 1916; *s* of Mendelsohn Bloch; *m*; one *s*. *Educ.:* German Colleges; Leeds College of Art (John Frank Kavanagh); Regent St. Polytechnic; and in Germany under Gerhard Priedigkeit. *Exhib.:* Berkeley Galleries, Cooling Galleries, Ben Uri Galleries, Leeds Art Gallery, Britain Can Make It. *Address:* 15 Eton Villas, London NW3. *Signs work:* "Gunther Bloch" or "G. Bloch."

BLOCH, Vitale, D.A., Moscow University; art critic; editor, Maandblad Voor Beeldende Kunsten, Amsterdam; *b* Moscow, Russia, 25 Feb., 1900. *Educ.:* Moscow University; *studied art* at Inst. of History of Art, Moscow University. *Publications:* contributions on Dutch and French paintings to Oud Holland, Maandblad Voor Beeldende Kunsten, Gazette des Beaux-Artes, Vita Artistica, Burlington Magazine, Paragone. Monographs on Fedotov (Russian 19th c. painter), Georges De La Tour (de Bussy, Amsterdam, 1950) and Il Milione, Milan (1953), Vermeer van Delft (Rizzoli, Milan, 1954) and Editions des 4 Chemins (Paris, 1966), Michael Sweerts (Boucher, The Hague, 1968), Rembrandt Today (van Gendt, Amsterdam, 1970). *Address:* The Hague, Riouwstr. 173.

BLOCKLEY, Gwillym John, R.I., P.S.; artist and designer; conducts private painting schools, lectures, demonstrations; *b* Knighton, Radnorshire, 1921; *s* of Thos. Blockley; *m* Margaret Blockley; two *d*. *Exhib.:* R.A., Mall Galleries, and many provincial galleries. *Publications:* John Blockley Water-colour Course (Pitman Correspondence College, Croydon), contributor to art magazines. *Address:* The Barn, Lower Swell, Cheltenham, Glos. *Signs work:* "G. John Blockley."

BLOND, Maxwell; artist in oil, water-colour, woodcut and etching; *b* St. Annes-on-Sea, 15 Feb., 1943; *s* of Leslie Blond; *m* Gabrielle Wilson; four *s*, one *d*. *Studied art* at Bath Academy, Corsham under Howard Hodgkin; Slade School of Art under Patrick George. *Exhib.:* London Group; one-man shows: Allerton Gallery, Liverpool (1974, 1975, 1976). *Address:* 13 Fulwood Pk., Liverpool 17. *Signs work:* "Blond."

BLUNT, Sir Anthony, K.C.V.O., C.V.O., F.B.A., F.S.A., Hon.D.Litt. (Oxford, Bristol, Durham and Paris); Adviser for the Queen's pictures and drawings; *b* 26 Sept., 1907. *Publications:* Artistic Theory in Italy (1940), François Mansart (1941); Catalogues of French and Italian Drawings at Windsor Castle (1945-71); The Drawings of Nicolas Poussin (1939-75); French Art and Architecture, 1500-1700 (1953); Philbert de l'Orme (1958); The Art of William Blake (1959); Picasso: the Formative Years (with Phoebe Poole, 1962); N. Poussin (1966-67); Sicilian Baroque (1968); Picasso's "Guernica" (1969); Neopolitan Baroque and Rococo Architecture (1975). *Address:* 45 Portsea Hall, Portsea Pl., London W2 2BW.

BLUNT, Wilfrid, A.R.C.A. (1923), F.L.S.; art master, Haileybury College (1923-38), Eton College (1938-59), curator of the Watts Gallery, Compton, from 1959; *b* 19 July, 1901; *s* of Rev. A. S. V. Blunt. *Educ.:* Marlborough College,

Worcester College, Oxford; *studied art* in Paris and R.C.A. *Publications:* Art of Botanical Illustration (Collins); Sweet Roman Hand, Pietro's Pilgrimage, Sebastiano and A Persian Spring (James Barrie); Of Flowers and a Village, Cockerell, The Dream King, The Golden Road to Samarkand, 'England's Michelangelo' (Hamish Hamilton); Omar (Chapman and Hall); Isfahan (Elek); John Christie of Glyndebourne (Geoffrey Bles), etc. *Address:* The Watts Gallery, Compton, Guildford.

BODEN, Leonard, F.R.S.A.; portrait painter; *b* Greenock, Scotland, 1911; *s* of John Boden; *m* Margaret Tulloch; one *d. Educ.:* Sedbergh; *studied art* at School of Art, Glasgow; Heatherley School of Art, London. *Exhib.:* R.P., R.S.A. *Official portraits:* Her Majesty Queen Elizabeth II, H.R.H. The Prince Philip, Duke of Edinburgh, K.G., K.T., G.B.E., His Holiness Pope Pius XII, Field-Marshal Lord Milne. G.C.B., G.C.M.G., D.S.O. *Work repro.:* The Connoisseur; The Artist; many periodicals in this country and abroad; and as Fine Art Prints. *Address:* 27 Warwick Gdns., Kensington, London W14. *Clubs:* Savage, Chelsea Arts. *Signs work:* "LEONARD BODEN."

BODEN, Margaret, F.R.S.A.; portrait painter; *b* Ecclesmachen, Scotland; *d* of A. P. S. Tulloch, M.A., B.D.; *m* Leonard Boden; one *d. Educ.:* Dowanhill; *studied art* at School of Art, Glasgow; Heatherley School of Art, London. *Exhib.:* R.P., R.O.I., Royal Inst. of Fine Arts, Glasgow; National Soc.; Summer Salon; Royal B'ham Soc. of Artists; City of Bradford A.G., etc. Honourable Mention, Paris Salon. *Work repro.:* The Times, The Artist, many magazines and periodicals, etc. *Address:* 27 Warwick Gdns., Kensington, London W14. *Signs work:* "MARGARET BODEN."

BOGART, Bram; 1970 Notionnalité Belge; painter; *b* Delft, Holland 12 July, 1921; *s* of Abraham van den Boogaart; *m* Abelina Sjoukje-Vos; one *s*, two *d. Studied art:* self-taught. *Work in permanent collections:* Gallery Gimpel Fils, London; Gallerie Rive Gauche, Paris; Galerie Internationale d'Art Contemporain, Paris; Gallerie Bleue, Stockholm; Galleria Senior, Roma; Galerie Françoise Mayer. *Address:* Manoir d'Ohain, Belgium.

BONE, Charles, R.I., A.R.C.A., F.R.S.A.; F.B.I. Award for Design; painter and designer; Council mem. R.I.; artist in water-colour, oil, variety of mediums including ceramic for murals; *b* Farnham, Surrey, 15 Sept., 1926; *m* Sheila Mitchell, A.R.B.S., A.R.C.A., sculptor; two *s. Studied art* at Farnham School of Art; Royal College of Art. *Work in permanent collections:* many mural paintings in public buildings and water-colours and oils in private collections. *Work repro.:* illustrated book on Puttenham by Ruth Dusmore; Critic for Arts Review. *Address:* Winters Farm, Puttenham, nr. Guildford, Surrey. *Club:* Chelsea Arts. *Signs work:* "BONE."

BONNER, George Gilbert; Membro Honoris, Tommasso Campanella Academy, Rome; painter in oils and acrylic; *b* Toronto, Canada, 1924; *s* of G. Bonner, surveyor, and Laura Bonner, musician. *Educ.:* St. Egbert's College, Chingford, and S.W. Essex Tech. College. Work included in over fifty mixed exhibitions, including R.A., New Vision Gallery, Towner Art Gallery, Casino Gallery, France, and University, Kent, etc. Five one-man exhibitions. *Work in permanent collections:* Towner Art Gallery (2), Battle Arts Collection. Represented in private collections in England, France, Germany, Italy, Sweden, Canada and U.S.A. Travelled in Europe, 1967. Member, Eastbourne Group. Freelance art critic for several papers. *Addresses:* 19A Cornwall Rd., Bexhill, Sussex, and 95 Silverdale, Paynton Rd., St. Leonards, Sussex. *Signs work:* see appendix.

BONNET, Philippe; artist in oil; *b* Paris, 24 Feb., 1927; *m;* one *d, Exhib.:*

Carnegie Institute, Pittsburgh, Maison de la Pensée Française, Paris, Arthur Tooth, London, Galerie Blanche, Stockholm, Prix Lissone, Milan, Berggruen et Cie, Paris. *Work in private collections:* Maus (Geneva), Sainsbury (London), Tezenas (Paris). *Work repro.:* Ph. Bonnet by Tristan Tzara (Ed. Berggruen, Paris), Cahiers d'Art (Paris), Vol. I, July 1952, Vol. II, 1953. *Address:* 10 rue Jacob, Paris. *Signs work:* see appendix.

BONNET, Rudolf; Knight in the Orde van Oranje Nassau (1955); artist in painting and drawing in tempera, conté and pastel; *b* Amsterdam, Holland, 30 Mar., 1895; *s* of Jean Bonnet, Jr. *Studied art* at State Academy of Arts, Amsterdam (1914-18), under C. L. Dake and J. Bronner; Arts and Craft School, Haarlem, and Amsterdam. *One-man exhib.:* The Hague (1925, 1928, 1962, 1964), Amsterdam (1927), Batavia (1932), Laren (1958, 1964), Utrecht (1960), Haarlem (1962), etc. *Works in permanent collection:* Singer Museum, Laren. *Publications:* Some studies about art of Bali. *Address:* Rosa Spier Stichting, Laren N.H., Holland. *Club:* Gooise Schildersvereniging, Laren. *Signs work:* see appendix.

BORDASS, Dorthy Trotman; painter and printer; *b* London, 19 Nov., 1905; *d* of Reginald W. Foster, coal contractor; *m* William H. Bordass; one *s,* one *d. Educ.:* South Hampstead High School, Northwood College; *studied illuminating* with Alberto Sangorski (1923-25); art at Harrow (R. T. Mumford), Julian, Paris (1926), Heatherley (Ian Macnab) (1927). *Exhib.:* throughout the world, 17 one-man shows: London, England, U.S.A., Malaysia. *Work in permanent collections:* State Gallery, Perth, Australia, Oriel College, Oxford, Ferens Art Gallery, S. London Gallery, Educational Authorities: Inner London and Nottingham, Abbot Hall Gallery. *Clubs:* R.S.P.E.E., W.I.A.C., F.P.S. *Address:* 30 Pretoria Rd., Cambridge CB4 1HE. *Signs work:* see appendix.

BORDUAS, Paul-Emile; artist in oil and water-colour; sculptor in wood; *b* Saint-Hilaire, Qué., 1 Nov., 1905; *s* of Magloire Borduas; *m* Gabrielle Goyette; one *s,* two *d. Educ.:* Sherbrooke, Montreal, Paris; *Studied art* at École des Beaux-Arts, Montreal, Atelier des Arts Sacrés, Paris. *Exhib.:* Montreal, Washington, Paris, New York, Pittsburgh Int., São Paulo Bienale, Venice Bienale. *Work in permanent collections:* Musée des Beaux-Arts, Montreal, Musée de la Province de Québec, National Gallery, Ottawa, Art Gallery of Toronto, Art Gallery of Vancouver, Museum of Modern Art, New York, Carnegie Institute, Pittsburgh. *Address:* 119E 17th Street, New York 3, N.Y., U.S.A. *Signs work:* "BORDUAS."

BORNFRIEND, Jacob; painter; *b* Zborov, Czechoslovakia; *s* of Isaak Bauernfreund; *m* Pippa Suenkens. *Educ.:* Prague; *studied art* at Academy of Fine Arts, Prague, under Prof. Willi Nowak (1930-35). *Work in permanent collections:* Contemporary Art Society, Tate Gallery, Auckland City Art Gallery, N.Z., Goeteborg Museum, Prague National Gallery, Bratislava Slovak National Gallery, Kosice Slovakian Museum, Moravia Museum, Leeds City Art Gallery, Bradford University, Lincoln College, Churchill College and Nuffield College Oxford, Southampton Art Gallery, Stockholm Modern Museum, Tel-Aviv Museum, Uppsala Konsthallen, Wakefield City Art Gallery, Wellington National Gallery, N.Z. *Work repro.:* Studio, Contact, Review, London; Zivot, Prague; Svenska Hem, Stockholm; Les Arts Plastigues, Quadrum, Brussels; Prisme des Arts, Paris. *Address:* 13 Ravenscroft Ave., London NW11. *Signs work:* "J. Bornfriend."

BORRIE: see HOPE HENDERSON, Eleanor.

BOSS, Marcus Arthur; oil and water-colour; *b* 2 June, 1891; *s* of Mark Boss (merchant). *Educ.:* Birkbeck College; Birkbeck School of Art, and Heatherley's

(1908-11); R.A. Schools (1911-16). *Exhib.:* R.A., R.I., R.O.I., R.B.A., R.P. and provinces, International Portraid Soc. *Address:* 2 Clifton Hill Studios, 95A Clifton Hill, St. John's Wood, London NW8. *Clubs:* Chelsea Arts and London Sketch. *Signs work:* "Marcus A. Boss."

BOSTOCK, James Edward, R.E. (1961), A.R.C.A. (Lond.) 1939; teacher, illustrator, wood engraver, painter; Academic Development Officer, Bristol Polytechnic; *b* Hanley, Staffs, 11 June, 1917; *m*; three *s*. *Educ.:* Borden Grammar School, Sittingbourne, Kent; *studied art* at Medway School of Art, Rochester (1933-36), Royal College of Art (1936-39). *Exhib.:* R.A., R.B.A., N.E.A.C., Crafts Centre of Great Britain, V. & A. Museum, Mignon Gallery, Bath, Van Dyck Gallery, Bristol; travelling exhbns. to Poland, Czechoslovakia, S. Africa, New Zealand and the Far East. *Work in permanent collections:* V. & A. Museum, British Museum, Wakefield Collection, Hunt Botanical Library, Pittsburgh, U.S.A. *Publications:* Roman Lettering for Students (Studio), 1959; articles in The Studio, The Artist, Guardian, Staffordshire Sentinel, Times Ed. Supp. *Address:* 16 Claremont Rd., Bishopston, Bristol, 7.

BOSWELL, William Aubrey, A.R.Cam.A., F.R.S.A.; town planner; part-time teacher; artist and illustrator in oil, pen and ink; Principal Design Officer, County Planning Clwyd; part-time teacher, Oswestry College Further Education; *b* Nottingham, 30 May, 1926; *s* of W. E. Boswell, F.T.I.; *m* Jessie; one *s*, two *d*. *Educ.:* Cottesmore, Nottingham; *studied art* at Nottingham College of Arts and Crafts (1942) under Alfred Foster; R.A.F. School of Art and Architecture; Heliopolis and Geniefa School of Art, Suez, Egypt. *Exhib.:* Annual Summer Exhbns., Royal Cambrian Academy of Art. *Work repro.:* illustrations, Ruthin, Town Conservation; Denbigh Town Trail. *Address:* 24 Hilltop View Rd., Borras Park, Wrexham, Clwyd. *Signs work:* "William A. Boswell."

BOSZIN, Endre; founded, Taurus Artists (1961), London; painter in oil and water-colour, sculptor in bronze, graphic artist; President, Sculptors Society of Canada (1971-73); *b* Hungary, 1923, U.K. subject since 1962; *s* of Julius Boszin, merchant; *m* Charlotte de Sarlay; one *s*, one *d*. *Studied art* at Budapest, École d'Indépendants, R.C.A. *Exhib.:* London Group; Festival of Visual Art at Harrogate, Edinburgh Festival; Grabovsky, Crane Kalman, Chiltern, Woodstock; Piccadilly Galleries, London, Gallery Raymond Creuze, Paris; International Medal Exhbns,: Madrid, Cologne, Helsinki, Prague. *Work in permanent collections:* Budapest, National Museum of Hungarian Art, Ujpest, City County Collection. *Address:* 39 Gilgorm Rd., Toronto, Canada. *Clubs:* Sculptors Soc. of Canada, Canadian Artists Representation. *Signs work:* "Boszin," Capital letters on oil and sculptures; ink sign on water-colours.

BOTHWELL, Dorr; painter, printmaker and teacher in oil, gouache, and serigraphic printing; Prof., Mendocino Art Centre, Sonoma State Coll.; *b* San Francisco, 3 May, 1902; *s* of John Stuart Bothwell. *Educ.:* Russ High School, San Diego; Univ of Oregon; *studied art* at Calif. School of Fine Arts and Rudolph Schaeffer School of Design, San Francisco. *Work in permanent collections:* Metropolitan Museum, Museum of Modern Art and Brooklyn Museum, N.Y.; Achenbach Foundation of Graphic Art, San Francisco; Bibliotheque Nationale, Paris; V. & A.; Fogg Museum, Cambridge, Mass.; Whitney Museum, N.Y.; San Francisco Museum of Art. *Address:* P.O. Box 27, Mendocino, California. *Signs work:* "Bothwell."

BOTTOMLEY, Peter, A.R.E. (Jan., 1952), A.R.C.A. (Lond., 1951); artist in water-colour, gouache, etching, aquatint, lithography; Principal, Southport College of Art; *b* Goole, Yorks, 26 Dec., 1927; *s* of Rowland Bottomley; *m* Mary

Ruth Foulger; two d. *Educ.:* Goole Modern School; *studied art* at Doncaster School of Art under T. A. Anderson, A.T.D. (1942-45), and R.C.A. under Robert Austin, R.A., R.E., R.W.S. (1948-52), *Exhib.:* R.A., R.P.E. (1952-70). *Address:* College of Art, Mornington Rd., Southport., Merseyside. *Signs work:* "P. Bottomley."

BOUFFARD, Pierre; Ancien Maire de Genève, délégué aux beaux-arts, Directeur du Musée d'art et d'histoire, Genève, et professeur a l'Universite, Directeur des Editions Bonvent S.A. et de Rosepierre S.A. *Educ.:* Geneva and Basle; *studied art* at Basle for doctorate in the history of art under Prof. J. Gantner, H. Reinhardt, K. Schefold. *Address:* 1254 Jussy Ge. *Club:* Société des antiquaries de France et Société française d'archéologie. *Speciality:* Moyenâge, sculpture et peinture.

BOURNE, John Frye; painter in oil, water-colour; *b* Hampstead, 1912; *s* of Rev. Arthur A. Bourne; *m* Norah Hett. *Educ.:* Bishop's Stortford College; *studied art* at R.A. Schools under Sir Walter Russell, R.A. (1929-34). *Exhib.:* R.A., R.Cam.A., R.I., R.W.S., R.P., S.G.A. *Work repro.:* Royal Academy Illustrated (1950). *Address:* Rose Hill, Sidbury, nr. Sidmouth, Devon. *Club:* Chelsea Arts. *Signs work:* "J. F. BOURNE" (oils), "John Frye Bourne" (other works).

BOWEN, Denis, A.R.C.A. (1949), Mem. A.I.C.A.; painter; directed The New Vision Centre (1956-66); Premio Internationale Europa Arte (1964) Silver Star with Antonioni Pasolini; visiting Associate Prof., University of Victoria, B.C., Canada (1969-71); *b* Kimberley, 5 Apr., 1921. *Studied art* at King James I Grammar School, Almondbury; Royal College of Art (1946-49). Works in fluorescent media and black light co-ordinated with music and dance, first shown at Greater Victoria Art Gallery, B.C., Canada (1971) and since with Continuum at Studio 3, I.C.A., the Playhouse, Harlow, Loggia Gallery, Kinetic Art Glynn Vivian A.G., Swansea, Talbot Rice Art Centre, Edinburgh. *Exhib.:* 1st retrospective Bede 1300 Festival, Bede Gallery, Jarrow (1973), and internationally. *Publications:* illustrated, A Concise History of English Painting by William Gaunt (Thames & Hudson, 1964), Dream of Icarus by Kenneth Coutts-Smith (Hutchinson, 1969), Etching and Engraving by John Brunsdon (Batsford, 1969), Art since 1945 by Herbert Read; critical writings in Art International Lugano, D'Ars Milano, Arts Canada Toronto, R.S.A. Journal and Arts Review, London. *Address:* 4 Seymour Pl., London W1H 5WF.

BOWEN, Thomas Alfred Edwin, F.R.S.A., M.S.I.A.; fore-edge book painter; medal designer in gold and platinum (Canterbury Tales); government artist; art director (publicity); engineering draughtsman; industrial designer; lithographer, photo-lithographer; violin-maker; *b* Clapham, London, 2 Feb., 1909; *s* of Thomas Edward Bowen; *m* Mary Dorothy Brooker; two *s*. *Educ.:* St. John's Bowyer School; *studied art, colour printing and lithography* at London School of Printing, Bolt Court School of Photo-Engraving, Clapham School of Art. *Exhib.:* R.W.S., London, Coventry and Bristol, Olympia. *Work in permanent collections:* Warsaw Museum, Poland, and New York (illuminated MSS.), over 100 fore-edge paintings in Canada—America. *Address:* 9 Crescent Grove, Southside, Clapham Common, London SW4. *Signs work:* "BOWEN" (underlined, with year below line), and see appendix.

BOWES, John, R.C.A. (1965); artist in oil, water-colour, pen and ink; *b* Oldham, Lancs., 29 Dec., 1899; *s* of Robert Bowes, M.D. *Educ.:* Manchester Grammar School. *Exhib.:* R.A., R.S.A., R.I., R.O.I., R.B.A., N.S., S.G.A., London Group, R.Cam.A., R.W.A., R.S.W., Paris Salon. *Work in permanent collections:* Rutherston Collection, Newcastle-upon-Tyne, Salford, Liverpool and Southport. *Address:* 1 Cumberland Rd., Southport. *Clubs:* Manchester Academy,

Liverpool Academy, Manchester Soc. of Modern Painters, Lancs Group of Artists. *Signs work:* "J. Bowes."

BOWETT, Druie; painter in oil, gouache, mixed media; *b* Ripon, Yorks., 3 Jan., 1924; *d* of S. A. W. Glover; *m* John Bowett; three *s. Educ.:* Queen Margaret's School; *studied art* at Harrogate College of Art, later under Jean-Georges Simon. *Exhib.:* one-man shows, Midland Group, Austen Hayes Gallery, York, Cooper Art Gallery, Wakefield City Art Gallery, Sheffield University, Durham, Abbot Hall, Kendal, Nottingham Playhouse, Vaccarino, Florence, 359 Gallery, Nottingham. *Work in permanent collections:* County College, Derbyshire; Education Authorities of Sussex, Rochdale, Leicestershire and Nottinghamshire; Wakefield and Kendall Galleries; John Players Ltd.; British Nylon Spinners Ltd.; Glass Bulbs Ltd.; Sheffield Twistdrill Ltd.; Tetley's Brewery. *Work repro.:* Art News and Review, B.B.C. Television (1963), Young Artists of Promise. *Address:* Wilton Lodge, Blyth, nr. Worksop, Notts. *Signs work:* (paintings) "Bowett"; (drawings) "D.B."

BOWEY, Olwyn, A.R.A. (1970), A.R.C.A., R.B.A.; painter in oil, watercolour, pencil; *b* Stockton, Tees-side, 10 Feb., 1936; *d* of James Bowey, industrial chemist. *Educ.:* William Newton School, Co. Durham; *studied art* at West Hartlepool School of Art, Royal College of Art. *Work in permanent collections:* Tate Gallery, Carlisle Art Gallery, Shell Building, Royal Academy Collection, Somerset and Leicester Education Authorities. *Publications:* Shell Agricultural Journals, The Engagement (Bryan Guinness). *Address:* 8 Winthorpe Rd., Putney, London SW15. *Signs work:* "Olwyn Bowey."

BOWMAN, Betty; artist in oil, etching, pastel, pen and ink; *b* Ealing, 19 Nov., 1923; *m* D. J. Garrard, F.R.I.C.S. *Educ.:* Heaverton House, St. Augustus Convent; *studied art* at Central School of Art (1943) under Ruskin Spear, R.A., St. Martin's Art School (1945), Regents St. Polytechnic (1952) under N. Blamey, City and Guilds of London Art School (1967-70) under Rodney Burn, R.A., Robin Guthrie, R.A., Henry Wilkinson, A.R.E., Bernard Dunstan, A.R.A.; also privately with Stanley Spencer, R.A. *Work in permanent collections:* Prague Museum, Southend Municipal, Hastings Municipal, Oxford Hospital Regional Board, Talisman Prints, U.S.A., Courtaulds. *Address:* Dean Mill, Dean, Spelsbury, nr. Charlbury, Oxon. *Signs work:* "Bowman."

BOWNESS, Alan, M.A.; art historian; Reader in the History of Art at Courtauld Inst. of Art in the University of London; *b* London, 11 Jan., 1928; *s* of George Bowness; *m* Sarah Hepworth Nicholson; one *s,* one *d. Educ.:* University College School, Downing College, Cambridge, and Courtauld Inst. of Art. *Publications:* William Scott: Paintings (Lund Humphries, 1964); Modern Sculpture (Studio Vista, 1965); Henry Moore: Sculpture, 1955-64 (Lund Humphries, 1965); Alan Davie (Lund Humphries, 1968); Gauguin (Phaidon, 1971); Complete Sculpture of Barbara Hepworth 1960-69 (Lund Humphries, 1971); Modern European Art (Thames & Hudson, 1972); Ivon Hitchens (Lund Humphries, 1973). *Address:* 91 Castelnau, London SW13.

BOYCOTT-BROWN, Hugh, R.S.M.A. (Council mem.); mem. Wapping Group; marine artist in oil; *b* Bushey, Herts., 27 Apr., 1909; *s* of A. R. Brown; *m* Lesley Thain; three *s. Educ.:* Trent College, Derbyshire; *studied art* at Watford School of Art, Heatherleys' School of Art, Cotswold School of Landscape Painting. *Exhib.:* R.A., Paris Salon, N.E.A.C., R.I., R.O.I., R.B.A., N.S., S.G.A., R.S.M.A., R.S.A., Royal Glasgow Inst. Fine Arts, Ashbarn Gallery, Petersfield, Tunbridge Wells Gallery, Phoenix Gallery. Lavenham, Deben Gallery, Woodbridge, Reade's Gallery, Aldeburgh. *Address:* 1 Lavender Cottages, Post Office

Rd., Knodishall, Saxmundham, Suffolk. *Club:* Festival (Aldeburgh). *Signs work:* "Hugh Brown" (pre-war); now "Hugh Boycott Brown" or "H.B.B."

BOYD, Arthur Merric Bloomfield; painter in oil, graphics, ceramic; *b* Murrumbeena, Australia, 1920; *s* of William Merric Boyd; *m*; one *s*, two *d*. *Educ.:* State School, Murrumbeena, Victoria, Australia; *studied art* with parents. *Work in permanent collections:* Australian National collections, V. & A. *Publications:* Monograph by Franz Phillipp (1967), illustrated St. Francis by T. S. R. Boase, Lysistrata (1970). *Address:* c/o Commercial Bank of Australia Ltd., 34 Piccadilly, London W1.

BOYD, G., A.T.D. (1951); painter and sculptor; senior lecturer in painting at Wall Hall College; *b* Bristol, 1928; *s* of Herbert Leslie Boyd; *m* Pauline Lilian S. Andrew; *d* Sophie. *Educ.:* Watford Grammar School; *studied art* at Watford School of Art and London University Inst. of Education. *Exhib.:* Young Contemporaries, Daily Express Artists under 35, London Group, John Moores (1957, 1967, 1969), R.A. (1968, 1973, 1975), A.I.A. Big Pictures (1958); one-man shows: A.I.A. (1962, 1969), Molton Gallery (1963), Oxford Gallery (1970, 1972), Arts Council of N. Ireland, Belfast 68, Shapes in Spaces, Woburn Abbey (1970), Summer Studio I.C.A. (1973), Int. Drawing Biennale 1975, Middlesborough, slides of work viewable at A.I.R. Burlington House. *Public collections:* Walker Gallery, Oxford Centre for Management Studies. *Address:* Blackapple, Scatterdells Lane, Chipperfield, Herts. *Signs work:* "G. BOYD."

BOYD, James Davidson, D.A. (Glas.), F.M.A., F.S.A.Scot., F.R.S.A.; director Dundee Art Galleries and Museums (1949—); curator on staff of Glasgow Art Galleries and Museums under Dr. T. J. Honeyman (1946-49); artist in oil and water-colour; enamellist; *b* Glasgow, 10 Aug., 1917; *m* Elizabeth A. Ogilvie, D.A. (Glas.). *Educ.:* Falkirk High and Technical Schools; *studied art* at Glasgow School of Art (1936-40). *Publications:* articles on art and history in various publications. *Addresses:* Dundee Art Galleries, Albert Sq., Dundee, and 16 Strips of Craigie Rd., Dundee.

BOYD, John G.; teacher and painter in oil; *b* Stonehaven Kincardineshire, 7 Apr., 1940; two *s*. *Educ.:* Mackie Academy, Stonehaven; *studied art* at Gray's School of Art (1958-62) under R. H. Blyth; Hospitalfield College of Art (summer 1961) under James Cummings. *Exhib.:* Present Gallery, Lanark (1975), Armstrong Gallery, Glasgow (1970), New St. Gallery, Edinburgh (1967), R.S.A., R.G.I., Glasgow Art Club. *Address:* 4 Devonshire Terr., Glasgow G12 0XE. *Club:* Glasgow Art. *Signs work:* "Boyd."

BOYDELL, Bertha Stanfield; Mem., Society of Portrait Sculptors; sculptress and potter in clay, stone and wood; *b* Cobridge, Staffs., 25 Apr., 1899; *d* of William Stanfield White; *m* Phillip Boydell; one *s*, one *d*. *Educ.:* various schools in the Potteries; *studied art* at School of Art, Hanley (1916-20) under Mr. Light, Goldsmiths College of Art (1920-22) under Mr. Marriot, assistant to Charles Vyse, potter (1922-23). *Exhib.:* R.A., R.B.A., S.P.S., etc. *Address:* 9 Chartfield Sq., London SW15 6DR. *Signs work:* "B.S.B."

BOYDELL, Phillip, A.R.C.A., F.I.P.A.; artist in oil and water-colour, designer, typographer; Art Master, Croydon and Blackheath Schools of Art; R.C.A. (1923-26); Art Director and Creative Director, London Press Exchange (1926-61); Governor, Central School of Arts and Crafts; and Ealing College of Art (1952-54); President, Advertising Creative Circle (1951); designer, typeface "Festival" for Festival of Britain (1951); *b* Tyldesley, Lancs., 21 May, 1896; *s* of Oliver Boydell; *m* Bertha Stanfield White; one *s*, one *d*. *Educ.:* various schools in Tyldesley and Leigh, Lancs.; *studied art* at Manchester School of Art and R.C.A.

(1919-23) under Sir William Rothenstein and Robert Anning Bell, R.A. *Exhib.:* R.A., R.B.A., etc. *Work in permanent collections:* Trinity College, Oxford, Imperial War Museum, and private collections in America, France and the U.K. *Work repro.:* various national press and poster campaigns, book jackets and illustrations, Art and Industry, etc. *Publications:* The Artist in Advertising. *Address:* 9 Chartfield Sq., London SW15 6DR. *Signs work:* see appendix.

BOYDEN, John, B.A.(Lond.); Curator, Hove Museum of Art (1974-); *b* Tunbridge Wells, 1942; *s* of G. J. Boyden, M.A. *Educ.:* Rugby School; Universities of London and Manchester; *studied art* at Dept. of Art History, University of Manchester (Diploma 1972). *Address:* 7 Norfolk Terr., Brighton, Sussex. *Club:* Royal Overseas League.

BOYLAN, Hugo; self-taught artist in oil; *b* Dublin, 17 Nov., 1942; *m*; one *s*, one *d*. *Educ.:* Catholic University School and University College, Dublin. *Exhib.:* Davis Gallery, Arts Club, Project Galleries, Dublin; Mall Galleries, Studio Shows, London. *Work in permanent collection:* Arts Council of Ireland. *Address:* Edbury, Theydon Mount, Epping, Essex. *Club:* United Arts, Dublin. *Signs work:* "Hugo."

BOYLE, Alicia; painter; *b* Bangkok; childhood in Ireland and London; *studied art* at Byam Shaw School of Drawing and Painting under F. Ernest Jackson. *Exhib.:* Leger and Leicester Galleries, Arts Council of Northern Ireland etc. *Work in permanent collections:* Arts Council of N. Ireland; Ulster Museum; Irish Arts Council; Nottingham Castle Art Gallery; Herbert Art Gallery, Coventry; Lake District Art Gallery, Kendal; Northampton Art Gallery; North West Art Trust, N.I.; Cork A.G., Education committees and private collections in Great Britain, Republic of Ireland, U.S.A., Sweden, etc. *Work repro.:* Apollo, Studio, Arts Review. *Address:* Reenacappul, Durrus near Bantry, Co. Cork. *Signs work:* "BOYLE" and "AB."

BRABANT, Rosemary, M.F.P.S. (1970); artist in oil, impressionist-abstract; Mem. Westminster Visual Arts Com.; *b* Cottesloe, W. Australia, 28 June, 1915; *d* of Cecil Grave; *m* William Brabant; one *d*. *Educ.:* Presentation Convent, Windsor; *studied art* at Melbourne National Gallery; Hammersmith College of Art; Atelier, Florence, Italy. *Exhib.:* one-man shows, London: Woodstock Gallery, New Vision Centre, Loggia Gallery, International Arts Centre, Elephant & Castle, The Place, Cockpit Theatre; Brighton: Vincitore Gallery; Italy: New Medusa Gallery, La Spezia, Palazzo dei Priori, Volterra; group shows: A.I.A., National, F.P.S., Chelsea, Kensington, Paddington, St. Albans, Westminster, Royal Overseas League, Sussex & Kent Artists, City of London Guild. *Work in private collections:* worldwide. *Address:* 36 Arundel Gdns., London W11. *Club:* W.I.A.C. *Signs work:* "R. Brabant."

BRABY, Dorothea; wood-engraver, portrait painter, book illustrator, commercial artist; *b* London, 1909; *studied art* in London, Florence and Paris. *Exhib.:* S.W.A., Hampstead Artists, Festival of Women at Wembley, Arts Council Exhbn., N.B.L., Society of Wood Engravers. *Work repro.:* in Studio, Radio Times, Times Literary Supplement, Observer, I.C.I. Magazine. *Publications:* Studio How to Do It series: The Way of Wood Engraving; Golden Cockerell Press: 91st Psalm, Lottery Ticket (Lorca), Mabinogion, Labyrinth (Komensky), etc.; Folio Society: Keats Poems, Semi-Attached Couple (Eden), Lord Arthur Savile's Crime; F. Lewis: The Commandments. *Address:* 28 Willow Rd., London NW3 1TL. *Signs work:* "BRABY."

BRADBERY, Ian Westwood, F.S.I.A.; typographer and designer of exhbn. stands, showrooms, etc.; design teacher, Willesden Technical College (1947-48), Central School of Arts and Crafts (1949-50), London School of Printing and

Graphic Arts (1955); *b* London, 31 Dec., 1918; *s* of John James Bradbery. *Educ.:* Mill Hill School; *studied art* at Central School of Arts and Crafts (1939). *Work repro.:* Architectural Review, Architects Journal, Domus, Typographica, Designers in Britain, Neue Möbel, Wood, Architect and Building News, S.G.M., Stile Industria, Display, Architectural Design, Idea, Graphik, Graphis Annual, Photographis, etc. *Address:* 217-218 Tottenham Court Rd., London W1. *Signs work:* "Ian Bradbery."

BRADBURY, Arthur, A.R.W.A.; artist in oil, water-colour, pastel; *s* of H. M. Bradbury; *m* Evelyn; one *d.*; *studied art* at St. John's Wood Art School, R.A. Schools. *Exhib.:* R.A., R.O.I., R.B.A., R.I., R.W.A. *Work in permanent collections:* Imperial War Museum (Huddersfield); Russell Cotes A.G., Bournemouth; Bournemouth Town Hall; Maritime Museum, Guernsey. *Work repro.:* Swan Lake, A Colonial Clipper, A British Windjammer (Medici Soc.); Aristides, Loch Torridon (Brown, Son and Ferguson); illustrations for Come Boating With Me (Frederick Muller), Dorset Year Book, Yachting Monthly, Illustrated London News, Sphere, Islands of England (Batsford), Water-colour (Studio). *Address:* Yellow Sands, Sandbanks, Poole. *Club:* Bournemouth Arts. *Signs work:* "ARTHUR BRADBURY."

BRADFORD, Dorothy; artist in oils, inks, water-colours, etching, aquatint; art assistant, C.E.M.A. (1942-45), official artist to New Philharmonia Orchestra on tour in U.S.A. (1971); *b* Cockermouth, Cumberland, 2 Apr., 1918; *d* of S. H. Bassadona, school teacher; *m* R. D. Bradford; one *s,* two *d. Studied art* at Liverpool College of Art, Leeds College of Art, Central School of Art, London, St. Martin's School of Art, London. *Exhib.:* one-man shows: Lincoln Center, N.Y., Mermaid Theatre, Royal Festival Hall, U.S. Embassy, London, Liverpool, Ilkley, Belfast, Preston, Leeds, Manchester, Menston, Cardiff, Nottingham, etc. *Addresses:* 19 Brows La., Formby, Liverpool; studio: 19 Bluecoat Chas., Liverpool 1. *Club:* Liverpool Architectural Soc. *Signs work:* "Bradford."

BRADFORD, Robert, M.A.(R.C.A.), 1970; artist in acrylic resin and film-maker (16mm film); part-time lecturer, Maidstone College of Art; *b* London, 4 Dec., 1945; *m*; two s, one *d. Educ.:* Beckenham Grammar School; *studied art* at Beckenham School of Art (1961-63); Ravensbourne College of Art (1964-67); Royal College of Art (1967-70) under Alan Green, Brian Fielding, Roger Hill. *Exhib.:* I.C.A. (1975), Arnolfini Gallery, Bristol (1975), Bath Festival Gallery (1975), S.W.A. Touring Show (1974, 1975). *Address:* 6 Windsor Terr., Clifton, Bristol BS8 4LW. *Signs work:* drawings are signed "R. Bradford" or rubber stamped; paintings are stencil sprayed "R.B." or left blank.

BRADLEY, Frank, R.C.A.; painter and theatrical designer; *b* Manchester, May, 1903; *s* of Frank Bradley; *m* Constance Mary Davey, M.A. *Studied art* at College of Art, Manchester, Manchester Academy of Fine Arts, Newlyn School of Painting. *Exhib.:* Utd. Soc. of Artists, V. & A., City Art Gallery, Manchester, Lancashire Artists, Cheshire Artists, R.Cam.A., Paris Salon etc., and in Norway and Germany, one-man show Salford Art Gallery (1958). Mem. Royal Cambrian Academy, Manchester Academy of Fine Arts and The Lancashire Group. *Work repro.:* La Revue Moderne and other journals. *Address:* Spring Cottage, Maynestone Rd., Chinley, Derbyshire. *Signs work:* see appendix.

BRADSHAW, Brian; Prof. of Fine Art, Rhodes University, Grahamstown, S. Africa (July, 1960); Silver Medal, R.C.A. (1951); A.R.E. (1951), Prix de Rome (Engraving, 1951), A.T.D. (1948); painter and etcher; *b* Bolton, Lancs, 22 Mar., 1923; *s* of Hubert George Bradshaw; *m* Maureen E. M. Keating; two *s. Work in permanent collections:* Manchester City Art Gallery, Whitworth Art

Gallery, Bolton Art Gallery, Salford Art Gallery, Walker Art Gallery, Rutherston Collection and the Ashmolean Museum, Oxford. Author of the Culture Plan and Art and Totality. *Addresses:* Rhodes University, Grahamstown, South Africa; Haulgh Hall, Bolton, Lancs; and Cae Canol, Fachwen, Caernarvon. *Signs work:* "Brian Bradshaw."

BRADSHAW, Kathleen M.; painter of flowers and portraits in oil and water-colour; mem. com., St. Ives Soc. of Artists; *d* of Capt. A. A. Slatter, B.S.A.P.; *m* George F. Bradshaw, D.S.O., S.M.A.: one *s*, one *d*. *Studied art* in St. Ives. *Exhib.:* St. Ives Soc. of Artists. *Address:* "Penylan", Hellesvean Cl., Higher Stennack, St. Ives, Cornwall. *Signs work:* "Kathleen Bradshaw."

BRADSHAW, Laurence, F.R.B.S.; sculptor, painter, engraver; mem. of the Association of Internationale des Critiques d'Art; Master, Art Workers' Guild (1958); *b* Cheshire, 1899; *s* of Peter Bradshaw, author. *Educ.:* privately and Liverpool University; *studied art* at Liverpool College of Art (1916), in Sir Frank Brangwyn's studio (1920-1925), and sculpture in London and Paris. *Exhib.:* St. George's Gall., Alpine Gall., Whitechapel A.G., Godfrey Phillips Gall., R.W.S. Gall., Society of Portrait Sculptors, San Francisco; one-man shows at Architectural Association Gall., Budapest, Moscow Academy of Arts, Prague. *Work in permanent collections:* V. & A. (theatre designs), Marx Engels Museum, Moscow, Pushkin Museum, Moscow; sculpture for civic buildings: at Cambridge Guildhall, Radcliff Maternity Home, Oxford, Watford Town Hall, Doncaster Grammar School, Cleveland Girls' Grammar School, Redcar, Brompton Oratory, Westminster Cathedral, King's College, Taunton, Worthing Town Hall and Sports Pavilion. Memorials: Karl Marx Memorial, Highgate, Royal Army Catering Corps Memorial, Aldershot, Portrait bust Capt. Pitt Rivers, Pitt Rivers Museum, Dr. W. E. B. Dubois, Mass. University, U.S.A., Hannan Swaffer bust, Press Club, London, Lenin Memorial plaque, Marx Memorial Library, London, Harry Pollitt Memorial bust on M.V. *Harry Pollitt*. *Publications:* works illus. in Robes of Thespis, Studio Year Book, Apollo, Architectural Review, Architectural Journal, Studio Magazine, Art Work, 1928 and periodicals in Europe and U.S.A. *Address:* 2 St. Oswald's Studios, London SW6. *Signs work:* "Laurence Bradshaw."

BRADSHAW, Maurice Bernard, F.R.S.A.; specialist in organizing art exhbns.; director, Art Exhbns. Bureau; director Goupil Galleries; director Arts News Agency; Secretary General, Federation of British Artists; organizing director, Empire Art Loan Exhbns. Soc.; sec., Royal Soc. of Portrait Painters; sec., Society of Wildlife Artists; sec., Society of Portrait Sculptors; sec., Royal Institute of Painters in Watercolours; sec., Pastel Society; sec., Society of Women Artists; Soc. of Mural Painters and Senefelder Group of Lithographers; mem., Museum Assoc.; *b* 7 Feb., 1903; *s* of John Bradshaw; *m* Gladys Harvey-Frost; one *d*. *Educ.:* Christ's College, N. London. *Addresses:* 17 Carlton House Terr., London SW1Y 5BD; Flat Two, 110 Elm Pk. Gdns., Chelsea, London SW10. *Clubs:* Army and Navy, Chelsea Arts.

BRADSHAW, Raymond Henry, A.T.D.; draughtsman, portrait and figure painter in oil, crayon and ink; Head of Art Dept. and Housemaster, Bancroft's School; vice-president, Hesketh Hubbard Art Soc. (Federation of British Artists); *b* 9 Jan., 1918; *s* of Herbert Edward Bradshaw; *m* Marjorie Bayliss; two *d*. *Educ.:* Bancroft's School; *studied art* at West Ham School of Art (1935-36); Westminster School of Art (1936-38) under Mark Gertler, Bernard Meninsky, Mervyn Peake and Adrian Hill; Hornsey School of Art (1938-39). *Exhib.:* R.B.A., R.A., R.P., V. & A., etc. Work in private collections. *Publication:* illustrated, Introducing Local Studies (Dent). *Address:* Little Monkwood Lodge, Baldwins Hill, Loughton, Essex. *Signs work:* "Raymond H. Bradshaw."

BRAMMER, Leonard Griffiths, A.R.C.A. (Painting) 1929, Travelling Scholar (Engraving) R.C.A. (1930), R.E. (1956); painter and etcher in oil, watercolour, etching, engraving; *b* Burslem, Stoke-on-Trent, 1906; *s* of Frederick William Brammer, designer and builder of pottery ovens and kilns; *m* Florence Barnet; one *d. Educ.:* Park High School, Burslem and privately; *studied art* at Burslem School of Art (1923-26); R.C.A. (1926-1930) under Sir William Rothenstein, Malcolm Osborne, Robert Austin, Job Nixon, E. Constable Alston, Gwyn-Jones, Gordon M. Forsyth. *Exhib.:* R.A., R.P.E. *Work in permanent collections:* Tate Gallery, V. & A., Ashmolean, Oxford, Wedgwood Museum, Stoke-on-Trent A.G., Carlisle A.G., University of Keele, British Council. *Address:* "Sŵn-y-Wylan", Morfa Bychan, Porthmadog, Gwynedd. *Signs work:* "L. G. Brammer."

BRANNAN, Noel Rowston, N.D.D., A.T.D. (1951, 1952); painter, potter; art master, South Wigston High School; *b* Tynemouth, 25 Dec., 1921; *s* of the late Edward Eaton Brannan, artist; *m* Mavis Annie (*née* Leitch); one *s,* one *d. Educ.:* Humberstone Foundation School, Clee, Lincs.; *studied art* at School of Art, Lincoln (1947-51), College of Art, Leicester (1951-52). *Exhib.:* R.A., R.B.A., New English, A.I.A., etc. *Work in permanent collections:* Usher A.G., Lincoln, Fison's Fertilizer Works, water-colour (1948), Farmhouse at Wolvey, gouache (1960), Lincolnshire Association, Cloudesley Bush, drawing (1966). *Address:* Athelstan, Hinckley Rd., Burbage, Leics. LE10 2AG. Full member A.I.A. *Signs work:* "Noel Brannan."

BRANNAN, Peter Arthur, R.B.A. (1960), N.D.D., painting (1952); artist in oil, water-colour, etc.; *b* Cleethorpes, 13 Dec., 1926; *s* of the late Edward E. Brannan, artist. *Educ.:* Humberstone Foundation School, School of Art, Grimsby, and Leicester College of Art. *Exhib.:* R.A., R.B.A., N.E.A.C., etc.; six one-man shows, Trafford Gallery, Mount St., London. *Work in permanent collections:* Usher Art Gallery, Lincoln, G.L.C., Manchester College of Art, Grundy Gallery, Blackpool, Notts. and Kesteven Ed. Committees. *Addresses:* Manor Cottage, Welbourn, Lincoln, and 1 Mount Lane, Newark, Notts. *Clubs:* R.B.A., Lincolnshire Artists' Soc. *Signs work:* "PETER BRANNAN."

BRATBY, John Randall, A.R.A. (1959), A.R.C.A. (1st Class); Mem. of the London Group; painter in oil, on canvas and hardboard; *b* 19 July, 1928; *s* of George Alfred Bratby; *m* Jean Cooke. *Educ.:* Tiffin Boys' School, Kingston, Surrey; *studied art* at Kingston Art School. *Exhib.:* Pittsburgh International, I.C.A. Exhibition, Six Young Painters; Southport Spring Exhbn., St. Edmund's College, Ware, Cartwright Hall, Bradford, Arts Council Exhbn.; Blackburn Art Gallery, Carlisle, Bromley Art Soc. Exhbn. *Work in permanent collections:* Arts Council, British Council, Tate, Carlisle A.G., Walker A.G., Contemporary Art Society, King's College, Newcastle. *Address:* 7 Hardy Rd., London SE23. *Signs work:* "John Bratby" or "Bratby" in white capitals.

BRAUND, Allin, M.S.I.A.; painter, printmaker; lecturer, Middlesex Polytechnic; *b* Northam, Devon, 1915; *s* of Ralph Braund; *m* Lena Cann; three *s,* one *d. Educ.:* Bideford Grammar School; *studied art* at Bideford School of Art. *Exhib.:* R.A., Venice Biennale, International Biennale, Cincinnati, São Paulo, New York, Redfern, Zwemmers, R.E., St. George's, Paris, Lubljana. *Official purchases:* Ministry of Works Atomic Energy Commission, S. London Gallery, British Council, Arts Council, V. & A., Leicester Art Gallery, Museum of Modern Art, New York, C.A.S., National Art Gallery, New Zealand, Boston Art Museum, Cincinnati Museum. *Work repro.:* Studio. *Address:* 48 Bidwell Gdns., London N11. *Signs work:* "BRAUND."

BRAY, Phyllis; painter in oil and water-colour, lithographer; *b* 30 Aug., 1911;

d of William Bray; *m* Eric Phillips; two *s,* one *d. Educ.:* Queenwood, Eastbourne; *studied art* at Slade; Slade Scholarship. *Exhib.:* R.A., Leicester Galleries, London Group, Sydney, etc.; one-man shows, Drian Gallery (1975), London Gallery, Wildenstein, Mignon Gallery, Bath (1975). *Work in permanent collections:* Walker A.G., Blackpool A.G., C.A.S., St. Crispin's Church, Bermondsey. *Work repro.:* The Golden Road (Dent), Children's books (O.U.P., Faber, Dent, Evans Bros.). *Address:* 46 Platt's La., London NW3. *Signs work:* "Phyllis Bray."

BRAYER, Yves; painter; Member of Académie des Beaux-Arts, Paris; Officer Légion d'Honneur; *s* of General Victor Brayer. Born at Versailles, France, on 18 Nov., 1907, he showed a great individuality from the start of his career and is now one of the best-known French painters of his generation. He studied art in Montparnasse academies, then in the National School of Arts. In 1927, he was deeply impressed by a first trip to Spain, but the Prix de Rome, which he won in 1930, led him to make a prolonged stay in Italy. He also visited Greece, Constantinople and Morocco. Attracted by the quality of the light, he likes working in Provence and in Camargue (since 1945), and it marks a new stage in his development. He has designed sets and costumes for the operas of Paris, Amsterdam and Monte Carlo, and designed tapestries for Gobelins and Aubusson. He illustrated luxury editions, including texts from Henry de Montherlant, André Gide, Ernest Hemingway and Paul Claudel. The Paris Museum of Art Moderne, many museums in France and foreign countries and many collectors have bought his works. *Address:* 22 rue Monsieur le Prince, Paris, 6°. *Signs work:* "Yves Brayer."

BRAZDA, Jan; abstract painter, stained glass artist and stage designer, working in oils, tempera, stained glass, mosaic, church textiles, fresco, stage décor and costumes (*inter alia* Covent Garden), Lyric Opera, Chicago, Staatsoper, Munich; *b* Rome, 4 Dec., 1917; *s* of Oki Brazda. *Studied art* at Academy of Fine Arts, Prague, 1st Prize, Triennale, Milan, and Biennale, Venice. *Work in permanent collections:* National Museum, Prins Eugen Gallery (Stockholm), Art Museums of Gothenburg, Malmö, Röhsska Konstslöjd Museum, Archive Museum at Lund University. *Work repro.:* Svenska Konsntnärer, Allhems, Armitage Stained Glass. Member of National Organisation of Swedish Artists (K.R.O.). *Address:* Rindögatan 44, Stockholm, Sweden.

BRAZIER, A. Keeley, B.W.S., A.I.A.L. (1959); artist in water-colour, oil and pastel; *b* 22 Apr., 1894; *s* of Edwin Brazier; *m* Lily Doris Pane; two *s,* one *d. Educ.:* Barmouth Grammar School; *studied art* at Coalport China Works as apprenticed ceramic artist, Coalbrookdale School of Art under W. H. Gates, A.R.C.A. (1911-15), Birkenhead School of Art, Hammersmith School of Art. *Exhib.:* R.W.A., R.C.A., S.M.A. Utd. Soc. of Artists, R.B.S.A., North Wales Group, etc. *Official purchase:* poster for Barmouth Publicity Association (1965). *Work repro.:* Liverpool Daily Post, etc. *Address:* The Gables, Barmouth, Merioneth. *Signs work:* "A. Keeley Brazier."

BRENT, Ralph Richard Angus; land and seascape painter in oil and water-colour; *b* 5 Oct., 1903; *studied art* St. Martin's, London, under Bertram Nicholls, P.R.B.A. *Exhib.:* R.A., R.B.A., Fine Art Soc., Newlyn Soc. of Artists, Bladon Art Gallery, Hurstbourne Tarrant. *Invited exhib.:* Southport, Blackpool, Bolton, Bradford, Exeter, Devon Art Soc., Torquay, Auckland Soc., and Christchurch, N.Z., Beaulieu Gallery, Southampton Art Soc., Bournemouth Art Soc., etc. *Address:* c/o Lloyds Bank, Ltd. (Belgrave Rd. Branch), 68 Warwick Sq., London SW1. *Signs work:* see appendix.

BRESSLERN-ROTH, Norbertine von; prof.; animal painter, oil, water-colour, graphic wood-cuts; *b* 13 Nov., 1891; *m* George von Bresslern. *Educ.:* Akad d. Bild. Künste Wien (Prof. Schmutzer), Landeskunstschule, Graz (Prof. v. Schrötter). *Exhib.:* Albertina Wien; National Gallery; V. & A. Museum; National Galleries, Sydney, Hobart, Dunedin, Colonial-museum Rom, Kupferstichkabinett and Landes Bildergalerie, Graz, Styria. *Work repro.:* The Studio, etc. *Address:* Graz, Styria, Langegasse 29. *Club:* Künstlerbund Graz. *Signs work:* "Br.-Roth," "B.-Roth," "N.B.-Roth."

BRETT, Mary Elizabeth; artist in water-colour, pen, pencil; *b* Croydon; *d* of Capt. J. V. Brett, M.B.E. *Work repro.:* greetings cards, postcards, children's book illustrations (Medici Soc., Brockhampton Press, Wm. Collins & Sons, Frederick Warne). *Publications:* author and illustrator of Robin Finds Christmas, Tom Tit Moves House, A Surprise for Dumpy, The Untidy Little Hedgehog, The Forgotten Bear, Two in a Tent, Flip Flop's Secret, Paddy Gets into Mischief, Jiggy's Treasure Hunt, Midget and the Pet Shop, The Hare in a Hurry. *Address:* Chimes Cottage, Horsell Vale, Woking, Surrey. *Clubs:* Woking and Guildford Art Soc., Society of Authors. *Signs work:* "MOLLY BRETT."

BRIDGE, Muriel Elisabeth (Mrs. M. Taylor); N.D.D. Graphic Design; artist in water-colour and oils, part-time lecturer; *b* Rome, 20 March, 1934; *d* of Robert Bridge, President of Royal Numismatic Soc.; *m* John Taylor; one *s*, two *d*. *Educ.:* Private schools in Worcestershire; *studied art* at St. Martins School of Art under Mr. Rowe, John Minton, Ruskin Spear. *Address:* The White House, Horndean Rd., Emsworth, Hants. *Signs work:* "M. Bridge."

BRIDGEMAN, John, A.R.C.A. (1949), F.R.B.S. (1960); sculptor in stone, concrete and bronze; Head, Dept. Sculpture, Birmingham College of Art; *b* Felixstowe, Suffolk, 2 Feb., 1916; *s* of Bernard John Bridgeman, soldier; *m* Irene Dancyger, writer; one *s*, one *d*. *Educ.:* Colchester; *studied art* at Colchester School of Art (1936-39); under Barry Hart and Edward J. Morss (1939-40); Royal College of Art, under Frank Dobson (1947-49). *Work in permanent collections:* sculptures at St. Helen's, Birmingham, churches at Birmingham and Rugby, private gardens, private collections, Messrs. Petrofina. *Publications:* Journal of Institute of Landscape Architects (Feb., 1961), Concrete Quarterly (Sept., 1962), Architect and Builder (Dec., 1960). *Address:* Glebe House, Ufton, Warwickshire. *Signs work:* see appendix.

BRIDGWATER, Barbara Helen, A.T.D. (1941), A.I.I.D. (1948); on staff of Malvern School of Art (1941-48), Greenmore College (1950-56); senior lecturer at City of Birmingham College of Education (1956-75); Birmingham Polytechnic Centre for Education (1975—); embroideress; *b* 2 Dec., 1919; *d* of Harold G. Brunt; *m* Alan Bridgwater, A.R.B.S.; one *d*; *studied art* at Birmingham College of Art (1936-41). *Exhib.:* R.A., N.E.A.C., R.S.A., R.B.A., etc. *Address:* 107 Gough Rd., Edgbaston, Birmingham, 15. *Signs work:* "Barbara H. Bridgwater."

BRIERS, Irene A., A.I.C.A., Editorial Board, The Artist, Artist's Guide and Art Review (until 1975); Editor, Pictures and Prints (1957-75); supervisor of Studies, Famous Artists Schools, Associate Editor, The Artist's Handbooks; *b* London, 6 Mar., 1933; *d* of A. Briers. *Educ.:* Trinity. *Publications:* frequent contributions in The Artist, Artist's Guide, Art Review and other art publications and national papers; Editor, Leisure Painter and Craftsmen. *Clubs:* Studio, I.C.A., Chelsea Arts, Wig and Pen. *Address:* 41 Parker St., London WC2B 5PB.

BRILL, Reginald; artist in oil and water-colour; late Principal, Kingston School of Art; *b* London, 1902; *m* Rosalie. *Studied art* at Slade School (Prof. Tonks, 1921-24), British School at Rome (1927-29). *Publications:* Modern Painting (Avalon Press), Art as a Career (Batsford). *Address:* The

Little Hall, Lavenham, Suffolk. *Clubs:* The Arts, Chelsea Arts. *Signs work:* see appendix.

BRILLIANT, Fredda, F.R.S.A., F.I.A.L., S.P.S.; sculptress; *b* Lodz, Poland; *m* Herbert Marshall. *Exhib.:* R.A., Arcade, Leicester, A.I.A., R.W.S., R.I., Whitechapel and Ben Uri Galls., India House, Kominsky Galls. (Melbourne), Moscow Mus. of Fine Arts, New Delhi, Bombay, St. Louis, U.S.A. *Work in permanent collections:* Nat. Art Gall., New Delhi, Schevchenko and Mayakovsky Museums, U.S.S.R., Southern Illinois University. *Official purchases:* H.H. the Maharajah of Baroda, Mahatma Gandhi Memorial for Tavistock Sq., Sir Isaac Hayward in Hayward Gallery, Prof. Buckminster Fuller, South Illinois University, Sir Maurice Bowra, Oxford University. *Address:* 1204 Chautauqua St., Carbondale, Illinois, 62901, U.S.A. *Signs work:* "Fredda Brilliant."

BRIMMELL, Ronald Arthur (Max); artist in water-colour, pastel, black and white; *b* Wimbledon, 27 Apr., 1917; *s* of Arthur Brimmell, accountant; *m*; one *s*. *Educ.:* Wandsworth County School, Clark's College; *studied art* at Putney School of Art under Francis E. Hodge, R.O.I., J. Bowyer, E. Bately. *Exhib.:* P.S., R.B.A., United Soc. Artists, Britain in Water-colours Exhbn., Royal Institute of Water-colour Painters, R.S.M.A. *Address:* 9 High Wickham, Old Town, Hastings, Sussex TN35 5PB. *Signs work:* "Max Brimmell" (underlined).

BRINE, John Nicholas, R.B.A., A.R.C.A. (1949); artist in oils and acrylic; head of School of Fine Art, Ravensbourne College of Art and Design, Chislehurst; *b* 25 June, 1920; *s* of George Edward Brine. *Studied art* at Clapham School of Art (1935-1939) under Pitchforth; R.C.A. (1946-49) under Moynihan and Minton. *Address:* 87 Widmore Rd., Bromley, Kent. *Signs work:* "BRINE."

BROADFIELD, Aubrey Alfred (Alan), M.A. (1934); librarian and author; art teacher at Alleyn's School, Dulwich (1936-37), librarian since 1938; *b* Doncaster, 1910; *s* of Rev. A. L. Broadfield; *m* Robina Margaret Hedley. *Educ.:* Manchester Grammar School; New College, Oxford; Birmingham University; *studied art* at Loughborough College, Slade School under Randolph Schwabe (1935-36), Courtauld Inst. *Author of:* Philosophy of Classification (1946), Philosophy of Librarianship (1949), Leicester as it was (1972); contributions to T.L.S., World Review, National and English Review, Bookseller, etc. *Address:* 99 Station Rd., Glenfield, Leics. *Signs work:* "AB."

BROADFIELD, Robina Margaret; artist in oil, water-colour, tempera; mem. of Council, Leicester Soc. of Artists (1954); *b* Hebburn-on-Tyne; *d* of Francis Hedley; *m* A. Broadfield, M.A. (Oxon.), librarian and author. *Educ.:* Grammar School, Jarrow; High School of Commerce, Toronto; *studied art:* mainly self-taught. *Exhib.:* Wiesbaden, Leicester. Nottingham Castle, Galleria Europa Arte, Ancona, Italy, Annuale Italiana D'Arte Grafica, Mostra Internazionale (1968) (Medaglia e Diploma d'Onore), Bienalle delle Regioni (1968-69), Mostra Confronto Internazionale (Medaglia e Diploma di Menzione Onorevole). *Address:* 99 Station Rd., Glenfield, Leicester. *Signs work:* "R.M.B."

BROADIE, Barry; artist in acrylics, water-colour and inks; art tutor, Basil Paterson Tutorial College; *b* Manchester, 20 Oct., 1940; *s* of Frederick Broadie, Ph.D., B.A., M.A. *Educ.:* George Heriot's School, Edinburgh. *Exhib.:* R.S.A., R.S.W., R.G.I., Demarco Gallery, Scottish Gallery; regular one-man shows in Edinburgh. *Work in permanent collections:* Royal Edinburgh Hospital, Argyle County Council, Hopetoun House, Edinburgh Danish Institute. *Address:* 4 Leslie Pl., Stockbridge, Edinburgh. *Signs work:* "Barry Broadie."

BROCKBANK, Russell., Art Editor, Punch (1949-60); *b* Niagara Falls,

Canada, 15 Apr., 1913; *s* of Clarence Brockbank, F.C.I.C., A.M.I.E.; *m* Eileen Mary Hames; one *s*, one *d*. *Educ.:* Ridley College, Ontario, Canada; *studied art* at Buffalo N.Y. School of Art, and at Chelsea School of Art under Williamson (1931-32). *Exhib.:* S.G.A. *Work repro.:* in Punch, The Motor, Automobile Jahr, Road and Track. *Publications:* Round the Bend, Up the Straight, Over the Line, Manifold Pressures, Move Over, The Brockbank Omnibus. *Address:* Badgers, Thursley, Surrey. *Clubs:* Savage, B.A.R.C. *Signs work:* see appendix.

BROCKLEHURST, Phillips: see PHILLIPS BROCKLEHURST, C. D. F.

BROCKWAY, Michael Gordon; artist in oil and water-colour; *b* 11 Apr., 1919; *m* Margaret, *d* of Sir William Harris, K.C.V.O., D.Mus.; two *s*. *Educ.:* Stowe and Peterhouse, Cambridge; *studied art* at Farnham School of Art (1946-50), Cheltenham School of Art (1950), and Ruskin School of Drawing, Oxford (1951-54). *Exhib.:* R.A., R.I., R.B.A., N.E.A.C. *Publication:* Charles Knight, R.W.S., R.O.I., 1952. *Address:* New Place, Farmington, Northleach, Glos. *Signs work:* "MICHAEL BROCKWAY."

BRODY, Frederick J., A.V.C.M. (1931), A.R.C.A. (1937), M.S.I.A. (1946), F.I.A.L. (1952), F.R.S.A. (1960); lecturer in art, interior designer, silversmith, cabinet-maker, painter in tempera; *b* Sheffield, 31 May, 1914; *s* of Solomon Brody, master cabinet manufacturer; *studied art* at Sheffield College of Art (1929-34); R.C.A. (1934-37) under Prof. Tristram, Sir William Rothenstein, John Nash, Bawden, Ravilious, Spencer, Barnett Freedman. *Exhib.:* London, provinces, International Exhbn. (Paris, 1937), B.I.F. exhbns., Britain Can Make It exhbn. Festival of Britain (1951) and U.S.A. *Work repro.:* silverware at Sheffield and London, furniture in own furniture factory. *Address:* 15 Cherry Tree Drive, Sheffield 11. *Signs work:* see appendix.

BROKMAN DAVIS, William David, A.R.E., F.I.A.L.; painter and etcher. *Official purchases:* British Council; Contem. Art Soc.; British Museum; Gothenburg Museum, Sweden; National Museum, Stockholm; Scottish Arts Assoc.; National Gallery, Cardiff; Art Inst., Chicago; Artists' Advisory Council; Manchester, Birmingham, Glasgow, Bradford, Newport, Stoke Art Galleries. *Address:* Tudor Cottage, Longfield Drive, West Parley, Dorset. *Club:* Chelsea Arts.

BRONDUM-NIELSEN, Birgitte, R.I., S.S.W.A.; Diplome d'Honneur, Vichy (1964); artist in water-colours; illustrator; *b* Copenhagen, 1917; *d* of Dr. E. Bocher; *m* H. Brondum-Nielsen. *Educ.:* Copenhagen; *studied art* at College of Arts and Crafts, Copenhagen. *Exhib.:* group shows: R.A., R.S.A., S.S.A., R.S.W., Pitlochry Festival Theatre, Charlottenborg (Copenhagen), Salon International de Vichy, Brighton Art Gallery, Royal Glasgow Institute of Fine Arts; one-man shows: Bristol, Stirling, Edinburgh (two), Roskilde (Denmark), Edinburgh Festival. *Work in permanent collection:* Glasgow Art Gallery. *Work repro.:* illustrations for songbooks for children (Danish), De Smaa Synger; Fairytales from many Lands; Switzerland, etc. *Address:* 36 Claremont, Alloa, Scotland. *Signs work:* "BITTE B-N."

BROOK, Peter, R.B.A.; painter in oil; teacher, Sowerby Bridge Grammar School; *b* Holmfirth, Yorks., 6 Dec., 1927; *s* of Hildred Brook; *m* Margaret Thornsby; two *d*. *Studied art* at Goldsmiths' College, London University. Works in many public and private collections in this country, Switzerland, U.S.A., South Africa and Australia. Exclusive agent, Agnew & Sons Ltd. *Address:* 43 Old Bond St., London. *Signs work:* "PETER BROOK."

BROOKE, Anne Isabella, A.T.D.; landscape painter; *b* nr. Huddersfield, 1916. *Studied art* at The Byam Shaw, Chelsea and Huddersfield Schools of Art and London University Institute of Educ. *Exhib.:* R.A., R. Scottish A., N.E.A.C., Paris

Salon, R.B.A., R. Cambrian A., R.O.I., W.I.A.C., R.I. Salon, United Artists, National Soc. and many provincial exhbns. *Official purchases:* Herts Educ. Com., Lincs. Educ. Com., Harrogate A.G., Bristol Educ. Com., Wakefield A.G., Keighley A.G., Northumberland Educ. Com., The Beecroft A.G., Southend-on-Sea. *Address:* 3 Oak Terr., Harrogate. *Signs work:* "A. Brooke."

BROOKE, Geoffrey Arthur George, D.S.C., R.N. (retd.); oil painter; *b* Bath, 25 Apr., 1920; *s* of Capt. J. Brooke, D.S.C., R.N. (retd.). *Educ.:* R.N. College, Dartmouth; *studied art* under Miss Sonia Mervyn, 28 Roland Gdns., SW7 (1949-50). *Exhib.:* Army Art Soc. exhbns. *Address:* Beech House, Balcombe, Sussex. *Club:* Army and Navy. *Signs work:* "G.A.G.B."

BROOKE, James Leslie, F.I.B.D.; artist in oil, water-colour, gouache, picture restorer; *b* Huddersfield, 28 May, 1903; *s* of Alfred Brooke. *Educ.:* Birkby School; *studied art* at Huddersfield College of Art under J. R. Gauld, A.R.C.A., Paris, Florence, Rome, Naples, New York, etc. *Exhib.:* R.A., R.B.A., Paris Salon, United Artists, Yorkshire Artists Exhbn., Bradford Spring Exhbn., W. Riding Artists, etc.; one-man shows, Huddersfield and Dewsbury Municipal Art Galleries. *Work in permanent collections:* Huddersfield, Dewsbury. *Publications:* in Architectural Review, Yorkshire Life Illustrated, Dalesman, Journal of Decorative Art, etc. *Address:* 33 Birkby Lodge Rd., Huddersfield. *Signs work:* "JAMES L. BROOKE."

BROOKE, Thomas Humphrey, C.V.O.; First Class Hons. (Mod. History) Oxford (1935), B.Litt. (1937); asst. keeper, Public Record Office (1937-46); served on Monuments, Fine Arts and Archives Sub-Commissions in Italy and Austria (1944-46); asst. keeper, Tate Gallery (1946-48). deputy keeper (1948-49); principal, Min. of Town and Country Planning (1949-51); sec., Royal Academy of Arts (1952-68); *b* nr. Huddersfield, 31 Jan., 1914; *s* of Major Thomas Brooke; *m* Nathalie Benckendorff (*d.* of Count Benckendorff, D.S.O.); one *d.* (one *s*, one *d.* dec'd.). *Educ.:* Wellington College and Magdalen College, Oxford. *Address:* 8 Pelham Cres., London SW7. *Club:* Chelsea Arts.

BROOKER, William; painter in oil; Principal, Wimbledon School of Art; *b* Croydon, Surrey, 26 June, 1918; *s* of C. F. Brooker. *Educ.:* Royal Masonic School, Bushey, Herts.; *studied art* at Croydon School of Art (1936-39), Chelsea School of Art (1947-49). *Work in permanent collections:* Tate Gallery, Arts Council, National Gallery of Canada, National Gallery of New Zealand, National Gallery of South Australia, Castle Museum, Nottingham, Glynn Vivian Museum, Swansea, Oldham Art Gallery, Rotherham Art Gallery, Aberdeen Art Gallery, City Art Gallery, Manchester, Southampton Art Gallery, Contemporary Art Society, Museum of Modern Art, Belo Horisonte, Brazil. *Address:* c/o A. Tooth & Sons Ltd., 31 Bruton St., London W1. *Signs work:* "Brooker."

BROOKES, Ronald E., F.S.I.A.; consultant industrial designer; *b* 26 Aug., 1920. *Educ.:* Bedford, Bath. *Exhib.:* London, Paris, New York, Tokyo, Amsterdam, Milan, etc. In Designers in Britain, 2, 3, 4, 5, 6 and 7, Architectural Review, Design, etc. *Address:* 12 Lansdown Pl. East, Bath.

BROOKS, Louie (Mrs. L. Grimshaw), M.A.F.A. (1943); housewife and artist in oil; *b* Manchester, 1 Aug., 1900; *d* of Harold Brooks; *m* Donald P. Grimshaw. *Educ.:* Convent of Notre Dame, Wigan, Namur; *studied art* at Manchester College of Art under A. W. Dodd and J. Millard. *Exhib.:* R.S.P.P., R.B.A., M.A.F.A., Salford. *Work repro.:* Studio, Cheshire Life. *Address:* 29 Llandudno Rd., Colwyn Bay. *Signs work:* "L. Brooks."

BROOKS, Mary, A.R.C.A., W.I.A.C.; portrait and landscape painter in oils;

art mistress, Cambridge County School (1924-28); *b* Barnsley, 1897; *d* of Walter Brown; *m* J. C. V. Brooks; one *s*. *Educ.:* Barnsley High School; *studied art* at Leeds School of Art and Royal College of Art under Sir W. Rothenstein (1920-24). *Exhib.:* R.A., R.B.A., W.I.A.C., Leger Gallery and London Group. *Address:* Four Winds, Cornwallis Ave., Tonbridge, Kent. *Signs work:* "MARY BROOKS."

BROOKS, Mary Eileen; self-taught artist in oil and acrylic; Hon. Director, Loggia Gallery, London; P.R.O. of F.P.S.; *b* London, 8 May, 1906; *d* of Henry George Chandler, banker; *m* Edward James Brooks, writer (dec'd.). *Educ.:* Clapham High School, London. *Exhib.:* one-man shows in London and the provinces, San Francisco, California and Paris. *Address:* 64 Kings Ct., Ravenscourt Pk., London W6 0RW. *Club:* F.P.S. *Signs work:* "Mary Brooks" or "M. Brooks."

BROUGHTON, Aya, N.S., M.F.P.S., W.I.A.C., S.W.A.; artist in water-colour and oil, mural painter; Associate, Société des Artistes Français; Paris Salon silver medal (1972); *b* Kyoto, Japan; *d* of Dr. T. Kumagai (M.D.); *m* B. L. Broughton, M.A. (Oxon). *Educ.:* Kyoto Furitsu Daiichi High School and the College, Kyoto, Japan; *studied art* at Newton Abbot School of Art and Dartington Adult Centre. *Exhib.:* R.A. (1958), W.I.A.C., N.S., R.B.A., R.I., R.O.I., London Group, Paris Salon, United Soc., R.W.S. Exhbn. Flower Painting, Festival of Women, Wembley, London, Exhbn. of Living British Women Artists, Flower Painters of the World (1971). *Work collected privately* in U.K., Japan, Switzerland, America, New Zealand. *Work repro.:* La Revue Moderne, Western Morning News, Herald Express and Torquay Times, TV BBC1 Peninsula. *Publications:* Article on Buddhism and Japanese Art (The Mahabodhi Journal). *Address:* Greylands, 14 Cleveland Rd., Torquay, Devon. *Signs work:* "AYA"; see appendix.

BROWN, Deborah; *b* Belfast, 1927. *Studied art* in Belfast, Dublin, Paris. *Exhib.:* France, Germany, Scandinavia, Gt. Britain, U.S.A. and Ireland. Ten one-man shows since 1951. *Work in private and permanent collections* in Gt. Britain, Ireland and U.S.A. Mem. of the Women's International Art Club and Free Painters and Sculptors, London. *Commission:* 1965, by Ferranti Ltd., a series of eight panels for the interior of their building at Hollinwood, Manchester. *Prizes:* 1970 First Prize Carroll Open Award, Irish Exhibition of Living Art, Dublin; 1970 Subsidiary Prize Open Painting Arts Council of N. Ireland. *Address:* 115 Marlborough Pk. Sth., Belfast. *Dealer:* The David Hendriks Gallery, 119 St. Stephen's Green, Dublin.

BROWN, Mary Rachel; Mem. National Society Literature and the Arts; self-taught artist in oil; *b* New York City, 24 Sept., 1921. *Educ.:* New York University. *Exhib.:* Paris, New York, Switzerland. *Work in permanent collections:* Jean Aberbach, Theodora Settele. *Address:* 33 W. 67th St., New York 10023, N.Y. *Signs work:* "Marais."

BROWN, Neil Dallas, D.A. (Drawing and Painting, 1958); major prizewinner, Arts Council of N. Ireland Open Painting Exhibition (1970); painter in oil; part-time tutor, Duncan of Jordanstone College of Art, Dundee; *b* Elgin, 10 Aug., 1938; *s* of Robert Duncan Brown; *m*; two *d*. *Educ.:* Bell Baxter High School, Cupar, Fife; *studied art* at Dundee College of Art (1954-59), Alberto Morrocco), Royal Academy Schools (1960-61, Peter Greenham). *Work in permanent collections:* Scottish Arts Council, Dundee City Museum, Skopje Museum, Yugoslavia, Nottingham City Art Gallery, Scunthorpe Education Committee, Hertfordshire County Council, Schools Collection, Walker Art Gallery, Liverpool, Kingsway Technical College, Dundee. *Address:* Tayside, 55 Cupar Rd., Newport-on-Tay, Fife. *Signs work:* see appendix.

BROWN, Percy, A.R.C.A.; sculptor and potter; *b* Oct., 1911; *m* Ursula Moynihan; *studied art* at R.C.A. *Exhib.:* R.A., Leicester Galleries, Gimpel Fils. *Official purchases:* City of Leicester A.G. and Educ. Com., Blackburn Corp., Leeds Corp., British Transport Commission, L.C.C. Works in private collections. *Work repro.:* Studio, The Modern Potter. *Address:* 27 St. George's Rd., St. Margaret's-on-Thames, Middx. *Signs work:* see appendix.

BROWN, Philip; painter; *b* London, 4 Nov., 1925; *s* of Leslie Norman Brown, M.A.; *m* Gounil; five *d. Educ.:* St. Paul's School, London, and Christ Church, Oxford; *studied art* at Slade School (1945-47); Académie de la Grande Chaumière, Paris (1948); Ateliers d'Art Sacré, Paris (1949-50). *Stained glass work* in St. John's Cathedral, Umtata, South Africa; St. Mark's, Regent's Park; St. Paul's Church, Crofton; St. Edmund's, Twickenham; St. Ambrose, Speke, Liverpool; Catholic Church, Pershore; Spode House, Hawkesyarde Priory; Holy Infants, Bolton; Holy Name, Fazackerly, Liverpool; Chapel, St. Patrick's Open-air School, Hayling Island; Holy Souls, Scunthorpe; St. Gregory, Eastbourne; Baptist Church, Brighton, etc. *Address:* Calle de la Residencia 7, S.L. de El Escorial (Madrid), Spain.

BROWN, Ralph, R.A., A.R.C.A.; sculptor; *b* Leeds, 24 Apr., 1928. *Educ.:* Leeds Grammar School; *studied art* at Leeds School of Art, Hammersmith School of Art, R.C.A. and Paris. *Work in permanent collections:* Tate, Rijksmuseum Kröller-Müller, Holland, A.G. of New South Wales, Arts Council collections, Contem. Art Soc., Leeds A.G., Aberdeen A.G., Cardiff A.G., Huddersfield A.G., Southport A.G., West Riding Ed. Com., Norfolk Contem. Art Soc., Peter Stuyvesant Foundation. *Public commissions:* Harlow New Town, Brussels World Fair (1958), L.C.C. School, Tulse Hill, Hatfield New Town, Loughborough College of Advanced Technology. *Address:* Mas de Guérit, Saumaul 30125, Gard, France. *Signs work:* see appendix.

BROWN, William George Baldwin, F.L.A.; borough librarian and curator, public libraries, museum and art gallery, Kingston upon Thames; *b* 28 Nov., 1920. *Address:* Central Library, Museum and Art Gallery, Fairfield Rd., Kingston-upon-Thames.

BROWNBRIDGE, John, M.S.I.A.; designer of packaging and posters; *studied art* at St. Martin's; Reimann (Austin Cooper) and abroad. *Address:* Flat 6, 115 Finchley Rd., London NW3. *Signs work:* see appendix.

BROWNE, Clive Richard; landscape painter in oil; *b* Keelby, 27 July, 1901; *s* of Canon Neville Lord Browne; *m* Edna Mary Garrard; one *s,* one *d. Educ.:* St. James' Secondary School, Grimsby; St. John's College, York; *studied art* at Grimsby Art School and under H. Rollett, R.B.A. *Exhib.:* R.A., R.Scot.A., R.H.A., R.Cam.A., R.W.E.A., R.B.A., R.O.I., N.S., British Empire Soc. Arts, W.A.G., Paris Salon, and provinces. *Work in permanent collections:* Usher Art Gallery, Lincoln. *Work repro.:* in Salon, Illustrated. *Address:* Kirkdale, Waltham, Grimsby, Lincs. *Clubs:* N. Lincs. Art Soc., Lincs. Art Soc. *Signs work:* see appendix.

BROWNE, Richard, F.R.B.S.; sculptor in stone, bronze, glass fibre; Mem., Society of Portrait Sculptors; *b* London, 1921; *s* of Reginald Browne; *m* Janice Browne; one s, one *d. Studied art* at Wimbledon (1948-52), Slade (1953). *Work in permanent collections:* bronze family group, Crawley New Town; Guildford Cathedral; Hotel Intercontinental, Kabul; City of London University; New Central Synagogue, London; British and Foreign Bible Society, etc. *Address:* 43 Trinity Rise, London SW2. *Signs work:* "Richard Browne."

BROWNING, Amy Katherine, R.P., R.O.I., A.R.C.A., gold medal, silver medal, h.c. Paris Salon; oil, pencil, chalk; *m* the late T. C. Dugdale, R.A. *Educ.:* privately; *studied art* at R.C.A. (Gerald Moira) and in Paris. *Exhib.:* R.A., N.E.A.C., R.P., R.O.I., Pittsburgh, Vienna, Paris, Wellington, Sydney, Ghent, Salon des Artists Français, many provincial galleries. *Official purchases:* Glasgow, Manchester, Wolverhampton, Wellington (N.Z.), National Gallery, French Govt. for Luxembourg Gallery (Gold Medal and Hors Concours), Southport, Luton. *Work repro.:* Studio, Artist, Apollo, etc. *Address:* 58 Glebe Pl., London SW3. *Signs work:* "A. K. Browning" (in caps. on paintings, written on drawings).

BROWNING, Stephen James, B.A. Oxon. Modern History (1974); artist in oil and water-colour; Theatre Manager, Greenwich Theatre; Director, Greenwich Theatre Art Gallery; *b* London, 2 Feb., 1953; *s* of Leslie John Browning, T.D., F.C.I.S. *Educ.:* Marlborough College (1966-70); Trinity College, Oxford (1971-74); *studied art* at Putney School of Art (1971); Byam Shaw (part-time 1971) under Peter Garrard. *Exhib.:* Mall Galleries, London, Oxford, Cornwall, Redruth; group show: F.P.S. Work in private collections. *Address:* 40 Victoria Rd., Kensington, London W8. *Signs work:* "S. J. Browning."

BROWSE, Lillian; partner in firm of Roland, Browse, and Delbanco, 19 Cork St. W1; editor and writer of books on art; former ballet critic, Spectator; organized wartime loan exhbns. at National Gallery, London (1940-45); also exhbns. for C.E.M.A. and British Inst. of Adult Education. *Publications:* Augustus John Drawings (Faber & Faber, 1941); Sickert (Faber & Faber, 1943); Degas Dancers (Faber & Faber 1949); general editor of Ariel Books on the Arts, published for the Shenval Press by Faber & Faber; William Nicholson (Rupert Hart-Davis, 1955); Sickert (Rupert Hart-Davis, May, 1960). *Address:* 19 Cork St., London W1.

BRUCE, George J. D., elected R.S.P.P. (1969), Hon. Sec. (1970); portrait painter and painter of landscapes, still life, flowers etc. in oil; *b* London, 28 Mar., 1930. *Educ.:* between terms at Westminster; *studied art* at Byam Shaw School of Drawing and Painting (Brian D. L. Thomas, O.B.E., Patrick Phillips, R.P., Peter Greenham, R.A.). *Address:* 6 Pembroke Walk, Kensington, London W8. *Signs work:* see appendix.

BRUCE, Matt, D.A. (Edin.), R.I., M.P.S.; teacher of painting and crafts, artist in all media, teacher at Victoria College, Jersey, Varndean School for Boys, Brighton, and Brighton College of Art evening classes; *b* Shanghai, China, 17 Nov., 1915; *s* of M. W. Bruce, C.P.A.; *m* M. F. Bruce; one *s. Educ.:* Dollar Academy, Scotland; *studied art* at Edinburgh College of Art (1932-39) under W. Gillies and J. Maxwell. *Exhib.:* R.A., R.I., R.B.A., Brighton. *Address:* The Coach House, Old London Rd., Brighton BN1 8XQ. *Club:* Chelsea Art. *Signs work:* "Matt Bruce."

BRUCE LOW, Mabel, R.B.A. (1919); water-colours, colour prints (woodcuts); vice-pres., Soc. of Women Artists; *d* of Robert Bruce Low, C.B., M.D.; *m* Alexander Chisholm. *Educ.:* Dulwich High School and Dresden; *studied art* at Westminster Art School (Mouat Loudon and Walter Sickert), Edinburgh College of Art (Robert Burns, R.S.A.), London Art School (Richard Jack, R.A.). *Exhib.:* R.A., R.S.A., International Soc., N.E.A.C., R.I., etc. *Official purchases:* Contemp. Art Soc. for British Museum (colour print), Sunderland (colour print), Bournemouth (three water-colours). *Publications:* colour print—A Country Bouquet (Warren Johns, Ltd.) and Summer Flowers. *Address:* 14 Burford Ct., Manor Rd., Bournemouth. *Signs work:* "M. Bruce Low."

BRUNN, Peter, M.S.I.A. (1952); designer of furniture, interiors, shops, displays, etc.; *b* Berlin, 25 June, 1928; *s* of Max Brunn, foreign representative.

Educ.: Bolton County Grammar School; *studied art* at Bolton School of Art (1945-49). *Exhib.:* I.C.A., Arts and Crafts Exhbn. Soc., Cotton Board, Crane Gallery. *Work repro.:* British Furniture Today, Decorative Art, House and Garden, Mobili Tipo, Interiors, Domus, Designers in Britain. *Address:* 22 Margaretta Terr., London SW3. *Signs work:* "Peter Brunn."

BRUNSDON, John Reginald, A.R.C.A. (1958); printmaker (etchings and aquatints on steel) and painter in oil on canvas; in charge of printmaking at St. Albans School of Art; *b* Cheltenham, 1933; *s* of John Robert Brunsdon; *m* Heather; one *s*, two *stepsons*. *Educ.:* Cheltenham Grammar School; *studied art* at Cheltenham College of Art (Principal, S. G. Dent), Royal College of Art (Julian Trevelyan). *Work in permanent exhibitions:* New York Museum of Modern Art, Scottish Museum of Modern Art, Rochester Memorial Museum of Modern Art, Arts Council of Gt. Britain, V. & A. Museum. *Publication:* Etching and Engraving (B. T. Batsford Ltd.). *Address:* 17 Bedford St., Woburn, nr. Bletchley, Bucks. *Signs work:* "John Brunsdon."

BRUNSKILL, Ann, Assoc. of Royal Society of Painter Etchers (1969); painter and printmaker; *b* London, 5 July, 1923; *d* of Hugh George Edmund Durnford, M.C.; *m* John Brunskill; three *s*, one *d*. *Educ.:* Langford Grove School; *studied art* at Central School of Arts and Crafts, Chelsea College of Art. *Work in permanent collections:* V. & A., Bibliothèque Nationale, University College, Oxford, South London Collection of Original Prints, Lib. of Congress, Washington, U.S.A., J. Lessing Rosenwald Alverthorpe Coll., U.S.A., Universities of Princeton, Yale, U.S.A., National Library of Australia, Canberra. *Address:* 1A Oliver's Wharf, 64 Wapping High St., London E1 9PJ. *Signs work:* "Ann Brunskill."

BRYANT, Dena; artist in oils on polyfilla, scraper-board, water-colour; gallery owner and restorer; *b* Gloucester, 19 Mar., 1930; three *s*. *Educ.:* Red Maid's School, Westbury-on-Trym, Bristol; *studied art* at Royal West of England College of Art (5 years part-time) under Paul Feiler. *Exhib.:* St. Albans Gallery (1975), St. Albans Museum (1970). *Work in permanent collection:* New England Street Gallery, St. Albans. *Address:* 27 Lower Dagnall St., St. Albans, Herts. *Signs work:* "D.B.", "Dena" or a snail.

BRYCE, Gordon, D.A. (Edin.), A.R.S.A., R.S.W.; Arts Council Awards (1968, 1970) five national awards for painting; painter in oil, lecturer in printmaking; *b* Edinburgh, 30 June, 1943; *m* Margaret Bryce; two *s*. *Educ.:* Watsons College, Edinburgh Academy; *studied art* at Edinburgh College of Art (1960-65), Andrew Grant scholar. *Exhib.:* Richard Demarco Gallery (1971), New 57 Gallery (1965, 1966), Bath Festival, R.S.A., S.S.A., R.S.W. and group shows throughout Britain. *Work in permanent collections:* Scottish Gallery of Modern Art, Arts Council, Aberdeen A.G., Leeds A.G., Watson Trust, Arbroath Town Council, Fife Educ. Authority, Lothian Region, Grampian Region, British Petroleum, Aberdeen, Sussex, and Stirling Universities, Royal Edinburgh Hospital. *Address:* 67 Malcolm Rd., Culter, Aberdeen.

BUCHANAN, Elspeth, D.A. (Edin.); painter in oil; mem. of Council of S.S.W.A. (1956-59), S.S.A.; *b* Bridge of Weir, 29 Nov., 1915; *d* of John Buchanan. *Educ.:* St. George's School for Girls, Murrayfield, Edinburgh; *studied art* at Edinburgh College of Art (1933-38) under Wellington. *Exhib.:* R.A., R.Scot.A., S.S.A., S.S.W.A., G.I., N.E.A.C.; first one-man show, Great King St. Gallery. *Publication:* illustrated Land Air Ocean (Duckworth). *Address:* 2 Learmonth Terr., Edinburgh. *Club:* Soroptomist, Edinburgh. *Signs work:* "Elspeth Buchanan."

BUCHANAN-DUNLOP, Brigadier Archibald Ian, C.B.E. (1958), D.S.O.

(1944), retired 1960; principal, Scottish Office, retired 1975; artist in water-colour, indian ink; *b* Whitefield, Lancs., 3 Mar., 1908; *s* of Lt.-Col. A. H. Buchanan-Dunlop, O.B.E., of Drumhead; *m* Renée Frances Caroline Serjeant; one *s*, one *d*. *Educ.:* Loretto; Sandhurst. *Exhib.:* R.S.W.S., R.W.S. Art Club and other exhbns. *Work repro.:* occasional illustrations and cartoons in various publications. *Address:* The Coach House, Colinton, Edinburgh 13. *Clubs:* Army & Navy, United Hunts, R.W.S. Art Club. *Signs work:* "Ian Buchanan-Dunlop" (water-colour), "Bian" (pen-work).

BUCK, John Sandford, B.W.S. (1944); oil, water-colour, black and white; *b* Minehead, 13 Apr., 1896; *s* of Thomas Buck; *m* Ellen Elizabeth Wiggins. *Educ.:* Monmouth School; *studied art* at Bristol (etching under R. E. J. Bush, R.E., R.W.A.). *Exhib.:* R.I., R.B.A., R.W.A., R.B.S.A., B.W.S. *Official purchases:* Newport (Mon.) Art Gallery; mural painting, Monmouth Methodist Church. *Address:* Holborn Hse., Brains Green, Blakeney, Glos. *Clubs:* Gloucestershire Society of Artists, Wye Valley Art Society. *Signs work:* "J. SANDFORD BUCK."

BUCKLEY, Charles Edward, M.A. (Harvard, 1948), B.F.A. (Chicago Art Inst., 1940); Director, St. Louis Art Museum, Missouri (since 1964); Director, The Currier Gallery of Art, Manchester, New Hampshire (1955-64), Curator, Wadsworth Atheneum, Hartford (1951-55); keeper of W. A. Clark Collection of Corcoran Gallery of Art, Washington (1949-51); *b* South Hadley Center, Mass., 29 Apr., 1919. *Educ.:* Universities of Chicago and Harvard; *studied art* at Chicago Art Inst. School and Harvard University. *Address:* City Art Museum, Forest Park, St. Louis, Missouri.

BUCKLEY, Howard, M.A., A.R.C.A.; artist in water-colour, etcher; *b* Croydon, 1909; *s* of Thomas Buckley, A.M.I.E.E.; *m* Margaret Schaeffer; one *s*, one *d*. *Educ.:* John Ruskin School, Croydon; *studied art* at Croydon School of Art, R.C.A. *Exhib.:* R.A., R.W.E.A., Chicago International exhbn. and many provincial galleries. *Work in permanent collections:* Southampton and Brighton Municipal A.G.'s, etchings; Worthing Pier Pavilion, murals. *Work repro.:* Apollo, Studio, several textbooks. *Address:* Kiln Cottage, Westfield La., Wheatley, Oxford. *Signs work:* "Howard Buckley."

BUCKLEY, Sydney, artist in water-colour, oil, etcher and engraver; on staff of Oldham School of Art (1927-32); *b* Oldham, Lancs., 16 Apr., 1899; *s* of Isaac Bradburn Buckley. *Educ.:* Oldham Hulme Grammar School; *studied art* at Oldham School of Art (Principal, W. H. Helm, A.R.C.A.). *Exhib.:* R.I., R.S.A., R.S.W., Manchester Academy of Fine Arts (mem.), Lake Artists' Soc. *Work in permanent collections:* 100 book plates in Picton Library Collection, Liverpool; small selection of book-plate designs in British Museum. *Publications:* cover drawings and chapter headings for official handbook, Hardknot, for H.M. Forestry Commission. *Address:* Cartmel Gallery, Cartmel, Grange-over-Sands, Cumbria. *Signs work:* "S. Buckley."

BUCKMASTER, Ann Devereaux, M.S.I.A. (1951); freelance artist in pen; *b* London, 27 Mar., 1924; *d* of Arthur D. Buckmaster; *m* Anthony Gilbert. *Educ.:* Bromley High School; *studied art* at Beckenham School of Art, Bromley College of Art. Illustration and fashion drawing for magazines and advertising. *Address:* 14 South Hill Rd., Bromley, Kent.

BUDAY, George, Dr. (Szeged University, 1934), A.R.E. (1938), R.E. (1953), Fellow Soc. of Wood Engravers (1954); artist, wood engraver, author; lecturer on graphic arts, Franz Joseph University, Hungary (1934-41); *b* Hungary, 1907; *s* of Prof. A. Buday, archæologist. *Educ.:* Kolozsvar and Szeged University; *studied* *art* in Hungary, Italy. *Exhib.:* R.A., R.S.P.E., etc. *Work in permanent collections:* B.M., V. & A., etc. *Official purchases:* by Contemp. Art Soc., Arts Council of Gt. Britain, etc. *Work repro.:* Studio, T.L.S., etc., and large number of book illustrations. *Publications:* G. Buday's Little Books (annually 1943-56 and 1968); The History of Christmas Cards (1954 and 1964); G.B.'s Wood-engravings (1970); Multiple Portraiture (1975). *Address:* Downs House, Netherne, P.O. Box 150, Coulsdon, Surrey CR3 1YE. *Signs work:* see appendix.

BUDD, Kenneth George, A.R.C.A. (1950); mural designer; *b* London, 16 Oct., 1925; *s* of Henry Walter Budd; *m* June Casburn (1956); two *s*, one *d*. *Studied art* at Beckenham School of Art (1941-44) and R.C.A. (1947-50). *Murals designed and produced* include Boys' Grammar School, Kettering (mosaic); College of Science and Technology, Derby (sand and resin); Birmingham Corporation Inner Ring Road (murals); Colmore Circus (mosaics); Horse Fair (mosaics); Priory Ringway (brass and lead relief); St. Chad's Circus, 300-ft. long mural in mosaic, brass and aggregate (History of Snow Hill/G.W.R.); Kennedy Memorial (mosaic and quartzite); Savoy, Birmingham (silver relief); Church of Good Shepherd, Brighton (stained glass); Newport Street, offices Swindon (mosaic); Old Green Interchange, Newport, Mons. (landscaping, surfaces, 164-ft. mosaic and concrete mural and two 20-ft. bronze sculptures of heraldic beasts). *Address:* Caragana, Trotts La., Westerham, Kent. *Signs work:* see appendix.

BUFFET, Bernard; artist in oil; Prix de la Critique (1948); *b* Paris, 1928. *Studied art* at École des Beaux Arts, 1944. *Exhib.:* Salon d'Automne, 1947. *Work in permanent collections:* Musée d'Art Moderne, Paris; Museum of Modern Art, New York; Musée de Grenoble. *Publications:* Le Cirque, by Bernard Buffet (1955); Bernard Buffet, by Pierre Bergé (1958). *Address:* c/o Maurice Garnier, 6 Ave. Matignon, Paris, 8. *Signs work:* "Bernard Buffet."

BÜHLER, Curt F., B.A. (1927), Ph.D. (1930), Litt.D. (1947); librarian; Research Fellow Emeritus, Pierpont Morgan Library (1948—); mem., Dept. of Printed Books, Pierpont Morgan Library (1934-48); *b* N.Y., 11 July, 1905; *s* of Conrad Bühler; *m* Lucy Jane Ford; one *s*. *Educ.:* Hill School and Universities of Yale, Dublin (Trinity College) and Munich. *Publications:* The Melk Salbenkrämerspiel, Dicts and Sayings of the Philosophers, Standards of Bibliographical Description, Sources of the Court of Sapience, 15th Century Books and the 20th Century, The Epistle of Othea, The History of Tom Thumbe. *Address:* 33 E. 36th St., New York, N.Y. *Clubs:* Devonshire (London), University (Dublin), Royal Dublin Soc., Grolier (N.Y.), Gutenberg Gesellschaft (Mainz).

BULLARD, Paul, A.R.C.A. (1947); lecturer in art. Woolwich Polytechnic (1948-58), Head of Department of Foundation Studies at Camberwell School of Arts and Crafts (since 1966); *b* London, 1918; *s* of Arnold Robert Bullard; *m* Jeanne Fenner; two *s*. *Educ.:* Central Foundation Grammar School; *studied art* at Clapham School of Art (1934-38) and R.C.A. (1938-47). *Exhib.:* R.A., N.E.A.C., London Group, etc. *Address:* 7 Orchard Drive, Blackheath, London SE3. *Signs work:* "Paul Bullard."

BULLEN, Maud, F.P.S.; artist in water-colour; *b* Dorking, 14 Feb., 1906; *d* of George Batts; *m* Stanley Bullen; one *s*. *Educ.:* St. Paul's, Dorking; *studied art* at Rentwood Occupational Therapy Centre, Fetcham, Leatherhead under Ursula Hulme. *Exhib.:* one-man shows: Loggia Gallery, Liberty's; group shows: Dickins & Jones, Post Offices (London), Mall Galleries, Folkestone Da Carlo Restaurant, Art Centre and others. *Work in permanent collection:* Liberty's, London. *Address:* 30 Hart Rd., Dorking, Surrey. *Clubs:* Rentwood Occupational Therapy Centre, Sticks & Wheels, Darby & Joan. *Signs work:* "M. Bullen."

BULLEY, Edward Stanley, A.R.C.A., F.R.S.A.; calligrapher and teacher (retired); *b* London, 1906; *s* of William George Bulley, jeweller; *m* Olive Mary White; one *s,* one *d. Educ.:* Salesian School, Farnborough; St. John's College, Wonersh; *studied art* at Medway School of Art (1928-29), R.C.A. *Work in permanent collections:* Roll of Honour, Bedford School; MS. book, Tiverton School, MS. books at St. John's, Wonersh, and Westminster Cathedral. *Address:* 11 Grosvenor Ave., Carshalton, Surrey.

BULLOCK, Jean; Mem. Society of Portrait Sculptors; sculptor and graphic artist; *b* Bristol, 27 Apr., 1923; *m* John Bullock, artist and lecturer. *Educ.:* Bishopshalt, Hillingdon, Middx., George Watsons Ladies College; *studied art* at Watford College of Art under Guido Belmonte, Camberwell School of Art under Dr. K. Vogel. *Exhib.:* R.A., Soc. of Portrait Sculptors, Singapore Art Society, Art Exhbns., Bureau Travelling Exhbn. *Work in permanent collections:* Min. of Defence. *Address:* The Old School, Ashwell, Oakham, Rutland. *Signs work:* "JEAN BULLOCK."

BUMPHREY, Nigel; schoolmaster, gold and silversmith, and furniture maker; *b* Norwich, 22 Feb., 1928; *s* of Herbert Bumphrey. *Educ.:* The City of Norwich School and Loughborough College; *studied art* at Central School of Arts and Crafts and Norwich Art School. *Exhib.:* Blakeney Guild of Many Crafts. *Address:* 28G Jessopp Rd., Norwich. *Signs work:* see appendix.

BUNTING, John Joseph, F.R.B.S. (1972), A.R.C.A. (1954); sculptor in wood, stone and bronze; *b* 3 Aug., 1927. *Educ.:* Ampleforth College, Oriel College, Oxford; *studied art* at St. Martin's School of Art (1949-51); R.C.A. (1951-54). *Exhib.:* one-man shows at Paris (1965), Billingham (1972). *Work in permanent collections:* Churches: St. Michael and All Angels (Oxford), War Memorial Chapel (Hambledon), St. Aidan's Church (Oswaldkirk); schools: St. Wilfrid's (Featherstone), St. Thomas à Becket (Wakefield), St. Bernard's (Rotherham). *Work repro.:* Monthly Report (1958-60), illustrations to Partage de Midi Paul Claudel (1963), Stages of the Cross (1972), John Bunting, sculptor (Paris, 1966). *Address:* Oswaldkirk, York.

BURFORD, Doreen Elaine, A.S.I.A., C. & G. Fin. Emb., A.T.D. (1950); designer woven textiles and embroidery; Head of School of Fashion, College of Art, Bournemouth, since 1951; *b* Derby, 11 Apr., 1925; *d* of A. R. Barnett, A.I.I.A., A.C.I.S.; *m* Philip R. Burford. *Educ.:* Parkfields Cedars Secondary School, Derby; *studied art* at Derby College of Art, Leicester College of Art. *Exhib.:* Derby A.G., Manchester Cotton Board, Leeds City A.G., Leicester City A.G., British Man-made Fibres Fed. *Work repro.:* Art and Industry, Design. *Address:* Harewood Ave., Bournemouth. *Signs work:* "Burford."

BURKE, Joseph T., C.B.E. (1946), M.A., London, Yale and Melbourne; Herald Prof. of Fine Arts, University of Melbourne; Pres. Australian Academy of the Humanities; Trustee, the Felton Bequest; mem., Australian Council for Industrial Design; private sec. to successive Lords President of the Council (1942-45) and to Prime Minister (1945-46); *b* London, 14 July, 1913; *s* of R. M. J. Burke, decd.; *m* Agnes Middleton; one *s. Educ.:* King's College; Courtauld Institute of Art, University of London; Yale University, U.S.A. *Publications:* Hogarth and Reynolds: A Contrast in English Art Theory, Ed. William Hogarth's Analysis of Beauty and Autobiography, The Paintings of Russel Drysdale. *Address:* 807 Toorak Rd., Melbourne E3, Australia. *Clubs:* Athenæum (London), Melbourne (Melbourne).

BURLAND, Cottie A., F.R.A.I. (1941); writer and lecturer on art and primitive religions; *b* Notting Hill Gate, London, 1905; *m* Maud, *née* March; one *s,* one *d. Educ.:* Portobello Rd. L.C.C. School, St. Mark's, Kensington, Regent St. Polytechnic. *Publications:* Magic Books from Mexico (King Penguin, 1950); series of children's books on history of civilization (Hulton Educational Press, 1958-65); The Selden Roll (Mann, Berlin, 1955); Mexican Codices (Graz, 1965-68); Myths of the North American Indians (Hamlyn, 1965); The Arts of the Alchemists (Weidenfeld & Nicholson, 1967); The Exotic White Man (Weidenfeld & Nicholson, 1969); Echoes of Magic (Peter Davies, 1972); The Gods of Mexico (Eyre & Spottiswoode, 1967); Montezuma (Weidenfeld & Nicholson, 1973); Myths of Life and Death (Macmillan, 1974); contributor, Arts Review, Man, etc. *Address:* 246 Molesey Ave., West Molesey, Surrey.

BURLEY, David W., M.S.I.A. (1944); artist in water-colour, oil, lino-cut, etc.; tutor, Galleon Sketching Holidays and Adult Art Education; *b* 28 Apr., 1901; *studied art* at Goldsmiths' School of Art. *Exhib.:* R.A., R.I., R.B.A. and provinces. *Address:* 25 Alpha Rd., Birchington-on-Sea, Kent. *Signs work:* "D. W. Burley."

BURN, Rodney Joseph, R.A. (1962), Hon. A.R.C.A., N.E.A.C. (1924), S.M.A. (1958); landscape and figure painter; senior tutor, R.C.A.; hon. sec., N.E.A.C.; *b* London, 11 July, 1899; *s* of Sir Joseph Burn, K.B.E. (decd.); *m* Dorothy Sharwood Smith; one *s*, two *d. Educ.:* Harrow School; *studied art* at Slade School (1918-22) under Prof. Henry Tonks. *Exhib.:* R.A., N.E.A.C., London and provinces. *Work in permanent collections:* Tate Gallery, B.M. (print room), Brighton, Bristol. *Official purchases:* Chantrey Bequest (1953), Contemp. Art Soc. *Address:* 1 The Moorings, Strand on the Green, Chiswick, London W4. *Club:* N.E.A.C. *Signs work:* "R. J. Burn."

BURNAND, Robert Alan Lewis, A.R.E. (Jan., 1968), A.T.D. (July, 1949); artist in wood-engraving and water-colour and teacher; *b* Malacca, Malaya, 19 Feb., 1929; *s* of John Robert Burnand, A.I.S.P., F.I.R.I.; *m* Wendy June; one *s*, two *d. Educ.:* Slough Grammar School for Boys; *studied art* at College of Art, High Wycombe, College of Art, Harrow, Middx., College of Art, Brighton (Morgan Rendle, Frederick Herrick). *Publications:* She (Rider Haggard), Longmans, Green; Let's Look It Up (school textbook), Chatto & Windus. *Address:* Avon Water, Aller, Langport, Somerset. *Club:* Somerset Society of Artists. *Signs work:* "R. Burnand."

BURR, Victor; artist in oil; *b* Wandsworth, 5 July, 1908; *s* of James Burr; *m* Elizabeth Tidy. *Educ.:* Honeywell Rd. School, Battersea; *studied art* at West Sussex School of Painting and Drawing under R. O. Dunlop, R.A. *Exhib.:* R.A., R.O.I., R.P., N.E.A.C., Brighton Art Gallery, etc. *Address:* 38 East Park, Crawley, Sussex. *Signs work:* "Victor Burr."

BURROUGH, Helen Mary (Mrs.), A.R.W.A.; artist in oil, water-colour, sepia and wash; *b* Ceylon, 17 Feb., 1917; *d* of Axel J. Austin Dickson; *m* T. H. B. Burrough; two *s. Educ.:* St. George's, Ascot; *studied art* at Miss McMuns Studio, Park Walk, Chelsea (1937), Prof. Otte Skölds' Ateljé, Stockholm (1938-39). *Address:* The Old House, Frenchay, nr. Bristol BS16 1ND. *Club:* Royal Commonwealth Society. *Signs work:* "Helen."

BURROUGH, Thomas Hedley Bruce, T.D., R.W.A., F.R.I.B.A.; chartered architect, artist in drawing and water-colour; Special Lecturer (Architecture), University of Bristol; Pres. Bristol and Glos. Archaeological Soc.; *b* Newport, Mon., 30 Apr., 1910; *m* Helen Mary Dickson, A.R.W.A.; two *s. Educ.:* Clifton College; *studied art* at R.W.A. School of Architecture (1928-32) (G. D. Gordon-Hake). *Work in permanent collections:* R.W.A., Bristol City Art Gallery, Red Lodge. *Publications:* An Approach to Planning (Pitman), South German Baroque (Tiranti), Bristol Buildings (Studio Vista). *Address:* The Old House, Frenchay, nr.

Bristol BS16 1ND. *Clubs:* Royal Empire Soc., Bristol Savages. *Signs work:* see appendix.

BURROUGHS, Victor Hugh Seamark, R.M.S., S.WL.A., F.R.S.A., S.M.; Associate, Société des Artistes Français, Paris Salon (Gold Medallist 1974, Silver Medallist 1973); admitted to Freedom of the City of London, Freeman and Liveryman of the Worshipful Company of Painters—Painters Stainers; artist in water-colour and oil; *b* London, 1900; *s* of William R. Burroughs (decd.), artist and dealer in antiques; *m* Grace E. Hayward; three *s,* two *d. Educ.:* Lyndhurst Grove School, London; *studied art* at Camberwell School of Arts and Crafts, Southampton Row School of Design, Goldsmiths' College, Reading University under Prof. A. Betts. *Exhib.:* R.A., R.I., R.M.S., S.WL.A., S.M., Société des Artistes Français, Paris Salon, R.Cam.A., Augustine Gallery, Holt, and many other provincial galleries. *Address:* 46 Westlands Ave., Shinfield, Reading, Berks RG2 8EN. *Signs work:* "Victor H. S. Burroughs" on oils and water-colours; and see appendix.

BURROWS, Roy, A.R.Cam.A., A.T.C., F.R.S.A. (1951), Royal Aeronautical Society's "Elliot Memorial" Prize (1940); Senior Master, Cartref Melys School, Conway; W.E.A. Lecturer, Tutor (summer schools) Coleg Harlech; landscape artist in oil, acrylics, dyes and inks; *b* Crewe, 17 Mar., 1922; *s* of Frederick William Burrows, farmer/councillor; *m* Joan Nielston; one *s,* two *d. Educ.:* Chester City Grammar School; Nottingham University; *studied art* at St. Peter's College, Peterborough (1947-48); Nottingham College of Arts and Crafts (1948-50). *Exhib.:* one-man shows: Peterloo Gallery, Manchester, Pentagon, Stoke-on-Trent, Royal Cambrian Academy, Birmingham, Mold & Pwhelli, N. Wales, N. Staffs. Art Soc. *Work in permanent collections:* Stoke-on-Trent A.G. and Museum, N.A.S.A. America, Manchester City Council. *Address:* Woodford, 53 Brompton Ave., Colwyn Bay, Clwyd. *Clubs:* Cheshire Artists, N. Wales Assoc. of the Arts. *Signs work:* "Roy Burrows."

BURTON, Ralph Molyneux, A.R.B.S., A.R.C.A.; sculptor in wood, cold cast resin, bronze; tutor, Adult Education Centre, Tunbridge Wells; *b* Cheshire, 1922; one *d. Educ.:* King's School, Macclesfield; *studied art* at R.C.A. (1947-50) under Frank Dobson, A.R.A., and John Skeaping, A.R.A. *Work in permanent collections:* various commissioned works sited in London, the Midlands and the Home Counties. *Address:* 30 Sunnyside, Rose Hill, Ticehurst, Sussex TN5 7AJ. *Signs work:* "Ralph M. Burton."

BURY, Adrian, R.W.S.; water-colour painter, poet and writer on art; *b* 6 Dec., 1891; nephew of Sir Alfred Gilbert, R.A.; *studied art* in London, Paris and Rome. *Exhib.:* R.A., R.P., N.E.A.C., Leger Gall. *Official purchases:* Contemp. Art Soc., B.M., V. & A., Birmingham, Edinburgh, Wolverhampton, Newcastle, London Museum, Leamington, Hereford and Southport A.G. *Publications:* Water-colour Painting of Today; Oil Painting of Today; Thomas Collier, R.I.; John Varley of the "Old Society"; Richard Wilson, the Grand Classic; Thomas Rowlandson; Two Centuries of British Water-Colour Painting; Sir Alfred Gilbert, R.A.; Syon House; Joseph Crawhall; Francis Towne, Just a Moment, Time—autobiography. *Address:* 37 Eashing Point, Roehampton, London SW15.

BUSHE, Frederick; Scottish Arts Council Award (1971, 1973); sculptor, lecturer, Aberdeen College of Education; *b* Coatbridge, Scotland, 1 Mar., 1931; *m* Rosemary R. Beattie; three *s,* one *d. Studied art* at Glasgow School of Art (1949-53), University of Birmingham (1966-67). *Exhib.:* 57 Gallery Edinburgh (1962), Bluecoat Gallery, Liverpool (1966), Demarco Gallery, Edinburgh (1971); Glasgow University (1964), Grosvenor Gallery, London (1966), International Sculpture, Dunfermline, Art-in-a-City, I.C.A., London (1967), Sculpture in a City Arts Council (1968), Ledlanet, Kinross (1970), Arts Spectrum (1971), Awards to Artists exhibition (1972), Scottish Sculpture (1975). *Work in permanent collections:* Scottish Arts Council, Liverpool University, Aberdeen University, Aberdeen A.G. *Work repro.:* Apollo Magazine, Art-in-a-City—John Willette, Whither Scotland, ed., article by Cordelia Oliver. *Address:* Glenburn House, Tomaveen, Torphins, Aberdeen.

BUSSELL, Jan (John Garrett); puppet master (The Hogarth Puppets); author; theatrical, radio, television producer; maker and exhibitor of marionettes, glove puppets, shadow puppets, owner of Muffin the Mule, director, Sheffield Repertory Theatre (1932-33); B.B.C. North Regional drama producer (1933-35); B.B.C. television producer (1937-48); Sub-Lieut., R.N.V.R. (1944-46); *b* Oxford, 20 July, 1909; *s* of Rev. John Garrett Bussell of Marlborough College; *m* Ann Hogarth; one *d. Educ.:* Marlborough and Brasenose. *Publications:* Plays for Puppets, Faber; The Art of Television, Faber; Puppet's Progress, Faber; Through Wooden Eyes, Faber; Pegasus Book of Puppets, Dobson. *Address:* 16 Riverside, Egham, Surrey.

BUTLER, Alice Caroline, R.M.S. (1960); miniaturist in water-colour and pen and ink; *m* Maurice H. Bizley; one *d. Educ.:* private and State schools; *studied art* at St. Albans School of Art. *Exhib.:* St. Ives Society of Artists, Royal Society of Miniature Painters, Sculptors and Gravers. *Publications:* author and illustrator of The Slate Figures of Cornwall; illustrated Friendly Retreat (M. H. Bizley), Cornish Windmills (H. L. Douch, B.A.). *Address:* St. Annes, Tywarnhayle Rd., Perranporth, Cwll. *Signs work:* see appendix.

BUTLER, Anthony, R.C.A. (Cambrian, 1960), A.T.D. (1950); schoolmaster; artist in oil and gouache; head of art, Birkenhead School; *b* Liverpool, 1927; *s* of George Butler; *m* Jean; two *s,* one *d. Educ.:* Liverpool Institute; *studied art* at Liverpool School of Art (1944-45, 1948-50) under Martin Bell, Alfred Wiffin, Alan Tankard. *Exhib.:* R.A., New Burlington, Agnews, Northern Young Contemporaries. *Work in permanent collections:* Walker Art Gallery, Liverpool; Whitworth Art Gallery, Manchester; Williamson Art Gallery, Birkenhead; and various county educational collections; ceramic decoration commissioned by Dudley C.C. for new shopping precinct. *Address:* 4 Princes Ave., West Kirby, Ches. *Signs work:* "BUTLER."

BUTLER, Auriol; associate mem., Société des Artistes Français (1972); artist in oil, pastel, water-colour; *b* Pitney, Somerset; *d* of Alexander Ross Biddle, B.A.; *m* Richard Butler; one *s,* one *d. Educ.:* Copplestone House School, Budleigh Salterton; Lausanne, École Cantonale; *studied art* at Byam Shaw School under Ernest Jackson and at Slade School, pastel with Mlle. Landau in Paris, also worked at L'Académie de la grande Chaumière, Paris. *Exhib.:* Pastel Soc., London, R.B.A., S.W.A., Kenn Group, London Group, Paris Salon, United Society, etc. *Work repro.:* La Revue Moderne. *Address:* Glebe Studio, Cornwood, Ivybridge, Devon. *Signs work:* "A. Butler." or "Auriol."

BUTLER, George, R.W.S., R.B.A., N.E.A.C.; painter in oil and water-colour; *b* Sheffield, 17 Oct., 1904; *m* Kcenia; one *s,* one *d. Educ.:* King Edward VII School, Sheffield; *studied art* at Sheffield College of Art (1922-23), Central School of Arts and Crafts (1923-26). *Work in permanent collections:* Graves Art Gallery, Maplin Art Gallery. *Address:* Riversdale, Bakewell, Derbyshire. *Clubs:* Arts, Chelsea Arts. *Signs work:* "George Butler."

BUTLER, James; R.A. (1972); sculptor in bronze and stone; *b* Deptford, 25 July, 1931; *s* of Walter Arthur Butler; *m* Angela Berry; two *d. Educ.:* Maidstone

Grammar School; *studied art* at Maidstone School of Art (1948-50); St. Martin's School of Art (1950-52). *Major commissions:* twice life size portrait statue of President Kenyatta of Kenya, Nairobi; monument to Freedom Fighters of Zambia, Lusaka, Zambia. *Address:* Old School House, High St., Greenfield, Bedford MK45 5OB. *Signs work:* surname and year.

BUTLER, Reg.; sculptor; *b* 1913. *Address:* Ash, Berkhamsted Pl., Berkhamsted, Herts.

BUTLER, Richard Gerald Ernest; painter, graphic designer; senior lecturer, Central School of Art and Design; *b* Essex, 31 Dec., 1921; *s* of Major Gerald Butler, A.P.T.C.; *m* Mary Driscoll; three children. *Studied art* at Salisbury School of Art. *Exhib.:* R.A., Arts Council Touring Exhbns., etc., one-man shows: Walker Galleries (1956-58). *Address:* 32 Denne Rd., Horsham, Sussex. *Signs work:* "Richard Butler."

BUTLER, Vincent; sculptor, figurative, bronze; associate, Royal Scottish Academy; teacher, Edinburgh College of Art; *b* Manchester, 1933. *Exhib.:* one-man shows: Crestine Gallery, Edinburgh (1963), New Grafton Gallery, London (1969), Birley Gallery, Manchester (1973), Goosewell Gallery, Bradford (1974). *Address:* 17 Dean Park Cres., Edinburgh 4. *Signs work:* see appendix.

BUTTERFIELD, Ron, S.C.C.; sculptor, woodcarver and designer in wood, stone, bronze and precious metals; *b* Sheffield, 4 May, 1920; *s* of Randolph Lloynd Butterfield; *m* Audrey Beatrice Butterfield; one *s,* two *d. Educ.:* Hunter's Bar School; *studied art* at Sheffield College of Art (1934-35 full-time, 1935-40 part-time) under J. A. Sands, A.R.C.A., J. Clarkson, A.R.C.A. *Work in permanent collections:* hanging rood: St. Catherine's Church, Houghton on Hill, Leics.; St. John's Church, Troedyrhiw; SS. Mary and John, Nuneaton; rood beam with figures: Bradwell, Derbys., St. Elidyr's Church, Crunwere; eagle lecterns: Pontnwynnydd, Saltney, Radcliffe, Sheffield, Skegby, Melksham, Ropsley, Windsor, Ontario, Saundersfoot. *Address:* 57 Rustlings Rd., Sheffield S11 7AA. *Clubs:* Society of Church Craftsmen, London; Guild of Yorkshire Craftsmen, York. *Signs work:* "Ron Butterfield" and see appendix.

BYRNE, John (Patrick); artist in oil; *b* Paisley, 1940; *s* of Patrick Byrne; *m*; two children. *Educ.:* Glasgow; *studied art* at Glasgow School of Art. *Work in permanent collections:* Contemporary Arts Society, London; Museum of Primitive Art, Ecuador; Lobel Gallery, Stockholm; Friesner Art Institute, N.Y.; Fasler Collection, Hartford, Conn.; Scottish Arts Council. *Publications:* Modern Primitives, Oto Behalji-Merin; Ways of Communicating, Donald J. Tighe. *Address:* 278 Paisley Rd., Renfrew, Scotland. *Signs work:* "Byrne" or "Patrick."

BYWATER, Marjorie, A.R.C.A. (1930); lecturer in art, Southampton R.C. Training College, Charlton Kings Cheltenham (1943-45); artist in oil and watercolour; *b* Ealing; *d* of William Bywater; *m* Bernard Stanton, Editor of the Medical Directory. *Educ.:* Haberdashers' Aske's School, Acton, and Stoney Green Hall, Prestwood, Bucks.; *studied art* at R.C.A. (1927-30) under the late Sir William Rothenstein, Prof. E. W. Tristram, and Reco Capey, and at the Slade School of Art (1935-36) under Polunin. *Exhib.:* R.A., R.I., Paris Salon. *Address:* 11 East Cl., London W5. *Signs work:* see appendix.

C

CADENHEAD, William Collie Milne, D.A., cert.R.A.S., Bronze Medal R.A. Schools (1957), David Murray Landscape Scholarship (1957), elected prof.

member S.S.A. (1969); painter in oil and water-colour; lecturer in drawing and painting, Duncan of Jordanstone College of Art, Dundee; *b* Aberdeen, 8 Oct., 1934; *s* of A. L. Cadenhead, L.D.S., R.C.S. Edin.; *m. Educ.:* Aberdeen Grammar School; Forfar Academy; *studied art* at Dundee College of Art (1951-55) under Alberto Morrocco; Florence, Rome, Paris (1956); Hospitalfield Art College, Arbroath; R.A. Schools, London (1957-61) under Peter Greenham. *Exhib.:* R.S.A., S.S.A., R.S.W., R.S.P.P. Savage Gallery, Compass Gallery, Montrose Festival, Royal Overseas League, Edinburgh Festival (1968), etc. *Work in permanent collections:* (Stations of the Cross), St. Fergus, Forfar; Meffan Institute, Forfar; Steel Company of Wales and private collections in U.K. and U.S.A. *Address:* The Rowans, Muir of Lownie, Forfar, Angus. *Signs work:* "Cadenhead."

CADMAN, Michael Lawrence, A.R.C.A. (1945), R.I. (1970); painter in oil and gouache of landscape, natural history subjects; Instructor, Epsom School of Art (1946-69); *b* Epsom, 9 Nov., 1920; *m* Ann Burden. *Educ.:* Epsom; *studied art* at Wimbledon School of Art (1937-40) under Gerald Cooper; Royal College of Art (1942-45) under Gilbert Spencer. *Exhib.:* seven one-man shows London, etc.; annually, R.I. (Mall Galleries). *Work in permanent collections:* banks, boardrooms, colleges, etc. *Work repro.:* Paul Hamlyn, B.P., Royle Publications, etc. *Address:* Tolmennor Studio, Trew, Breage, Helston, Cornwall. *Signs work:* "–Michael–Cadman–."

CAINE, Osmund, M.D.C.S., A.S.M.G.P., mem. Craft Centre, A.S.I.A.; teacher, painter in oil, water-colour, illustrator, lithographer, artist in stained glass and mosaic; Principal Lecturer, Graphic Design, Twickenham College of Technology (1962); *b* Manchester. *Studied art* at Birmingham College of Art (1930-37) and in Italy (1938). *Exhib.:* R.A., N.E.A.C., R.B.A., R.B.S.A., V. & A., Craft Centre, Lambeth Palace, Guildhall, and Walker, Adams, Piccadilly Galleries, Leicester, Whitworth Gallery, R.I.B.A., Southwell-Brown Gallery, Richmond, Hampton-Hill & Ashbarn Gallery, Petersfield, London; one-man exhbns.: 1961, Walker's Gallery, Richmond Hill Gallery; 1966, 1969, Canaletto Gallery, Foyles' Art Gallery. *Official purchases:* St. Gabriel's Church, Cricklewood; St. Paul's Church, Kingston; Erdington Abbey, St. Cuthbert's Church, Portsmouth; St. Augustine's, Edgbaston (1953); Min. of Transport (1955); St. Luke's Church, Wellington, N.Z. (1961); St. Keyne's Church, Liskeard (1973). Films: The Glastonbury Giants (in conjunction with Mary Caine), (1966); The Ruskin Country (1966). *Address:* 25 Kingston Hill, Kingston-on-Thames. *Signs work:* see appendix.

CAINS, Gerald Albert, N.D.D. (Painting S.L. 1953), A.T.D. (1957), A.R.W.A. (1969), A.D.A.E. (University of Wales, 1975); painter and set designer in oil and water-colour; *b* Stubbington, Hants., 11 May, 1932; *s* of Albert George Cains; *m* Ruth Lillian Blackburn; one *s,* one *d. Educ.:* Gosport County Grammar School; *studied art* at Southern College of Art, Portsmouth (1949-53). *Work in permanent collections:* Lancashire Museum Service, R.W.E.A., Walsall Art Service. *Address:* 1 Broadway Cottages, Broadway Lane, Clandown, nr. Bath, Som. *Signs work:* "G. A. CAINS."

CAIRNS, Huntington; lawyer, writer on art, etc.; secretary, treasurer and general counsel, National Gallery of Art, 1943-65; *b* Baltimore, Md., 1 Sept., 1904; *s* of James Duncanson Cairns; *m* Florence Faison Butler. *Educ.:* Baltimore City College, University of Maryland. *Publications:* Law and the Social Sciences, The Theory of Legal Science, Invitation to Learning, Masterpieces of Painting from the National Gallery of Art, The Limits of Art, Legal Philosophy from Plato to Hegel, Great paintings from the National Gallery of Art, Lectures in Criticism. *Address:* 2219 California St., N.W., Washington, D.C. 20008. *Clubs:* Hamilton

Street (Balt.), Maryland (Balt.), Wranglers (Balt.), Cosmos (D.C.), 1925 F Street (D.C.).

CALLAM, Edward, R.O.I., F.R.S.A., M.S.I.A. (1950); artist in oil, watercolour, black and white; designer and typographer; hon. sec. Army Art Soc. (1951); *b* Great Kimble, Bucks.; *m* Marion Norwood, F.S.C.A. historian and genealogist. *Exhib.:* R.A., Société des Artistes Français, R.O.I., R.B.A., Foyles, R.G.I., Imperial Institute, Russell-Cotes, Bournemouth, Brighton A.G., Worthing A.G. *Official purchases:* Maidstone Corporation (1958); Richter Bequest (1959); Luton Art Gallery (1964); Luton Corpn., 30 ptgs. (1969). *Work repro.:* Sphere, Tatler, Penguin and Pelican books, The Christian Science Monitor. *Address:* The Studio, Collington La. W., Bexhill, Sussex. *Signs work:* see appendix.

CAMBRON, Ghislaine; artist, painter, ceramist; Professeur de Dessin, Academie de Mollenbeek, Brussels; Grand Prix de Belgique (1954), Grand Prix de Decoration (1955), Grand Prix de Belgique (1956), Prix de L'État Belge (1942), Distinction-Prix Europe Peinture (1962); *b* St. Amand-les-Eaux, 6 July, 1923; *m* Mariee. *Studied art* at Académie de Bruxelles. *Work in permanent collections:* Musée Art Moderne, Brussels, Centre Culturel, Uccle, Musée de Molenbeek, Timbres-Poste du Congo (Serie Masques). *Address:* Dréve Angevine, Domaine de la Motte, Bousval 1488, Brabant, Belgique. *Signs work:* "Cambron, Ghislaine."

CAMERON, Gordon Stewart, R.S.A. (1971); painter in oil; senior lecturer, School of Drawing and Painting, Duncan of Jordanstone College of Art, Dundee; *b* Aberdeen, 27 Apr., 1916; *s* of John Roderick Cameron; *m* Ellen Malcolm, A.R.S.A. *Educ.:* Robert Gordon's College, Aberdeen; *studied art* at Gray's School of Art, Aberdeen (1935-40) (Dr. D. M. Sutherland, R.S.A., Robert Sivell, R.S.A.). *Work in permanent collections:* Aberdeen Art Gallery, Perth Art Gallery, Royal Scottish Academy, Dundee Art Gallery. *Publication:* illustrations for Lockhart's Anatomy of the Human Body. *Address:* 7 Auburn Terr., Invergowrie, Perthshire. *Club:* Scottish Arts, Edinburgh. *Signs work:* "G. S. CAMERON."

CAMP, Ann, A.R.C.A. (1946); freelance calligrapher and lettering designer; instructor at Digby Stuart College and Marylebone Institute; *b* London, 1924; *d* of Instructor/Capt. John Camp, R.M. *Studied* at Hampstead Garden Suburb Inst. and R.C.A. *Work in permanent collections:* loan collections of V. & A., L.C.C. and National Museum of Wales; Book 4, R.A.F. Book of Remembrance in St. Clement Dane's Church; lettering on stamps, murals, etc. *Publication:* Pen Lettering (Dryad Press). *Club:* Soc. of Scribes and Illuminators. *Address:* 115 Bridge La., London NW11. *Signs work:* "Ann Camp."

CAMP, Jeffery Bruce, A.R.A., D.A. (Edin.) 1943, Andrew Grant awards (1944), (1945); painter; lecturer, Slade School; Mem. London Group; *b* 1923. *Exhib.:* John Moores, Liverpool (1959, 1961, 1963, 1975), Beaux Arts Gallery (1959, 1961, 1963), New Art Centre (1968), Retrospective Exhbn. (1973), ICA Apollinaire Exhbn. (1969), R.A. (1970, 1971), British Art, Hayward Gallery (1974), Chichester National (1975). *Work in permanent collections:* Arts Council collection, Norwich Castle Museum. *Official purchases:* Norfolk Contem. Art Society, Chantrey Bequest, C.A.S., Arts Council, Ministry for the Environment, altar-piece for St. Alban's Church, Norwich. *Address:* 78 Forthbridge Rd., London SW11. *Signs work:* see appendix.

CAMPBELL, Alexander Buchanan, A.R.S.A. (1972), B.Arch. (1937), F.R.I.B.A. (1955), F.R.I.A.S. (1955); architect; *b* Findochty, 14 June, 1914; *s* of Hugh Campbell, master mariner; *m* Sheila Smith; one *s,* one *d. Studied architecture* at Glasgow School of Architecture (Strathclyde University) (1930-37) under

Prof. T. Harold Hughes, Dr. J. A. Coia. *Address:* 1 Royal Cres., Glasgow. *Clubs:* Art, R.S.A. *Signs work:* "A. Buchanan Campbell."

CAMPBELL, Felicity, A.I.A.L., R.I.; commercial artist; painter in oil and miniature from photograph or life, animals a speciality, family portraits copied; *d* of Vere and Josephine Campbell; *m* J. Walsh. *Studied art:* London, Paris, Rome. *Exhib.:* R.A. (1961-62), R.I. (1962-63). *Work in permanent collection:* (murals) Adventures of Sherlock Holmes at Windlesham. *Publications:* illustrated Seven Deadly Sins by Marjorie Bowen, Rosemary Books by N. Purvis. *Address:* Laughing Cat Studio, Friars Hill, Guestling, Sussex. *Club:* I.C.A. *Signs work:* see appendix.

CAMPBELL, George F., R.H.A. (1954); artist in oil and water-colour; *b* Arklow, Ireland, 29 July, 1917; *s* of Matthew Campbell; *m* Margaret McNeil. *Educ.:* Richview School, Dublin; *studied art:* mainly self-taught, with some weeks at Grande-Chaumière, Paris. *Work in permanent collections:* Dublin Municipal Gallery, Belfast Municipal Gallery, Abbot Collection (Boston), C.E.M.A., Internat. Post Office (Berne), Belfast University, Beaverbrook Art Gallery, Trinity College, Oxford, Leicester Educ. Comm. *Official purchases:* Irish Nat. Collection, Haverty Trust, Arts Council N. Ireland, Arts Council Republic of Ireland, Bank of Ireland, Duchess of Westminster, Duke of Westminster, Museum of Fine Arts, Málaga, Museum of Fine Arts, Antequera. *Address:* David Hendriks Gallery, 119 St. Stephen's Green, Dublin 2, Ireland. *Signs work:* "Campbell."

CAMPBELL-QUINE, Nina; Jane Plotz scholarship; painter in water-colour, gouache, oil, enamel; designer (interior architecture, furniture, theatre, etc.), enamellist; *b* Pretoria, Transvaal, 17 July, 1911; *d* of Alexander John Arbuckle, M.I.Mech.E/M.I.M.E.; *m* William Campbell-Quine. *Educ.:* by private tutors; *studied art* at School of Art, Johannesburg (1926-28) under Prof. Winter-Moore and Prof. Armstrong. *Work in permanent collections:* Anton Rupert and Schlesinger. *Address:* 79 Third Rd., Hyde Pk., Sandton, Tvl. 2196. *Club:* Johannesburg Country. *Signs work:* "Nina."

CANEY, Eric, A.R.I.B.A., F.R.S.A.; architect and illustrator in pencil, ink, water-colour; *b* London, 22 Mar., 1908. *Exhib.:* R.A., N.S., R.I., R.B.A., Artists of Chelsea. *Address:* 10 Harvey Rd., Guildford, Surrey. *Signs work:* "Eric Caney."

CANNELL, Edward Ashton, N.D.D., A.T.D., F.R.S.A.; painter and illustrator; formerly Head of Art Dept., Rutherford School, London; Senior Art Assessor for Metropolitan Regional Examinations Board; representative of the National Society for Art Education on the Art Advisory Panel of the I.L.E.A.; *b* Isle of Man, 12 Sept., 1927. *Educ.:* King William's College; *studied art* Isle of Man School of Art, Liverpool College of Art. *Exhib.:* R.I., R.B.A., R.S.M.A., Paris Salon (Silver Medal 1973, Gold Medal 1975), Thackeray Gallery, Archer Gallery, Francis Iles Gallery, Ditchley Gallery (U.S.A.). *Work in private collections:* U.S.A., Canada, South Africa, Japan, Saudi Arabia and most European countries. *Publications:* freelance work for various publications, W. & G. Foyle, Cassell, Bass International, British Petroleum. *Address:* Studio House, 52 Dyne Rd., London NW6 7DS. *Clubs:* Langham, London Sketch, Wapping Group, United Society of Artists, R.W.S. Art. *Signs work:* "Ashton Cannell" (paintings), "Ash" (commercial work).

CANNEY, Michael Richard Ladd, A.T.D., N.D.D.; Senior Lecturer in Painting, Bristol Polytechnic; artist in all media and TV documentary film-maker; Curator, Newlyn Art Gallery (1956-64); Director, Fore Street Gallery, St. Ives, and Porthleven Art Gallery; Visiting lecturer, University of California, Santa

Barbara; Director, University Art Gallery (1965-66); freelance TV film-maker since 1962; *b* Falmouth, 16 July, 1923; *s* of Canon W. R. Ladd Canney; *m* Madeleine Harvey Body; one *s*. *Educ.:* King's College, Taunton; *studied art* at Goldsmiths' School of Art (1947-51); Redruth, Penzance and St. Ives (1939-42). *Exhib.:* Waddington Galleries, Piccadilly Gallery, A.I.A., Royal West of England Academy, London Group, Ostend, Chicago, Santa Barbara, Plymouth City A.G., Exeter, Newlyn and St. Ives, Arnolfini, Bristol, Bath Festival. *Publications:* The Early Newlyn School 1880-1900, art criticism in Painter and Sculptor, Art International, Manchester Guardian, Art News, Western Morning News, West Briton, Cornishmen, The Listener, BBC radio and World Service of BBC. *Address:* Yew Tree Cottage, Clapton-in-Gordano, Bristol BS20 9RH.

CANNON-BROOKES, Peter, M.A., Cantab., Ph.D., Lond., F.R.S.A., F.M.A.; museum curator; Keeper of the Department of Art, City of Birmingham Museum and Art Gallery; Vice-President of the Royal Birmingham Society of Artists; occasional lecturer, Courtauld Institute of Art; *b* London, 23 Aug., 1938; *s* of Victor Montgomery Cannon-Brookes, solicitor; *m* Caroline Aylmer, *née* Christie-Miller; one *s*, one *d*. *Educ.:* Bryanston School, Trinity Hall, Cambridge, Courtauld Institute of Art, London. *Publications:* European Sculpture (1964), in collaboration with H. D. Molesworth; Baroque Churches (1969), in collaboration with C. A. Cannon-Brookes, Lombard Painting (1974). *Address:* Keele House, 33 St. Mary's Rd., Harborne, Birmingham 17. *Clubs:* Athenaeum, Union (Birmingham).

CAPLAN, David, F.S.I.A., F.S.T.D.; freelance artist, designer and typographer; *b* London, 15 July, 1910; *s* of Isaac Caplan; *m* A. W. Stewart; one *s*, two *d*. *Educ.:* elementary schools; *studied art:* self-taught. *Exhib.:* R.A., A.I.A., Whitechapel Art Gallery, etc., and in U.S.A., Paris, Berlin, Vienna, Budapest, Lisbon. *Work in permanent collections:* B.M. (Print Collection), Coventry (Herbert Mus.). *Work repro.:* Graphis Annual, Design magazine. International Poster Annual, Graphis, Designers in Britain, Modern Publicity, The Studio, Art et Metiers Graphique, etc. *Publications:* author, British Trade Marks and Symbols; Editor, Designers in Britain. *Address:* 5 Pearces Meadow, Nettlebed, Henley-on-Thames, Oxon, RG9 5AF.

CAPRARA, Julia Rosemary, N.D.D., A.T.C. Lond. (1961), M.S.D-C.; designer in embroidery and fabric collage; *b* London, 27 Feb., 1939; *d* of John I. L. Jenkins; *m* A. C. Caprara; one *s*. *Educ.:* Perse School for Girls, Cambridge; Henrietta Barnett School, Hampstead Garden Suburb; *studied art* at Hornsey College of Art (1955-61). *Exhib.:* one-man show of Embroidery at Commonwealth Institute A.G.; group shows: Guildford House, National Museum of Wales, Congress House, Foyle's A.G. Australia. *Work in permanent collection:* National Museum of Wales, Cardiff. *Address:* 119 Eastcote Rd., Pinner, Middx. *Signs work:* "Julia Caprara."

CARMI, Mrs. Z.; see ROSENAU, Helen.

CARO, Anthony; sculptor; part-time teacher of sculpture, St. Martin's School of Art; *b* London, 8 Mar., 1924; *s* of Alfred Caro; *m* Sheila Girling; two *s*. *Educ.:* Charterhouse School and Christ's College, Cambridge; *studied art* at Regent Street Polytechnic and R.A. Schools. *Exhib.:* Venice Biennale (1958, 1966), Battersea Park Open-air Sculpture (1963, 1966), Pittsburgh International, Carnegie Inst. (1958, 1967); one-man shows: Whitechapel Gallery (1963), Kasmin Gallery, London (1965, 1967), Hayward Gallery (1969), André Emmerich Gallery, New York (1964, 1966, 1968, 1970, 1972, 1973, 1974), Washington Gallery of Modern Art (1965), Mirvish Gallery, Toronto (1966, 1971), Kroller-Muller Museum, Holland (1967), Norfolk and Norwich Triennale (1973), Kenwood House, Hampstead (1974), Museum of Modern Art, N.Y. (1975), Walker Art Centre, Minneapolis, Museum of Fine Arts, Houston, Boston Museum of Fine Arts (1976). *Address:* 111 Frognal, Hampstead, London NW3.

CARPREAU, Willem Henri; Dutch & British Teacher's Certificates; artist in oil and acrylic; *b* Bandoeng, 20 Oct., 1923; *s* of W. A. P. Carpreau, accountant; *m* Elizabeth; two *d. Educ.:* Grammar School and School of Philology, The Hague; *studied art* at Culham College, Abingdon (1951-53) and College of Art, Bournemouth. *Address:* 11 Ravendale Rd., Sunbury-on-Thames, Middx. *Signs work:* "Carpreau."

CARRICK, Desmond, R.H.A.; artist in sculpture, oil, water-colour and tempera, lithography, stained glass and ceramics; secretary, Royal Hibernian Academy of Arts; *b* Dublin, 18 Dec., 1928; *s* of Henry Carrick. *Educ.:* Synge St. School; *studied art* at Dublin National College of Art. *Exhib.:* R.H.A., Oireachtas Art Exhbn., Waterford Art Exhbn., Dublin Painters Exhbn., Exhbn. of Irish Contemporary Painters organized by the Cultural Relations Com. of Ireland, Exhbn. of English and Canadian Contemporary Painters, Exhbn. of Living Art; one-man shows: Dublin. *Commissions:* Murals in the Guinness Visitors' Waiting Room (Dublin). *Address:* "Studio," Woodtown, Rathfarnham, Co. Dublin. *Signs work:* see appendix.

CARRUTHERS, Derek William, B.A. (Hons., Fine Art); head of Fine Art, Trent Polytechnic, Nottingham; *b* Penrith, Cumberland, 13 May, 1935; *s* of William Edward Carruthers; *m* Eileen Carruthers, B.A.; one *s,* one *d. Educ.:* Penrith and the Royal Grammar School, Lancaster; *studied art* at Dept. Fine Art, King's College, Newcastle-upon-Tyne (1953-57). *Address:* 14 Sandown Rd., Leicester. *Signs work:* "Carruthers."

CARRUTHERS, Joe, F.R.S.A. (1939), A.R.P.S. (1962), A.I.I.P. (1970); Former Instructor-in-charge of typography, Huddersfield School of Art; *b* 1 Feb., 1909; *s* of John Carruthers; *m. Educ.:* Hillhouse School; *studied art* at Huddersfield School of Art; former "Survey of Specimens" critic, The British Printer. *Publications:* A History of Type Design (film-strip) (Common Ground Ltd.), An Approach to Pen Lettering (Holme Valley Press). On Yorkshire Photographic Union's Judges and Lecturer List. *Address:* 24 Grange Ave., Birkby, Huddersfield. *Signs work:* "CARRUTHERS" (usually block characters).

CARRUTHERS, Rose; see ELLENBY, Rose.

CARSTENSEN, Thelma (Mrs. Phillips), W.I.A.C., Slade Diploma; painter in oil and gouache; *b* 6 Sept., 1906; *d* of A. Carstensen, Norwegian timber agent; *m* Alastair Phillips; two *s. Educ.:* Crouch End High School, London, N8; *studied art* at Hornsey School of Art (1924-27) under J. C. Moody; Slade School (1927-30) under Prof. Schwabe. *Exhib.:* R.A., London Group, R.B.A., Walker's Art Gallery, Bond Street (one-man show, 1957). *Address:* Morton House, Brightwell-cum-Sotwell, Berks. *Club:* W.I.A.C. *Signs work:* "Thelma Carstensen."

CARTER, Charles, B.Sc. (1st class hons., Leeds, 1924), M.Sc. (Leeds, 1925), F.S.A.(Scot.), F.M.A.; director, Aberdeen Art Gallery since 1939; hon. president, Scottish Federation of Museums and Art Galleries (1946-50); mem. Council of Museums Assoc. (1938-41, 1947-50, 1953-56, 1959-61); hon. treas. Museums Assoc. (1961-66); President, Aberdeen Artists' Society (1965—); *b* 3 Mar., 1903; *s* of Charles Morris Carter; *m* Elsie Simpson; one *d. Educ.:* Archbishop Holgate's School, York; Leeds University. *Publications:* The Easter Story in Art (Epworth, 1936); Etchings and Dry-points by James McBey (from 1924). *Address:* 100 Cornhill Rd., Aberdeen. *Club:* Aberdeen Business and Professional (President, 1950).

CARTER, John Kelvin, M.S.I.A., F.I.B.D., R.B.A., R.I.; designer and artist in gouache and oil; formerly Manager, Heal Design Studio; *b* London, 1910; *s* of Herbert Carter, electrical engineer; *m* Barbara Prudence Carter. *Educ.:* Mill Hill; *studied art* at Regent Street Polytechnic; Central School of Arts & Crafts and St. Martin's School of Art (1925-1930). *Address:* 33B Chalcot Sq., Regents Park, London NW1. *Signs work:* "M. Carter."

CARTER, Mary; artist in oil; *b* 19 Feb., 1909; *d* of C. B. Ramsden, yarn agent; *m* Major D. G. Carter, R.A.P.C. (decd.); one *s,* one *d. Educ.:* Bury Grammar School; Queen Elizabeth College, London; *studied art* at The Heatherley and Sir John Cass Schools of Art. *Address:* 26 Gloucester St., London SW1V 2DD. *Clubs:* I.C.A., F.P.S. *Signs work:* "Mary Carter."

CARUANA, Gabriel; sculptor, painter, ceramist; *b* Malta, 7 Apr., 1929; *s* of Anthony; single. *Educ.:* Government School of Art, Malta; *studied art* at School of Arts and Crafts, Detroit, Mich., U.S.A., Istituto Statale per la Ceramica, Faenza, Italy. *Exhib.:* Commonwealth Institute (London, 1967), Demarco Gallery (Edinburgh, 1970), Galleria Internazionale Città Della (Ascona), Munich (1969), International Exhbn. of Ceramic Art (Faenza, 1966, 1967, 1968, 1969, 1970, 1972, and at Cervia, 1968), Libya and Australia, and in the Malta Pavilion, Expo 70 (Japan, 1970), Expo 72, Mostra Artigianato (Amsterdam, 1973); one-man shows: National Museum of Malta (Valletta, 1969), Mazaron Art Galleries (Malta, 1969), Peterloo Art Gallery (Manchester, 1970), Galleria la Cittadella (Ascona), Grande Albergo Ambasciatori (Torino, 1972), Sette Sculture alla First National City Bank (Milano, 1972), Malta Hilton (1973). *Addresses:* Dr. Zammit St., Balzan, and 26 Providence St., Balzan, Malta. *Signs work:* "Gabriel Caruana."

CARTLEDGE, William, R.I. (1955), R.S.M.A. (1962), D.F.A. (Lond., 1914), F.R.S.A. (1934), F.S.A.E. (1949); pres., National Soc. for Art Education (1948-49); vice-pres. Soc. of Staffs. Artists (1944-51); art master (retd.); artist in oil and water-colour; *b* Manchester, 30 Jan., 1891; *s* of William Cartledge; *m* Kathleen Annie, *d* of J. H. Nidd, M.P.S. *Educ.:* Hulme Grammar School, Manchester; *studied art* at Slade School. *Exhib.:* R.A., R.I., R.B.A., R.S.M.A., etc. *Work in permanent collections:* Manchester, Hanley, Stafford, Brierley Hill (Staffs.). *Address:* St. Mary's Cottage, Birdham, nr. Chichester, Sussex. *Signs work:* written signature (water-colours), "Wm. Cartledge" (oils).

CASIMIR, Ann, B.A., M.F.P.S.; sculptor in wood, stone and resin, screen-printer; *b* Montreal, 1935. *Educ.:* McGill University; *studied art* at Montreal Museum of Fine Arts; Bellas Artes, Madrid; Sir John Cass School of Art. *Exhib.:* two one-man shows in London, various in London, etc. *Work in permanent collections:* Montreal, Barcelona and London. *Address:* 63 Upper Pk. Rd., London NW3 2UL. *Clubs:* Inner Eye, H.A.C., F.P.S., A.I.R., A.U. *Signs work:* "Ann Casimir."

CASSON, Sir Hugh Maxwell, Kt. (1952), M.A., R.A., R.D.I., F.R.I.B.A., F.S.I.A.; Hon. Dr. R.C.A. (1975); architect; director of architecture, Festival of Britain (1951); Prof. Environmental Design, R.C.A. (1953-75); *b* London, 23 May, 1910; *s* of Randal Casson, I.C.S.; *m* Margaret Macdonald, A.R.I.B.A.; three *d. Educ.:* Eastbourne College; St. John's College, Cambridge; *studied architecture* at Cambridge, British School at Athens, Bartlett School, University College, London. *Work repro.:* in Architectural Review, Architects' Journal, Alphabet and Image, Country Life, Contact, Housewife, Leader, Picture Post, Vogue, Future, etc. *Publications:* Homes by the Million, Victorian Architecture, New Sights of London, Nanny Says. *Address:* 35 Victoria Rd., London W8.

CASTLE, Eva, F.R.B.S.; founder mem. Soc. of Portrait Sculptors (1953); 4th prize Constance Fund Comp. for fountain in Hyde Park; sculptor, designer, potter in terracotta; guest artist at Chelsea Pottery (1956-57); *b* Aarhus, Denmark, 6 Dec., 1922; *d* of K. Skytte Birkefeldt, organist; *m* Tony Britton; one *s. Educ.:* Marselisborg School, Aarhus; *studied art* at Royal Academy, Copenhagen under Prof. Johannes Bjerg (1945-47), Slade School under Prof. Gerrard and Mr. MacWilliam (1948-50). *Exhib.:* R.A. most years since 1951, City of Bradford, Football and Fine Arts, all main London and provincial galleries. *Work in permanent collections:* St. John's Church, Newbury, textile designs in Denmark and Britain. *Address:* 39 Limerston St., Chelsea, London SW10. *Signs work:* "EC." or "Eva Castle."

CATTERMOLE, Lance, R.O.I. (1938); painter in oils and water-colours; *b* 19 July, 1898; *grandson* of George Cattermole, painter, illustrator of The Old Curiosity Shop and other works by Charles Dickens; *m* Lydia Coles, B.A. *Educ.:* Holmsdale Hse., Prep. School, Worthing; Odiham Grammar School, Hants.; *studied art* at Central School of Arts and Crafts, Slade School of Fine Art (Prof. Tonks, P. Wilson Steer, 1923-26). *Exhib.:* R.A., R.P., R.O.I., R.B.A., Liverpool, Brighton, Bournemouth, etc. *Work repro.:* in The Studio and numerous periodicals. *Address:* Horizon, 17 Palmers Way, High Salvington, Worthing, Sussex. *Signs work:* "Lance Cattermole."

CAVANAGH, John; couturier (retd. Sept. 1974); *b* Belmullet, 28 Sept., 1914; *s* of Cyril Cavanagh. *Educ.:* St. Paul's School; *trained* with Molyneux and Balmain in Paris. *Exhib.:* Munich, 1954 (Gold Medal); designed Wedding Dress for H.R.H. Duchess of Kent (June, 1961); designed Wedding Dress for H.R.H. Princess Alexandra (April, 1963). *Work in permanent collections:* V. & A., Museum of Costume, Bath. *Address:* 11 Pembridge Gdns., London W2. *Signs work:* "JOHN CAVANAGH."

CAWS, Alfred Walter Richard, N.S. (1967); R.S.A. Award, Poster Design (1931); painter in oils; further education teacher, painting and drawing (part-time); *b* Bembridge, I.O.W., 12 Feb., 1912; *s* of W. B. Caws; *m* Maude Ellen; one *d. Educ.:* Elmslie Prep. and Ryde Cent.; *studied art* at Heatherley School of Fine Art (Fredric Whiting, R.P., Patrick Larking, R.O.I.). *Exhib.:* 8 London galleries and over 30 public and private galleries throughout the country. *Work repro.:* in various art and commercial publications. *Address:* 102 Carter Ave., Shanklin, I.O.W. *Signs work:* "CAWS."

CHADWICK, Enid M.; church decorator, calligrapher, children's book illustrator, artist in oil, indian ink and wash; *b* Basingstoke, 26 Oct., 1902; *d* of J. H. Chadwick, priest-headmaster. *Educ.:* St. Michael's School, Oxford; *studied art* at Exeter under W. B. Morrell and Brighton under L. Ginnet and L. Preston. *Work in permanent collections:* murals and other work in shrine of Our Lady of Walsingham; murals in St. Margaret's, Liverpool; screen decoration in Kettlebaston Church, Suffolk; altar panels, Howick, also in U.S.A. and S. Africa. *Publications:* My Book of the Church's Year, Come and Worship, The Seven Sacraments. *Address:* Cobbles, Walsingham, Norfolk. *Signs work:* "E.M.C." and see appendix.

CHADWICK, Hulme, A.R.C.A. (1934), A.R.Ae.S. (1945), F.S.I.A. (1953), Hon. D.A. (Man.) (1956), A.R.I.B.A. (1957); National Scholar (1930); R.C.A. Travelling Scholar (1934); Ford Foundation E.S.U. Travel Grant (1957); C.O.I.D. Design Award (1957, 1958, 1964); Gold Medallist, Internationale Triennale (1960); Silver Medallist, Internationale Triennale (1964); consultant designer, Liberty & Co., Ltd. (1949-56); consultant designer, Marshall & Snelgrove (1956-60); consultant designer, Wilkinson Sword, Ltd. (1952—); chief camouflage officer, A.M. (1938-44); *b* 1910; *m*; two *s*, one *d. Educ.:* N. Manchester Central School, Manchester School of Art (1925-26 and 1929-30), R.C.A. *Address:* 26 Eccleston St., London SW1. *Clubs:* Arts, Hurlingham. *Signs work:* "Hulme Chadwick."

CHADWICK, Lynn, C.B.E.; 1st Prize, Venice Biennale (1956); sculptor, chiefly in iron; *b* London, 24 Nov., 1914; *s* of V. R. Chadwick, J.P.; *m* Eva Reiner; two *s,* two *d. Educ.:* Merchant Taylors. *Exhib.:* Stedelijk Museum (Amsterdam, 1957), Palais des Beaux Arts, Bruxelles (1957), Arts Council of G.B. (London, 1957). *Work in permanent collections:* Tate, Museum of Modern Art (N.Y.), Allbright Art Gallery (Buffalo), The Kroller-Müller Museum (Otterlo). *Work repro.:* Contemporary British Art (Herbert Read), Sir Herbert Read, Lynn Chadwick (Bodensee Verlag, Amriswill, Swiss), Pelican, Lynn Chadwick (Dr. J. P. Hodin, Zwemmer), Lynn Chadwick (Alan Bowness, Methuen). *Address:* Lypiatt Pk., Stroud, Glos.

CHAFFEY, Douglas H.; self-taught professional artist in oil and water-colour; proprietor, Trinity Art Gallery, Wareham; *b* Poole, Dorset, 21 Feb., 1924. *Exhib.:* one-man shows in many galleries throughout Britain. *Work in permanent collection:* Trinity Art Gallery. *Address:* 43 Shaftesbury Rd., Poole, Dorset. *Signs work:* "Douglas H. Chaffey."

CHAGALL, Marc; artist, illustrator, designer of Carnegie Prize, 1939; consultant on fine arts for Vitebsk, founded School; *b* Vitebsk, Russia, 7 July, 1887 *m* Bella (decd. 1944). *Studied art* at Imperial School of Fine Arts, St. Petersburg. *Exhib.:* Berlin, Paris, New York, Basle, Amsterdam, Tate, Zürich, Berne, Israel, Nice, Turin, Munich, Hamburg. *Work in private collections:* Nell Warden, Krous-Lange, Hermann Lange, Arensberg, Gretzer, Vicomtesse Charles de Noailles, Bernheim-Jeune, Ivon Sterenberg, Tel Aviv, Miss M. E. Johnstone, Mrs. C. B. Goodspeed, L. E. Stern, A. A. Juviler, J. S. Newberry, Galerie Maeght, Galerie Rosengart. *Address:* c/o Galerie Maeght, Paris. *Signs work:* see appendix.

CHAMBERLAIN, Trevor, R.O.I. (1972), R.S.M.A. (1970), N.S. (1968); marine, town and landscape painter in oil and water-colour; *b* Hertford, 13 Dec., 1933; *s* of Frederick Joseph Chamberlain; *m* Elaine Waterfield; one *s. Educ.:* Ware Central School. *Work in permanent collections:* Guildhall Art Gallery, London, Government House, N. Ireland, National Maritime Museum, Greenwich. *Work repro.:* The Connoisseur, Studio International, La Revue Moderne. *Address:* Braeside, Goldings La., Waterford, Hertford, Herts. *Signs work:* "T. Chamberlain."

CHAMBERS, Basil, M.I.P.A.; artist in water-colour; advertising designer; senior art director; *b* 14 Aug., 1920. *Studied art* at Chelsea School of Commercial Art, Hornsey College of Art, Beckenham School of Art. *Address:* Summerford Farm, Fairwarp, Uckfield, Sussex. *Signs work:* "B. H. A. Chambers."

CHAMOT, Mary, University of Lond. Dip. in Fine Art (1922); Asst. Keeper, Tate Gallery (1950-65); London University Extension Lecturer; *b* Strelna, Russia, 1899. *Educ.:* privately; *studied art* at Slade School of Art. *Publications:* Modern Painting in England (1937); Russian Painting and Sculpture (1963); Gontcharova (Paris, 1972). *Address:* Flat 1, 57 Melbury Rd., London W14 8AD.

CHANCE, Ivan Oswald, C.B.E.; Chairman, Christie, Manson & Woods (1958-74); Chairman, Christies International (1974); Chairman, Georgian Group since 1968; *b* 23 June, 1910; *s* of the late Brig.-Gen. O. K. Chance, C.M.G., D.S.O.; *m* Pamela Martin Smith. *Educ.:* Eton. *Address:* 38 Belgravia Ct., Ebury St., London SW1. *Clubs:* Brooks's, Brook (New York), White's.

CHANDRA; artist in oils, coloured inks, glass murals, fibre-glass murals; *b*

Simla, India, 28 Aug., 1931; *m* Premlata, artist; one *d. Studied art* at Polytechnic, Delhi. *Work in permanent collections:* National Gallery of Modern Art, New Delhi, Tate Gallery, V. & A. Museum, Arts Council of Great Britain, Ashmolean Museum, Oxford, Musée National d'Art Moderne, Paris, Ulster Museum, Belfast, Gulbenkian Museum of Oriental Art, Durham, City Art Gallery, Birmingham, Whitworth Art Gallery, Manchester, Museum of Modern Art, Haifa, Punjab Museum, Chandigarl. *Address:* 24 Willoughby Rd., London NW3. *Signs work:* "AVINASH" ("Avinash").

CHANG, Chien-Ying, B.A. (1935); artist in water-colour; mem. of R.I., R.W.A. and Soc. of Women Artists; *b* 27 June, 1915; *d* of Peh-Sung Chang; *m* Cheng-Wu Fei, artist. *Educ.:* National Central University, China, and Slade School of Fine Art. *Exhib.:* R.A., R.I., R.B.A.; one-man shows at Leicester Gallery (1951, 1955, 1960). *Work in permanent collections:* London University; St. John's College, Oxford; R.W.A., Bristol; Grave's Gallery, Sheffield; Derby Art Gallery. *Work repro.:* Studio, Art News and Review, Future, Picture Post, La Revue Moderne, Kunst, etc. *Address:* 52 Dollis Pk., London N3. *Signs work:* see appendix.

CHANG, Dai-Chien; painter, calligrapher and poet, working with Chinese brush, ink, colour paper and silk; *b* Nei-kian, Szechuan, China, 10 May, 1899; *s* of Houai-Chung; *m* Hsu Wen-Pu, painter; four *s,* two *d. Educ.:* at home and in Chungking, Shanghai and Kyoto. *Exhib.:* Peking, Nanking, Shanghai, Chungking, Chengtu, Hongkong, Tokyo, Paris, New Delhi, London, Geneva, Prague, Buenos Aires, Cologne. *Work in permanent collections:* Musée Jeu de Paume (Paris), Musée Cernushchi (Paris), Musée d'Art Moderne (Paris), etc. *Addresses:* Caixa Postal 249, Mogi das Cruzes, São Paulo, Brazil; P.O. Box 3543, Carmel, Calif. 93921, U.S.A. *Club:* Prof. Mem. International Fine Arts Council. *Signs work:* see appendix.

CHANNING-RENTON, Captain Ernest Matthews; Regular Army officer (retired); late British Vice-Consul; *Palmes d'Academie; Officier de l'Instruction Publique; Croix d'Honneur du Merite Franco-Britannique;* artist in oils, water-colours, Indian ink, charcoal, and author; *b* Plymouth, 30 July, 1895; *s* of Thomas S. Matthews, late H.M. Civil Service, author of "Channing—a Study," etc.; *m* (1st) Helen, daughter of late Brigade Surgeon Lieut-Colonel David Renton, M.D., 15th Hussars, Barrister-at-Law (Inner Temple); (2nd) Alice, daughter of Mme. et. M. Victor Iehl of Paris; one *d. Educ.:* Jesus College, Cambridge; Army schools; *studied art* at Plymouth School of Art under Babb (before 1914), John Hassall, R.I. (after 1918). *Exhib.:* Royal Soc. of British Artists, London (1947); Musée Massena, Nice (1948); Bulawayo (1948); Salisbury (1952, 1965, 1966); Rhodes National Gallery (1964-65); National Gallery of Rhodesia (1973); one-man shows: Umtali and Gwelo (1964); Bulawayo (1964); Inyanga (1965); Salisbury (1965, 1966). First Prize, with cash award, Arts and Crafts section, Inyanga Show (1965); Honours, with cash award, at Rhodesia Institute of Allied Arts Exhibition (1965); Troutbeck Silver Cup, trophy for Art, Inyanga Show (1966 and again 1967). *Official purchases or acquisitions:* Arthur Gray, M.A. (published work and sketches of Jesus College, Cambridge); Rt. Hon. Sir Roy Welensky, P.C., K.C.M.G., Federal Prime Minister, Rhodesia and Nyasaland (oil painting); Dr. K. H. Barnes ("Wintry Scene," National Gallery, Rhodesia); Sir Patrick Hennessy ("L'Automne" and "Bush Fire, Rhodesia," purchased 1964); Hon. Ian Douglas Smith, M.P. ("Night Operations, Somme, 1916," official residence of Prime Minister, Rhodesia); Hon. J. J. Wrathall, M.P. (two oil paintings, priv. coll. of Deputy Prime Minister and Finance Minister, Govt. of Rhodesia); Hon. A. P. Smith, M.P. (oil-painting, priv. coll. of Minister of Education, Govt. of Rhodesia);

President of Rhodesia (oil painting, now hanging in Government House, Salisbury, 1973). *Work repro.:* Dawlish and District Official Guide, Home and Abroad, and other periodicals. *Publications:* Jesus College, Cambridge, in Black and White. Trilogy: "Pot-Pourri"; I. Early Days; II. Between the Wars; III. Later Years; From An Artist's Portfolio; At Random (1973); En Passant (in preparation). *Address:* Channings, Sanyatwe, Rhodesia. *Clubs:* Life member of R.U.S.I., and Cambridge Union Society. *Signs work:* see appendix.

CHAO, Shao-An; painter in water-colour; International Art Gold Medal awarded by Belgium Centenary Independence World Fair, Brussels (1930); *b* Canton, China, 6 Mar., 1905. *Studied art* under Kao Chi-Feng, founder Lingnan School of Chinese arts. *Exhib.:* Sino-Japanese Joint Art Exhbn., Hangchow; All-China Arts Exhbn., First Shanghai (1929), Second Nanking (1937), Third Chungking (1943); one-man shows: China, Hongkong, New Zealand, Portugal, Macao, Singapore, Malaysia, Switzerland, France, England, U.S.A., Canada, West Germany, Australia (1934-73). *Work in permanent collections:* Boston Fine Art Museum; Washington County Museum; Nanyang University Museum, Singapore; etc. *Publications:* Charming Cicadas Collection (1 volume), Collection of Shao-An's Paintings (20 volumes), Recent works of Chao Shao-An (3 volumes). *Address:* 295-A Prince Edward Rd. (2nd floor), Kowloon, Hongkong. *Signs work:* "Chao Shao-An" and see appendix.

CHAPLIN, Bob, Dip.A.D., A.T.D., S.P.C.; printmaker in photography, screen, etching, lithography; lecturer, Eastbourne and W. Sussex Colleges of Art; *b* Hastings, 22 May, 1947; *m* Susannah Chaplin; one *s,* one *d. Studied art* at Ravensbourne and Brighton Colleges of Art (1965-73). *Exhib.:* one-man shows: Manor House Gallery, Ilkley (British Print Biennale 1976), Gardner Centre Gallery, Brighton (1975), University of East Anglia (1970); group shows: Fifth British Print Biennale (Prize-winner), Sixth British Print Biennale, Florence Biennale, A.I.R. Artist's Prints, Premio Internazionale Biella Per l'Incisione, Italy. *Work in permanent collections:* British Council, S.E.A.A., various Art Centres, Universities, Education Authorities, and private collections in Europe, U.S.A. and Canada. *Address:* 23 Sun St., Lewes, Sussex, BN7 2QB. *Signs work:* "Bob Chaplin."

CHAPLIN, Michael James, N.D.D., F.R.E.; artist in etchings, lithographs; lecturer, Maidstone School of Art and Kingston Polytechnic; *b* St. Neots, 19 Sept., 1943; *s* of A. B. Chaplin; *m* Gaynor Lloyd. *Educ.:* St. Albans Boys' Grammar School; *studied art* at Watford College of Art (Peter Schmidt, 1961-64), Brighton College of Art (1967-68), post-graduate under Jennifer Dickson. *Work in permanent collections:* Redbridge Art Centre, Sussex education authorities and private collections. *Publications:* Connaught Rooms Review (illustrations). *Address:* Ivy Cottage, 4 Weavering St., Maidstone, Kent. *Signs work:* "Michael Chaplin."

CHAPMAN, Anthea, A.T.D. (1954); painter in oil; part-time member of staff of Eastbourne School of Art; *b* Sussex, 4 Sept., 1933; *d* of Bernard Crabb; *m* David Chapman, painter and lecturer of art; two *s,* one *d. Educ.:* Convent of Sacred Heart, Hove, Sussex; *studied art* at Brighton College of Art and Crafts (1949-55, R. T. Cowern, Charles Knight, Herbert Holt). *Work in permanent collections:* Stoke-on-Trent Museum and Art Gallery, Tel Aviv, Israel, Museum and Art Gallery, Nuffield Scheme for Pictures in Hospitals, I.L.E.A., Scunthorpe and Yarmouth education authorities. *Address:* Higham Farmhouse, Herstmonceux (Hailsham), Sussex. *Clubs:* Eastbourne Group, Chelsea Arts. *Signs work:* "Anthea C."

CHAPMAN, Max; painter, critic; *b* Dulwich, 24 Feb., 1911; *s* of Joshua Chapman, M.A. *Educ.:* Dulwich College; *studied art* at Byam Shaw Art School and by travelling scholarship in Italy. *Educ.:* one-man shows, Storran, Leger, Gallery One, New Vision Centre, Molton, London; shared exhbns.: Paris, Zürich, Grabowski Gallery, London Forum, Bristol; group shows, R.A., Glasgow, London Group, Bradford A.G., Drian, Towner, Bladon, Commonwealth Biennial, etc. *Work repro.:* Quadrum, Apollo, Arts Review, Times, Architects' Journal, Connoisseur. *Address:* c/o Molton Gallery, London. *Signs work:* "Chapman."

CHAPMAN, Ronald George, M.A.; Assistant Librarian, Bodleian Library; *b* Compton, Surrey, 21 Sept., 1917; *s* of Michael Chapman, M.C.; *m* Teresa Watkin; two *s*, two *d*. *Educ.:* Eton and New College, Oxford. *Publications:* Laurel and the Thorn, a study of G. F. Watts (Faber, 1945), Scenes from the life of Christ in English manuscripts (Bodleian picture books, 1951), Watts (Medici Soc., 1955), Father Faber (Burns Oates, 1961), The Education of Davey Porteous (novel) (Collins, 1969), This is My Winter (poems) (Mitre Press, 1973). *Address:* 18 Park Town, Oxford.

CHARAGEAT, Marguerite, *b* Paris, 1894. Conservateur hon. au Musée du Louvre; Prof. honoraire section du Paysage (Ec. Sup. d'hort. de Versailles); Diplomée de L'Ecole du Louvre, Chev. de la Légion d'Honneur, Chev. Inst. publique; Off. Mérite Agr; Lauréat de l'Institut de France; Membre des Comités de: Soc. Hist. art français; Société des Amateurs de jardins; Membre de la Commission du Vieux Paris; de l'Academi d'Arras. *Publications:* L'Art des jardins, Ognon et Raray, Jardins de France en Pays d'Ouest, La Sculpture en Bas-Limousin au XVème siècle; André Lenôtre et ses dessins, l'optique en son temps; articles in: Construction Moderne, Bul. de soc. d'histoire art français, Bul. monumental, etc. *Address:* 10 rue du Pré aux clercs, 75007 Paris.

CHARLES, Agnes E.; designer and maker of stained-glass windows for ecclesiastical and secular buildings under name of St. Crispin's Glass; also glass mosaics, sculpture with mosaics; landscape and portrait painter in oil; *d* of the late A. P. Charles. *Educ.:* Kensington High School; *studied art* at R.A. schools. *Exhib.:* R.A., Leicester Gallery, Leger Gallery, Heals, Foyles, Alpine Gallery, provinces. *Permanent exhbns.:* in records of Council for Places of Worship, 83 London Wall, EC2; in Craftsman's Index of Crafts Council of Great Britain Ltd., 47 Victoria St., SW1. *Address:* 28 St. Albans Rd., Codicote, Herts. *Signs work:* "A. Charles."

CHARLES, Bernard Hugh, A.T.D.; potter, industrial designer specializing in tiles and architectural ceramics; teacher at Reading Technical College (1955-57), and at Poole School of Art, now Bournemouth and Poole College of Art (since Sept., 1957); Director of Design, Kinson Pottery Ltd.; *s* of Albert Hugh Charles; *m* Doris Mary Jones. *Educ.:* Oswestry High School for Boys; *studied art* at Leicester and Stoke-on-Trent Colleges of Art. *Address:* 10 Kimberley Rd., Parkstone, Poole, Dorset. *Signs work:* see appendix.

CHARLES, Robert Lonsdale, M.C. (1942), J.P., M.A., F.M.A.; Keeper, Department of Art, National Museum of Wales; *b* Lostwithiel, 1916; *s* of the late R. H. Charles, C.B.E.; *m*; one *s*, two *d*. *Educ.:* Shrewsbury School and Corpus Christi College, Oxford. *Publications:* Continental Porcelain of the Eighteenth Century (1964); articles and reviews. *Address:* Fieldings, Penmark, Barry, Glam.

CHARLESTON, Robert Jesse, M.A., F.S.A., F.M.A.; keeper at V. & A. since 1963; *b* 3 Apr., 1916; *s* of S. J. Charleston, M.A.; *m*; one *s*, one *d*. *Educ.:* Berkhamsted School, Herts.; New College, Oxford. *Publications:* Roman Pottery (1955); (ed.) English Porcelain, 1745-1850 (1965); (ed.) World Ceramics

(1968); (with J G Ayers) The James A. de Rothschild Collection at Waddesdon Manor; Meissen and Oriental Porcelain (1971); Some Early Egyptian Draw-Loom Weavings (with C. J. Lamm, 1939); A Group of Near Eastern Glasses (1942); Han Damasks (1948); Michael Edkins and the Problem of English Enamelled Glass (1954), etc. *Address:* 1 Denbigh Gdns., Richmond, Surrey.

CHARLTON, George, N.E.A.C. (1925); on staff of Slade School (1919-62), on staff of Willesden School of Art (1949-59), examiner for University of London Gen. School Exams since 1931, Governor of Camberwell School of Art, Farnham School of Art (1950-), and Trent Park College; mem. New English Art Club (1926) and Hon. Treas. (1958); *b* 1899. *Studied art* at Slade School of Fine Art (commenced 1914). *Exhib.:* one-man shows at Redfern Gallery and Beaux Art Gallery (1951). *Official purchases:* Tate Gallery, Contemp. Art Soc., C.E.M.A. and provincial galleries. *Publications:* illustrations in Anatomy for Artists, by Wolff; articles on Prof. Frederick Brown and Prof. Henry Tonks in Dict. of National Biography. *Address:* 40 New End Sq., Hampstead, London NW3.

CHAROUX, Siegfried, R.A. (1956); sculptor; *b* 15 Nov., 1896; *s* of Joseph Charoux; became British subject (1945); *m. Educ.:* Vienna; *studied art* at Academy of Fine Arts and Kunstpreis der Stadt, Vienna. *Exhib.:* R.A., Glasgow Academy of Fine Arts. *Official purchases:* Engineering College, Cambridge, Vienna, Cambridge, Hull, Liverpool, South Bank Festival Hall, L.C.C., Belfast Art Gallery, Southport Art Gallery, Chantry Bequest, Tate Gallery (1963). *Work repro.:* Studio, Art News, Picture Post, London Illustrated News. *Publications:* Dekorative Vorbilder, Kunst und Kuenstler. *Address:* 26 Temple Fortune Hill, London NW11. *Clubs:* Chelsea Arts, Arts. *Signs work:* "Charoux."

CHART, Daphne; painter and teacher at Chelsea School of Art; *m* Dunbar Marshall. *Studied art* at Chelsea School of Art. *Gallery:* Grabowski, 84 Sloane Ave., SW3. One-man exhibition there in April-May, 1964. *Address:* 17 Broomhouse Rd., London SW6. *Signs work:* "D. Chart."

CHATTERTON, George Edward, F.R.S.A., F.I.A.L.; Mem. Artists' League of Great Britain (London); artist, cartoonist and photographer; *b* Kidderminster, 15 July, 1911; *s* of Benjamin Chatterton; *m* Iris Betty Wilce; two *s. Educ.:* Toronto; *studied art* at Kidderminster School of Art; *photography* at School of Photography, Farnborough. *Work repro.:* since 1932 in leading London and Dundee illustrated journals, including London Opinion, Weekend, Daily Mirror, Daily Sketch, Everybody's, Blighty, Weekly News, Picturegoer, Boy's Own Paper, R.A.F. Review, etc. Strip creations include "Chad, by Chat" (1938, continuing), "Sheriff Shucks" (Amalgamated Press), "Leo CV", etc. *Address:* Canal Cottage, Ryeford, Stonehouse, Glos. *Signs work:* see appendix.

CHATZIDAKIS, Manolis, I.C.O.M., A.I.C.A., C.I.H.A.; Hon. Director of the Benaki Museum, Athens (since 1941); hon. director of Byzantine Museum (since 1960); sec. of the Christian Archaeol. Soc. (Athens); *b* Candia, Crete, 1909; *s* of Gerasimos A. Chatzidakis; *m* Eugenie Chatzidakis, ex-assist. curator in the Benaki Museum; one *s*, one *d. Educ.:* Athens; *studied history of art:* Athens, Paris and Berlin. *Publications:* on Islamic, Byzantine and Modern Greek Art and art criticism. *Address:* 32, Odos Dimokzitou, Athens.

CHAUVIN, Enid; Board of Educ. art dip. (1934), elected M.A.I.A. (1948), M.S.G.A. (1969); artist in oils, lithography and water-colour; art teacher; awarded Medal and Diploma of Merit, Annuale Italiana d'Arte Grafica (1968), Medal and Honourable Mention, Biennale degli Regioni, Ancona (1968); Diplome Palme d'Or des Beaux Arts (1969); elected Conseiller Culturel of International Arts Guild (1969); Hon. Vice-President L'Internazionale de Centro Studi e Scambi

Internazionali; *b* Blackheath, 21 June, 1910; *d* of Laurence Chauvin, electrical engineer; *m* Victor Patrick Law; one *s*. *Educ.:* Blackheath High School; *studied art* at Blackheath School of Art and at Goldsmiths' College. *Exhib.:* R.A., R.B.A., R.O.I., A.I.A., United Artists, S.W.A., R.P., N.S., Senefelder Group, Redfern and Heal's Galleries, Kensington Gallery, Mercury Gallery, Piccadilly Gallery, Curwen Gallery, Furneau Gallery, Ganymed Editions, one-man exhbn. Maison de la Culture, Ajaccio (1971), Bastia (1972, 1975), Calvi (1972, 1973, 1974). *Work purchased* by Southampton Education Authority. *Work repro.:* Circus Horses in Children's Oxford Ency., biography and reproduction in La Femme dans L'Art Contemporain (1972). *Address:* Place de L'Ormeau, Santa Reparata-di-Balagna, 20220 Ile-Rousse, Corsica. *Signs work:* see appendix.

CHEESMAN, Harold, A.R.W.S. (1964), A.R.C.A. (1938), F.R.S.A. (1970); J. Andrew Lloyd Scholar (Landscape); painter in oil, water-colour, gouache, and teacher; Head of Department of Painting, West Surrey College of Art and Design; *b* Rye, Sussex, 16 Apr., 1915; *s* of Herbert Cheesman; *m* Doreen Knight; three *s*, one *d*. *Educ.:* The Grammar School, Rye; *studied art* at Hastings School of Art (George Graham), Royal College of Art (Gilbert Spencer, Paul Nash). *Exhib.:* R.A., N.E.A.C., R.W.S., Roland, Browse and Delbanco, Leicester Galleries; one-man exhbns.: Zwemmer Gallery (1958, 1961, 1964); mural on Scottish liner Glenogle. *Work repro.:* and article in Studio (Oct., 1961). *Work in permanent collections:* Towner Art Gallery, Eastbourne, Nottingham City Art Gallery, Plymouth City Art Gallery, Melbourne City Art Gallery, Australia. *Address:* Minadhu, Rowledge, Farnham, Surrey. *Signs work:* "Harold Cheesman."

CHEN, Chi; water-colour artist; *b* Wushih, China, 2 May, 1912. *Studied art* at Hsin Hua College of Fine Arts, Shanghai; Gold Medals: National Arts Club (1954, 1956, 1966, 1967, 1968), Audubon Artists (1956, 1963, 1968), The Allied Artists of America (1960), American Water-colour Society (1966), and many other prizes. *Work in permanent collections:* Wilmington Art Centre, Arnot Art Gallery, Metropolitan Museum of Art, Dallas Museum of Fine Arts, etc. *Publications:* Aquarelles de Chen Chi (Shanghai, 1942); A portfolio of Chen Chi's Paintings, Limited Edition, (New York, 1965); Sketchbook of Chen Chi (New York, 1969). *Address:* 23 Washington Sq. North, New York, N.Y. 10011, U.S.A. *Clubs:* Philadelphia Water-colour, American Water-colour Society, The Allied Artists of America, etc. *Signs work:* "Chen Chi."

CHESSER, Sheila; prize-winner, Festival of the Church and the Arts, Nottingham; painter in acrylic; *b* Cheshire, 21 Feb., 1915; *d* of John Blayney-Jones; *m* Dr. Eustace Chesser. *Educ.:* Howells School, Denbigh; *studied art:* no formal art training. *Exhib.:* Leicester Gallery, Redfern Gallery, Whitechapel Gallery, W.I.A.C., Art Council, Northern Ireland, Municipal Gallery Modern Art, Dublin, Bradford City Art Gallery, Royal Scottish Academy; one-man shows; Midland Group Gallery, Nottingham, Thames Gallery, Eton, Greenwich Theatre Gallery. *Work in permanent collection:* Leicester University. *Publication:* Through a Glass. *Address:* 17 Wimpole St., London W1. *Clubs:* W.I.A.C., H.A.C., F.P.S. *Signs work:* see appendix.

CHEVINS, Hugh Terry, M.S.I.A.; artist, oil, gouache, commercial and book illustrator, poster, mural painter, portrait painter; R.A. Bronze Medal (1953), Paris Salon Medaille d'Argent (1955, 1956); *b* Retford, 2 July, 1931; *s* of K. C. Chevins. *Educ.:* Gunnersbury Grammar School; *studied art:* Twickenham School of Art, Paris, R.A. Schools. *Exhib.:* R.A., R.B.A., United Artists, Glasgow Academy, Paris, Piccadilly Gallery, Brighton Art Gallery, Bournemouth. *Work in permanent collections:* Rijksmuseum, Amsterdam, Science Museum, London. *Work repro.:* Imperial Chemical Industries, Reed Paper Group, Shell, John Laing.

Club: London Sketch. *Address:* 2 Gaston Way, Shepperton, Middx. *Signs work:* "HUGH CHEVINS."

CHIA, Yu-Chian; artist in oil, water-colour and pastel; *b* Kota Tinggi, Johore, Malaysia, 1 Sept., 1936. *Educ.:* Chinese Primary School, Kota Tinggi; Chinese High School, Singapore; *studied art* at Ecole Nationale Superieure des Beaux Arts, Paris (1959-62) under Prof. Chaplain-Midy. *Exhib.:* one-man shows: Johore Bahru (1956), Singapore (1957, 1963), Kuala Lumpur (1958, 1962), Penang (1958, 1961, 1969, 1970, 1971), Paris (1959, 1960), Hanover (1960), New Delhi (1960), Calcutta (1960), Bombay (1960), Madras (1960), London (1960), Madrid (1961), Ipoh (1966), Bangkok (1972), etc.; group shows: Singapore Art Society Annual Exhbn. (1954-57), Singapore Art Exhbn. in Australia, Sydney (1957), Salon des Artistes Français (1951-61), Salon des Independants (1959-61), Salon des Nationale (1960-61), Salon d'Automne (1960-61), Salon Français (1960-61), Salon Berruyer, Bourges (1960-61), Johore State Art Exhbn., Johore Bahru (1966), Asian Mobile Exhbn. (1974). *Work in permanent collections:* National A.G. and University of Malaya Museum, Kuala Lumpur; University of Singapore Museum and Raffles Museum, Singapore; State Gallery, Penang; Boston A.G.; Sonnenberg International Centre, Hanover, etc. *Address:* 1107 Selanggor Mansion, Jalan Melayu, Kuala Lumpur, Malaysia. *Clubs:* Penang Art Society, Malaysia Art Council. *Signs work:* "CHIA Yu-Chian" and see appendix.

CHIANG, Yee, B.Sc., F.R.A.S., H.L.D. (Hof.), D.Lit. (Canberra), D.Art. (Rider College), Member of American Academy of Arts and Sciences; artist, writer and painter in water-colour; Professor of Chinese Studies at Columbia University, New York; *b* Kiukiang, China, 19 May, 1903; *s* of Chiang Ho-An. *Educ.:* National South-Eastern University, Nanking; *studied art* at home under his father. *Work in permanent collections:* Fogg Art Museum, Cambridge, Mass., and Fish Happiness, Utah State University, Logan, etc. *Publications:* The Chinese Eye; Chinese Painting; Chinese Calligraphy; A Chinese Childhood; and The Silent Traveller in Lakeland, London, Wartime, the Yorkshire Dales, Oxford, Edinburgh, New York, Dublin, Paris, Boston, Japan, etc. *Address:* 520 West 123 St., New York, 27, N.Y. *Signs work:* "Chiang Yee."

CHILD, Heather, M.B.E.; painter in pen and ink, water-colour, calligrapher; chairman, Federation of British Crafts Societies. *Educ.:* St. Swithun's School, Winchester; *studied art* at Chelsea College of Art (exhbn. to R.C.A.). *Work in permanent collections:* V. & A., Harvard University Library, Boston Public Library, U.S.A. *Publications:* Decorative Maps (Studio Ltd., 1956), The Armorial Bearings of the Guilds of London (Warne, 1960), Calligraphy Today (Studio Vista Books, 1963), Heraldic Design (G. Bell & Sons, 1969), Formal Penmanship (Lund Humphries, 1971), Christian Symbols (G. Bell & Sons, 1971). *Address:* 188 Cromwell Rd., London SW5 0SJ. *Clubs:* Soc. of Designer-Craftsmen, Soc. of Scribes and Illuminators.

CHINCHWADKAR, Vasant Narayan, B.A. (1958), G.D.Arts; artist in oil, water-colour, collages; *b* 7 May, 1934. *Educ.:* Holker College, Indore (M.P.), India; *studied art* at Art College, Indore, under Mr. D. J. Joshi, Mr. V. D. Chinchalkar, Mr. Kirkire. *Exhib.:* Delhi, Bombay, India, London, Cambridge, Maldon. *Work in permanent collections:* Trinity College, Oxford, U.N.I.C.E.F., Art College, Indore. *Address:* 39 Market Hill, Maldon, Essex. *Signs work:* see appendix.

CHOAT, Herbert William, F.R.S.A.; commercial artist, painter in oil and water-colour; *b* Southsea, 20 Aug., 1912; *s* of Frederick A. Choat; *m* Mary Sherwin; two *s*. *Educ.:* Portsmouth Southern secondary school; *studied art* at

Portsmouth School of Art (1928-33). *Exhib.:* R.A., London and provinces. *Address:* 83 The Fairway, South Ruislip, Middx. *Club:* London Sketch. *Signs work:* "Herbert Choat" (written).

CHOU, Lien-Hsia; artist, paintress in water-colour and poetess; Vancouver Golden Jubilee Chinese Carnival Honorary Prize, Canada (1936); All-China Grand Prize for Female Figure Painting in Academic School, Peking (1953); National Art First Prize for the best work of the year, Shanghai (1956); *b* Luling, China, 15 Oct., 1909. *Educ.:* at home by her parents; *studied art* under a scholar-tutor. *Work in permanent collections:* Shanghai Art Gallery; State Palace, Djakarta; Presidential Palace, Bogor; etc. *P ublications:* Cradle Song, etc. *Address:* 1/383 Chü-Lu Rd., Shanghai. *Clubs:* China Women's Calligraphy and Painting Association and China Society of Fine Arts, Shanghai. *Signs work:* "CHOU Lien-Hsia" and see appendix.

CHRISTOPHER, Ann, Dip.A.D.; sculptor in bronze; *b* Watford, Herts., 4 Dec., 1947; *d* of Wm. Christopher; *m* K. Cook. *Educ.:* Watford Girls' Grammar School; *studied art* at Harrow School of Art (1965-66), West of England College of Art (1966-69) under Ralph Brown, R.A., and Robert Clatworthy, R.A. *Work in permanent collection:* Bristol City Art Gallery. *Address:* 7 Belgrave Terr., Camden Rd., Bath. *Signs work:* "AC."

CHRISTOPHERSON, José, F.I.A.L., M.A.F.A. (1961); painter in oil, gouache and water-colour; *b* 23 Feb., 1914; *d* of Joseph Christopherson. *Educ.:* Manchester High School for Girls; *studied art* at Manchester School of Art and Grosvenor School of Modern Art. *Exhib.:* R.A., Piccadilly Gallery, Salford Art Gallery, Little Gallery, Manchester Art Gallery, provinces and Winnipeg; one-man shows, Tib Lane Gallery, Manchester, Crane Gallery, Manchester, Blackburn Art Gallery, Rivington Art Gallery, Bolton. *Official purchases:* Manchester Art Gallery, Salford Educ. Comm. *Work in permanent collections:* Salford Art Gallery, John Moore and Bernard Lovell Collections, Blackburn Art Gallery, School of Architecture, Stoke-on-Trent. *Address:* 25 Linden Lea, Brooklands Rd., Sale, Ches. *Signs work:* "José Christopherson."

CHUGG, Brian J., A.T.D. (1951); painter in oil, etc., author; lecturer, North Devon College (1953); *b* Braunton, Devon, 3 Nov., 1926; *s* of John Chugg, F.R.G.S.; *m* Mary Bryan Cooper. *Educ.:* Challoners School, N. Devon; *studied art* at Bideford Art School (1946-49), Camberwell Art School under Martin Bloch and Karel Vogel (1950). *Exhib.:* Westward Ho! Art Soc., annual exhbns., one-man exhbns., Barnstaple (1953, 1958). *Address:* 5 Shorelands Rd., Barnstaple, N. Devon. *Signs work:* "BRIAN CHUGG."

CIPRIANI-BOND, Douglas (exhibits: Douglas Cipriani), A.R.D.S., L.S.I.A.; painter in oil and acrylic, designer and design consultant own practice in London; U.K. National Art Comm. for UNESCO (International Association of Art); *b* London, 12 June, 1928; *s* of Lt. D. G. Cipriani-Bond. *Educ.:* Collegiate and St. Martha's College, Feltham; *studied art* at Twickenham College of Art (1942-46) under F. Coulson-Davies. *Exhib.:* one-man show: Sussex University; group show: 'Invasion Artistique', exchange exhbns. France/Britain, Pittsburgh, U.S.A., New Burlington, Suffolk St., Mall Galleries, Loggia Gallery, 'Today's Art', Brighton, 'Modern Art', Bath Festival, Cambridge, Surrey and Southampton Universities, 'Painting South East 1975', International Arts Centre (touring exhbn.). *Work in permanent collection:* Feltham Council, and private collections in Canada, Holland and Britain. *Publications:* designs and illustrations for B.B.C. Publications 'Time & Tune' and Radio Times. *Biography and work repro:* Studio Vista, Graphis International (Zurich), General Press & Art Magazines. *Address:* Delroy

House, 14 Melville Rd., Hove, Sussex. *Clubs:* R.D.S., I.A.A., S.I.A., F.P.S. *Signs work:* "Cipriani."

CITRON, Minna Wright (Mrs.); painter in oil and collage and etcher, print-maker and teacher; joined staff, Pratt Institute Manhattan Center (1971); *b* Newark, N.J., U.S.A., 15 Oct., 1896; *d* of Simon and Lena Wright; *m* D.; two *s*. *Educ.:* Brooklyn Institute of Arts and Sciences; C.C.N.Y., Art Students' League, N.Y.; Atelier 17, N.Y.; and Paris. *Exhib.:* New York, England, France, Germany, Cuba, Brazil, Yugoslavia, Spain. *Work in important private and public collections:* U.S.A., France, England, Holland, Israel, Yugoslavia, Cuba, Brazil and Germany. *Address:* 32 Union Sq., New York, 3. *Clubs:* numerous art organizations. *Signs work:* "Minna Citron."

CLAESSEN, George; artist in oil and graphic media; *b* Colombo, Ceylon, 5 May, 1909; *s* of Granville Claessen. *Educ.:* St. Joseph's College, Colombo; *studied art:* self-taught. *Exhib.:* R.B.A., London, Kensington Gallery, London, Utd. Soc. of Artists, London, Imperial Inst., London, Hampstead Arts Council, Petit Palais (Paris), S.G.A., A.I.A., New Vision Gallery (London), Venice Bienale (1956), hon. mention (plaque) V Biennial, São Paulo, Brazil (1959). *Work in permanent collection:* Lionel Wendt Coll., Ceylon. *Publication:* Book of drawings (1946), Poems of a Painter (Mitre Press, London, 1967). *Address:* 5 Spencer Rise, London NW5. *Club:* Free Painters and Sculptors. *Signs work:* "Claessen" and "G.C."

CLARK, Alan Nicholas, F.R.S.A. (1963), Cert. of Fine Art (Oxon.); artist in oil, water-colour, pastel; school teacher; head of art; Mem. National Soc. of Art Education; sec. 65 Group, Public School Art Masters (1974); *b* Leeds, 10 Aug., 1939; *s* of Edwin George Clark, bank manager; *m* Elisabeth Sherras Clark; two *s*. *Educ.:* Worksop College; *studied art* at Ruskin School of Fine Art (1959-63) under Percy Horton, Richard Naish, Geoffrey Rhodes. *Address:* Briar Cottage, 9 Lombard St., Rawdon, Leeds, Yorks. *Club:* Public Schools. *Signs work:* "Alan N. Clark."

CLARK, Bruce Michael; painter in oil; Head of Art Dept., Barton Court School, Canterbury; *b* Bedfont, 17 July, 1937; *s* of William Henry Clark, artist in water-colour; *m* Jill Clark; two *s*. *Educ.:* Strodes School; *studied art* at Bath Academy of Art, Corsham (1958-60) under Gwyther Irwin, William Crozier. *Exhib.:* one-man shows: Chiltern Gallery, Compendium Galleries, Birmingham, Worcester City A.G.; group shows: Walker's Gallery, Woodstock Gallery, Kootenay Gallery, Canada, Assembly House, Norwich, Festival de Provence, France, Minotaur Gallery, Toronto, Calgary Arts Council, Canada, Piccadilly Gallery, London. *Address:* 40 St. Michael's Pl., Canterbury, Kent. *Signs work:* "Clark."

CLARK, Elisabeth Sherras, N.D.D., Cert. Fine Art (Oxon); painter in oil, water-colour, pastel; teacher; *b* Surbiton, Surrey, 30 Aug., 1936; *d* of Francis E. Sherras; *m* Alan N. Clark; two *s*. *Educ.:* Arts Educational Trust School, London; *studied art* at Ruskin School of Fine Art (1961-64) under Percy Horton, Richard Naish, Geoffrey Rhodes. *Work repro.:* illustrated: Some Sieges by Allington (Blackwell); Fossil Catalogue (British Museum). *Address:* Briar Cottage, 9 Lombard St., Rawdon, Leeds, Yorks. *Signs work:* "Sherras Clark."

CLARK, Jean Manson, R.W.S. (1972), N.E.A.C. (1952); artist in water-colour and oil; *b* Sidcup, Kent, 6 Aug., 1902; *d* of Daniel William Wymer, engineer; *m* Cosmo Clark, R.A. (decd.); one *d*. *Educ.:* Merton Court School, Sidcup; *studied art* at Sidcup School of Art, R.A. Schools. *Exhib.:* R.A., member N.E.A.C. *Murals* in Hadfield Hall, Cutlers' Hall, Sheffield (1954), Bankers' Clearing House, Carpenters' Hall, London. *Ceiling painting* in Woodford Green

United Free Church; *three murals* for Corpus Christi Church, Weston-super-Mare (1967). *Address:* 2 Church Cottages, Church La., Shottisham, Woodbridge, Suffolk IP12 3HH. *Club:* Hon. Mem. Chelsea Arts. *Signs work:* "Jean Clark."

CLARK, John M'Kenzie, D.A. (Dundee, 1950); N.D.D. (Painting) St. Martin's (1956); artist in oil, water-colour, ink; winner of Punch scholarship; *b* Dundee, 29 Nov., 1928; *s* of James Clark, commercial artist. *Educ.:* Harris Academy, Dundee; *studied art* at Dundee College of Art (1945-50), Norwich Art College (1950-51), Hospitalfield Art School (1953), St. Martin's Art School (1955-56). *Exhib.:* R.A., R.S.A., R.S.W., S.S.A., R.G.I., United Soc. of Artists, one-man shows at Dundee, Edinburgh (1960). Mem. Royal Glasgow Institute of Fine Art. *Official purchase:* City of Dundee Permanent Collection (1961). *Work repro.:* in Glad Mag. *Address:* 2 Birchwood Pl., Dundee. *Signs work:* "J. M'KENZIE CLARK."

CLARK, Lord, C.H. (1959), K.C.B. (1938); keeper of fine art, Ashmolean Museum, Oxford (1931-33); director of National Gallery (1934-45); Slade Prof. of Fine Art, Oxford University (1946-51); chairman, Arts Council of Gt. Britain (1953-60); trustee, British Museum; *b* 13 July, 1903; *s* of Kenneth McKenzie Clark; *m* Elizabeth Martin; two *s*, one *d*. *Educ.:* Winchester and Trinity College, Oxford. *Publications:* The Gothic Revival (1929), Leonardo da Vinci (1939), Last Lectures by Roger Fry (edited, 1939), Piero della Francesca (1951), The Nude (1956), Looking at Pictures (1960), Ruskin Today (1964), Rembrandt and the Italian Renaissance (1966), Civilisation (1969); and over sixty television programmes on art. *Address:* The Garden House, Saltwood Castle, Kent. *Club:* St. James's.

CLARK, Michael, P.R.B.S.; sculptor in stone, wood, bronze; President of The Royal Society of British Sculptors, Vice Pres. Society of Catholic Artists; *b* Cheltenham, 19 Dec., 1918; *s* of P. Lindsey Clark, D.S.O., F.R.B.S.; *m* Catherine Heron; five *s*, three *d*. *Educ.:* Blackfriars School, Laxton; *studied art* at Chelsea School of Art (1935-37), at Kennington (1947-50). *Exhib.:* R.A., Catholic Artists' Guild exhbn., I.F.A. and many provincial art galleries. *Work repro.:* The Times, Telegraph, Observer, The Catholic Herald. *Address:* Studio 14, Caroline Terr., Sloane Sq., London SW1. *Signs work:* "Michael Clark."

CLARK, Norman Alexander, R.W.S.; Royal Academy Schools Gold Medallist and Edward Stott Scholar in Historical Painting (1931), Armitage Bronze Medallist in Pictorial Design (1931), Landseer prize-winner in Mural Decoration (1932), Leverhulme Scholar (1935); painter in oil and water-colour; Senior Lecturer, Faculty of Art and Design, Brighton Polytechnic; *b* Ilford, Essex, 17 Feb., 1913; *s* of Hugh Alexander Clark (decd.); *m* Constance Josephine Barnard; one *d*. *Educ.:* Bancroft's School, Woodford; *studied art* at Central School, London (1929), R.A. Schools (1930-35). *Exhib.:* R.A., R.W.S. *Work in permanent collections:* Harris Museum and Art Gallery, Preston, Lancs., and in private collections. *Address:* Mountfield, Brighton Rd., Hurstpierpoint, Sussex. *Signs work:* "Norman Clark."

CLARK, Peter Christian; Oxford University Certificate of Fine Art; professional painter in polymer, black and white, etching and oils; *b* Bingley, Yorks., 19 Apr., 1950; *s* of T. H. Clark, A.C.P., A.R.D.S., F.R.S.A., art director, St. Aldate's College, Oxford. *Educ.:* Clifton House School, Harrogate, H.M.S. Conway, Anglesey, N. Wales; *studied art* at Ruskin School of Drawing and Fine Art under Richard Naish, M.A. *Address:* Flat 7, Wytham Abbey, Oxford. *Signs work:* "Peter C. Clark" and "Christian Clark."

CLARK, Thomas Humphrey, A.C.P., A.R.D.S., F.R.S.A.; art director, St.

Aldate's College, Oxford; artist in polymer, black and white, water-colour, oils; *b* Manchester, 30 Jan., 1921; *s* of Edwin George Clark; *m* Betty Whitley Clark; two *s*. *Educ.:* Leeds Grammar School, Ordination College; *studied art* at Bradford Regional College of Art under Frank Lyle, A.T.D., Fred C. Jones, A.T.D., R.B.A. *Work repro.:* in medical pamphlets. *Address:* Chagford, 8 Lucerne Rd., Oxford. *Club:* N.S.A.E. *Signs work:* "T. H. Clark."

CLARKE, Audrey M.; painter and draughtsman in oil, pen and ink, gouache; occasional illustrator and stage designer; *b* Huncote, Leics., 15 Dec., 1926. *Educ.:* Hinckley Grammar School, Leics.; *studied art* at Leicester College of Art (1943-48). *Exhib.:* City of Leicester Art Gallery. *Address:* 42 Forest Rd., Huncote, Leicester. *Signs work:* see appendix.

CLARKE, Dora, R.B.A.; sculptor in wood, stone, ivory, etc.; *b* Harrow, Middx.; *d* of Joseph Thatcher Clarke; *m* Admiral Gervase B. Middleton, C.B., C.B.E. *Studied art* at Slade School under Havard Thomas and Tonks. *Exhib.:* R.A., R.B.A. *Work in permanent collections:* Manchester Art Gallery and Ashmolean Museum, Oxford. *Official purchases:* Joseph Conrad Memorial Library (N.Y.), Conrad Memorial Hall (Bishopsbourne, Kent), Fletcher Memorial, Nat. Inst. Medical Research (Mill Hill), Min. of Information Nat. War Records. *Address:* Studio 3, 95A Clifton Hill, London NW8. *Signs work:* "D.C."

CLARKE, Geoffrey, A.R.A., A.R.C.A.; artist; *b* 28 Nov., 1924; *s* of John Moulding Clarke and Janet Petts; *m*, 1947, Ethelwynne Tyrer; one *s*. *Educ.:* Royal College of Art (Hons.). *Work in permanent collections:* (stained glass) Coventry and Lincoln Cathedrals, Taunton, Ipswich, Crownhill Plymouth; (sculpture) Coventry and Chichester Cathedrals; Cambridge (Churchill, Homerton, Newnham), Exeter, Liverpool, Newcastle, Manchester and Lancaster Universities; Bedford, Chichester and Winchester Colleges. *Other Principal Work:* Castrol House, Thorn Electric, Newcastle Civic Centre, Nottingham Playhouse, Culham Atomic Energy, Guard's Chapel, Birdcage Walk, Aldershot Landscape, St. Paul Minnesota. *Address:* Stowe Hill, Hartest, Bury St. Edmunds, Suffolk.

CLARKE, Joan; potter, stoneware; *b* Leicester, 28 Dec., 1913; *d* of H. Harvey Clarke, landscape painter and etcher. *Educ.:* Wyggeston Grammar School for Girls, Leicester; *studied pottery* at Loughborough College of Art under David Leach. *Address:* Little Orchard, Ludham, Norfolk. *Clubs:* Norfolk Rural Craftsmen's Guild, Guild of Many Crafts. *Signs work:* "Joan Clarke, Ludham."

CLARKE, Richard Cambridge; water-colour artist; *b* Ilford, Essex, 29 Nov., 1909; *m* Titia Faber (decd.); one *d;* *m* Ursula Davies (1955). *Educ.:* Bishop's Stortford College (1921-26), Regent St. Polytechnic (part-time: 1937-38). *Publications:* various books illustrated for Heinemann, Longman, Nelson, etc. *Address:* Studio, Farnham Green, Bishop's Stortford, Herts. *Signs work:* "Richard C. Clarke."

CLARKSON, Jack, A.R.C.A. (1930); Principal, School of Art, Newcastle, Staffs.; artist in wood, bronze, terra-cotta, oils; retd. teacher; head of sculpture dept., Sheffield College of Art (1930-44); *b* Silsden, Yorks., 7 July, 1906; *s* of Samuel Clarkson, leather merchant; *m* (1st) Rhoda Southwell, divorced (1960); (2nd) Vera Woolridge (1964); one *d*. *Educ.:* Silsden Modern School; *studied art* at Keighley School of Art, R.C.A. *Exhib.:* R.A., Glasgow, Sheffield, Hanley. *Work in permanent collections:* Hanley Art Gallery, Newcastle Art Gallery. *Official purchases:* Silsden Parish Church, County Hall, Newport, I.O.W. *Address:* 5 Clumber Ave., Clayton, Newcastle, Staffs. *Signs work:* "J. Clarkson."

CLATWORTHY, Robert, R.A. (1973); sculptor; mem. Fine Art Panel of

National Council for Diplomas in Art and Design (1961-71); head of Fine Art, Central School of Art and Design; *b* 1 Jan., 1928. *Studied art* at West of England College of Art, Chelsea School of Art, The Slade. *Exhib.:* Hanover Gallery (1954, 1956), Waddington Galls. (1965), Holland Park Open Air Sculpture (1957), Battersea Park Open Air Sculpture (1960, 1963), Tate Gallery British Sculpture in the Sixties (1965), Basil Jacobs Gallery (1972), British Sculpture '72, Burlington House. *Work in permanent collections:* Arts Council, Contemporary Art Society, Tate Gallery, V. & A., G.L.C. *Address:* 1 Park St., London SE1.

CLAUGHTON, Richard Bentley, F.R.B.S.; sculptor; senior lecturer in sculpture, Slade School; *b* London, 28 Feb., 1917; *m*; one *s*. *Educ.:* Woodford House School, Birchington; *studied art* at Slade School under Professor Schwabe (1946-49). *Exhib.:* Open-air, Battersea, London Group, R.B.A., New English, and in Holland, London and provincial galleries. *Sculpture* on buildings in London, provinces, and work in Lagos Cathedral and in private collections in Britain, Iraq and America. *Address:* 8 The Mall, London SW14.

CLEAVER, James, A.R.C.A. (1937), M.S.I.A.; painter and illustrator in B/W, oil, water-colour, lithography; *b* 5 Dec., 1911; *s* of Frederick Richard Cleaver, merchant; *m* Helen von Rabenau. *Educ.:* Southwark County School; *studied art* at Camberwell School of Art (1930-34) and R.C.A. (1934-38). *Exhib.:* R.A., and other London and provincial galleries. *Work repro.:* in Radio Times, Observer. *Publications:* The Theatre Through the Ages (Harrap, 1946, Hart, 1967), The Theatre at Work (Puffin Picture Book, 1947), A History of Graphic Art (Peter Owen, 1963). *Address:* Alderside, Egham Hill, Surrey. *Club:* Authors. *Signs work:* "James Cleaver."

CLEMENT SMITH, Winifred May; final diplomas in art subjects; artist in oil, water-colour and pastel; *b* Tunbridge Wells, 26 Nov., 1904; *m* Clement Smith, architect. *Educ.:* Tunbridge Wells; *studied art:* Regent St. Polytechnic, London. *Exhib.:* S.W.A., R.I., R.O.I., and P.S., and provincial galleries. *Address:* 14 Queens Rd., Tunbridge Wells.

CLEMENTS, Keith, N.D.D., A.T.D., D.A.E.; senior lecturer in Art, Eastbourne College of Education (1965—); painter, illustrator; art director, Man and Religion series, Pergamon Press; *b* Brighton, 9 May, 1931; *s* of Cecil Clements; *m* Jackie Sinclair; one *s*, one *d*. *Educ.:* Varndean Grammar School, Brighton; *studied art* at Brighton College of Art (1947-53), Birmingham School of Art Education (1964-65). *Exhib.:* Alwin Gallery, R.A., R.E., Young Contemporaries, Arts Council tours. *Address:* Eastbourne College of Education, Sussex. *Signs work:* "Keith Clements."

CLEMENTS, Raymon John, F.I.A.L. (1957), A.T.D. (1951), Mem. Nat. Soc. Art Educ. (1951), N.D.D., painting (1950); painter in oil and sculptor; Director, Creative Studies, Rowley Regis College, Warley, W. Midlands; visiting specialist, Leamington School of Art (1951-52); lecturer Birmingham College of Technology; Housemaster, Rowley Grammar (1956-74); *b* Dudley, Worcs., 19 July, 1927; *s* of John Alfred Clements, A.M.I.Mech.E., engineer; *m* Hazel Tite; one *s*. *Educ.:* Dudley Grammar School; *studied art* at Birmingham College of Arts and Crafts under Harold Smith, Bernard Fleetwood-Walker, R.A., etc. *Exhib.:* Birmingham, Glasgow, S. America, Europe (touring exhbn.). *Address:* 44 Tennyson Rd., Dudley, W. Midlands. *Signs work:* "Clements."

CLEMENTS, William Charles; portrait and landscape painter; adult art tutor; *b* London, 9 Nov., 1903; *s* of William Henry Clements; *m* Elsie Florence Bennett; one *s*, one *d*. Work in private collections. *Address:* 17 Silverthorn Gdns., Chingford, London E4. *Clubs:* London Sketch (President 1975), Essex Art (Past Chairman). *Signs work:* "W. Clements" (early), now "William C. Clements."

CLEVELAND, Sydney Dyson, O.B.E. (1955), Hon. M.A. (Manc., 1963), Hon. D.A. (Manc., 1958), F.M.A. (Pres., 1950-52); Director, Manchester Art Galleries (1952-62) (Deputy, 1937-52); keeper, Rutherston Loan Collection (1927-37); *b* Manchester, 11 Apr., 1898; *m* Helen Plant; two *s*. *Educ.:* Manchester Central Grammar School; *studied art* at Manchester College of Art and abroad. *Publications:* Guide to the Manchester Art Galleries, History of the Royal Manchester Inst.; Heaton Hall, Heaton Park; contributions to Studio, Connoisseur, Museums' Journal, etc. *Address:* 6 Highfield Pk., Heaton Mersey, Ches.

CLIFFORD, Clare Lady, A.R.M.S.; artist in water-colour, mediums for miniatures; *b* Hythe, 1894; *d* of Capt. J. G. Mayne, C.B.E., chief constable, E. Suffolk; *m* 1st, the late Charles S. W. Ogilvie; 2nd, Lord Clifford of Chudleigh; one *s*, one *d*. *Educ.:* privately; *studied art* with Lindsay, pres. R.M.S. *Exhib.:* R.M.S., Exeter Art Soc. *Address:* Lyde Mill, Newnham, Hants. *Signs work:* "Clare M. Clifford" and previously "Clare M. Ogilvie."

CLOUGH, Thomas Collingwood, A.R.C.A. (1930); artist in oil, water-colour; art master; camouflage officer, Middle East (1941); art master, Edmonton Latymer's School (1945); now lecturer, Sir John Cass School of Art; *b* Glen Conway, Denbighshire, N. Wales; *s* of Thomas Clough, artist; *m* Kathleen Clough; one *s*. *Educ.:* Rydal, Colwyn Bay; *studied art* at Slade School under Prof. Henry Tonks (1925-27), under Prof. William Rothstein (1928-30). *Exhib.:* R.A., London Group. *Address:* 46 Redcliffe Rd., London SW10. *Club:* Chelsea Arts. *Signs work:* "Colin Clough."

CLUTTERBUCK, Jan; painter in oils, mixed media, and printmaker; teacher of painting, Cassio College, Watford; Chairman, Women's International Art Club; *b* Newton, Mass., 16 July, 1919; *d* of Sier Diefendorf, Greenwich, Conn.; *m* Jeremy R. H. Clutterbuck; one *s*, one *d*. *Educ.:* Greenbrier College, West Virginia; *studied art:* self-taught; studied printmaking under Michael Rothenstein. *Exhib.:* R.A., N.S., American Embassy. *Work in permanent collections:* Gloucester Education Committee, Coventry Education Committee. *Address:* White House, Chandlers Cross, Rickmansworth, Herts. *Club:* W.I.A.C. *Signs work:* "Jan Clutterbuck."

CLUYSENAAR, John, Prix de Rome, Prix Godecharles; sculptor and painter in water-colour and oil; *b* Brussels, 26 Sept., 1899; *s* of Andre Cluysenaar, portrait painter; *m* Jacqueline Collier; one *d*. *Educ.:* Marlborough. *Work in permanent collection:* Museums of Brussels, Antwerp, Liège, Mons, La Louvière, Maaseik. *Monuments:* at Brussels, Daelhem, Teddington (England). *Address:* 5054 Noville sur Mehaigne, Belgium. *Signs work:* "Cluysenaar."

CLYNE, Henry Horne, D.A.(Edin.), Harkness Fellow; sculptor in steel, stone, wood, ceramics and bronze; Head of Sculpture Dept., Winchester School of Art; *b* Caithness, Scotland, 5 Mar., 1930; *s* of W. A. Scott Clyne, farmer and shorthorn breeder; *m* Elaine Clyne; one *s*. *Educ.:* Wick High School, Scotland; *studied art* at Edinburgh College of Art under Eric Schilsky, Maxwell Allan, William MacTaggart, Charles Pulsford, Leonard Rosoman. *Exhib.:* New York, Manchester (V.T.); Edinburgh, Festival Shows at Aldeburgh, Brighton, Stroud; Diaglihev Exhbn. (1954); Structure 1966 (Cardiff); Leicester Galleries. *Work in permanent collections:* Scottish Arts Council, University of E. Anglia and private collections in U.K. and U.S.A. *Publication:* West Goes East (1967).

Address: Sunnymede, Horsebridge Rd., Kings Somborne, Hants. SO20 6PT. *Signs work:* "Henry H. Clyne" and see appendix.

CLYNE, Thora, M.A.Hons. in Fine Art (1960); artist in oil, water-colour, pastel, pen and ink; part-time lecturer in drawing and painting at Edinburgh College of Art; *b* Wick, Caithness, 10 Nov., 1937; *m* Robin Philipson (divorced). *Educ.:* Edinburgh University; *studied art* at Edinburgh College of Art (1955-61) under W. G. Gillies, R.S.A. and John Maxwell, R.S.A. *Exhib.:* one-man shows: The Open Eye Gallery, Edinburgh (1975), Loomshop, Lower Largo, Fife (1971); group show: The Scottish Gallery, Edinburgh (1976). *Work in permanent collections:* Edinburgh Corporation Schools, Ross & Cromarty Educ. Authority, First Scottish-American Trust Co., Ltd. *Address:* 7 Strathearn Pl., Edinburgh. *Signs work:* "Thora Clyne."

COATE, Peter, A.T.D., R.W.A., Chelsea Dip. (1950); painter in oil, water-colour, and teacher; Director, Mendip Painting Centre; *b* Nailsea, Som., 9 Mar., 1926; *s* of Redvers Coate, cidermaker; *m* Margaret Bickerton; one *s*, one *d*. *Educ.:* Sherborne; *studied art* at Chelsea under Robert Medley. *Exhib.:* London Group, R.A., S.WL.A., R.W.E.A., six West Country exhbns. of Somerset and Suffolk landscapes. *Work in permanent collections:* R.W.A., Hertfordshire and Cumberland County Councils, Nuffield Foundation. *Address:* West End House, Blagdon, nr. Bristol. *Signs work:* "Peter Coate."

COATMAN, Maureen Margaret; sculptress in clay, stone, fibre-glass; Mem. Portrait Sculptors Soc. (1968); *b* Woking, Surrey, 7 Nov., 1919; *d* of Col. Noel Hudson, D.S.O., M.I.C.E., M.I.E.E.; *m* J. S. B. Coatman, A.R.I.B.A.; two *s*. *Educ.:* Sherborne School for Girls; *studied art* privately from 1937 till joining forces in 1940 with William T. Wood (oil painting), and Enid Fenton-Smith (sculpture). *Work in permanent collections:* in churches: Living Christ, Sonning Common, nr. Reading; St. Dunstan and the Devil, Monks Risborough, nr. Aylesbury; external mural in fibre-glass, St. Edward's School, Windsor. *Address:* Brook Cottage, Askett Lane, Askett, Aylesbury, Bucks. *Signs work:* "MMCOATMAN" or "MMC."

COBB, David, R.O.I., R.S.M.A.; marine and industrial artist in oil, gouache, black and white; *b* Bromley, Kent, 13 May, 1921; *s* of A. Cobb; *m* Jean Main, S.W.A.; one *d*. *Educ.:* Pangbourne. *Exhib.:* R.O.I., R.B.A. S.M.A., Paris, Canada, U.S.A., Bermuda, etc. *Work repro.:* Players, Brit. Rlys., Vickers Armstrong, Imperial Oil, B.A.T., Radio Times, Shell-Mex, Esso, Marconi, Anchor Line, G.P.O., Wellworthy, Thornycroft, Whitbread, Fairey, Vosper, Brit. Aluminium, Iliffes, Temple Press, etc. *Address:* Woodis, Setley, Brockenhurst, Hants. *Signs work:* "DAVID COBB."

COBBETT, Hilary Dulcie, S.W.A.; artist in oil, water-colour; teacher (1927-33); *b* Richmond, Surrey, 1885; *d* of W. V. H. Cobbett, solicitor. *Educ.:* privately; *studied art* at Richmond School of Art (1903-5, 1924-27). *Exhib.:* R.A., R.B.A., R.P.S., R.O.I., R.I., S.M.A., S.W.A., etc. *Address:* 43 Queens Ct., Queens Rd., Richmond, Surrey. *Signs work:* "HILARY COBBETT."

COCHRANE, John Peter Warren; with Arthur Tooth & Sons (Director) since 1951 (formerly Director, Redfern Gallery); specialist in painting of 19th and 20th centuries for private and public collections, particularly such artists as Appel, Dubuffet, Sam Francis, Paul Jenkins, Jorn, Riopelle, Tapies; agent for William Brooker, Richard Eurich, Tristram Hillier, Peter Kinley, Howard Hodgkin, Felix Kelly; member, N.A.C.F., C.A.S., Soc. London Art Dealers; Vice-President, Fine Art Provident Inst.; *b* Ash, Surrey, 15 Oct., 1913; *s* of Col. E. W. W. Cochrane,

D.S.O. *Educ.:* Wellington College and R.M.C. Sandhurst. *Address:* 31 Bruton St., London W1. *Club:* Savile.

COCKERELL, Sydney Morris, F.S.A.; bookbinder; developed marbling on paper for book production (Cockerell Papers); visiting lecturer to University College, London; *b* London, 6 June, 1906; *s* of Douglas Cockerell, O.B.E., R.D.I., bookbinder; *m* Elizabeth Cowlishaw; one *s*, two *d*. *Publications:* The Marbling of Paper (Russell, Hitchin); article in Encyclopaedia Britannica; article for Junior Oxford Encyclopaedia; Appendix to Bookbinding and the Care of Books (Pitman); The Repairing of Books (Sheppard Press). *Address:* Riversdale, Grantchester, Cambridge.

CODNER, John Whitlock, R.W.A. (1947); artist in oil, portrait painter; asst. master, Sir John Cass College, School of Art (1947-51); *b* Beaconsfield, 1913; *s* of Maurice Codner, R.P. (hon. sec.), R.O.I.; *m* Rachael Notley; two *s*. *Studied art* at Polytechnic School of Art, Regent St., under Harry Watson (1930-32). *Exhib.:* R.A., R.P., R.W.A., etc. *Work in permanent collections:* Royal West of England Academy, Office of Works, Bristol Corp., Bristol University, Essex County Council, The Institution of Civil Engineers, Malaya, Canada, Mexico, Spain. *Work repro.:* Illustrated (1954), Press, etc. *Address:* Breadstone House, nr. Berkeley, Glos. *Clubs:* Arts, Bristol Savages. *Signs work:* "JOHN CODNER."

COHEN, Dr. Harry, surgeon; Pres. International Fine Arts Council; Pres., American International Academy; Chancellor, Philathea College; Vice-Pres., Chatham Hill College, etc.; Chairman, Section of Medicine and Science, Encyclopedia Judaica; *b* Austria, 10 Jan., 1885; *s* of Samuel Cohen; *m* Flora Cohen; two *s*. *Educ.:* Cornell University; *studied art* at most of the art galleries of the world. *Publications:* Simon Bolivar and the Conquest and Liberation of South America; The Story of the Taj Mahal. *Clubs:* Navigators', N.Y. Power Squadron, Mem. of Metropolitan Museum of Art. *Address:* 7 Lexington Ave., New York City, 10. *Signs work:* "Dr. Harry Cohen."

COHEN, Mary; artist in oil, pen and wash, water-colour; *b* London, 21 Nov., 1910; *d* of the late Ernest M. Joseph, C.B.E., F.R.I.B.A., architect; *m* Cdr. Kenneth Cohen, C.B., C.M.G., R.N.; one *s*, one *d*. *Studied art:* Florence, Slade under Prof. Tonks and Prof. Schwabe (1928-31), and Euston Road School. *Exhib.:* Leicester Galleries Mixed Exhbns., R.A., R.B.A., N.E.A.C., London Group, Roland, Browse and Delbanco, New Grafton Gallery, etc. *Address:* 33 Bloomfield Terr., London SW1. *Signs work:* "Mary S. C."

COLDSTREAM, Sir William Menzies, Kt., C.B.E., Hon. D.Litt. (Nottingham), Hon. D.Litt. (Birmingham); painter; Slade Professor of Fine Art, University College, London (1949-75); *b* Belford, Northumberland, 1908; *s* of G. P. Coldstream, M.B., C.M.; *m* (1st, 1931), Nancy Culliford Sharp (marriage dissolved, 1942); two *d*; (2nd, 1961), Monica Mary Hoyer *d* of A. E. Monrad Hoyer; one *s*, two *d*. *Educ.:* privately; *studied art* at Slade. *Work in permanent collections:* Tate, National Gallery of Canada, etc. *Address:* Slade School, University College, Gower St., London WC1. *Signs work:* "William Coldstream."

COLE, Arthur Bertram, Jr., F.C.A.D., L.S.I.A., F.I.A.L.; industrial designer and consultant; managing director, Design Industries, Cole Associates, Le-Roye Productions; Industrial Design Partnership (1938-40); *b* Wallasey, Ches., 19 Mar., 1920; *s* of Arthur Bertram Cole, snr., prof. of music; *m* Hazel Joyce; one *s*, two *d*. *Educ.:* Wallasey Grammar School, Wrigley's College; *studied sculpture* under John Cole and Henry Carr, A.R.C.A., Beckenham Art School. *Addresses:* Manor House, 34 Wickham Rd., Beckenham, Kent; office and studios: Royal London House, 171 High St., Beckenham, Kent. *Signs work:* "A. B. COLE."

COLE, A. Ernest; sculptor, draughtsman; prof. of Sculpture, R.C.A. South Kensington (1924-26); *b* Greenwich, 9 July, 1890; *s* of John Stickland Cole; *m* Dr. Laurie Manley. *Studied art* at Goldsmiths' College School of Art. *Sculptures* on London County Council Hall, Westminster. *Bronze Monument:* Perth, Scotland (A. Lisle). *Work in permanent collections:* B.M., Fitzwilliam Museum, Cambridge, Canadian National Gallery, etc. *Work repro.:* Studio (1919), Country Life, Print Collectors' Quarterly. *Address:* Studio, Kingston, nr. Canterbury, Kent. *Signs work:* "Ernest Cole."

COLEBORN, Keith, A.R.C.A., A.T.D., F.R.S.A., M.S.I.A.; principal, Ravensbourne College of Art and Crafts; regional art principal, N.W. Kent; principal, Bromley College of Art (1946-62); principal, Stourbridge School of Art (1937-40); principal, Wallasey School of Art (1940-46); *b* Portsmouth. *Address:* Downe Hall Farm, Downe, Kent.

COLEMAN, Alan, F.R.B.S. (1961), R.B.A. (1952), A.R.C.A. (1st Class, 1951); sculptor; *b* Croydon, Surrey, 1920; *m* Joan Bradley, M.B., C.H.B., M.R.C.Psych.; three *s*, one *d*. *Studied art* at Goldsmiths' College School of Art, R.C.A. *Address:* Derrysbourne, Wonersh, Guildford, Surrey.

COLLINGBOURNE, Stephen; sculptor in steel, stainless steel, aluminium and wood; *b* Dartington, 15 Aug., 1943. *Educ.:* Dartington Hall School; *studied art* at Dartington College of Art (1960-61); Bath Academy, Corsham (1961-64). *Exhib.:* W.A.G. and Bluecoat, Liverpool; British Council, Malaya; Arts Centre, Aberystwyth; Chapter, and Oriel, Cardiff; Zella 9, Fisher Gallery and Serpentine, London; Kettles Yard, Cambridge. *Work in permanent collections:* Southampton and Leicester Art Galleries, Welsh Arts Council, Leicester University, Devon and Hereford Educ. Authorities. *Address:* Melindwr, Gwaith Goginan, Aberystwyth, Dyfed. *Signs work:* "Stephen Collingbourne."

COLLINS, Cecil; *b* Plymouth, Devon, 1908; *m* Elisabeth Ramsden. *Educ.:* R.C.A. *Exhib.:* Bloomsbury Gallery (1935), Lefevre Gallery (1944, 1945, 1948), Ashmolean Museum (1953), Whitechapel Gallery (1959), Carnegie International Exhibition, Pittsburgh, U.S.A. (1964), Tooth Gallery (1965-71), Hamet Gallery (1972). *Work in permanent collections:* Tate Gallery, V. & A. Museum, British Museum, Museum of Fine Arts, Boston, U.S.A., and various private collections in England, Italy and America. *Publications:* British Art since 1900, Sir John Rothenstein (Phaidon Press, 1962), The Vision of the Fool (1947). *Address:* 35 Selwyn Gdns., Cambridge. *Signs work:* see appendix.

COLOM, Maria Josefa; painter and engraver; Prize, Castro Gil (1965); Prize, National School of Graphic Arts (1966); Hon. Prize of A.E.B. (1967); Dip. of the Great International Prize, Monte Carlo (1967); Hon. Mem. Spanish Association Engravers (1964); Prize, Ciudad de Cuenca, National Exhibition (1968); President, Comite Promotor 1 Muestra Internacional de Grabado y Litografia, Barcelona (1969); Mention, National Exhibition (1970); National Prize Engraving, Madrid (1960); Silver Medal, Paris (1959); Medal, National Exhibition (1960); Medal, Royal Academy of Fine Arts, Barcelona (1956); Prize, Barcelona Corporation (1954); Juan Sedo Peris Mencheta Prize (1956); 2nd National Prize, Engraving, Madrid (1958); Dip. Huesca Prize (1962); Professor of Engraving, Conservatorio Artes Libro, Barcelona; *b* Cervera, 1926; *d* of Francisco Colom Guix; *m* C. Vives. *Educ.:* Verdaguer Institute; *studied art* at Barcelona, Rome, Paris; St. George Higher School of Fine Arts. *Work in permanent collections:* Barcelona Modern Art Museum, Madrid, Vienna, Duran Saupere Museum, Secretariate of Fine Arts, Madrid. *Address:* Travesera de las Corts 348, Barcelona, Spain. *Signs work:* "M. J. Colom."

COLQUHOUN, Ithell; Slade Summer Composition Prize (1929); painter and poet; lecture-demonstrations in Automatic Processes, Oxford, Cambridge, London. *Studied art* at Slade School, Paris and Athens. *Exhib.:* C.A.S., Living Art, Fantasmagie, Hamet Gallery, Harvare Gallery, Paris, Belgium, Germany, Czechoslovakia, W. Berlin, London (Leva); one-man shows: London Gallery, Mayor Gallery, Gallery I, Heffer Gallery (Cambridge), Newlyn Gallery (Cornwall), W. Berlin, Hamburg, Bristol, Exeter, Penzance, Plymouth. *Publications:* The Crying of the Wind (1955); The Living Stones (1957); Goose of Hermogenes (1961); Grimoire of the Entangled Thicket (1973); Sword of Wisdom (1975). *Address:* Stone Cross Cottage, Paul, Penzance. *Signs work:* "ITHELL COLQUHOUN" on back; since 1962 by a monogram (see appendix).

CONEY, John J.; artist in slipware and stoneware; lecturer (ceramics), College of Art, Portsmouth, 1947-71 (retired); *b* Batcombe, Somerset, 5 Dec., 1907; *s* of Gerald Coney, independent means; *m* Merle Dempsey. *Educ.:* St. Edward's School, Oxford; *studied art* at St. Ives under Bernard Leach (1925-26), R.C.A. under Prof. Staite Murray (1929), Camberwell School of Art under Hopkins brothers. *Address:* 56 Hulbert Rd., Bedhampton, Hants. *Signs work:* "J Coney" and date.

CONGDON, William; artist in oil and water-colour; *b* Providence, Rhode Island, U.S.A., 15 Apr., 1912; *s* of Gilbert M. Congdon (decd.). *Educ.:* Yale University; *studied art* at George Demetrios (sculpture); Henry Hensche, Provincetown. *Prizes:* R.I. Mus. Annual (1948-49), P.A.F.A. Temple Gold Medal (1951), Corcoran, Washington, Clark Award (1953); Univ. Illinois Purchase Prize (1952); Gold Medal, 1st International Sacred Art, Trieste (1961). *Exhib.:* America, Italy, England and Japan. *Work in permanent collections:* Museums in America and Italy; Benedictine Monastery, Subiaco, Italy; and others. *Addresses:* Vicolo Bovi 1, Assisi (Pg), and Subiaco (Rome). *Signs work:* see appendix.

CONNEW, Joan V., M.B.E., S.S.I.; artist and calligrapher; *b* Sydenham SE26; *d* of Charles Connew. *Educ.:* private school, Burgess Hill, Sussex; *studied writing and illuminating* at Brighton School of Art under Mrs. A. Gasston; *art* (drawing and painting) at Beckenham School of Art under Henry Carr; *calligraphy* at the Central School of Arts and Crafts (L.C.C.) under M. C. Oliver. *Exhib.:* R.A., R.B.A., R.S.M.A. *Address:* 118 Farnaby Rd., Shortlands, Bromley, Kent. *Club:* R.W.S. Art. *Signs work:* "CONNEW."

CONNON, William John, D.A. (1959), post-Dip. (1960); mem. S.S.A.; painter in oil, draughtsman, teacher; lecturer in drawing and painting at Grays School of Art, Aberdeen; *b* Turriff, 11 Dec., 1929; *s* of Albert Connon; *m* Margaret R. Mair; one *s*, one *d*. *Educ.:* Turriff Academy; *studied art* at Grays School of Art under R. Henderson Blyth, R.S.A., Ian Fleming, R.S.A. *Exhib.:* R.S.A., S.S.A., A.A.S. *Work in permanent collections:* Aberdeen A.G., Scottish Arts Council, City of Edinburgh Art Centre. *Address:* 8 Fonthill Rd., Aberdeen. *Signs work:* "wjconnon."

CONRAN, George Loraine; director, City Art Galleries, Manchester (1962); curator, The Iveagh Bequest, Kenwood (1950); curator, Southampton Art Gallery (1938-50); deputy director, Walker Art Gallery, Liverpool (1936-38); asst., Birmingham City Museum and Art Gallery (1934-36); president, Museums' Assoc. (1967), hon. sec. (1959-64); hon. sec., Contemporary Art Soc.; *b* 29 Mar., 1912; *s* of Col. G. H. M. Conran; *m* Jacqueline O'Neill Roe; one *s*, one *d*; divorced 1970; *m* E. Johnston, 1970; one *d*. *Educ.:* R.N. College, Dartmouth. *Address:* 9 Churchwood Rd., Didsbury, Manchester 20. *Club:* Athenæum.

CONWAY, Frances Ruth, N.D.D., A.R.W.A.; painter in oil conté, water paint, collage; *b* Bristol; *m*; two *s*, one *d*. *Educ.:* College of Commerce, Bristol; *studied art* at West of England College of Art, Bristol, under George Sweet, Robert Hurdle, Francis Hoyland, William Townsend. *Publications:* The Adventures of Mary-Jane, written and illustrated. *Address:* 37 Cornwallis Cres., Clifton, Bristol. *Club:* R.W.A. *Signs work:* "Frances Conway."

COOK, Sir Francis Ferdinand Maurice (Bt.), A.R.B.A. (1938, rtd. 1947), F.R.S.A. (1940); mem. St. Ives Soc. Artists, Cornwall (1938); mem. Royal Institution of Cornwall (1947); mem. Jersey Soc. of Artists (1949); the Chelsea Arts Soc. (1953); Jersey Artists Group (1963); gold medallist, Bentalls Exhbn. (1934-35); oil painter and tempera, pastel, pencil artist of portraits and landscapes, allegories, religious, still life, animals, children; research worker and expert on mediums and methods of old masters, with rediscovery and proofs of lost techniques; critic and writer on art; *b* London, 21 Dec., 1907; *s* of Sir Herbert Frederick Cook (Bt.), M.A., F.S.A. (decd.); *m*; one *s*, one *d*. *Educ.:* privately and Bradfield College, Berks.; *studied art* under Harold Speed (1926-32); Sir J. Arnsby Brown, R.A. (1932-34); S. J. Lamorna Birch, R.A. (1935-36), and others. *Exhib.:* R.A., R.O.I., R.B.A., N.E.A.C., United Artists' Exhbn. at R.A., London Portrait Soc., London Group, Renaissance Gallery, A.I.A. Salon, Bournemouth, Walker Art Gallery, Southport, Brighton, Ferens Art Gallery, Hull, Bolton, Southampton, etc. *Work in permanent collections:* Walker Art Gallery, Manchester, Northampton. *Publications:* in the Bulletin of the Russell Cotes Art Gallery and Museum Bulletin, Bournemouth. *Addresses:* Le Coin, La Haule, St. Aubin, Jersey, C.I.; The Augrés Foundation of Fine Art, Augrés, Trinity, Jersey, C.I. *Clubs:* R.A.C., Arts, Victoria Club, Jersey. *Signs work:* see appendix. Some works from 1952 unsigned, particularly tempera. Some drawings unsigned, or *on drawings* sometimes "F. Cook 69" or "FMC 69" with own catalogue number on reverse side of work.

COOK, Frederick T. W., R.W.A.; landscape, marine and flower painter in oil, gouache; official war fireman-artist; *b* London; *m* M. Anyon, portrait painter. *Studied art* at Hampstead School of Art. *Exhib.:* R.A., R.W.A., R.S.A., Redfern, Leicester and Trafford Galleries. *Work in permanent collections:* Imperial War Museum, R.W.A., Art Gallery, Plymouth. *Official purchases:* for the National Collection, R.W.A. and Plymouth. *Work repro.:* in Studio, Artist, Tatler, Sphere, Time and Life, Standard History of the Second Great War. *Address:* Harbour Studio, Polperro, Cornwall. *Club:* English Speaking Union. *Signs work:* "Frederick T. W. Cook."

COOK, Jennifer, Dip.A.D.(Central) 1969; art teacher, textile designer, artist/illustrator of children's books, greetings cards using poster, water-colours and inks; *b* Eastbourne, 5 July, 1947; *d* of Robert Arthur Cook. *Educ.:* Chichester High School for Girls; *studied art* at West Sussex College of Art and Design, Worthing (1958-64) under Mr. Spedding; Central School of Art and Design (1966-69) under Gilbert Harding Green, Gordon Baldwin, John Colbeck and Dan Arbeid. *Publication:* illustrations for a Childrens' Book of Poetry by Sarah Clarke. *Address:* 573 Romford Rd., Forest Gate, London E7. *Signs work:* "J" within a "C."

COOK, Jennifer Martin, N.D.D., A.T.D.; painter in transparent oil paint on perspex; *b* Preston, Lancs., 1942; *d* of Albert J. Heathcote, local government officer; *m* John H. Cook, glassmaker and designer. *Educ.:* Casterton School; *studied art* at Harris College, Preston (1960-65); Leicester College of Art (1965-66). *Exhib.:* R.A. Summer Exhbn. (1975); three-man shows: Yew Tree Cottage Gallery, Derbys., Oxford Gallery (1975). *Work in permanent collections:* in

England and abroad. *Address:* 28 Castle St., Whitwick Leics. LE6 4AG. *Signs work:* "Jenny Cook."

COOKE, Anthony R., R.A.S. Cert.; landscape and portrait painter in oil, drawing instructor; mem. of Foundation Studies, West Sussex College of Design; *b* London, 1933; *m* Christine Frances, S.R.N.; two *s,* two *d. Educ.:* St. Johns, Leatherhead; *studied art* at Royal Academy Schools under Henry Rushbury, Peter Greenham, also studied under Carel Weight and Ruskin Spear. *Work in permanent collections:* Batley, Nottingham, Leicester, Worthing and Preston Municipal Galleries; Ministry of Works, J. Walter Thompson Ltd., Trust Forte Ltd. *Address:* 25 Ravens Rd., Shoreham-by-Sea, Sussex. *Signs work:* "A.R.C."

COOKE, Jean, R.A., N.D.D., R.B.A.; painter; lecturer, Royal College (1965-74); *b* London, 18 Feb., 1927; *d* of A. O. Cooke; *m* John Bratby; three *s,* one *d. Educ.:* Blackheath High School; *studied art* at Central School of Arts and Crafts, Goldsmiths' College of Arts, Camberwell School of Art, City and Guilds, Royal College. *Exhib.:* one-man show: Farnham (1962, 1964, 1973), Establishment (1963), Leicester Gallery (1964), Bear Lane, Bladon Gallery (1966), Phoenix (1970), New Grafton (1971); mixed show: R.A., Zwemmer, London Group, R.B.A., Arts Council, Young Contemporaries, Royal College of Art, Upper Grosvenor, Arundel, Furneaux (1968), Agnew (1974). *Work in permanent collections:* R.A., R.C.A., Tate. *Address:* 7 Hardy Rd., Blackheath, London SE3. *Signs work:* "Jean E. Cooke."

COOKE, Stanley; artist in oil and water-colour; *b* Mansfield, Notts., 11 Jan., 1913; *s* of John Cooke; *m* Anne M. Clayton; one *s. Educ.:* King Edward School, Mansfield; *studied art* at Mansfield School of Art (1924-32) and The Press Art School. *Exhib.:* R.A., R.I., R.O.I., Britain in Water-colours exhbns., provinces; one-man shows at Drian Galleries, London and Mansfield Art Gallery. *Work in permanent collection:* Quarry at Mansfield, Mansfield Art Gallery. *Work repro.:* in Apollo, Arts Review and greeting cards. *Address:* Broadlands, Grasmere Cl., Guildford. *Signs work:* see appendix.

COOKSON, Delan, F.S.D-C., Gold Medal (Vallauris, 1974), Churchill Fellow (1966); lecturer in ceramics; in charge of ceramics dept., High Wycombe College of Technology and Art; licentiateship secretary of Soc. of Designer-Craftsmen; *b* Torquay, 13 Sept., 1937; *s* of W. R. Cookson; *m* Judith; two *s. Educ.:* Bournemouth School; *studied art* at at Bournemouth College of Art, Central School of Arts and Crafts. *Exhib.:* Oxford Gallery, British Crafts Centre, Craftsman Potters Assoc., Design Centre, Midland Group Gallery; one-man show: Salix, Windsor. *Work repro.:* Ceramic Review, Decorative Art in Modern Interiors. *Address:* 5 Mole Run, High Wycombe, Bucks. HP13 5JJ. *Club:* International Academy of Ceramics.

COOLIDGE, John, A.B. (Harvard University, 1935), Ph.D. (New York University, 1948); director, Fogg Art Museum (1948-68); Prof. of Fine Arts, Harvard University (1955–); *b* Cambridge, Mass., 16 Dec., 1913; *s* of Julian Lowell Coolidge, Prof. of Maths., Harvard University; *m* Mary Welch Coolidge; one *d. Educ.:* Groton School, Harvard and New York Universities. *Publication:* Mill and Mansion (Columbia University Press, 1943). *Address:* Fogg Art Museum, Quincy St. and Broadway, Cambridge, Mass.

COOPER, Emmanuel; potter in stoneware, clay; visiting lecturer (ceramics), Middlesex Polytechnic (Hornsey College of Art); *b* Derbyshire, 12 Dec., 1940. *Educ.:* Tupton Hall Grammar School, Derbyshire. *Exhib.:* British Crafts Centre, London, many other one-man and mixed exhbns. here and abroad. *Work in permanent collection:* V. & A. *Publications:* A Handbook of Pottery, A History of

Pottery (Longman); Taking up Pottery (Arthur Barker); New Ceramics (with E. Lewenstein); Pottery (Macdonalds), co-editor with Eileen Lewenstein of Ceramic Review. *Address:* 38 Chalcot Rd., London NW1. *Signs work:* see appendix.

COOPER, Francis Glanville, M.S.I.A., F.I.A.L., Nat. Dip. Pottery (1949); artist in water-colour and pottery (slipware and stoneware); lecturer in Pottery, Sheffield College of Art, Maidstone College of Art (1949), Southend School of Art (1949-52); *b* Portsmouth, 10 Feb., 1918; *s* of Arthur Richard Cooper. *Educ.:* Francis Avenue Senior School; *studied art* at Kingston School of Art, Burslem School of Art, Woolwich Polytechnic. *Exhib.:* London Arts and Crafts Exhbn. Soc., Manchester, Red Rose Guild of Craftsmen, Design Centre. *Work in permanent collections:* Exhibits at Craft Centre of Gt. Britain; London County Council; Royal Academy Volksmuseum, Holland; Wakefield City Art Gallery. *Publications:* in Future, S.I.A. Journal *Address:* 15 Glentilt Rd., Sheffield, 7. *Signs work:* see appendix.

COOPER, John Hubert, B.A., R.D.S., F.R.S.A., Oxford University Sec. Teachers Art Cert., M. of Ed. Cert. in Industrial Design; Mem., of the College of Craft Education; artist in water-colour and oil; Adult Education Art Tutor; Head of Art Dept., Gosport County Grammar School and Bay House School, Gosport (1936-75); *b* Pemberton, Wigan, 15 Aug., 1912; *s* of Thomas Cooper; *m* Josephine Masterman; two *s*. *Educ.:* Wigan Grammar School, Liverpool University Dept. of Educ. and Open University; *studied art* at Wigan School of Art. Designer for acid etched windows for Council Chamber, Gosport Town Hall. *Exhib.:* Paris Salon, Lancashire Spring Exhbn., British Water-colour Soc., Hampshire Artists Exhbn., Wessex Artists Exhbn. *Address:* 53 Jellicoe Ave., Alverstoke, Hants. *Signs work:* see appendix.

COOPER, Josephine Mary, S.M. (1974), U.A. (1975) for miniatures, Silver Medallist, Paris Salon (1974); artist in oil and water-colour; *b* Brighton, 8 Aug., 1932; *d* of Everard Frisby; *m* Tom Cooper; one *s*, one *d*. *Studied art* at St. Albans School of Art under Kathleen Pargiter; Mid-Herts. College of Further Education under Kenneth Haw. *Exhib.:* R.M.S., R.I., S.G.A., U.A., S.M.; one-man shows: St. Albans, Gordon Maynard Gallery, Welwyn Garden City. *Address:* 27 Parkfields, Welwyn Garden City, Herts. *Clubs:* Welwyn Garden City Art, Hertford Art Soc. *Signs work:* "J. M. Cooper."

COOPER, Rosamund Le Hunte: see LE HUNTE-COOPER, Rosamund.

COOPER, William Alwin, R.W.A. (1973); housemaster, Sherborne School; self-taught artist in oil and collage; *b* Merthyr Tydfil, 2 June, 1923; *s* of L. H. Cooper, M.B.E.; *m* Dorothy Tustain, G.R.S.M.; one *s*, two *d*. *Educ.:* Westminster School, Corpus Christi College, Cambridge. *Exhib.:* one-man shows: Drian Gallery (1971), Albany Gallery, Cardiff (1972), Hambledon Gallery, Blandford. *Work in permanent collections:* Bryanston School, Staffordshire Educ. Com. *Publication:* illustration in History of Corpus Christi College, Cambridge. *Address:* Westcott House, Sherborne, Dorset. *Signs work:* "Cooper."

COOPER, William Heaton, R.I.; landscape painter; elected R.I., 1953; *b* Coniston, 1903; *m* Ophelia Gordon Bell, sculptor; two *s*, two *d*. *Educ.:* Kelsick School, Ambleside; *studied art* under father, A. Heaton Cooper, and at R.A. Schools (1922-25). *Exhib.:* R.A., R.I., R.B.A., etc., three London exhbns. and several in other cities. *Work repro.:* wrote and illustrated Hills of Lakeland (1938, 1947), Lakeland Portraits (1954), The Tarns of Lakeland (1960, 1970), The Lakes (1966, 1970), illustrated Lakeland Prose and 10 climbing guides; publishes colour prints. *Address:* Studio, Grasmere, Westmorland. *Club:* Fell and Rock Climbing. *Signs work:* "W. Heaton Cooper."

COPELAND, Lawrence Gill, Cranbrook Medal, U.S. State Dept. Purchase Award, Y.S.C. First Prize, National Merit Award, Craftsmen, U.S.A.; designer in metal; assoc. prof., Art Dept., City College of City University of New York; *b* Pittsburgh, Pa., U.S.A., 12 Apr., 1922; *s* of Lloyd D. Copeland, college professor; *m* Mary Cuteri; two *s*, one *d*. *Educ.:* Ohio State Univ., Cranbrook Academy of Art, Univ. of Stockholm, Univ. of Paris; *studied art* at Stockholm (1947-48, Baron Erik Fleming), Paris (1948-49, Emeric Gomery). *Work in private collection:* National Gallery, Washington, D.C. *Address:* 442 Hamilton Pl., Hackensack, N.J., U.S.A.

COPLANS, John; art editor, art critic; *b* London, 24 June, 1920. Editor-at-large, Artforum Magazine (1962-66), associate editor (1966-70, editor 1971–); director, art gallery, University of California, Irvine (1965-68); curator, Pasadena Art Museum (1967-70); organiser of numerous exhbn. and catalogue essays. *Awards:* Guggenheim Fellow (1969), Frank Jewitt Mather (1974), National Endowment Arts Fellow (1975). *Publications:* author: Cezanne water-colours (Ward Ritchie Press, 1967), Serial imagery (N.Y. Graphic, 1968), Andy Warhol (N.Y. Graphic, 1971), Roy Lichtenstein (Praeger, 1972), Ellsworth Kelly (Abrams, 1972), Decisions, Decisions (Norton, 1975); contributor: Artforum, Art News, Art in America, Art International *Address:* c/o Artforum, 667 Madison Ave., New York, N.Y. 10021.

COPNALL, John; painter in acrylics; *b* Slinfold, Sussex, 16 Feb., 1928; *s* of Bainbridge Copnall, sculptor. *Educ.:* Churcher's College; *studied art* at R.A. Schools (1950-55). *Exhib.:* one-man shows: Piccadilly Gallery, Bear Lane Gallery, Oxford, Stone Gallery, Newcastle, I.C.A. (London), Ikon (Birmingham), Sala Vayreda (Barcelona), Wolfgang Gurlitt (Munich), Boisserée (Cologne), Universa-haus (Nuremberg), Institut für Auslandsbeziehungen (Stuttgart); mixed shows: R.A., Hamilton Gallery, John Moores of Liverpool, A.I.R. shows in Glasgow, Edinburgh, Harlow; Art Spectrum, London, Wildenstein, Camden Art Centre. *Work in permanent collections:* Bristol and York Universities, St. John's College, Oxford. *Official purchases:* Herts, Hull, Leicestershire and W. Riding of Yorkshire Educ. Com.: Nuffield Foundation. *Work repro.:* Studio International, Arts Review. *Address:* 2 Sycamore St., London EC1. *Signs work:* Does not sign on front of paintings, "john copnall" on back of canvas.

COPSON, Horace, N.S.P.S.; Hon mem., Paris Salon (1965); artist in water-colour and designer; *b* Bedford, 19 Jan., 1903; *s* of Joseph John Copson, shoe designer; *m* Phyllis Caroline Elizabeth. *Educ.:* St. Giles' School, Northampton; *studied art* at Northampton Art and Technical School, then privately. *Exhib.:* R.I., R.O.I., R.B.A., R.B.S.A., R.W.S., Paris Salon, London Guildhall, provincial and private galleries; one-man shows were held Feb., 1968, at Northampton Town Art Gallery; May, 1968, at Corby Civic Centre; Aug., 1968, at Herbert Gallery, Coventry; May, 1969, at Halford House, Bourton-on-the-Water; Sept., 1969, at Arts Unlimited, London; Feb., 1970, at Kettering Art Gallery; June, 1970, at Northampton; July, 1971, at Letchworth; 1972-73 at Worcester, Northampton, Grosvenor St., London, Leamington and Tewksbury; Alfred East Gallery, Kettering (1974); Woburn Abbey (1975). *Work in public and private collections:* in England, U.S.A., Canada and New Zealand. *Designs:* several accepted by Council and Industrial Design and at Trienali di Milan o. *Work illustrated:* in Paris Art Journals, La Revue Moderne and Boomerang, and in English newspapers. *Address:* 36 Elmhurst Ave., Northampton. *Clubs:* N.S., R.W.S. (Council mem.), Ridley Art Soc. (Council mem.). *Signs work:* see appendix.

CORDEN, Cyril; sculptor in stone and marble, specializing in architectural carving and lettering; *studied art* at Central School of Arts and Crafts under Alfred

Turner, R.A., and Richard Garbe, R.A. *Address:* 7 Densley Close, Welwyn Garden City, Herts. *Signs work:* "C. Corden."

CORFIELD, Alfred James; artist in water-colour, oil, pastel; designer of textile machinery; lecturer on water-colour; *b* Portsmouth, 17 Sept., 1904; *s* of Alfred Corfield; *m* Olive Mary Vickerstaffe; one *s*, two *d*. *Educ.:* Swindon, Horich and St. Mary Rd. School, Newton Heath, Manchester; *studied art:* mainly self-taught, privately under J. White (1919-21) and E. Benton (1933-34). *Exhib.:* Stockport A.G. (1936 to 1954), Salford A.G. (1953-54), Oldham A.G., Manchester Ballet Club and Arts Club, Saddleworth Art Guild, Colin Jellicoe Gallery (1972), one-man show, Gibbs Bookshop, Manchester, 1956. *Publication:* Random Remarks of a Water-colourist. *Work repro.:* Calendar (1957), J. Chadwick & Co., Manchester. *Address:* 183 Culcheth La., Newton Heath, Manchester. *Clubs:* Stockport Art Guild, Oldham Soc. of Artists, Saddleworth Art Group. *Signs work:* "A. J. Corfield" with date.

CORFIELD, Charles Collingwood, A.R.C.A. (1933); travelling scholarship (1934); portrait painter; *s* of T. H. Corfield; *m*. *Educ.:* Leeds College of Art; R.C.A.; Académie des Beaux Arts; Louvre; Prado. *Exhib.:* R.S.P.P. *Address:* Old Oast Cottage, Selling, nr. Faversham, Kent. *Club:* Chelsea Arts. *Signs work:* "Colin Corfield."

CORISH, Joseph R.; specializing in marine painting; graduated from Boston University (1932); awarded an Adjunct in Arts Degree from Harvard (1938); Art Director, Castle Hill Foundation (1958-62); artist in residence, U.S. First Naval District; guest lecturer at Harvard and at various colleges, museums and art associations; did paintings for Boston University's Case Memorial Center; *b* Somerville, Mass., 9 Apr., 1909; *s* of John W. and Sarah A. Corish; *m* Cecelia; one *d*. *Exhib.:* one-man shows: Harvard, Yale, Boston University, Connecticut, University of Arkansas and other colleges; Boston Museum of Fine Arts; Harvard's Busch Reisinger Museum; Jasper Rand Museum; Bergen (Norway) Stofartsmuseum; Barcelona (Spain) Museum; Bertrand Russell Centennial Exhibition, London (England); Etajima Museum (Japan); the XX Olympic Art Exhibition "Man and the Sea", Kiel (Germany); Holyoke (Massachusetts); Columbus (Ohio); Newburyport and Birmingham (Alabama) Museum of Art; United States Naval Academy Museum; group shows: American Artists Professional League Grand National Exhibition; Jordan Exhibition Contemporary New England Artists; Paris Salon; R.S.M.A.; and other museums and exhibitions where they have won several awards. *Work in permanent collections:* British, German, Japanese, American, Portuguese, and Spanish Navies, Boston University, Connecticut College, U.S. Naval Academy Museum of Art, London (England) Museum, the U.S. Naval War College, court houses, State Capitols, foreign embassies, banks and other public and private institutions on three continents and in ward rooms of naval ships on the seven seas. *Work repro.:* full colour magazine covers for the Naval War College Review and nationally circulated magazines. *Address:* 421 Highland Ave., Somerville, Mass., U.S.A. *Signs work:* "CORISH."

CORLEY, John Elmer, Dip.A.D. Fine Art (Cant.) 1973; painter in acrylics on canvas, glass, staining, enamelling, lithography; working on restoration of stained-glass windows at Canterbury Cathedral; *b* Peterborough, 24 June, 1950; *s* of Martin Corley, engineer. *Educ.:* St. John Fisher R.C. Sec. Mod., Peterborough; Salvatorian College, Chester; *studied art* at Northampton School of Art (1968-70) under Peter Pretsell, Frank Cryer and Henry Bird; Canterbury College of Art (1970-73) under Thomas Watt, Stass Paraskos, Noel Forster, Geoffrey Rigden. *Exhib.:* Northampton A.G. (1974), New Metropole Gallery, Folkestone (1973).

Address: Lower Venson Farm, Tilmanstone, Deal, Kent CT14 0JY. *Signs work:* "J. E. Corley."

CORNELL, David, F.R.S.A., A.R.B.S., mem. Society of Portrait Sculptors (1970); sculptor and engraver of medals, portrait sculpture, bas relief, equestrian painter; Director of Art, John Pinches, London; *b* Enfield, 18 Sept., 1935; *s* of Henry Arthur Cornell, engineer; *m* Marie Anne; two *s*. *Educ.:* Essendene School, London; *studied art* at Central School of Art (1951-56) under F. Fryer, Friend, Kavanagh; Harrow School of Art (1959) under P. Turner; Academy of Fine Art, University of Pennsylvania (1968) under Prof. R. B. Hale; Royal Mint, London. *Work in permanent collection:* Franklin Centre, U.S.A. *Address:* The White Cottage, 47 Heathfield Rd., Keston, Kent. *Signs work:* "CORNELL."

CORNWELL, Arthur Bruce, S.G.A. dip. (1947); illustrator in gouache, oil, water-colour, indian ink; *b* Vancouver, B.C., 11 Feb., 1920; *s* of Arthur Redfern Cornwell; *m* Peggy Brenda Huggins; one *s*. *Educ.:* Palms Public School, and Page Military Academy, California; *studied art* at Art Centre School, Los Angeles, Regent St. Polytechnic, London, Heatherly's, London, Academy Julien, Paris. *Exhib.:* R.A., N.E.A.C., S.M.A., S.G.A., Sunderland Gallery, Bolton Gallery. *Work in permanent collection:* Diploma Gallery, R.A. *Official purchase:* Stott Bequest, R.A., The Coaster. *Work repro.:* Yachting Monthly, Macmillan teach-visuals. *Publications:* The Ship's Crew. *Address:* Westways, 132 Eastcote Rd., Ruislip, Middx. *Signs work:* see appendix.

CORTLANDT, Lyn, F.I.A.L., F.R.S.A.; artist; *b* New York. *Studied art* at Los Angeles, California: Chouinard and Jepson Art Institutes; New York: Arts Students' League, Pratt Inst., Columbia University, Hans Hofmann School, China Inst., followed by private instruction. *Exhib.:* internationally, including Belgium, France, Greece, Holland, Italy, Japan, Portugal, South America, Switzerland, U.S.A., etc. *Work in permanent collections:* Musée National d'Art Moderne, Paris; Stedelijk Museum, Amsterdam; Metropolitan Museum, Museum of Fine Arts, Boston; Fogg Museum; Brooklyn Museum; Baltimore Museum; Cincinnati Art Museum, Springfield Museum of Fine Arts, etc. *Address:* 1070 Park Ave., New York, 10028. *Signs work:* see appendix.

COSMAN, Milein, Slade Diploma Fine Art; painter, graphic artist; *b* Gotha; *d* of Hugo Cosmann; *m* Hans Keller. *Educ.:* Düsseldorf; International School, Geneva; *studied art* at Slade School. *Exhib.:* Berkeley Galleries, Matthiesen, Molton Gallery, City of London Festival, Camden Arts Centre, Everyman Cinema; mixed shows: Roland, Browse & Delbanco, A.I.A., Hampstead Artists Council, etc. *Books:* Musical Sketchbook (Bruno Cassirer, Faber & Faber, 1957), Stravinsky at Rehearsal (Dobson, 1962), Strawinsky Dirigiert (Ullstein, 1962). *Book illustrations:* Penguin Music Magazine, A Composer's Eleven (Cardus, Cape), etc. *Work in numerous private collections and repro.:* Radio Times, Sunday Times, Observer, The Times, Sunday Telegraph, national and foreign press, art and musical magazines. Series of Educational Programmes on Drawing for ITV. *Address:* 3 Frognal Gdns., Hampstead, London NW3. *Clubs:* A.I.A., Hampstead Artists Council.

COSTALL, Brian, N.D.D. (Painting and Etching, 1964), M.Art R.C.A. (1967); visiting art teacher; artist in oil and acrylic on canvas and board, also etching; *b* London, 3 Oct., 1943; *s* of Sidney A. Costall; *m* Barbara Loftus. *Educ.:* Percy School; *studied art* at Harrow School of Art (1959-64), R.C.A. (1964-67) under Peter Blake, Carel Weight, R.A. *Address:* c/o The Trafford Gallery, 119 Mount St., London W1Y 5HB. *Signs work:* "B. S. Costall."

COTTERILL, Allan, A.T.D. (1938); painter, sculptor and teacher; art master,

Kent College, Canterbury, first asst., Carmarthen School of Art, lecturer, Cardiff College of Art; *b* Southport, Lancs., 23 Mar., 1913; *s* of Arthur A. Cotterill; *m* Edna Jane Oakes; one *d. Educ.:* King George V School, Southport; *studied art* at School of Art, Southport; Liverpool College of Art; L.C.C. Central School of Art and Crafts. *Exhib.:* London and provinces. *Address:* The White House, Colebrook St., Winchester. *Signs work:* "Allan Cotterill."

COULOURIS, Mary Louise, A.R.E. (1973); Dip. A.D. (London) (1961); Post Grad. Scholarship, Slade School (1962); French Government Scholarship (1963); Mem. Printmakers Council; artist and printmaker; *b* New York, 17 July, 1939; *d* of George Alexander Coulouris, actor; *m* Gordon Wallace; one *s*, one *d. Educ.:* Parliament Hill School; *studied art* at Slade School, London University (1958-62) under Antony Gross; Ecole des Beaux Arts, Paris (1963-64); Atelier 17, Paris (1963-64) under William Hayter. *Exhib.:* R.A. (1966, 1971, 1972, 1973); one-man shows: London, Oxford, Paris. *Work in permanent collections:* Bibliotheque Nationale, Paris, New York Public Library, Nuffield Trust, Trinity College, Oxford. *Address:* 4 Chalcot Sq., London NW1. *Signs work:* "Mary Louise Coulouris."

COURTNEY, Frederic E., F.S.A.E., A.T.D.; artist in wood engraving, water-colour; Principal, College of Art, Bournemouth, to 1966; Principal, Mansfield (1933-37), Northampton (1937-47); *b* Menston-in-Wharfedale, 25 Mar., 1901; *s* of W. F. Courtney; *m* Marjorie Wormald (decd.); Elsa Cleonice Rose; one *s. Educ.:* Aireborough Grammar School; *studied art* at Leeds College of Art under H. H. Holden, H. E. Simpson, Owen Jennings (1923-28). *Exhib.:* R.A., Leeds, Liverpool, etc. *Work in permanent collections:* Leeds, Northampton, Bournemouth. *Work repro.:* Puffin Picture Book (lithography). *Address:* High Hedges, Studland, Dorset. *Club:* Bournemouth Constitutional. *Signs work:* "Frederic E. Courtney."

COUTTS-SMITH, Kenneth; painter and critic; *b* 24 Sept., 1929. *Educ.:* St. Paul's and Shoreham Grammar School; *studied art* at at Heatherleys. *Exhib.:* nine one-man exhibitions since 1952, most recent at New Vision Centre, London. Group exhibitions in public and commercial galleries in England, France, Germany, Scandinavia, Italy, U.S.A., etc. *Work in permanent collections:* Derbyshire Education Committee; School Loans Collection, Leeds City Art Gallery; Isaac Delgado Museum and Art Gallery, New Orleans; Towner Art Gallery, Eastbourne; Museum of Modern Art, Skopje. *Publications:* art criticism in various periodicals; The Dream of Icarus (Hutchinson); Dada (Studio Vista). Member of A.I.C.A. *Address:* 4 Seymour Pl., London W1. *Signs work:* "Coutts-Smith."

COUTU, Jack, A.R.E., A.R.C.A.; printmaker and sculptor; etching and engraving on copper, miniature carving in boxwood and ivory; lecturer in print-making, West Surrey College of Art and Design; *b* Farnham, Surrey, 1924; *s* of Herbert Coutu. *Educ.:* Farnham Grammar School; *studied art* at Farnham School of Art (1947-51), R.C.A. (1951-54). *Work in permanent collections:* King Gustave of Sweden, Museum of Fine Art, Boston, Mass., Bradford City Art Gallery, V. & A., Arts Council of Great Britain. *Address:* Bramblings, 22 Quennels Hill, Wrecclesham, Farnham, Surrey. *Signs work:* "Coutu" and see appendix.

COUVE DE MURVILLE-DESENNE, Lucie-Renée, F.I.L., F.I.A.L.; portrait, flower and marine painter, oil; *b* Majunga, Madagascar, 15 Apr., 1920; *d* of J. L. E. Couve de Murville, artist and engineer; *m* F. H. Desenne; one *s*, one *d. Educ.:* Paris; *studied art* in Paris as private pupil of E. Ruff. *Exhib.:* Wakefield, Bradford, London, R.W.A.; one-man show: R.W.A. (1975). *Address:* 12 Leigh Rd., Clifton,

Bristol 8. *Clubs:* Fellow of the Institute of Linguists, Fellow of the International Institute of Arts and Letters, mem. Friends of the Bristol Art Gallery, Hon. Pres. Bristol French Circle, Presidente UF de G.B. (Sud-ouest). Chevalier de l'Ordre des Palmes Academiques. *Signs work:* see appendix.

COVENTRY, Frederick Halford; mural painter, glass, metal, etc.; *s* of Harry Coventry; *m*; one *s*, one *d*, one *step-d. Educ.:* Julian Ashton Art School, Sydney, and Grosvenor School of Art. *Exhib.:* R.A.; N.Z. Hse., London; C.O.I.D.; Macquarie Gallery, Sydney; Soc. of Artists, Sydney; Imperial Inst., London; N.Z. Academy. *Official purchases:* B.M.; Imperial War Museum; Campion Hall, Oxford; National Gallery, N.S.W.; N.Z. Govt.; Plymouth Guildhall; Queensland Govt.; Methodist Church, Plymouth; C.O.I. *Address:* 49 Brunswick Gdns., London W8. *Club:* Chelsea Arts. *Signs work:* "F. H. COVENTRY" (block caps).

COVERLEY-PRICE, Victor, M.A. (Cantab.), F.R.G.S.; self-taught artist in oil and water-colour; writer; Mem. H.M. Diplomatic Service (1925-46); *b* Winchester, 31 Jan., 1901; *s* of Dr. A. E. Price (decd.); *m* Mary Cecilia Galpin. *Educ.:* Harrow and Pembroke College, Cambridge. *Exhib.:* R.A., R.B.A., R.I., R.P., United Soc. of Artists, etc.; London and provincial galleries; one-man shows in London and provinces, Cairo, Ottawa and Mexico City. *Work repro.:* in The Sphere, The Artist, etc. *Publication:* An Artist Among Mountains (Robert Hale, Ltd.), and illustrated books for children (O.U.P.). *Address:* Ashcroft, Baunton La., Cirencester, Glos. GL7 2LN. *Signs work:* "V. Coverley-Price."

COWERN, Raymond Teague, R.A. (1968), A.R.A. (1957), R.W.S., R.E., A.R.C.A. (London), R.W.A.; painter, etcher, draughtsman, illustrator; Assoc. Director and Dean of Faculty of Art and Design, Brighton Polytechnic; *b* 12 July, 1913; *s* of George Dent Cowern and Elsie Ellen Teague; *m* Margaret Jean Trotman; one *s*, two *d. Educ.:* King Edwards Grammar School; *studied art* at Central School of Art, Birmingham, R.C.A. (1931-35), British School at Rome (1937-39). *Work in permanent collections:* B.M., Glasgow, Liverpool, Birmingham, Oxford, Cambridge, Bristol and museums abroad. *Address:* Church Lodge, Church Hill, Patcham, Brighton BN1 8YE. *Signs work:* "R. T. Cowern."

COX, Gertrude Florence Mary; water-colour and oil painter, etcher; *d* of William Cox, of Exeter. *Educ.:* The Bishop Blackall School, Exeter; Exeter University; under R. Kirkland Jamieson, R.B.A. *Exhib.:* R.I., R.O.I., R.B.A., Paris Salon, R.W.A., Britain in Water-colour (1970). *Official purchase:* Exeter from Exwick (etching) by Municipal Art Gallery, Exeter. *Address:* 13 Queen's Cres., Exeter. *Signs work:* "G. F. M. Cox."

COX, Hebe; City and Guilds London Advanced Embroidery Exam.; Council mem., Soc. Designer Craftsmen; embroiderer and designer; *b* Cheshire; *m* G. R. W. Portway; one *s. Educ.:* French convent; *studied art* at Central School of Arts and Crafts, London. *Work in many public and private collections* in England and Australia. Has had two one-man shows in London and exhibited in Italy, United States of America, and Australia. *Publications:* Simple Embroidery Design, Fifteen Craftsmen on Their Crafts (part author), Embroidery Technique and Design, Canvas Embroidery. *Address:* Cricketers, Forward Green, Stowmarket, Suffolk. *Signs work:* with a swan.

COX, Sir Trenchard, C.B.E., D.Litt., M.A., F.S.A., F.M.A., Chevalier de la Légion d'Honneur; formerly director, V. & A. Museum, London; *b* 31 July, 1905; *s* of the late William Pallet Cox; *m* Mary Desirée Anderson (*d.* 1973). *Educ.:* Eton and King's College, Cambridge. *Publications:* The National Gallery, a Room-to-Room Guide (1930); Jehan Foucquet, Native of Tours (1931); part editor of Catalogue to Exhbn. of French Art at Burlington Hse. (1932); The Renaissance in

Europe (1933); A General Guide to the Wallace Collection (1933); A Short Illustrated History of the Wallace Collection and its Founders (1936); David Cox (1948); Peter Bruegel (1951); Pictures: a Handbook for Curators (1956). *Address:* 33 Queen's Gate Gdns., London SW7. *Clubs:* Athenæum, Beefsteak.

COXON, Raymond James, A.R.C.A.; painter, lithographer and writer; officially commissioned war artist; mem., London Group; *b* Hanley (Stoke-on-Trent), 18 Aug., 1896; *m* Edna Ginesi. *Educ.:* Leek High School, R.C.A. *Exhib.:* London, Leicester Galleries, International Exhbn. Brussels, Pittsburgh, New York, Tokio. *Official purchases:* B.M., V. & A., Tate, Chantrey Bequest, Courtauld Inst., National Gallery of Wales, Univ. of South Tennessee, Columbia Museum, S. Carolina, and principal provincial public galleries. *Publications:* Art (Pitman, 1932); Critic for World of Art Illustrated (1938). *Addresses:* 10 Hammersmith Terr., London W6, and Mill Studio, Rowfant, Sussex. *Signs work:* "R. COXON."

CRABBE, Richard Markham, A.R.C.A. (1951), F.R.S.A.; painter; senior lecturer in painting, Portsmouth Polytechnic dept. of Fine Art; exchange teacher, Eastern Illinois University (1975); *b* Horley, Surrey, 1927; *s* of Sidney Charles Crabbe; *m* Peggy Crabbe; three children. *Studied art* at Croydon School of Art and Royal College of Art. *Exhib.:* R.A. London Group and other mixed shows, 38 × 11 Manchester City Art Gallery (1965); one-man show: Hiscock Gallery (1971), Openfield (1973), City Art Project (1974). *Work in permanent collections:* Portsmouth Museum, Staffordshire Educ. Com., Wigan Educ. Com. and private collections. *Address:* 22 Andover Rd., Southsea. Rarely signs work.

CRAMP, Jonathan David, A.T.D., A.R.W.S., F.R.S.A.; painter; Head of Art Dept., Fishguard C.S. School; *b* Ninfield, Sussex, 29 Jan., 1930; *s* of David Cramp; *m* Elizabeth (painter); one *d*. *Educ.:* Huish Grammar School, Taunton, Bexhill Grammar School; *studied art* at Hastings School of Art (1949-51) (Vincent Lines). *Work in permanent collections:* Welsh Arts Council, Contemporary Art Society for Wales, Pembrokeshire County Museum, Schools Service, National Museum of Wales, Cartrefle and Caerleon Colleges of Education, various education authorities. *Address:* Heatherdene, Windy-Hall, Fishguard, Pembs. *Signs work:* see appendix.

CRAMPTON, Seán, M.C. (1943), G.M. (1944), A.R.B.S. (1953), F.R.B.S. (1965), P.R.B.S. (1966-71); sculptor, silversmith, mosaicist; Professeur de sculpture, Anglo-French Art Centre (1946-50); *b* Manchester, 15 Mar., 1918; *s* of Joshua Crampton, L.R.I.B.A.; *m;* five children. *Studied art* at Vittoria Junior School of Art, and Central School of Art, Birmingham; Paris. *Exhib.:* R.A., R.S.A., London Gallery, Leicester Gallery, Ashley Gallery, R.I. and R.I.B.A. Galleries, S.P.S., etc. *Works now handled* by Alwin Gallery, 9-10 Grafton St. W1X 4DA. *Work repro.:* Studio International, Sculpture International, Architectural Review, Builder, Liturgical Arts (N.Y.), Sphere, Art News, etc. *Address:* The Coach House, The Butts, Brentford, Middx. *Club:* Chelsea Arts. *Signs work:* "Seán Crampton" or "SC" within circle.

CRANE, Doris Martha Alice (Miss), M.B.E., R.M.S. (1958); sculptor in wood and ivory; *b* Clapham SW4, 20 Feb., 1911; *d* of Sydney Charles Crane. *Educ.:* Belmont House Private School, Clapham, St. George's College, Red Lion Sq., London; *studied art* with late W. Everatt Gray, A.R.B.S. *Exhib.:* R.A., R.S.A. and Paris Salon. *Address:* 6 Upperfield Drive, Old Felixstowe, Suffolk. *Signs work:* see appendix.

CRAWFORD, Joan Margaret Caldwell: see FAITHFULL, Joan Margaret Caldwell.

CRAWLEY, James, M.A., F.M.A.; ex-director, Public Art Gallery, Museum and Libraries, Sunderland (1939-60). *Educ.:* St. Cuthbert's Grammar School, Newcastle-on-Tyne. *Address:* 5 Elwin Terr., Sunderland.

CRAWSHAW, Alwyn; artist in acrylic, water-colour and oil; director (partner), Russell Artists Merchandising Ltd., Kingston-upon-Thames, Surrey; lecturer and demonstrator on acrylic painting for George Rowney & Co., Ltd. Bracknell, Berks; *b* Mirfield, Yorks., 20 Sept., 1934; *s* of Fred Crawshaw; *m* June Crawshaw; one *s,* two *d. Educ.:* Hastings Grammar School for Boys; *studied art* at Hastings School of Art (1949-1951) under Vincent Lines. *Exhib.:* one-man shows: Harrods, St. Paul's Gallery, London, Marina Gallery, Weybridge, Barclay A.G., Chester, Guildford Galleries, Guildford. *Work sold* in galleries in Europe, Australia and Canada. *Publications:* Painting with Acrylic Colours (George Rowney & Co., Ltd.) now in German, Italian and Finnish. *Address:* Bembridge, Hook Heath Ave., Hook Heath, Woking, Surrey. *Signs work:* "Alwyn Crawshaw."

CRAXTON, John; artist in oil, tempera, conté crayon; *b* London, 3 Oct., 1922; *s* of Harold Craxton, O.B.E., pianist, composer, teacher. *Educ.:* various private schools; *studied art* at Goldsmiths' College and Academie Julian. *Exhib.:* Leicester Galleries, London Gallery, Galerie Gasser, Zürich, British Council, Athens, Retrospective, Whitechapel (1967). *Work in permanent collections:* Tate Gallery, City Art Gallery, Bristol, Manchester and Birmingham A.G., Melbourne A.G., British Council, Arts Council, Victoria and Albert Museum, Ministry of Works. *Work repro.:* John Craxton, by Geoffrey Grigson, Horizon (1948), The Poet's Eye (1944: 16 lithographs), sets and costumes for Royal Ballet, Daphnis et Chlöe (1951), Apollo (1966). *Addresses:* 14 Kidderpore Ave., London NW3, and Moschon 1, Canea, Crete. *Signs work:* "Craxton."

CREE, Alexander, D.A.(Edin.) 1950; art teacher in oil, pastel and water-colour; Head of Art Dept., Dunbar Grammar School; *b* 24 Feb., 1929; *s* of John Cree. *Educ.:* Dunfermline High School; *studied art* at Edinburgh College of Art (1946-52) under Sir William Gillies, R.S.A., Adam Bruce Thomson, R.S.A. *Exhib.:* Richard Demarco Gallery (1968, 1976), Shed 50 (1974), Loomshop Gallery (1969), Scottish Lyceum Club (1957). *Work in permanent collections:* Scottish Arts Council, Nuffield Foundation. *Address:* Braeheads Loan, E. Linton, E. Lothian, Scotland. *Signs work:* "A. Cree."

CREFFIELD, Dennis; artist in oil and charcoal; mem. Borough and London Groups; *b* London, 29 Jan., 1931; *s* of Donald Creffield. *Educ.:* Colfes Grammar School; *studied art* at Borough Polytechnic (1948-51), Slade School (1957-61); Gregory Fellow in Painting at the University of Leeds (1964-67). *Exhib.:* Arcade Gallery; Brasenose and Keble Colleges, Oxford; Gummeson's Gallery, Stockholm; Grabowski Gallery; A.I.A. Gallery; Parsons Gallery; Heffer's Gallery, Cambridge; London Group; Young Contemporaries; Arts Council Travelling Exhibition, Six Young Painters (1961); Towner Art Gallery, Eastbourne (Resolution 42); Park Sq. Gallery, Leeds; Gardner Arts Centre, University of Sussex. *Address:* 45 Marine Parade, Brighton. *Signs work:* "D. Creffield."

CROCKER, Barbara; painter and illustrator in oil, water-colour, lithography; *b* London, 4 Feb., 1910; *d* of George Ashcombe Crocker; *m* Eric Whelpton. *Educ.:* Putney High School; *studied art* at the Slade School (1927-30), France and Italy. *Work repro.:* illustrations for L'Air de Londres, by Jean Queval (Paris), Collins Pocket Guide Series, wall decorations for London offices. *Publications:* Barbara Whelpton, The Florentine Portrait (trans. from Jean Alazand), French Tapestry (trans. from Jean Lurçat), Myths and Legends Series (trans. from French, Burke), Unknown Ireland (Johnson), Unknown Austria, 3 vols. (Johnson), Art Appreciation Made Simple (W. H. Allen); drawings for national press and magazines. *Address:* West Watch, Traders' Passage, Rye, Sussex. *Signs work:* "B. Crocker."

CROFT, Ivor John, M.A. (Oxon. and Lond.); painter in oil and civil servant; head of research unit, Home Office; *b* 6 Jan., 1923; *s* of Oswald Croft. *Educ.:* Westminster School; Christ Church, Oxford; Institute of Education, University of London; London School of Economics and Political Science. *Exhib.:* group shows: Piccadilly Gallery (1958); John Whibley Gallery (1963); Camden Arts Centre (Survey of Abstract Painters, 1967); Bear Lane Gallery, Oxford (1968); John Player Open Exhbn. (1968, 1969); Covent Garden Gallery (Critical Discoveries, 1973); one-man shows: Gardner Centre for the Arts, University of Sussex (1970); University of Warwick (1971). *Work repro.:* Art and Artists. *Address:* 4A Phillimore Ct., London W8. *Clubs:* Athenæum, Reform. *Signs work:* "John Croft."

CROFT, Richard John, N.D.D., A.T.C., Royal Ulster Academician; artist in oil, perspex constructions and kinetics; head of Art Dept., Annadale Grammar School, Belfast; *b* London, 1935. *Exhib.:* Young Contemporaries, London and Dublin, Irish Exhibition of Living Art (Dublin, 1962-70), N.I. Arts Council Open Painting Exhibition; one-man shows: Arts Council of N. Ireland (1961, 1966, 1970), Oxford University, Queen's University, Belfast. *Work in permanent collections:* N.I. Arts Council and various public and private collections in Ireland, England, Scotland and America. *Address:* 44 Casaeldona Pk., Belfast BT6 9RB, N. Ireland. *Signs work:* see appendix.

CROFT-MURRAY, Edward, C.B.E., F.S.A. (1940); late keeper, Dept. of Prints and Drawings, British Museum; *b* Chichester, 1 Sept., 1907; *s* of Bernard Croft-Murray; *m* Jill Whitford-Hawkey. *Educ.:* Lancing College and Magdalen College, Oxford. *Publications:* (with Paul Hulton) Catalogue of British Drawings in B.M., Vol. I, 1961; Decorative Painting in England, 1537-1837, Vol. I, 1962, Vol. II, 1970; also papers in Walpole Soc., Burlington Magazine and Country Life. *Addresses:* 4 Maids of Honour Row, Richmond Green, Surrey; Croft Castle, Herefordshire. *Clubs:* Athenæum and Beefsteak.

CRONYN, Hugh Verschoyle, G.M., F.R.S.A.; artist in oil, water-colour, lithography, mural painter, director of art, A.A. School of Architecture (1946-49); painting instructor, Colchester School of Art since 1949; Lt.-Cdr. R.N.V.R. (1939-45); *b* Vancouver, B.C., Canada; *s* of V. F. Cronyn; *m* Jean Harris, M.A.; two *d*. *Educ.:* Ridley College; *studied art* at Ontario College of Art; Art Students' League, New York; American School of Fine Arts, Fontainebleau; various Paris academies. *One-man exhbns.:* London, Colchester, Montreal, Toronto, Victoria. *Work in permanent collections:* England, Sweden, Canada, and U.S.A. *Address:* Studio 3, St. Peter's Wharf, Hammersmith Terr., London W6.

CROSBY, Theo, F.R.I.B.A. (1968), F.S.I.A. (1962); architect, author and sculptor; partner, Pentagram Design Partnership; *b* Mafeking, S. Africa, 3 Apr., 1925; *s* of Nicholas John Crosby; *m* Anne Buchanan; one *s*, one *d*. *Educ.:* University of Witwatersrand, Johannesburg; *studied art* at Sir John Cass School (1947), Central School (1950-54), St. Martin's School (1956-58). *Publications:* Architecture: City Sense (1965); The Necessary Monument (1970); How to play the Environment Game (1973); edited: This is Tomorrow (1956), Le Corbusier (1959), The Architecture of Technology (1961), five issues of Uppercase; three issues of Living Arts with John Bodley. *Address:* 10 Rutland Grove, London W6.

CROSS, Nicolette Elizabeth, Mem. Utd. Soc. Artists (1952); artist in oil, water-colour, tempera; *b* London, 1 Feb., 1930; *d* of Michael Cross, company director; *m* G. B. McIntosh. *Educ.:* Hampden House and Burgess Hill P.N.E.U.

School; *studied art* at Byam Shaw School of Drawing and Painting under Patrick Phillips, Brian Thomas and Peter Greenham (1947-52). *Exhib.:* Utd. Soc., R.B.A., R.W.A., N.S., N.E.A.C., S.G.A., and Brit. Council Black Hall (Oxford), etc. *Address:* 6975 Adera St., Vancouver, B.C., Canada. *Signs work:* "Nicolette Cross" and date.

CROSS, Roy, S.A.A. (1960); industrial and fine artist, author and marine painter in gouache and oils; *b* London, 1924; *m* Rita May; one *s*. *Exhib.:* Malcolm Henderson Gallery (1973). *Past commissions* for many industrial concerns including B.E.A., Hunting Group, B.A.C., London Transport, Shell, Brooke Bond. *Publications:* Jet Aircraft of the World, Military Aircraft 1939-45, Great Planes and their Pilots, Spitfire, etc. *Address:* Squirrels, Hither Chantlers, Langton Green, Tunbridge Wells, Kent TN3 0BJ. *Signs work:* "Roy Cross."

CROSSLEY, Bob; painter in oil, gouache, printmaker; *b* Northwich, 1912; *s* of Edwin Crossley, engineer; *m* Marjorie; one *s*, two *d*. *Educ.:* Heybrook School, Rochdale; *studied art:* largely self-taught. *Exhib.:* 8 one-man shows: Crane Gallery, Manchester (1959), Reid Gallery, London (1960, 1964), Gallery Bique, Madrid (1965), Reid, Guildford (1966), Curwen Gallery, London (1972), Singers Fridden Division, Stevenage (1972), John Player & Sons, Nottingham (1972); group shows: Rochdale, Manchester, Preston, Bury, St. Ives, Newlyn, Bristol, London, Spotorno, Turin, Milan, Catania, Belfast. *Work in permanent collections:* Contemporary Art Society purchase (1964), Rochdale Art Gallery, Municipal Art Gallery, Durban, S.A., Winnipeg Art Gallery, Canada, College of Advanced Education, Port Elizabeth, S.A., Summerfield College, Kidderminster, Hereford Art Gallery. *Work repro.:* in art journals and newspapers. *Addresses:* 3 Spencer Walk, Putney, London SW15; No. 7, Porthmeor Studios, St. Ives, Cornwall. *Clubs:* Manchester Academy, Penwith Soc. of Arts. *Signs work:* "Bob Crossley."

CROSSLEY, Harold; sculptor, painter in oils and water-colour and etcher; *b* Thornton, Bradford, Yorks., 10 Apr., 1900; *s* of Jesse Crossley. *Educ.:* Thornton National School; *studied art* at Bradford Art School under Prof. Stephenson (1915-19). *Exhib.:* Cartwright Memorial Hall, Bradford, Preston A.G., Walker A.G., Liverpool, Manchester A.G. *Work repro.:* Medici Soc. Ltd. *Address:* 87 Links Rd., Knott-End-on-Sea, Lancs. *Signs work:* "Harold Crossley."

CROWCROFT, Ronald Bryan; artist in oil; writer; *b* Hastings, 7 Apr., 1953; *s* of George Henry Ronald Crowcroft. *Educ.:* St. Michael's, Nicosia, Cyprus; St. John's Episkopi, Cyprus; Chichester High School, Sussex; *studied art* at W. Sussex College of Design, Worthing (1972-73) under Anthony Cooke; Leeds Polytechnic (1973-) under Jeff Nuttall, Glynn Williams, Ken Rowatt, Miles McCalinden, Kate Barnard. *Exhib.:* Crossley Hall, Selsey, Sheffield College of Art, Whitworth Spring Exhbn., Leeds University Gallery. *Work in permanent collection:* Leeds City A.G. *Publications:* Instant Herring (writing, poetry and drawings), Table Manners (drawings), Poems and Drawings by . . . *Address:* 56 Woodsley Rd., Leeds 3, Yorks. *Signs work:* "Ron Crowcroft."

CROWTHER, Hugh Melvill; artist in oil, pastel; *b* Newby, nr. Scarborough, Yorks., 25 June, 1914; *s* of Guy Fenwick Crowther, civil engineer; *m* Margaret Steele Wainey. *Educ.:* St. John's, Tutshill, Chepstow; *studied art* at Newport Technical College, Gwent. *Exhib.:* Royal Glasgow Institute of Fine Arts, Cardiff, Newport, Monmouth, Hereford, Gloucester, London. *Work in permanent collection:* Newport Museum, Gwent. *Work repro.:* Chepstow Castle, Village Smithy, Naturalist's Collection, all in La Revue Moderne. *Address:* Meadow End, Tidenham, Chepstow, Gwent. *Clubs:* West Gloucestershire Art Soc., Wye Valley Art Soc., Gloucestershire Soc. of Artists. *Signs work:* see appendix.

CROWTHER, Stephen, A.R.C.A., R.B.A.; mem. Contemporary Portrait Society (1971); artist in oil, charcoal, conté; lecturer in charge of drawing and painting courses, Hartlepool College of Art; *b* Sheffield, 23 Aug., 1922; *s* of Henry Crowther; *m* Sheila Maria Higgins; two *s*, one *d*. *Educ.:* De la Salle College, Sheffield; *studied art* at Sheffield College of Art; Royal Scholarship to Royal College of Art (1941); war service (1941-46); R.C.A. (1946-49). *Exhib.:* R.A., R.B.A., Royal Society of Portrait Painters, Contemporary Portrait Society, Leicester Galleries, Stone Gallery, Newcastle; one-man shows: Gray Art Gallery, Hartlepool; Billingham Art Gallery; Zaydler Gallery, London (1973). *Work in permanent collections:* Gray Art Gallery, Derbyshire and Hartlepool Education Committees. *Work repro.:* in Young Artists of Promise, by Jack Beddington, C.B.E. (Studio, 1957). *Address:* 5 The Cliff, Seaton Carew, Hartlepool TS25 1AB. *Signs work:* see appendix.

CUBA, Ivan; professor extraordinary of art, proclaimed for distinguished service, Dictionary of International Biography, Vol. V (1968); elected Fellow, Institut des Arts et des Lettres, Switzerland (1963); The Temple of Arts Museum award U.S.A. (1970); developed educational composite painting and sculpture, segment painting and aluminium engravure, discovered colour-balancing by mathematics and weight changes in matter contributory to Einstein's theories, decorations include six diplomas, two sets of letters and two silver medals. *Studied* at University of Auckland, N.Z. *Exhib.:* U.K., U.S.A., N.Z. *Publications:* The Science of Painting, Evolution of Segmentation, Realms of the Spiral Stairway, etc. *Address:* P.O. Box 5199, Auckland, N.Z.

CUDWORTH, Nick, Dip. A.D. (1969); artist in pencil and pastel, musician, postman; *b* Derby, 4 Oct., 1947; *s* of Kenneth Cudworth, N.R.D., F.R.S.A.; *m*; one *s*, one *d*. *Educ.:* Derby College School; Henry Cavendish School, Derby; *studied art* at Derby College of Art (1964-66) under Brian Mills, Bob Girling; Chelsea School of Art (1966-69) under Edward Wright, Bob Chapman. *Exhib.:* Treadwell Gallery, Arnolfini Gallery; one-man shows: Thumb Gallery, London, Collection Gallery, Birmingham; mixed shows: Angela Flowers, Burlington House, Vintage Gallery, Cheltenham. *Work in permanent collections:* Arnolfini Gallery, Bristol, Nicholas Treadwell Gallery, London. *Address:* 27 Bath Rd., Stroud, Glos. *Signs work:* "Nick Cudworth."

CUMMING, Alexander A., Museums Assoc. Diploma; president, Museums Assoc. (1972-73); Director, Plymouth Museums and Art Gallery since 1939; *b* Accrington, Lancs., 15 Jan., 1912; *s* of the late Capt. A. S. Cumming; *m* Margaret Hobson; two *d*. *Educ.:* Bacup and Rawtenstall Grammar Schools, Manchester University; *studied art* at London, Amsterdam and Cologne. *Publications:* various official catalogues, etc. *Address:* Buckland Abbey, nr. Yelverton, Devon. *Club:* Athenæum.

CUNEO, Terence Tenison, R.G.I., P.I.P.G.; portrait and figure painter, ceremonial, military and engineering subjects; *b* 1 Nov., 1907; *s* of Cyrus Cuneo; *m* Catherine Mayfield Monro; two *d*. *Educ.:* Sutton Valence School; *studied art* at Chelsea and Slade; mem. War Artists Advisory Com. *Exhib.:* R.A., R.P., R.O.I.; one-man shows: R.W.S. Galleries (1941-58), Sladmore Gallery (1971-73). *Official purchases:* Coronation of Queen Elizabeth II in Westminster Abbey, portrait of H.M. Queen as Col.-in-Chief, Grenadier Guards, on Imperial, Royal Academy (1963), The Ceremony of the Garter at Windsor (June, 1964), first official portrait of Prime Minister Edward Heath (1971), portrait of Field Marshal Montgomery (1972), H.M. the Queen, opening New Stock Exchange (1973), portrait of H.M. the Queen as Patron of Kennel Club (1974). *Address:* 201 Ember Lane, East Molesey, Surrey. *Club:* Junior Carlton. *Signs work:* see appendix.

CUNLIFFE, Mitzi, B.S., M.A., Hon. Men. Prix de Rome (1947), George B. Widener Gold Medal, Penn.; professional mem. Architectural Assoc.; sculptor in stone, wood, metal, clay, plaster; designer of textiles, tiles, pottery and jewellery; lecturer and writer; lecturer in design, School of Architecture, Thames Polytechnic, Hammersmith, London; *b* N.Y., 1 Jan., 1918; *d* of Abraham Solomon; *m* 1949, divorced 1971; one *s,* two *d. Educ.:* Columbia University; *studied art* at Art Students' League, N.Y. (1930-33), Columbia University (1935-40). *Exhib.:* one-man shows in Brussels 1973 and in 1967 at American Embassy, London, Sussex University, Brighton Art Gallery, etc. *Work in permanent collections:* University of Liverpool, University of Leeds, Lewis's, Liverpool, University of Manchester, Sunderland Technical College, Scottish Life House, London. *Work repro.:* articles in Royal Town Planning Institute Journal, New York Times, Times Higher Education Supplement, etc. *Address:* 77 Cadogan Sq., London SW1X 0DY.

CUNNINGHAM, Mrs. Ruth Helen, B. of E. exams. in drawing and industrial design; artist in water-colour; visiting teacher, Harrow School of Art (1933-44), Watford School of Art (1936-40), St. Albans School of Art (1936-40); *b* Uxbridge, Middx., 12 Mar., 1909; one *s. Studied art* at Harrow School of Art. *Exhib.:* Guernsey Eisteddfod (1950, 1951, certs. of Honour and Merit), Mahy Gallery, Winchester and Oxford. *Address:* Bell Cottage, Hampton Poyle, Oxford OX5 2QD. *Signs work:* "RUTH WOODBRIDGE."

CUNNINGTON, E. B. (Mrs. N. E. C. Attrill), M.A. (Oxon., 1940); artist in sculpture, principally modelling, and in water-colour; *b* London, 13 July, 1914; *d* of W. A. Cunnington, M.A., D.Sc., Ph.D., A.R.C.S., F.L.S.; *m* N. E. C. Attrill, B.A. *Educ.:* Clapham High School; Somerville College, Oxford; *studied art* at Slade School (1936-39). *Exhib.:* N.S., S.S.W.A., Utd. Soc. of Artists, Reading Guild of Artists. R.A., R.B.A., S.W.A., Observer exhbn. of Children's Portraits. *Address:* 1 Woodlands Cottages, Bayworth La., Boars Hill, Oxford. *Signs work:* "E. B. Cunnington."

CURMAN, Billy, B.F.A. (1973), U.W.M./Editor Wisconsin Art Guild News; artist in mixed media; Director, Broadway Galleries, Ltd.; *b* U.S.A., 1949. *Educ.:* Guild Workshop; University of Wisconsin. *Exhib.:* one-man shows: Minneapolis (1974), Milwaukee (1970, 1971); three-man show: New York (1972); four-man show: Milwaukee (1973-74); group shows: 19th Annual Sidney Rothman, N.J. (1976), 18th National, El Paso (1974-75), Accordian Post Card show, N.Y. (1973), 57th Wisconsin Painters/Sculptors, Milwaukee (1972), 8th Tyler National, Texas (1972), Paula Insel Annual, N.Y. (1972), Graphics U.S.A., Chicago (1971), Artists' Proposals for Human Environment, Milwaukee (1971). *Address:* c/o Broadway Galleries, 630 N. Broadway, Milwaukee, Wisconsin 53202, U.S.A. *Clubs:* Wisconsin Art Guild, National Art Workers Community, Art Information Registry. *Signs work:* "Billy Curman."

CURTIS, Anthony Ewart, A.R.W.A., M.F.P.S.; experimental and landscape artist in P.E.P., oils, inks, gouache, charcoal, pencil, flo-master; sculptor; interest in pottery; Head of Visual Arts Department, Cressex School, High Wycombe, Bucks; *b* Wakefield, Yorks, 7 July, 1928; *s* of G. E. Curtis, M.R.S.H., F.A.P.H.I. (retired 1966); *m* Joyce Isabel (*née* Yates); three *s*, one *d. Educ.:* Kingswood Grammar School, Bristol, Loughboro' College (1948-50); Diploma Course in Art Education, London University (1974-75); *studied art* at Bath Academy of Art (1950-51) under Potworowsky, William Scott, Lanyon, Wynter, Russ, Cliffe, Armitage, Helen Binyon. *Exhib.:* Redfern, Daily Express Young Painters (1955), London Group, R.W.A., Arts Council Modern Stained Glass (1960-62), Free Painters and Sculptors (1962, 1963, 1967), joined group 1967, full member 1969, local organizer, Group Show, High Wycombe Festival (1968), Bear Lane,

Century Gallery and Scopas, Henley; first one-man, Bear Lane, Oxford (1959), 2nd, in Seven Young Artists, Reading Art Gallery (1961), 3rd, in Cookham (1964). *Official purchases:* Bristol Education Committee, Art Service. *Work repro.:* Young Artists of Promise (Jack Beddington, C.B.E., 1957). Sand-blasted glass screen for Church of St. Andrew, High Wycombe (Feb., 1961). *Address:* Oak Tree House, Heath End, Flackwell Heath, High Wycombe, Bucks. *Signs work:* "Anthony Curtis" with date, or see appendix.

CUTNER, E., R.B.A. (1939), hon. mem., Paris Salon (1936); Slade Diploma and Scholarship, eleven prizes, including summer exhbn. competition; Clayden Travelling Scholarship (1929); oil and water-colour painter, magazine illustrator; teacher of water-colour, Hampstead Garden Suburb Institute; *d* of Witford G. Smith; *b* Woodbridge, Suffolk; *m* Herbert Cutner; one *d*. *Educ.:* Ipswich High School; *studied art* at Ipswich School of Art under G. R. Rushton; Slade School under Prof. Tonks (1925-29). *Exhib.:* R.A., Paris Salon, R.B.A., R.O.I., R.P., London Portrait Soc., N.E.A.C., R.W.A., W.A.G., Ipswich, Doncaster, Derby, Manchester, Liverpool. *Address:* 1 Temple Fortune La., London NW11. *Signs work:* "E. CUTNER."

CZIMBALMOS, Magdolna Paal, S.I. Museum, N.Y., Gold Med. (1958, 1960, 1962, 1963, 1966); personal letter from President J. F. Kennedy for portrait of Jacqueline Kennedy (1961); Italian Culture Award, N.Y. (1967); Szinyei Merse Gold Med., N.Y. (1971); several Silver Med. and Hon. Men.; artist in oil; *b* Esztergom, Hungary; *m* Kalman Sz. Czimbalmos; one *d*. *Studied art* under Prof. A. Bayor pr. Art Sch. Esztergom, Hung., Radatz pr. Art Sch. Germ. *Exhib.:* Paris, Germany, Monaco, Canada, U.S.A., several one-man and group shows. *Work in permanent collections:* S.I. Museum, N.Y., International Inst., Detroit, Carnegie International Cent., N.Y., Bergstrom Art Cent., Ill. *Address:* 31 Bayview Pl., Ward Hill, Staten Island, New York, 10304. *Clubs:* S.I. Museum, N.Y., World Fed. of Hung. Artists. *Signs work:* "Magdolna Paal Czimbalmos" and see appendix.

CZIMBALMOS, Szabo Kalman, Hung. Roy. Acad. Pr. (1933), S.I. Museum, N.Y., Pr. Gold Med. (1950, 1956, 1962, 1963, 1967), St. Stephen Gold Medal, N.Y. (1971), several Silver Med. and Hon. Men.; M.F.A., painter-educator, Dir. Czimbalmos Pvt. Art Sch., N.Y.; owner, Czimbalmos Fine Art Studio, S.I., N.Y.; artist in oil, water-colour, tempera; *b* Esztergom, Hungary, 1914; *s* of Janos Czimbalmos; *m* Magdolna Paal Bohatka; one *d*. *Studied art* at Royal Academy of Fine Art, Budapest (1936) under Prof. J. Harahghy, E. Domanowsky; postgrad. Vienna, Munich, Paris, Rome. *Exhib.:* Munchen, Paris, Monaco, Canada, U.S.A.; several one-man and group shows. *Work in permanent collections:* S.I. Museum, N.Y., S.I. Com. Coll. N.Y., Bergstrom Art Center, Ill., City Museum, Esztergom, Hung., etc.; murals in churches, convents and private inst., U.S.A. *Address:* 31 Bayview Pl., Ward Hill, Staten Island, New York, 10304. *Clubs:* Bavaryan Fine Art Soc., S.I. Museum, N.Y., World Fed. of Hung. Artists. *Signs work:* "K. Sz. Czimbalmos" and see appendix.

D

D'AGUILAR, Michael, gold, silver and bronze medals, Royal Drawing Soc., Armitage and silver medal, R.A. (1949); artist in oil and lithograph; *b* London, 11 May, 1924. *Educ.:* privately in Spain, Italy and France; *studied art* at R.A. Schools under Henry Rushbury, R.A., Fleetwood-Walker, A.R.A., William Dring, R.A. (1948-53). *Exhib.:* R.A., R.B.A., N.E.A.C., Irving Galleries, Gimpel Fils, Leicester Galleries, Young Contemporaries; one-man shows, Gimpel Fils,

Irving Galleries, New Grafton Gallery. *Work repro:* Artist, Studio, La Revue Moderne des Arts. *Publications:* articles in Diario de Tarragona, La Revue Moderne, The Artist, Studio. *Address:* Studio 4, Chelsea Farm House, Milmans St., London SW10. *Signs work:* "M. D'Aguilar."

D'AGUILAR, Paul; artist in oil, water-colour, pen and ink, lithographer; 1st prize for drawing at R.A. schools (1949); gold, silver and bronze medals, R.D.S.; *b* London, 9 Sept., 1927. *Educ.:* privately in Spain, Italy and France; *studied art:* R.A. schools (1948-53) and privately under Prof. Barblain Oskar (Siena). *Exhib.:* R.A., Redfern, Young Contemporaries, Leicester Galleries, Daily Express Young Artists Exhbn., R.B.A., N.E.A.C., Irving Gallery (1952), Sindicato de Iniciativa, Tarragona (Spain), Temple Gallery (1960), and New Grafton Gallery. *Work in permanent collection:* Lord Rothermere. *Work repro.:* Artist, Studio, Collins Magazine, La Revue Moderne, Drawing Nudes (Studio Vista). *Address:* 11 Sheen Gate Gdns., London SW14. *Club:* Reynolds. *Signs work:* "P. D'Aguilar."

DAHL, Chrix; draughtsman, graphic arts, painter; head teacher, graphic arts, Statens Håndverks og Kunstindustriskole, Oslo; *b* Oslo, 5 Jan., 1906; *s* of Christian Dahl, commander, Navy; *m* Ellen Olsen. *Educ.:* Frogner skole; Håndverks og Kunstindustriskole; Statens Kunstakademi in Oslo; *studied art* under H. Strøm, Axel Revold, Olaf Willums and self-taught. *Exhib.:* Oslo, U.S.A., Rio, Rome, Paris, London, Scandinavia. *Work in permanent collections:* National Gallery, Oslo; Museums of Art in Bergen; Trondheim; Stockholm; Copenhagen; Helsinki; Praha. *Work repro.:* illustrations for Voltaire's Candide (1946), O. S. Anderssen: Hjemme i Oslo, Geraldy: Mannen og Kjaerligheten, etc. *Address:* Smestad, Oslo, Norway. *Signs work:* "Chr. D.", "Chr. Dahl."

DAI-CHIEN, Chang: see CHANG, Dai-Chien.

DAINTREY, Adrian Maurice, R.W.A.; painter and draftsman; *b* London, 1902. *Studied art* at Slade School, and in Museums. *Works in public and private collections:* at home and abroad. *Publications:* art critic to Punch 1953 for 7 years; I Must Say (1963); Le Billet Doux by Fragonard (1969). *Address:* 20 Randolph Rd., London W9 1AH. *Signs work:* "Adrian Daintrey," "A.D." and "A.M.D."

DAKEYNE, Gabriel; Associé Société des Artistes Français (1974); artist in collage, pen and ink, oil paint, water-colour; *b* Marske-by-the-sea, Yorkshire, 23 Feb., 1916; *d* of Cecil R. B. Dakeyne, Clerk in Holy Orders; *m* Wing-Cdr. Jack Brain, Retd.; two *d*. *Educ.:* home; *studied art* at Swindon School of Art (Mr. Dearden, 1934), The Hague, Holland, Press Art School (1953). *Exhib.:* S.W.A., Graphic Artists and Flower Paintings, R.A. (1966), R.W.E.A. (1971, 1972), Hon. Men. Paris Salon (1972-75), 9th Grand Prix de la Cote D'Azure Cannes (1973). *Work repro.:* La Revue Moderne. *Address:* Sadlers Cottage, Sadlers Lane, Winnersh, Wokingham RG11 5AL. *Signs work:* see appendix.

DALBY, Claire, A.R.W.S.; E. T. Greenshields Memorial Scholarship (1961), David Murray Studentship (1966); artist in pen and ink, water-colour and wood-engraving; *b* St. Andrews, Scotland, 1944; *d* of Charles N. Longbotham, R.W.S.; *m* D. H. Dalby, Ph.D. *Educ.:* Haberdashers' Aske's School, Acton; *studied art* at City and Guilds of London Art School (1964-67). *Exhib.:* R.A., R.W.S., R.E., N.E.A.C.; one-man shows: Clarges Gallery, London (1968, 1972), Camberley (1975). *Work repro.:* Arts Review, Country Life. *Address:* 132 Gordon Rd., Camberley, Surrey GU15 2JQ. *Signs work:* see appendix.

DALE, Antony, B.Litt., M.A. (Oxon.), F.S.A.; Chief Investigator of Historic Buildings, Dept. of the Environment; enrolled solicitor (1938); hon. treasurer, Regency Soc. of Brighton and Hove (1945-48), hon. sec. since 1948; *b* Walton-on-the-Hill, 12 July, 1912; *s* of Major Claude Henry Dale, C.M.G., O.B.E.; *m* Yvonne Chevallier Macfie; one *d*. *Educ.:* Brighton College and Oriel College, Oxford. *Publications:* James Wyatt, Fashionable Brighton, 1820-60; The History and Architecture of Brighton; About Brighton. *Address:* 33 Roedean Cres., Brighton 7. *Club:* The Athenæum.

DALE, William Scott Abell, M.A. (Toronto, 1946), Ph.D. (Harvard, 1955); Professor of Fine Arts, University of Western Ontario; Deputy Director, National Gallery of Canada (1961-67); director, Vancouver Art Gallery (1959-61); curator Art Gallery of Toronto (1957-59); Nat. Gallery of Canada (1951-57); mem. College Art Assoc. of America, R.S.A.; research fellow, Dumbarton Oaks, Washington (1956-57); *b* Toronto, 18 Sept., 1921; *s* of Prof. Ernest A. Dale, M.A. (Oxon); *m* Jane Gordon Laidlaw; three *s*. *Educ.:* University of Toronto Schools; Trinity College, Toronto; Harvard University. *Address:* University of Western Ontario, London, Canada.

d'ANDREA, Albert Philip, F.R.S.A., Benjamin Franklin Fellow of the Royal Society of Arts, Accademico d'Onore, Perugia, Phi Beta Kappa, Townsend Harris Medal, Lindsey Morris Prize; artist and teacher; Emeritus Prof. of Art, Chairman of Art Dept., City College, N.Y. City; *b* Italy, 27 Oct., 1897; *s* of Gregory d'Andrea; *m* Rose E. d'Andrea; two *s*. *Educ.:* City College, N.Y. (A.B., 1918); *studied art* at National Academy of Design, Universita di Roma. *Work in permanent collections:* Hall of Fame, N.Y., Library of Congress, Smithsonian Institution. *Official purchases:* chiefly medallic art. *Clubs:* Audubon Artists, National Sculpture Society. *Address:* 2121 Bay Avenue, Brooklyn, N.Y., U.S.A. *Signs work:* "Albert d'Andrea."

DANIELS, Alfred, A.R.W.S., A.R.C.A., F.R.S.A.; artist in oil, water-colour and acrylic; art instructor, Hornsey College of Art at Middlesex Polytechnic; *b* London, 8 Oct., 1924; *s* of Samuel Daniels; *m* Margot Hamilton Hill. *Educ.:* George Greens School; *studied art* at Woolwich Polytechnic, R.C.A. *Exhib.:* R.A., Zwemmer Gall., Portal Gall., Gallery 359, Nottingham. *Work in permanent collections:* G.L.C., Cambridgeshire Educ. Com., Leicester Educ. Com., Bradford A.G., Leeds University, Bezalel Museum, Israel, Nottingham A.G. *Official purchases:* Hammersmith Town Hall, British Rail, O.U.P. *Publications:* Drawing and Painting (1961), Drawing Made Simple (1963), Enjoying Acrylics (1975), Visible Thinking (1976). *Work repro.:* Studio International, The Artist, Art and Artists, R.A. Illustrated, Arts Review. *Address:* 24 Esmond Rd., London W4. *Signs work:* "Alfred Daniels."

DANIELS, Harvey Morton, Slade Dip. F.A. (Lond.), A.T.D.; artist in oil, lithography, mixed media, printmaker, art lecturer; lecturer in charge of printmaking, Brighton College; part-time extra-mural lecturer, London University; *b* London, 17 June, 1936; *s* of Charles S. Daniels; *m* Judy Stapleton, painter. *Studied art* at Willesden College of Art (1951-56), Slade School of Fine Art (Ceri Richards, Lynton Lamb, 1956-58), Brighton College of Art (1958-59). *Work in permanent collections:* Museum of Modern Art, New York, Metropolitan Museum, New York, V. & A., University of Sussex. *Address:* 10 Powis Rd., Brighton BN1 3HJ, Sussex. *Club:* Printmakers' Council of Great Britain. *Signs work:* "Harvey Daniels."

DANIELS, Jeffery, M.A. (Oxon.); Mem., International Consultative Committee for Mostra di Sebastiano Ricci, Udine (1976), mem., A.I.C.A., Assoc. of Art Historians; Curator, Geffrye Museum, London since 1969; *b* 13 July, 1932; *s* of John Henry Daniels. *Educ.:* Milford Haven Grammar School; Balliol College, Oxford. *Publications:* Architecture in England, 1968; Biography and Catalogue raisonné of Sebastiano Ricci, 1976; contrib. The Times, The Connoisseur, Apollo, Art & Artists, The Burlington Magazine, Art News (U.S.A.). *Address:* 5 Edith Grove, Chelsea, London SW10 0JZ. *Clubs:* Society of Authors, Motor Sports.

DARGIE, Sir William Alexander, Kt., O.B.E., F.R.S.A.; portrait and landscape painter. Mem. Commonwealth Art Advisory Board; Official War Artist (1941-46); Head, National Gallery of Victoria Art Schools (1946-53); *portraits painted:* H.M. Queen Elizabeth II for Parliament House, Canberra; members of the Royal Family; scientists, artists, politicians, and distinguished citizens; *b* Melbourne, 1912; *s* of Andrew Dargie; *m* Kathleen Howitt; one *s*, one *d*. *Studied* under A. D. Colquhoun. *Exhib.:* R.A., R.S.P.P., one-man shows. *Represented in permanent collections:* U.K., U.S.A., Australia and N.Z. *Publications:* On Painting a Portrait. *Addresses:* 19 Irilbarra Rd., Canterbury, Victoria, Australia; 9 Wimpole Mews, London W1. *Clubs:* Melbourne, Savage and Yorick (Melb.). *Signs work:* "Dargie."

DAUBAN, Mrs. May Lilian, gold medallist, Calcutta (1936-37); painter in water-colour; *b* Worthing, 29 Oct., 1907; *d* of Sir Claude Ricketts, Bt. (decd.); *m* Colonel Dauban, R.A., rtd.; one *s,* two *d. Educ.:* St. Michael's, Guildford, Surrey; *studied art* at St. Michael's, Guildford, and privately, Paris under Mr. Zebrofska. *Exhib.:* Plymouth, all main Pakistan and Indian exhbns., Darlington, R.W.S. Art Club, R.B.A. Galleries. *Address:* Meavy, 102 Farley Rd., Selsdon, Surrey. *Signs work:* "M. L. DAUBAN."

DAVEY, Leonard John, D.A. (Edin.) (1949); potter and ceramic sculptor in stoneware clay; *b* Nottingham, 1913; *s* of John Wright Davey; *m* Kathleen Margaret Frost; one *s,* two *d. Educ.:* County Schools, Leicester; *studied art* at Leicester College of Art (1926-28) under Roberts, Christopherson, Miss Roberts, Miss Windley; Edinburgh College of Art (1945-49) under John Maxwell, Sir Adam Bruce Thompson, Sir W. MacTaggart, Eric Schilsky, Kathleen Horsman, A.R.C.A. *Exhib.:* Scottish Crafts (1971), Crafts Biennale, Scotland (1974). *Work in permanent collections:* Royal Scottish Museum, Edinburgh, Leicester Museum, Shipley A.G., Gateshead. *Address:* Old Bridge Pottery, Bridge of Dee, Castle Douglas, Kirkcudbrightshire, Scotland. *Signs work:* see appendix.

DAVIDSON, Ian Stuart, N.D.D. (1962), Cert. R.C.A. (1966), A.R.B.S. (1972); sculptor, lecturer, bronze caster; guest lecturer in Sculpture, Rochdale College of Art; visiting lecturer, Winchester and Exeter; *b* Sheffield, 13 July, 1936; *s* of H. H. Davidson (Dave), painter and illustrator; divorced; one *s. Educ.:* Boys' High School, Durban, Natal; *studied art* at Camberwell School of Art (1960-61), Chelsea College of Art (1962-63), Central School of Art (1964), Post Graduate, R.C.A. (1965-66), Post Graduate Certificate R.C.A. under Prof. Meadows. *Work in permanent collections:* Manchester Loan Collection, private collections in Germany, France, England. *Address:* 73 Northview Rd., Brixham, Devon. *Clubs:* Ocean Cruising, R.A.F. Assoc. *Signs work:* "ID" with date, or "Davidson" with date.

DAVIDSON-HOUSTON, Aubrey Claud; portrait artist in oil, pencil; *b* Dublin, 2 Feb., 1906; *s* of Lt.-Col. W. B. Davidson-Houston, C.M.G.; *m;* one *d. Educ.:* St. Ronan's School, W. Worthing; St. Edward's School, Oxford; Royal Military College, Sandhurst; *studied art* at St. Martin's School; Slade School. *Exhib.:* R.S.A., R.C.A., R.P., R.B.A., R.O.I., N.S., United Artists, Paris Salon. *Work repro.:* Sketch, Woman's Journal, etc. *Addresses:* Hillview, West End Lane, Esher, Surrey, and 4 Chelsea Studios, 412 Fulham Rd., London SW6. *Clubs:* Naval and Military, Buck's. *Signs work:* see appendix.

DAVIES, Antoni Douglas, D.A. (Edin.) (1970), post dip. (1971); lecturer and potter in clay; mem. Scottish Craft Council; *b* Haroldwood, Essex, 29 Nov., 1946. *Educ.:* Boroughmuir, Edinburgh; *studied art* at Edinburgh College of Art (1966-71) under Katie Horsman, Helen Turner. *Exhib.:* group shows: Scottish Craft Centre, Salzburg Festival; one-man shows: various Edinburgh Festivals, Scottish Society of Artists. *Work in permanent collections:* Edinburgh University, Austrian Ministry of Culture and private collections. *Address:* c/o Glasgow School of Art, Renfrew St., Glasgow. *Signs work:* a double D for Douglas Davies.

DAVIES, Arthur Edward, R.B.A. (1939), R.C.A. (1942); artist in water-colour, oil, black and white, etc.; *b* Pontrhydgroes Ystrad Meurig, Cardiganshire, June, 1893. *Educ.:* Carmarthen Old College School, Tredegar County School; *studied art* at Metropolitan School of Art, Dublin (George Aikinson, R.H.A.). *Exhib.:* R.A. (1936-67), R.S.A., R.W.A., Brighton, Derby, Bradford Galleries, Société des Artistes Français Salon (1962) (Mention Honorable). *Work in permanent collection:* National Library of Wales, Aberystwyth. *Address:* Studio, 331 Earlham Rd., Norwich, Norfolk NOR O3G. *Signs work:* see appendix.

DAVIES, Emrys, M.P.S. (1928); artist in pastel, water-colour; retail pharmacist; *b* Pontrhydygroes; *s* of David Davies, woollen factory proprietor; *m* A. E. V. Davies; one *s*. *Educ.:* Council School, Tregaron County School; *studied art:* self-taught. *Exhib.:* N.S., P.S., Musée D'Art Moderne, Paris. *Address:* 23 Fernley Ct., Harrow La., Maidenhead, Berks. *Signs work:* "Emrys Davies."

DAVIES, John A., O.B.E. (1945), R.S.M.A. (1967), Paris Salon Silver Medal (1968); artist in water-colour and oil; chairman, Wapping Group; *b* Ware, 22 April, 1901; two *s*. *Educ.:* Clifton College; Royal Military Academy, Woolwich; *studied art* at Heatherley's, and privately with Jack Merriott and others. *Work in permanent collections:* National Maritime Museum, Greenwich; Oregon Historical Society. *Address:* Limes, Therfield, Royston, Herts. *Clubs:* Langham Sketch, R.W.S. Art, Army & Navy, Royal Ocean Racing, Little Ship. *Signs work:* "J. A. Davies."

DAVIES, Stephanie Joyce, F.I.A.L., F.R.S.A.; painter, designer, art costume historian; *b* Bristol; *d* of Stephen Curtis, Customs and Excise, Bristol; widow of D. T. Davies, Llandyrnog, N. Wales; one *d*. *Educ.:* privately, Bristol Art College and University. *Exhib.:* U.S.A., British Isles, Europe; *Awards:* Finaliste Laureat Grand Prix International, Côte d'Azur 72; Finaliste Laureat Grand Prix International, Deauville 72; Diplome d'Honneur Palme d'or des Beaux Arts, I.A.G. Monte Carlo 69; Paris Salon M.H. 65; also Salon Bosio, M.C. 69; Salon d'Art Belge, Brussels; Salon Internationale di Pittura, Rome 72; L'Albatros, Roma 72; Lond. S.M.A., Ind. P., S.W.A., V.A., N.S., R.B.A.; *one-man shows:* University of York 71; Giffard, Worcester 72, 73; Swan Theatre, Worcester; Malvern Festival Theatre; Malvern Girls' College; Tudor House and Owen Owens, Chester; S.W. University, Exeter; Old Vic, Bristol; *group shows:* provinces, R.W.A., M.A.F.A., R.Cam.A., Brighton, A.E.B. Exhbns. *Address:* 50 Meadow Rd., Malvern Link WR14 2SD. *Signs work:* "Stephanie Davies" in perpendicular line.

DAVIES, Thomas; artist in water-colour and oil; *b* Colwyn Bay, Denbighshire, 31 Aug., 1899; *s* of R. J. Davies, saddler; *m* Elizabeth Ann Williams; two *s*, one *d*. *Educ.:* H.G. School, Colwyn Bay; *studied art* privately under Robert Evans Hughes, F.R.S.A., F.I.A.L. *Exhib.:* Denbighshire Art Soc., Flintshire Art Soc., N. Wales Group, Odeon Festival Exhbn., one-man exhbn., Gwrych Castle. *Address:* Glenthorpe, 20 Glanrafon, Abergele, Cl wyd. *Signs work:* "T. DAVIES" and see appendix.

DAVIS, Brian: see FFOLKES, Michael.

DAVIS, Derek Maynard; Artist in Residence, University of Sussex (1967); potter; Mem. Arts Panel, Southern Arts Assoc., Mem. International Academy of Ceramics, Mem. Crafts Centre, Craftsmen's Potters Assoc. Design Centre; *b* London, 1926; *s* of James A. Davis, craftsman; *m* Ruth; one *s*. *Educ.:* Emanuel School, Wandsworth; *studied painting* at Central School of Arts and Crafts, London, under Keith Vaughan, Robert Buhler. *Exhib.:* Istanbul, Munich, Toronto, Zurich, Tokyo, Paris, Primavera (London and Cambridge). *Work in permanent collections:* Paisley Museum, Oxford and Woodstock Museum, Portsmouth Museum, Prinsenhof, Holland, Southampton Museum, University of Sussex, Bradford Museum, V. & A. *Address:* Duff House, Maltravers St., Arundel, Sussex.

DAVIS, Elizabeth Cathrine; Viscontea Prize, Milan, Italy (1970), B.B.C. Poster Design Prize (1970); restorer, painter in oils, water-colour; constructions in wood, metal and plaster; director of gallery; *b* Johannesburg, S.A., 1921; *m* A. K. Davis; two *s*, one *d*. *Educ.:* St. Cathrine's Convent, Pretoria. *Exhib.:* one-man shows; Galleria Pater, Milano, Italy (1969), Woodside Gallery (1972); group shows: Bari, Italy (1970), R.H.O., Italy (1970-71). *Work repro.:* Catalogo Bolaffi d'Arte Moderna, Torino, Italy (1970). *Address:* Woodside Gallery, 211 Fir Tree Rd., Epsom Downs, Surrey. *Signs work:* "Elizabeth Davis."

DAVIS, James, L.I.F.A.; Freeman the Worshipful Company Painter-Stainers (1972); Freeman of the City .of London (1973); sculptor and stone-carver in stone, marble and bronze; *b* London, 16 July, 1926; *s* of James E. Davis, engineer; *m* Joan Davis; one *s*, one *d*. *Educ.:* Eastbrook Boys School, Dagenham, Essex; *studied art* at Sir John Cass School of Art (1949-53) under Bainbridge and Copnal. *Exhib.:* Guildhall; Leighton House, Royal Exchange, Mall Galleries. *Work in permanent collections:* Painters Hall, Chelsea and Kensington Town Hall, Community Centre, Shoeburyness. *Address:* 9 Rembrandt Cl., Friars Meadow, Shoeburyness, Essex. *Signs work:* "J. Davis."

DAVIS, John Warren, M.C., A.T.D.; sculptor in wood, stone and metal; *b* Christchurch, 24 Feb., 1919; *s* of Capt. J. Warren Davis, M.C.; *m* Evelyn Ann; three *s*, one *d*. *Educ.:* Bedford School; *studied art* at Westminster School of Art (1937-39), under Bernard Meninsky and Mark Gertler; Brighton College of Art (1948-52), under James Woodford, R.A. *Work in permanent collections:* Cardiff, Leeds, Southampton, New York. *Address:* Northfields Farm, Eastergate, Chichester, Sussex.

DAWLSON, Sidney, M.F.P.S., H.H.A.S.; proof reader for Hansard; artist in oil, acrylic and collage; *b* London, 16 Sept., 1917; *m* Charlotte Dawlson. *Educ.:* Hugh Myddelton School; *studied art* at Central School of Arts and Crafts (1937-38). *Exhib.:* one-man shows: Loggia Gallery (1975, 1976), N. London (1975, 1976); group shows: R.I. Galleries, Suffolk Street Gallery, Mall Galleries, Chenil Gallery, Guildhall A.G., R.B.A., R.O.I., N.S., U.S.A., R.S.M.A., C.A.S., Southampton University, Surrey University, Culham College and various other provincial exhbns. *Address:* 2 Morven Rd., Upper Tooting, London SW17 7NA. *Club:* London Ballet Circle. *Signs work:* "Sidney Dawlson."

DAWSON, Gladys, A.R.C.A. (1943), R.C.A. (1946), F.R.S.A. (1952), A.S.W.A. (1953), S.W.A. (1955); artist in water-colour, pastel, black and white; writer and illustrator of children's books; *b* Castleton, Rochdale; *d* of Ernest Jacques Dawson; *m* Ronald G. Woodruff, Mines and Geology Dept., Nairobi, Kenya. *Educ.:* private schools; Heatherley's (1936-39) (R. O. Dunlop, Frederick Whiting, Paul Drury). *Exhib.:* R.C.A., R.I., R.W.A., S.W.A., Lancashire Artists, Preston, Walker Art Gallery, Liverpool, etc. *Work repro.:* Textile designs, book jackets, greeting cards, etc. *Address:* 10 Courtlands Cres., Banstead, Surrey. *Signs* *work:* "G. Dawson" (G and D linked together, horizontal stroke of G into top of D).

DAWSON, Patricia Vaughan; printmaker, sculptor and writer; *b* Liverpool, 23 Jan., 1925; *d* of Theodore James Wright, army officer; *m* James N. Dawson; one *s,* two *d. Educ.:* Chroham Hurst School; *studied art* at Croydon School of Art (1941-45) under Reginald Marlow and Ruskin Spear. *Exhib.:* Bear Lane Gallery. *Work in permanent collections:* B.M., Bibliothèque Nationale. *Publication:* The Artist Looks at Life (a series of books and slide strips published by Visual Publications introducing art to children). *Address:* 34 Rouse Gdns., Dulwich, London SE21.

DAY, Lucienne, R.D.I., A.R.C.A. (1940), F.S.I.A.; textile designer; Royal Designer for Industry (1962); *b* Coulsdon, Surrey, 1917; *d* of Felix Conradi; *m* Robin Day; one *d. Educ.:* Convent of Notre Dame de Sion, Worthing; *studied art:* Croydon School of Art (1934-37), R.C.A. (1937-40). *Exhib.:* London, Manchester, Zürich, Amsterdam, Milan, Dublin, Oslo, Bergen, Stavanger, Washington, Toronto, Bulawayo. *Work in permanent collections:* V. & A., museums of Cranbrook, Michigan, Museum of Industrial Design (Trondheim). *Address:* 49 Cheyne Walk, Chelsea, London SW3. *Signs work:* "Lucienne Day."

DAY, Robin, A.R.C.A., F.S.I.A., R.D.I.; designer; *b* High Wycombe, Bucks., 1915; *studied art* at High Wycombe School of Art and R.C.A. *Exhib.:* Museum of Modern Art, New York, I.C.A., Triennale, Milan (1951), Copenhagen, Oslo, Stavanger, Bergen, Zürich, Canada. *Work in permanent collections:* Museum of Modern Art, New, York, Trondheim Industrial Art Museum. *Work repro.:* most architectural and design publications here and abroad. *Address:* 49 Cheyne Walk, Chelsea, London SW3. *Club:* Arts, Dover St.

DEAKINS, Cyril Edward, A.R.E. (1948), M.S.I.A. (1961-71), A.T.D. (1947), F.R.S.A. (1951-71); painter in oil, tempera and water-colour, etcher, wood-engraver and illustrator; *b* Bearwood, nr. Birmingham, 5 Oct., 1916; *s* of Charles H. Deakins; *m;* one *s,* one *d. Educ.:* Christ's College, Finchley; *studied art* under J. C. Moody, Norman Janes, at Hornsey School of Art. *Exhib.:* R.A., N.E.A.C., R.E., R.B.A., provincial galleries, S. Africa and U.S.A. *Official purchase:* Print Collectors' Club, presentation print, 1948. *Work repro.:* four postage stamp designs for Govt. of Bermuda, 1953, book and magazine illustrations. *Address:* Smallcorner, 1 Mill Lane, Dunmow, Essex. *Signs work:* "C.D." or "Cyril Deakins."

DEAN, Beryl, M.B.E. (1975), A.R.C.A. (1937), F.S.D-C. (1970); freelance designer, author, lecturer, embroideress in fabrics with gold thread; Tutor, I.L.E.A.; *b* Bromley, 1911; *d* of Herbert Charles Dean; *m* W. M. Phillips; two stepsons. *Educ.:* Bromley High School, G.P.D.S.T.; *studied art* at Bromley School of Art (1932) under M. E. G. Thomson; Royal School of Needlework (1929) under M. Randall; Royal College of Art (1935) under Prof. E. Tristram. *Exhib.:* one-man shows, Ecclesiastical Embroidery: St. Paul's Cathedral, St. Andrew's Church, London, and abroad; Embroidery: British Colour Council. *Work in permanent collections:* V. & A., Collection of the Embroideries Guild, London, etc. *Publications:* Ecclesiastical Embroidery, Ideas for Church Embroidery, Church Needlework, Creative appliqué. *Address:* 59 Thornhill Sq., London N1 1BE.

DEAN, Ronald Herbert, R.S.M.A. (1970), F.C.I.I. (1965); self-taught painter in water-colour and oil; Insurance broker; *b* Farnborough, Hants., 1929; *s* of Herbert Dean, B.E.M.; *m* Audrey Grace Payne; two *d. Educ.:* Farnborough Grammar School. *Exhib.:* R.S.M.A., R.I., R.B.A., Biarritz, National Maritime

Museum. *Address:* 5 Barchester Way, Tonbridge, Kent. *Club:* Tonbridge Art Group. *Signs work:* RONALD DEAN" printed.

de FRANCIA, Peter; painter in oil, author; Principal, DFA, School of Art, Goldsmiths College, University of London; *b* Beaulieu, Alpes Maritimes, France, 25 Jan., 1921; *s* of Fernand de Francia. *Studied art* in Paris, Academy of Brussels, Slade School. *Work in permanent collections:* Society for Contemporary Art, National Gallery of Modern Art, Prague, private collections in U.K., and U.S.A. *Publications:* Fernand Léger (Cassells, 1968-69); in preparation: Fernand Léger (Gerd Hatje, Stuttgart) German and English edition 1972/73. *Address:* 44 Surrey Sq., London SE17 2JX. *Club:* Architectural Association. *Signs work:* see appendix.

DE GOEDE, Julien Maximilien, Diploma, Honours, High School, Nijmegen; painter in P.V.A.; *b* Rotterdam, Holland, 20 May, 1937; *s* of Maximilien Julien de Goede, builder. *Educ.:* High School, Nijmegen; *studied art* at Academie voor Beeldende Kunsten en Kunstnijverheid, Arnhem (1953-55). Eindhoven School of Art (1955-56), Julian Ashton School of Art, Sydney (1957-58), Orban School of Art, Sydney (1958-59), Canberra School of Art (1959-61). *Exhib.:* Three one-man shows, Canberra, four one-man shows, Grabowski, London. *Work in permanent collections:* Australian National University, Leicestershire Education Committee, Contemporary Art Society, Newcastle City Gallery. *Address:* S.P.A.C.E., 71 Stepney Green, London E1. *Signs works:* "Jules de Goede."

DEKK, Dorrit (Mrs.), F.S.I.A. (1962); free-lance advertising designer and illustrator in water-colour, gouache, and pen and ink; poster designer; *b* Brno, Czechoslovakia, 18 May, 1917; *d* of Fuhrmann, industrialist; *m* Dr. Leonard Klatzow (decd.) and *m* K. V. Epstein, Aug., 1968. *Educ.:* Vienna and Switzerland; *studied art* at Vienna, Kuntstgewerbe Schule; Reinhardt School (stage design) (1936-39); Reimann School, London (commercial art). *Work repro.:* in Graphis, Studio, Designers in Britain, Modern Publicity, press and magazines and commercial publications. *Address:* 9/16 Airlie Gdns., London W8. *Signs work:* "Dekk."

DE LA FOUGÈRE, Lucette, R.B.A., R.O.I., N.S.; painter in oil, water-colour, gouache, and sculptor in ceramics; *b* London. *Educ.:* both in Touraine, France, and London; *studied art* under Leopold Pascal. *Work in permanent collections:* The National Museum of Wales, Cardiff. *Exhib.:* R.A., Royal Society of British Artists, Royal Institute of Oil Painters, N.S.P.S., New English Art Club; one-man show: Mall Galleries; works permanently on tour in Great Britain and U.S.A. *Work repro.:* articles and works reproduced in the Artist (1966). *Address:* The Studio, 20 Lower Common South, Putney, London SW15. *Club:* Chelsea Arts. *Signs work:* "FOUGÈRE."

DELLAR, Ronald Peter; painter in oil, water-colour, gouache, charcoal, etc.; portraits and murals; mem. Contemporary Portrait Soc. (1970); *b* South London, 30 Apr., 1930; *s* of Frederick Dellar, company director. *Studied art:* self-taught. *Exhib.:* one-man shows: Archer Gallery (1952), Düsseldorf (1956), Young Contemporaries (R.B.A. Galleries, 1953), Daily Express Young Artists (1955), Artists of Fame and Promise, Leicester Gallery (1958), New Art Centre, Sloane St. (1958), Royal Society of Portrait Painters (1968-69), Hackney Borough Council (1970), Düsseldorf (1971), Neuss (1974-75). *Work in private collections:* England, Germany, France, Belgium, Switzerland, America. *Address:* The Studio, Cowden, Kent.

de MAJO, Willy M., M.B.E., F.S.I.A., Hon. G.V.N., Hon. A.B.C.D. (S.A.F.F.T.), Hon. C.B.G.; graphic and industrial designer; founder and Past Pres., I.C.O.G.R.A.D.A.; co-ordinating designer, Festival of Britain, N.I. (1951);

consultant designer to: Charles Letts & Co., John Millar & Sons, Cronmatch Ltd., Tape Industries Ltd., *b* Vienna, 25 July, 1917; *s* of Maks de Majo; *m* Veronica Mary Booker; three *d. Educ.:* Commercial Academy, Vienna; auto-didact. *Exhib.:* Vienna, Belgrade, Paris, London, Belfast, Brussels, Bulawayo, U.S.A., Japan and Canada. Recipient of 1969 S.I.A.D. Design Medal for outstanding services to international design. *Address:* 99 Archel Rd., London W14 9QL. *Signs work:* "W. M. de MAJO," or "de MAJO."

DEMARCO, Richard, R.S.W. (1966), S.S.A. (1964); painter in water-colours, pencil, pen and ink, gouache and illustrator; director of the Richard Demarco Gallery; director, Edinburgh Arts Summer School; visiting lecturer in over 50 North American and European art schools and universities; *b* Edinburgh, 1930; *s* of Carmine Demarco; *m* Anne. *Educ.:* Edinburgh College of Art (1949-53). *Work in permanent collections:* Scottish National Gallery of Modern Art, V. & A., Arts Council of Scotland, City of Sheffield Art Galleries, and the Universities of Glasgow, Durham, Krakow. *Publications:* Edinburgh Arts Catalogues (1974 and 1975), Architectural Review. *Address:* 29 Frederick St., Edinburgh, 2. *Club:* Scottish Arts. *Signs work:* "Richard DEMARCO."

DEMEL, Richard, Art Diploma (1948). M.I.L.Incorp.Linguist (Pol, Eng. It.), F.R.S.A.; Mem. Assoc. Polish Univ. Prof. London; Accad. di Merito Accad. de "i 500", Accad. Tiberina, Accad. Gent. P. Pacem, Legion d'Oro, Rome; Counsellor Nat. Univ. of Canada, Toronto; art master, lecturer, writer; lecturer: Istit. di Stato, Abano, Liceo Ling., Univ. Coll. Padova, Univ. of Venice; stained glass artist (transparent mosaic method inventor), painter, engraver; *b* Ustron Poland, 21 Dec., 1921; *s* of Joseph (artist) and Anna (née Bieta); *m* Anna Parisi; one *s*, one *d*. *Educ.:* Andrychow and Biala-Bielsko; *studied art* at Accad. d. Belle Arti e del Nudc (1945-47), Rome, Polish Accad. Art Centre, Rome, London (1945-49); London University Slade School (1949); LCC Central School of Art (1949-51); asst. to J. Nuttgens (St. Etheldreda's Church windows); asst. lecturer to Prof. M. Bohusz-Szyszko. *Exhib.:* 12 one-man and 95 collective; ITV film (1961), BBC TV on pupils' work (with Miró 1962). *Biography and work repro.:* in 36 art encyclopaedias and art publications. *Address:* Via S. Bartolomeo 13,-35030 Tencarola, Padova, Italy. *Signs work:* see appendix.

de MERIC, Rosalie, F.F.P.S.; painter in acrylic; Lecturer in Art Hist., Croydon College of Art; *b* Weymouth, 1916; *d* of V. E. de Meric, Royal Engineers; *m* Thomas Blackburn; one *d. Educ.:* Putney High School; York University; *studied art* at Central School (1941-43) under Bernard Meninsky, St. Martin's (1943-45), Medway School of Art (1945-48). *Exhib.:* Drian Gallery, London, Nova Fine Art, Copenhagen, Environment, Harrogate, Hoya Gallery, London. *Address:* Cambria Lodge, 2c Oakhill Rd., Putney, London SW15. *Club:* W.I.A.C. *Work* not signed.

DEMPSTER: see JONES, Thomas DEMPSTER.

DEMUS, Otto, Ph.D., Dr. L.C., M.A. (Camb.); Em. Pres. Austrian Monuments and Fine Arts Service, Prof. in History of Art at Vienna University; writer on art, particularly Byzantine and Western Mediaeval Art; mem. of British Academy, Society of Antiquaries, London, of Austrian and Mainz Academy, Académie Française and of Austrian Archaeological Palermo Institute; *b* Harland, Austria, 4 Nov., 1902; *s* of Carl Demus, M.D.; *m* Margarethe Quatember, Ph.D.; two *s*. *Educ.:* Vienna University; *studied art* under Strzygowski, v. Schlosser, Glück, Menghin, Reisch, Keil (History of Art, Prehistory, Archaeology). *Publications:* several books and many papers on Byzantine mosaics, Romanesque Art; papers on Austrian art. *Address:* Kunsthistor Institut, Universitatsstr, 7, Vienna, 1.

DENMAN, Gladys, R.M.S. (1960); artist in oil and water-colour, miniature painter; *b* Hampstead, 1900; *d* of Adrian Denman-Jones, electrical engineer. *Educ.:* King Alfred School, Hampstead, King's College for Women, Campden Hill; *studied art* at Slade School (1919-23) under Henry Tonks, Wilson Steer, and W. W. Russell. *Exhib.:* R.P., R.M.S., R.I., R.O.I. *Address:* 36 Rotherwick Rd., London NW11 7DB. *Club:* Hampstead Golf. *Signs work:* see appendix.

DENNES, Noel; painter in oil and tempera and engraver; Chairman of Norfolk and Norwich Art Circle (1961-62); *b* Lowestoft, 25 Dec., 1908; *s* of Rev. F. B. Dennes. *Educ.:* Hitchin Grammar School and Bracondale School, Norwich; *studied art* at Norwich School of Art and under E. H. Whydale A.R.E. *Exhib.:* R.B.A., R.O.I., N.S., R.E., City Art Gallery, Birmingham, R.A. Exhbn., Blackpool, Norwich Castle Museum; municipal galleries at Southgate, Guildford, Wolverhampton, Stafford, Stretford and Scarborough; one-man shows, Assembly House, Norwich, etc. *Address:* St. Annes, 196 Dereham Rd., Costessey, Norfolk. *Signs work:* "NOEL DENNES."

DENT, Aileen Rose; artist in oils; portrait and still-life painter in realistic and tonal manner; *b* Victoria, Feb., 1891; *d* of H. Dent. *Educ.:* Methodist Ladies' College, Melbourne; *studied art* at Melbourne National Gallery School (1915-20) under W. B. McInnes, F. W. McCubbin and L. B. Hall. *Exhib.:* in annual one-man shows in Melbourne; portraits hung in Archibald Prize, Sydney, also exhib. Victorian Artists' Society. *Work in permanent collections:* Melbourne National Gallery, National Library, Canberra, Latrobe Library, Melbourne. *Address:* c/o Mrs. P. E. Tom, Batley's Creek, Parkes, 2870, N.S.W., Australia. *Signs work:* "Aileen Dent" or "A. R. Dent."

DENT, Richard, F.R.S.A., M.F.P.S.; self-taught artist, repousse worker in copper and enamel; *b* Hereford, 1902; one *s*. *Exhib.:* Free Painters Society (1976, 1977), Loggia Gallery (1971), Hanna Holmes Gallery (1967). *Address:* 15 Moreton Pl., Westminster, London SW1. *Signs work:* "R. Dent."

DENT, Robert Stanley Gorrell, A.R.C.A. (Lond.) (1933), R.E. (1946), R.W.A. (1953), A.S.I.A. (Ed.) (1967); Principal, Glos. College of Art and Design, Cheltenham, and Stroud (1950-74); etcher and water-colour painter; Mem. Fine Art Panel and National Council for Diplomas in Art and Design (1962-65); Min. of Educ. Intermediate Assessor (1957-60); G.C.E. Chief Examiner, A level; *b* 1 July, 1909; *m* Doris Wenban; two *s*. *Educ.:* Newport School of Arts and Crafts, R.C.A. *Exhib.:* R.A.; R.S.A.; International Exhbn. of Etching and Engraving, Chicago; International Printmakers' Exhbn., California. *Address:* Wenbans, Ashley Road, Battledown, Charlton Kings, Glos. *Signs work:* "R. S. G. Dent."

de QUIN, Robert, N.D.D., N.S., F.F.P.S.; artist using mainly welded metal sculpture and some wood; art teacher; Head of Faculty of Design; Vice-chairman, F.P.S.; mem. Westminster Arts Council Visual Arts Sub-Committee; *b* Namur, Belgium, 1927; *m*; two *d*. *Educ.:* Hornsey College of Art (1945-50). *Exhib.:* many group shows in this country and abroad; one-man shows: Mall Galleries, Old Bakehouse Gallery, Sevenoaks. *Address:* 42 Grosvenor Rd., Muswell Hill, London N10 2DS. *Clubs:* H.A.C., F.P.S., N.S. *Signs work:* "Robert de Quin" usually etched in the metal followed by year.

DERRINGER, Kenneth, A.T.D. (1949), travelling schol. (1948); painter, designer; Principal, College of Art and Design, Warrington; *b* Liverpool; *s* of Thomas Derringer; *m* Dr. Evelyn Roberts; one *s*. one *d*. *Educ.:* Oulton Grammar School, Liverpool; *studied art* at Liverpool University School of Architecture and Liverpool College of Art. *Exhib.:* Arts Council of Great Britain, Walker A.G., Manchester A.G., Preston A.G., Williamson A.G., R.Cam.A. *Work in permanent* *collections:* Walker A.G. *Address:* 9 Croxteth Rd., Liverpool 8. *Clubs:* Sandon Studios, Liverpool Academy, Wirral Art Soc., Inst. of Amateur Cinematographers. *Signs work:* "KENNETH DERRINGER."

DE SALAS, Xavier, Dr. of History (1930), L.D. in Laws (1932); Great Cross of the order of Civil Merit, Knight Commander of the O. of Isabel La Catolica, etc.; Cultural Attaché to Spanish Embassy in London; Director of Institute of Spain (London, 1947); Deputy Director, Museo del Prado, Madrid (1960); Director, Museo del Prado (1969); *b* 4 June, 1907; *s* of Francis Javier de Salas; *m* Carmen de Ortueta; three *s,* one *d. Publications:* Marcos Antonio de Orellana, Biographia Pictorica Valentina, La Familia de Carlos IV (Barcelona, 1945), El Bosco en la Literatura Española (Barcelona, 1945), Velazquez (London, 1963), Appendix to Las pinturas negras de Goya (Milano, Barcelona, 1963). *Address:* Pedro de Valdivia 4, Madrid 6.

de SAULLES, Mary, A.R.I.B.A. (1948), A.A. dip (1947), F.S.I.A. (1959); architect and designer, interior, exhbn., display; deputy to chief officer of specialized design section, L.C.C. Architects' Dept. (1950-52); partnership with John Lunn, F.S.I.A. (1951-55); Industrial Designer, British European Airways (1959); private practice (1960), interiors, exhibitions, housing, etc.; *b* Westcliff-on-Sea, 1925; *d* of Curzon Harper; *m* Patrick de Saulles, A.A.dip. *Educ.:* St. Monica's, Clacton-on-Sea; *studied* architecture at the Architectural Assoc. School of Architecture. *Work repro.:* Designers in Britain, Nos. 4 and 5, Architectural Review. *Address:* 8 Belmont, Shrewsbury. *Club:* Architectural Assoc. *Signs work:* "Mary de Saulles & Associates."

DE SOUZA, Pascoal, R.O.I., R.B.A.; de Lazlo Award (1959); artist in oil; *b* Goa, 1 June, 1928; *m;* two *s. Studied art* at Sir John Cass and St. Martin's Schools of Art. *Exhib.:* R.A., Paris Salon, etc.; 4 one-man shows, Trafford Gallery, London; 1 at Alwin Gallery, London. *Address:* 10 Heron Rd., St. Margaret's, Twickenham, Middx. *Signs work:* "Pascoal de Souza."

de TOLNAY, Charles (Erich), Ph.D. (Vienna, 1925), Lauréat de l'Académie des Inscriptions et Belles-Lettres (Paris, 1937), Guggenheim Fellow (1948-53); D. in Lettere h. c, (1964); art historian; Director, Casa Buonarroti, Florence (since 1965); *b* Budapest, 27 May, 1899; *s* of Arnold de Tolnay; *m* Anna Marie Reps. *Educ.:* Budapest and the universities of Vienna, Berlin and Frankfurt-on-Main. *Publications:* Werk und Weltbild des Michelangelo (Zürich, 1949), Michel-Ange (Paris, 1951; Florence, 1951), Michelangelo (Princeton Univ. Press, 1943-60, 5 vols.); H. Bosch (London, 1965). *Address:* Casa Buonarroti, Via Ghibellina 70, Florence.

DE VASCONCELLOS, Josephina, F.R.B.S., A.W.G.; sculptor in stone, bronze, wood, perspex, lead; *b* Molesey-on-Thames; *d* of Hippolyto De Vasconcellos; *m* Delmar Banner. *Educ.:* Bournemouth High School; *studied art* at Regent St. Polytechnic; Florence; Paris. *Exhib.:* R.A., Salon. *Work in permanent collections:* National Gallery, Rio de Janeiro; Glasgow A.G.; Southampton A.G.; Sheffield A.G.; Gloucester Cathedral; Liverpool Cathedral; National Memorial to the Battle of Britain, Aldershot; Mary and Child, St. Paul's Cathedral. *Address:* Bield, Little Langdale, Ambleside, Westmorland. *Club:* The Reynolds. *Signs work:* see appendix.

DEVEY, Phyllis, R.D.S., R.B.S.A., N.D.D.; artist in oils (especially portrait); Director of Art, Windylow School, Solihull (1956-62); teacher of life and painting, Handsworth School of Art, Birmingham (1952-55), and at Bournville School of Art (since 1954); Vice-President Royal Birmingham Society of Artists (1969); *b* Birmingham, 27 Feb., 1907; *d* of Wilfred E. Busby; *m* H. Robert Devey. *Educ.:*

Moseley Ladies' College; *studied art* at Birmingham College of Arts and Crafts. *Exhib.:* Paris Salon, R.O.I., R.B.A., N.S., S.W.A., R.C.A., R.B.S.A., Birmingham, Bournemouth, Hull, Nottingham, Sheffield, Wolverhampton, Worcester. *Club:* Soroptomist Club of Stratford-upon-Avon. *Address:* Applegarth, Bearley Cross, Wootton Wawen, Solihull, W. Midlands. *Signs work:* "PHYLLIS DEVEY."

DEVLIN, George, R.S.W. (1964); painter in oil, water-colour, etching and ceramics; Head of Art, Hermitage, Helensburgh; *b* Glasgow, 8 Sept., 1937; *s* of George Devlin. *Educ.:* Albert Secondary School, Glasgow; *studied art* at Glasgow School of Art (1955-60) under David Donaldson. *Exhib.:* many one-man shows; Belfast Open 100, 2nd British Biennale of Drawing, Contemporary Scottish Painting (Arts Council), etc. *Work in permanent collections:* Scottish National Gallery of Modern Art, Arts Council, Aberdeen A.G., Essex County Council, Leicester and Strathclyde Universities, Edinburgh City Collection, Argyle County Council. *Publications:* illustrations for Scotsman and Maclellan Publishers. Designed set and costumes for new ballet by Walter Gore (1973) and presented by Scottish Ballet. *Address:* 5A Churchill Drive, Glasgow G11 7LQ. *Signs work:* "George Devlin."

de WINTER, Carl: deputy Sec. Gen., Federation of British Artists: director, Art Exhbns. Bureau: sec. Royal Society of Marine Artists: sec. Royal Society of Miniature Painters, Sculptors and Gravers; sec. National Society of Painters, Sculptors and Printmakers; sec. New English Art Club; sec. Royal Institute of Oil Painters; sec. United Society of Artists; keeper, Royal Society of British Artists; asst. sec. Royal Society of Portrait Painters; *b* 18 June, 1934; *s* of Alfred de Winter; *m* Lyndall Bradshaw; one *s*, one *d*. *Educ.:* Pangbourne. *Addresses:* 17 Carlton House Terr., London SW1Y 5BD; Dalewood Cottage, Mickleham, nr. Dorking.

DEXTER, James Henry; designer; *b* 23 July, 1912; *s* of James Badby Dexter; *m* Marjorie Ellen Gurr. *Educ.:* Leicester College of Art. *Exhib.:* N.E.A.C., R.A., London Group, various provincial galleries. *Official purchases:* Corporation of Leicester. *Address:* 52 Scraptoft Lane, Humberstone, Leicester. *Signs work:* "James Dexter."

DEYKIN, Henry Cotterill; painter in oil and teacher; art master, Warwick School (1935-65); Army camouflage officer in late war; *b* Edgbaston, 31 May, 1905; *s* of W. Cotterill Deykin; *m* Barbara Gordon Fife; one *s*. *Educ.:* King Edward's School, Birmingham; *studied art* at Birmingham College of Art, Slade School. *Exhib.:* R.A., Whitechapel A.G., Birmingham A.G.; sponsored one-man exhbns. at Eton, Harrow, Shrewsbury, Wycombe Abbey School, Norwich and Cambridge Art Schools, Assembly House, Norwich, Hurlingham Club, London, Leamington A.G., and Bristol A.G. *Work repro.:* Times Educ. Supplement. *Address:* 68 Binswood Av., Leamington Spa, Warwickshire.

DICKSON, Jennifer, A.R.A., R.E.; printmaker, painter; *b* Piet Retief, S. Africa, 17 Sept., 1936. *Studied art* at Goldsmiths' College School of Art (University of London, 1954-59) and Atelier 17, Paris, under S. W. Hayter. Professor, Faculty of Fine Arts, Concordia University, Montreal, Canada. *Work in permanent collections:* V. & A.; National Gallery of Canada; Hermitage, Leningrad; Cleveland Art Institute, etc. *Published* 11 major suites of original prints. *Address:* c/o Galerie Dresdnere, 130 Bloor St. West, Toronto 5.

DI GIROLAMO, Romeo, R.B.A., N.D.D.; artist in oil; Bucks Architectural Competition (1953, 1954); Bucks Art Scholarship (1954-59); Granada Theatre National Painting Prize (1957); David Murray Travelling Scholarship awarded by R.A. (1959); formerly Head of Art Depts., Gt. Marlow Secondary, Slough Grammar for Boys, The Radcliffe Comprehensive; at present Head of Painting

Dept., Amersham College of Further Education and School of Art (formerly High Wycombe School of Art); mem. of the Academic Board and Governor of the College; *b* Civitella Casanova, Italy, 1939; *s* of Paolo Emilio di Girolamo; *m* Megan, A.T.C. *Educ.:* Quainton and Waddesdon secondary schools; *studied art* at High Wycombe School of Art (1954-59). *Exhib.:* R.A., R.B.A., Art Bureau Travelling exhbns. and many one-man shows. *Work in permanent collections:* private collections in many countries. *Address:* Bridge Bend, Nash Lee Rd., Wendover, Bucks. *Signs work:* "Romeo di Girolamo."

DINKEL, Ernest Michael, R.W.S., A.R.C.A., R.I.B.A. Owen Jones Scholarship (1926); designer, artist in oil, water-colour, tempera, stained glass, glass engraver; assistant to Prof. Tristram (R.C.A., 1925-40); princ. School of Art, Stourbridge (1940-47), head of School of Design, Edinburgh College of Art (1947-61); *b* Huddersfield, 24 Oct., 1894; *s* of Charles Dinkel; *m* 1st, Kathleen Hanks; 2nd, Emmy Keet; three *s*, two *d*. *Studied art* at Huddersfield School of Art, R.C.A. (1921-24), Italy, France, etc. *Exhib.:* N.E.A.C., R.A., R.Scot.A., R.W.S. *Work in permanent collections:* Laing Art Gallery, Newcastle, Tate Gallery, Dudley Art Gallery. *Official purchases:* see above. *Address:* The Grange, Bussage, nr. Stroud, Glos. *Signs work:* see appendix.

DIXON, Rex Matthew, Dip. A.D. (1971), A.T.D. (1972); visual arts officer, Midlands Arts Centre; part-time lecturer, Stourbridge College of Art; *b* London, 1939. *Studied art* at School of Art, Newton Abbott (1966-68), Stourbridge College of Art (1968-71). *Exhib.:* one-man shows: Ikon Gallery, Birmingham (1971), Midlands Arts Centre (1973, 1974), Dudley Art Gallery (1976). *Address:* 3 Brook St., Stourbridge, Worcs. *Signs work:* Canvases titled and dated on stretcher.

DOBBS, Honor, F.P.S.; painter in oil and water-colour; *d* of James J. Bowman; *m* Brig. N. C. Dobbs, R.A.; one *s*, one *d*. *Studied art* at Beckenham Art and Crafts under Lawrence Norris, R. G. E. Pickering, N.D.D., A.T.D., A.R.B.A., P.S. *Exhib.:* Loggia Gallery, Fairfields Hall, Croydon, F.B.A., Mall Galleries, R.W.S., R.A. (1964); one-man show: Bromley Arts Council. *Addresses:* Barkmore, Wilderness Rd., Chislehurst, Kent, and Portnagolan, Cushendall, Co. Antrim, N. Ireland. *Clubs:* Camden Place, Chislehurst, Cushendall Golf, Ballymena. *Signs work:* "Honor Dobbs."

DOBINSON, Eric Arthur, A.T.D. (1951), D.A.E. (1954); schoolmaster, furniture designer, book illustrator; senior art master, King Edward VI School, Nuneaton (1951-55); teacher of cabinet-making and furniture design, Nuneaton School of Art (1951-53); senior art master, Chichester High School for Boys (1955-58); director of art, Seaford College, since 1958; *b* Llandudno, 8 Mar., 1927; *s* of Ivor Dobinson, constructional engineer; *m* Meriel June Perkes; one *s*, one *d*. *Educ.:* John Bright School, Llandudno; *studied art* at Liverpool College of Art (1945-50), and furniture and interior design in Stockholm and Copenhagen (1950-51). *Address:* Seaford College, Petworth, Sussex. *Signs work:* "E.A.D."

DOBSON, Mary: see THORNBERY, Mary.

DODD, Alan, Cert. R.A.S. (1966); painter, interior designer, muralist; *b* Kennington, Ashford, Kent, 23 Nov., 1942. *Studied art* at Maidstone College of Art, Royal Academy Schools. *Exhib.:* R.A. Bicentenary Exhibition (1968); one-man shows: New Grafton Gallery (July, 1969, Nov., 1970, Oct. 1972), 'Four English Painters' Galleria Estudio Cid, Madrid (Nov., 1970). *Work in permanent collections:* in private collections in England, U.S.A., Australia, Spain, Portugal. *Addresses:* 295 Caledonian Rd., London N1, and New Grafton Gallery, 1A Grafton St., London W1. *Signs work:* "Dodd."

DODDS, Andrew, M.S.I.A. (1950), N.D.D. (1949); freelance illustrator and painter; lecturer, Ipswich School of Art; *b* Gullane, Scotland, 5 May, 1927; *m* Rachel Foster. *Studied art* at Colchester School of Art (1942-45), L.C.C. Central School of Arts and Crafts (1947-50). *Exhib.:* R.A.; one-man exhib.: Drawn from London, Mermaid Theatre (1961), Minories, Colchester (1968). *Work repro.:* Designers in Britain, Radio Times and other national publications. Has illustrated 25 books. *Address:* Bourne Mill, Bourne Rd., Colchester, Essex. *Signs work:* "Andrew Dodds."

DOLBY, James Taylor, R.E. (1957), A.R.C.A. (1932), S.W.E.; engraver and illustrator; head, Blackburn School of Art, 1947-69; *b* nr. Haworth, Yorks. *Educ.:* Keighley Grammar School; *studied art* at Keighley School of Art and Royal College of Art under Profs. Malcolm Osborne, R.A., and Robert Austin, R.A. *Exhib.:* R.A., R.S.P.E., Soc. Wood Engravers, Senefelder Club, R.B.A., R.S.M.A., Western Europe, U.S.A., S. Africa, Australia, London, provinces. *Work in permanent collections:* V. & A. Museum, Whitworth Art Gallery, Manchester, Blackburn, Portsmouth, Blackpool, Southport and Keighley. *Publications:* Various. *Address:* 1A River View Rd., Southampton. *Club:* Brook House, Southampton. *Signs work:* "James Dolby."

DONIACH, Thea, N.D.D. (1952), A.T.D. (1954), A.R.W.A. (1968); artist in water-colour, gouache, ink; part-time Tutor, Oxford; *b* Chevreuse, France, 1907; *d* of Leopold Pilichowski, artist; *m* Nakdimon Doniach, O.B.E.; two *d. Educ.:* Lycée Français de Londres; *studied art* at St. Martin's School of Art under Freddie Gore (1951-53), Goldsmiths' College (1953-54). *Work in permanent collections:* R.W.E.A., St. Cyprien: Fondation François Desnoyer, Corpus Christi College J.C.R., Oxford, University College J.C.R., Oxford, City of Oxford Education Committee. *Address:* 11 West St., Osney-Town, Oxford. *Club:* Oxford Art Society. *Signs work:* "Thea Doniach."

DONINGTON, Mary; sculptor; *b* London, 1909. *Educ.:* Mary Datchelor School and R.A.M.; *studied art:* mainly self-taught, but one year under Frank K. Dobson (1945-46). *Exhib.:* R.A., N.S., W.I.A.C., etc. *Publications:* music for children. *Address:* Lashen, Furze Hill Rd., Headley Down, Hants.

DONNE, Leonard David, N.D.D., A.T.D. (1951); artist in oil, water-colour and etching; Head of Art, Cheshunt School; *b* Leicester, 19 June, 1926; *s* of W. D. B. Donne, local government officer; *m* Elizabeth Donne; one *s,* two *d. Educ.:* Wyggeston School, Leicester; *studied art* at Leicester College of Art under D. P. Carrington. *Exhib.:* one-man shows: Gordon Maynard Gallery (1974), Loggia Gallery (1973), F.P.S. and various provincial and London galleries. *Address:* 4 Jeffries Rd., Ware, Herts. *Club:* F.P.S. *Signs work:* "D.D."

DORF, Barbara, D.F.A. London (1962); painter in oil and water-colour; art historian; examiner G.C.E. London University; visiting tutor, Ruskin School, Oxford; *b* London, 1933; *d* of John Stahlheim Dorf. *Educ.:* North London Collegiate School; *studied art* at Central School, Slade School (1959-62) under Sir Tom Monnington, Sir William Coldstream, Sir Ernst Gombrich, Prof. Haskell. *Exhib.:* R.A., Royal Portrait Society, several London, Paris and Belgrade galleries. *Work in permanent collections:* B.M., St. Edmund's Hall, Oxon., Lady Margaret Hall, Oxon., University College, London. *Publications:* Beginners Guides to: Oil Painting, Water-colour, the Nude, the Portrait (Pelham Books); articles in The Artist and Arts Review. *Address:* 11 Pembridge Villas, London W11. *Clubs:* Oxford Union, Newman. *Signs work:* "Dorf."

DOUBLEDAY, John; sculptor mainly in bronze; *b* Langford, Essex, 1947; *s* of G. V. Doubleday, farmer; *m* Isobel J. C. Durie. *Educ.:* Stowe; *studied art* at

Goldsmiths' College (1965-68) under Ivor Roberts-Jones. *Exhib.:* one-man shows at Manchester (1967), Waterhouse Gallery, London (1968), Waterhouse, Galerie Sothmann, Amsterdam (1969), Waterhouse (1970), Sothmann, Waterhouse (1971), Galerie 6, Dusseldorf (1972), Richard Demarco Gallery, Edinburgh, Laing Museum and A.G., Newcastle (1973), Alwin Gallery, London (1974), Touring Exhib. from Bowes Museum (1974-75), Braintree Festival and Sothmann (1975). *Commissioned portraits* include P.M. of Fiji, Archbishop of Canterbury, King of Norway, Earl Mountbatten, Lord Olivier and Golda Meir. *Work in public collections* include Dorman Museum and Ashmolean Museum. *Address:* Lodge Cottage, Great Totham, Maldon, Essex.

DOUDNEY, Henry Eric John, F.R.B.S. (1935), M.S.I.A. (1947); industrial designer, sculptor; *b* Watford, 28 Dec., 1905; *s* of Cecil H. Doudney; *m* Patricia Nicholls; three *s. Educ.:* Isleworth Central School, Acton and Chiswick Polytechnic; *studied art* at Richmond School of Art, R.A. School of Sculpt., Kennington School of Art. *Exhib.:* R.A., R.B.A. *Work in permanent collections:* London, Carlisle, Durham, Derby and Christchurch, Hamilton and Hastings, N.Z. *Publications:* Colour slide sets with notes on History of Architecture and Sculpture (Budek Films & Slides Ltd., U.S.A.). *Address:* Governors Bay, Lyttelton R.D. 1, N.Z. *Signs work:* "E.J.D."

DOUGLAS, Marguerite France, C.I.A.L.; farmer; artist in oil and watercolour; *b* 12 July, 1918; *d* of Edouard Dommen, Swiss engineer; *m* John Haig Douglas; one *s*, three *d. Educ.:* Cheltenham Ladies' College; *studied art* at Derby, Lausanne (1935) and R.A. Schools under Russell and Monnington (1936-39). *Exhib.:* S.S.A., R.S.W., Ancona. *Address:* Glendearg, Galashiels, Selkirkshire. *Signs work:* "M.F.D."

DOWN, Avril; artist in oil, pastel, gouache; taught at local schools, Bishop's Stortford; *b* Penang, Apr., 1900; *d* of C. W. Anderson, M.I.C.E., civil engineer; *m* John Thornton Down, decd.; one *s*, one *d. Educ.:* High Schools, London, Sunderland, Stockton-on-Tees; *studied art* at Slade School under Henry Tonks, Wilson Steer, W. W. Russell. *Exhib.:* Utd. Soc. of Artists, R.I., Sutton Coldfield, Bishop's Stortford, Calcutta and Simla. *Work in permanent collections:* mural paintings, Tower House and New Empire Theatre, Calcutta, Letchworth, Sutton Coldfield and Stansted factories. *Address:* Tye Green, Elsenham, Bishop's Stortford, Herts. *Club:* Bishop's Stortford Art Soc. *Signs work:* "Avril Down," "A.D." or "A. Down."

DOXFORD, James; D.F.A. (Durham), A.T.Dip. (1926), R.W.A.; formerly Principal, Bridgwater Art and Tech. School, Principal, Barnstaple Art and Tech. School, Head, Art Dept., Gateshead Grammar School; artist in oil and watercolour; *b* North Shields, 8 Sept., 1899; *s* of James Doxford, schoolmaster; *m* Norah Elizabeth. *Educ.:* Royal Jubilee School, North Shields, The High School, South Shields; *studied art* at Dept. of Fine Art, Durham University (1922-26) under Prof. R. G. Hatton, Prof. E. M. O'R. Dickey. *Work in permanent collections:* R.W.A., Municipal Art Gallery, Newcastle upon Tyne, Shipley Art Gallery, Gateshead-on-Tyne. *Address:* 1 Tyler Close, Canterbury, Kent. *Signs work:* "DOXFORD."

DREISER, Peter, A.R.M.S.; glass engraver and designer; sealstone engraving and copper-wheel engravings on glass; *b* Cologne, 11 June, 1936; *m* Jovita M-Torner; one *s*, two *d. Educ.:* Brühl Secondary School; *studied art* at Glass Technical School, Rheinbach, Bonn (1951-54) under Prof. A. Dorn, Prof. O. Pietsch, Prof. O. Lippert. *Work repro.:* article on copper wheel engraving in Engraving and Decorating Glass by Barbara Norman (David & Charles).

Address: 18 Rowland Ave., Kenton, Middx. *Signs work:* "P. Dreiser, 1973" and see appendix.

DREW, Pamela, S.M.A., S.A.A.; artist in oil, pastel, chalks and oils or polymer on aluminium; Official Artist, R.A.F. Coronation Review (1953); tour of M.E.A.F. as Air Ministry accredited artist (1955), in Port Said and Suez (Nov., 1956) (war artist); *b* Burnley, 11 Sept., 1910; *d* of John M. Drew, calico printer; *m* (1st) Lord Rathdonnel, M.C. (decd.); one *s*, three *d*; (2nd) Hugh C. Massy. *Studied art* under Dorothy Baker, Christchurch, Hants, Iain MacNab, Grosvenor School of Modern Art, and Roger Chastel, Paris. *Exhib.:* one-man, Wexford Festival (1972), Cork Arts (1975), London and Nairobi. *Work repro.:* R.A.F. Coronation Review; R.S.M.A. diploma work in National Maritime Museum, Greenwich. *Work in permanent collections:* City A.G., Belfast, Imperial War Museum, London, R.A.F. Museum (1972) Hendon, Port of London Authority. *Official purchases:* Fighter Command, R.A.F.; Min. of Works. *Address:* The Studio, Ballinatray, Youghal, Co. Cork, Ireland. *Signs work:* "Pamela Drew." "P. Drew" or "P.D."

DREWITT, Geoffrey Crellin, A.T.D., F.R.S.A.; painter; Senior Art Master, Pinner County School (1947-49); City of Norwich School (1949-56); Part-time instructor, Norwich Art School (1950-56); Head of Dept., Gateacre Comprehensive School, Liverpool (1956-66); Art Adviser, Northumberland County (1967-); *b* Little Gaddesden, 6 May, 1921; *s* of Ivan C. Drewitt; *m* Pauline Julian, S.R.N., C.M.B.; three *d. Educ.:* Berkhamsted School; *studied art* at Westminster School of Art, Central School of Art (1938-40), University of London Inst. of Educ. (1946-47). *Exhib.:* R.A., R.O.I., R.B.A., N.S. *Official purchase:* Little Gaddesden, Herts., School (mural decorations). *Address:* 38 Mitchell Ave., Newcastle upon Tyne, 2. *Signs work:* "G. C. Drewitt."

DREYFUS, John Gustave, M.A. (1945), F.S.I.A. (1957), F.R.S.A. (1970); typographer; *b* London, 15 Apr., 1918; typographical adviser to the University Press, Cambridge (since 1958), having been Assistant Printer (1949-58); typographical adviser to the Monotype Corporation Limited since 1955; European consultant to the George Macy Companies Inc. (since 1956); President of Assoc. Typographique Internationale (1967-73), now Hon. Pres.; Chairman of the Printing Historical Society; director of the Curwen Press (1970); *m* Irène Thurnauer; one *s*, two *d. Educ.:* Oundle; Trinity College, Cambridge. *Address:* 169 Queen's Gate, London SW7. *Clubs:* Garrick, Double Crown.

DRING, James, A.R.C.A., R.O.I.; painter in oil and water-colour; teacher at St. Martin's School of Art (1943-72); *b* London, 8 Oct., 1905; *s* of William Henry Dring; *m* Olive Stacey; one *s*, one *d*; *studied art* at Clapham School of Art (1920-27) and R.C.A. under Sir William Rothenstein (painting). *Exhib.:* R.A., R.O.I., R.B.A., Wertheim Gallery, Paul Alexander Gallery, Galerie Apollinaire, provincial galleries, Paris, Brussels, Sweden, U.S.A. *Work in permanent collections:* V. & A., Southampton Art Gallery, Mons and Brussels Museums. *Official purchases:* Contemporary Art Soc. *Work repro.:* Medici Soc. *Address:* 20 Grange Rd., Barnes, London SW13. Member of I.A.L. and R.O.I. *Signs work:* see appendix.

DRING, Lilian M., A.R.C.A. (1929); F. Soc. Designer-craftsmen; designer-embroiderer, specialist in hand-machine stitched applique; *b* Surbiton, 15 Mar., 1908; *d* of G. R. Welch; *m* James Dring (divorced 1946); one *s*. *Studied art* at Kingston School of Art under A. J. Collister (1922-26), R.C.A. under Profs. Tristram and Reco Capey (1926-29). *Official purchases:* Modern Church Embroidery (Council for Care of Churches), includes sets of vestments for Gloucester Cathedral, cope for Kew Church, etc. Specializes in fabric house-portraits (including Hovingham Hall, etc.). *Address:* 6 Devoncroft Gdns., Twickenham, Middx. *Signs work:* see appendix.

DRING, W., R.A. (1955), R.W.S.; painter; *b* 26 Jan., 1904; *s* of W. H. Dring; *m*; one *s*, two *d*. *Educ.:* Slade School of Fine Arts (1922-25). *Address:* Windy Ridge, Compton, Winchester. *Club:* Arts. *Signs work:* see appendix.

DRINKWATER, G. Nevin, B.Sc. (London, 1928); Diploma of Museums Assoc. (1933); Fellow (1952); Pres. Northern Federation of Museums and Art Galleries (1951, 1952), Curator, Teaching Museum, Royal Dental Hospital, London (1924-26); Deputy Curator, Sunderland Museum, Art Gallery and Libraries (1929-46); Curator, Shipley Art Gallery and Saltwell Park Museum, Gateshead (1946-69); *b* London, 4 Feb., 1904; *s* of Dr. Ernest Harold Drinkwater; *m* Isabel Hailes McDonald. *Address:* Tigh Aisling, 20 Church St., Bradford-on-Avon, Wilts.

DRLJACHA, Zorica, A.R.B.S.; awarded First Prize British Institute in Sculpture (1961), anatomy drawing competition (1962), Landseer Scholarship, first prize and silver medal (1963), Catherine Adeline Sparkes prize; sculptress in bronze, aluminium, resin, ciment fondu; *b* Yugoslavia, 14 July, 1942; *d* of Ilija Drljacha, detective sergeant; *m* Mladen; two *d*. *Educ.:* Grammar school (Yugoslavia), Luton College of Technology; *studied art* at Goldsmiths' College under H. W. Parker, F.R.B.S., R. Jones, R.A.; R.A. Schools under C. Mahoney, R.A., Sir Arnold Machin, O.B.E., R.A., Sir Henry Rushbury, K.C.V.O., C.B.E. *Exhib.:* R.A. summer exhbns., R.B.S., Alwyn, Chelsea, Forty Hall, Portrait Society, open-air Holland Park, Davies St., Ealing, Chiswick, etc. *Commissions:* figures for "Battle of Trafalgar" at Madame Tussauds (1966), Expo '67 (Canada). *Work in permanent collections:* England, U.S.A., Yugoslavia, Germany, Italy, France. *Address:* 152 Sutton Ct. Rd., Chiswick, London W4.

DRUMMOND, V. H.; artist and author of children's books; water-colour painter; *b* London, 1911; *d* of D. R. Drummond; *m* A. C. Swetenham. *Studied art* at St. Martin's (1930). *Exhib.:* Upper Grosvenor Gallery. *Publications:* Library Association's award (1957) best illustrated children's book, Mrs. Easter and the Storks, Mr. Finch's Pet Shop, Mrs. Easter and the Golden Bounder, Lady Talavera, Tidgies Innings, Little Laura, Mrs. Easter's Parasol (Faber), Miss Anna Truly and the Christmas Lights, The Flying Postman, Phewtus the Squirrel (Longmans). Drawings for B.B.C. animated film Little Laura. *Address:* 24 Norfolk Rd., St. John's Wood, London NW8. *Signs work:* "V. H. Drummond."

DRURY, Paul Dalou, P.R.E. (1970); painting, drawing, etching, Principal Goldsmiths' College School of Art (1967-69); visiting lecturer Sir John Cass College School of Art; *b* 14 Oct., 1903; *s* of Alfred Drury, R.A.; *m* Enid Solomon, painter; one *s*. *Educ.:* Westminster School; Goldsmiths' Coll. Sch. of Art (Clive Gardiner, Stanley Anderson, R.A., 1920-25); B.I.Schol. in Engraving, 1924. *Exhib.:* R.A., Leicester Galls., Royal Soc. Painter-Etchers, etc. British Council exhbns. abroad. *Official purchases:* British Museum, Ashmolean Museum, Contemp. Art Soc., Toronto, Stockholm, etc., War Artists' Com. *Work repro.:* various periodicals, Print Collector's Quarterly (1929). *Address:* Rangers Cottage, Nutley, Uckfield, Sussex. *Club:* Arts. *Signs work:* "Paul Drury."

DUBUFFET, Jean, painter in oil; Founded, Society for the Collection of l'art brut; *b* Le Havre, 1901. *Exhib.:* New York (1947); I.C.A., London (1955); Arthur Tooth (1958, 1960); Retrospective Exhbn., Musée des Arts, Paris (1960-61). *Work in permanent collections:* Museum of Modern Art (New York); Tate Gallery. *Publications:* Prospectus aux Amateurs de tout Gemre (1946); L'Art Brut preféré aux arts culturels (1951); Dubuffet Drawings by Danial Cordier

(1960); L'Art Brut de Jean Dubuffet, by Georges Limbeur (1953). *Address:* c/o Arthur Tooth & Sons Ltd., 31 Bruton St., London W1. *Signs work:* "Jean Dubuffet."

DUCKETT, Ernest John, P.S. (1951); portrait painter in oil, pastel and water-colour; *b* Much Wenlock, Shropshire; *s* of E. L. Duckett; *m* A. P. J. Wyse. *Educ.:* Much Wenlock and Birmingham; *studied art:* Shrewsbury Art School under M. S. A. Daynes and at Stoke-on-Trent. *Exhib.:* R.A., Paris Salon, R.P., R.O.I., R.B.A., N.S., and provincial galleries. *Address:* The Orchard, London Rd., Southborough, Kent. *Club:* Imperial Arts League. *Signs work:* "E. John Duckett."

DUCKWORTH, Barbara, F.M.A.A., A.I.M.B.I., S.R.N.; medical artist, artist in water-colour, conté, black and white, oil and pastel; *b* Wallasey, Ches., 31 Oct., 1913; *d* of William Duckworth, solicitor. *Educ.:* Sandford Private School, Blundellsands; *studied art:* Liverpool College of Art (1934-38). *Exhib.:* Walker Art Gallery, Liverpool; Liver Sketching Club; medical work at B.M.A. House, London, and Med. Institution, Liverpool. *Work in permanent collection:* Fundus and eye paintings, St. Paul's Eye Hospital, Liverpool. *Work repro.:* many illustrations in medical journals; medical text-books. *Address:* 131 Milner Rd., Heswall, Wirral, Ches. L60 5RX. *Signs work:* "Barbara Duckworth."

DUDENEY, Wilfred, F.R.B.S. (1952); sculptor; Vice-President: Royal Society of British Sculptors (1971-75); Head of Dept. of Art, Crafts and Liberal Studies, Isleworth Polytechnic, Middx. (1959-71); asst. Prof. National College of Art, Dublin (1938-39); *b* Leicester, 30 Sept. 1911; *s* of Leonard Dudeney, journalist; *m* Dorothy Stephenson; one *d*. *Educ.:* St. Paul's School; *studied art* at L.C.C. Central School of Arts and Crafts under Alfred Turner, R.A. (1928-33). *Exhib.:* R.A., R.H.A., N.E.A.C., London and provinces. *Address:* Woodroffe House, Chiswick Mall, London W4. *Signs work:* "W.D." or "Wilfred Dudeney."

DUDLEY, Colin Joseph, D.F.C., A.T.D. (1948); painter, sculptor, designer and teacher of art; Head of Art at Christ Church College, Canterbury (teacher training) since 1963; Head of Foundation School and teacher training at Loughborough College of Art (1957-63); Senior Lecturer in Art to Loughborough Training College (1954-57); Art Master at Collyer's School (1948-49), Deal Boys' Secondary (1949-51), Loughborough College School (1951-54); *b* Greenwich, 13 Apr., 1923; *s* of Joseph Dudley, musician. *Educ.:* Eltham College; *studied art* at Sidcup School of Art and Goldsmiths' College. *Exhib.:* R.A., R.B.A., N.E.A.C., S.E.A., London Group, Midland Group. *Official purchases:* Derbyshire Educ. Com., L.C.C., Loughborough College. *Address:* Wye College, Canterbury Cathedral.

DUFFY, Evelyn Arthur Joseph, M.F.P.S. (1973); entomologist; esoteric painter in coloured inks; *b* Croydon, 1916. *Educ.:* Croydon High School for Boys. *Exhib.:* one-man shows: Loggia Gallery (1975), Woodstock Gallery (1972, 1974, 1975, 1976), Paris Salon (1975). *Work repro.:* Athena Reproductions Ltd., Science Fiction Monthly (Mar., 1974). *Address:* c/o British Museum (N.H.), London SW7. *Signs work:* "Dy."

DUFTY, Arthur Richard, C.B.E. (1971), A.R.I.B.A. (1935), F.S.A. (1946); Sec. (1962-73) to Royal Commn. on Historical Monuments (England) and (1964) National Monuments Record, incorporating National Buildings Record; Master of the Armouries, H.M. Tower of London (1963); Sec. to Soc. of Antiquaries (1954-64), Vice-Pres. (1964-67, 1975-); Vice-Pres. (1962-65) of Council for British Archaeology: Editor (1952-56) to Royal Archaeological Institute, Vice-Pres. (1960-64); Chairman, Corpus Vitrearum Medii Aevi (1970-); Vice-Chairman, Cathedrals Advisory Committee (1964-); mem. of Ancient

Monuments Board for England (1962-73); Chairman of Governors of Farnham Art School (1953-64); *b* 23 June, 1911; *s* of T. E. Dufty; *m* Kate Brazley Ainsworth; one *s*, two *d*. *Educ.:* Rugby, Liverpool School of Architecture. *Work repro.:* Drawings in Commission Inventories, etc. *Publications:* on architecture, W. Norris and Kelmscott, etc. *Address:* 46 Trafalgar Ct., Farnham, Surrey. *Clubs:* Athenæum, Arts. *Signs work:* see appendix.

DUMMETT, Edwin James, R.C.A.; painter; *b* Castle Cary, Som., 15 July, 1906. *Educ.:* Bristol. *Exhib.:* R.C.A. *Address:* Noddfa, Coed Gwydyr, Trefriw, Gwynedd. *Signs work:* "Ted Dummett."

DUNCAN, Joseph; painter in oil and gouache; *b* Ireland; *s* of Ewart John Duncan; *m* Manja Alexandra; two *s*. *Educ.:* Mayfield College; *studied art* at Slade School under Profs. Gerrard and Schwabe. *Work in museums:* Dublin, Ireland; St. Etienne, Fr.; Bahia, Brazil; Stedelijk, Amsterdam; Borås and Halmstad, Sweden; Maisons de la Culture, Le Havre and Grenoble, France; Phoenix, Arizona; Santa Fé, New Mexico; Providence, Rhode Island; Boston University, U.S.A.; Air France Air Terminal, Les Invalides, Paris; commissioned painting 144 sq. ft. for French Pavilion, Montreal World's Fair (1967). *Exhib.:* frequently Europe, the Americas, and Japan. *Addresses:* 21 rue Michel le Comte, Paris 3°, and Le Mazert, Barjac, 30, Le Gard. *Signs work:* "Duncan."

DUNCAN, Marjorie; artist in oil; *b* London, 4 May, 1905; *d* of Charles F. Duncan. *Educ.:* Lady Margaret School and Froebel Ed. Inst.; *studied art* under Bernard Adams, R.O.I., R.P., N.S. *Exhib.:* R.O.I., R.B.A., N.S., Chelsea Artists, S.W.A. *Club:* The Eastbourne Group. *Address:* Winton Cottage, Alfriston, Sussex. *Signs work:* "MARJORIE DUNCAN."

DUNCAN, Ruth (Mrs. Robert Duncan); F. American Artists Professional League, N.Y.C., Mem. Coppini Academy of Fine Arts, River Art Group, Society of Western Artists; landscape painter; *b* Greeley, Colorado, 19 Feb., 1908; resident of San Antonio, Texas since 1945; *d* of Edwin Starkey; *m* Robert Duncan; two *s*. *Studied art* with Harold Roney and Simon Michael; A.A. Stephens College, Columbia, Mo., B.F.A. Univ. of Okla. *Exhib.:* National Galleries, Smithsonian Institution; Exhibn. Intercontinentale, Congres des Palais, Monaco. Selected San Antonio Artist of the year (1971). *Work in permanent collections:* Stephens College, Royal-Globe Building, Dallas, Texas. *Address:* San Antonio, Texas. *Clubs:* Delta Gamma, P.E.O. Sisterhood. *Signs work:* "RUTH DUNCAN," see appendix.

DUNCAN, Terence Edward; picture framer and artist in oil and water-colour; *b* Herts., 17 Aug., 1947. *Educ.:* Manland Secondary Modern, Harpenden; *studied art* at St. Albans School of Art; Harpenden Art Centre. *Exhib.:* St. Albans Gallery (1971), Amateur Artists' Exhbn., London (1967), Batchwood Hall, St. Albans. *Publication:* article, Hertfordshire Countryside. *Address:* 27 Lower Dagnall St., St. Albans, Herts. AC3 EPS. *Signs work:* "Terry" with date.

DUNDAS, Douglas Roberts, M.B.E., N.S.W. travelling art scholar (1927); painter; draughtsman; lecturer; writer on art; ret. Head of Nat. Art School, Sydney; ret. Vice-Pres. of Trustees of Art Gallery of N.S.W.; *b* Inverell, N.S.W., 25 Jan., 1900; *s* of Robert Dundas; *m* Dorothy Thornhill; one *s*. *Studied art* under Julian Ashton, N.S.W. (1922-27), and at Regent St. Polytechnic (1928). *Exhib.:* R.A., Paris Salon (1929), annually at Soc. of Artists' Exhbn., Sydney. *Work in permanent collections:* all State galleries of Australia; Teachers' College, Armidale. *Work repro.:* in Art in Australia, Studio, Present-day Art in Australia, Society of Artists' Book. *Address:* 316 Jersey Rd., Woollahra, Sydney, N.S.W., Australia. *Signs work:* "D. R. DUNDAS."

DUNDERDALE, Philip, F.L.A. (1934); Chief Librarian and Curator, Grundy Art Gallery, Blackpool; *b* Preston, 24 Feb., 1913. *Educ.:* Preston Grammar School. *Address:* 1 Settle Pl., Lytham St. Annes FY8 3QY.

DUNHAM, Peter Browning, Dip., architecture, London (1933), Donaldson medallist (1933), F.R.I.B.A.; architect and painter in oil and water-colour; *b* Luton, 9 Oct., 1911; *s* of F. W. Dunham; *m* Constance Young; one *s,* one *d. Educ.:* Malvern College; *studied art* at Bartlett School of Architecture. *Exhib.:* R.A. (oils, water-colour and architecture). *Principal architectural works:* Luton and Dunstable Hospital; schools in Hertfordshire and Bedfordshire; Housing. Winner of several awards in open architectural competitions, housing medals and Civic Trust awards. *Work repro.:* illustrated in technical press. *Address:* Gladley House, Rushmere, Leighton Buzzard, Bedfordshire. *Signs work:* "PETER DUNHAM."

DUNKLEY, Keith, A.R.W.S.; David Murray Studentship, B.I. Fund Award, Landseer Drawing Prizes, Armitage Prize and Silver Medal, Leverhulme Scholarship; artist in oil and water-colour and lecturer; *b* Corbridge, Northumberland, 14 July, 1942. *Educ.:* Royal Grammar School, Guildford; *studied art* at Kingston College of Art (1960-64), R.A. Schools (1964-67) *Exhb.:* R.A., R.W.S., F.B.A., Expo 67, The Stirling Gallery, Drew Smith Gallery, Toronto. *Work repro.:* in periodicals. *Address:* Bettyfield, Kelso, Roxburghshire, Scotland. *Signs work:* "Keith Dunkley."

DUNN, Albert Anthony; artist in oil (landscape); *b* Farnborough, Hants, 3 Apr., 1908; *s* of Reginald Cumming Dunn; *m* Sylvia Jannie; one *d. Educ.:* St. John's School, Newcastle upon Tyne; *studied art* at Newcastle upon Tyne (William Fenton) (1925-30). *Exhib.:* R.A. Summer Exhibitions: 3 one-man shows in Malvern Art Gallery, 1 in Langford's Hotel, Hove. *Address:* St. Michael's, 1 Powyke Court Close, Powick, Worcester. *Club:* Worcester Art Society, Malvern Art. *Signs work:* "A. Dunn."

DUNN, Alfred, A.R.C.A. (1961); artist; Tutor, Royal College of Art and Royal Academy Schools; *b* Wombwell, Yorks., 4 Oct., 1937; *s* of George Simeon Dunn; *m* Janet Dunn; one *s,* one *d. Educ.:* Wath-upon-Dearne Grammar School; *studied art* at Royal College of Art (1959-61). *Exhib.:* Galerie Buchhandlung Claus Lincke, Dusseldorf (1976), Monika Beck Gallery, Hamburg (1976), Redfern Gallery, London (1965, 1966, 1969, 1971, 1975), L'Umo del Arte, Milan (1971). *Address:* Little Moss Farm, Trawden, nr. Colne, Lancs. *Signs work:* "Alf Dunn."

DUNN, Anne; painter in oil, gouache, collage; *b* London, 4 Sept., 1929; *d* of Sir James Dunn, Bt.; *m* Rodrigo Moynihan; two *s. Studied art* at Chelsea School of Art. *Exhib.:* 6 one-man shows, London; 2 in New York; 1 in Paris. *Work in permanent collections:* Arts Council, Contemporary Art Society, Ministry of Works, Carlisle City Art Gallery, Columbus Gallery of Fine Arts, Beaverbrook Art Gallery, N.B. *Publication:* Editor, Art and Literature (1964-68). *Address:* Domaine St. Esteve, Lambesc, B.D.R., France. *Club:* W.I.A.C. *Signs work:* "Anne Dunn."

DUNN, Rev. Reginald George, F.I.A.L., Life Fellowship and Diploma (1967); artist in oil and pastel; *b* Windsor, 29 Apr., 1907; *s* of Reginald C. Dunn. *Educ.:* All Nations Missionary College, London; *studied art* under Professor Iatrou, Athens (1944), and Torquay School of Art (1949-50). *Exhib.:* R. Camb. Academy. Wing Chaplain, Devon Air Training Corp. *Address:* 1 St. Paul's Rd., Paignton, S. Devon. *Signs work:* "R. G. Dunn."

DUNNE, Berthold; Mem. Water-colour Soc. of Ireland (1951); artist in water-colour; *b* Dublin, 21 Sept., 1924; *s* of Michael D. Dunne. *Educ.:* Christian

Brothers Schools, Synge Street; *studied art* at National College of Art, Dublin, under John Keating, P.R.H.A., and Maurice MacGonigal, R.H.A. (1946-51). *Exhib.:* R.H.A., Oireachtas Art Exhbn., Water-colour Soc. of Ireland. *Address:* Goa, Shrewsbury Rd., Shankill, Co. Dublin. *Signs work:* "Berthold."

DUNSTAN, Bernard, R.A. (1968), N.E.A.C., R.W.A.; oil painter; *b* 19 Jan., 1920; *s* of the late Dr. A. E. Dunstan; *m* Diana Armfield; three *s*. *Educ.:* St. Paul's School; *studied art* at Byam Shaw School (Ernest Jackson), Slade School of Fine Arts. *Exhib.:* R.A., etc., one-man exhbns. at Roland, Browse and Delbanco, Agnew's, etc. *Work in permanent collections:* Bristol, Rochdale, Coventry, National Gallery of New Zealand, London Museum, National Portrait Gallery, etc. *Official purchases:* Contemporary Art Soc., Arts Council. *Publications:* Learning to Paint (Watson-Guptill), Starting to Paint Portraits, Starting to Paint Still-life, Composing Your Pictures (Studio Vista). *Address:* 10 High Pk. Rd., Kew, Surrey. *Signs work:* "B.D."

DURANTY, Charles Henry; artist in water-colour; publisher's representative; *b* Romford, Essex, Feb., 1918; *s* of W. H. Duranty, M.C. (retired); *m* Vivian Marguerite. *Educ.:* St. Lawrence College, Ramsgate, Kent. *Exhib.:* Leicester Galleries, Roland, Browse & Delbanco, New Grafton, Mercury, Heal's, Zwemmers, Medici, Thackeray Gallery, London; outside London: Ashgate, Farnham, Rye Art Gallery, Sussex, Brighton Art Gallery, Sussex, Guildford House and Reid's Gallery, Guildford; and in Johannesburg, S.A. *Publication:* Audition (poetry). *Address:* Blue Horses, Levylsdene, Merrow, Guildford, Surrey. *Signs work:* "Charles Duranty"; sometimes "C.H.D."

DURBIN, Leslie, M.V.O. (4th class, 1943), Hon. LL.D. (Cambridge, 1963); liveryman of Worshipful Company of Goldsmiths (1943); *b* Fulham, London, 21 Feb., 1913; *m* Phyllis Ginger, R.W.S.; one *s*, one *d*. *Studied art* at Central School of Arts and Crafts. *Work in permanent collections:* Goldsmiths' Company, Fishmongers' Company, Corpus Christi College, Oxford. *Official purchases (commissions):* principal part in making Stalingrad Sword to Prof. R. M. Gleadowe's design (1943); New College, Oxford; Gloucester Cathedral; Bath Abbey; Coventry Cathedral; Winchester Cathedral; South Carolina University, S.C.; Smithsonian Institution, Washington, D.C.; St. George's Chapel, Windsor. *Address:* 62 Rochester Pl., London NW1 9JX.

DURRANT, Roy Turner, N.D.D. (1952), F.R.S.A. (1953), F.F.P.S., A.I.A., Cambridge Society of Painters; painter in oil, gouache and water-colour; *b* 4 Oct., 1925, *s* of Francis Henry Durrant and Edna May, *née* Turner; *m* Jean, *née* Lyell; four *s*. *Educ.:* Lavenham, privately and Camberwell School of Art (1948-52); served in Suffolk Regt. (1944-47). *Exhib.:* R.A., Artists of Fame and Promise (Leicester Galleries), London Group; one-man shows: Lavenham (Suffolk); Guildhall (1948); Cromwell Gal. (1949); Beaux Arts Gal. (1950); Playhouse Theatre, Kidderminster (1951); Kensington Art Gal. (1951); Coffee House, Trafalgar Sq. (1952); Parson's Gal. (1953); Everyman Cinema, Hampstead (1953); Roland, Browse and Delbanco (1954); County Cinema, Sudbury (Suffolk) 1954; New Vision Art Centre (1957); A.I.A. (1957); Everyman Cinema, Hampstead (1958); Grabowski Gal. (1959); New Gal., Ipswich (1960); Phoenix Gal., Lavenham (1960); New Vision Gal. (1960); Gainsborough's House, Sudbury (1961); A.I.A. Gal., London (1969); Dept. of Biochemistry, Cambridge (1969); St. John's Wood Library (1972); Old Fire Engine House Gal., Ely (1972, 1974); Manor Gal., Royston (1973); Loggia Gal., London (1973, 1975); Cambridge Art and Design Gal. (1974); Cambridge Arts Assoc. (1975). *Work in permanent collections:* Carlisle Museum and Art Gal.; Castle Museum,

Norwich; Southampton Art Gal.; Bury St. Edmunds Cornhill Gal.; Leeds University; Bradford City Art Gal.; Grenville College, Stoke-by-Clare, Suffolk; Holywell Manor, Oxford; Pembroke College, Oxford; Trinity College, Cambridge; Balliol College, Oxford; Kettles Yard College, Cambridge; University of Adelaide, Australia; Western Australian Art Gall., Perth; University of Massachusetts, U.S.A.; and in private collections in Britain, U.S.A., and Europe. *Work repro.:* Studio, The Artist, Art Gazette, Oblicze Tygodni, etc. *Publication:* A Rag Book of Love (Scorpion Press, 1960). *Addresses:* 38 Hurst Pk. Ave., Cambridge CB4 2AE.; High St., Lavenham, Suffolk. *Signs work:* see appendix.

DUVAL, Dorothy Zinaida; mem. United Society of Artists (1960); silver medal, Paris Salon (1959), art merit, Stock Exchange Art Soc., (1969, 1973); oil painter, teacher of art; *b* Ipplepen, Newton Abbot, Devon, 26 Sept., 1917; *d* of Frederick William Hecht (decd.), mem. London Stock Exchange. *Educ.:* Bedford Park High School; *studied art* at Slade School. *Exhib.:* R.A., R.P., N.E.A.C., R.B.A., R.O.I., R.Scot.A., R.W.S., London Group, C.I.A.D., Manchester, Chenil Galleries, Paris Salon; one-man show: Saffron Gallery, Saffron Waldon. *Official purchases:* Grenadier Guards, H.Q., (Harry Nicholls, V.C.). *Address:* 166 Percy Ave., Kingsgate. *Signs work:* "D. Z. Duval."

DYKE, John C. A.; Curator of the Lundy Museum and editor and illustrator of the island magazine The Illustrated Lundy News (quarterly) and designer of the Island's local stamps; *b* Rossett, E. Denbighshire, 16 May, 1923; *m* Beatrice Joan Leach; one *s*, one *d*. *Educ.:* Holly Bank, Chester; *studied art* at Chester School of Art, principal, A. J. Mayson, A.R.C.A.; awards, Westminster Gold Medal and Randolph Caldecott Memorial Prize for book illustration (1937-41). *Address:* Signal Cottage, Lundy, Bristol Channel, via Ilfracombe. *Signs work:* see appendix.

DYNEVOR, Lady (Lucy Catherine King); Mem. Arts Committee, National Museum, Wales; Mem. Arts Committee, Welsh Arts Council; partner in the firm of Dunluce and Rothenstein, picture restorers; *d* of Sir John Rothenstein; *m* Lord Dynevor; one *s*, three *d*. *Educ.:* The Convent of the Holy Child, Mayfield; The Ruskin School of Drawing, Oxford; and with Mr. Helmut Ruhemann. *Addresses:* 18 Brook Green, London W6; Dynevor Castle, Llandeilo, Carmarthenshire.

DYRENFORTH, Noel; artist in batik; *b* London, 17 June, 1936; one *s*. *Educ.:* St. Clement Danes, London. *Exhib.:* one-man shows: Primavera, Cambridge (1965), Commonwealth Inst., London (1967), Little Gallery, Detroit, U.S.A. (1968), Mansard, London (1969), Craft Centre of G.B., London (1969), Herbert Art Gallery, Coventry (1970), Lane Gallery, Bradford (1970), Loughborough School of Art (1970), Mansard Art Gallery, Heal's, London (1971), Oxford Gallery, Oxford (1971, 1973), 359 Gallery, Nottingham (1973), Atmosphere, London (1975), Oxford Gallery (1976), Scopas (1976). *Work in public collections:* V. & A. Museum and six others. *Publication:* Noel Dyrenforth "batik" by John Houston (Orbis Publishing Co. Ltd., 1975). *Address:* 11 Shepherds Hill, Highgate, London N6.

DYSON, Douglas Kerr, A.R.C.A. (1949); painter and draughtsman; lecturer, Department of Visual Studies, Faculty of Art and Design, Manchester Polytechnic; *b* Halifax, 11 Dec., 1918; *s* of Coningsby Dyson; *m* Sylvia Varley (Sylvia Dyson, illustrator); one *s*. *Educ.:* Royds Hall Grammar School, Huddersfield; *studied art* at Huddersfield School of Art (1935-39), R.C.A., under Gilbert Spencer and Rodrigo Moynihan (1946-49). *Exhib.:* R.A., Manchester Academy. *Work in permanent collections:* The Manchester Education Committee, The Manchester City Art Gallery; Co-operative Insurance Society; private collections. *Address:* 32 Broomfield La., Hale, Cheshire. *Signs work:* "Dyson."

E

EAGAR, Richard Michael Cardwell, M.A. (Oxon, 1942), Ph.D. (Glas., 1944), D.Sc. (Glas., 1969), F.G.S., F.M.A., F.R.S.A.; Keeper of Geology since 1945, Manchester Museum, University; status of Reader since 1971, artist in oil and pen and ink; *b* Thornhill, Yorks., 26 Nov., 1919; *s* of G. F. F. Eagar, M.I.Min.E., F.R.S.A.; *m* Enid Mary Parris; one *s*, one *d*. *Educ.:* Shrewsbury and Magdalen College, Oxford; *studied art:* self-taught. *Exhib.:* West Riding, Yorks. Artists, St. James Art Soc. *Work repro.:* The Artist, technical drawings (pen and ink) in palaeontological scientific papers. *Publications:* articles in the above. *Address:* Highfield House, Schools Hill, Cheadle, Ches. *Signs work:* "Michael Eagar" or "RMCE."

EAGLETON, Aileen C., S.G.A.; painter in oil, water-colour; wood-engraver; *d* of Leonard Osborne Eagleton, solicitor. *Educ.:* Oak Hill House, Earley; *studied art* under Louis Thomson. Member, Society of Graphic Artists. *Exhib.:* R.A., R.O.I., R.I., Paris Salon, etc. *Address:* 1A Grove Rd., East Molesey, Surrey. *Signs work:* "Aileen Eagleton."

EARLE, Donald Maurice, A.T.D., D.A.E., F.R.S.A.; artist in oil, water-colour, etc.; Middle East College, Egypt (1948-49); Quakers' Yard Grammar School (1951-55); Churchfields Comprehensive School (1955-61); head of Junior School, Hassenbrook School (1961-65); head of Wing, Great Baddow Comprehensive School (1965); *b* Melksham, Wilts., 15 Aug., 1928; *m* Jennifer Mary Isaac. *Educ.:* Trowbridge (Wilts.) Boys' High School; *studied art* at W. of England College of Art, Bristol (1944-47, 1949-51). *Exhib.:* R.W.A., R.B.S.A. *Work repro.:* illustrations and designs for national magazines. *Address:* 37 High Rd., Rayleigh, Essex. *Signs work:* "D. M. Earle."

EASTOP, Geoffrey Frank, N.D.D. (1951), A.T.D. (1952), M.S.D-C. (1972); lecturer, potter in ceramics; *b* London, 16 Jan., 1921; *s* of Charles Alfred Eastop; *m* Patricia Eastop; three *s*, one *d*. *Educ.:* St. Olave's Grammar School; *studied art* at Goldsmiths' College (1949-52) under Kenneth Martin (painting), Kenneth Clark (pottery); Academie Ranson, Paris (1952-53) guidance of Francois Desnoyer. *Exhib.:* National Museum of Wales (1976), Marjorie Parr Gallery (1974), Whiterose Gallery (1973), Reading Museum (1961), V. & A. (1959), Heal & Son (1958). *Work in permanent collections:* Durham Museum, Southampton Museum A.G., Reading Museum. *Address:* Lindley, Victoria Rd., Mortimer, Berks. *Clubs:* Craftsmen Potters' Assoc. of Gt. Britain, S.D-C. *Signs work:* see appendix.

EAVES, John, R.W.A.; Art Teacher's Certificate (3 years) (1952), Distinction in Ceramics; lecturer in painting and ceramics, Bath Academy of Art, Corsham, Wilts; *b* Bristol, 10 Nov., 1929; *m* Cecily Edith; two *s*, two *d*. *Educ.:* Bembridge School, Bembridge, I.O.W.; *studied art* at Bath Academy of Art, James Tower (ceramics), William Scott (painting) (1949-52). *Work in permanent collections:* Arts Council, City Art Gallery, Bristol, L.C.C., Leicestershire Education Authority, Royal West of England Academy, Derbyshire Education Authority, South West Arts. *Work repro.:* in Henry Cliffe's Lithography (Studio Vista, 1965). Awarded Winston Churchill Travelling Fellowship to U.S.A. (1966), Print Prize, Westward TV Open Art Competition. *Address:* 2 Belgrave Pl., Bath, Som. *Signs work:* "Eaves '75."

ECCLESTON, Harry Norman, R.E. (1961), A.R.E. (1949), A.R.C.A. (1950), A.T.D. (1947), A.R.W.S. (1964); engraver in all processes; artist in oil and water-colour; *b* Bilston, Staffs., 21 Jan., 1923; *s* of Harry Norman Eccleston; *m*; two *d*. *Educ.:* Wednesbury County Commercial College; *studied art* at

Birmingham College of Art (1939-42) and R.C.A. (1947-51). *Exhib.:* R.A., R.E., R.W.S., etc. *Address:* 110 Priory Rd., Harold Hill, Romford, Essex. *Club:* Chelsea Arts. *Signs work:* "H. N. Eccleston."

EDGCUMBE, Ursula; sculptor in stone and wood until 1940, painter in oil; *b* Sandy, Beds., 1900; *d* of Sir Robert Edgcumbe. *Studied art:* Slade School (1916-21) under Prof. Havard Thomas. *Exhib.:* R.B.A., W.I.A.C., London Group, Leicester Galleries; one-man shows; sculpture at Leger Galleries (1935); bird compositions in oil, Kingly Gallery (1949). *Works include:* War Memorial at Zennor (St. Ives), stone carvings and plaster ceiling at Bibury Court (Glos.), also carved tombstones. *Work repro.:* in The Art of Carved Sculpture (Kineton Parkes), Modern Architectural Sculpture (Aumonier). *Address:* 36 Parsons Green La., London SW6. *Signs work:* "URSULA EDGCUMBE" in incised capitals on carvings; on paintings and drawings, U E interlaced.

EDVI ILLES, George; painter, sculptor and medallist in oil, pastel, acrylic; *b* Budapest, Hungary, 29 Sept., 1911; *s* of Aladar Edvi Illes, painter; *m* Emma Edvi Illes; one *s*, two *d*. *Educ.:* Fine Art Academy, Budapest; Academy of Applied Arts, Budapest; Vienna, Paris, Munich and Florence under Stephen Bosznay, Bertalan Karlowszky, Oszkar Glatz, Lajos Kunffy, Ede Telcs, Stephen Szentgzorgyi, Luis Bory. *Work in permanent collections:* Chamber of Lawyers, Chamber of Physicians, Capitolium of Caracas, Historical Library in Táchira, Venezuela, Fine Art Museum, Budapest, Hungarian National Museum, Weimar Liszt Museum. *Address:* 436 Londonberry Rd., N.W. Atlanta, Ga. 30327, U.S.A. *Club:* Chatahoochi Plantation Country Club, Atlanta. *Signs work:* see appendix.

EDWARDS, Carl J.; liveryman, Worshipful Company of Glaziers; Studio, Apothecaries Hall, Black Friars Lane, EC4; governor, Harrow Technical College and School of Art (1949-51); *b* London, 1914; *m* Kathleen Margaret; two *d*. *Studied art* at Polytechnic School of Architecture, Central School of Arts and Crafts, Harrow School of Art. *Exhib.:* V. & A., Empress Hall. *Work in position:* Liverpool Cathedral, Cairo Cathedral, House of Lords and Temple Church, Mossley Hill, Liverpool, Portsmouth Cathedral, Lambeth Palace Chapel, R.A.F. Church, St. Clement Danes, St. David's Cathedral. *Work repro.:* Studio. *Address:* The Glasshouse, 11 Lettice St., London SW6 4EH. *Signs work:* "C.E." (usually).

EDWARDS, Iorwerth Eiddon Stephen, C.M.G., C.B.E., Litt.D., F.B.A.; Keeper, Dept. of Egyptian Antiquities, B.M. (1955-74); Vice-President of Egypt Exploration Soc.; Visiting Prof. in Egyptology, Brown Univ., Providence, R.I., U.S.A. (1953-54); *b* London, 21 July, 1909; *s* of Edward Edwards, M.A.; *m* Elizabeth Lisle; one *s* (decd.), one *d*. *Educ.:* Merchant Taylors' School and Gonville and Caius College, Cambridge. Pioneered and chose objects for Tutankhamun Exhibition in London (1972). *Publications:* The Pyramids of Egypt, Hieratic Papyri in the B.M., Fourth Series, Treasures of Tutankhamun, joint editor of the Cambridge Ancient History (3rd edition). *Address:* Morden Lodge, Morden, Surrey. *Club:* Athenæum.

EDWARDS, John Colin, R.P.; Cert. R.A. Schools; Elizabeth T. Greenshields Memorial Foundation Award; Silver and Bronze Medallist R.A. Schools; freelance figure, portrait, landscape, sporting and wildlife painter and sculptor in oil, bronze, pencil, chalk, etc.; *b* Kidderminster, Worcs., 23 Aug., 1940; *s* of A. R. Edwards; *m* Patricia Rose; two *d*. *Exhib.:* R.A., R.P., Society of Portrait Sculptors; one-man exhbns. at the F.B.A., Chesterville and Moorland Galleries, etc. *Studied art:* Pietro Annigoni in Florence, Royal Academy Schools. *Work in permanent collections:* Kidderminster, Scunthorpe, Oxford University Press, St. John's, Balliol and Nuffield Colleges, Oxford, W. D. & H. O. Wills; *private collections:* in

England, Europe and U.S.A. *Address:* Chesterville Gallery, 163 Chester Rd. North, Kidderminster, Worcs. DY10 1TP. *Signs work:* "John Edwards" and "Edwards."

EDWARDS, Ralph, C.B.E., B.A., F.S.A.; Keeper, Dept. of Woodwork, Victoria and Albert Museum (1945-54); adviser on works of art for Min. of Works and Historic Buildings Council of England and Wales; *b* 24 June, 1894; *s* of Rev. W. A. Edwards; *m* Marjorie Ingham Brooke; three *s. Educ.:* privately; Hertford College, Oxford (War Degree). *Publications:* Dictionary of English Furniture, with the late Percy Macquoid, 2nd ed. revised and enlarged by Ralph Edwards (1954); concise ed. (1964); Georgian Cabinet Makers, 3rd ed. (1955), with Margaret Jourdain; Introduction, R.A. Cat. (1955); many articles and official publications; Early Conversation Pictures (1954). *Address:* Suffolk House, Chiswick Mall, London W4. *Club:* Athenæum.

EDWARDS, Victor E., M.S.D-C.; lecturer, weaving consultant, designer of looms and fabric; consultant and designer to Harris Looms, Ltd. and The Harris Centre as Weaving Teacher; adviser to many Colleges of Art throughout Gt. Britain and world-wide; *b* Cranbrook, Kent; *s* of W. E. Edwards; *m*; one *s. Educ.:* Cranbrook; *studied art* at Tunbridge Wells School of Art under M. Sutton. *Exhib.:* numerous. *Work in permanent collections:* The Harris Centre, Etchingham Church (wood turning). *Address:* 2 Sandrock Bungalows, Cranbrook Rd., Hawhurst, Kent. *Signs work:* "Victor E. Edwards."

EGGINTON, Frank, R.C.A.; landscape painter in water-colour and oils; *b* 10 Nov., 1908; *s* of W. Egginton, R.I., R.C.A.; *m*; one *d. Educ.:* Newton College. *Exhib.:* Most public exhbns. *Address:* Dunfanaghy, Co. Donegal, Ireland. *Signs work:* "Frank Egginton."

EGONU, Uzo, L.S.I.A., F.R.S.A.; painter, graphic artist, illustrator and designer; *b* Onitsha, Nigeria, 1931; *s* of Chukuma Egonu. *Educ.:* Holy Trinity School, Onitsha, Sacred Heart College, Calabar; *studied art* at Camberwell School of Arts and Crafts, London (1949-51). *Exhib.:* consistently in one-man, mixed and group exhbns. in Europe, Africa and America. *Prizes:* First Prize (oil painting), B.B.C. Morning Show Competition (1970); Bronze Medal (graphics), Les arts en Europe (1971), Brussels; Cup of the City of Caserta (oil painting), ITALIA 2000, Naples (1972); Second Prize (oil painting), African Arts, University of California, Los Angeles (1972). Public and private collections. Member of Printmakers Council, London,; Graphics Society, Hollis, U.S.A. *Address:* 32 Coniston Gdns., South Kenton, Wembley, Middx.

EICHLER, Richard W., holder of "Schiller-Preis" (1969); art writer and critic; *b* Liebenau, Bohemia, 8 Aug., 1921; *s* of Richard H. Eichler, printer; *m* Elisabeth Eichler (*née* Mojr); one *s,* six *d. Educ.:* Gymnasium at Reichenberg; *studied art* at Vienna, Munich (history of art). *Publications:* Könner-Künstler-Scharlatane (Munich, 1960; 6th ed., 1968), Künstler und Werke (Munich, 1962; 3rd ed., 1968), Der gesteuerte Kunstverfall (Munich, 1965; 3rd ed., 1968), Die tätowierte Muse (Velbert, 1965), Viel Gunst für schlechte Kunst (Munich, 1968; 2nd ed., 1969), and many papers. *Address:* Steinkirchner Strasse 15, D-8000 München 71, Bundesrepublik Deutschland.

EISELIN, Louise, A.I.A.L.; artist-painter; *b* Zürich, 2 Mar., 1903. *Individual shows:* Internat. Inst. of Arts and Letters, Lindau; Galérie Ror Volmar, Paris; Fondazione Europa, Milano. *Group shows:* Helmhaus, Zürich; Annuale Italiana d'Arte Grafica, Mostra Internazionale, Ancona (Medal of Honour); Biennale delle Regioni e Mostra Confronto Internazionale, Ancona (Medal of Honour); Bertrand Russell Centenary Int. Art Exhib., Nottingham, England. *Work repro.:* Internat.

Inst. of Arts and Letters (1958), La Revue Moderne, Paris (1968), Guida all'Arte Europea (1969), Rivista Internazionale degli Artisti (1969). Assoc. Member, Internat. Inst. of Arts and Letters. *Address:* Kapperlergasse 13, 8001 Zürich, Switzerland.

EISELIN, Rolf; Architect SIA dipl. EPF, reg. arch. State of Illinois, U.S.A.; *b* Zürich, 6 Nov., 1925. Architect with Skidmore, Owings & Merrill, Chicago (in team for U.S. Air Force Academy design), and other firms in New York, Boston, Paris. *Exhib.:* group shows: sculpture: Oakland Art Museum; painting: Univ. California; prints: U.S. National Museum, Washington; Royal Ontario Museum, Toronto; Kunsthaus, Zürich; England; Japan; one-man show, prints: San Francisco Museum of Art; Honour Medal, Nat. Exhib., Jersey City Museum. *Work in permanent collections:* San Francisco Museum of Art, Legion of Honour, San Francisco, Graphische Sammlung, ETH, Zürich. *Address:* Résidences de La Côte 60, 1110 Morges, Switzerland.

EISENMAYER, Ernst; sculptor in steel, bronze, stone and painter; *b* Vienna, 18 Sept., 1920; *m*; two *d*. *Educ.:* High School, Vienna; *studied art* at Camberwell School of Art (1947) (Victor Pasmore). *Exhib:* Mercury Gallery, Marjory Parr. *Work in permanent collections:* Nottingham, King's Lynn, Leicester, Sheldon Swope Mus., Ind., U.S.A., Secession, Vienna. *Commissions:* Large sculpture for Brit. Pavilion Expo '70 Japan; Forma Viva 1970, Yugoslavia. *Address:* 1 White Hart La., London SW13. *Signs work:* "EISENMAYER" on paintings and drawings; "E.E." and date on sculpture.

ELDRIDGE, Harold Percy, A.R.C.A. (1950), artist in oil, mural painter; *b* London, 8 June, 1923; *s* of Horace Frank Eldridge; *m* Sheila May Smith; one *s*, two *d*. *Studied art* at Camberwell School of Arts and Crafts and R.C.A. *Exhib.:* R.A., R.B.A., London Group. Murals at European Patisserie (S. Kensington), Mortlake Primary School (Surrey). *Work repro.:* in The Sketch. Also illustrations, scale models and historical reconstructions for Schools Television Programmes. Teaches art at school in Coventry. *Address:* 42 Beechwood Ave., Coventry.

ELDRIDGE, Mildred E., A.R.C.A., A.R.W.S., A.S.M.P., F.R.S.A.; recording Wales for Pilgrim Trust (1944-46); artist in oil and water-colour; book illustrator; *b* Wimbledon, 1 Aug., 1909. *Studied art* at Wimbledon School of Art, R.C.A., British School at Rome. *Exhib.:* R.A., R.Scot.A., R.Cam.A., R.H.A., R.W.S., etc. *Work in permanent collections:* V. & A., Birmingham Arts Council, L.C.C. Schools, National Museum, Cardiff, Sheffield, Oldham Corporations, 120-ft. mural in dining-hall of Nurses' Home at Robert Jones and Agnes Hunt Orthopædic Hospital, Gobowen, Oswestry, etc. *Work repro.:* drawings for Culpepper Soc. Herbals, Star-born Three Royal Monkeys, Wales, and other publications. *Address:* Aberdaron Vicarage, Pwllheli, Gwynedd. *Signs work:* see appendix.

ELLENBY, Rose, M.S.I.A., William Atkinson award, Queen's prizeman; painter and book illustrator in oil, water-colour, black and white; *b* London; *m* R. J. Carruthers. *Studied art:* Central School of Arts and Crafts. *Exhib.:* V. & A. and New Burlington Galleries. *Work in permanent collection:* V. & A. *Publications:* Edible Fungi (King Penguin), Poisonous Fungi (King Penguin), Gold Coast Fishes (Colonial Office), numerous contributions in botanical and gardening books and magazines. *Address:* 67 Kempe Rd., London NW6 6SN. *Signs work:* "Rose Ellenby" or "Rose Carruthers."

ELLIOTT, Martha Beggs; fine artist in portraiture, landscape and still life; *b* 17 Dec., 1892; *d* of John Phillip Beggs, manufacturer; mother, artist; *m* Vann S. Elliott; one *d*, Jane (Mrs. Mandeville Smith). *Educ.:* Birmingham, Ala. schools;

Samford College; *studied art* with Louise Cone, Birmingham (1930), in N.Y. with Wayman Adams, N.A. (1935-36-37); in Europe, Paris, Academies Julien and La Chaumier (1949-68); western U.S.A. and Hawaii (1968-69). *Exhib.:* one-man shows: Montgomery, Ala. (1939), Pensacola (1940), Guild Hall, E. Hampton, Long Is., N.Y. (1943), Dallas (1950), Panama City, Fla. (1960), retrospective show, Panama City Gallery of Art (1973). *Work in permanent collections:* I.B.M., Ala. Archives and History, Montgomery Museum, Washington, D.C., Wild Life Foundation, Fla. House of Representatives, Edward Benjamin Collection of New Orleans, La. *Publications:* Illustrations in Ala. Homes by Huger, War Bond Poster, U.S.A. (1945). *Address:* Studio, 240 Bunker's Cove Rd., Panama City, Fla. 32401. *Signs work:* see appendix.

ELLIS, Harold; draughtsman and artist in polymer, water-colour, line; *b* Baildon, 10 Apr., 1917; *s* of Frederick Ellis, rating officer; *m* Margaret Lovatt; one *s*, one *d*. *Educ.:* Bradford Grammar School; *studied art* as apprentice in commercial art studio, Messrs. Field, Sons & Co., Lidget Green, Bradford (1933-39). *Exhib.:* Bradford City A.G. *Work repro.:* cartoons, general anonymous commercial work. *Address:* 5 Whitelands Cres., Baildon, Shipley, Yorks. *Club:* Bradford Arts. *Signs work:* "H. Ellis" or "ELLIS."

ELLIS, Lionel, N.S. (1930), A.R.C.A. (London, 1924), Travelling Scholar (1926), F.R.S.A. (1952); figurative painter, sculptor and engraver; *b* Plymouth, 7 Feb., 1903; *s* of Frederick John Ellis. *Educ.:* Plymouth School of Art; Royal College of Art; Paris; Florence; Rome. *Exhib.:* N.E.A.C., R.A., National Soc., Whitechapel, etc.; retrospective exhbn., City of Plymouth Art Gallery (1973). *Official purchases:* British Museum; V. & A.; Newnham College; Bradford Art Gallery. *Work repro.:* Medici Soc., Pallas Gallery, Studio, various magazines. *Publications:* engravings for Delighted Earth, Theocritos, Catullus. *Address:* Stubbs Oak, Headley, Surrey. *Signs work:* "Lionel Ellis."

ELLIS, Noel, A.R.C.A. (1948); painter in oil and printmaker; *b* Plymouth, 25 Dec., 1917; *s* of George Ellis; *m* Linda Zinger. *Educ.:* Sutton High School, Plymouth; *studied art* at Plymouth School of Art, R.C.A. *Exhib.:* R.A., R.O.I., R.B.A., N.E.A.C., London Group, Grundy A.G., Blackpool, Plymouth A.G. *Address:* 95 Bennerley Rd., Battersea, London SW11 6DT. *Signs work:* "NOEL ELLIS."

ELLIS, Norman Ernest, A.I.O.B., A.R.S.H.; lecturer, artist in oil and water-colour; *b* Leicester, 9 Nov., 1913; *s* of John Henry Ellis; *m* Helena Ellis. *Educ.:* Moat Rd. Intermediate School, Leicester; *studied art* at Leicester College and Lincoln College of Art. *Exhib.:* R.B.A., R.O.I., Nottingham Castle, Leicester and Birmingham Art Galleries. *Work in permanent collection:* Leicester Corporation Art Galleries. *Address:* 300 Victoria Pk. Rd., Leicester. *Clubs:* Leicester Soc. of Artists and Leicester Sketch. *Signs work:* "Ellis."

ELLIS, William John; artist in oil, water-colour, crayon; insurance inspector; *b* Rhyl, 21 Sept., 1944; *s* of John Ellis; *m* Gaynor Ellis; one *s*, one *d*. *Educ.:* Glyndwr Secondary Modern, Rhyl; *studied art* at Glyndwr Secondary and later under Robert Evans Hughes. *Exhib.:* Rhyl Town Hall. *Address:* 69 Russell Rd., Rhyl, Clwyd. *Clubs:* Clwydian Art Society, Clwyd Assoc. for the Visual Arts, Prestatyn 57 Group, Flint and Deeside Art Society. *Signs work:* "B. Ellis."

ELWYN, John, A.R.C.A. (prizeman); artist in oil; assistant lecturer at Portsmouth College of Art (1948-53); lecturer, Winchester School of Art; *b* Newcastle Emlyn, Carms., 20 Nov., 1916; *m* Gillian Butterworth, pianist. *Educ.:* Llandyssul Grammar School; *studied art* at Carmarthen Art School (1935-37), West of England College of Art, Bristol (1937-38), R.C.A. (1938-40, 1946-47). *One-man* *exhbn.:* Leicester Galleries (1965, 1968). *Official purchases:* Leeds University; Southampton University; Glynne-Vivian Art Gallery, Swansea; Contemporary Art Soc. for Wales; National Museum of Wales (Cardiff); National Eisteddfod Com.; several Educ. Com.; Arts Council Welsh Collection; King Alfred College, Winchester; Milton Training College, Portsmouth; Aberystwyth University; Newport Art Gallery; Nuffield Foundation; Pembroke College, Cambridge; and many private collections. Commissioned work for Shell, G.P.O., Radio Times. Gold Medallist, National Eisteddfod (1956). *Address:* 5 Compton Rd., Winchester. *Signs work:* "JOHN ELWYN."

EMERY, Arthur George Stevenson, D.F.A. (Slade School, 1948); artist in oil, water-colour, pen and ink; merchant navy officer, retd.; *b* Penmaen, Glam., 16 July, 1896; *s* of Rev. George Emery, B.A. (London), Mus.Bac. (Oxon); *m* Edith Alkin; one *s*. *Educ.:* St. Edmund's School, Canterbury; *studied art* at Slade School, Oxford (1939-40), London (1946-48) under Profs. Randolph Schwabe and Allan Gwynne-Jones, D.S.O. *Exhib.:* R.A. (1948), R.Cam.A. (1952, 1953, 1956, 1958). *Work repro.:* covers for parish magazines, illustrations, school magazine, cover for Army instruction booklet, Christmas cards. *Address:* Ael-y-Bryn, Bodfean, Pwllheli, Gwynedd. *Signs work:* "Arthur Emery."

EMERY, William Walter, R.I.B.A., F.R.S.A.: chartered architect, partner in Wood, Goldstraw & Yorath; *b* Hanley, Stoke-on-Trent, 22 May, 1913; *s* of Enoch Emery, potter; *m* Marjorie Pemberton; one *s*, one *d*. *Principal works* include restorations, industrial and commercial premises. *Address:* Churchill House, Regent Rd., Hanley, Stoke-on-Trent.

EMETT, Rowland; artist and inventor. *Address:* Wild Goose Cottage, Ditchling, Sussex. *Tel.* Hassocks 2459. *Signs work:* see appendix.

EMMS, John Victor, A.T.D. (1948); artist in oil, water-colour and art teacher; art teacher, Raine's Foundation Grammar School, E1, Woolwich Polytechnic Secondary Art School; *b* Borden, nr. Aldershot, 13 Feb., 1912; *s* of John Emms, Army (ranks); *m*; one *d*. *Studied art* at Woolwich Polytechnic Art School under A. Buckley, L. S. M. Prince (1930-34), Hornsey School of Art under A. S. H. Mills, F. Mitchell (1946-48), Goldsmiths' College School of Art (1948-49). *Exhib.:* R.A., Surrey, South Coast and London galleries. *Address:* 3 Clinton Rd., Leatherhead, Surrey. *Signs work:* "John V. Emms."

EMSLIE, Rosalie, R.B.A., Hon. Mention, Carnegie Inst., Pittsburgh; artist in oil, black and white; *b* London, 26 Jan., 1891; *d* of A. E. Emslie, R.W.S. *Educ.:* privately; *studied art* at R.A. (1913-18); Paris, Florence, and Madrid. *Exhib.:* R.A., R.B.A., Paris Salon, Venice International Exhbn., London Group, N.E.A.C., Goupil Galleries, Carnegie Inst., Pittsburgh, and provinces. *Work in permanent collections:* Buffalo, U.S.A., Toronto. *Official purchases:* Canadian Government. *Work repro.:* The Times, Daily Telegraph, Studio, etc., and U.S.A. journals. *Address:* 2 Yorke Gdns., Reigate, Surrey. *Club:* Reynolds. *Signs work:* "Rosalie Emslie."

ENGLAND, Frederick John, N.D.D., A.T.C. (Lond.), I.A.G., M.F.P.S., Norwegian Scholarship (1960), Medaille d'Argent, Paris Salon (Gold Medal, 1975), Diploma d'Honneur, International Arts Guild, Monte Carlo; painter in oil, lithograph, etching, water-colour; lecturer in painting and design at Leek School of Art; director, England's Gallery, Ipstones, nr. Stoke-on-Trent; *b* Fulham, London, 5 Mar., 1939; *s* of Frederick Thomas England; *m* Sheelagh Jane. *Educ.:* Deacons School; *studied art* at Brighton College of Art and Crafts (1956) under Sallis Benney, R.O.I., R.W.S., Charles Knight, R.O.I., R.W.S., R. T. Cowen, Principal; Hardanger Folkschule, Norway (1960) under Oddmund J. Aarhus; London

University (1961) under Ronald Horton. *Exhib.:* Paris Salon, Arts Council of N. Ireland, R.B.A., R.I. Summer and Winter Salon, R.B.S.A., Manchester Academy, Bradford Open Exhibition, Trends Free Painters and Sculptors, R.W.E.A., S.I.A. (travelling shows included). Open Exhibition Stafford, Society of Staffordshire Artists; one-man shows: England's Gallery, Burlington Gallery, Buxton, Schaffer Gallery, Market Drayton, Galerie für Zeitgenössische Kunst, Hamburg, Galerie Bernheim-Jeune, Paris, I.A.G. Monte Carlo, Zilina, Czechoslovakia, Octagon Gallery, Bolton, University of Keele. *Work in permanent collections:* Nicholson Institute, Leek, Staffs., Goritz Coll., Fenning Coll., Geneva, City of Stoke-on-Trent Art Gallery. *Reviewed work* in La Revue Moderne, Les Journal des Jeunes, Boomerang (Paris Salon Edition of One Hundred Young European Painters), Dictionnaire des Artists, Repertorium Artis, Dictionnaire International d'Art Contemporain. *Addresses:* 5A Union St., Leek, Staffs. ST13 6DY, and England's Gallery, 12 High St., Ipstones, Stoke-on-Trent ST10 2LU. *Signs work:* "England."

ENGLESMITH, George, B.Arch., Liverpool, A.R.I.B.A., M.R.A.I.C., M.S.I.A., A.C.I.D., F.R.S.A.; Coronation Medal (1953); architect, industrial design and planning consultant; Lecturer in Architecture, Toronto University (1946-51); founder (1st Pres.) Assn. Canadian Industrial Designers; charter-director, Can. Industrial Design Council; Advisory Committee, Houston University (1957—); Hon. Sec.-Treasurer, British Benevolent Fund; Executive Director (founder), Frederick Delius Soc. (Texas); *b* Liverpool, 31 May, 1914; *m* Lydia Johnson-Briet; one *s* (Tejas), one *d* (Suzelle). *Educ.:* Private and public schools, Texas; architecture and civic design, Liverpool University. *Publications:* works and articles in U.K., Canada, Italy, Japan and U.S.A. *Addresses:* (business) Suite 600, W. Loop S., Houston, Texas 77401; (residence) 7839 Fondren, Houston, Texas, 77036. *Clubs:* Architectural Assn., London; Rudi's, Houston.

ENGLESMITH, Tejas; curator; Curator of Contemporary Art (1969—), The Jewish Museum, New York; formerly Assistant Director, Whitechapel Gallery (1963-69); *b* Darlington, 28 Nov., 1941; *s* of George Englesmith, B.Arch (Liverpool). *Educ.:* public schools, Toronto, Canada, Houston, Texas, University of St. Thomas, Houston, Texas; *studied art history* at University of St. Thomas under Dr. Jermayne MacAgy. *Addresses:* The Jewish Museum, 1109 Fifth Ave., New York, N.Y., 10028, U.S.A., and 339 East 87th St., New York, N.Y., 10028. *Club:* I.C.A., London.

ENTHOVEN, Roderick Eustace, F.S.A. (1957), A.A.Dip. (1924), A.R.I.B.A. (1925), F.R.I.B.A. (1932); architect; Pres., Architectural Assoc. (1948-49); Vice-Pres., R.I.B.A. (1951-53); F.R.S.A. (1964); partner, Enthoven & Mock; *b* Seal, Kent, 30 May, 1900; *s* of Ernest James Enthoven, underwriter; *m* Cecilia Mary Le Mesurier; three *s*. *Educ.:* Clifton College; *studied art* at Architectural Assoc. School of Architecture under Robert Atkinson and Howard Robertson (1919-24). *Exhib.:* R.A. *Work repro.:* Architectural Review, Architects' Journal, Building. *Address:* 4 Raymond Buildings, Gray's Inn, London WC1. *Club:* Athenæum. *Signs work:* "R. E. Enthoven."

ERNI, Hans; painter in tempera and oil; gold medal for ceramics at Expos. Internat. "Les chefs-d'œuvres de la céramique moderne" (Cannes, 1955); *b* Lucerne, 21 Feb., 1909; *s* of Gotthard Erni; *m* Doris Kessler; one *s*, two *d*. *Educ.:* State School, Lucerne; *studied art* at Lucerne School of Arts and Crafts (1927-28), Academie Julien, Paris (1928-29), Berlin Vereinigte Staatsschulen für freie und angewandte Kunst under Klewer (1929-30). *Exhib.:* throughout the world. *Official purchases:* Musée d'Ethnographique, Neuchâtel; World Exhbn. Brussels, Swiss Pavilion; World Health Organization; Nestlé, Vevey (Café). Murals in mosaic, fresco and graffito technique in different banks and industries in Switzerland. Designs for the execution of tapestries in official buildings. Designs for 7 medals. Postage-stamps for Switzerland and the Principality of Liechtenstein. Posters for social and cultural occasions. Illustrations for several bibliophile Editions. *Publications:* sketchbooks: Africa, Israel and India after studies in the countries. *Bibliography:* C. J. Burchkardt Hans Erni, Editions Ernst Scheidegger, Zurich and Rencontre, Lausanne; Zeitgenossen sehen Hans Erni, Editions Kunstkreis, Lucerne. *Address:* Meggen/Lu., Switzerland. *Clubs:* Schweizischer Werkbund, A.G.I., Société Europeénne de Culture. *Signs work:* see appendix.

ERTE-DE TIRTOFF, Roman; painter in gouache and pen and ink for illustrations, theatre and fashion designs, three-dimensional sculpture/paintings; *b* St. Petersburg, Russia, 1892; *s* of Admiral Peter De Tirtoff. *Educ.:* St. Petersburg; *studied art* at St. Petersburg with Repine and Lossewsky. *Exhib.:* World representatives: Grosvenor Gallery, London (1st exhbn. 1967, 1970, 1972); Paris (1926, 1929, 1964, 1965, 1966, 1967, 1969, 1971, 1972); New York (1925, 1929, 1935, 1967, 1970, 1972 (entire collection purchased by Metropolitan Museum, New York in 1967 and exhib. 1968); Brussels (1927); Chicago (1968, 1969); Milan (1965, 1966, 1971); Turin (1967); Brescia (1967); Venice (1968); Mexico City (1970); Rome (1971); Hamburg (1968); Bologna (1971); Palermo (1971); Parma (1971); Detroit (1972); New Orleans (1973); 1970 and 1972 costumes and sets for Casino de Paris. *Address:* 21 rue Gutenberg, Boulogne-sur-Seine, France. *Signs work:* see appendix.

EULER, Margaret Ida; painter; R.A. Silver Medal, Creswick Prize; Board of Education Art Diploma (1938); *b* London; *d* of Louis H. Euler, M.I.E.E. *Educ.:* Lewisham Prendergast School; *studied art* at Goldsmiths' College, New Cross, R.A. Schools, under Sickert, Sir George Clausen, R.A., Sir Walter Russell, R.A., Clive Gardiner, James Bateman, R.A. *Exhib.:* R.A., Paris Salon, R.B.A., Pastel Society, New Burlington Galleries, N.E.A.C.; invited Hull, Derby, Bradford, Brighton. *Address:* 6 Curzon Ct., Beckenham Grove, Shortlands, Kent. *Signs work:* "Euler" or "Margaret Euler."

EURICH, Richard Ernst, R.A. (1953), A.R.A. (1942), N.E.A.C. (1943); painter in oil; *b* Bradford, 14 Mar., 1903; *s* of F. W. Eurich, M.D.; *m* Mavis Pope; one *s,* two *d. Educ.:* St. George's School, Harpenden; Bradford Grammar School; Bradford School of Arts and Crafts; Slade School. *Exhib.:* R.A., N.E.A.C., London Group, Redfern Gallery, Pittsburgh International Exhbns., etc. *Official purchases:* Tate Gallery, Chantrey Bequest, Contemporary Art Soc., Imperial War Museum, Nat. Maritime Museum, Nat. Gallery of Victoria, Canadian War Museum, Eton College. *Address:* Appletreewick, Dibden Purlieu, Southampton. *Signs work:* "R. Eurich."

EVANS, Garth; artist and teacher; instructor at Camberwell School of Art, St. Martin's School of Art and Slade School; *b* Cheadle, Cheshire, 23 Nov., 1934; *s* of Cyril John Evans. *Studied art* at Regional College of Art, Manchester and Slade School. *Work in permanent collections:* Arts Council of Great Britain; Tate Gallery; City Art Gallery, Bristol; Museum of Modern Art, N.Y.; Power Gallery of Contemporary Art, Sydney, Australia; V. & A.; Contemporary Arts Soc. of G.B. *Address:* 109 Regent's Pk. Rd., London NW1. *Signs work:* "GARTH EVANS."

EVANS, Ray, R.I., A.R.Cam.A.; painter and illustrator in water-colour and mixed media; Council Mem., R.I.; *b* 19 Apr., 1920; *s* of Evan Price Evans; one *s*, one *d. Studied art* at Manchester College of Art (1946-48), Heatherleys under Iain Macnab. *Exhib.:* one-man shows: Furneaux, Thackeray, Galerie France and

Medici, London, Ashbarn Gallery, Hampshire. *Work in permanent collections:* Hampshire Education Authority; Gulbenkian Foundation; Aberystwyth University; Winchester Guildhall Gallery and many private collections in Britain and abroad. *Work repro.:* Wide range book publishers, magazines and newspapers, advertising and TV. *Address:* Bradford House, 106 Stockbridge Rd., Winchester, Hants. *Club:* Chelsea Arts. *Signs work:* see appendix.

EVANS, Sybil Charlotte. *Educ.:* The College, Pontypool; Newport College of Art; Hornsey College of Art. *Exhib.:* R.A., New English Art Club, etc. *Address:* Grove Hill, Shipway Ave., Torquay. *Signs work:* "Evans."

EVANS, William Charles, R.B.A., R.P.; *b* London, 1911; *m* Barbara Prince; one *s*. *Studied art:* Hammersmith School of Art and R.A. Schools. *Exhib.:* R.A., R.B.A., R.P., Contemporary Portrait Society. *Work in permanent collections:* London, Oxford, Cambridge, Reading, Charterhouse; private collections in Britain and U.S.A. *Address:* The Studio, Hackhurst La., Abinger Hammer, Dorking, Surrey RH5 6SE. *Signs work:* "Evans."

EVE, Esmé Frances, A.R.C.A.; book illustrator, commercial and industrial designer. *Studied art* at Croydon College of Art, R.C.A. *Publishers* include Blackie, Nelson, Warne, Hamlyn, Lutterworth, Oxford University Press, Odhams, Child Education, Longmans, Macdonald, Chatto, Boyd and Oliver, T.V. Annuals, etc. Educational and encyclopaedic work, poetry books, fabric designs, laminates and greetings cards for the Medici, Christian Action, Oxfam and other charities. *Address:* Southernwood, Meads Rd., Seaford, Sussex BN25 1SY.

EVERETT, Mrs. Roberta G., A.T.D.; sculptor in clay and stone; Principal Lecturer (retd.) Brentwood College of Education, Essex; Examiner for the Associated Examining Board (retd.); *b* Surrey, 29 May, 1906; *d* of Robert and Alice Hatcher; *m* John Garwood Everett, B.Sc., Ph.D., F.R.I.C., M.I.Ch.E. (decd.); one *s*, two *d*. *Educ.:* Wallington County School for Girls, Goldsmiths' College; *studied art* at Goldsmiths' School of Art and City and Guilds of London Art School. *Exhib.:* R.A., Paris Salon, G.I., Bradford City Art Gallery. *Official purchases:* Lancs. Educ. Com. *Address:* 45 Merton Rd., Harrow, Middx. HA2 0AA. *Signs work:* see appendix.

EVETTS, Leonard Charles, M.A., AR.C.A.; stained glass artist, letterer, watercolour painter; Master of Design, Department of Fine Art, University of Newcastle upon Tyne (retd.); *b* 12 Jan., 1909; *s* of C. H. Evetts, lettering craftsman; *m* Joan C. M. Macdonald. *Educ.:* Royal College of Art (Prof. E. W. Tristram, Edward Johnson, 1930-33), student demonstrator under Edward Johnston. *Exhib.:* R.A. *Publications:* Roman Lettering (Pitman, 1938); numerous articles on English stained glass and Roman inscriptions in periodicals and archæological journals. *Address:* The Stead, Woolsington Bridge, Newcastle upon Tyne. *Club:* Pen and Palette. *Signs work:* "L. C. Evetts" or "Leonard Evetts."

EYTON, Anthony, Mem. London Group, N.D.D., Abbey Major Scholarship in Painting (1950); artist in oil, part-time lecturer, Camberwell School of Arts and Crafts (since 1956) and Royal Academy Schools; asst. lecturer, Dept. of Fine Art, Durham University (1953-54); *b* Teddington, 17 May, 1923; *s* of Capt. John Eyton, I.C.S., author. *Educ.:* Twyford School (1932-37), Canford School (1937-41); *studied art:* Reading University (1941); Camberwell School of Arts and Crafts (1947-50). *Exhib.:* London Group, R.A.; one-man shows: St. George's Gallery, Galerie de Seine, New Art Centre. *Official purchases:* Arts Council (1955), Plymouth Art Gallery (1968). *Address:* 166 Brixton Rd., London SW9. *Signs work:* "A. Eyton."

F

FAIRCLOUGH, Bernard Peake, A.T.D., D.A., Manc., F.R.S.A., Head of Department, School of Art, Darlington; artist in oil, gouache; *b* Glossop, Derbyshire, 5 Dec., 1915; *s* of Leonard Fairclough; *m* Patricia Mary Poulton; one *s*, one *d*. *Educ.:* Glossop Grammar School; *studied art* at Manchester School of Art, principal, R. C. Dawson, A.R.C.A., painting, L. R. Baxter. *Exhib.:* Manchester, Salford, Birmingham, Derby municipal galleries, Whitechapel A.G., private galleries in London, Arts Council Travelling exhbn. *Official purchases:* Manchester Educ. Com. for Schools Collection. *Address:* c/o School of Art, Darlington. *Signs work:* "Fairclough."

FAIRCLOUGH, Michael, R.E. (1946), A.T.D. (1962), Rome Scholar in Engraving (1964-66); painter and printmaker; lecturer, West Surrey College of Art; *b* Blackburn, 16 Sept., 1940; *s* of W. Fairclough, Principal, Kingston College of Art; *m* Mary Malenoir; two *d*. *Studied art* at Kingston College of Art, British School at Rome, Atelier 17, Paris. *Work in permanent collections:* Various public and private collections in U.K., U.S.A., etc. *Mural commissioned:* By Dept. of Environment (1971). *Address:* White Lion House, 37 Red Lion La., Farnham, Surrey. *Signs work:* "Michael Fairclough."

FAIRCLOUGH, Wilfred, A.R.C.A. (1934), R.E., A.R.W.S. (1961), R.W.S. (1967); Rome Scholar (engraving, 1934), R.E., 1946; artist engraver; Principal, Kingston College of Art (1962-69); Assistant Director, Kingston Polytechnic (1970-72); *b* 13 June, 1907; *m;* one *s*, one *d*. *Educ.:* All Saints, Blackburn; Royal College of Art (1931-34); British School at Rome, Italy (1934-37). *Exhib.:* R.A., R.E., R.S.A., Bradford, Brighton, Chicago, Los Angeles, Copenhagen, Stockholm, Madrid. *Official purchases:* Contemporary Art Soc. *Work repro.:* Fine Prints of the Year, Recording Britain, Londoner's England. *Publications:* paintings, etchings, engravings. *Address:* 12 Manorgate Rd., Kingston-on-Thames. *Signs work:* "W. Fairclough."

FAIRER, Frederick Park, N.D.D. (1951); portrait artist in oil; *b* Hull, E. Yorks., 1910. *Educ.:* Hull; *studied art* at Borough Polytechnic under David Bomberg (1948), Kennington (1950), Middleton Todd and Robin Guthrie, Central School of Arts and Crafts under Hans Tisdale, Leslie Cole (1951-53). *Exhib.:* R.A., R.P., N.E.A.C., and New Zealand, one-man show Elizabeth Gallery. *Publications:* in The Hippodrome Art News and Review. *Address:* 9 Craven Hill, London W2. *Signs work:* "F. P. Fairer."

FAIRGRIEVE, James Hanratty, D.A. (Edin.), R.S.W., A.R.S.A.; part-time lecturer, painter in acrylic; *b* Prestonpans, E. Lothian, 17 June, 1944; *s* of Andrew D. G. Fairgrieve, ex-miner; *m* Margaret Fairgrieve; two *s*, one *d*. *Educ.:* Preston Lodge Senior Secondary School; *studied art* at Edinburgh College of Art. *Exhib.:* Hawarth A.G. (1974), Triad Arts Centre (1974), Scottish Gallery (1974), Scottish Arts Club (1973), New 57 Gallery (1969, 1971). *Work in permanent collections:* Edinburgh Corp., Scottish Arts Council, National Bank of Chicago, Milngavie A.G., H.R.H. The Duke of Edinburgh, Argyll Schools. *Address:* Main St., Gordon, Berwickshire, Scotland. *Signs work:* "James H. Fairgrieve."

FAIRHURST, Jack Leslie, A.R.C.A. (1926); portrait painter, draughtsman, landscape, flower painter; *b* London, 1905; *s* of Enoch Fairhurst, R.M.S.; *m* Barbara Domaire; two *s*, one *d*. *Studied art* at Camberwell School of Art and R.C.A.; hon. sec. London District National Soc. Art Educ. (1937-43); hon. sec. Old Students' Association R.C.A. (1946-51). *Exhib.:* R.A., R.P.S., many London and provincial galleries; one-man shows in London and Suffolk. Art master at

Shene School, acting head, Richmond School of Art (1941-57); chairman, Richmond and Fulham Art Groups; mem. Ridley Art Soc. *Work repro.:* Radio Times, Star, Church Times. *Address:* Dallinghoo, Woodbridge, Suffolk. *Signs work:* see appendix.

FAIRLEY, Dorothy M., Mem. S.G.A.; wood-engraver, etcher, painter and stone-carver; *b* 18 Mar., 1894; *d* of William Fairley, M.I.C.E. *Educ.:* Ellerker College, Richmond, Surrey; Richmond Art School; Regent St. Polytechnic. *Exhib.:* R.A., R.S.A., Liverpool, Sunderland, Glasgow, Paris Salon, Chicago Inst. of Fine Art, London galleries; one-man exhbn. Nov., 1946, at Walker Galleries, Bond St. *Official purchases:* Sunderland. *Address:* Homehurst, Knelle Rd., Robertsbridge, Sussex. *Signs work:* "Dorothy M. Fairley."

FAIRLEY, George, D.A. (Edin.); painter, sculptor, and lecturer; *b* Dunfermline, 16 Dec., 1920; *s* of Robert Fairley, quarry labourer; *m* Elizabeth Mary Sergent; three *s*, one *d*. *Educ.:* Dunfermline High School; *studied art* at Edinburgh College of Art under David Alison, R.S.A., W. G. Gillies, R.S.A., and A. B. Thomson, R.S.A. *Exhib.:* Gimpel Fils, Redfern Gallery, Galerie de France, Paris, London Group, Bear Lane Gallery, Oxford, Glynn Vivian Gallery, Swansea, New Vision Art Centre, Brooklyn Museum, John Moores, Liverpool, etc. *Official purchases:* Arts Council, C.A.S. for Wales, University College, Swansea, Worcesster College, Oxford, Westminster Bank. *Address:* 25 Kings Rd., Horsham, Sussex.

FAIRWEATHER-WALKER, Dorothy; artist in oils, water-colours, charcoal; landscape painter, exhibition director, agent; president, Soroptimist Club of Sevenoaks (1973-74); chairman, Hesketh Hubbard Art Society; sec., Guild of Kent Artists; *b* Folkstone, 4 Aug., 1915; *d* of Benjamin Stewart, F.A.I.; *m* James Fairweather-Walker, B.Sc., F.R.I.C., M.I.Biol., A.M.Inst., W.P.C.; one *s*. *Educ.:* privately; Folkestone School of Art (1930-34) under John Robinson, E. Studd; *studied art* at Folkestone School of Art and Liverpool School of Art (1942-44) under Mr. Whiffen. *Exhib.:* nine one-man shows 1958-72; group shows, Industrial Painters (1966, 1967), Pastel Soc. (1963, 1964, 1965), United Soc. (1962, 1964), National Soc. (1971), R.B.A. (1963, 1969, 1970), Trends (1968, 1969, 1970, 1972), Gallérie Jules Salle, Nimes (1969) and many others. *Work in permanent collections:* Stockwell College of Further Education, Walthamstow Hall, and public and private collections in Britain, Kenya and U.S.A. *Publications:* articles for newspapers, magazines including Arts Review. *Address:* Lanterns, 4 Cade La., Sevenoaks, Kent. *Clubs:* Soroptimist, F.P.S., H.H. Art Soc. *Signs work:* "DFW '73."

FAITHFULL, Joan Margaret Caldwell (née Crawford); potter; mem. Scottish Craft Centre since 1953; *b* E. Linton, E. Lothian, 17 May, 1923; *d* of William Caldwell Crawford, artist, former president of S.S.A. *Educ.:* St. Trinnean's, Edinburgh; *studied* at Edinburgh College of Art under Katie Horsman. *Exhib.:* S.S.A., S.S.W.A. *Address:* 16 Park Rd., Eskbank, Midlothian. *Signs work:* "J.F."

FALCON, Roland, A.R.M.S. (1945), A.R.P.S. (1938), F.R.S.A. (1947); photographer and carver in wood, ivory, perspex; official sculpture photographer, Tate Gallery; *b* Marienfelde, 7 Apr., 1914; *s* of Karl Federn, LL.D., historian and author; *m* Helen Brasen; one *d*. *Educ.:* Copenhagen, Berlin, London. *Exhib.:* R.M.S. (1945-52), Contemporary Sculpture, Russell Cotes A.G. (1948, 1952), Foyles A.G., R.S.A., London Salon, R.P.S. *Publications:* Official sculpture postcards, Tate Gallery. *Address:* 46 Glendale Ave., Edgware, Middx. *Signs work:* "Roland Falcon."

FARÉ, Michel; Conservateur en chef du Musée des Arts Decoratifs de Paris;

Prof. at L'Ecole Nationale Superieure des Arts Decoratifs, Docteur ès lettres; Chevalier de la Légion d'Honneur, Croix de Guerre. *Educ.:* Paris University; *studied art* at L'Institut d'Art et d'Archéologie and at L'École du Louvre (Dip.). *Address:* 28 Avenue de Lamballe, Paris XVIe.

FARLEIGH, Elsie; landscape and portrait painter in oil; Mem. London Group, and Contemporary Portrait Soc.; *b* London, Jan., 1900; *d* of Richard Wooden; *m* John Farleigh; one *d. Educ.:* Hornsey High School; *studied art* at Central School of Arts and Crafts (1917-21) under B. Meninsky, J. Grant. *Exhib.:* Bradford, Brighton, Bristol, Leicester Gallery, Redfern Gallery, etc. *Work repro.:* in Black on White by Arnold Haskell. *Address:* 36 Belsize Grove, London NW3. *Signs work:* "Anne Neville."

FARR, Dennis Larry Ashwell, M.A., F.R.S.A., F.M.A.; Director, Birmingham City Museums and Art Gallery; Senior Lecturer in Fine Art and Deputy Keeper, University of Glasgow (1967-69); Curator Paul Mellon Collection, Washington, D.C. (1964-66); Asst. Keeper, Tate Gallery, London (1954-64); *b* Luton, 3 Apr., 1929; *s* of Arthur Farr; *m* Diana Pullein-Thompson, writer; one *s,* one *d. Educ.:* Luton Grammar School; *studied art* at Courtauld Inst. of Art, University of London (1947-50). *Publications:* articles and reviews in Apollo, Burlington Magazine, contributions to Encyclopaedia Britannica, William Etty (1958), Catalogue of the Modern British Paintings, Drawings and Sculpture in the Tate Gallery (with M. Chamot and M. Butlin, 1964-65), etc. *Address:* City Museums and Art Gallery, Birmingham B3 3DH. *Clubs:* Athenæum, I.C.A. *Signs work:* "Dennis Farr."

FASTNEDGE, Ralph William, D.F.C., B.A.; curator, The Lady Lever Art Gallery, Port Sunlight, Merseyside; *b* London, 16 Apr., 1913. *Educ.:* University College School; Worcester College, Oxford; Courtauld Inst. of Art. *Publications:* English Furniture Styles (1500-1830), Penguin Books, 1955; Sheraton Furniture, Faber; Shearer Furniture Designs, Tiranti; Regency Furniture (revision), Country Life. *Address:* The Lady Lever Art Gallery, Port Sunlight, Merseyside.

FAULKNER, Howard, A.R.C.A. (1922), Royal Exhibitioner (1914), designer; artist in water-colour; *b* Birmingham, 1 May, 1894; *s* of Joseph Faulkner; *m* Dorothy Edith Todd; one *s,* two *d. Educ.:* George Dixon's Secondary School, Birmingham; *studied art* at Dudley School of Art (1910-14), R.C.A. (1919-22). *Work in permanent collections:* V. & A. print coll. (joint with Elfie Parry); Towner A.G., Eastbourne; Municipal A.G., Dudley, designs for fourteen Stations of the Cross carved in English oak in the crypt of the Roman Catholic Cathedral, Liverpool. *Official purchase:* monochrome drawing, Towner A.G., Eastbourne. *Work repro.:* Studio, The Artist. *Address:* 51 Manvers Rd., Eastbourne. *Club:* Eastbourne Soc. of Artists. *Signs work:* "HOWARD FAULKNER" in Roman Capital Italics.

FAULKNER, Robert Trevor, A.R.C.A. (1955), A.R.B.S. (1966); sculptor in direct welding in ferrous and non-ferrous metals (wild-life and architectural); Lecturer, Sheffield School of Art; *b* Sheffield, 17 Sept., 1929; *m* Brenda Flowers; one *d. Educ.:* Penistone Grammar School; *studied art* at Sheffield School of Art (1946-50) under George Mason, Ray Stone; R.C.A. (1952-55) under Frank Dobson, John Skeaping. *Exhib.:* Moorland Gallery, Cork St., John Hutton Gallery, Peterboro, Kolberg's, Elgin, U.S.A. *Work in permanent collections;* Ulster Museum. Derbyshire, Oxfordshire, Lancashire and Sheffield Educ. Authorities. *Work repro.:* Wildlife. *Address:* 4 Birchitt Cl., Bradway, Sheffield. *Signs work:* "TREVOR FAULKNER."

FAUSSET, Shelley, Dip. F.A. (Lond.), (1954); sculptor in stone, metal, wood and resin, and teacher; head of dept., Central School of Arts and Crafts, London; *b* Newbury, Berks, 5 Apr., 1920; *s* of H. I'A. Fausset, author; *m* Ann; five *d*. *Educ.:* Friends' School, Saffron Walden; *studied art* at Chelsea School of Art (1948-52), Slade School, University College (1952-54). *Work in permanent collections:* Arts Council of Wales and numerous private collections; Herts and Derbyshire Education Committees, etc. Represented by Mercury Gallery, London. *Address:* 20 High St., Pirton, Hitchin, Herts. *Signs work:* "Shelley Fausset."

FAUST, Pat; artist in oil, water-colour, pastel, theatrical designs, murals; *b* Lancs.; *d* of the late William Faust. *Educ.:* Culcheth Hall, Ches.; *studied art* at Manchester Regional College of Art; Crescent Theatre, Birmingham. *Exhib.:* R.A., R.G.I., Manchester Academy, Birmingham A.G., Sewerby Hall, Bridlington, Scarborough A.G. and Town Hall, Ferens A.G., Hull, Beverley, Cartwright Hall, Bradford, Pannett, Whitby, R.B.A., S.W.A., R.Cam.A., U.A.S., Leeds City A.G., Paris Salon, Gallery Vallombreuse Biarritz, Brye A.G., Glaisdale, City Gallery, Darlington, Francis Phillips Gallery, Sheffield; one-man shows: Marshalls, Scarborough, Hull University. *Work in permanent collections:* Scarborough A.G., Scarborough Town Hall, Menston Hospital and private collections. *Official purchase:* painting of Scarborough A.G. (hung R.A.) by Scarborough Corp. *Address:* Sea-Point, Upper Flat Cliffs, nr. Filey. *Clubs:* Leeds Fine Art, Scarborough Arts Soc. *Signs work:* "Pat Faust."

FAVORSKY, Vladimir, Hon. Artist of R.S.F.S.R.; engraver, xylographist, book designer, painter and theatrical designer; *b* Moscow, 1886; *studied art* at Moscow and Munich Universities. *Work repro.:* illustrations to Jen-shen (by M. M. Prishvin), The Lay of the Host of Igor, Boris Godunov (by Pushkin). *Address:* Moscow, Gogolevskyi bul. 10, The Union of Soviet Artists.

FAWSSETT, Ann, R.A.S. (1961); painter in water-colour and ink; tutor, Beaford Centre; *b* Lindfield, Sussex, 1937; *d* of Capt. A. C. Fawssett, D.S.O., R.N.; *m* Ron Atkin; two *s*. *Educ.:* Burgess Hill P.N.E.U.; *studied art* at Brighton College of Art (1954-58); Royal Academy Schools (1958-61). *Exhib.:* Young Contemporaries, Beaford Centre, Crane Arts Ltd. *Address:* The Old Rectory, W. Putford, Devon EX22 7XE. *Signs work:* "FAWSSETT" and "Ann Salaman."

FEDDEN, Mary; Scholarship and Slade Diploma of Fine Arts, A.R.W.E.A.; artist in oil, teacher of painting at Royal Coll. of Art (1958-64); Yehudi Menuhin School (1965-70); *b* Bristol, 14 Aug., 1915; *d* of Vincent Fedden; *m* Julian Trevelyan. *Educ.:* Badminton School, Bristol. *Exhib.:* Leicester Gallery, Heals Gallery, Gimpel Fils, R.W.E.A., London Group, Edinburgh, Dublin, Brighton, Bristol; six one-man shows, Redfern Gallery; three at Hamet Gallery; one at New Grafton Gallery. *Work in permanent collections:* H.M. The Queen, Bristol, Hull, Carlisle, Edinburgh, Melbourne. *Official purchases:* Contemporary Arts Soc., Yorkshire C.C., Leicestershire C.C., Hertfordshire C.C., Min. of Works, Orient Line and Bristol Educ. Com. *Address:* Durham Wharf, Hammersmith Terr., London W6. *Signs work:* "Fedden."

FEENY, Patrick A., F.M.G.P.; ecclesiastical artist; *b* Harrow, Middx., 30 Nov., 1910. *Educ.:* Stonyhurst College. *Address:* Lightwoods Pk., Hagley Rd. West, Warley, West Midlands B67 5DP. *Signs work:* see appendix.

FEI, Cheng-Wu; painter; Prof. (1941-46), College of Fine Art, National Central University, China; *b* China, 30 Dec., 1914; *s* of Mai-Chu Fei, poet, prof. of Chinese literature; *m* Chien-Ying Chang, artist. *Educ.:* National Central University, China (1930-34), Slade School of Fine Art (1947-50). *Exhib.:* R.A., R.I., R.W.A., R.W.S., N.E.A.C.; one-man shows at Leicester Galleries. *Work in permanent collections:* Royal West of England Academy, Universities' China

Committee, Grave's Gallery, Sheffield, Derby A.G., etc. *Work repro.:* Studio, Art News & Review, La Revue Moderne, Kunst, etc. *Publication:* Brush Drawing in the Chinese Manner (Studio). *Address:* 52 Dollis Pk., London N3. *Signs work:* see appendix.

FEILER, Paul; painter; *b* 30 Apr., 1918; *s* of Prof. E. Feiler, M.D.; *m* Catharine Armitage; three *s,* two *d. Educ.:* Canford School, Dorset; *studied art* at Slade School of Fine Art. *Exhib.:* one-man shows since 1953. Redfern Gallery, London, Grosvenor Gallery, London, U.S.A. *Public collections:* Tate Gallery, Arts Council, British Council, Liverpool, Manchester, Warwick, London, Oxford, Cambridge, Newcastle Universities; galleries in England, U.S.A., France, Austria, Canada and New Zealand. *Address:* Kerris, nr. Penzance, Cornwall.

FELKEL, Carl F., S.G.A., A.I.A.; *b* 18 Jan., 1896; *m. Educ.:* Vienna; Munich (W. Thor); Academy of Fine Art, Vienna (Master Class Bacher). *Exhib.:* Vienna, Paris, Rome, London, R.A. Travelled extensively in U.S.A. and all countries of Europe, painting portraits and landscapes. *Official purchases:* Manchester and Derby Public Galleries; Vienna Albertina. *Address:* 70 Holland Park, London W11. *Club:* National Society, Society of Graphic Artists. *Signs work:* "C. Felkel."

FELL, Sheila Mary, F.R.S.A. (1973), R.A. (1974); painter in oil; teacher, Chelsea School of Art; *b* Aspatria, nr. Carlisle, 20 July, 1931; *d* of John Fell. *Educ.:* Thomlinson Grammar School, Wigton; *studied art* at Carlisle School of Art; St. Martin's School of Art under John Napper, V. Pitchforth, F. Gore. *Exhib.:* Arts Council, Contemporary Art Society, Tate Gallery, Municipal Galleries of Carlisle, Liverpool, Middlesborough, Southport, Sunderland, Swindon and Newcastle (Laing), Abbott Hall, Kendal, Eastbourne. *Publication:* contributor to Breakthrough edited by Ronald Goldman (Routledge & Kegan Paul Ltd.). *Address:* 41 Redcliffe Sq., London SW10. *Club:* Colony Room. *Signs work:* "Fell."

FENDT, René; painter-impressionism in oil and acrylics on canvas, printmaking, murals; Tutor, School of Art and Crafts, Basle (1968-73); *b* Basle, 4 Feb., 1948; *s* of Max Fendt, graphic designer; *m* Germaine Waeber. *Educ.:* Realschule, Basle; *studied art* at School of Art and Crafts, Basle (1963-68). *Exhib.:* 14 group and one-man shows. *Work in permanent collections:* Zem Specht Gallery, Basle, A.I.R., S.E.A.A. *Address:* Lower Venson Farm, Tilmanstone, Deal, Kent. *Signs work:* "R. Fendt" or "R.F."

FENTON, Katherine; artist, enamellist and painter in oils; previously Social worker and Student Services Officer; *b* London; *m* Roland Fenton; one *s. Educ.:* Brondesbury & Kilburn High School, London; external student London University: Diploma Social Studies. *Exhib.:* Second Biennale Internationale '73, L'Art de L'Email, Limorges, F.P.S. Trends at Mall Galleries and Loggia Galleries, Artist Enamellers at Chenil Gallery and Alpine Gallery (1971-1974); one-man shows: Hornsey (1969, 1970). *Address:* 54 Oakfield Ct., Haslemere Rd., Hornsey, London N8 9QY. *Club:* F.P.S. *Signs work:* "Fenton," "KF" or "F."

FEREDAY, Joseph, Diploma in Fine Art, Slade School, Slade School drawing and etching prizes; Senior Lecturer, Portsmouth College of Art and Design; *b* Dudley, 9 Feb., 1917; *s* of Joseph Fereday, manufacturer; *m* Ida Mary Jones; two *d. Educ.:* privately and Dudley Grammar School; *studied art* at Wolverhampton and Birmingham College of Art, Slade School (1946-48). *Work in permanent collections:* Plymouth A.G., Bilston A.G., St. Mary's College, Twickenham, Portsmouth Corp., Seely Library, Ryde, I.O.W., British Embassy, Helsinki, Galerie Alphonse Marré, Chartres; one-man shows: Woodstock Gallery, London,

Hiscock Gallery, Portsmouth, Galerie de Vallombreuse Biarritz. *Address:* Yarborough House, New Rd., Brading, I.O.W.

FERGUSON, Dan, R.O.I. (1958); artist in oil, water-colour and colour print; awarded Médaille D'Argent, Paris Salon (1961); *b* Motherwell, 1910; *s* of Archibald Ferguson, master builder. *Educ.:* Dalziel High School, Motherwell; *studied art* at Glasgow School of Art. *Exhib.:* R.S.A., R.O.I., R.S.W., R.G.I., R.I. Summer Salon, Paris Salon, Awarded Hon. Mention Paris Salon, 1956. *Official purchases:* Glasgow Art Gallery (Flowers in a Jug), Paisley Art Gallery (Sheldrakes). *Address:* Red Yett, Motherwell, Lanarks. *Signs work:* "DAN FERGUSON."

FERGUSON, Malcolm Alastair Percy, A.R.W.A. (1965), Diploma in Fine Art (Lond., 1950); religious landscape and figure painter; visiting teacher; *b* Blackwater, Hants., 19 Dec., 1913; *s* of P. F. H. Ferguson; *m* Joy Rosemary Holdsworth; one *s*, one *d*. *Educ.:* Durham School, R.M.A., Sandhurst; *studied art* at Croydon School of Art (1936-39), Slade School (1939, 1948-51). *Exhib.:* R.A., N.E.A.C., R.P., R.I., R.W.A., Paris Salon, Nat. Gall. of Wales (Cardiff), Bradford, etc. *Work repro.:* in La Revue Moderne and Art News and Review (1951-55). *Official purchases:* Plymouth City Art Gallery (1965), George M. Whiley (1963), R. W. A. Talboys Bequest (1969). *Address:* Lower Cleeve, Minehead. *Signs work:* "Malcolm A. P. Ferguson."

FERGUSON, Roy Young, S.S.A. (1943), R.S.W. (1945); artist in water-colour, wash, black and white; caricaturist and illustrator in black and white and writer on natural history; poetry published P.E.N. Anthology (1965), also Scotsman, Glasgow Herald, Scottish Field, etc.; *b* Motherwell, 1907; *s* of Archibald Ferguson. *Educ.:* Dalziel High School, Motherwell; *studied art* at Glasgow School of Art. *Exhib.:* R.A., N.E.A.C., R.B.A., R.S.A., R.S.W., Paris Salon (1951), etc.; tour of Holland with R.S.W.; France, Holland, Canada, awarded Silver Medal Paris Salon (1952). *Official purchases:* Glasgow Art Gallery; Newport, Wales, Corporation. *Address:* Redyett, Motherwell, Lanarks. *Signs work:* (paintings) "R. Y. FERGUSON," (caricatures) "eff."

FERRAN, Brian, A.T.C. (1962); art administrator, painter and teacher; Exhibitions Officer, A.C. of N.I.; *b* Derry, N.I., 19 Oct., 1940; *s* of Bernard Ferran; *m* Denise Devine; one *s*, one *d*. *Educ.:* St. Columb's Coll., Derry; *studied art* at St. Mary's and St. Joseph's Colls., Belfast. *Exhib.:* Royal Hibernian Academy, Royal Ulster Academy, Oireachtas Exhibitions, Minnesota, U.S.A., Ulster Museum, Dublin (1969), Newcastle-on-Tyne. *Work in permanent collections:* Arts Council, Dublin; Arts Council of Northern Ireland; Kilkenny Design Centre; Haverty Trust; Belfast Education Committee; Magee University College; St. John Fisher College, New York, and Institution of Public Administration. *Work repro.:* Eire-Ireland, Ulster Painting 68. *Address:* 31 Skegoneill Ave., Belfast BT15 3JP. *Signs work:* see appendix.

FERRER-PERALTA, Magda; painter; Municipal Gold Medal (1959); *b* Barcelona, 2 Oct., 1931; *d* of Dr. Pedro Ferrer. *Educ.:* Barcelona University; *studied art* at High School of Fine Arts, Barcelona. *Exhib.:* Galeria Norte Sur, Caracas, Ateneo, Barcelona, Amadis, Madrid, Galerie Numero, Firenze; group shows: Taipeh, Lisbon, Paris, Caracas, São Paulo (Biennal), etc. *Work in permanent collections:* Museum of Modern Art, Barcelona, Arts Museum, Taipeh. *Work repro.:* 20 Years of Spanish Painting (C. A. Arean), Pintura Catalana (C. A. Arean), Aujourd-hui (J. E. Cirlot). *Address:* Rambla de Cataluna, 57, Barcelona. *Club:* Forum Verges, Rosellon 223, Barcelona. *Signs work:* "Magda F."

FERRY, James Alexander, Hon. R.U.A.; artist in oil, water-colour and pastel;

textile designer. *Studied art* in Northern Ireland, London and Paris. *Address:* 27 Brown St., Belfast, 13, N. Ireland. *Clubs:* R.U.A., Belfast Natural History and Philosophical Soc. *Signs work:* "FERRY."

FFOLKES, Michael (Brian Davis); F.S.I.A. (1968), N.D. painting (1948); illustrator, cartoonist; *b* London, 6 June, 1925; *s* of the late Walter Lawrence Davis, M.S.I.A.; *m* Mary Boxer; two *s,* one *d; m* Irene Ogilvy Kemp. *Educ.:* Leigh Hall College, Essex; *studied art* at St. Martin's School of Art under John Farleigh (1943), Chelsea School of Art under Ceri Richards, Robert Medley (1946-49). *Work repro.:* Punch, Daily Telegraph, Sunday Telegraph, Playboy, Pardon. *Address:* 34 Kelly St., London NW1. *Club:* Savage. *Signs work:* "ffolkes," "ff."

FIDLER, Alwyn G. Sheppard, C.B.E., M.A., B.Arch., Dip.C.D. (Liverpool), F.R.I.B.A., Dist.T.P., F.R.T.P.I., Rome Scholar in Architecture (1933), Victory Scholarship, R.I.B.A. (1933); architect and planning consultant; city architect of Birmingham (1952-64); chief architect, Crawley New Town (1947-52); *b* Holywell, Flintshire, 8 May, 1909; *s* of W. Ernest Sheppard Fidler; *m* Margaret Kidner; one *s. Educ.:* Holywell Grammar School; *studied art* at University of Liverpool School of Architecture and British School at Rome. *Exhib.:* R.A., British School at Rome, R.I.B.A. *Publications:* contributions to professional journals. *Address:* Woodcote Grove, Epsom. *Club:* R.A.C. *Signs work:* "A. G. Sheppard Fidler."

FIELD, Natalie; portrait painter in oil; Founder and First President, Transvaal Art Soc., now affiliated to the S.A. Assoc. of Arts; *b* South Africa, 1898; *m* J. A. Nash, wool buyer. *Educ.:* Princess Helena College, Ealing, England; *studied art* at Slade School of Art, under Profs. Brown, Henry Tonks, McEvoy, Walter Russell, Wilson Steer, and under Richard Sickert at Westminster. *Work in permanent collections:* South African National Gallery, Cape Town. *Official purchases:* for South African War Art and South African Railways collections. *Address:* St. Andrew's Hotel, Umkomaas, Natal, S.A. *Signs work:* "Natalie Field" (surname underlined).

FIELD, Peter L., A.T.D.; artist, teacher and lecturer, Paignton School of Art (1949-53), Swindon School of Art (1953-58); Birmingham College of Art and Design (now City of Birmingham Polytechnic) (Head of Department since 1958); *b* Winson, Glos., 7 Feb., 1920; *s* of W. W. Field; *m* Cynthia G. Barry; two *d. Educ.:* Rendcomb College; *studied art* at Cheltenham School of Art (1937-39) under A. Seaton-White, Goldsmiths' College School of Art (1946-49) under Clive Gardner. *Exhib.:* London and provincial exhbns. *Work in permanent collections:* Swindon Art Gallery. *Official purchases:* Swindon Corporation. *Address:* 264 Mary Vale Rd., Bournville, Birmingham, 30. *Signs work:* "Peter L. Field."

FIGGIS, Roberts Richmond, B.A. (Dublin); company director; mem. of the Arts Council of Ireland, of the council of the Royal Dublin Society and of the Friends of the National Collections of Ireland; a Governor of the National Gallery of Ireland; Committee member of the Irish Exhibition of Living Art; *b* Dublin, 26 Apr., 1900; *s* of Henry Wingfield Figgis; *m* Philippa Maria Young; one *s,* one *d. Educ.:* Earlsfort House School and Dublin Univ. *Address:* Farm Lodge, Ballybrack, Co. Dublin. *Club:* Kildare St., Dublin.

FINCH, William Robert, F.I.A.L. (1953), free-lance journalist; oils, watercolour, pencil, pastel, gouache, pen and ink; etcher; lecturer on art country life; late head art dept. Beal Grammar School, Ilford; founder-tutor, Over 40's Art Groups; lecturer rural architecture Extra Mural Dept., Cambridge University; *b* Lowestoft, 6 Apr., 1905; *s* of William Henry Austin Finch, master mariner; *m* Peggy Doreen Hill; two *s. Educ.:* Lowestoft Grammar School, College of St. Mark and St. John, Chelsea; *studied art:* self taught. *Exhib.:* R.A., East End Academy, Reading Art

Guild, Assembly Rooms, Norwich, Ilford Art Soc. *Work in collections:* Mrs. Lewis L. Douglas, New York; R. Hone, Esq.; Chigwell School, private Germany, France, etc. *Official purchases:* Ilford Libraries Com., Boy Scouts' Association, Westminster Bank, "Snowdrift" Lubricants. *Work repro.:* East Anglian Magazine, Quarterly Review Assoc. Agriculture, The Essex Countryside, Y.H.A. publications, etc. *Publications:* author/illustrator Journeying into Essex, In and Around Folkestone, Introducing Essex to America, Country Buildings, 100 years of Snowdrift Lubricants. *Address:* Waveney Cottage, Weybread, Diss, Norfolk. *Signs work:* "W. R. Finch" or "Finch."

FINDLAY, Sheila Anne Macfarlane, A.R.W.S., D.A.(Edin.), Post-Grad. (1950), Travelling Scholar (1951); artist and illustrator in water-colour and oil; *b* Auchlishie, Kirriemuir; *d* of William R. Findlay, farmer; *m* Alfred Hackney, A.R.W.S., A.R.E., D.A.(Edin.); two *d. Educ.:* Webster's Seminary; *studied art* at Edinburgh College of Art (1945-51) under John Maxwell, Sir William MacTaggart, Leonard Rosoman. *Work in permanent collections:* private collections. *Publications:* children's books illustrated for Faber & Faber, Adprint, Harrap, Odhams, Medici Soc. *Address:* Butt's Hill Cottage, Pilgrim's Way, Wrotham, Kent. *Signs work:* "Sheila Findlay."

FINLAY, Ian, C.B.E., M.A. (Hons.), H.R.S.A.; Liveryman, Worshipful Company of Goldsmiths, London; Professor of Antiquities to Royal Scottish Academy; formerly Director, Royal Scottish Museum and Secy. Royal Fine Art Commission, Scotland; *b* Auckland, N.Z.; *s* of W. R. Finlay, artist; *m* Mary Scott Pringle; two *s,* one *d. Educ.:* Edinburgh Academy, University of Edinburgh. *Publications:* Scotland (O.U.P.), Art in Scotland (O.U.P.), Scottish Crafts (Harrap), Scotland (Young Traveller Series; Phoenix House), History of Scottish Gold and Silver Work (Chatto), The Lothians (Collins), The Highlands (Batsford), The Lowlands (Batsford), Celtic Art (Faber). *Address:* Currie Riggs, Balerno, Midlothian. *Club:* Scottish Arts (Edinburgh).

FINLEY, David Edward; *b* York, S.C., U.S.A., 13 Sept., 1890; *s* of David Edward Finley and Elizabeth Gist; *m* (1931) Margaret Morton Eustis. *Educ.:* University of South Carolina (A.B.), George Washington Law School (LL.B.). European War (1917-18), 2nd Lt., U.S. Army; U.S. Treasury Dept. (1921-27); special asst. to Sec. of Treasury (1927-32); Hon. Counsellor, American Embassy, London (1932-33); Director, National Gallery of Art, Washington (1938-56; retd.); Pres., American Assoc. of Museums (1945-49); Chairman, National Trust for Historic Preservation (1949-62); Chairman, Commission of Fine Arts, Washington (1950-63). *Address:* 3318 "O" St., Washington, 7, D.C.

FIRTH, Sir Raymond William, M.A. (N.Z.), Ph.D.(Lond.), F.B.A., Emeritus Prof. of Anthropology, University of London; field research in Solomon Islands, 1928-29, 1952, 1966; Malaya, 1939-40, 1963; *b* Auckland, N.Z., 25 Mar., 1901; *m* Rosemary Upcott; one *s. Educ.:* Auckland University College, London School of Economics. *Publications:* Art and Life in New Guinea (Studio), 1938; The Social Framework of Primitive Art (ch. in Elements of Social Organization), (Watts, 1951), Tikopia Woodworking Ornament, (Man 40, 27), Tikopia Art and Society in Primitive Art and Society (ed. A. Forge) O.U.P. (1972). *Address:* 33 Southwood Ave., London N6.

FISCHLI, Hans; architect, sculptor and painter in oil; *b* Zürich, 9 Oct., 1909. *Studied art* at Bauhaus Dessau, Germany. *Work in permanent collections:* Musée d'Art Moderne, Paris, Museum, Oldenburg, Zürich Kunsthaus, Basel Kunstmuseum, Dr. Bechtler, Zürich, Elisabeth Feller Horgen, Dr. Staehelin Feldmeilen. *Official purchases:* Swiss National Exhibitions, Zürich (1939, adj. Chefarchitect);

co-founder and architect, Pestalozzi Children's Village, Trogen; Chefarchitect, Züka, 1947, Zürich. 1954-61, Dir. Kunstgewerbeschule und Museum, Zürich; Swiss Pavillon Triennale di Milano (1964, Commissaire and Architect). *Address:* Dufourstrasse 181A, 8008, Zürich. *Club:* B.S.A.

FISHER, Myrta, D.F.A.(Lond.) (1940); Certificates for design, painting and drawing, perspective and history of art (1st class at Henriques School, 1938); painter in acrylic and casein, part-time teacher; *b* Wimbledon, 28 Aug., 1917; *d* of Harold Fisher, woollen merchant and writer. *Educ.:* Roedean School; *studied art* at Huddersfield Art School; Slade School and Central School of Arts and Crafts. *Exhib.:* many shared and group exhbns.; one-man show Ansdell Gallery, London (1971). Work in many private collections. *Address:* 34 Meeching Rd., Newhaven, Sussex. *Signs work:* "M.F."

FISHWICK, Clifford, A.T.D. (1947); painter; Principal, Exeter College of Art; *b* nr. Accrington, 21 June, 1923; *s* of Norman Fishwick, draper; *m* Patricia Fishwick; two *s,* two *d. Educ.:* Chester Grammar School; *studied art* at Liverpool College of Art. *Exhib.:* (one-man) St. George's Gallery (1957), Dartington Hall Arts Centre, Exeter University, John Moores Exhbn., Bradford Art Gallery, Penwith Society, Plymouth City Gallery, Exeter Museum. *Official purchases:* Murals: S.W. Electricity Board and Schools, Plymouth, Bradford and Exeter Galleries; Christchurch, Oxford, Exeter University, Elmslie Philip Collection, Devon County. *Address:* Salisbury House, Monmouth St., Topsham, Devon. *Club:* Newlyn. *Signs work:* "Clifford Fishwick."

FLANDERS, Dennis, A.R.W.S., R.B.A, Hon. Freeman, Painter-Stainers' Co., water-colours and black and whites; *b* 2 July, 1915; *m* Dalma Darnley Taylor; one *s,* one *d. Educ.:* Merchant Taylor's School. *Exhib.:* R.A.; one-man shows in London galleries (1947, 1951, 1953, 1955, 1964, 1967). *Work in permanent collections:* Guildhall, National War Collection, Fitzwilliam Museum, Cambridge, Wolverhampton, Bury, Southport. *Work repro.:* Famous Streets in Sunday Times (1952-53); special artist to the Illustrated London News (1956-64); The Great Livery Companies of The City of London (1974), portfolios of Drawings. *Addresses:* 51 Gt. Ormond St., London WC1, and Baker's Cross House, Cranbrook, Kent. *Club:* Art Workers' Guild (Master, 1975). *Signs work:* see appendix.

FLATTELY, Alastair, R.W.A., D.A. (Edin.) 1949, Andrew Grant Fellowship in Painting (1953-55); artist in oil, water-colour and black and white; Head, Grays School of Art, Aberdeen; *b* Inverness, 20 Nov., 1922. *Educ.:* Maiden Erlegh School, Reading, and Glasgow Univ.; *studied art* at Edinburgh Coll. of Art. *Exhib.:* Wildenstein's; Parsons Gall.; Roland, Browse and Delbanco; Gallery One; Upper Grosvenor Gallery; Fieldborne Galleries; R.S.A.; S.S.A.; R.A.; R.W.A. *Work in permanent collections:* R.S.A.; R.W.A.; Nuffield Foundation; Aberdeen, Glasgow, Dundee and Cheltenham A.Gs. *Address:* Briar Lodge, Westerton Pl., Cults, Aberdeen. *Signs work:* "Alastair Flattely" or "Flattely."

FLEISCHMANN, Arthur John, F.R.B.S. (Brit.); sculptor in bronze, terracotta, acrylics, wood, cement, stone; *b* Bratislava, 5 June, 1896; *s* of Simon Fleischmann; *m* Cecile Joy Burtonshaw; one *s. Educ.:* University Budapest, Art Academy, Prague, Master School, Vienna, and in France, Italy. *Exhib.:* Vienna, Bratislava, Padua, U.S.A., Melbourne, Sydney, R.A., Paris Salon, Festival of Britain (1951), Brussels World Exhbn. (1958); one-man show, Los Angeles (1968), Expo '70, Japan, London Park (1972). *Work in permanent collections:* National Gallery of N.S.W. and South Australia, California, New York, Blackburn Art Gallery, Beaulieu Castle. *Official purchases:* Municipal, Vienna; Churches in Austria, Germany, Holland, Australia, Britain; Government House, Canberra; Botanical

Gardens, Sydney; Public Library of N.S.W.; Beda College, Rome; Scotts College, Rome; World Trade Centre, London; G.L.C. *Address:* 92 Carlton Hill, London NW8. *Signs work:* "ARTHUR FLEISCHMANN" or "A.F."

FLEMING, Ian, R.S.W. (1946), A.R.S.A. (1947), R.S.A. (1956); painter in oils and water-colour, etcher; senior lecturer, Glasgow School of Art (1931-47), Warden, Patrick Allan Fraser Art College, Arbroath, Angus, (1948-54); head of Gray's School of Art, Aberdeen (since 1954); *b* Glasgow, 19 Nov., 1906; *s* of John Fleming; *m* Catherine Weetch, D.A.; one *s,* two *d. Educ.:* Glasgow School of Art and Paris. *Exhib.:* R.A., R.S.A., Royal Glasgow Institute of Fine Art, Soc. Scottish Artists, Walker Art Gallery, etc. *Official purchases:* Belfast, Liverpool, Bradford, Glasgow and other municipal galleries; Thorburn Ross Memorial Fund, R.S.A. *Address:* 15 Fonthill Rd., Aberdeen. *Club:* Glasgow Art. *Signs work:* "Fleming."

FLETCHER, Henry; painter in oil and water-colour; sometime a teacher of drawing and painting at the regional College of Art, Bradford; *b* Bradford, 27 Jan., 1901; *s* of H. Fletcher, master tailor; *m* Kathleen M. Green; one *d. Educ.:* Marshfield and Grange Grammar School; *studied art* at Bradford College of Art under Charles Stephenson, A.R.C.A., and Fred Stead, A.R.C.A. (1915-18), Colarossi, Paris (1920), St. Martin's School of Art, London, under John E. Allen, A.R.C.A. (1921-22). *Exhib.:* R.A., R.B.A., Goupil Salon, New Burlington Galls. and provincial galleries. *Address:* 100 Wykeham Rd., Earley, Reading, Berks. *Signs work:* "H. Fletcher" or "Fletcher."

FLETCHER, Rosamund M B., F.R.B.S., M.G.L.C., Feodora Gleichen award (1948), Olympic Bronze Medal (1948), sculptor in stone and bronze; *b* Dorking, Surrey, 5 Aug., 1914; *d* of Blandford Fletcher, painter. *Educ.:* St. Joseph's Priory, Dorking; *studied art* at Ruskin School, Oxford, Slade School. *Work in permanent collections:* Richmond R.C. Secondary School; St. Teresa's Church, Princes Risborough; Woking R.C. Primary School; St. Mary's Convent, Ascot; Church of Our Lady Queen of Peace, E. Sheen; St. Mary's R.C. Primary School (Wimbledon); Samuel Slater Memorial, Mass., U.S.A.; Tyburn Shrine, London; Carmelite Monastery, Quidennum. *Address:* 305 Woodstock Rd., Oxford. *Signs work:* "Rosamund M. B. Fletcher."

FLINT, Francis Murray Russell, R.N.V.R., Lt.-Cdr. (1939); oil and water-colour artist; *b* 3 June, 1915; *s* of late Sir W. Russell Flint, R.A., P.R.W.S.; *m;* three *s,* two *d. Educ.:* Cheltenham College; H.M.S. Conway; Grosvenor School of Modern Art; R.A. Schools; Paris Schools. *Exhib.:* R.A., R.W.E.A., R.S.A., Birmingham, Bristol, U.S.A., Africa, Canada, etc. Official Admiralty Artist. *Official purchases:* Imperial War Museum; Rocket Ships off Walcheron, Holland. *Work repro.:* Illustrated London News, Sketch, Tatler, R.A. Pictures, Escape Episodes in Malaya. Specialises principally in marine subjects. *Publications:* in The Artist, Studio, Author: How To Paint In Water-colour; Water-colour Out of Doors. *Address:* Jesmond Dene, Silverdale Rd., Burgess Hill, Sussex. *Clubs:* R.N.V.R., Arts. *Signs work:* amended from "Francis R. Flint" as previously to "F. Russell Flint."

FOGEL, Seymour; artist, muralist, sculptor, teacher, writer; former Vice-Pres., Architectural League of New York; *b* New York City, 25 Aug., 1911; *s* of Benjamin Fogel; *m* Barbara Clark; one *s,* one *d. Exhib.:* in all national shows and in South America and England; executed 21 major mural commissions, the most recent of which are for the new U.S. Customs Court's Bldg., Foley Square, N.Y.C., Int. School 29, N.Y.C. and Gouverneur Hospital, N.Y.C., stained glass screen for lobby of new Bellevue Hospital, N.Y.C. (1973), work added to National Archives,

Washington, D.C. (1973); 17 one-man shows, including ones at Knoedler, Houston Museum of Fine Arts, and the Santa Barbara Art Museum. *Work owned* by Whitney, Dallas, Houston art museums and the Joseph Hirschhorn collection as well as many other major collections. Awards include First Prize, Gulf Caribbean International, Texas General, Silver Medal, Architectural League. *Address:* 68 Georgetown Rd., Weston, Connecticut 06880.

FOLKARD, Edward, F.R.B.S. (1955); sculptor, primarily a modeller; *b* London, 16 May, 1911; *s* of Charles James Folkard. *Educ.:* Eltham College; *studied art* at Goldsmiths' College and R.A. Schools. *Exhib.:* R.A., R.B.A., London Group, Glasgow Institute of Fine Arts, Arts Council (1951-53), Holland Pk. (1957). *Address:* 105 Princedale Rd., London W11. *Signs work:* "E.F." or "Folkard."

FOLKES, Peter Leonard, A.T.D., R.W.A., R.I.; painter in oil and water-colour; lecturer at Southampton College of Art; *b* Beaminster, 3 Nov., 1923; *s* of Leonard Folkes; *m* Muriel Giddings; two *s*. *Educ.:* Sexey's School Bruton; *studied art* at West of England College of Art, Bristol, under George Sweet (1940-42 and 1947-50). *Exhib.:* R.A., R.W.A., R.I.; one-man shows: Rumbold Gallery, Midhurst (1962), Crespi Gallery, New York (1965), University of Southampton (1965, 1973), Hamwic Gallery, Southampton (1966), Barzansky Gallery, New York (1967), and Alwin Gallery, London (1970). *Official purchases:* Arts Council of Great Britain, R.W.A. *Address:* 61 Ethelburt Ave., Swaythling, Southampton. *Signs work:* "Folkes."

FOOT, Victorine Anne, S.S.A., D.A.; artist in oil, mural painting; Directorate of Camouflage (1941-45); *b* Kent, 1 May, 1920; *d* of Major Hammond-Foot, R.E.; *m* Eric Schilsky, R.A., R.S.A. (decd.); one *d*, Clare. *Educ.:* Oakdene School; *studied art* at L.C.C. Central School of Arts and Crafts, Chelsea School of Art, Edinburgh College of Art. *Exhib.:* R.A., R.S.A., N.E.A.C., London Group, etc., exhbn. at Institut Français, Edinburgh (1949), Scottish Gallery, Edinburgh (1969). *Official purchases:* Arts Council (Scottish Committee), War Artists' Advisory Commn. (1943). *Address:* 16A Meadow Pl., Edinburgh EH9 1JR. *Signs work:* "Victorine Foot," "V.F."

FORBES, Ronald, D.A.; awarded Leverhulme Senior Art Fellowship, University of Strathclyde (1973-74); founder chairman, Glasgow League of Artists; mem., S.S.A.; painter in acrylic, film-maker; Head of Painting Dept., Crawford School of Art, Cork; *b* Braco, Scotland, 1947; *s* of William Forbes; *m* Ruth Forbes. *Educ.:* Morrison's Academy, Crieff; *studied art* at Edinburgh College of Art (1964-69) under Robin Philipson. *Exhib.:* one-man shows: Glasgow, London, Cork and Dublin. *Work in permanent collections:* Perth Council, Strathclyde and Glasgow Universities, Scottish Arts Council. *Address:* 41 Springmount Rd., Glanmire, Cork, Ireland. *Signs work:* "Forbes."

FORD, George Henry, F.R.B.S. (1955), G.M.C. (1947-62); sculptor; *b* 13 July, 1912; *s* of George S. Ford, builder. *Educ.:* Steyne School Worthing; Hornsey School of Art (Harold Youngman, F.R.B.S.). *Exhib.:* R.A.; R.S.A.; Walker Art Gallery, Liverpool; Glasgow; Bradford and other galleries in London and provinces. *Official purchases:* Eve, figure carved in teak, by Bradford Art Gallery; commissioned, Beasts for Coventry Cross (Architect: Helberg & Partners). *Work repro.:* Sculpture Today, by Arthur T. Broadbent, Studio, Illustrated London News, and other periodicals and trade magazines. *Address:* 105 Cranley Gdns., London N10 3AD. *Club:* R.W.S. Art. *Signs work:* "G. H. Ford."

FORD, Michael, free-lance artist in oils, water-colour, black and white; *b* 28 July, 1920; *s* of Major E. M. Ford, M.C. *Educ.:* privately; London University;

Goldsmiths' College Art School (Clive Gardiner, 1937-40). *Exhib.:* R.A., R.P., N.E.A.C., R.B.A., United Soc., P.S., Paris Salon, Russell Cotes Gallery, Towner Art Gallery, also touring exhbns. on loan, etc. *Official purchases:* Three oil paintings by M. of I. (War Artists' Exhbn.). *Works repro.:* Two paintings bought by M. of I.; portraits commissioned by magazines and newspapers. *Address:* Studio Cottage, Winsor Rd., Winsor, Southampton. *Signs work:* "Michael Ford."

FORD, Olga Gemes, M.S.I.A. graduated in arch. (Techn. University, Berlin); lecturer, The City of Leicester Polytechnic and School of Architecture; *d* of L. Gemes; *m* Oliver E. Ford, B.Sc. (London), Ph.D. (Zürich), F.R.I.C. *Educ.:* Realschule, Vienna; *studied architecture* at Vienna, Dresden, Berlin, Paris; under Prof. Poelzig. *Exhib.:* Britain Can Make It, Cotton Board, Manchester. *Work repro.:* in Architectural Review, L'Architecture d'Aujourd'hui, La Construction Moderne, Design, 46 Designers in Britain 2 and 4, Decoration, etc. *Addresses:* 30 Elmfield Ave., Stoneygate, Leicester; 12 Highgate Spinney, Crescent Rd., London N8. *Signs work:* "OLGA GEMES FORD" or "OLGA FORD."

FORD SMITH, James William, M.A. (1965), A.M.A. (1965), F.R.S.A. (1965), R.U.A. (Ext.) (1966), F.M.A. (1971); art historian and museum curator; *b* York, 16 May, 1939; *s* of James Ford Smith, M.A. *Educ.:* Wyggeston and Emmanuel College, Cambridge; Assistant Keeper of Art, Leicester City Museum and Art Gallery (1961-63); Deputy Director, Laing Art Gallery, Newcastle upon Tyne (1963-66); Keeper of Art, Ulster Museum (1966), Special Projects Officer (1972). *Publications:* a catalogue of water-colours and drawings; Leicester Museum and Art Gallery; "Brian King—sculptor" essay in The Irish Imagination (Dublin, 1971). *Address:* c/o Ulster Museum, Botanic Gdns., Belfast BT9 5AB.

FORESTIER-WALKER, Mollie; hon. mention, Paris Salon (1949); artist in oil, pastel, pencil; *b* Devon, 1 July, 1916; *d* of J. Clifford Wing, M.D.; *m* E. R. Forestier-Walker. *Educ.:* Duncan House, Clifton; *studied art* at West of England School of Art and under T. Percival Anderson. *Exhib.:* R.S.P.P., P.S., N.S., Paris Salon. *Work in permanent collection:* Imperial War Museum (portrait, Wing-Cdr. Guy Gibson, D.F.C., D.S.O.). *Official purchases:* above by War Artists Advisory Com. *Addresses:* Studio 6, Mallord St., Chelsea, London SW3; also studio at Captain's Cottage, St. Mawes, Cornwall. *Signs work:* see appendix.

FORGE, Andrew Murray; painter, writer, broadcaster; Tate Trustee (1964-71 and 1972-); Nat. Gall. Trustee (1967); President of the London Group (1965-71); *b* Hastingleigh, Kent, 10 Nov., 1923; *s* of Sidney Wallace Forge; *m*; three *d*. *Educ.:* Downs School and Leighton Park; *studied art* at Camberwell School of Art (1947-49) under Coldstream, Pasmore and Kenneth Martin. *Exhib.:* London Group, A.I.A., etc. *Official purchases:* Min. of Works, Arts Council of Great Britain, Tate. *Publications:* Paul Klee (1953), Soutine (1964), Rauschenberg (1970), and criticism in Listener, New Statesman, Studio International, B.B.C., etc. *Address:* c/o Tate Gallery. No signatures.

FORSTER, Juliana, A.R.B.S. (1970); sculptor in bronze and wood; *b* Dorchester, 20 Aug., 1943; *m* Kay Carslaw; two *d*. *Educ.:* Hanford (Blandford), Tudor Hall (Banbury); *studied art* at Chelsea Art College (1962) under Elizabeth Frink, Willi Soukop. *Exhib.:* Ewan Phillips Gallery, London, David Paul Gallery, Chichester. *Address:* Costers Farm, West Lavington, Midhurst, Sussex. *Signs work:* see appendix.

FORSYTH, James William Alexander; painter in oil and water-colour; *b* 11 June, 1910; *s* of Neil Forsyth, M.V.O. *Educ.:* Down House, Rottingdean, Corpus Christi College, Cambridge; *studied art* at Slade School under Prof. Schwabe (1932-33) and the Academy, Florence (1935). *Exhib.:* R.A., N.E.A.C., R.B.A.,

R.S.P.P., Leicester Galleries, and provinces. *Work repro.:* in La Revue Moderne. *Address:* Studio Cottage, Traders Passage, Rye, Sussex. *Signs work:* "J. Forsyth."

FORSYTH, Moira, A.R.C.A. (1930), F.M.G.P.; artist in stained glass; pottery; *b* Cresswell, 3 May, 1905; *d* of Gordon M. Forsyth, R.I., A.R.C.A.; *studied art* at Burslem School of Art, R.C.A. *Exhib.:* R.A., etc. *Official purchases:* windows in Norwich Cathedral, Eton College Chapel, Guildford Cathedral, St. Paul's Cathedral, Middle Temple, St. Columba's, Pont St., St. John's College, Oxford, King Edward's School, Birmingham, etc.; water-colours at Stoke-on-Trent and Bristol Museums; pottery figures at Museo Internationale delle Ceramiche, Faenza, Stoke-on-Trent and Brussels Museums. *Work repro.:* in Studio, Pottery and Glass Record, etc. *Address:* The Glass House, 11 Lettice St., London SW6. *Signs work:* see appendix.

FORTNUM, Peggy; book illustrator and designer; *b* Harrow-on-the-Hill, 23 Dec., 1919; *d* of Comdr. Arthur John Fortnum; *m* Ralph Nuttall-Smith, painter and sculptor. *Educ.:* St. Margaret's, Harrow; Central School of Arts and Crafts. *Work repro.:* textile designs, magazines, illustrations for eighty books, which include The Happy Prince and Other Stories (Oscar Wilde), The Reluctant Dragon (Kenneth Grahame), A Bear Called Paddington, 10 Books (Michael Bond), Thursday's Child (Noel Streatfeild), Robin (Catherine Storr), Little Pete Stories (Leila Berg), A Few Fair Days (Jane Gardam), Running Wild (Autobiography) (Chatto & Windus); drawings for television: Playschool, Jackanory. *Address:* 67 Churchfields, West Mersea, Essex. *Signs work:* "PEGGY FORTNUM" or "P.F."

FOSTER, Deryck, R.S.M.A.; marine artist in oil; *b* Bournemouth, 1 Mar., 1924; *m* Denise Chuter; two *d. Educ.:* King's School, Canterbury; *studied art:* Southern School of Art, Bournemouth (1939-42) (Geoffrey Baker, Lesley Ward), Central School of Art, Holborn (1946-47) (John Farleigh, Henrion, Laurence Scarfe, Jesse Collins). *Work in permanent collections:* Greenwich National Maritime Museum, Russell Cotes, Bournemouth. *Address:* Studio Cottage, South St., Yarmouth, I.O.W. *Clubs:* I.S.C., R.S.Y.C. *Signs work:* see appendix.

FOSTER, James W., Jr.; museum administrator; Director; Honolulu Academy of Arts, since 1963; Director, Santa Barbara Museum of Art, Calif. (1957-63); Asst. Dir., Baltimore Museum of Art (1947-57); Mem. Assoc. of Art Museum Directors, American Assoc. of Museums, and Western Assoc. of Art Museums; *b* Baltimore, Md., 4 Jan., 1920; *s* of James W. Foster; *m* Mary Page Foster; two *s*, one *d. Educ.:* Johns Hopkins University and the American University (B.A. degree); *studied art* at George Washington University, Washington, D.C., and the American University, Washington (1946-47). *Address:* Honolulu Academy of Arts, 900 S. Beretania St., Honolulu, Hawaii.

FOSTER, Marcia Lane; artist in chalk, water-colour, wood-engraver; *b* Seaton, Devon, 27 Aug., 1897; *d* of Henry Llewellyn Thomas Foster, M.I.C.E.; *m* Dudley Jarrett, artist and writer; one *d. Studied art:* St. John's Wood Art Schools, Central School of Arts and Crafts and R.A. Schools. Mem. A.R.E. (1957). *Exhib.:* R.A., Royal Soc. Painter-Etchers, Soc. Wood Engravers, S.W.A., Paris Salon, Art Inst. of Chicago. *Work in permanent collections:* B.M. *Work repro.:* The Woodcut of Today at Home and Abroad, The New Woodcut, The Modern Woodcut, Contemporary English Woodcuts, The Merrie Tales of Jacques Tournebroche, The Headswoman and many children's books. *Publication:* Let's Do It. *Address:* The Old Toll House, Bruton, Som. *Signs work:* "Marcia Lane Foster" or "Lane Foster."

FOULDS, Helen Shirley, Frobel Diploma; artist in oil and water-colour; *b*

Romiley, Ches., 20 Aug., 1902; *widow*; one *s*, one *d*. *Educ.:* Mount School, York; *studied art* at Camden Art Centre with Madeline Pearson. *Exhib.:* Camden Art Centre, R.S.A., Archer Gallery, R.W.S., S.W.A.; several one-man shows in London Post Offices. *Address:* 30 Ordnance Hill, London NW8 0NA. *Signs work:* "FOULDS."

FOWKES, David Reeve, B.A.; senior lecturer, Grays School of Art, Aberdeen; artist in oil; *b* Eastbourne, 15 Dec., 1919; *s* of A. F. Reeve Fowkes; *m* Lorna Fowkes; one *s*, one *d*. *Educ.:* Eastbourne Grammar School; *studied art* at Reading University (1938-40, 1946-48) under J. Anthony Betts. *Exhib.:* R.S.A., S.S.A.; one-man shows: Scottish Gallery (Dotts) Edinburgh (1973, 1976), Aberdeen University (1974), Douglas and Foulis Edinburgh (1970). *Work in permanent collections:* H.M. The Queen, Aberdeen A.G., Angus County, Maltby U.D.C., North of Scotland College of Agriculture, Rowntree, Seaforth Maritime Ltd. *Address:* Home Farm Cottage, Muchalls, Kincardines. AB3 2PP. *Signs work:* "FOWKES."

FOXELL, Maurice Frederic, K.C.V.O. (1964), M.A.; water-colour painter, woodengraver; *b* 15 Aug., 1888; *s* of Rev. W. J. Foxell, Ph.D., M.A.; *m*; two *s*, two *d*. *Educ.:* Christ's Hospital; Queen's College, Oxford. *Address:* The Homes of St. Barnabas, Lingfield, Surrey. *Club:* Athenæum. *Signs work:* "Maurice Foxell."

FRANCESCONI, Anselmo; painter in oil, acrylic on canvas, drawing and etching, sculptor in clay for bronze; *b* Lugo (Ravenna), Italy, 29 July, 1921; *s* of Cesare Francesconi; *m* Margherita Francesconi. *Educ.:* Lugo; *studied art* at Liceo Artistico, Ravenna; School of Fine Art, Bologna; Brera, Milan. *Exhib.:* one-man shows: Catherine Viviano, N.Y., Engelberths, Geneva, Galleria d'Eendt, Amsterdam, Musée d'Art et d'Histoire, Geneva, Fine Art Faculty, University of Teheran, Iran, Galleria Toninelli, Milan, Galleria Giulia, Rome, Bedford House Gallery, London, etc. *Work in permanent collections:* Musée d'Art et d'Histoire, Geneva; Musée Cantonale de Lausanne; Cabinet delle Stampe, Castello Sforzesco, Milan; Museum of Fine Art, N.Y.; Museum of Fine Art, Buffalo. *Address:* 4 Macaulay Rd., Clapham, London SW11. *Signs work:* "Anselmo."

FRANCIS, Brian Jabez; associate, Société des Artistes Français (1974), Paris Salon Medallist, associate mem. (American) Soc. of Miniature Painters, Sculptors and 'Gravers (1972), F.N.S.A.E. (1971), R.M.S. (1969), A.R.M.S. (1966), S.G.A. (1966), S.I.P.E. (1966), F.R.S.A. (1965), O.C.S. (1963); artist in diamond point engraved glass; *b* Dersingham, Norfolk, 2 July, 1927; *s* of Jabez Francis; *m* Margaret Ena Greenwood. *Educ.:* King Edward School, King's Lynn; London University; Nottingham University; *studied art* at Canterbury College of Art; Exeter College of Art under Walter Dexter, R.B.A. *Address:* 5 Chestnut Drive, Thorney, Peterborough. *Signs work:* "B. Jabez Francis" and see appendix.

FRANCIS, Eric Carwardine, F.S.A., R.W.A., F.R.I.B.A.; architect; *b* St. Tewdric, nr. Chepstow, Mon., 30 Aug., 1887. *Educ.:* Malvern College; *studied art* at office of Sir E. Guy Dawber, R.A. *Exhib.:* R.A., R.W.A. *Work in permanent collection:* R.W.A. *Work repro.:* Architectural Review, Country Life. *Address:* Longmeadow, West Monkton, Taunton.

FRANCIS, Sir Frank Chalton, K.C.B., M.A., F.S.A., F.M.A., F.L.A., Hon. D.Litt., Hon. Litt. D.; museum director; formerly Director and Principal Librarian of the British Museum; *b* Liverpool, 5 Oct., 1901; *s* of Frank William Francis; *m* K. F. McClennon; two *s*, one *d*. *Educ.:* Liverpool Institute, Liverpool University and Cambridge University. *Address:* The Vine, Nether Winchendon, Aylesbury, Bucks. *Clubs:* Athenæum, Royal Commonwealth Society, Grolier, New York.

FRANCIS, Henry Sayles; formerly curator of painting, prints and drawings at the Cleveland Museum of Art, Cleveland, Ohio (1931-67); curator of prints, Cleveland (1927-29), retired, Apr., 1967; *b* Boston, Mass., 4 Mar., 1902; *s* of George Tappan Francis; *m* Frances Meriam Burrage; one *s*. *Educ.:* St. Paul's School, Concord, New Hampshire; Harvard University, A.B. (1924); *studied art* at the Fogg Art Museum, Harvard University. *Publications:* articles in the Bulletin, Cleveland Museum of Art, Gazette des Beaux-Arts, Print Collectors Quarterly, The Art Quarterly, Bulletin of the Medical Library Assoc. *Address:* Wentworth Rd., Walpole, New Hampshire 03608. *Signs work:* "Henry S. Francis."

FRANCYN (Dehn Fuller), F.F.P.S., W.I.A.C., N.S.; painter in oils and gouache; *b* Portsmouth; *d* of Walter Henry Fuller, lecturer; *m* Curt Dehn; one *s*, one *d*. *Educ.:* at home. *Exhib.:* one-man shows: Paris, The Hague, Utrecht, Sydney, London; group shows: Free Painters and Sculptors, W.I.A.C., Hampstead Artists, N.S., etc. *Work in private collections:* Holland, Germany, U.S.A., Australia. *Publications:* Poems, Man's Moment (U.S.A.), portfolio of folk-songs, collection of poems. *Address:* 6 Elsworthy Ct., Elsworthy Rd., London NW3. *Clubs:* I.C.A., Hampstead Artist, New Arts Theatre. *Signs work:* see appendix.

FRANKEL, Rudolf, F.R.I.B.A.; Prof. in charge of graduate study in Urban Design at Miami University, Oxford, Ohio, U.S.A. (since 1950); distinctions in exhbns. and competitions; architect-planner, Berlin (1924-33), Bucharest (1933-37), London (1937-50), Oxford, Ohio (since 1950); *b* 14 June, 1901; *s* of Louis Frankel; *m* Eva Tarrasch. *Educ.:* Berlin; *studied architecture and sculpture* in Berlin and Munich. *Work repro.:* theatres, cinemas; domestic, administrative industrial buildings, and city and urban renewal plans in various countries reproduced in textbooks, and in leading periodicals of England, France, Spain, Italy, Switzerland, Germany, Japan, U.S., etc. *Address:* 516 South Main St., Oxford, Ohio, U.S.A. *Signs work:* see appendix.

FRANKENTHALER, Helen; First Prize, Paris Biennale (1959); painter in oils, acrylics, on unsized cotton-duck; teacher, Yale, Princeton, New York Universities; *b* New York, 12 Dec., 1928; *d* of Alfred Frankenthaler, Supreme Court Justice. *Educ.:* Bennington College, Vermont, U.S.A. (B.A.). *Work in permanent collections:* Museum of Modern Art, N.Y.C., Whitney Museum, N.Y.C., Albright-Knox Art Gallery, Buffalo, N.Y., Met. Mus. of Art, N.Y.C., Venice Biennale, U.S. Pavilion (1966), Retrospective, Whitney Museum of American Art, N.Y. (1969), Art Institute, Chicago, Cleveland Museum of Art, San Francisco Museum of Art. *Address:* 173 East 94th St., New York, 28. *Signs work:* see appendix.

FRANKLIN, Ben, R.B.A.; sculptor in stone, bronze, wood, glass fibre; *b* Petworth, Sussex, 7 Feb., 1918; *s* of Frederick Franklin; *m;* two *s*, two *d*. *Educ.:* Reedham School, Surrey; *studied art* at Croydon School of Art under R. H. Marlow, Goldsmiths' College under H. Wilson Parker. *Exhib.:* R.A., R.B.A., London Galleries. *Official purchases:* Leicestershire County Council Educ. Com. and in private collections in U.S.A. and Europe. *Work repro.:* Architectural Review, Arts Review. *Address:* 29 Hale Rd., Farnham, Surrey. *Signs work:* "Ben Franklin."

FRASER, Donald Hamilton, A.R.A.; painter in oil; Fellow R.C.A.; Hon. Sec. A.G.B.I.; *b* London, 30 July, 1929; *s* of Donald Fraser, fine art dealer; *m* Judith Wentworth-Shields, illustrator; one *d*. *Studied art:* St. Martin's School of Art (1949-52) and in Paris. Holds regular exhibitions at Gimpel Fils Gallery, London; Paul Rosenberg & Co., New York; and Gimpel-Hanover Galerie, Zürich. *Work in public collections:* Museum of Fine Arts, Boston; Albright-Knox Gallery, Buffalo; Carnegie Institute, Pittsburg; City Art Museum, St. Louis; Wadsworth Atheneum,

Hartford, Conn.; Hirshhorn Museum, Washington; Yale University Art Museum; National Gallery of Canada, Ottawa; Felton Bequest, Melbourne; Nottingham City A.G.; Southampton City A.G.; Rutherstone Loan Coll. Manchester; Hull City A.G.; Arts Council and C.A.S. Colls. *Publications:* Gauguin's 'Vision after the Sermon' (Cassell, 1969). *Address:* c/o Gimpel Fils, 30 Davies St., London W1. *Signs work:* "Fraser" and see appendix,

FRASER, Elizabeth Bertha, Mem. Society of Portrait Sculptors; sculptor in wax, plaster, bronze, painter in oil; *b* Teddington, London, 1914; *d* of Arthur Marks, F.I.C., A.R.S.M., A.R.C.Sc., A.M.I.Mech.E.; *m* Lindley Maughton Fraser. *Studied art* at Birmingham School of Art, Central School of Art, London, Westminster School of Art, London, under Schilsky, Edinburgh College of Art under Schilsky. *Exhib.:* R.A.; one-man shows, London and Edinburgh, Tour of Britain Sculptors Society, Society of Portrait Sculptors Yearly Exhbn., Edinburgh Younger Academy. *Address:* The Studio, 7 Ridgway Gdns., London SW19. *Signs work:* "Liz Frazer," "Elizabeth Scott-Fraser" or "Elizabeth Fraser."

FRASER, Eric George, F.S.I.A. (1945); painter in oil and water-colour, pen and ink, stained-glass designer; teacher of figure composition and commercial design, Camberwell School of Art (1928-40); *b* 11 June, 1902; *s* of George James Fraser; *m*; three *s*, one *d*. *Educ.:* Westminster City School, SW1; Goldsmiths' College. *Exhib.:* R.A., S.S.A. *Work repro.:* in Harper's Bazaar, Vogue, Radio Times, Listener, Art and Industry, Studio, Lilliput, Nash's, Britannia and Eve, London Mystery Magazine, Leader, Folio Soc., Golden Cockerel Press, etc.; mural paintings for Babcock House (1957), Brussels Exhbn. (1958). *Address:* Penn's Pl., 9 Church St., Hampton, Middx. *Signs work:* "eric fraser" usually (lower-case letters—no caps.).

FRASER, Ian, N.D.D. (1953), A.R.C.A. (1958); artist in oil, litho, etching and art lecturer; instructor in printmaking, Hornsey College of Art; *b* Newcastle upon Tyne, 11 July, 1933; *m* Anna Dubenska, A.R.C.A.; two *s*, one *d*. *Studied art* at Leeds College of Art (1949-53), Royal College of Art (1955-58). *Address:* 94 Charlton Rd., Shepperton, Middx. *Signs work:* "Ian Fraser."

FRASER, Joseph Thompson, Jr.; Edn. B.S. in Architecture, University of Pennsylvania (1922); practising architect (1922-34); Fellow in American Institute of Architects; Curator of Schools, Pennsylvania Academy of the Fine Arts (1935-38); Director, Pennsylvania Academy of the Fine Arts (1938-69); *b* Philadelphia, 15 Sept., 1898; *m* Isabel Chism; one *s*, Joseph Thompson Fraser 3rd; one *d*, Sarah Ann. Mem. of Board of Directors, Fairmount Park Art Assoc., Franklin Inn Club. *Address:* 330 S. Camac St., Philadelphia, 7, Pa. *Signs work:* "Joseph T. Fraser, Jr."

FREDYNA, Katerina; freelance artist in gouache; *b* Kharkov, Russia, 21 Feb., 1906; *d* of M. Levenberg, estate manager; *m* Dr. Manfred Schwersenz, lawyer (decd.). *Educ.:* Jimnasium (Russia); *studied art* at St. Martin's School of Art, London (from 1956) under Muriel S. Pemberton, A.R.W.S. *Exhib.:* Galerie Creuze (1967), Salon Bosio, Monte Carlo (1962), Paris Salon (1960, 1961), Army & Navy Stores, London (1959); with W.I.A.C.; Camden Art Centre, Whitechapel Galleries, Queen Elizabeth Hall, F.B.A. Galleries, Leighton House, Drian Galleries. *Work in permanent collections:* Bibliothèque Nationale, Paris; and private coll. of H.R.H. Princess Alexandra of Kent. *Address:* Flat 19, Kings Gdns., West Lane, London NW6. *Clubs:* W.I.A.C. Camden Hill, F.P.S. *Signs work:* "K. Fredyna."

FREETH, H. Andrew, P.R.W.S. (1973), R.A. (1965), A.R.A. (1955), R.P. (1966), R.W.S. (1955), R.E. (1946), R.B.A.; on staff, St. Martin's School of Art

(1946); portrait painter and etcher; *b* Birmingham, 29 Dec., 1912; *s* of John Stewart Freeth; *m* Roseen Marguerite Preston; three *s,* one *d. Educ.:* College of Art, Birmingham; Rome Scholarship in Engraving. *Exhib.:* R.A., R.W.S., R.E., R.P., R.B.A., British Graphic Art, British Council Exhbns.; one-man shows, Colnaghi's, Oxford, Birmingham, Upper Grosvenor Gallery. *Official purchases:* by Contemporary Art. Soc. for B.M.; War Artists' Advisory Com.; Ashmolean and Fitzwilliam Museums, Sunderland, Bristol and Birmingham A.Gs., National Portrait Gallery. *Address:* 37 Eastbury Rd., Northwood, Middx. *Signs work:* "H. A. Freeth."

FRENCH, Dick, Dip. A.D., M.Art. R.C.A., Burston Award (1970), Harmstone Bequest (1967); resident artist, Lanchester Polytechnic, Coventry; artist in oil paint and latex rubber; *b* S. Shields, Co. Durham, 31 Jan., 1946. *Educ.:* Marlcliffe Secondary School, Sheffield; *studied art* at Sheffield College of Art (1962-67) under Robin Plummer, Dave Smith, Kevin Farrell; R.C.A. (1967-70) under Carel Weight, Cyril Reason, Peter Blake. *Work in permanent collections:* Kultureel Centrum, Ostend; Galérie Arcanes, Lille; Wolverhampton Art Gallery; Sheffield Art Gallery; Gallery Peter Robinson, Teheran, Iran; R.C.A. *Address:* 6 Church Hill, Leamington Spa, Warks. *Clubs:* Leamington Spa Wildlife Assoc., Commonwealth, Leamington Spa. *Signs work:* "Dick French" on back.

FRENKIEL, Stanislaw; painter and writer on art; Head of Art Dept., School of Education, University of London; *b* Cracow, 14 Sept., 1918; *s* of Dr. A. Frenkiel; *m* Anna; one *s,* one *d. Educ.:* Cracow Grammar School; *studied art* at Cracow Academy of Fine Arts, Académie des Beaux Arts, Beirut, Sir John Cass College and the Courtauld Institute, London. *Exhib.:* one-man shows: American University, Beirut (1947); Sheffield (1954); Grabowski Gallery, London (1960, 1962, 1965, 1969, 1970, 1973); Cracow (1965); Poznan (1965); Galerie Tamara Pfeiffer, Brussels (1973); mixed shows: London, Munich, Hamburg, Wroclaw, Cracow, Lyons. *Work in permanent collections:* London, Geneva, Paris, Brussels, N.Y. and Cleveland; Hampstead Hospital Memorial Collection, London; Polish Cultural Foundation, London; Gipsy Hill College, London; University of London, National Museum, Warsaw. *Publications:* articles and essays in Polish in Wiadomosci, Kontynenty, Oficyna Poetow i Malarzy (Poets' and Painters' Press) London. *Address:* Cedry, 6 Clement Rd., London SW19. *Signs work:* see appendix.

FREY-SURBEK, Marguerite; artist in oil and fresco, graphic artist; *b* Delémont, 1886; *m* Victor Surbek. *Educ.:* Berne; *studied art* in Paris with Vuillard, Valloton, Lucien Simon and Maurice Denis and at Berne with Paul Klee. *Exhib.:* Switzerland and other countries. *Work in permanent collections:* Fresco at Art School, Berne, other works in Swiss Museums. *Official purchases:* see above. *Work repro.:* in DU and other art periodicals. *Address:* Junkerngasse 51, Berne. *Clubs:* Art Socs. and Lyceum. *Signs work:* "Marg. Frey-Surbek."

FRIEDEBERGER, Klaus, A.S.T.C., F.S.I.A.; painter and designer; visiting tutor, London College of Printing; *b* Berlin, 1922; *m* Julie. *Educ.:* Quakerschool Eerde, Holland; *studied art:* E. Sydney Tech. College. *Exhib.:* one-man shows: London, Belfast; group shows since 1944; Europe Prize (1964), Ostende (Gold Medal). *Official purchases:* Mosman Art Prize (1949). *Work in permanent collections:* Australia, England, U.S.A. *Work repro.:* Graphis Annual, Designers in Britain, Art Directors' Annual, New York, Modern publicity, etc. *Address:* 16 Coleraine Rd., London SE3. *Signs work:* "Friedeberger."

FRIEND, William Albert, L.S.I.A. (1950); artist in oil, water-colour, scraperboard; designer of printed publicity; art editor of House magazine; design consultant; Managing Director, Graphic Designers Ltd.; *b* London, 21 Sept., 1926; *s* of David J. Friend; *m* Betty Curvin; one *d. Educ.:* Hendon County Secondary School; *studied art* at St. Martin's School of Art under J. Hadley-Rowe, S. M. Litten, Willesden School of Art, Bolt Court. *Work repro.:* national and international Press. *Address:* 4 Holly Park, London N3. *Signs work:* "FRIEND."

FRIERS, Ian, V.R.D.; sculptor in wood; former Academician, Vice-Pres. and Council Mem., R.U.A.; *b* Belfast; *s* of Wm. Friers (decd.); *m* Noreen; five children. *Educ.:* Belfast Model School and College of Art. Distinctive sculpture self-taught and developed and now teaching to others. *Exhib.:* one-man, dual Royal Dublin Soc., Bradford Exhbn. of Contemporary British Art, R.H.A., R.U.A., etc. *Official purchases:* C.E.M.A. (N.I.) *Address:* Keelong, Ballybeen, Dundonald, Co. Down, N. Ireland. *Signs work:* "Ian Friers" or see appendix.

FRIERS, Rowel Boyd, R.U.A. (1953); oil painter and cartoonist (Irish Times), stage designer, illustrator (TV. Graphics, B.B.C. & U.T.V.; *b* Belfast, 13 Apr., 1920; *s* of William Friers; *m* Evelyn Maude Yvonne Henderson. *Educ.:* Belfast; *studied art* at Belfast College of Art. *Exhib.:* London, R.H.A., Royal Ulster Academy. *Work in permanent collections:* Haverty Trust for Irish National Collection, Belfast Art Gallery. *Official purchases:* C.E.M.A. (N.I.) and Haverty Trust. *Work repro.:* in Dublin Opinion, Punch, London Opinion, Radio Times, Belfast Telegraph, Lines of Laughter, This is My Best Humour. *Publications:* Wholly Friers and Mainly Spanish, Riotous Living, Pig in the Parlour, Book of Friers and The Revolting Irish. *Address:* Millbank House, Victoria Rd., Holywood, Co. Down. *Signs work:* see appendix.

FRINK, Elisabeth, C.B.E. (1969); sculptor in plaster for bronze; *b* Thurlow, Suffolk, 14 Nov., 1930; *d* of Brig. Ralph Frink, D.S.O.; *m* Alexander Csáky; one *s. Educ.:* Convent of Holy Family, Exmouth; *studied art* at Guildford and Chelsea Schools of Art (1947-51). *Exhib.:* regularly at Waddington Galleries. *Work in permanent collections:* Tate Gallery, National Gallery of Australia, Melbourne, Museum of Modern Art, N.Y., etc. *Publications:* Art of Elisabeth Frink, illustrated; Canterbury Tales, Aesops Fables, Iliad & Odyssey for Folio Society. *Address:* 1303 Minsterhouse, St. James's Ct., Buckingham Gate, London SW1. *Club:* Arts. *Signs work:* "Elisabeth Frink."

FROBISHER, Lucy Marguerite, R.C.A. (1937), P.S., S.W.A.; artist and principal of the Frobisher School of Painting; painter in oils, water-colours and pastel; *d* of Dr. William Martin Frobisher, Leeds. *Educ.:* Leeds Girls' High School; *studied art* at Kemp-Welch School of Painting (Lucy Kemp-Welch, R.I.). *Exhib.:* R.A., R.I., R.O.I., P.S., Paris Salon and provinces; Paris Salon Award of Honourable Mention (1966). *Work repro.:* by Raphael Tuck, Forman, Medici Soc., The Artist. *Addresses:* Frobisher School of Painting, Glencoe Rd., Bushey; Kingsley, Bushey, Herts. (*private address*). *Signs work:* "Marguerite Frobisher."

FROHLICH, Caroline Lili Bume, Ph.D. (Vienna, 1910); *b* Vienna, 14 May, 1886; *d* of Ernst Bum, D.L.L. (Vienna), lawyer; *m* Otto Frohlich, D.L.L., Ph.D. (Vienna), art-dealer (decd.). *Studied art history* at University of Vienna under Wickhoff, Schlosser, Dvorak. *Publications:* co-operated at the International; Bibliografie der Kunstwissenschaft; Parmigianino und der Manierismusi; Ingres (Vienna and London); descriptive Catalogue of the drawings of the Albertina, Vols. 1 and 3; monograph, A. Schiavone in Vienna Museum Yearbook; many articles in yearbooks and magazines; London correspondent for Weltkunst (München). *Address:* 26 Parliament Ct., London NW3. *Club:* British Federation of University Women. *Signs work:* "Lili Frohlich-Bume" or "L. Frohlich-Bume."

FROST, Edith, King Christian medal, Denmark (1945); Board of Directors,

Frost & Reed Ltd.; past master, Fine Art Trade Guild, London; past master, Number 6 Branch, Fine Art Trade Guild; past pres., Soroptimist Club of Bristol; *b* Bristol; *d* of Walter Frost, governing director, Frost & Reed, Ltd. *Educ.:* Clifton High School; Charlotte Mason College, Ambleside; *studied art* at Ambleside and at museums and art galleries in Germany, Holland, Belgium, France, Italy and Austria. *Address:* Frost & Reed, Ltd., 10 Clare St., Bristol.

FROST, Kathleen Margaret; editor and author; formerly director of The Studio, Ltd. (London) (retired 31 Dec., 1958), a founder of The Studio Publications Inc. (New York); *d* of Alfred James Frost. *Educ.:* St. George's College, Palmers Green; under Geoffrey Holme, and through travel and books. *Publications:* first sub-editor Art and Industry and Gardens and Gardening; joint editor (1943-58) (with Rathbone Holme) Decorative Art; author of Furnishing the Small Home (pseu.: Margaret Merivale). *Address:* 10 Raglan Ct., Lansdowne Rd., West Worthing, Sussex BN11 5HA.

FROST, Shirley Jane, A.R.C.A., M.S.I.A., M.S.D-C.; freelance designer of limited production and one-off jewellery; ceramist; painter; senior lecturer, Dept. of Three Dimensional Design, Birmingham Polytechnic; *b* London, 8 Mar., 1935; *d* of Charles Frost; *m* Barrie Eccleston, Des.R.C.A., M.S.I.A. *Educ.:* Roedean, Johannesburg, S. Africa; Luckley, Wokingham, England; *studied art* at Worthing and Wimbledon Schools of Art, R.C.A. (1957-60). *Exhib.:* paintings, ceramics and jewellery, London Design Centre and many national and international jewellery exhbns. in Gt. Britain, Europe and N. America. *Address:* Birmingham Polytechnic. *Signs work:* Uses maiden name. Jewellery hallmark: B'ham/SF in rectangle; London/SF in diamond.

FROY, Martin, D.F.A. (1951); painter; Professor of Fine Art, University of Reading; *b* London, 9 Feb., 1926. *Studied art* at Slade School of Art. *Exhib.:* N.E.A.C., R.B.A., I.C.A., A.I.A., London Group, Wakefield City Art Gallery, University of Leeds, Hanover Gallery, Redfern Gallery, Leicester Gallery, Ashmolean Museum (Oxford), Riverside Museum (New York), Pittsburgh, Rome, Paris, Brussels. *Work in permanent collections:* Tate Gallery, Museum of Modern Art (New York), Chicago Art Institute, Arts Council, C.A.S., the city art galleries of Bristol, Carlisle, Leeds, Southampton and Wakefield. *Address:* Colham Mill Farmhouse, Castle Combe, Wilts.

FRUH, Eugen; C. F. Meyer prizeman (1943); oil painter and illustrator; *b* St. Gall, Switzerland, 22 Jan., 1914; *s* of Huldreich Fruh; *m* Erna Yoshida Blenk, artist. *Educ.:* Kunstgewerbeschule, Zürich (1928-32); *studied art:* self-taught. *Exhib.:* Kunsthaus Zürich (1940), Museum Winterthur (1944), Kunsthalle Bern (1947), Gallery Wolfsberg Zürich (1949), L'Athénée Geneva (1950), Kuenstler Haus Vienna (1950), Konsthallen Helsinki (1952), International Art Exhbn. Tokyo (1955, 1957), Kunstmuseum Zürich (1956), Kunsthalle Basle (1956), Helmhaus Zürich (1962). *Work in permanent collections:* Zürich, Winterthur, Basle and Geneva, etc. *Work repro.:* Art and You, Galerie und Sammler, Werk. *Address:* Romergasse 9, Zürich. *Club:* G.S.M.B.A. *Signs work:* see appendix.

FRUHMANN, Johann; painter; *b* Weissenstein a.d. Drau Kärnten, Austria, 22 Apr., 1928; *m* Christa Hauer. *Studied art* at Kunstgewerbeschule Graz with Prof. Silberbauer and Wickenburg (1943-48), Akademie der bildenden Künste Wien with Prof. Andersen and Prof. Gütersloh (1948-50). *Work in permanent collections:* Graphische Sammlung Albertina, Wien, Neue Galerie, Graz, Sammlung der Stadt Wien, Bundesminsterium für Unterricht, Art Museum, Cincinnati, Museum des 20. Jhd., Wien (1965), Österr. Sraatspreis for Painting. *Address:* Wien 1, Fischerstiege 1-7/II. *Signs work:* "JOH. FRUH." on back of painting.

FRY, Arthur Malcolm, H.R.W.S., F.R.S.A.; water-colour and oil painter; sec. R.W.S.; sec. R.E.; sec. S.M.; *b* 20 May, 1909; *s* of C. S. Fry; *m*; one *s*, one *d*. *Educ.:* Latymer Upper School; Bournemouth School of Art (Geoffrey Baker, Leslie Ward, R.E.). *Exhib.:* principal London galleries; one-man shows in Bavaria, London, Bournemouth, Salisbury, Swindon. *Official purchases:* water-colour, Bournemouth Corp. *Address:* Long Meadow, Church Rd., Chelsfield, Kent. *Club:* Athenæum. *Signs work:* "Fry."

FRY, Gladys Windsor, King's Prize Winner, design; City and Guilds Embroidery Honours; Board of Educ. art teacher's cert.; water-colour painter; art lecturer; *d* of F. Hardy-Syms; *m* H. Windsor Fry, R.B.A. *Educ.:* Heathfield House, Horsham; Horsham (Florence Davey); Chichester (G. H. Catt); London Art Schools. *Exhib.:* Arts and Crafts Exhbn. Soc., R.A., R.B.A., Hull, Leeds, Sydney, Festival of Britain, etc. *Official purchases:* Memorial brass to Thomas Thirlby, Bishop of Westminster, Norwich and Ely, in chancel of St. Mary's Church, Lambeth. *Publications:* Embroidery and Needlework (Pitman), and Working Drawings for Embroidery (Pitman). *Address:* 10 Somerhill Rd., Hove BN3 1RN. *Signs work:* "Gladys Windsor Fry."

FRY, James William; artist in oil, pastel, water-colour; *b* London, 23 Dec., 1910. *Studied art* at Watford School of Art under Arthur Scott, R.B.A. *Address:* Dollings Barn, 148 East St., Corfe Castle, Wareham, Dorset. *Signs work:* "JAMES FRY," more often "J.F."

FRYER, Stan; painter in oils, water-colour, pen and ink, etc.; *b* Manchester, 1906; *s* of George Fryer; *m* Doris A. Rothwell; one *s*, one *d*. *Educ.:* Manchester; *studied art* at Manchester School of Art, Italy, Africa. *Exhib.:* London and provinces. *Work repro.:* in national and local press. *Address:* 49 Mellington Ave., E. Didsbury, Manchester 20. *Signs work:* "Stan Fryer", "Fryer" or "F."

FULLER, Mrs. E. G.: see SAWYERS, Dorothy.

FULLER, Violet; Fellow of Free Painters and Sculptors; artist in water-colour, oil, pastel; *b* Tottenham, 26 July, 1920; *d* of Charles Fuller. *Studied art* at Hornsey School of Art (1937-40) under Russell Reeve, R.B.A, A.R.E., and H. Holzer; Stroud School of Art (1942-44) under Gwilym E. Jones, A.R.C.A. *Exhib.:* Paris, R.A., R.I., R.B.A., W.I.A.C., P.S., Whitechapel Art Gallery (1967), 9 painters of East London, Bath Festival (1967); one-man shows: Woodstock Gallery (1958, 1959, 1961, 1963, 1967, 1970), Ditchling Gallery, Old Bakehouse Gallery, Sevenoaks (1968, 1970), Hornsey Library (1968, 1973), New Gallery, Hornsey (1975), Forty Hall, Enfield (1974). *Official purchases:* London Borough of Haringey, London Borough of Enfield. *Address:* 27 Walpole Rd., Tottenham, London N17. *Signs work:* "VIOLET FULLER."

FURLONG, George Joseph, B.A., Ph.D. (Vienna), F.R.S.A.; director, National Gallery of Ireland, Dublin (1935-50); lecturer, National Gallery, London (1930-35); Hon. Member, Soc. Artistique des Amateurs, Paris; Vice-President, Friends of Nat. Collection of Eire. *Educ.:* Clongowes Wood College; University College, Dublin; University of Grenoble; *studied history of art* at the Sorbonne, Paris, and universities of Munich and Vienna. *Publications:* Articles in the Listener, Burlington Magazine. *Address:* 2 Thurloe St., London SW7. *Clubs:* Reform, London; Kildare St., Dublin.

FURNIVAL, John P., A.R.C.A.; artist in pen and ink and mixed media; lecturer, Bath Academy of Art; editor, Openings Press; *b* London, 29 May, 1933; *m* Astrid Furnival; two *s*, one *d*. *Studied art* at Wimbledon College of Art; Royal College of Art. *Exhib.:* Biennale des Jeunes, Paris; one-man show: Thumb Gallery, London; retrospective: Laing Gallery, Newcastle, Arnolfini, Bristol, plus various international exhbns. of visual and concrete poetry. *Work in permanent collections:* Arts Council of Gt. Britain, Arnolfini Trust, Munich Pinakothek. *Publications:* The Bang Book (Jargon Press), The Lucidities (Turret Books). *Address:* Rooksmoor House, Woodchester, Glos. *Club:* Dorothy's Umbrellas Dining Society (DUDS). *Signs work:* "John Furnival."

G

GABRIEL, Caroline S.; sculptress in stone and clay cast in cold bronze, etc; sculptor tutor to I.L.E.A. Evening Class; *b* London, 1916; *d* of Leon J. H. Gabriel, mining engineer. *Educ.:* North London Collegiate School; *studied art* at Regent Street Polytechnic; Camberwell College of Art; Slade School of Fine Art, University of London under Profs. Randolph Schwabe, George Gerrard and George Charlton. *Exhib.:* R.A., N.E.A.C., W.E.A.C., Society of Portrait Sculptors, etc. *Publications:* text books for schools and colleges. *Address:* 1 Midholm, The Studio, London NW11 6LL. *Signs work:* see appendix.

GAGE, Edward Arthur, R.S.W. (1963), D.A.(Edin.) (1950), Past President S.S.A.; painter in oil and water-colour, illustrator, journalist, broadcaster; art master, Fettes College (1952-68); Senior Lecturer, Napier College of Commerce and Technology; part-time lecturer, Edinburgh College of Art, art critic, The Scotsman; *b* Gullane, East Lothian, 28 Mar., 1925; *s* of Thomas Arthur Gage; *m* Valerie Alexandra; one *s*, two *d*. *Educ.:* Royal High School of Edinburgh; *studied art* at Edinburgh College of Art (1941-42, 1947-52) under Sir W. G. Gillies. *Work in permanent collections:* Scottish Arts Council, Glasgow Art Gallery, Edinburgh City Collection, Universities of Aberdeen and Edinburgh, Argyll County Council. *Work repro.:* Radio Times and B.B.C. Publications, and illustrations in books published by Bodley Head, Dents, Cassell, Michael Joseph, Longmans. *Address:* 6 Hillview, Edinburgh, 4. *Signs work:* "Edward Gage."

GAINEY, William Henry; interior decorator, oil painter; *b* Cardiff, 30 Nov., 1897; *s* of William Gainey; *m* Harriet Elizabeth Gainey; two *d*. *Educ.:* Cardiff Technical College (Mr. Wilson Jagger, A.R.C.A., 1928-30). *Exhib.:* S. Wales Art Soc.; Glyn Vivian Galleries, Swansea. *Official purchases:* in France. *Address:* 19 Lawrenny Ave., Cardiff. *Clubs:* Non-Political; Canton Liberal. *Signs work:* "GAINEY" (surname in rough block letters in keeping with general design of picture, sometimes letters beneath each other).

GAINSBOROUGH, John; Editor, Arts Review. *Educ.:* Lewes County Grammar School, Brighton College of Art (Architectural Dept.). *Address:* 8 Wyndham Pl., London W1H 2AY.

GALE, Richard John, Dip. A.D. (1968), M.A. (R.C.A., 1973); artist in oil; *b* Bristol, 8 Feb., 1946; *s* of C. L. Gale; *m* Francis Joan. *Educ.:* Weston-super-Mare Grammar School; *studied art* at Kingston upon Thames School of Art (1965-68), R.C.A. (1970-73). *Address:* 35 Gloucester Cres., London NW1. *Signs work:* "R. Gale."

GALLOWAY, Henry, Mem., Islington Art Circle; commission agent; artist in oil; *b* London, 12 Oct., 1901; *s* of John Galloway, artists' frame maker; *m* Florence Galloway. *Educ.:* Elementary and Secondary School, London; *studied art* under instruction by father in drawing and painting. *Exhib.:* Islington exhbns. *Address:* 86 Mildenhall Rd., Clapton, London E5. *Signs work:* "H. GALLOWAY."

GAMES, Abram, O.B.E., R.D.I., F.S.I.A.; graphic designer, War Office poster designer (1941-46); *b* 29 July, 1914; *s* of Joseph Games; *m;* one *s,* two *d. Exhib.:* one-man shows London, Stockholm, Brussels, Jerusalem, Tel Aviv, New York, Chicago, Rio de Janeiro. Represented Gt. Britain in poster exhibition at Museum of Modern Art, N.Y.; first prizes, British Trade Fair Poster Competitions, Helsinki, 1958, Lisbon, 1959, New York, 1960, Stockholm, 1962, Barcelona, 1964. Designed stamps for G.B. and Israel; Festival of Britain, B.B.C. television and the Queen's Award to Industry Emblems. Society of Industrial Artists Design Medal (1960), Royal Society of Arts Silver Medal (1962). *Address:* 41 The Vale, London NW11. *Signs work:* "A. Games."

GAMMON, Reginald William, R.W.A., R.O.I.; artist in oil and water-colour, formerly illustrations in line and colour; *b* Petersfield, 1894; two *s. Educ.:* Churchers College, Petersfield; *studied art* with Frank Patterson (1910-14). *Work in permanent collections:* R.W.A., Bath University, Bristol College of Art, and private collections. *Work repro.:* contributions and illustrations to News Chronicle, Cyclists Touring Club Gazette, Scout, and I.C.I. Industrial Press. *Address:* Mulberry Studio, Church St., Cannington, Bridgwater. *Signs work:* "Gammon."

GANLY, Rosaleen Brigid, A.R.H.A. (1928), R.H.A. (1935-69); artist in oil, water-colour, egg-tempera, pastels, pen and ink, etc.; *b* Dublin, 29 Jan., 1909; *d* of Dermod O'Brien, P.R.H.A., H.R.A., etc.; *m* Andrew Ganly; one *s,* one *d. Studied art* at Dublin School of Art under Sean Keatinge, Patrick Tuohy, Oswald Reeves, Oliver Sheppard and George Atkinson, and at R.H.A. School under D. O'Brien, Sean O'Sullivan, Richard Orpen, etc. *Exhib.:* R.H.A. (yearly since 1928), Waterford, Limerick, Galway, Cork, Berlin, America, Canada, Dublin Municipal Gallery of Modern Art, Royal Dublin Soc., Waterford, Blackrock (All Souls Church), murals in church, Ennis, Co. Clare. *Official purchases:* Haverty Trust. *Work repro.:* numerous book illustrations and dust jackets. *Address:* 5 Rus in Urbe, Lower Glenageary Rd., Dunlaoghaire, Co. Dublin. *Signs work:* "RBG" or "R. Brigid Ganly."

GAPPER, Robert Lambert, Hon. M.A. (1972), B.Sc. (1922), A.R.C.A.; travelling scholarship in sculpture, Federation British Industries Prize for Pottery (1930); Civic Trust Award, Group A (1971); sculptor and University teacher in charge of art dept. and curator of museum, U.C.W., Aberystwyth (1934-62); *s* of Robert Gapper; *m* Florence; two *s,* two *d. Educ.:* Grammar School, Pwllheli; U.C.L. Goldsmiths' College (1913-15); U.C.N.W., Bangor (1919-22); College of Art, Rugby; R.C.A.; Chelsea Polytechnic; Central School of Art. Worked on rock face, Trefor Granite Quarry. Works in diorite, slate, bronze, oak, metals, incl. precious. *Memorials* including St. Olaf, Pool of London Authority, H.M.S. Thetis Submarine, Holyhead, Admiralty, Capel Celyn and Quakers', Bala, Corp. City of Liverpool, Centenary Landing of Welsh in Patagonia. Inscribed slate slabs, many for colleges; church furniture; wrought iron work including firescreen for Queen Elizabeth II; badges, certificates, ornaments of office, crowns for Nat. Eist. Wales; bronzes of many famous Welshmen. *Address:* Meiros, Llanbadarn Rd., Aberystwyth.

GARDNER, Annette; painter in oil; Principal and Teacher, Wood Tutorial College NW3. (since 1972); Founder and Director, New End Gallery NW3.; *b* 11 June, 1920; *m* C. J. Wood, M.A., (decd.); one *s,* one *d. Studied art* at Twickenham Art School (1952-54); Hampstead Garden Suburb Institute (1954-56) under Mr. Gower; St. Martin's (1960-63) under David Tindle; principal teacher Walter Nessler. *Exhib.:* R.O.I., R.B.A., N.S., S.W.A., U.A.S., N.E.A.C., S.I.A., Contemporary Portrait Painters, W.I.A.C., Group H, Pictures for Schools, F.P.S.; travelling exhbns.: Camden, Cambridge, Harrow, Barnet, Westminster and Bath;

finalist, Woman's Journal Painting of the Year (1961). *Work in private collections:* Australia, England, U.S.A., Israel, Hungary. *Address:* The Studio, 18 Canons Drive, Edgware, Middx. *Clubs:* F.P.S., Ben Uri. *Signs work:* "A. Gardner."

GARDNER, Derek George Montague, V.R.D., R.S.M.A., Commander R.N.V.R.; marine artist in oil and water-colour; *b* Gerrards Cross, Bucks, 13 Feb., 1914; *s* of Alfred Charles Gardner, F.R.S.E.; *m* Mary neé Dalton; one *s,* one *d. Educ.:* Monkton Combe Junior School and Oundle School. *Exhib.:* R.S.M.A., United Artists, Bermuda, IPG; one-man shows, London (1972, 1975). *Work in permanent collection:* National Maritime Museum, Greenwich. *Address:* High Thatch, Corfe Mullen, Wimborne, Dorset. *Club:* Naval Club. *Signs work:* "Derek G. M. over Gardner."

GARDNER, Peter, N.D.D. (1949), A.T.D. (1952); artist in oil; Head of Art Dept., Plaistow Grammar School; Hon. Sec. Society of Fulham Artists; *b* London, 25 Oct., 1921; *s* of Ronald Gardner, Bacteriologist; *m* Irene Gladys, (neé Hill). *Educ.:* St. Matthias School, London SW5; *studied art:* Hammersmith College of Art (1935-39, 1946-50) under Harold Workman, R.B.A., R.C.A. and Herbert Holt, R.P. *Work in permanent collections:* Hammersmith Borough Council, York University. *Address:* c/o The Trafford Gallery, 119 Mount St., London W1Y 5HB. *Signs work:* "P.G." or "PETER GARDNER."

GARDNER, Stephen Reginald; engineer; artist in oils; *b* Preswich, 24 Apr., 1948; *s* of Charles E. Gardner, interior decorator; *m* Beryl Claire; one *s. Educ.:* Nicholls, High (Ardwick); *studied art* at High School of Art, Cheetham. *Exhib.:* Colin Jellicoe Gallery, Portfolio Gallery, Scunthorpe; open show: Brigg, Lincs. *Address:* 74 Landos Rd., Miles Platting, Manchester M10 7JL. *Signs work:* "R. S. Gardner."

GARDNER, William M., A.R.C.A., F.S.I.A., F.R.S.A., A.R.Hist.S.; designer, medallist, and letterer in private practice; member of Royal Mint Panel of Artists (1938), visiting professor, Colorado State University (1963), Churchill Fellow (1966), Leverhulme Fellow (1969); *b* 25 May, 1914; *m*; two *s*, one *d. Commissions for* Privy Council, House of Commons, Household Cavalry and Brigade of Foot Guards, Home Office, Colonial Office, Postmaster-General, London Transport Executive, Governments of New Zealand, Guyana, Nigeria, Algeria, Cyprus, Jordan, Nepal, Ceylon. Also for universities, presses, industrial and trading associations. *Address:* Chequertree, Wittersham, Tenterden, Kent. *Signs work:* "W. M. Gardner."

GARIN Ortiz de Taranco, Felipe Maria, Doctor of Philosophy in Literature, Presidente de la Real de Bellas Artes de San Carlos (Valencia), and director of Archivo de Arte Valenciano, Correspondiente de la Academia de la Historia and de la de Bellas Artes de San Fernando (Madrid); del Centro de Cultura Valenciana; *b* Valencia, Spain, 14 Feb., 1908; *s* of Dr. Felipe N. Garin; *m* Da. Maria Angeles Llombart Rodriguez; two *s. Educ.:* Universidad, Valencia; *studied art* at Valencia. *Publications:* Yañez de la Almedina (1953), Catalogo del Museo de Bellas Artes de Valencia (1955), Valencia Monumental (1959), El Museo de Valencia (1964), Vinculaciones universales del gotico valenciano, Valencia, (1969), etc. *Address:* Valencia 1. Calle Reloj Viejo, 9.

GARLICK, Kenneth John, M.A., Ph.D., F.M.A.; art historian; Keeper of Western Art, The Ashmolean Museum, Oxford; *b* Glastonbury, 1 Oct., 1916; *s* of David Ernest Garlick. *Educ.:* Elmhurst Grammar School, Street, Balliol College, Oxford, Courtauld Institute of Art, University of London. *Publications:* Sir Thomas Lawrence (Routledge, 1954), Sir Thomas Lawrence: a Catalogue

(Walpole Society, Vol. XXXIX, 1964). *Address:* 39 Hawkswell Hse., Hawkswell Gdns., Oxford. *Club:* Reform.

GARNETT, Eve; Carnegie Gold Medal (1938); painter, illustrator, writer; *d* of Lt.-Col. F. H. Garnett. *Studied art* at Chelsea (Polytechnic) School of Art; R.A. Schools (Creswick Prize and Silver Medal); and with Alexander Jamieson, A.R.A. *Exhib.:* Tate Gallery (photographs of mural decorations); N.E.A.C., Lefévre Gallery; Mural decorations, Children's House, Bow. *Work repro.:* in Penguin Books; T.L.S. *Publications:* (illustrated) The Family from One End Street; Is It Well with the Child?; In and Out and Roundabout; A Book of the Seasons; Further Adventures of the Family from One End Street; Holiday at the Dew Drop Inn; To Greenland's Icy Mountains: the Story of Hans Egede, explorer, colonizer, missionary; Lost and Found: four stories. *Address:* c/o Lloyds Bank, Lewes, Sussex.

GARRARD, Peter John, R.B.A., N.E.A.C.; painter in oil; *b* 4 Jan., 1929; *s* of Col. W. V. Garrard, M.B.E., T.D.; *m* Patricia Marmoy; one *s,* two *d. Educ.:* Magdalen College School, Brackley; *studied art:* Byam Shaw School of Drawing and Painting. *Work in permanent collections:* in public and private collections in England, America, Australia, Canada, Germany, etc. *Address:* 340 Westbourne Park Rd., London W11. *Signs work:* "P.J.G."

GARRATT, John Geoffrey, R.I.B.A. Schools Prize (1931); antiquarian bookshop manager; artist in water-colour, pen and ink, oils; *b* Wallasey, 20 Sept., 1914; *s* of Robert Garratt; *m* Dorothy Cartwright; one *d. Educ.:* Quarry Bank High School, Liverpool; *studied art* at Brighton College of Art. *Exhib.:* R.A., E. End Academy, Lewes, Hove, Brighton, Bolton, Blackpool, Eastbourne, Gloucester, Cheltenham, Imperial Institute, Horsham. *Work in permanent collections:* Farnham Museum, Library; Hove. *Publications:* Landscape Drawing in Pen and Ink; Westcountryman's England; Model Soldiers: a Collectors' Guide; Model Soldiers for the Connoisseur; A History of Bramber and Steyning; Collecting Model Soldiers. *Address:* 20 Marston Rd., Farnham. *Club:* British Model Soldier Soc. *Signs work:* "J. G. GARRATT" (form varies).

GARRETT, Albert Charles, R.O.I., F.R.S.A.; artist in oil, wood engraver and writer; senior art lecturer, Polytechnic of North London, School of Architecture (1963), president, Society of Wood Engravers, chairman, Mall Prints, F.B.A., Vice President, National Society, mem., Free Painters and Sculptors, Colour Group of Gt. Britain; Academie Internationale de Lutèce, Paris; *b* Kingsclere, Hants., 14 May, 1915; *s* of A. J. Garrett; *m* Jessie Iris; one *d. Educ.:* Camberwell School of Art (1947-49), Anglo French Art Centre (1949-50), Slade School of Fine Art (1950-51); *studied art:* painting under Sir William Coldstream; engraving under John Buckland-Wright. *Exhib.:* one-man shows, Gallery One (1954), Walkers Gallery (1961), Woodstock Gallery (1961), Mount Street P.O. (1970), Mall Galleries (1972). *Work in permanent collections:* Derby A.G., Hull Ferens A.G., Waikato A.G. Hamilton, Richter Trust, Polytechnic of North London, Portsmouth A.G. *International Exhib.:* Calgary Graphics International Printmakers (1968), Canadian International Printmakers, Winnipeg (1968), Palme d'Or des Beaux Arts, Monte-Carlo (1969-75), International Kunstmesse Art, Basel (1972), International Grafikart, Zürich (1972), International Markt fur aktuelle Kunst, Dusseldorf (1972), Art Contemporain International, Lyon (1973), Bertrand Russell Centenary International, London (1972-73), Paris Salon (1974), International Salon de Noel (1975), Galerie Vallombreuse, Biarritz. *Awards:* Diplome d'Honneur (engraving) (1969), Diplome de Selection (engraving (1970-75), International Arts Guild, Monte-Carlo (Silver medallist, 1974-75), Academie Internationale de Lutèce. Art director, film, Colour Today (1961).

Publications: author, Wood Engravings and Drawings of Iain Macnab, Midas; co-authorship: Colour in Architecture, Factory Building, Leonard Hill, Physical Working Conditions, Industrial Society, Colour 73, Adam Hilger; research papers: Colour in Motion, Automobile Engineer (1962-63), Colour Stimulus, Building Materials, (1967), Read paper, Diagnostic colour from natural and artificial light in dental hospitals, International Colour Association Congress, University of York (1973). Stroboscoping light sources and ultra-violet radiation survey, Federation of British Artists Quarterly (1972-73); articles published, Studio, Arts Review, Leonardo, Impulse, Office Magazine, Ophthalmic Optician, Works Management, Industrial Architecture, Screen Printing. *Address:* 10 Sunningdale Ave., Eastcote, Ruislip, Middx. *Signs work:* "A. C. GARRETT."

GARRETT, John: see BUSSELL, Jan.

GARROD, Violet Nellie, F.R.S.A. (1946); artist in oil, water-colour, conté, pastel, miniatures; Founder of Southbourne Art Soc. (1938) and New Milton Art Circle (1948), and the Palette Club, Lymington (1954), and the Milford-on-Sea Art Group (1958); *b* 19 Nov., 1898; *d* of H. W. Garrod. *Educ.:* Private schools; Central Inst., Hampstead Garden Suburb (Dudley Heath); St. John's Wood Art School (Leonard Walker, Fred Walean). *Exhib.:* R.A., Paris Salon (Silver Medallist), R.B.A., R.M.S., S.M., P.S., S.W.A., etc. *Official purchases:* Russell-Cotes Gallery, Bournemouth. *Address:* 12 Rabling Rd., Swanage, Dorset. *Signs work:* "V. N. Garrod"; "V. N. G." in rectangle on miniatures.

•**GARSTIN, Alethea,** R.W.A.; painter in oil; Mem., Penwith Society of Artists and Newlyn Society of Artists; *d* of Norman Garstin. *Studied art* under Norman Garstin. *Work in permanent collections:* Bristol, Plymouth. *Address:* Old Poorhouse, Zennor, St. Ives, Cornwall. *Signs work:* "ALETHEA GARSTIN."

GAUGUIN, Paul René, Médaille de la Résistance Française; works in graphics, collages, iron sculpture; *b* Copenhagen (Norwegian by nationality), 27 Jan., 1911; *s* of Pola Gauguin, writer; *m* Martha Poulsen; one *s*. *Educ.:* self-taught. *Exhib.:* Scandinavia, Germany, France, Tahiti, America, etc. *Official purchases:* V. & A., London; Bibliothèque Nationale, Musée d'Art Moderne, Paris; National Gallery and State Gallery, Oslo; State galleries of Bergen, Copenhagen, Stockholm, Berlin, Essen, Würzburg, Cincinnati, Tahiti, etc. *Work repro.:* Norsk Grafikk i det 20 Aarh., Ung Norsk Malerkunst, Norsk Billedkunst, Kunsten i Dag, Life Magazine, etc. *Address:* Solvaenget 10, 2100 Copenhagen. *Signs work:* see appendix.

GAUNT, William, M.A. (1926); writer and painter; *b* 5 July, 1900; *s* of William Gaunt, artist; *m* Mary Catherine O'Reilly. *Educ.:* Hull Grammar School; Worcester College, Oxford; Westminster School of Art. *Exhib.:* R.A., one-man exhbns. Redfern, Leger, Lefevre, Walker Galleries. *Publications:* London Promenade; Bandits in a Landscape; The Pre-Raphaelite Tragedy; The Aesthetic Adventure; The March of the Moderns; Victorian Olympus; Arrows of Desire (1956), Everyman Dictionary of Pictorial Art (1961), Concise History of English Painting (1964), The Impressionists (1970), The Great Century of British Painting (1971), The Restless Century, 1800-1900 (1972). *Address:* 35B Lansdowne Rd., London W11. *Signs work:* "W. Gaunt."

GAY, Barbara, A.R.W.A. (1958); artist potter in glazed, coloured stoneware, also painter in oils; *b* Bristol, 20 June, 1921; *d* of Henry Valentine Gay, B.Sc., F.R.G.S., schoolmaster. *Educ.:* privately; *studied art* at West of England College of Art (1936-46), Principal, Donald Milner, O.B.E., M.A., A.R.C.A. (Lond.), R.W.A., modelling master, Roy Smith, R.W.A., and Monkton Combe Pottery with Rachel Warner (1949). *Work in permanent collections:* Cast, stone statue of

St. George (1940) (War Memorial), statue of Madonna (1945), both in St. George, Brandon Hill, Bristol; painting War v. Healing (1945) in Medical Library, Pentagon, Washington, D.C.; also many sets of stoneware figures of Canterbury Pilgrims in private colls. in the U.S.A. *Address:* 12 Miles Rd., Clifton, Bristol BS8 2JN. *Clubs:* R.W.E.A., Clifton Arts, Portfolio Soc. *Signs work:* Paintings, "Barbara Gay," pottery, see appendix.

GAY, Bernard, H.M.I., A.S.I.A., F.R.S.A.; painter in mixed media, designer, writer, lecturer; H.M. Inspector of Schools; co-founder Camden Arts Centre, Chairman Camden Arts Trust, Trustee, Arkwright Arts Trust; *b* Exmouth, Devon, 11 Apr., 1921; two *s.* *Studied art* at Willesden School of Art (1947-51) under Maurice de Sausmarez and Eric Taylor. *Exhib.:* one-man shows I.C.A., Camden Arts Centre, Piccadilly Gallery, Wildenstein, Pace, John Whibley, Austen Hayes and other galleries. *Official purchases:* West Riding of Yorkshire Educ. Com., Oxford University, I.C.I., Essex C.C., Hertfordshire C.C., Nottingham C.C. *Publications:* The Art of Sandro Botticelli (Batchworth Press), Definitive Catalogue on the De Stijl Movement, numerous articles and reviews in the Arts Bulletin, Pictures and Prints, The Artist, Studio International, Art News, Design, Realism, etc. *Address:* Church Cottage, Cookley, Halesworth, Suffolk. *Signs work:* "Bernard Gay," "BG," "bg."

GEAR, William, D.A. (Edin.), F.R.S.A.; Head of Dept. of Fine Art, Birmingham Polytechnic (retd. 1975); Chairman, Fine Art Board, C.N.A.A.; Curator, Towner Art Gallery, Eastbourne (1958-64); R. Signals (1940-45); M.F.A. & A., Germany (1946-47); *b* Methil, Fife, 2 Aug., 1915; *m* Charlotte Chertok; two *s.* *Studied art* at Edinburgh (1932-37), Academie Fernand Leger, Paris (1937). Worked in Paris (1947-50). *Exhib.:* numerous one-man and group exhbns. in U.K. and abroad. *Work in permanent collections:* include Tate Gallery, V. & A., Arts Council, Scottish Arts Council, Arts Council of N. Ireland, British Council; Scottish Nat. Gallery of Modern Art, Nat. Gallery of Canada, Nat. Gallery of N.S.W., and at Aberdeen, Birmingham, Brighton, Buffalo, N.Y., Cambridge, Dundee, Eastbourne, Glasgow, Liege, Lima, Manchester, Nelson, N.Z., Newcastle, New York, Oxford, Southampton, Tel Aviv, Toronto, Toledo, etc. *Prizes and Awards:* Festival of Britain (1951), David Cargill Award (1967), Lorne Fellowship (1975). *Address:* 46 George Rd., Birmingham B15 1PL. *Signs work:* see appendix.

GENEVER, Margaret; artist in oil; *b* London; *d* of Charles T. Genever, architect and contractor. *Educ.:* privately and Southend-on-Sea Grammar School; *studied art* at St. Martin's School of Art, London (1945-55) under Otwell McConnell, Herbert Holt; Hammersmith School of Art under Carel Weight, R.A., and Ruskin Spear, R.A.; Central School of Art, London (lithography). *Exhib.:* R.A., A.I.A., F.P.S., various London and provincial galleries. *Work repro.:* La Revue Moderne des Arts et de La Vie. *Address:* Chilton Cottage, 1 Chesham Rd., Guildford, Surrey GU1 3LS. *Signs work:* "Margaret Genever."

GEORGE, Grace Courtenay, University of Oxford Secondary Teachers Art Cert.; artist in water-colour and lino and wood block; Head of Art Department, The Grammar School, Chipping Sodbury, nr. Bristol (1939-69); art mistress, Hereward School, March, Cambs. (1934-38); exchange teacher, South High School, Lima, Ohio, U.S.A. (1948); Mem. National Society of Art Education; *b* Bristol, 9 Sept., 1909; *d* of the late Frank Courtenay George, bookseller. *Educ.:* Hillside House School and Duncan House School, Clifton, Bristol; *studied art* at W. of England College of Art, Bristol, principal, R. E. J. Bush. *Address:* Middle Thatched Cottage, Lower St., West Harnham, Salisbury, Wilts. *Signs work:* "G. C. George."

GEORGE, Patrick; teacher, Slade School, University College; *b* Manchester, 1923; *m* June; four *d. Work in permanent collections:* Arts Council, Tate Gallery, Castle Museum, Norwich, Huddersfield Art Gallery, Ministry of Environment, etc. *Address:* 33 Moreton Terr., London SW1.

GERE, John Arthur Giles, B.A.; Keeper, Dept. of Prints and Drawings, British Museum, since 1973 (Assistant Keeper, 1946-66, Deputy Keeper, 1966); *b* London, 7 Oct., 1921. *Educ.:* Winchester and Balliol College, Oxford. *Publications:* Pre-Raphaelite Painters (1948); Catalogue of Drawings by Raphael and His Circle in the British Museum (jointly with Philip Pouncey, 1962); Taddeo Zuccaro: his Development studied in his Drawings (1970); I disegni dei maestri: il manierismo a Roma (1971); various exhibition catalogues and articles in Burlington Magazine, Master Drawings, etc. *Address:* 21 Lamont Rd., London SW10. *Club:* Athenæum.

GERSON, Horst, Dr. Phil.; Emeritus Professor, Department of History of Art, University of Groningen; *b* Berlin, 2 Mar., 1907; *studied history of art* at Universities of Berlin, Göttingen and Vienna. *Publications:* Philips Koninck (1936), Die Ausbreitung und Nachwirkung der holländischen Malerei des 17. Jahrhunderts (1942), Zes eeuwen Nederlandse schilderkunst (1962), (together with E. H. ter Kuile) Art and Architecture in Belgium (1960), the Age of Rembrandt (exhibition catalogue, San Francisco-Toledo-Boston, 1966-67), Rembrandt Paintings (1968), Rembrandt (the Complete Edition of the Paintings), by A. Bredius, revised by H. Gerson (1969). *Address:* Goeman Borgesiuslaan 65, Groningen.

GESSNER, Robert S.; painter in oil and tempera; lithographer; engraver on wood and copper; *b* Zürich, 20 Sept., 1908; *s* of Col. Karl Eduard Gessner, judge; *m* Selma Regula. *Educ.:* Zürich; *studied art:* self-taught painter; publicity design under Ernst Keller (Zürich). *Exhib.:* Zürich, Frauenfeld, Freiburg i.B., Schwenningen, Milano, Tokio, Birmingham, Basle, Berne, Geneva, Lucerne, Paris, Brooklyn, Köln, etc. *Address:* Seegartenstrasse 12, Zürich, 8. *Clubs:* G.S.M.B.A., Allianz. *Signs work:* "Rob. S. Gessner."

GHIKA, Niko; First Prize of Academy of Athens; painter in oils, water-colours, tempera, etc., engraver, theatrical designer (Persephone, Covent Garden), and writer; Emeritus Prof., Technical University of Athens; *b* Athens, 26 Feb., 1906; *s* of Alexander Hadjikyriaco, Admiral Commander in Chief of the Greek Fleet, Politician; *m* Barbara Warner (1961). *Educ.:* Lycee, Paris; *studied art* at Académie Ranson, Paris. *Exhib.:* 21 one-man shows and many group exhbns. *Work in permanent collections:* Musee National d'Art Moderne, Paris; Tate Gallery, London; Metropolitan Museum, New York; Cincinnati Museum, U.S.A.; Melbourne Museum, Australia; Le Musee de Carcassonne, France; The Pinacotheque, Cyprus; Rhodes Museum; Calamatamuseum; Pinacotheque of Athens; Theatrical Museum, Athens; Centre National d'Art Contemporain, Paris. *Publications:* Kazantzakis: The Odyssey (Simon and Schuster, N.Y.); Cavafy: Poems; Daphnis and Chloe, Poems by Elytis; India an album, all by Icarus Press. *Addresses:* 3 Kriezotou St., Athens, Greece; 27 Blomfield Rd., London W9. *Signs work:* "Ghika."

GIARDELLI, Arthur, M.B.E., M.A. (Oxon.); Chairman, 56 Group, Wales; painter in mixed media (wood, brass, burlap, oil, etc.) for wall panels, water-colour, and lecturer; Senior Tutor, University College of Wales, Aberystwyth; *b* London, 11 Apr., 1911; *s* of Vincent Giardelli; *m*; one *s*, one *d*. *Educ.:* Alleyn's School, Dulwich, Hertford College, Oxford; *studied art* Ruskin School of Art, Oxford. *Exhib.:* Amsterdam, Paris, Chicago, Washington, New York. *Work in permanent* *collections:* Arts Council of Great Britain, Welsh Arts Council, National Museum of Wales, National Library of Wales, Museum of Modern Art, Dublin, Keble College, Oxford, Estorick Collection, Grosvenor Gallery, London. *Publication:* The Delight of Painting (University College, Swansea). *Work repro.:* Anglo-Welsh Review, art magazines. *Address:* Golden Plover, Warren, Pembroke. *Signs work:* see appendix.

GIBBARD, Elizabeth; painter, wood engraver and sculptress; *b* 8 July, 1913; *d* of F. J. Miller; *m* Daniel George Gibbard; two *s*, one *d*. *Educ.:* Girls' Grammar School, Thame; Banbury School of Art; Bath School of Art. *Exhib.:* R.A., United Artists; one-man shows, Oxford. *Official purchases:* Herts County Council Education Dept. from R,A, (1946), Women's International Art Club (1960), Royal West of England Academy (1966). *Address:* 1 Malmesbury Rd., The Leigh, Cricklade, Wilts. *Signs work:* "Elizabeth Gibbard."

GIBBERD, Sir Frederick, C.B.E., R.A., F.R.I.B.A., F.R.T.P.I., F.I.L.A.; practising as architect and town planning consultant; p. Mem. Royal Fine Art Commission; p. Princ., A.A. School of Architecture; *b* 7 Jan., 1908; *s* of Frederick Gibberd, Kenilworth, Warwickshire; *m* 1938, Dorothy Phillips, died 1970; one *s*, two *d*; remarried 1972, Patricia Fox-Edwards. *Educ.:* King Henry VIII School, Coventry. *Principal buildings include:* London Airport, St. Albans and Leamington Spa Civic Halls, Belfast Hospital, Inter Continental Hotel, Hyde Park Corner, Arundel Great Court and Coutts Bank, the Strand, London, winner of open competition for Metropolitan Cathedral of Christ the King, Liverpool (1960), and The London Mosque (1970); Landscape Consultant for Derwent, Tryweryn and Kielder Reservoirs; Architect Planner, Harlow new town. *Publications:* Town Design (1953). *Addresses:* 8 Percy St., London W1, and at 19 The Rows, Stone Cross, Harlow, Essex. *Signs work:* see appendix.

GIBBON, Sidney, A.T.D., Lond., F.R.S.A.; artist in water-colour, oil, pen and pencil; headmaster, School of Art, Newark-on-Trent (1930-57); chairman, Notts. Puppetry Guild; *b* Leamington Spa, 6 May, 1895. *Educ.:* Leamington College; *studied art* at Leicester College of Art, Brighton College of Art. *Exhib.:* Nottingham Castle A.G., Municipal Museum, Newark-on-Trent, Scarborough A.G. *Work in permanent collections:* Forum Fantasy and Chanctonbury Ring (Newark Municipal Museum). *Work repro.:* Brixham Harbour (Artist). *Publications:* A Windmill by Inigo Jones (Architect), Georgian Architecture in Newark-on-Trent (Architectural Design and Construction). *Address:* 7B Scalby Beck Rd., Scarborough. *Signs work:* "S. Gibbon."

GIBBS, Evelyn, Rome Scholar in Engraving (1929), A.R.C.A., A.R.E.; painter in oil; etcher and engraver; *b* Liverpool; *m* Hugh Willatt. *Studied art* at Liverpool School of Art, R.C.A. and at the British School in Rome. *Exhib.:* Zwemmer Gallery, Leicester Galleries, Midland Group Gallery. *Work in permanent collections:* Castle Art Gallery (Nottingham), B.M. (Print Room), Ashmolean Museum, Oxford. *Official purchases:* Arts Council, L.C.C., War Artists Advisory Com., County Collections of Leicester, Derbys., Herts and Cambs. *Address:* 32 Marden Ave., London W2. *Signs work:* "GIBBS" (on paintings); "Evelyn Gibbs" (on engravings).

GIBBS, Timothy Francis, B.A. (Oxon., 1947), D.F.A. (Oxon, 1948); painter in oils and water-colour; deputy Ruskin master, Ruskin School of Drawing; *b* Epping, Essex, 21 Aug., 1923; *s* of G. Y. Gibbs; *m* Bridget; one *s*, two *d*. *Educ.:* Trinity College, Oxford; *studied art* at Ruskin School of Drawing (1947-48). *Exhib.:* one-man shows: Piccadilly Gallery (1955), Leicester Galleries (1962, 1963, 1966, 1969). *Work in permanent collections:* Ministry of Works, Atkinson

Art Gallery, Southport, Financial Times, Nottingham Education Authority, Hertfordshire Education Authority, mural Barclays Bank, Guildford. *Address:* 131 Elgin Cres., London W11. *Signs work:* "T. F. Gibbs."

GIBBS-SMITH, Charles Harvard, Hon. F.R.C.A., F.R.S.A., M.A. (Harvard, U.S.A.), Hon. Companion R.Ae.S., F.M.A., Chevalier, Order of the Dannebrog (Denmark); Keeper Emeritus V. & A. (asst. keeper, 1932); Research Fellow, Science Museum (from 1976); *b* 22 Mar., 1909. *Educ.:* Westminster and Harvard Univ. *Publications:* art criticism, etc., in various magazines; Ballooning; The Great Exhibition of 1851; Operation Caroline; A History of Flying; Yankee Poodle; Escape and Be Secret; The Bayeux Tapestry (part author); The Fashionable Lady in the 19th Century; The Aeroplane; Sir George Cayley's Aeronautics; The Invention of the Aeroplane, Clément Ader; Aviation; The Wright Brothers; The Bayeux Tapestry; The Art of Observation. *Address:* Victoria and Albert Museum, London SW7. *Club:* Naval and Military.

GIBSON, Alexander, R.I.B.A. (1932), A.A.Hons. Dip. (1931); in private practice and consultant to Design Research Unit; *b* Northampton, 23 Aug., 1906; *s* of George Langford Gibson; *m* Iona Reid, architect; two *s*, one *d*. *Educ.:* Shrewsbury School and A.A. *Exhib.:* offices, shops, restaurants, showrooms and domestic; work for International Distillers and Vintners, Co-operative Insurance Society, B.P., B.S.C., Mobil, Air India, etc. *Addresses:* 16 Downshire Hill, London NW3 1NT; 32 Aybrook St., London W1M 4BB.

GIBSON, Roland, Ph.D.; collector, especially of contemporary abstract art by Japanese, Italian and other European artists; Curator of Art, State University College at Potsdam, N.Y.; editor, catalogue of New England Sculpture travelling exhibition (1973), Japanese Art of the Sixties (1974); trustee, Potsdam College Foundation; *b* Potsdam, N.Y., 4 Feb., 1902; *s* of Fred E. Gibson. *Educ.:* Dartmouth College and Columbia University. *Address:* 9 Garden St., Potsdam, N.Y., U.S.A.

GIFFARD, Colin Carmichael, M.A. Cantab., Dip.Arch. London (A.R.I.B.A. 1947-57), A.R.W.A.; R.I.B.A. Schools Drawing Prize (1932), Rome finalist (Arch.) 1939; painter in oil, acrylic; lecturer, Bath Academy of Art, Sydney Place (1951-68); *b* London, 1915. *Educ.:* Charterhouse, Clare College, Cambridge, University College, London; *studied art* at Bath Academy of Art under William Scott, Peter Potworowski. *Exhib.:* R.A., R.W.A., London Group, Bristol City A.G.; one-man shows: Bath (1958-60), Woodstock Gallery (1966-68-69). *Official purchases:* Hertfordshire, Wigan Educ. Coms. (murals in schools), Architectural Association, St. Catherine's College, Cambridge, Newton Park College Bath, Bristol, Walsall Educ. Coms. *Address:* Little Mead, Freshford, Bath.

GIGGLE, Philip, Dip. A.D., M.F.P.S., L.H.O.O.Q. Paris; artist and illustrator in tempera, oil, water-colour and photography; part-time lecturer in art; *b* Cublington, 7 Oct., 1949; *s* of George Harry Giggle. *Educ.:* Aston Abbotts Wing Secondary Modern; *studied art* at High Wycombe (1968) under Di Girolamo; Ruskin, Oxford (1972) under Morsberger; Atelier Delafon, Paris (1973). *Exhib.:* Burleighfield House (1973), Open Mid. 25 (1972), Cross Keys (1970). *Work in permanent collection:* Trustee Savings Bank; private collections of L. Marsh, London, John Blakeway, Paris, T. Jenns, Amersham. *Work repro.:* Sunday Observer, Arts Review Directory. *Publications:* Riverside Shakespeare, Smoking, Sin or Sickness. *Address:* Old Post Office, Cublington, Bucks. *Signs work:* "P.G." and "Philip Giggle."

GILBERT, Anthony Allen, M.S.I.A. (1951); artist and designer in pen, gouache, monoprint; *b* Leamington Spa, 31 Mar., 1916; *s* of Theodore F. Gilbert;

m Ann D. Buckmaster. *Educ.:* Colfe's; *studied art* at Goldsmiths' College. *Work in permanent collections:* Tapestry, Kirkstall Abbey House, Leeds Museum. *Official purchases:* in South Bank Exhbn. (1951), tapestry depicting Norman Life in Britain; in Festival Pleasure Gdns., Battersea Park, decorative panels for stage, design for stage door (1951); Eight panels of English Kings (1953); stained-glass window in St. Philip's Church, Hove, drawing presented to Permanent Collection of V. & A. Museum (1954). *Address:* 14 South Hill Rd., Bromley, Kent. *Signs work:* "Anthony Gilbert."

GILBERT, Dennis, N.E.A.C., N.S.; painter; lecturer, Hammersmith College of Art; *b* London, 7 Jan., 1922; *s* of Gordon S. Gilbert; *m* Joan Gilbert, painter; three *s,* one *d. Educ.:* Weston-super-Mare; *studied art* at St. Martin's School of Art (1946-51). *Exhib.:* R.A., Paris Salon, R.B.A., N.E.A.C., S.E.A., Roland, Browse & Delbanco, Leicester Galleries, Redfern, O'Hana and Zwemmer Galleries, etc.; one-man show: F.B.A. Gallery (1968). *Address:* 91 Ashleigh Rd., London SW14. *Signs work:* "GILBERT."

GILBERT, Joan; painter; *b* India, 24 Jan., 1928; *d* of Harold Musker, O.B.E., M.C.; *m* Dennis Gilbert, painter; three *s*, one *d. Educ.:* Badminton School; *studied art* at St. Martin's School of Art (1945-50). *Exhib.:* R.A., Arts Council, R.B.A., S.E.A. and Zwemmer Gallery; one-man shows: Travers Gallery (1969, 1970). *Official purchases:* I.L.E.A., W. Riding Educ. Authority, Zoological Gardens, London. *Work repro.:* The Sketch; illustrations to Saints and Their Attributes. *Address:* 91 Ashleigh Rd., London SW14. *Signs work:* "Joan Gilbert."

GILBERT, Stephen, Diploma, Slade School (1935); sculptor and painter; *b* Fife, Scotland, 1910; *s* of Capt. F. G. W. Gilbert, R.N.; *m* Jocelyn Chewett; one *s*, one *d. Educ.:* University College School, University College, London. *Work in permanent collections:* Tate Gallery, Stedelijk Museum, Arts Council, British Council, Leicester Museum, Leicester University, Sheffield Museum, Norwich Museum, Alborg Museum, British Steel Corp., G.L.C. *Address:* 7 Impasse du Rouet, Paris, 14e. *Signs work:* "Stephen Gilbert."

GILBERY, Michael, A.R.C.A. (1935); portrait painter in oil; teacher, St. Martin's School of Art since 1945; *b* London, 18 Oct., 1913; *s* of Joseph Gilbery; *m* Adrianne Irene Roberts; one *d. Educ.:* Mile End Central School, E1; *studied art* at St. Martin's School of Art (1928-32) and R.C.A. under Pitchforth, Bramley, Sir William Rothenstein, and Gilbert Spencer. *Exhib.:* R.A., R.P.S., N.E.A.C., R.O.I., N.S. *Work in permanent collection:* Tel-Aviv Museum. *Work repro.:* Tatler and British and foreign Press. *Address:* 6 Rosecroft Ave., London NW3. *Club:* Chelsea Arts. *Signs work:* "Gilbery."

GILES, A. F. Lynton, A.R.W.A. (1970); artist, designer and art-master; silver medallist, Paris Salon (1948), Mem. Society of Sussex Painters (1971). *Studied art* under Stanley Anderson, James Bateman, and Vivian Pitchforth at Goldsmiths' College, St. Martin's School of Art. *Exhib.:* R.A., N.E.A.C., R.Cam.A., R.S.A., R.P., R.B.A., C.E.M., Arts Council, United Soc., Paris Salon, R.W.S., R.W.A., R.I., Bradford Open (1965, 1966), Sheffield Open (1964, 1966, 1968, 1970) and provincial galleries. Works in private collections and public collections. *Work repro.:* R.A. Illustrated, Medici Soc., Country Life, Courier Magazine. *Address:* 20 Dolphin Lodge, Grand Ave., Worthing, Sussex BN11 5AL. *Signs work:* "Lynton Giles."

GILES, Peter Donovan, N.D.D. (Special level Illustration) 1959, A.T.C. (Lond.) 1960; painter, graphic designer and sculptor in acrylic paint, mixed media for assemblages and plaster; senior art master, Frank Hooker School, Canterbury; Tutor, life drawing, Canterbury Adult Studies Centre; *b* Perivale, Middx., 15 Feb.,

1939; *s* of Donovan Eric Giles; *m* Elizabeth Ann Giles; one *s*, one *d*. *Educ.:* Castlehill College, Ealing; *studied art* at Ealing School of Art (1954-59) under Colin Sorenson, A.R.C.A.; Hornsey College of Art (1959-60) under Peter Green, A.T.D. *Exhib.:* All Hallows on the Wall, EC2; one-man shows in the provinces; lecture tours in the U.S.A. and Canada (1973 and 1975). *Work in permanent collections:* Lichfield City A.G., War Memorial Ely Cathedral. *Publication:* Right Irreverent, cartoons (1974). *Address:* Filmer House, Bridge, Canterbury, Kent. *Signs work:* "Peter Giles."

GILES, Phyllis Margaret, M.A. (Cantab., 1928), Fellow of Lucy Cavendish College, Cambridge, University of London School of Librarianship Diploma (1930); Librarian of Fitzwilliam Museum, Cambridge (1947-74); Asst. University of London Library (1933-43); Asst. Librarian, Min. of Town and Country Planning (1943-47); *b* London, 20 Jan., 1907; *d* of Charles Giles, parliamentary journalist. *Educ.:* Clapham High School and Girton College, Cambs. *Address:* 8 Park Pde., Cambs. *Club:* Cambridge Drawing Society.

GILIOLI, Emile; sculptor; *b* Paris, 10 June, 1911. *Studied art* at Beaux Arts, Paris, and privately. *Exhib.:* Galerie Louis Carré (Paris, 1958). *Work in permanent collections:* Museum of Modern Art, Paris, Tate Gallery, London, Museums of Grenoble and Nice, Musée Middleheim, Anvers, Musée de São Paulo; Helsingfors Kunsthall, Helsinki. *Official purchases:* Monument des Deportés de Grenoble, Monument des Gliére, etc. *Work repro.:* in various periodicals, particularly in Art d'aujourd'hui, XXe Siècle, Architecture d'aujourd'hui. *Publications:* chapter in Témoignage d'Art Abstrait (édition d'Art d'aujourd'hui), article in L'Oeil No. 16. *Address:* 4 rue Gager Gabillot, Paris 15e. *Signs work:* "GILIOLI."

GILL, Stanley Herbert, A.R.C.A., A.T.D.; art teacher, painter in oil, watercolour, gouache, lithographer; painting instructor, York and Dewsbury Schools of Art (1936-41); Head of Dept., School of Fine Art and Graphic Design, Salisbury College of Art (1947-72); *b* Leeds, 21 May, 1912; *s* of Fred Gill, lithographer; *m* Lavinia P. Leader; one *s*. *Educ.:* City of Leeds School; *studied art* at Leeds College of Art (1928-31), R.C.A. (1931-35) under Gilbert Spencer, Sir William Rothenstein, and H. Spear. *Exhib:* R.A., British Art Centre, Leeds, Yorkshire Artists, Bradford, York, Wakefield, Preston, Brighton, Southampton, Salisbury. *Address:* 1 Hadrian's Cl., Salisbury SP2 9NN. *Signs work:* "S. H. Gill" (plus date).

GILLEY, Leonard Christopher; free-lance artist in oil and water-colour; *b* Camberwell, 28 May, 1915; *s* of Christopher George Gilley, engineer; *m* Eleanor Betty Shadbolt. *Educ.:* Strand School, Tulse Hill; *studied art* at Camberwell School of Art. *Work repro.:* in magazines, Press, posters, etc., for national advertisers at home and overseas, also art galleries. *Address:* Little Moyle, Tupwood La., Caterham, Surrey. *Club:* Caterham Arts. *Signs work:* see appendix.

GILLHAM, Kenneth Geoffrey, A.R.B.S., N.D.D. (1954), R.A. Silver Medal, Landseer Scholarship (1958); sculptor, 3-D graphic design modeller in plastics, chrome, enamel, etc.; part-time lecturer; *b* London, 28 May, 1934; *m*; two *s*. *Educ.:* Sheppey Secondary School; *studied art* at Medway College of Art (1950-54), Royal Academy School of Sculpture (1956-58) under Maurice Lambert, R.A., Peter Greenham, R.A. *Exhib.:* Trade Fairs, etc., museums. *Address:* 14 Waldeck Rd., Chiswick, London W4. *Signs work:* "Ken Gillham."

GILLIGAN, Barbara; artist in oil; *b* London, 3 Feb., 1913; *d* of Lt.-Col. Gilligan; *m* David Carr; three *s*. *Educ.:* Langford Grove School; *studied art* at East Anglian School of Art under Cedric Morris and at Slade School under Polunin (stage design). *Exhib.:* one-man show, Leicester Galleries (1948). *Address:* Starston Hall, Harleston, Norfolk. *Signs work:* see appendix.

GILLISON, Margaret, M.C.S.P., Dip. Lond. (Phys. Ed.), Dip., Bedford P.T. College; painter and illustrator; design and display officer, Grosvenor Museum, Chester (1966-); *b* Warwick, 1916; *d* of Douglas Gillison. *Educ.:* Howell's School, Denbigh. *Exhib.:* R.Cam.A., N. Wales Group, S. Wales Group, S.E.A. Pictures for Schools, National Eisteddfod, etc. *Work repro.:* various medical textbooks, posters, book jackets, etc. *Publications:* A Histology of the Body Tissues, illustrated (E. & S. Livingstone, Edinburgh). *Address:* Pen-y-Llwyn, Llanarmon-yn-Ial, nr. Mold, N. Wales. *Signs work:* "M. GILLISON."

GILMORE, Sidney; sculptor in steel, wood, stone and glassfibre; *b* London, 3 June, 1923. *Educ.:* Willesden Grammar School; *studied art* at Willesden College of Technology. *Exhib.:* R.A., F.P.S., Chicago British Fortnight, U.S.A., Bradford A.G., Heals, London, etc. *Address:* 111 Sudbury Ave., N. Wembley, Middx. *Club:* F.P.S. *Signs work:* "S. B. Gilmore."

GILMOUR, Albert Edward; artist in oil, pen and ink; sec., Gateshead Art Club (1950-51); locomotive fireman; *b* W. Hartlepool, 31 May, 1923; *s* of A. E. Gilmour; *m* Elaine Bolton (*q.v.*); one *s*, one *d*. *Educ.:* Heworth and Felling Elementary Schools; *studied art:* courses at Gateshead Technical College, King's College, Newcastle. *Exhib.:* Federation of Northern Arts Socs. Exhbns., Artists of the Northern Counties Exhbns., Artists of Durham Exhbn., Gateshead Art Club Exhbns. *Work repro.:* Locomotive Express, British Railways Magazine, N.E. Region. *Address:* 11 Limewood Grove, Woodlands Pk., North Gosforth, Newcastle upon Tyne NE13 6PU. *Clubs:* Park Rd., and West End Group, Newcastle; Gateshead Art. *Signs work:* "GILMOUR."

GILMOUR, Elaine; University of Durham teachers' cert. with distinction in Art (advanced); artist in oil, collage; *b* Hetton-le-Hole, Co. Durham, 29 Apr., 1931; *d* of Albert William Bolton; *m* Albert E. Gilmour (*q.v.*); one *s*, one *d*. *Educ.:* Eppleton Infants', Junior Mixed and Modern School, Houghton-le-Spring Grammar School; *studied art* at Neville's Cross College, Durham, and Sunderland College of Art. *Exhib.:* Sunderland A.G., Shipley A.G., Laing A.G., Newcastle, Gateshead. *Work in permanent collections:* Sunderland A.G., Laing A.G., Newcastle. *Address:* 11 Limewood Grove, Woodlands Pk., North Gosforth, Newcastle upon Tyne NE13 6PU. *Club:* West End Art. *Signs work:* "Elaine Gilmour."

GINESI, Edna, A.R.C.A.; figure draughtsman and painter in oil; Mem. London Group, Mem. Chiswick Group; *b* Leeds, 15 Feb., 1902; *m* Raymond Coxon. *Educ.:* privately; *studied art* at Leeds College of Art, R.C.A. *Exhib.:* London and provinces, Canada and U.S.A. *Work in permanent collections:* Tate Gallery (2); Nat. Gallery of Wales, Leeds, Wakefield, Bradford and Manchester City Art Galleries. *Addresses:* 10 Hammersmith Terr., London W6; Mill Studio, Rowfant, nr. Crawley, Sussex. *Signs work:* "E. Ginesi" or "E. GINESI."

GINGER, Phyllis Ethel, R.W.S. (1958); free-lance illustrator and water-colour artist; *b* London, 19 Oct., 1907; *d* of Arthur James Ginger, civil servant; *m* Leslie Durbin; one *s*, one *d*. *Educ.:* Tiffin's Girls' School, Kingston-on-Thames; *studied art* at Richmond School of Art (1932-35), Central School of Arts and Crafts (1937-39) (John Farleigh, William Robins, Clark Hutton). *Work in permanent collections:* water-colours, Pilgrim Trust Recording Britain Scheme; drawings and lithographs in Washington State Library, Victoria and Albert Museum, London Museum, South London Art Gallery. *Publications:* Alexander the Circus Pony (Puffin Book); London and The Virgin of Aldermanbury, by Mrs. Robert Henrey. *Address:* 298 Kew Rd., Kew, Richmond, Surrey. *Signs work:* "Phyllis Ginger."

GLASS, Pauline, R.B.S.A.; painter in oils and gouache; subjects: flowers, landscape, portraits; *b* 17 Mar., 1908; *m* Dr. S. Glass, one *s. Educ.:* Lycée Emile Max, Academie des Beaux Arts, Brussels. Regular exhibitor at Summer Exhibition, R.A., since 1945. Vice-President, Royal Birmingham Society of Artists. *Paintings in private collections* in England, France, U.S.A., South Africa, Japan. Gives painting demonstration to art societies and private pupils. Collector of Early Staffordshire, papier-maché, and English water-colours. *Address:* 146 Lordswood Rd., Harborne, Birmingham, 17. *Club:* Soroptimist Club of Central Birmingham. *Signs work:* "Pauline Glass."

GLEDSTANES, Elsie, R.B.A. (1929), F.R.S.A., Mem.P.S.; artist in tempera, oil, pastel, water-colour. *Educ.:* Paris; Slade School of Fine Arts; Byam Shaw School of Art. *Exhib.:* R.A., R.B.A., R.P., S.W.A., P.S., etc.; Glasgow, Liverpool, Bournemouth, Leeds, Brighton, Hull, etc. *Addresses:* 61 Campden St., London W8; Glan y Gors, Prenteg, Portmadoc, N. Wales. *Signs work:* "GLEDSTANES" or "E. GLEDSTANES" or "E.G." (joined monogram).

GLOVER, John Ainsworth, D.F.A. (Lond.) (1972), A.T.C. (1973); painter in tempera, water-colour, silkscreen, teacher; part-time lecturer; *b* Maryland, U.S.A., 4 July, 1949; *s* of Joseph Glover, Lt. Col. U.S. Army; *m* Julia Naish. *Educ.:* King's School, Harrow; Chiswick Polytechnic; *studied art* at Ealing Art School (1968-69) under Derrick Hirst, Slade School of Fine Art (1969-72) under Keith Critchlow. *Exhib.:* mixed shows: U.S. Embassy, London (1971), C.C.B. Gallery, London (1971); one-man show, Amwell Gallery, London (1973). *Address:* 90A Essex Rd., London N1. *Club:* Research into Lost Knowledge Organisation. *Signs work:* "John A. Glover."

GLOVER, Louis Henry Horace, A.R.C.A., A.T.D.; artist in oil and potter; Principal, School of Art, and Art Adviser, County Borough of Barnsley; Hon. Director, Cooper Art Gallery; *b* Coventry, 4 Jan., 1912; *s* of W. H. Glover; *m* Grace T. Glover, A.R.C.A., A.T.D., F.R.S.A.; two *d. Educ.:* King Henry VIII School, Coventry; *studied art* at R.C.A. under Prof. Tristram and Staite Murray (1931-35). *Exhib.:* Warwickshire Soc., Yorkshire Soc. of Artists. *Publications:* author, Batsford Book of Dogs, Batsford Book of Poodles. *Work repro.:* Paintings of dogs, illustrations in Dog World. *Address:* Keresforth House, Barnsley, Yorks. *Signs work:* "GLOVER."

GOAMAN, Michael, F.S.I.A.; postage-stamp designer; *b* East Grinstead, 14 Feb., 1921; *s* of John F. Goaman; *m* Sylvia Priestley; three *d. Educ.:* Reading School; *studied art* at University of Reading School of Art (1938-39) and L.C.C. Central School of Arts and Crafts (1946-48). *Work repro.:* commercially and by Designers in Britain, Design, Graphis, Society of Industrial Designers of America, national and philatelic press and abroad. *Exhib.:* International Poster Exhbn., Stampex and abroad. *Address:* 22 St. George's Rd., St. Margaret's, Twickenham. *Signs work:* see appendix.

GODDARD, Michael; Salford Dip. of Associateship, Art and Design; graphic designer, artist in oil; Mem. Manchester Academy of Fine Art (1975); *b* Lancashire, 30 Jan., 1951. *Educ.:* Bridgewater Grammar School, Worsley; *studied art* at Salford College of Technology, Dept. of Art and Design (1967-71). *Address:* 4 Brook Rd., Heaton Chapel, Stockport, Ches. *Signs work:* "Goddard."

GODDARD, Preston; painter and designer; *b* Liverpool, 5 May, 1928; *m* Kathleen Fleming, picture restorer/business manager. *Studied art under* R. A. Wilson, A.R.C.A., at Croydon. *Exhib.:* foremost London and provincial galleries; one-man shows at Beaux Arts Gallery, Leicester Galleries, Somerville College, Oxford; British Art in Moscow. *Work in permanent collections:* Leicestershire

Education Committee, Surrey Education Committee, Oxford University. *Work repro.:* in leading art journals. *Work of special merit:* "Regatta" murals at Chambrun, 73 Eaton Sq., London. *Address:* Studio Hse., 46 Selborne Rd., Croydon. *Signs work:* "PRESTON GODDARD.'

GODWIN, Keith, A.R.C.A. (1947), R.B.A. (1950); sculptor; *b* Warsop, 17 Apr., 1916; *s* of Frederick Fuller Godwin, miner; *m* Mary Holloway; two *s*. *Educ.:* Brunts School (Mansfield); *studied art:* Mansfield Art School (1934-35), Nottingham College of Art (1935-36), Leicester College of Art (1936-39), R.C.A. (1939, 1946-48). *Exhib.:* R.A., R.B.A., Arts Council, London Group, London and provincial galleries. *Official purchases:* I.C.I., Span Developments, schools, Harlow New Town, Mullard, N.U.T. Building, Commonwealth Institute, Reed Paper Group, A.T.V., British Rail, Manchester Evening News and other architectural schemes. *Work repro.:* Architectural journals and Press. *Club:* Arts, Dover St., W.1. *Address:* Heywoods House, Bollington Cross, Macclesfield, Cheshire.

GOERLICH, Ernest Joseph, Doctor philosophiae (1930, Vienna); professor, writer, collector, critic; *b* Vienna, 16 Nov., 1905; *s* of John; *m* Mary; two *s*, one . *Educ.:* high schools. *Publications:* World History (also in Spanish language), History of Our Times, History of Austrian Literature, Austrian History (including Austrian art), History of Slavery and Bondage. *Addresses:* A-1103 Vienna (Austria), P.O.B. 106, and (in July and August), A-7453 Steinberg, 316 Burgenland, Austria, Villa Josephine. *Club:* Austrian P.E.N.

GOGAN, L. S., M.A.; vice-pres., Academy of Christian Art; Mem. Art Advisory Council Municipal Gallery; asst. Irish Antiquities Division, 1914; deputy keeper, 1929, keeper, Art and Industrial Division (1936-56, retd.); *b* 24 Oct., 1891; *m* 1st, the late Maire Forbes, four *s*, two *d;* 2nd, Nora M. O'Hea, B.A. *Educ.:* University College, Dublin. *Publications:* The Ardagh Chalice, Poems (6 vols.); art and archæological papers. *Address:* 18 Terenure Rd., E. Rathgar, Dublin.

GOLDEN, Grace, A.R.C.A. (1926); free-lance artist for reproduction, specializing in historical subjects; *b* 2 Apr., 1904; *d* of Henry F. Golden. *Educ.:* City of London School for Girls; Chelsea Art School (J. D. Revel); Royal College of Art (Sir W. Rothenstein). *Exhib.:* R.A. *Work in permanent collections:* Tate, Chantrey Bequest (1937, 1940). *Official purchases:* by War Artists' Advisory Com.; posters for R.S.P.A., G.P.O. and Government propaganda. *Publications:* Old Bankside (1951), illustrations in educational books. *Address:* 37 Laurier Rd., NW5. *Club:* Hesketh Hubbard Art Society. *Signs work:* "Grace Golden" or "Golden."

GOLDFINGER, Ernö, R.A., D.P.L.G., F.R.I.B.A.; architect and townplanner; Organising Sec. International Union of Architects (London, 1946); Mem. C.O.I.D. (1961-65); *b* Budapest, 11 Sept., 1902; *s* of Dr. Oscar Goldfinger; *m* Ursual Blackwell; two *s*, one *d*. *Educ.:* Budapest and Le Rosay (Switzerland); *studied architecture* at L'Ecole des Beaux-Arts (Paris). *Official works:* Le Touquet, Hampstead, Brussels, Hammersmith, Putney, Shoreditch and Ministry of Health headquarters, London, French Railways, 127 Champs Elysees, Paris, G.L.C. North Kensington and Tower Hamlets. *Work repro.:* in Architectural Review, Architects' Journal, Architectural Forum, The Times, L'Architecture d'Aujourd'hui, Studio Year Book, Architectural Design, The New Yorker, Architecture and Urbanisme, Tokio, Christian Science Monitor, Washington, Building Design, The Guardian, The Sunday Times, etc. *Publications:* Goldfinger Ernö by Prof. Major Akadémiai Kiado Budapest; County of London Plan Explained,

British Furniture Today, New Architecture of London. *Address:* 2 Willow Rd., London NW3 1TH.

GOMBRICH, Sir Ernst Hans, Kt. (1972), C.B.E. (1966), Ph.D. (Vienna, 1933), M.A. (Oxon, 1952; Cantab, 1961), F.B.A. (1960), F.S.A. (1961), Hon. D.Lit. (Belfast, 1963), LL.D. (St. Andrews, 1965), D.Litt. (Leeds, 1965), D.Lit. (Oxford, 1969), D.Lit. (Cambridge, 1970); Director of the Warburg Institute and Professor of the History of the Classical Tradition in the University of London; *b* Vienna, 30 Mar., 1909; *s* of Karl Gombrich, lawyer; *m* Ilse Heller; one s. *Educ.:* Theresianum and University, Vienna. *Publications:* Caricature (with E. Kris, 1940); The Story of Art (1950); Art and Illusion (1959); Meditations on a Hobby Horse (1963); Norm and Form (1966); Aby Warburg (1970), Symbolic Images (1972), articles in learned journals. *Address:* 19 Briardale Gdns., London NW3.

GOODALL, John Strickland, R.I., R.B.A.; draughtsman, artist in water-colour, pen and ink; *b* Heacham, 7 June, 1908; *s* of Joseph Strickland Goodall, M.B., M.R.C.P., F.R.C.S., F.R.S., M.S.A.; *m* Margaret Nicol; one *d. Educ.:* Harrow School; *studied art* under Sir Arthur Cope, R.A. (1923), J. Watson Nicol, Harold Speed (1924), R.A. Schools (1925-29). *Exhib.:* R.A., R.I., R.B.A., Walker Galleries. *Work repro.:* in Radio Times, books, magazines. *Address:* Lawn Cottage, Tisbury, Wilts. *Signs work:* "J. S. Goodall."

GOODCHILD, Mrs. A. V.: see WHITE, Ianthe.

GOODCHILD, Francis Philip, A.R.C.A. (1926), F.S.A.E. (1946), Royal Exhibitioner (1923); Princ., Tiverton School of Art (1934-47). Princ., Newton Abbot College of Art (1947-64); artist in water-colour; *b* Leyton, 12 Mar., 1904; *s* of Thomas Abraham Goodchild, of London; *m* Emily Grace Muton; one *d. Studied art* at High Wycombe School of Art under W. J. Stamps, A.R.C.A. (1919-23) and at R.C.A. under Sir William Rothenstein, Profs. Tristram and Bell (1923-26). *Exhib.:* R.W.A., Assoc. Devon Art Soc.; R.C.A. Old Students Arts Council of Gt. Britain Touring Collection and privately. *Address:* Spindlewood, Churston Cl., Churston Ferrers, Brixham, S. Devon. *Signs work:* "FRANCIS, PHILIP, GOODCHILD."

GOODE, Mervyn; full-time professional artist in oil; landscape artist known chiefly for depicting the Hampshire and surrounding countryside; *b* Peterborough, 27 July, 1948. *Educ.:* Farnborough Grammar School; Gloucester College of Art (environmental design). *Exhib.:* one-man shows: Southwell-Brown Gallery, Richmond (1976), Furneaux Gallery (1975), King St. Galleries (1974), Alpine Gallery (1970, 1971), Highton Gallery (1970); mixed shows: Southampton A.G., Reid Gallery, Guildford, Ash Barn, Petersfield, John Nevill, Canterbury, Burton Gallery, Somerset, Furneaux Gallery, Southwell-Brown Gallery; regular exhibitor R.I. *Work repro.:* Medici Society and Hampshire Magazine. *Address:* Stone House, Hawkley Hurst, Hants. *Signs work:* "Mervyn Goode."

GOODISON, Jack Weatherburn, M.A., 1928; asst. director, Fitzwilliam Museum, Cambridge, since 1939; deputy director since 1958; Senior Keeper, 1967; resigned, 1968; Controller, Monuments, Fine Arts and Archives Branch, Allied Commission for Austria (B.E.) (1944-46); Ehrenbürger, Technische Hochschule, Vienna (1946); Emeritus Fellow of Darwin College, Cambridge; *b* 17 Mar., 1903; *s* of late G. Goodison of Leeds. *Educ.:* Clifton College; King's College, Cambridge. *Publications:* Catalogue of Cambridge Portraits, Vol. I (1955), Fitzwilliam Museum, Catalogue of Paintings, Vol. I (1960, part author), Vol. II (1967, part author). *Address:* The Manor House, High St., Melbourn, Royston, Herts.

GORDON, (Alexander) Esmé, R.S.A. (1967), F.R.I.B.A. (1956), F.R.I.A.S. (1953), D.A. Edin. (1934), Hon. sec., R.S.A. (1973); architect, painter in watercolour; Owen Jones Scholar (1934); senior partner, Gordon & Dey, FF.R.I.B.A.; *b* Edinburgh, 12 Sept., 1910; *s* of Alexander Shand Gordon, W.S.; *m* Betsy McCurry; two *s,* one *d. Educ.:* Edinburgh Academy; *studied architecture* at Edinburgh College of Art (1928-34) under John Begg, John Summerson, E. A. A. Rowse and A. Bruce Thomson. *Publications:* A Short History of St. Giles Cathedral, Edinburgh; The Principles of Church Building, The Royal Scottish Academy 1826–1976. *Address:* 36 Heriot Row, Edinburgh. *Signs work:* see appendix.

GORDON, Susuan, City and Guilds Diploma in Fine Art (Sculpture); Theodora Gleichen Award to women sculptors; sculptor in metal, terracotta; part-time teacher; *b* Wembley, Middx., 23 Dec., 1942; *d* of Kenneth Sidney Gordon, company secretary. *Educ.:* Peterborough and St. Margarets High School, Harrow; *studied art* at Wimbledon School of Art (1965-66) under Miss Skinner, Hammersmith School of Art (1964-65), City and Guilds School of Art (1966-69) under Mr. Butler. *Exhib.:* one-man shows: Stoke Newington Library, R.A. Summer Exhibition, Mineral Gallery, Nicholas Treadwell Galleries. *Address:* 75 Glenarm Rd., Clapton, London E5. *Club:* R.B.S. *Signs work:* "S.G."

GORRARA, Mary, F.P.S., F.R.B.S. (1975); sculptor in clay, plaster, bronze, wood and stone; lecturer, Camden Arts Centre; *b* London, 1923; *d* of John Quin, stockbroker; *m* Primo Gorrara; one *s,* one *d. Educ.:* New Hall, Chelmsford; *studied art* at Camberwell School of Art; Kennington School of Art under Middleton Todd, Ronald Bisset; Sir John Cass School of Art. *Exhib.:* one-man shows: Studio Space Floral Hall, Covent Garden (1971), Camden Arts Centre, Hampstead (1972); mixed shows: Keats House, Kenwood House, Fenton House, Sculpture in the City, Richmond Festival, Lincoln Cathedral, R.A. *Work in permanent collections:* Camden Borough Council (sculpture lending library), Henderson Court, Hampstead, Teacher Training College, Doncaster (concrete fountain). *Address:* 29 Steeles Rd., London NW3. *Signs work:* "Mary Gorrara."

GOULD, Cecil Hilton Monk, Keeper and Deputy Director, National Gallery, since 1973 (Assistant Keeper, 1946); *b* London, 24 May, 1918; *s* of the late Lt.-Com. R. T. Gould, R.N. *Educ.:* Westminster School. *Publications:* An Introduction to Italian Renaissance Painting (1957), The Sixteenth-century Venetian School (1959), The Sixteenth-century Italian Schools (excluding the Venetian) (1962), Trophy of Conquest (1965), Leonardo (1975), National Gallery catalogues, articles in the main art journals in England and abroad. *Address:* 6 Palace Gate, London W8. *Club:* Reform.

GOURDIE, Thomas, M.B.E., D.A. (Edin.); Soc. of Scribes and Illuminators; art teacher, calligrapher, handwriting advisor; *b* Cowdenbeath, 18 May, 1913; *s* of Thomas Gourdie; *m* Lilias Taylor; one *s,* two *d. Studied art* at Edinburgh College of Art. *Official purchases:* Imperial War Museum; Kirkaldy A.G. *Publications:* Italic Handwriting and A Guide to Better Handwriting (Studio Vista), Puffin Book of Lettering (Penguin), Ladybird Book of Handwriting (Ladybird Books), Handwriting for Today and Improve your Handwriting (Pitman), I Can Write (Macmillan Educational). *Address:* 3 Doughlas St., Kirkaldy, Scotland.

GOURLEY, Alan Stenhouse, R.O.I. (1964), D.A. (Edin. 1932); artist in oil; Scottish mem. European Group (1974), mem. Chelsea Art Society (1975); *b* Ayr, 13 Apr., 1909. *Studied art* at Glasgow (1928) under Ancel Stronach, James Huck; Edinburgh (1929-31) under W. Gillies, Herbert Hendry; Slade (1945) under Randolph Schwabe, A. Gwynne-Jones; Ecole des Beaux Arts (Studio

Sabatti, 1938-40). *Exhib.:* one-man show, Mall Galleries (1974). *Work in permanent collections:* Port Elizabeth A.G., Luxembourg A.G. *Address:* 69 Freelands Rd., Bromley, Kent. *Signs work:* "A. S. Gourley."

GOVIER, James Henry, A.R.C.A. (1938); artist in oil, water-colour, engraver; art teacher; *b* Oakley, Bucks., 1 Aug., 1910; *s* of Harry Govier; *m* Freda Tye; one *s,* one *d. Studied art* at Swansea School of Art under Grant Murray, R.C.A., and Malcolm Osborne. *Exhib.:* R.A. *Official purchases:* Glynn Vivian A.G., Swansea, National Museum, Wales. *Address:* The Retreat, Hoxne Diss, Norfolk. *Signs work:* "GOVIER."

GRABOWSKI, Mateusz Bronislaw, M.Pharm. (Poland, 1931), Ph.C. (1948); pharmacist and art dealer; director of several companies; *b* Wizna, Poland, 15 July, 1904; *m*; two *s. Educ.:* Stefan Batory's University in Wilno. *Publication:* Pharmacy in Poland between Two Wars. *Address:* 86 Sloane Ave., London SW3 3AL.

GRADMANN, Erwin, Ph.D., o.Prof. E.T.H.; Ordinarius, art historian, director of Graphische Sammlung at the Technische Hochschule, Zürich, President of Gottfried Keller-stiftung; *b* 2 Aug., 1908; *s* of Arthur Gradmann, Ph.D.; *m* Maria Christine Gradmann. *Educ.:* at Vienna; *studied art* in Vienna under J. von Schlosser. *Publications:* Bildhauerzeichnung, Schweiz. Malerei und Zeichnung of 17th and 18th Century, Bau-Stilkunde, Urs Graf, French Drawings 18th Century, Phantastik und Komik, Aufsätze zur Architektur Indische Miniaturen, etc. *Address:* 82 Gloriastr., Zürich.

GRAHAM, David, R.B.A., R.P., A.R.C.A.; painter in oil; Senior Lecturer, Sir John Cass School of Art; *b* Hammersmith, 20 May, 1926; *s* of Philip Graham. *Educ.:* Latymer Foundation School; *studied art* at Hammersmith School of Art, St. Martin's School of Art, and R.C.A. *Exhib.:* R.A., R.P., Arts Council, Leicester Galleries, Brighton Art Gallery, etc. *Work in permanent collections:* Guildhall Art Gallery, I.L.E.A., Bristol Educ. Com., and private collections. *Address:* c/o Sir John Cass School of Art, City of London Polytechnic, Whitechapel High St., London E1. *Signs work:* "David Graham."

GRAINGER, Bernard Montague, A.R.C.A., F.R.S.A.; H.M. Corps Royal Engineers, Field Survey; artist, design consultant and engineer; *b* Paddock Wood, Kent, 16 July, 1907; *s* of William Montague Grainger; *m* Pattie Revell; two *s,* one *d. Educ.:* Ardingly College; *studied art* at Maidstone School of Art, R.C.A., Central School of Arts and Crafts. *Exhib.:* Paris, London and provinces. *Address:* Moorbrook, Bradwell, Derbyshire, via Sheffield, S30 2JJ. *Clubs:* Life member Sheffield University Mountaineering Club, Craven Pothole Club, Underground Survey Association, past-president of Derbyshire Pennine Club and Sheffield Society of Artists. *Signs work:* "B. M. GRAINGER."

GRANGE, Kenneth Henry, R.D.I., F.S.I.A. (1951); designer, display, typographical and industrial; *b* London, 1929; *s* of H. A. Grange. *Educ.:* Sir John Cass School and Wembley Hill Secondary; *studied art* at Willesden School of Art. *Address:* 7A Hampstead High St., London NW3. *Signs work:* "K. GRANGE."

GRANT, Duncan James Corrowr, R.D.I.; artist in oil and water-colour, draughtsman; *b* Rothiemurchus, Inverness, 21 Jan., 1885; *s* of Bartle Grant, army officer. *Educ.:* St. Paul's School; *studied art* at Westminster School of Art, Florence and at La Palette (Paris) under J. E. Blanche. *Exhib.:* many exhbns. at home and abroad. *Work in permanent collections:* Tate Gallery, Liverpool Art Gallery, Bucharest, Southampton, etc. *Work repro.:* in Penguin Painters by Raymond Mortimer and Modern English Painters by Roger Fry (Hogarth Press). *Address:* Charleston, Firle, Sussex. *Signs work:* "D. Grant."

GRANT, Ian MacDonald, D.A. (Glasgow, 1926), A.R.C.A. (1929), F.R.S.A.; oil and water-colour painter, pastel artist; art historian; *b* 6 Sept., 1904; *s* of H. M. Grant; *m* Margaret Gumuchian; one *d. Educ.:* privately; Glasgow School of Art (1922-26); Colorossi, etc., Paris (1927); R.C.A. (1927-30). *Exhib.:* one-man shows, Manchester, Salford, Winnipeg. *Official purchases:* Manchester Art Gallery, Salford Art Gallery, Rutherston Collection, Derby Art Gallery, Eccles Art Gallery. *Address:* Barrachnie, Aldersgreen Ave., High Lane, Stockport, Ches. *Club:* Lancs. and Ches. Car. *Signs work:* "IAN GRANT" (date below).

GRANT, John, F.S.I.A. (1956); Group Design Consultant, BP Trading Limited; previously Manager of the Council of Industrial Design's Designer Selection Service (1966-71); *b* Lewisham, 17 Dec., 1925; *s* of Robert Grant, Crown agent; *m* Sarah Harding; two *s. Educ.:* Southend High School. Joined E. K. Cole Group of companies in 1948, where he became deputy chief designer in 1957, specializing in radio, television, plastics, electronics, gas and electrical heating. Work exhibited in Europe and the United States, mainly under Ekco and Ferranti trade-marks. *Address:* 445 Woodgrange Drive, Thorpe Bay, Essex.

GRANT, Keith Frederick, A.R.C.A.; landscape painter and constructivist; teacher, St. Martin's School of Art, Camberwell School of Art; *b* Liverpool, 10 Aug., 1930; *m* Gisèle Barka (née Djouadi); one *d. Studied art* at Willesden School of Art (1952-55), Royal College of Art (1955-58). *Agent:* Roland, Browse & Delbanco, 19 Cork St., W1. *Address:* 6 Camden Studios, Camden St., London NW1 0LG. *Signs work:* "Keith Grant" or "K. F. Grant."

GRANT, Peter, A.N.C.A.; designer and sculptor; Taylour Scholarship, R.D.S. (1937), Nat. Art Scholarship (1935-38), 1st Prize Medal, Industrial and Pictorial Design; Asst. Prof. of Sculpture, Nat. College of Art, Dublin (1941-44); Founder-mem., Inst. of the Sculptors of Ireland; *b* Pomeroy, Co. Tyrone, N. Ireland, 5 Dec., 1915; *s* of James Grant, creamery manager; *m* Una Mac Eoin. *Educ.:* O'Connell's Schools, Dublin; *studied art* at Nat. College of Art, Ireland. *Exhib.:* R.H.A., Oireactas Institute of Sculptors, Gregynog Gallery, Wales, Holy Year exposition, Rome, Servite Arts Festival (1963), California International Sculpture Exhbn. (Municipal Gallery of Modern Art, Dublin). *Work in permanent collections:* Manannan, Coll. Brendan O'Regan; Warrior Statue, New York World Fair (1939); Ignatius Rice Memorial (Callan, Co. Kilkenny); bronze door design, Rome International Exhbn.; memorial to Fr. Manus Sweeney, Achill; wood carvings, Coll. Mrs. Conor Maguire, Servite Priory, Tyrone; Crucifix, life-size, Dungloe, Donegal, Sculpture models for Irish Room, Pittsburgh University, Sculpture, Roscrea Abbey, Ireland; 1916, Threshold of Freedom memorial (Ashbourne), Joseph Plunkett, bronze, Irish patriot, National Gallery, Dublin; Our Lady of the Sign of the Cross, Carrickmacross, Co. Monaghan. *Publications:* The Catholic Herald, The Universe, Art and Theatre, The World, etc. *Addresses:* Park Gate House Studio, 2 Nth. Cir. Rd., Dublin, 7, and 14 Seaview Ave., N. Clontarf, 3. *Signs work:* see appendix.

GRANVILLE-JACKSON, Alastair, Medallist in Art History (1951), B.A. Fine Arts (University of Cape Town, 1954), M.F.A. (Cranbrook Academy, U.S.A., 1967), F.R.S.A. (1971); sculptor in stone, wood, bronze, plastics, and lithographer; Prof. of Sculpture, Wayne State University; formerly Lecturer in Methods and Artists' Training, Brighton College of Art; Inaugurator of International Association of Plastic Arts in the Central African Federation; *b* Woodstock, South Africa; *y.s.* of William Jackson. *Educ.:* South African College and Sea Point; *studied art* at University of Cape Town (1951-54); Accademia di Belle Arti, Florence (1957), under Fazzini; Slade School (1957) under Reg Butler; Central School of Arts and Crafts (1963), bronze-casting; St. Martin's School of

Art (1962-63) under Caro; Cranbrook Academy of Art (1965-67) with Julius Schmidt. *Exhib.:* Yellow Window Studio, Johannesburg (1945), Arts Festival, Cape Town (1951), A.I.A. Gallery (1963. 1964), Heals' Art Gallery, London (1963), London Group (1964), Royal Birmingham Society of Arts (1965), Cranbrook Summer Exhibition (1967), 1st International Sculpture Exhbn., Blossom Centre, U.S.A. (1969), Michigan Biennial (1971), O. K. Harris Works of Art, New York (1972), Longridge, New York (1973). *Address:* Cranbrook Academy, Bloomfield Hills, Michigan, U.S.A. *Signs work:* see appendix.

GRASBY, Richard D., F.S.D-C., F.R.S.A.; lettering craftsman and artist; *b* Royal Tunbridge Wells, 19 July, 1934; *s* of E. D. Y. Grasby, M.D., F.R.C.O.G.; *m* Juliet; one *s,* one *d. Educ.:* Tonbridge Public School; *studied ar* at Tonbridge under Harvey Adams, and graphics and print at The Londcn School of Printing. *Address:* The Malt House, The Moor, Hawkhurst, Kent. *Club:* Naval & Military. *Signs work:* "Richard Grasby."

GRAVETT, Guy Patrick; picture maker (photographer and painter) in oil, water-colour and gouache; *b* Wye, Kent, 2 Nov., 1919. *Educ.:* Lewes County Grammar School; *studied art* at Brighton College of Art (1937-39) under Sallis Benney, Laurence Preston and Walter Bayes. *Exhib.:* various. *Publications:* History of Glyndebourne Opera (illustrated), various books on Wine. *Address:* Hope Lodge, Sussex Rd., Hurstpierpoint, Sussex BN6 9QL. *Club:* Royal Ocean Racing. *Signs work:* "Gravett" or "Guy Gravett" followed by year.

GRAY, Basil, M.A., C.B., C.B.E., F.B.A.; Keeper of Oriental Antiquities, B.M. (1946-69); deputy Keeper, 1940; *b* 21 July, 1904; *m* Nicolete Mary Gray (*q.v.*), née Binyon; two *s,* three *d. Educ.:* Bradfield; New College, Oxford. *Publications:* Writings on Islamic and Indian Painting and Chinese Ceramics and Japanese Woodcuts, etc. (1930-1975). *Club:* Savile. *Address:* Dawber's Hse., Long Wittenham, Abingdon, Oxon.

GRAY, Jane Campbell, N.D.D., A.R.C.A.; stained glass artist; *b* Lincoln, 1931; *d* of Archibald Denison Ross, M.A.; *m* Kiril Gray; two *d. Studied art* at Kingston School of Art (1948-52) under Reginald Brill; Royal College of Art (1952-55) under Lawrence Lee. Assisted Lawrence Lee with Coventry Cathedral nave windows (1955-58); designed for 'Heraldry Today', London, 4 years. Examples of own stained glass windows: St. Jerome's, Dawley; St. Mary's, Twickenham; St. Bernadette's, Hillingdon, Middx.; St. John's Episcopal, Perth; windows (26) in Hillingdon Hospital Chapel; and St. Peter's, Martindale, Cumbria; numerous coats-of-arms, decorative roundels, domestic windows and doors. *Address:* 117 Belmont Rd., Uxbridge, UB8 1QZ. *Signs work:* "Jane Gray," and see appendix.

GRAY, Milner Connorton, C.B.E., R.D.I., F.S.I.A., A.G.I., Hon. Des. R.C.A.; designer; founder partner, Design Research Unit; Master, Faculty of Royal Designers for Industry (1955-57); Pres., Soc. Industrial Artists and Designers (1943-49 and 1968); Master, Art Workers Guild (1963); mem. Royal Mint Advisory Committee; Artists' General Benevolent Inst.; *b* 1899; *s* of A. Campbell Gray; *m. Studied painting and design* at London University; Goldsmiths' College. *Publications:* The Practice of Design, Lund Humphries Ltd. (jointly with others); Package Design, Studio Ltd.; Lettering for Architects and Designers, jointly with Ronald Armstrong, Batsford Ltd. *Address:* 8 Holly Mount, Hampstead, London NW3. *Clubs:* Arts, Garrick.

GRAY, Nicolete; art historian and designer of lettering; Lecturer in Lettering. Central School of Art and Design; *b* Stevenage, 1911; *d* of Laurence Binyon; *m* Basil Gray (*q.v.*); two *s,* three *d. Educ.:* St. Paul's Girls' School, Lady Margaret Hall, Oxford, British School at Rome. *Publications:* 19th c. Ornamental Types and

Title Pages, 1938; Rossetti, Dante and Ourselves, 1947; The Paleography of Latin Inscriptions in Italy, 700-1000 A.D., 1948; Jacob's Ladder, a Bible Picture Book from English MSS. (1949); Lettering on Buildings (1960); Lettering as Drawing (1969). *Work:* lettering wall-relief in the Shakespeare Centre, Stratford. *Address:* Dawber's House, Long Wittenham, Abingdon, Berks.

GREAVES, Derrick, A.R.C.A. (1951); painter in oil; *b* Sheffield, 5 June, 1927; *s* of Harry Greaves, steelworker; *m* Mary Margaret Johnson; three children. *Educ.:* Elementary School and Junior Art Dept., Sheffield; *studied art:* R.C.A. (1948-52) and in Italy on scholarship (1952-54). *Exhib.:* Beaux Arts Gallery (1953, 1955), Pushkin Museum, Moscow (1957), Zwemmer Gallery (1958, 1960, 1962, 1963), London Galleries (1969, 1971), Whitechapel Art Gallery (1973), Belfast and Dublin (1972). *Work in permanent collections:* Tate Gallery, C.A.S., Arts Council, Ulster Museum, Walker Art Gallery, Leeds Art Gallery, Sheffield Art Gallery, Southampton Art Gallery, Municipal Gallery of Modern Art, Dublin, Art Gallery of S. Australia, Adelaide, etc. *Address:* 11 George St., Woburn, nr. Bletchley, Bucks. *Signs work:* "Derrick Greaves."

GREEN, Alan, A.R.C.A. (1958); artist in gravure; *b* London, 22 Dec., 1932; *s* of Frank J. Green, M.S.C., F.R.I.C.; *m* June Green; two *d. Educ.:* Colfes Grammar School, Lewisham; *studied art* at Royal College of Art (1955-58). *Exhib.:* Gallery de Gestlo, Hamburg (1975), Gallery Art in Progress, Munich (1974), Annely Juda Fine Art (1970, 1973, 1975). *Work in permanent collections:* McCrory Corp., N.Y., Power Gallery of Contemporary Art, Power Institute, Sydney, Veranneman Foundation, Belgium. *Address:* c/o Annely Juda Fine Art, 11 Tottenham Mews, London W1P 9PJ. *Signs work:* "ALAN GREEN" or "Alan Green."

GREEN, E. Helen: see BEALE, Elizabeth Helen.

GREEN, Jonathan, M.S.I.A., M.Illum.E.; environmental designer; *b* Liverpool, 1923; *m* Margaret Hart; one *s. Studied art* at Liverpool College of Art (1946-49), Sir John Cass Inst. (1949-50); exhibition design for B.B.C., EKCO, I.B.M., N.I.F.E. (1950-55); design consultant to I.B.M. in graphics, exhibition, interiors and computer centres (1955-59); developed artificial environment for County Laboratories (1959); New Century Concert Hall for C.W.S. (1960); offices for Armour Star, Beecham Group (1961-62). *Works published:* Design, Industrial Architecture, Light and Lighting, Times, Interior Design, Electrical Times. Graphic design for Rolls Royce, British Eagle (1965). Lighting design for Oil-Sheik palace Qatar (1966). Co-designer, Mandarin Hotel, Singapore (1969). Design Consultant, New Craigavon Hospital (1970-71), New Belfast City Hospital (1972). Lecturer in Lighting and 3D Design, Kingston Polytechnic (1966-72). *Clubs:* Nash House and No. 10. *Address:* Old Bartons, Whitchurch-on-Thames, Oxfordshire.

GREENBURY, Judith Pamela, A.R.W.A. (1971); painter in oil, water-colour; *b* Bristol, 17 Feb., 1924; *d* of Bernard Spielman; *m* C. L. Greenbury, M.D., three *s. Educ.:* Badminton School, Westbury-on-Trym, Bristol; *studied art* at West of England College of Art (1943-46) under George Sweet, Slade School (1946-47) under Prof. Schwabe. *Exhib.:* R.A., R.W.A., R.S.P.P., N.E.A.C., Bear Lane Gallery, Oxford, Mall Galleries, London. *Work in permanent collection:* R.W.E.A. *Address:* Milford Hse., 44 Chearsley Rd., Long Crendon, Aylesbury, Bucks. *Signs work:* "J.G."

GREENE, John A., A.R.C.A.; artist in oil and water-colour; lecturer at the Architectural Assoc. School. *Studied art* at R.C.A. *Exhib.:* R.A. *Official purchases:* Mural decorations at Morley College; for I.C.I.; for North-western

Electricity Board; paintings and designs for the British Transport Com mission and Alfred Holt & Co.; paintings and designs for the G.P.O.; architectural perspectives for Central Electricity Generating Board, Manchester University, I.C.I.; mural decoration for Manchester University; drawings and paintings in private collections. *Publication:* Elements of Drawing. *Address:* Greenbank, Wilsons Rd., Headley Down, Bordon, Hants.

GREENE, Patricia Margaret, A.R.C.A.; artist in water-colour. *Studied art* at R.C.A. *Work repro.:* drawings and designs for British Transport Commission and the G.P.O. *Work in private collections:* flower studies and collage embroideries. *Address:* Greenbank, Wilsons Rd., Headley Down, Bordon, Hants.

GREENHAM, Robert Duckworth, R.B.A. (1931), R.O.I. (1931); oil painter, black and white artist; *b* 6 Sept., 1906; *s* of the late George F. Greenham, M.B.E., M.I.E.E.; *m* 1st, Joan Benbow, two *d*; 2nd, Janet Williams (1964). *Educ.:* Dulwich College; *studied art* at Byam Shaw School of Art; R.A. Schools (British Inst. Scholarship, Landseer Scholarship, silver medal, bronze medals). *Exhib.:* R.A., N.E.A.C., R.P., London Group, R.I., R.B.A.; one-man show, New York City, 1937; R.B.A. Silver Medal (1948). *Official purchases:* Bathing Beach, by Australian Government; work mostly in private collections in G.B. and abroad. *Address:* Cheriton Manor, Gillingham, Dorset. *Signs work:* "Robert Greenham" (longhand); on work before 1938, "ROBERT D. GREENHAM"; or initials "R.D.G."

GREENMAN, Edwin, A.R.C.A., R.P., F.R.S.A.; artist in oils; head of dept., drawing, painting and design, Guildford School of Art; head of Sir John Cass School of Art, London; *b* Beckenham, Kent; *s* of Edwin Greenman; *m* Freda Johns; one *s*. *Studied art* at Beckenham School of Art (1926-29) under Henry Carr, R.A.; R.C.A. (1929-33) under Rothenstein, Spencer, Tristram and Malcolm Osbourne. *Exhib.:* engravings at World's Fair, New York (1938), and at Prague; paintings at R.A. Elected to Royal Society of Portrait Painters (1968). *Work in permanent collections:* V. & A. *Official purchases:* Contemporary Art Fund; Travelling Art Exhbns., Bureau Collections. *Address:* The Lilacs, Wield Rd., Medstead, Alton, Hants. *Club:* Chelsea Arts. *Signs work:* "Greenman."

GREENWOOD, Ernest, A.R.W.S. (1962), A.R.C.A. (1931-35), F.R.S.A.; artist in oil and water-colour; Inspector of Art Educ. for K.E.C.; *b* Welling, Kent, 12 Feb., 1913; *m* Eileen C. Greenwood; one *d*. *Educ.:* Gravesend Grammar School. *Exhib.:* R.A., N.E.A.C., R.I., R.B.A., Kensington Salon, Manchester; two-man show (with wife) at Kensington Gallery (1951 and 1953), Walker's (Nov., 1960), F.B.A. Gallery (1965), Zaydler Gallery (1971), Retrospective (Oct., 1972), New Metro Gallery, Folkestone. *Work in permanent collections:* Preston, Southend, Tate Gallery; private collections, U.S.A., Municipal Galleries of Brighton, Hastings, Hull. *Address:* Brushing Farm House, Broad St., nr. Hollingsbourne, Kent. *Signs work:* "Ernest Greenwood."

GREENWOOD, Sydney, A.T.D., A.R.W.A., F.R.S.A.; artist in lithography, water-colour, oil; vice-principal and head of dept. of Graphic and Fine Art, Southampton College of Art (1950-75); art master, Manchester Grammar School (1946-47); lecturer, Manchester Regional College of Art (1948-50); *b* Stalybridge, Ches., 11 Jan., 1913; *s* of Frederick Greenwood, textile designer; *m* Marjorie Olive Hernaman, M.A.; one *d*. *Educ.:* Manchester Municipal High School of Commerce; *studied art* under C. Hanney, later at Goldsmiths' College and Croydon School of Art. *Exhib.:* R.A., W. of England Academy, Redfern Gallery, Senefelder. *Publications:* Illustrations and Mural Paintings. *Address:* Cross Oaks, Sway. *Signs work:* "Sydney Greenwood."

GREG, Barbara, F.R.E.; artist in water-colour, engraver of wood and lino; *b*

Styal, Ches., 1900; *d* of H. P. Greg, industrialist; *m* N. T. Janes; one *s*, two *d*. *Educ.:* at Bedales; *studied art* at Slade School under Prof. Tombs, W. P. Robins; Central School, London. *Exhib.:* R.E., S.W.E., N.E.A.C. *Work in permanent collection:* Contemporary Art Society. *Publications:* illustrated, Fisherman's Log by Mayar Ashley Dodd, The Poacher's Handbook, Pastures New—Fresh Woods by Ian Niall, Enigmas of Natural History, More Enigmas of Natural History by Grant Watson. *Address:* 70 Canonbury Park South, London N1. *Signs work:* "Barbara Greg."

GRESTY, Kenneth H., F.R.S.A. (1971), F.I.A.L. (1966), A.T.D. (1951), D.A., Manc. (1950), N.D.D., painting (1950); Head of Visual Arts Dept., Smithills Schools Base, Bolton; Mem. Manchester Academy (1954); *b* Manchester, 17 May, 1928; *s* of Harry Gresty; *m* Marjorie Ingred Smith; four *s*. *Educ.:* Sale Grammar School; *studied art* at Manchester Regional College of Art under H. Williamson, R.W.A. (1944-46, 1948-51). *Exhib.:* R.A., Manchester Academy of Fine Arts. *Official purchase:* Rutherston Collection. *Work repro.:* in Cheshire Life, Lancashire Life, and local press. *Address:* Rowanhurst, Moss La., Sale, Ches. *Signs work:* "K. H. Gresty."

GRIBBIN, Lancelot Benedict, A.T.D. (1949); B.A. (Hons.) Hist. of Art (1953); painter in oil; lecturer, Victoria and Albert Museum; *b* Gateshead-on-Tyne, 7 Nov., 1927; *s* of L. B. Gribbin (senior), pharmacist; *m* Joanna Mary Satchell. *Educ.:* Dartford Grammar School; *studied art* at Sidcup School of Art under Ruskin Spear, A.R.A., Robin Guthrie, William Clause. *Exhib.:* R.A., N.E.A.C., London Group, National Soc.; one-man shows, Artists' House, Manette St., etc. *Address:* 8 Mile House La., St. Albans, Herts. *Signs work:* "L. B. GRIBBIN" (written with brush).

GRIFFIN, Frederick, R.O.I., N.S., S.G.A.; cartographer and designer; artist of landscape, architecture, travel, theatre, ballet and fashionable women in oil, gouache, acrylic; *b* Nottingham, 1906; *s* of John Griffin, civil engineer. *Educ.:* Nottingham Secondary School; *studied art* at Nottingham Art School under Mr. J. Else. *Exhib.:* R.A., Scottish R.A., R.B.A., R.O.I. (Mall Galleries), R.S.M.A. (Guildhall), R.I., N.E.A.C., N.S., London Group, S.G.A. *Work repro.:* Ideal Home, Good Housekeeping, Modern Woman, Designers in Britain, etc., Press advertisements, posters and Press ads. for B.O.A.C., B.T.A., British Railways, Shipping Cos., etc. *Address:* 182 Haverstock Hill, London NW3. *Club:* Arts Theatre. *Signs work:* "Frederick Griffin."

GRIFFING, Robert Perkins, Jr., B.A. (Yale University, 1935), M.F.A. (Princeton University, 1940), D.F.A. (Hon.), Univ. of Hawaii; Honorary Consultant, Berenice Bishop Museum, Hawaii; *b* Long Island, N.Y., 27 Mar., 1914; *m* Marjorie Lewis Griffing; one *s*, one *d*. *Educ.:* Phillips Academy, Mass. (1927-31), Yale University (1931-35), Princeton University (1936-39), University of Paris (1937). *Publications:* articles in Art Bulletin, Museum, Architectural Record, Bulletin of Honolulu Academy of Arts, The Barbara Hutton Collection of Chinese Porcelain, Honolulu (1956), The Art of the Korean Potter (New York, The Asia Society, 1968). *Address:* 3887 Owena St., Honolulu, 15. *Clubs:* Pacific (Honolulu), Elizabethan (Conn.).

GRIFFITHS, Tom; painter, designer and illuminator on vellum; Senior lecturer, Norwich School of Art (1942-49). *Educ.:* City of Norwich School; *studied art* at Norwich School of Art, Heatherleys' and The Grosvenor (London). *Exhib.:* R.A., R.O.I., N.S., and provincial art galleries; one-man shows of townscapes (Norwich). *Official purchases:* many illuminated vellums include Loyal Address (Norwich); Freedom Scrolls for H.M. Queen Elizabeth the Queen

Mother, Sir John Barbirolli (King's Lynn); the Royal Air Force and Regimental presentations and the County War Memorial Book of Remembrance, Norwich Cathedral. *Address:* 15 Essex St., Norwich. *Signs work:* "Tom Griffiths."

GRIGSBY, John Higham, N.D.D., A.T.D., A.R.E. (1973); artist in etching and water-colour; Head of Art Dept., Selhurst Girls' School, Croydon; *b* Newcastle-under-Lyme, Staffs., 18 Dec., 1940; *s* of Alfred Edward Grigsby; *m* Valerie Butler. *Educ.:* Longton High School, Stoke-on-Trent; *studied art* at Stoke-on-Trent College of Art, Leicester College of Art. *Exhib.:* Young Contemporaries, R.A., N.E.A.C., R.W.E.A., R.W.S. Galleries, Mall Galleries, F.B.A. Touring Exhbns., Woburn Abbey, Glasgow Institute. *Work in permanent collections:* Medici Gallery; City Gallery, Milton Keynes; Reading Museum, Whitgift Foundation; Graves Gallery, Sheffield; Open University; National Museum of Wales; Hertfordshire and Mid-Glamorgan Education Authorities; numerous private collections. *Address:* 127 Ravenscroft Rd., Beckenham, Kent. *Signs work:* "John Grigsby."

GRIMSHAW, Gladys, A.R.C.A. (1934); potter; awarded Medaille de Bronze, Paris Salon (1963); visiting lecturer, Oxford School of Art; lecturer for Wedgwood's; *b* Nelson; *d* of Harry Elliott, master printer; *m* Reginald Grimshaw, A.R.C.A., A.T.D.; two *s*. *Educ.:* Nelson Grammar School; *studied art* at Liverpool School of Art under George Marples (1928-31), R.C.A. (1931-34), Sir William Rothenstein and Staite Murray. *Exhib.:* R.A., R.B.A., Paris Salon, G.I., W.I.A.C. Awarded Mention d'Honneur, Paris (1957); religious sculpture exhbn., Edinburgh and Oxford and Cambridge. *Address:* The Old Rectory, Noke, Oxford. *Signs work:* "G. Grimshaw."

GRIMSHAW, Reginald, A.R.C.A., A.T.D., F.R.S.A.; head, Oxford School of Art; asst. teacher, Cheltenham School of Art (1934-35); Maidstone School of Art (1935-40); artist in oil and water-colour; *b* Farsley, Yorks., 27 Sept., 1910; *s* of Harry Grimshaw; *m* Gladys Grimshaw, A.R.C.A.; two *s*. *Educ.:* Pudsey Grammar School; *studied art* at Pudsey School of Art (1927-30), Leeds College of Art (1930-31), R.C.A. (1931-34) under Sir William Rothenstein and Prof. Tristram. *Exhib.:* R.A., R.B.A., A.I.A. *Address:* The Old Rectory, Noke, Oxford. *Signs work:* "R. Grimshaw."

GRINLING, Antony Gibbons, M.C. (1918), M.B.E. (1943); sculptor and director of companies; *b* 6 Jan., 1896; *s* of Gibbons Grinling; *m* Cicely Somers; one *s*, three *d*. *Educ.:* Harrow. *Exhib.:* R.A., G.I., Tooth's Galleries, Wildenstein's Galleries, Worthing and Leicester Art Galleries, Upper Grosvenor Gallery. *Address:* Estate Yard House, Dyrham, Chippenham, Wilts. *Club:* The Garrick. *Signs sculpture:* "A.G.G."

GRINSTEAD, John, A.R.C.A. (1950); designer; painter and senior lecturer at the Polytechnic, Kingston upon Thames; *b* Leeds. *Educ.:* Wakefield, Central School of Art and Design WC1, and R.C.A. *Exhib.:* R.A., R.B.A. Galleries and various public art galleries. *Official purchases* include presentations to H.M. the Queen Mother; H.R.H. the Princess Margaret and the late Duchess of Kent, and Earl Attlee. *Work repro.:* R.A. Illustrated catalogue, Book Design and Production, Odhams Press, etc. *Address:* 3 Riverbank, Hampton Court, East Molesey, Surrey. *Signs work:* "John Grinstead."

GROAG, Jacqueline, F.S.I.A. *Educ.:* Vienna Art Academy, after graduating several years in Paris. Field of design: printed textiles, wallpaper, laminated plastics, etc.; works now for various important British industries. *Work repro.:* House and Gardens, Ambassador, Vogue, Harpers, Studio, Designs, Domus, etc.

Exhib.: Vienna, Milan, Paris, London, New York. *Address:* 26 Clifton Hill, St. John's Wood, London NW8.

GROGAN, Michael Douglas, Dip. A.D. (Painting), M.A. (R.C.A.); painter in water-colour and oils, etcher, portraiture, illustrator; temp. illustrator, British Museum; *b* Lyndhurst, Hants., 23 Feb., 1947; *m* Lynne Fiona Kerridge, M.A. (R.C.A.). *Educ.:* School of Navigation, Warsash (1963); *studied art* at Winchester (1967-68), Liverpool (1968-71), Royal College of Art (1971-74), Cité Internationale des Arts, Paris (1973). *Exhib.:* one-man show: Gallery 273; mixed show: Jordan Gallery. *Publication:* contributed to Vol. II of Sutton Hoo Treasures. *Addresses:* 1 Linthorpe Rd., Stamford Hill, London N16; 106 Stannington Cres., Totton, Hants. *Signs work:* "Michael Grogan."

GROSVENOR, Stella Athalie (Mrs.), R.B.S., Society Portrait Sculptors, Slade Dip. Fine Art (1937); sculptor in bronze, resin, stone, wood, painter in oil; *b* Beaconsfield; *d* of Sidney Henderson; *m* Hugh N. W. Grosvenor, A.R.I.B.A. *Educ.:* St. Margaret's School, Hampstead; *studied art* at Slade School under Prof. Schwabe and Prof. Gerrard. *Exhib.:* group shows, Society Portrait Sculptors, Hampstead Artists Council, R.A., Travers Gallery, Erica Bourne Gallery; one-man show, Foyles, London (1968). *Publications:* Art Editor, National Trade Press; Illustrated, Caxton Publishing Co. *Address:* 35 Flask Walk, London NW3. *Club:* Hampstead Artists Council. *Signs work:* "A. Grosvenor."

GROVE, Leonard Robert Allen, B.A., F.S.A., F.R.E.S., F.M.A.; curator, Maidstone Art Gallery and Museum and Tyrwhitt-Drake Museum of Carriages (since 1948); *b* 27 Nov., 1910. *Educ.:* St. Olave's Grammar School, Tower Bridge; University College, London. *Publications:* contributor to: Antiquaries Journal, Archaeologia Cantiana, Berkshire Archæological Journal, Yorkshire Archæological Journal (Medieval Art, etc.), etc. *Address:* Chillington House, Maidstone.

GROVES, Lavender, R.O.I.; Nat. Dip. Design, Oil Painting (1 Aug., 1954); Inter. M. of E. Arts and Crafts (1 Aug., 1951); artist in oil and ceramics; *b* Manchester, 8 Oct., 1932; *d* of Michael Peer Groves, master brewer; *m* Mark Leo Beard (*q.v.*). *Educ.:* Privately; *studied art* at Chelsea School of Art. *Address:* Upton Pottery, 17 High St., Upton-upon-Severn, Worcs. *Club:* Budokwai. *Signs work:* "GROVES."

GROVES-RAINES, Ralph Gore Antony, B.A. (Camb.); *b* 8 June, 1913; *s* of Lt.-Col. Ralph Gore Devereux Groves-Raines, D.S.O. *Educ.:* Tonbridge School, Christ's College, Camb.; Munich (1930). *Address:* Killinchy, Co. Down, N. Ireland. *Signs work:* "A.G.R." or "ANTONY GROVES-RAINES."

GRUBB, Roy, F.R.H.S.; freelance artist specializing in botanical and still-life, black and white; official artist G.H.Q. India (1941-45); art editor, Army Educ. Publications, Bombay (1945-46); *b* London, 12 Oct., 1915; *s* of William Grubb; *m* Ann Cowley. *Educ.:* St. Egbert's, Chingford; *studied art* at Leyton School of Art. *Work repro.:* advertising illustrations in national Press; and in Graphis, Modern Publicity, Designers in Britain, etc. *Publications:* Backgrounds to Living (Studio), Selected Orchidaceous Plants (Grubb). *Address:* Lavender House, Chaldon Common Rd., Caterham, Surrey. *Signs work:* "Grubb."

GRÜNEWALD, Eleanor Mavis (née Wilson), Inter. Exam. in Art and Crafts (1949), N.D.D. Painting (1951), A.T.D. (1952); artist in oil, pastel, charcoal; art teacher (1956-58) at Heginbottom School of Art; *b* Stockton-on-Tees, 2 Mar., 1931; *d* of Harold Wilson. *Educ.:* Richard Hind School, Stockton; *studied art* at Middlesbrough School of Art, Leeds College of Art. *Exhib.:* Middlesbrough A.G., Macclesfield A.G., Frankfurt/Main in Haus Riederwald, Penthouse Gallerie,

Römer. *Official purchases:* Stadt Frankfurt; Stadt Wiesbaden; Middlesbrough Town Council. *Address:* Frankfurt/Main, Fahrgasse 21. *Club:* Berufsverband Bildender Künstler, Frankfurt. *Signs work:* "Mavis Wilson Grünewald."

GUEST, Alan Sexty; artist in oil; teacher, private tutor, lecturer, autodidact; teacher, Coventry City Council; *b* 11 Dec., 1920; *s* of Robert Sexty Guest, B.A., accountant; *m* Kathleen Guest; two *s,* five *d. Educ.:* Woodlands, nr. Doncaster. *Exhib.:* Nuneaton A.G., Coventry, Chalk Farm; two paintings selected by BBC Search for an Artist; TV appearances. *Commission:* by owner of L'escargot, now hanging in the Curragh. *Address:* 11 Sharp Cl., Holbrooks, Coventry. *Club:* Unicorn. *Signs work:* "A. Guest."

GUEVARA José; painter-ecrivain de théâtre; creator of the technique today known as "oil by combustion of the pigment"; *b* Puebla de Guzmán (Huelva), Espagne, 12 Mar., 1928. *Educ.:* Instituto de Segunda Enseñanza "La Rábida" de Huelva, Escuela Superior de Comercio de Sevilla; *studied art* at Academia Provincial de Bellas Artes (1939-40-41-42, Prof. Pedro Gómez y Enrique Garcia Orta), Atelier Guillermo Rodriguez (1955-56-57), Atelier Prof. Armando Balloni (1955-56-57-58); Armando Balloni has been only one teacher. Travelled through five continents and taken part in many international competitions, as the XXXI Bienal de Venecia, VII Bienal de São Paulo, II Bienal de Paris, VI Bienal de Alexandria, I Bienal de Arte Español de Paris, etc., etc.; 100 one-man shows and participated in 300 collective exhibitions. *Work in permanent collections:* Museo Español de Arte Contemporaneo, Madrid; Musée d'Art Moderne, Melbourne; Musée d'Art Contemporain, Moscow; Galleria Nacional de Art Moderna, Roma; Musée d'Art Moderne, Buenos Aires; Musée d'Art Moderne, Montevideo; Musée d'Art Moderne, Baghdad; Instituto de Arte Panameño, Panama; Pinacotheque Municipale de Jesi, Italia; Musée d'Art Moderne de Gallarate, Italia; Museo de Marsala, Italia; Musée de Arte Moderno del Altoaragon, Huesca; Musée Redondo del Riojana, Santander; Circulo de la Amistad, Cordoba; Club La Rábida, Sevilla; Universidad L. de Huesca. *Publications:* The Telephones, After the Escalade, The Revendiction of Judas, 1, 2, 3, 4, 5, 6, 7, 8, 9, 10, Aut! etc., etc. *Address:* 20 Rue de Penthièvre, Sceaux, 92, France. *Signs work:* see appendix.

GUGGENHEIM, Peggy, H.F.R.C.A.; Honorary Citizen of Venice and Commandatore; art collector, museum director and writer; director, own museum of modern art in Venice and formerly of Guggenheim Jeune, London (1938-39) and Art of This Century, New York (1942-47); *b* New York, 26 Aug., 1898; *d* of Benjamin Guggenheim, mining engineer; *m* Florette Seligman; two children. *Educ.:* privately tutored. *Publications:* Art of This Century (1942), Out of This Century (Dial Press, 1946), Una Collezionista Ricorda (Cavallino, Venice, 1956), Confessions of an Art Addict (Deutsch, London, Macmillan, New York, 1960, and Verlegt bei Kindler, Munich, 1962). *Address:* Palazzo Venier dei Leoni, Venice. *Signs work:* "Peggy Guggenheim."

GUISE, T. G. M.: painter in oil, emulsion, water-colour. *Address:* 25 Dean Bank Lane, Edinburgh EH3 5BS.

GUMUCHIAN, Margaret, D.A. (Manc.), A.T.D., F.R.S.A.; artist in oil, gouache and lithography; *b* Manchester, 8 June, 1927; *d* of Leon Gumuchian; *m* Ian MacDonald Grant; one *d. Studied art* at the Regional College of Art, Manchester. *Exhib.:* R.A., R.B.A., M.A.F.A., S.M.P. regional galleries, Paris, and Biarritz. *Official purchases:* School Loans Collection, Salford; Salford Art Gallery, Rutherston Loans Collection and various private collections. *Address:* Barrachnie, Aldersgreen Ave., High Lane, Stockport, Cheshire. *Signs work:* "Mgt. Gumuchian."

GUNN, James Thomson, F.I.A.L., A.I.P.D.; artist in oil, water-colour, gouache and designer; *b* Gorebridge, 9 Apr., 1932; *s* of late George J. T. Gunn, B.Sc.; *m* Mary Lang (née Linton); one *d. Educ.:* Dalkeith High School; *studied art* at Edinburgh College of Art (1953-56), awarded Andrew Grant Travelling Scholarship (1956), travelled in Holland, France, Germany, Austria, Switzerland and Italy; studied painting privately. *Exhib.:* R.S.A., R.S.W., S.S.A., Pitlochry Festival Theatre (1970), Hopetoun House (1970), and one-man shows. *Work in permanent collections:* Argyll Educ. Com., represented in private collections in Britain and Canada, executed mural paintings, magazine illustration and tapestry embroidery design. *Address:* 3 Park Cres., Easthouses, Dalkeith, Midlothian, Scotland. *Signs work:* see appendix.

GURR, George Albert; oil and water-colour artist; *b* 11 July, 1911; *m*; two children. *Studied art* at Leicester College of Art (Middleton Todd, A.R.A., 1932-37). *Exhib.:* N.E.A.C. (1937, 1946, 1948), Nottingham Castle, Leicester Soc. of Artists. *Official purchases:* Nottingham Educ. Com., and private collector. *Address:* 6 Westcotes Drive, Leicester. *Signs work:* "George Gurr."

GUTHRIE, Jane Gordon, A.R.C.A. (1950); painter in oil and water-colour; *b* Farningham, Kent, 1 May, 1927; *d* of Alexander Gordon Guthrie, A.M.I.Mech.E., retired company director; *m* John M. R. Best-Shaw; two *s,* one *d. Educ.:* St. Leonards School, St. Andrews, Fife; *studied art* at Sidcup Art School (1944-46), Goldsmiths' College Art School (1946-47) and R.C.A. under Ruskin Spear, Robin Guthrie, Leonard Appelbee and Carel Weight (1947-50), Oskar Kokoschka (1959). *Exhib.:* R.A., N.E.A.C., Young Contemporaries; first one-man show (1971), Upper Street Gallery. *Address:* The Stone House, Boxley, Maidstone, Kent. *Signs work:* "Jane G. Guthrie."

GUTHRIE, Kathleen; painter in oils; *d* of E. G. Maltby, M.D.; *m* 1st, Robin Guthrie, one *s*; 2nd, John Cecil Stephenson. *Educ.:* St. Michael's Hall, Hove; *studied art* at Slade School, Royal Academy Schools. *Exhib.:* one-man shows: Boston, U.S.A., Little Gallery, London, Kalman Gallery, Manchester, New End Gallery; Retrospective Exhibition, Drian Gallery (1966); retrospective: Brighton Gallery (1968), Trentham Gallery, Emsworth (1969), Erica Bourne Gallery (1972); mixed shows and group shows in England, France and Italy. *Address:* 6 Mall Studios, Tasker Rd., London NW3. *Signs work:* "Kathleen Guthrie."

GUTMAN, Nachum, F.I.A.L. (1959); painter in oils and water-colour; author; prize for water-colour at 3rd Biennale, São Paulo, Brazil (1955); Gold Medal, Int. Ex. Paris (1936); Hans Christian Andersen Honorary Prize (1962); *b* Telenesht, Russia, 15 Nov., 1898; *s* of Ben Zion (Gutman); *m* Dora Gutman; one *s. Studied art* at Bezalel Art School, Jerusalem, and at Vienna, Berlin and Paris (1920-27). *Exhib.:* Gallerie Billet (Paris, 1929); Centaur (Brussels, 1929); Biennale Venice; Museum of Modern Art, Boston; Metropolitan Museum, New York (1953); John Heller Gallery, N.Y. (1954); O'Hana Gallery, London (1955); Musée d'Art Moderne, Paris (1960). *Work repro.:* The Arts (Oct., 1928), The Studio (Feb., 1952). *Address:* Achad Haam 136, Tel Aviv, Israel. *Signs work:* see appendix.

GUYNET-PECHADRE, Madeleine; Chevalier de la Légion d'Honneur; Officier de l'Ordre des Arts et des Lettres; Officier de l'Ordre de Vasa; Conservateur du Musée National de Vallaures; appointed by the Directoire des Musées de France to the Musée du Louvre as Conservateur Chef du Services des relations exterieures (from 1 Oct., 1957); director of the Museums of Nice (1951); *b* Paris, 10 Feb., 1905; *d* of Adhemar Pechadre, Deputy, National Assembly; *m* Daniel Guynet; two *s. Educ.:* École du Louvre; University of Paris; *studied art* under Profs. Marcel Aubert, Robert Rey, Mauricheau-Beaupre, Gabriel Rouches. *Address:* Musée National de Vallaures 06220.

GWYNNE-JONES, Allan, D.S.O., R.A., R.P.; painter, etcher, ex-Professor of Painting, R.C.A.; subsequently Senior Lecturer, Slade School, till 1959; trustee, Tate Gallery, 1939-46; *b* 27 Mar., 1892; served as Lieut. in 1914-18 War in Welsh Guards; mentioned in despatches twice, wounded twice, D.S.O. (1916); *s* of Ll. Gwynne-Jones; *m* Elizabeth Rosemary Allan, 1937; one *d*. *Educ.:* Bedales School; Slade School. *Official purchases:* Chantrey Bequest; collections of H.M. the Queen, H.M. the Queen Mother, Tate Gallery, British Museum, V. & A. Museum, War Artists and in principal provincial galleries and national galleries of S. Africa and Australia. *Publications:* Catalogue of Portraits for Arts Council; Portrait Painters; A Way of Looking at Pictures; Notes for Art Students (Phoenix House); Introduction to Still-Life (Staples Press). *Address:* Eastleach Turville, Cirencester, Glos. *Club:* Athenæum. *Signs work:* "Allan Gwynne-Jones" or "A.GJ."

H

HACCURIA, Maurice; painter and sculptor; distinctions and mentions: Jeune Peinture Belge (1958), Prix Talens (1959), Prix de la Critique (1962), Prix Olivetti (1961), Prix Europe (1962); Fellow of Institut International des arts et des lettres (Kreuzlingen). Teacher; *b* Goyer, 13 Jan., 1919. Autodidact. *Exhib.:* (1951-65) Antwerp, Brussels, Rotterdam, Brugge, Ljubljana, Grenchen, Lausanne, Venice, Trieste, Vienna, Lille, Frankfurt-am-Main, Köln, Skopje, Ostend, Knokke. *Work in permanent collections:* Royal Library (Brussels), Belgian Government, Middelheim (Antwerp), Musée d'art contemporain de Skopje, Art Gallery Zodiaque (Brussels), public and private collections in Belgium, Rotterdam, Suisse, New York. *Address:* Stwg. op Gelrode 88, Rotselaar 15. *Signs work:* see appendix.

HACKETT, Frank, A.M.A.; Manager, Luton Museum and Art Gallery, Wardown Park, Luton, Beds.

HACKNEY, Alfred, R.W.S., A.R.E. (1951), D.A., Edin. (1950); artist in etching, engraving, pen and water-colour; senior lecturer, Medway College of Art, Rochester; free-lance illustrator and designer; *b* Yorks., 18 May, 1926; *s* of John Thomas Hackney. *Educ.:* Burslem School of Art, Stoke-on-Trent; *studied art* at Edinburgh College of Art and travelling scholarship to France and Italy. *Exhib.:* R.A., London Group, Soc. of Staffordshire Artists, S.E.A., R.E., R.S.A., S.S.A. *Work in permanent collection:* R.A., and numerous public and private collections. *Address:* Butts Hill Cottage, Pilgrims Way, Wrotham, Kent. *Signs work:* "Alfred Hackney."

HACKNEY, Arthur, V.P.R.W.S. (1973), R.E., A.R.C.A.; etcher; painter in oil and water-colour; Head of Dept. (Printmaking), West Surrey College of Art and Design; Mem. Fine Art Board, Council for National Academy Awards (1975); *b* Stainforth, Yorks., 13 Mar., 1925; *s* of John Thomas Hackney. *Educ.:* Stoke-on-Trent; *studied art* at Burslem School of Art and R.C.A. (travelling scholarship). *Exhib.:* R.A., R.E., R.W.S. *Work in permanent collections:* V. & A. Museum; Bradford City Art Gall.; G.L.C.; Russell Smith Trust; Nottingham Castle Art Gallery; Keighley Art Gallery; Wakefield City Art Gall.; Preston Art Gallery; Graves Art Gallery (Sheffield); Wellington Art Gallery (N.Z.); Stoke-on-Trent Art Gallery. *Address:* Woodhatches, Spoil La., Tongham, Surrey. *Signs work:* see appendix.

HADFIELD, Miles; illustrator and author; *b* Birmingham, 1903; *s* of Heywood Hadfield, solicitor. *Educ.:* Bradfield College; Birmingham University; *studied art* at Birmingham School of Art. *Publications:* The Gardener's Companion (1936), Everyman's Wild Flowers (1938), An English Almanac (1950), British Trees (1957), all published by Dent, Pioneers in Gardening (Routledge & Kegan Paul, 1955), Gardening in Britain: An Historical Outline (Hutchinson, 1960), The Twelve Days of Christmas (with John Hadfield) (Cassell, 1961), Gardens of Delight (with John Hadfield) (Cassell, 1964), The Art of the Garden (Studio Vista, 1965), Landscape with Trees (Country Life, 1967), Topiary and Ornamental Hedges (A. & C. Black, 1971). *Address:* 35 Laugherne Rd., Worcester WR2 5LP. *Signs work:* "M.H."

HAFFKIN, Arthur; Director, Rotunda Gallery, Hampstead. *Educ.:* Grocers, City University London; *studied art* at St. Martin's School of Art under Kenneth Martin, Ruskin Spear; Central School of Art. *Address:* The Penthouse, 116-118 Finchley Rd., London NW3 5HT.

HAGGAR, Reginald George, Hon. M.Univ. (Keele) (1972), R.I. (1952), A.R.C.A. (1928), F.R.S.A., Pres. Soc. of Staffordshire Artists (1945); water-colour painter and ceramic designer; Extension Lecturer, University of Keele Dept. Adult Education; Chairman, North Staffs Watercolour Group; Pres. Northern Ceramic Society; Pres. Mason Collectors Club; *b* 25 Dec., 1905; *s* of Ernest Edward Haggar; *m* Dorothy Frances Wood. *Exhib.:* R.A., R.S.A., R.I., R.W.A., R.B.A., R.A. Industrial Exhbn. (1935), and "Britain Can Make It" (1946). *Official purchases:* Watercolours purchased for Ipswich, Dudley, Yeovil, Stafford, Walsall, Leek, and Stoke-on-Trent Art Galleries. *Address:* 337 Stone Rd., Hanford, Stoke-on-Trent.

HAGUE, Jonathan, N.D.D., A.T.D., Netherland State Scholarship; *b* Llandudno, 18 Nov., 1938. *Studied art* at Liverpool College of Art (1957-63), Royal Academy of Fine Art, The Hague (1964-66). *Exhib.:* one-man shows: The Germeente Museum, The Hague; The Royal Institute Gallery, Piccadilly. *Address:* 21 Leam Terr., Leamington Spa, Warwicks. *Signs work:* "HAGUE."

HAIG, George Douglas (The Earl Haig), professional M.S.S.A.; painter in oil and water-colour; *b* London, 15 Mar., 1918; *s* of F.M. Earl Haig. *Educ.:* Stowe and Christ Church, Oxford; *studied art* at Camberwell School of Art (1945-47) under Victor Pasmore, and privately with Paul Maze. *Exhib.:* Redfern Gallery and in Edinburgh; paintings in collections of Arts Council and Scottish National Gallery of Modern Art. *Address:* Bemersyde, Melrose. *Signs work:* "Haig."

HAILSTONE, Harold William, cartoonist and illustrator in oil, water-colour, black and white; Flt. Lt. R.A.F. (1939-45); official artist, R.A.F. (1944-45); *b* London, 1897; *s* of William Edward Hailstone, dentist; *m* 1st, Olivia Henderson (decd. 1928); three *d. Educ.:* Sir Andrew Judd's School, Tonbridge; *studied art* at Goldsmiths' College School of Art. *Exhib.:* War Artists' Exhbn. *Work in permanent collection:* Imperial War Museum. *Official purchases:* War Artists' Advisory Com. *Work repro.:* in Punch, Illustrated London News, Strand Magazine, Pearsons', Humorist, Passing Show, Bystander, Tatler, Sketch, Britannia and Eve. *Address:* Corneys Cottage, Hadlow, nr. Tonbridge, Kent. *Signs work:* "Hailstone."

HAINAULT, June, M.F.P.S.; painter; on committee, Free Painters and Sculptors; *d* of Henry Lane Eno, of Princeton, U.S.A.; divorced; two *s. Studied art* at Regent St. Polytechnic; Heatherley School of Art under Ian Macnab and F. Whiting. *Exhib.:* one-man: Carnival '75, University of Manchester (1975), Loggia Gallery (1972, 1975), Upper St. Gallery, Islington (1972, 1975), Cockpit Theatre (1970), New Town Gallery, Uckfield (1969, 1976), Lightning Mark, Rye (1967), Il Traghetto Gallery, Venice (1966), St. Martin's Gallery, London

(1965). *Address:* The Oast House, Five Ashes, nr. Mayfield, Sussex. *Club:* Surrey and Kent Flying. *Signs work:* "Hainault."

HALE, Helen Margaret; painter and sculptor; *b* Harpenden, 18 Apr., 1936; *d* of Robert Hale; *m* Horne Shepherd. *Educ.:* St. George's School, Harpenden; *studied art* at St. Martin's School of Art and Sir John Cass School of Art. *Exhib.:* group shows: London, Edinburgh, Paris. *Address:* 15 Thurlow Rd., Hampstead, London NW3. *Clubs:* Free Painters and Sculptors, National Society, Women's International Art Club, Hampstead Artists' Council. *Signs work:* "HALE."

HALE, Sydney Thomas; Birmingham Art Circle (1940-47); artist in oil, pastel and pen and ink; teacher of Drawing and Painting (life and portraiture) at Birmingham College of Art and Coventry School of Art; *b* May, 1907; *m* Doris Frowen-Hale; one *s. Educ.:* Grammar School; Birmingham College of Arts and Crafts (B. Fleetwood-Walker, A.R.A., 1939-43). *Exhib.:* R.B.A., London Group, R.A., R.B.S.A.; one-man shows in Birmingham and W. Bromwich. *Work repro.:* Portraits in oils of A. P. Marshall, Judge Donald Hurst, Dr. Sworn, Sydney Hill, etc. *Address:* 180 Bromford La., W. Bromwich, W. Midlands. *Clubs:* Coventry and Warwicks. Art Soc. *Signs work:* "HALE" (followed by last two figures of date of year).

HALL, Arthur Henderson, A.R.C.A. (1930), R.E., R.W.S., Prix de Rome in Engraving (1931); painter in oil and water-colour; draughtsman, etcher and illustrator; *b* Sedgefield, Co. Durham, 25 June, 1906; *s* of Charles Hall; *m* Frances Bruce; one *s*, one *d. Studied art* at Accrington and Coventry Schools of Art, R.C.A., and British School in Rome. *Exhib.:* R.A., R.W.S., R.E.; London Group. *Official purchases:* B.M., Leamington Public Art Gallery, Cambridge University. *Work repro.:* History of Britain, Child Education, Penguin books on gardening, children's books, Readers' Digest, Library of Gardening. *Address:* 15 Church Rd., E. Molesey, Surrey. *Signs work:* "A. HENDERSON HALL."

HALL, Clifford, R.O.I., N.S. artist; *b* London, 24 Jan., 1904. *Educ.:* R.A. Schools, 1925-28; *studied art:* André l'Hôte, Paris, 1928. *Exhib.:* one-man shows, Roland, Browse and Delbanco and Leicester Galleries, R.A., R.P., R.O.I., N.E.A.C., R.B.A., London Group, N.S., Paris Salon, National Gallery, Some Contemporary British Painters, Wildenstein Gallery (1958), Fact and Idea, South London Gallery (1958). *Official purchases:* Birmingham, Darlington, Altrincham (Manchester), V. & A., S. Kensington, Official War Artists, Contemporary Art Soc., Brooklyn Museum, U.S.A., National Gallery of Wales, Melbourne (Felton Bequest), Sydney, National Gallery of New South Wales, Belfast, London Museum, Hertford College, Oxford, Brasenose College, Oxford, Nuffield Foundation, Hull University Art Collection, Hastings Art Gallery, Arts Council. *Address:* 24 Newton Rd., London W2. *Signs work:* "Clifford Hall."

HALL, Sir Julian, Bart., B.A.; formerly art critic of Truth; *b.* S. Africa, 22 Feb., 1907. *Educ.:* Eton; Balliol College, Oxford. *Address:* 33 Eaton Sq., London SW1.

HALL, Nigel John, M.Art R.C.A.; sculptor; Principal Lecturer, Chelsea School of Art; *b* Bristol, 30 Aug., 1943; *s* of H. J. Hall. *Educ.:* Bristol Grammar School; *studied art* at West of England College of Art (1960-64), Royal College of Art (1964-67), Harkness Fellowship (1967-69). *Exhib.:* one-man shows, Galerie Givaudin, Paris; Wilder Gallery, Los Angeles; Galerie Neuendorf, Hamburg and Cologne; Serpentine Gallery, London; Felicity Samuel Gallery, London; Primo Piano, Rome; Elkon Gallery, N.Y. *Work in permanent collections:* Tate Gallery, V. & A., Arts Council of Great Britain, Gothenburg Art Museum, Dallas Museum of Fine Art, Scottish Arts Council. *Address:* 1 Cahill St., London EC1. *Signs work:* "NIGEL HALL."

HALL, Patrick; artist in water-colour, black and white; *b* York, 16 Dec., 1906. *Educ.:* Sedbergh School. *Exhib.:* one-man shows, Waddington Galleries, London (4); Marjorie Parr Galleries, London (4); Victor Waddington, Dublin (4); Waddington Fine Arts, Montreal (2); Boston, U.S.A.; Thames Gallery, Windsor (3); Hilton Gallery, Cambridge; Fermoy Gallery, King's Lynn; Connell Gallery, Glasgow; Halesworth Gallery, Suffolk; Ashgate Gallery, Farnham; group shows, R.A., R.S.A., Paris Salon, N.E.A.C. *Work in permanent collections:* Imperial War Museum; National Gallery, Australia; National Gallery, N.Z.; Christchurch Art Gallery, N.Z.; Guildhall Art Gallery, London; Aberdeen, Bath, Bradford, Brighton, Coventry, Plymouth and York art galleries; Nuffield Foundation; Liverpool University; Sussex County Educ. Com.; Dean and Chapter, York and Winchester. *Work commissioned and purchased* by Albright and Wilson, Barrow Hepburn, Bass Charrington, British Steel, Hoover, Rowntree, Glaxo, Selfridge, Oxo, Whitbread, Plessey, Rank. *Work repro.:* From time to time. *Address:* Maison Dieu, Stone Hill, Sellindge, Ashford, Kent. *Clubs:* Arts, Chelsea Arts.

HALL, William Douglas, B.A., F.M.A.; keeper, Scottish National Gallery of Modern Art; deputy director, Manchester City A.G. (1958-61); Mem. Scottish Arts Council (1968-73); Mem. British Council Fine Arts Advisory Com.; *b* London, 9 Oct., 1926; *s* of William Bertram Hall, civil engineer; *m* Helen Elizabeth Ellis; one *s*, one *d*. *Educ.:* University College School, Hampstead; Courtauld Institute of Art, University of London. *Contributor to* Walpole Society Annual, various art journals. *Address:* 23 Dundas St., Edinburgh 3.

HALLETT, Ellen Kathleen, F.I.A.L., F.S.A.E.; qualified art teacher, Fairfield Grammar School, Bristol (retired); artist in oil, water-colour, etching, fabric collage, silverwork, embroidery; *b* Bristol, 21 Dec., 1899; *d* of Frederick Hallett. *Educ.:* Fairfield Grammar School, Bristol; *studied art* at West of England College of Art, Bristol, under the late Reginald E. J. Bush, R.E., A.R.C.A., R.W.A. *Exhib.:* R.A., R.B.A., R.E., R.Cam.A., R.W.A., R.B.S.A., S.W.A., S.G.A., S.E.A. (Pictures for Schools), Medici Soc., Foyles, Olympia, Embroiderer's Guild Open Exhbn., and the provinces. *Official purchases:* Cheshire County Training College (pencil drawing); Derbyshire Education Committee Museum Service (fabric collage). *Work repro.:* Ideal Home, B.B.C. Television, Fabric Pictures by Eugenie Alexander (Mills & Boon), Art and Craft (Evans Bros. Ltd.). *Publications:* Blue Print and Dyeline for Schools (Faber). *Address:* 3 Logan Rd., Bristol BS7 8DU. *Signs work:* see appendix.

HALLIDAY, Charlotte Mary Irvine, R.B.A. (1960), N.E.A.C. (1961), A.R.W.S. (1971); topographical artist; *b* Kensington, 5 Sept., 1935; *d* of Edward Halliday, C.B.E., P.R.P., P.P.R.B.A., A.R.C.A. *Educ.:* Wester Elchies, Francis Holland; *studied art* at R.A. Schools (1953-58). *Exhib.:* R.A., R.B.A., N.E.A.C., etc. *Address:* 36A Abercorn Pl., London NW8. *Signs work:* "Charlotte Halliday" or "CMIH."

HALLIDAY, Edward Irvine, C.B.E., P.R.P., P.P.R.B.A., A.R.C.A., Rome Scholar in Decorative Painting (1925); portrait painter; President, Royal Society of Portrait Painters; President, Artists' League of Great Britain; Chairman, Artists General Benevolent Institution; *b* Liverpool, 7 Oct., 1902; *s* of the late James Halliday; *m* Dorothy Lucy Hatswell, M.A. (Cantab.); one *s*, one *d*. *Educ.:* Liverpool College; *studied art* at Liverpool City School of Art, Académie Colarossi, Paris, R.C.A., British School at Rome. *Exhib.:* R.A., R.B.A., R.P., Paris Salon. *Work in permanent collections:* Walker Art Gallery, Rome, H.M. The Queen. *Work repro.:* in Studio, Illustrated London News, Times. *Publication:* (with Stanley Casson) Artists at Work. *Address:* 62 Hamilton Terr., St. John's

Wood, London NW8. *Clubs:* Athenæum, Arts, Chelsea Arts. *Signs work:* "Edward I. Halliday."

HALLIDAY, Irene May, R.S.W. (1955), D.A. (1952), Post Dipl. schol. (1952-53), travelling schol. (1953); artist in oil and gouache; principal lecturer, head of Art & Design Dept., Didsbury College of Educ., Manchester; *b* Kingsmuir, by Forfar, Angus, 26 Sept., 1931; *d* of Andrew W. Halliday, schoolmaster. *Educ.:* Kingsmuir School; Arbroath High School; *studied art* at Dundee School of Art (1948-53). *Exhib.:* R.A., R.S.A., R.S.W., Royal Glasgow Institute of Fine Arts; one-man shows Manchester and Edinburgh. *Address:* 5 Duncan Ave., Arbroath, Angus, Scotland. *Signs work:* "Halliday."

HALLIDAY, John Alexander, D.A. (1953); mural, portrait and landscape painter in oil and tempera; *b* Kirkcudbright, 14 July, 1933; *s* of Thomas Heron Halliday. *Educ.:* Glasgow School of Art (1949-53); Royal Scottish Academy Travelling Scholarships. *Exhib.:* one-man shows: Paris, Glasgow, Edinburgh, London. *Work in permanent collections:* Murals in Banks, Distilleries, Prestwick Airport and private houses in Scotland, England and Eire. *Address:* Studio, 4 Polwarth Terr., Edinburgh EH1 1NE. *Club:* Scottish Art. *Signs work:* "John A. Halliday."

HALLIDAY, Thomas Symington, M.B.E., F.R.S.A., F.I.A.L., Founder Mem. Guild of Aviation Artists; *b* Thornhill, Dumfriesshire, 1902; *studied art* at Glasgow. *Exhib.:* R.A., Soc. Portrait Sculptors, Paris Salon, R.S.A., G.I., R.S.W., S.S.A., N.E.A.C., R.S.M.A. *Work in permanent collections:* Derby Museum, Glasgow, Arbroath, Ayr, Imperial War Museum, United Services Museum, Edinburgh, Dundee, H.M. The Queen. *Official purchases:* Battle of Narvik in R.N. Dockyard, Rosyth; Warspite Opens Fire, by Cadet College, Frimley. *Work repro.:* in Studio, Scots Magazine, Life and Work, Wood. *Publications:* Scottish Sculpture. *Address:* 9 Hill Cres., Wormit, Dundee. *Signs work:* "T. S. HALLIDAY" or "HALLIDAY."

HAMILTON, Gavin, bursaries from R.S.A. (1948-49, 1969), F.R.S.A.; carpet designer with James Templeton & Co. Ltd., Glasgow; *b* Rutherglen, 19 Nov., 1923; *m* Irene Carmichael; two *d*. *Educ.:* Gallowflat School; *studied art* at Darlington School of Art (1945-46) and Glasgow Art School (1946-49). *Designed carpets* for Marlborough House, Empress of Britain, Empress of Canada, British Embassy, Warsaw, and Royal Festival Hall Restaurant. Designed British Carpet Centre symbol. *Address:* 5 Copthill Gdns., Mill Hill, London NW7. *Signs work:* see appendix.

HAMMOND, Hermione, Rome Scholar (Painting, 1938); *studied art* at Chelsea Polytechnic, R.A. Schools (Dip.). *Exhib.:* R.A.; one-man exhbns.: Bishopsgate Institute (1956); Colnaghi's (1957); Arthur Jeffress (1961); All Hallows, London Wall (1965); New Grafton (1970); Great King St. Gallery, Edinburgh (1972); Six Portfolios, Chelsea (1973). *Work in permanent collections:* ceiling decoration and collage panels, University of London, Guildhall collections, Fondation Custodia, Institut Néerlandais, Paris, Fitzwilliam Museum, Cambridge. *Work repro.:* Oxford Almanack, Arts Review, R.I.B.A. Journal, Country Life. *Address:* 2 Hans Studio, 43A Glebe Pl., London SW3. *Signs work:* "Hermione Hammond."

HAMPSON, Roger Hamer, A.T.D. (1950), D.A., Manc. (1950); artist in oil, lithography, monoprint, aquatint; graphic designer; Principal, Bolton College of Art and Design; President, Manchester Academy; *b* Tyldesley, Lancs., 25 Mar., 1925; *s* of Harry Hampson; *m* Elizabeth Mary Brown; one *s*, one *d*. *Educ.:* Leigh Grammar School; *studied art* at Manchester College of Art and Design under Paul W. Keen, A.R.C.A. (1946-51). *Exhib.:* London, Manchester, Salford, Bolton,

Plymouth, Altrincham, etc. *Work in permanent collections:* Manchester, Bolton, Keighley, Plymouth, Southport, etc. *Address:* 25 Devonshire Rd., Bolton, Lancs. *Signs work:* "Roger Hampson."

HANAUER, John Arno, M.S.I.A. (1952); joint Managing Director, W. Wood & Son Ltd. since 1951; asst. designer, J. B. Brooks & Co. Ltd. (1947-49); *b* Wurzburg, Bavaria, 17 Feb., 1929; *s* of Alfred Hanauer; *m* Jacqueline Cole. *Educ.:* Lady Owens School (1939-43); Northern Polytechnic School of Building and Architecture (1943-45); *studied art* at B'ham School of Arts and Crafts (1945-47). *Exhib.:* Rhodes Centenary Exhbn., Bulawayo (1953), National Exhbn., Canada (1953), St. Erik's Fair, Stockholm (1954), Milan Triennale (1964). *Work repro.:* Vogue, Queen, etc. *Publications:* articles in Leather Goods Journal. *Address:* 15 Kenneth Cres., Willesden Green, London NW2. *Signs work:* "J.A.H."

HANCERI, Dennis John, R.S.M.A. (1970); graphic designer, water-colour and gouache; *b* London, 7 June, 1928; *m* Jill; one *s,* one *d. Educ.:* St. Phillips Elem. School, Kennington Road; *studied art* at St. Martin's School of Art. *Exhib.:* one-man show, Denver, Colorado, U.S.A., Centaur Gallery and Dallas, Texas. *Address:* 97 Horncastle Rd., London SE12. *Club:* Wapping Group of Artists. *Signs work:* "Dennis John Hanceri."

HANDS, Freda; N.R.D., Mem. Soc. Scribes and Illuminators (1952); scribe, map draughtsman and commercial artist; *b* London, 1918; *d* of F. L. Hands, B.Sc.; *m* S/Sgt. W. F. Jones, R.A.S.C. *Educ.:* Clapham High School; *studied art* at Chelsea School of Art (1936-39). *Exhib.:* Crafts Centre, Arts and Crafts Exhbn. Soc., etc. *Work repro.:* Book Jackets, illustrations for children's official and scientific publications, etc. *Address:* 34 Pollard Rd., Morden, Surrey. *Signs work:* "HANDS."

HANLEY, Liam Powys; self-taught painter in oil on canvas, pen and ink; *b* S. Kensington, 4 Apr., 1933; *s* of James Hanley, novelist; *m* Hilary Hanley; one *s,* one *d. Educ.:* Wrekin College, Salop. *Exhib.:* Stone Gallery, Newcastle, David Paul Gallery, Chichester, Mermaid Theatre, Thackeray Gallery, London, R.A. *Publication:* The Face of Winter by James Hanley. *Address:* 21 Woodsome Rd., London NW5. *Club:* Chelsea Arts. *Signs work:* "Hanley."

HANLY, Daithi Patrick, K.L.J., B.Arch. (1940), F.R.I.A.I., F.R.I.B.A., F.R.T.P.I.; consultant architect, town-planner, landscape architect, sculptor; former Dublin City Architect; *b* Cavan, 11 Mar., 1917; *s* of Joseph Hanly, F.R.C.Sc.I., M.Sc.; *m* Joan Kennedy; one *s,* one *d. Educ.:* National University of Ireland, College of Art, Dublin. *Exhib.:* R.H.A., Oireactas, Tostal sculpture exhbn. *Publications:* papers on housing in Ireland at Zürich Conference (1948), Amsterdam (1950), etc. In 1966, U.N. expert in Geneva to edit report on Building Material, 1975, Architect to Royal Dublin Society for large Exhibition Conference, sales complex with restaurants, bars, etc. *Address:* San Elmo, Vico Rd., Dalkey, Co. Dublin. *Signs work:* "D. P. Hanly" or "D.P.H."

HANNEY, Clifford, A.R.W.A., F.S.A.M.; painter; *b* Pensford, Somerset, 1890; *s* of Albert Hanney; *m* Eirene Hutton-Seed, B.W.S. *Educ.:* Merchant Venturers and Bristol University; *studied art* at Southampton and Bristol Art Schools. War Service with Harwich and Dover flotillas; Senior Lecturer in Art, Cheshire County Training College (1930-50); President of Bristol Savages (1963). *Exhib.:* R.A., R.O.I., R.B.A., R.W.A., Walker, Manchester and various provincial galleries. *Official purchases:* Bristol Savages. *Work repro.:* Colour print, End of Day (Frost & Reed), repro. in black and white in The Year's Art

(1936). *Address:* 3 The Paragon, Clifton, Bristol. *Club:* Bristol Savages. *Signs work:* see appendix.

HARDEN, Gerald A. C., A.R.C.A., Cadet Forces medal (1951); artist in pencil, pen and ink, water-colour, oil, calligraphy and painted and enriched lettering, engraving; art master, Cambridgeshire High School, Cambridge (1938-71); art master, Grammar School, Maidstone (1932-38); *b* Charlton Kings, nr. Cheltenham, 2 Feb., 1909; *s* of Arthur Graty Harden; *m* Edith Eva Lampard; one *s,* two *d. Educ.:* Pate's Grammar School, Cheltenham; *studied art* at Cheltenham School of Arts and Crafts, R.C.A. *Exhib.:* Cheltenham, Maidstone, Folkestone, Rochester, London, Cambridge, R.A. and Tate Gallery (pictures for schools exhbn.). *Address:* 22 Hartington Grove, Cambridge. *Clubs:* Cambridge and County Bowling, County Badge. *Signs work:* see appendix.

HARDIE, Alexander Merrie, M.A. (Aberdeen, 1931), B.Sc. (1934), Ph.D. (1959), R.W.A. (1970); Professor of Physics; artist in oil, water-colour, gouache, pastel; professor, University of Bath; *b* 10 Feb., 1910; *s* of Alexander Hardie; *m* Phyllis Amy Auld; one *s,* one *d. Educ.:* Aberdeen Grammar School, Aberdeen University. *Exhib.:* Aberdeen A.G., R.W.E.A., R.S.A., R.S.W., one-man shows, Bristol and Bath. *Address:* 83 Parry's La., Bristol, BS9 1AN. *Club:* Bristol Savages. *Signs work:* "A. M. Hardie" in water-colours; "Hardie" in oils.

HARDIE, James Watterston, D.A.(Glas.) 1959; painter in oil, gouache, water-colour; lecturer, College of Education, Aberdeen; *b* Motherwell, 28 Apr., 1938; *s* of James W. Hardie, civil servant; *m* Ann Livingston; two *d. Educ.:* Larkhall Academy (1950-55); *studied art* at Glasgow School of Art (1955-59) under David A. Donaldon, LL.D., R.S.A., R.P. *Exhib.:* R.S.A., R.S.W., R.G.I., S.S.A.; one-man shows: Compass Gallery, Glasgow (1976), Present Gallery (1974), Nottingham Playhouse (1972), Aberdeen Arts Centre (1971), New Charing Cross Gallery (1966), Blythswood Gallery, Glasgow (1961). *Work in permanent collections:* Aberdeen A.G., Lanarkshire County Council, Scottish Arts Council, Fife County Council, Liverpool, Leicester and Stockholm Universities. *Film:* R.C.A. production Painters Landscape (Contemporary Films Ltd.). *Address:* Fetternear Schoolhouse, nr. Kemnay, Aberdeenshire. *Signs work:* "Hardie."

HARDY-HENRION, Daphne; sculptor in clay, stone, wood; *b* Amersham, 20 Oct., 1917; *d* of Clive Hardy, D.S.O.; *m* F. H. K. Henrion, M.B.E.; two *s,* one *d. Educ.:* Holland and France; *studied art* at R.A. Schools, awarded gold medal. *Exhib.:* Beaux Arts Gallery, Arts Council exhbns., R.A., A.I.A. *Official purchases:* Festival of Britain (1951), Hertfordshire schools. *Work repro.:* Observer, Manchester Guardian, Alphabet and Image, Architectural Review, Vogue, Harpers Bazaar. *Address:* Pope Mill, Sturmer, Haverhill, Suffolk. *Signs work:* "Daphne Hardy-Henrion."

HARNACK, Frederick Bertrand, R.S.M.A. (1950); artist in oil, water-colour and wood-cuts; *b* London, 22 July, 1897; *s* of Ernest Henry Harnack (decd.), pioneer X-ray specialist at London Hospital; *m* Edna May Ewbank. *Educ.:* St. Bonaventure's Grammar School, Forest Gate; *studied* under Arthur Briscoe. *Exhib.:* R.A., also at London, provincial and Continental galleries. *Work repro.:* in Yachting Monthly and various other magazines, All About Ships and Shipping (Faber). *Publication:* Sailing Ships Through the Ages (De La More Press). *Address:* Greenwood, W. Mersea, Colchester, Essex. *Club:* W. Mersea Yacht. *Signs work:* "F. B. HARNACK" or "FID HARNACK."

HARRIS, Geoffrey, A.R.C.A. (1954); sculptor; mem. London Group; Senior lecturer, Ravensbourne College of Art and Design; *b* Nottingham, 1928; *s* of Charles Frederick Harris, A.I.A.S.; *m* Gillian Farr, M.S.I.A., textile designer; two *s. Educ.:* Leeds Modern School; *studied art* at Leeds College of Art (1948-51), Royal College of Art (1951-54). *Exhib.:* Sculptors Today, Midland Group Gallery, Nottingham (1962), London Group, R.B.A. Galleries, London (1965), R.I. Galleries (1967), Canterbury Festival (1970); one-man shows: Leicester Galleries, London (1964), Queen Square Gallery, Leeds (1964). *Work in private collections* in Britain, Europe, U.S.A. *Public commissions:* Baildon Primary School, Yorkshire, L.C.C. Maitland Park Housing Scheme, St. Pancras. *Address:* 5 Queen's Rd., Faversham, Kent. *Signs work:* "Harris."

HARRIS, Josephine, A.R.W.S. (1967), N.E.A.C. (1968); artist in water-colour, drawing, etching; secretary to Royal Academy Schools; *d* of P. A. Harris, *Educ.:* privately; *studied art* at Plymouth College of Art (1948-52) under William Mann, A.R.C.A. *Official purchases:* Plymouth A.G., Graves A.G., Sheffield, South London A.G., I.L.E.A., K.C.C. *Address:* 37 Melville Rd., Barnes, London SW13. *Signs work:* "Josephine Harris" or "J.H."

HARRIS, Lyndon Goodwin, R.I., R.S.W., R.W.A., Dip. Fine Art (Lond.), A.T.D., Courtauld Certificate, Leverhulme, Pilkington, and Slade Scholar; Slade Anatomy Prizeman, Gold Medal Paris Salon (painting, 1956), Hon. Men. (painting, 1948) and Hon. Men. (etching, 1949); artist in oil, water-colour, stained glass; etcher; *b* Halesowen, Worcs., 25 July, 1928; *s* of the late S. E. Harris, A.C.I.S. *Educ.:* Halesowen Grammar School; *studied art* at Birmingham College of Art, L.C.C. Central School of Art and Crafts, Courtauld Inst., Slade School (Profs. Randolph Schwabe and Sir William Coldstream) and University of London Institute of Education. *Exhib.:* Paris Salon, R.A. (first exhib. at age of 13), R.S.A., R.I., N.E.A.C., R.B.A., R.S.W., R.G.I., R.W.A., Britain in Water-colour, Birmingham, Bradford, Wolverhampton, Bournemouth, Blackpool, Southport and other principal provincial galleries. *Work in permanent collections:* University College, London; Min. of Works; Birmingham and Midland Inst.; City of Worcester; stained-glass window, Gorsty Hill Methodist Church, Halesowen. *Work repro.:* Masters of Water-colour and Their Techniques (The Artist), Young Artists of Promise, Souvenir Handbook of Halesowen, Birmingham Post, etc. *Address:* The Uplands, Waxland Rd., Halesowen, Worcs. *Signs work:* "Lyndon G. Harris."

HARRIS, Mary Packer, D.A.; artist in water-colour, tempera, woodcuts; lecturer National Gallery S. Australia (1937-47); art mistress S. Australia School of Arts and Crafts; *b* Middlesbrough, 30 July, 1891; *d* of Clement Antrobus Harris, musician and author. *Educ.:* Crieff Academy, Perth Academy; *studied art* at Edinburgh College of Art under Sir Morley Fletcher, William S. Black, J. Campbell Mitchell. *Exhib.:* S.S.A., Soc. of Artists, Australia, Australian Academy of Arts. *Work in permanent collections:* National Art Gallery, S. Australia (The Spirit of Spring), The Timeless Time. *Publications:* Art: the Torch of Life, The Cosmic Rhythm of Art and Literature, In One Splendour Spun: autobiography of a Quaker Artist. *Address:* 116 Walkerville Terrace, Walkerville, Adelaide. *Club:* Adelaide Lyceum.

HARRISON, Claude, R.P., A.R.C.A.; artist in oil, egg tempera, oil and tempera, pen and wash, etc.; primarily a painter of conversation pieces and imaginative landscapes; *b* Leyland, Lancs., 31 Mar., 1922; *s* of Harold Harrison, engineer; *m* Audrey Johnson, painter; one *s. Educ.:* Hutton Grammar School, Lancs; *studied art* at Preston (1938-40), Liverpool (1940-41), R.C.A. (1947-49). *Exhib.:* R.A., R.S.P.P., R.S.A., R.B.A., etc. *Official purchases:* Murals at Ryedale County Modern School and at Nelson, Lancs., at St. Anne's, Lancs., and at David Whitehead Ltd., Rawtenstall. *Publication:* The Portrait Painters' Handbook (Studio Vista, 1968). *Address:* Easedale House, Grasmere, Westmorland. *Signs work:* "CLAUDE HARRISON."

HARRISON, Eric, A.R.C.A., M.S.I.A., A.T.I.; textile designer, woven and printed fabrics; designer for Henry Nathan & Co. Ltd. (1949-55), Floral Furnishing Fabrics Ltd. (1955-56), T. F. Firth & Sons Ltd. (1956-58). Lecturer in Textile Design and Colour, Inst. of Technology, Bradford, Yorks (1958-66), University of Bradford (Oct. 1966-70), senior lecturer (Apr., 1970); *b* Oswaldtwistle, Lancs., 5 Nov., 1919; *s* of John H. Harrison, cotton industry. *Educ.:* Accrington Grammar School; *studied art* at Accrington School of Arts and Crafts (1935-39), R.C.A. (1946-49). *Address:* 3 Temple Rhydding Drive, Baildon, Shipley, West Yorkshire, BD17 5PX.

HARRISON, Ian, B.A., T.Eng.(CEI), M.I.G.Tech.E., S.M.; lecturer in art history and art and design at Halton College of F.E., Widnes; artist in marine subjects and miniatures which include portraits; oil, ink and water-colour drawings, water-colour miniatures; special interest in Japanese Sumi-e brush techniques; *b* Staines, Surrey, 8 Apr., 1935; *s* of Austin M. Harrison, A.M.I.Mech.E., A.M.I.Prod.E., M.I.M.; *m* Pauline Brenda Harris; two *d. Educ.:* Stanley House School, Birmingham and Prince of Wales School, Nairobi, Kenya; *studied art* at Prince of Wales School, Nairobi, Kenya (1947-52) under MacLellan Simm. *Exhib.:* Hesketh Hubbard Art Soc., Mall Galleries (1972), R.M.S. (1972); one-man shows of marine paintings, Barley Festival (1972), North Herts. Arts Festival (1973), Woburn Abbey (1974, 1975). *Address:* Stuarton, Lime Ave., Northwich, Ches. *Signs work:* see appendix.

HARRISON, John Cyril; artist in water-colour; *b* Tidworth, Wilts., 11 Mar., 1898. *Studied art* at Slade School. *Publications:* Bird Portraits (Country Life), Illustrations for Pheasants of the World by Jean Delacour (Country Life), Illustrations for Eagles, Hawks and Falcons of the World by Leslie Brown and Dean Amadon (Country Life). *Address:* The Studio, Haynford, Norwich, Norfolk. *Signs work:* "J. C. Harrison."

HARRISON, Marguerite Hazel, National Froebel Foundation Diploma in Art; artist in oil, pen and wash, also potter in stoneware; *b* Llandudno, N. Wales, 7 Oct., 1927; *d* of Judge R. O. Roberts, d. 1929; *m* Michael Harrison; three *s,* two *d. Educ.:* Royal Masonic School, Rickmansworth, Herts.; *studied art:* mainly self-taught; tuition for a period under Kenneth A. Jameson. *Exhib.:* R.A., R.Cam.A., Wirral Soc. of Arts, Deeside. *Address:* 19 Kingsmead Rd. South, Birkenhead, Merseyside. *Signs work:* "Marguerite Harrison" and see appendix.

HARRISON, Mary Kent; oil painter; N.E.A.C., R.B.A.; *b* 29 Dec., 1915; *d* of Howard Marryat, M.I.E.E.; *m* G. Kent Harrison (surgeon); four *s,* three *d. Educ.:* privately and Kingston School of Art (1933-35), Slade School (1936-37), R.A. Schools (1937-38). *Exhib.:* R.A., R.S.A., N.E.A.C., R.B.A., R.P., Leicester Galleries, Wildenstein (1965), Brighton, Eastbourne, Bournemouth, etc. *Work repro.:* Britain in Pictures series; People of Britain, 1947; Nativity (Studio). Subject of an article in Studio, 1948: Mary Kent Harrison, by Michael Ayrton. *Publication:* How to Dress Dancers. *Address:* White Stones Farm, Bolton-le-Bowland, Clitheroe, Lancs. BB7 4PQ. *Signs work:* "MARY KENT."

HART, John; painter; *b* Manchester, 1921; *s* of Harold Hart; *m* Gwendoline Prichard; three *d. Educ.:* Merchant Taylors' School, Crosby; *studied art* at Liverpool College of Art and in Paris. *Exhib.:* Redfern, Beaux Arts, Zwemmers, Leicester Galls., I.C.A., Whitechapel, Molton, Hamilton, Marjorie Parr, Annely Juda, London Group, Art Spectrum London, Galleria Torbandena Trieste, John Moores, Bear Lane, Oxford, Camden Arts Centre, London, etc. *Official purchases:* Nottingham, Leicester, Birmingham, Liverpool, Granada TV, Universities of Liverpool, Manchester and York; mural at Daresbury Nuclear Physics Laboratory. *Address:* 134 Humber Rd., London SE3.

HARTAL, Paul; artist, theoretician, Founder of Lyrical Conceptualism; *b* Hungary, 25 Apr., 1936; descendant of Baron de Hatvanis Family; *m*; two *s*, one *d*. *Educ.:* Universities of Szeged, Jerusalem and Montreal. *Exhib.:* one-man shows: Montreal, Washington D.C., International Art Fair, Wash-Art 76, Argraf, Paris, Israel. *Work repro.:* Artists/U.S.A., Bicentennial Issue, Phil. (1976), A Manifesto on Lyrical Conceptualism by Paul Hartal, Montreal (1975), newspapers. *Publications:* author of A History of Architecture (1972); anthologized poems in Windfall (1975). *Address:* P.O. Box 1012, St. Laurent, Montreal, Quebec, Canada, H4L 4W3. *Signs work:* "Hartal."

HARTUNG, Hans; painter; *b*. Leipzig, 21 Sept., 1904; *s* of Curt Hartung, Dr. of Medicine and Philosophy; *m* Anna-Eva Bergman. *Educ.:* Dresden. *Exhib.:* Grand Prix International for Painting unanimously at the Biennale of Venice (1960); one-man show: Metropolitan Museum, N.Y. (1975). *Work in permanent collections:* Museums and private collections in France and abroad. *Publications:* Madeleine Rousseau, James Johnson Sweeney, Ottomar Domnick: Hans Hartung (Stuttgart, 1949), R.-V. Gindertael: Hans Hartung (Paris, Tisné, 1960); Will Grohmann: Hans Hartung, Aquarelle, 1922 (St. Gall, Erker-Verlag, 1966); Umbro Apollonio: Hans Hartung (Milan, Fratelli Fabbri, 1966). *Address:* c/o Musée National d'Art Moderne, Paris. *Signs work:* "HARTUNG," see appendix.

HARVEY, Jake, D.A. (1972); sculptor in forged, welded steel, cast brass, bronze; lecturer, Edinburgh College of Art; *b* Yetholm, Kelso, Roxburghshire, 3 June, 1948. *Educ.:* Kelso High School; *studied art* at Edinburgh College of Art (1966-72). *Exhib.:* R.S.A., S.S.A., Dunfermline, Border Arts Festival, Scottish Sculpture '75, Edinburgh, Leeds, Glasgow. *Work in permanent collections:* Grangemouth, Scottish Arts Council, Perth, E. Germany. *Address:* Maxton Cross, Maxton, Melrose, Roxburghshire. *Signs work:* see appendix.

HARVEY, Pat: see YALLUP, Pat.

HARWOOD, John Hammond, A.R.C.A. (1927), Hon. F.S.P. (Fellow of Sheffield Polytechnic) (1969), Freeman of Worshipful Company of Goldsmiths (1952); artist in oil, water-colour; princ. Gloucester School of Art (1939-45), princ. Sheffield College of Art (1945-64), now retired; *b* Darwen, 3 Dec., 1904; *s* of Thomas Hammond Harwood; *m;* one *s*, one *d*. *Educ.:* Ripon School, Yorks; *studied art* at Harrogate School of Art (1921-24) under Richard H. Parker, A.R.C.A.; R.C.A. (1924-28) under Sir W. Rothenstein. *Exhib.:* R.A., N.E.A.C., London Group, etc. *Work repro.:* illustrations for Puffin Books, Porpoise Books, Puffin Story Books, etc. *Address:* 32 Brooklands Ave., Fulwood, Sheffield, 10. *Signs work:* "John Harwood."

HASSALL, Joan, A.R.E. (1938), R.E. (1948), F.S.I.A. (1957), Master A.W.G. (1972), Bronze Medal: Salon (1973); painter in oil and water-colour, wood engraver and typographer; *b* 3 Mar., 1906; *d* of John Hassall, R.I. *Educ.:* Norland Pl. Day School, London; R.A. Schools; L.C.C. School of Photo-Engraving and Lithography. *Exhib.:* R.A., N.E.A.C., S.W.A., R.S.A., R.H.A. *Official purchases:* B.M.; Whitworth Gallery, Manchester; National Gallery of Canada. *Work repro.:* in Studio, Adventures in Monochrome, Devil's Dyke, Portrait of a Village, Cranford, Fifty-one Poems (Mary Webb), Our Village, Sealskin Trousers, Coronation Invitation (1953). *Address:* 88 Kensington Park Rd., London W11. *Signs work:* "Joan Hassall" also, for wood engravings, see appendix.

HATCH, Lionel Douglas; typographer, artist in pastel, monotype; *b* Bolton, Lancs., 20 Aug., 1949. *Educ.:* Castle Hill, Bolton; *studied art* at College of Art,

Bolton (1966-69) Principal, Roger Hampson. Work in various private collections. *Address:* 260 Bolton Rd., Atherton, Lancs. *Signs work:* "Lionel Hatch."

HATTS, Clifford Ronald, F.S.I.A., A.R.C.A. (Silver Medal, 1949); exhbn. and typographic designer; *b* London, 10 Nov., 1921; *s* of Harold Walter Hatts; *m* Barbara Helen Hatts; *studied art* at Woolwich (1935-41), and R.C.A. (1946-49). *Exhibition designs for:* Exhbn. Designer and Graphic Artist; freelance until 1957, now Head of Design with B.B.C. Television. *Work repro.:* in Designers in Britain. *Address:* 33 Upper Richmond Rd., Putney, London SW15.

HAUGHTON, Wilfred James, P.R.U.A. (1964), F.R.S.A. (1960), F.I.A.L. (1960), R.U.A. (1956); artist in oil, water-colour; vice-president, R.U.A. (1951); director, Frazer & Haughton Ltd.; *b* Hillmount, 14 Dec., 1921; *s* of J. Wilfred Haughton; *m* Priscilla Elizabeth McLaughlin; three *s,* one *d. Educ.:* Terra Nova School, Birkdale, Southport, Lancs.; Worksop College, Notts.; *studied art:* self-taught. *Exhib.:* R.H.A., R.U.A., Royal Scottish Water-Colour Soc., R.I., W.C.S.I. *Official purchases:* oil painting by C.E.M.A., oil painting by Thomas Haverty Trust (Dublin). *Address:* Kilconway, Hillmount, Cullybackey, Co. Antrim, N. Ireland. *Signs work:* see appendix.

HAWCROFT, Francis Wilson, B.A., F.M.A.; Keeper of the Whitworth Art Gallery and lecturer in art history, University of Manchester (1959-); *b* Kidderminster, 25 May, 1925; *s* of Joseph Collins Hawcroft. *Educ.:* Sebright School, Worcestershire; *studied art history* at Courtauld Institute of Art, University of London. *Publications:* A Visual History of Modern Britain: The Arts (1967), various exhbn. Catalogues including John Crome (1968), Water-colours by John Robert Cozens (1971), Thomas Girtin (1975). *Address:* 12 Beech Ct., Willow Bank, Manchester 14.

HAWKE, Marjorie, A.I.A.L.; painter and draughtsman; *b* London, 16 Jan., 1894; *d* of Frederick Hawke; *m* Laurie Tayler. *Educ.:* Threave House, Hampstead, and Switzerland; *studied art* at Heatherley, Central and Westminster Schools of Art. *Exhib.:* London Group, F.P.S., Leicester, O'Hana, F.B.A. and Gal. Creuse, Paris, Athens and Florence; one-man shows at A.I.A. Gal., Bear Lane, Oxford, New End, London, and Rotunda Gallery, London. *Work in private collections:* U.S.A., Australia, S. Africa, Holland, Sweden, Switzerland. *Address:* 16 Prince Arthur Rd., London NW3. *Clubs:* W.I.A.C., A.I.A., H.A.C. *Signs work:* "Hawke."

HAWKINS, Dennis, D.F.A.(Lond.) 1952, F.R.S.A., M.I.A.A., chairman, P.M.C. (1972); painter, printmaker; director of art, Repton School; *b* 15 Feb., 1925; *m*; two *s,* three *d. Studied art* at Ruskin School (1947-49) under Albert Rothenstein, Percy Horton; Slade School (1949-52) under Prof. Sir William Coldstream, Prof. R. Wittkower, Graham Sutherland. *Exhib.:* Arts Council, 4th International Print Biennale (Tokyo, 1964), 3rd International Print Biennale (Florence, 1972). *Work in permanent collections:* Arts Council; V. & A.; Boston Museum of Modern Art, Seattle Museum of Modern Art, U.S.A.; City Art Galleries of Birmingham, Exeter, Norwich, Liverpool, Portsmouth, Eastbourne, etc.; 22 Educ. Authorities in British Isles; Bezalel National Museum, Israel; N.S.W. Museum of Modern Art, Sydney. *Public commissions:* sculpture, large-scale concrete bas-reliefs and mural paintings for New Hospital, Netheredge, Sheffield (1964-68), 20 painted panels: Royal Children's Hospital, Liverpool (1969, 1975), Royal School for the Deaf, Derby (1973), 40 ft mural for CDFC, London (1975). *Address:* Askew Cottage, 23 Milton Rd., Repton, Derbyshire, DE6 6FZ. *Associations:* International Assoc. of Artists, Midland Group of Artists, Printmakers Council of Great Britain. *Signs work:* "Hawkins."

HAWTHORN, Raymond Humphrey Millis, A.T.D. (1940), A.R.E. (1960), R.E. (1975); lecturer, Laird School of Art and Crafts, Birkenhead; Medway School of Art and Crafts, Rochester (1946-47); wood engraver; *b* Poole, Dorset, 18 Mar., 1917; *s* of the late Wilfrid Charles Hawthorn; *m* Beryl Hine Moore; two *d. Educ.:* Bablake School, Coventry; *studied art:* Coventry School of Art (1935-39); Hornsey School of Arts and Crafts, London (1939-40). *Exhib.:* R.E., A.I.A., Soc. of Wood Engravers. *Work in permanent collections:* Atkinson Art Gallery, Southport. *Publications:* book illustrations for Folio Society Ltd. *Address:* 97 Wirral Gdns., Bebington, Wirral, Cheshire. *Signs work:* "Raymond H. M. Hawthorn," and see appendix.

HAYDEN, Reg Henry; Head of Fine Art, Liverpool Polytechnic; *b* 5 July, 1917. *Studied art* at Brighton College of Art and Slade School. *Work in private collections:* England and America. *Exhib.:* Leicester Galleries, London Group, Yorkshire Artists, Sussex University. *Address:* 17 Aigburth Dr., Liverpool 17. *Signs work:* "Reg Hayden."

HAY-EDIE, Mrs. Gerd, F.S.I.A.; craftsman designer, wool, cotton, linen, etc.; *b* Trondheim, 4 Nov., 1909; *d* of Com. Olav Bergersen; *m* A. W. Hay-Edie; two *s,* two *d. Studied art* at private and Government schools in Norway. *Exhib.:* Oslo, Zürich, Milan Triennale, Festival of Britain, Washington, Bulawayo, Copenhagen, Norway. *Work repro.:* designs for Rural Industries, Broadhead and Graves, Maharajah of Gwalior, designs for Mourne Textiles Ltd., founded in 1950. *Address:* Mourne Textiles Ltd., Killowen, Newry, Northern Ireland.

HAYES, Colin Graham, R.A., M.A.(Oxon.), Hon.A.R.C.A.; painter in oil and water-colour; reader, Royal College of Art; *b* London, 17 Nov., 1919; *s* of Gerald Hayes; *m* Jean Westbrook; three *d. Educ.:* Westminster School; Christ Church, Oxford; *studied art* at Bath School of Art; Ruskin School of Drawing. *Exhib.:* Marlborough, Agnews, Search, New Grafton. *Work in permanent collections:* Arts Council, British Council, Carlisle A.G. and others. *Publications:* Stanley Spencer, Renoir, Rembrandt, A Grammar of Drawing. *Address:* 26 Cleveland Ave., London W4. *Signs work:* "Hayes."

HAYLETT, Malcolm John, F.B.D.S., F.I.B.D., L.S.I.A.; portrait painter in oil; designer, illustrator, photographer, writer and broadcaster; Pres., St. Ives Arts Club (1951-52); *b* Montreal, 25 Sept., 1923; *s* of H. A. Haylett, printer; *m* Jean Haylett; two *d. Studied art* at Southend College of Art. *Exhib.:* St. Ives Soc. of Artists. *Work repro.:* in Britannia and Eve, Ideal Home, Display, Hotel and Catering Review, Sport and County, John Bull, House and Garden, Daily Mail, Sphere, Builder, Architect and Building News, Illustrated London News, etc. *Address:* The Warren Studio, St. Ives, Cornwall. *Club:* St. Ives Arts. *Signs work:* "MALCOLM HAYLETT" or "Malcolm Haylett."

HAYTER, Stanley William, C.B.E., Chevalier, Legion of Honour, Chevalier des Arts et Lettres; Grand Prix des Arts de la Ville de Paris (1972); artist, painter in oil and gouache, engraver and etcher, writer, and teacher of art; founder and director Atelier 17, New York and Paris (since 1927); *b* London, 27 Dec., 1901; *s* of William Harry Hayter; *m* (1) Edith Fletcher, (2) Helen Phillips, sculptor; two *s. Educ.:* Whitgift School; King's College, London; *studied art* at father's studio, Academie Julian, Paris. *Exhib.:* One-man shows, Paris, New York, London, Munich, San Francisco, Pasadena, Los Angeles, Dallas Liège, Tokyo. *Addresses:* 12 rue Cassini, 75 Paris 14e; Atelier 17, 63 rue Daguerre, 75 Paris 14e. *Signs work:* "S. W. HAYTER" on prints, "HAYTER" on paintings.

HAYWARD, John Forrest, B.A. (Oxon.), Officer of the Order of Leopold II of Belgium; Membre associé, Academie Royale d'Archéologie de Belgique; art historian; deputy keeper, V. & A. (1946-65); associate Director, Sothebys, since 1965; *b* 10 Feb., 1916. *Educ.:* St. Paul's and Magdalen College, Oxford. *Publications:* Viennese Porcelain of the Du Paquier Period (Rockliff, 1952), European Firearms (Stationery Office, 1955), Huguenot Silver in England (Faber, 1959), The Art of the Gunmaker (2 Vols., Rockliff, 1962-63), The Virtuoso Goldsmith and the Triumph of Mannerism (Sotheby Pubs. 1976); contributions to English and foreign art journals on Arms, Ceramics, etc. *Address:* 28 Chepstow Villas, Bayswater, London W11.

HAYWOOD, Mark, B.A. (Hons) Fine Art (1975); project artist in silkscreen and crayon; teacher of photography, Salford College of Art; *b* Oldham, 23 Nov., 1952; *s* of A. J. Haywood. *Educ.:* Counthill School, Oldham; *studied art* at Jacob Kramer College of Art, Leeds (1971-72); Medlock Fine Art Centre, Manchester (1972-75) under Wendy Smith, R.C.A., Brendan Neiland, R.C.A. and Keith Godwin, A.R.C.A. *Exhib.:* Oldham A.G., Portland Gallery, Manchester, Manchester Academy, Chenil Galleries, London. *Work in permanent collections:* Manchester Polytechnic, Wiltshire C.C. *Address:* 33A Wood Rd., Whalley Range, Manchester 16. *Signs work:* see appendix.

HAZELWOOD, David, M.F.P.S.; painter in oil, acrylic, collage; *b* Ipswich, 29 Feb., 1932; *s* of Wasley Gordon Hazelwood, printer; *m* Pauline Woodward; two *d. Educ.:* Northgate Grammar School, Ipswich; *studied art* part-time Ipswich School of Art under Colin Moss, A.R.C.A.; but mainly self-taught. *Exhib.:* Camden Arts Centre; one-man shows: Ipswich, Woodbridge, Cardiff, Richmond, Halesworth, Aldeburgh, University of London, Medici Gallery, F.P.S. Gallery; mixed shows: Hintlesham Festivals, Wills Lane Gallery, St. Ives. Participated in film Painters in the Modern World (1969). *Address:* 83 Arundel Way, Ipswich. *Clubs:* Ipswich Art Society (Executive Committee), Colchester Art Society. *Signs work:* "D. Hazelwood."

HEADLEY-NEAVE, Alice; painter in oil; *b* Hastings, 1903; *d* of Huckle A. H. Headley, M.R.C.S., L.R.C.P., D.P.H., barrister-at-law; *m;* two *s,* one *d. Educ.:* St. Hilary's School, Bexhill; *studied art* at Slade School, under Prof. Tonks and R.A. Schools under Sir Walter Russell (Landseer Prize). *Exhib.:* R.A., R.B.A., R.P., N.E.A.C., R. Scot. A., Paris Salon, W.I.A.C. *Address:* Baisden, Etchingham, Sussex. *Signs work:* "A. Headley Neave" (oil) or "A. H. Neave."

HEAL, John Christopher, M.A., F.S.I.A.; designer (chiefly furniture); director and drawing office manager, Heal & Son, Ltd.; *b* 2 Oct., 1911; *s* of Sir Ambrose Heal; *m* (1) Teresa Anstruther; two *s,* three *d;* (2) Olive Scarth. *Educ.:* Gresham's School, Holt and Sidney Sussex College, Cambs.; *studied art* at Central Schools of Arts and Crafts, Camb. University School of Architecture. *Exhib.:* Paris International Exhbn., 1937, Britain Can Make It Exhbn., 1946. *Address:* Heal & Son, Ltd., 196 Tottenham Ct. Rd., London W1. *Signs work:* "J. Christopher Heal."

HEALER, George, A.R.B.S. (1974); sculptor in clay, plaster, wood, cast aluminium, brass and bronze; *b* 25 Sept., 1936; *s* of John Healer; *m* Brenda Maureen Healer; one *s,* two *d. Educ.:* Bullion Lane School; *studied art* at Sunderland College of Art (1952-56) under Harry Thubron, A.R.C.A., and Robert Jewell A.R.C.A. *Exhib.:* R.A., R.G.I., Commonwealth Institute, Woolgate House, London, D.L.I. Durham City, Gulbenkian Gallery, Newcastle-upon-Tyne. *Work in permanent collection:* life-size figures of John and Josiphe Bowes, Bowes Museum, Barnard Castle, Co. Durham. *Publication:* article, Aluminium for Schools for the British Aluminium Federation. *Address:* 12 Melville St., Chester-le-Street, Co. Durham. *Signs work:* "HEALER" hammered into metal with flat chisel.

HEATH, Isobel Atterbury; artist in water-colour; portrait and romantic impressionist landscape painter; war artist with M.O.I. (1939-45); *b* Hull, Yorks; *d* of Sidney Heath, M.P.S.; widow of the late Marcello Prati, LL.D. *Educ.:* Canonesses of St. Augustine School, Hull; *studied art* at Collarossi's, Montparnasse, Paris, and under Wm. Ritson, A.R.C.A. *Exhib.:* R.S.A., R.S.S.W., Cam.A., R.O.I., R.I., Bradford Muncipal A.G., Britain in Water-colour, Artists of Fame and Promise, Leicester Gall., Custom House Studio, St. Ives; organizer, London exhbn., Cornish Experiment (1962). *Publications:* Passing Thoughts, and Love (1972-73). *Address:* Bosunsnest, St. Ives, Cornwall. *Clubs:* R.W.S. Art, Penwith Sy., St. Ives, St. Ives Soc. of Artists. *Signs work:* "Isobel Heath."

HEATHER, Marjorie Kate, Cert. of Fine Art (Oxford, 1948); artist in oil and water-colour of semi-caricature figure compositions. *Educ.:* Newbury Girls' High School; *studied art* at Ruskin School of Art, Oxford (1945-48) under Albert Rutherston; and at Byam Shaw School (1948-50). *Exhib.:* R.A. and R.P. and various galleries in Paris, London and provinces. *Address:* Airidh, Tydehams, Newbury, Berks. *Club:* E.S.U. *Signs work:* "Marjorie Heather."

HECHT, Godfrey, M.F.P.S., N.S.; painter in oil, gouache, ink or anything workable; experimenter; *b* London, 23 May, 1902; *s* of E. Hecht; *m* Kathleen Elles; one *s*. *Educ.:* Downside School. *Exhib.:* Free Painters and Sculptors (London and provinces), R.O.I. Winter Salon, N.S., S.G.A., Westminster Arts Council Woodstock Gallery (one-man), Loggia Gallery. *Address:* c/o Midland Bank Ltd., Holborn Circus, London EC1. *Club:* Reform. *Signs work:* see appendix.

HEIBERG, Jean; Commander of St. Olav's (1956); painter in oil; professor director, State Academy of Fine Arts, Oslo (1935-55); *b* Oslo, 19 Dec., 1884; *s* of Hjalmar Heiberg; *m* 1st, 1913, Sigri Welhaven; one *s; m* 2nd, 1922, the late Agnes Mannheimer; one *d; m* 3rd, 1954, Anna Cleve. *Educ.:* Higher School, Oslo; *studied art* at School of Arts and Crafts, Oslo, Heinrich Knirr Schule, München (1904) and at Henri Matisse's School, Paris. *Exhib.:* Oslo, Stockholm Gothenburg, Copenhagen, Helsingfors, Paris, London, The Hague, Brussels, Berlin, Munich, New York, Reykjavik. *Work in permanent collections:* National Gallery, Oslo; A. G. Bergen; Rasmus Meyers Coll. Bergen; Museum of Trondheim; National Museum, Stockholm; Art Museum, Gothenburg; Museum of Art, Copenhagen. *Publications:* H. Grevenor (1933), Bjarne Rise (1954), Terre d'Europe (1972), (Numero special, "Norvege"—Juin 1972). *Address:* Industrigate 15d, Oslo. *Signs work:* "J. Heiberg."

HEINONEN, Aarre, K. White Rose of Finland I (1946), Commander of Finnish Lion (1954), Commander of Pologna Resituta (1957), K. Leopold Order II (1938), Officer of Orange Nassau (Holland), Officer of Crown Order of Belgium, K. of Dannebrog I; painter in oil and water-colour; *b* Lahti, 31 July, 1906; *s* of Hugo Aleksanteri Heinonen; *m* Tuomi Kaarina Elmgren; one *s*, two *d*. *Studied art* at Helsinki University, Royal Academy of Fine Arts, Antwerp. *Exhib.:* Helsinki, Antwerp, Paris, Hamburg. *Work in permanent collections:* Fine Arts Gallery, Helsinki, French State, Antwerp Museum of Fine Arts, U.S.S.R. State Collection of Occidental Art. *Address:* Fredrikink, 19, Helsinki. *Signs work:* see appendix.

HEISE, Carl Georg, D.Phil.; director of Kunsthalle, Hamburg (1945-55), retd.; hon. prof. University of Hamburg; art historian; director, Lübeck Museum (1920-33); *b* Hamburg, 28 June, 1890; *m* Hildegard Neumann. *Educ.:* at Universities of Freiburg, München, Halle, Berlin, Kiel. *Publications:* Norddeutsche Malerei (1918), Overbeck und sein Kreis (1926), Fabelwelt des Mittelalters (1935), Franzosische Malerei des 19, Jahrh (1942), Hans Memling (1950),

Grosse Zeichner des 19 Jahrunderts (1959), Der gegenwärtige Augenblick (Gesammelte Aufsätze) (1960). Editor of Genius, Kunstbriefe and Werkmonographien. *Address:* Hamburg 50, Kriemwildstr 77.

HELLEBERG, Berndt; sculptor; *b* Stockholm, 17 Dec., 1920; *s* of Sigurd Helleberg, inspector of assurance; *m* Margareta Kinberg. *Educ.:* High School, Härnösand; *studied art* at Stockholm (1945-48), Konstfackskolan, Stockholm (1947-49), France (1950-52). Prize, The Unknown Political Prisoner, London (1953), first prize winner, competition of modern medals (Stockholm 1955), first prize winner 20,000 Sw. crowns, competition of underground station decoration (Stockholm 1960). *Exhib.:* Tate Gallery, London, Stockholm, Paris, U.S.A., etc. *Official purchases:* The underground station, Hornstull, Stockholm; Cathedral Window, Baptist Church, Stockholm; monument of Ludwig Nordstrom at Härnösand; several playground sculptures in Sweden; several sculptures in Stockholm and Sweden. *Address:* Saturnusu 7, 18400 Akersberga, Sweden. *Signs work:* "Berndt Helleberg."

HELLMAN, Glenn; winner of a national sculpture competition (1964); sculptor in steel; teacher at Morley College and Goldsmiths' College School of Art; *b* Walthamstow, 1 Mar., 1938. *Educ.:* D.Y.R.M.S., Dover; *studied art* at Walthamstow (1959-61), Hornsey (1961-64) asst. to Robert Adams (1964-66). *Exhib.:* one-man shows Leicester Gals. (1967, 1971). *Work in permanent collections:* Leeds Merrion Centre, Wakefield Education Authority. *Address:* 1 Mill Cottage, Millbank, Headcorn, Kent TN27 9RG. *Signs work:* "HELLMAN" (punched into the steel), and silver mark, see appendix.

HELSDON, Maureen Constance, A.T.D. (1950); designer of fabric collage and embroidery, wall-hangings, etc.; trained at Hornsey College of Art; teaches design and embroidery at Southampton College of Art; Fellow of Society of Designer Craftsmen. *Exhib.:* regularly in London; one-man shows at Crafts Centre, W1 (1960, 1965), and at Southampton University (1965, 1968). *Work in permanent collections:* Embroiderers' Guild, Leicester, London County Council, Southampton and other ed. committees. *Work in private collections:* in this country and U.S.A. *Commissions* for wall hangings from a number of architects for churches and public buildings. *Address:* 17 Welbeck Ave, Highfield, Southampton SO2 1ST.

HEMPTON, Paul Andrew Keates, M.A., R.C.A.; artist in oil paint and etching; part time lecturer, Dept. Fine Art, Reading University since 1974; Fellow in Fine Art, University of Nottingham (1971-73); *b* Wakefield, Yorks., 3 Oct., 1946; *s* of Revd. Canon G. B. Hempton, B.A.; *m* Margaret Helena; one *s*, one *d*. *Educ.:* King's School, Chester; *studied art* at Goldsmiths' College School of Art (1964-68) under Andrew Forge; R.C.A. (1968-71) under Prof. Carel Weight. *Address:* 9 West End, Minchinhampton, Stroud, Glos. GL6 9JA. *Signs work:* "P.H."

HENDERSON, Keith, O.B.E., R.W.S., R.S.W., R.O.I., P.S.; artist; *b* 17 Apr., 1883; *s* of George MacDonald Henderson, barrister-at-law; *m* Helen Knox-Shaw. *Educ.:* Marlborough, Slade and Paris. *Exhib.:* All principal exhbns. in U.K. and many abroad. *Official purchases:* Glasgow, Dublin, Manchester, Birmingham, Preston, Worthing, Newport, Leamington, Carlisle, Lancaster, Perth. *Work repro.:* in Studio, etc. *Publications with illustrations:* Letters to Helen, Conquest of Mexico, Palm Groves and Humming Birds, Burns by Himself, Pastels, etc.; and, with Stuart Piggott, Scotland before History; also many other illustrations to books. *Address:* 9 St. George's Terr., Regent's Park, London NW1. *Signs work:* "Keith Henderson."

HENDERSON, Sheila Scott; Landscape and portrait painter in oil; *b* 5 July,

1910; *d* of Walter Scott Henderson, F.S.A. *Educ.:* Downe House, Newbury, and Glendower School, London; Yellow Door Studio (F. Spenlove-Spenlove, R.I.; R. G. Eves, R.A., 1930-35). *Exhib.:* R.A., R.S.A., R.P., N.E.A.C., R.B.A., R.O.I., Paris Salon (Hon. Mention, 1957), etc. *Address:* Broadway, Seale Hill, South Park, Reigate, Surrey. *Signs work:* "Sheila S. Henderson" (with stroke beneath).

HENDIL, Birgitte, Art Dip.; miniature painter in gouache and ink of birds and people; *b* Copenhagen, 4 Sept., 1944; *d* of Axel H. Hendil, financial director. *Educ.:* Falkoner gardens Gymnasium; *studied art* at Edinburgh College of Art (1964-69) under Harry More-Gordon. *Exhib.:* Scottish Arts Council, Stirling Gallery, R.S.A. *Publication:* Old St. Paul's Missal. *Address:* c/o Stirling Gallery, 39 Broad St., Stirling, Scotland. *Signs work:* "Birgitte Hendil."

HENDRY, Archibald Hunter, professional M.S.S.A.; artist in oil, water-colour; *b* North Leith, Midlothian, 6 Feb., 1890; *s* of Archibald Hunter Hendry; *m* Jessie MacFarlane; two *s,* one *d. Educ.:* Canonmills; *studied art* at Royal High School, Edinburgh; Edinburgh College of Art (1916-23) under Campbell Mitchell, R.S.A., D. M. Sutherland, R.S.A., Adam B. Thompson, R.S.A., David Foggie, R.S.A. *Exhib.:* Edinburgh and Stirling Triennial, R.Scot.A., S.S.A., R.S.W. *Address:* 2 Borthwick Cas. Tc. Middleton, Midlothian. *Club:* Royal Scots. *Signs work:* "A. Hunter Hendry" (followed by year).

HENNES, Hubert, A.R.C.A. (1933); F.R.S.A. (1948); painter and draughtsman in oil and water-colour; teacher, Leicester College of Arts and Crafts (1934-41), Oxford School of Art (since 1945), senior lecturer drawing and painting (1951) (retd. 1972); *b* 5 Mar., 1907; *s* of William Hennes; *m* Hilary Miller, A.R.C.A.; two *s. Educ.:* Stanley Central Boys' School, London, St. Martin's School of Art (1928-30); R.C.A. (1930-34). *Exhib.:* R.A., R.B.A. *Address:* Cuckfield, Gidley Hill, Horspath, nr. Oxford. *Signs work:* H. Hennes."

HENRI, Adrian, Hons. B.A. Fine Art (1955); artist and author; President, Liverpool Academy of Arts; *b* Birkenhead, 1932; *s* of Arthur Maurice Henri; *m* Joyce Wilson (divorced). *Educ.:* St. Asaph Grammar School, N. Wales; *studied art* at Dept. of Fine Art, King's College, Newcastle. *Exhib.:* one-man shows: Wolverhampton City A.G. (1976), Williamson A.G. (1975), Art Net, London (1975), I.C.A. (1968); other shows: John Moores Liverpool (1962. 1966, 1968, 1974), John Moores £2,000 Prize (1972). *Work in permanent collections:* W.A.G., Williamson A.G., Birkenhead. *Publications:* Environments and Happenings (Thames & Hudson, 1974), plus a number of books of poetry. *Address:* 21 Mount St., Liverpool 1. *Signs work:* "Adrian Henri."

HENRION, F. Henri K., M.B.E. (1952), R.D.I., P.P.S.I.A., President, International Council of Graphic Design Associations (1968-70); member of Summerson and Coldstream Councils; general consulting designer; President Alliance Graphique Internationale (1963-66); Master of the Faculty of Royal Designers of the Royal Society of Arts; Ministry of Information (1941-43), consulting designer to U.S. Embassy and O.W.I. (1943-45), director of visual planning, Erwin Wasey, Ltd. (1954-58), consultant designer to K.L.M., G.P.O., the Blue Circle Group, B.E.A. and Volkswagen; *b* 18 Apr., 1914; *m* Daphne Hardy, sculptor; *studied art* in Paris. *Exhib.:* Museum of Modern Art, National Gallery, Stockholm; Stedelijk Museum, Amsterdam; Munich, New York, Tokyo, Warsaw, V. & A. *Publications:* With A. Parkin, Design Co-ordination and Corporate Image (1969). *Address:* 35 Pond St., London NW3. *Signs work:* "HENRION of HDA International."

HENTY-CREER, Deidre, F.R.S.A. (elected to Utd. Artists Council, 1947, 1952 and 1955); F.C.I.A.D. (1945); Artists of Chelsea (1961); Com. Chelsea Art Soc.; Com. Armed Forces Art Soc.; artist in oil; *b* Sydney, Australia; *d* of

Capt. Reginald C. F. Creer, R.N., retd. *Educ.:* privately; *studied art:* self-taught. *Exhib.:* R.A., R.O.I., R.B.A., N.E.A.C., N.S., U.A., Towner Art Gallery, Eastbourne, Russell-Cotes Gallery, Bournemouth, Williamson Art Gallery, Birkenhead, Municipal Galleries of Blackpool, Bolton, Bedford, Worthing, Wolverhampton, Worcester, Rotherham, Darlington, Submarine Museum, Gosport, H.M.S. Victory Museum, Portsmouth, etc. One-man shows, Fine Art Soc., Frost & Reed, Cooling Galleries, Bond St., Upper Grosvenor Gallery, Harrods, Palais Marie Cristine, Nice XIV Olympiad Sport in Art at Victoria and Albert Museum. *Work repro.:* The Artist, Cover of Studio, Medici Soc., T.A.V.R. Mag., Royal Sussex Regt. Mag., Poster for Municipality of Monaco, The Sphere, and in the U.S.A. *Address:* 5 St. Georges Ct., Gloucester Rd., London SW7.

HENTZEN, Werner, Mem., Academies of Perugia, Italy; Malaga, Toledo, Valencia, Spain; nomination as Commendatore by the Duca di Bedemar, Grande di Spagna; artist-painter; *b* Guldenworth, 25 Nov., 1900; *s* of Walter Hentzen; *m* Ilda Hoffman; one *s,* one *d. Studied art* at Dusseldorf Art Academy, Munich Art Academy, London. *Exhib.:* Florence, Italy, Berne, Thun, Switzerland, Vaduz, Liechtenstein, Berlin, Hamburg, Munich, Germany. *Work repro.:* book by Prof. Schaub-Koch, Geneva, Switzerland. *Address:* Chalet Monbijou, Hilterfingen, Lake of Thun, Switzerland. *Signs work:* "Werner Hentzen."

HEPPLE, Norman, R.A. (1961), A.R.A. (1954), R.P. (1948), N.E.A.C. (1950); *b* 1908; *m* Jillian Pratt; one *s,* one *d. Educ.:* Colfe's Grammar School, Blackheath; Goldsmiths' College; R.A. Schools. *Address:* 16 Cresswell Pl., London SW10. *Club:* Chelsea Arts. *Signs work:* "Norman Hepple."

HERBERT, Barry; artist/printmaker in silk-screen, etching, collage; lecturer; Warden of Grant House, University of Leeds (1969-73); Lecturer in Fine Art, University of Leeds; Secretary, Printmakers from Yorkshire; *b* York, 19 Mar., 1937; *m* Janet Herbert; one *s,* one *d. Educ.:* Archbishop Holgate's School, York; *studied art* at James Graham College (1959-61) under John Jones. *Exhib.:* one-man shows: Park Square Gallery, Leeds (1974), Victoria Gallery, Harrogate (1974), Northern Artists Gallery, Leeds (1973), Mappin A.G., Sheffield (1972), Galerie Brechbuhl, Grenchen (1972), Serpentine Gallery, London (1971), University Gallery, Leeds (1971), Gevim, Israel (1969), Nahal-Oz, Israel (1968), Manor House Gallery, Ilkley (1965); *print exhbns.:* Pratt Graphics Centre Gallery, N.Y. (1974), Photography into Art. London & Edinburgh (1973), International Triennale of Coloured Graphic Prints, Switzerland (commendation) (1970, 1973), First British International Print Beinnale (1968); numerous group and open exhbns. in Britain, Switzerland, Canada and Israel. *Address:* 43 Weetwood Lane, Leeds LS16 5NW. *Signs work:* "Barry Herbert."

HERKNER, Frederich, State Rome Prize for Sculpture (Vienna, 1929); ceramist; sculptor in stone and wood; Prof. of Sculpture at Dublin National College of Art since 1938; *b* Bruex, 25 Oct., 1902; *s* of Anton Herkner; *m* Maria Herkner; one *s,* two *d. Educ.:* Vienna; *studied art* at Vienna Academy of Fine Arts under Prof. Josef Müllner (1921-29). *Exhib.:* R.H.A., Vienna, Prague, Aussig, Leipzig, Dublin, New York World's Fair (1939) and London. *Work in permanent collection:* Prague Museum. *Work repro.:* in many British and European newspapers, magazines, etc. *Address:* National College of Art, Kildare St., Dublin. *Signs work:* see appendix.

HERMAN, Josef, Gold medal for services to Art in Wales (Llanelley, 1962); painter and draughtsman; *b* Warsaw, 3 Jan., 1911; naturalised British citizen (1948). *Educ.:* Warsaw, *Exhib.:* Warsaw (1932), Brussels (1939), Glasgow and Edinburgh (1942), Reid and Lefevre (1943), and since 1946 exhibits internationally, but chiefly with Roland, Browse and Delbanco; retrospective exhbn. Wakefield City A.G. (1955), Whitechapel A.G. (1956); surrealist Ballet of the Palette performed in Glasgow. *Work in permanent collections:* Arts Council, British Council, Stuyvesant Foundation, British Museum, Tate Gallery, V. & A., National Museum of Wales, Cardiff, Scottish National Gallery of Modern Art, Edinburgh, National Galleries of Melbourne, Wellington, Johannesburg, Ottawa, etc. *Publications:* Josef Herman Drawings by Basil Taylor (Jonathan Cape, 1956), Josef Herman, Paintings and Drawings by Edwin Mullins (Evelyn, Adams and Mackay, 1967). Related Twilights, notes from a painters diaries, by Josef Herman (Robson Books, 1975), Fifty Drawings by Herman from the Roland Collection (Graphic Press, 1975). *Films:* The Artist Speaks (BBC Television, 1960), Josef Herman by Anthony Roland (Paris, 1962), Private Lives—Josef Herman (Granada Television, 1975), A Day Eleven Years Long (BBC Wales, 1975). *Address:* 120 Edith Rd., London W14. *Agent:* Roland, Browse and Delbanco, London.

HERMAN, Sali, O.B.E.; Wynne, Sulman, Geelong, and Bendigo Prizeman; artist in oil; official war artist (1945-46); *b* Zürich, 12 Feb., 1898; *m* Paulette Briand; one *s,* one *d. Educ.:* at Zürich; *studied art* at Technical College, Zürich (1913-15), Rheinhard School, Zürich (1918) and at Melbourne under George Bell (1937-38). *Exhib.:* Kunsthaus Zürich, Melbourne, Sydney, N.Z. and London. *Work in permanent collections:* National Galleries; Melbourne, Sydney, Brisbane, Adelaide, Perth; Australian Legations, New York, Washington and Paris; Bendigo and Geelong Art Galleries, etc. *Official purchases:* as above. *Work repro.:* in Australian Artist, Art and Design, Contemporary Australian Art, Place, Taste, and Fashion, etc. *Publication:* Sali Herman by Daniel Thomas (1970). *Address:* 58 Palmgrove Rd., Avalon Beach, N.S.W. 2107, Australia. *Signs work:* "S. Herman."

HERMES, Gertrude, R.A. (1971), R.E.; sculptor and wood engraver; teacher, Royal Academy Schools of Art; *b* Bromley, Kent, 18 Aug., 1901; *d* of L. A. Hermes; *m;* one *s,* one *d. Educ.:* privately and Leon Underwood's School of Painting and Sculpture (1922-26). *Work in permanent collections:* B.M., V. & A., and other galleries at home and abroad. *Address:* 31 Danvers St., Chelsea, London SW3 5AY. *Signs work:* see appendix.

HERON, Hilary; three Taylor prizes; Mainie Jellet Travelling Scholarship (1948); sculptor in wood, stone, wrought metals; *b* Dublin, 27 Mar., 1923; *d* of James Heron; *m* Professor David Greene. *Educ.:* John Ivory's School; *studied art* at National College of Art, Dublin. *Exhib.:* Ulster Museum, Arts Council of Northern Ireland, Biennale Di Venezia (1956); one-man shows: Waddington Galleries, Dublin and London, Queen's University, Belfast; travelling group exhibitions to U.S.A., Scandinavia and Germany; regular exhibitor, Irish Exhibition of Living Art. *Address:* 2 Vico Terr., Dalkey, Co. Dublin. *Signs work:* see appendix.

HERON, Patrick; painter; *b* Leeds, 1920. *Exhib.:* one-man shows: Waddington Galleries, Bertha Schaefer Gallery (N.Y.), Galerie Lienhard (Zürich), São Paulo Bienal (1953 and 1965), Edinburgh, Oslo, Dublin, Rio de Janeiro, B. Aires, Santiago, Lima, Caracas, Waddington Fine Art, Montreal, Sydney, Melbourne, Toronto, etc. *Work in permanent collections:* Tate Gallery; Gulbenkian Foundation; National Portrait Gallery; Contemporary Art Society; V. & A. Museum; British Museum; Arts Council; British Council; Stuyvesant Foundation; Wakefield; Manchester; Cardiff; Aberdeen; Belfast; Eastbourne; Exeter University; Plymouth; Univ. of Warwick; Univ. of Stirling; Bedford; Oxford; Oldham; Leeds; Montreal; Toronto; Vancouver; Toledo, Ohio; Smith College, Mass,; Brooklyn; Albright-Knox, Buffalo; University of Michigan, Ann Arbor; Nat. Gall. of W.

Australia, Perth; Boymans Museum, Rotterdam; Power Collection, Sydney, etc. *Addresses:* Eagle's Nest, Zennor, St. Ives, Cornwall, and 12 Edith Mans., Edith Grove, London SW10.

HERRAGHTY, George Edward, D.A.; miniaturist and landscape artist in acrylic, oil, collage, graphite pencil; *b* Letterfourie, Buckie, Banffshire, 20 Mar., 1949; *s* of Edward A. Herraghty; *m* Fiona McDonald, B.Sc. *Educ.:* Carle Kemp Priory; Nairn Academy; Buckie High School; *studied art* at Duncan of Jordanstone College of Art, Dundee (1967-71) under Alberto Morrocco, R.S.A., David McClure, R.S.A.; Post-dip. (1971-72); S.E.D. Major Travelling Scholarship (1972); France, Italy, Spain and Portugal. *Exhib.:* S.S.A., R.S.A., Shed 50, Fife, New St. Gallery, Edinburgh, Galerie Tendenz, Sindelfingen, Germany. *Address:* 50 Seafield Rd., Dundee. *Signs work:* "G. HERRAGHTY."

HESSE, I. J. Berthe (Bertisme), Mrs.; full-time professional painter in oil on canvas (Bertisme); invented a totally new technique called Bertisme, hailed in the art world as the only serious new technique to emergy since Picassoism, involves the "sculpting" of a picture by tiny brush strokes on canvas out of enormous quantities of oil paint. No palette knife is used and a single painting can take a year to complete. Finished surface up to 2½ inches thick and takes several years to dry; *b* Paris, 4 Nov., 1925; *d* of J. Izapow, industrialist; *m* Adolph, one *d*. *Educ.:* Academie des Beaux Art, Paris; during the war, free classes. *Exhib.:* over 40, including Paris, Tel-Aviv and London. *Work in permanent collections:* Berthe Hess Museum, London; Les Amis d'I. J. Berthe Hess, Paris; and public collections. More than 200 important articles in national, local and international papers, antique and art magazines. *Address:* 34 Cathedral Pl., London EC4M 7ED. *Signs work:* "I. J. Berthe Hess"; fingerprint on back of canvas.

HEWISON, William, N.D.D., painting (1949), A.T.D. (1950), M.S.I.A. (1954); illustrator in ink; line and line and wash, and gouache; Art Editor, Punch; *b* South Shields, 15 May, 1925; *s* of Ralph Hewison; *m* Elsie Hammond; one *s*, one *d*. *Educ.:* South Shields High School; London University; *studied art* at South Shields Art School (1941-43), Regent St. Polytechnic Art School (1947-49). *Exhib.:* Whitechapel A.G. and in three Arts Council travelling exhbns., Young Contemporaries, Punch Exhbn. in U.S.A. (1953). *Work repro.:* illustrations and cartoons; Press advertisements, Punch; book jackets; books, Types Behind the Print, Mindfire. *Address:* 11 Seymour Rd., London SW19. *Signs work:* "Hewison" or "H."

HEWLAND, Elise Dalton, practising artist in oil, water-colour and gouache; Mem. of Medical Artists Assoc.; *b* 23 Nov., 1901; *d* of Robert Hewland, company director and accountant. *Educ.:* Sheffield Secondary School; Sheffield College of Art; R.A. Schools. *Exhib.:* R.A., R.W.S., Leicester Gallery, War Artists' Exhbn. (by special invitation). *Official purchases:* Nursery School for War Workers' Children, Schoolboys Learning to Drive a Tractor, Assembling Hawker Hurricanes, Typhoon Fly in Repair, Swinging the Compass and Test Flights, H-Hurricanes (National Collection of War Pictures). *Work repro.:* in Studio, Women's Institutes (Britain in Pictures), War Through Artists' Eyes, by Eric Newton. *Publications:* Fun on the Farm, Laddie Labrador (written and illustrated). *Address:* Ash Grove, Castle Rd., Ventnor, Isle of Wight. *Signs work:* see appendix.

HEY, Cicely; sculptor and modeller of miniature period figures; *b* 1896. *Studied art* at Central School of Arts and Crafts and Slade School. *Exhib.:* London Group, N.S., W.I.A.C., N.E.A.C., S.G.A., Lefevre Galleries ("Portraits of Art Celebrities." 1933), Inn Signs exhbn., Inn Crafts exhbn., Festival of Britain,

Geffrye Museum (Period Figures, 1964), etc. *Work in permanent collections:* portrait of D. S. McColl in B.M.; "Man-in-stock" Rural Life Mus., Reading University. *Official purchases:* Bob Hughes (terra-cotta) bt. by C.A.S. for Wales; ballad Singer bt. by Nat. Mus. of Wales. *Work repro.:* in Studio, Daily Telegraph, Radio Times, etc. *Address:* Tawelfryn, Llysfaen, Clwyd LL29 8UD. *Signs work:* "HEY."

HEYDENREICH, Ludwig H., Dr. Phil.; art historian; Fellowship, German Institute for History of Art, Florence (1928-34); priv. doz., University of Hamburg (1934-37); Asst. Prof., University of Berlin (1941); director, German Institute for History of Art, Florence (1943); director Zentralinstitut f. Kunstgeschichte, Munich (1947-70); Hon. Prof., University of Munich (1950); Member of the (Scientific) Academies of Florence, Munich, Vicenza and Vienna; *b* Leipzig, 23 Mar., 1903. *Educ.:* Universities of Berlin and Hamburg. *Publications:* Leonardo da Vinci (Berlin, 1944, 2nd ed. Basle, 1953, in German, English), Eclosion de la Renaissance, Italie 1400-1460 (Paris, 1972); Architecture in Italy 1400-1600 (with W. Lotz) (Baltimore, Md., 1974); many essays in various reviews. *Address:* Barerstrasse 11, Munich, Germany.

HEYWORTH, Alfred, R.W.S., R.B.A., N.E.A.C., A.R.C.A. (1949); Fourth Year Drawing Prize, French Government Scholarship (one year, Paris); painter in oil, water-colour, pastel; visiting teacher, Kingston College of Art; visitor, Epsom School of Art; *b* Birmingham, 1926; *s* of John Heyworth; *m* Sonia Marie; one *d.* *Educ.:* Clifton Road School, Birmingham; *studied art* at Moseley Junior Art School (1939-42), Birmingham College of Art (1942-46), Royal College of Art (1946-50), La Grande Chaumière (1950-51). *Work in permanent collections:* Birmingham Art Gallery, Sheffield Art Gallery, Bradford Art Gallery, Preston Art Gallery, Beecroft Art Gallery, Southend, Kent C.C. *Address:* 7 Cleveland Ave., Chiswick, London W4. *Club:* Chelsea Arts. *Signs work:* "Heyworth."

HIBBERT, Phyllis I., B.W.S., C.T.E.; artist in water-colour and oil of flowers; former art teacher, College of Further Education, St. Annes-on-Sea, Lytham St. Annes; *b* 10 Mar., 1903. *Studied art* at Preston School of Art, Liverpool College of Art. *Exhib.:* R.A., R.I., S.W.A., R.B.A. Gallery, R.Cam.A., Atkinson Gallery, Southport, Walker A.G., Liverpool, Manchester Academy. *Work in permanent collections:* Grundy A.G., Blackpool, Harris A.G., Preston. *Publications:* Weldon's Publications. *Address:* 59 Blackpool Rd., Ansdell, Lytham St. Annes. *Clubs:* B.W.S., Blackpool Sketch, Lytham St. Annes Art Soc. *Signs work:* "Phyllis I. Hibbert."

HICKLING, Edward Albert; artist in oil and water-colour; technical illustrator; *b* Nottingham, 2 May, 1913; *s* of A. Hickling. *Educ.:* Nottingham; *studied art* at Nottingham College of Art (1927-39) under A. Spooner, R.B.A. *Exhib.:* R.A., R.B.A., R.I., R.O.I., R.P. (1972, 1973), R.S.M.A. *Address:* 25 Wilsthorpe Rd., Breaston, Derbys. *Clubs:* Nottingham Soc. of Artists, Derby Sketching. *Signs work:* "E. A. Hickling."

HICKS, Anne, R.W.A., Slade Dip.; artist in oil and water-colour of portraits, murals, costume design, environmental design; Adult Education Avon and Visiting Lecturer, University Architects Dept., Bristol; *b* London; *d* of J. R. G. Hayward, C.Eng, F.I.E.E.; *m* Jerry Hicks; one *s*, one *d.* *Educ.:* Hampstead and Minehead; *studied art* at Slade School under Profs. Schwabe and Coldstream. *Exhib.:* R.W.A., British Women Painters Musée de l'Art Moderne, Paris (1967); two-man shows with husband: Bristol Biannual (1954-75), Cardiff (1969). *Work in private collections* in England, France, America, New Zealand. *Address:* Goldrush, Gt. George St., Bristol 1. *Work unsigned* unless requested.

HICKS, Jerry, A.T.D., R.W.A., Slade Dip., Judo 4th Dan; artist in oil, pastel, etc. of murals, stage design, portraits; head art dept., Cotham Grammar Bristol, Sports Council (S.W.); *b* London, 12 June, 1927; *s* of Algernon Hicks, actor; *m* Anne Hayward; one *s*, one *d*. *Educ.:* Actors' Orphanage and Rishworth, Halifax; *studied art* at Slade School under Prof. Coldstream, Freud, Bird, and with Walter Bayes. *Exhib.:* R.A., R.W.A., R.I.B.A.; two-man shows with wife; Bristol Biannual (1954-75), Cardiff (1969). Winner of Bristol 600 Competition (1973). *Work in private collections* in Britain, U.S.A., Canada, Jamaica, Germany, France, Australia, Japan. *Address:* Goldrush, Gt. George St., Bristol 1. *Work unsigned* unless requested.

HIGGINS, Charles S., B.Sc. (London); author and painter in oil and water-colour; *b* Belgrano, Buenos Aires, 18 Mar., 1893; *s* of William Higgins, O.B.E., shipping and company director; *m* the late Kate E. Olver. *Educ.:* Michael Charles Kickham's Academy, Belgrano, Malvern College and London University; *studied art* in London, Paris and Rome. *Exhib.:* Leading London Galleries, Rome, Paris, U.S.A. *Official purchases:* Contemporary Arts Soc., Johns Hopkins Inst., Boston. *Work repro.:* in The Queen, Studio, Moderns, Architectural Review, Arts Review etc. *Publications:* Noah's Wife, Here are Stones, Singing Waters, Sun Before Seven, One Man's Anthology (under pen-name "Ian Dall"). *Address:* 15 Hall Rd., London NW8. *Signs work:* "Pic."

HIGGINS, Francis Wilfrid, F.I.A.L.; portrait painter; served as Flight Lieut. in R.F.C. and R.A.F. in both World Wars; *b* Chester, 1893; *m* Margaret Helena Horton, *d* of William Horton, M.Sc., Liverpool. *Educ.:* Chester College, Chester Grosvenor Museum; *studied art* at Chester, London and Italy. *Exhib.:* R.A., R.S.A., R.H.A., Paris Salon, National Galleries of Ottawa, Toronto, New South Wales, Florence, Rome and most provincial and Continental galleries. Gold and Silver Medallist, Men. Hon. Société des Artistes Français. *Address:* 29 Selkirk Rd., Curzon Pk., Chester. *Clubs:* Devonshire, Arts, Royal Air Force, Chester City. *Signs work:* "WILFRID HIGGINS" ("Higgins" under "Wilfrid").

HILDER, Rowland, P.P.R.I., R.S.M.A.; painter; *b* 28 June, 1905; *m*; one *s*, one *d*. *Educ.:* Goldsmiths' College. *Exhib.:* widely in public and private collections; Furneaux Gallery, Wimbledon, London. *Work repro.:* illustrated editions of Moby Dick (Cape), Treasure Island (Oxford Press), Precious Bane (Cape), The Bible for Today (O.U.P.), The Shell Guide to Flowers of the Countryside (Phoenix House), British Wildflowers, Ladybird Books (in collaboration with Edith Hilder). *Publications:* Starting with Watercolour (Studio Vista); numerous large prints published by Royle Publications Ltd. *Address:* 5 Kidbrooke Grove, Blackheath, London SE3. *Signs work:* "Rowland Hilder."

HILL, Adrian Keith Graham, P.P.R.O.I., R.B.A., R.I., S.G.A.; painter in oil and water-colour; Hon. Artillery Coy. (1914); official War Artist (1917-18); Vice-Pres. of R.B.A. Art Club (1930); Vice-Pres., St. James Art Soc. (1948); Pres. Chichester Art Society (1969); *s* of Graham Hill; *m*; one *s*. *Educ.:* Dulwich, R.C.A. *Exhib.:* R.A., Paris Salon, U.S.A., Canada, S. Africa, U.S.S.R. *Official purchases:* V. & A. Museum, Brighton, Derby, Oldham, Northampton, Bradford, Leicester, Cork, Lever Art Gallery, Imperial War Museum. *Publications:* numerous books on drawing and painting. *Address:* Old Laundry Cottage, Midhurst, Sussex. *Signs work:* "Adrian Hill."

HILL, Anthony; artist, plastician and theorist: works in industrial materials; awarded Leverhulme Fellowship, Hon. Research Fellow, Dept. Mathematics, University College, London (1971-73); on staff of Chelsea School of Art; *b* London, 23 Apr., 1930; *s* of Adrian Hill, R.B.A. *Educ.:* Bryanston; *studied art* at

St. Martin's (1947-49), Central School (1949-51). *Exhib.:* Kasmin Gallery (1966, 1969). *Work in permanent collections:* Tate Gallery, Whitworth Art Museum, Arts Council, British Council, V. & A., McCrory Corp., N.Y., Gulbenkian Foundation, Stuyvesant Foundation, Kröller-Muller Museum, Otterloo. *Articles and work repro.:* in English, Continental and American publications since 1950. *Address:* 24 Charlotte St., London W1. *Signs work:* "Anthony Hill." and see appendix.

HILL, Derek; painter in oil and stage designer; director of Art, British School at Rome (1953-55 and 1957-59); organiser of Degas Exhbn. at Edinburgh Festival and Tate Gallery; *b* Southampton, 6 Dec., 1916; *s* of A. J. L. Hill. *Educ.:* Marlborough College; *studied art* at Munich, Vienna, Paris, and theatre design in Russia, China and Japan. *Exhib.:* Leicester Galleries, Whitechapel Gallery (1961). *Work in permanent collections:* Tate Gallery, Belfast Art Gallery, Dublin Municipal Gallery, Arts Council, National Gallery of Canada. *Publication:* co-author, Islamic Architecture—Its Decoration (Faber & Faber, 1964). *Address:* St. Colomb's, Churchill (Letterkenny), Co. Donegal, Ireland. *Club:* Travellers. *Signs work:* "D.H." in a circle when picture is signed.

HILL, Dorothy Kent, A.B. (1928), Ph.D. (1933), ΦBK; Fellow of Archæological Inst. of America at American School of Classical Studies, Athens (1930-31); archæologist; Research Assoc., Walters Art Gallery (1934-37), Assoc. curator (1937-42), curator since 1942; *b* New York, 3 Feb., 1907; *d* of Arthur Edward Hill, Prof. of Chemistry, New York University. *Educ.:* Vassar College and Johns Hopkins University. *Publications:* Catalogue of Classical Bronze Sculpture in the Walters Art Gallery (1949); articles in American Journal of Archæology, Hesperia, Journal of the Walters Art Gallery, etc., editor of book reviews, American Journal of Archæology (since 1957). *Address:* 249 West 31st St., Baltimore, Md., 21211.

HILL, Raymond A., A.R.C.A. (1939), N.R.D. (1940), F.R.S.A.; artist in water-colour, engraving, design for silver, lettering; head of Worcester School of Art (1947-50); head of Swindon School of Art (1950-53), head of Industrial Design, Liverpool College of Art (1953-64), restoration specialist, South Liverpool church; *b* Leicester, 11 Oct., 1916; *s* of Arthur C. Hill, minister of the Gospel; *m* Olive Haffenden; one *s*, three *d*. *Educ.:* Wyggeston Grammar School, Leicester; Skinners', Tunbridge Wells; *studied art* at Tunbridge Wells School of Art under E. Owen Jennings (1933-36), R.C.A. under Prof. Tristram (1936-40). *Exhib.:* Modern silverwork, Goldsmiths' Hall, 48th Church Congress, Arts and Crafts Exhbn. Soc., Artists' International Assoc., etc. *Address:* 31 Mossley Hill Rd., Liverpool L18 4PT. *Signs work:* see appendix.

HILL, Rowland, A.R.U.A.; landscape and portrait painter in oil and water-colour; *b* Belfast, 18 July, 1919; *s* of Thomas Hill; *m*; one *d*. *Educ.:* Belfast; *studied art* at Belfast College of Art under Fred Allen, Newton Penprase and Mr. Stoupe (anatomy). *Exhib.:* R.H.A., Dublin, London, Toronto, Belfast, R.U.A. (annual). *Address:* 18 Sycamore Dr., Jordanstown, Co. Antrim, N. Ireland. *Club:* Ulster Arts. *Signs work:* "Rowland Hill."

HILLIER, Tristram Paul, A.R.A. (1957), R.A. (1967); painter in oil; *b* Peking, 11 Apr., 1905; *s* of Edward Guy Hillier, C.M.G., banker; *m* 1st, Irene Rose Hodgkins (dissolved, 1935), two *s*; 2nd, Leda Millicent Hardcastle, two *d*. *Educ.:* Downside and Christ's College, Cambridge; *studied art* at Slade School under Prof. Henry Tonks and at Academie L'Hote. *Exhib.:* one-man shows at Galerie Barreiro, Paris (one), Langton Gallery (one), Reid & Lefévre Galleries (two) and at Arthur Tooth & Sons (eight). *Official purchases:* Tate Gallery, National Gallery of Canada (Ottawa), National Gallery of N.S.W. (Sydney), National Gallery of Victoria (Melbourne), National Gallery of S. Australia (Adelaide), Toronto Art Gallery, Manchester City Art Gallery, Ferens Art Gallery (Hull), Aberdeen Art Gallery, Leeds Art Gallery, Contemporary Art Soc., Southampton Art Gallery; U.S.A. (Public Collection), City of Belfast Art Gallery, City of Nottingham Art Gallery, Min. of Works (British Embassies Fund), W. Riding Educ. Com., Hamilton Bequest, City of Glasgow Art Gallery, Oldham Art Gallery, Preston Art Gallery, Rochdale Museum. *Publication:* Leda and the Goose, published by Longmans, 1954. *Address:* Yew Tree Cottage, E. Pennard, Shepton Mallet, Som.

HILLS, Peter Faber, N.D.D., R.A.Cert., A.R.B.S., Past Secretary of the 65 Group (Public School Art Masters); Churchill Fellow in Sculpture (1972); sculptor in clay, stone, wood; schoolmaster; Director of Art, Tonbridge School; *b* Bearsted, Kent, 4 Dec., 1925; *m* Ann-Mary Ewart (née Macdonald); two *s*, one *d*. *Educ.:* Tonbridge School; *studied art* at Bromley College of Art (1948-50), R.A. Schools (1950-55); assistant to Maurice Lambert, R.A. (1955-60), and worked for Sir Henry Rushbury, R.A., Sir Albert Richardson, P.R.A. *Work in permanent collections:* Lord Leighton Museum, Kensington, Skinner's Library, Tonbridge School. *Address:* 33 Yardley Park Rd., Tonbridge, Kent. *Signs work:* "HILLS."

HIPKISS, Percy Randolph, A.R.B.S.A. (1971); freelance artist in oil, water-colour and pastel; jewellery designer; president, Birmingham Water-colour Soc.; *b* Blackheath, Birmingham, 8 Aug., 1912; *s* of William Hipkiss, woodworker; *m* Dorothy Alice Boraston; one *s*, one *d*. *Educ.:* at Blackheath. *Work in permanent collections:* Dudley A.G., and in private collections throughout U.K., America, Australia, Belgium. *Address:* 18 Lewis Rd., Oldbury, Warley, Worcs. *Signs work:* "Hipkiss."

HISCOCK, Jeannette; Mem. Oxford Art Soc.; painter in water-colour and oils; *b* Oxford, 1895; *d* of John Manson Timms; *m* W. G. Hiscock, Hon. M.A.; one *d*. *Educ.:* Oxford and Ruskin School (Alexander MacDonald, 1918-20; S. Carline, 1927). *Exhib.:* Oxford Art Soc., R.I., Ryman's Galleries, Oxford, and Blackhall St. Giles (Oxford) (June, 1953), S.W.A., Renaissance Galleries, Russell-Cotes Gallery, Bournemouth, Halifax House, Oxford (Nov.), White Hart Hotel, Fyfield (1966, 1967). *Address:* 18 Squitchey La., Oxford. *Signs work:* "J. Hiscock."

HISLOP, Margaret, R.S.A. (1964); artist in oil, water-colour, etc.; one *d*, Vivien Mary Hislop, artist, Daily Mail Home Editor. *Studied art* at Edinburgh College of Art. *Work in permanent collections:* Edinburgh, Greenock, Glasgow, Dundee, Australia, etc. *Address:* 10 Inverleith Row, Edinburgh, 3. *Signs work:* "Margaret Hislop."

HITCHCOCK, Harold Raymond, F.R.S.A. (1972); Hon. Col. of State of Louisiana U.S.A. (1974); artist in water-colour and oil; *b* London, 23 May, 1914; *s* of Thomas R. Hitchcock; *m* Rose Hitchcock; two *s*, one *d*. *Studied art* at Working Mens College, Camden Town (1935-36) under Percy Horton, Barnett Freedman. *Exhib.:* one-man shows: Campbell & Franks (Fine Art) Ltd. (1975), Pilkington Glass Museum (1973), Hilton Gallery (1970), Upper Grosvenor Gallery (1969), Woburn Abbey (1967), Walker Gallery (1956); retrospective show: R.I. Galleries (1967); touring exhbn. in U.S.A.: New Orleans, Huntsville, Atlanta City, Daytona Beach, Corpus Christi and Winston Salem (opened by the Duke of Bedford, 1972). *Work in permanent collections:* Rowntree Memorial Trust, Lidice Memorial Museum, Czechoslovakia, Museum of Fine Art, N. Carolina, University of Louisiana. *Address:* Meadow View, Ugborough, Ivybridge, Devon. *Signs work:* see appendix.

HITCHENS, John; painter in oil; *b* Sussex, 1940; *s* of Ivon Hitchens, painter;

m; two *s. Educ.:* Bedales School; *studied art* at Bath Academy of Art. *Work in permanent collections:* W. Sussex Educ. Com., Brighton A.G., Leicestershire Educ. Com., W. Riding of Yorkshire Educ. Com., Nuffield College, Oxford, Ferens A.G., Hull, Leicester University, City of Leicester Museums and A.G., Nuffield Foundation for Paintings in Hospitals, Bradford City A.G., Towner A.G., Eastbourne, Bradford Institute of Technology, British Steel Corp., Hull Educ. Com. *Address:* The Old School, Byworth, Petworth, Sussex. *Signs work:* "John Hitchens."

HITCHENS, Sydney Ivon, C.B.E. (1958); painter; *b* London, 3 Mar., 1893; *s* of Alfred Hitchens; *m* Mary Cranford Coates; one *s. Educ.:* Bedales School; *studied art* at St. John's Wood School of Art and R.A. Schools. *Exhib.:* Mayor Gallery, Arthur Tooth & Son, L.A.A., Mansard Gallery, Lefévre Galleries, Leicester Galleries, Waddington Galleries, Rutland Galleries, Poindexter, New York; *retrospective exhbns.:* Temple Newsam, Leeds; Graves A.G., Sheffield; Leicester Galleries; Venice Biennale, 1956; Wiener Secession, Vienna; Mus. d'Art Moderne, Paris; Stedelijk Museum, Amsterdam; Tate Gallery, London (1963); 69-foot mural in Cecil Sharp House, Hampstead. *Represented in public collections,* including Gottenberg Museum, Sweden; N.G., Oslo; Museum d'Art Moderne, Paris; V. & A. London; Nat. Museum of Wales, Cardiff; British Council; Arts Council; American galleries; Australia; New Zealand; Canada; Ashmolean, Oxford; Fitzwilliam Museum, Cambridge; Tate Gallery, London; H.M. the Queen's private collection. *Monographs on his work:* Penguin Modern Painters by Patrick Heron; and Ivon Hitchens by Alan Bowness, introduced by T. G. Rosenthal (Lund Humphries). *Address:* Greenleaves, Petworth, Sussex. *Signs work:* see appendix.

HO, Kok-Hoe, M.S.I.A., F.R.A.I.A., F.R.I.B.A., A.P.A.M., A.R.A.S., A.R.P.S.; awarded St. Andrew's Gold (1935) and Bronze (1937); 2nd Inter-School Art gold medal (1939); architect; artist in oil and water-colour painting, pen and pencil drawing; art-photographer; president-director, Ho Kwong-Yew & Sons, Architects, Singapore; Chairman, Singapore Art Soc. (1953-70); *b* Singapore, 14 July, 1922. *Educ.:* St. Andrew's School, Singapore; graduated N.S.W. College of Architecture, Sydney. *Exhib.:* Sydney (1948-49); Singapore (1954-62); Kuala Lumpur (1960-62), etc. Photo salons: London (1957); La Coruna (1958); Hongkong (1958), etc. Architectural Work: National Museum, Kuala Lumpur, etc. *Publications:* Travel Sketches and Paintings, etc. *Clubs:* Royal Art Soc.; Royal Institute of Australian Architects; R.I.B.A.; Royal Photographic Soc. of Great Britain; Singapore Art Soc. *Address:* 9 Chamben Park, Singapore 11. *Signs work:* "Ho Kok-Hoe."

HOBART, John, B.Sc. (Lond.), R.C.A.; painter in oil and water-colour; senior lecturer in University College of North Wales, Bangor; *b* London, 27 May, 1922; *s* of P. J. Hobart; *m* Mair Roberts; one *s,* two *d. Educ.:* St. Dunstan's College and University College, London. *Exhib.:* North Wales Group, Royal Cambrian A.C.A.D., R.I. *Address:* Y Wern, Hwfa Rd., Bangor, N. Wales. *Signs work:* see appendix.

HOBBS, Henry William; industrial designer and artist; consultant and designer on aesthetics and mechanical principles of industrial equipment, domestic appliances, small machinery and scientific apparatus; *b* Ealing, 2 June, 1897. *Educ.:* Latymer Upper School, Hammersmith; London School of Economics; *studied art* at Chiswick School of Art under H. Schroder. *Address:* Spring Cottage, Marley Lane, Haslemere, Surrey. *Signs work:* "Hy. W. Hobbs."

HOBLING, Ronald Edward Wilton, F.I.A.L.; painter in oil, pastel and black and white (portraits); *b* London. *Studied art* at Hornsey School of Art under J. C.

Moody, A.R.E., R.I., H. J. Youngman, F.R.B.S., A.R.C.A., Russell Reeve, R.B.A.; finishing course in portraiture under Frank L. Emanuel, P.S.G.A. *Exhib.:* R.O.I., London Portrait Soc., R.I., Foyle's Gallery, Whitechapel Art Gallery, Parson's Gallery, Artists of Chelsea, and in provinces. *Work repro.:* Morning Post, Kensington News, La Revue Moderne, Mitre Press. *Address:* 6 Wimborne Rd., London, N17. *Signs work:* "HOBLING."

HOCKEY, James Morey, R.B.A., R.O.I., F.S.A.E.; pres. Farnham Art Soc.; painter in oil and water-colour, portraits, landscapes, flower pieces; etcher, engraver; *b* Clapham Park, 4 Mar., 1904; *s* of James Morey Hockey; *m* 1st, Winifred Gagen (d. 1959); 2nd Ethel Violet Fear (d. 1968); 3rd, Phyllis Shimield. *Educ.:* Alleyn's School, Dulwich; *studied art* at Goldsmiths' College School of Art (1922-27). *Exhib.:* R.A., N.E.A.C., R.B.A., R.O.I., etc. *Work in permanent collections:* Bournemouth Art Gallery (flower piece). *Official purchases:* Contemporary Art Soc. *Address:* 37 Guildford Rd., Farnham, Surrey. *Club:* Arts. *Signs work:* "JAMES HOCKEY."

HODGES, Cyril Walter, F.S.I.A. (1952); author, mural painter, illustrator, stage designer; *b* Beckenham, 1909; *m* Greta Becker; two *s. Educ.:* Dulwich College; *studied art* at Goldsmiths' College. *Work repro.:* advertisements, books, magazine illustrations in England and U.S.A. Special subjects: costume and period illustrations, theatre, Shakespeare. Designer of Mermaid Theatre (1951), Lloyd's 1951 Exhbn., executed mural painting for United Kingdom Provident Inst. (1957). *Publications:* Columbus Sails, The Globe Restored, The Namesake, Shakespeare's Theatre, The Overland Launch, Shakespeare's Second Globe, Playhouse Tales. Awarded Kate Greenaway Medal for Illustration (1964). *Address:* 36 Southover High St., Lewes, Sussex. *Signs work:* "C. Walter Hodges."

HODGKINSON, Terence William Ivan, C.B.E. (1958), B.A. (Oxon), 1935; Director, The Wallace Collection; *b* 1913 at Wells, Som.; *s* of Ivan Tattersall Hodgkinson, author. *Educ.:* Oundle School; Magdalen College, Oxford. *Publications:* Articles. *Address:* The Wallace Collection, Manchester Square, London.

HODGKINSON, Wilfred Philip, A.T.D.; artist, craftsman and author; Princ., Truro School of Art (1935-39); Princ., Bilston School of Art (1939-46); Curator, Bilston Art Gallery (1939-46); retd. Principal Art Lecturer; *b* 30 Apr., 1912; *m. Educ.:* King Charles I School, Kidderminster; Kidderminster School of Art; Birmingham College of Art. *Exhib.:* London, Truro, Wolverhampton, Bilston. *Work repro.:* by Austin Motors Ltd. (Milestones of Progress). *Publications:* The Eloquent Silence, The Kingdom is a Garden. *Address:* 90 Stanmore La., Winchester. *Signs work:* "W. P. Hodgkinson," or, on cartoons, "W.P.H."

HODIN, Josef Paul, L.L.D. (Prague), Ph.D. (Hon., Uppsala), D.S.M., 1st Class, Czech; Commander order of merit, Italian; St. Olav Medal, Norwegian; Grand Cross, order of merit, Austrian; Silver Cross of Merit, Vienna; author, art historian, critic; librarian of I.C.A. (1949-54); press attaché to the Norwegian Govt. (1944-45); director of Studies, I.C.A. (1949-54); co-editor of Quandrum, Brussels; mem. executive comm. British Society of Aesthetics; hon. mem. Editorial Council J.A.A.C., Cleveland; dir. foreign rel. Studio International, London; awarded intern. 1st prize for art criticism, 1954 (Biennale, Venice); *b* Prague, 17 Aug., 1905; *s* of Edouard D. Hodin; *m* Doris Pamela Simms; one *s*, one *d*. *Educ.:* Realschule, Realgymnasium, and Charles University, Prague; *studied art* at Dresden, Berlin, Paris and Stockholm, and at the Courtauld Institute of Art, London University. *Publications:* Monographs on Sven Erixson (1940), Ernst Josephson (1942), Edvard Munch (1948, 1951, 1963 and 1972), Isaac Grünwald (1949), Art and Criticism (1944), J. A. Comenius and Our Time (1944), The

Dilemma of Being Modern (1956 and 1959), Henry Moore (1956 and 1958), Ben Nicholson (1957), Lynn Chadwick (1961), Barbara Hepworth (1961), Alan Reynolds (1962), Oskar Kokoschka (1963, 1966, 1968 and 1973), Walter Kern (1966), Ruszkowski (1966), Bernard Leach (1967), Kafka and Goethe (1968), Emilio Greco (1970), Giacomo Manzù (1969), Modern Art and the Modern Mind (1972), Bernard Stern (1972), The painter Alfred Manessier (1972), Ludwig Meidner (1973), Hilde Goldschmidt (1973), Paul Berger-Bergner (1974), Kokoschka and Hellas (1976). Novels: Die Brühlsche Terasse (1970), Die Leute von Elverdingen (1974); contributor to Encyclopedia Universale dell' Arte, Rome; literary and art essays published in various periodicals in England and abroad. *Address:* 12 Eton Ave., London NW3.

HODSON, John; abstract and impressionist artist in oil; *b* Oxford, 19 Aug., 1945; *s* of Frank George Hodson, toolmaker. *Educ.:* Cardinal Hinsley School, London. *Exhib.:* one-man show London (1973). *Work in permanent collections:* Paris Salon, Salon des Independants. *Work repro.:* Modern Art Revue. *Address:* 2 Richborough Rd., London NW2. *Signs work:* "J. Hodson."

HOFER, Paul, Dr. Phil. (1938), Privatdocent Univ. Bern (1948), ao. Prof. (1956); Prof. of Ecole polytechnique, Univ. Lausanne (1962); Prof. Eidg. Techn. Hochschule, Zürich (1964, o. Prof., 1967); historian of Art; *b* Bern, 8 Aug., 1909; *s* of Friedrich Hofer; *m* Gertrud Wild, Dr. Phil. *Educ.:* Bern, Elementary School and Gymnasium; *studied art* history at Univ. of Bern under Prof. Artur Weese and H. R. Hahnloser, Univ. of Munich under Prof. Wilhelm Pinder. *Publications:* Die Italienische Landschaft im 16. Th. (1946), Die Kunstdenkmäler des Kantons Bern, Vol. I, Basle (1952), Vol. II, Basle (1959), Vol. III, Basle (1947), Vol. V, Basle (1968); Bern, Die Stadt als Monument (1953), Die Wehrbauten Berns (1953), Flugbildder Schweizer Stadt (with Prof. Hans Boesch, Univ. of Zürich, 1963), Palladios Eistling (1968), Fundplätze, Bauplätze (1970). *Address:* Halensiedlung 2, Bern-Stuckishaus.

HOFFER, Franz Peter Bernard, M.S.I.A.; architect/designer, painter; hon. sec., Society of Mural Painters (1948-51); designer, Glasgow Citizens' Theatre, Stratford-on-Avon, London; consultant architect designer, Reader's Digest; *b* Berlin, 1924; *s* of Dr. W. Hoffer; *m* Maria Pilar Perez Vales; three children. *Educ.:* Bunce Court School, Kent; *studied art* St. Martin's School of Art, Cambridge. *Exhib.:* R.B.A., Leicester Gallery, Arts Council, Amsterdam, Milan. *Work in permanent collections:* U.S. Theatre Library, Washington and private collections. *Work repro.:* Das Kunstwerk, Designers in Britain, Studio, Domus, Architectural Review. *Address:* Via Montebello 30, Milan. *Signs work:* "F. P. Hoffer."

HOFFMANN, Edith, Ph.D., Munich, 1934; art historian and critic; editorial asst., Burlington Magazine (1938-46); asst. editor of the Burlington Magazine (1946-50); lecturer, Hebrew University of Jerusalem (1960-61); art editor of the Encyclopaedia Hebraica (Jerusalem, 1953-65); *d* of Camill Hoffmann, author; *m* Dr. E. Yapou; one *d. Educ.:* in Berlin, Vienna, Munich. *Publications:* Kokoschka: Life and Work (1947); Chagall: Water-colours (1947); contributions to the Burlington Magazine, Apollo, Art News (New York), Phoebus (Basle), Studio, Manchester Guardian, Listener, New Statesman, Twentieth Century, Neue Zürcher Zeitung, etc. *Address:* Alfasi St. 27, Jerusalem, Israel.

HOFLEHNER, Rudolf; sculptor and painter; Professor an der Akademie der bildenden Künste, Stuttgart; skulpturen in Eisen, massiv; *b* Linz, 8 Aug., 1916; *s* of Johann Hoflehner; *m* Luse Schaffer. *Studied art* at Akademie der bild. Künste, Vienna. *Addresses:* Italien, Val d'Elsa, Podere Pantaneto, Provincia Siena.; atelier: Wien 2, Krieau Atelier 10; Stuttgart Nord, Akademie der bild. Künste, am Weissenhof 1. *Signs work:* see appendix.

HOGARTH, Arthur Paul, A.R.A., F.S.I.A., Dr. R.C.A.; illustrator and draughtsman; visiting lecturer, Royal College of Art; *b* Kendal, Cumbria, 4 Oct., 1917; *s* of Arthur Hogarth. *Studied art* at Manchester School of Art, London and Paris. *Official purchases:* Library of Congress, Washington, D.C., Brooklyn Art Museum, State Museum, Bucharest, Fitzwilliam Museum, Cambridge, National Museum, Warsaw, and works in various private collections. *Works in permanent collections:* Manchester, Newcastle, Bradford, Carlisle, Dudley, Bury and Blackburn, Whitworth Art Inst., Manchester, Trinity College, Cambridge. *Publications:* author of Artist as Reporter (London and New York, 1967), an historical study of the creative artist's involvement with journalism; Artists on Horseback (New York, 1972), a study of the Old West through the eyes of British artists; illustrator of Brendan Behan's Island and Brendan Behan's New York (with Brendan Behan); Majorca Observed (with Robert Graves); London à la Mode (with Malcolm Muggeridge); Russian Journey (with Alaric Jacob). Contributor to leading American and European periodicals including Fortune, Sports Illustrated and Daily Telegraph Magazine. *Address:* Ca'n Bi, Deya, Majorca. *Signs work:* "Paul Hogarth" or "P.H."

HOLDEN, Harold H., R.W.S., A.R.C.A. (Lond.), R.B.S.A.; painter in water-colour; retired teacher; Princ., Cheltenham School of Art; Princ., Leeds College of Art; Princ., Birmingham College of Art and Director of Art Educ. for Birmingham; *b* Settle, Yorks., 1885; *s* of Thomas H. Holden; *m* Elizabeth Corney; four *s*. *Studied art:* Settle Art Classes; Skipton School of Art; Leeds College of Art; R.C.A. London. *Exhib.:* R.A., R.W.S., other exhbns. at home and abroad. *Work in permanent collections* (*all official purchases*)*:* Cheltenham, Leeds, Birmingham, Brierley Hill, Chicago. *Work repro.:* in Studio. *Address:* 3 Southwood Drive, Westbury-on-Trym, Bristol. *Signs work:* "HAROLD H. HOLDEN."

HOLDEN, John H., A.R.C.A., A.T.D., Hon. A.D.F. (Manc.); deputy director, Manchester Polytechnic; formerly Principal, Manchester College of Art and Design; before that Principal, Wolverhampton College of Art; Vice Chairman, National Council for Diplomas in Art Design; past president, N.S.A.E., and A.A.I.; *b* Leeds, 5 May, 1913; *s* of H. H. Holden, A.R.C.A., R.W.S. (ex principal Birmingham College of Art); *m* Barbara Holden; one *d*. *Educ.:* King Edwards School, Birmingham; *studied art* at Birmingham College of Art, R.C.A. *Exhib.:* R.A. and provincial galleries. *Work repro.:* articles on art, design and education in journals. *Address:* 5 Kings Rd., Wilmslow, Ches.

HOLDEN-JONES, Mrs. Margaret Talbot, A.R.C.A., F.R.S.A., F.I.A.L., Hon. F.S.D.-C.; artist in water-colour, calligraphy, embroidery and other crafts; lecturer at Goldsmiths' College, North-Western Polytechnic (1934-45, 1945-58, retd.); *b* Liverpool; *d* of W. S. Holden, solicitor. *Educ.:* Belvedere School, G.P.D.S.T., Liverpool; *studied art* at Liverpool School of Art and Royal College of Art under Prof. W. R. Lethaby and Edward Johnston (1913-21). *Exhib.:* Arts and Crafts Exhbn. Soc. at R.A., Crafts Centre of Gt. Britain International Exhbn., Paris, U.S.A., New Zealand and other countries. *Work repro.:* Studio, Builder, Teacher's World, Christian Science Monitor, La Revue Moderne, Paris, etc., and work executed for the Trustees under the will of Mary Baker Eddy for publication in Christian Science Reading Rooms, script for War Records for Royal Inst. of Chartered Surveyors (1914-19) and (1939-45). *Publications:* The Embroideress, Christian Science Monitor, B.M. acquired two works in (1969), V. & A. acquired one work (1969), two works (1974). *Address:* 32 Bigginwood Rd., London SW16 3RZ. *Signs work:* "Margaret T. Holden-Jones."

HOLGATE, Margaret (Mrs.), A.R.C.A. (1940); teacher at Newport, (Mon.) School of Art (1941-45); *b* Caernarvon, 1917; *d* of David Greenfield; *m* James

Holgate. *Educ.:* Newport High School; *studied art* at Newport School of Art (1933-37) and R.C.A. (1937-40). Designs and makes souvenirs that she hopes are worth buying—mainly for the Welsh market. *Address:* 35 Southwood Ave., Highgate, London N6. *Signs work:* "Margaret Holgate."

HOLISTER, Frederick Darnton, M.A. (Cantab.) (1957), M.Arch. Harvard (1953), A.R.I.B.A., Wheelwright Fellowship, Harvard (1952); Fellow, Clare College, Cambridge; Director of Studies in Architecture, Clare College, Cambridge; University Lecturer, Department of Land Economy, Cambridge; architect in private practice; *b* Coventry, 14 Aug., 1927; *s* of F. D. Holister, M.I.Mech.E.; *m* Patricia Ogilvy Reid; two *s*, two *d*. *Educ.:* Bablake School; *studied art* at Birmingham School of Architecture under A. Douglas Jones (1944-46, 1948-51), Harvard University under Prof. Walter Gropius (1951-53). *Exhib.:* Corpus Christi, Texas. *Address:* Clare College, Cambridge.

HOLLAND, George H. B.; painter in oil of portraits, landscapes and still-life; *b* 28 Apr., 1901; *m* Beryl Lavinia Claridge. *Educ.:* Northampton Town and County School; Northampton School of Art; Leicester College of Art; Chelsea Polytechnic. *Official purchases:* Nat. Portrait Gallery, Birmingham School of Music, Northampton Art Gallery, National Library of Wales, Aberystwyth; Bedford Public Library, Royal Academy of Music, Keble College, Oxford, and Howard Payne College, Brownwood, Texas, U.S.A. *Work repro.:* various portraits and landscapes. *Address:* 28 East Pk. Parade, Northampton. *Signs work:* Sometimes "G. H. B. Holland" and sometimes just "Holland" (according to space on canvas).

HOLLAND, Vera Mary; artist in oil, embroideress and tapestry designer; *b* Sileby, Leics.; *d* of William Alfred Holland. *Educ.:* privately; *studied art* under Edgar Lander and at Loughborough School of Art. *Exhib.:* R.I., S.W.A., S.G.A., Salon, Wembley, Britain in Water-colours, R.W.S., Manchester Art Gallery, Leicester and Loughborough A.G., Loughborough Town Hall, R.I. Summer Salon, Bournemouth and Nottingham A.G. *Work repro.:* The Listener, The Countryman, Country Fair, Embroidery, and Artist. *Publications:* The Lady, Stitchcraft, Weldons' periodicals. *Address:* The Laurels, Sileby, Loughborough, Leics. Life Member of the International Inst. of Arts and Letters. *Signs work:* "Vera Holland" or "HOLLAND."

HOLLAWAY, Antony Lynn, A.T.D. (1953), A.R.C.A. (1956); painter, designer in mosaic, stained glass and metal; design consultant to the G.L.C. and other authorities; mem. Architectural Assoc.; *b* Kinson, Dorset, 8 Mar., 1928. *Educ.:* Poole Grammar School; *studied art:* Bournemouth College of Art (1948-53) and R.C.A. (1953-57), Royal Scholar. *Exhib.:* R.A., provincial galleries and in U.S.A. *Work in permanent collection:* V. & A. *Work repro.:* Architectural Press. *Official purchases:* mosaics, metal sculpture, stained glass and relief concrete for local authorities, housing, offices and schools. *Address:* Albert Wharf, 21 Hester Rd., Battersea, London SW11. *Signs work:* "HOLLAWAY."

HOLLICK, Kenneth Russell, F.S.I.A.; designer; mem. of the Designers and Art Directors Assoc. of London; *b* Essex, 5 Jan., 1923. *Studied art and design* at Central School of Arts and Crafts. *Work repro.:* trade marks, symbols, corporate identity programmes, vehicle livery booklets, packaging, exhibition stands. *Address:* Midford Hse., 1-5 Midford Pl., London W1P 9HH.

HOLLIES-SMITH, Roland George, F.R.G.S.; Mem. Soc. of Army Historical Research, Mem. Military Historical Soc., Mem. Royal United Service Inst., Mem. B.A.D.A., Mem. Company of Military Collectors and Historians, Washington, D.C.; specialist in military and historical paintings, prints and water-colours; director of the Parker Gallery; *b* London, 1910; *s* of George Hollies-Smith; *m*; one *d. Educ.:* Highgate. *Addresses:* Lindens. Broadstrood. Loughton. Essex; and 2 Albemarle St., London W1. *Club:* Cavalry.

HOLLOWAY, Edgar, R.B.A. (1947); painter and etcher; *b* 6 May, 1914; *m* Daisy M. Hawkins; three *s*, one *d. Educ.:* Doncaster Grammar School, Slade School of Fine Art. *Exhib.:* R.A., R.S.A., R.I., N.E.A.C., etc. *Official purchases:* B.M., V. & A., Ashmolean Museum, Oxford and provincial galleries. *Address:* St. Rose, Ditchling Common, Sussex. *Signs work:* "Edgar Holloway."

HOLLOWAY, Robert Charles, A.R.C.A. (1936); art master, King's College School; *b* Chelsea, 21 Apr., 1914; *s* of Leonard Henry, soldier; *m* Pamela Mary Jacob; one *s*, one *d. Exhib.:* R.A., R.B.A., N.E.A.C., A.I.A. *Work in permanent collections:* V. & A., B.M. *Address:* 80 Bracken Path, Epsom, Surrey.

HOLMAN, George Alfred, N.R.D. (1939), F.R.B.S. (1955), B.I. Scholarship for Sculpture (1931); sculptor, medallist; *b* 13 June, 1911; *s* of Charles Holman. *Educ.:* Brettenham Rd. Board School (Headmaster, W. Frewer, was first to show interest); Hornsey School of Art (H. J. Youngman, A.R.C.A., F.R.B.S., 1927-34); Hackney School of Art (1925-27). *Exhib.:* R.A. and various London and provincial galleries. *Work repro.:* in British Sculpture (1944-46), Monumental Journal and The Architect. *Official purchases:* Bas-relief stone carving, Broomfield Pk., Southgate Borough Council. *Address:* 250 Highlands Boulevard, Leigh-on-Sea, Essex. *Signs work:* "GEORGE A. HOLMAN," or "G. A. HOLMAN."

HOLME, Rathbone, F.I.A.L., F.R.S.A.; graphic and industrial designer; *b* 26 Oct., 1911; *s* of the late Charles Geoffrey Holme, former Chairman and Editor of The Studio; *m* Naomi Joan Phillips; one *s*, one *d. Educ.:* Oundle; *studied art* under E. M. O'R. Dickey and C. G. Holme. *Work repro.:* in Studio, Art and Industry. *Publications:* Editor: Art and Industry until 1958; Joint-editor with K. M. Frost, Decorative Art until 1958; Art Director, City Display Organization (1958-60). *Address:* 12A Marlborough Cres., Bedford Pk., London W4.

HOLMES, Kenneth, O.B.E., A.R.C.A. (Des., 1926), A.R.C.A. (Engrav., 1926), A.T.D., M.S.I.A., F.S.E.A., Hon. F.I.B.D.; etcher, painter, designer, design consultant from 1956; *m* M. B. W. Fenning; two *d. Educ.:* Ermysted's Grammar School and School of Art, Skipton, Leeds, and Royal College of Art; Principal, Leicester College of Art (1934-56); Head, Huddersfield School of Art (1932-34). *Exhib.:* national and provincial galleries. *Official purchases:* Leicester, Brighton, Huddersfield, Wakefield, Newcastle, American and Commonwealth galleries. *Address:* 4 Rozel, Mid Lincombe Rd., Torquay TQ1 2NF.

HOLT, Eric Stace; painter in tempera; *b* Surrey, 12 May, 1944; *s* of A. W. J. Holt; *m* S. Wrightson; one *s*, one *d. Educ.:* Sutton West Secondary and Sutton East Art Course; *studied art* at Epsom and Ewell School of Art (1959-62) under E. Rodway and L. Worth. *Exhib.:* R.S.B.A. (1970), R.A. Summer Exhbns. (1971, 1972, 1974, 1975); one-man shows, Maltzahn Gallery, London (1972, 1974), Düsseldorf International Art Fair (1973); Joint winner "U.S.A. Revolution 200" Exhbn. (1975). *Work repro.:* R.A. catalogue, magazines, newspapers and limited editions, signed reproductions. *Address:* 17 High St., Purley, Surrey. *Signs work:* "E.S. HOLT." (Brush roman capitals).

HOLT, Gwynneth, F.R.B.S., A.R.B.S.A. (Dec., 1952); sculptor in wood, ivory, bronze, terra-cotta; *b* Wednesbury, Staffs., 18 Jan., 1909; *d* of Benjamin Holt; *m* The Rt. Rev., Eric Gordon. *Educ.:* St. Anne's Convent, Birmingham; Wolverhampton School of Art. *Exhib.:* R.A., R.B.S.A., S.P.S. *Work in permanent collections:* Newport (Mon.) Art Gallery, Aberdeen Art Gallery, Wolverhampton Art Gallery, Hopkins Center, Hanover, N.H., U.S.A., Leamington Art Gallery; many churches in Essex, East Mission Stepney, London, Balsham Church,

Cambridge. *Address:* Cobden, Queen St., Eynsham, Oxon. OX8 1HH. *Signs work:* "GWYNNETH HOLT."

HOMES, Ronald Thomas John, D.F.C., F.S.I.A.; winner of R.S.A. industrial design bursaries (1948-49); Central School of Arts and Crafts Dip for Industrial Design; industrial designer, specialist in domestic equipment; director of Cone-light Ltd. and Yarborough-Homes Partnership Ltd.; *b* London, 3 Oct., 1922; *s* of Arthur Leopold Homes; *m* Ione Winifred Amelia; two *d. Educ.:* Willesden Technical College; *studied art* at Central School of Arts and Crafts. *Address:* Holloway Hse., East Knoyle, Wilts. *Signs work:* see appendix.

HOMESHAW, Arthur Howard, A.R.W.A., A.T.D.; artist in water-colour, pastel, colour prints; art master; Queen Elizabeth's School, Crediton, Devon; *b* 27 Nov., 1933; *m* Wendy Bennetto; two *s. Educ.:* Chipping Sodbury Grammar School; *studied art* at West of England College of Art (1951-54, 1956-57). *Exhib.:* R.A. and with Plymouth Society of Artists. *Work in permanent collections:* R.W.E.A., Bristol Education Comm., Devon County Hall, mural decoration in Temple Meads Station, Bristol, Chagford Galleries, Devon. *Address:* Arwen, Alexandra Rd., Crediton, Devon. *Signs work:* "HOMESHAW."

HONE, David, R.H.A., A.N.C.A.; portrait and landscape painter in oil; *b* Dublin, 1928; *s* of Joseph M. Hone, biographer; *m* Rosemary D'Arcy; two *s,* one *d. Educ.:* St. Columba's College; Univ. College, Dublin; *studied art* at National College of Art, Dublin (1947-50), under J. Keating and M. MacGonical. *Work in permanent collections:* National Gallery, Dublin, Cork Municipal Gallery. *Address:* 25 Lr. Baggot St., Dublin, 2. *Signs work:* "D. Hone."

HOODLESS, Harry Taylor, A.R.C.A. (1936), A.T.D. (1933), F.R.S.A. (1951); painter in oil, tempera and water-colour, etcher; Princ., Laird School of Art, Birkenhead (since 1946); *b* 29 June, 1913; *s* of William Hoodless; *m* Hilda Lilian Grimes; three *s. Educ.:* Leeds Central High School; Leeds College of Art (D. S. Andrews, A.R.C.A., S.G.A., 1929-33); R.C.A. (P. H. Jowett, A.R.C.A., E. W. Tristram, A.R.C.A., 1933-36). *Exhib.:* R.A. and provinces. *Official purchases:* W.A.G., Liverpool, Williamson Art Gallery, Birkenhead. *Address:* Craigroy, Village Rd., West Kirby, Ches. *Signs work:* "HOODLESS" (on oil and tempera) and "Hoodless" (water-colours and etchings).

HOOPER, George; Rome Scholarship in Mural Painting (1935), R.A. Gold Medal and Travelling Scholarship (1933); artist in oil and water-colour; lecturer at Brighton College of Art; *b* Gorakhpur, India, 1910; *s* of A. P. Hooper; *m* Joyce Gayford. *Studied art* at Slade School (1931-32), R.A. Schools (1932-35), Rome Scholarship (1935-38). *Exhib.:* R.A., New English Art Club, Leicester Galleries, Wildenstein's Gallery. *Official purchases:* Contemporary Art Soc., Recording Britain Pilgrim Trust Grant, V. & A., Towner A.G., Eastbourne, Brighton A.G., Ferens A.G., Hull, Hertford College, Oxford. *Publications:* articles in The Artist. *Address:* 16 Ridgeway Rd., Redhill. *Signs work:* see appendix.

HOPE, Rosa Somerville, A.R.E. (1923), retired, Fellow S.A. Soc. Artists; Fellow Natal Soc. Arts; etcher, painter and draughtsman; joined staff, Michaelis, Cape Town Univ. (1935-38); Snr. lecturer Natal University (1938-57); *b* Manchester, 8 June, 1902; *d* of H. Somerville Hope. *Educ.:* Slade School, Central School. *Exhib.:* R.A., N.E.A.C., R.E., S.G.A., N.S.A., S.A.A.S. and provinces, Chicago, Philadelphia, Stockholm, Vienna, S.A. Academy, Johannesburg and Union of S.A. *Official purchases:* British Museum; V. & A.; Manchester; National Gallery, Wales; Pietermaritzburg, S.A.; National Gallery, Cape Town; Pretoria; and Durban Art Gallery. *Address:* Box 41, Kokstad, Cape, S. Africa. *Signs work:* "Rosa Hope."

HOPE HENDERSON, Eleanor, D.A., S.S.A., Post Grad. Scholarship, Guthrie Award (1940); artist in oil; *b* Edinburgh, 1917; *d* of Major David A. Spence, farmer and land agent; *m* David Hope Henderson; two *s. Educ.:* St. George's, Edinburgh; *studied art* at Edinburgh College of Art under Sir William Gillies, Sir W. MacTaggart, Westwater, Maxwell. *Exhib.:* S.S.A., R.S.A., R.A., R.S.P.P., Dumfries Art Soc., Chelsea A.G., Kirkcudbright A.G.; one-man show: Woodstock Galleries. Work in private collections. *Address:* Achie, New Galloway, Kirkcudbrightshire. *Signs work:* "E. Hope Henderson", before marriage "BORRIE."

HOPKINS, Peter; Grant for Art (1950), American Academy of Arts and Letters and National Institute of Arts and Letters; Dean of Men, Emeritus, New York-Phoenix Schools of Design; painter in oils, educator, writer; Chairman, Dept. of Fine Arts, N.Y.-Phoenix Schools of Design (1961-73); art correspondent Christian Science Monitor (1973); *b* New York, 18 Dec., 1911; *s* of Charles R. Hopkins, actor, theatrical producer and director; *m* Gertrude Beach, actress. *Educ.:* Browning and Hotchkiss Schools, U.S.A.; Peiping Union Medical College, China; serviced internship under Rockefeller Foundation Grant (1936); *studied art* at Capri with Wilhelm Eggert (1944) with Reginald Marsh, N.A., Art Students League of N.Y. (1945-50), also sculpture with William Zorach; with Jacques Maroger, L. H., rtd. art conservationist, the Louvre (1950); with Kenneth Hayes Miller, Robert B. Hale, Harry Sternberg and William McNulty (1945-50); illustration with Frank Reilley (1947); anatomy with George Bridgman (1928). *Work in permanent collection:* Museum of the City of New York. *Exhib.:* one-man shows: St. George's Gallery, London (1957), Ward Eggleston Galleries, New York (1958-65), Grand Central Art Galleries, New York, National Academy of Design (1947), New York Public Library (1951), American Academy of Arts and Letters (1950) with John Sloan. *Publications:* The Essentials of Perspective; The American Heritage History of the 1920's and 1930's. *Address:* 36 Horatio St., New York, N.Y. 10014, U.S.A. *Clubs:* Art Students League of N.Y.; Metropolitan Museum of Art. *Signs work:* "Peter Hopkins."

HORN, Frederick Angus, M.I.P.A., Senior Mem. Advertising Creative Circle; consultant on design and typography; *b* Bradford, Yorks; *s* of Angus Horn, textile designer and painter; *m* Irene Quayle; *studied art* at Bradford College of Art. *Exhib.:* exhbns. of advertising and typographical design in Great Britain and abroad. *Publications:* Lettering at Work (Studio) and many articles on graphic art and typography. *Address:* Meadowcroft, Outwood Lane, Chipstead, Surrey. *Signs work:* "HORN."

HORNE, Cleeve, R.C.A., O.S.A., S.S.C.; pres. Ontario Soc. of Artists (1949-51); painter, sculptor and artist consultant; *b* Jamaica, B.W.I., 9 Jan., 1912; *s* of A. C. W. Horne; *m* Jean Horne (sculptor); three *s. Educ.:* England and Canada; *studied art:* sculpture under D. Dick of England (1928); painting at Ontario College of Art, Toronto (1930); R.A.I.C. Allied Arts Medal for 1963; Europe in 1936. *Exhib.:* Canada, U.S.A. and England. *Work in permanent collections:* portraits of leading Canadians; memorials and architectural sculpture. *Address:* 181 Balmoral Ave., Toronto, Canada. *Clubs:* Art and Letters (Pres., 1956-57), York Club. *Signs work:* "Cleeve Horne."

HORSBRUGH, Patrick B., R.I.B.A., M.R.T.P.I., C.I.P., A.A. (Hons.) Dipl., A.I.A., A.I.P., Fellow, British Interplanetary Society; Honorary Member, American Society of Landscape Architects; Honorary Member, American Institute of Interior Design; chartered architect; town planner and artist in ink, water-colour, gouache, etc.; (1915-54) with Sergei Kadleigh, designed High Paddington, co-designer of New Barbican; (1954-56) with Raglan Squire and Partners, extensive travelling in Middle East, India and Burma; Professor of Architecture, University of Nebraska, University of Texas; organized the Texas Conference on Our Environmental Crisis (1966) and the International Conference, Cities in Context, Cultural, Ethical and Natural (1968); *b* Belfast, 21 June, 1920; *s* of Charles B. Horsbrugh. *Educ.:* Canford and A.A. *Address:* Department of Architecture, University of Notre Dame, Indiana, 46556. *Signs work:* "Patrick Horsbrugh."

HORSNELL, Walter Cecil; painter in oil and watercolour of landscapes, figures and portraits; draughtsman in line; painting demonstrations to art societies; designer of art film production presentation; typographical designer and letterer; Photographic Reconnaissance R.A.F. (1941); Official Technical Illustrator Min. of Aircraft Production (1942-47); *b* Ware, Herts, 18 Dec., 1911; *s* of John Horsnell; *m* Kathleen Chappel (neé Leslie); two *s*, two *d*. *Educ.:* Musley Secondary School, Ware; *studied art* at St. Martin's and Bolt Court Schools of Art. *Exhib.:* R.A., R.B.A., National Portrait Gallery (1944), Municipal Galleries of Blackpool, Bradford, Brighton, Harrogate, Keighley, Leeds, Wakefield and other provincial galleries; one-man shows, Harrogate Festival of Arts 1970 and in various galleries. *Work in permanent collections:* Grundy Gallery Blackpool (oil) and private collections in Australia, British Isles, Canada, France, Germany, Holland, India, Italy, Kenya, New Zealand, United States of America, South Africa, Spain, Switzerland, Yugoslavia. *Official purchases:* Blackpool Corporation, Coal Board, Milk Marketing Board, Football Association, West Riding of Yorkshire Educ. Cttee. (Misterton School), Scargill House C. of E. Council (presentation: Archbishop of York), Ghyll Royd School Ilkley, National Westminster Bank, Barclays Bank, Midland Bank, Risparmio Bank Italy, Alliance Building Society, Wakefield Hospital Cttee., North-Eastern Electricity Board, Nidderdale R.D.C., Parents-Teachers Association (Bilton Grange School), British Poliomyelitis Fellowship. *Works include:* "Bishopthorpe, Palace of the Archbishop of York" (Dr. D. Coggan) (1970); "Wharfedale Landscape" (Sir Michael Blundell K.B.E.) (1971); "Croft Castle Kingsland" (Lord Croft) (1946); "Brocket Hall Bridge" (Dowager Lady Ann Brocket) (1947). *Work repro.:* in Ambassador Magazine, Ford Times, Marlbeck Annual, R.A.F. Supply Magazine, Evening Post, Yorkshire Post, First Prize Poster Design Min. of Defence 1975, publications for John Waddington, Gratton (Bradford), Thomas Smith, Rodley, Sampietro Italy, technical publications for H.M. Government. *Address:* Studio, 89 Knox Ave., Harrogate, Yorkshire. *Signs work:* "Walter Horsnell", see appendix.

HOSALI, Nina Moti, M.Sc. (Lond., 1922); painter in oils, mixed media; Fellow and Hon. Sec., Free Painters and Sculptors; *b* London, 23 Oct., 1898; *d* of Shivlinga Chanbasappa Hosali, B.A. *Educ.:* Park School, Glasgow, Regent St. Polytechnic, University College, London; *studied art:* privately. *Exhib.:* R.O.I., R.B.A., Bradford, Paris, Pittsburgh, U.S.A., W.I.A.C., Drian, etc.; one-man shows: London, Edinburgh, Glasgow, Belfast, Bergen. *Publications:* On Seismic Waves in a Visco-Elastic Earth, Children of Allah, A North African Diary. *Address:* 49 Sunningdale Ave., Biggin Hill, Kent. *Clubs:* Institute of Contemporary Arts, Royal Society of Arts. *Signs work:* see appendix.

HOSIASSON, Philippe; painter in oil; *b* Odessa, Russia, 15 Feb., 1898; French citizen since 1928. *Exhib.:* Martha Jackson Gallery (New York); Galerie Karl Flinker (Paris). *Work in permanent collections:* Musée National d'Art Moderne (Paris); Museum of Modern Art (New York); Moderna Museet (Stockholm); Museums of Buffalo, Boston, Phoenix, Exeter, Newark, Raleigh (U.S.A.), and Universities of New York, Columbia and Princeton (U.S.A.). *Work repro.:* in René Huyghe's Dialogue avec le Visible; Michel Seuphor's Dictionnaire de la Peinture Abstraite; Michel Ragon's Naissance d'Un Art Nouveau; and XXe

Siecle, Cimaise, Art News, Arts. *Address:* 26 rue Lacretelle, Paris, 15e. *Signs work:* see appendix.

HOSKIN, John; sculptor in steel; *b* Cheltenham, 8 Sept., 1921; *s* of Stanley Hoskin, tailor; *m* Doreen; three *d* (Caroline, Jane and Sophie). *Studied art:* self-taught. *Work in permanent collections:* Tate Gallery, Birmingham City A.G., V. & A., National Gallery of South Australia, National Gallery of New South Wales, Australia, Arts Council, British Council, Nuffield College, Oxford, St. Stephen's Church, Bristol, Darlington Town Centre, University of Lancaster, University of Kent, University of Georgia, U.S.A., Ravne, Yugoslavia, Peter Stuyvesant Foundation, Provincial Insurance Co., Kendal. *Exhib.:* Antwerp, Rotterdam, Middleheim, Rome, Japan, Sweden, India, London. *Work repro.:* Art Now (Herbert Read), Quadrum II, Motif 5, International Directory of Art, Concise History of Modern Sculpture, Apollo, Art and Artists (1969), British Sculpture (since 1945), Direct Metal Sculpture, Modern English Sculpture. *Address:* Studio: Upper Siddington, Cirencester, Glos. *Signs work:* "John Hoskin."

HOUSE, Wm. S., art scholarship (1925) with free pass to Senior Art School; artist in oil; *b* Islington, 8 June, 1909; *s* of F. House; *m* Mary Joan House; one *s*, one *d*. *Studied art* at Central School of Arts and Crafts under Spencer Price (1925-26), Bolt Court School of Art, Fleet St., under Mr. Boxius (1926-30). *Exhib.:* Islington Public Libraries, Barnet Art Centre, Hampstead Open-air Exhibition, Galerie Montaigne Sarlat, France. *Address:* Le Vignasses, Beynac et Cazenac, 24220 St. Cyprien, France. *Signs work:* see appendix.

HOWARD, Charles, B.A. (1921); painter in oil, gouache and india ink; visiting teacher, Camberwell School of Arts and Crafts; *b* Montclair, N.J., 2 Jan., 1899; *s* of John Galen Howard, architect; *m* Madge Knight. *Educ.:* Berkeley High School, California, and University of California; *studied art* with Louis Bouché, New York (private pupil). *Work in permanent collections:* Metropolitan Museum of Art, New York, Chicago Inst. of Art, Chicago, San Francisco Museum of Art, Museum of the Legion of Honor, San Francisco, National Gallery of Australia, Contemporary Art Society. *Address:* Granaiola, Bagni di Lucca (Ponte), 55 021-Lucca, Italy. *Signs work:* see appendix.

HOWARD, James Campbell, S.G.A.; part-time artist in oil and water-colour; *b* London, 26 Oct., 1906; *s* of James Wilson Howard; *m* Frances Maud Howard; two *s*. *Studied art:* self-taught. *Exhib.:* R.A., R.I. *Address:* Dormer Cottage, East End La., Ditchling, Sussex. *Club:* Langham Sketch. *Signs work:* "J. C. HOWARD" (followed by date).

HOWARD, Kenneth, A.R.C.A. (1958), N.E.A.C. (1961), R.O.I. (1965); artist in oil, gouache and etching; *b* London, 26 Dec., 1932; *s* of Frank Howard; *m* Ann Howard, dress designer. *Educ.:* Kilburn Grammar School; *studied art* at Hornsey College of Art (1949-53), Royal College of Art (1955-58) (Carel Weight, Ruskin Spear), Florence, British Council Scholarship (1958-59). *Exhib.:* one-man exhibitions, Plymouth (1955), John Whibley Gallery (1966-1968), New Grafton Gallery (1971); group shows: Wildenstein (1959, 1961, 1963), R.A., etc. *Work in permanent collections:* Guildhall Art Gallery, Plymouth City Art Gallery. *Address:* Meadowside, Albert Rd., Hampton Hill, Middx. *Signs work:* "Ken Howard."

HOWARD, Margaret Maitland, F.Z.S.; artist in oil, water-colour, black and white, pastel; *b* Friern Barnet, 31 July, 1898. *Educ.:* privately; *studied art* at Byam Shaw and Vicat Cole School, R.A. Schools (five silver medals; British Inst. scholarship, and R.A. cert.). *Exhib.:* R.A., R.P., R.O.I., N.E.A.C., S.W.A., Hull

Municipal Gallery, Bournemouth, etc. *Work repro.:* Several. *Publications:* Illustrations for Aesop's Fables, Dating the Past, Ancient India, Bones for the Archaeologist, The Making of Man, Animal Ancestors, The World of Ancient Man, Hunter's Moon, Ancient Britons, After Livingstone, Prehistoric Animals and their Hunters, The World of Ancient Man, Ice Ages, Through the Green Meadows, Rovers and Stay-at-homes. *Papers on* prehistoric cattle, dried cats, Nimrud ivory tablets, etc. *Address:* Flat 3, Ashwood House, 69 Grange Rd., Sutton, Surrey. *Club:* Campden Hill. *Signs work:* "M. MAITLAND HOWARD" (block letters).

HOWARD-JONES, Ray, Fine Art Dip. University of London, Slade Scholar; 1st class Hons. History of Art, R.C.A.; painter, poet, mosaics; *b* Lambourne, Berks., 30 May, 1903; *d* of Hubert Stanley Howard-Jones, R.A.V.C., M.R.C.V.S. *Educ.:* St. Hilda's, Penarth, London Garden School; *studied art* at Slade School, University of London (1921) under Henry Tonks, Wilson Steer, Elliot-Smith (anatomy), Tancred Borenius (History of Art); Postgraduate School of Painting, Arbroath. *Work in permanent collections:* National Museum of Wales, National Museum of S. Australia, Glynn Vivian Gallery Swansea, Contemporary Art Society, Museum and Gallery Glasgow, Imperial War Museum, Arts Council for Wales, M. of W., City Art Galleries of Aberdeen, Glasgow, Burton-on-Trent, large mosaic—exterior Thomson House Cardiff and Grang Church Edinburgh. *Work repro.:* various contributions to The Anglo-Welsh Review. *Addresses:* Studio House, 29 Ashchurch Park Villas, London W12; St. Martin's Haven, Marloes, W. Wales. *Clubs:* I.C.A., S.W.G., A.I.A. *Signs work:* "Ray."

HOWARTH, Charles Wilfred, R.C.A.; artist in line, water-colour and oil; *b* 1893; *s* of Samuel Howarth, manufacturer. *Educ.:* King Edward's, Sheffield; Sheffield School of Art (A. C. C. Jahn, Oliver Senior, 1910-12); Birmingham School of Art (1912-14). *Exhib.:* Sheffield Soc. of Artists, Birmingham, R.S.A., R.Cam.A. *Work repro.:* Illustrations in books, magazines and newspapers. *Address:* Cartref Melus Cottage, Llechwedd, Conway, N. Wales. *Signs work:* "Chas. W. Howarth" (with flourish to "C" and "t").

HOWARTH, Constance M., B. of E. intermed. (1946), N.D.D. (1947); artist in water-colour, textile designer of printed fabrics; fashion-designer, fabric and colour consultant; *b* Rochdale, Lancs., 14 May, 1927; *d* of Edward Howarth, retired executive civil servant. *Educ.:* Merchant Taylors' School for Girls, Crosby; Bolton School (Public); *studied art* at Manchester Regional College of Art. *Exhib.:* Rayon Industry Design Centre, London, Cotton Board Design Centre, Manchester. *Work in permanent collections:* V. & A. *Work repro.:* By leading British and American textile manufacturers, also in Ambassador. *Address:* 17 Upper Wimpole St., London W1. *Signs work:* "Constance Howarth."

HOWORTH, Nancy; landscape artist in oil; *b* 25 Mar., 1912; *d* of H. P. Peacock, M.A.; *m* John H. E. Howorth. *Educ.:* Eastbourne; *studied art* at Eastbourne School of Art (1930-32); and under Jon Peaty of Sussex (1963-66). *Exhib.:* one-man shows: Ditchling Gallery, Sackville Gallery, E. Grinstead; group shows: S.W.A., F.P.S., R.B.A.; Sussex galleries: Rye, Burwash, Ditchling, Seaford, Uckfield, etc. *Address:* Cornwells Cottage, N. Chailey, Sussex. *Clubs:* F.P.S., Assoc. of Sussex Artists, Attic, Ditchling, Adventurer's, Sussex.

HOWSE, Henrietta Rose Chicheliana, A.R.M.S.; artist in water-colour; *b* Waterford, Ireland, 20 Jan., 1892; *d* of Richard Chicheley Thornton, Col. (Middlesex Regiment); *m* Capt. H. F. Howse, R.N.; one *s*, one *d*. *Educ.:* in Brighton and Brussels: *studied art* in Brussels, London with S. Arthur Lindsay, P.R.M.S. *Address:* Woodholm, Lochwinnoch Rd., Kilmacolm, Renfrewshire.

Clubs: English-Speaking Union (London and Edinburgh), Western Club, Glasgow. *Signs work:* "Rose C. Howse."

HOWSON, Cherry; water-colour artist; *b* Tipton, Staffs., 29 Feb., 1912; *d* of the late W. J. Willis, county valuer and surveyor; *m* H. R. G. Howson; one *d. Educ.:* Harrogate College, Yorks.; Lancaster Art School (Charles Ripper, 1929); under G. Mortram Moorhouse of Kendal. *Exhib.:* W.A.G., R.S., Birmingham; Atkinson Art Gallery, Southport; Lake Artists' Soc., Lancashire Artists Exhbn. (Preston). *Address:* 18 Croft Rd., Evesham, Worcs. *Signs work:* "Cherry Howson."

HOYLE, Walter, A.R.C.A. (1946); mural painter, designer and printmaker; *b* Rishton, Lancs., July, 1922; *s* of Fred Hoyle; *m* Denise Colombo. *Educ.:* Beckenham; *studied art* at Beckenham School of Art, R.C.A. *Exhib.:* One-man shows, Leicester Galleries (1952), Zürich, Paris, Byzantine Institute Library (1951). *Work in permanent collections:* British Museum (Natural History), Faraday House, London, Fogg Museum and Seattle museums, U.S.A. *Official purchases:* M. of W. (1952), various schools and colleges, exhbn. paintings, Whitworth Art Gallery (1955). *Work repro.:* since 1965 produces limited editions of artists prints. *Address:* 94 High St., Bottisham, Cambridge CB5 9BA. *Signs work:* "Walter Hoyle."

HOYLES, Louis, M.S.I.A.; industrial designer, product designer and design consultant on electrical, mechanical and acoustic engineering design; sculptor, artist in ink, water-colour, ceramics, plastics, metal; *b* London, 13 Feb., 1914; *s* of Alfred Hoyles; *m* Madeline Kain; one *s,* one *d. Studied art and sculpture* under H. J. Youngman, F.R.B.S., A.R.C.A., and R. Reeve, R.B.A., A.R.E., D.F.A. Lond. *Exhib.:* B.I.F., International Machine Tool Exhbn., Medical Exhbn., British Plastics Exhbn., American Society of Industrial Designers Exhbn. *Work repro.:* British Plastics, Electrical Review, Idea 54. Idea 55, Designers in Britain 4, 5 and 6, Council of Industrial Design Index. *Address:* 62 St. Andrew's Drive, Stanmore, Middx. *Signs work:* see appendix.

HOYTON, Edward Bouverie, F.R.S.A., Rome Scholar in Engraving (1926), S.I.A. (1931), N.S. (1932); Princ., Penzance School of Art (1941-66); artist in dry-point and water-colour, etcher and engraver; *b* London; *m* Inez Hoyton. *Educ.:* Colfe Grammar School, Blackheath; *studied art* at University of London, Goldsmiths' College, British School in Rome. *Exhib.:* R.A., R.B.A., N.S., G.I., Leeds, Bradford, Newlyn, St. Ives. *Work in permanent collections:* London, Wakefield, Leicester, Glasgow, Liverpool, Belfast, Vienna, Dresden, Paris, Rome, Toronto, Baltimore, Los Angeles, Chicago, New York and Washington. *Work repro.:* Studio, Apollo. *Address:* Delmore House, Jack La., Newlyn, Penzance, Cornwall. *Signs work:* "E. BOUVERIE-HOYTON."

HOYTON, Inez Estelle (Mrs.), F.R.S.A.; painter, teacher, embroideress, weaver, designer; art teacher, Benenden School, Cranbrook, Kent (1942-46); art and craft teacher, Penzance School of Art (1946-68); Mem., St. Ives Society of Artists, Life Associate Mem., Penwith Society, St. Ives; *m* Edward Bouverie Hoyton, Rome scholar. *Educ.:* Queen Anne High School and privately; *studied teaching and art* at Leeds College of Art. *Exhib.:* R.A., London Galleries, Bradford, Wakefield, Leeds, Sheviock, Orion Gallery, Penzance; C.E.M.A. Travelling Exhbns. *Address:* Delmore House, Jack La., Newlyn, Penzance, Cornwall. *Signs work:* "Inez Hoyton" or "Inez B. Hoyton."

HSÜ, Chung-Ming; artist, writer and painter in oil and water-colours; Fellow of the Academy of Arts, Shanghai; secretary of the Society of Chinese Artists in Indonesia; lecturer, School of Oriental Studies in University of Indonesia; *b* Tegal,

Java, 31 July, 1914. *Educ.:* China Institute, Shanghai; *studied art* at Shanghai College of Fine Arts, Shanghai. *Publication:* associate editor, Paintings and Statues from the Collection of President Sukarno of the Republic of Indonesia (Tokyo, 1964), etc. *Address:* Jalan Cutnyakdin 3, Jakarta, Indonesia. *Clubs:* Federation of Art Circles in Indonesia, Academician Circle in Indonesia, and International Society of Sciences, Letters and Arts. *Signs work:* "C. M. Hsü."

HUBBARD, Robert Hamilton; Chief Curator, Nat. Gallery of Canada, Ottawa (since 1954); currently seconded as cultural adviser to Governor General of Canada, Government House, Ottawa; previously lecturer, University of Toronto; *b* Hamilton, Ont., 17 June, 1916. *Educ.:* McMaster University (B.A.), University of Paris, Musées Royaux, Brussels, University of Wisconsin (M.A., Ph.D.); Fellow of the Royal Society of Canada (1962); (Hon.) LL.D. (Mount Allison University) (1965). *Publications:* European Paintings in Canadian Collections, Anthology of Canadian Art, National Gallery Catalogues (1957-60); The Development of Canadian Art (1963); Rideau Hall (1967); (ed.) Scholarship in Canada (1967); Thomas Davies in Early Canada (1973); contributions to Art Quarterly, Art in America, Oxford Companion to Art, etc. *Address:* 200 Rideau Terr., Ottawa K1M 0Z3. *Clubs:* Athenæum, London; Rideau, Ottawa.

HUDSON, Eleanor Erlund, R.W.S. (1949), R.E. (1946), A.R.C.A. (1937); graphic artist, portraitist, figure subjects, costume designer, water-colour; costume designer, artistic advisor to Brooking Ballet School, Marylebone; *b* S. Devon; *d* of Harold Hudson and Helen Ingeborg Olsen. *Educ.:* Wentworth Hall, Surrey; *studied art* at R.C.A. (School of Engraving) under Professors Malcolm Osborne, R.A., R. S. Austin, R.A., Drawing Prize, 1936, Continuation Schol. (4th year) 1938, Travelling Schol. 1939. *Exhib.:* R.A. and international. *Work in permanent collections:* Boston Pub. Library, Fogg Museum, U.S.A. *Official purchases:* War Artist's Advisory Comm. *Address:* 6 Hammersmith Terr., London W6. *Signs work:* "ERLUND HUDSON."

HUDSON, Yvonne, Slade Dip. (painting 1946), (sculpture 1948), Richardson Scholar (1947), Slade Sculpture Prize (1948); sculptor in ceramic, stone and metal; part-time lecturer, Horsham School of Art; *b* Wanstead, Essex, 12 Jan., 1924; *d* of Henry Hudson; *m* John Rusbridge, farmer; one *s,* three *d. Studied art* at Slade School of Fine Art, London University under Prof. Gerrard, George Meldrum, MacWilliam. *Exhib.:* R.A., R.B.A., at Alwyn Gallery, Richmond Park, Isleworth Outdoor; 2 one-man shows at Chichester. *Work in permanent collections:* Worthing A.G., Bishops Chapel, Chichester; churches: Selsey, East and West Wittering. *Address:* The Manor House, Earnley, Chichester PD20 7JL. *Club:* R.B.S. *Signs work:* "Y. Hudson" and date, and see appendix.

HUGGLER, Max Melchior; Dr. Phil., Director of Museum of Fine Art, Berne; Director Kunsthalle Berne (1931); Director Kunstmuseum Berne (1944 until Mar., 1965); e.o. Prof. (since 1946) Univ. Berne; Mem. Federal Art Commission (1945-50); *b* Berne, 12 Oct., 1903. *Educ.:* Gym. Berne, Paris, Berlin. *Publications:* Schweizer Malerei im 19, Jahrhundert; Raoul Dufy; Paul Klee, die Malerei als Blick in den Kosmos, Huber Frauenfeld (1969), with 4 coloured and 34 black-and-white plates and 27 reproductions in the text. Catalogues of exhbns. Kunsthalle Berne and Berne Museum of Fine Art. *Address:* Sent CR (Switzerland).

HUGHES, Jim, D.A. (1954), S.G.A. (1972), Teacher's Technical Cert. (1955), Teacher's General Cert. (1956); artist/designer in poster and water-colour; teacher of art and design, Extra-mural Dept., Glasgow University; *b* Glasgow, 1935; *s* of Edward Hughes, engineer. *Educ.:* Ayr Academy; *studied art* at Glasgow School of Art (1950-54); Jordanhill College (1954-56) under Sam Black, D.A.,

R.S.W. *Work in permanent collection:* Glasgow Art Gallery (abstract), other work in private collections throughout the world. *Publications:* Graphic Design for S.S.A.E. and Ayr Area Further Educ. Booklets. *Address:* 32 Macadam Pl., Ayr KA8 0BZ. *Signs work:* initials on work, name on back, see appendix.

HUGHES, Malcolm, A.R.C.A., D.A. (Manc.); artist (painter) and lecturer; visiting lecturer at Bath Academy of Art, Corsham, Chelsea School of Art, Slade School of Fine Art, London; *b* Manchester, 1920. *Studied art* at Regional College of Art, Manchester, Royal College of Art, London. *Work in permanent collections:* Tate Gallery, Arts Council of Great Britain, Walker Art Gallery, Liverpool, etc. *Address:* 19 Oxford Rd., Putney, London SW15. *Signs work:* name written on the back of each work.

HULBERT, Thelma; painter in oils, water-colours; *b* Bath, 1913; *d* of Richard John Hulbert. *Educ.:* Bath; *studied art* at Bath School of Art; worked with Euston Rd. School painting. *Exhib.:* one-man shows, Cambridge, Leicester Gallery, Whitechapel Retrospective, Bristol City Museum, Bath City Museum, Cardiff City, Nottingham, Arts Council Tour, Redfern Gallery; group shows: English eye Malbough Gerson, New York, Whitechapel, Redfern, Bath. *Work in permanent collections:* Bath Victoria Art Museum, Bristol City Art Museum, Harris Museum Preston, Abbot Hall A. G., Arts Council of G.B., Contemporary Art Soc., Hallmark Collection, Kansas, America, Sydney National Gallery, N.S.W., Queensland National Gallery, Derbyshire Educ. Com., M. of W. for Embassy in Tehran; private collections in Zürich, Cape Town, Brazil, Italy, London. Film: Thelma Hulbert (Tempo) for television; Twentieth Cen. Women interview B.B.C.; B.B.C. in Town Today. *Address:* 2 Kelfield Gdns., London W10. *Signs work:* "Thelma Hulbert."

HULL, Norman Thomas Stephen, F.R.S.A. (1954), F.R.G.S. (1957), F.I.A.L. (1963), F.I.B.D. (1964), L.I.B.D. (1961), N.R.D. (1940), R.D.S. (1960), A.B.W.S. (1935), D.I.A., F.R.E.S. (1957), A.I.D. New York (1964); Design Associate Member, International Chapter, American Institute of Interior Designers, New York 22, N.Y. (A.I.D.); Liveryman and Freeman of the Worshipful Company of Glaziers and Painter of Glass of the City of London (1961); Freedom of the City of London (1959); Member of the Guild of Freemen of the City of London (1959); Member of the City Livery Club, City of London (1966); Member of the City of London Society (1959); Member-Accademia Internazionale, Rome; Life Governor, Royal Society of St. George; Member, International Academy of Literature, Arts, Science, Rome; Gold and Silver Medallist: Member-Associate, Société des Artistes Français, Paris (1971); late Member, Society of Industrial Artists (1942); Bronze Medallist, Paris Salon (1957); Hon. Mention, Paris Salon (1956); F.C.I.A.D. Board of Educ. Industrial Design Diploma (1928); awarded Certificate of Merit by the Dictionary of International Biography (1969) and the International Who's Who in Art and Antiques (1973) and Diploma of Honour (1975) by International Who's Who in Community Service; artist, designer, modeller in ceramics, oil, water-colour; past Managing Director, Honiton Art Potteries Ltd. and the Norman Hull Pottery, Devon; late asst. to Henri Creange, Art Director, Johnson Bros. Hanley Ltd.; Member British Ceramic Society (1960); Member, British Pottery Manufacturers' Federation; Ornamental Pottery Association; North Staffs. Chamber of Commerce (1949-53); Member, Ancient Monuments Soc.; lay Mem. Soc. of Aviation Artists; Fellow, the Royal Commonwealth Society; Examiner of the Incorporated Institute of British Decorators and Interior Designers; *b* Church Gresley, 14 Nov., 1901; *s* of T. Hull, engineer. *Studied art* at Nottingham College of Art (J. Else, F.R.B.S.), Derby College of Art (D. S. Andrews, A.R.C.A.), Stoke-on-Trent College of Art (G. M.

Forsyth, R.I.). *Exhib.:* R.I., R.C.A., Paris Salon (1954, 1955, 1956, 1957, 1958, 1959, 1960, 1961, 1962, 1966, 1967, 1968, 1969, 1970, 1971, 1972, 1973, 1974, 1975); Société des Artistes Français, Paris; Festival of Britain, Coronation Souvenirs Exhbn. (1953); Council of Industrial Design, Nottingham, Hanley, Exeter, Derby, Taunton, Bath, Reading, Cheltenham, Brighton, Worthing, Augustine Gallery, Holt, Norfolk, Galerie Internationale, New York. *Work in collections* of H.M. Queen Elizabeth, The Queen Mother, H.R.H. Princess Margaret, H.R.H. The Prince of Wales, The Countess of Halifax, Sir A. Penn, G.C.V.O., Rt. Hon. Harold Wilson, M.P., Sir Cedric Drewe, Monsieur Georges Labro, Past President, Paris Salon, Sir Winston Churchill, Sir E. Chapman-Andrews, Sir Eric Penn, K.C.V.O., Baroness Marcia Falkender. *Work repro.:* Illustrated Carpenter and Builder, Pottery Gazette, La Revue Moderne, Paris. Biography recorded also in Who's Who in the World, Who's Who in Europe, The Blue Book, International Directory of Arts, Internationales Kunst-Adressbuch, Men of Achievement, Who's Who in America, Marquis Who's Who, Inc., Who's Who in the City of London. *Address:* 36 Shermanbury Rd., Worthing, Sussex. *Clubs:* Designers Club International, New York, International Arts Guild, Monte Carlo, Sussex, Staffordshire, Somerset, Exeter and Civil Service Arts Socs., City Livery, Rotary. *Signs work:* "Norman T. S. Hull" or "N. T. S. Hull."

HULME, Ursula, N.R.D., F.P.S., B.A.A.T.; artist in oil, water-colour, pastel, felt pen and collage; textile designer; art therapist for the physically handicapped; *b* Cottbus, 5 Mar., 1917; *d* of Dr. Karl Neumann; *m* Ernest Hulme. *Educ.:* Berlin; *studied art* at Reimann School, Berlin under Maria May. *Exhib.:* 3 one-man shows: Woodstock Gallery, London; group shows: P.S., Mall Galleries, Loggia Gallery, Nimes. France, Leatherhead Theatre, Richmond Art Group, etc. *Publication:* entries in London Diary in book form from 1970-72. *Address:* 3 Beverley Cl., E. Ewell, Epsom, Surrey. *Signs work:* "Ursula Hulme."

HULTON, John; *b* 28 Dec., 1915; *s* of Rev. Samuel Hulton of Knaresborough; *m* Helen McFarlan; two *d. Educ.:* Kingswood School, Bath, Hertford College, Oxford, and Leeds University. Hon. Assistant, Leeds City Art Gallery (1937-38); Assistant, Brighton Art Gallery and Museum (1946-48); British Council, Fine Arts Dept. (1948), Director (1970), resigned (1975) to study landscape design. *Address:* 70 Gloucester Cres., London NW1 7EG.

HUMPHREY, Jack Weldon, LL.D. (U.N.B., 1951); Can. Govt.-R.S. Overseas Fellow (1952-53), Can. Council Senior Arts Fellow (1960); artist in oil, water-colour, etc.; *b* St. John, N.B., Canada, 12 Jan., 1901. Member Can. Gr. of Painters, Can. Soc. of Painters in Watercolour; Can. Soc. of Graphic Art. *Studied art* at Boston Museum School; National Academy, N.Y., and Provincetown under Hawthorne; with Hans Hofmann in Munich. *Exhib.:* throughout Canada, U.S.A. and abroad; honoured with retrospective exhbn. which opened at N.G. of Canada, Oct., 1966, and toured Canada for ten months. *Work in permanent collections:* Nat. Gall. of Can.; H.M. the Queen Mother; A.G. of Ontario; Hart House; major Can. galls., universities and noted private collections. *Address:* 10 Spruce St., Saint John, N.B., Canada.

HUMPHREYS, David, B.A. (Dunelm); Thomas Penman Scholar and State Scholar at Durham University (1958-62); painter and constructor; *b* London, 27 Oct., 1937; *s* of J. H. Ll. Humphreys. *Educ.:* Battersea Grammar School and King's College, Durham University (Dept. of Fine Art). *Work in permanent collections:* Arts Council, Leicester, Newcastle, London Universities, Ministry of Works, Bishop Otter College, Ashridge College, Nuffield Foundation, I.C.I., J. Sainsbury, Shell, C.W.S., P. & O., Financial Times. *Address:* Kingsmead House, Steyning, Sussex.

HUNDERTWASSER (Friedrich Stowasser); *b* Vienna, 15 Dec., 1928; Matura (1948). *Exhib.:* Art Club, Vienna (1952), Facchetti, Paris (1954), R. Cordier, Paris (1960), Tokyo Gallery (1961), Biennale, Venice (1962); itinerant show (1964-65): Kestner Gesellschaft, Hanover; Kunsthalle, Bern; Stedelijk Museum, Amsterdam; Moderna Museet, Stockholm; Museum XX Jahrh., Vienna; itinerant show (1967); Galerie Flinker, Paris; Hanover Gallery, London; Galerie Krugier and Georges Moos, Genève; Kunstverein, Berlin; itinerant show: United States (1969), New Zealand and Australia (1973). *Cassette of graphic works:* Look at it on a rainy day (1972), first Japanese colour woodcut portfolio Nana-Hyaku-Mizu (1973). *Manifestos:* Transautomatism (1954), Grammar of Vision (1957), Mouldiness Manifesto: Against Rationalism in Architecture (1958), Your right to windows—your duty to the trees (1972). *Publications:* Verlag Galerie Welz, Salzburg (1965), Buchheim Verlag, Feldafing (1965), Bruckmann Verlag, Munich (1972). *Lives:* on his ship "Regentag"; Normandie, France; Venice, Italy; Waldviertel, Austria. *Address:* P.O. Box 989, A-1011 Vienna, Austria.

HUNDLEBY, A. R., M.S.I.A., M.Inst.Pkg.; designer—packaging and graphics, artist in water-colour; *b* 1923; *m* Marion Smallshaw, A.T.D.; *studied art* at Lincoln and Leicester. *Work repro.:* Designers in Britain, Graphis, etc. *Addresses:* 35 Kelross Rd., London N5 2QS; Hill House, Binham, nr. Fakenham, Norfolk. *Signs work:* "HUNDLEBY."

HUNTLEY, Dennis, N.D.D. (1951), A.T.C. (1952), F.R.B.S. (1970); sculptor in bronze, plastics, stone, wood; educationalist; Head of Sir John Cass School of Art; Governor, City of London Polytechnic; *b* Weybridge, Surrey, 6 Dec., 1929; *s* of William Lanchbury Huntley, management executive; *m* Gillian Huntley; one *s*, two *d*. *Educ.:* Wallington Grammar School for Boys; *studied art* at Wimbledon School of Art (1947-51), Gerald Cooper (principal), London University Senior House (1951-52). *Exhib.:* several galleries. *Works permanently displayed:* 6 major works (4 stone, 2 wood) Guildford Cathedral, 7 ft. metal fig. for L.C.C. Patronage of the Arts Scheme at Henry Thornton School, Clapham, life-sized wood fig. of Anne Boleyn, London Borough of Sutton, awarded Sir Otto Beit medal in open competition for best work, 1967, in United Kingdom and Commonwealth. *Publications:* book reviews for L.C.C. and Studio Vista and various articles for Education. *Address:* The Studio, 30 Hawthorn Rd., Sutton, Surrey. *Clubs:* Arts, Chelsea Arts. *Signs work:* "D. W. Huntley" on prints and drawings, "D. HUNTLEY" on sculptured work.

HURDLE, Robert Henry, R.W.A.; painter; lecturer, Faculty of Fine Art, Bristol Polytechnic; *b* London, 1918; *s* of Arturer E. Hurdle, managing solicitor's clerk; *m* Frances; two *s*, one *d*. *Educ.:* East Sheen County School; *studied art* at Richmond School of Art (1935-37) under Holland, Badmin, Wilson; Camberwell School of Arts and Crafts under Coldstream, Passmore, Rogers, Townsend. *Exhib.:* one-man show, University College of Swansea, Faculty of Arts Gallery (June, 1969). *Work in permanent collections:* University College, Swansea, Bristol Corp., R.W.E.A., University of Bristol and various private collections. *Address:* 37 Cornwallis Cres., Clifton, Bristol BS8 4PH. *Signs work:* occasionally "Robert Hurdle."

HURFORD, Charles William; technical artist for Temple Press (Aeroplane, Motor, Motor Cycling, etc.); *b* 27 Sept., 1907; *s* of Henry Hurford, master printer; *m*; one *d*. *Educ.:* Harrow County School, Harrow School of Art; apprenticed to colour etching (process engraving). *Exhib.:* R.A. *Work repro.:* tech. journals, book illustrations, boats, antiques, motors, pubs. *Address:* 72 Park Cres., Harrow Weald, Middx. *Signs work:* "Charles Hurford."

HURTUNA, Josep Giralt; Mem. Saló de Primavera of Modern Art, Barcelona (1934). First Prize Xavier Nogués in engraving (1948). First Prize Exp. Municipal de Bellas Artes of Barcelona (1951). Great Prize III Bienal Hispanoamericana de Arte (1955). Prize Moncada (1958). Second Prize in engraving Exp. Nacional de Bellas Artes, Barcelona (1960). Prize Juan Gris in painting (1961). Prize Joan Miró in Drawing (1964). Prize Ynglada-Guillot in Drawing (1974). Organizer of the Salón de Octubre of Barcelona since its foundation; painter, engraver, and decorator on glass and ceramics; *b* Barcelona, 14 Apr., 1913; *s* of Ignacio Hurtana, civil engineer; *m* Maria Cristina Campanyá. *Educ.:* Escuela Superior de Bellas Artes, Barcelona; *studied art* in several workshops in Barcelona and Paris. *Exhib.:* Pers. Barcelona, Madrid, Rome, etc., I, II, III Bienales Hispanoamericanos de Arte; Biennale di Venezia; Bienal de São Paulo; Biennal of Alexandria, Biennal of Contemporary Colour Lithography of Cincinnati; Biennal of Prints in Tokio; Arts Council, London; 20 años de pintura española, Lisbon; Art Libre, Paris; Exhbn. of Occidental Artists, Taipeh (Formosa); International of Engraving, London; Salón de los Once, Madrid; Salón de Octubre and Salón de Mayo, Barcelona; Antologia de Pintura Catalana, Madrid, Barcelona; Obelisk Gallery, Washington; Gallery "A", Taos (N.M.); Galerie Kasper, Lausanne; Maestros del Siglo XX; Galeria Montevideo, Montevideo; Piccadilly Gallery, London; World Fair, New York (1964), and several towns of Europe and America. *Works in permanent collections:* in Barcelona, Madrid, Valencia, Paris, Rome, London, Stockholm, Buenos Aires, Pasadena, Brimfield, Washington, Würzburg, Beirut, Musée de Berne (Hommage à Paul Klee), Montevideo, Las Palmas, etc. *Official purchases:* Museo de Arte Comtemporáneo and Calcografia Municipal, Barcelona; Museo de Arte Contemporáneo and Calcografia Nacional, Madrid; Museo d'Arte di Pescia (Italy); Museo Nacional de Bellas Artes, Montevideo; National Museum of Fine Arts, Taipeh (Formosa); Museo de Villanueva y Geltrú and Museo de Arte de Valls (Catalónia), etc. *Work repro.:* Antologia española de Arte Contemporáneo, C. Rodriguez-Aguilera; Historia del Arte Español; Exponente de pintura moderna; Enciclopedia Espasa, Enciclopedia Universitas and Enciclopedia Salvat of Barcelona; La Pintura Catalana, A. Cirici Pellicer; Introducción a la pintura española, actual, J. M. Moreno Galván; Veinte años de pintura de vanguardia en España, C. A. Areán; Pintura Catalana Contemporánea, J. E. Cirlot; La escuela pictorica de Barcelona, C. A. Areán; and in various art magazines. *Publications:* Numerous mentions in art magazines, etc. *Address:* Avda. José Antonio 302, 3°, Barcelona, 4. *Club:* Circulo Artistico. *Signs work:* "Hurtuna" and see appendix.

HURUM, Per, King's medal of merit in gold; sculptor in bronze and granite; *b* Oslo, 2 June, 1910; *s* of Hans Hurum, merchant; *m* Asbjoerg Borgfelt; one *d.* *Educ.:* Academy in Oslo. *Exhib.:* São Paolo Biennale, Antwerp, Hanover. *Work in permanent collections:* National Gallery, Oslo, Riksgalleriet, Trondhiems Fastegaller, Lund Museum, Sweden. *Official purchases:* a fountain, Drammen; two fountains, City Hall Square, Oslo; memorial, Fredriksstad; memorial, Alta; portrait statues, Oslo and Gjoevik; park sculptures, Oslo, Porsgrunn, Skien, Arendal. *Articles:* Bonytt, Hjemmet, and other magazines. *Address:* Gabelsgt 18, Oslo. *Clubs:* Norsk Billedhogger Forening.

HUSON, Eric; landscape painter in oil, water-colour and ink; *b* Mitcham, Surrey, 10 Sept., 1930; *s* of B. S. J. Huson, insurance manager (retired); *m* Frances Farrer; two *s*, one *d.* *Educ.:* Alleyns School, Dulwich; *studied art* at Camberwell School of Art (1945-47) under John Minton, Claude Rogers, William Townsend; Shrewsbury School of Art (1947-48). *Address:* c/o The Trafford Gallery, 119 Mount St., London W1Y 5HB. *Signs work:* "Eric Huson" on reverse, title of work "Eric Huson" and date.

HUSSEY, Henry James, L.I.F.A. (1952); sculptor and stonemason; *b* London, 27 Oct., 1913; *s* of John Alexander Hussey; *m* (1st) Irene Margaret Rose; four *s*, three *d*; (2nd) Olive Lilian Hefford. *Educ.:* Townsend St. School, Elementary, Walworth; *studied art:* self-taught. *Exhib.:* R.A., I.F.A., R.S.B.A., R.I. Galleries, Guildhall Gallery, Leicester Galleries, Royal Glasgow Institute of Fine Arts, Ash Barn Galleries, Petersfield, Tryon Gallery, Moorland Gallery, S.WL.A. *Official purchases:* two stone carved figures on Senate House, University of London; commission for a relief carving of Robert Dover, the founder of the Cotswold Games, from an enlarged photograph of the portrait in Annalia Dubrenzia (1936); commission for figure of Warrior Putti for Lady Brunner, Greys Court (National Trust), nr. Henley-on-Thames. *Address:* 6 Felton House, Ryan Cl., Ferrier Estate, Kidbrooke, London SE3 9YN. *Signs work:* "H. J. Hussey."

HUSSEY, John Denis, A.R.W.A.; sculptor in steel, bronze and ceramics; principal lecturer, Bristol Polytechnic; *b* Slough, 26 Apr., 1928; *s* of F. W. Hussey; *m* Katherine Hussey; two *s*. *Educ.:* Slough Grammar School; *studied art* at Goldsmiths' College (1946-49) under K. Allen, M. Cowell and R. Fournier; Bristol Polytechnic (1969-70) under Ernest Pascoe, F.R.B.S., R.W.A. *Exhib.:* R.A., R.W.A., Welsh Pictures for Schools. *Work in permanent collections:* Tallboys, R.W.A. *Address:* The Rosery, 27 Henbury Rd., Westbury-on-Trym, Bristol. *Signs work:* "J. Hussey."

HUSTON, John I.; artist in oil, egg tempera, sculptures and the range of mixed media, rendered landscapes, portraits, figures, abstracts upon canvas, wood, masonite; writer; *b* Saltillo, Penna, U.S.A., 22 Jan., 1915; *s* of Harry E. Huston, merchant. *Educ.:* Juniata College and University Special Studies; *studied art:* completely self-trained via Commercial Art (retail), Industrial Art (design), Cinema Art (scenario and researches), Fine Art (oil, etc. 1971-76). *Work in private collection* only except as exhibited in book of the unfolding Apocalypse: The Art of Life as permanent. *Publication:* The Art of Life. *Address:* 107 Jackson Lick, Harrisburg, Pa. 17102. *Club:* International Directory of Arts. *Signs work:* see appendix.

HUTCHESON, Tom, D.A. (1949); artist in mixed media; film (cartoon); senior art lecturer; *b* Uddingston, Lanarkshire, 13 Nov., 1922; *m* Mary McKay. *Educ.:* Motherwell; *studied art* at Glasgow School of Art (1941-49) under Hugh Adam Crawford, R.S.A., David Donaldson, R.S.A. *Exhib.:* R.S.A., G.I., R.S.W., Moores; three one-man shows. *Work in permanent collections:* H.M. the Queen, H.R.H. Prince Philip, Arts Council, Liverpool and Glasgow Universities, Scottish Educ. Authorities. *Address:* 73 Woodend Dr., Glasgow G13. *Club:* Art, Glasgow. *Signs work:* "Tom Hutcheson."

HUTCHISON, Sidney Charles, M.V.O., F.S.A., F.M.A., F.R.S.A., London Univ. Dip. in Hist. of Art, Lt.-Cdr. (S), R.N.V.R.; Secretary, R.A. of Arts (since 1968); on administrative staff of R.A. since 1929 and Librarian, 1949-68; Sec. to Chantrey Trustees, British Institution Fund, E. A. Abbey Mural Painting and Scholarships Funds and E. Vincent Harris Mural Decoration Fund; Lecturer for Univ. of London Extension Courses (1957-67); *b* London, 26 Mar., 1912; *m* Nancy Arnold Brindley. *Educ.:* Holloway School, London. *Publications:* The Homes of the Royal Academy (1956), The History of the Royal Academy, 1768-1968 (1968). *Address:* 60 Belmont Cl., Mount Pleasant, Cockfosters, Herts. *Club:* Arts.

HUTTON, Clarke; book illustrator, designer and painter in all media; lithographer; lithographic teacher, L.C.C. Central School of Art and Design (1930-68); *b* London, 1898; *s* of H. Clarke Hutton, lawyer; *m* Marjorie Hewitt, artist; one *s*.

Educ.: secondary school, Gravesend, Kent; *studied art* at Central School of Art and Design (1927-30). *Exhib.:* R.A., London Group, etc. *Work in permanent collections:* B.M., V. & A. (lithographs). *Official purchases:* as above. *Work repro.:* illustrations for about fifty books (O.U.P., Chatto & Windus, Penguin Books Ltd., Houghton Mifflin Co., Boston, Mass.; Limited Editions Club, New York, etc.). *Address:* 41 Ladbroke Rd., London W11. *Club:* Double Crown. *Signs work:* "Clarke Hutton" or "C.H."

HUTTON, Dorothy, M.V.O.; Mem. Art Workers' Guild; Soc. of Scribes and Illuminators; artist and calligrapher, works in egg tempera, water-colour, lettering on vellum; *b* Bolton. *Studied art* at Central School of Arts and Crafts under F. Ernest Jackson and Graily Hewitt. *Exhib.:* R.A., N.E.A.C.; one of the official artists to the Crown Office. *Official purchases:* Metropolitan Police Roll of Honour; Barclays Bank Roll of Honour; Record for the Honourable Company Master Mariners; War Record, R.A.F., Coastal Command; Memorial to General Eisenhower. *Address:* 73 Campden St., Kensington, London W8. *Signs work:* "Dorothy Hutton."

HUYGHE, René, de l'Académie Française, Grand Officier de la Legion d'Honneur, Commander de l'Ordre de Leopold du Mérite de la Republique Italienne; Prof. at College de France (Psychologie des Arts Plastiques); Director, Museum Jacquemart-Andre; Laureate of the International Praemium Erasmianum, La Haye (1966); Conservateur en chef honoraire des Peintures et Dessins du Musée du Louvre (1930-50); President du Conseil de Musées de France; *b* Arras, 3 May, 1906; *s* of Louis Huyghe; *m* Lydie Bouthet; two *d*. *Educ.:* Sorbonne and l'École du Louvre. *Publications:* Dialogue avec le Visible (1955), L'Art et l'Ame (1960), L'Art et l'Homme (3 Vols., 1957-61), Delacroix ou le combat solitaire (1964), Les Puissances de l'Image (1965). Sens et Destin de l'Art (1967), L'Art et le Monde Moderne (2 vol., 1970-71), Formes et Forces (1971), La Relève du Réel (1974). *Address:* 3 rue Corneille, Paris, 75006.

HYATT, Derek James, A.R.C.A.; painter/designer/printmaker; Senior Lecturer, Department of Communication Design, Leeds Polytechnic; *b* Ilkley, Wharfedale, Yorkshire, 1931. *Educ.:* Ilkley Grammar School; *studied art:* Leeds College of Art (1948-52), Royal College of Art (1954-58). Edited ARK (1958). *Exhib.:* one-man shows, Waddington Galleries (1974), New Art Centre (1960, 1961, 1963, 1966), A.I.A. Gallery (1969), and in Bradford, Windsor, Leeds, Tampa (U.S.A.), Ilkley, York, Menston, Glasgow, Edinburgh (1963-73); group shows include John Moores, Cincinatti Bienniale, Arts Council Travelling Exhibitions. *Work in permanent collections:* Museum of Modern Art, New York, Contemporary Art Society, Carlisle, Hull, Keighley, Ilkley and Bootle Art Galleries and Nuffield Foundation. *Address:* Rectory Farm House, Collingham, Wetherby, Yorks.

I

I'ANSON, Charles, F.R.B.S., R.B.S.A., F.R.S.A.; sculptor; *b* Birmingham, 28 Oct., 1924. *Exhib.:* Paris, Monte Carlo, San Sebastian, Czechoslovakia and most major exhibitions in this country; included in several open-air exhibitions; one-man shows: Birmingham, Leeds, and Alwyn Gallery, London. *Work in permanent collections:* City of Birmingham Public Art Gallery; Wakefield City Gallery; Bradford City Gallery and Leeds University; group over main entrance, Midlands Arts Centre for Young People; fighting cocks, main entrance, R.A. Gamecock

Barracks; Nuneaton; pierced hand, Bristol University; Hollow Victory, Warmley R.D.C.; R.A.F. Central Flying School; Cardiff Civic Centre; and several public buildings. *Address:* Ashbrook, Heaton Grove, Bradford, 9.

INCHBALD, Michael, F.S.I.A.: Architectural and Interior Designer; *studied:* A.A.; twice married; two children. *Work includes* 1st Class Lounge "Queen's Room" and Library on Q.E.2, all Banquet, Ballroom Areas and "Le Perroquet" at Berkeley Hotel, all public areas Post House, Heathrow, Claridges' Penthouse, River Room, Lincoln Room and just completed American Bar at Savoy, Crown Commissioner's 3 houses in Carlton House Terrace, Stone's Chop House, Player's and Plessey's H.Q. Offices, Justerini and Brooks, Law Society's Lady's Annexe, Working on Dunhill's, Jermyn Street and Sydney, Moet & Chandon, Duke of St. Albans' London house. *Work repro.:* Architectural Review, Connaissance, Connoisseur, Designers in Britain. *Address:* 10 Milner St., Cadogan Sq., London SW3.

INGHAM, George Bryan, A.R.C.A., A.R.E.; painter/etcher; *b* Preston, Lancs., 11 June, 1936. *Educ.:* Nether Edge Grammar, Sheffield; *studied art* at St. Martin's School of Art (Bateson Mason, Peter Coker, Fredk. Gore, Vivian Pitchforth), R.C.A. (Prof. Carel Weight). *Work in permanent collections:* Arts Council, Exeter College, Oxford, Ashmolean, Oxford, Birmingham University, Graves A.G., Sheffield, Southampton A.G., Leeds City A.G., Rochdale A.G., Bowes Museum. *Commissions* include Department of the Environment, Dartington Hall Trust, Christies Prints, London, Print Collectors' Club. *Address:* Kynance Farm, The Lizard, Cornwall. *Signs work:* "Bryan Ingham."

INGLEFIELD, Sir Gilbert Samuel, G.B.E., T.D., M.A., D.Sc., A.R.I.B.A., A.A. Diploma, F.R.S.A., Hon. G.S.M., Hon. R.B.A., Hon. F.L.C.M.; director of companies; Governor, Royal Shakespeare Theatre; Trustee, London Symphony Orchestra; Chairman, City Arts Trust; *b* London, 1909; *s* of the late Admiral Sir F. S. Inglefield, K.C.B.; *m* Laura Barbara Frances; two *s,* one *d. Educ.:* Eton and Cambridge; *studied art* at Architectural Association. *Publications:* articles on music, architecture, etc. *Address:* Egginton House, Leighton Buzzard, Bedfordshire. *Clubs:* Athenæum, Arts, City Livery. *Signs work:* see appendix.

IRELAND, Mary; artist in silk textiles in fabric mosaics, stained glass, illumination on vellum, water-colour; writer and lecturer on English costume; collector of 18th and 19th century costumes; *b* Stockingford, Warwickshire, 1891; *d* of George Henry Morris. *Exhib.:* R.A., Walker, Arlington, Burlington and Royal Institute galleries; and in television and films. *Work in permanent collections:* Dover Patrol Book of Remembrance (Dover Town Hall), panel of St. George presented by R. Soc. of St. George (Malta), altar-pieces and reredos in various churches. *Address:* 27 Julian Rd., Folkestone, Kent. *Signs work:* see appendix.

IRVIN, Albert; painter; *b* London, 21 Aug., 1922; *s* of A. H. J. Irvin; *m* Beatrice Nicolson; two *d. Educ.:* Holloway County; *studied art* at Northampton and Goldsmiths' School of Art. *Exhib.:* New Art Centre; Skulima, Berlin; Lüpke, Frankfurt; 57 Gallery, Edinburgh; John Moores; Open 100; Griechenbeisl, Vienna; Jefferson Place, Washington; Edinburgh University; Contemporary British Painting, U.S.A.: S.P.A.C.E. in Berlin, Belfast, Dublin, Cambridge, Aberdeen, Glasgow, Edinburgh, London; Spectrum. *Official purchases:* Arts Council of G.B., C.A.S., Wolverhampton Art Gallery, Blackburn Art Gallery, Min. of Environment, Nuffield Foundation, Southampton University, St. John's, Oxford, Linz Gallery, Austria, Bucks Educ. Com., Herts Educ. Com., Cambridge Educ. Com. *Address:* 19 Gorst Rd., London SW11.

IRVINE, Robert Scott, R.S.W. (1934); painter in water-colour; principal art master George Watson's College; *b* Edinburgh, 16 Mar., 1906; *s* of Robert Irvine, art master; *m* Elizabeth Fielden Hollis, D.A. (1954); one *s,* Henry James Scott Irvine. *Educ.:* George Heriots, Edinburgh; *studied art at* Edinburgh College of Art (1922-27). *Exhib.:* R.S.A., R.S.W., S.S.A., etc.; provinces, America, Canada, etc. *Work in permanent collections:* Aberdeen Municipal Gallery, Dundee Municipal Gallery, R.S.A. Edinburgh. *Official purchases:* as above. *Address:* 5 Spence St., Edinburgh, 9. *Club:* Scottish Arts (Pres. 1951-53). *Signs work:* see appendix.

IRWIN, Gwyther; painter: wood, aluminium, oil paint, paper collage; Head of Fine Art at Brighton Polytechnic; *b* Cornwall, 7 May, 1931; *m* Elizabeth; two *s,* one *d. Educ.:* Bryanston; *studied art* at Goldsmiths' School of Art (1950-51), Central School of Art (1952-55). *Work in permanent collections:* Tate Gallery, British Council, Arts Council, Contemporary Art Soc., Arts Council of N. Ireland, Calouste Gulbenkian, City Art Gallery, Bradford, Albright-Knox, Yale University, Peggy Guggenheim, Peter Stuyvesant. *Address:* 21 Hillbury Rd., London SW17. *Signs work:* "Gwyther Irwin."

IRWIN, John C.; keeper, Oriental Dept., V. & A.; sec., R.A. Exhbn. of Indian Art (1947-48); UNESCO expert in Museum Development on mission to Indonesia (1956-57); *b* Madras, India, 5 Aug., 1917; *s* of J. W. Irwin; *m* Helen Hermione; three *s. Educ.:* Canford School, Wimborne. *Publications:* Jamini Roy (1944), Indian Art (Faber & Faber), 1947, in collaboration; Commemorative Catalogue of R.A. Exhbn. of Indian Art (1947-48, in collaboration); Shawls; A Study in Indo-European Influences (1955); Origins of chintz (1970); contributor to Burlington Magazine, Journal of Royal Asiatic Soc., etc. *Address:* Bellmans Green, Edenbridge, Kent TN8 6LU.

ISHERWOOD, James Lawrence, F.R.S.A., F.I.A.L. (Life Mem., Switzerland); silver medal, Rome (1971); artist in oils, water-colour, etc.; lecturer; *b* Wigan, 7 Apr., 1917; *s* of Harry Lawrence Isherwood (shoe manufacturer) and the late Lily Leyland (mother, who acted as model). *Studied art* at Wigan Technical College (School of Art) (1934-53). *Exhib.:* all over Great Britain in 154 one-man shows, thirteen in London and two in Canada. "England's only wandering artist" (The Times); ". . . he has gained for himself world-wide recognition" (Oxford Univ. Magazine, Scorpion). Has demonstrated on television and appeared with his paintings from Manchester, Anglia and Southampton ITV, and in plays. Has held fifty-one art shows at colleges in Cambridge and Oxford Universities. Showing with the Vice-Chancellor, Oxford University, May, 1965. *Official purchases:* Coventry City, Stoke City, H.R.H. Prince Charles, L. S. Lowry, R.A., Sir Wm. and Lady Hayter, Warden, New College; and St. Hugh's University and Oriel Colleges, Oxford University; Lady Wheare; Lady Strabolgi; Lord Newport (who exhibited his work at Cambridge University); also Caius, Emmanuel, Corpus Christi, Churchill and Pembroke Colleges, Cambridge. He was featured with Mother Lily on B.B.C. TV documentary (Apr., 1967) and in "It Takes All Sorts." B.B.C. Radio 4, June, 1969. Issued limited editions, 75 each, have been countersigned by Gracie Fields, Viscount Montgomery and Sir Francis Chichester (1972). *Address:* Scarisbrick Hotel, Lord St., Southport, Merseyside. *Signs work:* "Isherwood."

J

JACKMAN, Iris Rachel; Medallist, Royal Drawing Society; Full Diploma Charlotte Mason, P.N.E.U. College, University of Manchester; Diplome d'Honneur, Salon Internationale, Biarritz (1970); painter in oils, specialising in flower paintings; *d* of Capt. Maurice Anderson Ainslie, R.N., F.R.S., B.A.A., M.A.; *m* Lt.-Col. C. R. Jackman, O.B.E. *Studied* at Goldsmiths' College School of Art, University of London, and subsequently in Italy. *Exhib.:* one-man shows in Bournemouth and Guildford; now exhibiting at Mall Galleries, etc. *Work in permanent collections:* private collections. *Address:* Old Honeypots, Westfield Rd., Woking, Surrey. *Clubs:* Chelsea Arts, Society of Women Artists. *Signs work:* see appendix.

JACKSON, George William, A.R.C.A. (1938), A.T.D. (1935); artist in watercolour, gouache, wood engraving, etching, lithography; lecturer in illustration and industrial design; vice-principal, Chesterfield College of Art; *b* Leeds, 1914; *s* of George Jackson, engineer; *m* Joan Wells; one *d*. *Educ.:* Leeds Central High School; *studied art* at Leeds under D. S. Andrews, A.R.C.A., S.G.A. (1931-35), R.C.A. under P. H. Jowett, A.R.C.A., E. W. Tristram (1935-38), L.C.C. Central School (1936-38). *Exhib.:* London and provinces. *Work repro.:* illustrations in various trade journals. *Address:* 53 Cutthorpe Road, Chesterfield. *Signs work:* "G. W. JACKSON."

JACKSON, H. J., R.E., S.W.E., N.D.D.; commercial design studio manager, printmaker in lino; *b* Kings Lynn, Norfolk, 7 Dec., 1938; *s* of D. S. B. Jackson. *Educ.:* Melton Constable Secondary Modern School; *studied art* at Norwich School of Art (1954-58) under G. Wales, R.E. *Exhib.:* U.S.A., Bermuda, London, Norwich and various art exhibitions throughout east and south-east England. *Address:* 12 Whitehall Rd., Norwich NR2 3EW.

JACKSON, Muriel, Mem., Soc. of Wood-Engravers, Logan medal, International exhbn. of Lithography and Wood-engraving, Art Inst. of Chicago (1931); painter in tempera, wood-engraver, designer; *b* London, 9 Mar., 1901; *d* of Arthur Blomfield Jackson, F.R.I.B.A.; *m* Courtenay Mason, M.S., F.R.C.S.: one *s*, one *d*. *Educ.:* Ruskin House, Hampstead, private school; *studied art* at L.C.C. Central School of Arts and Crafts. *Exhib.:* R.A., N.E.A.C., Crafts Centre of Great Britain, Red Rose Guild of Art-workers, Manchester, Hull, Bournemouth, Art Inst. of Chicago, New York. *Work in permanent collections:* V. & A., Art Institute of Chicago. *Work repro.:* The Studio. *Address:* 14 Gainsborough Gdns., Hampstead, London NW3. *Signs work:* "Muriel Jackson."

JACKSON, Muriel Amy; artist in oil, black and white; specializing in flower paintings, child and architectural subjects; *b* London, 1902; *d* of the late A. E. Jackson, artist. *Educ.:* Berkhamsted High School; *studied art* at Hastings School of Art, L.C.C., under L. Badam, R.B.A., P. Cole, R.B.A., A.R.C.A. *Exhib.:* Highgate Artists Soc., Thames Valley Arts Club, E. Sussex Arts Club, Battle Arts Group and Bexhill Arts Society. *Work repro.:* flowers, illustrations to children's annuals, etc. *Address:* 33 Croft Rd., Hastings, Sussex. *Club:* E. Sussex Arts. *Signs work:* "MURIEL A. JACKSON."

JACQUES, Robin, F.S.I.A.; artist in pen and ink, oil, gouache; designer and book illustrator; principal art editor, C.O.I. (1950-51); art editor, Strand Magazine (1948-50); *b* Chelsea, 27 Mar., 1920; *s* of Robin Jacques, Capt., Royal Scots Fusiliers. *Educ.:* Royal Masonic Schools, Bushey, Herts.; no art school training. *Exhib.:* V. & A., provincial A.Gs. *Work in permanent collections:* V. & A. *Work repro.:* Alphabet and Image, Penrose Annual, Saturday Book, Vogue, Lilliput, Housewife, Strand, Radio Times. *Publications:* Don Quixote, Hans Andersen, Dubliners, Gulliver's Travels, Arabian Nights. *Address:* Paradou, 13, France. *Signs work:* "ROBIN JACQUES."

JADOT, Maurice; painter and sculptor; *b* Brussels, 23 Jan., 1893; *s* of Yvon Jadot, composer and conductor; *m* Margaret Crabb. *Educ.:* Athenée de Bruxelles;

studied art at Academie Royale des Beaux Arts, Brussels; architecture: Prof. Victor Horta (1910-14). Chairman the Belgian Cultural Centre in the United Kingdom; found-member and Fellow of the Free Painters and Sculptors. *Exhib.:* one-man shows: Drian Gallery, London (1958, 1959, 1960), Institute of Contemporary Arts, London (1961), Galerie d'Art du Faubourg, Paris (1962), Molton Gallery, London (1963, 1964, 1965), Palais des Beaux-Arts, Brussels (1964), City Museum and Art Gallery, Birmingham (1966), Queen's University, Belfast (1966), Laing Art Gallery and Museum, Newcastle (1967), Whibley's Gallery, Cork St., London (1968, 1971, 1973), City Museums Bolton, Accrington, Rochdale, Bury (1970); Belgian Ministry of Culture, travelling exhibitions in Belgium: Brussels, Liege, Namur, Luxembourg, etc. (1973-74-75). *Work in private and public collections:* Museum of Modern Art, Brussels, Art Museum, Malines (Belgium); Laing Art Gallery and Museum; Newcastle, Rutherston Collection, Manchester Museum; Leicester Education Authority, etc. *Address:* 90 Castellain Mansions, London W9 1HB.

JAENISCH, Hans; painter and sculptor; Prof., Hochschule fur bildende kunste, Berlin; *b* Eilenstedt, 9 May, 1907. *Exhib.:* Berlin, Paris, St. Gallen, Luzern, Köln, München, Düsseldorf, Hagen, U.A., Pittsburgh, New York, Detroit, London. *Work in permanent collections:* Museum XX century in Berlin; museum, Düsseldorf; Brooklyn Museum, New York; Albright Gallery, Buffalo; Köln, Pittsburgh (U.S.A.), Detroit, Richmond, Hartford. *Work repro.:* Das Kunstwerk, Freunde Zeitgenoss Kunst, Dr. E. Ruhmer: Sehen und Verstehen and Ulrich Gertz; Plastik der Gegenwarf; Aquarelle aus Amrum/Der Silberne Quell: Band 42, Dr. K. Hoyer: Jaenisch, Monogr., etc. *Address:* 1 Berlin 21, Bartningallee 12. *Clubs:* Deutscher Kunstler Bund, Berliner Neue Gruppe, Münchner Neue Gruppe. *Signs work:* see appendix.

JAFFÉ, Hans; Professor for Modern and Contemporary Art History, University of Amsterdam; Director, Jewish Historical Museum, Amsterdam; *b* Frankfurt, Germany, 14 May, 1915. *Address:* 17 Nieuwe Prinsengracht, Amsterdam.

JAFFE, Harold, F.I.P.D. (1965), A.S.A. (1973), F.A.E.D. (1974); artist in acrylic and mixed media; interior designer and muralist, teacher and antiquarian; Dean, Institute of Environmental Studies; *b* New York City, 26 Mar., 1922; *s* of Selig Jaffe; *m* Gisèle Jaffe; one *s*, one *d*. *Educ.:* Pratt Institute, Parsons School; *studied art* at Cape Ann, Gloucester under Maxwell Starr, Gilbert Golde. *Work in permanent collections:* Denton Greens Housing Development; *private collections:* Dr. C. MacCormick, Mr. and Mrs. S. Berman, Dr. D. Bernstein, Mr. and Mrs. B. Kornreich, Mr. and Mrs. A. Adler. *Work repro.:* Interiors Magazine, Years Work. *Address:* 5 Devon Rd., Great Neck, New York, U.S.A. *Signs work:* "Harold."

JAGGAR, Margaret Leah, R.Cam.A.; wood engraver, mural painter, commercial artist; *b* 9 July, 1907; *d* of Thomas Webster Blundell, cotton broker; *m* Major Robert Jaggar; one *s*, one *d*. *Educ.:* Cheltenham Ladies' College; Liverpool Art School. *Exhib.:* Soc. of Wood Engravers, etc. *Work repro.:* Murals in Architect, Building News, Architects Journal, Design; W. H. Smith and Sons, Ltd., etc.; murals for Cunard White Star Liner s.s. Caronia, National Trust, etc. *Address:* Croes Efa, Rhydwyn, nr. Holyhead.

JAMES, Herbert Norman, N.R.D., Dipl. Ing.; industrial design consultant, television and film director; *b* Rochford, Essex, 22 Oct., 1918; *s* of Herbert C. James, F.R.I.C.S., M.I.Struct.E.; *m* Justine Whateley, painter; one *s*, one *d*. *Educ.:* Royal Liberty School; *studied art* at West Ham School of Art, Pratt Inst., Brooklyn, N.Y., University of Bologna, Tech. Hochsch., Darmstadt. *Exhib.:* Tienniale, Turin; Museum of Modern Art, N.Y.; Cannes and Venice film festivals, etc. *Work repro.:* current design and scientific periodicals. *Address:* Central Ave., Frinton-on-Sea, Essex. *Signs work:* see appendix.

JAMES, Hywel Arthur, Dip.A.D.Hons., A.T.D.; painter in water-colour and acrylics, lecturer in art and design; Head of Foundation Studies, Dept. of Art and Design, Hastings College of Further Education; *b* Brighton, 12 July, 1944; *s* of Benjamin James. *Educ.:* Westlain Grammar School, Falmer, E. Sussex; *studied art* at Brighton College of Art (1962-66), painting and printmaking under Charles Knight, Ian Potts and Jennifer Dickson. *Exhib.:* Hastings A.G. (1976), R.I. (1975, 1976), Bedford A.G. (1973), R.E. (1965). *Work in permanent collections:* Leeds City A.G., Bedford A.G., Bedford School. *Address:* c/o Art & Design, Hastings College of Further Education, Archery Rd., St. Leonards, E. Sussex. *Signs work:* "Hywel James."

JAMES, Kim, M.A. (R.C.A.), N.D.D., A.T.C.; art educationalist; *b* Wollaston, Northants, 31 July, 1928; *s* of Christopher James; *m*; one *d*. *Educ.:* Wellingborough Grammar School; *studied art* at Borough Polytechnic under David Bomberg and Tom Eckersley; Royal College of Art. Special research field; The cognitive consequences of graphic activity in child development. Writings include critical essays on current theories of Perception and Philosophy (Leonardo, vols. 8, 9, 10). Teacher of visual research and sculpture, Depts. of Sculpture, Ceramics and Metalwork, Camberwell School of Art, London. Heads a team of teachers in research into the cognitive development of young children. Works in various media including films for education. *Exhib.:* R.A., Scottish Arts Council, Vision '68 Fontainebleau, Middleheim Biennale, Antwerp. *Work in permanent collections:* San Francisco Museum of Modern Art, Grosvenor Gallery, London, Louis Camu Banque de Bruxelle, Belgium. *Addresses:* 34 Marmora Rd., London SE22; "Jones' Farm", Hickmire, Wollaston, Northants. *Signs work:* "Kim James."

JAMES, Thomas K.; Assoc. of Nottingham Artists; *b* Nottingham, 29 Apr., 1906; *s* of Thomas James, railway engine driver; *m* Jessie James; two *s*. *Educ.:* Nottingham and S.A. Training College, London; *studied art* at Nottingham Soc. of Artists. *Exhib.:* Nottingham Festival of Britain exhbn., Nottingham Soc. of Artists exhbn., Beeston Library, Mansfield Public A.G.; also exhibited by B.R. at Euston, Swindon, Derby, Birmingham, etc.; exhib. fifty water-colours, oils and pastels, Nottingham (October, 1970). Painter in water-colour, oils and pastels. *Address:* 34 Stockhill Circus, Basford, Nottingham. *Club:* Nottingham Soc. of Artists. *Signs work:* "THOS. K. JAMES."

JAMESON, Kenneth Ambrose, R.C.A., R.D.S., F.R.S.A.; artist in oil and drawing; formerly, Art Inspector, I.L.E.A.; Vice-President, Pre-School Playgroups Assoc.; *b* Blackwell, Worcestershire, 21 May, 1913; *s* of Robert B. Jameson, timber merchant; *m* Norma M. Jameson. *Educ.:* King Edward VI Grammar School, Birmingham; *studied art* at Leicester College of Art, Bath Academy of Art. *Work in permanent collections:* Corporation Art Gallery, Birkenhead; extensively in colleges and educational establishments. *Publications:* Pre-school and Infant Art, You Can Draw, Flower Painting for Beginners, Starting with Abstract Painting, Junior School Art, Pre-School Play (all Studio Vista), Painting: A Complete Guide (Nelson). *Address:* 111 Hayes Way, Beckenham, Kent BR3 2RR. *Signs work:* see appendix.

JAMIESON, John S., D.A., F.R.S.A., F.I.A.L.; Resources Officer, Bradford College of Art and Technology; Vice-Principal, Regional College of Art, Bradford (1964-73); Head of Keighley School of Art (1959-64); taught at Harrow School of Art (1948-59) and Dundee College of Art (Sept., 1948 to Dec., 1948); commercial artist; letterer; textile designer and design consultant; worked with textile manufacturer (1938-39); *b* Forfar, Angus, 23 July, 1920, *m* Ines Healey; one *d. Educ.:* Forfar Academy; *studied art* at Dundee College of Art. *Address:* Timmourie Fell, The Lindens, Skipton Rd., Utley, Keighley, W. Yorks.

JAMILLY, Victor; painter, oil and water-colour; art gallery director; *b* 31 May, 1927; *s* of David Jamilly; *m* Audrey; two *s*, one *d. Educ.:* Highgate and Cranleigh Schools; *studied art* at St. Martin's School of Art. *Work in permanent collection:* Euston Gallery, London. *Exhib.:* New English Art Club, R.S.B.A., various group and gallery shows. *Address:* Wendover, 13 Hampstead Way, London NW11. *Signs work:* "V. Jamilly."

JAMISON, James Kenneth, D.A., A.T.D.; director, Arts Council of Northern Ireland; *b* Belfast, 9 May, 1931; *s* of William Jamison; *m* Joan (*née* Boyd); one *s*, one *d. Educ.:* Methodist College, Belfast; *studied painting and silversmithing* at Belfast College of Art (1949-53); Art Master, Annadale Grammar School (1961); Art Organiser, Arts Council of Northern Ireland (1962); Deputy Director (1966); Director (1969). Various short publications and reviews on aspects of the arts. *Address:* 64 Rugby Rd., Belfast BT7 1PT.

JANÀCÊK, Mirice: see MATTAROZZI, Mirella.

JANCO, Marcel, painter and teacher in art; founder and Mayor of the artists' village, Ein Hod, in Israel; *b* Bucarest, 1895; *s* of Zwi. *Educ.:* Polytechnicum, Zürich; one of the founders of Dada in Zürich. *Work in permanent and private collections:* Modern Art, New York; Art Institute, Chicago; Cleveland Museum; Tel Aviv Art Museum; Haifa Modern Art Museum. *Work repro.:* Monographie (Edition Masada, Tel Aviv), Marcel Janco (Dr. Mendelson), M. Janco (Michel Seuphor), Edition Bodensee (Suisse). Janco awarded Israel National Art Prize (1967). *Addresses:* Tel Aviv, reh. Glickson 9; Ein Hod, Artists' Village, nr. Haifa, Israel. *Signs work:* "Janco."

JANES, Norman, R.W.S., R.E., R.S.M.A.; painter, etcher, wood engraver; *b* 1892; *m* Barbara Greg; one *s*, two *d. Educ.:* Slade School; Central School of Art and Crafts. *Exhib.:* R.E., R.W.S., N.E.A.C., R.A., Soc. Wood Engravers, Soc. Marine Artists, Paris, U.S.A., Venice, Florence, Johannesburg, Beaux Arts Gallery (two one-man exhbns.). *Official purchases:* Contemporary Art Soc. for British Museum, V. & A., London Museum, National Gallery of New Zealand, National Art Collections Fund, British Council, Ministry of Works, City of London, Manchester (City Gallery), Sunderland, Manchester (Whitworth), Bradford, Brighton, New York, Brooklyn, etc. *Address:* 70 Canonbury Pk. South, London N1. *Signs work:* see appendix.

JANES, Violeta; portrait painter, still-life, artist in oil, pastel and water-colour; *b* Buenos Aires, Argentina; *d* of A. F. Janes and V. F. M. Coates. *Educ.:* Giffen School, Viña del Mar, Chile; *studied art* at Regent St. Polytechnic School of Art under S. Tresilian, Middleton Todd, E. Osmond. *Exhib.:* R.A., R.O.I., S.W.A., R.S.A., N.E.A.C., R.P. and the provinces; two-man show in the West End, one-man, Broomfield Museum. Member United Society of Artists. Directed art studies at Alma College, Ontario, Canada. *Address:* Studland, 111 Totteridge La., London N20 8DZ. *Signs work:* "Violeta Janes."

JANKOWSKI, Joseph Paul; painter in oil, encaustic and mixed technique; draughtsman and student of pre-Columbian civilizations; teacher of painting, drawing and design, The Cleveland Institute of Art (1953-); *b* Cleveland, Ohio, 12 Jan., 1916; *s* of Joseph J. Jankowski; *m* Felicia Mosinski; two *d. Educ.:* St. Mary's College, Orchard Lake, Mich.; *studied art* at John Huntington Polytechnic Inst., Art Students' League of New York. Bachelor of Fine Arts degree from Cleveland

Institute of Art. *Address:* The Cleveland Inst. of Art, Cleveland, 6, Ohio. *Clubs:* College Art Assoc., Art Students' League of New York, Cleveland Inst. of Art Alumni. *Signs work:* "J. Jankowski."

JANNASCH, Adolf, Dr. phil. (1923); art historian; director of the gallery of the 20th Century, Berlin; *b* Heidelberg, 7 June, 1898; *s* of Prof. Paul Jannasch; *m* Alice Breu; one *s*. *Educ.:* Grammar School, Heidelberg; *studied art* history at Universities of Heidelberg and Berlin under C. Neumann, A. Goldschmidt. *Publications:* Die niederländischen Maler des 17. Jahrhunderts (1940), Hans Meid (1943), Carl Hofer (1946), Renée Sintenis (1949), Heinrich Zille (1960), Max Beckmann als Illustrator (1969). *Address:* Berlin, 19, Nussbaumallee 42.

JANSON, Horst Woldemar, Ph.D. (Harvard, 1942); Editor-in-Chief, The Art Bulletin (1962-65); Charles Morey Award, College Art Assoc. (1952, '57); instructor, State University of Iowa (1938-41); assistant professor, Washington University (1941-48); professor and chairman of Department, Washington Square College, New York University (since 1949); *b* Leningrad, U.S.S.R., 4 Oct., 1913; *s* of Friedrich Janson; *m* Dora Jane Heineberg; three *s*, one *d*. *Educ.:* Harvard University (1935-38). *Publications:* Sculpture of Donatello (1957); Key Monuments of the History of Art (1959); History of Art (1962; rev. ed. 1970); articles and reviews in learned journals. *Address:* 29 Washington Sq. W., New York, N.Y. 10011.

JAQUES, Norman Clifford, D.A. (Manc., 1941), M.S.I.A. (1945); Sen. Lecturer, Manchester Polytechnic (litho. and eng.); free-lance artist in illustration; agent, R. P. Gossop, Ltd., London; *b* 23 Apr., 1922; *s* of John Clifford Jaques; *m* Marjorie Hovell; two *s*. *Educ.:* Manchester College of Art (J. M. Holmes, P. W. Keen, 1937-42); R. M. I. Heywood Prize; Proctor Travelling Scholarship (1940). Studio artist, Messrs. Rowlinson Broughton (1942-45). Member of Senefelder Club, Manchester Academy of Fine Art, Lancashire Artists. *Exhib.:* London, Manchester, Glasgow, Edinburgh, U.S.A. and Canada, etc. *Official purchases:* V. & A. Museum, Manchester City Art Gallery, B.B.C., Rochdale, Stoke, Manchester, Newcastle Education Committees, etc. *Commissions:* United Steel Co., Post Office, B.B.C., British Transport, Odhams, Macmillan, Harrap, etc. *Address:* 6 Wardle Rd., Sale, Ches.

JARAY, Tess, D.F.A. (Lond., 1960); painter in oil and etcher; *b* Vienna, 31 Dec., 1937; *d* of Francis F. Jaray, M.I.Chem.E.; *m* Marc Vaux. *Educ.:* Alice Ottley School, Worcester; *studied art* at St. Martin's School of Art (1954-57), Slade School of Fine Art (1957-60). *Work in permanent collections:* Stadtisches Museum, Leverkusen, Walker Art Gallery, Liverpool, Arts Council of Gt. Britain, Peter Stuyvesant Foundation, Tate Gallery, Graves Art Gallery, Sheffield, Warwick University. *Address:* 29 Camden Sq., London NW1. *Signs work:* "Tess Jaray."

JARVIS, Gloria, N.D.D.; artist in oil, water-colour, pastel, ink, gouache; lecturer on historic costume and instructor in costume drawing, Polytechnic, Regent St. (1950-63); *d* of R. V. Jarvis, artist; *m* A. Raymond Smith, B.A. (1964). *Educ.:* Heathfield-Norris School, Harrow; Aylesbury Grammar School; *studied art* at St. Martin's School of Art, London, under James Bateman, R.A., A.R.W.S., for drawing, painting and composition; the history of art at Florence University. *Exhib.:* R.A., N.E.A.C., N.S., Leicester Galleries; one-man show, Brussels (1970, 1971, 1972, 1973, 1975). *Work repro.:* Macmillan & Co. Ltd., Brussels Times. *Address:* 11 rue des Adriatiques, 1040 Brussels. *Signs work:* "Gloria Jarvis."

JEFFERSON, Alan, A.R.C.A.; painter; Senior Lecturer, Dept. of Fine Art, Portsmouth Polytechnic: *b* S. Kensington, 7 Apr., 1918; *s* of Arthur Edward

Jefferson; *m* Denise Audrey; one *s*, one *d*. *Educ.:* Mitcham County School; *studied art* at Wimbledon School of Art and R.C.A. *Exhib.:* Redfern, Piccadilly and provincial galleries; one-man exhibitions Bear Lane Gallery, Oxford and Hiscock Gallery, Portsmouth. *Work in private collections:* U.K., South Africa, U.S.A. *Official purchases:* Portsmouth Corp. *Address:* 22 Bell Rd., Cosham, Hants. *Signs work:* "ALAN JEFFERSON."

JEFFREY, Edward; artist in water-colour, black and white; *b* 17 Sept., 1898; *s* of George Jeffrey, decorator; *m*. *Educ.:* Newcastle upon Tyne; *studied art* at Armstrong College, Durham University, Newcastle upon Tyne. *Exhib.:* R.I., R.S.A., National Soc., R.B.A., Newcastle upon Tyne, Middlesbrough, Huddersfield, Kendal, Grasmere. *Work repro.:* general illustration, book jackets, greeting cards. *Address:* The Stables, Ravenstonedale, Kirkby Stephen, Cumbria. *Clubs:* Lake Artist Soc., Kendal Art Soc. *Signs work:* see appendix.

JELLICOE, Colin; painter in oil; art gallery director; *b* 1 Nov., 1942. *Educ.:* Heald Place School; *studied art* at Manchester Regional College of Art, now The Polytechnic. *Exhib.:* Monks Hall Museum; open shows: Haworth Art Gallery, first and second invited show; Stockport Art Gallery (1967, 1968), Bulls Eye Gallery (1971), Manchester Academy, City Art Gallery (1972, 1973). *Work in private collections:* Sheffield, Newcastle upon Tyne, Oxford, Wakefield, Manchester, London and North-West Arts Assoc. *Address:* 82 Portland St., Manchester 1. *Signs work:* "Colin Jellicoe."

JELLICOE, Geoffrey Alan, C.B.E., F.R.I.B.A., M.T.P.I., P.P.I.L.A., architect, town-planner, landscape architect; designer of Kennedy Memorial at Runnymede, etc.; late trustee, Tate Gallery; *b* London; *s* of George Edward Jellicoe; *m* Ursula Pares. *Educ.:* Cheltenham College; *studied art* at A.A. *Exhib.:* R.A., etc. *Publications:* Italian Gardens of the Renaissance (joint), Studies in Landscape Design, Vols. I. II and III: The Landscape of Man. *Address:* 19 Grove Terr., London NW5.

JENKINS, Eveline A., B.Sc. (Wales, 1919), F.R.S.A. (1951); artist in wax, black and white, oil and water-colour; Botanical Artist, National Museum of Wales, Cardiff (1936-59); *b* 6 June, 1893. *Educ.:* Newport Girls' High School; University College, Aberystwyth; *studied art* in spare time at various schools. *Exhib.:* Local exhbns. and S. Wales Group; models in National Museum of Wales. *Official purchases:* by Monmouthshire Educ. Cttee. and C.A.S. *Work repro.:* Botanical line drawings for official publications. *Publications:* The Preparation of Fungus Models (Mus. J. 38, 51-55, and 116-22, 1938); Some Welsh Fungi, pp. 50, Cardiff, 1948. *Address:* 32 Colum Rd., Cardiff. *Signs work:* "E.A.J." on line drawings, "Eveline A. Jenkins" on pictures.

JENKINSON, Geoffrey, R. Cam.A. (1947); professional artist in oil, water-colour, pencil and pastel; *b* Leeds, 31 Aug., 1925; *s* of William Jenkinson. *Educ.:* Kepler Council School, Leeds; *studied art* at Pudsey Grammar School (1940-48), (Fred C. Jones, R.B.A., A.T.D.). *Exhib.:* Hutchinson's Headrow Gallery, Leeds, Renoir Gallery, Harrogate. *Work in permanent collections:* water-colour drawing, West Riding Youth Academy of Art, water-colour drawing, Leeds and Airedale Beyond, Leeds City Art Gallery. *Address:* General Delivery, Tubac, Arizona, 85640, U.S.A. *Club:* Arizona Artists' Guild. *Signs work:* "GEOFFREY JENKINSON, R.C.A."

JENNETT, Seán; author, translator, photographer. free-lance designer; *b* 12 Nov., 1912; *m* Irene Lumley; one *s*, one *d*. *Publications:* Always Adam, The Cloth of Flesh, The Making of Books (Faber), Pioneers in Printing (Routledge), The Sun and Old Stones (Faber), Beloved Son Felix (translation, Muller), Journal of a Younger Son (translation, Muller), The Young Photographer's Companion

(Souvenir Press), Deserts of England (Heinemann), Munster (Faber), The Travellers Guides (Darton, Longman and Todd), Connacht (Faber), The Pilgrims' Way (Cassell), The Loire. *Address:* 3 The Dene, Chowns Hill, Hastings, Sussex.

JENNINGS, E. Owen, A.R.W.S. (1943), R.W.S. (1950), A.R.E. (1944), A.R.C.A. (1925), A.T.D. (1926); painter, etcher, engraver and illustrator; Principal of School of Art, Tunbridge Wells (1934-65); *b* 28 Dec., 1899; *s* of Wesley Jennings, J.P.; *m* May Cullingworth; one *s,* one *d. Educ.:* School of Art, Skipton, College of Art, Leeds, Royal College of Art. Silver Medallist, C. and G.; Logan Prize Winner, Chicago International; stained glass, Staplehurst Church. Examiner in three-dimensional design for Ministry of Education. President of R.W.S. Art Club. *Exhib.:* R.A., R.W.S., N.E.A.C., R.E., Paris Salon, New York, Chicago, Melbourne, Pittsburg, C.E.M.A. and British Council exhibitions in England, Russia, China, Poland, Antwerp. *Official purchases:* B.M., V. & A., Albertina, Vienna, Art Institute, Chicago, Brooklyn Museum, New York, Leeds, Birmingham, Wakefield. *Work repro.:* Fine Prints of the Year, Etchings of Today, New York Times, R.W.S. Annual Volumes. *Address:* Linton, Wilman Rd., Tunbridge Wells. *Club:* Chelsea Arts. *Signs work:* "E. OWEN JENNINGS."

JENNINGS, Philip O., A.R.E., A.R.C.A.; printmaker and painter; senior lecturer, Cardiff College of Art; Mem. Welsh Group; *b* Chiswick, London, 16 May, 1921; *s* of A. G. Jennings, secretary. *Educ.:* King's School, Harrow; *studied art* at Harrow School of Art and R.C.A. under R.S.Austin, R.A. *Exhib.:* R.A., London, Welsh Arts Council, provincial galleries, and in U.S.A. *Work in permanent collections:* National Museum of Wales, The Welsh Arts Council, University College, Cardiff, and a number of public and private collections. *Address:* 1 Kingsland Rd., Whitchurch, Cardiff, CF4 2EJ.

JENNINGS, Walter Robin; artist in oil; portraits, landscape, and equestrian pictures; *b* Old Hill, Staffs., 11 Mar., 1927; *s* of William Dennis Jennings; *m* Barbara Wilkinson. *Educ.:* Macefields Secondary School; *studied art* at Dudley and Staffordshire Art School, Brierley Hill School of Art, Birmingham School of Art. *Exhib.:* R.B.S.A., R.W.E.A., R.Cam.A., Royal Institute Galleries, Utd. Soc. of Artists, N.E.A.C., etc. *Work in permanent collections:* Allison House, Mr. H. Woodhouse; Enville Hall, Mr. and Mrs. J. Bissel. *Official purchase:* Brierley Hill A.G. *Publications:* Royle, Medici, Solomon and Whitehead, etc. *Address:* Kestrels, Caunsall, Cookley, nr. Kidderminster, Worcs. *Signs work:* see appendix.

JOBSON, Patrick; painter and draughtsman in oil, water-colour, tempera and pastel; illustrator in black and white; heraldic artist and designer. Signs for many of princ. London brewers. *Work repro.:* illustrations (O.U.P., Blackie, Macmillan), etc. *Address:* 117 Eton Ave., N. Wembley, Middx. *Clubs:* Langham Sketch, Wapping Group. *Signs work:* see appendix.

JOBSON, Richard Henry, M.B., Ch.B. (1934); artist in oil, water-colour, pastel, photography and cinematography; medical practitioner; *b* Urmston, Manchester, 3 June, 1910; *s* of Henry Jobson; *m* Ellen Pauline Murray. *Educ.:* Manchester University. *Exhib.:* Plas Mawr, Conway (Academy of Wales), Croft, Hereford; photography, London Salon, Royal Photographic Soc., Barcelona, Charleroi, Chicago, etc. *Address:* The Laurels, New Radnor, Presteigne, Radnor. *Signs work:* never.

JOHN, Anthony, M.A.I.A.; artist in oil, water-colour, gouache; paints mainly marine subjects; paints only to please himself, but likes to sell too; *b* Wales, 1905; *studied art* at Chelsea School under P. H. Jowett, and in Paris. *Exhib.:* one-man shows in Canada and S. Africa, Bloomsbury Gallery, Wertheim Gallery, Redfern Gallery. *Agent:* Moreton Street Gallery, 40 Moreton St., London SW1V 2PB.

Address: 26 Parkinson House, Tachbrook St., London SW1V 2QB. *Signs work:* "ANTHONY JOHN."

JOHNSON, Charles G., Mem. United Soc. Artists (1944); past pres. and hon. sec., Bishop's Stortford Art Soc.; artist in oil, water-colour, pastel, black and white; *b* Stansted, 9 Oct., 1902; *s* of T. R. Johnson; *m* Mary Christina; two *s. Educ.:* Stansted and R.N. Schools; *studied art:* self-taught. *Exhib.:* R.O.I., N.S., United Soc. Artists, Pastel Soc., Britain in Water-colours, Russell-Cotes Art Gallery, Bournemouth, Grundy Gallery, Blackpool, Middlesbrough, one-man show Bishop's Stortford, etc. *Work in private collections:* in England and U.S.A. *Work repro.:* Artist, commercial and technical illustrations. *Publications:* Introduction to Sketching, Silent World. *Address:* Highfields, High Lane, Stansted, Essex. *Signs work:* "C. G. Johnson" (scratched into paint on oils).

JOHNSON, Nowell Hewlett, A.R.C.A., J.P.; artist in oil, water-colour and black and white; *b* Crossens, Lancs., 1906; *d* of Rev. G. Z. Edwards; *m* Hewlett Johnson, Dean of Canterbury; two *d. Studied art* at Southport School of Art, and R.C.A. *Exhib.:* R.A., Artists for Peace, East Kent Art Soc. *Work repro.:* Illustrations to The Socialist Sixth of the World. *Address:* 24 New St., St. Dunstans, Canterbury. *Signs work:* "Nowell Hewlett Johnson" and "Nowell Johnson."

JOHNSTON, Duncan; sculptor in lignum vitae, bronze, ceramics; *b* Liverpool, 9 Mar., 1924. *Studied* commercial art Liverpool School of Art, self-taught sculptor since demobilisation in 1946, teacher trained 1948, Royal Academy Scholarship 1966, left teaching 1967. *Work in permanent collections:* Arts Council of Northern Ireland, O'Hana Gallery, London, Kingston-upon-Hull Education Committee, Lady Margaret School, St. George's Church, Museo Michelangelo, Tel Aviv Museum of Art. *Address:* 151 Craddocks Ave., Ashstead, Surrey. *Signs work:* see appendix.

JOHNSTON, George Bonar, D.A. (Edin.); artist in oil, gouache and water-colour; adviser in art, Tayside Educ. Authority; *b* Edinburgh, 14 June, 1933. *Educ.:* Bathgate Academy; *studied art* at Edinburgh College of Art (1951-56) under William Gillies, R.A., and Robin Philipson, A.R.A. *Exhib.:* regular exhibitor in R.S.A., R.S.W., R.G.I.; one-man shows: Perth, Kirkcaldy, Glasgow, Dundee; mixed shows: Paris, Toronto, Edinburgh, Aberdeen, etc. *Work in permanent collections:* Toronto, Glasgow, Strathclyde, Dundee. *Address:* Sandbraes, 10 Collingwood Cres., Barnhill, Dundee. *Signs work:* "Johnston."

JOICEY, Richard Raylton, G.M., V.R.D.; painter in oil and water-colour; *b* London, 5 Oct., 1925; *s* of Edward R. Joicey, M.C.; one *d. Educ.:* Harrow School; *studied art* at Sir John Cass College of Art (1967). *Publication:* A Mill in a Million. *Address:* The Old Mill, Langstone, Havant, Hants. *Signs work:* "Joicey."

JONES, Aldwyn Douglas, O.B.E., M.A., R.W.A., F.R.I.B.A.; architect; Diploma in Architecture with Distinction, Liverpool (1933); awarded R.I.B.A. Athens Bursary (1938); Royal West of England Academician; Professor Emeritus, University of Bristol; Consultant, Beardsworth Gallanaugh, Bristol; *b* Caernarvonshire, 1910; *m* Phyllis Catharine; two *s. Educ.:* Dragon School, Oxford, Malvern College; *studied* at Liverpool School of Architecture under Sir Charles Reilly. *Work repro.:* Ed. Colston papers: Communication and Energy in changing Urban Environments; contributor, Listener, R.I.B.A. Journal. *Address:* 32 St. Michael's Hill, Bristol BS2 8DX. *Signs work:* "A. Douglas Jones."

JONES, Allen, A.T.D. (1962); painter and printmaker; *b* Southampton, 1 Sept., 1937; *m* Janet Bowen; two *d. Studied art* at Hornsey School of Art (1955-59), Royal College of Art (1960-61). Prix des Jeunes Artistes, Paris Biennale (1963), Tarrarind Lithography Fellowship, Los Angeles (1966). Resident New York

(1964-65), now lives in London, but visits America. *Work in permanent collections:* many public and private, both home and abroad. *Publications:* sculpture, theatre and television projects and books. *Address:* 16B Edith Grove, London SW10.

JONES, Barbara, A.R.C.A.: painter, mural and exhibition designer; Mem., Soc. of Authors; Fellow, Royal Anthropological Institute; *studied art* at R.C.A. *Work in permanent collections:* V. & A. and private collections. Murals in Cheshire County Police Headquarters, Chester; Commonwealth Institute, London; New Cake House, St. James's Park, London. *Publications:* written and illustrated, The Isle of Wight, The Unsophisticated Arts, Follies and Grottoes, English Furniture at a Glance, Water-colour Painting, Design for Death, Popular Arts of the First World War (with Bill Howell); in preparation: Popular Arts Today. *Address:* 2 Well Walk, London NW3. *Signs work:* "Barbara Jones."

JONES, Edward Scott, R.C.A. (1964); artist in oil, water-colour, gouache; *b* Liverpool, 6 June, 1922; *m* Althea; one *s,* one *d. Educ.:* Anfield Road Elementary School; *studied art* at Liverpool College of Art. *Work in permanent collections:* Local History Department of Liverpool Corporation Libraries, County Borough of Bootle, Lancs., Cheshire Education Committee, Blackpool Corporation Art Gallery, Salford Art Gallery, Bolton Art Gallery. *Address:* 18 The Fairway, West Derby, Liverpool L12 3HS. *Signs work:* "E. Scott Jones."

JONES, Harold, A.R.C.A. (1928); illustrator in pen and ink, painter, and lithography; *b* 22 Feb., 1904; *s* of William Jones, F.Ph.S.(Eng.); *m*; two *d. Educ.:* St. Dunstan's College, Catford; R.C.A. *Exhib.:* Leicester Galleries, R.A., N.E.A.C., First Editions Club, etc. *Official purchases:* The Black Door (Tate Gallery); This Year, Next Year, by Walter de la Mare and Harold Jones (V. & A.) *Publications:* illustrations to Lavender's Blue (1954); The Water Babies, Kingsley (1961); The Hunting of The Snark, Carroll (1975); The Pied Piper of Hamelin, Browning (1962). *Address:* Doune Lodge, 27 Oxford Rd., Putney, London SW15. *Signs work:* "Harold Jones" (with stroke under "ones").

JONES, Harold Harris, B.Sc., Dip. Educ., F.R.S.A. (1951), D.P.A.; painter in oil and water-colour; *b* 13 Oct., 1908; *s* of David Jones; *m* Kitty M. Quigley; three *s,* two *d. Educ.:* Preston Grammar School, Reading University; *studied art* in Southport, Preston and St. Ives. *Exhib.:* R.A., R.O.I., R.I., R.B.A., N.S., R.P. *Address:* Loughrigg, 214 West Park Ave., Ashton, Preston, Lancs. *Signs work:* "Harold H. Jones."

JONES, Jonah Leonard; sculptor; Director, National College of Art and Design, Dublin (1974–); *b* 1919; *m* Judith Maro, writer; two *s,* one *d. Educ.:* Jarrow Secondary School; King Edward School of Art, Newcastle. *Exhib.:* retrospective exhbns. by Arts Council toured Wales (1961) and jointly with Keith Vaughan (1966), Magdelene Gallery, Cambridge (1974), Artist in School (1973), Artist at Work (1968). *Official purchases:* Welsh Arts Council, Contemporary Art Society for Wales, University of Ibadan, Ratcliffe College Chapel, Ampleforth College. *Address:* Minffordd, Penrhyndendraeth, Gwynedd. *Signs work:* "Jonah Jones."

JONES, Leslie, A.R.E., A.R.C.A., M.S.I.A., D.A.(Manc.), H.R.Cam.A., Rome Scholar; printmaker in etching and litho, illustrator; H.M.I. (Art Wales); taught at Hornsey, Kingston, St. Martin's Schools of Art (1961-67); *b* Tremadoc, 26 June, 1934. *Studied art* at Regional College of Art, Manchester (1951-55), Royal College of Art (1955-58), British School at Rome (1958-60); visitor at Belgrade Academy (1959). *Exhib.:* London, Rome, U.S.A., Austria. *Work in permanent collections:* V. & A., Arts Council, University of Oregon, University of Wales,

L.E.As. *Publications:* illustrated books for Lion & Unicorn, Longmans, University of Wales Press, Cambridge School Classics Project. *Address:* The Ferns, Old Highway, Colwyn Bay.

JONES, Olwen, R.A.S. (1968), A.R.E. (1974); part-time lecturer, Harrow School of Art; painter in oil and printmaker in relief and etching; *b* London, 1 Mar., 1945; *d* of William Jones; *m* Charles Bartlett. *Educ.:* Harrow School of Art (1960-65); *studied art* at Royal Academy Schools (1965-68), engraving under Gertrude Hermes. *Exhib.:* first one-man: Zaydler Gallery, London (1971). *Work in permanent collections:* National Museum of Wales, Norwich Castle Museum, Reading Museum, Nuffield Foundation. *Address:* St. Andrews, Fingringhoe, nr. Colchester, Essex CO5 7GB. *Signs work:* "Olwen Jones."

JONES, Peter; painter in oil, water-colour and designer of relief constructions; *b* London, 30 May, 1917; *m*; one *d. Studied art* at Richmond School of Art. *Exhib.:* London, Modern Art, Week-End, Redfern, Grosvenor Galleries, Molton Gallery, R.B.A., R.A., Demarco Gallery, Camden Arts Centre. *Work repro.:* in The Moderns, Famous Nudes by Famous Artists. *Official purchases:* V. & A., Temple Newsam, South London Art Gallery, London Borough of Camden. *Address:* Whitewood, 69A Pope's Ave., Twickenham, Middx. *Signs work:* see appendix.

JONES, Stanley Robert, A.T.D. (1950); painter and print-maker; *b* Birmingham, 9 June, 1927; *s* of George Jones, brewery departmental manager. *Educ.:* Elementary School; Yardley Grammar School, Birmingham; *studied art* at Birmingham College of Art under Harold Smith, B. Fleetwood-Walker, A.R.A. (1942-45, 1948-50), R.A. Schools under B. Fleetwood-Walker, A.R.A., Henry Rushbury, R.A. (1950-55). *Exhib.:* R.A., R.B.S.A., Blackpool, R.S.A., Glasgow, Dundee, Aberdeen Civic Galleries, Young Contemporaries, Bath and West Show, etc. *Work in permanent collection:* Graves Art Gallery, Sheffield. *Address:* 118 Totley Brook Rd., Sheffield S17. *Signs work:* see appendix.

JONES, Thomas DEMPSTER; International Gold Medallist; self-taught artist in oils, portrait, horses and landscape painter; President of Buckley Art Society; Associate Mem., Société des Artistes Française; *b* Harlech, North Wales, 18 Apr., 1914; *s* of a master tailor; *m* Catherine Hughes, A.L.C.M.; one s (Alwyn), one *d* (Carol). *Educ.:* Harlech College. *Exhib.:* R.A., Paris Salon (Hon. Mention 1967, Gold Medal 1970), R.B.A., R.I. Summer Salon, United Society of Artists, Bath, West and Southern Counties Society, Galerie Internationale, Madison Av., New York, R.Cam.A., Royal Nat. Eisteddfod of Wales (vested with Ovate Order in 1971), R.U.A., Welsh Arts Council Touring Exhbn. (1972-73). One-man exhibitions held in North Wales include: Civic Centre, Connah's Quay 1968; New Library Prestatyn 1968; New Exhibition Gallery, Civic Centre, Mold 1970. Also featured on television, B.B.C. and H.T.V. *Work repro.:* Daily Mail (1961, 1966), front cover of Deesider (colour), Chester Chronicle, Flintshire Leader, Liverpool Daily Post, La Revue Moderne, Paris Salon Catalogues, etc. *Work in permanent and private collections. Address:* Daisy Hill Studio, Buckley, Flintshire, North Wales. *Signs work:* see appendix.

JONZEN, Karin; sculptor (terracotta, bronze, and stone); *b* 1914; *d* of U. Lowenadler. *Studied art* at Slade School, Stockholm Royal Academy. Slade Scholarship and Diploma (1934); Prix de Rome (1939). *Work in permanent collections:* V. & A., Brighton, Bradford, Glasgow and Melbourne A.G. *Official purchases:* Arts Council; Selwyn College, Cambridge; L.C.C. housing estate at Lewisham (1960); St. Michael's Church, Golder's Green (1961); Guildford Cathedral (1962); World Health Organization Headquarters, New Delhi (1963), World Health Organization Headquarters, Geneva (1965). Exhibited three works for City of London Festival (1968), one work retained, Madonna and Child, purchased for St. Mary-le-Bow (1969). Exhibited New York, one torso acquired by Andrew White Museum, Cornell University (1969); life size bronze figure commissioned by London Co-operation for site at the Barbican (1970); Over life size group for Guildhall Square. Gift of Lord Blackford to London Co-operation (1972); $\frac{3}{4}$ life size Pièta for Swedish Church, Marylebone (1975). Portrait busts include: Malcolm Muggeridge, Sir Alan Herbert, Sir Hugh Casson, Eric Newton, Lord Constantine, Dame Ninette de Valois. *Address:* 6A Gunter Gr., London SW1 0UJ. *Signs work:* "K. Jonzen."

JOSEPH, Peter; painter in oil and acrylic paint and environmental constructions; *b* London, 18 Jan., 1929. *Educ.:* John Ruskin School; *studied art:* self-taught. *Work in permanent collections:* Manchester City Gallery, Arts Council of Great Britain, Ind Coope Collection. *Address:* 33 Clevedon Mansions, Lissenden Gdns., London NW5. *Signs work:* see appendix.

JOSSET, Lawrence Leon Louis, A.R.C.A. (1935), R.A. (1951); Mem., Art Workers' Guild; mezzotint engraver and etcher, portrait painter in water-colour and drawing; part-time art school teacher; *b* 2 Aug., 1910; *s* of Leon Antoine Hippolyte Josset. *Educ.:* Bromley County School; Bromley and Beckenham Schools of Art; R.C.A. (Sir W. Rothenstein, Malcolm Osborne, R.A., P.R.E., 1932-35). *Exhib.:* R.A., R.E., etc. *Publications:* Mezzotint engravings, after Fantin Latour, Ben Marshall, Constable, William Shayer, Boucher and Fragonard, Zoffany, etc. *Address:* The Cottage, Pilgrims' Way, Detling, nr. Maidstone, Kent. *Signs work:* "Lawrence Josset."

JOWITT, John Alan; painter in oil and water-colour; *b* 16 July, 1904; *m*; one *s*, one *d*. *Educ.:* Uppingham School; Yeovil School of Art (G. Mitchell, 1935-39). *Exhib.:* R.A. *Address:* Brook House, Chideock, Dorset. *Signs work:* "JOHN JOWITT."

JOYA, Jose, magna cul laude B.F.A., M.F.A.; artist in acrylic, oil and water-colour, pencil and drawing; Dean, College of Fine Arts, University of the Philippines (1970-); *b* Manila (Philippines), 3 June, 1931. *Educ.:* Mapa High School, Manila; *studied art* and graduated at School of Fine Arts, University of the Philippines, Quezon City (1949-53); Institute de Cultura Hispanics, Madrid (1954-55); Cranbrook Academy of Art, Michigan (1956-57). *Exhib.:* one-man shows: Philippine A.G. and Luz Gallery, Manila, Jackson Gallery, Hong Kong, etc.; group shows: Expo '70, Osaka, A.A.P. Annual Art Exhbns., Manila (1952-65), New York World Fair (1964), Seattle World Fair (1962), First International Art Exhbn., Hong Kong (1962) and Saigon (1962), Taipeh (1961), Biennales Hispano-Americanas de Arte, Havana (1953) and Barcelona (1955), Philippine Cultural Exposition, New York and Washington D.C. (1952), etc. *Work in permanent collections:* University of the Philippines Museum; Ateneo de Manila Museum, National Museum, Manila. *Address:* 8 Col. Martelino St., Quezon City, Philippines. *Club:* Art Assoc. of the Philippines (President, 1961-64). *Signs work:* "Joya" and see appendix.

JUKES, Edith Elizabeth, F.R.B.S., A.R.C.A. (1932), S.R.N. (Bart's, 1945), Mem., Society of Portrait Sculptors; sculptor in clay, wood, stone; teacher of sculpture, Sir John Cass College School of Art since 1947; *b* Shillong, Assam, 19 Dec., 1910; *d* of the late Capt. Andrew Monro Jukes, M.D., I.M.S. *Educ.:* Norland Pl. School, Kensington; *studied art* at R.C.A. (1928-32) under Profs. Richard Garbe, R.A., Henry Moore, and Herbert Palliser. *Exhib.:* R.A., etc. *Address:* The Studio, 347 Upper Richmond Rd., London SW15. *Club:* Ski Club of Gt. Britain. *Signs work:* see appendix.

JUMP, Mary Victoria; full Technological Certificate, City and Guilds of London; water-colour painter; *b* 31 Dec., 1897; *d* of Edward Jump. *Educ.:* Sefton Park County School, Liverpool; Liverpool Art School; Birkenhead Art School. *Exhib.:* R.Cam.A., Liverpool, Manchester and Southport Art Galleries, Williamson Art Gallery, Birkenhead, Lady Lever Art Gallery. *Address:* 15 Highcroft Ave., Bebington, Wirral, Merseyside L63 3EZ. *Club:* Wirral Society of Art. *Signs work:* "MARY V. JUMP," or "Mary V. Jump."

JUNG, Anastasia: see ANHALT, H. Highness Anastasia Prinzess of.

K

KAHANE, Anne; prize, Unknown Political Prisoner exhbn.; sculptor in wood; *b* Vienna, 1924. *Studied art* at Cooper Union Institute, New York (1945-46-47). *Exhib.:* Canadian Pavilion (Brussels, 1958), Canadian Pavilion (Venice Biennale, 1958), Pittsburg International (Pittsburg, U.S.A., 1959). *Work in permanent collections:* all major museums across Canada. *Work repro.:* Canadian Art, Vol. XIX, No. 4, 1962; The Arts in Canada, Ross (Macmillan, 1958); The Studio, Vol. 160, No. 807 (July, 1960); Vie des Arts, No. 69, Hiver, 1972-73. *Address:* 3794 Hampton Ave., Montreal 261, Que. *Signs work:* see appendix.

KAHN, Erich; painter and etcher; *b* Stuttgart, 25 Aug., 1904; *s* of Joseph Kahn. *Educ.:* Stuttgart Secondary School; *studied art* at Stuttgart Arts and Crafts School under Schneidler (1919-24), Paris under Leger (1926). *Exhib.:* Stuttgart, Berlin, Leger Galleries, Whitechapel A.G., Ben Uri A.G., Musée de l'art moderne (Unesco, 1946), Marzotto Europa (1969), Hampstead Arts Council, one-man shows Redfern (1956), Drian (1958), Institut fur Auslands Beziehungen, Stuttgart (1960), Erlangen (1960), Molton Galleries (1960). *Work in permanent collections:* Ben Uri A.G., Arts Museum, Tel Aviv. *Work repro.:* Imre Reiner, woodcut/-wood engraving (1947), Imre Reiner, Creative Desire (1949). *Address:* 1 Albert Studios, 20 Albert St., London NW1.

KALKHOF, Peter Heinz; painter, lecturer in fine art; *b* Stassfurt, Germany 20 Dec., 1933; *s* of Heinz Kalkhof, company secretary; *m* Jeanne The; two *s*. *Educ.:* Germany; *studied art* at School of Arts and Crafts, Braunschweig; Academy of Fine Art, Stuttgart; Slade School of Fine Art, London; Ecole des Beaux Art, Paris (1954-62). *Exhib.:* Annely Juda Fine Art (1970-74), Scottish Arts Council, Edinburgh, Glasgow. *Work in permanent collections:* Northern Ireland Trust, Arts Council of Gt. Britain, Leics. Educ. Authority. *Address:* c/o Annely Juda Fine Art, 11 Tottenham Mews, London W1P 9PJ. *Signs work:* "Peter Kalkhof."

KANIDINÇ, Salahattin; awarded High Moral Prize (1954); artist in pencil, pen, brush, ink, oil, polymer; letterer, calligrapher, designer, expert on historical writing systems (hieroglyphs to Roman alphabet) and modern letter forms; Chief Calligrapher, Naval Printing & Publishing House, Istanbul, Turkey (1950-61); lettering artist, Buzza-Cardozo, Anaheim, California (1962- 63); asst. art director, Rust Craft Publishers, Dedham, Massachusetts (1964); lettering specialist, Tiffany & Co., New York City (1964-72); owner-creative director, Kanidinç International; and consultant designer for major corporations; *b* Istanbul, Turkey, 12 Aug., 1927; *s* of Yahya Kanidinç; *m* Seniha Kanidinç; two *s*. *Educ.:* 22nd Elementary School of Uskudar, Uskudar 1st High School, Istanbul, Turkey; *studied art* at Defenbaugh School of Lettering, Minnesota (1954, under Roger I. Defenbaugh), Zanerian College of Penmanship, Ohio (1963, under John P.

Turner), State University of Iowa (1963, under Prof. Meyer), University of Minnesota (1964), University of California (1963-64). *Work in permanent collections:* Peabody Institute Library, Baltimore, Maryland; World Crafts Council, New York City; and in private collections. *Listed:* Who's Who in Turkey, Who's Who in the Middle East and North Africa, Who's Who in Europe, Who's Who in the East (U.S.A.), Who's Who in America, International Directory of Arts, Dictionary of International Biography, International Who's Who in Community Service, Community Leaders of America, Artists/U.S.A., International Year Book and Statesmen's Who's Who, The National Register of Prominent Americans and International Notables, The Two Thousand Men of Achievement, etc. *Publication:* participant designer, Alphabet Thesaurus, Vols. 2-3. *Addresses:* 62-34 99th Street, Rego Park, New York 11374, U.S.A., and Kanidinc International, 366 Madison Ave., New York, NY 10017, U.S.A. *Clubs:* Society of Scribes and Illuminators, The World Crafts Council, The International Association of Master Penmen and Teachers of Handwriting, The American Institute of Graphic Arts, The International Center for the Typographic Arts, National Advisory Board of the American Security Council. *Signs work:* see appendix.

KAPE, William Jack, A.R.C.A., A.T.D., F.S.A.E.; designer of furniture and light metalwork; previously Princ., London College of Furniture; *m*; one *s*. *Educ.:* Wycombe Grammar School; *studied art* at R.C.A. *Exhib.:* Water-colours; designer of Bilston Regalia, mace, coat of arms, Council Chamber furniture, etc. *Address:* 8 Blythwood Rd., Pinner, Middlesex HA5 3QB.

KAPP, Edmond X., B.A. (Cantab., 1913); painter, draughtsman; official war artist (1940-41); official artist to U.N.E.S.C.O. (1946-47); *b* London, 5 Nov., 1890; *m*; one *d*. *Educ.:* Owen's School; Christ's Coll., Cambridge; Paris, Rome. *Exhib.:* 35 one-man shows, London and provincial A.G.; Paris, Milan, Geneva, Buffalo, Toronto, etc.; represented in British Art since Whistler (N.G., 1945). 1938, unique sittings for only life-portrait of Picasso; Fifty Years Retrospective Exhib., Whitechapel Art Gallery (1961). *Official purchases:* Nat. Port. Gall.; V. & A.; B.M.; Imp. War Mus.; London Mus.; Fitzwilliam, Cambridge; Ashmolean, Oxford; Municipal Galleries at Manchester, Birmingham, Bradford, Leeds, Wakefield, Kendal, Kettle's Yard Museum of Modern Art, Cambridge, Israel Museums, Bibl. Nat. and Unesco, Paris, etc.; Contemp. Art Soc.; Caius and Christ's Colls., Cambridge; Merton and Exeter Colls., Oxford; portraits as stained-glass windows, Yale Law School; Barber Institute of Fine Arts, Birmingham, acquired 240 drawings (1969); private collections of H.R.H. the Duke of Edinburgh, Samuel Courtauld, Lord Clark, Sir Hugh Walpole, Edward le Bas, Sacha Guitry, Daniel de Pass, etc. *Publications:* Personalities (Secker), Reflections (Cape), Pastiche, Minims (Faber), Ten Great Lawyers (Butterworth). *Address:* 2 Steeles Studios, Haverstock Hill, London NW3. *Signs work:* "Kapp." *Telephone:* 01-722 3174.

KAPP, Helen; painter and illustrator in oil, water-colour, pen and wash; sometime wood-engraver; director, Abbot Hall A.G., Kendal (1961-67) and Wakefield City A.G. (1951-61); *b* London; *d* of Emil and Bella Kapp. *Studied art* at Slade School of Art, Central School of Arts and Crafts and in Paris. *Exhib.:* R.A., A.I.A., London Group, Soc. of Wood Engravers, etc.; one-man shows at Nicholson's Gallery (1939), Haifa (British Council, 1946). *Publications:* Enjoying Pictures (Routledge & Kegan Paul, 1975); numerous books illustrated for Dent, Gollancz, Routledge & Kegan Paul, Robert Hale, Medici Soc., etc. *Address:* 17 Carr Ave., Leiston, Suffolk. *Signs work:* "Helen Kapp."

KAUFFMANN, Arthur, Dr.phil.; Mem. Oriental Ceramic Soc., Mem. National Art-Collections Fund; art dealer and expert; *b* 11 June, 1887; *m* Tamara

Karp, M.D.; two *s. Studied art* at universities of Berlin, Erlangen, Heidelberg, and at the École du Louvre (Paris). *Official purchases:* European and overseas museums and art galleries. *Publications:* The Hugo Helbing (Frankfurt) Catalogues (1919-37). *Address:* 21 Grafton St., London W1.

KAWALEC, Witold Gracjan, F.F.P.S.; appointed sculptor to St. Christopher's Hospice; freelance sculptor in stone, wood and metal; *b* Wilno, Poland, 17 Nov., 1922; *s* of Romuald Kawalec, journalist and consul for R.P. Polska; *m* Danuta Kawalec; three *s*, one *d. Studied art* under private tutor in Poland and Rumania; Nottingham University College; Nottingham College of Art & Crafts. *Exhib.:* one-man shows: Stiffkey Studio, Norfolk (1975), Museum and A.G., Derby (1974), Royal Edinburgh Hospital (1973), Coventry Cathedral (1971), Carlton Forum, Nottingham (1970), Usher A.G. and Museum, Lincoln (1969), Edinburgh International Arts Festival (1967), St. Aidan's Church, Basford, Notts. (1967), Newark-on-Trent Museum (1966), Drian Galleries, London (1964), School of Physiotherapy, Sheffield (1960), Digest Art, Nottingham (1954). *Work in permanent collections:* St. Christopher's Hospice, London, Castle Museum and A.G., Nottingham. *Address:* c/o St. Christopher's Hospice. *Signs work:* "W. G. Kawalec."

KAY, Nora, A.R.C.A., M.S.I.A.; artist in cut paper, lino-cuts, calligraphy, italic writing, studio potter; designer for Yardley's, Jenners Ltd.; teacher at St. Martin's School of Art, Newland Park College, Maltman's Green School. *Educ.:* Wycombe High School, St. Martin's School of Art, R.C.A. *Exhib.:* R.B.A., N.E.A.C. *Work repro.:* General advertising work, London Transport posters, Christmas cards, book jackets. *Publications:* children's books. *Address:* Flat 5, Ethorpe Cres., Gerrards Cross, Bucks. *Signs work:* "N.K."

KEATES, John Gareth, A.T.D.; artist in oil, gouache and water-colour; Liverpool Council for Educ. (Inc.) Travel Award, 1958; principal lecturer, Liverpool Polytechnic; *b* Birkenhead, 18 Jan., 1915; *s* of John Willan Keates; *m* Margaret Bishop; two *d. Educ.:* Birkenhead Institute; *studied art* at Liverpool College of Art (1933-38), Central School of Art, London, under Bernard Meninsky (1946-47). *Exhib.:* Arts Council Gallery, F.P.S., London and provincial galleries and abroad; one-man exhibitions, 1964 and 1967. *Work in permanent collections:* Walker Art Gallery, Liverpool, Southport A.G., University of Liverpool; also in private collections. *Address:* 29 Saxon Rd., Birkdale, Southport, Lancs. *Club:* Liverpool Academy.

KEATING, John, Hon. R.A., Hon. R.S.A. (1950); painter; Prof. of anatomy at National College of Art; *b* Limerick, 28 Sept., 1889; *s* of Joseph Keating, accountant; *m* Mary Walsh; two *s. Educ.:* St. Munchin's College (Limerick); *studied art* at Limerick, Dublin, Met. School of Art, and London under Sir W. Orpen, R.A. *Exhib.:* R.A., R.S.A., R.H.A., Carnegie Trust, British Empire exhbns. abroad. *Work in permanent collections:* in Britain, Scotland, Ireland, Belgium, Italy, America. *Address:* Aitancuain, Ballyboden Rd., Rathfarnham, Dublin 14. *Signs work:* "KEATING."

KELL, Lorna Beatrice, S.G.A., F.R.S.A.; textile designer; wood-engraver; artist in water-colour; *b* London, 13 Jan., 1914; *d* of the late George and Beatrice Prince. *Educ.:* E. Finchley Grammar School; *studied art* at Hornsey School of Arts and Crafts under J. C. Moody, R.I., R.E., Miss E. Lindquist, Norman Janes, R.E., and Frank Winter, A.R.E. *Exhib.:* R.A., R.E., R.B.A., S.G.A., Guildhall, Paris Salon, and local exhbns. *Address:* 17 Dinsdale Ct., Great North Rd., New Barnet, Herts. *Club:* Print Collectors. *Signs work:* "Lorna B. Kell."

KELLEHER, Patrick Joseph; art historian and museum director; Fellow,

American Academy in Rome (1947-49); chief curator of Art, Los Angeles County Museum (1949); curator of collections, Albright A.G., Buffalo, N.Y. (1950-54); curator of European Art, William Rockhill Nelson Gallery of Art, Kansas City, Mo. (1954-59); director Art Museum and Prof. Art and Archaeology, Princeton University (1960-73); *b* Colorado Springs, Col., 26 July, 1917; *m* Marion Mackie. *Educ.:* Colorado College, Princeton University. *Publication:* The Holy Crown of Hungary (1951); numerous articles and exhbn. catalogues. *Address:* 176 Parkside Dr., Princeton, N.J. 08540.

KELLY, Charles Edward; cartoonist and painter in oil and water-colour; art editor, Dublin Opinion, since 1926; *b* Dublin, 15 June, 1902; *s* of David Kelly, municipal official; *m* Kathleen E. Hayden; three *s,* three *d. Educ.:* Christian Brothers' School, Synge St., Dublin; *studied art:* privately. *Exhib.:* Dublin Sketching Club and Water-colour Society of Ireland annual exhbns. *Work repro.:* Dublin Opinion and various newspapers and periodicals at home and abroad. *Address:* Carrickshinnagh, Westminster Rd., Foxrock, Co. Dublin. *Clubs:* Dublin Sketching, Water-colour Society of Ireland and P.E.N. *Signs work:* see appendix.

KELLY, Felix; artist in oil; *b* Auckland, N.Z., 1916. *Exhib.:* Lefévre Gallery (1943, 1944, 1946), Leicester Gallery (1950, 1952), Portraits Inc., N.Y. (1947), Charleston, S.C. (1948), Washington, D.C. (1949), Arthur Jeffress Gallery (1959-62), Arthur Tooth & Sons (1965, 1968, 1971), Kennedy Galleries Inc., N.Y. (1970), Delgado Museum of Art, New Orleans (1970). *Work in permanent collections:* Lord Rothermere, Sir Herbert Read, Lord Faringdon, Charles Engelhard, Esq., The Earl of Mountbatten, David Bruce, Esq., Chester Beattie, Esq., The Duke of Buccleuch, Walter Annenberg, Esq., John Hay Whitney, Esq., Lord Aberdare. *Publications:* Paintings by Felix Kelly, by Sir Herbert Read; illustrations for Longmans, Macmillans, Hutchinsons, Chatto & Windus. *Theatre sets* for Haymarket, Phoenix, Sadlers Wells, Old Vic. *Address:* 49 Princes Gate, London SW7. *Signs work:* "Felix Kelly."

KEMPSHALL, Hubert Kim, A.R.C.A. (1960), D.A. (Manc.) (1955); painter/printmaker in acrylic, water-colour, etching, lithography; Senior Lecturer in Fine Art Printmaking, Birmingham Polytechnic; *b* Manchester, 15 May, 1934; *m* Sylvia; one *s*, one *d. Educ.:* Stretford Grammar School; *studied art* at Manchester College of Art (1951-55); Royal College of Art (1957-60). *Exhib.:* R.A., Scottish Royal Academy, S.S.A., Scottish Printmakers, Arts Council, several one-man shows. *Work in permanent collections:* Edinburgh City Coll., Scottish Modern A.G., Aberdeen A.G., Dundee A.G. *Address:* Fenwick House, 135 Lordswood Rd., Harborne, Birmingham 17. *Signs work:* "K.K."

KENDALL, Alice R., D.A. (Edin.), F.R.Z.S. (Scot.), Vice-Pres., S.W.A.; founder and first editor (1972-74) F.B.A. Quarterly; artist and writer; *b* New York; *d* of Prof. James P. Kendall and Alice Kendall. *Educ.:* New York and Edinburgh; *studied* at Edinburgh College of Art. *Exhib.:* Paris Salon, R.A., R.S.A., R.B.A., etc.; private shows with the late Alice Kendall at Cooling Galleries (1948, 1956). *Official purchases:* murals for Brit. Council and Min. of Labour; portrait of father as P.P.R.S.E. (1957). *Work repro.:* in Scottish Field, La Revue Moderne, The Artist, The Voice of Youth. *Publications:* children's book, Funny Fishes; contrib.: Young Elizabethan, Poetry Review, Punch, etc. *Address:* 35 Beaufort Gdns., London SW3 1PW. *Signs work:* see appendix.

KENNEDY, Cecil; flower and portrait painter in oils; *b* Leyton, Essex, 4 Feb., 1905; *s* of T. R. Kennedy, artist; *m*; one *s. Studied art* in London, Paris, Antwerp, Zürich. *Exhib.:* R.A., R.S.A, R.H.A., Doncaster, Oldham, Bradford, Southport, etc., and many London galleries; also U.S.A. and S. African galleries. Awarded

Silver Medal, Paris Salon (1956) and Gold Medal, Paris Salon (1970). *Official purchases:* by H.M. Queen Mary, Merthyr Tydfil Art Gallery, Rochdale Art Gallery. *Work repro.:* Numerous. *Address:* Manor Garden House, 135 Fishpool St., St. Albans, Herts. AL3 4R7. *Signs work:* see appendix.

KENNEDY, Richard; book illustrator; artist in pen, pencil, wash, chalk, etc.; *b* Cambridge, 4 Sept., 1910; *s* of Capt. J. P. Kennedy, Scottish Rifles; *m* Olive Mary Johnstone; one *s,* two *d. Educ.:* Marlborough College and University College, London; *studied art* at Regent St. Polytechnic under Tressillian (1932-33) continued as evening student for considerable time, attending life classes. *Publications:* Written and illustrated: A Boy in The Hogarth Press; illustrations only: Peter Pan; Breton Fairy Tales; Pippi Longstocking; Inner Ring series; Martin Pippin in the Apple Orchard; Colette; and a wide range of children's books. *Address:* Woodcote, Ray Lea Rd., Maidenhead, Berks. *Signs work:* "Richard Kennedy."

KENNETT, James Smyth, B.Com.Sc. (1941); artist in oil and indian ink; harbour official; *b* Belfast, 10 Mar., 1915; *s* of James Kennett, manufacturer; *m* Sarah Waller Dodds. *Educ.:* Belfast Royal Academy; Queen's Univ., Belfast; *studied art* at London Art College under A. W. Browne (1947-48) and at R.U.A. *Address:* 20 Waterloo Pk. North, Belfast BT15 5HW, N. Ireland. *Signs work:* "J. S. KENNETT."

KENT, Leslie, R.B.A. (1940), R.S.M.A. (1939); oil painter; Mem. of Council of R.B.A. (1943-67); Mem. of Council of S.M.A. (1952-55); *b* 15 June, 1890; *s* of Col. H. H. Kent; *m* Margaret Schierwater; two *s. Educ.:* Bedales School; Leeds University; under Fred Milner, St. Ives (1918-20). *Exhib.:* R.A., R.O.I., R.S.A., N.E.A.C., Paris Salon, R.B.A., R.S.M.A., Glasgow and many provincial galleries. *Work repro.:* Several. *Address:* Bonds Cay, Radlett, Herts. *Signs work:* "LESLIE KENT."

KENT, Mary, see HARRISON, Mary Kent.

KENYON, Ley; art teacher, book illustrator, graphic designer, artist in oils, water-colour, black and white; *b* London, 28 Jan., 1913; *s* of A. K. Kenyon. *Educ.:* Marylebone Grammar School; *studied art* at Central School of Arts and Crafts (1931-34) under Meninsky, James Grant, William Roberts, Alfred Turner. *Exhib.:* Publishers Exhbns. *Official purchases:* War drawing, National Gallery. *Work repro.:* In Tatler, Illustrated London News, etc., book illustrations for Faber and Faber, Collins, Longmans-Green, Bodley Head, etc. *Address:* 37 Cranley Gdns., Kensington, London SW7. *Club:* Ex-Chairman, Chelsea Arts. *Signs work:* "Ley Kenyon."

KERNOFF, Harry; R.H.A. (1935); oil, water-colour, pastel, woodcuts, portraits; *b* 9 Jan., 1900; *s* of Isaac Kernoff. *Educ.:* College of Art, Dublin. *Exhib.:* R.H.A., R.A., Dublin, U.S.A., Glasgow, Holland, Paris, Moscow, Television (1957), Nova Scotia. *Official purchases:* Dublin, Waterford, Limerick, Galway, Castlebar, Belfast and Killarney Galleries; Large Oil, Berkeley Univ., Cal., U.S.A. (1966). *Publications:* Limited Editions of Woodcuts, Storyteller's Childhood, New Irish Poets, 1948, Tinker Boy. *Address:* 13 Stamer St., Dublin, Ireland. *Signs work:* "KERNOFF" on oils or water-colours, "K—" in woodcuts.

KESSELL, James Everett, F.R.S.A. (1954), R.B.S.A. (1968); artist and art tutor; Founder and Principal "The James Kessell School of Art" (founded 1969); *b* Coventry, 13 Oct., 1915; *s* of James Everett Kessell; *m* Myfanwy Lewis; three *s,* one *d. Educ.:* Stoke Boys' School; *studied art* at Coventry School of Art (1928-34 and 1945-52). *Exhib.:* R.A., R.B.A., R.O.I., R.S.M.A., R.B.S.A., Paris Salon (Hon. Mention, 1964), Arts Council; Waldorf-Astoria, New York; several one-man shows in England, including 130 works in the nave of Coventry Cathedral

(1973); many works in public and private collections in all parts of the world. *Official commissions* include portraits of leading church dignitaries: Bishop of New York, Rt. Rev. Horace Donegan (1970), Bishop of Coventry, Rt. Rev. Cuthbert Bardsley (1971), etc. Commissioned by A.T.V. to paint religious paintings for "Act of Worship" and supply paintings for "Morning Worship" (Television Religious Services, 1975). *Address:* "The Studios," Church La., Eastern Green, Coventry CV5 7BX. *Signs work:* see appendix.

KESTELMAN, Morris, A.R.C.A.; painter; Head of Fine Art Dept., Central School of Art and Design; Member of London Group and Mural Painters' Society; Vice-Chairman of U.K. National Branch, International Association of Art; *b* 1905; *m* Dorothy Mary Creagh; one *d. Studied art* at Central School of Arts and Crafts and R.C.A. *Works purchased:* Arts Council, C.A.S., V. & A., Leicester, Wakefield, Nuffield Foundation. *Commissions:* murals for Festival of Britain, South Bank. *Address:* 74B Belsize Park Gdns., London NW3. *Signs work:* "M. Kestelman."

KEY, Geoffrey, D.A. (1960); painter in oil, sculptor; teacher of painting, Withington Further Education; *b* Manchester, 13 May, 1941; *s* of George Key; *m* Judith. *Educ.:* High School of Art, Manchester; *studied art* at Regional College of Art, Manchester (1958-61), under Harry Rutherford, William Bailey. *Work in permanent collections:* Salford Art Gallery, Manchester City Gallery, Bolton Art Gallery, Manchester University, Monks Hall, Eccles. *Work repro.:* La Revue Moderne, Arts Review. *Address:* 59 Acresfield Rd., Pendleton, Salford 6. *Clubs:* Manchester Academy, Lancashire Group of Artists. *Signs work:* see appendix.

KHO, Khiem-Bing; artist in oil and water-colour; *b* Malang, Java, Indonesia, 14 Feb., 1907. *Educ.:* Methodist English School, Bogor; *studied art* at Academie des Beaux-Arts, Leuven (1931) under Willem Paerels; Academie Royale des Beaux-Arts, Brussels (1932-36). *Exhib.:* one-man shows: Brussels, Rotterdam, Jakarta, Paris, Antwerp, Gent, Tournai, Leige, etc. *Work in permanent collections:* Musee d'Art Moderne, Brussels, etc. *Address:* 19 Square Charles Maurice Wiser, 1040 Brussels, Belgium. *Signs work:* "Kho Khiem-Bing" and see appendix.

KIBART, James Henry; artist, designer and lecturer; consultant to Graphic Art Studio; *b* Leicester, 20 Sept., 1912; *s* of Sidney Augustus Kibart; *m* Beryl Doris Morgan; two *s*, one *d*. *Educ.:* Wyggeston Grammar School; *studied art* at Leicester College of Art. *Work in permanent Exhibitions:* Leicester Museum and Art Gallery, and in private collections inc. Leicester, London, Nottingham, Cambridge, Edinburgh. *Address:* 67 Dumbleton Ave., Leicester. *Clubs:* Leicester Society of Artists (past Pres.), Leicester Sketch (past Pres.). *Signs work:* "KIBART."

KIDD, Douglas Jessop; founder mem. Medical Artists' Assoc. of Gt. Britain; medical and scientific illustrator in water-colour, monochrome wash and line; artist to the Faculty of Medicine of the University of Liverpool (Retd.); *b* Liverpool, 3 Aug., 1903; *s* of William Beaumont Kidd; *m* Eveline Pover; two *s*, one *d*. *Educ.:* Holt High School, Liverpool; *studied art* at Liverpool School of Art. *Work in permanent collections:* Human Anatomy Dept., Liverpool University. *Work repro.:* numerous medical, surgical and scientific text-books and journals, etc. *Publications:* Preparing Illustrations for Half-tone Reproduction, Baillière's Atlases of Human Anatomy, etc. *Address:* 60 Almonds Green, Liverpool 12. *Signs work:* "Kidd,"

KIDNER, Michael, B.A.(Cantab); painter in oil and cryla; visiting lecturer since 1964 at Bath Academy of Art; *b* Kettering, 1917; *s* of Norman W. Kidner; *m* Marion Frederick; one *s*. *Educ.:* Bedales School; *studied art:* self-taught. *Work in* *permanent collections:* Tate Gallery, Arts Council of G.B., British Council, Walker Art Gallery, Huddersfield Art Gallery, Manchester City Art Gallery. *Address:* 18 Hampstead Hill Gdns., London NW3. *Signs work:* "Michael Kidner."

KINAHAN, Lady Coralie; artist in oil and water-colour; housewife; elected to Council R.U.A. (1957), Lady Mayoress of Belfast (1 June, 1959); *b* Bletchingley, Surrey, 16 Sept., 1924; *d* of Capt. Charles de Burgh, D.S.O., R.N.; *m;* two *s,* three *d. Educ.:* by 14 governesses and 4 schools; *studied art* at Miss Sonia Mervyn's private classes, 28 Roland Gdns., SW7 (1947-49). *Exhib.:* R.A., R.P., Olympic Exhbn., London, R.O.I., Darlington Painting Galleries, R.U.A.; exhibition of landscapes, portraits and horses, Belfast (1965, 1968, 1969, 1973, 1975), Dublin (1971). *Work in private collection:* Commissioned set of landscapes for Lord O'Neill (1963). *Official purchases:* Portrait of Lord Bishop of Durham, Dr. A. Williams, by Dean and Chapter of Durham; landscape, Glenariffe, purchased by Ulster Museum, Belfast (1965); portrait, Gen. Sir Ian Freeland, K.C.B., K.G.C., D.S.O. (1970). *Address:* Castle Upton, Templepatrick, Co. Antrim, N. Ireland. *Signs work:* "C. I. de B."

KINDBERG, Agnes Marie, A.T.D.; artist in oil (portraits), water-colour (flowers) and fabrics (embroidered collage); *b* Hartlepool, 11 Feb., 1906; *d* of C. R. Kindberg, master mariner. *Educ.:* Hartlepool, Newcastle and London; *studied art* at Hartlepool, Newcastle and London (1923-33) under A. J. Rushton, A.R.C.A. *Exhib.:* S.S.W.A., S.S.A., R.S.W., R.S.A., R.I., Scottish Craft Centre; one-man shows: Edinburgh Festival (1970-76), also at Studio Flat, 8 Chester St. *Work in private collections:* churches, regiments, etc. *Address:* 8 Chester St., Edinburgh EH3 7RA. *Clubs:* Ladies Caledonian, Lycium. *Signs work:* "AK" (collage), "A. Kindberg" (paintings).

KINDER, Joan, S.G.A. (1968), M.F.P.S. (1962); council mem. S.G.A.; artist in modern media; *b* Thornton le Dale, Yorks., 19 June, 1916; *d* of Leonard Arthur Marr; *m* Kenneth John Kinder, J.P., lecturer at London College of Printing; two *d. Educ.:* Bridlington High School for Girls; *studied art* at Scarborough College of Art (1932-36) principal, Edward Walker. *Exhib.:* London, provincial and International. *Official purchases:* L.C.C. Educ. Dept., Westminster Arts Committee. *Address:* 7 Ravens Wold, Hayes La., Kenley, Surrey. *Clubs:* S.G.A., F.P.S. *Signs work:* "Kinder."

KING, Dorothy, R.B.A. (1947); portrait painter in oil and pastel; Keeper, South London Art Gallery. *Educ.:* James Allens and Hornsey High School; *studied art* at Hornsey and Slade under Prof. Randolph Schwabe. *Exhib.:* R.A., R.B.A., N.E.A.C. *Work in permanent collection:* Met. Museum of Modern Art. *Address:* 38 Great Russell St., London WC1. *Signs work:* "Dorothy King."

KING, Edward S., M.F.A., (Princeton, 1927); art historian and museum director; Director, Walters Art Gallery, Baltimore (1951-66); Research Associate (1967—); Instructor, Bryn Mawr College, Pa. (1924-32); Instructor in History of Art, Princeton University (1928-29); Lecturer in Art, Johns Hopkins University (1935-36); Curator of Paintings and Far Eastern Art, Walters Art Gallery, Baltimore (1934-45); Acting Administrator (1945-46), Administrator (1946-51); *b* Baltimore, 27 Jan., 1900; *s* of Henry S. King, banker; one *s. Educ.:* Princeton University. *Publications:* articles in the Art Bulletin, Journal of the Walters Art Gallery, etc. *Address:* 4520 N. Charles St., Baltimore, 21210, Md.

KING, Laurence Edward, O.B.E., F.S.A., F.R.I.B.A., F.R.S.A., F.S.Scot.; architect; Mem. Art Workers Guild; *b* 28 June, 1907; *s* of Frederick E. King. *Educ.:* Brentwood School; London University. *Exhib.:* R.A. *Principal works:*

rebuilt Grey Coat Hospital; new buildings at Emanuel School, Sutton Valence School, Brentwood School; new churches: St. Mary's Church, S. Ruislip, St. Nicholas, Fleetwood, Ascension, Chelmsford, St. John's, North Woolwich; rebuilt Wren's Church of St. Magnus, London Bridge; rebuilt Wren's Church of St. Mary-le-Bow, Cheapside; completion and remodelling of Blackburn Cathedral; Consultant Architect for Exeter Cathedral. *Addresses:* 5 Bloomsbury Pl., London WC1A 2QA, and The Wayside, Shenfield Common, Brentwood, Essex. *Clubs:* Athenæum, Boodles. *Signs work:* "Laurence King."

KININMONTH, (Lady) Caroline Eleanor Newsam, D.A. (Edin.); painter in oil of flowers, landscapes, etc.; *b* 18 May, 1907; *d* of William Sutherland, F.C.I.I., P.P.R.S.A. (architect); *m* Sir William Kininmonth; one *d. Educ.:* Mary Erskine School, Edinburgh; *studied art* at Edinburgh College of Art (1926-30) under David Alison, R.S.A., Dr. D. M. Sutherland, R.S.A. *Exhib.:* R.S.A., S.S.W.A. *Work in permanent collections:* Scottish Arts Council, and numerous private collections. *Address:* The Lane House, 46A Dick Pl., Edinburgh 9. *Signs work:* "C. Kininmonth."

KININMONTH, Sir William Hardie, Kr. (1972), P.P.R.S.A. (1969), H.R.A. (196 9), H.R.S.W., F.R.I.B.A., F.R.I.A.S.; architect; President of the Royal Scottish Academy, Governor of Edinburgh College of Art; *b* Forfar, Scotland, 8 Nov., 1904; *s* of John Kininmonth; *m* Caroline Eleanor Newsam Sutherland; one *d. Educ.:* Dunfermline High School and George Watson's College, Edinburgh; *studied art* at Edinburgh College of Art (1924-29, John Begg, F.R.I.B.A.), Slade Atelier (Professor Albert Richardson). *Principal works:* Air Terminal Buildings, Renfrew, Royal Naval Air Station, Lossiemouth, Students' Hall of Residence, Edinburgh University, Mary Erskine Secondary School for Girls, Edinburgh, Redevelopment of Central Area, Linlithgow, Craigsbank Church, Edinburgh, Scottish Provident Institution Head Office, Edinburgh, Brunton Town Hall, Musselburgh, proposed New Opera House, Edinburgh. *Address:* The Lane House, 46A Dick Pl., Edinburgh 9. *Clubs:* New Club, Edinburgh, Scottish Arts.

KINMONT, David Bruce; Staff Tutor in Fine Arts, University of Bristol; *b* Westgate-on-Sea, Kent, 14 Nov., 1932; *s* of Duncan Bruce Kinmont; *m* Ann Marie Browne; three *s. Educ.:* Regional College of Art, Manchester, and St. John's College, Cambridge. *Address:* The Lent House, Clevedon Rd., Flax Bourton, Bristol. *Signs work:* see appendix.

KIRBY, Michael, M.F.P.S.; fine art restorer, artist in oil; *b* Farnham Common, Bucks., 30 Dec., 1949; *s* of H. Kirby, M.I.Nuc.E., L.R.S.H. *Studied art* at High Wycombe School of Art (1967-71) under G. G. Palmer, Romeo Di Gerolamo, R.B.A., Eric Smith, R.B.A., R.W.S., Henry Trivick, R.B.A. *Exhib.:* R.B.A., Open Salon, F.P.S., H.U.A.S. *Address:* 11 Stevenson Rd., Hedgerley, Bucks. *Signs work:* "M. Kirby."

KIRBY, Sarah, M.F.P.S. (1972), M.Sc. Lond. (1928), A.K.C. (1925); retired lecturer; self-taught artist in oil; *b* London, 5 Apr., 1903; *d* of C. H. Kirby, A.R.C.O. *Educ.:* James Allen's School, Dulwich; Mary Datchelor School, Camberwell; King's College, London; London Day Training College. *Exhib.:* R.A., Paris Salon; one-man show Bristol Arts Centre (1967); group show Loggia Gallery, London (1974). *Publication:* Nature Study for Schools (Methuen, 1957). *Address:* 28 Gay Street, Bath BA1 2PD. *Club:* F.P.S. *Signs work:* "S. K." or "Sarah Kirby."

KIRK, Douglas William, D.A., M.A.(RCA); painter and illustrator in oil, pencil and acrylic; *b* 22 Feb., 1949; *s* of Robert Kirk; *m* Jacqueline Susanne Kirk. *Educ.:* George Heriots. Edinburgh; *studied art* at Duncan of Jordanstone College of Art (1967-71); Royal College of Art (1971-74) under Peter Blake. *Exhib.:* Compass Gallery, Glasgow, Fruit Market, Edinburgh, 57 Gallery, Edinburgh. *Address:* 350 Leith Walk, Edinburgh 6. *Club:* S.S.A. *Signs work:* "Douglas Kirk."

KIRKWOOD, John Sutherland, D.A. post. Dip. Scholarship; artist, sculptor in mixed media, photography and etching; council of S.S.A. 57 Committee; *b* Edinburgh, 6 Apr., 1947; *s* of J. E. Kirkwood. *Educ.:* George Watson College, Edinburgh; *studied art* at Dundee College of Art. *Exhib.:* one-man shows: 57 Art Gallery, Edinburgh Printmakers Workshop; group shows: Fruit market Gallery, Dundee Museum, Triad Arts Centre, Bishops Stortford, Coal Utilisation Showroom, Edinburgh. Combat Room, Leith, Demarco Gallery. *Work in permanent collection:* S.A.C. Loan. *Address:* 16 Kirkhill Rd., Edinburgh. *Signs work:* "J SK."

KIRTLEY, E. W., A.L.A.; Acting-Director, Sunderland Public Libraries, Museum and Art Gallery since 1973. *Address:* c/o Museum and Art Gallery, Sunderland.

KITTS, Barry Edward Lyndon, N.D.D. (1964), F.R.S.A. (1972); landscape painter in gouache, topographical draughtsman and designer; *b* Bath, 18 Oct., 1943; *s* of George Edward Kitts. *Educ.:* Sutton East County Secondary School (Surrey Special Art Course under George Mackley, R.E.); *studied art* at Kingston School of Art (1959-61) under J. D. Binns, A.R.C.A., D.A. Pavey, A.R.C.A., Wimbledon School of Art (1961-64) under Gerald Cooper, A.R.C.A. *Exhib.:* N.E.A.C., R.B.A., Wessex Artists' Exhbn. Designed (with M. D. Moody): War Posters Exhbn. (1972), Yugoslav War Art (1973) at Imperial War Museum; sets for the film "Overlord" (produced by James Quinn and directed by Stuart Cooper, 1974). *Address:* 81 Worple Rd., Wimbledon, London SW19. *Club:* Folio. *Signs work:* "Barry Kitts."

KNAPP, Stefan, Knight's Cross of the Order of Polonia Restituta; Polish International Prize (1971); Churchill Fellowship (1970); Slade Diploma (1947-50); painter in oil on canvas and glass on steel; *b* Bilgoraj, Poland, 11 July, 1921. *Educ.:* High School, Lwow, Poland; *studied art* at Slade (1947-50). *Work in permanent collections:* Museo Nationale, Buenos Aires, National Museum of Helsinki, Finland, Museum of Fine Arts, Caracas, Dallas Museum, C.A.S., V. & A., Museum of Modern Art, Buenos Aires, Stedelijk Museum, Amsterdam, Museum of Modern Art, New York, Museum Naradowe, Warsaw, Copernicus University, Torun, Planetarium, Olsztyn, Lod Airport, Israel, Johnson Building, Amsterdam. *Work repro.:* The Square Sun (Museum Press). *Address:* 4 King's House Studios, 396 King's Rd., Chelsea, London SW10. *Signs work:* "S. Knapp."

KNEALE, Bryan, R.A. Rome Scholar; sculptor in steel and all metals, wood, etc.; Mem. C.N.A.A. Fine Arts Panel, Tutor, Royal College of Art, Chairman A.S.G.; *b* Douglas, I.O.M., 19 June, 1930; *s* of W. T. Kneale, newspaper editor; *m* Doreen Kneale; one *s*, one *d*. *Educ.:* Douglas High School; *studied art* at Douglas School of Art (1947) under W. H. Whitehead; R.A. Schools (1948-52) under Philip Connerd, Henry Rushbury. *Exhib.:* John Moores, Art d'aujourd'hui, Paris, Battersea Park, Whitechapel Retrospective, Cardiff, Leics. Educ. Com., Whitechapel, City of London, Peter Stuyvesant, Southampton, British Sculptors, R.A. Holland Park, Royal Exchange Sculpt., Hayward Gallery, R.A., London Group, Redfern Gallery. *Work in permanent collections:* Tate, Arts Council, C.A.S., Fitzwilliam, Cambridge, City Art Galleries of Manchester, Birmingham, Sheffield, Bradford, Wakefield, Leicester, York and Middlesbrough, Sao Paulo, Brazil, Museum of Modern Art, N.Y., National Galleries of N.Z., Queensland and S. Australia, Manx Museum and A.G., Abbot Hall Gallery, Cumberland, Beaverbrook Foundation, Frederickton, Bochum Museum, W. Germany, Bahia Museum, Brazil. *Address:* 7 Winthorpe Rd., London SW15. *Club:* Chelsea Arts. *Signs work:* "BRYAN KNEALE" (die stamp), "Bryan Kneale" (drawings, etc.).

KNEE, Howard; water-colour artist; *b* London, 1889; *m* Eileen Thompson. *Educ.:* Manchester Grammar School; *studied art* at School of Art, Dublin. *Exhib.:* R.A., R.H.A. *Work repro.:* by Armstrong & Co., Dublin; Samuel A. C. Todd, Ltd., Glasgow; Scholastic Production Co., Belfast. *Address:* Clovelly, Mount Tallant Ave., Terenure, Dublin. *Signs work:* "HOWARD KNEE."

KNEEBONE, Peter, M.A., F.S.I.A., F.S.T.D.; graphic designer, illustrator, visual communications consultant and design educator; Vice-President International Council of Graphic Design Associations and 1970 ICOGRADA President's Trophy; *b* Middlesbrough, 28 Apr., 1923; *m;* one *s,* three *d. Educ.:* University College, Oxford; autodidact. *Work repro.:* internationally, books illustrated and written. *Work exhib.:* New York, Tokyo, London, etc. *Address:* 25 Rue Vauvenargues, 75018 Paris. *Signs work:* "P.K." or "PETER KNEEBONE."

KNELLER, Frank, B.Sc. (1947); painter of horses and dogs of the Stubbs School; *b* Penrhyn Park, Bangor, Caerns., 2 July, 1914; *s* of J. Kneller, A.H.R.H.S. *Educ.:* University College of North Wales; *studied art* at Edinburgh School of Art under J. Murray Thompson, R.S.A., and dissected horses at Royal (Dick) Veterinary College, Edinburgh. *Exhib.:* R.Scot.A., R.Camb.A., United Soc., R.S.M.P., Artists of Chelsea. *Work repro.:* various cartoons. *Address:* 3 South Cliff Ave., Eastbourne. *Signs work:* see appendix.

KNIGHT, Charles, R.W.S., R.O.I.; landscape painter in water-colour and oil and designer; formerly Vice-Principal, Brighton College of Art; *b* Hove, 27 Aug., 1901; *s* of Charles Knight; *m* Leonora Vasey (decd.); one *s. Educ.:* Vardean Grammar School, Brighton; *studied art* at Brighton College of Art, Royal Academy Schools (Charles Sims, Keeper, Walter Sickert), Royal College of Art (Sir Frank Short). *Work in permanent collections:* B.M., Ashmolean, Oxford, Graves Art Gallery, Sheffield, Hull, Stoke-on-Trent, Brighton, Eastbourne. *Publications:* Monograph by Michael Brockway with 52 plates (Lewis pub., 1952). *Address:* Chettles, 34 Beacon Rd., Ditchling, Hassocks, Sussex. *Signs work:* "CHARLES KNIGHT" in caps.

KNIGHT, Lionel John; painter; *b* Romsey, Hants., 9 July, 1901; divorced 1972; *m* Marie-Jose Piguet. *Exhib.:* Arts Council of Gt. Britain, R.S.P.P., R.B.A., R.W.E.A.; one-man shows: Fontainebleau, London (1966), Bridgwater Art Gallery (1968). *Address:* 3 Cornwall Terr., Penzance.

KNOBLOCK, Joan, F.P.S., H.H.A.C.; portrait painter in oil; *b* London, 22 Apr., 1917; *d* of Julius Gluck; *m* Ernest Knoblock; one *s,* one *d. Educ.:* Southgate County School; *studied art* at Hornsey School of Art under Russell Reeve; Heatherley School of Art, also in Vienna and Berlin. *Exhib.:* one-man shows: Commonwealth Inst. Scotland (1969), Commonwealth Inst. London (1968), Lionel Wendt Gallery, Colombo (1967), British Council, Suva, Fiji (1964, 1966), Woodstock Gallery (1959, 1960, 1961), Rabat, Morocco (1958); group shows: Galerie Creuze, Paris, Contemporary Portrait Society, R.S.P.P., The Studio, Waresley, Beds. Work in various private collections. *Address:* 10 Ravenscroft Ave., London NW11. *Signs work:* "J.K."

KNOX, Harry Cooke, A.R.U.A. (1953); artist in oil, acrylic, water-colour and pastel, specialty portraits and murals; Pres., Ulster Arts Club (1955), vice-pres. (1951, 1952, 1953); vice-pres., R.U.A. (1950-52); *b* Newtownbutler, Co. Fermanagh; *s* of Andrew Knox; *m* Lila Mary Knox; two *s. Educ.:* Methodist College, Belfast; *studied art* at Belfast College of Art (1924-30). *Exhib.:* R.U.A., R.H.A.,

R.O.I. *Address:* 109 Marlborough Park South, Belfast 9. *Club:* Ulster Arts. *Signs work:* see appendix.

KNOX, John, A.R.S.A. (1972), D.A. (1957); artist in PVA and oil; Lecturer in Drawing and Painting, Dundee College of Art; *b* Kirkintilloch, 1936; *s* of Alexander Knox, Master Tailor; *m* Margaret K. Sutherland; one *s*, one *d*. *Educ.:* Lenzie Academy; *studied art* at Glasgow School of Art (1953-58) under Wm. Armour, R.S.A., David Donaldson, R.S.A., Paris under André Lhote. *Work in permanent collections:* Otis Art Institute, Los Angeles; Olinda Museum, Sao Paolo; National Gallery of Modern Art, Edinburgh; Scottish Arts Council; Contemporary Arts Society; Manchester City Art Gallery; Aberdeen Art Gallery, Dundee Art Gallery; Edinburgh Civic Collection; Royal Scottish Academy Collection; Nuffield Foundation; Dumfries C.C.; Edinburgh Educ. Authority; Borough of Camden; Universities of Aberdeen, Strathclyde, St. Andrews, Stirling. *Work repro.:* Studio International; Art International; Apollo; Burlington Magazine. *Address:* 15 Carlogie Rd., Carnoustie, Angus DD7 6DA. *Signs work:* "Knox."

KOBULADZE, Sergei, graduate of Tbilisi Academy of Art, professor of drawing of Tbilisi Academy of Art (rector 1952-59); corresponding member of Academy of Art of the U.S.S.R.; artist in oil, charcoal, gouache; Georgian; *b* Akhaltsikhe, Georgia, 1909. *Studied art* at Tbilisi Academy of Art under E. Lansere, I. Charlemagne and G. Gabashvili. *Work repro.:* Illustrations to King Lear, Rusthaveli's Knight in the Tiger Skin, The Lay of the Host of Igor, Tbilisi Opera-House curtain (tempera, 1961). *Address:* U.S.S.R., Tbilisi, ul. Kamo 4, apt. 49. *Signs work:* see appendix.

KOE: see KÖNEKAMP, Frederick Rudolph.

KOENIG, Ghisha; sculptor in terracotta and bronze, especially reliefs; *b* London, 12 Dec., 1921; *d* of Leo Koenig; *m* Dr. Emanuel Tuckman. *Studied art* at Hornsey (1939-42), Chelsea (1946-48) under Henry Moore, Slade (1949) under F. E. McWilliam. *Exhib.:* R.A., Whitechapel Art Gallery, Middleheim Biennale; one-man shows: Grosvenor Gallery, London, etc. *Work in permanent collections:* commissions include Festival of Britain, Ministry of Works, Edmonton Borough Council, Centre 42, Fulham High School, etc. *Publications:* Bibliog.: Architectural Review (1957), Engineering (1957), Times, N.Y. Times, Studio International, Observer, Jewish Chronicle, etc. *Film:* Ghisha Koenig, directed by Mike Casey (1968). *Address:* 27 Halfway St., Sidcup, Kent.

KOLB, Gideon, B.Com. (1934), F.R.S.A. (1974); portrait painter in oil and actor; *b* Vienna, 19 Aug., 1913; *s* late Hermann Kolb, director of finance; *m* Gerti Braun; one *s*, one *d*. *Educ.:* Academy of Commerce, Vienna; Sorbonne, Paris; *studied art* at Grande Chaumière, Paris; Polytechnic, Regent St., London; Chelsea College of Art. *Exhib.:* Redfern Gallery, R.I., Schoninger Gallerie, Munchen and many others in London and provinces; one-man shows: Loggia Gallery (1974), Drian Gallery (1968), Camden Institute (1967). *Work in permanent collections:* Financial Times, London and in private collections in England, France, Germany, U.S.A. and Israel. *Address:* 161 Hendon Way, London NW2 (residence and studio). *Clubs:* F.P.S., H.A.C., B.U.A.S. *Signs work:* "Kolb."

KOPEL, Harold; artist in oil and wood, teacher; lecturer, Further Education I.L.E.A.; *b* Newcastle upon Tyne, 9 Aug., 1915; *s* of Nathan Kopel. *Educ.:* Rutherford Grammar School, Newcastle, and University College, London; *studied art:* mainly self-taught and at Central School of Arts and Crafts. *Exhib.:* R.O.I., N.E.A.C., N.S., F.P.S., Ben Uri Art Soc., Guildhall, R.S.A., New Grafton Gallery, Radlett Gallery, Herts., Southampton, Surrey; one-man shows: Barnet

Borough Arts Council. Barnet Libraries Com., Ben Uri A.G., F.P.S., Upper St. A.G. *Work in permanent collections:* University College, London, Nuffield Foundation, Ben Uri A.G., I.L.E.A. *Address:* 13 Hampstead Gdns., London NW11. *Clubs:* Ben Uri Art Soc., F.P.S., Hampstead Artists Council. *Signs work:* "Kopel."

KORMIS, Fred J.; sculptor in bronze, terra-cotta, stone, wood; *b* Frankfurt, 20 Sept., 1896; *s* of Moritz Kormis; *m* Rachel Sender. *Educ.:* Frankfurt; *studied art* at Frankfurt Kunstschule under Prof. F. Hausmann. *Exhib.:* Frankfurt, Berlin, Hamburg, Weisbaden, Amsterdam, The Hague, R.A., R.I.B.A., etc. *Work in permanent collections:* British Museum, The Hague, Staedel'sche Museum, Frankfurt, Jewish Museum, New York. *Official purchases:* prisoners of war memorial, Tannenburg Memorial. *Work repro.:* in Das Kunstblatt, Berlin; Bouwkundig Weekbblad, The Hague. *Address:* Studio B, 3 Greville Pl., London NW6. *Signs work:* "KORMIS."

KORN, Halina (Miss), W.I.A.C.; sculptress and painter in oil; *b* Warszawa; *m* Marek Zulawski, painter; settled in London, 1940. Self-taught. *Exhib.:* R.A., London Group, W.I.A.C., A.I.A.; one-man shows; Mayor's Gallery, Beaux Arts Gallery, Gallery One; in New York and in Warsaw. *Work repro.:* Sketch, Studio, Vogue, Church of England Newspaper, Habitat (Brazil), and in Polish papers. *Address:* Greville Studio, 4A Greville Pl., London NW6. *Signs work:* "KORN."

KREEGER, Marianne; painter in oil, perspex, gouache; *b* Frankfurt, Germany, 17 Apr., 1929; *m* Lionel C. Kreeger; three *d. Studied art* at St. Martin's School of Art (1946). *Exhib.:* R.A., London Group, F.P.S., also 4 one-man shows in London. *Address:* 28 Heath Drive, London NW3. *Signs work:* "M K."

KROL, Stan, D.A., F.S.I.A., F.R.S.A.; graphic designer, typographer, art editor, consultant designer; *b* Warsaw, 13 June, 1910; *s* of Henryk Krol, industrialist; *m* Ingeborg le Vaye. *Educ.:* Mazovia School and University, Warsaw; *studied art* at Dundee College of Art. *Exhib.:* posters in several international poster exhbns. *Work in permanent collections:* posters at Stedelijk Museum, Amsterdam, and Poster Museum, Warsaw. *Work repro.:* posters, designs, etc., in several international journals, annuals and publications. *Work reviewed* in Publimondial (by Jean Picart le Doux), Gebrauchsgraphik (by Dr. Eberhard Hölscher), Graphik (by Geoffrey King and Anton Sailer), and others. *Address:* 7 Lowther Rd., London SW13 9NX. *Signs work:* see appendix.

KULESZA, Nel, Z.P.A.P. (Polish), R.M.S.; artist in tempera, water-colour, oil; miniaturist; *b* 6 Sept., 1916. *Studied art* at High School of Art, Warsaw (1934-39), diploma with distinction under Prof. Kokoszko (painting techniques), Prof. Radwan (graphic art). *Exhib.:* one-man shows: twice in Poland, Royal Soc. of Miniature Painters, London, Handwerkskammer Colonia, Gedok Gallery, Berlin, Fie Paris, etc. *Work repro.:* illustrated 18 children's books, 15 medical and ballet instructive books. *Address:* 01-884 Warszawa, Ul. Staffa 75, Poland. *Signs work:* "A and K" joined over date of work.

KUO, Nancy; director, choreographer, dancer, actress, designer, authoress, art critic and painter, gold medallist; visiting lecturer to universities, art colleges, art societies, women's societies, clubs and museums; *b* Shanghai, China. *Studied* western painting and traditional painting. *Exhib.:* in China, Hong Kong, Gambia, Burma, Afghanistan, France, Norway, Argentina and England. *Work repro.:* numerous newspapers and journals of various countries. *Work in permanent collections:* private collections all over the world, National Museum of Burma. *Publications:* author of Chinese Paper-cut Pictures; catalogue, Arts from China; contributions: poems, essays, plays, art reviews, etc. in Chinese and in English to newspapers and journals in China, Hong Kong, Burma, Afghanistan, Italy and England; 100 scripts for BBC Radio; TV appearances: ITV, BBC, France TV and Monte Carlo TV. Member of International P.E.N., International Association of Art Critics. *Address:* Orchid Studio, 51 Wise La., Mill Hill, London NW7 2RN. *Signs work:* "Nancy" in Chinese; see appendix.

KYNOCH, Kathryn Marie, D.A.: artist in oil; *b* Edinburgh, 18 Aug., 1942; *d* of William Haydn Kynoch, musician. *Educ.:* Gateway Grammar School, Leicester; *studied art* at Glasgow School of Art (1959-64) under Donaldson, Armour; Hospitalfield College of Art, Arbroath (summers of 1962 and 1963) under Cumming. *Exhib.:* '208' Gallery, Glasgow, Blythswood Gallery, Glasgow, R.G.I., Royal Scottish Academy, Adam Smith Building, Glasgow University, Close Theatre Club, Glasgow, Royal Scottish Academy of Music & Drama. *Work in permanent collections:* Glasgow Art Galleries, Edinburgh University, Glasgow University, University of Strathclyde. *Address:* 47 St. Vincent Cres., Glasgow, G3. *Signs work:* "K. M. Kynoch."

L

LACK, Barbara Dacia, A.R.C.A. Lond.: artist in oil, engraving, textile design, draughtswoman; *d* of Charles T. Lack, M.I.Mech.E., A.M.I.E.E. *Educ.:* Perse School, Camb.; *studied art:* Camb. School of Art, R.C.A. *Exhib.:* paintings and engravings, R.C.A. Assoc. Exhbn. at the R.A. (1948) and provinces; painting at Colchester Castle (1950); paintings in Leicester (1963); Norwich (1966); Peterborough (1969-1973); Sudbury (1969-1975); Cambridge, Ely, etc.; textiles, etc., in London, Edinburgh and Copenhagen. *Official purchases:* two purchased by Messrs J. and P. Coats (1945). *Work repro.:* Modern Embroidery, Embroideress, etc. *Address:* 12 Richmond Rd., Cambridge. *Signs work:* "B. D. LACK."

LACK, Henry Martyn, R.E. (1948), A.R.C.A. (1933); etcher; taught, Christ's Hospital, Sussex (1938-47), R.C.A. (1947-53), Hastings School of Art (1953-67); attached to Epigraphic Survey, Luxor, Egypt for University of Chicago; *b* Bozeat, Northants, 5 Dec., 1909; *s* of Arthur Henry Lack; *m* Phyllis Mary Hafford. *Educ.:* Wellingborough School; *studied art* at Leicester College of Art (Royal Exhbn.) 1926-30, R.C.A. (Student Demonstrator) 1930-34. *Exhib.:* R.A., R.E., and widely abroad. *Work in permanent collections:* V. & A., B.M., Reading University, S. London Art Gall. *Address:* 17 White Rock, Hastings, Sussex, TN34 1JY. *Signs work:* "Martyn Lack."

LA FONTAINE, Thomas Sherwood; painter in oil, water-colour and black and white of portraits and animal subjects; *b* 21 Dec., 1915. *Educ.:* Rottingdean and Tonbridge School; Regent St., Polytechnic (Harry Watson, S. Tresilian, since 1934); City and Guilds, Kennington (Innes Fripp, James Grant, Middleton Todd, since 1936); Spenlove School (Reginald Eves, since 1939). *Address:* East Cottage, Burton Hill, Malmesbury, Wilts. *Signs work:* in printed capitals.

LAIRD, E. Ruth; International Invitational 20th Annual Award, Syracuse; taught art, University of Houston (1958); Asst. Dean of Museum School, Houston Museum of Fine Arts (1958-68); *b* Houston, Texas, 1921; *d* of J. I. Laird. *Studied art* at Cranbrook Academy of Art, Bloomfield Hills, Michigan, U.S.A. (1953-55). *Exhib.:* Boston Museum, Metropolitan Museum, New York. *Work in permanent collections:* Cranbrook Museum, Bloomfield Hills, Children's Museum, Detroit,

Everson Museum, Syracuse, Iroquois China Co., Syracuse. Contemporary Crafts Museum, N.Y.C. *Address:* 1618 Cherryhurst, Houston, Texas, 77006, U.S.A. *Signs work:* see appendix.

LAIRD, Michael Donald, F.S.I.A., F.R.I.A.S., (McLaren Fellow 1956-58), R.I.B.A.; R.S.A. Architecture Medal (1968); Awards from Civic Trust, British Steel Corp., Saltire Society, etc.; architect and design consultant; Governor, Edinburgh College of Art; *b* 1928; *s* of G.D.S. Laird; *m* Hon. Kirsty Noel-Paton; two *s,* one *d. Educ.:* Loretto School; *studied art* at Edinburgh College of Art and University under Prof. R. Gordon Brown. *Buildings:* include Standard Life Assurance Head Office, Edinburgh University Kings Buildings Centre, Restoration, Maxwelton House and Blairquhan Castle. *Addresses:* 22 Moray Pl., Edinburgh, and Brock, Isle of Tiree, Argyllshire. *Club:* New (Edinburgh).

LAKE, Evelyn Frances Coote, Membre Associé de la Société des Artistes Français, A.R.M.S. (1947), S.M. (1967); prize for best drawing (portrait), Hesketh Hubbard Art Soc. Exhbn., 1968; painter (mainly of cats and birds) in water-colour, crayon, charcoal, pencil, pastel and oil; Mem. Council R.W.S. Art Club (1939-49, 1957-59); Mem. Council Ridley Art Club (1949-53, 1956-60); Vice-Pres., St. James' Art Soc. for the Deafened; Mem. Council Folklore Soc. since 1939; M.R.S.L., etc.; *b* London; *d* of Joseph Forsbrey Lake. *Educ.:* N. London Collegiate School, R.C.M. and L.S.E.; *studied art* at Camden and Hornsey Schools of Art and on Continent. *Exhib.:* nearly every open show in London; R. Cam. Acad.; R.W.E. Acad.; many municipal and provincial galleries; Paris Salon since 1938; one-man shows: Walker's Galleries, Bond St. (1949, 1951, 1953, 1955, 1958) and by invitation Blackhall Gallery, Oxford (1952), Cat's Protection League, London (1956, 1957, Caxton Hall), Augustine Gallery, Holt, Norfolk; Pittsburgh, Pa., Perth, W. Australia. *Commissioned to paint:* (cats) Champions Hendon Defendant and Barney of Bedale, etc. *Work repro.:* decorations for Cat Encyclopedia, by Kit Wilson (Internat. Cat. Judge; Ed. Cat Fancy); Woman's Journal. *Publications:* Hon. Editor section on Folk Life and Traditions in Folk-lore (quarterly) 1949-67; various articles; occasional verse. *Address:* 5 Hurst Ave., Highgate, London N6 5TZ. *Clubs:* Old Water-colour Soc., Hesketh Hubbard Art, R.W.S. Art, Ridley, Campden Hill, Lay mem. Wild Life Artists, Royal Commonwealth Soc., Nat. Cat Club, N.B.L. *Signs work:* "E. F. Coote Lake" or "Coote Lake."

LAMB, Lynton, F.R.S.A. (1953), R.O.I. (1975), London Group (1939); staff, Slade School of Fine Art (1950-71), lecturer, Royal College of Art (1956-71); *b* India, 15 Apr., 1907; *s* of Rev. F. Lamb; *m* Barbara Morgan; two *s. Educ.:* Kingswood School, Bath; *studied art* at L.C.C. Central School of Arts and Crafts. *Exhib.:* Leicester, Redfern, Wildenstein Galleries, R.B.A., Australia, Amsterdam, Dublin, Arts Council Festival Exhbn. *Publications:* The Purpose of Painting, County Town, Preparation for Painting, Editor, with Prof. Quentin Bell, Oxford Paperbacks, Handbooks for Artists. Drawing for Illustration, Materials and Methods of Painting. *Address:* Sandon, nr. Chelmsford. *Signs work:* "Lynton Lamb" or "L.L."

LAMBOURNE, Nigel, R.E. (1947), A.R.C.A., M.S.I.A.; draughtsman, lithographer, artist in all graphic mediums; *b* Nottingham, 30 May, 1919; *s* of Herbert Lambourne, M.A., M.Sc., F.I.C.; *m* Barbara Ward Standen, A.R.C.A.; one *s. Educ.:* Selhurst Grammar School, Croydon; *studied art* at Central School of Arts and Crafts, R.C.A. *Exhib.:* R.B.A., R.E., R.A. *Official purchases:* Arts Council, Nat. Gall. of Australia, Adelaide, Pierpoint Morgan Library (New York), Nottingham Castle Museum, Merton College (Oxford), Bradford City Gallery. *Address:* 3 The Cross, Enderby, Leicestershire. *Signs work:* "Nigel Lambourne."

LAMERAS, Lazaros, F.I.A.L., Ecole des Beaux Arts, first sculpture prize (1939), Unknown Political Prisoner prize; sculptor in coloured stones and marbles; Prof., Technical University, Athens; *b* Athens, 1918; *s* of John Lameras. *Educ.:* High School, Athens; *studied art* at the School of Fine Arts, Athens, under Thomopoulo, Ecole des Beaux Arts, Paris, on scholarship under Jean Boucher. *Exhib.:* São Paolo Biennale (1955), Salon de Touleine, Stockholm, Cairo, Tate, Greece, Venice Biennale (1960), Musée Rodin (1966), Geneve Musée Rath (1967), Expo 70, Osaka, Biarritz (1971). *Official purchases:* Athens. *Publications:* Plasti Ki (1969), Urban Survey of Modern Athens Contemporary Sculptures, Athens (1975). *Address:* 5 G. Trapezountiou 706 Str., Athens. *Signs work:* see appendix.

LANCASTER, Brian Christy; artist in marine and landscape painting also steam locomotives; mem. Princess Elizabeth and Dowty Locomotive Preservation Societies; helped complete restoration of a Sir William Stanier express engine, doing some painting and the whole relining and gold leaf lettering required; former mem. Canadian Artists Group; *b* 1931. *Studied art* at Bolton, Southport and Manchester Schools of Art. *Exhib.:* Atkinson A.G., Southport, Bristol Savages, and exhbns, sponsored by Messrs. Frost and Reed in Bristol, Birmingham and Bournemouth. *Address:* Ingle Cottage, Inglestone Common, Hawkesbury, Badminton, Glos. *Club:* Bristol Savages. *Signs work:* "BRIAN C. LANCASTER."

LANCELEY, Colin John, A.S.T.C. Painting (1960), Helena Rubinstein Scholarship (1964), Bronze Medal, Krakow (1968); painter in oil, wood construction, India inks, silkscreen, lithography; lecturer, Gloucestershire College of Art; *b* Dunedin, N.Z., 6 Jan., 1938; *s* of John Lassegue Lanceley, engineer; *m* Kay; two *s*, one *d*. *Educ.:* Naremburn, Sydney; *studied art* at National Art School, Sydney (1956-60), under Laverty, Passmore, Olsen, Miller. *Work in permanent collections:* Museum of Modern Art, N.Y., Art Gallery of N.S.W., National Museum of Warsaw, Musee Polonaise, Walker Art Centre, Minneapolis, Musee Silesienne, Michigan Museum, Kunstvrein, Hamburg, National Gallery of S. Australia, Newcastle Art Gallery, National Gallery of Victoria. *Address:* c/o Marlborough Fine Art, 6 Albemarle St., London W1. *Signs work:* "LANCELEY."

LANDER, Reginald Montague, M.S.I.A.; free-lance consultant and artist-designer in gouache, water-colour and black and white; Chief Designer and Studio Manager, Ralph Mott Studio (1930-39); *b* London, 18 Aug., 1913; *s* of M. Lander; *m* Panayota Spentzas. *Studied art* at Hammersmith School of Art. Freelance since 1946. *Work repro.:* for H.M. Ministries, B.T.C., British Railways, Co-operative Movement, etc. *Address:* 5 Grove Lodge, Hampstead La., London N6 4RT. *Signs work:* "Lander."

LANG, Wharton, R.S.M.A. (1948); sculptor in wood; Member of Selection Committee, Society of Wildlife Artists; *b* Oberammergau, Bavaria, 13 June, 1925; *s* of Faust Lang, wood sculptor; *m* Ingrid. *Educ.:* Newquay Grammar School; *studied art* at Leonard Fuller School of Painting (1946) and privately under Faust Lang (1946-49). *Work in permanent collections:* Ulster Museum, Belfast, R.S.M.A. Diploma Collection, National Maritime Museum, Greenwich. *Address:* Fauna Studio, Mount Zion, St. Ives, Cornwall. *Signs work:* "W. LANG" and "Wharton Lang."

LANGHORNE, Mary; designer, painter in oil and water-colour, teacher; *b* Exeter, 1909; *d* of the Rev. R. W. B. Langhorne, M.A. (Oxon.). *Educ.:* Queen Anne's School, Caversham; *studied art* at R.A.M. School of Art, Exeter (1928-30), Central School of Arts and Crafts (1930-32). *Exhib.:* R.W.E.A., R.I., R.S.A., and provincial galleries. *Work in permanent collections:* Royal West of England Academy, Bristol, and several libraries; also works in Exeter Cathedral, Diocese of Canterbury, Parish Churches of Chilton Foliat, St. Endellion, Exminster, Hartland and St. George's, Birmingham. Royal Arms in South Petherton Church, Somerset. *Address:* Nail House, Ferry Rd., Topsham, Exeter. *Signs work:* "Mary Langhorne."

LAPICQUE, Charles, Officier des Arts et Lettres (1960); artist in oil, gouache, encre and crayon; *b* Theize (Rhône), 6 Oct., 1898. *Educ.:* Paris; *studied art* at Académies Libres, Paris. *Work in permanent collections:* Musée d'Art Moderne, Paris, Museum of Modern Art, New York, Museum, Copenhagen, Musées Royaux des Beaux Arts, Brussels, Gallery of Living Art, New York, Museum Grenobles, Neue Staatsgalerie, Munich, Folkwarig Museum, Essen, Musée d'Historie et d'Art, Luxembourg. *Publications:* Jean Lescure, Lapicque (Paris, 1956); Charles Lapicque, Essais sur l'Espace, l'Art a la Destinée (1958); Jean Follain, Appareil de la Terre (Paris, 1961). *Address:* 4 rue Froidevaux, Paris. *Signs work:* "Lapicque."

LARDERA, Berto; sculptor in metal and graphic media; *b* La Spezia; 18 Dec., 1911; *s* of Carlo Lardera; *m* Cecile Corre; one *d. Educ.:* Florence; *studied art:* self-taught. *Over 50 works in art museums:* Paris, Brussels, Rome, Florence; Milan, Hamburg, Helsinki, Rio de Janeiro, San Francisco, Providence, Boston, Dallas, Hannover, etc.; 29 monumental works in Europe, U.S.A., Canada, etc. *Books on his work:* Lardera, by M. Seuphor (Ed. Griffon, Switzerland), J. Jianou and M. Brion (Arted Ed., Paris), Guy Robert (Ed. Songe, Montreal). Over 300 studies and articles quoted in Arted Ed. bibliography, by Haftmann, Degand, H. Read, Descargues, Dorfles, Giedion Welcker, Trier, Coates, Wember, Thwaites, Conil Lacoste, Huyghe, Kultermann, etc. *Address:* 9 Cité Falguiere, Paris, XV. *Signs work:* graphic works: see appendix.

LARKING, Patrick Lambert, R.P., R.O.I. (1951), N.S. (1947); elected Royal Portrait Society (1965); painter in oil, water-colour; teacher of painting Sir John Cass School of Art (1949); *b* Rudgwick, Sussex, 15 Apr., 1907; *s* of Capt. Lambert Larking, 1st Westminster Dragoons; *m* Betty Burnham. *Educ.:* Christ's Hospital; *studied art* at R.A. Schools (1923) under Charles Sims, R.A., F. Ernest Jackson. *Exhib.:* R.A., R.Can.A., R.P., N.S., R.O.I., R.B.A. *Address:* Greenways, Colyton, Devonshire. *Club:* Chelsea Arts. *Signs work:* "Patrick Larking."

LARMONT, Eric, N.D.D., A.T.C.; painter in oil; part-time art lecturer; *b* South Shields, 27 Sept., 1943. *Educ.:* South Shields Grammar; *studied art* at Sunderland College of Art (1963-65); Goldsmiths' School of Art (1965-66), Post-grad. Belgian Scholarship (1968-69). *Work in permanent collections:* Carlisle Corporation; private collections: various. *Prizes and awards:* Reeves Bicentenary Premier Award (1966); Second Non-purchase Prize, Northern Painters Exhibition (1966). *Address:* 30 Colville Terr., London W11. *Signs work:* see appendix.

LASDUN, Denys Louis, C.B.E. (1965), F.R.I.B.A. (1945), Hon. A.I.A. (1966), Hon. D.Litt. (U.E.A., 1974), Hon. F.R.C.P. (1975); Hoffman Wood Professor of Architecture, University of Leeds (1962-63); *b* 1914; *m*; two *s*, one *d*. *Educ.:* Rugby and Architectural Association. *Works* include housing schemes and schools for Bethnal Green and Paddington; flats at 26 St. James's Place (R.I.B.A. Bronze Medal, London Architecture, 1960); Royal College of Physicians (R.I.B.A. Bronze Medal, London Architecture, 1965); extensions to Christ's College, Cambridge; new University of East Anglia; University of London Redevelopment; work for Universities of Leicester and Liverpool; National Theatre, South Bank; new EEC headquarters, European Investment Bank, Luxembourg. *Address:* 50 Queen Anne St., London W1M 0DR.

LASUCHIN, Michael, B.F.A., M.F.A.; more than seventy awards and prizes since 1971; printmaker, teacher and artist in water-colour, acrylics, printmaking and drawing; Assistant Prof., Philadelphia College of Art; *b* Kramatorsk, U.S.S.R., 24 July, 1923. *Educ.:* Philadelphia College of Art; Tyler School of Art, Temple University; *studied art* at Rostow College of Art (1940-41) under Zownir, Tzymbal; Nachwuchsgruppe Bildender Künstler, Regensburg, Germany (1947-49) under Hauser, Wissner; Mahl & Zeichenschule 'Die Form', Munich, Germany (1950) under Konig; Pennsylvania Academy of Fine Art, Philadelphia (1968) under Lueders, Hanlen and Stumpfig. *Work in permanent collections:* Library of Congress, Philadelphia, Museum of Art, Free Library of Philadelphia, Springville, Museum of Art (Mis.), Allentown Art Museum, William Penn Memorial Museum, University of Pennsylvania, University of Delaware and more than thirty others. *Address:* 120 E. Cliveden St., Philadelphia, Pa. 19119, U.S.A. *Clubs:* The Print, Boston Printmaker, National Water-colour Soc., American Color Print Soc., Los Angeles Printmaking Soc., Philadelphia Water-color, Graphics Soc. *Signs work:* "Michael Lasuchin."

LAUDER, Kenneth Scott, A.R.C.A.; painter in oil, water-colour; lecturer; *b* Edinburgh, 1918; *s* of Duncan Fullerton Lauder; *m*; three *s*. *Educ.:* King Alfred's, Wantage under Albert Rutherston; *studied art* at Chelsea School of Art (1934) under Robert Medley, Royal College of Art (1936-39) under Gilbert Spenser. *Exhib.:* mixed: R.A., R.W.E.A., Agnews, Leicester Galls., Redfern Gall., Ruskin Gall., Bear Lane Gall., Oxford, Laing Gall., Newcastle, Walker Art Gall., Liverpool, Schloss Leopoldskron, Salzburg; one-man shows: Reid Gall., Waterhouse Gall. *Address:* 18 Eshe Rd. North, Blundellsands, Liverpool, L23 8UD. *Signs work:* "Lauder."

LAVENSTEIN, Cyril, R.B.S.A., portrait and landscape artist in oil, water-colour, pastel; *b* Birmingham, 11 Oct., 1891; *s* of Henry Lavenstein. *Educ.:* Birmingham College of Art (J. S. Wright Scholar). *Exhib.:* R.A. *Signs work:* "CYRIL LAVENSTEIN."

LAW, Enid: see CHAUVIN, Enid.

LAWRENCE, John, M.F.P.S. (1968); artist in oil and sculpture in bronze; *b* London, 25 Jan., 1934; *s* of Frederick Lawrence, furniture restorer; *m* Susan, artist; two *s*. *Educ.:* Bromley College of Art. *Exhib.:* London, Paris, New York, Nuffield Foundation, various art councils. *Work in permanent collections:* Walker Art Gallery, Manchester City Art Gallery, Bristol Art Gallery. *Address:* c/o Trafford Gallery, 119 Mount St., W1Y 5HB. *Signs work:* "J.L."

LAWS, Tony, Des.R.C.A., M.S.I.A., F.S.D.C.; silversmith designer/craftsman; part-time lecturer, silversmithing and jewellery, Hornsey College of Art; *b* London, 1935. *Studied art* at Gravesend School of Art (1951-53), Canterbury School of Art (1953-56), R.C.A. (1958-61), Silver Medallist. *Major commissions:* silver and metalwork for Coventry Cathedral, Royal Society, Royal Society of Arts, Sussex University, Melbourne University, and various industrial companies and private patrons; medals for Women's 9th European Gymnastics Championships. *Publications:* wrote and compiled the Conspectus on Silversmiths and Jewellers for magazine "Artifex". *Address:* 8 Garrick St., London WC2. *Signs work:* "TL."

LAWSON, Thomas, John Christie Prize, life drawing (1953); artist in oil and pencil; window-dresser; Cert. Fine Art, King's College, Newcastle-upon-Tyne (June, 1958); *b* Newcastle-upon-Tyne, 8 May, 1922. *Educ.:* Elementary school, and College of Art and Industrial Design, Newcastle-upon-Tyne (display); *studied art* at King's College, Newcastle-upon-Tyne, University of Durham, evening classes under Mr. Scott Campbell, drawing, and Mr. Tudor Davies, painting (1951-53). *Exhib.:* Federation of Northern Arts Socs. annual exhbn. (1952, 1953, 1969); Wallsend Art Club exhbn.; Artists of Northern Counties (Laing Art Gallery, Newcastle-upon-Tyne, 1960). *Address:* 11 Malcolm Ct., Monkseaton, Whitley Bay, Northumberland. *Club:* Newcastle Society of Artists. *Signs work:* "T. Lawson."

LAWSON DICK, Winifred; painter in oils; Freeman of the City of London; Freeman of the Worshipful Company of Painter-Stainers. *Studied art* at Chelsea School of Art (1950-55). *Exhib.:* R.O.I., London Group, City of London Guildhall, Festival Gdns. Exhbn.; one-man shows, Walker Galleries, New Bond St. (1953, 1955, 1959), Laniels, Knightsbridge (1955), Paris Salon, etc. *Work repro.:* Tatler, Britannia and Eve, Sketch, Harper's Bazaar, etc. *Address:* Flat 8, 92 Elm Park Gdns., London SW10. *Signs work:* "W. Lawson Dick" with year of date.

LAYCOCK, Norman, A.R.C.A. (1949); 2nd prize, Lord Mayor's Art Award (1975); artist in oil; art master Harrow School of Art and Isleworth Polytechnic; *b* Dewsbury, Yorks. 26 Feb., 1920; *s* of George B. Laycock. *Educ.:* Dewsbury Technical College; *studied art* at Dewsbury School of Art and Crafts (1934-39), R.C.A. (1946-49). *Exhib.:* Cairo, United Nations Art exhbn. (1944), Wakefield, Bradford, Leeds, Blackpool, Brighton, N.E.A.C., R.B.A., R.A., S.E.A., Pictures for Schools Exhbn.; one-man show, Walkers' Galleries (March, 1960). *Address:* 22 Little Common, Stanmore, Middx. *Signs work:* "Laycock."

LEA, Sheila; sculptor in plaster and bronze; *b* London, 16 Mar., 1901; *d* of Norman Maclagan; *m* C. A. E. Lea, C.B.E.; one *s. Educ.:* Grassendale, Southbourne; *studied art* at Bournemouth School of Art under B. Ingram and Herman Cawthra, Regent St. Polytechnic under H. Brownsword. *Exhib.:* R.A., Paris Salon, Bournemouth Arts Club, etc. *Work in permanent collection:* Russell-Cotes Loan Collection. *Official purchases:* Memorials to Lady Hawkins, Lyonshall; Sir Rudolf von Slatin Pasha, Omdurman; Sir Lee Stack, G.B.E., C.M.G., Khartoum. *Address:* 12 Berwick Rd., Bournemouth. *Club:* Bournemouth Arts. *Signs work:* "S. Lea."

LEACH, B., F.R.S.A., C.H. (1973). C.B.E., Hon. D.Litt., Order of the Sacred Treasure (2nd Class); American Ceramic Soc. Binns Medal (1950); potter, artist, author, lecturer; *b* Hong Kong, 5 Jan., 1887; *s* of Andrew John Leach, Puisne Judge, Straits Settlements; *m;* three *s,* three *d. Educ.:* Beaumont College, Slade School, London School of Art. *Exhib.:* Principal exhbns. England, Japan and Continent. *Work in permanent collections:* V. & A. National Art Collection, and many other English and overseas museums. *Publications:* A Potter's Book, A Potter's Portfolio, A Potter in Japan, Kenzan and his Tradition, Bernard Leach, a Potter's Work, The Unknown Craftsman—Soetsu Yanagi. *Address:* The Leach Pottery Ltd., St. Ives. *Signs work:* see appendix.

LEACROFT, Richard V. B., A.R.I.B.A., M.S.I.A., A.A. Hons. Dipl.; architect, stage designer, illustrator; *b* London, 16 July, 1914; *m* Helen Beal, actress; one *s,* one *d. Educ.:* Imperial Service College, Windsor; Architectural Assoc.; London Theatre Studio. *Official purchases:* National Gallery of Iraq, Leicester City Art Gallery. *Publications:* Building a House; Churches and Cathedrals; Historic Houses of Great Britain; Civic Theatre Design; The Theatre and You; The Theatre; Early Architecture in Britain; The Buildings of Ancient Egypt; Ancient Greece; Ancient Rome; Ancient Man; Ancient Mesopotamia; The Development of the English Playhouse. *Address:* Keven Lodge, Countesthorpe, Leics. *Signs work:* "Richard Leacroft."

LE BAS, Philip, R.B.A., N.E.A.C., A.T.D.; artist in oil; *b* St. Quentin de Baron,

France, 29 July, 1925; *s* of Major Herbert Arthur Le Bas, M.C. *Educ.:* Cardinal Vaughan School; *studied art* at Regent St. Polytechnic School (1948-51); Brighton College of Art (1951-52). *Exhib.:* R.A., R.B.A., Young Contemporaries. Walker's Gallery, Heffer's (Cambridge), Artists under 30, Trafford Gallery, Portal Gallery, London, also Madison 90 and Rehn, New York, and Danielli, Toronto. *Official purchases:* Min. of Works, B.E.A., the Church and many education committees. *Work repro.:* Art News and Review. *Address:* Combe Down, Shawford, nr. Winchester, Hants. *Signs work:* "P. Le Bas."

LE BAS, Rachel Ann, R.E., N.E.A.C.; Mem. A.W.G., Somerset Guild of Craftsmen; painter, line-engraver, etc.; *b* 9 Apr., 1923; *d* of Capt. R. S. Le Bas, Somerset Light Infantry (retd.). *Educ.:* W. Heath School, Sevenoaks; City and Guilds of London Art School (A. R. Middleton Todd, R.A., R.W.S., R.E.). *Exhib.:* R.A., N.E.A.C., R.B.A., London Group. *Address:* Winsford, nr. Minehead, Som. *Signs work:* "R. A. LE BAS."

LE BRETON, Edith, M.A.F.A. (1952), F.I.A.L. (1959); Manchester Academy of Fine Arts (1952); created and arranged first ever Le Breton International Children's Art for U.N.E.S.C.O., 2nd Exhbn. toured Gt. Britain (1972-73); first artist to discuss and show own paintings on experimental colour television; painter of industrial scenes and people; created original finger-paintings method in 1930, oils; *b* Salford, 26 Sept., 1912; *d* of Hugh Sapple, police officer. *Educ.:* Royal School of Art, Salford (1928-32); awarded scholarship, studentship and fellowship. *Exhib.:* one-man shows Salford Art Gallery, Medici London Gallery (1974, 1976), etc. Paintings in private collections Gt. Britain and overseas. *Address:* Magnolia, Thatched Cottage, School Lane, Dunham Massey, Altrincham, Cheshire. *Signs work:* see appendix.

LE BROCQUY, Louis, R.H.A. (1950), F.S.I.A. (1960), Hon. Litt.D., Dublin (1962), Chevalier de la Légion d'Honneur (1975); *b* Nov., 1916; *s* of Albert le Brocquy, M.A. *Educ.:* St. Gerard's, Bray, Ireland; *studied art:* self-taught. *Exhib.:* Gimpel Fils (London, Zürich, N.Y.); La Bussola, Turin; Robles (Los Angeles); Fondation Maeght; Venice Biennale (1956, prize-winner), etc. *Work in permanent collections:* Tate Gallery; V. & A. Museum; Arts Council; Carnegie Inst., Pittsburgh; Chicago Arts Club; Detroit Inst.; Albright Museum, Buffalo; Fort Worth Center, Texas; Foundation Maeght, St. Paul; Hirshhorn Foundation, N.Y.; Museo de Arte Moderna, São Paulo; municipal galleries of Dublin, Belfast, Sheffield, Leeds. *Books illustrated:* The Táin, trans. Thomas Kinsella (Dolmen Press, O.U.P., etc.), 1969. *Address:* c/o Gimpel Fils, 30 Davies St., London W1. *Signs work:* see appendix.

LEE, Erica, F.R.B.S., member, Portrait Sculptors; sculptor in clay or terra cotta; *b* Manchester; *d* of Walter Lee. *Studied art* under E. Whitney Smith, R.B.S., and Sir W. Reid Dick, R.A. *Exhib.:* R.A., R.S.A., W.A.G., G.I., Paris Salon. *Work in permanent collection:* The Nymph (bronze statuette) in Newport Art Gallery. *Address:* The Studio, 3A Acacia Rd., London NW8. *Club:* English Speaking Union. *Signs work:* "ERICA LEE."

LEE, Helen; awards: R.S.A. prize, Adam Bruce Thomson prize, John Moores prize; post graduate travelling scholar; artist in oil and water-colour; *b* Southport, 15 July, 1951; *d* of Vernon H. Lee, F.R.I.B.A. *Educ.:* Morrison's Academy for Girls, Crieff, Perthshire; *studied art* at Edinburgh College of Art (1970-76) under Robin Philipson, P.R.S.A., Alan Alexander. *Exhib.:* R.S.A. Galleries, Scottish Gallery, Edinburgh, W.A.G., Liverpool, R.A. *Address:* 15 Regent Terr., Edinburgh 7. *Signs work:* "Helen C. Lee."

LEE, Kah-Yeow; artist and antique collector; art teacher of the 12th and 13th

Provincial Middle Schools, Foochow (1923-25); Overseas Chinese High School, Singapore (1926-28); Chinese High School, Kuala Lumpur (1939), etc.; *b* Yungchun, China, 24 Apr., 1901. *Educ.:* Peking University; *studied art* at Shanghai College of Fine Arts. *Exhib.:* one-man shows: Amoy (1923); Kuala Lumpur (1962 and 1970); etc. *Work in permanent collections:* National Art Gallery, Kuala Lumpur; Nanyang University Museum, Singapore; Katesan House, Jakarta, etc. *Publications:* A collection of Kah-Yeow's painting and calligraphy (1956); A selection of Chinese Calligraphy and painting from the collection in Lee Kah-Yeow's villa (1970), etc. *Address:* 14 Bukit Ceylon, Kuala Lumpur, Malaysia. *Signs work:* "Lee Kah-Yeow."

LEE, Man-Fong; artist in oil and water-colours; Malino Scholarship for three years' study tour in the Netherlands (1947-49); court-painter at the Presidential Palaces of the Republic of Indonesia (1962-66); *b* Canton, China, 14 Nov., 1913; *m* Li Mu-Lan, pianist; one *s* (Lee Rern, painter); one *d* (Tory Lee Ie-Ling, printer). *Educ.:* St. Andrew's School, Singapore; *studied art:* self-taught. *Work in permanent collections:* National Art Gallery and Nanyang University Museum, Singapore; Merdeka and State Palaces, Jakarta; Presidential Palace, Bogor; etc. *Mural commissioned:* Ramayana Hall of Hotel Indonesia. *Publications:* Selected works of Indonesia overseas Chinese art Workers' mission (Peking, 1958); Paintings and Statues from the Collection of President Sukarno of the Republic of Indonesia (Tokyo, 1964); Paintings from the Collection of Dr. Ir. Sukarno, President of the Republic of Indonesia (Peking, 1965). *Address:* 51 Greenwood Ave., Singapore 11. *Clubs:* Federation of Art Circles in Indonesia and Federation neerlandaise des associations d'artistes professionels, Singapore Art Society and South-East Asia Art Assoc., etc. *Signs work:* "M. F. Lee" and see appendix.

LEE, Rern; painter in oil colour; *b* Jakarta, Indonesia, 19 Sept., 1938; *s* of Lee Man-Fong and Li Mu-Lan; *m* Siew Pui-Sam; one *d*. *Educ.:* Singapore and Jakarta; graduated at Nanyang Academy of Fine Arts, Singapore. Worked in father's studio under his guidance for several years, then travelled and worked in England, France, Italy, Holland, Germany and Singapore (1969-72). *Exhib.:* one-man shows: Singapore (1970), etc. *Work in permanent collections:* Nanyang University Museum, Singapore; Presidential Palaces, Jakarta and Bogor, etc. *Address:* Jalan Gedong 11-A, Jakarta, Indonesia. *Clubs:* Society of Chinese Artists in Indonesia and South-East Asia Art Assoc., etc. *Signs work:* "R. Lee."

LEE, Rosie, D.F.A. (1957), painter in oil, *b* Rotterdam, 23 Dec., 1935; *d* of James Peters; *m* Terry Lee; four *s*. *Educ.:* Abbeydale Girls' Grammar School, Sheffield; *studied art* at Sheffield College of Art (1953-55), Slade School (1955-58). *Work in permanent collections:* Walker Art Gallery (Schools Collection), Hull Educ. Authority, W. Riding of Yorks. Educ. Authority, Surrey Educ. Authority, Dept. of Environment, Coventry City Art Gall. *Address:* Calton Houses, Calton Lees, Beeley, Matlock, Derbyshire. *Signs work:* see appendix.

LEE, Terry Glyn, D.F.A. (Lond.), 1957; artist in oil and teacher; teaching Sheffield College of Art; *b* Sheffield, 28 Oct., 1932; *s* of G. W. Lee; *m* Rosemary Christina Peters; four *s*. *Educ.:* King Edward VII School, Sheffield; *studied art* at Sheffield College of Art; Slade School of Fine Art (1955-58); Sir William Coldstream. *Work in permanent collections:* Liverpool Art Gallery, Ferens Art Gallery, Hull, Coventry Art Gallery, Oldham Art Gallery, The Arts Council. *Address:* Calton Houses, Calton Lees, Beeley, nr. Matlock, Derbyshire. *Signs work:* "Terry Lee."

LEE-JOHNSON, Eric; painter; Founder and Hon. Life Mem. Waihi Arts Centre, Hon. Life Mem., Northland Art Soc.; *b* Suva, Fiji, 1908. *Art educ.:* Elam

School of Fine Arts (Auckland), London Central School. Represented all major New Zealand art galleries, Auckland and Victoria Univ. collections, Hocken (Dunedin) and Turnbull (Wellington) Libraries' collections. Awarded Assoc. N.Z. Art Societies' Fellowship (1954-55). Editor Arts in N.Z. Yearbook (1950-51). Hon. Keeper, Rutherford H.S. and Waihi College Collections N.Z. Art. *Publications:* Eric Lee-Johnson—a New Zealand Painter (E. H. McCormick, Pauls, and Phoenix House, 1956); Artist in Northland (National Film Unit documentary, 1957); As I See It—Drawings from North New Zealand (Collins, Auckland and London, 1969). *Address:* Snake Hill, Box 4194, Kamo, N.Z. *Signs work:* "Lee-Johnson."

LEESON, Laurence Joseph, A.T.D. (1953); painter and lecturer; *b* Leeds, 23 June, 1930; *s* of Frederick Leeson; *m;* three *d. Educ.:* Sandbach School, and Priory School for Boys, Shrewsbury; *studied art* at Shrewsbury Art School (1948-49), Birmingham College of Art (1949-53). *Exhib.:* Young Contemporaries, Arts Council, Café Royale, Bradford Spring Shows, Artists of Fame and Promise, University of Keele, Piccadilly Gallery, Brinken Gallery, Stockholm, Hull University; Gulbenkian Fellow, University of Keele (1963-64). *Official purchases:* H.R.H. the Princess Margaret, Countess of Snowdon, V. & A. Print Collection, University of Keele, Hanley Art Gallery, Plesch Collection, Granada Television, Yorks. Educ. Committee. *Address:* The Old School, Spring Rd., Market Weighton, Yorks.

LEFTWICH, Peter; painter in oil, tempera, fresco; *b* London, 13 Oct., 1913; *s* of Charles Gerrans Leftwich, C.B.E., I.C.S., retired; *m* Lorraine Ellis; two *s. Educ.:* privately; *studied art* at Durban School of Art; Michaelis School of Art, University of Cape Town under Prof. John Wheatley, A.R.A. and Mrs. Grace Wheatley (1932-36). *Exhib.:* R.A., R.P., Paris Salon (1960), Exhbn. of Dominion Art, R.I. Galleries (1936) and at all principal exhbns. in S. Africa; one-man shows in Durban and Johannesburg. *Work in permanent collections:* South African National Gallery, Durban Art Gallery. *Official purchases:* as above. *Address:* Backworth, Eston, Natal. *Club:* Arts, Dover St., London. *Signs work:* "Peter Leftwich."

LEGER, Harold Larmuth; art dealer; *b* 3 May, 1897; *s* of Joseph Leger, art dealer; *m*; three *d. Educ.:* Owen's, Islington. *Address:* 13 Old Bond St., London.

LEGG, Owen, F.F.P.S.; printmaker and artist in oil on board, lino-cut prints, abstract constructions; *b* London, 1 Aug., 1935. *Educ.:* Alleyns School, Dulwich; *studied art* at Tunbridge Wells Adult Education Centre. *Exhib.:* York University, Tunbridge Wells Library, Loggis Gallery. *Work in permanent collections:* Greenwich Library, Graphotek, Berlin. *Publication:* York Mystery Play—The Armourers Play. *Address:* 152 Hadlow Rd., Tonbridge, Kent. *Signs work:* "Owen Legg."

LE HUNTE-COOPER, Rosamund; artist in oil and pen and wash; teacher of art in London schools (1964-66) and at Runton Hill School (1950-51); *d* of Dr. Robert Le Hunte-Cooper, M.D., B.S., M.R.C.S., etc.; *studied art* at Heatherley's, London, under Frederick Whiting, R.P., R.W.S. *Exhib.:* Royal Society of Portrait Painters, Paris Salon, R.O.I., R.B.A., R.S.A., N.E.A.C., Marine Artists, S.W.A., private exhibition at Flint House Galleries, Norwich, and main galleries in England on tour exhibitions. *Work repro.:* in La Revue Modern, Paris. *Address:* Sea Horses, 14 St. Nicholas Pl., Sheringham, Norfolk.

LEIGH, Roger, B.Arch., M.C.D. (1947-53); sculptor in timber, steel and photomontage; Lecturer II, Exeter School of Art; *b* Broadwell, Glos., 15 Aug., 1925; *m* Patricia; one *s*, one *d. Educ.:* Radley; Liverpool University; assistant to

Barbara Hepworth (1954). *Exhib.:* one-man shows since 1964; *New* Vision Centre, Arnolfini, Bristol, Queen's Square, Leeds, Ulster, The Photographers, Oxford, and Portsmouth galleries. B.B.C. TV film "Volumes and Voids, No. 2." *Work in permanent collections:* Cornwall Education Committee, Leeds, Ulster and Portsmouth City Galleries, Exeter University. *Address:* Sorbus, Aldbourne, Wilts.

LEIGH-PEMBERTON, John, A.F.C.; painter in oil, tempera and gouache; *b* London, 18 Oct., 1911; *s* of Cyril Leigh-Pemberton; *m* Doreen Beatrice Townshend-Webster. *Educ.:* Eton; *studied art* in London, *c* 1928-32. *Exhib.:* R.A., R.O.I., N.S., and all principal London and provincial galleries and in the Commonwealth; past member R.O.I., N.S. *Work in permanent collections:* National Maritime Museum, Imperial War Museum, provincial galleries and many institutions; pictures for the Royal Navy, Royal Air Force, Brigade of Guards, etc.; also in Chicago, Washington, D.C. *Work repro. and publications:* Festival Almanack (Whitbread), Royal Progress (Shell-Mex), Whitbread Craftsmen (Whitbread), Shell Guide to Wild Life (Phoenix House), A Book of British Garden Flowers (Wills and Hepworth), A Book of Butterflies, Moths and Other Insects (Wills and Hepworth); many series of paintings, chiefly with natural history subjects, for Midland Bank Ltd., British Wildlife, Rarities and Introductions (Kaye and Ward) with Richard Fitter, Vanishing Wild Animals of the World (Kaye and Ward) with Richard Fitter, African Mammals, Australian Mammals, North American Mammals, European Mammals, Asian Mammals, South American Mammals (all pub. Wills and Hepworth). *Address:* 5 Roehampton Gate, London SW15. *Signs work:* "Leigh-Pemberton" or see appendix.

LEIGHTON, Clare; artist, wood-engraver, illustrator, author; *b* London, 12 Apr., 1901; *d* of Robert Leighton, author. *Educ.:* privately; *studied art* at Brighton School of Art, Slade School; Central School of Arts and Crafts. *Exhib.:* Venice, R.A., N.E.A.C., Soc. Wood-engravers, R.E. *Work in permanent collections:* B.M., V. & A., National Gallery of Canada, Art Inst. of Chicago, Boston, Cleveland, Baltimore, Los Angeles. *Designed* for Steuben Glass and Wedgwood; 33 windows St. Paul's Cathedral, Worcester, Mass.; 3 windows church on Cape Cod; 6 windows Lutheran Church, Waterbury, Conn.; mosaic Convent Chapel, Monroe. *Publications:* Four Hedges, The Farmer's Year, Country Matters, Southern Harvest, Sometimes Never, Give Us This Day, Woodcuts and Wood-Engraving, Wood-Engraving of the 1930's, Tempestuous Petticoat, Where Land Meets Sea, The Musical Box, The Wood That Came Back. *Address:* Woodbury, Conn., U.S.A. *Club:* Cosmopolitan, New York City. *Signs work:* see appendix.

LEISHMAN, Robert, D.A. (Edin., 1938), S.S.A. (1950), R.S.W. (1970); artist in oil, gouache and water-colour; *b* Inverkeithing, Fife, 30 Oct., 1916; *s* of Robert Leishman; *m* Patricia Stuart Edgar. *Educ.:* Dunfermline High School. War service, 1940-46. *Exhib.:* First Group Exhib. Art, Group 7 (Dunfermline, 1939); one-man shows: Glasgow (1951), St. Andrews (1950), Dundee (1952), Largo (1967), Edinburgh (1971); two-man shows: Edinburgh (1960, 1963, 1964), Glasgow (1964), exhibits annually in numerous mixed shows throughout the country and with several groups. *Address:* 15 Charleston Drive, Dundee DD2 2HF.

LE JEUNE, James George, A.R.H.A., R.S.M.A.; painter of portraits, landscapes and seascapes in oil, water-colour, pencil; freelance professional painter; *b* Saskatoon, Canada, 24 May, 1910; *s* of Anthony Le Jeune, musician. *Educ.:* in France, and Aston-le-Walls House, Northants; *studied art:* early training under Maitre Gregoire and Madame Guillaumot Adam of the Paris Salon, later at Heatherley's, Byam Shaw School and Students League, N.Y. *Work in permanent* *collections:* National Gallery, Dublin and Cardiff. *Address:* 38 Baggot La., Dublin, Eire. *Club:* United Arts, Dublin. *Signs work:* "LE JEUNE."

LEK, Karel, R.C.A., A.T.D., member Society of Wood-Engravers; artist in oil, water-colour and graphic media, and fine art dealer; *b* Antwerp, 7 June, 1929; *s* of Hendrick Lek, artist and fine art dealer. *Studied art* at Liverpool College of Art; *m;* two children. *Exhib.:* National Museum for Wales, R.A., R.C.A., Howard Roberts Gallery, Cardiff, Woodstock Gallery, W.1, Arts Council, Bangor Gallery. *Work in permanent collections:* University Coll. of N. Wales, Contemporary Art Soc. for Wales, Tegfryn Gallery, Anglesey Menai Bridge, Anglesey County Council, Flintshire Education Com. *Work repro.:* Football and the Fine Arts, Time Educ. Supp., Studio. *Address:* Studio House, Beaumaris, Anglesey.

LENG-SMITH, Barbara; Hon. Mention, Paris Salon, Silver Medal; portrait painter in oil, water-colour and pastel specialising in children; *b* Isle of Man, 7 Mar., 1922; *d* of E. Gibson Teare; *m* Ralph Leng-Smith; one *s,* four *d. Educ.:* Edinburgh and London; *studied art* at Manchester under Harry Rutherford. *Exhib.:* one-man show: Tibb Lane Gallery, Manchester; R.S.P.P., Paris Salon, R.S.A., Edinburgh, Manchester Academy of Fine Arts, Galerie Vallombreuse, Biarritz. *Address:* Miramar, Arthog Rd., Hale, Cheshire. *Club:* Société des Artistes Français. *Signs work:* "Leng-Smith."

LEONARD, Douglas Michael, painter and illustrator; *b* Bangalore, India, 25 June 1933; *s* of Maj. D. G. R. Leonard, IXth Jat Regt. *Educ.:* Stonyhurst College; *studied art* at St. Martin's School of Art (1954-57). *Exhib.:* English Explorations at Fischer Fine Art (Summer, 1972); first one-man show at Fischer Fine Art (1974). *Work repro.:* includes illustrations in magazines and books, book jackets, film posters, etc. in Britain, Europe and the U.S.A. *Address:* 30 Egerton Gdns., London SW3. *Signs work:* "LEONARD."

LESLIE, Cecil Mary; artist in aquatint, painter and illustrator; *b* 1900; *d* of Sir Norman Alexander Leslie, K.B.E. and Mimy Muriel Gambier; one adopted *d. Exhib.:* R.A., R.S.A., and London, provincial, and Continental exhbns. *Work in permanent collections:* B.M. (six aquatints). *Publications:* 35 illustrated books. *Address:* The Old School House, Blakeney, Norfolk. *Club:* Women's Provisional. *Signs work:* see appendix.

LESLIE, Ian Murray, C.B.E., Hon. F.R.I.B.A.; editor Building, formerly The Builder (1948-70), vice-chairman The Builder Ltd. (1970-75); mem. Editorial Advisory Panel (1975–); *b* 13 Mar., 1905; *s* of J. G. Leslie, M.B., C.M.; *m* (1) Josette Délétraz; one *s*; (2) Vivian Williams. *Educ.:* St. Paul's School. *Address:* 3/64 Hamilton Terr., London NW8 9UJ. *Clubs:* Savage, M.C.C., Architectural Association.

LESTER, M. A.: see LESZCZYŃSKI, Michal Antoni Lester.

LESTER, Peggy G. E.; *b* Walsall, Staffs., England; *d* of Alfred Davies, farmer. Art dealer in paintings, drawings, water-colour, prints, wood carvings and sculpture. Proprietress of Lester Art Gallery, established in 1955 in Montego Bay, Jamaica, West Indies. *Address:* Lester Art Gallery, 20 Market St., Montego Bay, Jamaica, W1. P.O. Box 590.

LESZCZYŃSKI, Michal Antoni Lester, F.R.S.A.; artist in oil, water-colours, drawings and mural paintings; Extra Master, Mariner Polish Merchant Navy and Master (Marine Board of Jamaica): 1939-45 Star, Atlantic Star, War Medal; *b* Dolina, Poland, 26 Mar., 1906; *s* of Franciszek Leszczyński, civil servant and industrialist; *m* Peggy Gertrude Emily Davies. *Educ.:* Warsaw, Krakow, and State Nautical College, Tczew, Chipin School of Music, Warsaw Konserwatorjum and

Academy of Art, Krakow, and privately in England. *Exhib.:* Zacheta Warsaw, R.A., London, R.I., N.S., and three one-man exhbns. in London (1938, 1946 and 1949), New York (1969). *Work in permanent collections:* in institutions in England, Poland and U.S.A. *Work repro.:* in several publications of England, Poland, U.S.A., France and Jamaica. *Publications:* How to Draw Sail and Sea (1944, 1946), Marine Perspective (1949), etc. *Address:* 20 Market St., Montego Bay, Jamaica, W.I. P.O. Box 590; and The Anchorage, Belmont, St. James, Jamaica. *Signs work:* see appendix.

LEVEE, John, B.A., Grand Prix, Academie Julian (1951); Grand Prix Biennal de Paris (1959); Ford Fellowship (1969); painter in oil, gouache, crayon; visiting Professor of Art, University of Illinois (1965), New York University (1967-68), University Southern California (1970-72); *b* Los Angeles, 10 Apr., 1924. *Educ.:* University Calif., New School for Social Research, N.Y.; *studied art* at New School. *Work in permanent collections:* Kunst Museum, Basle; Smith College Museum; Museum of Modern Art, N.Y.; Stedelijk Museum, Amsterdam; Musée du Havre; Towner Art Gallery; Baltimore Museum; Columbus Gallery of Fine Art; Whitney Museum, N.Y.; Musée d'art Moderne, Paris; Corcoran Gallery, Washington D.C.; Guggenheim Museum, N.Y. *Work repro.:* 16 Painters of Young, School of Paris, Abstract Art, Dictionary of Abstract Art, Concise History of Modern Art. *Address:* 119 rue Notre Dame des Champs, Paris, 6. *Signs work:* "Levee."

LEVENE, Ben, A.R.A.; painter (genre) in oils, water-colours; teaches part-time, Camberwell School of Art; *b* London, 23 Dec., 1938; *m* Jane; two *d. Educ.:* St. Clement Dane's Grammar School; *studied art* at Slade School (1956-61), Boise Scholarship (1961-62). *Address:* 26 Netherby Rd., Honor Oak, London SE23. *Signs work:* Usually signed on back.

LEWENSTEIN, Eileen, A.T.D., F.S.D-C.; potter in ceramics (stoneware and porcelain); co-editor, Ceramic Review; council mem., Craftsmen Potters Assoc.; *b* London, 1925; *m* Oscar Lewenstein; two *s. Educ.:* Red Maids School, Bristol; *studied art* at West of England College of Art under George Sweet; University of London Institute of Education under Clarence Waite. *Exhib.:* Vallauris Biennale (1974), Craftsman's Art V. & A. (1973), International Ceramics, Calgary (1973). *Work in permanent collections:* V. & A., Glasgow A.G. and Museum, Paisley Museum, Museum of Decorative Arts, Prague, Museum of Contemporary Ceramics, Bechyne. *Publication:* New Ceramics (Studio Vista 1974). *Address:* 11 Western Esplanade, Hove, Sussex, BN4 1WE. *Signs work:* "Eileen Lewenstein" and see appendix.

LEWIN, Keith K., F.R.S.A., A.R.D.S., Diploma of Membership International Society for Education through Art, D.F.A. (Hons.), London Art College; artist and portrait painter in oils, water-colours, pastels and other mediums, and teacher; *b* Jamaica, 19 Apr., 1931: *s* of Gerald Lewin, store employee; *m* Mary; one *s*, one *d. Educ.:* Government Technical High School; *studied art* at Jamaica School of Arts and Crafts, Dept., of Extra-Mural Studies, University of West Indies, Brooklyn Museum Art School, New York, Art Students' League of New York, School of Fine and Applied Arts. *Work in permanent collections:* galleries and museums in America, Europe, Trinidad, West Indies, Canada and Jamaica. *Work in private collections:* Lady Caradon, Mr. William L. Lassiter, Dr. Philip M. Sherlock, Sir Thomas and Lady Taylor of London, Dr. Hugh W. Springer, Mr. Robert McGregor, Sir Arthur A. Lewis, Mrs. Edna Manley, Mr. Charles J. Lewin. *Address:* 1865 52nd St., Brooklyn, New York, 11204. *Signs work:* "Keith Lewin."

LEWIS, Charles Walter Edward, A.R.C.A., F.R.B.S., A.W.G., Royal Exhibition and Continuation Scholarship (1946); sculptor in stone and wood; Head of Sculpture, Kingston Polytechnic; *b* Southsea, 18 July, 1916; *s* of Charles A. Lewis; *m* Margaret Parkinson; two *s,* one *d. Educ.:* Portsmouth Southern Secondary School; *studied art* at Portsmouth College of Art (1932-36), Royal College of Art, under Prof. Richard Garbe (1936-39). *Work in permanent collections:* sculpture commissioned by the Ministry of Public Building and Works, The G.L.C. and several private architects. *Address:* Nettlecombe Lodge, Chidgley, Watchet, Somerset TA23 OLT.

LEWIS, Dennis Reginald, A.R.W.A. (1965), A.S.I.A. (1969); artist in oil, acrylics, perspex; creative director (advertising); President, Bristol Savages (1973); *b* Bristol, 2 Apr., 1928; *s* of Francis George Henry Lewis; *m* Irene Margaret; one *s,* two *d. Educ.:* F.A.S., Bristol; *studied art* at No. 3 Army College, 1948, West of England College of Art, 1948-52. *Address:* Nutgrove, 5 The Dingle, Coombe Dingle, Bristol BS9 2PA. *Club:* Bristol Savages. *Signs work:* "Dennis Lewis."

LEWIS, John N. C., F.S.I.A.; typographer, designer and author; *b* 11 Dec., 1912; *m. Educ.:* Charterhouse School; Goldsmiths' College School of Art. *Publications:* Graphic Design (with John Brinkley) (Routledge); Typography: Basic Principles; and Illustration with Bob Gill (Studio Vista); Printed Ephemera (Cowell/Faber); The Twentieth Century Book (Studio Vista); Reproducing Art (with Edwin Smith) (Cowell/Faber); A Taste for Sailing (Adlard Coles); Anatomy of Printing (Faber); Small Craft Conversion (Adlard Coles); Heath Robinson (Constable); Vintage Boats (David & Charles). *Address:* Meadow Cottage, Great Bealings, Woodbridge, Suffolk. *Signs work:* "JOHN LEWIS."

LEWIS, Kathleen Margaret; painter in oil; *b* Lichfield, Staffs., 27 Sept., 1911; *d* of H. G. Fausset-Osborne, civil servant; *m* 1st, Morland Lewis, decd.; 2nd, Sir James Richards, formerly editor of The Architectural Review. *Educ.:* at home; *studied art* at Chelsea School of Art. *Exhib.:* London and provincial galleries and in America, one-man exhbn., Leicester Galleries (1953 and 1971). *Work in permanent collections:* Arts Council, National Museum of Wales, Cambridge and Sussex Schools, Carlisle City Art Gallery. *Address:* 29 Fawcett St., London SW10. *Signs work:* "KIT LEWIS."

LEWIS, Michael; senior lecturer in Fine Art at Croydon College of Art since 1961; *b* Cheltenham, 25 Oct. 1925; *s* of Rev. Ivor Lewis; *m* Dyné Hudson. *Studied art* at Regent St. Polytechnic School of Art. Chairman of Young Contemporaries (1953). Teaching posts held at Ealing, Shoreham, Worthing, Chichester and Cheltenham. *Exhib.:* Young Contemporaries, London Group, National Museum of Wales, R.A., R.B.A., R.O.I., R.S.W., R.G.I., S.E.A., etc.; one-man shows: Scunthorpe Art Gallery and Trafford Gallery. *Official purchases:* Essex, L.C.C., Swindon, Glamorgan, Monmouth, Northumberland Educ. Com., Hereford, Scunthorpe and New Zealand Art Galleries. *Publication:* A Sketchbook in Art History (Leonard Hill, 1968). *Address:* White Lodge, 53 Addiscombe Rd., Croydon CRO 6SB. *Signs work:* see appendix.

LEYDEN, John Michael; hon. mem., S.A. Assoc. of Draughtsmen; cartoonist in black and white; artist in water-colour and etching; staff cartoonist, Daily News, since 1939; *b* Grangemouth, Scotland, 21 Nov., 1908; *s* of Patrick Joseph Leyden; *m* Annabel Eugenie Wishart; one *s,* three *d. Educ.:* St. Aloysius College, Glasgow; *studied art* at Durban School of Art, Heatherley's, Central Schools of Arts and Crafts. *Exhib.:* Natal Soc. of Artists, Durban Art Gallery (one-man shows). *Work in permanent collections:* in Africana Museum, Johannesburg (cartoons). *Publica-*

tions: eleven books of cartoons. *Address:* 233 Nicholson Rd., Durban, Natal, S.A. *Club:* Patron, Natal Motorcycle and Car Club. *Signs work:* see appendix.

LEYGUE, Louis; Président de l'Académie des Beaux-Arts (1976); Membre de l'Institut; sculptor; Prof., head of studio, L'École Nationale Supérieure des Beaux-Arts since 1945; *b* Bourg-en-Bresse, Ain, 25 Aug., 1905; *s* of Albert Leygue; *m* Marianne Cochet, painter; two *s*. *Educ.:* Lycée Charlemagne, Paris; *studied art* at L'École Nationale des Arts décoratifs, Paris, L'École Nationale des Beaux-Arts, Paris, Villa Medicis, Rome. *Work in permanent collections:* Museum of Modern Art, Paris. *Official purchases:* Phenix Université de Caen, Auditorium Maison de la Radio, Paris, French Embassy, Ottawa, Fontaine des Corolles, Paris la Défense, Palais de Justice, Abidjan, Piave, Nantua. *Address:* 6 rue de Docteur Blanche, Paris XVIe. *Signs work:* "LOUIS LEYGUE."

LEYSHON, Thyrza Anne, S.M., Assoc. Mem. Société des Artistes Français, Paris Salon Medaille d'Argent (1968), Medaille d'Or and Prix Rowland Award (1973); *b* Swansea; *d* of Thomas Howell Leyshon. *Studied miniature painting* privately (after retirement from Civil Service) under the late Mrs. Ethol Court, A.R.M.S. *Exhib.:* Circle National Belge d'Art et Esthetique, Brussels (1963), Les Arts en Europe, Brussels (1964), then Member of Southall School of Miniaturists, Paris Salon (1962-65), R.A., R.M.S., R.S. Gall. Edinburgh, Glyn Vivian A.G., Swansea, Festival of Wales (Welsh Artists). *Address:* Wynn Edge, Killay, Swansea. *Signs work:* "Thyrza Anne Leyshon."

LILLEY, Geoffrey Ivan; painter in oil, author and illustrator in line and water-colour of seascapes, animal portraits, polar abstracts; *b* Cambridge, 1 May, 1930; *s* of Ernest Lilley; *m* Marguerite E.; one *d*. *Educ.:* Cambridge; *studied art* at Cambridge Technical College. *Exhib.:* St. Ives, Cornwall, and major galleries in Sussex; one-man shows at London, Oxford, Bourton-on-the-Water, and Seaford. *Work repro.:* Artist, Arts Review, Leisure Painter, etc.; author of several books and over 100 articles on art and craft subjects. *Address:* Roosters, Chiddingly, Lewes, Sussex. *Signs work:* see appendix.

LILLFORD, Ralph, A.R.C.A.; painter; taught at Slough College (1960-64); senior lecturer, Borough Road College (1964); visiting lecturer, Colleges of Art and V. & A.; *b* 6 Nov., 1932; *s* of Walter and Winefred Lillford; *m* 1st, B. M. Watson, divorced 1970; 2nd, M. G. O. Heritage; one *s*. *Studied art* at Doncaster School of Art (1948-52); Royal College of Art (1954-57); National Service (R.A.E.C.), Suez Canal Zone (1952-54). *Exhib.:* R.A., R.B.A., London and provincial galleries. *Work in permanent collections:* British Museum, Imperial War Museum, R.A., private collections: Holland, U.S.A., France, U.K. *Address:* 221 Jersey Rd., Osterley, Middx. *Signs work:* see appendix.

LIN, Richard Show Yu; First Prize, Open Painting Exhibition, N. Ireland (1966), William Frew Memorial Award, Pittsburgh International (1967); painter in oil; *b* Taiwan, 31 Jan., 1933; *m* Ann Lin; two *s*, three *d*. *Educ.:* Millfield, Somerset. *Work in permanent collections:* Tate Gallery, Leicester Museum, Whitworth Art Gallery, Albright-Knox Art Gallery, Walker Art Gallery, State Museum, Leverkusen, Gemeente Museum, Boymans Museum, Sao Paulo Museum, Ateneum Museum, Helsinki, Art Gallery of Ontario, Brooklyn Museum, N.Y., Carnegie Institute Pittsburgh. *Address:* Gwynfryn Hall, Taliesin, Machynlleth, Powys. *Signs work:* "RICHARD LIN," "LIN SHOW YU," "LIN."

LINDLEY, Kenneth Arthur, R.E., A.T.D., (1950), M.S.I.A. (1950), mem. Soc. of Wood Engravers; artist in engraving, drawing, collage, photography, writer; Principal, Herefordshire College of Art; *b* London, 28 June, 1928; *s* of Wilfrid Lindley; *m* Joyce Ruth; two *s*, one *d*. *Educ.:* St. Clement Danes Grammar School;

studied art at Ealing and Hornsey Schools of Art. *Exhib.:* one-man shows, London, etc. *Publications:* include Coastline (Hutchinson, 1967), Of Graves and Epitaphs (Hutchinson, 1965), Chapels and Meeting Houses (John Baker, 1969), Woodblock Engravers (David and Charles, 1970); also design, print and publish my own works under imprint, Pointing Finger Press. *Address:* 4 Sedgefield Rd., Hereford. *Signs work:* "Lindley."

LINDNER, Doris L. M.; sculptress in stone, bronze, concrete; modeller of horses and bulls for the Royal Worcester Porcelain Co.; *b* Llanyre, Radnorshire, 8 July, 1896; *d* of George M. Lindner; one *s*, adopted. *Educ.:* Norland Place School, Holland Park Avenue, W.; *studied art* at Caldrons Animal School, Kensington, St. Martin's School of Art, British Academy, Rome. *Exhib.:* R.A., Royal Glasgow Inst., London Group, W.I.A.C., International Faculty of Arts, R.B.A., Hampstead Artists Council. *Address:* Studio Cottage, Broad Campden, Glos. *Signs work:* "Doris Lindner."

LINDSAY, Daryl, Sir, K.B., LL.D. (Hons. Causa Aust. Nat. Univ.), A.R.W.S.; Mem. Commonwealth Art Advisory Board; painter in oil and water-colour; *b* Creswick, Victoria, 31 Dec., 1889; *s* of Robert Charles Lindsay, M.D.; *m* Joan A'Beckett Weigall. *Educ.:* State School and Grammar School, Creswick; *studied art* at Slade School. *Work in permanent collections:* V. & A., National Galleries of Victoria, S. Australia, N.S.W., W. Australia, Queensland and Hobart. *Publications:* Digger Book, Story of the Red Cross (with my wife), History of Felton Bequest, The Leafy Tree. *Address:* Mulberry Hill, Baxter, Victoria, Australia. *Clubs:* Melbourne, V.R.C. *Signs work:* see appendix.

LINFERT, Carl, Dr. rer. pol. (1924), Dr. phil. (1927); editor; asst. on Wallraf Richartz Museum (1928-29); art critic, Frankfurter Zeitung (1930-43), Kurier, Berlin (1946-49); Chief Editor Third Programme, Radio Cologne (1949-67); *b* Cologne, 14 July, 1900; *s* of Theodore Linfert, watchmaker; *m* Araca Linfert; one *s*. *Educ.:* Gymnasium. *Publications:* Die Grundlagen der Architekturzeichnung. In: Künstwissenschaftliche Forschungen, Band I, Heraüsg. von Otto Paecht. (1931), Albrecht Altdorfer, Die Enthüellung der Landschaft. (1938), Alt-Koelner Meister. (1941), Hieronymus Bosch (1959), Grundstoff der Bilder, Auswahlder Schriften von Julius Meier-Graefe (1959), Ueber die Zuschauer der Maler. Bild Eines Jahrzehnts (1966). *Address:* Cologne, Marienburger Str. 37.

LINNQVIST, Hilding Gunnar Oskar; Prins Eugen gold medallist (1945), St. Erik medal of Stockholm city; artist in oil, water-colour, frescoes, mosaic, tapestry-cartoons; *b* Stockholm, 20 Apr., 1891; *s* of Oskar Linnqvist; *m* Marta Delin. *Educ.:* Royal Academy, Stockholm. *Exhib.:* Stockholm, Paris, London, Berlin, Hamburg, Lubeck, Brussels, Carnegie Inst., Pittsburgh, Golden Gate Exhbn., San Francisco (1939). Biennale Venise, etc. *Work in permanent collections:* Stockholm, Paris, Gothenburg, Malmo, Oslo, Copenhagen, Helsingfors Museums. *Monumental tapestries:* City Library, Stockholm (1932), Swedish Parliament (1970); *frescoes:* Östersund Church (1940), Sophia Church, Stockholm (1951), Folklore Museum, Stockholm (1953), etc.; *mosaic:* Karlstad School (1960). *Publications:* Tankar om Konst (Stockholm, 1944), Grekisk Resa (1946), The Saga of Gösta Berling, by Selma Lagerlöf (illustrated by Hilding Linnqvist). *Address:* Bastugatan 21, Stockholm, Sweden. *Signs work:* see appendix.

LINTON, Robert George, D.A., A.T.D., A.R.U.A., Arts Council Travel Scholarship to Italy; artist in oil and bronze portraiture; Head of Grammar School Art Dept.; *b* Donegal, 4 Feb., 1930; *s* of the late Robert G. Linton; *m* Doreen Mary Shaw, B.A.; two *s*. *Studied art* at Belfast College of Art; London Central School of Art and Crafts. *Exhib.:* three Arts Council sponsored one-man exhbns.

in Belfast. *Address:* 100 Glenhead Rd., Limavady, Co. Londonderry. *Clubs:* Royal Ulster Academy, National Society for Art Education. *Signs work:* "Linton" followed by date.

LISHMAN, Walter, B.Sc. (Durham, 1926), D.Th.P.T. (Durham, 1927), M.R.S.T., Teacher's Cert., M.S.G.A.; Lecturer in Art, College of Venerable Bede, Durham; etcher and wood-engraver; *b* Wolviston, Stockton-on-Tees; *s* of Fred P. Lishman, schoolmaster; *m* 1st, Freda Piper (deceased); one *s*; 2nd, E. M. Hay. *Educ.:* Johnston Secondary School, Durham, and Armstrong College, Newcastle upon Tyne (Durham University); *studied art* at King Edward VII School of Art, Newcastle upon Tyne. *Address:* 7 Bainbridge, Holme Rd., Sunderland. *Club:* Sunderland Art. *Signs work:* "W. Lishman."

LISSIM, Simon, Hon. R.M.S. (1950), F.R.S.A. (1950); Honorary Corresponding Mem., U.S.A., R.S.A. (1955), Benjamin Franklin F.R.S.A. (1959), vice-pres. of Council (1960), Silver medal, Paris (1925), Gold medal, Barcelona (1929), Two grand dipl. d'honneur, Paris (1937), hon. fellow, American Scandinavian Foundation, U.S.A. (1954), mem., Salon d'automne, Soc. of Artists Decorators, Paris, Audubon Artists, New York; chairman, Nat. Selection Com. on Fulbright Awards in the Field of Painting, Sculpture and Graphic Arts (1956); artist-painter in water-colour, designer, educator, lecturer in art; formerly Prof. of Art, City College of New York; former head, art education project, New York Public Library; *b* Kiev, Russia, 24 Oct., 1900; *s* of Michel Lissim, banker; *m* 1st, the late Irene Zalchoupine (decd. 1945); 2nd, Dorothea Howson Waples. *Educ.:* Nauomenko School, Kiev; Sorbonne and École du Louvre, Paris; *studied art* in Russia and in Paris, with Leon Bakst, George Loukomsky, etc. *Exhib.:* Several International exhbns., at most Paris galleries, Audubon Artists, New York, Sadarbs, Riga, and more than 60 one-man shows in U.S.A. and in Europe. *Work in permanent collections:* in 62 European and U.S. Museums. *Official purchases:* French Government and City of Paris, Knight Cross, Academic Palms (French), 1958. *Work repro.:* in six monographs and many books. *Address:* 55 Magnolia Dr., Dobbs Ferry, New York, U.S.A. *Signs work:* "Simon Lissim" and year.

LISTER, Edward D'Arcy, A.R.C.A.; painter in oils, water-colour, gouache; colour prints; lecturer at Bournemouth and Poole College of Art; *b* Horsforth, 29 Oct., 1911; *s* of James D'Arcy Lister; *m* Sylvia Emily Dawson. *Educ.:* Aireborough Grammar School; *studied art* at Leeds College of Art (1928-33) and R.C.A. under Gilbert Spencer (1933-37). *Exhib.:* R.A. and provincial galleries. *Work in permanent collections:* V. & A. Museum, Southampton Art Gallery, Philadelphia Museum. Mural decorations: Percival Leigh Library, Leeds; Victoria Home, Bournemouth. *Work repro.:* in La Revue Moderne. *Address:* Cedar Cottage, Dunyeats Rd., Broadstone, Dorset. *Signs work:* see appendix.

LISTER, Raymond George, P.R.M.S. (1970), M.A. (Cantab.); President, Private Libraries Association (1971-74); President; Architectural Metalwork Assoc. (1975); Governor, Federation of British Artists (1972); Senior Research Fellow, Wolfson College, Cambridge; painter; author; *b* Cambridge, 28 Mar., 1919; *s* of Horace Lister; *m* Pamela Brutnell; one *s*, one *d*. *Educ.:* Cambs. High School; St. John's College Choir School, Cambridge; *studied art* privately. *Work in permanent collections:* New York Public Library, Brotherton Collection, Metropolitan Museum of Art, Russell-Cotes Museum. *Work repro.:* Raymond Lister, by C. R. Cammell and others (1963). *Publications:* Edward Calvert (1962), William Blake (1968), Samuel Palmer and His Etchings (1969), British Romantic Art (1973), Samuel Palmer, a biography; The Letters of Samuel Palmer; Infernal Methods (1975). *Address:* Windmill House, Linton, Cambridge. *Club:* Savile.

LITTEN, Maurice, R.S.P.P.; portrait painter in oil; *b* Hammersmith, 3 May, 1919; *s* of Sydney Mackenzie Litten, A.R.C.A., Vice-Principal, St. Martin's School of Art; *m* Alma; one *s*. *Educ.:* Skinners' School, Tunbridge Wells; *studied art* at Goldsmiths' School of Art (under James Bateman), St. Martin's School of Art (under Barry Craig). *Exhib.:* R.A., R.B.A., New English, R.S.P.P. Member of Artists of Chelsea. *Address:* Studio 6, 49 Roland Gdns., London SW7. *Club:* Chelsea Arts. *Signs work:* "Litten" or "LITTEN."

LITTLE, Margaret Isabel, M.R.C.S. (Eng.) (1927), L.R.C.P. (Lond.), M.R.C.Psych. (1971), M.F.P.S. (1963); medical practitioner; painter in gouache, oil and mosaic; *b* Bedford, 21 May, 1901; *d* of J. T. Little, M.A.; *m* Reginald Sizen, M.C. (decd.). *Educ.:* Bedford H.S.G.; Bedford College; St. Mary's Hospital; Institute of Psycho-Analysis; *studied art* privately under Miss G. Hylton-Hylton (1939-45); Sir John Cass College (1957-65) under John Bowles. *Exhib.:* W.I.A.C., R.B.A., U.A.S., F.P.S., S.W.A., etc.; one-man show at Sevenoaks (1971). *Work repro.:* Revue Moderne, Paris. *Address:* Rosemary Cottage, 102 Church Rd., Sundridge, Sevenoaks, Kent TN14 6EA. *Clubs:* F.P.S., Cass Art Group. *Signs work:* "Margaret I. Little."

LITTLEJOHN, William Hunter, D.A., R.S.A.; painter in oil; Head of the Dept. of Drawing and Painting, Gray's School of Art, Aberdeen; *b* Arbroath, Angus, Scotland, 16 Apr., 1929; *s* of the late William Littlejohn. *Educ.:* Arbroath High School; *studied art* at Dundee College of Art. *Work in permanent collections:* National Gallery of Modern Art, Edinburgh, Arbroath Art Gallery, Aberdeen Art Gallery, Arts Council Collection, Abbot Hall Art Gallery, Kendal, Edinburgh Civic Collection, Edinburgh Education Authority, Paisley Art Gallery, Towner Art Gallery, Eastbourne. *Address:* 16 Colvill Pl., Arbroath, Angus, Scotland. *Signs work:* see appendix.

LITTLEWOOD, Wilfred E.; artist in oil; restorer of paintings; part-time teacher, School of Art, 1927-38; *b* New Mill, Huddersfield, 7 Feb., 1899; *m*. *Educ.:* New Mill School; *studied art* at Huddersfield School of Art. *Exhib.:* R.A., Paris Salon, Wakefield, Leeds, Manchester, Harrogate, Austen Hayes Gallery, York. *Work in permanent collection:* Huddersfield Art Gallery. *Address:* 5 Syringa St., Huddersfield, Yorks. *Signs work:* "W. E. Littlewood."

LIU, Hai-Sou; artist in oil and water-colours (Chinese-painting), Director of the Academy of Arts, Shanghai; *b* Changchow, China, 16 Mar., 1896; *m* Hsia I-Chiao, paintress. *Studied art:* self-taught. *Work in permanent collections:* Musée du Jeu de Paume and Musées des Ecoles Etrangères Contemporaines, Paris; Museum für Ostasiatische Kunst, Berlin; Japanese Imperial Household Museum, Tokyo; Nanyang University Museum, Singapore; etc. *Publications:* Contemporary Famous Chinese Paintings (Berlin, 1934); Modern Movement in Painting (Shanghai, 1936); An Essay of Six Principles on the Art of Chinese Painting (Shanghai, 1957); etc. *Address:* 512 Fu-Hsing Road C., Shanghai, China. *Club:* China Art Society, Shanghai. *Signs work:* "Liu Hai-Sou" and see appendix.

LIUBA; sculptor in bronze; *b* Sofia, Bulgaria, 1923. *Educ.:* High School, Sofia; *studied art* at Academy of Fine Arts, Geneva (1943-44); and with Germaine Richier in Paris (1944-49). *Exhib.:* one-man shows: Paris, Rio de Janeiro, São-Paulo, London, Cannes, St. Paul de Vence, and many group shows. *Work in permanent collections:* Bienal of São-Paulo, Museum of Modern Art, Rio de Janeiro; Museum of Contemporary Art, São-Paulo; Museum of St. Paul de Vence. *Publications:* Art Aujourd'hui, XXe Siècle, Cahier d'Art, Galerie des Arts, Chef d'œuvre de l'art Studio International, Art News, Art and Artists, Sculpture International, Pictures on Exhibit, Dictionary of Brazilian Art, Art of Brazil

Today. *Addresses:* 16 rue Jacob, Paris 6e; Av. São Luiz 140-São Paulo. *Signs work:* "LIUBA."

LLOYD, Charles, A.R.E.; painter and printmaker in intaglio, relief and screen; lecturer, Goldsmiths' College; *b* Sydney, 1930; *s* of Charles Thomas; *m* Billie Gilligan. *Educ.:* Masonic School, Australia; *studied art* at Julian Ashton Art School, Sydney and Atelier 17, Paris under S. W. Hayter. *Exhib.:* London Biennales; Bradford, Ljubjana. *Work in permanent collection:* National Maritime Museum. *Address:* 40 Longton Gr., Sydenham, London. *Club:* Printmakers Council. *Signs work:* "Charles Lloyd."

LLOYD JONES, Audrey; painter in pastel, gouache, oils and water-colour; draughtsman in black and white; *b* Cambridge; *d* of the late Dr. E. Lloyd Jones, consultant physician. *Educ.:* Abbotshill, Malvern, and N. Foreland Lodge, Broadstairs; *studied art* privately with A. C. G. S. Amarasekara (1940-41). *Exhib.:* R.B.A., P.S., R.Cam.A., English Municipal Galleries, one-man show Cambridge. *Work in private collections:* Leeds and Cambridge. *Work repro.:* in Journal of British Grassland Soc., and other scientific and agricultural publications. *Address:* 1 Selwyn Rd., Cambridge CB3 9EA. *Signs work:* "Audrey Lloyd Jones."

LOBB, Howard Leslie Vicars, C.B.E., F.R.I.B.A., M.R.A.I.C., F.I.Arb., A.I.Struct.E., F.R.S.A., F.G.S.; Consultant to Howard V. Lobb and Partners, architects, London and Calgary; *b* 9 Mar., 1909; *s* of Hedley Vicars Lobb; *m* Charmian Reilly; three *s*. *Educ.:* privately and at Regent St. Polytechnic School of Architecture. *Architectural commissions* include numerous schools for County Authorities; British Pavilion, Brussels Expo 1958; H.Q. City and Guilds of London Institute; Newmarket, Doncaster and Leopardstown Racecourses; H.Q. British Council, Carlton House Terrace; Calgary Exhibition and Stampede; R.Y.A. National Yacht Racing Centre; Nuclear Power Stations at Dungeness, Hunterston and Iverkip. Mem. R.I.B.A. Council (1953-56); life vice-president (past chairman) London Building Centre; hon. sec. Architects' Benevolent Soc.; Deputy Master, Mason's Company; Freeman of City of London. *Address:* Black Hill, 18 Blackhills, Esher, Surrey KT10 9JW. *Clubs:* Athenæum, Arts, Royal Corinthian Yacht, Royal London Yacht, Island Sailing.

LOCKHART, David, R.S.W. (1969), D.A. (Edin.) (1944), M.S.S.A. (1959); artist in acrylics, oil and water-colour; principal teacher of art, Ballingry Junior High School; *b* Leven, Fife, 4 Nov., 1922; *s* of Thomas Lockhart, miner; *m* Jean Lockhart; one *s*, two *d*. *Educ.:* Beath High School, Cowdenbeath (1934-40); *studied art* at Edinburgh College of Art (1940-46). *Educ.:* Shed '50 (1974), Carnegie Dunfermline Trust Festival of Arts (1972), Douglas and Fowlis Gallery, Edinburgh (1963) with James Barclay. *Work in permanent collections:* Scottish Committee of the Arts Council, W. Riding of Yorkshire Educ. Authority, Carnegie Dunfermline Trust, Fife County Council, Dunbartonshire Educ. Authority, Harry Cruden Coll. (Pitlochry Festival Theatre). *Address:* West Green, 5 Main St., Hillend, Fife KY11 5ND. *Signs work:* "David Lockhart" (paintings), and see appendix.

LOCHHEAD, Thomas, D.A.; potter; *b* Milngavie, Glasgow, 28 Nov., 1917; *s* of Thomas Lochhead; *m* Anne T. Wilson; three *s*, two *d*. *Educ.:* Dumfries Academy; *studied art* at Edinburgh College of Art under Princ. Wellington, A.R.C.A., and Alick Wolfenden, A.R.C.A. *Exhib.:* S.S.A. *Official purchases:* Glasgow Art Gallery, Paisley Art Gallery. *Address:* Ashbank, Kirkcudbright. *Signs work:* "Lochhead."

LOCK, Anton, P.S.; oil, water-colour, etcher, wood engraver, illustrator (animal and pastoral); *b* 21 Jan., 1893; one *d*. *Educ.:* Millbank; Westminster

School, Vincent Sq. (Walter Sickert, 1910-12); School of Lithography, Bolt Ct. (Walter Seymour, Walter Bayes, 1912-14). *Exhib.:* R.A., Paris Salon, R.O.I., R.B.A., R.W.S., P.S., British Museum, Oslo, Stockholm; provincial galleries, one-man shows at Leger Galleries. *Official purchases:* British Museum, Contemporary Art Soc., British Council. *Work repro.:* Studio, Apollo, Colour, Saturday Review, Connoisseur, Sphere, Illustrated London News, Graphic, Sporting and Dramatic. Illustrated biographical articles Studio (1932), Apollo (1932-33), Colour (1932), Saturday Review (1932). *Address:* 14 Lancaster Rd., Wimbledon Common, London SW19. *Club:* Savage. *Signs work:* "Anton Lock," and see appendix.

LOCKWOOD, Dorothy, R.W.S. (1974), R.B.S.A. (1959); artist in water-colour; *b* Birmingham; *d* of A. R. Smith, craftsman in fine art woodwork; widow. *Educ.:* Birmingham College of Art, Moseley Art School; *studied art* under Harold H. Holden, R.W.S., A.R.C.A. (1930s), B. Fleetwood Walker, R.A., R.W.S. (1940s), Harold Smith, R.B.S.A. *Work in permanent collections:* London, Leamington, Seattle, New York, Detroit, Quebec. *Address:* 25 Chesterwood Rd., Birmingham B13 0QG. *Signs work:* "Dorothy Lockwood."

LOEBENSTEIN, Alphons, N.R.D., M.S.I.A., A.I.A.L. (Zürich and Lindau); industrial art designer; Designer D. Meredew, Ltd., Letchworth, Herts., since 1945; *b* Muehlhausen/Thuer, Germany, 18 May, 1888; *s* of Gustav Loebenstein; *m* Margarete Gottschling; one *s*, one *d*. *Educ.:* Grammar schools; *studied art* at Munich, Nuremberg and Museum of Arts and Crafts, Berlin. *Work repro.:* Country Life, Cabinet Maker, Studio Yearbook Decorative Art (1950-51), Design at the Festival of Britain (1951), Design (1954), Furnishing (1955), Innendekoration (Darmstadt), Pyramide (Berlin), Die Kunst (Munich). *Address:* Buckdene, 22 Redwoods Way E., Letchworth, Herts. *Signs work:* see appendix.

LOHSE, Richard Paul; Art Prize of the City of Zürich (1973); Sikkens Prize of the Netherlands (1971); painter; co-founder Allianz Vereinigung moderner Schweizer Künstler (1937); *b* Zürich, 13 Sept., 1902; *s* of Paul Richard Ferdinand Lohse; *m* Ida Dürner; one *d*. *Educ.:* Zürich Kunstgewerbeschule. *Exhib.:* one-man shows (1960-75) in Ulm (Kunstmuseum), Zürich (Kunsthaus), Amsterdam (Stedelijk Museum), São Paulo (8° Bienal), Buenos Aires (Instituto Torquato Di Tella), Rio de Janeiro (Museo di Arte Moderna), Bern (Kunsthalle), Munich (Kunstverein), Hannover (Kunstverein), Stockholm (Moderna Museet), Eindhoven (Van Abbemuseum), Den Haag (Gemeentemuseum), Venice (36° Bienal), Düsseldorf (Kunstmuseum) (Kunsthalle). Participated in important museums and galleries in Europe, U.S.A., South America, Japan. Since 1964 to 1975: London, Tate Gallery (A Decade, 1954-64); Amsterdam, Stuttgart, Bern (New Shapes of Colour); St. Paul, Foundation Maeght (Dix ans d'art vivant, 1955-65); Montreal (Art et Mouvement); Buffalo (Plus × Minus: Today's Half-century); Venice, 34° Bienal (Linee della ricerca contemporanea); Kassel (4. documenta); Nürnberg Biennale (Konstruktive Kunst: Elemente + Prinzipien); Nürnberg Biennale (Künstler—Theorie—Werk); Dublin (Rosc. '71); New York (Swiss Avant Garde); Warszawa (Zeitg. Schweizer Malerei); Stuttgart (Konstruktivismus und seine Nachfolge). *Work in permanent collections:* in museums and collections. *Murals:* Ebnat-Kappel, Lenggis/Rapperswil. *Editor:* Vordemberge-Gildewart, Teufen 1959. *Co-editor:* Almanach neuer Kunst in der Schweiz, Zürich (1940). *Publications:* articles in Abstrakt/Konkret (Zürich, 1944 and 1945); Allianz Catalogue (Kunsthaus, Zürich, 1947); transformation (New York 1/3, 1952); Vision and Value Series by Kepes (New York, 1966; Standard Series Module); DATA (London, 1968; Elementarism Series Modulus). *Literature:* Lohse by H. P. Riese (Circular 5A Bonn); Richard Paul Lohse (Du Mont-Schauberg, Cologne, 1973, texts by E. Gomringer, F. W. Heckmanns, H. H. Holz, R. Kallhardt, J.

Leering, H. P. Riese, W. Sandberg); Richard Paul Lohse (Niggteufen, 1962); Karl Gerstner Fli Kalte Kunst? (Teufen, 1957); Künstler Lexikon der Schweiz (Frauenfeld, 1965, Dr. Eduard Plüss); Constructivism by George Rickey (Braziller, New York, 1967); Studio International Feb. 1968, London (Kenneth Martin: Richard Paul Lohse: an appreciation); Art International Sept. 1970 (Hans-Peter Riese: Richard P. Lohse); Plan 6, 1971, Amsterdam (Eugen Gomringer: lohse: wetmatigheden door middel van vorm en kleur). *Address:* Stockerstr. 32, 8002 Zürich/Switzerland.

LOM, Josephine: see LOMNICKA, Azdia Josephine.

LOMNICKA, Azdia Josephine, A.C.I. (1962), M.S.D-C. (1968); textile designer and technologist, teacher, illustrator, portrait painter and sculptor; senior lecturer in art, Digby Stuart College of Education; *b* Poland; *d* of Stanislaw Szymański; *m* Adam Lomnicki (divorced); one *d. Educ.:* Dabrowka, Gimnazium and Liceum, Poznan, Poland; Garnett College (1956); *studied art* at Staatliche Kunst Academie, Kassel under Prof. K. Van Nebel; Liverpool School of Art (1946). *Exhib.:* one-man show: Battersea Library, London; group shows: Commonwealth Institute, Bristol, Coventry, Oxford, Southampton, Bath Museum, Lincoln Cathedral, Royal Exchange, Building Centre, London. *Work in permanent collection:* Wilts. C.C. Museum and Library, Trowbridge. *Publication:* Step-by-Step Collage (David and Charles, 1975). *Address:* 20 Girdwood Rd., London SW18 5QS. *Signs work:* "Josephine Lom."

LONGBOTHAM, Charles Norman, R.W.S.; artist in water-colour and other media, modelmaker (specialist in landscape models); Mem. A.W.G.; *b* Carlton, Notts., 6 July, 1917; *s* of George N. Longbotham, mining engineer; *m* Eleanor (*née* Nairn-Allison), artist; one *d. Educ.:* Portsmouth Grammar School and H.M.S. *Conway*, Birkenhead. *Exhib.:* R.A., R.W.S. Galleries, and other London exhbns.; one-man exhbns. London and provinces. *Work in permanent collections:* Commonwealth Inst., Shell Museum, Pilkington Glass Museum, St. Helens, Imperial War Museum, etc. *Addresses:* Tunbeck Cottage, Alburgh, Norfolk IP20 0BS; c/o Royal Society of Painters in Water-colours, 26 Conduit St., London W1. *Club:* R.W.S. Art (President). *Signs work:* see appendix.

LOPEZ-REY, Jose, Ph.D. (Madrid, 1935); art historian; Prof. of Fine Arts, Inst. of Fine Arts, New York University; Vice-President, International Foundation for Art Research, N.Y.; *b* Madrid, 14 May, 1905; *s* of Leocadio Lopez Arrojo, M.D. *Educ.:* Universities of Madrid, Florence, and Vienna. *Publications:* Antonio del Pollaiuolo y el fin del Quattrocento; Realismo é impresionismo en las artes figuratives españolas del siglo XIX; Goya y el mundo a su alrededor; Goya's Caprichos: Beauty, Reason and Caricature; A Cycle of Goya's Drawings: The Expression of Truth and Liberty; Velázquez: A Catalogue Raisonné of his *oeuvre*; Goya and His Pupil, Maria del Rosario Weiss, Velazquez' Work and World (1968). *Address:* Box 574, Wilton, Conn. 06897, U.S.A.

LORIMER, Hew, R.S.A. (1957), R.B.S.; sculptor in stone; *b* Edinburgh, 22 May, 1907; 2nd *s* of the late Sir Robert Lorimer, architect; *m* Mary McCleod Wylie; two *s*, one *d. Educ.:* Loretto; *studied art* at Edinburgh College of Art and under Eric Gill. *Exhib.:* R.S.A., etc. *Address:* Kellie Castle, Pittenweem, Fife. *Club:* Scottish Arts. *Signs work:* unsigned.

LOUNDS, Stanley Samuel Alfred; priest, mem. of Community of the Resurrection; ordained priest (1930), worked in England, S. Africa and R.A.F., mem., C. of R. since 1947; artist in oils, water-colour, sepia, black and white; *b* Grantham, Lincs., 6 June, 1906; *s* of Arthur Lounds, coachbuilder. *Educ.:* Grantham Grammar School; Burgh Theological College. *Exhib.:* Huddersfield Art Soc. (1952-60),

Bradford Biennial (1959), Cardiff Art Society (1962). *Work repro.:* Religious periodicals and pamphlets. *Address:* House of the Resurrection, Mirfield, Yorks. *Signs work:* "S.L."

LOVE, Hazel, N.D.D. (1952), R.W.A. (1971); painter in oil and watercolour; *b* Hinton St. George, Somerset, 1923; *d* of Augustine Tutchen Love, agent to the Wyndham Estate. *Educ.:* Gardenhurst School, Burnham-on-Sea, Som.; *studied art* at West of England College of Art (1946-52). *Exhib.:* R.W.A., A.I.A., Somerset Soc. of Artists, and other mixed shows. *Work in permanent collection:* Royal West of England Academy. *Address:* Little Bullington, Sutton Scotney, nr. Winchester, Hants. *Clubs:* Hampstead Artists' Council, Bristol Manuscript. *Signs work:* see appendix.

LOVEGROVE, James William, A.R.E. (1952), A.R.C.A. (1952); sometime artist (drawing and etching), writer and seaman; Winchester District Councillor; *b* Hong Kong, 29 Sept., 1922; *s* of Brigadier C. G. Lovegrove, M.I.Mech.E. (decd.) and Marjorie Alice (*née* Freeman); *m* Jean Margaret Connell; two *s*, two *d*. *Educ.:* county Grammar School in Kent; *studied art* at Woolwich Polytechnic (1945-48) and Royal College of Art (1949-52). *Publications:* historical journals, magazines and reviews. *Address:* Marlands, Headbourne Worthy, nr. Winchester, Hants., SO23 7JJ. *Club:* Hampshire.

LOVELESS, John; painter in acrylics, murals and silk-screen; designer, University of Bristol, Ava Unit; *b* Bristol, 14 Aug., 1943; *s* of Jack Loveless; *m* Jennifer Kathleen Loveless; one *s*, one d. *Educ.:* Queen Elizabeth's Hospital School; *studied art* at Royal West of England College of Art (1963-65) under John Epstein, Frank Fennel, Robert Hurdle, Ron Fuller. *Exhib.:* Festival Gallery, Bath (1974), Dartington Hall (1972), Arts Council, Serpentine Gallery (1971), Camden Arts Centre (1970), Arnolfini Gallery (1967, 1969, 1972). *Work in permanent collections:* Bristol City A.G., Grabowski Gallery, London, Universities of Bristol, Sussex and Southampton, Arnolfini Gallery Trust, South Western Arts Assoc. *Address:* Drove Cottage, Rookham, Wells, Som. *Signs work:* "John Loveless."

LOVELL, Margaret, Dip. F.A. (Slade, 1962), F.R.B.S. (1973), R.W.A. (1972); sculptor in bronze, marble, slate; *b* Bristol, 7 Mar., 1939; *d* of Harold Lovell. *Educ.:* Kingswood Grammar School, Bristol; *studied art* at West of England College of Art, Bristol (Ernest Pascoe, 1956-60), Slade School of Fine Art (Professor A. H. Gerrard, 1960-62), Academy of Fine Art, Florence (1962-63), Greek Government Scholarship (1965-66). *Exhib.:* City Art Gall., Bristol, Arts Council of Great Britain, Marjorie Parr Gall., (4 one-man shows, 1965, 1968, 1970, 1972), Plymouth City Art Gall., also one-man shows at Park Square Gall., Leeds (1968, 1971), Fermoy Art Gall., King's Lynn (1970), Univ. of Bath (1973), Bruton Gall., Somerset (1973), 1st retrospective Plymouth City Art Gall. (1972). *Address:* Manor House Farm, North Stoke, Bath. *Signs work:* "M. Lovell" or "Margaret Lovell."

LOVELY, Maureen Patey, A.R.C.A.; painter, engraver, and designer in egg tempera and oils, etc.; for posters, textiles, china, carpets, book-jackets, etc.; *b* Oxton, Ches., 18 May, 1906; *d* of P. G. Patey Eyre; *m* (1) Philip A. Proudman; two *s*; *m* (2) 1974. *Educ.:* Godolphin, Salisbury; *studied art* at B.A. (Rome); R.C.A. (London). *Exhib.:* Rome, Simla, Burlington House, Leicester Galleries, Walker Art Gallery, and provincial galleries. *Work repro.:* 70-ft. poster for Messrs. Yardley Industrial World (1931); poster Jodhpur Fort for Indian State Railways; also used as cover of magazine (1937); tempera (Mousehole), Artist (1938). *Address:* 5 Brook Ct., Middlebridge St., Romsey, Hants. *Signs work:* "M. EYRE PROUDMAN."

LOVETT, Eleanor Selwyn; R.A. Dip., City of London Award (1968); painter in oil; *b* Bromley; *d* of E. R. Lovett. *Educ.:* Sydenham High School; *studied art* at Goldsmiths' School of Art, Epsom School of Art; pupil of Hans Tisdale. *Exhib.:* N.E.A.C., R.O.I., Whitechapel Art Gallery, Mall Galleries, Burlington House, St. John's Wood Art Centre, R.B.A., South London Group, Cert. Merit, S.E. Group Summer Exhbn., Guildhall (1958, 1971), Leicester Gallery mixed exhbns. *Work in permanent collection:* landscapes and murals, Robert Fleming (Merchant Bankers). *Address:* 18 Elgin Rd., East Croydon, Addiscombe, Surrey. *Club:* Reynolds. *Signs work:* unsigned.

LOW, Jack; artist in oil and water-colours, stone- and wood-carver, carpet designer; L.C.C. art instructor (1945-48); *b* Brondesbury, 17 Oct., 1903; *s* of Charles Abbot Low; *studied art* at City & Guilds School (1941-42), and Goldsmiths' School of Art (1946-50) under Adrian Ryan. *Exhib.:* R.A., R.B.A., A.I.A., Northbank Artists, Leicester Gallery, Redfern Gallery, John Neville Gallery, Canterbury, one-man show, Theatre Club (Shaftesbury Avenue, 1953), etc. *Work in permanent collections:* England, France, Rome, Germany, America. *Address:* Little Stour Cottage, West Stourmouth, nr. Canterbury, Kent.

LOWE, Ronald, A.T.D. (1955); painter, lithographer, mural painter and stage designer; H.M.I. (Art Wales); *b* Skipton, Yorks., 10 Feb., 1932; *s* of Ernest Lowe; *m* Frances Ceridwen Doble; two *s*. *Educ.:* Ermysted's Grammar School, Yorkshire; *studied art* at Leeds College of Art (1949-55) under Richard Macdonald and Keith Lucas, and in London. *Exhib.:* Howard Roberts Gallery, Cardiff (1962, 1965, 1969), Dillwyn Gallery, Swansea (1963, 1964, 1966), R.A., A.I.A., Free Painters Group, Five Artists from Wales, Queen Square Gallery, Leeds, Argus Gallery, Madison, New Jersey, Bear Lane Gallery, Oxford and Albany Gallery, Cardiff. *Work in permanent collections:* Arts Council of Wales, National Museum of Wales, Contemporary Art Society, University of Wales, Pembroke College, Cambridge, Steel Company of Wales, G.L.C., County Collections of Essex, Lincoln, Glamorgan, Dyfed, Clwyd, Gwent, Bristol, and Leeds, Education Committees, Newport Art Gallery, St. Edmund Hall, Oxford, Bradford University, British Petroleum Co. *Address:* Maesyderi House, Abercrave, Brecons. *Signs work:* "Lowe," usually in bottom left of painting.

LOWNDES, Alan; painter in oil; *b* Stockport, 23 Feb., 1921; *s* of S. B. Lowndes; *m* Valerie Lowndes; one *s*, two *d*. *Educ.:* Christchurch School, Stockport; *studied art* at Stockport College (1945-49) under Emmanuel Levy (evening classes). *Exhib.:* Crane Gallery, Manchester; Prospect Gallery, London; Rutland Gallery, London; OsbornGallery, N.Y.; Magdalene Gallery, Cambridge; Crane Kalman Gallery, London. *Work in permanent collections:* Manchester, Liverpool, Coventry, Balliol College, Oxford, Plymouth, Huddersfield, Arts Council. *Address:* Downside, Ashmed Green, Dursley, Glos. *Club:* Chelsea Arts. *Signs work:* "Alan Lowndes."

LOXTON KNIGHT, Edward, R.B.A.; artist in oil, pastel, water-colour, gouache, woodblock printing; *b* Long Eaton, Notts., 12 July, 1905; *s* of Samuel Knight; *m* Jill Malins (25 Aug., 1952); one *d*. *Educ.:* Grammar School, Long Eaton; *studied art* at Nottingham School of Art under Joseph Else (1924-29). *Exhib.:* R.A., R.B.A., R.I., Paris Salon, London, Glasgow, New York, Nottingham, Johannesburg, Derby, Dublin. *Work in permanent collections:* municipal galleries of Nottingham, Derby, Preston, Adelaide, Wanganui (N.Z.). *Work repro.:* in Studio, Artist, Colour, etc. *Address:* 20 Breedon St., Long Eaton, Notts. *Signs work:* see appendix.

LOXTON PEACOCK, Clarisse; painter in oil; *b* 7 May, 1926; *m* G. Loxton

Peacock; one *s*, one *d*. *Educ.:* Budapest University; *studied art* at Chelsea School of Art (Dip. course); Central School of Arts and Crafts (Post. Grad. course); St. Martin's School of Art. *Exhib.:* W.A.G., Grosvenor Gallery, O'Hana Gallery, Dusseldorf, New York Bodley, Frost & Reed. *Work in permanent collections:* U.S.A., Spain, Germany, England, S. Africa (Queen's Gallery). *Address:* 85 Bedford Gdns., London W8. *Signs work:* "C. Loxton Peacock."

LUBELSKI, Jan Stanislaw; Slade Dip. (1949), A.T.D. (1951); sculptor in bronze and stone (clay modelling), specialises in portraiture and animal sculpture; *b* Poznan, Poland, 5 Mar., 1922; *s* of Mieczyslaw Lubelski, sculptor; *m* Josephine G. Enock; two *s*; divorced; *m* 2nd (1964) Christina C. Sheppard; one *s*, one *d*. *Educ.:* Bonn Grammar School; Polish matriculation; Glasgow; Regent St. Polytechnic School of Art (1945-46); Slade School (Prof. Gerrard, 1946-49); and under Benno Elkan, O.B.E. (1940-41); worked on "New Testament" candelabrum, now in Westminster Abbey; Inst. of Educ. (1950-51). *Exhib.:* Forces Exhbn. at National Gallery; R.A.; Slade School Exhbn., Walker's Galleries; Fine Art Soc.; Royal Copenhagen Gallery, Bond St.; Young Contemporaries at R.B.A., Kingley Galleries, W1; Glasgow Inst. *Work in permanent collections:* St. Gabriel's College, Camberwell; Prof. Paul Glees, Göttingen and others. *Address:* 61 Claremont Rd., Highgate, London N6. *Signs work:* see appendix.

LUCAS, Eric, M.A.; Asst. Master, Winchester College (1935-51); Prof. of Educ., Makerere College, E. Africa (1951—); *b* Salford, Lancs., 22 May, 1911; *s* of Arthur Lucas. *Educ.:* Manchester Grammar School and Emmanuel College, Cambridge. Collector of contemporary English and French painting and sculpture, incl. Moore, Smith, Gerain, Singer, Hodgkins, Paul Nash, Ravilious. *Address:* Makerere University, P.O. Box 7062, Kampala, Uganda. *Club:* Royal Commonwealth Society, WC1.

LUCAS, Marjorie A., A.R.C.A. (1933), S.S.A. (1946), Soc. Artist Print Makers (1935); artist in line-engraving, wood-engraving, water-colour, embroidery and book plates; *b* 1911; *d* of S. B. Lucas, B.A.; *m* Murray M. Tod; one *s*, two *d*. *Educ.:* N. London Collegiate School; R.C.A. (Malcolm Osborne, R.A., R.E., Robert Austin, R.A., R.E.). *Exhib.:* R.A., R.S.A., G.I., British Council. *Address:* 2 Abbotsford Ct., Ettrick Rd., Edinburgh EH10 5EH. *Signs work:* "Marjorie A. Lucas."

LUCAS, Suzanne (née Craven), R.M.S., F.R.H.S., S.W.A., U.A.; Médaille de la Résistance; Grenfell Medal (1956), Silver Grenfell (1971, 1973); R.H.S. Gold Medal (1975); painter and miniaturist in water-colour; Vice President, Dorset Arts and Crafts Society; Hon. Sec., Royal Society of Miniature Painters; Councillor, Society of Miniaturists; *b* Calcutta, 10 Sept., 1915; *d* of S/Ldr. Alfred Craven, B.Sc.Eng. 1st Cl., M.I.Mech.E., M.I.E.E.; *m* Admiral Louis Lucas, C.B.E., Commandeur of Legion of Honour. *Educ.:* Roedean School, Edinburgh University; *studied art* at Munich and Grenoble Universities, Berlin School of Art and with Professor Schmidt. *Exhib.:* R.A., Paris Salon, R.I.; one-man shows in London: Cooling Galleries (1954), Sladmore Gallery (1973), Mall Galleries (1975). *Address:* Ladyfield, Bourton, Dorset SP8 5AT. *Signs work:* see appendix.

LUCIE-SMITH, John Edward McKenzie, F.R.S.L.; writer (poetry and art criticism); *b* Kingston, Jamaica, W.I., 27 Feb., 1933. *Educ.:* King's School, Canterbury; Merton College, Oxford. *Publications:* What is a Painting? (Macdonald, 1966), Thinking about Art (Calder, 1968), Movements in Art since 1945 (Thames & Hudson, 1969), A Concise History of French Painting (Thames & Hudson, 1971), Eroticism in Western Art (Thames & Hudson, 1972), Symbolist Art (Thames & Hudson, 1972), The Invented Eye (Paddington Press,

1974). World of the Makers (Paddington Press, 1974). *Address:* 24 Sydney St., London SW3.

LUNDQUIST, Evert, F.R.S.A.; Royal Medal of Prince Eughen; painter in oil; Professor, Royal High School of Fine Arts, Stockholm; mem., Royal Swedish Academy of Fine Arts; *b* Stockholm, 17 July, 1904; *s* of Ernst Lundquist, Chief, Bureau of Royal Swedish Railways; *m* Ebba Reutercrona, artist-painter; two *s*. *Educ.:* Academy Julian, Paris; *studied art* at Academy Julian, Paris (1924-25), Royal Swedish Academy of Fine Arts (1925-31) under C. Wilhelmson. *Work in permanent collections:* Museum of Modern Art, Stockholm; Tate Gallery; Musée de l'Art Modern, Paris; Museum of Modern Art, New York; Museo de l'Arte Moderna, São Paulo; National Museum, Melbourne. *Books written or illustrated:* Malar Pionjarer, Evert Lundquist, F.R.S.A. *Address:* Kanton, Drottningholm, Sweden. *Signs work:* "Evert Lundquist."

LUPTON, Lewis F.; preacher, writer, historian, painter in oil and water-colour; *b* London, 18 July, 1909. *Studied art* at Sheffield College of Arts (1923-30). Practised commercial art in Strand advertising agency before the war. Freelance since 1940. Exhibition designer during and just after the war. Many paintings in the R.A. at this period. Then turned to the illustration of Christian literature. Numerous exhibitions of own, and wife's work held in recent years. Publisher under the Olive Tree imprint of own History of the Geneva Bible (8 vols.) and other related literature. *Address:* 2 Milnthorpe Rd., London W4.

LUXMOORE, John M., M.A.F.A.; wood sculptor; *b* 12 May, 1912; *s* of L. A. Luxmoore; *m*; three *s*. *Educ.:* Loretto School and Magdalene College, Camb. *Exhib.:* R.A., R.B.A., Manchester, etc. *Work repro.:* in Studio (Sept., 1947). *Address:* Prospect, Ledward La., Bowdon, Altrincham, Ches. *Signs work:* see appendix.

LUXTON, Doris E., N.S.A.M. (1926), further exam. (1928), bronze and silver medals; artist in oil and water-colour; art mistress, Truro Art School (1925-29) and visiting art teacher for local schools; *b* Exeter, 30 Apr., 1908; *d* of Harry Stafford-Moass, dentist; *m* John Luxton; three *s*. *Educ.:* Truro County School; *studied art* at Truro Art School under Arthur Jackson. *Exhib.:* Royal Cornwall Polytechnic Art Exhbns., Bideford and Westward Ho Art Soc. Exhbns., North Devon Art Soc. Exhbns., annual one-woman exhbns. at Burton Art Gallery, Bideford. *Address:* 15 Allhalland St., Bideford, N. Devon. *Clubs:* Westward Ho! Arts, North Devon Arts, Royal West of England Arts. *Signs work:* "Doris E. Luxton."

LYNE, Charles Edward Michael; artist in oil and water-colour; *b* Upton Bishop, Herefordshire, 12 Sept., 1912; *s* of Rev. R. A. Lyne, M.A.; *m* Jessie Muriel; one *s*, one *d*. *Educ.:* Rossall; *studied art* at Cheltenham Art School under Gerald Gardiner. *Publications:* Horses, Hounds and Country, A Parson's Son, From Litter to Later On (written and illustrated); illustrated about 40 books, including The Horse in Action, Hounds, Horses and Country (Frances Pitt), Riding For Children, Treasury of Horse Stories, The Controversial Horse, etc. *Address:* Dunfield House, nr. Fairford, Glos. *Signs work:* see appendix.

LYON, Robert, M.A. (Dunelm), A.R.C.A., R.B.A., R.P., Rome Scholar (1924). *Studied art* at Liverpool School of Art, R.C.A. *Exhib.:* R.A., R.B.A., R.P.P.S., Brighton, Southport, Newcastle; recent murals (1962), Western General Hospital, Edinburgh and King's College Hospital (School of Dentistry), London. *Address:* 28 Arlington Rd., Eastbourne. *Signs work:* "R. Lyon."

LYRIA, Hado; painter in mixed technique and indian inks, writer; *b* Barcelona,

18 Mar., 1940. *Educ.:* America, Spain and Italy: *studied art* at Accademia di Brera, Milan (1959-62) under Cantatore and later under Achile Funi. *Exhib.:* one-man shows: Edinburgh Festival (1976), Venice (1976), Milan (1975), Barcelona (1975). *Work repro.:* in Panorama, Il Giono, Mondadori Publications, L'Espresso, El Correo Catalan, El Noticiero Universal, Gazetta Del Arte. *Reviews:* Il Giorno, Corriere Della Sera, Epoca, L'Europeo, Tele-Express, El Noticiero Universal, La Vanguardia Espanola, Barcelona and National Radios, El Correo Catalan, La Estafeta Literaria, Fotogramas. *Address:* Viale Piave, 17, Milan, Italy. *Signs work:* "Hado Lyria."

M

MACARRÓN, Ricardo, R.S.P.P. (1962); 1st prize National Fine Art Exhbn. (1962), Prize Direction of Fine Art (1954); artist in oil of figures, dead nature, landscapes, portraits; *b* Madrid, 9 Apr., 1926; *s* of Juan Macarron, art dealer; *m* Alicia; two *d. Studied art* at Fine Art School of San Fernando, Madrid (1942); scholarship to study in France by French Institute (1950). *Work in permanent collections:* Contemporary Art Museum, Madrid, University of Oslo, National Gallery (Cape Town), Güell Foundation (Barcelona), and several private collections. *Address:* Augustin de Bethencourt 5, Madrid 3, Spain. *Signs work:* see appendix.

MACCABE, Gladys, R.O.I., F.R.S.A., F.I.A.L.; Founder and Past-Pres. Ulster Society of Women Artists; painter in oil and water-colour and various other media; art lecturer, writer and broadcaster; *b* Randalstown, N. Ireland; *d* of George Chalmers; *m* Max Maccabe; two *s. Educ.:* Brookvale Collegiate School, and Ulster College of Art. *Exhib.:* London, Dublin, U.S.A., Canada, Belfast, Scotland, France, etc. *Work in permanent collections:* Imperial War Museum, Ulster Museum, Arts Council of Northern Ireland, The Queen's University, Belfast, Ulster Office, London, Longford County Library, Thomas Haverty Trust, County Dublin Educ. Authority, Cyril Cusack, Esq., Miss Beatrice Lillie, Lady Wakehurst, the late Adlai Stevenson, Esq., etc. *Work repro.:* Many important publications. *Address:* 19 Mountcharles, Belfast, BT7 1NY. *Signs work:* "GLADYS MACCABE."

MACCABE, Max, F.R.S.A., Mem. W.C.S.I.; painter in oil and water-colour; art critic and lecturer; *b* Belfast, 16 Aug., 1917; *s* of Matthew Henry Maccabe; *m* Gladys Chalmers; two *s. Educ.:* Royal Belfast Academical Inst. *Exhib.:* London, U.S.A., Canada, Scotland, Belfast, Dublin. *Work in permanent collections:* The Hon. Mrs. McClintock, The Countess of Antrim, Lady Clark, The Ana M. Berry Memorial Fund, Ernest Milton, Lady Wakehurst, Ulster Museum, Swan Hunter Tyne Shipbuilders, etc. *Work repro.:* The Listener, Irish Tatler and Sketch, Sunday Independent, The Studio, International Who's Who in Art and Antiques, etc. *Address:* 19 Mountcharles, Belfast, BT7 1NY. *Signs work:* "MAX MACCABE."

McCALL, Charles James, R.O.I. (1950), D.A. (Edin., 1935), N.E.A.C. (1957); artist; *b* 24 Feb., 1907; *s* of William McCall; *m* Eloise Jerwood. *Educ.:* Broughton; *studied art:* Edinburgh College of Art, Edinburgh University, Académie Colarossi (Paris), Europe (1937-38) *Exhib.:* R.A., R.S.A., N.E.A.C., London Group, Leicester Galleries, Waddington Galleries (Dublin), Duveen-Graham Galleries, N.Y., Belgrave Gallery (London), Ash Barn Gallery (Petersfield), Klinkhoff Gallery, Montreal. *Work in permanent collections:* Herts. Educ.

Authority. *Official purchases:* Contemp. Arts Soc., Scottish Modern Arts Assoc., Scottish Art Council, Ministry of Works, Paisley Gallery, Maidstone Gallery. *Work repro.:* Studio. *Address:* 1A Caroline Terr., London SW1W 8JS.

McCANNELL, Ursula Vivian, A.R.C.A. (1944); artist in oil, tempera, pastel; portrait painter; tutor at West Surrey College of Art and Design; *b* Hampstead, 11 June, 1923; *d* of Otway McCannell, artist; *m* Peter Rees-Roberts; three *s*. *Studied art* at R.C.A. in Painting and Design Schools. *Exhib.:* one-man shows, Redfern, Leger, Modern Arts, Gimpel Fils, 20 Brook St., Ashgate, Thackeray Galls., also at Leicester, R.A., R.P.S., London Group, Roland, Browse & Delbanco. *Work in permanent collections:* Manchester Art Gallery, National Gas Board, Electricity Council. *Work repro.:* in Studio, Art News, The Moderns. *Address:* Hawks Hill, Moor Pk., Farnham, Surrey. *Signs work:* "U. McC." (small "c" underlined.)

McCHEYNE, Alistair; painter, critic, teacher, diploma and major post-dip. scholarship in drawing and painting, Edinburgh (1939), travelling scholarship (1940), senior maintenance scholarship (1938), professional M.S.S.A.; B.B.C. art critic since 1950; principal art teacher, George Heriot's School, Edinburgh; former teacher of life drawing and painting, Lauder Technical School, Dunfermline; *b* Perth, 27 May, 1918; *s* of Martin McCheyne. *Educ.:* Perth Academy; *studied art* at Edinburgh (1935-40) under David Alison, London and Paris. *Exhib.:* R.S.A., S.S.A., etc. *Publications:* Listener, Scotsman, Saltire Magazine. *Address:* 14 Sciennes Gdns., Edinburgh. *Club:* Scottish Arts. *Signs work:* "McCheyne."

McCLOY, William Ashby; Henry B. Plant Prof., Connecticut College; painter, sculptor, printmaker; *b* Baltimore, Md., 2 Jan., 1913; *s* of Chas. H. McCloy; *m* Patricia C. *Educ.:* Phillips Academy, Andover, Mass., University of Iowa; *studied art* at University of Iowa. *Exhib.:* N.A., Whitney Museum of American Art, Pennsylvania Academy of Fine Arts, Chicago Art Inst., Carnegie Inst., Walker Art Centre, Kansas City Art Inst., Cincinnati Art Museum, Joslyn Mem. Art Museum, Library of Congress, Milwaukee Art Inst. *Address:* Connecticut College, New London, Connecticut. *Signs work:* "WILLIAM ASHBY McCLOY."

McCLURE, David, D.A. (Edin.), A.R.S.A. (1963), R.S.W. (1965), R.S.A. (1971); painter in oils and water-colours; teacher of painting, College of Art, Dundee; *b* Lochwinnoch, Scotland, 20 Feb., 1926; *s* of Robert C. McClure, M.M. and Margaret Helena Evans; *m* Joyce Dixon Flanigan; two *s*, one *d*. *Educ.:* Queen's Park School, Glasgow, Edinburgh Univ.; *studied art* at Edinburgh College of Art (1947-52), Travelling Scholarship (1952-53). Fellow of Edinburgh College of Art (1955-57). *Work in permanent collections:* Arts Council (Scotland), Dundee Art Gallery, Glasgow Art Gallery, Aberdeen Art Gallery, Scottish National Gallery of Modern Art, Towner Art Gallery, Eastbourne, Edinburgh and St. Andrew's University Staff Clubs, Queen's College, Dundee. *Address:* 16 Strawberry Bank, Dundee. *Signs work:* "D. McClure" or "McClure."

McCOMBS, John, N.D.D.; R.A. scholarship award and college prize; artist in oil; *b* Manchester, 28 Dec., 1943. *Educ.:* High School of Art, Manchester; *studied art* at St. Martin's School of Art (1962-67) under Frederick Gore, Alan Reynolds, Leon Kossoff. *Exhib.:* Manchester and Salford City Art Galleries, Upper St. Galleries, Chenil Gallery, Tib Lane Gallery, Portland Gallery, Oldham A.G. *Work in permanent collection:* Salford A.G. *Address:* 112 Stoneswood Rd., Delph, nr. Oldham. *Club:* Manchester Academy of Fine Art. *Signs work:* "J. McCombs", sometimes "JMc."

McCRACKEN, David, M.R.C.V.S. (1948); artist in water-colour; veterinary surgeon; *b* Glasgow, 30 Apr., 1925; *s* of Samuel McCracken; *m* Irene G. Lewis, three children. *Educ.:* Queen's Park, Glasgow; Marr College, Troon; Glasgow Veterinary College. *Exhib.:* Hereford. *Address:* 29 Balhousie St., Perth. *Signs work:* "David McCracken" or "McCRACKEN."

McCULLOUGH, George, M.S.Exc., hons. M. of E. dipl.; artist in oil, water-colour, gouache, pastel; *b* Belfast, 2 Oct., 1922. *Educ.:* Belfast College of Technology and Belfast College of Art (1940-47); *studied art* as above. *Exhib.:* R.U.A. *Address:* 20 Joanmount Drive, Carrs Glen, Belfast. *Signs work:* see appendix.

McCUTCHEON, John, D.A. Glas. (1933), R.O.I. (1970). Hon. mention Paris Salon, Assoc.-member Societé des Artistes Français (1970); artist in oil, water-colour and pen and ink; *b* Dalmellington, 1 June, 1910; *s* of Ivie McCutcheon; *m* Christina B. Weir. *Educ.:* Ayr Academy; *studied art* at Glasgow School of Art (1929-1933). *Exhib.:* Paris Salon, R.O.I., R.S.A., R.G.I. *Work in permanent collection:* Kelvingrove Art Gallery. *Address:* 12 Craigie Ave., Ayr, Scotland. *Club:* Ayr Sketch. *Signs work:* "Jn. McCUTCHEON."

MacDONALD, Alastair James Henderson, R.M.S. (1969), A.R.M.S. (1968), F.R.S.A. (1961), U.A.S. (1974); miniature painter in water-colour and gouache, and scribe; Council mem. R.M.S. (1973-74); *b* Tighnabruaich, Argyll, 5 July, 1934; *s* of Angus Graham MacDonald, licensed master grocer; *m* Juliet Anne Mead; two *s,* three *d. Educ.:* Pope Street School, New Eltham; *studied art* at Woolwich Polytechnic School of Art and Crafts under Heber Mathews and Joan Dawson. *Exhib.:* R.M.S., R.I., U.A.S. *Address:* 63 Somers Rd., North Mymms, Herts. *Club:* Safari. *Signs work:* see appendix.

McDONALD, John Patrick; sculptor, civil servant; *b* Denton, Lancs., 2 Nov., 1949. *Educ.:* Manchester Polytechnic. *Exhib.:* Portland Gallery, and North West Arts, Manchester. *Address:* c/o Portland Gallery, Manchester. *Signs work:* "J. Mc.D."

MACDONALD, Richard, A.R.C.A., R.W.A.; painter; *b* Yeovil, 1919; *s* of P. T. T. Macdonald, surgeon; *m* Edna Orchard; one *s. Educ.:* Dauntseys School; *studied art* at W. of England College of Art (1937) under Evan Carlton, R.C.A. (1939) under Gilbert Spencer. *Exhib.:* R.A., R.S.A., R.W.A., etc. *Work in permanent collections:* R.W.E.A. *Official purchases:* War Artists' Collection, Edward Stott Fund. *Publication:* And the Sailor Sang. *Address:* c/o Blinkhorn Lyon, Golding & Co., 14-16 Gt. Portland St., London W1N 5AB. *Club:* Chelsea Arts. *Signs work:* "R.M."

MacDONALD, Stuart Wyllie, D.A.; Italian Government Scholarship (1971); artist in acrylic, oil and water-colour; teacher, Mackie Academy, Stonehaven; *b* Dundee, 8 Sept., 1948; *s* of D. K. C. MacDonald; *m* C. A. Macdonald. *Educ.:* Morgan Academy, Dundee; *studied art* at Grays School of Art, Aberdeen under R. Henderson Blyth, R.S.A., R.S.W.; Hospitalfield College of Art; Aberdeen College of Educ. *Exhib.:* R.S.A., S.S.A., R.G.I., A.A.S. *Work in permanent collections:* H.R.H. the Duke of Edinburgh, Scottish Arts Council, Camden Public Libraries. *Publication:* S.S.A. Catalogue (1971). *Address:* 8 Union St., Montrose, Angus, Scotland. *Club:* A.A.S. *Signs work:* "S. W. MacDonald."

McFALL, David, R.A.; sculptor in stone and bronze; *b* Glasgow, 1919; *s* of David McFall, civil servant; *m* Alexander Dane, actress; one *d. Educ.:* English Martyrs, Spark Hill; *studied art* at Birmingham, R.C.A. and Lambeth. *Work in permanent collections:* Bullcalf (Tate), Churchill (Burlington House), Balfour (House of Commons), Vaughan Williams (Royal Festival Hall), Lord Attlee (Imperial War Museum), bronze study of Prince Charles (Buckingham Palace), Oedipus and Jocasta (W. Norwood Library), Pocahontas (Red Lion Square,

Holborn), etc. *Addresses:* Natura, Fairlight Cove, Sussex TN35 4DJ; and 19 Colehill La., London SW6; (Studio) 1 White Hart St., Kennington, London SE11. *Signs work:* see appendix.

MacFARLANE, Sheila Margaret, D.A. (Edin.) 1964; artist, printmaker and engraver; lecturer in printmaking, Duncan of Jordanstone College of Art, Dundee (1970-76); founder and director, Printmakers Workshop at Kirkton of Craig; *b* Aberdeen, 2 May, 1943; *d* of Alexander Stewart MacFarlane; *m* Michael Stuart Green, N.D.D., F.R.S.A., interior designer. *Studied art* at Edinburgh College of Art (painting 1960-64); Atelier 17, Paris (printmaking under S. W. Hayter 1967-68). *Exhib.:* one-man show: Printmakers' Workshop, Edinburgh (1970); group shows: R.A., R.S.A., S.S.A., 'Original Print' (1972, 1973, 1974, 1975), 'A Word on Prints' Scottish Arts Council Gallery (1975), 'Impress' Aberdeen A.G. (1975), '4 Printmakers' Aberdeen Arts Centre (1973), 'International Print Exchange' Compass Gallery, Glasgow (1972). *Work in permanent collections:* Scottish Arts Council, Glasgow University, Fife Educ. Dept., Aberdeen Educ. Dept. *Address:* Kirk Tower House, Kirkton of Craig, Montrose, Angus, Scotland. *Signs work:* "Sheila M. MacFarlane."

McGLASHAN, Archibald A., R.S.A. (1939); Mem., Soc. of Eight; artist in oil; *b* Paisley, 16 Mar., 1888; *s* of John McGlashan; *m* Teresa; one *s*, two *d*. *Educ.:* Glasgow and Paisley; *studied art* at Glasgow School of Art under Fra. H. Newbery and Maurice Greiffenhagen, R.A. *Exhib.:* R.A., R.Scot.A., Royal Glasgow Inst. of Fine Arts, etc. *Work in permanent collections:* Scottish Modern Arts Assoc.; Glasgow University; Glasgow, Aberdeen, Dundee, Paisley, Newcastle upon Tyne, Berwick, Edinburgh and Belfast Corporations, Arts Council of Gt. Britain, Perth; many private collections. *Work repro.:* Studio, Artist, Colour, etc. *Address:* Gayfield, Serpentine Rd., Rothesay, Bute. *Club:* Glasgow Art. *Signs work:* see appendix.

Mac GONIGAL, Maurice Joseph, R.H.A. (1933), Hon. R.A. (1964), Hon. R.S.A. (1966), LL.D., Hons Causa, N.U.I. (1970); artist in oil, water-colour and the point; President, Royal Hibernian Academy of Arts; Governor and Guardian, National Gallery of Ireland; *b* Dublin, 22 Jan., 1900; *s* of Francis Mac Gonigal, church decorator; *m* Aida Kelly; two *s*. *Educ.:* Christian Brothers Schools, Dublin; *studied art* at Metropolitan School of Art, Dublin (1924-27). *Work in permanent collections:* National Gallery of Ireland, Municipal Gallery of Modern Art, Dublin, Cork Art Gallery, G. S. Hotels, Arts Council, Dáil and Senate Chambers, National Museum, etc. *Address:* Kendor, Shankill, Co. Dublin. *Signs work:* "Mac Con'gal."

McGRATH, Raymond, B.Arch., R.H.A., F.R.I.B.A., F.R.I.A.I., F.S.I.A.; architect, Prof. of Architecture, Royal Hibernian Academy; Past-President, Society of Designers in Ireland; *b* 7 Mar., 1903; *m*; one *s*, one *d*. *Educ.:* Fort St. High School, Sydney; University of Sydney; Clare, Camb.; drawing under Datillo Rubbo and Julian Ashton in Sydney; Westminster School of Art. *Exhib.:* Sydney, London, Dublin, New York, etc. (mainly water-colours, landscape and topography). *Official purchases:* aircraft production drawings (Ministry of Information). *Work repro.:* Various book illustrations. *Publications:* Twentieth Century Houses (Faber); Glass in Architecture and Decoration (Architectural Press). *Address:* Somerton Lodge, Rochestown Ave., Dublin. *Signs work:* "Raymond McGrath" (with long stroke under surname).

MacGREGOR, David Roy, M.A. (Cantab), 1948; F.R.Hist.S., A.R.I.B.A.; architect, ship draughtsman, author, artist in oil, water-colour and pen; *b* Fulham, 1925; *s* of Lieut.-Col. W. W. MacGregor, D.S.O. *Educ.:* Eton and Trinity College,

Cambridge; *studied art* under Cdr. G. F. Bradshaw, R.N., D.S.O., S.M.A. *Exhib.:* R.O.I., N.E.A.C., R.B.A., S.M.A., Camb. *Work repro.:* illustrations to his own books, The Tea Clippers (1952), The China Bird (1961), Fast Sailing Ships 1775-1875 (1973), and to The Merchant Schooners, by Basil Greenhill. *Address:* 99 Lonsdale Rd., London SW13. *Signs work:* "D. R. MacGregor."

McGUGAN, Ian Joseph; bronze 'medaille' from Council of Municipalim d'Antony, France (1974); artist in oil on canvas; *b* Toronto, Canada, 21 June, 1932; *s* of Duncan Fletcher, B.Eng.; *m* Myra McGugan; one *s*, one *d*. *Educ.:* Toronto; *studied art* at Ontario College of Art, Toronto. *Work in permanent collections:* Canada Arts Council 'Art Bank' Canada (Ottawa), and over 100 works in private collections. *Address:* 9 Selwyn Ct., Blackheath Village, London SE3 9SZ. *Signs work:* "McGugan" and year.

McGUINNESS, Norah, D.Litt. (Trinity College, Dublin); *b* Derry, 1903. *Educ.:* Londonderry High School; *studied art* at National College of Art, Dublin; Chelsea Polytechnic; André Lhote, Paris. *Exhib.:* Leicester Galls.; Paul Rheinhart, New York; Waddington Gall., Dublin; Dawson Gall., Dublin. *Work in permanent collections:* Municipal Gallery, Dublin; National Gall., Belfast; Cork Gall.; Trinity College, Dublin; Irish Arts Council. *Work repro.:* illustrations of books by W. B. Yeats and Elizabeth Bowen; costumes, masks and sets, Abbey Theatre. *Address:* 53 York Rd., Dun Laoghaire, Dublin. *Club:* Irish Club, London. *Signs work:* "Norah McGuinness."

McGUIRE, Edward Augustine, F.R.S.A.I.; Mem. Irish Senate (1948-65); Mem. The Arts Council (Ireland, 1951-56); Mem. Advisory Com. on Industrial Art; Mem. Board of Governors of National Gallery of Ireland; Mem. Visitors Com. to National Museum of Ireland; Mem. Cultural Relations Com. Dept. Ex. Affairs (1949-53); Mem. Com. Dublin Theatre Festival; artist in oil and water-colour; *b* Tramore, Co. Waterford, 1901; *s* of John F. McGuire; *m* Brigid Patricia Neary; two *s*, two *d*. *Educ.:* Clongowes Wood College, Douai Abbey School and National University of Ireland; *studied art* in Dublin. *Work in permanent collections:* Waterford, Limerick and Tralee A.G. *Work repro.:* Crucifixion. *Address:* Newtown Park, Blackrock, Co. Dublin. *Clubs:* Royal Irish Yacht, Fitzwilliam (Dublin), International Club of Gt. Britain, etc.

McINTYRE, Donald, R.I., R.C.A.; landscape painter in oil and water-colour; *b* Yorkshire, 1923; *s* of Dr. Donald McDonald McIntyre; *m* Gaynor Wyn; one *d*. *Educ.:* Scarborough College, Skipton Grammar School; *studied art* at studio of James Wright, R.S.W. *Work in permanent collections:* H.R.H. Duke of Edinburgh, Birkenhead Art Gallery, Newport (Gwent) Art Gallery, Merthyr Tydfil Gallery, Welsh Contemporary Art Soc. *Address:* Pen Llyn, Tregarth, nr. Bangor, Gwynedd. *Signs work:* see appendix.

MACKAY, Arthur Stewart, R.O.I. (1949); artist in oil; former lecturer, Hammersmith College of Art and Building; *b* Dulwich, London, 25 Feb., 1909. *Educ.:* Wilson's Grammar School, Camberwell, Regent St. Polytechnic School of Art; *studied art* at Regent St. Polytechnic School of Art. *Exhib.:* R.A., R.S.A., Paris Salon and London galleries. *Work in permanent collections:* in many private collections in Britain and Australia. *Publications:* articles on figure painting and outdoor sketching written for the publication, Artist. *Address:* 4 Dog Kennel Hill, East Dulwich, London SE22. *Club:* Denmark Lawn Tennis, Dulwich. *Signs work:* "A STEWART MACKAY" or "STEWART MACKAY."

MACKAY, Donald Cameron, Lieut.-Cdr., R.C.N. (Retd.); D.F.A., F.N.S.C.A., F.R.S.A.; Princ. N.S. Coll. of Art (1945-71); lecturer in Fine Arts, Dalhousie Univ.; artist in oil and water-colour; illustrator in graphic media; Past

Pres. N.S. Soc. Artists, Can. Soc. Education Through Art; V.P. Can. Soc. Graphic Art, N.S. Museum Fine Art; Can. Arts Council; *b* Fredericton, N.B., 1906; *m* (1st) Alice Mary Mackay, A.O.C.A., deceased; (2nd) Margaret Virginia MacNeil; one *d. Educ.:* Halifax Acad. and Dalhousie Univ.; *studied art* at N.S. Coll. of Art, Chelsea School of Art, Academie Colorossi, Toronto Univ. *Address:* 5883 Inglis St., Halifax, N.S. *Clubs:* United Services Inst. (Canada), Saraguay Club. *Signs work:* "Donald C. Mackay."

McKAY, Eric Bruce, F.R.S.A.; artist in oil, pastel, gouache, and interior decorator; owner Carmelite Studio, Fleet St. EC4 (1935-40); *b* Hampstead, 25 Sept., 1907; *s* of Frederick Bruce McKay; *m* Jessie Ellen Haslam; one *d. Educ.:* St. Mary, Finchley; *studied art* at Hampstead School of Art, L.C.C. School of Art, and in Florence. *Exhib.:* N.E.A.C., R.O.I., R.B.A., Canada and U.S.A. *Work in permanent collections:* Towner Gallery, Eastbourne; mural paintings for London boroughs. *Address:* Camden House, Camden Rd., Eastbourne. *Club:* Eastbourne Arts. *Signs work:* see appendix.

McKELVEY, Frank, R.H.A. (1930); portrait and landscape painter in oil and water-colour; *b* Belfast, 1895; *s* of William McKelvey; *m* Elizabeth Murphy; two *s. Educ.:* Belfast; *studied art* at College of Art, Belfast. *Exhib.:* London, New York, Musée d'Art (Brussels), G.I., Dublin, Belfast. *Work in permanent collections:* National Collection of Ireland (1938), Belfast, Dublin, Cork, Limerick, Waterford, The Queen's University, Boston College Library (Mass., U.S.A.), National Maritime Museum, Greenwich. *Official purchases:* by Haverty Trust, Dutch Royal Collection (presented to Princess Juliana from Dutch Residents in Eire as wedding gift). *Work repro.:* Falcaragh. *Publication:* Twelve Irish Artists. *Address:* Studio, St. Clair, My Lady's Mile, Holywood, Co. Down, N. Ireland. *Clubs:* Dublin Arts, Ulster Arts. *Signs work:* see appendix.

McKENNA, Laurence; artist in chalk, water-colour, pencil and oil; postal official; *b* 20 Nov., 1927; *s* of Charles J. McKenna; *m* Carmel Beattie; two *s*, one *d. Educ.:* St. Kevin's, Belfast; *studied art:* self-taught. *Exhib.:* Belfast, Dublin, Cork, London, U.S.A. *Work repro.:* Revue Moderne, Paris (drawing, 1947), Sunday Independent, Dublin (drawing, 1956), Irish News (drawing, 1958), Ulster Illustrated (drawing, 1958), Sunday Independent (drawing, 1965). *Address:* 7 Riverdale Pk. North, Belfast. *Signs work:* "LAURENCE McKENNA."

MACKENZIE, Alexander, N.D.D. (1949); painter; Head of Dept. Fine Art, Plymouth College of Art and Design; *b* Liverpool, 9 Apr., 1923; *s* of Dr. A. E. Mackenzie, F.R.C.S., L.R.C.P.; three *d. Educ.:* Pannal Ash College, Harrogate; *studied art* at Liverpool College of Art (1947-51). *Exhib.:* City A.G., Plymouth (1975); Waddington Galleries (1959, 1961, 1963); Durlachers, N.Y. (1960, 1962); Six painters (Waddington Galleries, 1962); Marzotto European Exhbn. (1963); Northern Artists (1960); Brooklyn, N.Y.; International Water-colour Exhbn. *Work in permanent collections:* Gulbenkian Foundation, Contemporary Art Society, Plymouth A.G., Nuffield Foundation, Arts Council of G.B., Bishop Suter Gallery, Nelson, N.A., National Gallery of N.S.W., West Riding, Cornwall C.C., Brazenose College, York, Oldham and Leamington A.G. *Address:* Trefrize, Linkinhorne, Callington, Cornwall. *Signs work:* "Alexander Mackenzie" (signed on the back).

McKENZIE, Alison, R.S.W., D.A. (Glas.), Fra Newbery medallist; gouache and oil painter and wood engraver; taught at Dundee College of Art for 10 years; *b* 30 Aug., 1907; *d* of George McKenzie, architect. *Educ.:* Prior's Field; Glasgow School of Art; Grosvenor School of Modern Art (Iain MacNab). *Exhib.:* R.S.W., S.S.W.A., R.S.A., etc. *Work in permanent collection:* Dundee, Ottawa. *Address:* 3

Playfair Terr., St. Andrews, Fife. *Signs work:* "Alison McKenzie" (followed by short stroke).

MACKENZIE, Keith, Slade Diploma, Punch Scholarship in Humorous Art (1947); caricaturist and illustrator using water-colour, etching, lithography; *b* London, 16 July, 1924; *s* of James Mackenzie, E. India Merchant; *m* Zelma Blakely. *Educ.:* Rugby School; *studied art* at Chepping Wycombe School of Art (1941-43) under J. C. Tarr, A.R.C.A., and Slade School under Prof. Randolph Schwabe. *Exhib.:* R.A., W.A.G., Senefelder Club. *Work in permanent collections:* University College, London. *Address:* 28 Ladbroke Grove, London W11. *Signs work:* "K. McK." or "Keith Mackenzie."

MACKENZIE, Phyllis Edith; Slade Dip. in Fine Arts; artist in oil, pastel, water-colour, pen and wash, sanguine, pencil, gouache; *b* Salvington, Sussex, 3 Aug., 1911; *d* of F. H. Fawkes; *m* K. E. Mackenzie; one *s*. *Educ.:* Cheltenham Ladies' College; *studied art* at Slade School of Art. *Address:* 24 London Rd., Datchet, Slough, Bucks. SL3 9JN. *Clubs:* East India, Sports and Public Schools. *Signs work:* "Phyllis Mackenzie."

McKENZIE, Winifred, D.A. (Glas.); for fourteen years taught in Dundee College of Art; artist in oil; wood-engraver; *b* Bombay, 23 Aug., 1905; *d* of George McKenzie, architect. *Educ.:* Prior's Field; *studied art* at Glasgow School of Art and Grosvenor School of Modern Art under Iain MacNab. *Exhib.:* R.S.A., S.S.W.A., etc. *Work in permanent collections:* Liverpool, Belfast, Cork. *Official purchase:* Modern Arts Assoc. *Work repro.:* in Studio, Image. *Address:* 3B Playfair Terr., St. Andrews, Fife. *Signs work:* "Winifred McKenzie."

MACKIE, George, D.F.C., R.D.I., R.S.W., F.S.I.A.; Head of Design, Grays School of Art, Aberdeen; Graphic Designer to Edinburgh University Press; *b* Cupar-Fife, 17 July, 1920; *m* Barbara Balmer, A.R.S.A., R.S.W.; two *d*. *Studied art* at Dundee College of Art (1937-40), Edinburgh College of Art (1946-48). *Exhib.:* R.S.A., R.S.W., S.S.A. *Work in permanent collections:* H.R.H. The Duke of Edinburgh, Scottish Arts Council, Edinburgh University, Aberdeen Art Gallery. *Work repro.:* Gebrauchsgraphik, and Graphis. *Addresses:* 7 Park Rd., Cults, Aberdeen; 37 Queensferry St., Edinburgh. *Signs work:* "GM" or "G Mackie."

MACKIE, Sheila Gertrude, 1st Class Hons. B.A. (Fine Art, 1950); artist in oil and pencil, pen and ink, and scraperboard; art mistress, Consett Grammar School; *b* Chester-le-Street, Co. Durham, 5 Oct., 1928; *d* of James W. B. Mackie. *Educ.:* Durham High School; *studied art* at King Edward VII School of Art, Durham University. *Exhib.:* R.A., Laing Art Gallery (Newcastle upon Tyne). *Work in permanent collection:* Shipley Art Gallery, Gateshead. *Official purchases:* Shipley Art Gallery, Gateshead; Dept. of Educ., King's College, Newcastle upon Tyne; Ministry of Works. *Work repro.:* The Studio. *Address:* Benachie, Pelaw Bank, Chester-le-Street, Co. Durham. *Signs work:* "S. G. MACKIE."

MACLAGAN, Dorothea F., R.A. Silver and Bronze medallist (1917-22); artist in oil and water-colour; *b* Greenoch, 1895; *m* Philip D. Maclagan, landscape painter. *Studied art* at Byam Shaw School of Art (1914-16), R.A. Schools (1917-22). *Exhib.:* R.A., R.O.I., N.E.A.C., etc.; one-man shows: Cambridge (1947), Dartington Hall (1975). *Address:* 1 Hembury, Bridgetown, Totnes, Devon. *Clubs:* Reynold's, Devon Art, Campden Hill. *Signs work:* "D.F.M."

MACLAREN, Neil, B.A. (Hons.); Deputy Keeper, National Gallery, until 1962; Associate Director, Sotheby & Co.; *b* 20 Dec., 1909; *s* of Neil MacLaren; *m* Nina Tarakanova. *Educ.:* Malvern College; University College, London; Courtauld Inst. of Art. *Publications:* Contributions to principal art publications; The

Spanish School (National Gallery, 1952); The Dutch School (1960). *Address:* 49 Maze Hill, Greenwich.

McLAREN, Sally; Central School of Art Diploma, Etching; French Government Scholarship; painter and printmaker; taught at Goldsmiths' School of Art, etching (1964-65); *b* London, 21 Sept., 1936; *m* David Webster; three *s*. *Studied art* at Central School of Art and Design, London (1960-63), Atelier 17. Work in many important international collections. *Exhib.:* one-man show of prints, Bear Lane, Oxford, studio prints, London; widely in group shows in England and abroad; Llubjana Print Biennale, Seoul Biennale; North-west Printmakers U.S.A.; Edinburgh Festival; Atelier 17 Group Show, Paris, etc. *Address:* 18 Downshire Hill, Hampstead, London NW3. *Clubs:* Printmakers' Council, R.E. *Signs work:* "Sally McLaren."

McLEAN, Henry, D.A. (1946); picture-restorer; Conservator of Paintings at Glasgow Art Gallery; *b* Glasgow, 4 Oct., 1927. *Educ.:* Glasgow; *studied art* at Glasgow School of Art under Hugh Adam Crawford (1942-46). *Publications:* articles in Scottish Art Review. *Address:* 122 Main St., Carnwath, Lanarkshire. *Club:* Glasgow Art.

MACLEAN, W. J., D.A.; teacher of art in drawing, constructions and oil; *b* Inverness, 12 Oct., 1941; *s* of John Maclean, master mariner; *m* Marian Maclean; one *s*, one *d*. *Educ.:* Inverness Royal Academy, H.M.S. *Conway*, N. Wales; *studied art* at Grays School of Art, Aberdeen (1961-66); British School at Rome (1966). *Exhib.:* one-man shows: Edinburgh, New 57 Gallery, Richard Demarco Gallery; group shows: Scottish Arts Council, Marjory Parr Gallery. *Work in permanent collections:* Aberdeen A.G., Scottish Arts Council, Contemporary Art Society, Hull A.G., British Transport. *Address:* School House, Gateside, Strathmiglo, Fife, Scotland. *Signs work:* "W. J. Maclean."

MACLEOD, Flora, B.W.S. (1951-56), S.S.W.A. (1955-67), S.W.A. (1960); *b* Forres, 24 Mar., 1907; *d* of Colonel Norman MacLeod. *Educ.:* privately. *Exhib.:* R.B.A. (Open Assembly), R.I., R.S.W., S.S.W.A., S.W.A., R.G.I., R.W.S. Art Club, Ridley Art Club, R.B.S.A., Paisley Art Inst., Aberdeen Artists, Britain in Water-colours. *Address:* Dalvey, Forres, Morayshire. *Signs work:* "FLORA MACLEOD."

MACLEOD, Margaret Henderson, D.A. (Edin.), M.S.S.A.; artist in oil and water-colour; art teacher, Dunoon Grammar School; *b* Barnet, 26 Sept., 1922; *d* of Alexander Doig, C.A.; *m* Rev. Allan Macleod; two *s*. *Educ.:* Elgin Academy; *studied art* at Edinburgh College of Art (1940-44) under W. G. Gillies, W. M. MacTaggart. *Exhib.:* R.S.A., R.S.W., S.S.A. *Address:* The Manse, 103 Auchamore Rd., Dunoon.

MACLUSKY, Hector John; Slade Dip. (London); painter; illustrator; L.C.C. lecturer (1948-50); art master, Highgate School (1948-50); *b* Glasgow, 20 Jan., 1923; *s* of W. B. McLusky, M.C. *Educ.:* Roundhay and Warwick Schools; *studied art* at Leeds College of Art (1939-40) and Slade School (1945-48). *Exhib.:* R.A., R.B.A., London and provinces. *Work in private collections:* in America and Australia. *Work in permanent collection:* Leighton House Art Gallery (London). *Work repro.:* in books, journals and posters; free-lance cartoonist and illustrator for Press and television. *Address:* Hollybush House, Baines Lane, Datchworth, Herts.

MACMARTIN, John Rayment, D.A. (Glasgow), F.R.S.A. (London); Industrial Design Consultant and Architectural Designer; Lecturer in Industrial Design and Art; artist in oils, wood carvings, metal sculpture; *b* Glasgow, 3 Oct., 1925; *s* of John Menzies Macmartin, works manager; *m* Evelyn Margaret Lindsay Macmartin, embroideress; two *s*, one *d*. *Educ.:* Allan Glen's Sen. Sec. School, Glasgow; *studied art* at Glasgow School of Art (1946-50) under Mr. McCrumb, Design; Mr. Beno Schotz, Sculpture; Mr. Crawford, Painting; Mr. Adams, Architecture; Past President, Glasgow School of Art Graduates' Association. *Work in permanent collections:* Lanarkshire Public Libraries, Clydesdale Bank, History of East Kilbride (in oils), Lanarkshire Educ. Authority, designed scheme for Seaborne Centre for Scotland at Irvine, that the Development Corp. are developing. *Address:* Rosebank, 2 Markethill Rd., East Mains, East Kilbride. *Club:* East Kilbride Art. *Signs work:* "John Rayment Macmartin."

MacMIADHACHÁIN, Pádraig; artist, paints mostly in Romania, Poland, Canaries and his Dorset home; Travelling Prize to Moscow (1957), British Council Scholarship to Poland (1961); *b* Downpatrick, Ireland, 2 Mar., 1929; *s* of Jim McMechan, bank manager; *m* Hazel McCool; two children; divorced; *m* Ann Slacke, one child. *Educ.:* Bangor Grammar School, Bangor; Portoria Royal School, Enniskillen; *studied art* at Belfast College of Art (1944-48), National College of Art, Dublin (1948-49). *Exhib.:* one-man: Belfast, London, Madrid, Krakow; Arts Council, R.A., Design Centre, Gorky Park Galleries, Moscow, Irish Exhbn. of Living Art. *Work in collections:* Arts Council, Ronald Alley, Sam Wanamaker, Chris Chataway, Peter Sellers, Bob Monkhouse, Asa Briggs, etc. *Publications:* two collections of poems, Spanish Cook-Book (jointly with wife, Anna Davey, 1973). *Address:* Studio 7, Swanage, Dorset. *Signs work:* see appendix.

McMILLAN, Ian Douglas, D.A. (Glasgow); Director, Glasgow League of Artists; artist in oil on canvas and timber mixed media constructions; *b* Glasgow, 2 June, 1946. *Educ.:* Hillhead High School, Glasgow; *studied art* at Glasgow School of Art (1964-68). *Exhib.:* one-man shows: Third Eye Centre (1975), New 57 Fruit Market Gallery (1975); group shows: Project Gallery, Dublin (1975), Liverpool Academy of Arts (1974), Edinburgh Festival (1973, 1974, 1975), Aberdeen A.G. (1973), Arts Council Gallery, Belfast, Contemporary Scottish Artists, Edinburgh Arts Centre. *Work in permanent collections:* Scottish Arts Council, Fife C.C. *Address:* 2 Caledon St., Glasgow, G12 9DX. *Signs work:* "Ian D. McMillan."

McMILLAN, William, C.V.O. (1956), R.A. (1933), A.R.A. (1925), Hon. LL.D. (Aberdeen, 1957); sculptor; *b* Aberdeen, 31 Aug., 1887; *m* Dorothy Williams. *Studied art* at Grays School of Art and R.C.A. *Principal works:* George V (Calcutta); Earl Haig (Clifton College, Bristol); Hugh Oldham (Manchester Grammar School); Beatty Memorial Fountain, Trafalgar Sq.; Constance Lund Fountain (Regents Pk.); Memorial to Alcock and Brown (London Airport); King George VI (Carlton Gdns., London); and various models and busts; works in Tate Gallery, etc. *Address:* 65 Glebe Pl., London SW3. *Club:* Chelsea Arts.

MACMURRAY, Elizabeth Hyde, M.A. (Aberdeen, 1915); painter in oil; *b* Banchory, Kincardineshire, 23 Dec., 1891; *d* George Campbell; *m* Prof. John Macmurray, M.C., LL.D. *Educ.:* University of Aberdeen; *studied art* privately in London with Roy de Maistre and Martin Bloch. *Exhib.:* R.S.A., S.S.A., S.S.W.A. *Address:* 8 Mansionhouse Rd., Edinburgh, EH9 1TZ. *Signs work:* "E. Hyde Macmurray."

McNEILL, Mary, F.S.D-C.; City and Guilds Dress Design and Making 1st class; Mem. Crafts Centre London and Edinburgh; professional handweaver in wool, cotton, raffia, consultant; *b* Newcastle-upon-Tyne, 9 May, 1913; *d* of George Nelson Wetherell; *m* Thomas Cragg McNeill; three *s*. *Educ.:* Lemington Grammar School, Northumberland; *studied weaving* with Dorothy Wilkinson and

Mother (professional court dressmaker and weaver). *Exhib.:* Textiles '68, London, Weaving Today, London, S.D-C., London, Lincoln Cathedral, Southampton A.G., Bath. *Work in permanent collections:* Reading Museum, Edinburgh Weavers' Guild, Berkeley Museum, California. *Publications:* articles, such as Handweaver & Craftsman, U.S.A. *Address:* 32 Parkstone Av., Southsea, Hants. PO4 0QZ. *Signs work:* "Mary McNeill."

MACPHAIL, Ian S., F.I.P.R.; artist in typography and print design; Director-General, World Wildlife Fund; free-lance typographer and editor; asst. music controller, E.N.S.A., specializing in publicity; asst. music director, Arts Council of Gt. Britain, responsible for all printing and publicity design; *b* Aberdeen, 11 Mar., 1922; *m* Michal Hambourg; one *s*, one *d*. *Educ.:* Aberdeen Grammar School; *studied art* with Charles W. Hemmingway. *Exhib.:* Exhbns. of posters, Council of Industrial Design. *Work repro.:* British Printer. *Publications:* You and the Orchestra (McDonald & Evans), editor and designer of Dexion News, Good Company and The Griffith Graph, designed literature for the first world conference on gifted children (1975). *Address:* 35 Boundary Rd., St. John's Wood, London NW8. *Club:* Savile. *Signs work:* "Ian Mac. Phail."

MACPHERSON, George Gordon, D.S.C., A.R.B.S.; sculptor in metal, wood, clay, and painter in oil and water-colour; Head of Dept. of Sculpture, Liverpool College of Art (1954-71); *b* London, 10 May, 1910; *s* of G. Gordon MacPherson, accountant; *m* Hilda Heap; two *s*. *Educ.:* Oldershaw Grammar School, Wallasey; *studied art* at Liverpool College of Art (1927-32) under W. C. Penn, Central College of Art, London (1936-38), under Sir Alfred Turner and William Roberts. *Exhib.:* W.A.G., Liverpool Academy, Bluecoat Gallery, Whitworth Gallery, Manchester, Bradford Art Gallery, Royal Cambrian Society, Suffolk Galleries, London. *Address:* Ty Gwyn, Llannefydd, Denbighs. *Club:* Liverpool Academy. *Signs work:* "Gordon MacPherson" or letter M in circle surmounted by horns.

MACPHERSON, Hamish, A.R.B.S., M.S.I.A.; sculptor; industrial designer; teacher, Central School of Arts and Crafts, London (1948-52), Sir John Cass School of Art, London (1948-53); *b* Hartlepool, 20 Feb., 1915. *Educ.:* New Zealand; *studied art* at Elam School of Art, Auckland, N.Z. (1930-32), Central School of Arts and Crafts, London (1934-39). *Exhib.:* one-man exhbns., Picture Hire, Ltd., London (1938), Chelsea Gallery, London (1947), Apollinaire Gallery, London (1950, 1952), Alwin Gallery, London (1968), London Group, N.S., New York, Paris, the Colonies and provinces; work for Festival of Britain (1951). *Address:* Alpha, The Ridge, Winchelsea Beach, Sussex. *Signs work:* "Hamish Macpherson."

MacTAGGART, Sir William, Kt. (1962), P.P.R.S.A., H.R.A. (1959), H.R.S.W. (1959), LL.D. (1961), F.R.S.E. (1967), R.A. (1973), Chevalier de la Legion d'Honneur (1968), H.F.R.I.A.S. (1968); artist in oils; Pres. Royal Scottish Academy (1959-69); *b* Loanhead, Midlothian, 15 May, 1903; *s* of Hugh Holmes MacTaggart, engineer; *m* Fanny Margaretha. *Educ.:* privately; *studied art* at Edinburgh College of Art and abroad. *Work in permanent collections:* Tate Gallery, and in major public galleries in Scotland, England, U.S.A. and Australia. *Address:* 4 Drummond Pl., Edinburgh EH3 6PH. *Club:* Scottish Arts. *Signs work:* "W. MacTaggart."

McWILLIAM, F. E., C.B.E. (1966), Hon. Dr. of Lit., Belfast (1964); Fellow U.C.L. (1972); sculptor; *b* Banbridge, Ireland, 30 Apr., 1909; *s* of Dr. W. N. McWilliam; *m* Elizabeth Crowther; two *d*. *Educ.:* Campbell College, Belfast; *studied art* at Slade School. *Exhib.:* London Gallery, Hanover Gallery, Battersea Park, Glasgow, Antwerp, Holland Park, Sonsbeeck, Musée Rodin, Stockholm,

Gothenberg. *Official purchases:* Tate Gallery; V. & A. Museum; Arts Council of Gt. Britain; Contemporary Arts Soc.; National Gallery, S. Australia; Art Inst., Chicago; Antwerp; Belfast; New Zealand; Toronto. *Address:* 8A Holland Villas Rd., London W14. *Signs work:* "McW." *Agent:* Waddington Galleries.

MADDOX, Ronald, R.I., F.S.I.A., S.G.A., P.S.; consultant designer, illustrator, artist in water-colour, line, gouache, acrylic; *b* Purley, Surrey, 5 Oct., 1930; *s* of H. G. Maddox; *m* Camilla Farrin; two *s. Studied art* at St. Albans School of Art, London School of Print and Graphic Arts. Design/art direction advertising (1951-61), freelance from 1962. *Exhib.:* R.A., R.I., S.G.A., Mall Galleries, Wapping Group, one-man shows. *Work in permanent collections:* Britain, Germany. *Work repro.:* Post Office stamp designs/telephone directories, C.O.I., B.R., B.B.C., B.T.A., publishing, advertising. *Address:* Herons, 21 New Rd., Digswell, Welwyn, Herts. *Signs work:* "RONALD MADDOX" or "MADDOX."

MAER, Stephen, M.S.D-C., Mem. British Crafts Centre, C.A.C. Index of Craftsmen, Design Council Register of Designers; designer jeweller; part-time lecturer, Central School of Art & Design, Sutton College of Liberal Arts; *b* London, 1933; *s* of Mitchel Maer; *m* Janet Eddington; one *d. Educ.:* Clayesmore School; *studied art* at R.C.A. under Prof. R. Goodden. *Exhib.:* one-man show: Ashgate Gallery, Farnham; group show: Toronto, San Francisco, London: Design Centre, Cameo Corner, Crafts Centre, Goldsmiths Hall. *Address:* 18 Yerbury Rd., London N19. *Signs work:* "SM" (hallmark).

MAGOR, William Laurence, A.R.C.A. (1939), A.T.D. (1940); Principal, Berkshire College of Art (since 1960); artist in water-colour; *b* Mountain Ash, S. Wales, 30 Apr., 1913; *s* of L. L. Magor; *m* Marie Alexander; one *s*, two *d. Educ.:* Crypt Grammar School, Gloucester; *studied art* at Gloucester Art School (1932-36) and R.C.A. (1936-39) under E. Bawden, Paul Nash. *Exhib.:* R.A. *Address:* 10 Laburnham Rd., Maidenhead, Berks. *Signs work:* "W. L. Magor."

MAHLER, Marianne, N.R.D., F.S.I.A.; book illustrator, free-lance designer (textiles, etc.), qualified art teacher, etc. *Educ.:* Vienna, and grammar school; Kunstgewerbeschule, Vienna (Prof. Josef Hoffmann, architect); R.A.; prize, Paris Exhbn.; under contract David Whitehead Furnishing Fabrics. *Exhib.:* Paris Exhbn. (1936), Vienna, London, Manchester, New York. *Work repro.:* Textiles, furnishing fabrics, wallpapers, posters, show cards, etc.; designs in Vogue, Studio, Design in Britain, British Textiles, British Achievement in Design. *Publications:* Children's books (written and illustrated, signed Marian). *Address:* 11 Weech Rd., London NW6.

MAHONEY, Dorothy Louise, A.R.C.A.; calligrapher; teacher of calligraphy at R.C.A. (1934-53), teacher of calligraphy at the Stanhope Institute, Mem. Soc. Scribes and Illuminators, and Soc. of Designer Craftsmen; *b* Wednesbury, 1902; *m* Charles Mahoney, R.A.; one *d. Studied art* at Ryland Memorial School of Art, W. Bromwich; R.C.A. (Sir W. Rothenstein, 1924-28). *Exhib.:* Soc. of Designer Craftsmen Exhbns., and Crafts Centre. *Publications:* articles on Lettering in Art Magazines. *Address:* Oak Cottage, Wrotham, nr. Sevenoaks, Kent. *Signs work:* "Dorothy Mahoney."

MAKEPEACE, John, F.S.I.A.; furniture designer and craftsman in wood; member of various committees for the Crafts Advisory Committee; *b* Solihull, 1939; *m* Ann Sutton. *Educ.:* Denstone College, Staffs.; *apprenticed to* Keith Cooper. *Exhib.:* 1975: Philadelphia, Tokyo, London, Dusseldorf. *Work in permanent collections:* V. & A., Leeds Museum, Cardiff Museum. *Featured in* House & Garden (July 1975), Domus (Aug. 1975), Vogue (Jan. 1976); filmed for "Aquarius", produced and directed by Peter Hall (1975). *Publication:* Decorative

Art and Modern Interiors (1975/76). *Address:* Parnham House, Beaminster, Dorset. *Signs work:* "John Makepeace."

MAKINSON, Prof. Trevor Owen; portrait and landscape painter; visiting lecturer, Glasgow School of Art and Glasgow University; Director of Moglia-Makinson Gallery, Glasgow; *b* Southport, 8 June, 1926; *s* of Owen Makinson. *Educ.:* privately; *studied art* at Hereford Art School, Slade School. *Exhib.:* R.A., R.B.A., R.P., R.S.A., United Soc. of Artists, Soc. of Scottish Artists, R.G.I., Wye Valley Art Soc., Herefordshire Arts and Crafts; one-man shows at Hereford Art Gallery (1944, 1946, 1949, 1955), Buxton (1948), Worcester (1951), Nottingham (1953), Worthing (1954). *Official purchases:* Hereford, Salford, Stoke-on-Trent, Stockholm, Nat. Mus. of Wales, Worthing, Newport A.G., Glasgow A.G., Glasgow University College, Buxton A.G. *Address:* c/o Glasgow School of Art (Staff), 167 Renfrew St., Glasgow C3. *Signs work:* "Makinson" or "MAKINSON."

MAKLOUF, Raphael; sculptor in bronze; painter; *b* Jerusalem, 10 Dec., 1937. *Studied art* at Camberwell School of Art (1953-58) under Dr. Karel Vogel. *Official purchases:* Tower of London, Carnegie Hall, N.Y., etc. *Address:* 3 St. Helena Terr., Richmond, Surrey. *Signs work:* see appendix.

MALCLES, Jean-Denis; Mem. Salon d'Automne, Salon des Artistes Décorateurs, Salon de l'Imagerie, Chevalier ordre des Arts et Lettres; painter in oil, gouache and pastel; lithographer; stage and costume designer; *b* Paris, 15 May, 1912; *s* of Laurent Malcles, sculptor; *m* Martine Malcles. *Educ.:* École Boulle and Académies Peinture; *studied art* under Louis Sognot and Rulhmann. *Work in permanent collections:* Musée d'Art Moderne. *Official purchases:* City of Paris, French Government. *Work repro.:* Vogue, Femina, Plaisir de France, Graphis, Ballets des Champs-Elysées, Art et Style, Style en France. *Theatre decor:* Opéra de Paris, Comedie-Francaise, Scala de Milan, Opéra de Hambourg, Cie Renaud-Barrault, Festival musique d'Aix en Provence, Le Théâtre de Jean Anouilh, Covent Garden. *Publications:* Bel Ami, Lettres de Mon Moulin, La Muse au Cabaret, Affiches. *Address:* 152 rue L. M. Nordmann, Paris 13. *Signs work:* see appendix.

MALCOLM, Ellen, A.R.S.A. (1968), Guthrie Award (1952); artist in oil; teacher; *b* Grangemouth, 28 Sept., 1923; *d* of John Malcolm; *m* Gordon S. Cameron, R.S.A. *Educ.:* Aberdeen Academy; *studied art* at Gray's School of Art, Aberdeen (1940-44) under Robert Sivell, R.S.A., and Dr. D. M. Sutherland, R.S.A. *Work in permanent collections:* Perth City Gallery, Art Gallery, Southend, Lillie Gallery, Milngavie, Edinburgh City Collection, Palace of Holyrood House, Thorburn-Ross and Dr. Arnott Hamilton Collections, Edinburgh. *Address:* 7 Auburn Terr., Invergowrie, Perthshire. *Signs work:* "E. Malcolm."

MALEŠ, Miha; artist in oil, monotype, engraving on wood and metal, linoleum, lithography, lithogravure, etching, fresco; *b* Jeranovo, Slovenia, 6 Jan., 1903; *s* of Franc Maleš; *m* Olga Čibej; one *d. Studied art* at Academy of Fine Arts, Zagreb; private Art School of St. Anna, Vienna; Academy of Fine Arts, Prague. *Work in permanent collections:* National Picture Gallery, Ljubljana, Modern Picture Gallery, Ljubljana, Modern Picture Gallery, Milano, Rome, Leningrad, Zagreb and Belgrade. *Work repro.:* Makedonija, Moderna galerija, Dom in Svet, Arhitektura, Mladika, Umetnost-Ljubljana, Les Arts, Nouvelles Litteraires, Studio, Rhein-Neckar Zeitung, Monografija, Slovenski lesorez, Slovenski slikarji. *Address:* Ljubljana, Vošnjakova 9, Yugoslavia. *Signs work:* "Miha Maleš."

MALET, Guy, R.B.A. (1936), Soc. of Wood Engravers (1947); painter in oil and water-colour, engraver; *b* 6 Aug., 1900; *s* of the late Major John Warre Malet; *m* Dorothy Coxon. *Educ.:* Downside School; R.M.C., Sandhurst; London School of Art; Grosvenor School of Art. *Exhib.:* R.A., R.B.A., R.E., Wood Engraving Soc., N.E.A.C., Printmakers Soc. of California. *Official purchases:* B.M., V. & A., Liverpool, Harrogate, Edinburgh College of Art, National Gallery of Canada, Contemp. Art Soc. *Address:* Fairmead, North End, Ditchling, Sussex. *Club:* Arts. *Signs work:* "Guy Malet" (on water-colours), "GUY MALET" (on oils and prints).

MALINS, Margery Helen, A.T.D., D.A. (Reading), R.C.A., F.P.S. (Assoc.), Assoc. Liverpool Academy; artist in oil, water-colour, screen print; *b* Reading; *d* of Dr. E. W. Squire, M.B., B.S. (London); *m* F. M. Malins, A.T.D., D.A., R.C.A.; four *s. Educ.:* Abbey School, Reading; *studied art* at Reading University under Prof. A. Betts and Walter Bayes, Liverpool College of Art. *Address:* Kings Mill Lodge, Kings Cross La., South Nutfield, Redhill. *Signs work:* "M. H. Malins."

MALLET, Violet Sanders: see SANDERS, Violet.

MALTHOUSE, Eric; painter; *b* Birmingham, 1914; *s* of J. W. Malthouse; *m* Anne Gascoigne; one *s*, two *d. Educ.:* King Edward's, Birmingham; *studied art* at College of Art, Birmingham (1931-37). Founder of the 56 Group. Mural Paintings: Wales Gas Board, Penylan Hostel and L. G. Harris & Co. Ltd. *Exhib.:* Ten-year Retrospective (1959), Growth of Two Paintings (1963), Paintings, New Vision Gallery (1965), Small Paintings, A.I.A. (1969), Bangor Art Gallery (1970), Oxford Gallery (1971), Exeter Univ. (1975). *Work in permanent collections:* National Museum of Wales, Welsh Arts Council, Swansea and Newport Art Galleries. *Address:* Marlais, Church La., Cargreen, Saltash, Cornwall. *Signs work:* see appendix.

MANDL, Anita, A.R.W.A. (1970), R.S.M.A. (1971), A.R.B.S. (1972), Ph.D. (1951), D.Sc. (1960); sculptress, formerly University Reader, Medical School, Birmingham; carvings in wood (mainly tropical timbers) and stone (alabaster, marbles); *b* Prague, 17 May, 1926; *m* Dr. Denys Jennings. *Studied art:* part-time at Birmingham College of Art. *Exhib.:* R.A., R.B.A., R.W.A., R.S.A., R.G.I.F.A., R.S.M.A., R.U.A., Leicester Gall., London. *Work in permanent collection:* Ulster Museum. *Work repro.:* Exploring Sculpture by Jan Arundell (Mills and Boon, 1971). *Address:* 21 Northview Rd., Budleigh Salterton, Devon. *Signs work:* Mostly unsigned. (Highly polished carvings are marred by signature.)

MANESSIER, Alfred; painter, designer; *b* St. Ouen, France, 5 Dec., 1911. *Educ.:* Lycée and École des Beaux Arts, Amiens. *Exhib.:* Paris, Luxembourg, Frankfurt, Stuttgart, Constance, Toronto, Dublin, Stockholm, Gotenbourg, Pittsburgh, London, Bâle, Vienna, New York, Kassel, Valencia, Venezuela, Tel-Aviv, Munich, Geneva, Milan, Turin, Lissone, Venice, Dortmund, Ljubljana, Tokyo, Kyoto, Brussels, New York, Stockholm, Copenhagen. *Work in permanent collections:* Art Moderne, Paris, Le Havre, Rouen, Amiens, Nantes, Brussels, Eindhoven, Bâle, La Chaux de Fonds, Turin, Oslo, Stockholm, Malmö, Carnegie Institute, Pittsburgh. *Address:* c/o Galerie de France, 3 Faubourg Saint Honoré, Paris.

MANLEY, Edna; sculptor in wood; *b* England, but since youth lived and recognized as Jamaican, 28 Feb., 1900; *d* of Rev. H. G. Swithenbank; *m* N. W. Manley, politician and lawyer; two *s. Educ.:* W. Cornwall College; *studied art* at St. Martin's and Regent St. Polytechnic, London. *Exhib.:* London Group, Germany and Guyana; one-man show, French Gallery, Goupil Gallery, Atlanta, U.S.A., Canada, Puerto Rico, Cuba, Haiti, Jamaica. *Work in permanent collections:* Eve and Dance in Sheffield. *Public statues:* Holy Cross Church (Mary), All Saints Church (Crucifix), Kingston Parish Church (Angel), Court House, Morent Bay and George VI Park, Kingston (Paul Bogle). *Official purchases:* University

College of the West Indies, Institute of Jamaica. *Work repro.:* in Studio. *Address:* Regardless, Washington Dr., Kingston 10, Jamaica, W.I. *Signs work:* see appendix.

MANN, Alex; artist in acrylic, Gallery Director; *b* Ayr, Scotland, 23 Feb., 1923; *s* of Charles Rob Mann; *m* Joyce; four *d. Educ.:* Polockshield Academy; *studied art* at Sidcup School of Art under Mr. Saunderson. *Work in permanent collection:* Leamington Art Gallery. *Address:* The Old Mill, Clifford Chambers, Stratford on Avon, Warks. *Signs work:* "A. Mann."

MANN, Paul Bevington, F.R.S.A. (1947); since 1956 painted almost exclusively in cellulose cols., developing new techniques for use of this medium on all surfaces; *b* Kettering, 16 Feb., 1907; *s* of Lewis William Mann; *m* three times, second wife killed in road accident; two *s* first marriage and one *s* and one *d* by second. *Educ.:* Kettering Central School; *studied art* at Wellingborough Technical College. *Exhib.:* many galleries in England, last one-man shows Luton Art Gallery (1966), Gallery 33 (1969), also many galleries in U.S.A., Canada, Brussels, Rome and work in many private collections. *Work repro.:* Studio and Penguin Books. *Publications:* How to Draw Locomotives (Studio) and others, now out of print. *Address:* Calgary House, Sherington, Newport Pagnell, Bucks. *Signs work:* "Paul Mann."

MANZU, Giacomo; artist in all materials; mem. of various academies; hon. professor of sculpture, Academy of Fine Arts of Brera, Milan; *b* Bergamo, 24 Dec., 1908; *s* of Fu Angelo Manzu; one *s. Educ.:* self-taught. *Exhib.:* all the principal exhbns. *Work in permanent collections:* Museums at home and abroad. *Official purchases:* various governments. *Work repro.:* in several publications. *Publications:* various. *Address:* Campo del Fico, Ardea, Roma. *Signs work:* see appendix.

MAPP, John Ernest, A.R.C.A. (1948); head of creative arts, Grey Court Comprehensive School, Ham, Richmond, Surrey; artist in oil, water-colour, freelance designer, etc.; *b* Northampton, 26 Mar., 1926; *s* of E. Mapp; *m* Margaret Trayler; one *s,* one *d. Educ.:* Eaglehurst College, Northampton; *studied art* at Northampton School of Art (1941-45), R.C.A. (1945-48) under Barnett Freedman and Gilbert Spencer. *Exhib.:* R.A. *Address:* 64A Vineyard Hill Rd., Wimbledon Pk., London SW19. *Signs work:* see appendix.

MARAIS: see BROWN, Mary Rachel.

MAREK: see ZULAWSKI, Marek.

MAREK, Jerzy; self-taught primitive painter in oil; *b* Poland, 1925; *m* Margaret Marek; one *s. Exhib.:* Portal and Grosvenor Galleries, London, Great House Gallery, Rivington, Lancs.; also in a number of International and Arts Council Exhbns. for primitive painters. *Work in permanent collections:* Salford A.G., Bolton A.G., Abbotts Hall Museum, Kendal, Sydney Janis Coll., N.Y. *Publications:* postcards by Kirkpatrick Cards, London. *Address:* 155 Watling Street Rd., Preston PR2 4AE. *Signs work:* "J. Marek."

MARGRIE, Victor; potter in porcelain; secretary, Crafts Advisory Committee; *b* London, 29 Dec., 1929. *Studied art* at Hornsey College of Art. *Work in permanent collections:* V. & A., and private collections. *Work repro.:* in various books, magazines and journals. *Publications:* written contribution to The Oxford Companion to The Decorative Arts. *Address:* Red House, Hempstead La., Potten End, Berkhamsted, Herts. *Signs work:* see appendix.

MARIAN: see MAHLER, Marianne.

MARINI, Marino; sculptor, engraver, titolare, Cattedra di Scultura, Academy of the Brera, Milan, since 1940, Hon. Academician Accademia Florentina della

Arti (1932), Corres. Academ. Accademia Albertina, Bologna (1947), Mem. Royal Flemish Academy, Brussels (1950), Hon. Academ. Akademische Kollegium, Munich (1951), Mem. Accademie Royale des Beaux Arts, Stockholm (1952), Hon. Mem. Mark Twain Soc. (1954), Gran Premio for Sculpture Venice Biennale (1952), Gran Premio Internazionale of Accademia Lincei (Rome, 1954); *b* Pistoia, 25 Feb., 1901. *Studied art* at Academy of Fine Arts, Florence. *Work in permanent collections:* Florence, Turin, Milan, Brussels. *Address:* 2 Piazza Mirabello, Milan. *Signs work:* "Marino Marini."

MARKS, Claude; painter and author; *b* London, England, 13 Nov., 1915 (went to U.S., 1937; became U.S. citizen); *m*; one *s*. *Educ.:* Harrow and Cambridge (M.A. Honours). Served U.S. Air Corps (1942-45). M.F.A. Degree in Painting at State Univ., Iowa (1950). Article, Calling On Craig, Theatre Arts Magazine (1957). Designed sets for off Broadway productions, Tanglewood and New York Shakespeare Festival. *Exhib.:* F.A.R. Gallery, N.Y. (1961); American Embassy, London (June, 1965); The Room, Greenwich, London (1970); Lincoln Center, New York (1971); theatre drawings and pastels. *Publications:* From The Sketchbooks of the Great Artists (Crowell, N.Y., 1972); Pilgrims, Heretics and Lovers (Macmillan, N.Y., 1975). Guest lecturer on art, Metropolitan Museum of Art, N.Y. *Address:* 315 Central Park West, N.Y. 10025.

MARKS, Peggie; sculptress; *b* Oldham, Nov., 1914; *d* of Vivian Bethel, physical culturist; *m* Charles Marks; one *s*. *Educ.:* Werneth Grange Convent; *studied art* at Manchester Regional College of Art. *Exhib.:* Oldham A.G., Manchester A.G., Salford A.G., Galerie Vallombreuse Biarritz, Houses of Parliament, N. Regional travelling exhbn., Saddleworth Art Soc. Rooms. *Address:* (studio), 18 Waterloo St., Oldham. *Clubs:* Oldham Artists, Saddleworth Art Soc., Rochdale Sculptors. *Signs work:* "Peggie Marks,"

MARR, Leslie, M.A. (1947); artist in oil, water-colour and charcoal; Secretary, Borough Group (1947-49); *b* Durham, 14 Aug., 1922; *s* of Col. J. Lynn Marr, O.B.E., T.D. *Studied art* at Borough Polytechnic under David Bomberg. *Exhib.:* one-man shows: Everyman Gallery, Drian Galleries, Laing Art Gallery, Newcastle upon Tyne, Artemis Gallery, Woodstock Gallery, Maddermarket Theatre, Norwich, Fermoy Gallery, Kings Lynn. *Work in permanent collection:* Laing Art Gallery, Newcastle upon Tyne. *Address:* The Pottery House, Binham, Fakenham, Norfolk. *Signs work:* see appendix.

MARRIOTT, John Oakes; artist in oil; *b* London, 2 Apr., 1921; *s* of Maj.-Gen. Sir John Marriott. *Educ.:* Eton College; *studied art* at Chelsea Polytechnic (1948) and privately under Oskar Kokoschka (1950). *Exhib.:* two one-man shows and group shows, Trafford Gallery, London. *Address:* c/o Trafford Gallery, 119 Mount St., London W1Y 5HB. *Signs work:* "J. M."

MARSHALL, Brian Roberts, Des. R.C.A. (Silver Medal, 1960), F.S.D.C. (1963), F.R.S.A. (1968); industrial designer, silversmith and jeweller; gallery owner; director of The Design Mine, Truro, Cornwall; com. mem. Society of Design Craftsmen, Cornwall Crafts Assoc.; *b* London, 27 Feb., 1935; *s* of W. O. R. Marshall; *m* Sally; one *s*, one *d*. *Educ.:* Gravesend Technical College; *studied art* at Gravesend School of Art (1952-54), Canterbury College of Art (1954-56), R.C.A. (1957-60). *Official purchases:* H.M. Govt. Independence gifts to Malaysia (silver centrepiece, 1963), H.M. Govt. Independence gift to Trinidad and Tobago (silver centrepiece, 1964). *Address:* Roche House, Roche, nr. St. Austell, Cornwall. *Signs work:* "B. R. Marshall."

MARSHALL, Francis, F.S.I.A.; illustrator in black and white and water-colour, and author; Admiralty Camouflage Officer (1941-45); *s* of F. M. Marshall,

M.I.M.M., mining engineer; *m* Margaret Simpson. *Educ.:* H.M.S. Worcester; University College, London; Slade. *Exhib.:* Walker Galleries, Bond St. *Work repro.:* in Vogue, Harpers Bazaar, Woman's Journal, Studio, Art and Industry, Daily Mail, The Sketch, etc. *Publications:* Fashion Drawing; London West; An Englishman in New York; Sketching the Ballet; The London Book; The Londoner's Week-end Book; Drawing the Female Figure; Magazine Illustration. *Address:* Ashbury Villa, 25 Dury Rd., Hadley Green, Herts. *Signs work:* "F.M."

MARSHALL, John: landscape painter in water-colour; *b* Colchester. *Educ.:* Rugby School; *studied art:* pupil of Cedric John Kennedy (1898-1968). *Exhib.:* British Art Centre, New York, Leicester Galleries, London; *one-man exhbns.:* Leicester Galleries, London (1956, 1959, 1962). *Work in permanent collections:* Wadsworth Atheneum, U.S.A., Columbia Museum of Art, U.S.A., Norwich Castle Museum. *Official purchases:* Hull Education Committee. *Work repro.:* The Studio (July, 1956, Feb., 1960); monographs: Arts Review (June, 1956), The Studio (Feb., 1960). *Publications:* Cedric Kennedy memorial Catalogue and Monograph (1969 and 1972). *Address:* 41 Campden Hill Rd., London W8. *Signs work:* "John (J) Marshall."

MARSHALL MALAGOLA, Dunbar, R.B.A.; painter; Fellow of Free Painters and Sculptors; mem. Salon d'Automne, Paris (1972); Secretary-General of International Association of Art, U.N.E.S.C.O.; *b* Florence, 1918; *m* Daphne Chart. *Studied art* at Westminster and Chelsea Schools of Art under Gertler, Meninsky, Robt. Medley, Ceri Richards. *Work in permanent collections:* Mus. of Contemp. Art, Skopje, Yugoslavia; Academy of Savignano, Italy; University of Liverpool, etc. *Address:* 17 Broomhouse Rd., London SW6 3QU. *Signs work:* "Dunbar Marshall." *Gallery:* Grabowski, 84 Sloane Ave., London SW3. One-man exhbns. there in 1961 and 1964.

MARTIN, David McLeod, D.A. (Glasgow), R.S.W. (1961), Professional Member, S.S.A. (1949), Member, R.G.I. (1961); artist in oil and gouache; principal teacher of art; Past Vice-Pres., R.S.W.; *b* Glasgow, 30 Dec., 1922; *s* of Allan McLeod Martin; *m* Isobel A. F. Smith; four *s*. *Educ.:* Glasgow; *studied:* Glasgow School of Art, 1940-42 (R.A.F., 1943-46), 1946-48 under Hugh Adam Crawford, R.S.A. *Exhib.:* one-man shows: R.G.I. Gallery (1958), 57 Gallery (1958), Crestine Gallery (1965), Stone Gallery (1965), Pitlochry Festival Theatre Exhbn., Mansard Gallery, London. *Work in permanent collections:* Scottish Arts Council, Argyll Educ. Authority, Edinburgh Educ. Authority, Dunbartonshire Educ. Council, Edinburgh Corp. Council Chamber, and several private collections, including U.S.A. *Address:* The Old Schoolhouse, 53 Gilmour St., Eaglesham, Glasgow G76 0LG. *Signs work:* "DAVID M. MARTIN."

MARTIN, Frank Graeme, F.R.B.S., Dip. R.A.S.; sculptor in stone, wood, bronze, metal; teacher; Head of the Sculpture Dept., St. Martin's School of Art, London; *b* Portsmouth, 27 Dec., 1914; *m* Edna Joan; two *s*, two *d*. *Educ.:* Technical School, Portsmouth; *studied art* at School of Art, Portsmouth, Royal Academy Schools, London. *Address:* Cockle Rythe Cottage, 53 Southwood Rd., Hayling Island, Hants. *Signs work:* "Frank Martin."

MARTIN, Kenneth, O.B.E.; *b* Sheffield, 1905; *m* Mary Balmford (d. 1969); two *s*. *Studied:* Sheffield School of Art and Royal College of Art. First abstract works 1948. Since 1951 developed "Screw mobiles" and kinetic constructions. First "Chance and order" works 1969). *Exhib.:* I.C.A. (with M.M.) 1960, Waddington (1970, 1974), Whitechapel (with M.M.) 1971, Galerie Swart, Amsterdam (1974), Tate retrospective (1975), many international group exhbns. *Work in permanent collections:* Tate, Arts Council, British Council, New Orleans

Museum, McCrory Foundation, Kroller-Muller. *Commissions:* Brixton College of Further Education, Engineering Dept., Cambridge, Gorinchem Holland. *Publications:* Chance and Order (1973), Tate retrospective catalogue (1975). *Address:* 9 Eton Ave., London NW3.

MARTIN, Mabel L. I., Board of Educ. diploma, medallist; painter, oil, watercolour, miniaturist; art teacher (retd.); *b* Dover, 1887; *d* of Frederick Martin. *Educ.:* G.P.D.S.T.; *studied art* at Regent St. Polytechnic (1918-24) under Harry Watson, Bolt Court Lithography, Hornsey College (1932-34), Westminster (1938), privately Paris. *Exhib.:* R.A., Paris Salon, R.B.A., R.O.I., W.I.A.C., S.W.A., E. Kent Art Soc., Walker's and Whitechapel. *Work repro.:* poster of Dover, poster Girls' Club, London, postcards of Dover, Plate 4 in book, St. Edmund's Chapel, Dover, and in Les Artistes d'aujourd'hui La Revue Moderne. *Work in permanent collections:* portrait of Worshipful Masters in Bank of England Masonic Lodge, Dover Museum. *Address:* 2 Castlemount Rd., Dover. *Signs work:* "Mabel L. I. Martin."

MARTIN, Pierre Noël; artist, kinetic sculptor and painter in wood, metal, paper and paint; *b* London, 18 Dec., 1920. *Educ.:* Hackney Technical Institute. *Exhib.:* Hampstead Artists Council, F.P.S., Mall Galleries, Chelsea Artists, Gallery Petite. *Address:* 17 Princes Ave., London N10 3LS. *Club:* Hampstead Artists Council. *Signs work:* "Pierre Noël Martin."

MARTIN, Robert Russell; artist in oil of portraits, landscapes and still life; *b* Cleveland, Ohio, 9 June, 1918; *s* of Charles James Martin; *m* Kay Ackerman Martin. *Educ.:* Superior Grade School; Kirk Junior High; Shaw High School, Cleveland; *studied art* at Cleveland School of Art under Carl Geartner; Academie de la grande Chaumiere, Paris under Yves Breyer; Art Students League, N.Y. under Sidney Dickinson; Old Mill School, N.Y. under Jossey Bilan. *Work in permanent collections:* Schrafft's Restaurants: New York, Bal Harbour, Beverly Hills; Somerset Inn: Troy, Michigan; Plaza Madrid, Reading, P.A.; Win Schuler's Restaurants, Michigan; many private collections and one-man shows. *Address:* 3287 S. Weymouth Rd., Medina, Ohio 44256, U.S.A. *Signs work:* "Robert Martin."

MARTIN, Ronald Arthur, F.S.I.A., S.G.A., F.R.S.A.; graphic artist, painter and designer in water-colour, acrylic, lithography, engraver on wood; *b* Eastbourne, 6 Dec., 1904; *s* of Frank Martin, builder; *m* Hephzibah Relf; one *s*. *Educ.:* Eastbourne; *studied art* at Eastbourne School of Art (1921-24) under F. Reeve Fowkes, A.R.C.A.; L.C.C. School of Art and Graphic Reproduction (1926-31). *Exhib.:* R.A., R.B.A., R.I., S.G.A., R.S.M.A., London and provincial galleries; several one-man shows. *Work in permanent collections:* Hove Museum and Art Gallery, London Collections. *Publications:* Illustrating With The Airbrush. *Work repro.:* Admiralty, A.E.R.E., Harwell, Ministry of Defence, Ministry of Information, Designers in Britain, For Industry, National and Overseas. *Address:* 16 Valverde House, Eaton Gdns., Hove, Sussex BN3 3TU. *Club:* Sussex Painters. *Signs work:* see appendix.

MARTIN, Timothy Stuart, Hon. Major, Alderman, F.R.S.A., A.Coll.H., M.R.S.T., C. and G., Lond.; illustrator; Art and Crafts master, Queen Elizabeth's Grammar School for Boys, Mansfield; Hon. Sec., National Soc. for Art Education, E. Midland Area (1937-52); Chairman (1953-56); advisor, C. and G., since 1952; sometime examiner, N.S.A.M. and U.L.C.I.; *b* Bolsover, 18 Mar., 1908; *s* of John Martin; *m* Ann Johnson; one *s*, one *d*. *Educ.:* University College, Nottingham; *studied art* at Chesterfield and Nottingham. *Work repro.:* Parthenon, Building Times, Illustrated Builder and Carpenter; Editor, Boys' Practical Aid

(1937-40). *Address:* Westwood, 323 Chesterfield Rd. South, Mansfield, Notts. *Club:* Conservative. *Signs work:* "T. Stuart Martin," v for u.

MARTINEZ, Coqué; painter in tempera, oil, acrylic; *b* Navarra, Spain, 1928; *s* of Tirso Martinez Castillo, engineer. *Educ.:* Escuela Normal, Bilbao; *studied art* at Croydon School of Art and Crafts (1942-46) under G. F. Hinchliff (Principal), R. Marlow, R. Spear. *Exhib.:* one-man shows at the Spanish Institute, Archer Gallery, Arthur Jeffress Gallery, A.I.A. Gallery, Trafford Gallery. *Address:* c/o Trafford Gallery, 119 Mount St., London W1Y 5HB. *Signs work:* "COQUÉ MARTINEZ."

MARX, Enid C. D., R.D.I. (1942), F.S.I.A. (1946); designer of textiles to the Board of Trade Utility Furniture Design Com.; *b* 20 Oct., 1902; *d* of Robert Marx, consulting engineer. *Educ.:* Roedean School, Central School of Arts and Crafts, Royal College of Art. *Exhib.:* Burlington House, Paris, Leipzig, Boston Museum. *Official purchases:* Arts Council, V. & A., Leipzig, U.S.A. *Work repro.:* in Graphis, International Textiles, Listener, Vogue, Design 46, Architectural Review, House and Garden, Studio Year Book. *Publications:* Popular and Traditional Art in England (with Margaret Lambert); Victorian Scrapbook (with Margaret Lambert); and some twelve children's books. *Address:* The Studio, 39 Thornhill Rd., Barnsbury Square, London N1.

MASON, John, F.R.S.A. (1949); bookbinder, printer and publisher; co-founder mem. of Gregynog Press (Wales); manager of Shakespeare Head Press (Stratford-on-Avon, 1921-30); teacher at Leicester College of Art (1930-60); founded Twelve by Eight Paper Mill (1954); *b* Hammersmith, 26 Apr., 1901; *s* of J. H. Mason, R.D.I., typographer and teacher of printing. *Educ.:* Upper Latimer Secondary School, Hammersmith; *studied art* at Central School of Arts and Crafts (1915-21). *Publications:* Papermaking as an Artistic Craft, etc. (Twelve by Eight Press, Leicester). *Address:* 2 Ratcliffe Rd., Leicester. *Clubs:* Arts and Double Crown.

MASON, Michael Dean, N.D.D. Painting, A.T.D.; art teacher, Colyton Grammar School, Devon; painter in oils and water-colours; *b* Brooklands, Ches., 26 May, 1930; *s* of John D. Mason; *m* Françoise Pointis (30 Dec., 1965); one *s*. *Educ.:* Crediton Grammar School, Devon; *studied art* at Exeter College of Art (1947-51, 1953-55). *Exhib.:* Roland, Browse and Delbanco (1959, 1961); Retrospective Exhbn., University of Exeter (1963-64); Exeter, New Jersey, U.S.A. (1967); University of Leicester (1967), University of Exeter (1969). *Work in permanent collections:* Plymouth City Art Gallery (Devon). *Address:* 3 Cranford House, Denver Rd., Topsham, Exeter, Devon. *Signs work:* "MASON '67."

MASSON, Henri, C.G.P., C.S.P.W.C., L.L.D.; painter in oil and water-colour; art instructor Queen's University, Kingston, Ont. (1948-) and children's teacher at Canadian National Gallery; *b* Namur, Belgium, 7 Jan., 1907; *s* of Armand Masson; *m* Germaine Masson; two *s*, one *d*. *Educ.:* Athénée Royale, Brussels; *studied art* at Brussels and Ottawa, but mostly self-taught. *Exhib.:* London, Paris, Rome, Brazil, U.S.A. and Canada. *Work in permanent collections:* National Gallery, Ottawa, National Gallery, Caracas, Venezuela, Toronto Art Gallery, Vancouver Art Gallery, and ten other provincial galleries. *Address:* 1870 Ferncroft Cres., Ottawa, Ont. *Signs work:* "Henri Masson."

MATCHWICK, Beryl A., Hon. R.M.S.; artist in oil and water-colour; *b* London, 1907; *d* of W. Guildford Matchwick; *m* Anthony M. Tew. *Educ.:* privately; *studied art* at Redhill School of Art under W. Todd-Brown, R.O.I. *Exhib.:* R.A., R.I., R.M.S., R.S.A., Paris Salon, Hull, etc. *Address:* Springmead, Ramsbury, Marlborough, Wilts. *Signs work:* "Matchwick."

MATHESON, Gertrude A., M.S.S.A.; painter in oil, water-colour and pencil; *b* Edinburgh; *d* of Augustus Alexander Matheson, M.D., F.R.C.P.E.; *m* Alfred Badenoch, M.B., C.H.B. *Educ.:* Canaan Park, Edinburgh; *studied art* at Edinburgh College of Art (5 years). *Exhib.:* Paris Salon, R.S.A., S.S.A., S.WL.A., Coolings, R.B.A.; one-man shows: Edinburgh, W.A.G., Bradford, R.G.I. Summer Salon, London; two-man shows: Alnwick, Galerie Vallombreuse, Biarritz, Vallombreuse A.G., Palm Beach. Work in small private collections. *Address:* Newbarn, nr. Stenton, Dunbar, Scotland. *Signs work:* "Gertrude A. Matheson."

MATHEWS, Benjamin Kenny Ollard, R.O.I., P.N.S.; painter in oil and gouache; President of the National Society of Painters, Sculptors and Engravers; Hon. Secretary, Royal Institute of Oil Painters; *b* Duston, Northampton, 1889; *s* of the Rev. B. Mathews. *Educ.:* The Nautical College, H.M.S. *Worcester*; *studied art:* architecture in London, pupil of Eustace Frere; Qualified Associate, R.I.B.A. (1922); painting in Paris at Académie Moderne under Othon Friesz and Fernand Léger (1924, 1925); lived and worked principally in France until 1939. *Address:* 415 Abingdon Pk. Parade, Northampton. *Clubs:* Chelsea Arts, Savage. *Signs work:* "B. Mathews" or "B.M."

MATTAROZZI DI THARASH, Mirella (Mirice Janàcêk); artist-painter, fine arts professor, writer; Diploma, Istituto Belle Arti di Bologna, Accademia di Belle Arti di Bologna; *b* Bologna; *d* of Adelmo. *Exhib.:* Italy, Europe, South America. *Work in permanent collections:* museums, Palazzo Vecchio, Firenze, Castello Sforzesco, Milano, Museo S. Matteo, Pisa, etc. Associate of Incisori d'Italia (I.D.IT.), Ex Libristi d'Italia (E.L.D.IT.). *Publications:* Il Comanducci, Annuario Internazionale di Belle Arti (Berlin), Guida all'arte Italiana, Who's Who in Europe, ed. Feniks, etc., Knight of the Tommaso da Vico Order; Academician of the Accademia dei 500, Rome. Lady-in-waiting of the Corporazione Internazionale della Stella Croce d'Argento (C.I.S.C.A.) dei Cavalieri del Bene. *Address:* via Emilia Ponente No. 20-40133, Bologna, Italy.

MATTHEWS, H. Philip; portrait and landscape painter; Head of Fine Art, Camberwell School of Arts and Crafts; *b* 16 May, 1916; *s* of Harold Matthews, Army officer; one *d*. *Educ.:* Dauntsey's School, Wilts, Maidenhead School of Art; Euston Road School; privately, William Coldstream. *Exhib.:* London Group, R.A., Leicester Galls., etc. *Work in private collections:* purchases by Arts Council, Ministry of Works, etc. *Address:* 47 Elgin Cres., London W11.

MATTHEWS, Peter Jolyon Ellis, Dip.A.D. (1973), M.F.A. (1975); Fellowship at Gloucestershire College of Art; artist; *b* Prittlewell, 31 Aug., 1948. *Studied art* at Farnham College of Art (1967-70); Bristol Polytechnic (1970-73); Reading University (1973-75). *Exhib.:* one-man shows: Art Ngt London, South Hill Park, Bracknell, Festival Gallery, Bath. *Address:* 67 Langtoft Rd., Stroud, Glos.

MAY, Gwendolen Marie, R.E.; etcher, wood engraver, water-colour painter; formerly Heraldic painter at the College of Arms, London; *b* London, 14 July, 1903; *d* od Joseph Horsnell May, M.I.E.E., F.C.S. *Educ.:* Hornsey College of Art. *Exhib.:* R.A., R.E., R.B.A., N.E.A.C., W.I.A.S., S.G.A., A.I.A., U.A.S., provincial galleries, S. Africa and U.S.A. *Official purchases:* Wardrobe Room, Old Vic Theatre, by Bradford Permanent Collection; The Thames, Rotherhithe, Outskirts of London by Nottingham Castle Art Gallery; The Old Bridewell by Liverpool, Hornsey Borough Council, etc. *Works* in Ashmolean, Oxford; New York, Lisbon. *Address:* 21 Donovan Ave., Muswell Hill, London N10. *Signs work:* "Gwen May."

MAY, William Edward, Comdr. R.N. (emergency list); F.R.Inst. of Navigation; Deputy Director, National Maritime Museum (1951-68); Naval Asst.,

Compass Dept., Admiralty, and Curator, Admiralty Compass Museum (1929-51); *b* Tilehurst, Berks., 10 Nov., 1899; *s* of Edmund May, solicitor; *m* Mary Elspeth Margaret James. *Educ.:* R.N. Colleges, Osborne and Dartmouth. *Publications:* Compass Adjustment (1951); From Lodestone to Gyro Compass (1952); Dress of Naval Officers (1966); Swords for Sea Service (with P. G. W. Annis, 1971); A History of Marine Navigation (1973); articles in Encyclopædia Britannica and numerous periodicals. *Address:* 58 South Audley St., London W1.

MAYERSON, Anna; painter and sculptor; *b* Austria, 24 May, 1906; *d* of H. Kaphan. *Educ.:* Switzerland; *studied art* at Kunstgewerbe Museum, Zurich; Vienna Academy; Slade School. *Exhib.:* one-man shows: 5 exhbns. Leger Gallery; 3 exhbns. Hanover Gallery; 1 exhbn. Modern Art; 1 exhbn. Galleria Odyssia, Rome; 1 exhbn. Annely Juda Fine Art Gallery (1972); four-man shows with Sutherland, Ubac, Adler, Redfern Gallery; A.I.A. Exhbn. (4 Freedoms); UNESCO, Paris; selected group exhbn.: Central Institute of Art and Design, Hartford School, Arts Council, London Group, Arcade Gallery, Bradford (Yorks), Art Gallery and Museum, St. George's Gallery, Leicester Gallery, Hanover Gallery. *Publication:* illustrated Truman Capote's The Grass Harp (1951). *Address:* 9 Albert Bridge Rd., London SW11 4PX. *Signs work:* see appendix.

MAYES, Reginald Harry Duncan, M.S.I.A., painter in oil and water-colour; chief staff artist L.M.S. Railway (1936-46); Art Director, West One Studios; *b* 4 July, 1900; *s* of Herbert Henry Mayes; *m*; one *s*. *Educ.:* Priory School, Gt. Yarmouth; Regent St. Polytechnic (Harry Watson, Harold Brownsword); Goldsmiths' College (Clive Gardiner). *Address:* 32 Royal Esplanade, Westbrook, Kent. *Signs work:* "Reginald Mayes."

MAYES, W. Philip, Dip. of Museums Assoc., F.S.A. (Scot.), F.M.A.; keeper of Art Dept., Imperial War Museum (1950-67); asst., Leicester Museum and Art Gallery (1930-34); deputy curator, Royal Albert Memorial Museum, Exeter (1934-36); director, Paisley Museum and Art Galleries (1936-50); *b* Liscard, Ches., 25 Nov., 1907. *Educ.:* Wyggeston School, Leicester; *studied art* at Leicester School of Art and abroad. *Publications:* articles on art and kindred subjects in the Press; catalogues, guides and lectures. *Address:* 2 Berwick Rd., Saltdean, Sussex.

MAYO, Eileen; printmaker, illustrator and writer. *Studied art* at Slade School and Leger, Paris. *Exhib.:* R.A., many shows in London and U.K., also U.S.A., Canada, Australia, N.Z., Leipzig, Lugano, Tokyo, etc. *Work in permanent collections:* B.M. Print Room, V. & A., art galleries in U.K., U.S.A., Australia and N.Z. *Wrote and illustrated:* The Story of Living Things, and other books on natural history. *Designer of Postage Stamps:* Australia, Mammals and Barrier Reef series; N.Z., Capt. Cook Bicentenary; Fishes and Moths Definitives; Chatham Islands; Antarctic Treaty; U.N.I.C.E.F.; Alpine Plants, etc. *Address:* 11 Berwick St., Dunedin, N.Z. *Signs work:* "Eileen Mayo."

MAYS, Douglas Lionel; painter and illustrator in oil, water-colour and black and white; *b* 4 Aug., 1900; *s* of Adam Mays; *m* Janet Duff; four *d*. *Educ.:* Tiffins (Kingston-on-Thames); *studied art* at Goldsmiths' College (1920-23). *Exhib.:* R.A., R.B.A., S.G.A., Bournemouth, Blackpool and Canadian National Exhbn. *Work in permanent collection:* National Gallery of Canada (Ottawa). *Work repro.:* in Punch, John Bull, Tatler; and for Blackie & Son, John Murray, Odhams, Amalgamated Press, Heinemann, Newnes, Macmillan, Collins, Hurst & Blackett, Lutterworth, Nelson, Royle Publications, etc. *Address:* Mount Whistle, Ashton, Helston, Cornwall. *Club:* A.W.G. *Signs work:* "MAYS," "mays," and see appendix.

MEADOWS, Bernard, A.R.C.A.; sculptor; Prof. of Sculpture, Royal College of Art, London; *b* Norwich, 19 Feb., 1915; *s* of William Meadows; *m* Marjorie Payne; two *d. Educ.:* City of Norwich School; *studied art* at R.C.A., Norwich School of Art, and as asst. to Henry Moore. *Exhib.:* London, New York, Venice, Antwerp, Arnhem, São Paulo, Pittsburgh, Zürich, Dublin. *Official purchases:* Arts Council of Gt. Britain, Tate, V. & A., Contem. Art Soc., Arts Council, British Council, Museum of Modern Art, N.Y., Hertfordshire Education Committee. *Address:* 34 Belsize Gr., London NW3.

MEESON, Philip, N.D.D. (1951), A.T.D. (1952), Travelling Scholarship (1952-53), F.S.A.E. (1966), F.R.S.A. (1969); artist in oil, pen and wash and art teacher; *b* Liverpool, 14 Feb., 1932; *s* of F. J. Meeson, representative. *Educ.:* Holt High School, Liverpool; *studied art* at Liverpool College of Art under N. M. Bell, A.R.C.A., W. L. Stevenson, O.B.E. *Exhib.:* Walker A. G., Liverpool. *Address:* Brighton Polytechnic, Faculty of Art and Design ATD Dept., 2 Sussex Sq., Brighton, Sussex. *Signs work:* "P. Meeson."

MEISTERMANN, Georg; painter in oil and of murals, and designer of stained-glass windows; professor at Kunstakademie Karlsruhe; *b* Solingen, 16 June, 1911; *s* of Arthur Kaufmann; *m* Professor Ir. Edeltrud. *Educ.:* University, Cologne; *studied art* at Matare, Nauen (Academie of F. A. Düsseldorf). *Work in permanent collections:* German museums, private collections, churches, official houses, etc. *Address:* Karlsruhe, Stefanienstr. 82. *Signs work:* "G.M."

MELHUISH, George William Seymour; artist in oil, philosopher; *b* Bristol, 26 Aug., 1916; *s* of G. B. Melhuish, R.N. (retd.). *Educ.:* Tellisford House School; *studied art* in London and Paris. *Exhib.:* R.A., National Gallery (War Artists 1940-45), Arts Council exhbns.; one-man shows in London and Paris (1944-59), also Bristol R.W.A. (1962, 1971), Cheltenham Art Gallery (1950), Gloucester Art Gallery (1972). *Work in permanent collections:* Bournemouth, Bristol City, Gloucester, Walsall and Worcester Art Galleries. *Official purchase:* Imperial War Museum. *Work repro.:* in Studio, Connoisseur, The Artist, Queen, Arts Review (Paris), Art News and Review, Studio International. *Publications:* George Melhuish (1945); Image (1949); The Paradoxical Universe (1959); Guide (1973); The Paradoxical Nature of Reality (1973). *Address:* St. Vincent's Priory, Sion Hill, Clifton, Bristol BS8 4DQ. *Signs work:* "Melhuish."

MELLAND, Sylvia, R.E.; painter-etcher; *b* Altrincham; *d* of Brian Melland, M.D., M.B. (Lond.); *m* Brian Mertain Melland; one *s*. *Educ.:* Altrincham Grammar School; *studied art* at Manchester College of Art, Byam Shaw, London, Euston Road, Central School (Graphics). *Exhib.:* one-man shows, Wertheim Gallery, Manchester, Jackson's Gallery, Manchester, Zwemmer Gallery, London, Galleria S. Stefano, Venice, Galerie Maurice Bridel, Lausanne, Galerie Bürdeke, Zürich. *Work purchased:* Rutherston Collection, S. London Art Gallery, N.Y. Library, Leeds Art Gallery, Brighton Museum, Coventry Educ. Council, Twickenham Educ. Council, Greenwich Library, Ferens Art Gallery, Hull, V. & A., R.A. (Stott Foundation). *Address:* 68 Bedford Gdns., London W8. *Signs work:* prints, "Sylvia Melland," oils, "S.M."

MELLIS, Margaret; *b* Wu-King-Fu, China; *d* of Rev. D. B. M. Mellis, M.A.; *m* 1st, Adrian Stokes (1938); one *s*; 2nd, Francis Davison (1948). *Studied art:* Edinburgh (S. J. Peploe); Paris (André Lhote); Fellowship, 1937. *Exhib.:* Scottish and Demarco Galleries, Edinburgh; Waddington, Hamilton and Grabowski Galleries, London. *Official purchases:* Derbyshire, Leicestershire and Nottingham (Trent Bridge) Educ. Committees, Ferens Gallery, Hull, Arts Council of Gt. Britain, Cornwall County Council, Nuffield Foundation, Tate Gallery, Contemporary Art Society, Dept. of the Environment, Scottish Gallery of Modern Art. *Address:* Church Farm Cottage, Syleham, Diss, Norfolk.

MELVILL, Harald, scenic designer, portrait painter (pastel) and playwright; Lecturer on Scenic Design, Manchester University (1961). *Educ.:* The Hall, Hampstead; Ovingden, Brighton; Highgate. *Exhib.:* Dowdeswell; Maddox Street; Chester Galleries. *Work in permanent collections:* Glasgow; Delavigne, Paris. *Publications:* Designing and Painting Scenery for the Theatre, Theatrecraft, The Magic of Make-up, Complete Guide to Amateur Dramatics, Historic Costume for the Amateur Theatre, and How to Make it, Stage Management in the Amateur Theatre (Barrie & Rockliff). *Addresses:* 263 Hampstead Rd., London NW1; and Melvill Cottage, St. Agnes, Cornwall.

MENDEL, Renée; sculptor and potter; *b* Elmshorn, 22 Sept., 1908; *d* of Oscar Mendel, leather merchant. *Educ.:* Lichtwark School, Hamburg; universities of Berlin, Frankfurt, Paris; *studied art* at Berlin under Ernest de Fiori, Paris under Pablo Gargallo. *Exhib.:* Salon d'automne, Paris, R.A., Hertford House; one-man show at Royal Copenhagen Porcelain Co., 6 Bond St., Heal & Son Exhbn. Sculpture for the Home, Camden Arts Centre. *Work repro.:* The Studio, Evening Standard, Semaine à Paris, Artistes d'aujourd'hui, Hampstead and Highgate Express and News. *Address:* 27 Onslow Gdns., London N10. *Signs work:* "Renée Mendel."

MENZIES, Gordon William, D.A.; Josef Sckalski Award for Printmaking; Head of Pottery Dept., Community Centre, Edinburgh; freelance illustrator, pottery teacher in printmaking, etching, linocuts, ceramics and stoneware; *b* Motherwell, Scotland, 9 Jan., 1950; *s* of David M. Menzies, storekeeper. *Educ.:* Dalziel High School, Motherwell; *studied art* at Duncan of Jordanstone College of Art, Dundee (1969–73) under Sheila Green, Ron Stenberg; Atelier 17, Paris (1974) under S. W. Hayter. *Exhib.:* Compass Gallery, Glasgow, Montpelier Art Institute, France, R.S.A., S.S.A., Edinburgh, Printmakers Workshop, Edinburgh, many others within Edinburgh and surrounding area. *Publication:* books illustrated mainly within Children's Educational area. *Address:* 2 Salisbury Rd., Edinburgh 16.

MEREDITH, Norman, A.R.C.A., M.S.I.A.; book illustrator in gouache, watercolour and pen and ink; G.L.C. visiting lecturer; lecturer in Art, University of Aberystwyth (1935); war service, technical illustrator, M. of A.P. (Farnborough); *b* Liverpool; *s* of Jane Ann Meredith; *m* Violet Mary Brant. *Studied art* at Liverpool College of Art and R.C.A., and in Italy, Germany, Holland and France. *Official purchases:* by H.R.H. the Duke of Gloucester, etc. *Work repro.:* Punch, Tatler, Sketch, Bystander; books illus. for Odhams Press, Methuen, O.U.P., Illustrated History of England (Allman), Macmillan, Newnes, etc. Evening Standard strip cartoonist. *Address:* 35 Gayfere Rd., Stoneleigh, Ewell, Surrey. *Signs work:* see appendix.

MERTON, John Ralph, M.B.E., Military (1942), Legion of Merit (1945), late Lt.-Col., Air Photographic Reconnaissance Research; portrait painter; *b* London, 7 May, 1913; *s* of Sir Thomas Merton, C.B.E., F.R.S.; *m* Penelope von Bernd; three *d*. *Educ.:* Eton and Balliol; *studied art* at Ruskin School, Oxford, and in Italy. *Exhib.:* Colnaghi (1938), R.A., R.P. *Works include:* Mrs. Daphne Wall (1948); The Artist's Daughter, Sarah (1949); The Countess of March (silver point), altarpiece (1952); The Countess of Dalkeith (1958); A Myth of Delos, bought for the Huntington Hartford Museum, N.Y. (1959); Lady Georgina Pelham (1970); and drawing of Duke of Kent (1971). *Addresses:* The Grange, Enford, Pewsey, Wilts., and 50 Cadogan Sq., London SW1. *Signs work:* paintings unsigned.

MERVYN, Sonia, A.R.C.M., S.W.A.; oil, water-colour and pastel artist; Mem., Council of Ridley Art Soc.; on staff of Maidstone Art School (1943-45). *Exhib.:* R.A. for 17 years, all other galleries in London and provinces and abroad (through Arts Council and Art Exhbns. Bureau); one-man shows: Milford (1972, 1975). *Work in permanent collections:* Australia, New Zealand, S. Africa, Indonesia, North and South America, Canada. *Work repro.:* in R.A. Illustrated, Studio. *Address:* 42 Keyhaven Rd., Milford-on-Sea, Hants. *Club:* Chelsea Arts. *Signs work:* see appendix.

MESHAM, Isabel Beatrice; Paris Salon Medallist; artist in oil, etching, aquatint; *b* Gorey, Eire, 1896; *d* of the late Charles Mesham, officer, British Army. *Educ.:* St. John's College and abroad. *Exhib.:* Royal Academy, Paris Salon (medal), Lisbon Academy (medal), London galleries; one-man: England and abroad. *Work repro.:* Revue Moderne Les Arts, Boomerang, Artists Aujourdhui, etc. *Address:* St. Mary's Guest House, Priory Rd., St. Marychurch, Torquay. *Signs work:* "I. B. Mesham."

MESSELET, Jean; Conservateur honoraire du Musée Nissim de Camondo; *b* Paris, 22 Feb., 1898. *Educ.:* Lycée Louis le Grand; *studied art* at École du Louvre. *Publications:* monographs on French painters; articles in Archives de l'Art Francais, Beaux-Arts, Bulletin Monumental, Bulletin des Musées, etc. *Address:* 2 rue Léonce-Reynaud, Paris XVIe.

MESSENT, Charles; painter in oils, enamels and water-colours; *b* Felixstowe, 1 Mar., 1911; *s* of Malcolm Z. Messent; *m* Eveline. *Studied art* at Regional College of Art, Manchester, and with Sief el din Wanly, Alexandria. *Exhib.:* Paris Salon, New English Art Club, Foyles, Whitechapel Gallery, Cooling Gallery, Black Hall, Oxford, Midland Regional Artists and Designers Gallery, Nottingham, Salford City Art Gallery, Manchester City Art Gallery, Bluecoat Chambers, Liverpool. *Official purchases:* Museum of Modern Art, Cairo; New Zealand Government; Longford Hall, Stretford. *Address:* The Paddock, London Rd., Friars Oak, Hassocks, Sussex. *Clubs:* Hampstead Arts Council; Founder Member of Manchester Group. *Signs work:* see appendix.

MICHIE, David Alan Redpath, R.S.A. (1972), A.R.S.A. (1964); vice principal, Edinburgh College of Art; lecturer in painting, Grays School of Art, Aberdeen (1958-62); *b* 1928; *s* of the late James Michie and Anne Redpath, O.B.E., A.R.A., R.S.A., LL.D.; *m* Eileen Michie; two *d. Studied painting* at Edinburgh College of Art (1946-53), Italy (1953-54). *Exhib.:* one-man shows: Mercury Gallery, London (1967, 1969, 1971, 1974). *Address:* 17 Gilmour Rd., Edinburgh EH16 5NS.

MICKLEWRIGHT, Robert Flavell, D.F.A. (London), A.R.W.S., F.S.I.A.; graphic designer, illustrator, painter in oil, water-colour; *b* Staffordshire, 1923. *Studied art* at Croydon School of Art (1939), Wimbledon School of Art (1947-49), Slade School (1949-52). *Work in permanent collections:* regular exhibitor in London, provinces and U.S.A.; pictures in private collections. *Publications:* illustrated numerous books. Work reproduced in the following reference books: Artists of a Certain Line (Bodley Head), Designing a Book Jacket (Studio), Designers in Britain, 5, 6 7 (Andre Deutsch), Drawing for Radio Times (Bodley Head), Illustrators at Work (Studio), Royal Academy Illustrated. *Address:* Mount Hill, Mogador, Tadworth, Surrey.

MIDDLETON, Michael Humfrey, C.B.E., Hon. F.R.I.B.A., F.S.I.A.; Assistant Editor/Editor of Picture Post (1949-53); Lilliput (1953-54); House and Garden (1955-57); Deputy Director, the Civic Trust (1957-69), Director (1969—); art critic, Spectator (1946-56); *b* London, 1 Dec., 1917; *s* of Humfrey

Middleton; *m* Julie Hamson; one *s*, two d. *Educ.:* King's School, Canterbury; Heatherley's. *Publications:* Group Practice in Design; contributor to many periodicals, etc., on art and design. *Address:* 46 Holland Park Ave., London W11.

MIEG, Peter, D.Phil. (1933); composer and painter in water-colour; *b* Lenzburg, Switzerland, 5 Sept., 1906. *Educ.:* Aarau, Basle, Zürich, Paris; *studied art* in Paris. *Exhib.:* Basle, Lausanne, Aarau, Zürich, Winterthur, Lenzburg, Paris, New York, Dallas, Mexico City (Expositions, 1972-73). *Publications:* studies in Modern Water-colour Painting (1933), and numerous articles on modern art in Swiss Press. *Address:* Lenzburg, Switzerland. *Signs work:* "P.M."

MILES, June, R.W.A.; artist in oil; Mem., Newlyn Society of Artists and Penwith Society of Artists; lecturer, Bristol Folk House; *b* London, 4 July, 1924; *d* of William George Hilary Miles, Lt. Col Royal Marines (decd.); divorced; one *s*, two d. *Educ.:* Portsmouth High School; *studied art* at Slade (1941-43) under Randolph Schwabe. *Exhib.:* one-man shows: Durham University, Plymouth City A.G., Mignon Gallery, The Minories, Colchester. *Work in permanent collections:* Van Mildert College, Durham University, Sussex Educational Committee, Bristol City A.G., Plymouth City A.G., Nuffield Foundation, paintings in Hospitals. *Address:* Boswadden Cottage, Cape Cornwall, St. Just, Penzance, Cornwall, TR19 7NJ. *Signs work:* "June Miles" (on back of painting).

MILLAR, Jack Ernest, A.R.C.A. (1950), R.B.A. (1954); artist in oil; Head of Fine Art, Kingston Polytechnic; *b* London, 28 Nov., 1922; *s* of Ernest Woodroffe de Cauze Millar, stage designer; *m* Pamela Izzard, artist; one *s*, two *d*. *Educ.:* Sellincourt; *studied art* at Clapham School of Art (1939), St. Martin's School of Art (1941), Royal College of Art (1948-50). *Work in permanent collections:* Royal Academy (work purchased by President and Council shown at London Group), Leicester Galleries, Piccadilly Gallery, Trafford Gallery, Brighton Art Gallery, Roland, Browse and Delbanco (one-man show), Rumbold Gallery. *Address:* 10 Overhill Rd., East Dulwich, London SE22. *Signs work:* "J. Millar."

MILLAR, Sir Oliver Nicholas, K.C.V.O., F.B.A., F.S.A.; Surveyor of H.M. The Queen's pictures; *b* Standon, Herts., 26 Apr., 1923; *s* of Gerald Millar; *m* (1954) Delia Dawnay; one *s*, three *d*. *Educ.:* Rugby, Courtauld Inst. *Publications:* English Art (1625-1714), with Dr. M. D. Whinney; Abraham van der Doort's Catalogue; Tudor, Stuart and early Georgian Pictures in the Collection of H.M. the Queen; Zoffany and His Tribuna; Later Georgian Pictures in the Collection of H.M. the Queen; Inventories and Valuations of the King's Goods; catalogues and articles in various journals. *Address:* c/o Lord Chamberlain's Office, St. James's Palace, London SW1.

MILLER, Clive Beverley, Cert. R.A.S. (1964); Rome and Abbey Scholarship (1963); painter in oil; musician, Brothers Grimm; teacher of painting, Sheffield College of Art (specialist in life drawing), also Medway College of Design; R.A.F. (1957-60); *b* Bexley, 24 May, 1938; *s* of Bertram William Miller; *m* Shirley Margaret; two *s*, one *d*. *Educ.:* Hurstmere, Sidcup School of Art (1955), Bromley College of Art (1956), Royal Academy Schools (1960-64). *Work in permanent collections:* mural, Wildearath, Germany, Peter Cochran (Tooths, London); private collection: Lee Nordise (New York), Mrs. D. Martin (Brighton), Neil Miller (connoisseur in porcelain and antiques), Tenterden, Kent, Mr. R. Ganowski, 22 New Bond St., London, also agent, Welsh Arts Council. *Address:* Widegate, Cheriton, Gower, South Wales. *Clubs:* R.A.S., Renolds. *Signs work:* see appendix.

MILLER, David T., D.A. (Edin.), F.R.B.S., Latimer Award, R.S.A. (1961), Prof. Member S.S.A.; sculptor on wood, stone, bronze, steel, fibreglass resin;

lecturer, Moray House College; council member, R.B.S.; *b* Bo'ness, 1931; *s* of Robert Miller; *m* Morag Macmurray; one *s*, one *d*. *Educ.:* Mortlach School, Dufftown; *studied art* at Gray's School of Art, Aberdeen, Edinburgh College of Art (Eric Schilsky), Paris, Vallauris. *Work in permanent collections:* public sculpture in Edinburgh, Selkirk, Dalkeith, Alyth, Linwood, Moray House, Scottish Arts Council. *Address:* Northend House, Pathhead, Ford, Midlothian. *Signs work:* see appendix.

MILLER, Harry Vye; art teacher; President, Otago Art Soc. (1964-65) artist in oil, water-colour and lettering; *b* Lawrence, N.Z., 1907; *m* Vesper da Silva; one *s*, two *d*. *Studied art* at Dunedin School of Art under W. H. Allen, A.R.C.A., and R. N. Field, A.R.C.A. (1928). *Work in permanent collections:* Hocken Library Collection, National Gall., Dunedin Art Gall. and Invercargill Civic Collection. *Work repro.:* in N.Z. Arts Year Book, Studio. *Publications:* A History of Art in Otago (1948) and History Dunedin School of Art (1970); columnist for Evening Star, Dunedin. *Address:* 158 Rolla St., Dunedin, NE1, N.Z. *Signs work:* "H. V. Miller."

MILLER, James, R.S.A., R.S.W.; painter in oil and water-colour; *b* 25 Oct., 1893; *s* of William Miller; *m*. *Educ.:* Glasgow (M. Greiffenhagen, R.A., R. Anning Bell, R.A.). *Exhib.:* Glasgow, Edinburgh. *Official purchases:* Melbourne Art Gallery, Edinburgh Art Gallery, Glasgow Art Gallery, Bradford, Newport, Dundee. *Work repro.:* in Studio, Scotsman. *Address:* Tigh-na-Bruach, Dunvegan, Isle of Skye. *Club:* Glasgow Art. *Signs work:* "James Miller."

MILLS, Edward David, C.B.E., F.R.I.B.A., F.S.I.A., R.I.B.A., Alfred Bossom Research Fellow (1953); Churchill Fellow (1969); architect and design consultant in private practice; *b* London, 19 Mar., 1915. *Studied arch.* at Polytechnic School of Architecture, London; Chairman of the Architecture Faculty, British School at Rome. *Exhib.:* R.I.B.A., F.O.B. (1951), R.A., A.I.A., etc. *Work repro.:* architectural journals, etc. *Publications:* The Modern Factory (1951), Architect Details (1952-61), The New Architecture in Gt. Britain (1953), The Modern Church (1956), Factory Building (1957), The Changing Workplace (1971), Planning (9th Edition) (1975). *Address:* 9-11 Richmond Buildings, Dean St., Soho, London W1. *Signs work:* "Edward D. Mills."

MILLS, Enid Sybil, R.M.S. (1961); illuminator, scribe, portrait painter in water-colour and oil; *d* of Edwin James Smith, consulting engineer; *m* Frederick W. Mills; two *s*, one *d*. *Educ.:* City of London School; *studied art* at St. Martin's School of Art, Central School of Arts and Crafts (Meninsky, Con Lomax, Walter Bayes). *Exhib.:* R.W.S. Galleries, Suffolk Street Galleries, R.I. Galleries, Mall Galleries, Pittsburgh and Perth, W. Australia. *Publications:* children's books and magazines. *Address:* Woodlands, Wormley, Godalming, Surrey. *Signs work:* "Enid Mills."

MILLS, John FitzMaurice, F.S.A., F.I.I.C., R.D.S., F.R.S.A.I., F.R.S.A.; painter, picture-restorer, lecturer, broadcaster and author; *b* Cheam; *s* of Herbert FitzMaurice Mills; *m* Lucilla Margaret; one *s*. Educ.: Cothill, Bryanston, and Architectural Association; *studied art* privately; painting, picture-restoration, and artists' techniques and materials. *Exhib.:* R.B.A., R.O.I., R.I., N.S., Paris Salon and United States. *Publications:* The Practice and History of Painting, Instructions to Young Artists, Look at Pictures, Oil Painting, Flower Painting, Sketching, Art for Fun, Careers through Art, The Painter and His Materials, The Care of Antiques, Dictionary of Art Terms, Acrylic Painting, Studio and Art Room Techniques, The Growth of Child Art with R. R. Tomlinson. Fine arts correspondent to The Irish Times, external lecturer for the institute of education,

Oxford University. *Address:* Poulstone Ct., King's Caple, Herefords. *Signs work:* "Mills."

MILNE, Andrew John, Croix de Guerre and Star (1944), F.S.I.A.; industrial design consultant; *b* Dublin, Apr., 1916; *s* of Andrew Henry Milne; *m* Elizabeth Testar; one *s*, one *d*. *Educ.:* Prince Henry's Grammar School, and St. Mary's College, Aberystwyth; *studied art* at Cheltenham School of Art and Regent St. Polytechnic. *Exhib.:* Scottish Industries (1949), Festival of Britain (South Bank, 1951), Live Architectural Exhbn. (Poplar, 1951), etc. *Work repro.:* Various British and foreign publications. *Address:* Cherry Hinton, Watermill La., Beckley, nr. Rye, Sussex. *Signs work:* "Andrew J. Milne."

MILNE, John Erskine, N.D.D. (Sculpture), Salford University (1951), associateship of same (1951), F.R.S.A. (1950); sculptor in stone, wood, bronze, fibreglass; major sculpture prize, Westward Television Open Art Competition (Sept., 1971); *b* Eccles, Lancs., 1931; *s* of James Alexander Milne; *m* Isabel Batcheller, divorced 1973. *Educ.:* Salford School of Art, University of Salford; *studied art* at Academie de la Grande Chaumière, Paris; assistant to Barbara Hepworth (1952). *Work in permanent collections:* Lancashire County Council, Cornwall County Council, Truro, British Electricity Authority, Whitworth A.G., Manchester, Darlington, Arts Council of Great Britain, Leicestershire Education Authority, Contemporary Arts Society, Imperial Chemical Industries, English Calico, London Ltd., Whitly Inns Ltd., Plymouth City A.G., Tate Gallery, J. Lyons Ltd., London, Skyline Hotel, London, City A.G., Coventry, City A.G., Birmingham, John Player's Ltd., Nottingham, Hertford College, Oxford, Joseph Lucas Ltd., Birmingham, Royal Embassy of Morocco, London, Salford City A.G., Camden Borough Council, London, Royal Embassy of Iran, London, Konstmuseum, Gotenburg. *Address:* Trewyn, St. Ives, Cornwall. *Signs work:* "J.E.M."

MILNER, Donald Ewart, O.B.E., M.A. (Hon., Bristol University), A.R.C.A. (1921), R.W.A., elected Vice-Pres. R.W.A. (1970), President (1974); artist in oil and water-colour and stained glass; Chairman, Arts Com. Glos. Community Council; *b* Huddersfield, 19 May, 1898; *s* of J. H. Milner, artist; *m* Mildred Milner, R.W.A.; two *s*. *Educ.:* Royal College of Art. *Work in permanent collections:* Bristol City Art Gallery, City of Gloucester Art Gallery, R.W.E.A.; stained glass windows at Ivy Hatch, Leicester, Thames Ditton, Courts of Justice, Bristol, and University of Bristol. *Address:* Oakfield House, Ellerncroft Rd., Wotton-under-Edge, Glos. *Signs work:* "D. E. Milner."

MILWARD, Frith, A.R.C.A.; painter in oil and water-colour; *b* Worcester Pk., Surrey, 14 Apr., 1906; *m* Peggy Lydia Rogenhagen, D.F.A. (Lond.). *Educ.:* Epsom College and King's College, Taunton; *studied art* at Wimbledon Art School under G. Cooper (1931); Kingston Art School under Prof. A. Betts (1932); R.C.A. under Sir William Rothenstein (1933-35). *Exhib.:* London Group, Kingston Group, Staffs Art Soc., Manchester Art Club. *Address:* Belfield House, Newtown Longnor, nr. Buxton, Derbys. *Signs work:* "Frith Milward."

MINERS, Neil; artist in oil, water-colour and linocuts; *b* Redruth, Cornwall, 19 June, 1931; *s* of Charles Arthur Miners; *m* Wendy Miners; two *d*. *Studied art* at Falmouth School of Art (drawing only part-time); painting privately under Jack Chalker (1948). *Exhib.:* three one-man shows and various in Cornwall. *Work in permanent collections:* H.R.H. Prince Charles, Royal National Lifeboat Institution. *Publication:* book of Falmouth and Penryn (contributor), designs of medals, illustrated book and flags for Tall Ships start from Falmouth. *Address:* Studio, 13A Church St., Falmouth, Cornwall. *Signs work:* see appendix.

MIRÓ, Joan; painter, designer, lithographer, illustrator; Internation Prize of the

Guggenheim Foundation (1959); *b* Barcelona, 20 Apr., 1893. *Studied art* at Barcelona School of Fine Arts; Gali Academy. *Exhib.:* Galerie Maeght (Paris, 1948, 1953, 1956, 1960, 1967); Pierre Matisse Gallery (1946, 1953, 1956, 1961). *Official purchases:* Plaza Hotel, Cincinnati (1947); UNESCO; St. Gall Univ.; Guggenheim Museum (1967). *Work repro.:* fifty lithographs for Parler Seul by Tzara (1950); décor and costumes for: Roméo et Juliette (with Max Ernst), Russian Ballet (1925); Jeux d'Enfants for Monte Carlo Ballet (1933); decorations on Artigas' pottery from 1940. *Address:* c/o Galerie Maeght, Paris. *Signs work:* see appendix.

MITCHELL, Charles, M.A., B.Litt. (Oxon.), Litt.D.; Bernheimer Prof. of the History of Art, Bryn Mawr College, since 1960; asst., Nat. Maritime Museum, Greenwich (1935-45); lecturer, Warburg Institute, Univ. of London (1945-60); Tallman Prof., Bowdoin College, U.S.A. (1956-57); Art Historian in Residence, American Academy in Rome (1965-66); *b* London, 25 Jan., 1912; *s* of Stanley Mitchell; *m* 1st, Prudence Yalden-Thomson; 2nd, Jean Flower; two *s*. *Educ.:* Merchant Taylors' School; St. John's College, Oxford. *Publications:* A Book of Ships, Seaman's Portrait, Hogarth's Peregrination, A Fifteenth Century Italian Plutarch, Pirro Ligorio's Roman Antiquities (with E. Mandowsky), ed. A. P. Oppé, *Raphael*, numerous articles. *Addresses:* Woodhouse Farmhouse, Fyfield, Abingdon, Oxon.; Bryn Mawr College, Pa., U.S.A.

MITCHELL, Enid G. D., A.R.B.S.; Visual Arts Diploma, London University; Ghilchrist Prize; sculptor of portrait and figures in clay both fired and modelled for casting, cast cement and resin, carved stone and wood; *d* of R. J. Mitchell, B.A. Hons., Lond., J.P.; one *s*, two *d*. *Educ.:* Lady Elenor Holles School, Hampton, Middx.; *studied art* at Ealing School of Art (sculpture tutors, Tom Bailey and Robert Thomas, F.R.B.S., A.R.C.A.). *Work in permanent collections:* Leamington Spa, Islip Manor Primary School, Drayton Green Primary School, various private collections. *Address:* Flat 3, 17 Powis Terr., London W11 1JJ. *Clubs:* Royal Society of British Sculptors, Society of Portrait Sculptors. *Signs work:* "MITCHELL" or "Enid G. D. Mitchell."

MITCHELL, John, R.S.W. (1967); lecturer and teacher; artist in water-colour, silkscreen; *b* Glasgow, 21 Dec., 1937. *Educ.:* Glasgow Academy, Royal High School of Edinburgh; *studied art* at Edinburgh College of Art (1956-61). *Work in permanent collections:* Fife Education Com., British Transport Hotels. *Address:* West Gowanbrae Temple, Lower Largo, Fife. *Signs work:* "JOHN MITCHELL."

MITCHELL, Leonard Victor; professional artist, portrait, figure, still-life, landscape, painter-etcher and sculptor; Scholarship, Wellington Technical College School of Art; Inaugural Kelliher Prize for Landscape Painting (twice awarded); National Bank of New Zealand Prize for Mural Painting; Netherlands Government Art Fellowship; Honorable Mention, Bronze, Silver, Gold Medals, Paris Salon; Prize-winner, Arun Art Centre, J. Barcham Green Water-colour Competition; Laureate 2nd, Grand Salon International de Charleroi; Grand Prix des Editeurs Beaux-Arts, Monte Carlo (1970); *b* New Zealand; *s* of L. C. Mitchell, artist, illustrator, international stamp-designer; *m* Patricia Marianne Nickalls; *studied art* at father's studio, Wellington Technical College School of Art (later taught life drawing, painting, graphics), Coulls Somerville Willkie, printers, N.Z.; studio-trained, studios of Frederic V. Ellis, A.R.C.A., painter-etcher, Alexander R. Fraser, A.R.C.A., A.R.B.S., sculptor, Nugent Welch, O.B.E., painter; Pacific and European travels. *Exhib.:* one-man and group exhibitions, New Zealand; exhibited group exhibitions, Sydney, Far East, London, Paris, Monte Carlo, Belgium, New York, Paris Salon, R.A. *Work in permanent collections:* Wellington Technical

College Library, Lower Hutt City War Memorial Library murals, Australia and New Zealand Bank mural, Alexander Turnbull Library, National Gallery, Wellington, N.Z., National Bank of New Zealand, London, Ashmolean Museum, Oxford; world private collections. *Publications:* illustrated New Zealand Journey, official New Zealand Royal Tour Book, 1960-70—10 Ans d'Arts Graphiques (Monte Carlo); many New Zealand publications, La Revue Moderne, Flammes Vives, Paris, Art Libre, Repertorium Artis, Monte Carlo, La Femme et à l'Erotisme. *Address:* The Rood House, Bridge St., Coggeshall, Essex. *Clubs:* Artist Member, New Zealand Academy of Fine Arts; Royal Society of Arts, London; Associate, Société des Artistes Française, Paris; Member, International Arts Guild, Monte Carlo; Silver Medal and Member Honoris Causa Academia 'Tommaso Campanella,' Rome; Hon. Mem. Haute Academie Litteraire et Artistique de France. *Signs work:* see appendix.

MITCHELL, Robert James, elected A.R.B.S. (1967); Beckwith Travelling Scholarship Diploma of Merit; sculptor in stone, marble, bronze, resin and wood; Teacher of Sculpture, Kennington School of Art; *b* 2 Nov., 1930. *Educ.:* Ayds School, Dulwich; *studied art* at Camberwell School of Art under Professor Carl Vogel, and Kennington School of Art under David McFall, R.A. *Work in permanent collections:* Bolton Art Gallery, T.U.C. Congress House. *Address:* 2 Digswell House, Monks Rise, Welwyn Garden City, Herts. *Signs work:* "R. J. Mitchell."

MITCHELL, S. M., N.D.D., A.R.C.A., S.P.S., A.R.B.S.; sculptor in clay, wood, stone, fibreglass, resins, concrete, bronze; *b* 24 Nov., 1926; *d* of Squadron Leader L. J. Mitchell; *m* Charles Bone, artist; two *s*. *Educ.:* Seager House School, Farnham G.G.S.; *studied art* at Farnham School of Art (1946), under Charles Vyes, Guildford School of Art (1947), under Willi Soukop, R.A., Royal College of Art (1948-51), under Frank Dobson, R.A., John Skeaping, R.A., Edward Folkard, F.R.B.S. *Exhib.:* R.A., S.P.S., N.E.A.C., W.I.A., Ashgate Gallery, Furneaux Gallery, Canaletto Gallery, Bladon Gallery; six shared one-man exhbns., Ashgate Gallery, Farnham, Gainsborough's House, Sudbury, University of Surrey, Guildford House, Malta, G.C. *Portrait commissions* in bronze, terracotta. *Designer* ceramic sculpture, including Royal Worcester Porcelain. *Address:* Winters Farm, Puttenham, nr. Guildford, Surrey. *Signs work:* "S. Mitchell," sometimes (B) after signature.

MITCHELL, William George, Des. R.C.A. (Hons.), A.I.B.D.I.D., 4th year scholarship, silver medal, Abbey Award; design consultant, sculptor in plastics, concrete, wood, marble, brick; mem. Design Advisory Board, Hammersmith College of Art and Trent Polytechnic; Formwork Advisory Com., Concrete Society; *b* London, 30 Apr., 1925; *s* of Charles G. Mitchell; *m* G. A. Mitchell; one *s*, three *d*. *Educ.:* usual elementary schools; *studied art* at Southern College of Art, Portsmouth (G. Gaydon), R.C.A. (Prof. R. D. Russell), British School at Rome (Abbey Award). *Work repro.:* work illustrated in many international journals and technical publications, together with lecture papers delivered to educational and other professional bodies. *Address:* 243 Baring Rd., London SE12. *Club:* Arts. *Signs work:* see appendix.

MITFORD-BARBERTON, Ivan, C.L.J., A.R.C.A., A.R.B.S.; sculptor, author and herald; works in wood, stone, bronze and ivory; several large bronze works including 1820 Group (12′) in Grahamstown and many portrait busts; *b* 1 Feb., 1896; *m* 1st, Cecile Hoole; two *s*, one *d*; 2nd, Pamela Gibbs; one *s*, one *d*. *Studied art* at R.C.A. (1923-25), Italy (1926). *Work in permanent collections:* in most S.A. galleries and museums, also Nairobi, Livingstone and Nottingham. In Cape Town a granite frieze 285 ft. long; Jan Smuts (bronze 9′), and other architectural sculpture. *Work repro.:* in many publications. *Publications:* author of seven books on the 1820 Settler Period. *Address:* Castleton, Orange St., Hout Bay, Cape, S. Africa. *Signs work:* "I. Mitford-Barberton."

MOGGRIDGE, Helen, F.F.P.S. (1972); painter in acrylic, oil, ink and litho; *d* of Allan MacNab Taylor, ship broker; *m* Lt. Col. Harry Weston Moggridge, CMG, Chevalier de la Legion d'Honneur; two *s. Educ.:* Eothen School, Surrey; *studied art* at the Slade under Henry Tonks, Wilson Steer, Walter Russell. *Exhib.:* Leicester Galleries, R.A., R.B.A., Towner Gallery, etc.; one-man shows: Drian Gallery and Woodstock Gallery. *Address:* 1 Oak Cottages, Piddinghoe, Sussex. *Clubs:* F.P.S., Eastbourne Group. *Signs work:* initials "HM" joined.

MOLENKAMP, Nicolaas Ferdinand, Willink van Collem Prize, Amsterdam (1950), Laurens Meeusprize for Painting, Belgium, Silver Medal, Europe, Prize for Painting, Osten (1962); painter; head of department (painting), Academy of Fine Arts, Tilburg; *b* Enschede, Netherlands, 6 Dec., 1920; *s* of Gerrit Jan Molenkamp; *m* Maria de Mast; one *s*, three *d. Studied art* at Academy of Art, Tilburg, and Academy of Fine Art, Antwerp. *Exhib.:* Amsterdam, Schiedam, Tilburg, Gt. Yarmouth, Brussels, Baghdad; van Abbe Museum, Eindhoven, Contour Delft. *Work in permanent collections:* Central Museum, Utrecht; Print Room, Antwerp. *Address:* Koningshoeven 30, Tilburg, Netherlands. *Clubs:* Federated Holland Societies of Artists. *Signs work:* "Molenkamp."

MOMPOU, Jose; painter in oil; *b* Barcelona, 9 Feb., 1888. *Studied art* at Barcelona and Paris. *Exhib.:* London (British Council, 1956), Venice Bienale (1955), Bonn Museum (1957), Rome, New York, Toledo, Pittsburgh, Amsterdam, Buenos Aires, Madrid, Barcelona. *Work in permanent collections:* Museums in Paris, Toledo (U.S.A.), Barcelona. *Work repro.:* Gaceta de les Arts, 1929; Art, 1934; Catalogue of European paintings, Toledo Museum of Art, U.S.A., 1939; Mensaje de Pintura, 1949; Bénézit Dictionnaire des Peintres, Paris, 1953; Diccionario Biografico de Artistas de Cataluna, Barcelona, 1951; Goya Art Review, Madrid, 1956. *Address:* Av. Republica Argentina 218, Barcelona (Spain). *Signs work:* "mompou."

MONGAN, Agnes, A.B. (1927), M.A. (1929), L.H.D. (1941), Litt.D. (1953), Dr.F.A. (1970); art historian, curator, lecturer, writer and museum director, Fogg Art Museum (1928-71); Timken Gallery, San Diego, California (1971-72); *b* Somerville, Mass., 1905; *d* of Dr. Charles E. Mongan, M.D. *Publications:* author or editor of numerous catalogues of museum collections and exhibitions, articles in periodicals, reviews, etc. *Address:* Drawing Dept., Fogg Art Museum, Harvard University, Cambridge, Mass. 02138. *Clubs:* Harvard Faculty, Cosmopolitan, N.Y.

MONKMAN, Percy; artist in water-colour, oil and gouache; Chairman, Bradford Arts Club; *b* Bradford, 11 Aug., 1892; *s* of Edwin Monkman; *m* Doris Northrop; two *s, one d. Studied art* at Bradford College of Art, Bradford Arts Club. *Exhib.:* R.B.A. and R.I. Galleries, London, Birmingham, Bradford, Leeds, Sheffield, York, Wakefield, Harrogate; one-man shows, Harrogate, Skipton, Batley, Middlesbrough. *Work in permanent collections:* Bradford A.G. (1958), Peterborough, Canada (1965), Roubaix, France (1969). *Work repro.:* Cartoons and caricatures, Yorkshire Evening Post, Bradford Telegraph and Argus; water-colour, The Artist; Textile Journal; The Dalesman, Bradford Pictorial. *Address:* 25 Springfield Rd., Baildon, Shipley. *Club:* Bradford Arts. *Signs work:* see appendix.

MONTANÉ, Roger; painter in oil; Prix Bethouard (1948); *b* Bordeaux, 21 Feb., 1916; *m*; two *s. Educ.:* Toulouse; *studied art:* self-taught. *Exhib.:* Chicago

(1964), New York (1965), Musée de Toulon (1965). *Official purchases:* Musée d'Art Moderne (Paris), Musées de la Ville (Paris), de St. Denis (Paris), Musées de Toulouse, de Lyon, d'Albi, Musée Ishibashi (Tokyo), Groupe International d'Art Figuratif (Japan, 1960), Exposition Particulière la Maison de Lapensee Française, Paris (1961), Aberdeen Museum and Art Gall., Musées de Valence, de Rodez, de Sete, de Bagnols s/Cèze, Wellington Museum (N.Z.), de Grenoble. President, Salon d'Automne (1966-68), Musées de Narbonne (Prague), Musée des Sports (Paris). *Address:* 33 rue Charcot, Paris 13. *Signs work:* see appendix.

MOODY, Michael David, Dip.A.D., Graphic Design (2nd Class Hons.) (1967); artist in mixed media, designer; museum assistant/exhibition designer, Art Dept., Imperial War Museum; *b* Newcastle upon Tyne, 9 Aug., 1946. *Educ.:* Skerry's College, Newcastle upon Tyne; *studied art* at College of Art and Industrial Design, Newcastle upon Tyne (1962-67) under John Crisp, Gilbert Ward, Peter Welton, George Ratcliffe. *Designed:* Ephemera 1914-18 Exhbn. (1970), co-designed The War Posters Exhbn. (1972) and Yugoslav War Art Exhbn. (1973) both with Barry Kitts, N.D.D., F.R.S.A. at Imperial War Museum. Set designs for the film 'Overlord' (Stuart Cooper, 1975) with Barry Kitts. *Publications:* The First World War; Ephemera, Mementoes, Documents with Maurice Rickards, M.S.I.A. (Jupiter Books, 1975). *Address:* 43 Fernhurst Rd., Fulham, London SW6. *Club:* William Norris Soc. *Signs work:* "M." and see appendix.

MOODY, Ronald, Mem. Council, Society of Portrait Sculptors (elected, 1959); sculptor in wood, bronze, concrete, terra-cotta, etc.; *b* Kingston, Jamaica, 12 Aug., 1910; *s* of Charles E. Moody; *m* Helene, *née* Cowan. *Educ.:* Calabar College, Kingston, Jamaica, and King's College, London; *studied art* in London and Paris. *Exhib.:* London, Paris, Amsterdam, New York, Boston. *Work in permanent collections:* The Nehru Memorial Museum, Delhi; the late Madame van Beuningen, Tiele, Holland; Professor A. L. Cochrane, Wales; Professor John Pilley, Edinburgh; Mrs. David Hussey, London; Miss Marie Seton, London. *Official purchases:* Colonial Office, London; Livingstone House, Westminster; Harmon Foundation, New York; University College West Indies, Jamaica. *Work repro.:* Beaux Arts (Oct., 1937; July, 1939); Nouvelles Litteraires (Oct., 1937); L'Intransigeant (Dec., 1938); De Telegraff, Amsterdam (Jan., 1940); Town and Country, N.Y. (Dec., 1940); France Libre, London (Dec., 1946); Studio (Feb., 1947; Jan., 1950; Sept., 1950; Feb., 1959; Nov., 1960); Punch (June, 1949); Corona (Aug., 1950); Guardian (Dec., 1950; July, 1953; Apr., 1960; Nov., 1960); Sphere (Dec., 1950); Chicago Defender (June, 1950); Star (Jan., 1951); Our World (Feb., 1951); Sketch (Feb., 1959); Negro in Art (Feb., 1940); Arts Review (Oct., 1961); Evening Standard (June, 1961); Times (Aug., 1962; 22 and 28 Aug., 1964); Yorkshire Post (Aug., 1964); Kensington Post (Dec., 1964); Daily Gleaner, Jamaica (Sept., 1961; June, 1964; Oct., 1964); Sunday Gleaner (Jan., 1950; Sept., 1964); Times of India Weekly (Sept., 1970). *Addresses:* (studio) 3 Fleming Close Studios, Winterton Place, London SW10; (home) 78 Redcliffe Sq., London SW10. *Signs work:* see appendix.

MOODY, Victor Hume, A.R.C.A., R.B.S.A., F.R.S.A.; painter of easel pictures; headmaster, Malvern School of Art (1935-62); *b* Clapham, London, 10 Nov., 1896; *s* of John Moody; *m* May Olive Willoughby; one *d*. *Educ.:* Raleigh College, London; *studied art* at Battersea Polytechnic, R.C.A. under Sir William Rothenstein. *Exhib.:* R.A., Goupil Gallery, R.S.A., R.B.S.A. *Work in permanent collection:* Harris Museum, Preston. *Work repro.:* The Studio, The Sphere. *Address:* Lorne Lodge, Sling La., Malvern, Worcs. *Signs work:* "V. H. Moody" occasionally.

MOON, Tennant, A.R.C.A., F.S.A.E., A.S.I.A., F.R.S.A., Principal, Carlisle College of Art and Design; Principal, Gravesend School of Art and Crafts (1949-57); Lecturer, Leicester College of Art (1946-49); President, National Society for Art Education (1972-73); Chairman, Standing Advisory Committee for Art & Crafts, Associated Examining Board; *b* Penarth, S. Glamorgan; *m* Barbara Ovenden; one *s,* one *d. Studied art* Cardiff School of Art, Royal College of Art under Sir William Rothenstein and Gilbert Spencer, R.A. *Exhib.:* R.A., Leicester Galleries, National Museum of Wales, South Wales Group, Newport (Gwent) A.G., Leicester A.G., etc. *Work in permanent collection:* Cumbria Educ. Comm. and private collections. *Address:* 29 Norfolk Rd., Carlisle, Cumbria CA2 5PQ. *Signs work:* "Tennant Moon."

MOORE, C. Rupert, A.R.C.A., Fellow B.S.M.G.P., Companion of Royal Aeronautical Society; *b* 2 Aug., 1904. *Exhib.:* R.A., Hammond Museum, N.Y. *Stained glass designs:* heraldic windows, seventeen for Lincoln's Inn, containing 309 arms, Royal Courts of Law, Gray's Inn, in London and four panels for Chequers. *Subject windows:* include Ely Cathedral, Dulwich College, Boston Grammar School; many for New Zealand, including nine for Napier Cathedral and three for Auckland Cathedral; many for U.S.A., Canada, South Africa and four for Casablanca. *Work in permanent collections:* King's College, Cambridge; a MS. book of Lincoln's Inn heraldry; Aeronautical paintings: Imperial War Museum, Royal Aeronautical Society, B.O.A.C. *Address:* Tykesditch, Oakridge Ave., Radlett, Herts. WD7 8ER.

MOORE, Harry; Captain, Sherwood Foresters (1914-18); won Military Cross and numerous Mentions in Dispatches, and Order of St. John; Art Teachers' Cert. (24 Nov., 1910, No. 7,633); artist in water-colours and oil; *b* Derby, 12 Oct., 1883; *s* of Henry Moore, audit/accountant, L.M.S. *Educ.:* Municipal Secondary School, Derby; *studied art* at Derby School of Art (now known as D.C.A.) under Mr. Simmonds (Head, 1905). *Work in permanent collections:* Derby Sketching Club. Additional to war service, acted as personal topographist to Field-Marshal Earl Douglas Haig, sketching trenches and enemy dug-outs, etc. Sec. Derby Sketching Club (1912-40). *Address:* Holbroke, 14 Newton Rd., Swanage, Dorset. *Signs work:* "H. Moore" and year.

MOORE, Henry, C.H. (1955), O.M. (1963), Hon. D.Litt. (Oxon, 1961); artist/sculptor; Hon. Assoc. of Royal Inst. of British Architects, 1948; awarded International Sculpture prize of the twenty-fourth Venice Biennale, 1948; Hon. Mem. of the American Academy of Arts and Letters and the Nationale Institute of Arts and Letters (May, 1961); Hon. Mem. of the Akademie der Kunste, Berlin (July, 1961); awarded the Feltrinelli Prize in Italy (1963); elected Fellow of the British Academy (1966); awarded the Erasmus Prize for 1968, in Holland; *b* 30 July, 1898; *s* of Raymond Spencer Moore; *m*; one *d. Educ.:* Castleford Grammar School; Leeds College of Art (1919-21); R.C.A. (1921-25). *Address:* Hoglands, Perry Green, Much Hadham, Herts. *Signs work:* "Moore."

MOORE, Ken; painter in oil; director, Commonwealth Biennale of Abstract Art London (1963); awarded Silver Medal of the Tommaso Campanella International Academy Rome (1970); *b* Melbourne, Australia, 1923; *s* of Albert Edward Moore, teacher of painting Geelong Grammar School. *Studied art* at St. Martin's School of Art (1956) under Derrick Greaves, Kenneth Martin, Russell Hall. *Work in permanent collections:* New Britten Museum, Connecticut, Phoenix Art Museum Arizona, Ceda Rapids Art Museum, Iowa, Keppe Gallery, Denmark, Lynam Allen Museum, Connecticut, Finch College Museum, N.Y., Tweed Gallery, Minneapolis, Witchita University, Kansas, Bertrand Russell Foundation, H.R.H. Princess Margaret. *Address:* 43 Bernard Ave., Yorkville, Toronto, Canada.

MOORE, Leslie Lancelot Hardy, R.I.; artist in water-colour; *b* Norwich, 1907; *m* daughter of Col. J. Plunkett; two *s. Educ.:* City of Norwich School, University of Reading; *studied art:* mainly self-taught, otherwise University of Reading and Norwich School of Art. *Exhib.:* R.A., N.E.A.C., Mall Galleries, Furneaux Gallery, Wimbledon, Mandells Gallery, Norwich. *Work repro.:* in colour commercially. *Publications:* illustrated Old Guns and Pistols, Norwich Inns, Call Me at Dawn. *Address:* 60 Intwood Rd., Cringleford, Norwich NOR 59D. *Signs work:* "Leslie L. H. Moore."

MOORE, Mona; illustrator and designer in pen and ink, water-colour and gouache; *b* London, 20 Mar., 1917; *d* of Thomas William Moore; *m* P. R. Bentin; one *s. Educ.:* St. Martin's-in-the-Fields; *studied art* at St. Martin's School of Art and Central School of Art (1931-39). *Exhib.:* Leicester Galleries; Tate, Whitechapel, National Gallery, London; Leger Gallery, etc. *Work in permanent collections:* V. & A., National Museum of Wales, Cardiff, etc. *Official purchases:* M.O.I., L.C.C. Schools, Recording Britain Scheme. *Work repro.:* in Radio Times, Listener, Good Housekeeping. *Address:* 19 Heath View, London N2. *Signs work:* "Mona Moore."

MOORE, William Stanley; artist and stage designer in oil, ink and water-colour; managing director, Stage Décor Ltd.; *b* London, 4 Feb., 1914; *s* of William Moore, farmer; *m* Nadine Hughes. *Educ.:* Shrewsbury; *studied art:* mainly self-taught. *Exhib.:* R.W.S., R.B.A., Redfern Gallery, Chelsea Artists, one-man shows at Lyric and Embassy Theatres (London); York, Shrewsbury, Bradford, Halifax, etc.; retrospective one-man show of 70 pictures Mall Galleries (1973). *Work in permanent collections:* Shrewsbury Art Gallery and Technical College; Kensington Palace. *Work repro.:* in La Revue Moderne. *Address:* Hedgerow Cottage, Tisman's Common, Rudgwick, Sussex RH12 3BN. *Signs work:* "W. Stanley Moore."

MORDUE, Truda, R.M.S. (1957), S.W.A. (1965); artist in water-colour, pastel and pencil, wildlife painter; teacher, miniature and general art, Isleworth Polytechnic, Ealing Adult Educ. classes (1960-67); *b* Hursley, Hants., 1909; *d* of William Rivers; *m* John Mordue (1936). *Studied art:* Poole Art School, Bournemouth College of Art (1927-32), Camberwell School of Art (1935-37) under R. Vivian Pitchforth, R.A., Eric Fraser, F.S.I.A. *Exhib.:* R.A., R.I., R.W.S., F.B.A., travelling exhbns., etc. Works included in private collections, home and abroad. *Work repro.:* by Medici Society: greetings card, post card, notelet designs; also publishers, childrens' picture-story book The Lonely Kitten. *Address:* 29 Kings Rd., Sherborne, Dorset DT9 4HU. *Signs work:* "TRUDA MORDUE," and see appendix.

MORGAN, Gwenda, R.E., N.S., Mem. Soc. of Wood Engravers; *b* Petworth, 1 Feb., 1908; *d* of the late William David Morgan, J.P., and the late Mary Morgan. *Educ.:* Brighton and Hove High School; *studied art* at Goldsmiths' College School of Art and at the Grosvenor School of Modern Art under Iain Macnab. Women's Land Army (1939-46). *Exhib.:* London, provincial and foreign exhbns. *Official purchases:* V. & A. Museum and Brighton Art Gallery. *Address:* Ridge House, Petworth, Sussex. *Signs work:* see appendix.

MORGAN, Robert; Diploma in Education and Teaching Certificate; painter in oil, water-colour, pastels, etc., designer; schoolmaster; Head of Remedial Dept., Secondary School; *b* Glamorgan, 1922; *s* of William Henry Morgan, mining engineer; *m* Jean Elizabeth Florence; two *d. Educ.:* Glamorgan Technical College; Fircroft College, Birmingham; College of Education, Bognor Regis; and Southampton University; *studied art* at College of Education, Bognor Regis

(1951-53) under Charles Woolaston. *Exhib.:* one-man shows, Surrey University, Hiscock Gallery, Portsmouth, Winchester Museum (organised by Southern Arts Council), Selbourne Gallery, etc. *Publications:* The Night's Prison (Rupert Hart-Davis, 1967), Poems and Extracts (Exeter University Press, 1968), On the Banks of the Cynon (Arc Publications, 1973), cover designs for Planet, Anglo-Welsh Review, Poetry Nation, etc. *Address:* 44 Martin Ave., Denmead, Portsmouth, Hants. PO7 6NS. *Signs work:* "R. Morgan."

MORGAN, Ronald; draughtsman, painter in water-colour, black and white, oil and pastel, illustrator, linguist, teacher; draughtsman, Borough Planning Dept., Tower Hamlet, E3; *b* Landywood, Staffordshire, 28 Feb., 1936; *s* of J. Morgan. *Educ.:* Landywood Junior School, Great Wyrley Secondary School, Staffordshire; *studied art* at Walsall School of Art (1951-53, George Willott, A.R.C.A.). *Exhib.:* R.A., R.I., R.B.A., N.E.A.C., S.G.A., R.B.S.A., R.S.M.A., R.O.I., Paris Salon, Britain in Water-colours and touring exhibitions, etc. *Work in permanent collections:* London Borough of Islington. *Work repro.:* La Revue Moderne (Paris, 1963, 1965). *Address:* 62 Clarendon Rd., Tottenham, London N15. *Signs work:* "R. MORGAN. 1968."

MORGAN-JONES, David Sylvanus, M.R.C.S. Eng., F.R.C.S., Edin. (1926); surgeon; artist in oil; *b* London, 7 Feb., 1900; *s* of John Morgan-Jones; *m* Catherine Mary Spencer; three *s,* one *d. Educ.:* Llandovery College; London University; *studied art* at St. Albans School of Art under William Lismore, C. Sanders, R.A. (1936-39). *Exhib.:* R.A., R.O.I., etc. *Address:* Farm Cottage, St. Margarets, Hemel Hempstead, Herts. *Signs work:* "D. MORGAN-JONES" or "DAVID VOEL."

MORLEY, John, Cert. R.A.S., R.B.A., N.E.A.C.; artist in oil; visiting lecturer, Epsom School of Art and Design; assistant art master, Westminster School; *b* Beckenham, 12 Sept., 1942; *s* of the late William John Morley; *m* Diana Rosemary Howard; one *d. Studied art* at Beckenham School of Art, Ravensbourne College of Art, R.A. Schools. *Exhib.:* R.A. Bicentenary Exhbn. (1968), R.A., R.B.A., Paris Salon. *Address:* Stoven North Green, nr. Beccles, Suffolk. *Signs work:* "John Morley" or "J.M." followed by year.

MORRIS, Anthony, N.D.D. (1958), Cert. R.A.S. (1961), R.P. (1971); David Murray Scholarship (1959-60-61), Leverhulme Scholarship (1961); painter and illustrator in oil and water-colour; *b* 2 Aug., 1938; *s* of F. V. Morris; *m* Aileen S. Griffiths. *Educ.:* Headington School; *studied art* at Oxford College of Art (1954-58) under R. Grimshaw, A.R.C.A., R.A. Schools (1958-61) under P. G. Greenham, R.A., R.P., the late Sir Henry Rushbury, C.V.O., R.A., the late B. Fleetwood-Walker, R.A. *Exhib.:* R.A. Summer Exhbn., R.S.P.P., Mall Galleries, R.A. Bicentenary Exhbn. (1968), Bodleian Library, Oxford, *Work repro.:* Open University course books, B.B.C. Television, Wild Life Fund publications. *Address:* Wenham Holt, Church Way, East Claydon, Buckingham MK18 2NB. *Signs work:* "A. Morris."

MORRIS, Charles Alfred, A.R.W.S. (1943), R.W.S. (1949), R.B.A. (1947); Pres., Society of Sussex Painters; Vice-Pres, R.W.S. (1957-60); Vice-princ., Brighton College of Art (1950-59); Princ., County School of Art, Worthing (1943-46); painter in oil, water-colour; *b* Portsmouth, 5 Sept., 1898; *m* Alice Muriel Drummond; one *s,* two *d. Studied art* at Brighton College of Art, R.A. Schools. *Exhib.:* R.A., R.W.S., R.B.A., R.O.I., provinces. *Work in permanent collections:* at Birkenhead, Eastbourne, Brighton, Worthing and Blackburn. *Address:* Hillside Cottage, Burpham, Arundel, Sussex. *Clubs:* R.W.S., Brighton Arts, Soc. of Sussex Painters. *Signs work:* "C. A. Morris."

MORRIS, James Shepherd, A.R.S.A., M.L.A., F.R.I.A.S., A.R.I.B.A.; architect and landscape architect; Mem. Arts Council of Gt. Britain, Scottish Arts Council, Arts Council Enquiry into Community Arts (1974), former Chairman, Scottish Arts Council Art Panel; Partner, Morris and Steedman, Architects and Landscape Architect, Edinburgh; Mem. Council of the Cockburn Assoc., Edinburgh; one time mem. Committee of Management of the Traverse Theatre, Edinburgh; past Council Mem. R.I.A.S., and Edinburgh Architectural Assoc. (1969-1971); *b* St. Andrews, Fife, 22 Aug., 1931; *s* of Thomas S. Morris, A.R.I.B.A., A.M.T.P.I.; *m* Eleanor Kenner Smith; two *s,* one *d. Studied art* at Edinburgh College of Art, University of Pennysylvania, Philadelphia. *Commissions:* Countryside Commission, Battleby (RIBA Award 1974, Heritage Year Award), Edinburgh University Students Centre, Refectory, Health Centre, Princess Margaret Rose Orthopaedic Hospital, Clinical Unit, Boilerhouse, Operating Theatre Suite; Wolfson Bio-Engineering Centre, Strathclyde University; Institute of Terrestrial Ecology, Bush Estate, Penicuik; houses: Mr. and Mrs. P. G. Nicol; Mr. and Mrs. P. E. G. Balfour (Civic Trust Award). *Address:* Woodcote Pk., Fala, Midlothian, Scotland. *Clubs:* New Edinburgh, Scottish Arts, Edinburgh Sports.

MORRIS, Stanley William, M.Ed. (1976), A.T.D. (1951), A.R.B.S.A., M.F.P.S.; lecturer; head of Curriculum studies, Madeley College of Education; *b* 1922. *Studied art* at Birmingham College of Art. *Work in permanent collection:* Midlands Arts Centre. *Exhib.:* Paris Salon, R.O.I., N.E.A.C., U.A.S., R.B.S.A. *Address:* c/o Madeley College of Education.

MORRISON, James, A.R.S.A., R.S.W., D.A.; painter in oil and water-colour; lecturer, Dundee College of Art; *b* Glasgow, 1932; *m*; one *s,* one *d. Educ.:* Hillhead High School, Glasgow School of Art. *Work in permanent collections:* Glasgow, Dundee and Aberdeen Art galleries, Arts Council, Argyll Educ. Comm., Glasgow, Edinburgh and Stirling Universities. *Address:* 3 Melville Gdns., Montrose, Angus. *Signs work:* "Morrison" and date.

MORROCCO, Alberto, R.S.A. (1963), D.A. (1937); painter in oil, tempera and water-colour; Head of School of Painting, Dundee College of Art; *b* Aberdeen, 14 Dec., 1917; *s* of Domenico Antonio Morrocco; *m* Vera Cockburn Mercer; two *s,* one *d. Educ.:* Aberdeen; *studied art* at Gray's School of Art, Aberdeen (1932-38) under Robert Sivell, R.S.A., James Cowie, R.S.A., and D. M. Sutherland, R.S.A.; travelled in France, Italy, Switzerland (1939). *Work in permanent collections:* Aberdeen, Dundee, Glasgow, Perth, Paisley and Bristol A.G., Scottish Modern Arts Assoc., Scottish National Gallery of Modern Art, Edinburgh. *Address:* Binrock, 456 Perth Rd., Dundee. *Club:* Scottish Arts, Edinburgh. *Signs work:* "Morrocco."

MORSS, Edward James, R.B.A., R.O.I., A.R.C.A. (1930); artist in oil; Principal (retd.) St. Martin's School of Art, 109 Charing Cross Rd., WC2, formerly, Colchester School of Art; and Maidstone College of Art; *b* Exmouth, Devon, 24 Jan., 1906; *s* of Edward Alexander Morss, engineer; *m* Dorothy Cullen; one *d. Educ.:* Orme's School; *studied art* at at Sheffield College of Art, R.C.A. (1927-31). *Exhib.:* Various London, Paris and provincial galleries. *Address:* 5 Kinnaird Ave., Chiswick, London W4. *Signs work:* see appendix.

MORTON, Cavendish, R.I., R.O.I., Hon. S.G.A., Hon. N.S.; painter of landscape, marine, country houses, motor racing, flowers, illustrations in oil, water-colour, black and white; Chairman, Gainsborough's House Society, Vice-Pres., Norfolk Contemporary Arts Society; *b* Edinburgh, 17 Feb., 1911; *s* of Cavendish Morton; *m* Rosemary Britten; one *s,* two *d. Exhib.:* R.A., R.B.A., U.S.A., Canada, Australia, Bermuda; one-man shows: London, York University, Norwich, King's

Lynn, Sudbury, Ipswich, Aldeburgh. *Work in permanent collections:* B.M., Norwich Castle Museum, Wolverhampton Art Gallery, Contemporary Arts Society. *Publications:* illustrations for Dorothy Hammond Innes' Occasions (Michael Joseph, 1972). *Address:* Stanley House, Castle St., Eye, Suffolk. *Signs work:* "MORTON" (until 1949), "CAVENDISH MORTON."

MOSS, Hugh, A.R.C.A. (1926), F.R.S.A.; art teacher; artist in calligraphy; Principal, Gloucester College of Art (1945-68); asst., Medway School of Art (1927-34); asst., Wakefield College of Art (1934-45); *b* Uxbridge, Middx., 20 Jan., 1904; *s* of Robert Moss; *m* Sylvia Hewitt; two *d. Educ.:* Royal Masonic School for Boys; *studied art* at Harrow School of Art (1921-23), R.C.A. (1923-27). *Work in permanent collections:* In Memorial Chapel, Gloucester Cathedral, Rolls of Honour, Gloucestershire County (1914-18 and 1939-45), Gloucestershire Hussars (1939-45), Gloucestershire Regiment (1939-45). *Address:* Half-Acre, Northwood Green, Westbury-on-Severn, Glos. *Signs work:* "Hugh Moss."

MOXLEY, Raymond, F.R.I.B.A., A.R.W.A., F.R.S.A.; architect and partner multi-professional practice; Vice-President, R.I.B.A. (1971-74), Hon. Librarian, R.I.B.A.; President, Wessex Association of Architects; Chairman, Association of Consultant Architects; *b* Sheffield, 28 June, 1923; *s* of Rev. H. R. Moxley, M.A.; *m* Jacqueline; one *s*, two *d. Educ.:* Caterham School; *studied art and architecture* at Oxford School of Architecture (1940-42, 1946-49) under Arthur Korn. *Exhib.:* R.W.A. annual exhibitions 1960 onwards. *Publications:* Elementary Building Construction (Batsford) and various articles in the professional press. *Addresses:* 77 Eaton Terr., London SW1W 8TN and 7 King St., Bristol BS1 4EJ. *Clubs:* R.A.C., Landsdown. *Signs work:* "R. Moxley."

MOYA, Hidalgo, R.I.B.A., A.A. Dip. (1943); architect in partnership with Philip Powell and Peter Skinner; *b* 5 May, 1920; *s* of Hidalgo Moya; *m* Janiffer Hall; one *s*, two *d. Educ.:* Oundle; *studied art* at Royal West of England College of Art and architecture at A.A. *Works include:* Churchill Gardens Housing, Pimlico; Skylon; Mayfield School, Putney for L.C.C.; British Pavilion, Expo '70; Hospitals at Swindon, Slough, High Wycombe and Wythenshawe; new buildings at Brasenose College, Oxford, Christ Church and Corpus Christi, Oxford and St. John's College, Cambridge; Chichester Festival Theatre; Wolfson College, Oxford. *Address:* 30 Percy St., London W1.

MOYNIHAN, Rodrigo, C.B.E. (1953), A.R.A. (1944); painter; Prof. of Painting at Royal College of Art (1948-57); official War Artist, 1943-44; *b* 17 Oct., 1910; *s* of Herbert Moynihan; *m* Elinor Bellingham Smith. *Educ.:* University College School, London, and in U.S.A.; *studied art* at Slade School (1928-31), Slade Scholar. *Exhib.:* Redfern and Leicester Galleries. *Work in permanent collections:* Manchester, Belfast, Leicester. *Official purchases:* Chantrey Bequest, C.A.S., War Artists Advisory Com. *Address:* 70 Avenue du Léman, Lausanne, Switzerland. *Clubs:* Chelsea Arts, Beefsteak.

MOYSE, Arthur; artist in collage, water-colour, pen and ink; art critic for Freedom Press, London Correspondent for Chicago Industrial Worker; *b* London, 21 June, 1914; *s* of Arthur Moyse, able seaman. *Educ.:* Addison Gardens L.C.C. Primary School. *Exhib.:* Angela Flowers Gallery, Woodstock and others. *Work in permanent collection:* Transport Museum. *Publications:* More in Sorrow, Zero One, Revolutionary Manifesto, Peterloo. *Address:* 39 Minford Gdns., W. Kensington, London W14 0AP. *Signs work:* "Arthur Moyse."

MUIR, Jane, M.A. Oxon. (1950), F.S.I.A. (1974), M.S.D-C. (1971), Dip. Architectural Decoration (1969); artist-craftsman in mosaic in glass and natural stones, charcoal and pastel drawings; visiting tutor, West Dean College,

Chichester; *b* London, 11 Apr., 1929; *d* of H. I. Pinches, M.D.; *m* A. W. E. Muir; two *s. Educ.:* Rye St. Antony School, Oxford; Oxford University; *studied art* at Teesside College of Art (1965-68) under Joan Haswell, specializing in mosaic and stained glass. *Exhib.:* Woburn Abbey Art Centre (1976), City Gallery, Milton Keynes (1975), Little Missenden Festival (1974-75), Upper Street Gallery, Islington (group) (1973), Billingham Civic Centre (1969). *Work in permanent collections:* exterior mosaic, St. Anne's College, Oxford, Thomas Woolfe Ltd. Birmingham, Constantine College of Technology, Teesside, Oxfordshire and Buckinghamshire Educ. Authorities; and private collections. *Address:* Butcher's Orchard, Weston Turville, Aylesbury, Bucks. *Club:* Art Workers' Guild. *Signs work:* "Muir."

MULLALY, Terence Frederick Stanley, Cavaliere Ufficiale of the Order "Al Merito della Repubblica Italiana" (1964) for services to Italian art; M.A. (Cantab.); Faculty Member, Finch College (New York), Intercontinental Study Plan; art historian and critic, art critic for the Daily Telegraph since 1958; Pres. British Section, International Assoc. of Art Critics 1968; *b* Quetta, India, 14 Nov., 1927; *s* of Col. B. R. Mullaly; *m* Elizabeth Helen Burkitt. *Educ.:* Privately in India and in Japan and Canada, and at Downing College, Cambridge. *Publications:* Numerous articles in The Burlington Magazine, The Economist, Apollo, The Studio, etc., and in Italian publications; B.B.C. talks. *Address:* 74 Greencroft Gdns., Hampstead, London NW6.

MULLEN GLOVER, Sybil, R.I. (1962), R.S.M.A. (1964), R.W.A. (1965); artist in water-colour; *b* Cheshire; *d* of W. T. C. W. Jeffery, step-daughter of Capt. A. J. C. Moore, O.B.E., R.N.; *m* Dr. W. E. Glover, Colonial Medical Service, Retd. *Educ.:* privately; *studied art* at St. Martin's School of Art and private tutors. *Exhib.:* R.A., N.E.A.C., R.O.I. and most leading galleries, including U.S.A. and Sweden. *Work in permanent collections:* Brighton Art Gallery, National Maritime Museum, Sweyne School and Walsall. Gold and silver medals, Paris Salon. *Address:* Park Place, 108 Molesworth Rd., Stoke, Plymouth. *Club:* Chelsea Arts. *Signs work:* "Sybil Mullen Glover."

MULLINS, Gwen, O.B.E.; weaver in wool and linen with natural dyes; co-director of Graffham Weavers; *b* London, 10 Apr., 1904; *d* of Augustus Phillip Brandt, merchant banker; *m* Claud Mullins; one *s*, one *d. Exhib.:* Tea Centre (1965), Craft Centre, Red Rose Guild; Designer–Craftsmen yearly exhbn. in Graffham. *Work in permanent collection:* V. & A. *Address:* Shuttles, Graffham, Petworth, Sussex. *Clubs:* British Crafts Centre, S.D-C., Red Rose Guild, London Guild of Weavers, Spinners & Dyers. *Signs work:* "Gwen Mullins."

MUMFORD, Lewis, Hon. LL.D. (Edinburgh); Hon. Dr. Arch. (Rome); Hon. Mem. R.I.B.A. (1942); Hon. Mem. T.P.I. (1946); Award of Merit, Philadelphia Art Alliance (1971); Prof. of Humanities, Stanford University (1942-44); Prof. of City Planning, University of Pennsylvania (1951-56); visiting Bemis Prof. M.I.T. (1957-60); Ford Research Prof. University of Pennsylvania (1959-61); Abrams Visiting Prof. M.I.T. (1973-75); writer; *b* Flushing, Long Island, N.Y., 19 Oct., 1895; *s* of Lewis Mumford; *m* Sophia Wittenberg; one *s* (killed Italy, 1944), one *d. Educ.:* The City College of New York and Columbia University. Art Critic, New Yorker (1932-37). *Publications:* The Golden Day (1926); The Brown Decades (1931); Art and Technics (1952); The City in History (1961); The Myth of The Machine (1967); The Pentagon of Power (1970); Interpretations and Forecasts, 1922-72, (1973); Findings and Keepings (1975), etc. *Address:* Amenia, New York.

MUNDY, Henry; painter in various media; *b* Birkenhead, 13 Jan., 1919; *s* of

James Mundy; *m* Gillian Ayres (painter); two *s*. *Educ.:* St. Hugh's School, Birkenhead; *studied art* at Laird School of Art, Birkenhead, Camberwell School of Art and Crafts, London (Coldstream, Pasmore). *Work in permanent collections:* Tate Gallery, Carnegie Institute, Pittsburgh, U.S.A., National Gallery of Canada, Nuffield Foundation, Brooklyn Museum, U.S.A., National Gallery of Victoria, Australia, Arts Council of Northern Ireland, Belfast, San Francisco Museum of Art. *Address:* 14 Beverley Rd., Barnes, London SW13.

MUNRO, Charles Alexander, M.B.E., M.S.I.A.; artist and designer; Principal of Charles Munro Associates; *b* 9 June, 1913; *m*; one *s*, two *d*. *Educ.:* Manor House, Felixstowe, and Acton College of Technology, London; *studied art* at Ealing College of Art (1929-31). Designer with Greenleys Advertising (1932-34); freelance artist and designer (1934-37); Art Editor and Political Cartoonist of the Civil and Military Gazette, Lahore, India (1937-40); Indian Army (Sappers) (1940-46); designer, Exhbns. Division, C.O.I. (1946-52), where he was responsible for the design of many major Government pavilions. In private practice (1952–); designer of exhbns. in all parts of the world, designer of Section 1, British Pavilion for Expo 70 World Fair, held in Osaka, Japan; designer of Doddington Carriage Museum. *Exhib.:* R.A. Mural works for business organisation and private individuals. *Publications:* Two books of political cartoons, periodicals, newspaper articles, etc. *Address:* Bywater Pl., Lymington, Hants. *Clubs:* London Sketch, Royal Lymington Yacht, Auriol Rowing, R.A.C. *Signs work:* "MUNRO."

MUNTZ, Elizabeth, G.M.C., Mem. of London Group; Mem. Purbeck Marblers and Stone Cutters; sculptor in stone, wood, bronze, etc., painter in oil, tempera, etc.; *b* Toronto, Canada, Oct., 1894; *d* of Rupert Muntz. *Educ.:* Bishop Strachan's School, Toronto; *studied art* at Ontario College of Art, Academie Grande Chaumière, Paris (Bourdelle), and privately under Frank Dobson. *Exhib.:* London, Paris, New York, Montreal, Berlin, Leipzig. *Work in permanent collections:* Manchester Art Gallery (Erda; bronze group); Stone Head of T. F. Powys in Bristol Art Gallery. *Publication:* The Dolphin Bottle (Gollancz, 1965). *Address:* Apple Tree Cottage, Chaldon Herring, Dorchester, Dorset. *Signs work:* "Elizabeth Muntz."

MURGATROYD, Keith, P.P.S.T.D., M.Inst.Pkg.; Director of Royle/Murgatroyd Design Associates Ltd.; Chairman of the North-Western Region of the S.I.A.D. (1967-68); Treasurer and Vice-President of the International Council of Graphic Design Associations (1968-74); President of the Society of Typographic Designers (1969-73). *Work repro.:* Design Magazine, Print Magazine, Graphic Annual, Modern Publicity, Design Magazine, etc. *Exhib.:* at Monotype House, London, British Embassy, Washington, D.C., and numerous art and design colleges. 59 Design Awards. *Address:* 48 Ridge Cres., Hawk Green, Marple, Ches.

MURISON, Neil, A.T.D. (1951), A.R.W.A. (1971); lecturer; painter in oil and acrylic; Director of Studies, Dept. of Foundation Studies, Bristol Polytechnic; previously art master, Queen Elizabeth's Hospital, Bristol (1952-61); *b* Bath, 10 Oct., 1930; *s* of William Murison, M.P.S., Ph.C.; *m* Valerie Elizabeth John; one *s*, one *d*. *Educ.:* Bristol Grammar School; *studied art* at West of England College of Art (1946-51). *Work in permanent collections:* Nuffield, Wills Tobacco Co., Skopje Modern Art Museum, Yugoslavia, Trumans Breweries, Bridgwater Public Library, Bristol, Devon, Leeds, Herts., Hull, Leics., Liverpool, Surrey and West Riding of Yorks. Educ. Authorities. *Address:* 10 Hartington Pk., Redland, Bristol BS6 7ES. *Signs work:* "Murison."

MURPHY, Diana, A.R.C.A.; R.C.A. Travelling Scholarship; artist in line and wash; *b* London; *m* A. E. Poulter, A.R.C.A., F.R.S.A., decd. *Educ.:* L.C.C. Trade

School; *studied art* at Clapham and R.C.A. *Exhib.:* R.A. Arts Council Exhbns., Leicester, Chenil, Drian, Camden Centre Galleries, Mall Galleries with N.E.A.C., N.S., S.G.A., F.P.S. *Work in collections:* Earl of Iddesleigh, W. B. Yeats, Hon. R. D. Denman, Richard Llewellyn, Ian Lubbock, Brian Melland, etc. *Official purchases:* Whitworth and Carlisle Galleries. *Work repro.:* Studio, Magazines. *Address:* 116 Stanley Rd., Teddington, Middx. *Clubs:* W.I.A.C., F.P.S., Campden Hill Art.

MURPHY, Seamus, R.H.A. (1954), LL.D. (1969); Prof. of Sculpture R.H.A. (1964); sculptor in stone, bronze, marble; *b* Mallow, Co. Cork, 1907; *m* Maigread Higgins; one *s*, two *d*. *Studied art* at School of Art, Cork, and in Paris. *Exhib.:* Ireland, England, France, U.S.A. *Work in permanent collections:* Gibson Gallery, Cork, City Hall, Cork, U.S. Embassy, Dublin, National Gallery, Dublin, etc. *Commissioned work* in Arus an Uachtarain and in many churches, etc. *Address:* 6 Wellesley Terr., Wellington Rd., Cork, Ireland. *Signs work:* "Seamus Murphy."

MURRAY, Donald, B.A., D.A., M.S.S.A.; artist and designer in calligraphy, water-colour and pastel; teacher of art, Robert Gordon's College, Aberdeen; *b* Edinburgh, 1940; *s* of Capt. James Murray; *m* Mary F. Low; one *s*. *Educ.:* George Heriot's School, Edinburgh; *studied art* at Edinburgh College of Art (1958-63) under Stuart Barrie, D.A., M.S.I.A., M.S.T.D. *Exhib.:* R.S.W., S.S.A., Aberdeen Artists' Society; group shows: Pitlochry Festival Theatre. *Work in permanent collections:* Heriot-Watt University, Edinburgh (calligraphic title page), Edinburgh District Council (calligraphic panels). *Publications:* Growing up in the Church (illustrations), numerous book jacket designs for Oliver & Boyd. *Address:* Manorlea, 41 Commerce St., Insch, Aberdeens. *Signs work:* "Donald Murray" (bottom right or left).

MURRY, Richard Arthur Crossthwaite; sec., Art Workers' Guild (1962—); sec., N.E.A.C. (1925-28); art master, A.A. (1928-30), Surbiton County Grammar School (1930-38), librarian, Central School of Art and Design (1938-67); artist in oil, water-colour, pencil, etching; *b* Dulwich, 8 May, 1902; *s* of John Murry, staff clerk, Inland Revenue. *Educ.:* Emanuel School; *studied art* at Central School of Art and Design (L.C.C. Scholar, 1922), Slade School of Art (Robert Ross Scholar, 1925, etc.). *Exhib.:* London Group, R.B.A., N.E.A.C., Leger Gallery, etc. *Work repro.:* in Studio. *Address:* 8 Edenhurst Ave., London SW6. *Signs work:* "R. Murry" (plus abbreviated date).

MUSGRAVE, Clifford, O.B.E., Hon. D.Litt., (Sussex); director, Brighton Art Gallery and Museum and Royal Pavilion (1939-68); Mem. Com. Le Siècle de l'Elegance Exhbn., Louvre (1959); Mem. Com. 18th-Century English Taste Exhbn., Burlington House (1955-56); Hon. Mem. Georgian Group; Mem. Advisory Council of V. & A. Museum (1957-69); Hon. Mem., Regency Soc.; *b* 1904; *m* Margaret Meakin; two *s*. *Publications:* Royal Pavilion (1959), Sussex (1957), Regency Furniture (1961), Adam and Hepplewhite Furniture (1965), Life in Brighton (1970). *Address:* 25A St. Peter's Rd., Seaford.

MUSIC, Zoran Antonio; painter, designer, engraver, lithographer; *b* Gorizia, Italy, 1909. *Studied art* at l'Académie des Beaux Arts at Zagreb. *Exhib.:* Salon de Mai (since 1953), Venice, Milan, Rome, Zürich, Geneva, Munich, Turin, Copenhagen, Pittsburgh, Vienna, Dortmund, Ljubljana, London, Minneapolis, Tokyo, New York, Nantes, Amiens, Aix-en-Provence, Grenoble, Rennes, Nice. *Work in permanent collections:* Musées d'Art Moderne, Amsterdam, Bâle, New York, Paris, Rome, Venice, Pittsburgh, Havre, Wellington. *Address:* c/o Galerie de France, 3 Faubourg Saint Honoré, Paris.

MUSZYNSKI, Leszek Tadeusz, R.B.A., D.A. (Edin.); artist in oil, drawing, lithograph; senior lecturer in painting, West Surrey College of Art and Design; *b* Poland, 19 Apr., 1923; *s* of Alexander Muszynski; *m* Patricia; one *s*. *Educ.:* in Poland; *studied art* at Edinburgh College of Art (W. Gillies, J. Maxwell, W. MacTaggart); Travelling Scholarship to Paris, Florence, Arezzo, Assisi. *Work in permanent collections:* Museum of Art, Dallas, Texas, Museum, Durban, S. Africa. *Exhib.:* Roland, Browse and Delbanco; one-man shows: London, Edinburgh, Copenhagen, Denmark, Basle, Dallas, Texas, Lavenham, Petersfield. *Address:* Holybourne Lodge, Holybourne, Alton, Hants. *Signs work:* see appendix.

MUSZYNSKI ZNICZ-, Tadeusz, N.D.D.; painter in oil, portrait and graphic art; art master; *b* Warsaw, 25 Sept., 1921; *s* of Antoni; *m* Giovanna; two *d*. *Educ.:* High School, Warsaw; Bologna University (1946-47); S.M.G. School of Art, Kingswood (1947-48) and Sir John Cass College, School of Art (1948-52). *Exhib.:* Munich, Hamburg, Florence and Rome; one-man shows: Related Arts Gallery, Grabowski Gallery, Galleria Numero (Florence), Barrett Gallery; group exhib.: Group 49, Chelsea Artists, F.P.S.; galleries: Kingley, Walker, Grabowski, Numero, New Vision, International Exhbn. Ronchi di Massa, Cassel, Clare College, Cambridge, Festival of Edinburgh, Olimpiade D'Arte e Cultura, Italy (1966), 1st prize, gold medal. F.P.S. in Nimes and Avignon (1967), Festival of Arts Lyon (1970), The Mall, Drian, Municipal Travelling Exhibition in South of England (1971-72), A.P.A. exhbn. Centaur Gal., winner of the Garby Prize (1975). *Address:* 14 Lilyville Rd., London SW6. *Signs work:* "ZNICZ-MUSZYNSKI."

MYERSCOUGH-WALKER; architect, writer, painter; *b* Knaresborough, Yorks., 30 Oct., 1912; *m*; four *s*, one *d*. *Educ.:* Architectural Asssoc., London; *studied* under Sir Howard Robertson. Finalist Tite Prize; Victory Scholarship; Prix de Rome. *Exhib.:* R.A., Leicester Gallery. *Publications:* Stage and Film *Décor* (Sir Isaac Pitman); Choosing a Modern House (Studio International); The Perspectivist (Sir Isaac Pitman); in preparation: Age & England. *Address:* Chilgrove, nr. Chichester, Sussex.

MYNOTT, Derek G., R.B.A. (1953), D.F.A. (Lond.); painter in oil and watercolour; *b* London, 27 Nov., 1926; *s* of G. E. Mynott; *m* Patricia Barton, designer and illustrator; two *s*, one *d*. *Studied art* at Slade School of Fine Art (1946-50) under Randolph Schwabe and Sir William Coldstream. *Exhib.:* R.A., R.B.A., etc.; one-man shows: R.B.A. Galleries (1953), Trafford Gallery (1959), Gstaad (1968), Jasper Galleries, Houston (1973), Mall Galleries (1975), Lord Mayor of London's Annual Art Award (1972), Medaille d'argent (1974), De Laszio Medal (1974). *Work in permanent collections:* in Galleries, Embassies, Ministries and private collections in Europe, America, S. Africa, etc. *Address:* 23 Mount Park Rd., London W5. *Club:* Chelsea Arts. *Signs work:* see appendix.

MYNOTT, Patricia, A.Z.S.; Mem. Association of Illustrators; artist in watercolour, line and gouache, illustrator of marine biology and natural history, film designer; *b* London, 1927; *d* of Carel Bartoniček, L.D.S., R.C.S. (Eng.); *m* Derek Mynott, R.B.A.; two *s*, one *d*. *Educ.:* Dominican Covent, Chingford; *studied art* at South West Essex School of Art (1945). *Films:* British Animated Productions, National Screen Service, National Savings, Film Producers Guild. *Prints:* Solomon & Whitehead. *Publications:* illustrated, Guide to the Seashore, Beaches and Beachcombing, Folklore of Fossils, The Curious Lore of Malta's Fossil Shark's Teeth; Childrens' books, Encyclopedias, Educational, Initial Teaching Alphabet; *publishers:* Michael Joseph, Blackies, Macmillan, Readers Digest, Macdonalds, Paul Hamlyn, Pitmans. *Address:* 23 Mount Park Rd., London W5. *Signs work:* "Mynott" or "Barton."

N

NAIMASTER, John Lynch; chairman and joint managing director, The Fine Art Society, Ltd.; joined Walker's Galleries, Ltd, 1924, director 1949-62; specialist in early English water-colour drawings; Vice-Pres., Fine Arts Provident Inst.; Mem., Exec. Com. The Old Water-colour Soc's Club; Hon. Treasurer, The Society of London Art Dealers; Mem., Artists Rifles (1923-39); Oxford and Bucks L.I. (1939-45); Vice-Pres., The Artists Rifles Association; *b* London, 23 May, 1905. *Educ.:* St. Paul's School. *Publications:* editor, Artists Rifles Gazette (1933-37), editor, Artists Rifles Assoc. Chronicle (1945-50). *Address:* 148 New Bond St., London W1. *Club:* Garrick.

NALECZ, Halima, Dip. U.S.B. (Wilno), Dame Chevalier d'Honneur (18 May, 1957); Bronze Medal, Europe prize for painting, Kursaal, Ostend, Belgium (1969, 1971); painter in oils and mixed media; Founder and Director of Drian Galleries, London; *b* Wilno, Poland, 2 Feb., 1917; *d* of Antoni Kzrywicz-Nowohonski, landowner; *m* Zygmunt Nalecz, writer. *Educ.:* Lycée, Wilno; *studied art* under Professor Roube, Professor Szyszko-Bohusz, Professor Zahorska, and in Paris under H. J. Closon. *Exhib.:* most municipal and public galleries in England, and W.I.A.C., A.I.A., Free Painters and Sculptors, London Group, Salon de Réalités Nouvelle, Galerie Collette Allendy, Salon des Divergences, Galerie Creuze (Paris); one-man exhbns. at Walker Galleries, London (1956), New Vision Centre, London (1957, 1959), Ewan Phillips, London (1967), County Town Gallery, Lewes (1967), Drian Galleries, London (1968-69), R.A. Summer Exhbn. (1967, 1968, 1969), S.S.W.A., Edinburgh. *Work in permanent collections:* Britain, France, Spain, Italy, Germany, Australia, U.S.A., Sweden, Nuffield Foundation, London, National Gallery of Israel, Bezalel, Jerusalem. *Work repro.:* Quadrum, Apollo, Arts Review, Art and Artists, Wiadomosci, Art International, etc.; prefaces to catalogues by Denis Bowen and Pierre Rouve. Paintings featured in film, The Millionairess. *Address:* 5-7 Porchester Pl., Marble Arch, London W2. *Clubs:* A.I.A., W.I.A.C., Hampstead Artists Association, Free Painters and Sculptors, Polish Hearth. *Signs work:* see appendix.

NAPIER, Charles Goddard, R.S.W. (1912); painter in water-colour, black and white; *b* Edinburgh, 1 Aug., 1889; *s* of Andrew Nelson Napier, herbalist; *m* Hazel May Eadie. *Educ.:* George Watson's College, Edinburgh; *studied art* at Edinburgh College of Art (1911-14) and Dutch Galleries (1927).*Exhib.:* R.S.A., R.S.W., G.I., U.S.A., Canada, N.Z., London, Oxford, British Council, water-colours (1949, 1952), etc. *Work in permanent collections:* by Scottish Modern Arts, Edinburgh (Marlborough, in Wiltshire, In Wells Harbour, Norfolk). *Official purchases:* as above. *Publications:* illustrated contributions to Studio.*Address:* 6 St. Margaret's Rd., Edinburgh, 9. *Signs work:* see appendix.

NAPPER, John; *b* 1916. *Exhib.:* One-man shows: Leicester Galleries (1949, 1961, 1962), Adams Gallery (1957, 1959), Retrospective Exhbn., Liverpool, Walker Art Gallery (1959), La Maison de la pensée française, Paris (1960), Galerie Lahumière, Paris (1963), Galerie Hervé et Lahumière, Paris (1965), the Larcada Gallery, New York (1968, 1970, 1972, 1975), Kingpitcher Gallery, Pittsburgh (Pa) (1973). Visiting Professor of Fine Arts, Southern Illinois University, U.S.A. (1968-69). Awarded prize at The International Exhbn. of Fine Arts, Moscow (1957); awarded the Critic's Prize (1961). *Address:* Steadvallets, Bromfield, Ludlow, Shropshire.

NARDINI, Peter Anthony, D.A. (1974); Cargill Award, Post. D.A. (1975).

travelling scholarship; art teacher in lithography, etching and painting; *b* Glasgow, 16 Aug., 1947; *s* of Gino Nardini, grocer; *m* Allison Nardini; one *s,* one *d. Educ.:* Holy Cross, Hamilton; *studied art* at Glasgow School of Art (1970-75) under Philip Reeves, Michael Roslau. *Exhib.:* R.S.A., Edinburgh, Art Centre, Edinburgh, Print Workshop, Glasgow. *Publication:* Short Story Triptich. *Address:* 63 Tinto View, Eddlewood, Hamilton, Lanarkshire. *Signs work:* "Peter Nardini."

NARRAWAY, William Edward, R.P., R.B.A., N.E.A.C., V.P.S.P.S.; portrait painter and sculptor; works in oil, water-colour, pastel; portraits, landscapes, genre, etc.; *b* 1 Feb., 1917; *s* of William Ewart Narraway; *m;* two *s. Educ.:* Yorkshire. *Exhib.:* R.A., R.S.P.P., London Group, N.E.A.C., R.B.A., P.S., Soc. Portrait Sculptors, provincial galleries; one-man show Guildford House, Guildford, Gold Medallist Paris Salon (portrait, H.M. the Queen, 1971, H.R.H. The Princess Anne, 1973, H.M. The Queen, 1973, Sir Malcolm Sargent, Sir Ralph Vaughan Williams) over 500 portraits. *Private collections:* H.M. The Queen, England, Scotland, France, Holland, Germany, America, Mexico, Australia, Portugal, Ireland, Italy. *Work repro.:* R.A. Catalogue, Magazines, national and provincial press, etc. *Address:* Limnery, Holmbury St. Mary, Dorking. *Club:* Chelsea Arts. *Signs work:* see appendix.

NASH, Arthur, M.I.P.A., M.S.I.A. (1953); Management Services Director; typographer; Leo Burnett Ltd. (1930-75); *b* London, 27 Sept., 1916; one *s,* one *d. Educ.:* L.C.C. Schools; *studied art* at London School of Printing and Graphic Arts, Camberwell School of Arts and Crafts. *Address:* 119 St. Mary's Drive, Crawley, Sussex RH10 3BG. *Signs work:* "Arthur Nash."

NASH, John Northcote, C.B.E. (1964), R.A. (1951), A.R.A. (1940), Hon. Fellow R.C.A.; painter and illustrator; formerly senior asst., Teacher of Design, R.C.A.; Pres., Colchester Art Soc.; *b* 11 Apr., 1893; *m* Dorothy Christine Kuhlenthal. *Educ.:* Wellington College. *Exhib.:* London Group, R.A., various provincial art galleries; Carnegie Inst., Pittsburgh, Brussels, etc. *Official purchases:* Contemporary Art Soc., National Gallery, Millbank, V. & A., Manchester, Sheffield, Glasgow, Aberdeen, Dublin, Bristol, Bath, Nottingham, Northampton, Pietermaritzburg, etc. *Work repro.:* Medici Society, Frost and Reed. *Address:* Bottengoms Farm, Wormingford, nr. Colchester, Essex. *Signs work:* "John Nash."

NASH, Tom, A.T.D., R.C.A.; artist in oil, P.V.A., gouache, collage, murals in retroreflective plastics, etc.; awarded the Geoffrey Crawshay Memorial Travelling Scholarship; West Wales Association for the Arts, Research Award; *b* Ammanford, 1931; *s* of William Nash; *m* Enid Williams; two *d. Educ.:* Llandeilo; *studied art* at Swansea, Paris, Provence; associated with Paul Jenkins in Paris. *Exhib.:* one-man and mixed exhibitions in London, provinces, Washington, D.C., Argentine, Toronto. *Work in permanent collections:* National Museum of Wales, Nuffield Foundation, Arts Council, Clare, Churchill, Pembroke Colleges, Cambridge, various county collections, Caerleon College of Education, Glynn Vivian Art Gallery, Swansea, Steel Company of Wales, C.A.S., Caiman Museum, Argentina, Wadham College, Oxford, University of Wales, India Rubber Co., Macco Corp., California, Brasenose College, Oxford, Trinity College of Education, 3M United Kingdom Limited, University of Bradford, Church of Wales Collection; private collections in Britain, France, Germany, U.S.A., Canada, New Zealand. *Address:* Clydfan, Llandeilo, Dyfed, Wales. *Signs work:* "Tom Nash."

NAYLOR, Clifford; artist, theoretician, portrait painter in multi-media (principally oil), batiks and constructions; *b* Derby, 27 Jan., 1953; *s* of Clarence Samuel

Naylor, N.C.P.S. *Educ.:* Mortimer Wilson, Alfreton; *studied art* at Derby College of Art (1971) under R. Selby; Birmingham College of Art (1972-74) under William Gear. *Exhib.:* Joint show at Kenning Gallery. *Publications:* articles Living Art and My Thoughts. *Address:* 40 Colin St., Alfreton, Derbys. OE5 7HT. *Signs work:* "C. Naylor."

NEAGU, Paul; draughtsman, sculptor, painter in pencil, gesso, wood, etc.; teacher, Hornsey College of Art, London; *b* Bucharest, 22 Feb., 1938; *s* of Tudor Neagu, minister. *Educ.:* Institute 'N. Grigorescu', Bucharest; *studied art* at Bucharest (1959-65); Kulturbehörde Hamburg; Musee Cantonal de Beaux-Arts, Lausanne. *Exhib.:* Oxford Museum of Modern Art (1975), Serpentine Gallery, London (1973), Richard Demarco Gallery (1969). *Work in permanent collections:* Aberdeen A.G., Ulster Museum, Belfast, Arts Council of Gt. Britain. *Address:* 73A Highbury New Pk., London N5. *Signs work:* "P. Neagu" or "Neagu P."

NEAL, James, A.R.C.A. (1939); artist; lecturer, Regional College of Art, Hull; *b* Islington, 18 Jan., 1918; *s* of James Abram Neal; *m* Doreen Barnes; two *s,* one *d.* *Educ.:* St. John Evangelist; *studied art* at St. Martin's School of Art; R.C.A. *Exhib.:* R.A., R.S.A., N.E.A.C., London Group, Redfern Galleries; one-man shows Trafford Gallery, Wildensteins, etc. *Official purchases:* Nottingham Art Gallery, Wakefield Art Gallery, Ferens Art Gallery, Hull, Beverley Art Gallery, London County Council, Hull Educ. Com., W. Riding Educ. Com., East Riding Educ. Com., Derbyshire Educ. Com., Durham Educ. Com., etc. *Address:* 205 Victoria Ave., Hull, N. Humberside. *Signs work:* "James Neal."

NEAVE, Alice Headley: see HEADLEY-NEAVE, Alice.

NEGRI, Nina; 3 prizes, oil painting, Société Lorraine; Auvers (commemoration Van Gogh), 1st Biennale, Bordeaux (1958); Lauréate engraving Palme d'Or, Monaco (1969), Painting Prix, Deauville (1970), IV Biennale, Cannes (1971); abstract painter and engraver; *b* Argentina; *d* of Sir Victor Negri. *Educ.:* England, B. Aires, Paris; *studied art* (Léger, Ozenfant, Hayter). *Exhib.:* most European countries, U.S.A., Mexico, Sao Paulo, etc.; one-man shows: N.Y. (1953), Milan, Paris (1959), Strasbourg; museums: Amsterdam; Brussels; Ville de Paris, l'État (Français); Toulon; Bibliothèque Nationale; Guggenheim, N.Y.; public and private collections. *Publications:* Seuphor, Hayter, Von Konow, Marinelli, Vrinat, etc. *Address:* 4 rue du Gros Caillou, Paris 7. *Signs work:* "Negri."

NELLENS, Roger; painter in oil on canvas; *b* Liege, Belgium, 11 May, 1937; *s* of Gustave Nellens; *m* Fabienne; one *s,* two *d.* *Educ.:* College St. Michel et St. Louis, Brussels, and London Academy; *studied art* privately under René Magritte and Paul Delvaux. *Work in permanent collections:* Collection de l'état Belge, Musée d'ostende, Boymans Museum, Rotterdam, Musée de St. Étienne, France. *Address:* Fort St. Pol, 202 Ave. du Zoute, 8.300 Knokke, Belgium. *Signs work:* see appendix.

NERELLE, Coral; J.H.A.M.I. (1949); portrait painter in oil; *b* Sydney, Australia; *d* of Alfred Edward White; *m* John Bill, A.R.W.A. *Educ.:* Sydney College of Art, Australia; Johns Hopkins University, U.S.A.: Byam Shaw School of Art; under G. Raynor Hoff, Stanislav Rembsky, Peter Greenham, R.A. *Work in permanent collections:* Johns Hopkins University, Baltimore (medical illustrations); Royal Australasian College of Surgeons, Melbourne (portraits) and in private collections in U.S.A., England, Wales and Ireland. *Address:* Flat 2, Salperton Pk., nr. Cheltenham, Gloucs. *Club:* English Speaking Union. *Signs work:* "Coral Nerelle."

NESCH, Rolf; prizes in Graphik: São Paulo (1955), Lichtwarckpreis, Hamburg (1958), Triennale, Greuchen (1958), Biennale, Venice (1963); painter, printmaker; *b* Oberesslingen, Württemberg; *s* of August Nesch; *m* Ragnhild Hald. *Educ.:* Academy, Dresden. *Work in permanent collections:* V. & A., Bibliotheque National, Scandinavia, Switzerland, Germany, U.S.A., Italy. *Work repro.:* Rolf Nesch, Graphik Materialbilder Plastik, Alfred Hentzen, Kornelinspreis, Düsseldorf (1965), Retrospective Ausstellung Akademie d. Künste, Berlin (1966), Grafik, Ausstellung Günther Franke, München (1966), Grafik, Ausstellung Galerie Maerklin, Stuttgart (1967), The Graphic Art of Rolf Nesch, Detroit Inst. of Arts (1969), Jan Askeland: Rolf Nesch, Oslo (1969). *Address:* Aal, Norway. *Signs work:* "Rolf Nesch."

NESSLER, Walter H.; Gold and Silver Medal, Academy Campanella, Rome; landscape painter in oil, polyester resin, reliefs; teacher; *b* Leipzig, 19 Jan., 1912; *m*; one *s*. *Studied art* at Castelli, Italian Art School at Dresden (1933-35), and self-taught. *Exhib.:* R.A., R.B.A., Leger Galleries, Redfern Gallery, Arcade Gallery, Twenty Brook St. Gallery, Galerie des Beaux-Arts (Paris), Bradford City Art Gallery, New Vision Gallery, Gallery One, Obelisk Gallery, John Whibley Gallery, O'Hana Gallery, Molton Gallery, Hendon Group, New End Gallery, Madden Galleries, Harlow Festival, Alwin Gallery, Gallery Petit, Rotunda Gallery, Erica Bourne Gallery. *Work in permanent collections:* C.A.S., Municipal Museum, Leicester, Ein Harod Museum (Israel); and private collections in America, S. Africa, England, Norway. *Address:* 16 Somali Rd., London NW2. *Club:* C.A.S. *Signs work:* "Nessler."

NEURATH, Marie; director Isotype Inst.; *b* Brunswick, 27 May, 1898; *d* of Dr. Hans Reidemeister; *m* Dr. Otto Neurath. *Educ.:* University of Göttingen; *studied art* at Art School, Brunswick. *Publications:* Visual History (3 vols.), Visual Science (6), Living with One Another, an Introduction to Social Studies, A New Look at World History (3), A New Look at Science (5), The Wonder World of Nature (16), Wonders of the Modern World (11), Junior Colour Books (8), They Lived Like This (20). Filmstrips: History (16), Government (4), Science (1). *Address:* 3A Eldon Grove, London NW3. *Signs work:* see appendix.

NEW, Vincent Arthur; M.A.W.G. (1938); freelance topographical illustrator, handprinter, water-colour painter in black and white, drypoint, water-colour etc.; retd. Royal Naval Staff Illustrator (1943-67); *b* Bromley, 27 Apr., 1906; *s* of Frederick William New, produce surveyor (cargo); *m* Dorothy Gertrude New; one *s*, five *d*. *Educ.:* Bromley County School; *studied art* at Bromley and Beckenham Art Schools (1926-29) under Mr. Schofield, H. A. Budd, Baylis Allen, Roland Gill; Camberwell School of Art (1931) lithography under Mr. Moore. *Work in permanent collections:* Napier, N.Z. *Publication:* 75 Villages of Kent, drawn for the Kentish Times and Kent and Sussex Courier (1931-1933). *Address:* Overdale Meadow, Brasted Chart, Westerham, Kent TN16 1LR.

NEWBURY, Bertram, F.R.S.A., Mem. B.A.D.A., Mem. Fine Arts Provident Inst.; Associate Mem., Royal Institute of Naval Architects; specialist in marine and military prints and paintings, old ship models, etc.; Chairman and Managing Director of the Parker Gallery; *b* London, 19 May, 1913; *s* of E. G. Newbury; *m* Gina Mary Fiorentini; one *s*, one *d*. *Educ.:* Middlesex College. *Address:* Tudorende, Great North Rd., Brookmans Park, Herts. *Club:* Naval.

NEWCOMB, Barbara; printmaker, etching, engraving, drypoint; *b* Arlington, Virginia, U.S.A., 23 June, 1936; *m* William D. Carter. *Educ.:* Syracuse University, Syracuse, N.Y.; *studied art* at Syracuse University (1954-58), Central School of Arts and Crafts, London (1960-62), Atelier 17, Paris (1962-63) (S. W.

Hayter). *Work in permanent collections:* Victoria and Albert Museum, Los Angeles County Museum, Brooklyn Museum, New York, Bibliotheque Nationale, Paris, Arts Council of Gt. Britain. *Address:* 182 Shaftesbury Ave., London WC2. *Club:* Printmakers Council, Royal Soc. of Painter-etchers and Engravers. *Signs work:* see appendix.

NEWCOMB, Mary, painter in oils; B.Sc. in Natural Sciences (1943); *b* Harrow, Middx., 25 Jan., 1922; *m* Godfrey Newcomb; two *d. Address:* Wood Farm, Linstead Magna, Halesworth, Suffolk. *Signs work:* "Mary Newcomb."

NEWICK, John; lecturer in education, University of London Institute of Education (1968-); Sidcot School (1947-52); lecturer in art education, Birmingham College of Art and Design (1952-62, 1964-65); visiting lecturer and subsequently reader in art education, Faculty of Art, University of Science and Technology, Ghana (1962-64); lecturer, Faculty of Education, Makerere University College, Uganda (1965-66); West of England College of Art (1966-67); staff exchange autumn 1969 School of Education, University of California, Berkeley; taught summer quarters: University of British Columbia (1970) and Stanford University California (1973); *b* Bristol, 30 Nov., 1919. *Educ.:* The Grammar School, Bristol; *studied art* at West of England College of Art. *Address:* University of London Institute of Education, Malet St., London WC1E 7HS.

NEWLAND, Anne; Edwin Abbey Major Scholarship (1938); *b* Wilts., 11 Jan., 1913. *Educ.:* Byam Shaw Art School (1934-38). *Address:* 4 Vaughan Rd., London SE5.

NEWMAN, Thomas, F.R.S.A.; artist in oil; President, Assoc. of Devon Art Societies; *b* London, 29 May, 1906; *s* of Robert Lydston Newman, Director of Bank of England; *m* Helen Newman; one *s,* two *d. Educ.:* Eton; Christ Church, Oxford; Downham School; *studied art* under Jack Merriatt. *Exhib.:* Cooling Gallery, Alpine Gallery, Quantas Gallery. *Publication:* The History of Aryton. *Address:* Widdicombe House, Kingsbridge, S. Devon. *Club:* Chelsea Arts. *Signs work:* "T. Newman."

NEWTON, Irene Margaret, N.R.D. (1940), F.R.S.A. (1940), F.I.A.L. (1958); woven textile designer (handweaving and machine), artist in oils, black and white, water-colour; senior lecturer in art and crafts at Elizabeth Gaskell College of Education, Manchester; asst. at Stourbridge School of Art (1949-59); asst. at Hereford School of Art (1946-49); *b* 23 Dec., 1915. *Educ.:* High School for Girls, Truro, Cornwall; *studied art* at Truro School of Art. *Exhib.:* Hereford, Wolverhampton, R.B.S.A., Worcester, Paris Salon, R.B.A. and United Soc. *Work repro.:* in La Revue Moderne. *Address:* 119 Garstang Rd., Southport. *Signs work:* "I. M. Newton", or see appendix.

NGUYEN, Tân-Phuoc; Mem. Confédération Internationale des Associations des Experts et de Conseils auprès de Conseil Economique et Social de l'Onu; Director, Galerie Arts Anciens de Chine et Extrême-Orient; art expert on Asiatic archaeology, historian, writer; *b* 10 Nov., 1931; *s* of Van-Phùng Nguyen, mandarin; *m* Hélène Gerber; two *s. Educ.:* Saigon, S. Vietnam, and Paris; *studied art* at l'Institut Hautes, Etudes Indochinoises, and Ecole du Louvre. *Publications:* Archéologie asiatique, Netzuke, La Culture de Ban-Chiang (Siam) 7.000-5.000 ans, Fouilles archéologiques à Ban-Chiang. *Address:* 16 rue de l'Hotel de Ville, Genève 1204. *Clubs:* Club Alpin Suisse, Musée d'Ethnographie, Musée des Collections Baur-Duret, Union Internationale des Experts, Croix Rouge Suisse, Intérêt de Genève, U.I.F.E., Kiwanis International.

NICHOLS, Patricia Mary, R.M.S. (1966); portrait painter in pastel and sanguine, miniaturist in oil; Council Mem. Royal Society of Miniature Painters,

Sculptors and Gravers; *b* 27 Sept., 1923; *d* of the late W/Cdr. E. T. Carpenter, A.F.C., R.A.F.; *m* John Trevor Nichols, M.C.I.T.; one *s*, one *d*. *Educ.:* innumerable private schools; *studied art* at Central School of Arts and Crafts under Ruskin Spear, R.A., William Roberts, John Minton. *Exhib.:* Suffolk St. Galleries, R.I., Camberwell Art Gallery, Mall Galleries. *Work repro.:* The Artists, illustrated county magazines and newspapers. *Address:* Sealand, Wodehouse Rd., Old Hunstanton, Norfolk. *Signs work:* "Patricia Nichols."

NICHOLS, Richard William; self-taught artist in oil, acrylic and gouache; *b* La Porte, Indiana, 18 June, 1930. *Educ.:* De Pauw University; Indiana University; Illinois University; American Conservatory of Music, Sorbonne, Ecole Normal de Musique. *Exhib.:* Opus Gallery, R.B.A., Trends (1968, 1970-72). Work in private collections. *Address:* 50 Tite St., London SW3 4UA. *Club:* F.P.S. *Signs work:* "R.W.N."

NICHOLSON, John Hobson, R.I. (1951), F.I.B.D. (1948); painter in water-colour and pastels; proprietor private art gallery and art shop; on staff, Douglas School of Art, Crafts and Technology; *b* Douglas, I.O.M., 23 Apr., 1911; *s* of the late Frank Nicholson. *Educ.:* Douglas High School; *studied art:* self-taught. *Exhib.:* London regularly. *Work in permanent collections:* Manx Museum and Art Gallery, Wolverhampton Public Art Gallery. *Official purchases:* designed Manx Regional Postage Stamps, Manx Government £5, £1, 10s. Banknotes, Manx £5, Sovereign and half-sovereign gold coins, eight Manx Revenue stamps. *Address:* 82 Strand St., Douglas, I.O.M. *Club:* President, Isle of Man Art Society. *Signs work:* "JOHN H. NICHOLSON."

NICHOLSON, Winifred; artist and painter in oil; *b* Oxford, 1893; *d* of Charles Roberts; *m* Ben Nicholson; two *s*, one *d* (Kate Nicholson). *Educ.:* Byam Shaw School of Art; *studied art* in Paris, Lugano, India and the Hebrides. *Exhib.:* Pittsburgh, Venice, London, Paris, Edinburgh, S. Africa. *Work in permanent collections:* Arts Council, I.C.I. *Official purchases:* Manchester, Bradford, Bristol, Adelaide and Melbourne art galleries. *Address:* Banks Head, Brampton, Cumbria. *Signs work:* "Winifred Nicholson."

NICOLSON, Benedict, C.B.E. (1971), M.V.O. (1947); Editor, Burlington Magazine; Dep. Surveyor of King's Pictures (1939-47); *b* 6 Aug., 1914; *s* of Sir Harold Nicolson. *Educ.:* Eton; Balliol, Oxford. *Publications:* The Painters of Ferrara (Paul Elek, 1950); Hendrick Terbrugghen (Lund, Humphries Ltd., 1958); Wright of Derby, Painter of Light (Mellon Foundation and Routledge, 1968); The Treasures of the Foundling Hospital (O.U.P. 1972); Courbet's Studio of the Painter (Penguin Books, 1973); Georges de La Tour (in collaboration with Christopher Wright) (Phaidon Press, 1974). *Address:* 45B Holland Park, London W11. *Club:* Brooks's. *Signs work:* "Benedict Nicolson."

NIELSEN, Bent Rosenkilde, Mem. Danish Authors Assoc. (since 1951); author, journalist, art critic; art critic to Danish papers and periodicals; *b* Copenhagen, 20 June, 1904; *s* of L. C. Nielsen, writer, poet, editor. *Educ.:* Academia Sorana (The High School of Soroe); *studied art* in Paris (1929-31), Italy (1958-59), Spain (1962-68). *Publications:* Danish Pioneers on the Pacific Ocean (1945), All About All Countries (1947), Ujuats Diary From East-Greenland (1950), Books for children; published in the last thirty years, numerous articles about art in Europe, Greenland, the South Sea Islands, Australia, Ethiopia, Congo, Morocco, Haiti and Sweden, based upon travels in these countries and studies in France, Italy and Spain. Several radio talks about art in Denmark. *Address:* Rolfsvej 10/3, Fasan: 5051 Giro: 17 77 24 2000F, Copenhagen, Denmark. *Signs work:* "Don Benito."

NIVEN, Margaret Graeme, R.O.I. (1936), N.S. (1932); painter of landscapes, flowers and portraits; *b* 1906; *d* of William Niven, F.S.A., J.P., A.R.E. *Educ.:* Prior's Field, Godalming: Heatherley School of Fine Art, and under Bernard Adams, R.P., R.O.I. *Exhib.:* R.A., R.P., R.O.I., National Soc., Artists of Chelsea, Leicester Galleries, Wildenstein's, etc. *Official purchases:* Bradford Municipal Art Gallery; Homerton College, Cambridge; Ministry of Works, Bedford College, London. *Work repro.:* flower pieces. *Address:* Broomhill, Sandhills, Godalming, Surrey, GU8 5UF.

NOAKES, Michael, V.P.R.O.I., R.P., C.P.S., Cert. R.A.S., N.S., N.D.D.; portrait painter; Chairman, Contemporary Portrait Society; art critic (1964-68), B.B.C. Television; *b* Brighton, 28 Oct., 1933; *m;* two *s,* one *d. Educ.:* Downside; *studied art* at R.A. Schools. *Exhib.:* R.A., R.O.I., R.P., R.B.A., Young Contemporaries, National Society, Contemporary Portrait Society, etc. *Work in permanent collections:* numerous public and private collections. *Work repro.:* widely in newspapers, art journals, etc. *Publication:* A Professional Approach to Oil Painting (Pitmans, 1968). *Address:* The Studio, Doods Park Rd., Reigate, Surrey. *Signs work:* "Michael Noakes," with date underneath.

NOBLE, John Rushton; painter, illustrator, designer and art teacher; fine arts tutor, Gateshead Technical College (1950-53); *b* Gateshead, 7 Oct., 1927; *s* of Robert Noble; *m* Dorothy Hass; one *s,* two *d. Educ.:* James I Grammar School, Bishop Auckland, and Hookergate Grammar School, Durham; *studied art* at King Edward VII School of Art, University of Durham, under Robin Darwin and L. C. Evetts (1944-46). *Exhib.:* R.I., R.B.A. Galleries, London and provincial galleries, also Europe and the Americas. *Work repro.:* Drawings in line and wash in Northern journals and periodicals, etc. *Address:* Northfields, Todhills, Newfield, Bishop Auckland, Co. Durham. *Signs work:* see appendix.

NOGUCHI, Yataro; Mem. Independent Art Society; painter in oils; Professor of Japan University, Faculty of Arts; *b* Tokyo, 1 Oct., 1899; *s* of late Yazo Noguchi, Managing Director, Dai-Ichi Bank, Ltd., Tokyo; *m* Kikue; one *s. Educ.:* Kansei Gakuin High School; *studied art* in Paris. *Work in permanent collections:* Museum of Modern Arts, Tokyo; French Government bought picture, Café on the Harbour. *Publications:* Art Collections of Y. Noguchi. *Address:* 117 Jomyoji, Kamakura City. *Signs work:* "Y. Noguchi."

NOLAN, Sidney Robert, C.B.E., Hon. Dr. Laws, N.U.A., Hon. Dr. Univ. of York, Hon. Dr. Lit. London Univ., M.B.A.; artist; *b* Melbourne, 22 Apr., 1917; *s* of late Sidney Henry Nolan; *m* Cynthia Hansen. *Educ.:* Victoria State and Technical Schools, National Art Gallery School, Victoria. *Exhib.:* London, Paris, New York, Rome, Venice, Pittsburgh, Australia. *Work in private collections:* Tate, Museum of Modern Art, New York, Australian national galleries, C.A.S. and A.C. of Great Britain. *Publications:* Kenneth Clark, Colin Macinnes, Bryan Robertson, Nolan (1961); Robert Melville, Ned Kelly (1964); Elwyn Lynn, Sidney Nolan: Myth and Imagery (1967); Cynthia Nolan; A Sight of China; Paradise Gardens (1971), Sidney Nolan. *Address:* c/o Bank N.S.W., 9 Sackville St., London W1.

NOLAND, Kenneth C.; artist; *b* Asheville, N.C., U.S.A., 10 Apr., 1927. *Educ.:* Black Mountain College (1946-51), Paris (1948). *Work in permanent collections:* Museum of Modern Art, Guggenheim Museum, Whitney Museum, Tate Gallery, Stedelijk Museum, Amsterdam, Zurich Kunsthaus, Art Institute of Chicago, Fogg Museum, Museum of Fine Arts, Boston, and others. *Address:* South Shaftesbury, Vermont. *Signs work:* "Kenneth C Noland."

NORDEN, Gerald, A.R.C.A. (1937); Principal, Folkestone and Dover School of Art (1948-71); painter in oil; *b* London, 28 June, 1912; *s* of Alfred Van

Noorden, merchant; *m* Lilian; one *s,* two *d. Educ.:* St. Lawrence College Ramsgate; *studied art* at Thanet School of Art under John Moody, Royal College of Art under Gilbert Spencer, Percy Horton. *Publications:* A Practical Guide to Perspective (Pitman). *Address:* c/o Trafford Gallery, 119 Mount St., London W1Y 5HB. *Signs work:* "Norden."

NORFIELD, Edgar George, F.R.S.A.; painter in oil and water-colour; humorous draughtsman and book illustrator; *m* Elsie Georgina Russell. *Studied art* at Cambridge School of Art, and in London and Paris. *Work repro.:* contributor to Punch and leading magazines; illustrated many books, including a considerable number for children. *Address:* 3 Well House Place, Lewes, Sussex. *Clubs:* Savage, London Sketch. *Signs work:* see appendix.

NORMAN, John Henry, M.M. (1918), R.O.I.; oil painter; founded Coventry Art Circle and chairman since 1934; *b* 9 Sept., 1896; *s* of John Henry Norman, artisan; *m* Dorothy Smith; two *s,* one *d. Educ.:* St. Annes Secondary School, Nottingham; Coventry School of Art (W. H. Milnes, R.B.A., A.R.E., A.R.C.A.) (1919-24). *Exhib.:* R.A., Paris Salon, R.B.A., R.O.I. *Official purchases:* Birkenhead Art Gallery, Coventry Art Gallery. *Address:* 1 Glendower Ave., Coventry. *Signs work:* "J. H. NORMAN."

NORRIS, Edith; Fellow Red Rose Guild of Designer-Craftsmen (1955); Associate, B.S.M.G.P. (1949); Mem. Bolton Art Circle; stained glass and mosaics; *b* Bolton; *d* of James Walsh, engineer; *m* Harry Norris, master craftsman, *Studied art* under Ernest Hartley, A.R.C.A. *Exhib.:* Burlington House, R.R.G.C., R.I.B.A. and many Lancs. art galleries. *Address:* 371 Bury Rd., Bolton, Lancs. BL2 6DE. *Signs work:* initials in Old English letters.

NOSWORTHY, Ann Louise, N.D.D. (1952), A.T.D. (1953); painter in oil, gouache, pastel and charcoal; *b* Stonehaven, Scotland, 24 Aug., 1929; *d* of Col. J. M. Savege, R.A.M.C.; *m* T. L. Nosworthy; one *s. Educ.:* Beacon School, Bridge-of-Allan, Scotland; *studied art* at Harrogate and Leeds Art College (1948-53) under J. Simon. *Exhib.:* one-man shows: Redcar, Yorks. (1968), Castel de Vide, Portugal (1966). *Work in permanent collection:* Municipal Art Gallery, Port Allegre, Portugal. *Address:* Brackengarth, Lealholm, Whitby, Yorks. *Signs work:* "A. L. Nosworthy."

NOVOTNY, Fritz, Prof., Dr.; director of Österreichische Galerie, Vienna (1960-68); Prof. of the University of Vienna since 1939; asst. in art history, Institute of Vienna University (Lehrkanzel Strzygowski) (1927-39); *b* Vienna, 10 Feb., 1903; *s* of Franz Novotny. *Educ.:* University of Vienna, school Jos. Strygowskis; *studied art* at Vienna University, Institut Strzygowski. *Publications:* Cézanne und das Ende der Wissenschaftlichen Perspektive (1938; reprint 1970), Die Monatsbilder Pieter Bruegels d.Ä. (1948), Der Maler Anton Romako, 1832-1889 (1954), Painting and Sculpture in Europe; 1780-1880 (The Pelican History of Art) (1960; second edition 1971); Toulouse-Lautrec (1969). *Address:* Linke Wienzeile 168, Vienna 6. *Signs work:* "Fritz Novotny."

NOWAK, Krysia Danuta, B.A. Gen. (1970), Dip. Ed. (1973); lecturer/painter in oil, ink and gouache; Education Officer for Sheffield City Art Galleries; President, Worksop Society of Artists; *b* 18 Mar., 1948; *d* of Wladystaw Jan Nowak. *Educ.:* Ealing Technical College; Garnett College, London; *studied art* under Prof. Bohusz-Szyszko (1967–70) and Marek Zulawski (1974). *Exhib.:* one-man shows: Drian Gallery, London (1974), Waterloo Gallery, Stoke-on-Trent (1974); group shows: Camden Town Arts Centre, Centaur Gallery, London, Worksop, Sheffield. *Work in permanent collection:* Nottingham Loans Collection. *Address:* 6 Hardy St., Worksop, Notts. *Clubs:* F.P.S., W.I.A.C., A.P.A. *Signs work:* "Krysia D. Nowak."

NUBEL, Basil, N.D.D. (1949), A.R.C.A. (1954); landscape, artist in oil, water-colour, pastel, ink; *b* Gt. Yarmouth, 1923; *s* of Albert Nubel, engineer. *Educ.:* Leeds; *studied art* at Leeds College of Art under Alfred Daniels and Maurice de Sausmarez, Royal College of Art under Rodrigo Moynihan, Carel Weight and Robert Buhler. *Exhib.:* R.A., R.B.A., etc., one-man shows: Woodstock Gallery (1967), Gallery Petit, London (1969, 1970, 1971), Upper St. Gallery (1972, 1973), New Gallery Hornsey Library (1973). Argonaut Gallery (1974); Art Jury Service:—Printers Art Club Exhbn. (1973, 1975). *Work in permanent collections:* Leeds Education Committee, Emanuel Bierer, Elizabeth Galambas. *Work repro.:* Young Artists of Promise, by Jack Beddington, C.B.E. (Studio Publications, 1957), print 'Summer Joy,' Solomon & Whitehead (Guild Prints) Ltd. *Address:* 11 Bellamy St., Clapham South, London SW12. *Signs work:* "BASIL NUBEL" in cursive hand, usually.

NUNAN, Philip Alan Widdrington, N.D.D. (1949), A.T.D. (1950), M.S.I.A.; graphic designer; manager, Design Services British Steel Corporation; artist in water-colour, pen and wash; *b* Southport, Lancs., 8 July, 1925; *s* of Frederick Denis Nunan, civil servant. *Educ.:* Wandsworth Secondary Grammar School; *studied art* at Polytechnic, Regent St. (1942–44 and 1947-49) under S. Tresilian and Henry Trivick. *Work repro.:* Gebrauchsgraphik, S.I.A. Journal, The Artist, Ingot Magazine, British Steel. *Address:* 44 Wakefield Gdns., Upper Norwood, London SE19. *Signs work:* "Nunan."

NUTTALL, Harold, B.W.S.; artist in water-colour and black chalk; *b* Oldham, 9 July, 1896; *s* of Henry Nuttall; *m* Edith Needham; one *s,* one *d. Educ.:* Oldham Municipal Secondary School. *Exhib.:* R.B.A., B.W.S., Mansfield Art Gallery, etc. *Work repro.:* cartoons and caricatures, etc. *Address:* Field View, Hodge Lane, Hartford, Northwich, Ches. *Signs work:* "H. Nuttall."

O

OAKESHOTT, Walter Fraser, M.A. (Oxon.), Hon. LL.D., F.B.A., F.S.A.; Headmaster, Winchester College (1946-54); Rector of Lincoln College, Oxford (1954-72); Vice-Chancellor, Oxford University (1962-64); *b* Lydenburg, Transvaal, S. Africa, 1903; *s* of Walter Oakeshott, M.D.; *m* Noel R. Moon; two *s,* two *d. Educ.:* Tonbridge School, Balliol College, Oxford. *Publications:* The Artists of the Winchester Bible, The Sequence of English Medieval Art, The Classical Tradition in Medieval Art (1959); Mosaics of Rome, Third to Fifteenth Centuries (1967); Sigera: Romanesque Artists in Spain and the Artists of the Winchester Bible (1972); editor, Faber Gallery of Medieval MSS. *Address:* The Old School House, Station Rd., Eynsham, Oxford. *Club:* Roxburghe.

OATES, Bennett, N.D.D. (1946); painter in oil and resin varnishes; Design Director, Pinewood Fabrics and Co., Ltd.; *b* London, 1 Jan., 1928; *s* of Joseph Bennett Oates, F.P.E.; *m* Phyllis Mary Bennett, senior lecturer in Art History and Designer A.R.C.A.; two *d. Educ.:* Raynes Park Grammar School; *studied art* at Wimbledon School of Art (1943-46) under Gerald Cooper; R.C.A. (1948-51) under Robin Darwin and Ruskin Spear. *Work in permanent collection:* Stacy-Marks Galleries. *Addresses:* Studio and principal address: Hazelwood House.

Coltishall, Norwich, NOR 65Y; and 14B Lower Teddington Rd., Hampton Wick, Kingston, Surrey. *Signs work:* "Bennett Oates."

OATES, Christine Tate, A.R.C.A., A.T.D.; artist in oil and water-colour; teacher at Ely High School (1939-43), Lancaster Girls' Grammar School (1943-45), Truro High School (1945-70); *b* Bradford, 13 Jan., 1913; *d* of Herbert Johnson Oates. *Educ.:* Bradford Girls' Grammar School; Bradford Regional College of Art under H. Butler (1930-35); Royal College of Art (1935-39). *Official purchases:* V. & A. (textiles) and other material for circulation to schools. *Address:* 6 The Parade, Truro, Cornwall. *Clubs:* Soc. for Educ. through Art, National Soc. for Art Educ., R.C.A. Old Students' Assoc. *Signs work:* "C. T. Oates."

OBRIEN, Kitty Wilmer, A.R.H.A.; Taylor Art Scholarship (1933), Douglas Hyde Gold Medal and Arts Council Award (1964), Associate R.H.A. (1968); housewife and artist in oil, water-colour, gouache; President, Water-colour Society of Ireland; *b* Quetta, Pakistan, 7 Aug., 1910; *d* of the late Major Harold Gordon Wilmer (14th Sikhs); *m* Brendan E. OBrien, M.D., F.R.C.P.I.; two *s. Educ.:* Nightingale Hall, Dublin, St. Stephens, Folkestone; *studied art* at Hibernian Academy School under Dermod OBrien, P.R.H.A., National College of Art, Dublin, under Maurice MacGonigal, P.R.H.A. (1929-33), Slade School under Prof. Schwabe (1934), André Lhote (1951). *Work in permanent collections:* Cork A.G., Arts Council of Ireland, Waterford A.G., Haverty Trust. *Address:* 26 Herbert Pk., Dublin 4, Eire. *Club:* Kildare Street. *Signs work:* "K. OBRIEN."

O'BRIEN, Robert John; Central School of Art and Design Diploma (1961); *b* Southampton, 24 May, 1939. *Educ.:* Folkestone, Kent; *studied art* at Central School of Art and Design, London; spent two years living in Greece. *Exhib.:* various group shows in London, Bradford, Liverpool, Cambridge (1965, 1966, 1967, 1968); one-man show in Cambridge, Benet Gallery (1965); two one-man shows at Grabowski Gallery, London (1965-67); represented at Expo 67. Work in private and public collections. *Work repro.:* in newspapers and journals. *Address:* 2 Great Ormond St., London WC1. *Signs work:* "R. O'Brien."

O CEALLACHAIN, Diarmuid, A.N.C.A. (1940); Bronze Medal, Paris Salon; artist, teacher; *b* Cork, 1915; *s* of Ellen and Patrick O Callaghan, R.N.; *m* Joan O Sullivan; one *s*, one *d. Educ.:* St. Patrick's and North Monastery; *studied art* under John Power and John Keating. *Exhib.:* Salon, R.H.A., Oireactas, Europe, U.S.A.; holds one-man shows. Painted in Athens and Holy Land (1971). *Address:* Gartan, Farranlea Pk., Model Farm Rd., Cork, Eire. *Signs work:* see appendix.

OCKENDON, Kathleen Ursula, A.T.D.; medical artist, illustrator and letterer; *b* London, 9 Aug., 1913; *d* of William Ockendon, railwayman. *Educ.:* Romford County High School, Ealing and Hornsey Schools of Art. Teacher at Kilburn Poly. J.T.S., Ealing School of Art and Ealing Technical College (1935-68). *Publications:* Your Penmanship (Sylvan P., 1951), Illustrations to Modelmaking in Cardboard by T. Bayley (Dryad P., 1959); film strip: Decorative Penmanship (V.P., 1964). *Exhib.:* R.A., R.I., New English A.C., etc. *Address:* 83 Islip Manor Rd., Northolt, Middx. *Signs work:* see appendix.

O'CONNELL, Michael, M.S.I.A.; Batik murals, craft dyeing expert; *b* 7 Aug., 1898; *s* of P. O'Connell, poet and civil servant; *m*; one *s. Educ.:* Ushaw College. Work influenced by primitive art studies in Africa, Polynesia, etc. *Exhib.:* Paris International (1937), Hambro House of Design, New York (1949), Festival of Britain (1951), Beaux Arts, London (1953), Zürich (1957), Johannesburg (1958), Ibiza (1960), Milan (1962), Interiors International, London (1963). *Work in permanent collections:* V. & A. Museum, Stratford Theatre, Reading

University. *Work repro.:* in principal art journals. *Address:* Perry Green, Much Hadham, Herts. *Club:* I.C.A. *Signs work:* "Michael O'Connell."

O'CONNOR, John, A.R.C.A., R.W.S.; painter and illustrator; visiting lecturer, Colchester and Glasgow Schools of Art; *b* Leicester, 11 Aug., 1913; *s* of Vernon Feargus O'Connor, instrument maker; *m* Jenny Tennant; one *s*. *Educ.:* Wyggeston School, Leicester; *studied art* at Leicester School of Art (1931-33); Royal College of Art (1933-37). *Exhib.:* one-man shows: Minories (1973, 1976), New Grafton Gallery (1970, 1972, 1974), Zwemmer Gallery (six shows between 1955 and 1968), Clare College, Cambridge (1965); mixed shows: New Grafton, R.A. *Work in permanent collections:* N.Y. Public Library, Columbia University; public galleries, Oxford, Cambridge and other Universities and Colleges. *Publications:* written and illustrated: Canals, Barges and People (Shenval Press), A Pattern of People (Hutchinson); books illustrated for Golden Cockerel Press, Rodale Press, Kynoch Press, Dropmore Press, Boston Imprint, Limited Editions Club of N.Y., Hutchinson and Bodley Head; technical: Landscape Paintings (Studio Vista), Technique of Wood Engraving (Batsford), Relief Printing (Batsford), Landscape Drawing (Batsford). *Address:* Craigmore, Parton Castle, Douglas, Kirkcudbrightshire. *Club:* Double-Crown. *Signs work:* "John O'Connor."

O'CONNOR, Michael Anthony, R.B.S., Granada Arts Fellow, York University; sculptor/teacher; works in rosewood, stone, direct carving; Master of Sculpture, Eton College; *b* Seven Kings, Essex, 11 Sept., 1944; *s* of C. P. O'Connor, Chief Factory Inspector; *m* Jennifer O'Connor, teacher. *Educ.:* Oak Park School for Boys, Havant, Hants., Shoreditch College of Education, Egham; *studied art* at Shoreditch College of Education (1963-66). Work in private collections. *Address:* Eton College, Eton, Windsor, Berks. *Signs work:* "M. O'Connor."

OFFICER, David Adrian, B.A. Fine Art (Dunelm), M.A. Fine Art (E.S.C.); F.R.S.A., A.T.D. (Scotland); Associate Royal S.A. Society of Arts (1973); artist and late art lecturer-tutor Harrow School of Art, London; recently Head of Art Dept., Rhyl Grammar School, N. Wales; television art lecturer, A.B.C.-TV, Melbourne and Sydney, C.B.C.-TV, Vancouver, C.B.S.-TV, Washington, and U.TV, Belfast (1960-64); *b* Belfast, N. Ireland; *s* of Adrian Charles Officer. *Educ.:* Hutcheson's Grammar School, Glasgow; *studied art* at King Edward VII College of Art and Faculty of Fine Art, Durham University, and Edinburgh University. *Exhib.:* London, Paris, Sydney, Melbourne, Vancouver, etc. *Work in permanent collections:* Melbourne, Durban, Newcastle. *Publications:* Art and Travel, New Gazette Ltd. and A.B.C.-TV pamphlets, Painting for Pleasure. *Work repro.:* in journals, magazines, newspapers and exhbn. catalogues. *Address:* "Riverslea," 12 Southfield, Hessle, E. Yorks. *Club:* Scottish Modern Artists' Assoc., Edinburgh. *Signs work:* see appendix.

OHL, Gabrielle, painter in oil, indian ink, engraving; *b* Diego-Suarez, Madagascar; *d* of René Ohl (decd.); *m* Serge Pesquès. *Educ.:* Couvent des Oiseaux, Hanoi; *studied art* at Madrid Beaux Arts (1950-51), Paris Academie Julian (1949-50, 1953-43), Melbourne Technical College of Arts (1951-53), Paris. *Exhib.:* Paris salons: Independents, Marine, Automne, Femmes Peintres; Maison de l'Alsace. One-man shows: Brussels, London, Biarritz, Italy, Malaya, Gent, Luxemburg. Medaglia e diploma di segnalazione per opere di avanguardia (Annuale d'Arte Grafica, 1968), Italy; Medaglia "Nuova Critica Europea" e diploma di menzione (Biennale delle Regioni) Italy (1969); Diplome d'Honneur, Salon International Noel (1970), Galerie Vallombreuse, Biarritz (1970); Diploma of Honour, Paternoster-Corner Academy, London (1971). *Address:* 10 Rue des Halles, Paris. *Signs work:* see appendix.

OLIVER, Charles William, A.R.C.A. (1933), Liverpool Academy (1938); artist in oil; Vice-Principal, Laird School of Art, Birkenhead; *b* Youngstown, Ohio, U.S.A., 21 Apr., 1911; *s* of Charles Oliver; *m* Ena Landon Davies; two *s. Educ.:* Wade Deacon Grammar School, Widnes, Lancs.; *studied art* at City School of Art, Liverpool, and at R.C.A. under Sir W. Rothenstein (1930-34). *Exhib.:* R.P.S., Senenfelder Club (lithographs), R.B.A., R.Scot.A., Liverpool Academy of Arts, Southport, R.Cam.A., Wirral Soc. of Arts. *Work in permanent collections:* Liverpool, Birkenhead A.G. *Publications:* Anatomy and Perspective (Studio Vista, 1972). *Address:* 1 South Bank, Oxton, Birkenhead. *Signs work:* "C. W. OLIVER" and date.

OLIVER, Kenneth Herbert, A.R.W.S., A.R.E., A.R.C.A., R.W.A.; etcher, lithographer, artist in water-colour; teacher at Gloucestershire College of Art; *b* Norwich, 7 Feb., 1923; *s* of Herbert B. Oliver; *m* Joyce Margaret Beaumont, A.R.C.A.; three *d. Educ.:* King Edward VI Grammar School, Norwich; *studied art* at Norwich School of Art and R.C.A. *Exhib.:* R.W.S., R.W.A., Bristol, R.A., R.E., Cheltenham Group of Artists, etc., and abroad. *Work in permanent collections:* Royal West of England Academy, Bristol. *Address:* 69 Shaw Green Lane, Prestbury, Cheltenham. *Signs work:* "KENNETH H. OLIVER."

O'MALLEY, Mrs. Peter Diarmuid: see WARBURTON, Joan.

OMAN, Charles, M.A. (1927); asst. keeper, Dept. of Metalwork, V. & A. (1924), Keeper (1945-66); *b* 5 June, 1901; *s* of the late Sir Charles Oman, K.B.E.; *m* Joan Trevelyan; one *s,* one *d. Educ.:* Winchester; New College, Oxford; British School at Rome. *Publications:* English Domestic Silver (1934); English Church Plate (1957); Golden Age of Hispanic Silver (1968); Caroline Silver, 1625-1688 (1971). British Rings, 800-1914 (1974). *Address:* 13 Woodborough Rd., Putney, London SW15.

OMAN, Julia Trevelyan, F.S.I.A.; Royal Scholar, R.C.A.; Des.R.C.A. 1st Class; Silver Medal R.C.A.; Designer of the Year Award (1967); designer for films, theatre, television, books; Director, Oman Productions Ltd.; *b* Kensington, 11 July, 1930; *m* Dr. Roy Strong, Director, V. & A. *Educ.:* R.C.A., London. *Exhib.:* design of productions for: National Theatre, Royal Opera Covent Garden, Royal Ballet, Royal Shakespeare Co., Hamburg State Opera, West End Theatres, B.B.C. Television, films. *Work in permanent collections:* V. & A., designs and model for Brief Lives. *Publications:* Street Children (photographs); Elizabeth R (design); Mary Queen of Scots (design); Merchant of Venice (Folio Society). *Address:* c/o London Management, 235/241 Regent St., London W1A 2JT. *Signs work:* "Julia Trevelyan Oman."

O'REILLY, Faith, N.D.D., Cert. R.A.S., A.T.C.; oil painter and portraitist, lecturer in Art and Educational Technology; *b* Boston, Mass., U.S.A., 6 Aug., 1938; *d* of Eileen O'Reilly. *Studied art* at Berkshire College of Art, Royal Academy Schools, and Hornsey. Helped to found Stanley Spencer Gallery. *Exhib.:* group: R.S.P.P.; one-man shows: Midland Group Gallery, 273 Gallery; shows in Universities, Audley Gallery, Salisbury. *Address:* 28 Beaconsfield Rd., Brighton, Sussex. *Signs work:* "Faith O'Reilly."

ORGAN, (Harold) Bryan, Dip.R.A. Schools; Hon. M.A. Loughborough University; painter in acrylic, oil and gouache; *b* 31 Aug., 1935; *s* of Harold Victor Organ; *m* Elizabeth Waters. *Educ.:* Wyggeston Boys School, Leicester; *studied art* at Loughborough College of Art (1952-55); Royal Academy Schools (1955-59). *Exhib.:* Third International Exhbn., Drawings, Darmstadt (1970), Mostra Mercatao d'Arte Contemporea, Florence (1969), Kunstalle, Darmstadt (1968), Gadsby Gallery, Redfern Gallery (1967, 1969, 1971, 1973, 1975), Leicester Museum and A.G. (1959-1965). *Address:* Manor Farm House, Castlethorpe, Wolverton, Bucks. *Signs work:* "Bryan Organ."

ORMEROD, Stanley Horton, N.S., S.G.A., S.W.E., A.I.A.L., F.Z.S.; wildlife artist, painter, etcher, engraver, lithographer, graphic artist; *b* Morecambe/Lancaster, 29 July, 1918; *s* of Lawrence Ormerod, cotton manufacturer; *m* Dorothy Barbara Bell; two *s. Studied art* at Accrington and Göttingen. *Exhib.:* New York, Royal Cambrian Academy, Manchester Academy of Fine Art; London: R.E., S.G.A., N.S., S.W.E., Soc. Wildlife Artists; many touring exhibitions and Art in Post Offices exhibitions; provincially: Preston, Southport, Manchester, Milngavie, Glasgow, Wolverhampton, Southend, Scarborough, Liverpool, Accrington, Blackburn, Bolton, Hereford, Walsall, Hastings, Warwick, Derby, Stockport, Rotherham, Rochdale, Bury, Batley, Stoke Newington, Stretford, Swindon, Bridlington, Nottingham, Gloucester, Rivington, Leigh. *Work repro.:* La Revue Moderne (1969), folio of twenty lithos Steam in the North, joint author Erzählt es mir. Lithographs for racing, sports, vintage car museums, safari parks, railway societies, historical castles, etc. *Address:* 21 Somerset Rd., Heaton, Bolton. *Signs work:* see appendix.

ORPEN, Bea; art teacher, lecturer and painter in gouache; art teacher, St. Peter's National School, Drogheda (1949-74), Drogheda Technical School (1943-74); lecturer under Charlotte Shaw Bequest and Arts Council; *b* Carrickmines, Co. Dublin, 7 Mar., 1913; *d* of Charles St. George Orpen; *m* Chalmers E. F. Trench; three *s*, one *d*. *Educ.:* French School, Bray, Co. Wicklow, and Alexandra College, Dublin; *studied art* at R.H.A. Life Schools and Slade. *Exhib.:* R.H.A., Water-colour Soc. of Ireland, Oireachtas Exhbn., Cork, Clonmel and Waterford Art Galleries. *Address:* Killrian, Slane, Navan, Co. Meath, Ireland. *Clubs:* R.I.A.C. (Dublin), Dublin Painters, Soroptimist Club of Drogheda. *Signs work:* "BEA ORPEN."

O'RYAN, Fergus, R.H.A., A.N.C.A.(Design) 1942, Douglas Hyde Gold Medal for Painting (1956); painter in oils and water-colour, wood engraver and lithographer; teacher at National College of Art, Dublin; *b* Limerick, 13 Mar., 1911; *s* of John O'Ryan, painter; *m* Mary E. Fitzgerald; *studied art* at National College of Art (Dublin, 1935-42), at Limerick School of Art, and in Germany (1936-38), Paris (1939, 1947-49), Spain (1950) and Italy (1951). *Exhib.:* London, New York, Boston, Toronto, Melbourne, Amsterdam. *Work in permanent collections:* all Irish public galleries. *Official purchases:* Fogg Art Museum, Harvard University, Boston Public Library, Irish Govt., Haverty Bequest, President of Ireland. *Address:* Avondale, Bird Ave., Clonskeagh, Co. Dublin. *Signs work:* "FERGUS O'RYAN."

OSBORNE, Denis Henry, N.D.D., A.R.U.A.; Purchase Award, Hamilton Art Gallery, Ontario (1957), invitation 20th Biennial International Water-colour Exhbn., Brooklyn Art Museum, New York (1959); painter in oil and water-colour; art master; Head of Art Dept. Sec. School; *b* Portsmouth, 23 Dec., 1919; *s* of Ernest Edward Osborne, R.N.; *m* Maureen; one *d*. *Educ.:* Kingsbury School, Middx.; *studied art* at Camberwell School of Art and Crafts (1946-50) under Sir William Coldstream, Victor Pasmore. *Exhib.:* R.A., N.E.A.C., R.B.A.S., O.S.A., Montreal Museum, Winnipeg and Hamilton Art Galleries, Dublin, Living Art Exhbn.; two one-man exhbns. Ulster Arts Council Gallery. *Work in permanent collections:* Hamilton Gallery, Ontario, Art Council, Belfast. *Address:* 34 Riverside Drive, Harmony Hill, Lambeg, Co. Antrim, N. Ireland. *Signs work:* "D. H. OSBORNE."

OSBORNE, Stuart John, A.R.B.S., A.R.C.A., A.T.D.; sculptor, runs own three-year sculpture course at Stafford College of Further Education; *b* Weston-s-Mare, Somerset; *s* of H. T. Osborne; *m* Margaret Cole; one *d*. *Educ.:* Kingsholme School, Weston-s-Mare; *studied art* at W. of England College of Art, Bristol, and Royal College of Art, London. *Exhib.:* societies: Royal Society of British Sculptors; Portrait Sculptors; Free Painters and Sculptors, and exhibits each year with the Wildlife Society; galleries: Ror Volmar, Paris, Vallombreuse, Biarritz, International, New York, Mall, London. *Address:* 64 Burton Manor Rd., Stafford. *Signs work:* "Osborne."

OSCAR, A., Diplôme (Société Lorrain, 1939); Prix Pierre Brune (1961); *b* Plymouth, 1919. *Exhib.:* Wertheim (1937), Ward (1937), Zak (1937), Leicester Gals. (1946), Couleur des Temps (1949), Broadway (1962), Kaplan (1962), Brook Street (1962), Obelisk (1953), Les Templiers (1961), Philippe Erre (1961), Miroir (1961), St. Martin's (1962), Chiltern (1963), Les Surindependants (1939), Grosvenor (1964), Drian (1964), Gemini Trust (1965), Hasenclever, Cologne (1965), Harlow Arts Festival (1965), Renée Laporte, Antibes (1965), Jardin Botanico, Rio (1973). *Public collections:* Ateneo Dominicano, Musée d'Art Moderne de Cèret, Musée d'Art Moderne Skopje, Berkshire Museum (Pittsfield), Sztuka Museum (Lodz). *Address:* Studio C, 404 Fulham Rd., London SW6. *Signs work:* "Oscar."

OSMAN, Louis, B.A.(Arch.) F.R.I.B.A.; architect, goldsmith and jeweller; *b* Exeter, 30 Jan., 1914; *s* of Charles Osman; *m* Dilys Roberts; one *d*. *Educ.:* Hele's School, Exeter; London University; *studied art* at Bartlet School of Architecture, The Slade. *Work in permanent collections:* Goldsmiths Hall, London; National Museum of Wales. *Exhib.:* one-man shows: London, Tokio and elsewhere in Europe and U.S.A., International Exhbn. of Modern Jewellery (1961), Gold Treasures of Europe (1972), Europalia 73, Brussels, etc. *Address:* Canons Ashby, Northamptonshire. *Signs work:* see appendix.

OSMOND, Edward, A.T.D., M.S.I.A.; artist in oils, wash, line, illustrations, commercial drawing and book design; *b* 1900; *m* C. M. ("Laurie") Osmond, sc. and painter. *Address:* Downland Cottage, Lullington Cl., Seaford, Sussex. *Signs work:* in full, block caps.

OSOSKI, Gerald, R.B.A., A.R.C.A., F.I.B.D.; awarded R.B.A. de Laszlo Medal (1972); landscape and figure artist; artist in chalk, wash, gouache and textural techniques; *b* London 1903; *s* of Edward Ososki; *m* Della; one *s*, one *d*. *Educ.:* St. Luke's, Chelsea; *studied art* at St. Martin's School of Art (1917-22), R.C.A. under Sir William Rothenstein. *Exhib.:* R.A., N.E.A.C., R.B.A.; Leicester, Goupil, Redfern and Leger Galleries, Ben-Uri Soc.; one-man exhbns., Claridge Gallery (1930), Mall Galleries (1973), Seventeen Collectors Exhbn. (Tate Gallery), U.S.A. *Work in permanent collections:* Ben-Uri Soc., Lord Methuen, R.A. *Work repro.:* in Colour, The Times. *Address:* 7 Heath Hurst Rd., Hampstead, London NW3. *Club:* Chelsea Arts. *Signs work:* "Ososki."

OSTLE, Roy John, N.D.D. (Painting 1950), A.T.D. (Liverpool 1951), council member R.Cam.A.; art lecturer, artist in oil, acrylic and mixed media (graphic work); senior lecturer in art, St. Mary's College, Bangor, N. Wales; lecturer in art appreciation, Extra Mural Dept., University College of North Wales, Bangor; *b* Chester, 3 July, 1930; *s* of Harry Ostle; *m* Margery; one *s*, two *d*. *Educ.:* Chester Grammar School; *studied art* at Chester School of Art (A. J. Mayson, A.R.C.A.), Liverpool College of Art (A. Tankard, A.T.D.). *Exhib.:* Welsh Arts Council, Tegfryn Art Gallery (Menai Bridge, Anglesey), Peterloo Gallery, Manchester, Ashbarn Gallery, Petersfield, New Art Centre, London, Gorstage Gallery (Weaverham, Cheshire), Edinburgh Festival. *Address:* Plas Penisarnant, Nant

Ffrancon, nr. Bethesda, Caerns., N. Wales. *Clubs:* R.Cam.A., Conwy. *Signs work:* "Roy Ostle."

OSWALD, Adrian, M.A. (Oxon.), F.S.A., F.M.A.; Hon. Sec., Roman London Excavation Council (1945-49); Hon. Sec., Midland Regional Group, Council of Archaeology (1950-52), Chairman, 1955; Vice-Pres. Birmingham Archaeological Soc.; Mem. of English Ceramic Circle; Keeper of Archaeology, City of Birmingham Museum (1950-64); *b* Nottingham, 3 Aug., 1908; *s* of Felix Oswald, D.Sc., B.A., F.S.A., F.G.S.; *m* D. M. Wheatley; one *s,* one *d. Educ.:* Nottingham High School and Exeter College, Oxford; *studied archaeology* in British and Continental museums. *Publications:* Economic History and Archaeology of English Clay Tobacco Pipes; No. 11 Ironmonger Lane; Connoisseur and the journals of learned socs. *Address:* 13 Chapel Rise, Avon Castle, Ringwood, Hants. *Club:* Athenæum.

OUSEY, Harry; painter in oil, water-colour, ink; *b* England, 1915; *m* Susie. *Educ.:* privately; *studied art* at various schools in London (1937 and also 1942-44) under Buckley, Ronald Allen, Heber Matthews. *Exhib.:* one-man shows: Lincoln Gallery, London (1963), Drian Galleries, London (1964), Ashgate Gallery, Farnham (1964), Watters Gallery, Australia (1965), Hamet Gallery, Fieldborne Gallery (1971-72), Harlow Arts Festival (1965), Questors Theatre, London (1970); many mixed exhibitions and one-man shows from 1940-66 and 1970. *Work in permanent collections:* Musée d'Art Moderne, Skopje, Yugoslavia. *Address:* Trevorrian House, Breage, Helston, Cornwall. *Signs work:* see appendix.

OXENBURY, Thomas Bernard, C.Eng., F.I.Mun.E. (1944), F.R.T.P.I. (1943), R.I.B.A., distinction in town planning; town-planning consultant; artist in water-colour and woods (marquetry); *b* Totnes, 5 Mar., 1904; *s* of Thomas Henry Oxenbury, business director; *m* Muriel Helen Oxenbury; one *s,* one *d. Educ.:* King Edward VI Grammar School, Totnes; *studied art* at school. *Exhib.:* Ipswich Art Club exhbns. *Publications:* in Architects' Journal, Planning Survey of Suffolk, T.P.I. Journal. *Address:* South Hill Cottage, South Hill, Felixstowe. *Club:* Ipswich Art. *Signs work:* "TBO."

OXLEY, Ursula; Board of Educ. drawing exam. (1937); artist in black and white, crayon, conte, pastel and water-colour; specialist in child portraiture; *b* Ealing, 4 May, 1918; *d* of Lawrence Deller, portrait painter; *m* Laurence Oxley; one *s,* one *d. Educ.:* privately; *studied art* at Winchester School of Art under E. E. Anderson, A.R.C.A. (1935-39). *Exhib.:* P.S., N.S., S.W.A., R.I. (Summer Exhbn.); Hampshire Artists' Exhbn., Southampton, etc. *Publications:* illustrated 1971 edition of History of Alresford. *Address:* The Studio Bookshop, Alresford, Hants. *Signs work:* "Ursula Oxley" (underlined).

OXTOBY, David Jowett Greaves, D.A., B.P.D., R.A.S.C.; artist in drawing, painting and prints; *b* Horsforth, nr. Leeds, 23 Jan., 1938; *s* of John Henry Oxtoby, managing representative for carpet factors. *Educ.:* Horsforth Council School; *studied art* at Bradford College of Art (1950-57) under John Fleming; R.A. Schools (1960-64) under Sir Henry Rushbury. *Exhib.:* 14 one-man shows including Redfern Gallery, London, I.C.A. London, Nordness Gallery, N.Y., Alexander Postan Fine Art, etc., various mixed exhbns. *Work in permanent collections:* Tate Gallery, Museum of Modern Art, N.Y., Minneapolis Institute of Art, Sheffield City A.G., Fundacao des Museum Regionais da Bahia, V. & A., Towner Gallery, Eastbourne, Bradford City A.G. *Publication:* A Short History of Black Magic (1957). *Address:* 46 St. Stephen's Gdns., London W2. *Clubs:* Imperial Arts League, Bag O'Nails. *Signs work:* "D. J. G. Oxtoby."

OYLER, Judith Audrey Allenby, Oxford Sec. Teacher's Art Cert.; landscape artist in water-colour; art teacher, retired, Christ's Hospital Girls' High School, Lincoln; previously at Harrogate School of Art; *b* Wychbold, Worcs.; *d* of George Oyler. *Educ.:* King Edward VI Girls' Grammar School, Louth; Princess Helena College, Ealing; *studied art* at Grimsby School of Art and Leicester College of Art under G. Ingles, J. Pettinger and S. R. Watson. *Exhib.:* R.A., R.B.A., Goupil Gallery, R.I., etc. *Address:* 2A Greestone Pl., Lincoln. *Signs work:* "Judith A. A. Oyler."

P

PACE, Stephen; artist in oil and water-colour; *b* Charleston, Mo., U.S.A., 18 Dec., 1918; *s* of John C. Pace; *m* Palmina Natalini Pace. *Studied art* at Art Students' League with Cameron Booth and Morris Cantor (1948-49), Grande Chaumière, Paris (1950), Instituto d'Arte Statale (1951), Hans Hofmann (1952). *Work in permanent collections:* Whitney Museum of American Art, Evansville (Ind.) Museum, Walter Chrysler Museum, Provincetown, Mass., Walker Art Centre, Minneapolis, Minn., University of Illinois Collection, James Michener Foundation, Norfolk (Va.) Museum of Arts and Sciences, Hallmark Collection, Des Moines Art Centre. *Address:* 345 W. 29th St., New York, 1, N.Y. *Signs work:* "Stephen Pace."

PACKARD, Gilian E., Des.R.C.A. (1963), F.R.S.A. (1975); first woman freeman of Goldsmith's Company by special grant (1971); designer in jewellery, gold, silver and stones; *b* Newcastle upon Tyne, 16 Mar., 1938; *d* of John L. Packard. *Educ.:* Claremont School, Esher; *studied art* at Kingston-upon-Thames School of Art (1955-58), Royal College of Art (1959-62). *Work in permanent collections:* Goldsmiths Hall, De Beers. *Address:* 8·2 Stirling Ct., 3 Marshal St., London W1V 1LQ. *Signs work:* "G.E.P." within oval, (Hallmark).

PACKER, Frederick, N.D.D.; painter and teacher; senior lecturer i/c cine-animation unit and postgraduate studies in graphic design, Central School of Art and Design; *b* Lewisham, 9 Jan., 1925. *Studied art* at College of Rhine Army (1946), Chelsea School of Art (1947-51). *Exhib.:* R.A., Young Contemporaries, London Group, John Moore's Liverpool Exhbn., etc. *Address:* 8 High St., Hastings, Sussex. *Signs work:* "packer."

PAGE, Evelyn; artist in oil; *b* Christchurch, N.Z.; *m* Prof. Frederic Page, Wellington University; one *s*, one *d*. *Studied art* at Canterbury College School of Art under Richard Wallwork, Cecil Kelly and Archibald Nicholl and at London and Paris. *Exhib.:* N.Z. Academy of Arts, Coll. of N.Z. Art in London. *Work in permanent collections:* public art galleries of all main centres of N.Z., Wellington National Gallery (organiser Retrospective Show (1970) purchasing for permanent collection). *Official purchase:* portrait of the late principal, Victoria University College, Wellington. *Work repro.:* Art in N.Z., Landfall. *Publication:* Landfall. *Address:* 20 Hobson St., Wellington, N.I., N.Z.

PAGE ROBERTS, James; painter in oil, sculptor, and artist in black and white; *b* Silchester, 5 Feb., 1925; *s* of Frederick William Page-Roberts; *m* Barbara Page Roberts, Ph.D. *Educ.:* Wellington College, and Taft, U.S.A.; *studied art* at Central School of Arts and Crafts under Bernard Meninsky, and Old Vic School of Theatre Design under Margaret Harris. *Exhib.:* one-man shows at Galerie de Seine, Reid Gallery, Kintetsu Gallery, Osaka, Qantas Gallery. *Official purchases:* M.O.W. *Work repro.:* The Tatler, The Studio, Daily Telegraph, The Antique Dealer and Collectors' Guide, What's on in London, Osaka Shinyukan. *Address:* c/o National

Westminster Bank Ltd., 250 Regent St., London W1. *Signs work:* "P R" and "PAGE ROBERTS."

PALMER, Garrick Salisbury, N.D.D. Painting and Engraving (1955); Cert. R.A.S. (1959); R.E.; Royal Academy Gold Medal and Edward Stott travelling scholarship (1958); teacher, painter in oil and water-colour and wood engraver; Head of Foundation Dept., Winchester School of Art; *b* 20 Sept., 1933; *s* of S. D. Palmer; *m* Ellis Palmer; three *d. Educ.:* St. John's College, Southsea; *studied art* at Portsmouth College of Art, Royal Academy Schools. *Work in permanent collections:* Eastbourne, Portsmouth, Brighton, Wakefield and Johannesburg Art Galleries; G.P.O. *Publications:* Three stories, by Herman Melville (Folio Society); The Sea and the Jungle (Imprint Society), U.S.A.; Moby Dick (Folio Society) (wood engravings). *Address:* 8 Firs Ave., Cowplain, Portsmouth PO8 8RS. *Signs work:* "Garrick Palmer."

PALMER, Herbert Ralph, awarded Scholarship of Art, Johannesburg, S. Africa (1932-36); A.R.B.S.; sculptor in all known media and painter in oil and water-colour; working in the Art Dept., V. & A.; art teacher, Tower Bridge Institute, London (1950-51); *b* Richmond, Surrey, 13 Dec., 1916; *s* of Herbert Jesse Palmer, Professor of Music, and the late Marie Menges, the well-known violinist and 'cellist. *Educ.:* Christian Brothers College, Pretoria, S. Africa; *studied art* at Johannesburg Art School, and one-time pupil of Anton Van Wouw and P. H. Jowett. *Exhib.:* in twenty leading galleries in London, New York, South Africa, Portugal. *Work in permanent collections:* (1947) worked with Sir William Reid Dick, K.C.V.O., R.A., on the Roosevelt Monument. *Work repro.:* numerous commissions, including two ecclesiastical figures, St. James Church, Fulham, London; bronze Mother and Child, South Africa House, London; Dr. Basil Merriman Bronze, Carter Foundation, London, etc. *Hobby:* Violin-making. *Address:* The Studio, 61A Britannia Rd., London SW6. *Club:* Chelsea Arts. *Signs work:* "Ralph H. Palmer" and "R. Palmer."

PANCANI, Azeglio, Jr., International Fine Arts Council; architect in firm of Gerber and Pancani (1951-71); firm of Azeglio T. Pancani, Jr., A.I.A., architect since 1971; senior architectural draughtsman, Bureau of Agricultural Engineering, Washington, D.C. (1935-38); Board of Education, New York (1938-45); in charge of architectural firm of Erwin Gerber, Newark, N.J. (1945-51); *b* St. Louis, Mo., 16 Nov., 1910; *s* of Azeglio Pancani, artist and wood-carver; *m* Çesarina; *w* Matilda; one *s*, one *d. Educ.:* N.Y. University; Columbia University; *studied art* at Art Students League, N.Y. *Address:* 3 Briar Hills Circle, Springfield, N.J. *Signs work:* "A. Pancani, Jr."

PANNETT, Juliet, S.G.A.; graphic artist and painter; *b* Hove, Sussex. 15 July, 1911; *d* of Chas. Somers; *m* Major M. R. D. Pannett; one *s*, one *d. Educ.:* Wistons, Brighton; Brighton College of Art. *Work in permanent collections:* National Portrait Gallery, Hove Art Gallery. Special artist to the Illustrated London News from 1958-64. Official artist Qantas Inaugural Jet Flight, London-Sydney (1959). *Work repro.:* Illustrated London News, The Times, Daily Telegraph, Radio Times, Birmingham Mail, Law Guardian. *Address:* Pound House, Angmering Village, Sussex. *Club:* Press. Awarded freedom of Worshipful Company of Painter Stainers; Freeman of City of London (1960). *Signs work:* "Juliet Pannett."

PARBURY, Kathleen Ophir Theodora, Dip. of Fine Art, University of London (1924), F.R.B.S. (1966); sculptor; *b* Boreham Wood, Herts., 23 Aug., 1901; *d* of Walter Key Parbury. *Educ.:* Bedford High School; *studied art* at Slade School, University of London (1920-24) under Prof. Henry Tonks and Prof. Havard Thomas. *Work in permanent collections:* works in churches in London, Salisbury,

Southampton, Beds., nr. Coventry, Sutton Coldfield, Cumberland, Co. Durham, Northumberland, Tipperary, Ireland, Nigeria, Canada and museums in New Zealand and Ohio, U.S.A.; portrait sculpture in London, Oxford, Leeds and many private collections. *Publications:* historical book on The Saints of Lindisfarne, Star of the North. *Address:* St. Bedes, 89 Longstone Cl., Beadnell, Northumb. *Signs work:* "K.O.T.P."

PARISH, David Alexander; professional artist, painting in oil, sculptor in sterling silver, wood, also jewellery designer; part-time instructor (evening classes) for jewellery; *b* Southend-on-Sea, 8 Jan., 1941; *s* of Walter Parish; *m* Jill Parish. *Educ.:* Wentworth High School; *studied art* at Southend College of Art (1965-67) for sculpture and life study under W. Threef and (1975) for jewellery, but mainly self-taught. *Exhib.:* Warwick Gallery, Vancouver, Chenil Gallery, Chelsea, Mason Gallery, California, International Art Centre, London. *Work in permanent collections:* Gallerie Internationale, N.Y.; sculpture in private collections of Mr. Andy Williams and Mr. Telly Savalas. *Address:* 158 Fleetwood Ave., Westcliff-on-Sea, Essex. *Signs work:* "David A. Parish."

PARK, Alistair, D.A. (Edin.), Post-Graduate (1952); artist; teacher, Newcastle upon Tyne Polytechnic, Fine Art Dept.; *b* Edinburgh, 22 Apr., 1930; *s* of William Park; *m* Sara Lawrence; two *s,* one *d. Educ.:* Kirkcaldy High School; *studied art* at Edinburgh College of Art (1947-52). *Exhib.:* Rowan Gallery, Demarco Gallery, Scottish Gallery, '57 Gallery, Stone Gallery, Hayes Gallery, York, Gallery House, London, Ceolfrith, Sunderland. *Work in permanent collections:* National Gallery of Modern Art, Edinburgh, Abbot Hall Art Gallery, Kendal and Collection of Arts Council, Scotland. *Address:* 55 Woodbine Rd., Gosforth, Newcastle upon Tyne. *Club:* Scottish Arts. *Signs work:* "A. Park" or "Alistair Park."

PARKER, Agnes Miller, D.A. (Glasgow), R.E.; artist in oil, tempera and wood; *d* of William McCall Parker, analytical chemist. *Educ.:* Whitehill Higher Grade School, Glasgow; Glasgow School of Art (Maurice Grieffenhagen, R.A., D. Forrester Wilson, James M. Dunlop, Prof. Baltus, 1914-19). *Exhib.:* Soc. of Wood Engravers, Royal Society of Painter Etchers and Engravers, International Exhbn. in Chicago, etc. *Official purchases:* art galleries in Britain and abroad (prints). *Publications:* illustrations for numerous books. *Address:* Cladach, King's Cross, Isle of Arran. *Signs work:* "A. Miller Parker."

PARKER, Constance-Anne, A.T.D., S.W.A.; Assistant Librarian, Royal Academy of Arts (since 1958); Landseer Scholar, Sir David Murray Scholarship, Leverhulme Scholarship; painter in oil, sculptor in wood and clay, wood engraver; *b* London, 19 Oct., 1921. *Educ.:* privately; *studied art:* Polytechnic School of Art and Royal Academy Schools (four silver and three bronze medals). *Exhib.:* R.A., R.B.A., R.P., N.E.A.C., and provinces. *Work repro.:* in The Artist. *Publication:* Mr. Stubbs the Horse Painter (1971). *Address:* 88 Philbeach Gdns., London SW5 9EU.

PARKER, Harold Wilson, A.R.C.A., Rome Scholar in sculpture (1927), F.R.B.S.; Vice-Pres., R.B.S. (1953); sculptor in wood, stone, bronze; *b* 6 May, 1896; *m* Constance M. Howard, A.R.C.A.; one *d. Educ.:* Sir George Monoux Grammar School, Walthamstow; *studied art* at Walthamstow School of Art, St. Martin's School of Art, Central School of Arts and Crafts, Sir John Cass School of Art, R.C.A. (1924-27). *Exhib.:* R.A., Arts and Crafts En. Soc. *Official purchases:* memorial to George Lansbury (commissioned Min. of Works); medals: Sir Charles Reilly, the Moynihan Medal, Cobbett Medal, reverse Imperial Farthing, Indian Gen. Service Medal, Civil Defence Medal; architectural bronzes, Nuffield

Orthopaedic Centre, Oxford. *Address:* 43 Cambridge Rd. South, Chiswick, London W4 3DA. *Signs work:* "H. Wilson Parker," and see appendix.

PARKER, Walter F., A.R.C.A. (1938), A.T.D. (1939), L.S.I.A. (1940), F.R.S.A. (1955), college of art principal; printmaker, graphic designer, painter in water-colours; Educ. Officer, R.A.F. (1940-46), Second Master, School of Art, Preston (1946-48), Senior Master, Hastings School of Art (1948-53); Head of Fine Art, Hartlepool College of Art (1953); Principal, Hartlepool College of Art (1954); *b* Carlisle, 11 May, 1914; *m* Joy E. Turk. *Educ.:* Carlisle Grammar School (1922-30); *studied art* at Carlisle School of Art (1930-35), R.C.A. (1935-38), Courtauld Inst. of Fine Art, Goldsmiths' College (1938-39). *Address:* 19 The Cliff, Seaton Carew, Hartlepool, Cleveland TS25 1AP. *Signs work:* "Walter F. Parker."

PARKIN, Michael Robert; art dealer; chairman/managing director, Michael Parkin Fine Art Ltd.; *b* London, 1 Dec., 1931; *s* of Frank Robert Parkin; two d. *Educ.:* Mill Hill and St. George's Schools; Magdalen College, Oxford. *Exhbns.:* at Parkin Gallery, 11 Motcomb St., SW1. Cover British Art 1840-1940, have included The Cafe Royalists, Four for Whistler, The Fitzrorians, Claude Flight, etc. *Publications:* Old Chelsea (Newson, London 1975), in preparation: Walter Greaves with Sir John Rothenstein, A Life of Charles Augustus Howell. *Address:* Studio 4, 1-6 Sloane Sq., London SW1. *Clubs:* Beefsteak, S.F.T.A., Chelsea Arts, P.E.N. International.

PARKIN, Trevor, N.D.D. (1955); teacher, painter, illustrator in water-colour, oil, gouache and ink; *b* S. Normanton, Derby; *s* of Mervyn Parkin; *m* Elizabeth Anne Parkin; one *s*, one *d. Educ.:* Heanor Grammar School; *studied art* at Derby and District College of Art under Richard Sharpe, A.R.C.A. *Exhib.:* one-man shows: Woodbridge, Suffolk, Nottingham. *Work in permanent private collections* in U.K., U.S.A. and S. Africa. *Publications:* illustrated numerous children's and educational books and magazines. *Address:* 16 Laxton Gdns., Pinchbeck, nr. Spalding, Lincs. *Signs work:* "T. Parkin" or "Trevor Parkin."

PARKINSON, Frederick C. D.; Consultant Editor Leisure Painter, Consultant Editor, Craft Book Society (1975-); managing editor, The Artist, Art Review, Artist's Guide (1950-75); general editor, The Artists' Handbooks; director, The Heatherley School of Art, (1957-75); member A.I.C.A.; *b* London, 28 May, 1916; *s* of the late F. C. Parkinson; *m* Alexa St. Clair Ross; three *s. Educ.:* Ewell Castle. *Publications:* A Guide to Type Identification; frequent contributions to The Leisure Painter, The Artist, Artist's Guide, and other art publications. *Addresses:* Knolly's Cottage, Willesborough Lees, nr. Ashford, Kent and Marignac 30, Uzes, France. *Clubs:* Arts, Chelsea Arts, Cinque Ports Y.C.

PARKINSON, Gerald; painter in oil, gouache and water-colour; *b* Shipley, Yorks., 5 Nov., 1926; *s* of Edward Parkinson; *m* Sylvia Mary; one *s*, one *d. Educ.:* Woodhouse Grove School, nr. Leeds; *studied art* at Bradford College of Art (1951-54). *Exhib.:* R.A., West of England Academy, John Moores, Sussex Artists, Yorks. Artists, S.E.A.; one-man shows: London, Bologna, Stockholm, Brighton, York, Bristol, Monte Carlo, Lewes, Bradford, Hove, Tunbridge Wells. *Work in permanent collections:* Glasgow, Brighton, Leicestershire C.C., L.C.C., Surrey C.C., West Riding C.C., Mural for National Provincial Bank (1968). *Address:* The Gate House, Wootton Manor, Polegate, Sussex. *Club:* A.I.A. *Signs work:* "Gerald Parkinson."

PARRY, Richard; painter, designer, lecturer in fine art; *b* Liverpool, 6 May, 1936; *s* of Bryn and Phyllis Parry. *Educ.:* Liverpool Junior School of Art; *studied art* at Liverpool College of Art (art scholarship, 1953-55), Goldsmiths' College

School of Art (1956-59). Designer for Bromley Theatre, Kent (1960-62); art lecturer Tate Gallery, National Gallery and Greenwich Adult Institute (1963-68); art teacher at Christ's College, Blackheath (1969 onwards). *Work in permanent collections:* South Africa, Vienna, Nuffield Foundation, South London Art Gallery, Liverpool Echo, The Jewel Houses Ltd., London. *Address:* 11 Crooms Hill Grove, Greenwich Park, London SE10. *Signs work:* "PARRY."

PARSONS-IRWIN, Maureen, N.D.D. (1955), R.D.S. (1959); artist in pen and ink, gouache, collage, polished stone collage; art and craft specialist of an Art and Craft Centre, Special School; taught in Schools of Art, Brighton College of Art, Secondary Modern Fenland School and Evening Institutes; *b* Guildford, Surrey, 25 May, 1935; *d* of Edward Raymond Parsons; two *s. Educ.:* Convent of Ladies of Mary, Merrow Grange, Guildford; *studied art* at Hastings School of Art (1951-55) under Vincent Lines, principal. *Exhib.:* three one-man shows; R.A.; work selected from R.A. for travelling exhbn. *Publications:* written and illustrated articles; designed and embroidered articles for House Beautiful, Homes and Gardens, Home Notes, etc. *Address:* 27 Croft Rd., Hastings, Sussex. *Signs work:* "Mia."

PARTRIDGE, John Arthur; antique dealer; Chairman, Partridge (Fine Arts) Ltd.; *b* London, 6 July, 1929; *s* of the late Claude A. Partridge; *m*; two *s,* one *d. Educ.:* Elstree and Harrow. *Address:* 144-146 New Bond St., London W1.

PASCOE, Ernest, F.R.B.S., D.F.A.(Lond.), R.W.A.; sculptor and painter; Head of Fine Art, Bristol Polytechnic; Chairman, Royal West of England Academy; Member of Faculty, British School at Rome; *b* 1922; *m* Jane Denwood, four *d. Studied art* at Carlisle (1937-41), R.A.F., 1941-45, Slade School (1945-48). *Exhib.:* Arts Council, R.A., London Group, etc. *Address:* 7 Goldney Rd., Bristol 8. *Signs work:* "E. Pascoe" or "Ernest Pascoe."

PASMORE, Victor, C.B.E. (1959), M.A.Dunelm (1956); painter, architectural designer, teacher; working in oil, cellulose, collage, wood, Perspex and formica; master of painting in dept. of fine art, Durham University (1954-61); consulting architectural designer, S.W. area, Peterlee New Town (since 1955); *b* 3 Dec., 1908; *s* of the late E. S. Pasmore, M.D., M.R.C.P.; *m* Wendy; one *s,* one *d. Educ.:* Harrow School; *studied art* privately and at Central School of Arts and Crafts. *Work in permanent collections:* Tate Gallery, National Galleries of Canada, Melbourne, Sydney, Brisbane and Adelaide, Allbright Gallery, Buffalo (U.S.A.). *Club:* I.C.A. *Address:* 12 St. German's Pl., Blackheath, London SE3. *Signs work:* see appendix.

PASMORE, Wendy; painter in oils; teacher of painting at Sunderland College of Art, 1955-58, and at Leeds College of Art since 1958; *b* Dublin, 1915; *d* of J. Lloyd Blood; *m* Victor Pasmore; one *s,* one *d. Educ.:* privately; *studied art:* privately. *Work in permanent collections:* Tate Gallery, Arts Council, Leeds Education Committee. *Address:* 12 St. German's Pl., Blackheath, London SE3. *Signs work:* "Wendy Pasmore."

PASS, Derek Percy; artist in ceramic enamels, water-colour; ceramic artist, Coalport China (Wedgwood Group); *b* Newcastle, Staffs., 19 Apr., 1929; *s* of Frank Pass; *m* Doreen Odell; two *d. Educ.:* Knutton Elementary School; Burslem School of Art; *studied art* at Stoke-on-Trent College of Art (1942) under Gordon Forsyth, R.I. and Reginald Haggar, R.I. *Exhib.:* Trends, Britain in Water-colours, N.S. *Work in permanent collection:* Wedgwood Rooms, U.K. *Address:* 12 Thirlmere Pl., Clayton, Newcastle, Staffs. ST5 3QJ. *Clubs:* F.P.S., Society of Ceramic Artists. *Signs work:* "Derek Pass," "D. Pass" (ceramic).

PATERSON, G. W. Lennox, V.R.D., A.R.E., Guthrie Award, R.S.A. (1946); painter and wood engraver; Deputy Director, Glasgow School of Art; *b* 7 Jan., 1915; *s* of George Andrew Paterson, F.R.I.B.A.; *m* Jean Patrick Martin, D.A.; two *s*, one *d*. *Educ.:* Glasgow Academy, Glasgow School of Art. *Exhib.:* R.S.A., G.I., R.E., Soc. of Artist Printmakers. *Official purchases:* various galleries. *Publications:* various. *Address:* Cairnsmore, 16 Queen St., Helensburgh. *Club:* Glasgow Art. *Signs work:* "G. W. Lennox Paterson."

PATERSON, Mary Viola; painter in oil, lithographer and colour printer; *b* 19 Feb., 1899; *d* of Alex. N. Paterson, M.A., A.R.I.B.A., A.R.S.A. *Educ.:* St. Bride's School, Helensburgh; Glasgow School of Art (Maurice Grieffenhagen, 1919-21); Académie de la Grande Chaumière (Lucien Simon Bésnard), Académie L'Hôte (André l'Hôte). *Exhib.:* R.A., R.S.A., Soc. of Artist Printmakers, G.I., S.S.A., Artists of Chelsea, International Faculty of Arts. *Official purchases:* Contemporary Art Soc. (three-colour prints), V. & A., National Gallery of Canada. *Work repro.:* Colour wood types in Studio. *Address:* The Long Croft, Helensburgh, Scotland. *Signs work:* "Viola Paterson," or sometimes "V̧. Paterson."

PATERSON, Michael Hugh Orr, B.A. (1951), Diploma of the Museums Association, F.R.S.A., F.M.A.; Curator of Museums and Art Gall., London Borough of Enfield; art restorer; lecturer for L.E.A. Adult Education Service, The National Trust; Wedgwoods; trainee, City A.G., Birmingham (1953-54); asst., City A.G., Hereford (1954-55); asst.-in-charge, Municipal A.G., Oldham (1956); asst. keeper, City A.G., Leicester (1957-58); Curator, Russell-Cotes A.G. and Museums, Bournemouth (1958-66); *b* London, 7 Dec., 1927; *s* of G. E. Paterson, engineer. *Educ.:* Kirkcudbright Academy; Cranleigh School; Manchester and Edinburgh Universities; *studied art* at Manchester, Edinburgh colleges of art (part-time). *Address:* Forty Hall, Enfield, Middx. EN2 9HA.

PATON, Frances Mary Richmond, D.A.(Edin.), S.S.A., A.A.S.; painter in oil; *b* Hareshawmuir, Ayrshire, 1920; *d* of E. Richmond Paton, B.A.(Cantab.), F.Z.S. *Educ.:* Overstone, Northants, Switzerland, Germany; *studied art* at Edinburgh (1947) under W. G. Gillies, William MacTaggart, Leonard Rosoman. *Exhib.:* R.S.A., R.G.I., S.S.A., A.A.S., Arts Council. *Work repro.:* reviewed in La Revue Moderne, Paris. *Address:* Rathen Lodge, 137 Fraserburgh, Aberdeenshire, AB4 5UL. *Signs work:* "Mary Paton."

PATRICK, J. McIntosh, R.S.A., R.O.I., A.R.E., LL.D.; oil and water-colour painter and etcher; *b* 1907; *s* of A. G. Patrick, architect; *m* Janet Watterston; one *s*, one *d*. *Educ.:* Dundee, Morgan Academy; Glasgow School of Art. *Exhib.:* R.A., R.S.A., Pittsburgh. *Official purchases:* Chantrey Bequest; Manchester; Glasgow; Aberdeen; National Gallery of S. Africa; British Museum; Carnegie Inst., Pittsburgh; National Gallery, S. Australia; W.A.G.; Lady Lever Gallery; Dundee; Scottish Modern Arts Assoc.; Pilgrim Trust, etc. *Work repro.:* Many paintings reproduced as large-scale prints. *Address:* c/o Fine Art Soc., Ltd., 148 New Bond St., London W1. *Club:* Scottish Arts. *Signs work:* "McINTOSH PATRICK."

PAVEY, Donald Adair, F.R.A.I., F.S.A.E., A.R.C.A.; colour consultant designer; editor of "Athene"; senior lecturer at Kingston Polytechnic; Founder of the Junior Arts and Science Centres (D.E.S. L244507/1), London, Surrey and Liverpool. *Studied art* at R.C.A. (medal of special distinction, the painting prize, architecture prize) and London University, history and psychology (distinctions for special research). *Publications:* First Facts about Colour (E.P.), Colour and Illusion (E.P.), Colour and History (E.P.), Colour Archetypes (ARK 22); edited the Methuen Handbook of Colour and Colour Dictionary, etc. *Societies:* Colour Group (Great Britain), Computer Arts Society. *Address:* 30 Wayside, London SW14.

PAYNE, Edward Raymond, A.R.C.A., A.B.S.M.G.P.; stained glass artist, painter in oil and water-colour; *b* 10 Nov., 1906; *s* of Henry A. Payne, R.W.S.; *m*; one *s*, one *d*. *Educ.:* St. George's School, Harpenden; R.C.A. (Sir W. Rothenstein, 1924-27); studied stained glass under father, windows made for many churches in Glos. and Lincs. *Exhib.:* R.A., N.E.A.C. *Official purchases:* Carlisle Art Gallery, Cheltenham Art Gallery, Imperial War Museum. *Work repro.:* Drying Clothes and Bedding (pen and wash drawing). *Publications:* Soldiers (Oxford, 1943). *Address:* Triangle, Box, Nr. Stroud, Glos. *Signs work:* "Edward R. Payne."

PAYNE, Margaret A., N.D.D. (1959), A.T.C. (1960), R.E.; graphic artist, painter in oil, etcher; lecturer at Digby Stuart College of Education, Roehampton, London; *b* Southampton, 14 Apr., 1937; *d* of G. E. B. Payne, M.D., D.P.H. *Educ.:* St. Helen's School, Northwood, Middx.; *studied art* at Harrow School of Art (1955-59), Goldsmiths' College (1959-60). *Exhib.:* R.A., R.E., Paris Salon, Society of Women Artists, Young Contemporaries, R.I. Galleries. *Work in permanent collections:* Sheffield and Nottinghamshire C.C., Pictures for Schools circulation. Designs decorative posters, record sleeves and programme covers. *Address:* 160B Murray Rd., S. Ealing, London W5 4DA.

PAYTON, Sheila Marguerite; Intermediate Exam. in Art and Crafts, Cert. in Education; artist in oil and ink of tigers, the cat family and orchids (large paintings); formerly Head of Art Dept. at Secondary Modern School (7 yrs.), Grammar School (6 yrs.); *b* Henley-on-Thames, 15 Sept., 1932; *d* of H. N. P. Payton, banker; *m* Richard Clifford Smith. *Educ.:* Henley Grammar School; *studied art* at University of Reading under Prof. Betts; Bath Academy of Art under Jack Smith, Peter Lanyon, Bryan Winter. *Exhib.:* R.A., R.B.A., S.WL.A., N.E.A.C., two Wildlife Exhbns. touring England, Campbell and Franks, Wessex Contemporary Artists, Salisbury, Petersfield, Oxford and other shows in London and the Home Counties. *Publication:* Heart Beat, book of poetry. *Address:* The Thatch, Appleshaw, nr. Andover, Hants. SP11 9BN. *Clubs:* Friend of the Federation of British Artists, World Wildlife Fund, Fauna Preservation Soc., Marwell Zoological Soc., Friends of the Earth, R.H.S., Beauty without Cruelty. *Signs work:* "Payton."

PEACE, David Brian, F.S.A. (1975), R.I.B.A. (1938), F.R.T.P.I. (1948); architect, town planner, glass engraver, lettering designer; Master, A.W.G. (1973); first Chairman, Guild of Glass Engravers (1975); Council, Royal Town Planning Institute (1961-62 and 1972-73); Council for British Archaeology (1965-); *b* Sheffield, 13 Mar., 1915; *s* of Herbert W. F. Peace; *m* Jean Margaret Lawson, A.R.C.A.; two *d*. *Educ.:* Mill Hill: University of Sheffield; *studied art* under Clarence Whaite. *Exhib.:* 7 one-man shows. *Work in permanent collections:* V. & A., Fitzwilliam Museum, Kettle's Yard, Cambridge, Manchester, Birmingham, Norwich, Royal Scottish Museum, Corning Museum, N.Y.; engraved windows include Manchester Cathedral, churches at Hemingford Abbots, Cambs., Trusley, Derbys., Ansty, Wilts.; Gunnersbury R.C. School; memorial tablet to G. M. Hopkins, Westminster Abbey. *Address:* Abbots End, Hemingford Abbots, Huntingdon, Cambs. *Club:* Arts. *Signs work:* see appendix.

PEACOCK, Carlos (Charles Hanbury), B.A.(Cantab.); writer and art critic; *s* of W. E. Peacock, M.D. *Educ.:* Uppingham and Cambridge. *Publications:* Painters and Writers (Tate Gallery), co-author (with John Rothenstein) of essay on Tate Gallery in The Nations Pictures (Chatto and Windus, 1951), John Constable (John Baker Ltd.), Samuel Palmer (John Baker Ltd.). *Arranged:* Constable Exhbn. at Aldeburgh Festival (1948), Pre-Raphaelite Exhbn. at Bournemouth (1951). *Addresses:* 26 Brompton Sq., London SW3, and Olivers, Toppesfield, Halstead, Essex.

PEARCE, Edward Holroyd, Lord, R.B.A. (1940), Hon. R.B.S.; painter in oils; *b* 1901; *s* of J. W. E. Pearce, M.A.; *m* Erica Priestman; two *s*. *Educ.:* Charterhouse. *Exhib.:* R.A., R.B.A., N.E.A.C., etc.; one-man show of landscapes, Mall Galleries (1971, 1973). *Address:* Sweethaws, Crowborough, Sussex. *Club:* Athenaeum.

PEARSON, James E.; artist in oil, clay, bronze; William Boyd Andrews, Best of Show, 1961; Gold Keys, 1951, 1954, 1956; Scholastic Art Awards, Carnegie Institute; art instructor, Woodstock Comm. High School, Woodstock, Illinois, U.S.A.; Bachelor of Science in Education (1961), Master of Science in Education (1962), Master of Fine Art (1964); *b* Woodstock, Illinois, U.S.A., 12 Dec., 1939; *s* of John C. Pearson. *Educ.:* McHenry Community High School, McHenry, Illinois; Northern Illinois University, Dekalb, Illinois; *studied art* at Northern Illinois University, Dekalb, Illinois. *Work in permanent collections:* Northern Illinois University; over 100 private collections (company and individual). *Publications:* McHenry County, 1832-1968. *Address:* 5117 Barnard Mill Rd., Ringwood, Illinois, 60072, U.S.A. *Signs work:* see appendix.

PÉE, Herbert, Dr. phil. (1937); director, Staatl. Graphische Sammlung, 8 Muenchen, Germany; *b* Halberstadt, 7 July, 1913. *Studied art* at Universities of Berlin and Goettingen under Prof. Graf Vitzthum. *Address:* Staatl. Graphische Sammlung, 8 Muenchen, Germany.

PEILE, Misomé; foundation mem. Penrith Soc. of Arts in Cornwall and of Taurus Artists, London, mem. Newlyn Society; worked with Royal Marine Commandos, 29th U.S. Inf. Div., Ballet Rambert, etc.; *b* Southsea, Hants, 1907. *Exhib.:* Dominions, London and provinces; one-man show, R.W.S. Galleries (1949); Drian Four Sculptors, Two Painters (1958), Chiltern Gallery (one-man) (1961-63); with Taurus Artists graphic tour of Canada, to Provence Festival, and to Minotaur Gallery, Toronto (1963), South American work, Newlyn Gallery (1970), Malta (April, 1971); sponsored exhbn. with Denis Mitchell, National Museum Valletta (May, 1973). *Address:* Stanmar, Ursuline Sisters St., G'Mangia, Malta, G.C. *Signs work:* "MISOMÉ PEILE."

PELL, Robert Leslie, N.D.D. (Painting) (1948), R.B.A. (1958), F.R.S.A. (1968); painter in oil and polymer and lecturer; Lecturer in Fine Art, North Oxfordshire Technical College and School of Art, Banbury; *b* Northampton, 24 Nov., 1928; *s* of Harry Pell; *m* Pamela Crake; one *s*, one *d*. *Educ.:* Technical High School, Northampton; *studied art* at Northampton School of Art (1944-49). *Exhib.:* R.C.A. Galleries, R.B.A., Foyle's Gallery, Canaletto Gallery, Leicester Gallery (Artists of Fame and Promise), Piccadilly Gallery, Bear Lane Gallery, Oxford. *Work in permanent collections:* University College and Balliol College, Oxford, Leicestershire, Reading, Surrey and Northumberland Education Committees, The John Lewis Organisation, Northampton Art Gallery, Coventry City Art Gallery, private collections in England, America and Finland. *Work repro.:* La Revue Moderne, Art Review, The Artist, The Oxford Magazine, The Studio. *Address:* The Studio House, 141 High St., Brackley, Northants. *Clubs:* Royal Society of British Artists, Royal Society of Arts. *Signs work:* "Pell" (written in italic script).

PELLING, John Arthur, A.R.C.A.; painter in oil on canvas; clergyman, Church of England, Vicar of St. Saviours, Hammersmith; Visiting Tutor at Sir John Cass School of Art, London; *b* Hove, 9 Aug., 1930; *s* of Arthur Robert Pelling; *m* Françoise; four *s*. *Educ.:* Brighton, Hove and Sussex Grammar School; *studied art* at Brighton College of Art and Crafts (1946-49) and Royal College of Art Painting School (1951-55), under Rodrigo Moynihan, John Minton, Carel Weight. *Exhib.:* six one-man shows, London, Sussex University, Manchester.

Work in permanent collections: Nuffield Foundation, Vittorio 'de Sica private collection, Italy. *Address:* The Vicarage, Cobbold Rd., London W12 9LN. *Signs work:* "PELLING" (on paintings), "John Pelling" (on drawings).

PEMBERTON, Muriel A., F.S.I.A., A.R.W.S., A.R.C.A., W.I.A.C.; painter in water-colour, oil, chalk, ink, etc., designer; Head of Faculty, Royal College of Art; formerly Head of Faculty, Fashion/Textiles, St. Martin's School of Art; *b* Stoke-on-Trent, 1909; *d* of Thoma Henry Pemberton, photographer; *m* John Hadley Rowe, A.R.C.A. *Educ.:* Brown Hills High School, Tunstall; *studied art* at Burslem School of Art, Royal College of Art under Prof. Tristram, Sir William Rothenstein. *Exhib.:* R.A., Rochdale A.G., Sheffield A.G., Hanley Museum and Art Gallery; one-man show: Leicester Gallery (1952), Worthing Museum, etc.; group-shows at the following galleries: Leger, Gimpel Fils, Beaux Arts, Whitechapel and many other galleries in London and the Provinces; British Council touring exhbn., New York, U.S.A., Italy, France, S. Africa, China, Japan, Canada, etc. *Work repro.:* by Unicef in America, Artist News Chronicle (1945-52), drawings in Arts Review. *Address:* The Croft, Maresfield, Sussex. *Signs work:* "Muriel A. Pemberton."

PENNEY, Victor E.; graphic artist in black and white, colour for reproduction; illustrator of children's books, Christmas cards, book wrappers, etc.; poster designer; *b* Dublin, 8 July, 1909; *m* Eileen C. Penney; one *s*, one *d*. *Educ.:* High School, Dublin; *studied art* at College of Art, Dublin. *Exhib.:* Hibernian Academy of Arts, Dublin. *Work repro.:* in ordinary commercial journals, newspapers, etc. *Address:* Studio, 2 Lower O'Connell St., Dublin. *Signs work:* "Victor E. Penney."

PEPLOE, Denis Frederic Neil, R.S.A. (1966); painter in oil; teacher at Edinburgh College of Art; *b* Edinburgh, 25 Mar., 1914; *s* of Samuel Peploe, R.S.A.; *m* Elizabeth; one *s*, one *d*. *Educ.:* Edinburgh Academy; *studied art* at Edinburgh College of Art (1931-36). *Work in permanent collections:* Glasgow, Kirkcaldy, Perth, Edinburgh, Arts Council. *Address:* 5 McLaren Rd., Edinburgh. *Signs work:* "denis P."

PEPYS, Rhoda Gertrude, N.A.T.C. (South Africa); artist, portrait painter, teacher; *b* Port Elizabeth, 12 Mar., 1914 (née Kussel); *m* Prof. Jack Pepys (1938); two children. *Educ.:* Collegiate and School of Arts and Crafts, Port Elizabeth; Municipal Silver Medal (1934). *Exhib.:* one-man shows: S.A.: Cape Town, Port Elizabeth; Europe (London): Hampstead Art Cellar (1961, 1963); (Italy): Sperlonga (1962, 1965); (Paris): Galerie Tedesco (1962); (London): Woolwich Polytechnic (1965), Mermaid Theatre (1966), Studio 36 (1967, 1970, 1973); group shows in London: H.A.C., Leicester Gall., W.I.A.C., R.W.S., Guildhall, R.A., R.S.P.P. *Address:* 36 Ferncroft Ave., London NW3. *Clubs:* H.A.C., Florentine Artists Assoc., Italy. *Signs work:* "Pepys" and "Rhoda Pepys."

PEPYS, Sandra Lynn, B.A. (Hons.), London; artist, art historian and art teacher; *b* Cape Town, 27 Jan., 1942; *m* A. Heidecker (1969). *Educ.:* South Hampstead and S.O.A.A.S., Univ. of London; awarded 1st Prize, Univ. of London Exhib. (1964, 1966). *Exhib.:* one-man shows: Hampstead Art Cellar (1962); London: Everyman (1963); Oxford: Halifax House (1963); Paris: Galerie Tedesco (1962); Italy: Sperlonga (1962, 1965); Rome: Galleria Coppella (1965); London: Mermaid Theatre (1966), Studio 36 (1966, 1967, 1969, 1972); group shows: H.A.C., W.A.C. Univ. of London, Guildhall, R.A. Summer Exhbn. (1973) *Commissions:* mural paintings for London University (1966) and British Railways (1967). *Address:* 36 Ferncroft Ave., London NW3. *Clubs:* H.A.C., Florentine Artists Assoc., Italy. *Signs work:* "Sandra Pepys."

PERCIVAL, Maurice Marshall, A.R.C.A., F.R.S.A.; art master, Downside

School (1961-68), Harrow School (1945-54), Malvern College (1939-45); artist in oil, pen and ink, mural painting, Shakespearian theatre design; *b* London, 8 May, 1906; *s* of F. P. Percival. *Educ.:* Hurstpierpoint College; *studied art* at Central School of Art, R.C.A. *Exhib.:* R.A. *Work repro.:* illustrations to Moonlight at the Globe, On Producing Shakespeare, Macbeth (O.U.P.) (all by Ronal Watkins), also English Two (school textbook, Heinemann), Exhibition "Roman Sketch Book," 200 drawings. *Address:* 5 Sudbrook Cottages, Ham Common, Richmond, Surrey.

PERRE, Hugo A. J. van de: author, critic and broadcaster; mem. of P.E.N., Critics' Circle and F.P.A.; Hon. Member F.P.S.; London Corresp. Vincent van Gogh Archives at Antwerp; *b* Antwerp, 24 Jan., 1914; *s* of the late Dr. A. van de Perre, Mem. of Belgian Parliament. *Educ.:* Antwerp and Louvain. *Publications:* various books and essays in English, French and Dutch on art, literature and history, e.g., Présences belges à Londres: Petit discours sur la contribution belge à l'histoire de la Capitale anglaise (Brussels-Aldington, 1954); Dutch Guide Book for London (Antwerp, 1958, revised edit. 1974); Contemporary Flemish Literature (India); John Osborne, boze jonge man (Tielt/The Hague); Five Belgian Painters from London (publ. in English, French and Dutch, London and Belgium, 1961); Vier Belgische Schilders uit Londen, Bruges (1968), co-editor Focus on English III (1972) and IV (1973, both Louvain). Also poems and fiction. *Address:* 95 Black Lion La., London W6 9BG.

PERRET, Julien Bernard; chairman and managing director, Delomosne & Son, Ltd.; past pres., British Antique Dealers' Assoc.; mem. Executive Com. and past chairman, Antique Dealers' Fair and Exhbn.; specialist in English and Irish glass, English and Continental porcelains; *b* Richmond, 17 May, 1898; *s* of Julien Auguste Perret, prof. of French; *m* Marcia E. Perret. *Educ.:* Latymer Upper School. *Address:* 4 Campden Hill Rd., London W8.

PERRY, Ernest Thomas; portrait painter; joint principal, St. John's Wood Art Schools (1933-38), principal (1939); *b* Belfast, 14 Nov., 1908; *s* of Ernest Perry, schoolmaster; *m* Nina Rawson; one *s*, one *d*. *Educ.:* Brighton College; *studied art* at Heatherley's and R.A. Schools under Sir W. Russell and F. Ernest Jackson. *Exhib.:* N.E.A.C., London Group, R.A., R.P. *Address:* 34 Downshire Hill, London NW3. *Signs work:* "E.P." with date.

PERSSE, K. M., Associate, Paris Salon (1971), artist in pastel, water-colour; art teacher African C.M.S. Schools, Froebel examiner Kenya; *b* Loughrea, Co. Galway, 22 Dec., 1899; *d* of William Arthur Persse; *m* Edmund Maturin Persse. *Educ.:* Heathfield School, Ascot; *studied art* at Byam Shaw and Vicat Cole School of Art. *Exhib.:* P.S., R.I., Paris Salon, United Artists Soc., Beaux Arts Gallery, London, Cooling Gallery, Related Arts Centre. Awarded Medaille D'Argent Salon (1965). *Work repro.:* in Crown Colonist. *Address:* Bridge House, Hillcrest Rd., Hythe, Kent. *Clubs:* Ridley Art, Camden Hill, R.W.S. Art, Hesketh Hubbard Art Soc. *Signs work:* "K. M. PERSSE."

PESKETT, Eric Harry, A.T.D. (1934), A.R.C.A. (1938), R.C.A. travelling scholar (1939), F.R.B.S. (1961); sculptor; principal lecturer, Ravensbourne College of Art; *b* Guildford, 31 Jan., 1914; *s* of Charles John Peskett; *m* Marjorie Ayling; one *s*. *Educ.:* Brighton, Hove and Sussex Grammar School; *studied art* at Brighton College of Art (1929-35), R.C.A. (1935-39). *Official purchases:* fountain, Cement and Concrete Ass., Wexham Springs; Borough Polytechnic, SE1; brick reliefs, Congress Theatre, Eastbourne; crucifix, St. Mary's Church, Denton, Lancs. *Work repro.:* in Architectural Review, Wood, R.I.B.A. Journal, The Architect, Book of Garden Ornament (1974). *Address:* 12 Court Bushes Rd., Whyteleafe, Surrey. *Club:* Architectural Association. *Signs work:* "Peskett."

PETER, Robert Charles, R.E.; painter in oil, engraver in mezzotint; *b* London, 5 May, 1888; *s* of Theodore Peter, chromo-lithographer; *m* Marie Louise; one *s*, one *d*. *Educ.:* privately; *studied art* at Bolt Court, Fleet St., Central School of Arts & Crafts, under Cecil Rea, Walter Seymour, W. P. Robins. *Work in permanent collections:* British Museum, Fitzwilliam Museum, Cambridge. *Address:* 65 Ennerdale Rd., Kew Gardens, Surrey. *Club:* Chelsea Arts. *Signs work:* "R. C. Peter."

PETHERBRIDGE, Deanna, B.A.F.A. (Wits) 1959; painter in pen and ink; *b* Pretoria, 11 Feb., 1939; *d* of Harry Schwartz, Attorney; *m* Guy Petherbridge. *Educ.:* Pretoria High School for Girls; University of the Witwatersrand, Johannesburg; *studied art* at University of the Witwatersrand (1956-59) under Profs. Heather Martiensson and Charles Argent. *Exhib.:* Second British International Drawing Biennale (1975), Whitechapel Gallery, London; 1973: Aurora Galerie, Geneva, Angela Flowers Gallery, London, First British International Drawing Biennale, Middlesbrough, Warehouse Gallery, London. *Work in permanent collections:* American Telephone & Telegraph Co., Chicago; San Francisco Museum of Modern Art, San Francisco. *Publication:* The Iron Siege of Pavia (etchings illustrating text) 1975. *Address:* Radnor Studio, Holmbury St. Mary, Surrey. *Signs work:* see appendix.

PETO, Michael James, B.A. (Arch.) (Lond.), A.R.I.B.A., R.I.B.A. Donaldson Medal (1950), Dip. T.P. (1952), F.R.S.A.; architect; artist in water-colour, ink; *b* Jaffna, Ceylon, 9 Feb., 1928; *s* of the Rev. Henry Peto. *Educ.:* St. John's, Leatherhead; *studied art* at Canterbury School of Art under Robert W. Paine and Gerald Norden (1944-45); Bartlett School of Architecture, London University, under Prof. H. O. Corfiato (1945-51). *Exhib.:* Canterbury, St. John's Wood, Rhodesia. *Work repro.:* Christmas cards, etc. *Address:* P.O. Box 270, Salisbury, Rhodesia. *Signs work:* "James Peto."

PETTS, John; painter, sculptor, engraver, designer-craftsman in stained glass, mosaic, metal and plastics; *b* London, 1914; *s* of Ernest Petts, tailor; *m* Margery ("Kusha") Miller; two *s*, one *d*. *Studied art:* Hornsey Coll. of Art, Central School, Royal Acad. Schools (Brit. Inst. Scholar). *Exhib.:* widely, inc. tours by Arts Council and British Council. *Work in permanent collections:* Britain and abroad, also in many churches, public buildings. Internationally acclaimed for his large window for the bombed Negro church where four children were killed in Birmingham, Alabama, a goodwill gift from the people of Wales (1965). Best-known works in Britain: sculpture, "The Risen Christ," welded steel, St. Robert's Church, Manchester; glass, East windows, 40 ft. wide, Brighton and Hove New Synagogue, memorial to the Jews killed by the Nazi régime. Wood-engravings for The Golden Cockerel Press etc. Films of works featured by BBC (notably "Out of the Rock" and "The Affirmative Way") and ITV. Churchill Fellow 1967, U.S.A. and Mexico. Guest artist (exhbn.) 1970 Birmingham Festival of Arts, Ala., U.S.A. Retrospective Exhbn., 1975, Glynn Vivian Gallery, Swansea. Hon. R.C.A. 1975. *Address:* Cambria Hse., Llansteffan, Dyfed. *Signs work:* "John Petts."

PETZSCH, Helmut Franz Günther, D.A. (Edin.) 1951; F.S.A. Scot.; art teacher and painter in oil and water-colour; principal teacher of art, Castlebrae H.S., Edinburgh; *b* Berlin, 13 Dec., 1920; *s* of Max Leberecht Petzsch; *m* Catherine Oag; one *s*, two *d*. *Educ.:* Hamburg and London; *studied art* at Edinburgh College of Art (1947-51) under Sir William G. Gillies, C.B.E., R.S.A. *Exhib.:* R.S.A., S.S.A., '57 Gallery, Edinburgh. *Publication:* author of Architecture in Scotland (Longman). *Address:* 32 Canaan Lane, Edinburgh EH10 4SU. *Club:* Scottish Arts. *Signs work:* "Helmut Petzsch."

PEVSNER, Sir Nikolaus, C.B.E., M.A., Ph.D.; Emeritus Prof. of the History of Art, Birkbeck College, University of London; *b* 30 Jan., 1902; widower; two *s*, one *d*. *Educ.:* St. Thomas's Leipzig; Universities of Berlin, Leipzig and Munich. *Publications:* Pioneers of Modern Design (Penguin ed., 1960), Industrial Art in England (C.U.P., 1937), Academies of Art, Past and Present (C.U.P., 1940), An Outline of European Architecture (Penguin Books, most recent edition), High Victorian Design (1951), The Englishness of English Art (1956), Studies in Art, Architecture and Design (1968), The Buildings of England (1951-71). *Addresses:* 2 Wildwood Terr., North End, London NW3, and 12 Bloomsbury Sq., London WC1.

PHILIPSON, Robin, P.R.S.A. (1973), A.R.A., Hon. R.A. (1973), R.S.W.; 3rd Prize, John Moores Exhbn. (1959); Cargill Award, G.I. (1966); painter in oil and water-colour; Secretary, R.S.A. (1969); Member of Royal Fine Art Commission for Scotland; Member of Council, Edin. Festival Society; Fellow of the Royal Society of Arts; Head of School of Drawing and Painting, Edinburgh College of Art; Visiting Professor of Painting, Summer School, University of Colorado, Boulder, U.S.A. (1963); *b* Broughton-in-Furness, 17 Dec., 1916; *s* of James Philipson; *m* (1st) Brenda Mark (1947), (2nd) Thora Clyne (1962). *Educ.:* Dumfries Academy; *studied art* at Edinburgh College of Art. *Exhib.:* London and Edinburgh. *Work in permanent collections:* art galleries in England and Scotland. *Address:* 23 Crawford Rd., Edinburgh 9. *Club:* Scottish Arts. *Signs work:* "R. Philipson."

PHILLIP, Albert, A.R.E. (1956), A.R.C.A. (1940), R.C.A. Drawing Prize, Sir Frank Short Prize Award; art lecturer and practising artist in water-colour and oil, printmaking; art lecturer, Lancaster and Morecambe College of Art; *b* Skipton, Yorks., 28 Jan., 1915. *Educ.:* St. Stephen's R.C., Skipton; *studied art* at Skipton Science and Art School (1934) under Col. E. H. Llewellyn, M.C., A.R.C.A., and Dan Binns, C. & G. Silver Medal, Royal College of Art (1937) under Malcolm Osborne, O.B.E., R.A., R.E., Robert Austin, R.A., R.E., Frank Dobson, R.A. *Exhib.:* R.A., R.E., U.S.A., and many other galleries. *Address:* 5 West St., Greaves, Lancaster. *Signs work:* "A. Phillip, A.R.E., A.R.C.A."

PHILLIPS, Aubrey R., A.R.W.A., P.S., U.A., Gold Medal, Paris Salon; artist/teacher in pastels, water-colour and oil; director of own Painting Courses; *b* Astley, Worcs., 18 June, 1920; *m*; three *s*. *Studied art* at Stourbridge and Kidderminster Schools of Art. *Exhib.:* F.B.A. London (two-man show), National Library of Wales, Civic Galleries in Worcester Gloucester and Hereford. *Work in permanent collection:* Worcester City A.G. *Publications:* illustrated articles contributed to Art Magazines. *Address:* 2 Sandhampton, Astley, Stourport-on-Severn, Worcs. *Signs work:* "Aubrey R. Phillips."

PHILLIPS, Ewan Godfrey, M.A. (Lond.), History of Art (1938); private dealer, art historian and dealer in nineteenth- and twentieth-century paintings and sculpture, Mem. International Association of Art Critics, Association of Art Historians, I.C.A.; *b* London, 16 Mar., 1914; *s* of Godfrey Phillips, late owner of Godfrey Phillips Galleries. *Educ.:* Epsom College and Courtauld Institute of Art (Univ. of London); *studied art* at Goldsmiths' College of Art, Courtauld Institute of Art under Sir Anthony Blunt, Professor W. G. Constable, Professor T. S. R. Boase, etc. *Publications:* Thesis, English Expressionist and Artists in the Nineteenth Century (see note in "William Blake", by Dr. Bronowski). *Address:* 60 Credition Hill, Hampstead, London NW6. *Club:* The Savile.

PHILLIPS, John Henry, A.T.D., M.C.C.Ed. (1947), F.R.S.A.; finalist, City and Guilds (handicrafts), Lond. (1948); artist in oil, water-colour; Administrator,

School Examinations Dept., University of London, responsible for art, technical subjects; Head of Art, Handicraft, Harold Hill Gram. Sch., Romford (1957-65), Chatham House Gram. Sch., Ramsgate (1952-57), Luton Gram. School (1947-52); *b* Horsham, Sussex, 26 May, 1920; *s* of E. H. E. Phillips, M.Coll. H.; *m* Gladys Phillips, S.R.N.; one *s*, one *d*. *Educ.:* Gram. Sch., Cowbridge, Glam.; *studied art:* College of Art, Cardiff, from 1936, under Evan Charlton, William Pickles. *Exhib.:* New Herts. Art Soc., Ramsgate Art Soc. *Address:* 3 Priory Rd., Harold Hill, Romford, Essex. *Signs work:* "J. Phillips."

PHILLIPS, Patrick Laurence; specialist in 19th- and 20th-century art; Joint Managing Director of Ernest Brown and Phillips Ltd., Proprietors of the Leicester Galleries, 22A Cork St., W1; Agents for Epstein since 1917, Russell Drysdale since 1950, and responsible for a great number of first exhibitions in England; organiser of the 1964 Festival exhbn., Henry Moore at King's Lynn, held throughout the town; *b* London, 1 July, 1912; *s* of Cecil Laurence Phillips, co-founder of the Leicester Galleries, Leicester Square, in 1902; *m* Margaret Elinor Chapman; two *s*. *Educ.:* Stonyhurst College; *studied art* in the museums of Europe. *Addresses:* 164 Coleherne Ct., London SW5, and Brandon House, Horn Hill, Dartmouth.

PHILLIPS BROCKLEHURST, C. D. F., B.A. (Oxon.); Chairman of Trustees, Wallace Collection; Trustee, Lady Lever Art Gallery; Governor, Whitworth Art Gallery; Hon. Curator, Macclesfield Museum and Art Gallery. *Educ.:* Eton, Christ Church (Oxford) and Vienna. *Addresses:* Hare Hill, Macclesfield, Ches., 3 West Eaton Pl., London SW1. *Clubs:* Whites, Beefsteak.

PHILLIPS-HAYTER, Helen; sculptress-engraver; Museum of Art Purchase Prize and Phelan Travelling Fellowship (San Francisco, 1936); Walter Sculpture Prize (1934); Pluegger Sculpture Prize (1947); International Awards; Unknown Political Prisoner representing France; Copley Foundation Award (1958); sculptress in stone, architecture multiples; *b* Fresno, Calif., U.S.A., 3 Mar., 1913; *d* of Louis H. Phillips; *m* Stanley W. Hayter; two *s*. *Studied art* at California Institute and Atelier 17, in U.S.A. and Paris. *Work in permanent collections:* San Francisco Museum of Art; Achenbach Coll.; Dallas Museum of Contemporary Sculpture; Albright-Knox Museum; V. & A., etc. *Addresses:* 737 Washington St., N.Y.C.; 36 rue Boissonade, Paris 14. *Signs work:* "Helen Phillips" or "Helen Phillips Hayter."

PIC: see HIGGINS, Charles S.

PICART LE DOUX, Jean; painter, tapestry designer, lithographer; Hon. Prof. Ecole Nat. Sup. des Arts Décoratifs, Paris; hon. pres. Assoc. des Peintres Cartonniers de Tapisserie; hon. pres. Alliance Graphique Internationale; *b* Paris, 31 Jan., 1902; *s* of Charles Picart le Doux, painter; *m* Annie Bellier. *Educ.:* Lycée Condorcet, Paris; *studied art* at private schools. *Exhib.:* Galerie de France, Maison de la Pensée Française, Musée Galliera, Galerie La Demeure, Galerie du Passeur, Galerie Verrière, Salon d'automne, Salon des Artistes Dècorateurs, Paris; Lausanne, Zürich, Berlin, Copenhagen, Rome, Florence, Hagen, Cologne, São Paulo, Milan, Bruxelles, Montréal, Moscow, Vienna, London, and thirty museums in U.S.A. *Address:* 163 avenue Victor-Hugo, Paris 16. *Signs work:* "Jean Picart le Doux."

PICHÉ, Roland, 1st Class N.D.D., A.R.C.A., Medal for Work of Distinction, R.C.A.; sculptor in resin, fibreglass and stainless steel; lecturer in sculpture; Senior Lecturer, Maidstone College of Art; *b* London, 21 Nov., 1938; *m* San-San; two *d*. *Educ.:* Romsey College, Embley Park, Hants,; *studied art* at Hornsey College of Art (Mr. C. Anderson, A.R.C.A., 1956-60), Royal College of Art (Mr.

B. Meadows, A.R.C.A., 1960-64). *Work in permanent collections:* The Arts Council of Great Britain and Wales, São Paulo Museum, Gothenburg Museum, Sweden, National Gallery of Western Australia. *Publications:* Private View (B. Robertson and T. Armstrong-Jones), Dada, Surrealism (W. S. Rubin). *Address:* Victoria Studios, Tollesbury, Essex. *Signs work:* see appendix.

PICKARD JENKINS, Perçy, F.S.I.A.; designer and teacher, package design, advertising and stained glass; designer, Metal Box Co. Ltd. (1936-40); draughtsman (war production), Metal Box Co. Ltd. (1940-45); art director, J. Walter Thompson Co. Ltd. (1945-50); freelance since 1950; lecturer, London School of Printing and Graphic Arts (1951-54); consultant designer, Metal Box Co. Ltd. (1954-58); head of Department of Graphic Design, Croydon College of Art (1961-71); *b* Swansea; *s* of William John Jenkins and Sarah Jane Pickard; *m* Elsa Lewis. *Studied art* at Swansea College of Art. Designer of Pickard Tuscan Type-Face for W. S. Cowell. *Work repro.:* International Design Publications. *Address:* 241 Pentregethin Rd., Manselton, Swansea, W. Glamorgan. *Signs work:* "P. Pickard Jenkins" or "P.P.J."

PICKEN, Mollie, N.D.D. (1963), A.T.C. (1964); freelance artist in pen and ink, embroidery and fabric collage; part-time teacher, North Oxon Technical College and School of Art; *b* 13 Oct., 1940. *Studied art* at Goldsmiths' College School of Art (1959-64) under Constance Howard and Betty Swanwick. *Work in permanent collections:* various Education Authorities. *Publications:* illustrated, Inspiration for Embroidery by Constance Howard; Colour in Embroidery by Constance Howard. *Address:* The Old Post Office, Sibford Gower, Banbury, Oxon. *Clubs:* British Craft Centre, S.D-C., Embroiderers' Guild, New Embroidery Group.

PICKING, John, N.D.D. (1960), D.A. Edin. (1962), A.T.D. (1966); painter and lecturer; Mem. Manchester Academy; Senior Lecturer in Fine Art, Manchester Polytechnic. *Studied art* at Wigan School of Art, 1956-60 (Governors Medal); Edinburgh College of Art, 1960-63 (Postgrad. Scholarship); Goldsmiths' College, London, 1965-66. *Exhib.:* regularly with Scottish Gallery, Edinburgh, Colin Jellicoe Gallery, Manchester, Mercury Gallery, London, Galleria 32, Milan. *Work in permanent collections:* Salford University, Edinburgh Corp., private collections in many parts of the world. Often living and painting in Sicily; interested in peasant-type communities, Sicily to Lapland to Armenia; gives illustrated talks to societies, etc. *Address:* c/o Colin Jellicoe Gallery, 82 Portland St., Manchester 1.

PIECH, Paul Peter, F.I.A.L., F.S.T.D. (1959); artist in lithography, woodcuts, water-colour, oil; *b* 11 Feb., 1920; *s* of Makary Piech; *m* Irene Tompkins; one *d.* *Educ.:* elementary schools and Brooklyn College, N.Y.; *studied art* at Cooper Union College of Art, N.Y.; Chelsea Polytechnic and School of Art; Central School of Art, London. *Official purchases:* Museum of Modern Art, N.Y., Philadelphia Museum of Art, Florida State College of Art, Cincinnati Museum of Art, Library of Congress, Washington D.C., U.S.A. *Publications:* War and Misery, Christ—Words and Wisdom of Martin Luther King; De Profundis—Sayings of Christ; John F. Kennedy—Profile of Courage; William Blake's "AMERICA." *Address:* Brooklyn, 2 Willow Dene, Bushey Heath, Herts. *Clubs:* A.I.A., Soc. of Typographic Artists, International Inst. of Arts and Letters. *Signs work:* "Paul Peter Piech."

PIERCE, Charles E., R.I.; artist in oil, water-colour, pastel, scraper board, wood engraving, etching, pen and ink, etc.; *b* Edinburgh; *s* of W. J. Pierce; *m* Dorothy Bell; one *s.* *Educ.:* George Heriot's School, Edinburgh; *studied art* at Edinburgh College of Art and R. Scot. Academy schools. *Exhib.:* R.A., R.S.A., etc. *Work repro.:* in The Studio, The Artist, etc. *Address:* 2 Harewood Row, London NW1. *Clubs:* Savage, Chelsea Arts, London Sketch. *Signs work:* PIERCE, and sometimes with a P only, and see appendix.

PIERCE, Norman F., A.R.C.A., F.R.B.S.; sculptor; mem. Soc. Portrait Sculptors; teacher, St. Thomas's Further Education Centre; *b* Lewisham, 1915; *s* of Charles F. Pierce; *studied art* at Reading University School of Art under Prof. A. W. Seaby, Prof. A. Betts, Albert C. Carter, F.R.B.S. (1931-35), and under Prof. R. Garbe, R.A. (1935-38). *Exhib.:* R.A. and Paris Salon. *Public works:* eight heraldic coats of arms, new county offices, Winchester; figures of Christ, Christchurch Grammar School, Highcliffe; bronze plaque portrait of Dr. Palmer, founder of the Science of Chiropractic. *Address:* 4 Wessex Drive, Winchester. *Signs work:* "Norman Pierce."

PILE, Albert Thomas, M.S.M., F.R.S.A., S.G.A.; illustrator, etcher, lithographer, painter; official artist, Min. of Inf. (1942-44); art teacher at Huddersfield Technical College; radio broadcaster; *b* London, 15 Aug., 1882; *s* of Matthew Henry Pile, engraver; *m* Ethel Stott. *Educ.:* King's College, London; *studied art* at Central School of Art under W. P. Robins, Camberwell School of Art under R. Schwabe, R. V. Pitchforth and I. Strang, Goldsmiths' College of Art under S. Anderson, J. Bateman, J. G. Platt, Bournemouth College of Art under L. M. Ward. *Exhib.:* Paris Salon, R.S.A., R.H.A., R.W.A., S.G.A., National Gallery, S. Kensington Museum, Leeds University and provincial galleries. *Work in permanent collections:* V. & A. (paintings and drawings). *Work repro.:* illustrations for Recording Britain, Shropshire Hills; Brighouse: Portrait of a Town; Early Timbered Buildings of the Huddersfield District, York's Golden Fleece, The Manor, Lordship and Castle of Danby. *Address:* Valmiki, 16 Stakesby Rd., Whitby, Yorks. YO21 1HS *Signs work:* "ALBERT T. PILE" (handwriting or block letters); and "PILE" (block letters).

PILKINGTON, Richard Godfrey, M.A. (Cantab.); art dealer and publisher; owner, Piccadilly Gallery, 16A Cork St., W1, since 1953; vice-chairman of Society of London Art Dealers; editor The Art Bulletin (1951-60); *b* Stafford, 8 Nov., 1918; *s* of Guy R. Pilkington; *m* Evelyn (Eve) Vincent; two *s*, two *d*. *Educ.:* Clifton and Trinity College, Cambridge. *Address:* 45 Barons Court Rd., London W14.

PILLEY, Vivien, F.R.B.A., M.S.I.A.; industrial artist and interior decorator in private practice; *b* Chevreuse, Seine-et-Oise, France, 28 Sept., 1907; *s* of Leopold Pilichowski, painter; one *d*. *Educ.:* Lycée Français: St. John's, Hurstpierpoint, and under Dr. Fritsh; *studied architecture* at A.A., Bedford Sq., WC1. *Publications:* Architectural Review, Architects' Journal, Architectural Illustrated, Architecture d'aujourd'hui, The Builder, House and Garden, Home and Garden, Ideal Home, The Studio Year Book (Decorative Art), Design, etc. *Address:* 45 Shepherd's Hill, Highgate, London N6. *Signs work:* see appendix.

PILLOW, Lorna Mary Carol, A.R.C.A.; Sir Frank Warner Memorial Medal; textile and graphic designer; taught, Croydon and Berkshire Colleges of Art; full-time lecturer, West Surrey College of Art and Design; *d* of W. Farquhar Pillow; *widow* of Peter John Palmer; one *s*. *Educ.:* Wolverhampton and Leeds; *studied art* at Leeds, Hull and the Royal Colleges of Art. *Exhib.:* Beverley Art Gallery, Ferens Art Gallery, Guildhall, R.W.S. Galleries Britain Can Make It Exhibition, R.S.A. Travelling Exhibition, Design Centre, London. *Work repro.:* International Textiles, Cabinet-maker; illustrated Geography of Flowering Plants. *Address:* 33 Havelock Rd., Maidenhead, Berks. *Signs work:* "Lorna Pillow."

PINDER, John Michael. D.A.(Manc.), Dip.A.D. (1970), M.S.D-C. (1974);

teacher/craftsman in jewellery; lecturer in jewellery, Isleworth Polytechnic; *b* Windsor, Berks., 30 Apr., 1948; *s* of A. T. Pinder, F.I.G.C.M., F.Inst.L.Ex. *Educ.:* Windsor Grammar School; *studied art* at Manchester Polytechnic (1966-70) under D. Frost and R. Semple; Gillian E. Packard's Workshop, London (1970-73); Stig Berg's Workshop, Copenhagen (1973-74); Tony Law's Workshop, London (1974). *Exhib.:* V. & A., Goldsmiths Hall, British Crafts Centre, Kunstindustrimuseum, Copenhagen, O'Keefe Centre, Toronto. *Address:* 87 Bedfont La., Feltham, Middx. *Signs work:* "J. M. Pinder."

PINKS, G. A. (Miss); Hon. mem., Salon des Artistes Français (1929); artist in oil and water-colour, specializing in children's portraits; *b* 1 Sept., 1890; *d* of E. C. Pinks, F.S.I. *Educ.:* The Study, SW19; *studied art* at Grosvenor Studio under Walter Donne (1909-12), and in Paris under Lucien Simon (1912-13). *Exhib.:* R.A., R.I., S.W.A., W.I.A.C., R.P., Salon des Artists Français, Canadian Soc. of Artists, Ontario Soc. of Artists, and English provincial galleries. *Work repro.:* several. *Address:* 12 Bedford Gdns., London W8. *Signs work:* "G. A. Pinks" (surname underlined).

PIPER, John, C.H.; painter, theatrical designer, author, mem. Royal Fine Art Commission (since 1960), mem. of Oxfordshire Diocesan Advisory Com. (since 1950); trustee, Tate Gallery (1946-60); *b* 13 Dec., 1903; *m* Myfanwy Evans, author; two *s*, two *d*. *Educ.:* Epsom College; *studied art* at R.C.A. *Work in permanent collections:* Tate Gallery, V. & A., decorations for British Embassy, Rio de Janeiro, etc. *Official purchases:* Tate Gallery, C.A.S., water-colours of Windsor Castle commissioned by H.M. the Queen Mother, many stage designs for ballet and opera at Royal Opera House, Glyndebourne, Scala, Milan, etc. Designed stained glass (executed by Patrick Reyntiens) for Plymouth, Oundle School, Coventry (Baptistery), etc. *Address:* Fawley Bottom Farm House, Henley-on-Thames, Oxon.

PITCHFORTH, Roland Vivian, A.R.C.A., R.A., R.W.S.; artist in water-colour; *b* 23 Apr., 1895; *s* of Joseph Pitchforth, shopkeeper; *m* Edith Brenda Pitchforth. *Educ.:* Wakefield Grammar School; *studied art* at Leeds School of Art (1913-15, 1919-21); Royal College of Art (1921-25) under Leon Underwood. *Exhib.:* London Artists Assoc., Wildenstein, Leicester Gallery, Redfern, Lefevre. *Work in permanent collections:* Tate, V. & A., Leeds, Bradford, Southport, Rochdale, Aberdeen, Helsinki, Glasgow, Manchester, Salford, Portsmouth, Wakefield, Huddersfield. *Address:* Flat 17, No. 7 Elm Park Gdns., London SW10 9QG. *Club:* Chelsea Arts. *Signs work:* "Pitchforth."

PITFIELD, Thomas Baron, N.R.D., Hon. F.R.M.C.M.; artist in water-colour, reed-pen, lino-cut, lettering; composer; art master; *b* Bolton, Lancs., 5 Apr., 1903; *s* of Thomas Baron Pitfield; *m* Alice Maud Astbury. *Educ.:* Bolton and Manchester; *studied art:* Municipal School of Art, Bolton (apprenticed in Engineer's drawing-office). *Exhib.:* R.A., Northern Academy of Fine Arts, and various one-man exhbns. *Work repro.:* Artist, Countryman, and other periodicals, calendars, etc. *Publications:* Junior Course in Art Teaching, Senior Course in Art Teaching, The Poetry of Trees, Recording a Region, and a large number of musical compositions. *Address:* Lesser Thorns, 21 East Downs Rd., Bowdon, Ches. *Signs work:* see appendix.

PITMAN, Primrose Vera, S.G.A. (1953), L.R.A.M., Gold Medal for Design; painter in water-colour, commercial artist in pencil; etcher; *d* of James L. Pitman. *Educ.:* St. Hilda's School; *studied art* at Royal Albert Memorial School of Art under Burman Morrall and James Sparks. *Exhib.:* R.W.E.A. and provincial galleries. *Work in permanent collection:* Royal Albert Memorial Museum. *Official* *purchases:* City of Exeter. *Publications:* Etchings and pencil drawings in This Jewel Remains (1942). *Work repro.:* repro. of pencil drawing of Exeter Cathedral for Preservation Fund organized by Mayor of Exeter. *Address:* Marlands, 4 Victoria Park Rd., Exeter. *Clubs:* Exeter Art Soc., Kenn Group. *Signs work:* "Primrose V. Pitman."

PLANASDURÁ, E., I.I.A.L. (Zürich); painter in oil; founder-mem. of Grupo Lais in Real Circulo Artistico de Barcelona, and signatory of Primer Manifiesto Negro (1949); mem. Grupo de Altamira (1949); mem. Cercle Maillol, Barcelona (1947); Founder-Mem. Asociación de Artistas Actuales (1956); Mem. of Jury. Los Premios Juan Gris and Julio Gonzales a perpetuidad (1957); Com. for Exhbn. of Spanish Art in London; *b* Barcelona, 2 Oct., 1921. *Exhib.:* Barcelona (1944, '45, '46, '48, '49, '50, '51, '61, '63); Exp. Palma de Mallorca (1962); official exhbns., Madrid, Paris, Colombia, Panama, Santander, Switzerland, Italy, Bogota, Medellin, Chile, Brazil and corresponding Biennials and trade shows; Brussels, Munich, Buenos Aires, Finland. *Address:* Canuda 13.3.2, Barcelona. *Signs work:* see appendix.

PLANTE, George, F.R.S.A., M.S.I.A.; creative director SSC & B—Lintas International Ltd.; creative director (1945-61), Young & Rubicam, Ltd.; art director, Political Intelligence Dept. of Foreign Office; Middle E. Forces (1943-45); *b* 18 Sept., 1914; *m*; one *s*. *Educ.:* George Heriot's School, Edinburgh; College of Art, Edinburgh (1929-33); Contempora, Berlin (1933). *Exhib.:* British American Art Centre, New York, and leading American galleries. *Official purchases:* War Artists' Advisory Com. *Work repro.:* in New York Times, Art News, etc. *Address:* Studio House, Templewood Ave., London NW3. *Club:* Pres. of Advertising Creative Circle (1955-56). *Signs work:* "PLANTE."

PLATT, Eric Warhurst, A.R.C.A., Silver Medallist (1940); artist in line and wash, water-colour, etching, lettering, and creative cut card relief; Vice-Principal, Doncaster College of Art; *b* Cudworth, Yorks., 2 May, 1915; *s* of John R. Platt, A.V.C.M.; *m* Mary Elizabeth; one *s*, one *d*. *Educ.:* Wakefield and Doncaster School of Art; *studied art* at R.C.A. under Malcolm Osborne, R.A., and Robert Austin, R.A. (1937-40). *Exhib.:* R.A., Brighton, West Riding Artists exhbn., Yorkshire Artists exhbn., Doncaster A.G., Feren's Gallery, Hull, Graves Gallery, Sheffield., etc. *Address:* 73 Grenville Rd., Balby, Doncaster. *Signs work:* "Eric Platt."

PLATT, John Gerald, A.R.C.A. (1924), A.R.E. (1924); princ., Harrow Technical and Art School (1930-47); princ., Hornsey College of Art (1947-57); chief assessor, M. of E. art examinations (1956-66); artist in oil, wood-engraving, etching; *b* Bolton, Lancs., 21 Dec., 1892; *s* of Thomas Platt (decd.); *m* Doreen May Hewison; one *s*. *Studied art* at King Edward VII School of Art, Armstrong College, Newcastle upon Tyne, Leicester College of Art (1919-20), R.C.A. (1920-24). *Exhib.:* R.A., R.P., Old International Soc., Paris, Stockholm, Canada, America. *Work in permanent collections:* V. & A., Manchester Art Gallery, Bolton Art Gallery, Los Angeles Museum, Welsh National Library. *Address:* 30 Kersey Rd., Flushing, Falmouth, Cornwall. *Signs work:* "John G. Platt" or "John Gerald Platt" or "J. G. Platt."

PLATT, Michael, A.R.C.A.; painter; taught painting at Southampton College of Art (1945-53); Birmingham College of Art (1953-55); head of art dept., Mayfield School, Putney (1960-63); Senior lecturer in art, N.W. Polytechnic, NW5 (1967-69); *b* 29 Sept., 1914; *s* of John Platt, A.R.C.A., F.S.A.M.; *m* Joan Dickson, A.R.C.A.; one *s*, two *d*. *Exhib.:* London Group, Brighton, Arts Council. *Special interests:* light and movement, painting. *Official purchases:* paintings by

L.C.C. *Address:* The Loft (Studio), Ashley Lane, Lymington, Hants. *Signs work:* "Michael Platt."

PLATT, Stella; artist in oil, water-colour, pastel and black and white (industrial scenes of Lancashire and the Pennines); *b* Bolton, 11 Sept., 1913; *d* of Henry Woodcock, constructional engineer; *m* John Kenworthy-Platt, B.A., solicitor; two *d. Educ.:* Heaton Academy, Bolton; Bolton School of Art. *Exhib.:* R.S.A., R.B.A., R.O.I., R.I., Paris Salon, S.G.A., S.W.A., Manchester, etc. *Work in permanent collections:* Blackburn, Bolton, Bury, Manchester (Rutherston Collection), Salford, Eccles, Lancaster, Oldham. *Work repro.:* in Art for Today and Textile Recorder. *Address:* Tanglewood, Dimples Lane, Garstang, nr. Preston. *Clubs:* Manchester Academy, Lancs Group of Artists, etc. *Signs work:* see appendix.

PLAZZOTTA, Enzo Mario; sculptor in bronze and marble; *b* Mestre (Venice), 29 May, 1921; *s* of Silvio Plazzotta; *m* Gillian Antonia Beamish; two *s,* one *d. Educ.:* Academia di Brera; *studied art:* sculpture with Giacomo Manzu, architecture at the Politecnico in Milan (1938-46). *Commissioned work:* The Lewes Memorial, Lewes. *Exhib.:* one-man exhbns. Grosvenor Gallery, London, Marjorie Parr Gallery, London, Acquavella Galleries, New York, G.A.M., Paris, Bruton Gallery, Somerset, Compendium Galleries, Birmingham, Galerie Rolly-Michaux, Boston, John Gage Gallery, Eastbourne, Edinburgh Festival, Ladlane Gallery, Dublin, Hogarth Gallery, New Orleans, Kovler Gallery, Chicago, Galerie Chedel, Geneva, Jewish Museum, Israel, Queensland Art Gallery, Brisbane, David Jones Art Gallery, Sydney, Artarmon Gallery, N.S.W., Australia; open air exhbns. Stowe, Cirencester Park, King's Lynn Festival, Birmingham Tulip Festival, Lewes Festival. *Address:* 6 Upper Cheyne Row, London SW3. *Signs work:* "PLAZZOTTA."

PLENDER, Donald James; painter, designer; exhibits internationally; P.E., Commonwealth of Massachusetts; *b* New York, 1932; *s* of Paul A. Plender. *Educ.:* M.A. (1960), San Francisco State College, B.Sc. (1953), Union College, New York, California School of Fine Arts, University of California, American University, Corcoran School of Art. *Address:* 8 Albert Studios, Albert Bridge Rd., London SW11 4QD.

POLLOCK, (Sir) George F., Bt., M.A. (Cantab.), F.R.S.A., F.R.P.S.; artist-photographer; Vice-President, Royal Photographic Society; retired solicitor; *b* 13 Aug., 1928; *s* of Sir John Pollock, Bt., M.A., Barrister-at-Law, Officer Legion of Honour (etc.); *m* Doreen Mumford *née* Nash; one *s,* two *d. Educ.:* Eton College and Trinity College, Cambridge. *Exhib.:* Photokina (1966, 1974), New Vision Centre (1965), Musée de St. Paul, France, I.P.E.X. (New York), City Library, The Hague, F.P.S. *Work in permanent collections:* British Council, R.P.S., National Gallery of Victoria, Musée de Photographie, Bièvres, Towner A.G., Eastbourne, Texas University, University of Surrey. *Publications:* books illustrated, Gernsheim's Shorter History of Photography, Focal Encyclopaedia of Photography, Penguin's Colour Photography. *Address:* Netherwood, Stones Lane, Westcott, Dorking, Surrey. *Clubs:* Landsdowne, Ski Club of G.B., Downhill Only. *Signs work:* "George F. Pollock."

POMERANCE, Fay; painter, wood-carver; *b* 1912; *d* of Sol Levy; *m* Ben Pomerance; one *d. Educ.:* King Edward's High School, College of Art, Birmingham. *Exhib.:* one-man shows: "Theme of Lucifer" and other works; (1949-72) Archer and Ben Uri Galleries, London; Liverpool, Wakefield, Batley, Derby, Middlesbrough, Newcastle, Gateshead municipal galleries, R.B.S.A., Birmingham, Oxford, Sheffield, Nottingham, Leicester University centres; group shows: London and provinces, Canada, New Zealand; represented London exhbns.,

Leicester, Redfern, Molton, S.W.A., P.S. *Work in permanent collections:* Batley, Gateshead municipal galleries, Ben Uri, Israel Museum, Hull and Stafford Educ. Comm., stained-glass window: Birmingham Synagogue. *Address:* 21 Clarendon Rd., Sheffield S10 3TQ. *Signs work:* "Fay Pomerance."

POOLE, Monica, A.R.E. (1967), R.E. (1975); Central School Diploma (1949); Member of the Art Workers' Guild; wood engraver and illustrator; *b* Canterbury, 20 May, 1921; *d* of C. Reginald Poole; *m* Cmdr. A. G. M. Small, R.N., F.I.H.V.E. *Educ.:* Abbotsford, Broadstairs; *studied art* at Central School of Arts and Crafts (1945-49). *Exhib.:* R.A., R.E., Society of Wood Engravers, etc. *Work in permanent collections:* V. & A., Ashmolean Museum, Museum Boymans van Beunegen, Rotterdam, Hunt Botanical Museum, Pittsburgh, U.S.A., Pistoia Art Gallery, South London Art Gallery, Essex County Council, K.C.C. *Address:* 67 Hadlow Rd., Tonbridge, Kent. *Signs work:* "MONICA POOLE."

POPE, Perpetua, D.A.(Edin.) 1947; painter in oil; lecturer in visual arts, Moray House College of Education (1968-73); *b* Solihull, Warwicks., 29 May, 1916; *d* of John Robert Pope. *Educ.:* Albyn School, Aberdeen; *studied art* at Edinburgh College of Art under W. G. Gillies, John Maxwell, Leonard Rosoman. *Exhib.:* one-man shows: Scottish Gallery, Edinburgh; mixed shows: R.A., R.S.A., S.S.A., S.S.W.A., Aberdeen Artists, Stirling Gallery. *Work in permanent collections:* Scottish Arts Council, Nuffield Trust, Argyll County Council. *Address:* Weavers Cottage, Carlops, nr. Penicuik, Midlothian. *Signs work:* "Perpetua Pope."

POPE-HENNESSY, Sir John, C.B.E. (1959), F.B.A.; Director, British Museum; *b* 13 Dec., 1913; *s* of Major-Gen. L. H. R. Pope-Hennessy. *Educ.:* Downside; Balliol College, Oxford. *Publications:* Giovanni di Paolo (1937), Sassetta (1939), Sienese Quattrocento Painting (1948), A Sienese Codex of the Divine Comedy (1948), The Drawings of Domenichino at Windsor Castle (1949), Paolo Uccello (1950), Fra Angelico (1952), Italian Gothic Sculpture (1955), Italian Renaissance Sculpture (1958), Italian High Renaissance and Baroque Sculpture (1963), Italian Sculpture in the V. & A. (1964), The Portrait in the Renaissance (1967), The Frick Collection: Sculpture (1970), Raphael (1970), etc. *Address:* 41 Bedford Gdns., London W8.

PORTCHMOUTH, Roland John, A.T.D.; author, artist, poet; *b* London, 1923; *m* Susan. *Studied art* at Harrow and Hornsey Art Colleges. *Exhib.:* R.B.A., R.A., R.O.I., other London and Municipal Galleries; one-man shows: Bath, Bristol. *Official purchases:* R.A., R.B.A., Education Authorities, National Trust, American Museum, Bath, Canadian Pacific Railway. *Publications:* Creative Crafts for Today; All Kinds of Papercrafts; Working in Collage (Studio Vista, Viking); Secondary School Art (Studio Vista, Van Nostrand Reinhold); How to Make Things from the Beach (Studio Vista); Poetry (Wylderness Press). Broadcaster on art education and poetry. *Address:* 17 Crossland Cres., Peebles, Scotland. *Signs work:* "Portchmouth."

PORTEOUS-WOOD, James, R.S.W. (1945); portrait, mural and landscape artist in oils, water-colour, black and white; chief artist and designer to Aspreys; *b* Edinburgh, 1919; *m*; one *s*. *Educ.:* George Heriot's School; *studied art* at Edinburgh College of Art, 1936-40 (Travelling Scholarship), under R. H. Westwater, R.S.A., W. F. Rayner, also with Sir D. Y. Cameron, R.A., R.S.A. *Exhib.:* R.A., R.S.A., R.S.W., G.I., several one-man shows, murals in Royal Palace, Kathmandu, and private residences. *Publications:* Midland Riches (Hancock), Yorkshire Dales (Harrison), also several private editions with miniatures (including Calligraphy). *Work repro.:* numerous editorial drawings mainly architectural, industrial, landscape and portrait in national Press and colour magazines. *Address:* 165 New Bond St., London W1. *Signs work:* "Porteous Wood."

PORTNER, Alexander Manrico; artist and portrait painter; designer of lithographs, specializing in the Regency period; originator of Organic-wood-painting, a process by which oil paint is applied translucently *into* planed wood so that the grain becomes part of the painting, transferring to it the feeling, intrinsic to wood of being organic and thereby part of life, in particular where skin textures are concerned. The Organic-wood-painting technique was originated by Alex Portner in 1950, first exhibited in 1960 and has been recorded under his name at the Frick Art Reference Library, New York, in 1973; *b* Berlin; *s* of Polish father, Dr. E. Portner, surgeon, and of White-Russian mother, Marussa Portner. *Studied art* in Amsterdam under Riskine, in Paris under Soutras, in Berlin under Kaus. Served in the British Army (1940-43). *Exhib.:* R.A.; group shows: Wildenstein Gallery; Royal Portrait Society; one-man shows: New Art Gallery (1960); Walton Gallery (1965); Gallery Petit (1969); Hilton Art Gallery (1971); Madden Gallery, London (1974); F.N.B. Galleries, Palm Beach, U.S.A. (1971); Whalespout Gallery and Hemingway Gallery, Nantucket, U.S.A. (1971); Selected Artists Galleries, New York (1973). *Pictures in permanent collections:* St. John's College, Oxford; private collections: The Abraham-Curiel Collection, London; The Mr. and Mrs. Patrick Vaughan Collection, London; The Maria Pollitt Collection, London; The Dr. and Mrs. Robert Schneider Collection, Bredon; The Immanuel Bierer Collection, London; The Flagler-Matthews Collection, Palm Beach, U.S.A. *Address:* 16 Bolton Studios, Gilston Rd., London SW10. *Signs work:* see appendix.

PORTSMOUTH, Delia; painter of landscapes, portraits, flowers, birds, wildlife in oils; *b* Mottram, Ches., 6 Aug., 1939; *d* of Edward Ford, farmer; *m* A. C. Portsmouth; four *d. Educ.:* Hyde and Bala Grammar Schools; *studied art:* self taught. *Exhib.:* R.O.I., Hesketh Hubbard, Flower Painters' Summer Salon; one-man shows: Chester, Lampeter, Bala, Brantwood, St. Davids, Usher Gallery, Lincoln. *Work in permanent collections:* National Library of Wales, National Museum of Wales, Liverpool Corp. and numerous private collections worldwide. *Address:* Cwmhwylfod, Cefnddwysarn, Bala, Gwynedd. *Club:* founder member, Modern Millais Association. *Signs work:* "Delia Portsmouth."

PORTWAY, Douglas Owen; European painting prize (Belgium) Bronze Medal (1969), Gold Medal (1971); taught at Witwatersrand School of Art and Witwatersrand University (1941-46); delegate to Ford and Rockefeller Foundations International Art Programme (1952); painter in oil on canvas and paper; *b* Johannesburg, 1922, (British Citizenship, 1960); *m* Caroline Shackell (1966); two *s*, one *d. Educ.:* mainly self-educated; *studied art* at Witwatersrand School of Art, S.A. (1940-41). *Exhib.:* one-man shows: Spain, Germany, Paris, Africa and England; retrospective: Pretoria Art Museum (1967); mixed: Venice Biennale (1956), John Moores (1961), Musée d'Art Moderne, Paris (1965). *Work in permanent collections:* Tate Gallery, V. & A., Scottish National A.G., Stuyvesant Foundation, Musée des Beaux Arts, Belgium, School Art Loans, Leeds, Manchester City A.G., Nuffield Foundation, Tatham A.G., Durban A.G., Schlesinger Organization, S. African National Gallery, King George VI A.G., Sandton A.G., Johannesburg A.G., University of Witwatersrand, Anglo-American Corp. *Work repro.:* in Contemporary British Art by Herbert Read (Pelican Publications) and a monograph Douglas Portway by George Butcher (20th Century Masters Publishing Co.). *Addresses:* Salubrious House, St. Ives, Cornwall; and "Le Sage", Razac D'Eymet, 24500 Eymet, France. *Signs work:* "Portway."

POSNETT, David Wilson, M.A.; art dealer; director, Leger Galleries; *b* 6 May, 1942. *Educ.:* The Leys, and Trinity College, Cambridge. *Address:* 13 Old Bond St., London.

POTTER, Donald, F.R.B.S.; sculptor in stone, wood and ivory; *b* Newington, Kent, 21 Apr., 1902; *m* Mary Potter; one *s*, one *d*. *Studied art:* pupil of Eric Gill. *Official purchases:* Sculptures in St. George's Chapel, Windsor, St. Paul's Cathedral, Zomby Cathedral (Nyasaland), The Baden-Powell Statue (Queens Gate), Winchester College. *Address:* Bryanston, Blandford, Dorset. *Signs work:* see appendix.

POTTER, Frank Hayden; *studied art* at the Slade under Henry Tonks, Wilson Steer and Randolph Schwabe; Central School, Westminster under Walter Bayes and typography under H. W. Thomas at the Baynard Press; formerly Head Art Dept., Pocklington, St. Peter's York, and Whitgift School, Croydon; sometime Chief and Senior Examiner G.C.E. Oxford, Cambridge, Oxford & Cambridge, London and Wales. *Exhib.:* 1928 onwards: R.A. (on the line), Paris Salon, London Group, New English, Royal Society of Portrait Painters and National Society. Served both wars, France 1914-18, 11th Hussars 87th Foot and 8th Hussars. *Address:* 22 Raglan Rd., Reigate. *Clubs:* Savage, Chelsea Arts. *Signs work:* "Potter" in italics.

POTTER, Mary; artist in oil and water-colour; *b* Beckenham, Kent, 9 Apr., 1900; *d* of J. A. Attenborough, solicitor; *m* Stephen Potter (marriage dissolved); two *s*. *Educ.:* private school; *studied art* at Slade School (Slade Scholar). *Exhib.:* one-man shows, Bloomsbury Gallery (1931), Redfern Gallery (1934-49), Tooth's Gallery (1939 and 1946), Leicester Galleries (1951, 1953, 1954, 1957, 1961, 1963), Retrospective, Whitechapel A.G. (1964), New Art Centre (1967, 1969, 1972, 1974). *Work in permanent collections:* Tate Gallery, Arts Council, Manchester City A.G., Contemp. Art Soc., Ferens A.G., Hull, and galleries in New York, Canada and Australia. *Address:* Red Studio, Aldeburgh, Suffolk. *Signs work:* "Mary Potter" or "MP."

POUNCEY, Philip Michael Rivers, F.B.A., M.A. (Cantab.), Hon. Attaché, Fitzwilliam Museum, Camb. (1931-33); asst., National Gallery (1934-45); asst. keeper, Dept. of Prints and Drawings, British Museum (1945), deputy keeper (1954-66); visiting prof., Columbia University, New York (1958), New York University (1965); director, Sotheby & Co. (1966); *b* 15 Feb., 1910; *s* of Rev. G. E. Pouncey; *m* Myril Gros; two *d*. *Educ.:* Marlborough; Queens' College, Camb. *Publications:* Catalogues of Italian Drawings in the British Museum, 14th and 15th c. (with A. E. Popham), Raphael and his Circle (with J. A. Gere); contributions to Burlington Magazine, etc. *Address:* 5 Addison Gdns., London W14.

POUNTNEY, Albert, A.R.C.A., Prix de Rome, F.R.B.S.; sculptor in stone, fibreglass, metals, cements; Head, School of Fine Art City of Leicester Polytechnic; director, Pountney Wright and Ford, Design Consultants, Ltd.; *b* Wolverhampton, 19 Aug., 1915; *s* of William Pountney, panel beater, sheet metal worker; *m* Jane Pountney, designer; one *d*, graphic designer, illustrator. *Studied art* at Wolverhampton Art School (1931-35) under R. J. Emerson, Royal College of Art (1935-38) under Prof. Garbe, British School at Rome (1938-39). *Publications:* Modelling a Figure from Life (Alec Tiranti). *Address:* The Lodge, Bitteswell, nr. Rugby.

POWELL, John, A.R.C.A.; painter and teacher of drawing and painting; Principal, Portsmouth College of Art and Design; *b* Nottingham, 27 Aug., 1911; *s* of William Powell; *m* Freda Heathcote; one *d*. *Educ.:* Trent Bridge School, Nottingham; *studied art* at R.C.A. under Gilbert Spencer (1935-39) and Nottingham College of Art (1932-35). *Exhib.:* R.A., R.B.A., R.O.I., N.E.A.C., London Group, S.M.A., N.S., Kensington Art Gallery, United Artists, and many provincial galleries. *Official purchases:* Bristol Educ. Com. (The Harbour, Tenby),

Manchester Educ. Com., oil paintings (A Child at Breakfast, A Fair at Twilight). *Address:* Fishbourne Farmhouse, Old Fishbourne, Chichester, Sussex. *Signs work:* "John Powell."

POWELL, Sir Philip, O.B.E., A.R.A., F.R.I.B.A., A.A. Dip. (Hons.) 1943, S.A.D.G. Bronze Medallist (1942); Member, Royal Fine Art Commission; architect in partnership with Hidalgo Moya and Peter Skinner; *b* Bedford, 15 Mar., 1921; *s* of Rev. Canon A. C. Powell, M.A.; *m* Philippa (*née* Eccles). *Educ.:* Epsom College; *studied architecture* at A.A. *Works include* Churchill Gdns., Pimlico; South Bank Skylon; British Pavilion, Expo. '70, Osaka; Mayfield School, Putney; Plumstead Manor School; Hospitals at Swindon, Slough, High Wycombe and Wythenshawe; Wolfson College, Oxford; new buildings at Brasenose, Christ Church and Corpus Christi, Oxford, and St. John's and Queens' Colleges, Cambridge; Chichester Festival Theatre. *Address:* 30 Percy St., London W1.

PRASSINOS, Mario, Croix de Guerre (1940), Chevalier des Arts et Lettres; painter, etcher and designer of tapestry; *b* Istanbul, 30 July, 1916; *s* of Lysander Prassinos, professor; *m* Yolande; one *d. Educ.:* Ecole des Langues Orientales, Faculte des Lettres, Paris. *Work in permanent collections:* Musée d'Art Moderne, Paris, Athens Pinacothek, Turin Museum, Wellington Museum, Stedelijk Museum, Amsterdam, Musée d'Antibes, Musée de la Chaux de Fonds, Kunst und Museumsverein, Wuppertal, Museum of Modern Art, New York, Guggenheim, New York, Gemeente Museum, Arnhem, Museum fur Kunst und Gewabe, Hamburg, etc. *Work repro.:* Heresiarque et Cie., Instant Fatal, Le Mur, The Raven, etc. *Address:* 18 villa Seurat, Paris, 14. *Signs work:* see appendix.

PRATT, Derrick Edward Henry, A.R.C.A. (1922); artist in oil, water-colour; principal, Llanelli School of Art (1923-60); *b* Walsall, 18 Dec., 1895; *m* Edith O'Brien (1926); one *d. Educ.:* Acton County School; *studied art* at Leeds College of Art (1910-15), R.C.A. (1919-23). *Exhib.:* R.A. and S. Wales Art Socs., S. Wales Group. *Work in permanent collections:* Landscape Swansea, and Llanelli. *Address:* 3 Bloomfield Rd., Harpenden, Herts. *Signs work:* "D. E. H. Pratt."

PRETSELL, Peter, D.A. (Edin.); artist in etching, lithography, painting; lecturer in printmaking, Nene College, Northampton; *b* Edinburgh, 1942; *s* of William Pretsell; *m* Philomena Pretsell; two *s. Educ.:* George Heriots School, Edinburgh; *studied art* at Edinburgh College of Art (1960-65). *Exhib.:* New St. Gallery, Printmakers Workshop, S.S.A. (Edinburgh), Northampton, Birmingham, Newcastle, Kettering, Bedford. *Work in permanent collections:* V. & A., Scottish Arts Council, Edinburgh Corp., Northampton A.G. *Address:* 91 Clarence Ave., Northampton. *Signs work:* "Peter Pretsell."

PRICE, E. Jessop, S.W.A. (1951), Mem. of Council (1956); painter in oils; *b* Ashby-de-la-Zouch; *d* of J. N. Moxon; *m* Rev. A. Jessop Price; four *s. Educ.:* Ashby and Versailles. *Studied art* at St. Ives School of Art (Leonard Fuller), St. Martin's School of Art (Archibald Zeigler), Heatherley's (Iain Macnab). *Exhib.:* one-man show at R.W.S. Gallery (1949), S.W.A., R.O.I., Bradford Art Gallery, City of London Guildhall, etc.; awarded Freedom of the Worshipful Company of Painter Stainers in 1957. *Official purchases:* St. Paul's Cathedral, Chase National Bank, N.Y., Newton Chambers, etc. *Work repro.:* The Soho Gallery, Daily Telegraph, etc. *Address:* Sefton, Stade St., Hythe, Kent. *Signs work:* "E. Jessop Price."

PRIDDEY, James, P.R.B.S.A. (1974), S.G.A., F.R.S.A.; Silver Medal, Paris Salon (1949); hon. secretary, R.B.S.A. (1966); artist, engraver, publisher, etchings, aquatints, dry-point, water-colour, etc.; *b* Handsworth, Birmingham, 19 Apr., 1916; *s* of James Priddey, mechanical engineer, violin-maker and collector of

Chinese porcelain; *m* Marguerite Joan Sykes-Waller; one *s. Educ.:* Moseley School of Arts and Crafts, Moseley, Birmingham; Birmingham College of Art (H. Holden, A.R.C.A., A. E. Harvey, A.R.C.A., 1931-35). *Exhib.:* R.B.A., R.B.S.A., R.E., R.S.A., R.Cam.A., R.W.A., S.G.A., S.M.A., S.G.P., Paris Salon (bronze medal, 1948), Bradford City Art Gallery, Atkinson Art Gallery, Southport, one-man show Bilston Art Gallery, R.A. (1967), East, West Gallery, New York. *Official purchases:* South London Art Gallery, Camberwell, and Brierley Hill Art Gallery. *Work repro.:* Birmingham Post (drawings), illustrations for book Heart of England (100 drawings) pub. Robert Hade, drawings for Birmingham Telephone Directory. *Address:* 22 Fellows La., Harborne, Birmingham 17. *Signs work:* "James Priddey."

PRIDE, Phyllis Elsie, R.C.A. (1956), S.W.A. (1969), Associate Mem. Society des Artistes Francaise (1971), Medaille d'Or, Paris Salon (1960), Medaille d'Argent (1955), hon. mention, Paris Salon (1954), L.R.A.M. (pianoforte); portrait painter in oil and water-colour; *d* of W. H. Wedlock, company director; *m* Eric Pride; two *s. Studied art* at Heatherley's (1938) with R. G. Eves, A.R.A. *Exhib.:* R.A., R.Scot.A., Paris Salon, N.E.A.C., R.P.S., R.B.A., S.W.A., R.O.I. *Address:* 1 Petyt Pl., Chelsea, London SW3. *Signs work:* "P. E. Pride."

PRIEST, Margaret Diane, M.Art, R.C.A.; John Minton Scholarship, Silver Medal; artist in pencil and water-colour, part-time lecturer; *b* Tyringham, Bucks., 15 Feb., 1944; *d* of Arthur Edmund Priest; *m* Tony Scherman; one *s. Educ.:* Dagenham County High School; *studied art* at South West Essex School of Art (1963-64); Maidstone College of Art (1964-67); Royal College of Art (1967-70). *Exhib.:* Hommage to John Constable, Tate Gallery (1976), British Exhbn., Basel (1975), Garage Art Ltd., London (1974), Critics Choice, Tooth's Gallery (1974), Arnolfini Gallery (1970, 1974). *Work in permanent collections:* Arts Council of Gt. Britain, British Council, Dallas County Museum, Texas. *Address:* 185 Ashley Gdns., Emery Hill St., London SW1. *Signs work:* "M. D. Priest."

PRINCE, Alison Mary, Slade Dip. (1952), A.T.D. (Distinction) (1955), A.R.E. (1956); freelance writer and illustrator in pen and ink and etching; *b* Beckenham, Kent, 26 Mar., 1931; *d* of Charles Prince; *m* Goronwy Siriol Parry; two *s*, one *d. Educ.:* Beckenham Grammar School; *studied art* at Slade School (1948-52) under Coldstream, Goldsmiths' College (1954). *Publications:* Joe—a children's television series, War Stories for Jackanory (B.B.C. TV); written and illustrated The House on the Common and The Red Alfa (children's books, Methuen), and articles for The Times Ed. Supp.; illustrated Let's Explore Mathematics and Jessica on Her Own. *Address:* 28 Hawes Rd., Bromley, Kent. *Signs work:* "Prince."

PRINET, Jean; Conservateur en chef à la Bibliothéque Nationale, Paris (1935); *b* Rambouillet, France, 15 May, 1912. *Educ.:* Lycée Henry IV, Sorbonne and Ecole du Louvre; *studied history of art* under H. Focillon, René Schneider, P. Lavedan, P. Vitry, G. Brière (1929-34) and at Marburg-Lahn under R. Hamann (1934). *Publications:* Le Portrait gravé, La Photographie et ses applications, Les illustrations de J. E. Laboureur, Constitution d'archives photographiques d'œuvres d'art, U.N.E.S.C.O. (1951), Collaboration au livre de Jean Laran l'Estampe (2 vols., P.U.F., 1959), Directeur (1959-62) de la collection Kiosque (Les Faits, La Presse, L'Opinion), Nadar (1966). *Address:* 72 rue de Seine, Paris, 6e.

PRINSEP, Anthony; artist in oil, gouache, water-colour, sculptor in wood and illustrator; *b* Shenstone, Staffs., 1908. *Educ.:* Durham School, Royal Military College, Sandhurst, Royal Veterinary College, London; *studied art* at L.C.C.

Central School of Art (1931-35) and other London art schools. *Exhib.:* London Group (1935), Leicester Gallery, Wildenstein, Mayor, Redfern, St. George's, S.E.A., Painter's Progress Exhbn., Whitechapel Gallery; one-man shows: Aldeburgh Festival, Beaux Art Gallery, Drian Gallery (1963, 1965). *Work in private collections:* in G.B., America, Sweden, Denmark, Portugal. *Work repro.:* Colonial Office, Corona Library volumes on Uganda, Nyasaland and Sierra Leone. *Address:* Tjørnevej 9A, Snekkersten, Denmark. *Signs work:* "Prinsep."

PRITCHARD, Arthur, A.R.I.C.S. (1957), A.R.Cam.A. (1969); Chartered Surveyor; artist in oil and tempera; Princ. Assistant, Highways Dept., Anglesey C.C.; *b* Llanystumdwy, 12 May, 1927; *s* of H. Ivor Pritchard; *m* Pauline; two *s*. *Educ.:* Portmadog Grammar. *Exhib.:* Arts Council, Wales, Contemporary Art Society, Wales, Howard Roberts Gallery, Cardiff, Tegfryn Gallery, Menai Bridge, Plas Mawr, Conway. *Address:* Garreglwyd, Lon Tudur, Llangefni. *Signs work:* "Arthur Pritchard."

PRITCHARD, Gwilym, R.C.A. (1960); artist in oil and tempera; art master, Friars School, Bangor, (retd. from teaching, 1973); *b* Llanystumdwy, Caerns., 4 Mar., 1931; *m* Claudia Williams, portrait painter; three *s,* one *d. Educ.:* Portmadog Grammar School; *studied art* at Bangor, Birmingham School of Art (1950-54). *Exhib.:* Mansard A.G., London. *Work in permanent collections:* Arts Council, Contemporary Art in Wales, Newport A.G., Nuffield Foundation, Educ. authorities of England and Wales. Commissioned to paint 25th Field Regiment Royal Artillery in Belfast (1975). *Address:* Plas Gwyn, Kingston Rd., Weobley, Hereford. *Signs work:* "GWILYM PRITCHARD."

PROCKTOR, Patrick; painter and stage designer; *b* Dublin, 12 Mar., 1936; *m* Kirsten Benson, *née* Bo-Andersen (1973). *Studied art* at Slade School (1958-62). Works represented in numerous public collections. *Publications:* author of One Window in Venice, publ. 1974 (16 water-colour views, published by Galleria Cavallino, Venice). *Address:* 26 Manchester St., London W1.

PROCTER (née PALMER), Marjorie, A.T.D. (1940); artist in water-colour, pencil and wash; art teacher, Ealing School of Art (1943-74); art teacher. Liverpool Inst. for Boys (1941-43); *b* Birmingham, 17 Feb., 1918; *d* of the late W. H. Palmer, B.A.(Cantab.), M.I.Chem.E., F.R.I.C.; *m* Kenneth Procter, painter (1964). *Educ.:* Wade Deacon Grammar School, Widnes; *studied art* at Liverpool City School of Art (1935-40). *Exhib.:* R.A., R.I., R.B.A., Nat. Soc., United Soc. of Artists, S.M.A., S.W.A., R.I. Summer Salon, Britain in Water-colour. *Address:* Spring Cottage, Woonton, Almeley, Herefordshire. *Signs work:* "Marjorie Procter," either written or in block capitals.

PROCTOR, Brenda, B.A. (Fine Art) (Hons.) 1970, Grad.C.E. (1971); painter in oil, collage, mixed media; director, Portfolio Gallery, Scunthorpe; *b* Manchester 9 June, 1948; *d* of Frank Cuttle, electrical engineer; *m* John Wilson Procter, agricultural fieldsman. *Educ.:* Thomas St. Primary, Central Grammar, Manchester; *studied art* at University of Newcastle upon Tyne (1966-70) under Kenneth Rowntree, Ian Stephenson. *Exhib.:* Hatton Gallery, Newcastle, Laing Gallery, Newcastle, Haworth Gallery, Accrington. *Work in permanent collections:* Colin Jellicoe Gallery, Manchester, Portfolio Gallery, Scunthorpe. *Address:* Old Police House, Appleby, nr. Scunthorpe, Lincs. *Signs work:* "Brenda Procter."

PROPHET, William Harry Marsden, F.R.S.A.; artist in oil; *b* St. Ives. *Educ.:* Rugeley School, Staffs., and Deytheur Grammar School, Llansantffraid, Mont.; *studied art* at Penzance School of Art under Bouverie Hoyton, R.S., F.R.S.A. (1944), Huddersfield School of Art (1950), Education Centre, Spandau, Berlin under Almuth Gittermann (1951), also studied as only pupil of T. Heath Robinson. *Exhib.:* oil painting reproductions and official water-colour impressions, Post Office Tower, London. 200 paintings reproduced as prints, designs and executes specialised interiors. *Address:* Warren House, Clarence St., Penzance, Cornwall. *Club:* The Penzance. *Signs work:* see appendix.

PROUDMAN, M. Eyre; see LOVELY, Maureen Patey.

PUHN, Franklin; sculptor in stone, wood, plastic; *b* Erfurt, Germany, 20 May, 1925; *m* Regina-Maria Kittel; two *d. Educ.:* Elementary and High School, Erfurt; Schiffbaupraktikant, Hamburg; *studied art* at Holzbildhauerei, Erfurt (1948-52) and at Akademie d.b. Kunste, Stuttgart under Prof. Otto Baum, sculptor. *Exhib.:* Stuttgart (1952), Berlin (1952), London (1953), Dusseldorf (1953), Ulm (1968), Aalen (1969), Göppingen (1970), Paris u. Biarritz (1971). *Official purchases:* various commemorative medals, Wurttemberg (1952-53). *Address:* 792 Heidenheim. Teckstr. 15, Germany. *Clubs:* Wurttemberg, Verband d. bild., Kunstler Stuttgart. *Signs work:* see appendix.

PULLAN, Margaret Ida Elizabeth; Paris Salon: Gold Medal (1972), Silver Medal (1967); artist in oil; *b* Saharanpur, U.P., India, 6 Nov., 1907; *d* of Ayrton George Popplewell Pullan, M.A.(Oxon), late I.C.S. *Educ.:* Highfield, Oxhey Lane, Watford, Herts; *studied art:* privately. *Exhib.:* Paris Salon (1957-58, 1963 (hon. mention), 1965-71), R.P., R.B.A., Leicester Galleries, Bournemouth, Bradford, Cartwright Memorial Hall, United Soc. of Artists. *Work in permanent collections:* Rugby A.G. *Address:* The Dene, Forest Way, Tunbridge Wells, Kent. *Signs work:* see appendix.

PULSFORD, Charles, A.R.S.A.; painter and three-dimensional; was art teacher now freelance artist; *b* 8 June, 1912; *m* L. Bronwen Gordon, artist; two *s*, one *d. Educ.:* Aberdour, Dunfermline High School; *studied art* at Edinburgh C. of A. *Exhib.:* R.S.A., S.S.A., London Group, Gimpel Fils Gallery, Scottish Gallery, Demarco Gallery (Edinburgh), New Charing Cross Gallery (Glasgow), Ledlanet (Scotland), Ikon Gallery (Birmingham), Stirling University etc.; also in France and U.S.A. *Work in permanent collections:* Arts Council (Scottish Committee). *Publication:* The Creative Cell (1973), thesis, limited subscription edition. *Address:* The Green, Abbots Bromley, Staffs. *Signs work:* see appendix.

PUOKKA, Jaakko Ilmari, GrFenO, D.Ph.; author in History of Fine Art; *b* Helsinki, 5 July, 1915; *s* of Waino Puokka; *m* Terttu; six *d. Educ.:* Helsinki University. *Publications:* Finnish Graphic Art (1945), Gunnar Finne, Sculptor (1948), Magnus Enckell, Painter (1949), Ten Essays of Art (1953), Hattula Medieval Church (1956), Greece of Gods and People (1959), The Art of Drawing in Finland (1966), Erkki Tanttu, Wood engraver (1967). *Address:* Laivurinkatu 25, Helsinki.

PYE, William, A.R.C.A. (1965); sculptor in stainless steel, film; *b* 16 July, 1938; *s* of Sir David Pye, M.A., Sc.D., F.R.S., C.B.; *m* Susan; one *s*, two *d. Educ.:* Charterhouse; *studied art* at Wimbledon School of Art (1958-61) under Freda Skinner, R.C.A. Sculpture School (1961) under Prof. B. Meadows. *Work in permanent collections:* Arts Council, Museum of Modern Art, N.Y., Contemporary Art Soc., G.L.C., University of Warwick, Leicester Educ. Authority, Royal Albert Memorial Museum, Exeter, Graves City A.G., Sheffield, Camden Borough Council, Middlesbrough City A.G. *Address:* 43 Hambalt Rd., Clapham, London SW4. *Signs work:* see appendix.

Q

QUICK, George Graham; carpet designer; with Carpet Trades, Ltd., Kidderminster (1928-32), Blackwood Morton & Sons, Ltd., Kilmarnock, since 1932; *b* Kidderminster, 2 May, 1911; *s* of Sydney Quick; *m* Lilian Mabel Tree; one *d*. *Educ.:* King Charles I School, Kidderminster; *studied art* at Kidderminster School of Art under W. E. Daley, carpet design under Harold Davies. *Exhib.:* Manchester Textile Centre, S.I.A. Textile Exhbn. (1949), Enterprise Scotland (1948), Design Centre, Gold Medal Award, Sacramento (1962), S.I.A. Exhibition, Whitworth Gallery, Manchester (1963). *Address:* 39 Wilson Ave., Troon, Ayrshire. *Signs work:* "G. Graham Quick."

QUIGLY, Elizabeth Pauline; designer, writer, environmentalist, book reviewer; *b* Limpsfield, Surrey, 1916; *d* of the late R. F. Quigly. *Educ.:* Old Palace School, Croydon; *studied art:* work influenced by extensive study of Asian art. *Exhib.:* Arts and Crafts Exhbn. Soc., Embroiderers' Guild, Oxted Eisteddfod, Guild of Many Crafts, Aldeburgh Festival. *Work in permanent collections:* Embroiderers' Guild; *designs purchased by:* Thomas de La Rue, Embroiderers' Guild, Hulton Press, etc. *Work repro.:* playing cards (De La Rue), etc. *Publications:* Embroidery Stitches (1948); Some Observations on Libraries, Manuscripts and Books of Burma, 36-pp. illus., A. Probsthain, London, 1956; Asian Design in Transmigration (in preparation). *Permanent address:* c/o Grindlays Bank, 13 St. James's Sq., London SW1. *Signs work:* see appendix.

R

RAACH, Richard; sculptor in stone and wood; *b* Reutlingen, Wurttemberg, 21 Jan., 1906; *s* of Gottlob Raach, sculptor; *m* Hildegard Hammer. *Educ.:* four years under father; *studied art* at Art School, Stuttgart. *Exhib.:* Christliche Kunst unserer Zeit, Freiburg (1949); Kirchliche Kunst der Gegenwart, Stuttgart (1952); Bildende Hande, Stuttgart (1952); Malerei u. Plastik aus Württemberg, Hohenzollern Touring exhbn. of the Ministry of Culture (1952); Der unbekante politische gefangene, Berlin-London (1952-53). *Official purchases:* Reutlingen and Rottweil, Local Authority, Caln, Architectural sculpture, religious and secular, Bauten. *Address:* Reutlingen, Württemberg. *Signs work:* "Raach."

RAE, John; tutor to Diploma in Architecture, University College London; *b* Exeter, 1931. *Address:* 15 Heath Hurst Rd., Hampstead, London NW3.

RAEBURN, Kenneth Alexander, D.A.(Edin.) (1966); Post Grad. Scholarship (1966-67); sculptor in bronze, resins and wood, of free-standing figures, portraits and relief murals; principal teacher of art, Comprehensive School; *b* Haddington, E. Lothian, 9 June, 1942; *s* of Francis James Raeburn; *m* Helen Raeburn; one *s*, one *d*. *Educ.:* Trinity Academy, Edinburgh; *studied art* at School of Sculpture, Edinburgh College of Art under Eric Schilsky. *Exhib.:* R.S.A., S.S.A., various group exhbns. in Scotland, Dunkeld A.G., Mews Theatre Gallery, Livingston. *Work in permanent collections:* commissioned panel depicting Baptism of Christ by St. John, in St. John the Baptist Primary School, W. Lothian (awarded Saltire Society Commendation, 1972); work in numerous private collections in U.K. *Address:* c/o 40 Netherby Rd., Trinity, Edinburgh. *Signs work:* "Raeburn."

RÀKÒCZI, Basil Ivan; painter, sculptor, writer; *b* London, 31 May, 1908; *s* of Ivan Ràkòczi. *Studied art:* Brighton School of Art and under Ossip Zadkine. *Exhib.:* Molton Gallery, Galerie Suillerot. Foundation member of White Stag Group. *Work in permanent collections:* Auckland City A.G., National Coll. Queensland and Barbados, V. & A., Hull, Leeds. *Work repro.:* Three Painters, Adventure in Art, The Painted Caravan, Song Book of Idiot Boy, The Caged and the Free, In the Beginning, Yarrow Cards of Destiny. Contributor to Man, Myth and Magic. *Clubs:* Gypsy Lore Soc., Folk Lore Soc., Société des Amis. *Address:* 5 rue Georges Bouzerait, 92 Montrouge, France. *Signs work:* "Ràkòczi."

RAMBISSOON, Sonnylal, A.C.P. (1959), N.D.D. (1964), A.T.C., London (1965), A.R.E. (1968); 1959 Trinidad Scholar in Fine Art; printmaker; art teacher; lecturer, Extra Mural Dept. University of West Indies; art critic; advisor, Trinidad and Tobago Stamp Committee; *b* Trinidad, W.I., 5 Apr., 1926. *Educ.:* Government Training College, Port of Spain; Brighton College of Art; Goldsmiths' College, London; Atelier 17, Paris; Art Students League, New York. *Exhib.:* London, New York, Washington, São Paulo, Cali, Caracas, San Juan and Port of Spain. *Address:* P.O. Box 1, Sanfernando, Trinidad, W1. *Signs work:* see appendix.

RAMIS, Julio; painter in wax and lacquer; *b* Soller, Majorca, 20 July, 1910; *m* Joan Foster; one *s*, four *d*. *Educ.:* Soller; *studied art* from age of 16 at Barcelona, Madrid; at free centres. *Exhib.:* First Biennial Hispano-Americano, Madrid (1952), Orient-Occident, Paris (1957), Museo Arte Moderno, Madrid (1959), 30th Biennial, Venice (1962), New Vision Centre, London (1965), Galeria Durán (1971), Casablanca (1971), Palma de Mallorca (1971), Beca (Prize) Fundación Juan March, Madrid (1971). *Work in permanent collections:* Museo Arte Contemporaneo, Madrid; Musée, Lyons; Musée d'Arte Moderne, Paris. *Publications:* Pintura (text, Paul Bowles), Julio Ramis (text, André Lubac), 20 Años de Pintura (Arean), España: 30° Bienal, Venecia, Primera Bienal Hispano-Americano. *Address:* 4 rue Marco Polo, Tangier. *Signs work:* see appendix.

RAMSDEN, Eric, N.D.D. (1950), A.R.E. (1960), Fellow, Society of Wood Engravers; artist in gouache, oil, wood engraving; *b* Runcorn, Cheshire, 22 June, 1927; *s* of William Ramsden; *m* Anna Maria; one *s*. *Educ.:* Runcorn County Grammar School; *studied art* at Liverpool College of Art (1943-45, 1948-50) (H. P. Huggill, A.R.E., R.C.A., Geoffrey H. Wedgwood, R.E., A.R.C.A., Will Penn, R.O.I., R.P.). *Exhib.:* R.A., R.W.S. Galleries, South London Gallery, provincial galleries, Liverpool Walker Art Gallery. *Work in permanent collections:* private collections in America and England. *Address:* The Priory, Freefolk, Whitchurch, Hants. *Signs work:* "Eric Ramsden."

RANKIN, Stella, Dip. in painting, Goldsmiths' College (1960), F.P.S.; painter in oil; Mem., West Wales Artists and Designers Group; *b* London, 1915; *d* of William Bartlett; *m* A. C. Rankin; one *d*. *Educ.:* St. John's Priory, Banbury; *studied art* at St. Martin's School of Art (1958-59) under Kenneth Martin; Goldsmiths' College (1959-61). *Exhib.:* one-man shows: Studio Club, W.I., Library U.S.A.A.F. Base, Lakenheath; group shows; Suffolk Gallery, A.I.A., Festival Hall, Guildhall, Loggia Gallery, Galerie Internationale, N.Y. *Address:* 7 Brynymor Terr., Aberystwyth. *Signs work:* "S.R."

RASCH, Lady (Catherine Margaret), J.P.; artist in oil and pastel; *b* London, 29 May, 1891; *d* of the Hon. John Boscowen; *m* 1st, Lionel, 16th Lord Petre (d of wounds, 1915); one *s*, one *d*; 2nd, Col. Sir Frederic Carne Rasch, Bt. *Educ.:* privately; *studied art* at Byam Shaw and Slade Schools of Art. *Exhib.:*

Paris Salon, R.O.I., P.S. *Address:* 9 Trevor St., London SW7. *Signs work:* "C. M. Rasch."

RASMUSSEN, Steen Eiler, R.D.I., corresponding mem. R.I.B.A.; architect; Prof. at Royal Academy of Arts, Copenhagen (1938-68); *b* Copenhagen, 9 Feb., 1898; *s* of Gen. Eiler Rasmussen; *m* Karen Margrete Schrøder; two *d. Educ.:* Metropolitanskolen, Copenhagen; *studied architecture* at Royal Academy of Arts, Copenhagen. *Publications:* London, the Unique City (1937), Towns and Buildings (1951), Experiencing Architecture. *Address:* Dreyersvej 9, Rungsted Kyst, Denmark.

RATCLIFF, John, O.B.E. (1952), F.R.I.B.A. (1955), F.R.T.P.I. (1972), F.F.P.S. (1959); architect and painter in oil on canvas; partner in Howard V. Lobb & Partners, architects for British Pavilion, Brussels International Exhibition (1958), City and Guilds of London Headquarters, Portland Place, W1, Hunterston and Dungeness B Nuclear Generating Stations, etc.; *b* Mirfield, Yorks., 22 Jan., 1914. *Educ.:* Shrewsbury School, Dijon and Göttingen Universities, Architectural Association School of Architecture (General Honours Diploma). *Address:* Terrace Cottage, 132 Richmond Hill, Richmond TW10 6RN. *Club:* Reform. *Signs work:* see appendix.

RATHBONE, Perry Townsend; Hon. Dr. of Arts degree, Washington University, St. Louis; director, Museum of Fine Arts, Boston (1955-72); Trustee: American Federation of Art, Rhode Island School of Design, New England Conservatory of Music; mem. visiting committee Fogg Art Museum, Harvard U., Pres. Assoc. of Art Museum Directors (1960, 1970); *b* 3 July, 1911; *s* of Howard Betts Rathbone; *m* Euretta de Cosson; one *s,* two *d. Educ.:* Harvard University. *Address:* Christie's U.S.A., 867 Madison Ave., N.Y., U.S.A. *Clubs:* Century Association, New York; Club of Odd Volumes, Boston; Harvard Club of Boston; Tavern Club, Boston; Massachusetts Historical Society; The Colonial Society of Massachusetts.

RATHMELL, Thomas Roland, A.R.C.A.; Mem. European Group; painter of figure subjects and portraits in oil and drawing mediums; Head of Dept. of Fine Art, Newport (Mon.) College of Art (1963-72); *b* Wallasey, 3 Sept., 1912; *s* of Bernard Rathmell, consulting engineer. *Educ.:* Wallasey Grammar School; *studied art* at Liverpool College of Art; R.C.A. *Work in permanent collections:* Welsh Arts Council, Contemporary Art Soc. for Wales, public galleries in Cardiff, Newport and Swansea. *Address:* 2 Fairfield Cl., Caerleon, Mon. NP6 1DR. *Signs work:* "T. RATHMELL" or "THOMAS RATHMELL."

RAVERA, John, A.R.B.S. (1968); sculptor in clay, glassfibre and resin; *b* Surrey, 27 Feb., 1941; *m* Daphne. *Educ.:* Camberwell Junior School of Art (1954-57); *studied art* at Camberwell School of Art (1957-62) under C. Vogal, assistant sculptor to F. Mancini, A. Nemon. *Exhib.:* Walberswick (1960, 61, 62), Ealing Abbey (May, 1970), Guildhall (City) (June 1970), Richmond Park (May, June, 1970), Whitegift Galleries (Sept., 1970), York Open Air Show (July, 1971), Rye (July, 1971), Augustine Gallery (Nov., 1971, Aug., 1972), Hounslow Festival Sculpture (June, 1972), R.A. (1975). *Address:* Studio, 82 Latham Rd., Bexleyheath, Kent. *Signs work:* "John E. Ravera."

RAWLINS, Darsie, A.R.C.A. (1934), F.R.B.S. (1961); sculptor in stone, wood, bronze; *b* Kentmere, 27 Mar., 1912; *s* of G. E. H. Rawlins, designer and craftsman in metalwork; *m* the Hon. Rachel Elizabeth, eldest daughter of the late Lord and Lady Boston; two *s,* two *d. Educ.:* Bembridge School; *studied art* at R.C.A. *Exhib.:* R.A. *Commissions* include sculpture on Denbighshire Technical College, Wrexham; Church of St. John Fisher, Rochester; Princesshay, Exeter; St.

Andrew's Church, Roxbourne; Hampshire County Offices; Tewkesbury Abbey; Royal Tank Regiment Memorial, St. Peter-upon-Cornhill; Staines Municipal Offices. *Address:* Red Tiles, Kingswood Ave., Penn, Bucks.

RAWLINS, Janet, N.D.D. (Illustration), A.T.D., artist/designer, fabric collage, gouache, water-colour, wall-hangings; *b* Horsforth, Leeds, 3 May, 1931; *d* of E. J. Rawlins; *m* Kenneth Parfitt (died 1971); one *s. Educ.:* Gt. Moreton Hall, Ches.; *studied art:* Leeds College of Art. *Exhib.:* R.A. Many one-man shows in northern galleries. *Official purchases:* Bradford, Harrogate and Batley Art Galleries, Leeds, Huddersfield, West Riding, Leicester and Essex Education Committees, Leeds Permanent Building Society, International Wool Secretariat, I.C.I. *Work repro.:* Design, House and Garden, Dalesman, Waddingtons. *Address:* Unicorn House, Bainbridge, Wensleydale, N. Yorks. *Signs work:* "Janet Rawlins."

RAWLINSON, William Thomas, A.T.D. (1945) Médaille d'or Paris Salon (1960), S.W.E. (1971); painter, engraver, art teacher; official war artist (1943-46); *b* Liverpool, 12 Jan., 1912; *s* of Thomas Rawlinson, schoolmaster; *m* F. E. Patricia Martin. *Educ.:* Quarry Bank High School; *studied art* at Liverpool College of Art (1929-35) under Will C. Penn, R.O.I., Geoffrey Wedgewood, R.E.; Senior City Art Travelling Scholarship (1932) studied abroad in France, Italy, Czechoslovakia, Austria and Germany. *Exhib.:* R.E., Paris Salon, R.A., R.C.A., R.S.A. *Work in permanent collections:* Imperial War Museum, Ashmolean Museum Oxford (Dept. of Western Art), Liverpool Walker Art Gall., Appleton Gall., N.Y., Brighton Art Gall., Letchworth Art Gall. *Address:* Scargill, Myatt's Field, Harvington, Evesham. *Signs work:* "William T. Rawlinson."

RAWNSLEY, Brenda Mary; Director, Colour Print Gallery, School Prints Ltd., Motcomb Frames Ltd.; Master of Fine Art Trade Guild (1961-62); *b* Cowley, July, 1916; *d* of Ll. A. Hugh-Jones; *m* (1st) D. L. Rawnsley (*d* 1943); (2nd) G. Keighley, O.B.E. (*d* 1966); one *s. Address:* 2 Motcomb St., London SW1.

RAY: see HOWARD-JONES, Ray.

RAY, Edith, A.M.C. (1925), S.W.A. (1955); art teacher; artist in oil, water-colour, wood engraving; *b* 7 July, 1905; *d* of the late John E. Ray, F.R.Hist.S., solicitor. *Educ.:* Hastings High School (1918-24) and Portsmouth College (1925-27); *studied art* under Philip W. Cole, R.B.A., A.R.C.A. *Exhib.:* R.I., R.B.A., R.S.A., R.E., Paris Salon, Doncaster, Wakefield, Brighton, Hastings, Tunbridge Wells art galleries. *Address:* Trewent, 36 Springfield Ave., Tenterden, Kent. *Clubs:* East Sussex Arts, S.W.A. *Signs work:* see appendix.

RAY, Peter, F.S.I.A.; designer and typographer in private practice; hon. sec., S.I.A. (1943-49, 1962-64); Senior Member Advertising Creative Circle; principal lecturer in typography, Leicester College of Art; *b* 1917; *m*; three *d. Educ.:* Christchurch, Bournemouth, Poole and Birmingham Schools of Art. *Publications:* numerous. *Address:* 18 St. Catherine's, Broxbourne, Herts. *Signs work:* "PETER RAY."

RAYNER, Donald Lewis, R.B.A. (1957), R.I. (1966), F.R.S.A. (1948); artist in water-colour; Hon. Secretary, Manchester Academy of Fine Arts (1956—); *b* Halstead, Essex, 27 Feb. 1907; *s* of George Lewis Rayner; *m*; one *s,* two *d. Studied art:* privately in Essex and Manchester School of Art. *Work in permanent collections:* Manchester, Warrington, Stoke-on-Trent, Stockport. *Address:* Gadenne, 83 Station Rd., Marple, Cheshire SK6 6NY. *Signs work:* "D. L. RAYNER."

READ, Edwin Alfred; stonemason; artist in oil, water-colour, cryla; *b* Tooting, 27 Feb., 1918; *s* of Alfred Edwin Read, foreman bricklayer; *m* Stella Jane Cload; one *s*, one *d*. *Educ.:* Singlegate Central School; *studied art* at Wimbledon Art School (commercial art), 1938-39. *Exhib.:* Valetta, Naples, Wimbledon, Camberwell Green, Monmouth, Ross, Cardiff, Newport, Swansea, Bangor, Hereford, Laugharne. *Address:* Laugharne Castle, Laugharne, Carms. *Club:* Wye Valley Art Soc. *Signs work:* "E. A. READ."

READE, Brian Edmund, M.A.; formerly deputy keeper, Dept. of Prints and Drawings, V. & A. 1958-73, (asst. keeper since 1936); *b* 13 Jan., 1913; *s* of the late Thomas Glover Reade; *m* Margaret Tennant Ware. *Educ.:* Clifton; King's College, Cambridge. *Publications:* Edward Lear's Parrots (1949); The Dominance of Spain (Costume of the Western World, 1951); Regency Antiques (1953); Edward Lear (Arts Council, 1958); Art Nouveau and Alphonse Mucha (1963); Aubrey Beardsley (1966); with Frank Dickinson, Catalogue of Beardsley Exhbn. V. & A. (1966); Ballet Designs and Illustrations (1967); Beardsley (1967); Sexual Heretics (Ed.) (1970); Eye of a Needle (1971); Louis Wain (1972). *Address:* 6 Abingdon Villas, Kensington, London W8.

READER, Charles Arthur; mem. of Antique Dealers' Assoc., Fine Art Trade Guild, Antiquarian Book Sellers Assoc.; specialist in old engravings, prints, drawings, paintings; proprietor, Arthur Reader, 71 Charing Cross Rd., WC2 (estb. 1750); *b* London, 1908; *s* of Arthur Reader; *m*; one *s*, one *d*.

REDDICK, Peter, D.F.A. (Slade, 1951), R.E.; printmaker and wood-engraver; freelance illustrator; Lecturer in Illustration at Bristol Polytechnic, Faculty of Art and Design (West of England College of Art); *b* Essex, 5 June, 1924; *s* of G. W. Reddick; *m* Joan Elizabeth Dawson; two *s*, one *d*. *Educ.:* Royal Liberty School, Romford, Essex; *studied art* at Slade School of Fine Art (1948-51). *Publications:* illustrated Crotchet Castle, Thos. Love Peacock (Folio Society, 1964), The Mayor of Casterbridge, Thos. Hardy (Folio Society, 1968), Poems of Robert Browning (Limited Editions Club, New York, 1969), The Return of the Native, Thos. Hardy (Folio Society, 1971). *Address:* 18 Hartington Park, Bristol, 6. *Signs work:* "Peter Reddick."

REDPATH, Barbara, D.A. (Edin.); artist in oil and water-colour; teacher, Education Dept., Kelvingrove Museum and Art Galleries, Glasgow; *b* London, 1924; *d* of William Lawford, clerk; formerly *m* T. K. Redpath; two *s*. *Educ.:* Streatham Secondary School; *studied art* at Edinburgh College of Art (Andrew Grant Scholar) (1942-44, 1945-47) under W. G. Gillies, P.R.S.W., W. MacTaggart, P.R.S.A., John Maxwell; Travelling Scholarship, Italy (1948). *Exhib.:* R.S.A., S.S.A., S.S.W.A., R.G.I.; one-man shows: Edinburgh, Glasgow, Alnwick; group shows: Pitlochry Festival, London, Cannes, Stirling University, Galashiels. *Work in permanent collections:* University of Glasgow, University of Strathclyde. *Address:* 32 Glasgow St., Glasgow, G12. *Signs work:* "Babs Redpath."

REECE, Alan, R.M.S.; portrait and vignette engraver, painter, specialist jeweller, designer, illustrator, etcher in gold, silver, steel, oils, inks; *b* London, 14 Nov., 1938; *s* of H. Reece, scientific glassblower; *m* Chérie Rosaland. *Educ.:* Priory Senior Boys' School, Taunton; *studied art* at Central School of Arts and Crafts (1954-56) engraving, etching; School of Fine Arts, Madrid (1962-63) under Senor Camilo Delohm; Sir John Cass College (1968-69) engraving under F. Fryer. *Exhib.:* Mall Galleries, Goldsmiths Hall, London. *Address:* 7A Hornton St., London W8. *Signs work:* paintings: "A. REECE", engravings and etchings: see appendix.

REED, Stanley, R.C.A.; portrait and genre painter; *b* Ullock, Cumberland, 5 Apr., 1908; *s* of John William Reed, blacksmith; *m. Educ.:* Nelson Grammar, Wigton; Liverpool College of Art (Will C. Penn) with Scholarship to Italy. *Exhib.:* R.S.P.P., R.A., M.A.F.A., R.C.A., National Portrait Gallery (portraits of Dr. Downey, Archbishop of Liverpool, and Prof. Sir Cyril Clarke, President of The Royal College of Physicians). *Official purchases:* provincial permanent collections; Lord Mayoral portraits; for Liverpool University: portraits of the late Professor E. C. C. Baly, F.R.S., the late Sir Richard Armstrong (Pro-Chancellor) and Professor R. A. Morton, F.R.S.; for Upholland College: portrait of The Rt. Rev. Monsignor J. Turner (rector) and the late Dr. Downey, Archbishop of Liverpool; for Royal College of Obstetricians: portrait of Sir Arthur Gemmell (Pres., 1952-55); for Rydal School: portrait of Headmaster, Donald Hughes, for Capper-Neil Ltd., portrait of President, W. H. Capper, O.B.E. *Work repro.:* Studio (1952), Lancashire Life (1953), etc. *Address:* 9 Grove Park, Liverpool, 8. *Club:* Sandon Studios Soc. *Signs work:* "Stanley Reed."

REES, Gladys Mary (Mrs. Teesdale), S.W.A.; painter in water-colour and oil; *b* London; *d* of Joseph Edward Rees; *m* John Pickworth Teesdale; two *s*, one *d*. *Studied art* at Chelsea School of Art (Board of Educ. painting dip.). *Exhib.:* R.A., N.E.A.C., R.I., S.W.A., etc. *Work repro.:* in Underground posters, Sphere, children's books, book jackets, etc. *Address:* Melbourn House, Ryhall, nr. Stamford, Lincs. *Signs work:* "G. REES TEESDALE" and "REES."

REEVE, Marion José, N.D.D. (1953), M.F.P.S. (1968); landscape painter in acrylic and gouache; civil servant, Building Research Establishment; life mem. International Assoc. of Art; *b* Watford, 26 Sept., 1926; *d* of Richard John Reeve, *m* Albert Edward Butcher. *Educ.:* St. Joan of Arc Convent, Rickmansworth; *studied art* at Watford College of Technology, School of Art (1947-53) under Alexander Sutherland, M.A. *Exhib.:* one-man show: Loggia Gallery (1974); Young Contemporaries (1954), F.P.S. Annual and Travelling exhbns. at Kings Lynn Festival, South of France, etc. *Work in permanent collection:* St. Michael and All Angels Church, Watford (Stations of the Cross). *Address:* 15 Elm Grove, Watford, Herts. *Club:* Watford and Bushey Art Soc. *Signs work:* "M. Reeve" and date.

REEVES, David Louis; engineer; *b* London, 1913; *s* of Albert John Reeves; *m* Elizabeth Paine; two *s*, one *d*. *Educ.:* Stowe School, Jesus College, Cambridge; Ecole Boulle, Paris. *Publications:* Furniture: An explanatory History (Faber & Faber, 1947). *Address:* Further Fields, Leeds, Maidstone, Kent.

REEVES, Philip Thomas Langford, A.R.C.A. (1954), R.E. (1963), R.S.W. (1959), A.R.S.A. (1971); painter-etcher; Senior Lecturer, Glasgow School of Art; *b* Cheltenham, 7 July, 1931; *s* of Herbert John Reeves, printer; *m* Christine MacLaren; one *d*. *Educ.:* Naunton Park Senior Secondary School, Cheltenham; *studied art* at Cheltenham School of Art (1945-49), Royal College of Art (1951-54). *Work in permanent collections:* Arts Council of Gt. Britain, Gallery of Modern Art, Edinburgh, Glasgow A.G., Glasgow University Print Collection, Aberdeen A.G., Paisley A.G., Milngavie A.G., Edinburgh University, Stirling University. *Address:* 13 Hamilton Drive, Glasgow G12. *Signs work:* "Philip Reeves."

REIACH, Alan, O.B.E., A.R.S.A., F.R.I.B.A., A.M.T.P.I.; architect; Mem. Royal Fine Arts for Scotland; Senior Partner, Reiach & Hall, Edinburgh; *b* London, 2 Mar., 1910; *s* of Herbert L. Reiach, naval architect, editor and publisher; *m*; one *s*, one *d*. *Educ.:* Edinburgh Academy; *studied art* at School of Architecture, Edinburgh College of Art. *Work repro.:* Architectural Review,

Architects' Journal, Building. *Publications:* Building Scotland, with Robert Hurd (1940). *Address:* 6 Darnaway St., Edinburgh 3. *Club:* Scottish Arts.

REICH, Tibor, F.R.S.A., A.T.I., F.S.I.A.; textile designer, fabric constructor, printed and woven fabrics; industrial and tapestry designer and colour consultant; *b* Budapest, 1916; *s* of Jeno Reich; *m* Freda Reich, L.R.A.M.; two *s*, two *d*. *Educ.:* Academy of Commerce, Budapest; Textile School, Vienna; Leeds University; *studied art* at Budapest, Vienna, College of Art, Leeds. *Work in permanent collections:* Shakespeare Centre, Stratford-on-Avon, Arts Council, London, Contemp. Section, V. & A., London Airport, Liners Vaal, Windsor Castle, Q.E.2. Planes, Concorde. *Addresses:* Clifford Mill, Stratford-on-Avon; (home) 23 Avenue Rd., Stratford-on-Avon. *Clubs:* various. *Signs work:* see appendix.

REID, John, Dip. Arch. (Distinction), A.R.I.B.A., P.P.S.I.A., F.Illum.E.S.; architect and general consultant designer, Dean of the Faculty of Art and Design, Middlesex Polytechnic; *b* 1 Dec., 1925; *m* Sylvia Reid, Dip. Arch., A.R.I.B.A., F.S.I.A. *Educ.:* Wellingborough Grammar School; *studied architecture* at Polytechnic School of Architecture, W1. *Address:* 5 The Green, Southgate, London N14 7EG. *Signs work:* "John and Sylvia Reid."

REID, Sir Norman Robert, Kt. (1970), D.A. (Edin., 1937), D.Litt., F.M.A., F.I.I.C., joined Tate Gallery, 1946; appointed Director, 1964; Chairman, British Council Fine Arts Committee; Member, Institute of Contemporary Arts Advisory Panel; Member, Contemporary Art Society Committee; Member of the Council, Friends of the Tate Gallery; Fellow and Vice-Chairman, International Institute for Conservation of Historic and Artistic Works; Member, British National Cttee. of I.C.O.M.; Mem. Culture Adv. Cttee.; President, Council of the Rome Centre; *b* London, 27 Dec., 1915; *s* of Edward Reid; *m* Jean Bertram; one *s*, one *d*. *Educ.:* Wilson's Grammar School; *studied art* at Goldsmiths' College, Edinburgh College of Art (1933-38) and Edinburgh University. *Address:* The Tate Gallery, Millbank, London SW1.

REILLY, Freda E., P.S. (1931); pastel artist; *d* of Frederick Reilly. *Educ.:* Woodridings School, Pinner; Chateau d'Aïre, Geneva. *Exhib.:* P.S., United Artists, Lake Artists. *Address:* Tigh-na-Sith, South Ledaig, by Connel, Argyll. *Signs work:* see appendix.

REILLY, Michael Leeds-Paine, M.S.I.A.; landscape painter and commercial designer; *b* 21 Aug., 1898; *s* of Walter Reilly; *m* Edith Alice Maude; one *s*. *Educ.:* Bishop Vesey's Grammar School, Sutton Coldfield; Central School of Arts and Crafts, Birmingham (1923-26). *Exhib.:* R.A., Paris Salon. *Official purchases:* Leeds Art Gallery, Dudley Art Gallery, and Russell-Cotes Art Gallery, Bournemouth. *Work repro.:* Big Bush Farm, Medici Soc. (most of work now sold in U.S.A.). *Address:* 12 Pages Close, Sutton Coldfield. *Signs work:* "Michael Reilly."

REILLY, Sir Paul, M.A. (Oxon, 1933), Hon. Des. R.C.A., Hon. F.R.I.B.A., Hon. F.S.I.A.; director, Design Council; on editorial staff of News Chronicle, 1936-40; *b* 29 May, 1912; only *s* of late Prof. Sir Charles Reilly, O.B.E., LL.D., F.R.I.B.A.; *m* 1st, Pamela Foster, ballet dancer; one *d*; 2nd Annette Stockwell, journalist. *Educ.:* Winchester, Oxford, L.S.E., London University. *Publications:* An Introduction to Regency Architecture, Art and Technics, 1948; British Catalogue of Plastics (co-editor), National Trade Press, 1948. *Address:* 3 Alexander Pl., London SW7. *Club:* Athenæum.

REINGANUM, Victor, F.S.I.A.; illustrator, painter; *b* 13 Sept., 1907; *m* Ethelwyn Sheppard; two *s*. *Educ.:* Self-educated in Paris and London (1925-30).

Work repro.: Since 1928 has been regular producer of books and magazine illustrations, murals, advertisements, etc. *Address:* Church St., Hartfield, Sussex. *Agents:* Alexander Postan Fine Art, London. *Signs work:* see appendix.

REMFRY, David; painter in oil; paints portraits for the portrait centre, New Grafton Gallery; *b* Sussex, 30 July, 1942. *Studied art* at Hull College of Art (1959-64). *Exhib.:* one-man shows: New Art Centre, Folkestone (1976), Ferens Art Gallery, Hull (1975), Fire Engine House, Ely (1975), Editions Graphiques (1974), New Grafton Gallery (1973). *Address:* 8 Lordship La., Dulwich, London SE22 8HN. *Signs work:* "David Remfry."

REMINGTON, Mary, A.R.C.A. (Lond., 1933), N.E.A.C. (1954), R.O.I. (1962), N.S. (1970); painter in oil; *b* Reigate, Surrey, June, 1910; *d* of William Beard; *m* George Edward Remington; one *s*. *Educ.:* privately; *studied art* at Redhill School of Art under William Todd-Brown, R.O.I.; Royal College of Art under Sir William Rothenstein; Académie de la Grande Chaumière, Paris. *Exhib.:* R.A., N.E.A.C., R.O.I., R.B.A., Arts Council and principal provincial galleries. *Work in permanent collections:* Grundy Art Gallery, Blackpool; Kensington Public Library; Brighton Art Gallery. *Address:* White Post Studio, 13 Stanley Rd., Sutton, Surrey. *Signs work:* "Mary Remington."

RENTON, Joan, D.A. (1957), Post.Dip., Travelling Scholarships; artist and teacher in oil, water-colour, pen and wash; *b* Sunderland, 1935; *d* of F. R. Biggins; *m* R. S. Renton, D.A.; two *s*, one *d*. *Educ.:* Hawick High School; *studied art* at Edinburgh College of Art under R. Lyon, Sir William Gillies, Sir William MacTaggart, John Maxwell, Robin Philipson, James Cumming, Charles Pulsford, Donald Moodie. *Exhib.:* one-man shows: Edinburgh, R.S.A., S.S.A., R.S.W., Sheffield, 57 Gallery, John Moores, S.S.W.A., travelling exhbns., etc. *Work in permanent collections:* H.R.H. the Duke of Edinburgh, Yorkshire West Riding, Scottish Hospital Board, Edinburgh Corp. *Address:* 9 Lennox Row, Edinburgh 5. *Signs work:* "Joan Renton."

REUSS, Albert; artist in oil and sculptor; *b* 2 Oct., 1889; *m* Rosa. *Educ.:* Vienna; *studied art:* self-taught. *Work in permanent collections:* Albertina, Vienna, B.M., Print Cabinet, Moscow, in museums at Birmingham, Cheltenham, Newcastle, Gateshead, Fitzwilliam Museum, Tel Aviv Museum, Oesterreichische Gallery im Belvedere, Vienna, etc., portrait in bronze of a town councillor (commissioned by the Town Hall, Vienna); portrait in plaster of the late M.P., Lipson (Library, Cheltenham); portrait in bronze of the artist's wife (Jerusalem Museum). *Bibliography:* Albert Reuss by N. Wyckes-Joyce (1971). *Address:* Arra, Mousehole, Cornwall. *Signs work:* see appendix.

REUTER, Erich F.; sculptor; sen. Prof. of Plastic Arts, Faculty of Architecture, Technical University, Berlin; guest-prof., Technical University, Istanbul (1966-68); *b* Berlin, 2 Sept., 1911; *s* of Gustav Reuter; *m* Bärbel Astfalk; one *s*. *Educ.:* Köllnisches Gymnasium, Berlin; *studied art* at Kunstgewerbeschule, Charlottenburg, and Kunstakademie, Berlin. *Examples of work in German and foreign museums and private collections:* portraits of actors, Schiller-Theater, Berlin, entrance-relievo, German pavilion, World Fair, Montreal, now Technical University, Berlin, Graundmosaiks in the new buildings of Philharmonie and Staatsbiblicthek in Berlin, Röntgendenkmal Giessen. *Exhib.:* Berlin, Hamburg, Galerie Gerd Rosen. *Official purchases:* Technical University, Berlin; Memorial Library, Berlin. *Publications:* Kunstwerk, Plastik der Gegenwart, Deutsche Kunst der Gegenwart, European Plastic Today. *Address:* Berlin-Grunewald, Caspar-Theysstr., 14. *Clubs:* Der Ring, Deutscher Künstlerbund. *Signs work:* "E. F. Reuter."

REWALD, John, Ph.D., 1936 (Docteur-ès-Lettres de l'Université de Paris), Prix Charles Blanc, Académie Française, 1941; Knight of the Legion of Honor, 1954; Prof., University of Chicago, 1963, City University of New York, 1971; author (art historian); *b* 12 May, 1912; *s* of Bruno Rewald, Ph.D.; div.; one *s;* remarried to Alice Bellony, 1956. *Educ.:* Hamburg and Frankfurt Universities; Sorbonne, Paris. *Publications:* Cézanne, sa vie, son oeuvre, son amitié pour Zola; Gauguin; Maillol; Georges Seurat; The History of Impressionism; Pierre Bonnard; Post-Impressionism—From van Gogh to Gauguin; Cézanne, Geffroy, Gasquet; Pissarro; Manzu. *Address:* 1075 Park Ave., New York, 10028. *Signs work:* "John Rewald."

REYCHAN, Stanislas, M.B.E. (1944); Paris Salon Bronze Medal (1958); Paris Salon Silver Medal (1960); sculptor and potter; *b* 8 Oct., 1897; *s* of S. Reychan, painter and illustrator; *m* Anna Szmidt. *Educ.:* Continental schools; *studied art* at St. Martin's School of Art (Walter Marsden), Central School of Arts and Crafts (Dora Billington). *Exhib.:* R.A., R.I., N.S., Paris Salon, Div. Crafts Exhbn. *Work in permanent collections:* Manchester Art Gallery, Leicester Art Gallery. *Address:* Garden Studio, 3 Acacia Rd., London NW8. *Signs work:* see appendix.

REYNARD, Ian David, N.D.D.; Guinness Travel Prize (1963); artist in oil and polymer, part-time teacher; *b* Leeds, 20 Aug., 1942; *s* of C. A. Reynard, F.I.H.V.E., M.Cons.E. *Educ.:* Lancaster Royal Grammar School; *studied art* at Lancaster and Morecambe College of Art (1960-65). *Work in permanent collections:* Euston Gallery, London NW1. *Address:* Arran, St. Michael's Pl., Barton, Preston, Lancs. *Signs work:* "Ian Reynard" or "IAN D. REYNARD" (before 1969).

REYNOLDS, Bernard Robert, A.R.B.S., D.A.E.; lecturer in sculpture, Ipswich School of Art; *b* 2 June, 1915; *s* of Edward Bernard Reynolds; *m* Gwynneth Jane Griffiths; one *s.* three *d. Educ.:* City of Norwich School; *studied art* at Norwich School of Art (1932-37), L.C.C. Westminster School of Art. *Exhib.:* regularly at Norwich, Aldeburgh, Ipswich and Colchester (sculpture). *Commissions* include pair 20-ft. pylons in aluminium for Ipswich Civic College, 25-ft. window for St. Matthew's School, and fountain sculpture for Ipswich Civic Centre which won the Sir Otto Beit Award given by the R.B.S. (1972). *Address:* 20 Anglesea Rd., Ipswich.

REYNOLDS, Graham, B.A. (1935); keeper, Dept. of Prints and Drawings, and Paintings, V. & A. (1959-74); *b* 10 Jan., 1914; *s* of Arthur T. Reynolds; *m* Daphne Dent. *Educ.:* Highgate School and Queens' College, Cambridge. *Publications:* Twentieth-century Drawings (1946), Nicholas Hillard and Isaac Oliver (1947), Elizabethan and Jacobean Costume (1951), English Portrait Miniatures (1952), Painters of the Victorian Scene (1953), Catalogue of the Constable Collection, Victoria and Albert Museum (1960), Constable, the Natural Painter (1965), Victorian Painting (1966), Turner (1969), A Concise History of Water-colours (1971). *Address:* The Old Manse, Bradfield St. George, Suffolk.

REYNOLDS, Maureen; painter in oil, water-colour; fine arts artist; *b* Thames Ditton, 3 Oct., 1926; *d* of T. Reynolds, artist. *Educ.:* St. Joseph's; *studied art* at St. Martin's School of Art under James Bateman, R.A. (1943-49). *Exhib.:* R.A., Horniman Museum, Leicester Galleries, Piccadilly Galleries, Lord Mayor Show, City of London, St. Mary's Crypt, Battersea (1965), Duncan Gallery (1966), Siri Colvin Gallery, London (1968), Petite Gallery, London (1970), Bond St. Antique Centre (1971-72), and provinces. *Official purchase:* by St. Martin's School of Art. *Work repro.:* in Revue Moderne, Paris. *Address:* 22 Victoria Cres., London SE19. *Signs work:* "M. Reynolds."

REYNOLDS, Ruth Evelyn Millicent; artist in oil, water-colour and sculpture; Com. Mem., Bucks. Art Society; *b* Wellington, Madras, India, 4 Oct., 1915; *d* of Lt.-Col. C. E. W. S. Fawcett, R.A.M.C.; *m* Lt.-Col. D. L. C. Reynolds, O.B.E.; one *s,* two *d. Educ.:* abroad and Conamur, Sandgate, Kent; *studied art* at Guildford School of Art (1932-33) under Victor Burnand, A.R.C.A., Prof. Arthur Pan, of Academie Authentique, Budapest (1969-70), Wycombe School of Art (1959-75). *Exhib.:* one-man shows: Halifax House, Oxford University Graduate Centre (1965), English-Speaking Union (1967), County Museum, Aylesbury (1976). *Work in permanent collections:* Anne Duchess of Westminster's Arkle Coll., Rev. J. Studd, M.A., The Paddocks, Princes Risborough. *Address:* Chiltern Retreat, Princes Risborough, Bucks. *Societies:* Contemporary Portrait, Ridley Art, Armed Forces Art. *Signs work:* "RUTH REYNOLDS" or "R.R."

REYNTIENS, Nicholas Patrick, D.A. (Edinburgh), F.Brit. Soc. M.G.P. (1958); artist in stained glass, metal, gouache; *b* London, 11 Dec., 1925; *s* of Nicholas S. Reyntiens, O.B.E.; *m* Anne Mary Bruce, painter; two *s,* two *d. Educ.:* Ampleforth; *studied art* at Regent Street Polytechnic, Edinburgh College of Art, Andrew Grant Fellowship. *Work in permanent collections:* stained-glass windows at Plymouth, Coventry Cathedral, Eton College Chapel, Oundle, Llandaff, Leyland, St. Leonard's, Southampton, Hucknall, Nottingham and Metropolitan Cathedral, Liverpool. *Publication:* The Technique of Stained Glass (Batsford, 1966). *Address:* Burleighfield House, Loudwater, Bucks. *Club:* Garrick. *Signs work:* "Reyntiens."

RHOADES, Geoffrey H.; artist in oil; *b* London, 27 Nov., 1898; *s* of Walter Rhoades, author and civil servant; *m* Joan; one *s. Educ.:* Dulwich College; *studied art* at Clapham Art School (1916), Slade School (1919-23) under Tonks and Wilson Steer. *Work in permanent collections:* Tate Gallery, Ashmolean Museum, V. & A., B.M., Leeds City A.G., Sheffield City A.G., Carlisle City A.G., Wye College, University of London. *Address:* Seven Stars, Cuddington, Aylesbury, Bucks. *Signs work:* "GHR," or surname in full.

RHODES, Marion, R.E., F.R.S.A., S.G.A. (Hon. Life Member), Paris Salon, Hon. Mention, bronze, silver and gold medals, Silver Medal and Diploma, Rome (1970), Associate Artistes Français (1971); artist in black and white, water-colour, oil; *b* Huddersfield, 1907; *d* of Samuel Rhodes, woollen manufacturer. *Educ.:* Greenhead High School, Huddersfield Art School, Leeds College of Art, Central School of Arts, London. *Exhib.:* R.A., Paris Salon, R.S.A., W.A.G. and provincial galleries, S. Africa and U.S.A. *Work in permanent collections:* British Museum print room, Bradford A.G., South London A.G., Brighouse A.G., and Huddersfield A.G. *Address:* 2 Goodwyn Ave., Mill Hill, London NW7 3RG. *Club:* E.S.U. *Signs work:* "Marion Rhodes."

RICE, Bernard; painter in oil, fresco, portrait sculptor, wood-engraver; *b* Innsbruck, Austria, 28 June, 1900; *s* of Bernard Rice, stained-glass painter. *Studied art* in Innsbruck, at R.C.A. and R.A. schools. *Work in permanent collections:* B.M. (Print Room), V. & A. (Print Room), Cairo Modern Art Gallery. *Address:* c/o Midland Bank Ltd., 337 Kings Rd., Chelsea, London SW3. *Signs work:* see appendix.

RICHARDS, Frances, A.R.C.A.; artist; *b* Stoke-on-Trent, 1903; *m* Ceri Richards; two *d. Studied art* at Burslem School of Art, Stoke-on-Trent; Royal College of Art, London. *Exhib.:* London Galleries (1945, 1949, 1951, 1952, 1954, 1964, 1967) and others. *Work in permanent collections:* Tate Gallery, V. & A., National Museum of Wales. *Publication:* illustrated Book of Revelation (Faber). *Address:* 12 Edith Grove, Chelsea, London SW10. *Signs work:* "F.R."

RICHARDSON, John Frederick, A.T.D. (1932), Dip. in Art History (London) 1956; artist in water-colour, pastels, oil and all drawing media, retd. art master; Head of Art Dept., Emanuel School, London (1951-74), Hove Grammar School (1938-50), East Sheen (1937-38), University College School (1934-37); *b* London, 23 Apr., 1912; *s* of E. W. Richardson. *Educ.:* Wilson's Grammar School, Camberwell; *studied art* at Camberwell School of Art and Crafts (1928-31) under Cosmo Clark, R.A., J. Gilroy, A.R.C.A., R. Schwabe; London Day Training College (1931-32) under Sir Percival Nunn, Clarence Waite. *Exhib.:* R.A., R.S.P.P., R.S.M.A., International Boat Show, R.S.A., R.H.A., P.S., R.S.W., Flower Show, R.W.S. Galleries, South London Group, Croydon Art Society; one-man show: Ickworth (1973). *Address:* 33 Downsway, Sanderstead, Surrey. *Club:* Croydon Art Society. *Signs work:* "J. F. Richardson."

RICHMOND, Donald Edward, N.D.D., painting (1952), A.T.C., London (1953); painter and theatrical designer; hon. treas. (1952), hon. adviser (1953), Young Contemporaries; art master, Luton Grammar School (1953-56); Senior Art Master, Borehamwood Grammar School (1956-63); Head of Art Dept., Stockwell Manor School, SW9 (1963-66); senior lecturer in stage design, West Midlands College (since 1966); *b* Ilford, Essex, 13 Aug., 1929; *s* of H. J. Richmond. *Educ.:* Ilford County High School; *studied art* at S.W. Essex Technical College and School of Art (1946-48 and 1950-52), Brighton College of Art (1952-53). *Exhib.:* Young Contemporaries, R.B.A. galleries (1952-53). *Designer:* Tower Theatre, N.1 (1956-61); Taming of the Shrew, British Council, Teheran (1963); English première Goyescas (Granados), Morley College (1965-66). *Address:* 6 Morven Close, Potters Bar, Herts. *Signs work:* "DON RICHMOND."

RICHMOND, Douglas Arthur Robert, A.T.D., F.R.S.A.; artist in oil; head of the Art and Crafts Dept., Trent Park College, Barnet, Herts. (since 1950); formerly mem. of the examining panel in art, London University General Cert. of Educ., teacher of drawing and painting, Chesterfield Art School and at Sheffield College of Art (1935); art master to Mirfield and Rastrick Grammar Schools, Yorks. (1937); art master, Chingford County High School (1945); *b* Chesterfield, 27 July, 1911; *s* of Arthur Richmond; *m* E. Louise Smith. *Educ.:* Chesterfield Grammar School; *studied art* at Slade School under Prof. Randolph Schwabe, and at Chesterfield Art School. *Exhib.:* N.E.A.C. and R.P. *Address:* Trent Park College, Barnet, Herts. *Club:* Chelsea Arts. *Signs work:* "DOUGLAS RICHMOND."

RICHMOND, Oliffe; sculptor in bronze and wood; visiting tutor, Chelsea School of Art; *b* Tasmania, 8 Nov., 1919; *s* of Robert Lawrence; *m* Waehlin Richmond. *Educ.:* Friends' School, Hobart; *studied art* at East Sydney Technical College (1946-48) under Lyndon Dadswell. *Exhib.:* Commonwealth A.G., London (1976), Australian Sculpture Centre, Canberra (1968), Hamilton Galleries, London (1965), Terry Dintenfass Gallery, N.Y. (1964), Molton Gallery, London (1962). *Work in permanent collections:* Kroller Muller Museum, Otterlo, Holland, New South Wales A.G. *Address:* 9 Pembroke Studios, Pembroke Gdns., London W8. *Signs work:* "Oliffe Richmond" (drawings), "O. R." (sculpture).

RICHTER, Gisela Marie Augusta; hon. mem. of the Hellenic Soc.; Fellow, British Academy (1946); Hon. Fellow, Soc. of Antiquaries (1947); Mem. of American Philosophical Soc. (1942); Fellow of Pontificia Accademia Romana di Archaeologia (1955); Hon. Fellow Somerville College (1953); Hon. Fellow Girton College (1955); Accademia Nazionale dei Lincei (1966); former Curator of Greek and Roman Dept., Metropolitan Museum of Art, New York; *b* 15 Aug., 1882; *d* of Jean Paul Richter, art historian. *Educ.:* Girton College, Camb.; British School of Archaeology, Athens, Greece. *Publications:* books and articles on Greek sculpture, pottery, engraved gems, etc. *Address:* 81, Viale delle Mura Gianicolensi, Rome.

RICKARD, Stephen, F.R.B.S. (1960), F.S.D.C. (1959), R.A.S.Dip. (1948), Gold and Silver Medals; freelance sculptor in clay for bronze sculpture and glass engraver in hollow glass vessels (NOT flat glass); *b* Carshalton, Surrey, 9 May, 1917; *s* of Aubrey Rickard, company sec.; *m* Lyn Loring; two *s*, two *d*. *Educ.:* Berkhamstead School, Herts.; *studied art* at Kingston-on-Thames (1936-39) under Reg. Brill and H. Wilson Parker, R.A. Schools (1939-40, 46-48) under Wm. McMillan, R.A. (Keeper Sir Walter Russell). *Work in permanent collections:* portrait of Dr. Margaret Murray in Univ. Coll. Lon. Library, portrait of Lord Fairhaven and figure of Orpheus at Anglesey Abbey, Cambs., Nat. Trust; glass in Corning Museum of Glass, Corning, N.Y., U.S.A., and V. & A. travelling coll. *Work repro.:* in many articles, books, etc. *Address:* The Old Vicarage, Vicarage Park, Plumstead, London SE18. *Club:* Savage. *Signs work:* "Stephen Rickard" and date; and see appendix.

RICKMAN, Philip; artist in water-colour; *b* Richmond, Surrey, 31 Jan., 1891; *s* of Commander Philip Howard Rickman, R.N.; *m* Letitia Needham-Smith. *Educ.:* Bradfield College, Theale, Berks.; *studied art* at 5 The Studios, Thurloe Sq., S.W., under George E. Lodge. *Work in permanent collections:* Glenbow Foundation, Calgary, Canada. *Work repro.:* Birds of Sussex (J. Walpole-Bond) and Game Birds. *Publications:* The Handbook of British Birds (Witherby); A Bird Painter's Sketch-book; Sketches and Notes from a Bird Painter's Journal. *Address:* Priory Pl., Wilmington, Polegate, Sussex. *Signs work:* see appendix.

RIDDLE, Hugh Joseph; artist in oil; *b* Beaconsfield, Bucks., 24 May, 1912; *s* of Hugh Howard Riddle, M.D.; *m* Joan Claudia Johnson; one *s*, two *d*. *Educ.:* Harrow and Magdalen; *studied art* at Slade School of Art under Profs. Tonks and Schwabe, Byam Shaw School of Art, etc. *Exhib.:* R.A., R.O.I., R.S.P.P., etc.; elected to the Royal Soc. of Portrait Painters, Dec., 1960. *Address:* c/o Mrs. P. Wigan, 12 Kelmscott Rd., London SW11. *Signs work:* "HUSEPH RIDDLE."

RIESER, Dolf Eric, D.Sc., F.R.E.; painter, etcher, engraver and lecturer; *b* S. Africa, 1898; *s* of E. Rieser, manufacturer; *m* B. Dyer; two *s*. *Educ.:* Polytechnic Zurich, Lausanne University; *studied art* at Hoffmann, Munich; Hayter's Atelier 17, Paris; Hecht, Paris. *Exhib.:* Gallery Bonjean, Paris, Beaux Arts Gallery, London, Carlton College, Minnesota, Adler Gallery, Johannesburg, Arts Council, Capetown, I.C.A. London, Surrey University, Oxford Gallery, Chris Drake Gallery, London and many group shows. *Work in permanent collections:* Arts Council, Imperial War Museum, V. & A., Bibliothèque Nationale, Paris, National Gallery Rosenwald Coll., U.S.A. National Gallery, Capetown, Public Library, N.Y. *Work repro.:* Fraternité (1939), Africa folder (10 engravings) (1939) printed J. Hecht, Salvo for Russia folder (1940), Two Tales of the Congo folder (10 engravings) (Folio Soc. 1952), illustrated Roy Campbell's Mamba's Precipice (Muller, 1953), Res Naturae folder (7 colour engravings). *Publication:* Art and Science (Studio Vista). *Address:* 98 Sumatra Rd., London NW6. *Signs work:* "Dolf Rieser."

RILEY, Bridget, C.B.E. (1972), A.R.C.A.; 1st English painter to win the major Painting Prize at Venice Biennale (1968); painter; *b* London, 1931; *d* of John Fisher Riley. *Educ.:* Cheltenham Ladies' College; *studied art* at Goldsmiths' College of Art; Royal College of Art. *Work in permanent collections:* Arts Council, Tate Gallery, Victoria & Albert Museum, British Council, Museum of Modern Art, New York, The Albright Knox, Buffalo, Pasadena Museum, California, Gulbenkian Foundation, Art Gallery of Victoria, Stuyvesant Foundation,

Melbourne, Ferens Art Gallery, Hull, Chicago Institute, Whitworth Art Gallery, Manchester, Power Gallery of Contemporary Art, Sydney, Walker Art Gallery, Liverpool. *Address:* The Rowan Gallery, 31A Bruton Pl., London W1X 7AB. *Signs work:* "Bridget Riley" or "Riley."

RILEY, Reginald; painter of topographical subjects in oil and water-colour; *b* 9 July, 1895. *Educ.:* W. Bridgford High School, Notts.; St. Albans Art School (Christopher Sanders, R.A.). *Exhib.:* R.A., R.I., Paris Salon, etc. *Address:* c/o Antelope Gallery, 20 George St., St. Albans. *Signs work:* "REGINALD RILEY."

RIOPELLE, Jean-Paul; painter in oil; *b* Montreal, 1923. *Exhib.:* Galerie Creuze (1949); Galerie Pierre (1952); Galerie Rive Droite (1954); Galerie Jacques Dubourg (1956); New York (1954); London (1956, 1957, 1959). *Work in permanent collections:* Tate Gallery, National Gallery of Canada. *Work repro.:* in L'Oeil (June, 1956). *Address:* c/o Arthur Tooth & Sons Ltd., 31 Bruton St., London W1. *Signs work:* "riopelle."

ROBB, Brian; painter and illustrator in oil and black and white; teacher, Royal College of Art; *b* Scarborough, Yorks., 7 May, 1913; *s* of Andrew Robb; *m* Barbara Robb. *Educ.:* Malvern College; *studied art* at Chelsea School of Art (1930-34) and Slade School of Art (1935-36). *Exhib.:* London Group, etc. *Official purchases:* Arts Council, Contemporary Art Soc. *Work in permanent collections:* Carlisle, Southampton and Leicester A.G. *Publications:* My Middle E. Campaigns (1945); illustrated The Golden Asse of Apuleius (1946). Twelve Adventures of Baron Munchausen (1947), Fables of Aesop (1954). *Address:* 10 Hampstead Grove, London NW3. *Signs work:* see appendix.

ROBBINS (Lord), Lionel Charles, Baron, C.H. (1968), C.B. (1944), M.A., B.Sc. (Econ.), F.B.A. (1942), L.H.D. (Columbia), D.Litt. (Dunelm and Exeter), LL.D. (Cantab. and Strasbourg), LL.D. (Leicester, 1961), Hon. D.Litt. (Sheffield and Heriott-Watt); trustee National Gallery (1952-59, 1960-67, 1967—); chairman (1954-59, 1962-67); trustee Tate Gallery (1953-59, 1962-67); director of Royal Opera House since 1956; President of the British Academy, 1962; mem. Accademia dei Lincei, American Philosophical Soc.; *b* 22 Nov., 1898; *s* of Rowland Richard Robbins; *m* Irish Elizabeth Gardiner; one *s*, one *d*. *Educ.:* Southall County School; University College, London; London School of Economics. *Address:* 10 Meadway Close, London NW11. *Club:* Reform.

ROBERTS, Gladys Gregory, A.R.Cam.A.; artist in oil and acrylic; secretary, Penrhyn Painting School; *b* Rhyl; *d* of C. Wesley Haslam, surveyor; *m* Prof. E. J. Roberts, M.A., M.Sc. (decd.); one *d*. *Educ.:* Pendre Private School, Prestatyn; *studied art* at Bangor Technical College (1959-63). *Exhib.:* Tegfryn Gall., Menai Bridge, Anglesey. *Address:* Gorad-y-Gyt, Bangor. *Club:* Anglesey Art Soc. *Signs work:* "G. Roberts."

ROBERTS, John Vivian, R.E., A.R.W.S., A.R.C.A., R.C.A.; Principal Lecturer, Faculty of Art and Design, Liverpool Polytechnic; artist in acrylic, mixed intaglio media, water-colour; *b* Tredegar, Mon., 26 Jan., 1923; *s* of Goronwy Roberts; *m* Gwendoline Thomas; one *s*, one *d*. *Educ.:* Cathays High School, Cardiff; *studied art* at Cardiff School of Art (1939-42), Royal College of Art (1947-51), Engraving School under Prof. Robert Austin. *Work in permanent collections:* Arts Council, Nat. Mus. of Wales. *Publications:* books illustrated for a variety of publishers. *Address:* 135 Raven Meols Lane, Formby, nr. Liverpool. *Signs work:* "John Roberts."

ROBERTS, Marguerite Hazel: see HARRISON, Marguerite Hazel.

ROBERTS, Phyllis Kathleen, R.O.I. (1961); Paris Salon Silver Medal (1959) and Gold Medal (1964); portrait and landscape painter in oil, and sculptor; *b* London, 11 June, 1916; *d* of Ernest Hart Aspden; *m* A. Gwynne Roberts, F.C.I.I. *Educ.:* Clifton College, London; *studied art* at Hornsey College of Art. *Exhib.:* R.A., Paris Salon, R.O.I., N.E.A.C., R.B.A., R.P., Contemporary Portrait Society, and principal provincial municipal art galleries, etc. *Address:* Clarendon Cottage, Station Rd., Hythe, Kent. *Signs work:* see appendix.

ROBERTS, Walter James; artist in water-colour, oil, polymer and black and white; retired civil servant; mem. Doncaster Art Club (1926-45), Scarborough Sketch Club (1934-35), Newcastle Soc. of Artists (1946-59) (chairman, 1956-57), Agricola Art Club (1956—), Soc. of Staffordshire Artists (1961—), chairman, Crewe Music and Arts Soc. (1964-75); further education tutor, Cheshire; *b* Doncaster, 10 Dec., 1907; *s* of J. H. A. Roberts; *m* Edith Wareing; two *s*. *Educ.:* Doncaster Grammar School; *studied art* at Doncaster School of Art under F. J. Glass. *Exhib.:* London and provincial galleries. *Work in permanent collections:* Stoke-on-Trent. *Address:* 591 Crewe Rd., Wistaston, Crewe CW2 6PU. *Signs work:* see appendix.

ROBERTS, Will, R.C.A.; Byne-Stamper Prize (awarded by Lord Clark, 1962); Welsh expressionist painter; draws and paints figures in landscape, religious themes, flowers; born and lives in Wales; *m*; one *d*. *Studied art* at Swansea School of Art (1930's); began painting after war service in R.A.F. *Exhib.:* first one-man shows, London (1954); Arts Council tour (1962-63); London Group, John Moores, Bradford Spring; retrospective exhbn. Llandaff Festival (1973). *Work in permanent collections:* National Museum of Wales, City of Coventry, City of Hereford, Contemporary Art Soc., Arts Council, Steel Corp., B.P. Llandarcy, B.P. Chemicals, and private collections; film feature B.B.C. *Address:* 10 Bilton Rd., Neath. *Signs work:* "Will R."

ROBERTS-JONES, Ivor, A.R.A. (1969); sculptor; teacher, Goldsmiths' College School of Art; *b* 2 Nov., 1913; *s* of William Roberts-Jones, solicitor and Welsh International footballer. *Educ.:* Worksop College; *studied art* at Goldsmiths' College and Royal Academy Schools. *Exhib.:* R.A., R.B.A., R.S.P.S.; one-man exhbn., Beaux Arts Gallery. *Work in permanent collections:* Tate Gallery, Beaverbrook Foundation, New Brunswick, Arts Council, Welsh Arts Council; National Museum, Cardiff. *Public commissions* include Augustus John Memorial (Fordingbridge), Sir Winston Churchill (Parliament Sq.). *Work repro.:* British Art since 1900 (John Rothenstein), British Sculptors (Tiranti), Architectural Review, etc. *Address:* 31 St. James Gdns., London W11. *Signs work:* see appendix.

ROBERTSON, Alexander, D.A., Edin.: artist; Art Department, Two Cities Films Ltd. (1946-47); art master, Acklam High School, Middlesbrough; *b* Tomintoul, Banffs., 8 Sept., 1916; *s* of William Robertson; *m* Rose Mary Sacco; three *s*. *Educ.:* Holy Cross Academy, Edinburgh; *studied art* at Edinburgh College of Art under H. L. Wellington, W. G. Gillies, R. H. Westwater, Dartington Hall under Hein Heckroth and Willi Soukop. *Exhib.:* R.S.A., S.S.A., London Group, Apollo Gallery, Brussels. *Address:* 10 Eastbourne Rd., Linthorpe, Middlesbrough. *Signs work:* "Robertson."

ROBERTSON, Barbara Janette, D.A. (1970), S.S.A. (1974), Lily MacDougall, S.S.W.A. (1975); printmaker in linoprint, part-time lecturer; *b* Broughty Ferry, Dundee, 16 Aug., 1945; *d* of James Fleming Robertson, innkeeper; *m* Kenneth Wilson, D.A. *Educ.:* Blairgowrie High School; *studied art* at Duncan of Jordanstone College of Art, Dundee (1965-71) under Ron Stenberg, Josef Sekalski. *Exhib.:* Aberdeen Art Centre, Print Exchange, Reiver Gallery, Galerie Tendenz; Contributor R.S.A. (1973-75), Prints in Folios of Compass

Gallery, Glasgow, Upstairs Gallery, Winchester, Galerie Tendenz, Stuttgart. *Work in permanent collections:* Leeds, Aberdeen, Glasgow, Stirling, Angus. *Publication:* illustrated The Cuckoo's Nest by Carl McDougall. *Address:* 10 The Row, Douglastown, Forfar, Scotland. *Signs work:* "Barbara Robertson."

ROBERTSON, Prof. Giles Henry, M.A.; Watson Gordon Professor of Fine Art, University of Edinburgh; *b* Cambridge, 16 Oct., 1913; *s* of Prof. Donald Struan Robertson, Regius Professor of Greek, University of Cambridge; *m* Eleanor Clark; four *s*, one *d*. *Educ.:* Leys School, Cambridge, New College, Oxford. *Publications:* Vincenzo Catena (Edinburgh, 1954), Giovanni Bellini (Oxford, 1968). *Address:* 4 Saxe-Coburg Pl., Edinburgh EH3 5BR. *Club:* Scottish Arts.

ROBERTSON, Richard Ross, D.A. (1938), A.R.B.S. (1951), F.R.B.S. (1963), A.R.S.A. (1969); sculptor in clay, wood, stone, bronze; lecturer, Gray's School of Art, Aberdeen; *b* Aberdeen, 10 Sept., 1914; *s* of Rev. R. R. Robertson, M.A., B.D.; *m* Kathleen May Robertson; two *d*. *Studied art* at Glasgow School of Art (1933-34), Gray's School of Art, Aberdeen (1934-39) under T. B. Huxley-Jones, F.R.B.S. *Work in permanent collections:* Aberdeen Corp., Peterhead Museum, Aberdeenshire Educ. Authority, Princeton University, U.S.A. *Address:* 7 Polmuir Rd., Aberdeen. *Signs work:* "R. R. Robertson."

ROBERTSON, Seonaid Mairi, Diploma in Design and Crafts, Edinburgh (1935), A.T.D., Post-Graduate Diploma in Psychology, London University (1947); educationist, lecturer, potter; fellow of Edinburgh College of Art (1945-48), lecturer Goldsmiths' College (1945-46), asst. art adviser, W.R.C.C. and senior lecturer in art, Bretton Hall (1949-56); Research Fellow (1953-54), Senior Research Fellow in Educ. (1957-59), Leeds University; *b* Perth, Scotland, 27 Jan., 1912; *d* of Theodore Robertson, farmer. *Educ.:* Perth Academy, Edinburgh Univeristy and College of Art; *studied art* at Edinburgh College of Art and on Continent. *Exhib.:* A.C.E.S., S.S.A., Art and Crafts Soc. (London), Red Rose Guild (Manchester). *Address:* Goldsmiths' College, London SE14. *Signs work:* "S.M.R."

ROBERTSON, Sheila Macleod, R.S.M.A. (1969), Mem. United Society of Artists (1956), St. Ives Society of Artists (1970); artist in oil, water-colour and animal studies in wire sculpture; *b* London, 1927; *d* of A. L. Robertson, chartered accountant. *Educ.:* St. Michael's School, Leigh-on-Sea; *studied art* at Watford Art School, Central School of Arts and Crafts. *Exhib.:* R.O.I. *Work in permanent collection:* National Maritime Museum. *Address:* The Nucleus, Berks Hill, Chorleywood, Herts. *Signs work:* "S. M. ROBERTSON."

ROBINSON, Basil William, M.A., B.Litt. (1938); museum curator; deputy keeper, Victoria and Albert Museum (1954), keeper (1966), Keeper Emeritus (1972); President, Royal Asiatic Society (1970-73); *b* London, 20 June, 1912; *s* of William Robinson, Life Assurance sec.; *m* 1st., Ailsa Mary Stewart (decd. 1954); 2nd, 1958, Oriel Hermione Steel; one *s*, one *d*. *Educ.:* Winchester, Corpus Christi (Oxford). *Publications:* A Primer of Japanese Sword Blades (1955), Descriptive Catalogue of the Persian Paintings in the Bodleian Library (1958) and other books, booklets, articles and reviews on Persian and Japanese Art. *Address:* 41 Redcliffe Gdns., London SW10.

ROBINSON, Bay; painter, illustrator in water-colour, gouache, lithography; *d* of Charles Robinson, R.I., illustrator of Child's Garden of Verses, Secret Garden, etc. *Educ.:* N. London Collegiate School; *studied art* at Hornsey College of Art. *Exhib.:* One-man show, Walkers Galleries, London (9 April, 1958, and March, 1961), R.A., R.B.A., R.I., S.G.A., Arts Council Exhbn. of Women Painters. *Work* *in permanent collection:* lithograph in Frank Emmanuel Memorial. *Address:* 7 Hillcrest Ave., Whyteladies La., Cookham, Berks. *Signs work:* "Bay Robinson."

ROBINSON, Ivor, M.D.E., F.R.S.A., awarded Silver and Bronze Medals, Prix Paul Bonet (1971); bookbinder in fine bindings; Lecturer in Bookbinding at Oxford Polytechnic (since 1959); President, Designer Bookbinders (1969-73); *b* 28 Oct., 1924; *m;* one *s,* one *d. Studied art* at Bournemouth College of Art (1939-41). *Exhib.:* one-man shows: Hantverket, Stockholm (1963), Galleria del Bel Libro, Ascona (1969). *Work in permanent collections:* B.M., V. & A., Swedish Royal Library, Danish Royal Library, Röhsska Museum, Gothenburg. *Publications:* Introducing Bookbinding (Batsford, 1968). *Address:* Trindles, Holton, Oxford. *Signs work:* "IR" and date.

ROBINSON, Kenneth John; journalist; assistant editor, Architects' Journal (1949-58); promotion officer, Council of Industrial Design (1958-60); *b* Ealing, 26 Apr., 1925; *s* of Bertram Henry Robinson; *m* Joan Mary Hargreaves; one *s,* one *d. Educ.:* Ealing Grammar School. *Publications:* contributions on design and architecture in Spectator, Punch, Observer, The Architect, Thames Television and B.B.C. *Address:* 3 Beech Row, Ham Common, Richmond, Surrey. *Signs work:* "Kenneth Robinson."

ROBINSON, Margaret Nancy, Royal Exhib. (1933), A.R.C.A. (1936); artist in oils, water-colours, ink, also pottery; *b* Trowbridge, Wilts., 17 Mar., 1912; *d* of E. P. Bartlett; *m* Hugh Robinson; one *s,* two *d. Educ.:* Solent House School, Cowes; *studied art* at Cheltenham School of Art (1929-33), R.C.A. (1933-36). *Address:* Park Crescent Farm, Emsworth, Hants. *Signs work:* "Bartlett."

ROBINSON, Oliver J.; Art Editor, National Magazine Co. (1930-46); Editor-in-Chief. Good Housekeeping (1947-67); Production Director, National Magazine Co.; *b* 7 Apr., 1908; *s* of Heath Robinson, artist; *m. Educ.:* Cranleigh School. *Address:* 92 Charlbert Ct., London NW8. *Club:* Savage.

ROBINSON, Peter Michael, N.D.D. (1966); artist on canvas in oil paint, resins, silk screen; lecturer, Stockport College of Technology; lecturer, painting and 3-dimensional design; *b* Leeds, 9 Aug., 1945; *s* of John Robinson, instrument artificer; *m* Pauline, teacher; two *d. Educ.:* Harrogate School of Art (1961-64); *studied art* at Derby College of Art (1964-66). *Exhib.:* Portland Gall., Manchester. *Address:* 1 Woodsmoor La., Stockport, Ches. *Club:* Hillgate Group Painters' Stockport. *Signs work:* "Peter Robinson."

ROBOZ, Zsuzsi; painter in oils, pencil and charcoal, sculptor in clay; *b* Budapest; *m. Studied art* at Regent St. Polytechnic, R.A. under Peter Greenham, and in Florence under Annigoni. *Work in permanent collections:* Museum of Fine Arts, Budapest, National Portrait Gallery, London, Bradford Museum, Graves A.G., Sheffield. *Publications:* Eux et Elles, Dix ans d'Arts Graphiques, La Femme dans l'art contemporain, Les Arts en Europe, Women and Men's Daughters, Chichester 10—Portrait of a Decade. *Address:* The Studio, 76 Eccleston Sq. Mews, London SW1. *Signs work:* "Roboz."

ROBSON, Hugh Mather; artist in oil, gouache, pen and ink; *b* Hinckley, Leics., 28 June, 1929; *s* of John McKenzie Robson, 2nd Engineer (marine); *m* Barbara Ann. *Educ.:* Hinckley Grammar School; *studied art* at St. Martin's School of Art (1945) under William Craig, Russell Hall; Slade School of Art (1949-53) under Lucien Freud, Sam Carter (tutor). *Publications:* illustrated Roses in History; House and Garden Book of Garden Decoration. *Address:* c/o Trafford Gallery, 119 Mount St., London W1Y 5HB. *Club:* Marylebone Rifle and Pistol. *Signs work:* "HUGH ROBSON." or "H. M. ROBSON."

ROCHE, Laurence, N.D.D., D.A.(Edin.), Post. Grad. scholarship, Edinburgh, A.T.C.; painter in acrylic and oil; art teacher, Cirencester School; *b* Goodwick, Pembs., 1 May, 1944; *s* of James Roche; *m* Helen Pollock, D.A.(Edin.). *Educ.:* Fishguard County Secondary School; *studied art* at Swansea College of Art (1962-65); Edinburgh College of Art (1965-68) under Robin Philipson, R.S.A., R.S.W., James Cumming, R.S.A., R.S.W. *Exhib.:* R.S.A., R.W.A., S.S.A., R.S.W., and various one-man shows. *Work in permanent collections:* Brecon County Council, University of Wales, Swansea, Coventry Educ. Authority, Surrey and Leicester Educ. Authorities. *Address:* 16 Belmont Rd., Stroud, Glos. *Signs work:* "Laurence Roche."

RODMELL, Harry Hudson, R.I., R.S.M.A., F.R.S.A., National Medallist; marine and landscape artist in oil, water-colour, etc.; *b* 1896; *s* of Henry Rodmell; *m* Dorothy Thelma Fisher. *Studied art* at Hull College of Art. *Exhib.:* R.A., R.I., S.G.A., R.S.M.A., R.B.A., Salon de la Marine, Paris, and provincial galleries; one-man show of Posters and Shipping Publicity, Hull. *Work repro.:* in Sphere, Graphic, Illustrated London News, Bystander, Shipping Wonders of the World; illustrations to The Lookoutman, by David W. Bone. *Official purchase:* National Maritime Museum. *Address:* Arnecliff, Atwick Rd., Hornsea, N. Humberside. *Signs work:* see appendix.

RODWAY, Eric, A.R.C.A. (Silver Medallist and continuation scholarship); draughtsman, painter in oil; lecturer, Guildford School of Art (1946-47), Epsom and Ewell School of Art since 1947; *b* Birmingham, 3 Aug., 1914; *s* of George Percival Rodway; *m* Evelyn Evans; one *s,* one *d. Educ.:* Sebbon School, Canonbury; *studied art* at Wimbledon School of Art (1933-37) under Gerald Cooper, James Hockey, Robert Baker; R.C.A. (1937-40) under Gilbert Spencer, Barnett Freedman, Percy Horton. *Exhib.:* R.A., R.B.A., N.E.A.C., S.L.G., etc. *Official purchases:* Office of Works, etc., Arts Theatre Club. *Address:* Garden Cottage, The Street, Fetcham, Leatherhead, Surrey. *Signs work:* "Eric Rodway."

ROE, Frederic Gordon, F.S.A. (1943), F.R.Hist.S. (1933); author, sometime Editor of The Connoisseur; *b* 24 Sept., 1894; *s* of Fred Roe, R.I., R.B.C.; *m;* one *d. Educ.:* Westminster School; under father; Chelsea School of Art. *Publications (excluding earlier):* Cox the Master (1946); English Period Furniture (1946); Rowlandson (1947); Sea Painters of Britain (1948); Old English Furniture (1948); English Cottage Furniture (1949: 3rd ed., 1961); Britain's Birthright (1950); Victorian Furniture (1952); Windsor Chairs (1953); The Victorian Child (1959); The Georgian Child (1961); The British Museum's Pictures (with J. R. F. Thompson, 1961); Home Furnishing with Antiques (1965); Victorian Corners (1968); Women in Profile (1970); innumerable articles and reviews. *Address:* 19 Vallance Rd., London N22 4UD.

ROGERS, Claude, O.B.E., Fellow, University College London; President, the London Group. Represented in the Tate Gallery, V. & A., Ashmolean, Fitzwilliam, and in many provincial, dominion and foreign galleries and collections. One-man exhbns.: Leicester Galleries, 1940, 1947, 1953, 1960. Retrospective, 1955, and Whitechapel, 1973. Portraits include Professor Tawnay, Lord Birkett, Professor Haldane and Lord Blackett. Professor of Fine Art, University of Reading, Professor Emeritus 1973. Sometime lecturer, Slade School of Fine Art, Chairman, Fine Art Panel, National Council for Diplomas in Art and Design. Vice-Chairman, U.K. Branch, International Association of Art. *Address:* 36 Southwood La., Highgate Village, London N6.

ROLAND, Henry M., Ph.D.; art historian and dealer, partner of Roland, Browse and Delbanco; mem. Soc. of London Art Dealers; Contemporary Art Soc.,

Inst. for Cont. Art; *b* Munich, 31 Dec., 1907; *m;* one *s. Educ.:* Universities of Berlin, Paris, Munich. Private collection. *Publications:* Der Junge Van Dyck, and contributions to Cicerone, Free Europe, Phoebus, etc. *Addresses:* 19 Cork St., Old Bond St., London W1, and Tyle Ct., Hockering Gdns., Woking, Surrey.

ROLFSEN, Alf; painter in oil, buon fresco; *b* Oslo, 28 Jan., 1895; *s* of Nordahl Rolfsen, author; *m* Ingrid Platou; two *s,* one . *Educ.:* Aars and Voss School, Oslo; *studied art* at the Academy of Copenhagen under P. Rostrup-Boyesen (1913-16). *Work in permanent collections:* National Galleries of Oslo, Copenhagen, Stockholm. *Official purchases:* buon fresco wall paintings, Telegraph Building, Oslo (1922); Soc. of Craftsmen, Oslo (1927); Choir of Church of Stiklestad (1930); new crematorium, Oslo (1932-37); Town Hall, Oslo (1940-50); Hansa Brewery, Bergen (1967); decorations, Town Hall, Haugesund (1953-54); church of Ullensaker (1957-58). *Publications:* Billedspråk (1960), Kunsten Skifter Ham (1974). *Address:* Vinderen, Oslo. *Signs work:* "Alf Rolfsen."

ROMER, Philippa Maynard; portrait painter in oil; *b* Hitchin, Herts; *d* of Maynard Tomson, M.C., F.R.I.C.S.; *m* M. L. R. Romer. *Educ.:* Queen Anne's School, Caversham; *studied art* at Cambridge School of Art and R.A. Schools. *Exhib.:* R.A., R.P., R.B.A., N.E.A.C., S.W.A. *Address:* The Old Vicarage, Braughing, Herts.

ROPER, Geoffrey John; painter in oil and water-colour; *b* Nottingham, 30 July, 1942; *s* of Tom Roper, O.B.E., political agent. *Educ.:* Manvers School, Nottingham Sec. Art School; *studied art* at Nottingham College of Art (1958-60); Edinburgh College of Art (1960-65) under Robin Philipson, P.R.S.A. *Exhib.:* Fine Art Society (1974, 1975), Teesside A.G. (1972), Great King St. Gallery, Edinburgh (1970, 1971, 1972), Middlesbrough Civic A.G. (1968), King St. Gallery, Dublin (1968), David Letham, Edinburgh (1968, 1969), Doogas Foulis Gallery, Edinburgh (1967), William St. Gallery, Edinburgh (1964, 1965, 1966), Silver Coin Gallery, Harrogate (1965, 1966). *Work in permanent collections:* Middlesbrough Civic Art Galleries, Edinburgh New Town Conservation Com., New University of N. Ireland. *Address:* c/o The Fine Art Society, Ltd., 12 Gt. King St., Edinburgh. *Signs work:* see appendix.

ROSE, Diana Cecilia, M.F.P.S. (1976); artist in oil; *b* Chiswick, 12 June, 1921; *d* of H. V. Base; *m* Donald Rose. *Educ.:* Lourdes Mount Convent, Ealing and Westcliff High School for Girls, Westcliff-on-Sea; *studied art* at Southend-on-Sea Art School (1948-60 part-time) under Leo Hardy; St. Martin's Art School (1946-47) under A. Ziegler. *Exhib.:* Whitechapel A.G., Mall Galleries, Trends, Beecroft A.G., Southend-on-Sea. *Work in permanent collection:* Old Leigh Art Centre, Leigh-on-Sea. *Work in private collections* in Britain, U.S.A. and Sweden. *Address:* 19b Cliff Parade, Leigh-on-Sea, Essex. *Signs work:* "Diana Rose."

ROSE, Muriel (Miss), RO.I. (1966), R.B.A. (1968), W.I.A.C. (1967), F.F.P.S., N.S.; painter in oils, designer, printmaker, ceramic sculptor, potter; Lecturer in ceramics and painting in Adult Education; Mem. of Executive Committee of International Association of Art (UNESCO); *b* London, 1923; *d* of H. C. Rose, F.C.A. *Educ.:* Richmond Grammar School, Surrey; *studied art* at Richmond School of Art, pottery at Hammersmith College of Art. *Exhib.:* R.A., R.B.A., R.O.I., Royal Scottish Academy, Paris Salon, Gallery Creuze, Paris, U.S.A., South Africa, National Museum of Wales, Glasgow Institute of the Fine Arts. *Work in permanent collections:* Oxford, Nottingham E.C., Herts E.C., Welsh E.C., Univ. of Texas A.G., Danish Court of Justice, Lady Docker, Mrs. Michael Foot, etc. *Address:* 9 Temple Sheen, London SW14. *Signs work:* "Muriel Rose."

ROSEN, Ismond, M.B., B.Ch. (1946), D.P.M. (1951), Witwatersrand M.D.

(1954), Associate Mem. British Institute of Psycho-analysis (1959), (Member, 1971), F.R.C.Psych. (1971); psychiatrist, sculptor, painter; *b* Johannesburg, S. Africa, 2 Aug., 1924; *s* of Harry Rosen. *Educ.:* Witwatersrand University; *studied art:* mainly self-taught and at Academie Julien and Ecole des Beaux Arts, Paris (1952), Regent St. Polytechnic. *Exhib.:* S. African Academy; private shows, Johannesburg (1949); Pretoria (1951); one-man shows: John Whibley Gallery (1972), "Genesis" Borough of Camden, Camden Arts Centre, (1974), R.A. *Address:* Charlecote, 3 Hampstead Hill Gdns., London NW3 2PH. *Club:* Fellow Soc. of Portrait Sculptors. *Signs work:* "Ismond Rosen."

ROSENAU, Helen, Dr.Phil., Ph.D.; art historian; formerly reader, University of Manchester; lecturer, Univ. of London, Central Polytechnic, London; *b* Monte Carlo. *Educ.:* privately and universities in Germany, France, Italy, England. *Publications:* Der Kölner Dom (1930), Design and Medieval Architecture (1934), Woman in Art (1944), The painter J. L. David (1948), A Short History of Jewish Art (1948); Boullée's Treatise on Architecture (1953); The Ideal City (1959, 1974); Social Purpose in Architecture, Paris and London Compared (1970); Burlington Magazine, R.I.B.A. Journal, Gazette des Beaux Arts, Architectural Review, The Bulletin of the John Rylands Library, etc. *Address:* 84A Ridgmount Gdns., London WC1. Member of P.E.N., British Society of Aesthetics, Assoc. of Art Historians, etc.

ROSOMAN, Leonard, A.R.A. (1960), R.A. (1970); artist and teacher; teacher of illustration, Camberwell School of Art; teacher of mural decoration, Edinburgh College of Art; tutor at the Royal College of Art, London; *b* Hampstead, London, 27 Oct., 1913; *s* of Henry Rosoman. *Educ.:* Deacons School, Peterborough; *studied art* at King Edward VII School of Art, Durham University; Central School of Arts and Crafts; R.A. School. *Exhib.:* Roland, Browse & Delbanco, Leicester Galleries, Leger Gallery, St. George's Gallery, Sheffield, Bradford, Edinburgh, Dublin, and provincial galleries, and Lincoln Center, N.Y., State University of New York at Albany. *Address:* 7 Pembroke Studios, Pembroke Gdns., London W8. *Signs work:* "Leonard Rosoman."

ROSS, Alastair Robertson, D.A., A.R.B.S., M.S.P.S., F.S.A.Scot., F.R.S.A., O.L.J.; sculptor in clay, metal and perspex; Lecturer in Sculpture at Duncan of Jordanstone College of Art, Dundee, Graduated D.A. (Dundee) 1965; post-graduate (1966); elected to Membership of Society of Portrait Sculptors (1966); elected F.R.S.A. (1966); elected to Associateship Royal Society of British Sculptors (1968); elected Prof. Member Society of Scottish Artists (1969); elected Membre Associé Société des Artistes Francais (1970); elected F.S.A. Scot (1971); elected Prof. Member Scottish Arts Club (1971); elected Member of Council Society of Scottish Artists (1972-75); elected Scottish Representative and Member of Council Royal Society of British Sculptors (1972–); Officer Companion of Order of St. Lazarus of Jerusalem (1972); *b* Perth, Scotland, 8 Aug., 1941; *s* of Alastair James Ross, F.S.A. Scot; *m* Kathryn Margaret Greig Wilson. *Educ.:* St. Mary's Episcopal School, Dunblane, McLaren High School, Callander; *studied art* at Edinburgh College of Art (1960, Eric Schilsky, R.S.A., R.A., late Norman J. Forrest, A.R.S.A., F.R.B.S.), Duncan of Jordanstone College of Art, Dundee (1960-66, Hugh Adam Crawford, R.S.A., Scott Sutherland, R.S.A., F.R.B.S.), also Vienna, Florence, Rome, Amsterdam and Athens on extensive travel/study abroad. *Exhib.:* R.S.A., R.B.S., S.S.A., Paris Salon, International Sculpture Exhibition, Madurodam, Holland (1966), Society of Portrait Sculptors, Commonwealth Arts Festival Exhibition, Royal Overseas League, Edinburgh International Festival (1968), Montrose Festival, Stirling Gallery, etc. *Work in permanent collections:* Scottish Arts Council, also represented in private collections in Austria, Switzerland, U.S.A., Norway and Bahamas as well as this country. *Awards:* Dickson Prize for Sculpture (1962), Scottish Education Department Travelling Scholarship (1963), Royal Scottish Academy Chalmers Bursary (1964), Royal Scottish Academy Carnegie Travelling Scholarship (1965), Duncan of Drumfork Scholarship (1965), Scottish Education Department Postgraduate Scholarship (1965-66); award winner in Sculpture Paris Salon Exhibition (1967), Société des Artistes Français Médaille de Bronze (1968), Société des Artistes Français Médaille d'Argent (1970). *Address:* 67 Dalcraig Cres., Dundee DD4 7QX. *Clubs:* Scottish Arts, Royal Overseas League. *Signs work:* see appendix.

ROSS, Marvin Chauncey; historian of Byzantine, mediaeval and nineteenth-century art; curator of Decorative Arts, Walters Art Gallery, Baltimore, Md. (1934-52); chief curator of Art, Los Angeles County Museum (1952-55); writer on art history since 1955; curator, Hillwood, Washington, D.C.; deputy advisor, Monuments, Fine Arts and Archives, S.H.A.E.F. (1944-45); *b* Moriches, N.Y., 21 Nov., 1904; *s* of William E. Ross; *m* Lotus Robb Ross. *Educ.:* Universities of Harvard, New York and Berlin. *Publications:* Catalogue of the Byzantine Antiquities in the Dumbarton Oaks Collection, Vol. I (1962), Vol. II (1965), Faberge and His Contemporaries; Collection of Mrs. Merriweather Post (Norman, 1965); The West of Alfred Jacob Miller (Second Edition, Norman, 1967); Russian Porcelain (Hillwood Collection) (Norman, 1967) etc.; articles in The Burlington Magazine, Connoisseur, Pantheon, etc. *Address:* 4155 Linnean Ave., Washington 8, D.C.

ROSS-CRAIG, Stella, F.L.S.; artist in water-colour, pencil, and pen and ink; *b* Aldershot, Hants, 19 Mar., 1906; *d* of John Ross-Craig, M.P.S.; *m* J. Robert Sealy, B.Sc., F.L.S. *Educ.:* privately; *studied art* at Thanet Schools of Art, and botany at Chelsea Polytechnic. *Work in permanent collections:* Reference Collection, Herbarium of Royal Botanic Gdns., Kew (approx. 500 water-colours, several hundred pen-and-ink and pencil drawings); Hunt Botanical Library, Pittsburgh, Penn., U.S.A. *Work repro.:* in Hooker's Icones Plantarum, Botanical Magazine, and many other scientific publications. *Publications:* Drawings of British Plants. *Address:* c/o The Herbarium, Royal Botanic Gdns., Kew, Surrey. *Signs work:* "SR-C" or "Stella Ross-Craig."

ROSSELET, André, V.S.G., O.E.V.; graphic designer, painter, postage stamp designer, illustrator, typographical book designer; director, Ides et Calendes publications; *b* Neuchâtel, 24 Aug., 1915; *m* Joan Jackson-Sytner; three *d.* *Studied art* at Zürich (Kunstgewerbeschule, 1934-36), Paris under Paul Colin (1936-37), Othon Friesz (1937-38), André Lhote (1938-39); studied the typographic arts with Daragnes. *Exhib.:* London (Purpose and Pleasure), Paris, Zürich, Lausanne, Austria, Geneva, Neuchâtel. *Address:* Auvernier, Neuchâtel, Switzerland. *Signs work:* "R."

ROSSITER, Anthony, M.S.I.A. (1963), R.W.A. (1964), Arts Council awards, Literature (1967, 1970), T.V. James Mossman's Review (1970); painter in oil and water-colour, writer, lecturer; Lecturer, Bristol Polytechnic; *b* London, 29 Mar., 1926; *s* of Leonard Rossiter; *m* Anneka; one *s,* one *d.* *Educ.:* Eton; *studied art* at Chelsea Polytechnic (1947-51). *Work in permanent collections:* V. & A., Bristol City Art Gallery, Reading City Art Gallery, London Transport, John F. Kennedy Centre, Smithsonian Institute, U.S.A., Ministry of Works, etc. *Publications:* The Pendulum (Gollancz, 1966), The Golden Chain (Hutchinson, 1970), The Pendulum, A Round Trip to Revelation (Garrett Publications, U.S.A.; Foreword W. H. Auden). *Address:* Dalesford House, Litton, nr. Bath, Somerset. *Signs work:* "A.R."

ROSZAK, Theodore; sculptor in base metal and alloys, draughtsman in indian ink, pen and brush; mem. of Advisory Committee on Art and Government; mem. Advisory Council Internat. Education and Exchange Program; mem. of University Council on Art and Architecture, Yale University; mem. National Advisory Com., Drawing Soc.; trustee Tiffany Foundation; *b* Posen, Poland, 1 May, 1907; *s* of Kasper Roszak; *m* Florence Sapir; one *d*. *Educ.:* James Monroe Grammar School, Chicago; Hoffman and Karl Schurz High School, Chicago; Columbia University, N.Y.; *studied art* at Art Inst. of Chicago; Nat. Academy of Design, N.Y. *Addresses:* One St. Luke's Pl., New York City, N.Y.; and c/o Pierre Matisse Gallery, 41 East 57th St., New York City, N.Y. *Signs work:* see appendix.

ROTHENSTEIN, Lady, Elizabeth Kennard; *d* of Charles Judson Smith (decd.); *m* Sir John Rothenstein (*q.v.*); one *d* (Lady Dynevor (*q.v.*)). *Educ.:* Univerity of Kentucky (B.A.), Art Students' League, New York. *Publications:* Stanley Spencer (Phaidon British Artists, 1945), Impressionist Paintings (1950), The Virgin and the Child (1951), Stanley Spencer (1961-62); contributions to The Dictionary of National Biography, Vogue, Month, etc. *Addresses:* Beauforest House, Newington, Dorchester, Oxon.; 8 Tryon St., Chelsea, London SW3.

ROTHENSTEIN, Sir John Knewstub Maurice, C.B.E., Ph.D., Hon. LL.D. (New Brunswick and St. Andrews); *b* London, 1901; *e.s.* of Sir William Rothenstein; *m* Elizabeth Kennard Smith (*see* Rothenstein, Lady). *Educ.:* Worcester College, Oxford (Honorary Fellow, 1963), University College, London. Director, Tate Gallery (1938-64); Rector, University of St. Andrews (1964-67); Professor, Art History, Fordham University, New York (1967-68); Agnes Scott College, Georgia (1969-70); Distinguished Professor, City University of New York (1971-72). *Publications:* An Introduction to English Painting (1933), Modern English Painters, I (1952), II (1956), III (1973); Summer's Lease (autobiography, I, 1965), Brave Day, Hideous Night (II, 1966), Time's Thievish Progress (III, 1970), etc. *Addresses:* Beauforest House, Newington, Dorchester, Oxon.; 8 Tryon St., Chelsea, London SW3. *Clubs:* Athenæum, Chelsea Arts (Hon. Mem.).

ROTHENSTEIN, Michael; maker of prints and constructions. *Exhib.:* Llubljana Biennial (1959, 1963, 1965); Tokio Biennial of Prints (1964, 1966); International Exhibition, Lugano (1964); Graven Image Award (1963); one-man exhbns.; Zwemmer Gallery, Grabowski Gallery, Hamilton Gallery, Ohio University, U.S.A. *Work in permanent collections:* B.M., V. & A., Tate Gallery, Museum of Modern Art, New York, Nat. Gall. of Victoria, Australia, Museum of Fine Art, Brussels, Arts Council, British Council. *Publications:* Frontiers of Printmaking, 1966. *Addresses:* Columbia House, Stisted, Braintree, Essex, and 113 Beaufort St., London SW3.

ROTTER, Vilem, F.S.I.A. (1957), Ing.; exhbn. and interior designer and consultant; managing director, Publicity Planning Ltd. (since 1943); founder and princ., Rotter School of Industrial Art, Prague (1934-39); exhbn. adviser to Czechoslovak Govt., London (1941-44); hon. adviser to Dept. of Public Information in relation to Graphic Art for U.N., New York; *b* Brno, Czechoslovakia, 28 May, 1903; *s* of Dr. John Rotter, lawyer; *m* Alzbeta Rotter; one *s*. *Educ.:* Technical University, Brno; *studied art* in Paris. *Work in permanent collections:* Steel Gallery, Science Museum. *Work repro.:* in Designers in Britain. *Publications:* Display, Conferences and Exhbns., Design. *Address:* 8 Hillbrow, Richmond, Surrey. *Signs work:* "Rotter" or "Ro."

ROTTERDAM, Paul (Paul Zwietnig-Rotterdam); painter in oil, resin; Lecturer on Visual Studies, Harvard University, Cambridge, Mass,; *b* Wr. Neustadt, Austria, 12 Feb., 1939; *s* of Peter Zwietnig-Rotterdam; *m* Dr. Heidrun Zwietnig-

Rotterdam; one *d. Educ.:* Academy of Fine Arts, Vienna, University of Vienna; *studied art* at Academy of Fine Art, Guetersloh, Academy of Applied Art. *Work in permanent collections:* Graphic Collection Albertina, Vienna; Busch-Reisinger Museum, Cambridge, Mass.; Museum Joanneum, Graz, Austria; Kunstverein Freiburg, Germany; Museum des 20. Jhd's, Vienna. *Addresses:* private and studio: 388 Broadway, New York City, N.Y. 10013; office: Carpenter Center for the Visual Arts, Harvard University, Cambridge, Mass. 02138 U.S.A. *Signs work:* "Paul Rotterdam."

ROWAN, Evadné Harris, M.S.I.A. (1952), A.I.A. (1949); free-lance artist in pen and ink, water-colour, oil, lithography; *b* Warsash, Hants; *d* of Capt. F. H. Rowan; *m* F. H. Paul. *Studied art:* Gloucester School of Arts and Crafts and Central School of Arts and Crafts, Southampton Row. *Exhib.:* Senefelder Club and Artists International Assoc. *Work repro.:* Heinemann, Macmillan, Penguin Books, Methuen, Harvill Press, Rupert Hart-Davis, Odhams, Collins, Putnams, G.P.O., Dents, O.U.P., Michael Joseph, Ward Lock, Longmans, B.B.C. *Publications:* work in Radio Times, Sunday Times. *Address:* Flat 7, 35 Elm Pk. Gdns., London SW10. *Signs work:* "Evadné Rowan."

RUSCOE, William, N.R.D., M.S.I.A.; lecturer (retired) College of Art, Exeter; asst., Burslem School of Art (1938-42), master-in-charge, Stoke School of Art (1942-44), instructor in pottery, R.C.A. (1939-40); artist in ceramics and painting; *b* Stoke-on-Trent, 20 June, 1904; *s* of William Ruscoe, potter; *m* Olga Stanley Harris, N.R.D.; two *s. Studied art* at Stoke-on-Trent under Gordon M. Forsyth. *Exhib.:* one-man shows: Exeter University, R.A.M. Museum and Art Gallery, Plymouth Civic Centre, Stafford Art Gallery. *Work in permanent collections:* Stoke-on-Trent Museum, Exeter Museum; private collections: America, France, New Zealand. *Publications:* English Porcelain Figures (Tiranti), A Manual for the Potter (Tiranti). *Address:* 46 Birchy Barton Hill, Exeter. *Signs work:* "William Ruscoe."

RUSK, William Sener; Phi Beta Kappa Assoc.; Prof. of Fine Arts Emeritus, Wells College; visiting prof. of Fine Arts (1965-66), Univ. of Richmond; sometime lecturer at Columbia Univ. and Univ. of California (Los Angeles), summer sessions, Cornell Univ., 2nd semester (1958-59); *b* Baltimore, Md., 29 Sept., 1892; *s* of Dr. George Glanville Rusk; *m* Evelyn T. Carroll. *Educ.:* Princeton and Johns Hopkins Univ., Harvard; schools in Paris, Rome, etc. *Publications:* William Henry Rinehart, Sculptor, Methods of Teaching the Fine Arts (editor), Monuments and Memorials (Art in Baltimore), Art in Its Environment. *Address:* Aurora, N.Y.

RUSSELL, Edwin John Cumming, A.R.B.S., Cert. R.A.S., R.A. Gold Medal; sculptor in bronze, stone, wood; *b* Heathfield, 4 May, 1939; *m* Lorne McKean, sculptor; two *d. Studied art* at Brighton College of Art and Crafts (1955-59), Royal Academy Schools (1959-63) under Arnold Machin, R.A., A. J. J. Ayres, F.R.B.S., R.A. Gold Medal for Sculpture. *Work in permanent collections:* Stanley-Bridges (Battersea); Crucifix, and St. Michael, St. Paul's Cathedral; St. Katherine, Westminster Abbey; Woodes-Rogers, Nassau; Billy Smart, Winkfield; Suffragette Memorial, Westminster. *Address:* Lethendry, Hindhead, Surrey. *Signs work:* "E. J. C. RUSSELL" (roman capitals).

RUSSELL, John; author and journalist; Sunday Times Art Critic since 1951; *b* 22 Jan., 1919. *Educ.:* St. Paul's School and Magdalen College, Oxford. *Publications:* Shakespeare's Country (1942), British Portrait Painters (1944), From Sickert to 1948 (1948), Portrait of Logan Pearsall Smith (1950), Switzerland (1950), Erich Kleiber (1957), Braque (1959), Paris (1960), Seurat (1965), Private View (with Bryan Robertson and Lord Snowdon; 1965), Henry Moore (1968),

The World of Matisse (1968), Ben Nicholson (1969). Pop Art Redefined (with Suzi Gablik, 1969), Francis Bacon (1971), Vuillard (1971). *Address:* c/o The Sunday Times, Thomson House, Gray's Inn Rd., London WC1.

RUSSELL, Kathleen Barbara, D.A.Edin. (1962); artist in oil and water-colour, teacher; *b* Edinburgh, 1940; *d* of John Sandilands Russell; *m* John Caskey. *Educ.:* The Mary Erskine School for Girls; *studied art* at Edinburgh College of Art (1958-63) under Sir Wm. Gillies, R.A., R.S.A. and Robin Philipson, P.R.S.A. *Exhib.:* one-man shows in Edinburgh since 1965; R.A., R.S.A., S.S.A., S.S.W.A. *Work in permanent collections:* Watson Coll., Edinburgh Corp. Schools Coll. *Address:* 113 Laleham Rd., Catford, London SE6. *Signs work:* "K" or "Kathleen Russell."

RUSSELL, Pat, F.S.D-C., M.S.S.I., M.A.W.G.; textile artist in fabric collage, designer, calligrapher (specialising in Manuscript books); *b* Wembley, 17 Aug., 1919; *d* of Herbert Cooch; *m* Birrell Russell; one *s*, one *d*. *Educ.:* Farnborough Hill; *studied art* at Chelsea College of Art under M. C. Oliver. *Exhib.:* Oxford Gallery and various group exhbns. *Work in permanent collections:* V. & A., Oxford City and County Museum, Reading Museum. *Publications:* Lettering for Embroidery (Batsford). *Address:* 48 East Saint Helen's St., Abingdon OX14 5EB. *Signs work:* "Pat Russell."

RUSSELL, Richard Drew, R.D.I. (1944), F.S.I.A. (1947); Professor of Furniture Design, Royal College of Art (1949-64), Professor Emeritus (1964); consultant industrial designer; *b* 1903; *s* of S. Bolton Russell; *m*; two *s*, one *d*. *Educ.:* Dean Close School, Cheltenham; Architectural Assoc., London. *Work in permanent collections:* Greek and Oriental galleries and prints and drawings in British Museum, etc. *Work repro.:* in Architectural Review, etc. *Address:* Charley Farm, Willingale, Essex CM5 0PZ.

RUSSELL, Sir (Sydney) Gordon, Kt. (1955), C.B.E. (1947), M.C. (1917), R.D.I. (1940), F.S.I.A. (1945), Hon. Des. R.C.A. (1952), Hon. A.R.I.B.A. (1953), Hon. Fellow (1965), Hon. A.I.L.A. (1955); furniture designer; mem. C.O.I.D. (1944-47), dir. (1947-59), mem. (1960—); pres., Design and Industries Association (1959-62); mem. Design Panel, British Railways Board (1956-66); mem. of Council of R.C.A. (1952-63); mem. of National Council for Diplomas in Art and Design (1961-68); *b* London, 20 May, 1892; *s* of Sydney Bolton Russell; *m* Constance Elizabeth Jane Vere Denning; three *s*, one *d*. *Educ.:* Campden Grammar School. *Publications:* The Story of Furniture; The Things We See: Furniture, autobiography, Designer's Trade. *Address:* Kingcombe, Chipping Campden, Glos. *Club:* Arts.

RUSSELL-FLINT, Francis Murray: see FLINT, Francis Murray Russell.

RUSSELL-HALL, Hugh, R.O.I. (1959); painter in oil; painting tutor, St. Martin's School of Art; *b* 28 Feb., 1905; *s* of Rev. William R. Hall, M.A. *Educ.:* Dundee High School; *studied art* at Dundee School of Art and in Paris in the studio of Emile Othon Friesz. *Exhib.:* R.A., R.S.P.P., R.O.I., and British provincial galleries. *Address:* 13 Maple Rd., London E11. *Club:* Chelsea Arts. *Signs work:* "Hugh Russell Hall."

RUSSON, Agatha; artist in oil, water-colour, crayon; *b* Raymond, Wisc., U.S.A., 1903; *d* of G. Lipinski, D.Med.; *m* Leslie Russon. *Studied art* under Mabel Wickham, R.I., Bernard Adams, R.P., R.O.I., and F. D. Daniels, A.R.C.A. *Exhib.:* Portsmouth, Southampton, R.B.A., R.O.I., Ashmolean Mus., Oxford, N.S. *Work repro.:* Flowers in Window. *Address:* 41 Hocombe Rd., Chandlers Ford, Hants. *Signs work:* see appendix.

RUSZKOWSKI, Zdzislaw; artist in oil, water-colour, etching; *b* Tomaszow, Maz., Poland, 5 Feb., 1907; *s* of Waclaw Ruszkowski, artist; *m* Jenifer McCormack; one *s*, one *d*. *Educ.:* Kalisz Grammar School; *studied art* at Krakow Academy (1924-29), Warsaw Academy (1930-32), Paris (self-taught, 1934-39). *Exhib.:* Warsaw, Paris; since 1940, London, Edinburgh, and provincial galleries. *Work repro.:* in Beaux Arts, Studio, Listener, Times Literary Supplement, Scotsman, Polish Literary News. *Publications:* Aquatints for River of Singing Fish (Hodder and Stoughton), Monograph by J. P. Hodin (Cory, Adams and Mackay. 1966). *Address:* 11 St. Thomas Gdns., Queens Cres., London NW5. *Signs work:* "Ruszkowski."

RUTHERFORD, Alexa, D.A., one year Post Dip.; illustrator in water-colour and inks, and lino printing; designer with printing and stationery firm; *b* Fife, 24 May, 1952; *d* of Thomas Rutherford, A.R.I.B.A.; *m* John Dewar. *Educ.:* Bell Baxter Senior High; *studied art* at Duncan of Jordanstone College of Art, Dundee (1969-74) under Ron Stenberg. *Exhib.:* R.S.A.; Edinburgh, Dundee Grampian Exhbn. *Publications:* Reader 5 Text Book (Oliver & Boyd), stationery products, 'Terston' Notes, etc., magazine illustrations. *Address:* 60 Raeburn Pl., Edinburgh EH4 1HJ. *Signs work:* "Alexa Rutherford."

RUTHERFORD, Eric; painter, printmaker, theatre designer, teacher in England and U.S.A. *Exhib.:* over twenty one-man shows in England, U.S.A., Canada, Spain; including Leicester Galleries, London, Indianapolis Museum, U.S.A., Michael Wyman Gallery, Chicago, U.S.A., Pollock Gallery, Toronto, Canada. *Work in permanent collections:* Arts Council of Great Britain, National Museum of Wales, Financial Times Collection, Museo d'arte Contemporaneo, Madrid, Museo Biblioteca Luis-Arango, Bogota, S.A., South Carolina University, U.S.A., J. B. Speed Museum, Louisville, U.S.A., Indianapolis Museum, U.S.A., Corcoran Gallery, Washington D.C., U.S.A. Producer of first All-African feature film now in National Film Archive, London and Museum of Modern Art, N.Y. *Address:* Ashgate Gallery, Farnham, Surrey. *Signs work:* "Rutherford."

RUTHERFORD, Harry; painter in oil; appeared on B.B.C. TV as illustrator and commentator; teaching staff, Regional College, Manchester (1952-69); President, Manchester Academy of Fine Arts (1960-69); *b* Denton, Lancs., 7 Jan., 1903; *s* of William Robert Rutherford; *studied art* at Manchester School of Art and as pupil of W. R. Sickert and Ernest and Dod Proctor. *Exhib.:* R.A., N.E.A.C., Paris Salon, R.B.A., R.P. *Official purchases:* Stott Bequest, R.A., Manchester, Stockport, Southport, Hyde, Oldham, Lords, Manchester Regiment Regimental Headquarters. *Address:* 17 Nelson St., Hyde, Ches. *Club:* Chelsea Arts. *Signs work:* "H. Rutherford."

RUTTER, Ruth: see ASPDEN, Ruth Spencer.

RYAN, Adrian; painter in oil, water-colour; teacher, Goldsmiths' School of Art since 1948; Cambridge School of Art since 1969; *b* Hampstead, 3 Oct., 1920; *s* of Vivian D. Ryan, painter; *m* 1st, Peggy Rose, one *d*; 2nd, Barbara Pitt, two *d*. *Educ.:* Eton; *studied art* at Slade School. *Exhib.:* R.A., London Group, Tate, etc. *Work in permanent collections:* Tate Gallery, V. & A., Belfast Art Gallery, Manchester Art Gallery, National Gallery of New Zealand, Plymouth Art Gallery, etc. *Official purchases:* Gulbenkian Foundation, Chantry Bequest, Arts Council of G.B., Contemp. Art Soc., etc. *Addresses:* 8 Camden Studios, Camden St., London NW1, and Hill House, Holbrook, Suffolk.

RYAN, John Gerald Christopher; freelance artist in oil, water-colour, pen and ink, mural painter; asst. art master, Harrow School (1948-54); *b* Edinburgh, 4 Mar., 1921; *s* of Sir Andrew Ryan, K.B.E., C.M.G. *Educ.:* Ampleforth College;

studied art at Regent St. Polytechnic (1945-48). *Exhib.:* R.A., Trafford Gallery, Royal Pavilion (Brighton). *Work repro.:* humorous drawings for advertisements and children's magazines and books, Radio Times and animated cartoons for B.B.C. television and overseas education. *Address:* 12 Airlie Gdns., London W8. *Signs work:* "RYAN."

RYAN, June; portrait painter, miniaturist and graphic artist in pastel, oil, water-colour and pencil; *b* London; *d* of Harry Ryan, actor. *Educ.:* St. Elizabeth's Convent, Walthamstow; *studied art* at S.W. Essex Technical College and Polytechnic, Regent St., W1. *Exhib.:* P.S., R.M.S., R.P., R.B.A., etc. *Publications:* author and illustrator of Ballet History (Methuen, 1960); illustrations for Ballet Annual, Ballet Today, Child Education, etc. *Address:* 22 Berkeley Sq., Worthing, Sussex BN11 5AF. *Signs work:* "June Ryan."

RYDER, Margaret Elaine, R.M.S., S.W.A., S.M., Member of the Royal Society of Miniature Painters, Sculptors and Gravers (1963); portrait, flower and landscape painter in oil, pastel, and water-colour, and miniaturist on ivory; for 20 years a freelance commercial artist; *b* Sheffield, 1908; *m* Norman Vint. *Educ.:* Sheffield High School; *studied art* at Sheffield College of Art; numerous scholarships. *Exhib.:* R.A., Paris Salon, Pastel Society, Royal Institute, Exhibition of Flower Painters, Manchester Academy, Aberdeen Society of Arts, Sheffield Society of Artists, Australia, U.S.A.; five one-man shows in Sheffield. *Address:* 26 Bents Dr., Sheffield, 11. *Signs work:* see appendix.

S

SABELIS, Huibert; painter in acrylics, Indian ink; *b* Wageningen, the Netherlands, 28 Feb., 1942; *m* Evangelina Quinto; three *s,* two *d. Studied art* at Technical School Apeldoorn (1957-60) under Mr. Bloothoofd; Instruction Schools include Minneapolis (drawing) (1964); lino printmaking with Henk Krijger (Sengig) (1973). *Exhib.:* one-man shows: Shute Inst., London, Ontario (1967-71), Ingenu Gallery, Toronto, Galt Public A.G., Philippine National Museum (1972), Manila Hilton A.G. (1973), Richmond Arts Centre, B.C. (1973), Kar Gallery, Toronto (1973), Niagara Falls A.G. (1973), Isetan Gallery, Tokyo (1974), Cowansville Arts Centre, P.Q. (1974), Oakville Centennial A.G., Sir Sandford Fleming College, Peterborough (1974), Gallery Heritage, Toronto (1974), Victoria University, Toronto (1975), A.G. at Thomas Elgin, Canada (1975). *Work in permanent collections:* Royal Ontario Museum, National Museum of the Philippines, Niagara Falls A.G. and Museum, Cowansville Arts Centre, Oakville Centennial A.G., Unesco of Japan, Canadian Embassy, Philippines, Dutch Consulate, Toronto, H.R.H. Prince Bernard of the Netherlands. *Address:* 276 Kristin Grove, Mississauga, Ontario, Canada. L5A-3E8.

SACK, Bertha; artist in acrylic, gouache and ink, sculptor; *b* London. *Studied art* at St. Martin's School of Art (1956) under R. V. Pitchforth, R.A. *Exhib.:* R.A., Lord Mayors, R.B.A., H.A.C., F.P.S. *Work in permanent collections:* Canada, U.S.A., Israel and London. *Address:* 60 Farley Ct., Allsop Pl., London NW1. *Signs work:* "B. Sack."

SAHAI, Virendra, Dip.T.P., A.R.I.B.A.; painter; *b* Shahjehanpur, India, 25 June, 1933; *s* of Dr. Girwar Sahay. *Educ.:* trained as an architect and townplanner,

Polytechnic, Regent St., London; *studied art* at Central School of Art. *Exhib.:* one-man shows: New Vision Centre and Biggins Gallery, London (1961), Commonwealth Institute, London (1966), Galerie Suzanne de Coninck, Paris (1967), Bear Lane Gallery, Oxford (1967); group and mixed exhbns.: Redfern Gallery, London, Commonwealth Biennale of Abstract Art (1961-67), Reading Museum, Bradford Museum, Brighton Museum, Beaune Gallery, Paris, and several others. *Work in permanent collections:* Bradford Museum, Councils for Art Education, Leicester and Oxford. *Private collections:* in England, Nigeria, U.S.A., Canada, Germany, Hong Kong and Spain. *Work repro.:* Guardian, Art International. *Address:* 68 Church Rd., Abbots Leigh, Bristol BS8 3QU. *Signs work:* see appendix.

SAILO, Nina; sculptor and designer; *b* St. Petersburg, 26 July, 1906; *d* of Albert Stunkel, architect; *m* Alpo Sailo, sculptor (*died* 6 Oct., 1955); three *s*, one *d*. *Studied art* at Drawing School, Viipuri (1921-24), Technical school in Harrow-on-the-Hill (1930-31), pupil of Alpo Sailo from 1932. *Exhib.:* Kalevalatalo, Helsinki. *Work in permanent collections:* Kalevala Ladies' Soc., Helsinki, in museums (Finland) and in Sweden; memorial medals in Finland and in Sweden. *Official purchases:* public monuments at Helsinki and Tornio. *Address:* Iltaruskontie 4 A 2 Tapiola, Finland. *Clubs:* Charter mem. of Kalevalatalo Foundation, mem. of Kalevala Ladies' Soc. *Signs work:* "N. Sailo."

SALAMAN, ANN: see FAWSSETT, Ann.

SALAMAN, Christopher; artist in oil, bronze and resin bronze; *b* Dorking, 4 Nov., 1939; *s* of Easton Salaman, A.R.I.B.A.; *m*; one *s*. *Educ.:* Bedales School; *studied art* at Camberwell School of Art and Crafts under Karel Vogel. *Exhib.:* Woodstock Gallery, Upper Street Gallery, Mall Galleries. *Address:* West Park Lodge, High Ongar, Essex. *Signs work:* "Christopher Salaman."

SALAMAN, Michael Jonathan; artist in oil, pencil and pen and ink; visiting teacher at Camberwell and Chelsea Schools of Art; *b* Porlock, Somerset, 8 May, 1911; *s* of Michel Hewitt Salaman; *m* Natalie Borisoff; three *d*. *Educ.:* Stowe; *studied art* at Slade School (1928-30) under Prof. Henry Tonks; Ruskin School of Art (1930-31) under Prof. Albert Rutherston; Académie Ranson, Paris (1933-34) under Prof. Bissière. *Work in permanent collections:* oil-painting, Camberwell Borough Council; drawings, V. & A.; and in private collections. *Address:* 271 Goldhawk Rd., London W12. *Signs work:* "Michael Salaman" or "M. Salaman."

SALMON, James Marchbank, D.A. (Edin., 1937), M.S.I.A.; artist in oil, water-colour, pen and ink; potter and lithographer; Princ. Lincoln School of Art (1947-60); Princ. Croydon College of Art (1960-73); Dean, University of Calgary, Alberta (1973—); President N.S.A.E. (1968-69); Chairman Assoc. of Art Institutions (1972-73); M.O.I. artist (1940-43); lecturer, St. Paul's Training College, Cheltenham (1938-47); *b* Edinburgh, 1916; *s* of George Salmon; *m* Margaret Hodges; one *s*, one *d*. *Educ.:* George Watson's Boys' College, Edinburgh; *studied art* at Edinburgh College of Art, Berlin Art Academy, Berlin Textil und Modesschule, Reimann School (Berlin). *Exhib.:* R.A., R.S.A., S.S.A., R.S.W., Berlin Academy, etc. *Address:* 11 Haling Pk. Rd., S. Croydon, Surrey. *Signs work:* "SALMON" (oils), and see appendix.

SALMON, Thomas Graham, M.A., LL.B., J.P., S.S.C.; formerly Sec. and Treas., Soc. of Scottish Artists, Scottish Soc. of Women Artists, Sec. and Treas. Edinburgh Architectural Assoc., Sec., Edinburgh and S.E. of Scotland Section, Cinematograph Exhibitors' Assoc., since 1936; Chairman, Board of Governors, Davidson Clinic, Edinburgh, since 1953; *b* 21 July, 1910; *s* of the late George Salmon, solicitor, Supreme Courts of Scotland; *m* Nancy, *d* of Sir George A.

Waters, LL.D., J.P., former editor of Scotsman; two *s*, one *d*. *Educ.:* George Watson's Boys' College, Edinburgh; Edinburgh University. *Address:* 31 Albany St., Edinburgh.

SALTZMAN, William, B.S. Education, University of Minnesota (1940); easel and mural painter, designer, teacher; Director-resident artist, Rochester Art Centre, Rochester, Minn. (1948-63), Freelance Studio, Minneapolis, Minn. (since 1963); Prof. of Art, Macalester College, St. Paul, Minn. (since 1966); currently painting and designing stained glass for many architectural commissions; exhibiting paintings widely coast to coast; mem. National Society of Mural Painters; *b* Mpls., Minn., 9 July, 1916; *s* of Jacob Saltzman; *m* Muriel; one *s*, two *d*. *Educ.:* University of Minnesota; Art Students League, N.Y.C.; *studied art* as above. *Address:* 5140 Lyndale Ave., S., 55419, Minneapolis, Minnesota. *Signs work:* see appendix.

SALVINI, Roberto; Prof. of the History of Art in the University of Florence since 1963, and art critic; superintendent, Fine Arts, Sicily (1939-43); superintendent, Fine Arts, Modena and Reggio, and director the Galleria Estense, Modena (1943-51); director of the Uffizi Gallery, Florence (1951-56); Professor in the University of Trieste (1958-63); *b* Florence, 6 Feb., 1912; *s* of Stefano Salvini; *m* Katja Rasceva, decd. (1946); one *s*, two *d*. *Educ.:* Florence, Munich, Berlin. *Publications:* books and essays on Agnolo Gaddi, Giotto, Cimabue, Michael Pacher, Byzantine Mosaics in Sicily, Romanesque Sculpture, Contemporary Art, Modern Art Criticism, Botticelli, Flemish Painting, German Painting, etc. *Address:* Via Goffredo Mameli 12, Florence.

SAMPE, Astrid, Hon. R.D.I., London (1949), S.I.D., Dame of the Order of Vasa (1961); Member of A.I.D., New York (1963); designer; director, A.B. Nordiska Kompaniet's design studio since 1937; designer for contract interiors, textile designer for industries making carpets, curtains, upholstery; *b* Stockholm; *d* of Otto Sampe, textile manufacturer, decd.; *m*, divorced; one *s*, one *d*. *Educ.:* Konstfackskolan, Stockholm; R.C.A., London; *studied art* at Atelier Vignal, Paris (1933), and on scholarship to Germany (1934), Italy (1936). *Publication:* Textile Bilderbok, with Vera Djurson (1948). *Address:* Consult Interior and Industrial Design, Karlaplan 4, Stockholm, Sweden. *Club:* Society of Swedish Industrial Designers. *Signs work:* "Astrid Sampe, S.I.D."

SANCHA, R. P.; portrait painter in oil; *b* London, 27 Apr., 1920; *s* of Luis Sancha y Lengo, B.A.; *m* Sheila Neal Green; two *s*, one *d*. *Educ.:* Lindisfarne College; *studied art* at Central School of Arts & Crafts under Rodrigo Moyniham, A.R.A., J. Grant; Byam Shaw School under Patrick Philips, R.P. *Exhib.:* R.A., R.P. *Address:* 8 Melbury Rd., London W14.

SANDBERG, Dr. Willem; former director city museums of Amsterdam; chairman executive, Israel Museum, Jerusalem; typographic designer; *b* Amersfoort, Holland, 24 Oct., 1897. *Address:* Dirk Schäferstraat 37, Amsterdam.

SANDERS, Christopher Cavania, R.P. (1968), R.A. (1961), A.R.A. (1953), A.R.C.A. (1928); painter; gold medallist, Paris Salon (1955); *b* 1905; *m* Barbara Stubbs, A.R.C.A. (1928, *d* 1967); two *s*, two *d*. *Educ.:* Ossett Grammar School (1917-22); Wakefield School of Art (1922-24); Leeds School of Art (1924-26); R.C.A. (1926-29). *Exhib.:* R.A. (thirty-seven exhbns.), R.P.; most art galleries in England. *Address:* 6 Firs Drive, Cranford, Hounslow, Middx. *Signs work:* "Sanders."

SANDERS, Henry; artist, painter of figures, landscapes, animals in oil and water-colour, lithograph, lino-cut; *b* Dresden, Germany, 27 Mar., 1918; *s* of Eugen Salomon, antique dealer; *m*. *Educ.:* Odenwaldschule, Germany; *studied art* at Hornsey College of Art (1935-39), course after war (1945), John Moody, Russell Reeve, H. Holzer. *Work in permanent collection:* Ben Uri Art Gallery. *Work repro.:* Connoisseur, Arts Review. *Address:* 170 Wightman Rd., London N8. *Club:* Ben Uri Art Society.

SANDERS, Violet, S.G.A.; wood-engraver, painter, heraldic artist, illuminator, modeller; *b* Mexico City, 1904; *d* of J. McConnell Sanders, F.C.S., F.I.C.; *m* Major A. J. Mallet (decd.). *Educ.:* Blackheath High School; Eastbourne (Senior Cambridge dipl); Willesden Technical College; dipl. Royal Exhibition standard Board of Educ. spec. wood-engraving, College of Arms (1936-39). *Exhib.:* R.A. (1937, 1939, 1949). Sold work from R.A., Derby Art Gallery by invitation. Art work for I.C.I. *Address:* Violet Lodge, "Sixteenpaws," Upper Hillcrest, Perranporth, Cornwall. *Signs work:* "Violet Sanders Mallet."

SANDERSON, C. J.; 1st prize Corfu Landscapes (1967); Dip. d'Honneur Salon International Biarritz (1974); artist in oil, acrylic, water-colour, pastel, gouache, pencil, etching, Indian ink, stone, clay and wood; *b* London, 18 Aug., 1949; *s* of James Comber Sanderson, printer. *Educ.:* Millfield; *studied art* at Byam Shaw School of Art (1967-71) under Maurice de Sausmarez and Ruskin Spear, R.A. *Exhib.:* one-man shows: Woodstock Gallery (1974), Gallery Vallombreuse (1974), Gallery Mouffe (1974); mixed shows: John Neville (1974), Ashgate Gallery (1973, 1974), Paris Salon (1974), R.A. (1970, 1972, 1973). *Work in permanent collections:* D. J. Redwood White, London, and Paris. *Address:* 7 Gordon Pl., London W8 4JD. *Club:* The Organ. *Signs work:* "C. J. Sanderson."

SANDFORD, Christopher, M.A.(Cantab.); book designer and publisher; learned printing at Chiswick Press; published books under imprints of Boar's Head Press and Golden Hours Press (1930-33); Proprietor, Golden Cockerel Press (1933-59); *b* Cork, 5 Dec., 1902; *s* of Arthur Sandford, M.D., M.Ch.; *m* Lettice Sandford; one *s*, two *d*. *Educ.:* Cheam; Marlborough; Corpus Christi, Cambridge; Sorbonne, Paris. *Exhib.:* book exhbns. throughout the world. *Work in permanent collections:* princ. national and municipal libraries. *Publications:* articles on book-production and illustration in various journals; bibliographies; short stories. *Address:* Eye Manor, Leominster, Herefordshire.

SANDWITH, Noelle; artist in egg tempera, water-colour, line, etching, oil; *d* of Francis Sandwith. *Educ.:* Carshalton House, Surrey; *studied art* at Kingston-on-Thames, Croydon and Heatherley's. *Exhib.:* R.A., R.B.A., S.W.A., Waldorf Astoria, New York; one-man show: Foyle's Art Gallery. *Work repro.:* The Times, Sydney Morning Herald, R.A. Illustrated, Revue Moderne, Frost & Reed. etc. *Work in permanent collections:* Royal Naval College, Greenwich, Starr Commonwealth, Albion, Michigan, U.S.A. *Address:* 17 Addison Rd., Wanstead, London E11. *Club:* H. Hubbard Art Society. *Signs work:* "Noelle Sandwith."

SANFORD, Roy; graphic and consultant designer; own private freelance practice; senior part-time lecturer in graphic design and advertising, Southampton College of Art; *b* 14 Sept., 1914; *s* of Frederick Berkeley Sanford, M.A.; *m* Sheila; three *s*. *Educ.:* Oakdene School, S. Croydon; *studied art* at St. Martin's School of Art (London). *Work repro.:* Graphis Annual, Designers in Britain, Modern Publicity, etc. Joint owner of Gallery 24, with Sheila Sanford. *Address:* Gallery 24, Bimport, Shaftesbury, Dorset. *Signs work:* see appendix.

SANFORD, Sheila; freelance illustrator; *b* Singapore; *d* of A. E. Thornley-Jones; *m* Roy Sanford; three *s*. *Educ.:* Brentwood School, Southport; *studied art* at St. Martin's School of Art. *Work repro.:* book jackets and magazine and newspaper illustrations, portrait painting; in private practice with Roy Sanford and joint owner with him of Gallery 24. *Address:* Gallery 24, Bimport, Shaftesbury, Dorset. *Signs work:* see appendix.

SANZ-PASTOR Fz. de PIÉROLA, Consuelo, Doctor of History; Mem. of Faculty of Cuerpo de Conservadores de Museos; Encomienda con placa de la Orden de Alfonso X (1950); Lazo de Dama de la Orden Isabel la Catolica (1964); Medalla de Plata del Mérito Turistico (1969); Mem. Hispanic Society of America (1959); Directora del Museo Cerralbo (1942); Inspectora de Museos de Bellas Artes (1963); *b* Madrid. *Educ.:* Royal College of Assomption, Madrid; *studied art* at Universities of Zaragoza and Madrid. *Publications:* Guia del Museo Cerralbo (2nd ed. 1969), Catálogos de las Exposiciones A. Berruguete (1960), San Pablo en el Arte (1963), Francisco de Zurbarán (1964), Museos y Colecciones de España (2nd ed. 1972). *Address:* Ventura, Rodriguez 17, Madrid, 8.

SARGENT, John; sculptor; *b* London, 21 July, 1910. *Exhib.:* R.A., Paris Salon, Méd d'Or (1962). *Address:* 22 Church St., Great Wilbraham, Cambridgeshire.

SATO, Key; prize, Tokyo Salon National (1932), prizes of Biennale de Menton (1964); painter in oil and gouache; Founder Member, Sinseisaku, Japan; Member of the Committee of Museum of Modern Art, Kamakura; *b* Oita, Japan, 1906; *m*; one *s*, one *d*. *Educ.:* Oita; *studied art* at Ecole de Beaux Arts, Tokyo (Diploma). *Work in permanent collections:* Musée National d'Art Moderne de Paris, Musée d'Arts Moderne de Ville de Paris, Musée National d'Art Moderne, Tokyo, Musée d'Art Moderne de Kamakura, Tokyo, Japan, Oeuvres acquises par l'Etat, France, Biblioteque Nationale, France, Contemporary Arts Society, Tate Gallery, London, Musée d'Art Moderne d'Helsinki, Finland, Musée de Verviers, Belgium. *Publications:* Theatre de Kabuki in Tokyo; Festival d'Art d'Avant-garde (Paris, 1952). *Address:* 49 Rue de la Procession, Paris 15e. *Signs work:* "Key Sato" and date.

SAUL, Isabel, R.M.S., F.R.S.A.; artist in water-colour, etching, tempera illumination and miniature portraits; *b* Southbourne; *d* of Wm. Osborne Saul, chemist. *Educ.:* Bournemouth High School (now known as Talbot Heath); *studied art* at Bournemouth Municipal College. *Work in permanent collections:* York Minster: illuminated ecclesiastical charts, plan of the Minster, Old Testament panels in the great east window, world map of the provinces and dioceses of the Anglican Communion; Salisbury Cathedral: the Diocese of Salisbury (unsigned); Carlisle Cathedral: The Border Regiment (legend of the colours). *Address:* Sibsey, 254 Iford La., Southbourne, Bournemouth. *Signs work:* see appendix.

SAUTER, Rudolf Helmut, R.B.A., R.W.A.; landscape, portrait, still-life and abstract painter, illustrator, poet and author; *b* May, 1895; *s* of Prof. George Sauter and Lilian Galsworthy; *m* Viola Ada Emily Wood. *Educ.:* Harrow; *studied art* in London and Munich. *Regular exhib.:* London and provinces; one-man shows: London, New York, San Francisco, Cincinnati and elsewhere. *Work in permanent collections:* National Portrait Gallery, Hull, R. West of England Academy and other collections. *Publications:* illustrations to definitive edition of Galsworthy's works, etc.; author of Galsworthy the Man—an Intimate Portrait (1967). *Address:* Fort William, Butterrow, Stroud, Glos. Fellow of International P.E.N. *Signs work:* see appendix.

SAVAGE, Francis B.; artist in oil and water-colour; *b* Wallasey, 6 Jan., 1908; *s* of Ernest A. Savage, Hon. LL.D., P.P.L.A.; *m* Margaret C. McKechnie; one *s*, one *d*. *Educ.:* Bablake School (Coventry) and George Watson's College (Edinburgh); *studied art* in Edinburgh and Bristol. *Exhib.:* R.A., Paris Salon, R.I., R.O.I., R.S.W., G.I., etc. *Address:* Helford, Herbert Rd., Salcombe, Devon. *Club:* Chairman, Salcombe Art. *Signs work:* see appendix.

SAVERYS, Albert, Officier de l'Ordre de Leopold (1935), Officier de l'Ordre de la Couronne (1930), Officier de l'Ordre du Leon Blanc (1936), Officier de l'Ordre des Trois Etoile (1932), Officier de l'Ordre du Grand Duc Geaermies (1936); prof. Nationael Hoger Instituut, Antwerp; Mem. Flemish Academy; landscape, still-life, flower painter in oil and water-colour; *b* Deinze, 12 May, 1886; *s* of Alf. Saverys, painter; *m* Irene de Milt; two *s*, three *d*. *Educ.:* Akademie, Ghent; *studied art* under Prof. Minne George. *Exhib.:* Brussels, Ghent, Antwerp, Luik, London, Paris, Pittsburgh, N.Z., Holland, Prague, Rome, Venice, Moscow, Budapest, Helsinki, Stockholm, Riga, etc. *Address:* Alb. Saverys, Deime, Belgium. *Signs work:* "Savery."

SAWYER, Charles Henry; Director of Museum of Art and Prof. of History of Art at the University of Michigan (1957-72); director, Addison Gallery of American Art, Andover, Mass. (1930-40); director, Worcester Art Museum (1940-47); Director, Division of the Arts, and Dean of the School of Fine Arts, Yale University (1947-57); *b* 20 Oct., 1906; *m* Katharine Clay, 1934. *Educ.:* Yale University, Harvard Law School, Harvard Graduate School. *Address:* Museum of Art, University of Michigan, Ann Arbor, Michigan, U.S.A. *Clubs:* Century, New York; American Antiquarian Soc.; American Academy of Arts and Sciences.

SAWYERS, Dorothy (Mrs. E. G. Fuller), Board of Educ. drawing, painting and industrial design cert., British Institutional Schol. (1927), Turner Gold Medal (1927), Edward Stott Travelling Schol. and Gold Medal (1929); artist in oil and water-colour; teacher, Worthing College of Art (1931-42); *b* Brighton, May, 1904; *d* of Walter Sawyers; *m* Edgar George Fuller; two *s*. *Educ.:* Brighton Secondary School; *studied* at Brighton College of Art (1919-26), R.A. Schools under Sir Walter Russell (1926-29), travelled abroad (1929-30). *Exhib.:* R.A., Brighton A.G., Hove A.G. *Address:* 38 Springfield Rd., Brighton BN1 6DA. *Club:* Reynolds. *Signs work:* "Dorothy Fuller."

SAYCE, Harry H., F.I.A.L., N.D.D.; painter; Head of the Art Department, Paddington School; *m* Oonagh McCarthy; one *s*, three *d*. *Educ.:* Trent Park College; *studied art* at Hammersmith School of Art; lithographic artist with the R.E. Field Survey (Reproduction Unit) in North Africa and Italy, Colchester School of Art (1942), Harrow School of Art (1938), Instituta Delle Arte, Florence (1945). *Exhib.:* R.A., R.B.A., New Burlington Galleries, Square and Mirror, A.I.A., Football and the Fine Arts, Arts Council Tours, Portsmouth, Worthing, Graves Gallery, Sheffield, Brighton, Piccadilly Gallery. *Address:* 9 Brackley Rd., Chiswick, London W4. *Club:* Chelsea Arts. *Signs work:* "Sayce."

SAYER, Harold Wilfred, A.R.C.A. (1936), A.R.E. (1936), A.T.D. (1937), R.W.A. (1957); artist in water-colour, etching; principal lecturer in design, St. Paul's Trng. College, Cheltenham; *b* Isleworth, Middx., 26 May, 1913; *s* of Henry Sayer; *m* Nancy Margetts Bradfield, A.R.C.A.; one *d*. *Educ.:* Isleworth County School; *studied art* at Willesden Art School (1930-33), R.C.A. (1933-36), Goldsmith's College, University of London (1936-37). *Exhib.:* R.A., R.E., London galleries, provincial galleries, travelling exhbns. Wife is author of Costume in Detail, 1730-1930, and Historical Costumes of England under maiden name, Bradfield. *Address:* Elm Cottage, Far End, Sheepscombe, Stroud, Glos. *Signs work:* "H. W. Sayer."

SCARFE, Laurence, A.R.C.A., F.S.I.A.; painter, graphic artist, writer. *Studied* mural painting Royal College of Art. *Exhib.:* West End and provincial galleries, U.S.A., Italy. *Murals for exhbns.:* B.C.M.I., B.I.F., Festival of Britain; coronation mural for I.C.I., Brussels. For s.s. *Orcades* and *Oriana*; Jamestown Museum, Virginia, U.S.A.; Beecham House, London; Royal Garden Hotel, London;

Penthouse mural, New York; mosaic, Scarborough Grammar School, etc. *Publications:* Rome (1950), Venice (1952), Alphabets (1954), Italian Baroque (Motif, 1961); sometime art editor for The Saturday Book, and contributor. *Designer* for C.O.I.; B.B.C.; G.P.O., etc.; ceramic tiles for Carters; prints for Curwen Gallery. Works in V. & A., Imperial War Museum, Science Museum, etc. Lecturer, London Central School of Art & Design (1945-70), now Faculty of Art, Brighton Polytechnic. *Address:* 13 Powis Villas, Brighton.

SCHAEFER, Carl Fellman, R.C.A. (Canada, 1964), F.I.A.L. (1958), C.S.G.A. (1932), C.S.P.W.C. (1933), C.G.P. (1936); Head of Drawing and Painting Dept., Ontario College of Art (1956); Chairman Emeritus (1968-69); Canada Centennial Medal (1967); Queen Elizabeth II Coronation Medal for contributions to Canadian painting; awarded J. S. Guggenheim memorial fellowship for creative painting (1940); painter in oil, water-colour and oil-tempera, printmaker, engraver and lithographer; *b* Hanover, Ontario, 30 Apr., 1903; *s* of John D. Schaefer; *m* Lillien Marie Evers; two *s*. *Educ.:* Hanover, Ontario and Toronto; *studied art* at Ontario College of Art. *Address:* 157 St. Clement's Ave., Toronto, Ontario M4R 1H1. *Signs work:* "C. Schaefer."

SCHAEFFER, Mrs. H. S.; art dealer; specialising in paintings and drawings of 15th to 19th c.; Pres. Schaeffer Galleries. *Address:* 983 Park Ave., New York, N.Y. 10028.

SCHEIDEGGER, Alfred; doctor's degree in history of art; Sec., Swiss Section of Intern. Assoc. of Art Critics; Mem. Swiss Soc. of Art History; Mem. Assoc. Intern. Council of Museums; Mem. Board of Directors of the Museum of Arts, Berne; art critic of Der Bund (Berne); collaborator on Bernhard Geisers Picasso, peintre-graveur; Sec. of the Gottfried Keller-Foundation; *b* Berne, 2 June, 1914; *s* of Siegfried Scheidegger; *m* Elsa Scheidegger-Matti; two *d*. *Educ.:* Berne; *studied art* at Berne University (1937-40). *Address:* Rosenweg, 41 Berne, Switzerland.

SCHIFFNER, Fritz; painter and draughtsman; *b* Graslitz (Czechoslovakia), 26 Aug., 1910; *s* of Franz Schiffner, headmaster. *Educ.:* two schools of art in Czechoslovakia; *studied art* at Academy of Art, Prague (1937-41) under Nechleba and Honich. *Exhib.:* Prague, Berlin, Stuttgart, R.A., provinces. *Work in permanent collections:* wall paintings, mosaics on big buildings, in schools, hospitals, swimming pools, and churches in Germany. *Official purchases:* Minister of Public Worship and Instruction, Prague. *Address:* Stockstadt/Main, nr. Aschaffenburg, Germany.

SCHILSKY, Mrs. Eric: see FOOT, Victorine Anne.

SCHJELDERUP, Gerik; artist-painter in oil, pastel, conté drawing, drypoint, and actor (theatre, B.B.C., films, TV); seven years Life Class, Hampstead's Artists Council; *s* of Gerhard Schjelderup, Norwegian opera composer; *m* Natalie Moya, actress. *Educ.:* Oslo; *studied art* at Oslo, Munich; scenic design, Jens Wang, Oslo; drawing and painting, Heymann Schule, Munich. *Exhib.:* N.S. *Work in permanent collections:* Oslo University (Music Dept.); most work in private collections. *Publications:* translated Bergliof Ibsen's The Three Ibsens (Hutchinson), B.B.C. Features on Nansen and Amundsen, lectures on Edvard Munch. *Address:* 32 Seafort Ave., Dublin, Eire. *Signs work:* "Gerik."

SCHMALENBACH, Fritz, Ph.D.; Hon. Prof. Universität Kiel (1970); Director of the museums of Lübeck (1956-74); Curator, Berne Kunstmuseum (1950-55); authority on 18th, 19th and 20th century History of Art and on Theory of Art; *b* Cologne, 13 July, 1909; *s* of Eugen Schmalenbach; *m* Susanna, Bing. *Studied art* under H. Jantzen, A. E. Brinckmann, Heinrich Alfred Schmid.

Publications: Jugendstil (1935), Kunsthistorische Studien (1941), Neue Studien über Malerei des 19. und 20. Jahrhunderts (1955), Käthe Kollwitz (1965), Oskar Kokoschka (1967); Studien über Malerei und Malereigeschichte (1973); Die Malerei der, Neuen Sachlichkeit' (1974). *Address:* Lübeck, Wakenitzstr. 32, Germany.

SCHMID, Alfred A., Dr. Ph. (Basle, 1946); chargé de cours at Fribourg University (1946), Mem. Federal Commission of the Gottfried Keller Foundation (1948), Vice-Pres. (1957), Mem. Swiss National Commission U.N.E.S.C.O. (1949-60), Full Prof. of History of Art at Fribourg University (1949), Mem. Federal Com. of Historical Monuments (Pres., 1964); Keeper of the Fine Arts Museum (Musée d'art et d'histoire), Fribourg (1952-56); Mem. C.I.H.A., Mem. of the Executive Board (1969); Mem. of the Executive Board of I.C.O.M.O.S. (1964); *b* Lucerne, 29 Mar., 1920; *s* of François Schmid. *Educ.:* Lucerne, Zürich University, Basle University. *Publications:* Buchmalerei (with Prof. Boeckler, in Handbuch der Bibliothek-swissenschaft, Vol. I, 1950), Die Buchmalerei des 16. Jh. in der Schweiz (1954), Die Bibel von Moutier-Grandval (Brit. Mus. Add. MS. 10546), with E. Beer, A. Bruckner, I. Duft, B. Fischer and others (Berne 1972). *Address:* Fribourg, Boulevard de Pérolles 59.

SCHMID, Fritz; portrait painter in oil; Mem. of National Soc. for Art Educ. and College Art Assoc. of America; Slade School prizeman; *b* Basle, 11 Sept., 1898; *s* of J. Schmid-Paganini, D.Ph., scientist. *Educ.:* Basle and Zürich; *studied art* at Slade. *Exhib.:* N.E.A.C., New York, Paris, Basle, Zürich, Switzerland. *Work in permanent collections:* Oeffentliche Kunstsammlung, Basle, Dr. H. Burckhardt Collection, Basle. *Publications:* The Practice of Painting, The Technique of Goya, Portrait Thomas Mann. *Address:* 25 Anwandstr., Zürich, Switzerland.

SCHMOLLER, Hans Peter; director of production, Penguin Books, Ltd.; *b* Berlin, 9 Apr., 1916; *s* of Hans Schmoller, M.D.; *m* 1st, Dorothée Wachsmuth (*d*. 1948); one *d*; 2nd, Tatyana Kent; one *s*. *Educ.:* Berlin; *studied* design, typography and calligraphy at Berlin School of Graphic Arts. *Work repro.:* Designers in Britain, Penrose Annual, Who's Who in Graphic Art, Printing Review, etc. *Publications:* articles in Penrose Annual, Signature, The Times Printing Supplement (1955), The Times Literary Supplement, Philobiblon, Motif, etc. Gold medallist, International Book Design Exhbn., Leipzig (1971). *Address:* Steading, Down Pl., Windsor, Berks. *Clubs:* Arts, Double Crown.

SCHOFFER, Nicolas; sculptor; *b* Kalocsa, Hungary, 6 Sept., 1912 (French nationality); *s* of Joseph Schoffer, advocate; *m* Marie-Rose. *Educ.:* College of Jesuits, Kalocsa, Budapest University (doctorat en droit); *studied art* at Ecole de Beaux Arts, Budapest (1930-35), Ecole de Beaux Arts, Paris (1937-39). *Work in permanent collections:* Musée d'Art Moderne, Paris, Musée d'Art, Buenos Aires, Salisbury Museum, S. Rhodesia, Brussels Museum, Knox-Albright Museum, Buffalo, Museum of Modern Art, New York. *Work repro.:* Nicolas Schoffer (Griffon, Neuchâtel), Le Spatiodynamisme Art d'Aujourd'hui Boulogne-sur-Seine. *Publications:* La Ville Cybernetique, Le Nouvel Esprit Artistique, La Tour Lumiere Cybernetique (Editions Denoel, Paris); Entretiens avec Nicolas Schöffer (Editions Belfond, Paris). *Address:* 15 rue Hegesippe Moreau, Paris, 18e. *Signs work:* "Schoffer."

SCHOTZ, Benno, R.S.A., LL.D., B.Sc., Hon.F.R.I.A.S.; sculptor in most materials; Her Majesty's Sculptor in Ordinary for Scotland; *b* Arensburgh, Estonia, 10 Sept., 1891; *m* Milly; one *s*, one *d*. *Educ.:* Pernu, Estonia, and Glasgow College of Science and Technology; *studied art* at Glasgow School of Art. *Work in permanent collections:* Kelvingrove Art Gallery, Glasgow; National Portrait Gallery, Edinburgh; Royal Scottish Academy, House of Commons; Modern Art

Association, Aberdeen, Belfast, Dundee, Paisley, Perth, Stoke-on-Trent, Jerusalem and Tel-Aviv Art Galleries. *Address:* 2 Kirklee Rd., Glasgow G12. *Club:* Glasgow Art. *Signs work:* "Benno Schotz."

SCHREIBER, Mrs. Gaby, F.S.I.A.D.; general consultant designer for industry; specialist in colour consultancy and interiors; Chairman: Gaby Schreiber & Associates; Convel Ltd.; *d* of Gunther George Peter Wolff; *m* Leopold Schreiber (d. 1961). *Educ.:* studied art, stage and interior design in Vienna, Florence, Berlin and Paris. Interior design consultant to: National Westminster Bank Ltd.; Westminster Foreign Bank, Brussels (1972-73); Chairman's offices, G.H.P. Group Ltd. (1974); President's offices Gulf Oil-Eastern Hemisphere (1973-74), etc. Has broadcast and appeared on TV. *Publications:* contribs. on industrial and interior design and on colour to art and technical publications; her work has appeared in international books and journals on design. *Recreations:* gardening, farming, golf, paintings, drawings. *Address:* 9 Eaton Sq., London SW1.

SCHULTZ, Alexander; artist, painter in oil; Prof. of Norwegian State Academy (autumn, 1955), Director-General (1958); prize winner, 1er Festival International de la Peinture (1969); *b* Oslo, 25 May 1901; *s* of Eugene Schultz, prof. of zoology; *m* Else Nygaard; two *s*, one *d*. *Studied art* in Paris under Henrik Sorensen, Othon Friesz (1919-29). *Exhib.:* Salon d'automne, Paris (1969), Oslo, Stockholm, Copenhagen, Paris, The Hague, Lausanne, Mentone, Pittsburgh, International exhbn.; San Francisco, Basle, Helsinki. *Work in permanent collections:* National Gallery, Oslo; Art Museum, Bergen; Art Museum, Trondheim; National Museum, Stockholm; Art Museum, Copenhagen; Norwegian State Gallery. *Publications:* Konstrevy, Stockholm, Kunst og Kultur, Oslo, Kunsten Jdag nr. 1 (1963), Morsk Bildende Kunst. *Address:* Myrhaugen 15, Oslo 7. *Signs work:* "Alexander Schultz."

SCHWARTZMAN, Arnold Martin; elected to Alliance Graphic Internationale (1974); artist in pencil and wash, graphic designer, film director; external assessor: The Royal College of Art for Masters Degrees and the National Council for Academic Awards for B.A. (Hons.); Director: The White Elephant Gallery; *b* London, 6 Jan., 1936; *s* of David Schwartzman, company director; *m* Marilyn Schwartzman; one *d*. *Educ.:* Shoreham Grammar School; *studied art* at Thanet School of Art and Crafts (1951-53); Canterbury College of Art (1953-56) under Stanley Hickson. *Exhib.:* New York, Tokio, Paris, Milan, Brussels, Amsterdam, etc. *Address:* 27 Curzon St., London W1. *Signs work:* "A. M. Schwartzman."

SCOTT, Douglas, F.S.I.A.; industrial designer; former D.S. Associates Ltd. (1957); *b* 4 Apr., 1913; *s* of Edward Scott, engineer; *m* Kathleen Tierney; one *s*, one *d*. *Educ.:* L.C.C. Central School of Arts; Birmingham College of Art; started career in drawing office of Osler and Faraday, Ltd., electric light fitting manufacturers, then at Birmingham works; joined G.V.D. Illuminators as chief designer in 1933; joined Raymond Loewy, Hon. R.D.I., in 1936; war years spent at de Havillands, Edgware, in aero engine dept.; instructor at L.C.C. Central School in industrial design; formed Scott Ashford Associates with F. C. Ashford, M.S.I.A. (1949). *Address:* 100 Gloucester Pl., London W1. *Clubs:* Studio, Merries.

SCOTT, Gerald, D.F.A. (Slade), F.R.B.S., R.W.A.; sculptor in bronze, wood, stone, resin and painter; principal lecturer Faculty of Art and Design, Bristol Polytechnic; *b* Hersham, Surrey, 9 Feb., 1916; *m* Jessica (*née* Cosson); one *s*, one *d*. *Educ.:* Tiffin Boys' School, Kingston-on-Thames; *studied art* at Kingston School of Art (1946-49), Slade School, University College, London (1949-52, Professor A. H. Gerrard). *Work in permanent collections:* R.W.A., L.C.C., Bristol Corporation, Lancs. C.C. *Address:* 20 Aberdeen Rd., Redland, Bristol, BS6 6HU. *Signs work:* "Gerald Scott" and date.

SCOTT, Ian William Ligertwood, D.A.(Aber.) 1961, Post. Grad. (1962), Latimer Award, R.S.A. (1965), Benno Schotz Prize, R.S.A. (1966), F.R.B.S. (1972); painter and sculptor in clay, final casts in cement fondu, fibre-glass resin, portrait work in bronze; *b* Ronaldsay, Orkney Islands, 23 Apr., 1940; *s* of Sydney Scott, farmer. *Educ.:* Kirkwall Grammar School, Orkney; *studied art* at Gray's School of Art, Aberdeen under Leo Clegg, D.A., D.S.C. *Exhib.:* one-man shows: Edinburgh, Aberdeen, King's Lynn, Norfolk, Thorshavn, Faeroe Islands; mixed shows: London, Graves A.G., Sheffield, Madurodam, Holland, S.A.C., Scottish Arts Council, Royal Scottish Academy. *Work in permanent collections:* Scottish Arts Council, Linacre College, Oxford, Oxford University, Orkney County Library. *Address:* Antabreck, N, Ronaldsay, Orkney Islands. *Signs work:* "Ian Scott."

SCOTT, John Edward, A.T.D., R.C.A., F.R.S.A.; lecturer, School of Art, Clwyd, N. Wales; artist in oil; *b* Beckenham, Kent, 21 Apr., 1934; *m* Nina. *Educ.:* Windsor Grammar School; *studied art* at Reading University School of Fine Art (1954-57); painting under Prof. J. Antony Betts. *Work in permanent collections:* Royal Cambrian Academy,works privately owned in Europe, esp. London. *Address:* Drws-y-Nant, Bronwylfa Rd., Legacy, Wrexham, Clwyd, N. Wales. *Signs work:* "John Scott."

SCOTT, Marian D., A.R.C.A.; mem. Société des Artistes Professionnels du Quebec, and C.A.R., former member of Canadian Group of Painters (group no longer in existence); painter in acrylic polymer; teacher and housewife; *b* Montreal, 26 June, 1906; *d* of R. J. Dale; *m* Frank R. Scott; one *s*. *Studied art* at Art Assoc. of Montreal, Ecole des Beaux-Arts (Montreal), Slade School. *Exhib.:* N.Y. World's Fair (1939), Canadian National Exhbn., O.S.A., Canadian Group, and in U.S.A., Brazil, Australia, South Africa, London. *Work in permanent collections:* Montreal Museum of Fine Arts, Quebec Provincial Museum, Toronto Art Gallery, National Gallery of Canada, Vancouver Art Gallery, Bezalel Museum (Jerusalem), Beaverbrook Museum (Fredrickton, N.B.), Thomas Moore Institute, Dept. of External Affairs (Montreal), Toronto Dominion Bank. *Address:* 451 Clarke Ave., Westmount, Montreal. *Signs work:* "M. Scott."

SCOTT, Sir Peter Markham, C.B.E., D.S.C. and Bar, LL.D.; painter; Director and founder of The Wild Fowl Trust, Slimbridge, Glos.; 1st Vice-Pres. and Chairman, World Wildlife Fund; *b* 1909; *s* of Capt. R. F. Scott; *m* 1st, Jane Howard, one *d*; 2nd, Philippa Talbot-Ponsonby, one *d*. *Educ.:* Oundle and Trinity College, Cambridge; Munich State Academy, R.A. Schools. *Address:* The New Grounds, Slimbridge, Glos. *Clubs:* Royal Yacht Squadron; Island Sailing; Cambridge University Cruising; Savile; Cambridge University Pitt.

SCOTT-MOORE, Elizabeth, R.W.S., N.E.A.C.; portrait and landscape painter and illustrator; *b* Dartford, Kent; *d* of Henry Brier, M.I.M.E.; *m* John Scott-Moore, F.S.S., F.S.A.A. *Educ.:* Dartford, Kent; *studied art* at Goldsmiths' School of Art, Central School of Art. *Exhib.:* R.A., R.W.S., R.P., N.E.A.C.; awarded Gold Medal for Painting, Paris Salon (1962), 1st Prize for water-colour, Glastonbury, Conn., U.S.A. *Work in many private and permanent collections* in America, Italy, Norway and British Isles. *Work repro.:* illustrated numerous children's books for Oxford University Press, Nelson, Blackies, Cassells, etc. *Official purchases:* Min. of Works; Hull Corp. *Address:* Brier Cottage, Wentworth, Virginia Water, Surrey. *Club:* Chelsea Arts. *Signs work:* "Elizabeth Scott-Moore."

SCOTT-TAGGART, Elizabeth Mary Josephine, N.D.D.; sculptor working in bronze, aluminium, ceramics; stone and wood-carver; *b* nr. Croydon 10 Oct.,

1927. *Educ.:* Old Palace School, Croydon; *studied art* at Central School of Arts and Crafts, and St. Martin's, London (1945-49). *Exhib.:* R.A.; group shows: R.B.A., Trends at Mall Galleries, Loggia Gallery, Wooburn and Cookham Festivals; two-man show: Threehouseholds Gallery, Chalfont St. Giles. Work to be seen at Kaczynski Gallery, Hampstead Way, NW11. *Address:* 96 Gregories Rd., Beaconsfield, Bucks. *Signs work:* "est."

SCRYMGEOUR WEDDERBURN, Janet, A.R.B.S. (1975), R.S.A. Ottillie Helen Wallace Scholarship (1972), R.S.A. Benno Schotz Prize (1973), Paris Salon bronze medal, silver medal; sculptor in clay and bronze, stained glass window designer; *b* Winchester, 14 Aug., 1941; *d* of Lt. Col. the Hon. David Scrymgeour Wedderburn, D.S.O.; *m* Mervyn Fox-Pitt; one *s,* two *d. Educ.:* Kilgraston, Convent of the Sacred Heart, Bridge of Earn, Perthshire; *studied art* with Alastair Ross, F.R.B.S. (1970-1971). *Exhib.:* R.S.A. (1971-76, sculpture); Paris Salon (1972, 1973, sculpture). *Work in permanent collection:* East Window of the Episcopal Church of St. James the Great, Cupar, Fife. *Address:* Grange Scrymgeour, Cupar, Fife. *Signs work:* "J.S.W."

SEABY, Wilfred A., F.S.A., F.M.A., Hon. M.A.; water-colour painter; Director, Ulster Museum, N. Ireland (1962-70); Chairman, Standing Committee, Arts Council of Northern Ireland (1962-64); Mem. Board of Arts Council of Northern Ireland (1961-72); *b* Reading, 16 Sept., 1910; *s* of Allen William Seaby (1867-1953), Professor of Fine Art, University of Reading (1911-33); *m* Nora Joyce Pecover; two *s,* one *d. Educ.:* Wycliffe College, Stonehouse, Gloucestershire; *studied art* at Reading School of Art (1926-27). *Publications:* papers on applied arts, antiquities and numismatics. *Address:* 36 Ladbrook Rd., Solihull, W. Midlands. *Signs work:* "W. A. Seaby."

SEAGER, Harry Abram, A.T.D. (Birm., 1955); sculptor in glass and steel; Senior Lecturer in Fine Art, College of Art, Stourbridge, Worcs.; *b* Birmingham, 9 May, 1931; *s* of Maurice Seager; *m* Marie Alfred; one *d. Educ.:* Holly Lodge Grammar School, Smethwick, Warley, Worcs.; *studied art* at College of Art and Crafts, Birmingham. *Work in permanent collections:* City Art Gallery, Leeds, C.A.S., London, Mineral Separations, London, Joseph H. Hirshorne Coll., U.S.A.; collected in U.K., Canada, U.S.A., Holland, Italy; Leicestershire E.C. (in progress, 1969), Shenstone Training Coll., Bromsgrove, Worcs. *Work repro.:* in commercial journals, newspapers, Domus, Art and Artists, Harper's Bazaar, Apollo, etc. Interviewed on TV Française (Fondation Maeght), 1968. B.B.C. TV film, 1969. *Address:* 1 Baylie St., Stourbridge, Worcestershire. *Signs work:* "H. Seager."

SEARLE, Ronald, F.S.I.A., A.G.I.; *b* Cambridge, 3 Mar., 1920; *studied* Cambridge School of Art (1936-39). *Exhib.:* Leicester Galleries (1948, 1950, 1954 and 1957); Kraushaar Galleries, New York (1959); Bianchini Gallery, New York (1963); Kunsthalle, Bremen (1965); Wilhelm-Busch Museum, Hanover (1965); 3rd Biennale, Tolentino, Italy (1965); Haus am Lützowplatz, Berlin (1965); Galerie Münsterberg, Basle (1966); Wolfgang Gurlitt Museum, Linz, Austria (1966); Galerie La Pochade, Paris (1966, 1967, 1968, 1969, and 1971); Galerie Gurlitt, Munich (1967, 1969, 1970, 1971 and 1973); Bibliothèque Nationale, Paris (1973), etc. *Address:* c/o 11 Jubilee Pl., London SW3 3TE. *Club:* Garrick. *Signs work:* see appendix.

SEDDON, Richard Harding, A.R.W.S. (1972), Ph.D. (1946), F.M.A. (1953), A.R.C.A. (1939); painter in oil and water-colour, writer and lecturer; Director of Liberal and Historical Studies, School of Design and Furniture, Bucks. College of Higher Education. *Educ.:* King Edward VII School and Reading University; *studied art* at R.C.A. (1936-39). *Exhib.:* R.A., R.W.S., and provincial galleries.

Work in permanent collections: V. & A., Imperial War Museum, Pilgrim Trust, Sheffield, Leeds, Southport, Derby and Reading official collections. *Publications:* The Artist's Vision, The Academic Technique of Oil Painting, A Hand Uplifted (war memoirs), Art Collecting for Amateurs, Yorkshire Post Art Critic (1974). *Address:* 6 Arlesey Close, London SW15.

SEGAL, Hyman, F.I.A.L., R.B.A.; artist, sculptor, designer; works in oil, charcoal, chalk, pastel, terracotta; *b* London, 26 May, 1914; *s* of Fredel Segal; *m* Lilla Beryl. *Educ.:* Elementary and Central School, London; *studied art* at St. Martin's School of Art, principally under Leon Underwood and Vivian Pitchforth. *Exhib.:* R.P., R.B.A., W.E.A., Imperial War Museum, Paris Salon, Bankfield Museum, Halifax, Batley, Swindon, Plymouth, Exeter, Rotherham, Hull, Nairobi, E. Africa, Russell Coates Gallery, Benuri Soc., Truro Art Gallery, International Club, Manchester, Whitechapel Art Gallery. *Permanent exhbn. in:* The Segal Room, Sloop Inn, St. Ives. *Address:* 10 Porthmeor Studios, St. Ives, Cornwall. *Signs work:* see appendix.

SENA, Antonio; C. Gulbenkian Scholarship (1966-67), 1st Prize, General Motors Art Exhbn., Lisbon (1968); painter in spray paint, oil, acrylic and pastels on canvas and paper, lithography and screen printing; *b* Lisbon, Feb., 1941. *Educ.:* Lisbon University (Sciences); *studied art* at St. Martin's School of Art, London (1966-67) under John Latham. *Exhib.:* 8th Tokyo Biennale (Japan, 1965), Art Portugais, Brussels, Paris, Madrid (1968), Apollinaire Celebration, I.C.A., London (1968); one-man shows: Lisson Gallery (1967) and Galerie Hachette (1971) in London. *Work in permanent collection:* C. Gulbenkian. *Work repro.:* Nothing doing in London, One (1966). *Address:* 1/713 Fulham Rd., London SW6. *Signs work:* "SENA."

SENIOR, Bryan; painter of figures, landscape, still-life; *b* Bolton, 1935. *Educ.:* Clifton College; Cambridge University (1954-57) *studied art* at Chelsea School of Art (1954). *Exhib.:* one-man shows include: Crane Kalman Gallery, London (1965, 1968, 1971). Demarco, Edinburgh (1970, 1973), Vaccarino, Florence (1968, 1970, 1975); Pucker-Safrai, Boston, U.S.A. (1968), Bolton Art Gallery (1961), Fieldborne Galleries, London (1972, acrylics), Ashgate Gallery, Farnham (1973, acrylics), Exeter Museum (1974), Exeter University (1975). *Work in permanent collections:* Bolton Art Gallery, Nuffield Foundation, C.A.S. of Wales, Financial Times. *Address:* 114 Priory Rd., London NW6 3NS.

SERPAN, Iaroslav; artist in oil, gouache, lithography and sculpture; poet; Docteur-ès-Sciences (Mathematical Biology); *b* Prague, 4 June, 1922; *s* of Eugen Serpan; *m* Lucienne; one *d. Educ.:* Lycée de Versailles and Paris University (Sorbonne). *Work in permanent collections:* Museum of Modern Art, New York; S. Guggenheim Museum, New York; Galerie Stadler, Paris; Galerie van de Loo, Munich; Galerie Lauter, Mannheim; Gutai Pinacothek, Tokyo, etc. Mural at the Besançon University, France (enamelled lava, 60 sq. m.). *Address:* 45 Avenue d'Aligre, 78230 Le Pecq, France. *Signs work:* "Serpan."

SERRA-BADUE, Daniel F.; Guggenheim Foundation Fellowships, N.Y. (1938, 1939); Walter Lippincott Prize, Penn. Acad. of Fine Arts, Philadelphia (1941); Purchase Prizes: II Bienal Hispano Americana, VII Salon Nacional, Havana (1954); Cintas Foundation Fellowships, N.Y. (1963, 1964); painter, graphic artist in oil and lithograph and art teacher; Instructor of Painting, Brooklyn Museum Art School, N.Y.; Associate Professor of Art History, St. Peter's College, Jersey City, N.J.; *b* Santiago de Cuba, 8 Sept., 1914; *s* of Daniel Serra y Navas, lawyer and educator; *m* Aida Betancourt Zabala; one *d. Educ.:* Universities of Barcelona and Havana; *studied art* at Escuela de Bellas Artes,

Santiago de Cuba (1924-26), Studios of Borrell-Nicolau and Muntané, Barcelona (1932-36), Escuela de Bellas Artes, Barcelona (1932-36), The Art Students League, The National Academy of Design, Columbia University, N.Y. (1938-40). *Work in permanent collections:* Museo Municipal, Santiago de Cuba, Museo Nacional, Havana, Metropolitan Museum, N.Y., Public Library, N.Y. *Publications:* The Visual Arts in Santiago de Cuba during the Colonial Period. *Address:* 15 West 72nd St., New York, N.Y., 10023. *Signs work:* see appendix.

SERVOLINI, Luigi, D.L., D.F.A., Accademico Arti del Disegno di Firenze. Mem. Royal Society of Arts (London), Secretary-General of the Assoc. Incisori d'Italia, Milan; artist, designer, wood engraver, lithographer, writer and art critic, journalist; head of the movement of the new wood-engraving of Italy; *b* Livorno, Tuscany, 1 Mar., 1906; *s* of Carlo Servolini, artist and etcher (*b* 1876, decd. 1948); *m*; two *s*. Prof. of the Craft of Engraving at the R. Istituto del Libro and Director of the University Library, Urbino (1930-39); Director of the Cultural and Artistic Insts. of Forli (1939-53); Director of the Rizzoli Inst. for Instruction in the Graphic Arts, Milan (since 1953); teacher of History of Art; Principal in stat. high schools (since 1965); Professor Spec. School "Storici d'Arte," Pisa University. Knight-Grand Officer Class Merit of Ital. Republic. *Exhib.:* six Biennales at Venice, seven Quadriennals at Rome; Chicago, London, Paris, Berlin, etc. *Work in permanent collections:* Represented in over seventy public galleries in Europe and America. *Addresses:* postal: piazza d.Liberta, 33, 57023-Cècina, (LI), Italy; via B. Borromei, 11, 57100-Leghorn, Italy.

SETCH, Terry, D.F.A. (Lond., 1959); painter, Senior Lecturer in Fine Art, Cardiff College of Art; *b* London, 11 Mar., 1936; *s* of Frank Arthur Setch, welder; *m* Dianne Shaw; one *d*. *Educ.:* Sutton and Cheam School; *studied art* at Sutton School of Art (1950-54), Slade School of Fine Art (1956-60). *Work in permanent collections:* Arts Council of Great Britain, Arts Council of Wales, University of Wales, Contemporary Arts Society of Wales, V. & A., University of London, Swansea University. *Address:* 111 Plymouth Rd., Penarth, Glamorgan, S. Wales. *Signs work:* "Setch."

SEUPHOR, Michel; writer, painter (in Chinese ink, and coloured Paper collage), art historian, poet; *b* Antwerp, 10 Mar., 1901; *m* Suzanne Plasse; one *s*. *Educ.:* Antwerp and University of Louvain. *Exhib.:* Galerie Berggruen, Paris; Galerie Denise René, Paris; Rose Fried Gallery, New York; Galleria Lorenzelli, Milan; Moderne Galerie, Basel; Galerie der Spiegel, Cologne; Documenta II, Kassel; Galerie St. Stephen, Wien; Galerie Saint Laurent, Brussels; Galerie Ziegler, Zürich; Robles Galleries, Los Angeles; Galerie Martano, Turin. Tapestries, mosaics and ceramics (Sèvres). *Address:* 83 avenue Emile Zola, Paris, XV. *Signs work:* see appendix.

SEVERIN, Mark, mem., National Reg. of Designers; mem., R.A. of Belgium and Belgian R.S.A.; Prof. of Engraving at Antwerp University of Art; Prof. of Plantin Inst. of Typography; Commander of Orders of Leopold and the Crown: of Order of Jap. Empire; painter, engraver; art director with London agency; freelance since 1938; *m* Nina Holme; two *s*. *Educ.:* Ghent and Oxford University. *Official purchases:* pictures by Belgian Govt.; stamp designs by G.P.O. and Belgian P.O.; pictures in V. & A.; many illustrations for British and foreign publishers. *Publications:* books on various art subjects. *Addresses:* c/o A. S. Knight Ltd., Chansitor House, Chancery Lane, London WC2, and Twinstead Old Rectory, Sudbury, Suffolk. *Signs work:* "SEVERIN."

SEWARD, Prudence Eaton, A.R.W.S., A.R.E., A.R.C.A., Rome Scholar; freelance artist in pen and ink, water-colour; *b* London, 1926; *d* of John Pearson

Seward; one *d. Educ.:* Northwood College, Northwood, Middx.; *studied art* at Harrow Art School (1945-47) under Heber Thompson, R.C.A. (1947-49), British School at Rome (1949-51) under Robert Austin, R.A. *Publications:* Children's books for Bodley Head, O.U.P., Collins, Hamish Hamilton, Nelson, Andre Deutsch, Methuen, Macmillan, Penguin, Longmans. *Address:* Syleham Hall Lane, Wingfield, Diss, Norfolk. *Clubs:* Rome Scholars Soc., R.W.S. *Signs work:* "P. Seward."

SEWTER, Albert Charles, B.Sc. (Econ.), M.A., F.M.A., F.R.S.A.; art historian; asst. Leicester Museum and Art Gallery (1935-39); editor, Burlington Magazine (1939-40); asst. director, Barber Inst. of Fine Arts, University of Birmingham (1940-49); absent on war service (1942-46); senior lecturer, University of Manchester (1949), Reader (1966); member of Whitworth Art Gallery Committee since 1953; retd. 1973; *b* 29 Nov., 1912; *m* 1st, Annie Beatrice Dibdin (d. 1941); 2nd Margarita Masters (div. 1964); two *s. Publications:* Glyn Philpot (Batsford, 1951), On the Relationship between Painting and Architecture (Tiranti, 1952), The Art of Fresco Painting (Tiranti, 1952), Modern British Woodcuts and Wood-engravings in the Whitworth Art Gallery (1962); I Disegni di G. B. Piazzetta, Rome (1969); Baroque and Rococo Art (Thames & Hudson, 1971); The Stained Glass of William Morris and his Circle (Yale U.P., 1974-75), etc. *Addresses:* The Cottage, Greenbank House, Albert Sq., Bowdon, Cheshire; Carmen, Ganu St., Birkirkara, Malta.

SEYD, Eileen, F.R.S.A., Member United Society of Artists; artist in oil, watercolour; *d* of Harold Seyd; *m* Hugh Jeaffreson. *Studied art* at Central School of Arts and Crafts. *Exhib.:* R.A., R.O.I., R.B.A., N.S., United Society of Artists, Paris Salon, Russell-Cotes Art Gallery, Société des Independants (Paris), Guildhall, Royal Exchange; one-man shows: Cooling Galleries, Parsons and São Paulo (1969). *Work repro.:* Revue Moderne. *Address:* Turnpidgeons, Oxhey Lane, Hatch End, Middx. *Clubs:* Hesketh Hubbard; Hon. Secretary and Founder Member of Stanmore Art Society; Member of British Association of Art Therapist working at Royal National Orthopaedic Hospital, Stanmore. *Signs work:* "Seyd."

SHACKLETON, Keith Hope, R.S.M.A., S.W.L.A.; artist in oil and black and white, writer, TV; *b* Weybridge, 16 Jan., 1923; *m* Jacqueline; two *s*, one *d. Educ.:* Melbourne, Australia, Oundle. *Work in permanent collections:* R.S.M.A. Diploma Collection, Maritime Museum, Greenwich. *Publications:* Wake, Tidelines, Wild Animals of Britain, My Favourite Stories of Wild Life, No Echo in the Sky, Highland Days and Nights, Varda, Ocean Birds, Birds of the Atlantic Ocean. *Address:* 28 Ladbroke Sq., London W11. *Signs work:* see appendix.

SHAPSHAK, René, Ph.D. (H.C.) St. Andrews, Scotland; International Fine Arts Council; Hon. Life Mem. American International Academy, Washington, D.C.; Chairman, Art Committee, American Intern. Institute, Washington, D.C.; recipient of the Titular de la Cruz de Eloy Alfaro (1961), Panama, Latin America T.C.E.A.; sculptor in wood, stone, marble, granite, ivory, iron, copper, aluminium, bronze; Curator, Philathea College Museum of Modern Art, London, Ontario, Canada; *b* 18 Apr., 1899; *s* of Arieh Shapshak; *m* Eugenie Palca; three *s. Educ.:* Ecole de la Roquette, Paris; *studied art* at Dalston School of Art (1915-17); Ecole des Vosges (1922-25); Ecole Julien (1923-26); Brussels (1925-26); Ecole des Beaux-Arts (1926-27). *Work in private collection:* Mr. and Mrs. Robert Williams. *Lectures:* Art Juror, Washington Sq., New York (1969, 1970, 1971). *Address:* Hotel Chelsea, 222 West 23rd St., New York, 11. *Clubs:* New Orleans; Member Adult Educ. Council, N.Y.C. *Signs work:* "René Shapshak."

SHARP, Miles, A.R.C.A. (Lond.), painting, engraving; Principal, Nuneaton

Art School (1925-52); oil and water-colour painter; *b* Brighouse, Yorks., 28 Nov., 1897; *s* of Miles Sharp; *m* Veda Kathleen Jenkinson. *Educ.:* Rastrick Grammar School; *studied art* at Bradford College of Art; Leeds College of Art; R.C.A., London. *Exhib.:* R.A., R.Scot.A., R.B.A., R.O.I., R.I., R.W.A., R.B.S.A.; one-man shows at 7 municipal art galleries, Warwick Gallery (Birmingham), Foyles' A.G., London. *Work in permanent collections:* Bath, Batley, Bradford, Bootle, Brighouse, Dewsbury, Exeter, Leicester, Middlesbrough, Nuneaton, Rotherham A.Gs. *Address:* 2 Dolforgan Ct., 2 Louisa Terr., Exmouth, Devon. *Club:* Chelsea Arts. *Signs work:* "MILES SHARP."

SHARROCKS, Alfred Burgess, P.P.R.C.A., M.B.O.U., N.D.D.; medallist, Landseer Scholarship in Painting, etc., R.A. Schools; artist, broadcaster, Fine Art writer, ornithologist; Pres., Cambrian Ornithological Soc. (1957); *b* Stockport, Ches., 27 Nov., 1919; *s* of Alfred Sharrocks, painter. *Educ.:* Stockport College, College of Technology, Manchester; *studied art* at Stockport College of Art, R.A. Schools. *Exhib.:* N.E.A.C., R.C.A. *Work in private and public collections:* National Museum of Wales, etc. *Address:* Cogwrn, Sychnant Pass, Conway, Gwynedd. *Agents:* R. P. Gossop Ltd., London. *Signs work:* "A. Burgess Sharrocks," or "A.B.S."

SHAW, Barbara, A.T.D. (1946); art teacher, artist in oil, engraver on wood; staff, Wimbledon School of Art (1945); staff, Wimbledon High School for Girls (G.P.D.S.T.) (1944); *b* Chiswick, 27 May, 1924; *d* of William Shaw, A.M.I.E.E. *Educ.:* secondary school; *studied art* at Wimbledon School of Art (1940-43) under Lionel Ellis, A.R.C.A.; also studied at Hornsey College of Art. *Exhib.:* R.A., N.S. *Work repro.:* by Medici Soc., Frost and Reed, Ltd., Pallas Gallery. *Address:* Sandbourne, Wayneflete Tower Ave., Esher, Surrey. *Signs work:* in copperplate.

SHAW, Margaret, A.R.C.A., R.W.S., N.E.A.C.; painter and lithographer; lecturer in the Dept. of History of Art at Sheffield Polytechnic; *m* Dr. E. D. Mackerness. *Studied art* at R.C.A. (1938-41). *Exhib.:* R.W.S., R.A.; one-man exhbns., Calouste Gulbenkian Gallery, Newcastle upon Tyne, and in Sheffield University. *Official purchases:* R.S.A., Graves Art Gallery, Derby Art Gallery, Ilkley Art Gallery; Sheffield, Leeds and Hull Education Committees. *Address:* 3 Peel Terr., Sheffield S10 2GU. *Club:* Chelsea Arts. *Signs work:* "MARGARET SHAW."

SHAW, Sax Roland, D.A. (1940); Head of Stained Glass Dept., Edinburgh College of Art; main work in tapestry, mural decoration, and concrete and stained glass; *b* Huddersfield, 5 Dec. 1916; *s* of Roland Wilfred Shaw; *m* Mary; two *s*. *Educ.:* Almondbury; *studied art* at Huddersfield School of Art, Edinburgh College of Art, and in Paris. *Work in permanent collections:* public buildings in Edinburgh, London and New York, and in private collections in Edinburgh and America. *Address:* 25 Howe St., Edinburgh. *Signs work:* "Shaw."

SHELDRICK, Albert William; curator, Ashwell Village Museum; *b* Ashwell, Herts., 2 Feb., 1911; *s* of Albert Sheldrick; *m* Winifred Sheldrick; two *d*. *Educ.:* Merchant Taylors' School. *Address:* Dixies Cottage, Ashwell, nr. Baldock, Herts.

SHELLEY, John, N.D.D. (1957), British Institute Fund Prize (1957); artist in oil; *b* Margate, Kent, 23 Feb., 1938; *s* of William Edward Shelley; *m* Sylvia Helen Elizabeth; one *s*, one *d*. *Educ.:* Sutton East County Sec. School; *studied art* at Wimbledon School of Art (1953-58) under Gerald Cooper, briefly at the Slade (1958). *Work in permanent collection:* Tate Gallery. *Address:* c/o Trafford Gallery, 119 Mount St., London W1Y 5HB. *Signs work:* "John Shelley."

SHEPHARD, Rupert, Hon. Academician, L'Accademia Fiorentina; R.P.,

N.E.A.C.; painter, etcher, lithographer, engraver; Slade Diploma; lecturer, Central School, St. Martin's School of Art (1945-48); Professor of Art, University of Cape Town (1948-63); *b* 12 Feb., 1909; *s* of William Henry Shephard; *m* 1st, Lorna Wilmott (decd., 1962); one *s,* two *d*; 2nd, Nicolette Devas (1965). *Exhib.:* one-man: Calmann Gall. (1939), Agnews (1962), Upper Grosvenor Gall. (1966, 1970), Kunsthalle, Bielefeld, Germany (1973), Collectors Gall., Johannesburg (1975), Patrick Seale Gall. (1975); Cape Town (seven) and Johannesburg (three) (1949-63); general: London: War Artists, R.A., R.P., N.E.A.C., London Group, Leicester Gall., Wildenstein Gall., New Grafton Gall., etc.; Venice Biennale (1958), São Paulo Bienal (1957), Ljubljana Biennale (1955, 1957, 1959, 1961), Cincinnati Lithographic (1956, 1958), Quadrennial South African Art (1956, 1960). *Work purchased:* C.E.M.A. British Museum, War Artists, National Portrait Gall., South African National Gall., Johannesburg Municipal Gall. *Illustrated books:* Capescapes (1954), Passing Scene (1966). *Address:* 68 Limerston St., London SW10. *Signs work:* "Rupert Shephard."

SHEPHEARD, Peter Faulkner, C.B.E. (1972), B.Arch., Liverpool (1936), P.P.R.I.B.A., A.M.T.P.I., P.P.I.L.A., R.I.B.A. Distinction in Town Planning; architect, town planner, landscape architect, draughtsman and illustrator. In private practice (Shepheard & Epstein) since 1948; Prof. of Environmental Design and Dean of the Graduate School of Fine Arts, University of Pennsylvania, Philadelphia (1971—); mem. National Parks Commission (1966-68), Countryside Commission (1968-71), Royal Fine Art Commission (1968-71); *b* Birkenhead, 1913; *s* of Thomas Faulkner Shepheard F.R.I.B.A.; *m* Mary Bailey; one *s,* one *d. Educ.:* Birkenhead School; *studied architecture* at Liverpool School of Architecture and Dept. of Civic Design. *Exhib.:* R.A., etc. *Publications:* Modern Gardens (Arch. Press, 1953), Gardens (C.O.I.D., 1969); illustr.: A Book of Ducks and Woodland Birds. *Address:* 60 Kingly St., London W1. *Signs work:* "Peter Shepheard."

SHEPHERD, S. Horne, D.A.(Glas.); painter, sculptor and printmaker in oil, water-colour and various graphic methods; *b* Dundee, 30 Dec., 1909; *s* of Thomas Shepherd; *m* Helen Margaret Hale. *Educ.:* Harris Academy; *studied art* at Glasgow School of Art. *Work in permanent collection:* V. & A. *Exhib.:* N.S., F.P.S., Rome, Washington, Boston and New York. *Address:* 15 Thurlow Rd., Hampstead, London NW3.

SHEPLEY, Clifford, D.A.(Edin.) 1932-33; founder member M.A.A. (1949), A.M.I. (1951), A.I.M.B.I. (1969); medical illustrator in pencil, pen, ink, water-colour and pastel; lecturer and supervisor, Dept. of Medical Illustration, Edinburgh University (1948-73); *b* Edinburgh, 5 Aug., 1908; *s* of Thomas H. Shepley, civil servant; *m* Sarah A. E. Geaton; one *s,* two *d. Educ.:* Edinburgh; *studied art* at Edinburgh College of Art (1928-32), Moray House Teachers' Training College (1932-33). *Exhib.:* R.S.A., M.A.A. *Publications:* author of Preparation of Drawings and Diagrams for Scientific Publications; Development of Medical Illustration. *Address:* 21 Joppa Rd., Edinburgh EH15 2HA. *Signs work:* "Clifford Shepley."

SHEPPARD, Faith Tresidder; landscape and marine subject painter in oils; *b* London, 4 June, 1920; *d* of Capt. R. L. Sheppard, O.B.E. *Studied art* under Nancy Huntly (twice Silver Medallist National Competition, mother); Byam Shaw School; Chelsea School of Art and R.A. Schools under Sir T. Monnington, P.R.A. *Exhib.:* R.A., Paris Salon (Mention Honorable Award for painting, 1970), R.O.I., R.P., N.E.A.C., R.B.A., R.S.M.A., International Boat Show (Earl's Court), Artists of Chelsea, Chelsea Art Society, R.G.I., Arundel Art Centre, and provincial municipal art galleries, etc. *Work in permanent collections:* H.M. Queen Elizabeth, the Queen Mother (Pentley Park in Spring). *Work repro.:* Backwater of the Roya, Bruges (Mansell & Co. Ltd.). *Clubs:* Reynolds, Chelsea Art Society, Ridley Art Society (publicity committee), R.G.I., W.G.C. Art, Caernarvon Art, etc. *Addresses:* 29 Digswell Rd., Welwyn Garden City, Herts. and "Bryn Ellen," Groeslon, Caernarvon, Gwynedd. *Signs work:* "Faith Sheppard."

SHEPPARD, Liz; Intermediate in Arts Crafts (1953), N.D.D. Painting (1955), A.T.D. (Lond.), Scholarship Pratt bequest (1956, to Italy); artist, print-maker in etching, lithography, painting; *b* Tonbridge, 20 Dec., 1933; *d* of D. O. Pearce; *m* Clive Sheppard, sculptor (decd.); two *s,* one *d. Educ.:* St. Albans Grammar School for Girls; *studied art* St. Albans School of Art (1950-52); St. Martin's College of Art (1952-55) under Frederick Gore, Derrick Greaves, Peter de Francia; London University Institute (1955-56). *Exhib.:* Digswell House, Bear Lane Gallery, Oxford, Casson Gallery, Zella 9, City Gallery, Milton Keynes, Gallery Facet, Amsterdam, Mall Galleries, Gallery Ploemp, Delft. *Work in permanent collection:* Digswell House. *Address:* 6 Leighton St., Woburn, Milton Keynes, MK17 9PJ. *Clubs:* Haagse Kunstkring, The Hague, Society of Designer Craftsmen. *Signs work:* "Liz Sheppard."

SHEPPARD, Maurice Raymond, A.R.W.S., M.A. (R.C.A.), Dip.A.D.; professional painter in oil and water-colour; *b* Llangwm, Pembrokeshire, 25 Feb., 1947; *s* of W. E. Sheppard. *Educ.:* Haverfordwest Grammar School; *studied art* at Loughborough College of Art; Kingston College of Art under Alfred Heyworth; R.C.A. under Hamilton-Fraser, Buhler, Spear, Weight. *Exhib.:* R.A. Summer Exhbn., Paris Salon, Colnaghi, New Grafton, Jonliegh Studio, Wonersh. *Address:* Holloway House, Holloway, Haverfordwest, Pembrokeshire, Wales. *Signs work:* "Maurice R. Sheppard."

SHEPPARD, Richard H., Hon. Dipl. A.A. (1935), F.R.I.B.A. (1944), C.B.E. (1964), R.A. (1973); principal partner, Richard Sheppard, Robson & Partners, Architects; Mem. R.I.B.A. Council; *b* Bristol, 1910; *s* of William Sheppard; *m* Jean Shufflebotham; one *s,* one *d. Educ.:* Bristol Grammar School; Architectural Association School of Architecture; R.W.A. School of Architecture, Clifton, Bristol. *Principal commissions* include City University, London, Brunel University, Uxbridge, Churchill College, Cambridge (Competition, 1959), and other educational and commercial buildings. *Publications:* Building for the People (1945), Prefabrication in Building (1946). *Address:* The Old Rectory, Little Berkhamsted, nr. Hertford, Herts. *Club:* Garrick.

SHERWIN, Frank, R.I. (1950), R.S.M.A. (1967); painter in water-colour and oil; *b* Derby, 19 May, 1896; *s* of Samuel Sherwin; *m*; two *d. Educ.:* Derby School; *studied art* at Derby School of Art and Heatherley's Art School (Henry Massey, 1920). *Exhib.:* R.A., R.I., etc. *Official purchases:* Derby Corporation Art Gallery. *Work repro.:* many prints of water-colours by British Railways, Medici Soc., Frost & Reed Ltd. *Publications:* articles in The Artist. *Address:* Goddans, High St., Cookham, Berks. *Signs work:* see appendix.

SHERWOOD, J. F. W., F.L.A., A.M.A.; City Librarian and Curator, Hereford Public Library, Museums and Art Gallery; *b* Holmfirth, Yorks, 1909; *m* Monica Distin; one *s,* one *d. Educ.:* King James's Grammar School (Almondbury). *Address:* c/o Museum and Art Gallery, Hereford.

SHETLAND, Ilric (alias), Hornsey Dip., S.I.A.D. (1969); artist in pencil, ink, sprayed pictorial sculpture, mixed media; *b* London, 24 Oct., 1946; *s* of John Preston; *m* Naurika Lenner. *Educ.:* Forest Hill Comprehensive School; *studied art* at Hornsey College of Art (1966-69). *Exhib.:* International Cultural Centre, Antwerp, Gamstyl, Brussels, Basle '75, Serpentine Gallery, London, Treadwell

o

Gallery, London, Patrick Seale Gallery, London. *Address:* 38 Chalcot Rd., London NW1. *Clubs:* A.I.R., A.M.P. *Signs work:* "Ilric Shetland."

SHIELD, George William, B.Sc., Lond.; sculptor, particularly in wood and concrete, terra-cotta, metal, plaster, little stone; head, Mexborough G.S.; *b* Leicester, 7 July, 1919; *s* of William Henry Shield; *m* Jean; one *s,* two *d. Educ.:* Gateway School; University College, Leicester; *studied art* at College of Art, Leicester, under A. Pountney and A. T. White (1948-52). *Exhib.:* R.A., R.S.A., R.B.A., R.I., Glasgow, S.S.A., Contemp. Artists, Bradford and local exhbns., Nottingham and Leicester. *Work in permanent exhibition:* Joan Farrier bust in Paisley Art Gallery. *Address:* 30 Lewes Rd., Conisborough, S. Yorks. *Clubs:* Midland Group, Leicester Soc. of Artists. *Signs work:* "SHIELD" inscribed with modelling tool.

SHIELS, Anthony Nicol; painter in oil and gouache; *b* Salford, 24 May, 1938; *s* of Thomas Daniel Shiels; *m* Mary Christine Price; two *s,* three *d. Educ.:* King Edward VII School, Lytham; *studied art* at Heatherley School of Art, London, under Gilmore Roberts (1954-56). *Exhib.:* one-man shows: Gallery Mingus and Rawinsky Gallery, London; group shows: London, Bristol, St. Ives, Colchester, Newlyn, Oxford, Bath, etc. *Publications:* three books on magic. *Work repro.:* Arts Review, Apollo, Link, International Times, etc. *Address:* 3 Vale View, Ponsanooth, Truro, Cornwall. *Clubs:* A.I.A. (London) and Penwith Society (St. Ives). *Signs work:* see appendix.

SHINER, Audrey, Slade Dip. (1926); portrait painter in oil and pastel, visiting teacher Winterbourne Collegiate School (1950-52), lecturer at evening classes since 1946; *b* Grays, Essex, 26 Apr., 1900; *d* of Christopher Mitchell Shiner, A.R.I.B.A., Chmn. Essex Chapter of Architects. *Educ.:* Palmer's Endowed School, L.C.C. Central School, and Slade (under Profs. Henry Tonks, Tancred Borenius, Eliot-Smith, Wilson Steer), and on the Continent. *Exhib.:* Bath Soc., W.E.A., Clifton Art Club. *Work in permanent collections:* Public Library, Palmer's School, St. John's Masonic Lodge, Grays, Essex. *Address:* Milestone Cottage, Chipping Sodbury, Bristol. *Signs work:* "AUDREY SHINER."

SHINN, Michael Lawrence, D.A. (Slade), A.R.W.A.; landscape and portrait painter in oil; artist and teacher; head of painting, Gloucestershire College of Art and Design; R.W.A. Council Member; *b* London, 5 Mar., 1934; *s* of F. E. Shinn; *m* Jennifer Margaret; one *s,* two *d. Studied art* at Wimbledon School of Art (1951-55), Slade School of Fine Art (1957-59) under Sir William Coldstream. *Work in permanent collections:* Royal West of England Academy, City Museum and Art Gallery, Plymouth, City Museum and Art Gallery, Gloucester, Cheltenham Art Gallery and Museum, Bristol Education Authority. *Address:* Old Gable House, Southam, nr. Cheltenham, Gloucs. *Signs work:* "Michael L. Shinn."

SHIPSIDES, Frank; painter in oil and water-colour, specialising in marine painting; President, Bristol Savages (1974-75); *b* Mansfield, Notts., 1908; *m* Phyllis; one *s,* one *d. Educ.:* King Edward School, Mansfield; *studied art* at Mansfield College of Art (1923) under Buxton; Nottingham College of Art (1925) under Else. *Publications:* Somerset Harbours. *Address:* 5 Florence Pk., Bristol BS6 7LS. *Club:* Bristol Savages. *Signs work:* see appendix.

SHIRLEY, Ralph Oakley, A.R.C.A. (1945); potter and painter in clays, metals, and acrylic paints; senior lecturer, Dept. of Three Dimensional Design, North Staffordshire Polytechnic; *b* Doveridge, Derbyshire, 2 May, 1918; *s* of William Shirley, cast-iron moulder; *m* Kathleen Mabel; one *s. Educ.:* Academic Department of Derby College of Art; *studied art* at Derby College of Art (1936-40). The Royal College of Art (1941-45). Professor Gilbert Spencer and Percy

Horton. *Work in permanent collections:* Student Union, Southampton University. *Address:* The Studio, 39 Uttoxeter Rd., Foston, Derby. *Club:* Chelsea Art. *Signs work:* "R. O. Shirley."

SHIRREFF, Jack Robert, N.D.D., A.T.D.; designer and lecturer; artist in etching, silkscreen, photoengraving, litho and enamelling; lecturer, Bath Academy of Art, Corsham, Wilts. (etching, photoengraving, photo fabrication); lecturer, Croydon College of Art (litho-process photography); *b* Colombo, Ceylon, 11 June, 1943; *m* Pauline. *Educ.:* Sutton Valence, Maidstone; *studied art* at Hastings College of Art under Vincent Lines and Martin Lack, Brighton College of Art, Art Teachers Training under Ronald Horton. *Work in permanent collections:* University of Sussex, Brighton College of Art, Kingston on Hull Educ. Authority. *Address:* Red House, Punnetts Town, Heathfield, Sussex. *Signs work:* "Shirreff."

SHORTLAND, Dorothy Frances, A.L.C.M., F.P.S., Membre Associe des Artistes Français; painter and teacher in oil, auto didactic; *b* Midlands, 1908. *Exhib.:* one-man shows: Mall Galleries, Blackfriars, Boston, Gallerie Majestic de Vallombreuse, Biarritz; group shows: Paris Salon, S.W.A., Lord Mayor's Art Award Show, Guildhall, R.S.M.A., R.B.A., R.I. *Work repro.:* The Globe, Paris Revue, French/Spanish dailies. *Address:* 2 Desborough Rd., Rothwell, Northants.

SHURROCK, Christopher, A.T.D. (Distinction) 1960; senior lecturer, art college; 2D and 3D constructs/prints, design; *b* Bristol, 1939. *Educ.:* Bristol Cathedral School; *studied art:* West of England College of Art (1955-59), Cardiff College of Art, A.T.D. (1959-60). *Work in permanent collections:* Welsh Arts Council, Contemporary Art Society for Wales, University College of Wales, National Museum of Wales, John Caroll University, Ohio. *Publications:* Space, Man and Structure, Architecture Wales No. 6. *Work repro.:* Studio International (June, 1966) D'Ars Agency N36-37 (1967), Arts and Artists (Jan., 1969), Art in Britain, 1969-70 (Dent). *Address:* 9 Min-y-Nant, Rhiwbina, Cardiff.

SILLMAN, Norman H., A.R.C.A., A.R.B.S.; mem. Midland Group; sculptor and designer in wood, stone, and cast metal and concrete; designer of coins, Royal Mint, and medals, various countries, ivory carver; Fine Art Dept. staff, Trent Polytechnic; *b* London, May, 1921; *m* M. Gillian; one *d. Educ.:* Pyramid Hill, Victoria, Australia; *studied art* at Blackheath Art School and Royal College of Art. *Exhib.:* R.A., R.B.A., London Group, S.E.A., Midland Group, Arts Council Sculpture in the Home Exhbn., R.C.A. Open Air Exhbn. *Work in permanent collections:* Derby Education Committee (two). *Address:* Swynford Cottage, Cottage La., S. Collingham, Notts. *Signs work:* "N. Sillman."

SIMCOCK, Jack; painter; *b* Biddulph, Staffs., 6 June, 1929; *m* Beryl Shallcross; one *s*, one *d. Educ.:* Stoke-on-Trent. *Exhib.:* 50 one-man shows, England, U.S.A., Italy, c/o Piccadilly Gallery, London; mixed shows, Britain, France, Italy, U.S.A., including John Moore's Liverpool, Edinburgh Open 100. *Official purchases:* Contemporary Art Society; public art galleries: Stoke-on-Trent, Coventry, Wakefield, Leicester, Salford, Wolverhampton, Oldham, Dudley, Liverpool, Rochdale; education authorities of Leicestershire, Yorkshire, Nottinghamshire, Hertfordshire, Durham, Surrey, Essex, Sheffield, Stoke-on-Trent, Hull; universities of Reading, Keele, Cincinnati, Ohio, U.S.A.; colleges (Oxford), Balliol, University, New; colleges (Cambridge), St. Catherine's and Newnham; Hockerill College, Herts.; St. Mary's College, Strawberry Hill; Dept. of the Environment; Nuffield Foundation; Granada TV; East Midlands Arts Association; also many private collectors at home and abroad. *Work repro.:* Arts Review, Time and Tide, The Listener, Das Kuntswerk, The Guardian, The Northern Echo, Birmingham Post, Woman's Journal Supplement, Country Life. Studio International, Cheshire Life, Apollo, The Daily Telegraph. *Publications:* Simcock, Mow Cop, an autobiography (1975), Midnight Till Three, a volume of poems (1975). *Address:* 13 Primitive St., Mow Cop, Stoke-on-Trent. *Signs work:* "Simcock."

SIMEON, Margaret, A.R.C.A. (1933), R.C.A. Travelling Scholar (1934), M.S.I.A. (1945); textile and wallpaper designer; teacher of Textile Design and Printing, R.C.A. (1936-40); teacher of textile design and history of art at Wimbledon School of Art (1934—); *b* 1910; *d* of Harry Simeon, ceramic designer. *Educ.:* Chelsea School of Art, R.C.A. *Exhib.:* International Exhbn. at Paris, Stockholm, New York, Arts and Crafts Exhbn. Soc. (1935-54), Britain Can Make It Exhbn. (1946), Festival of Britain (1951). *Work repro.:* in International Textiles, Architectural Review, Studio, Designers in Britain, Decorative Art. *Publications:* How to Draw Garden Flowers. *Address:* 2 Lodge Close, Stoke D'Abernon, Cobham, Surrey, KT11 2SG.

SIMPSON, Ian, A.R.C.A. (1958); Abbey Travelling Scholar (1958); artist in oil, acrylic and drawing media; Principal, St. Martin's School of Art (1972); *b* Loughborough, Leics., 12 Nov., 1933; *s* of H. W. Simpson, A.R.C.A.; *m* Joan, A.T.C.; two *s,* one *d. Educ.:* Bede Grammar School, Sunderland, Co. Durham; *studied art* at Sunderland College of Art (1950-53) (Harry Thubron); Royal College of Art (1955-58) (Prof. Moynihan, Prof. Carel Weight). *Work in permanent collections:* Glasgow City Art Gallery, Nuffield Foundation, Hull Education Authority, Northumberland Education Authority. *Publications:* Eyeline (B.B.C.), Picture Making (B.B.C.), Drawing: Seeing and Observation (Van Nostrand Reinhold). *Address:* 35 Slades Hill, Enfield, Middx. *Signs work:* "I. Simpson."

SINDALL, Bernard Ralph, Prix de Rome Sculpture (1950-52); sculptor in bronze, stone, wood and resins; *b* 24 Nov., 1925; *s* of Alfred Sindall, illustrator; *m* Jeanetta Sindall; two *s,* one *d. Educ.:* Kings', Canterbury and H.M.S. Worcester; *studied art* at Brighton College of Art (1946-50). *Exhib.:* R.A., New English, Trieste (1976), Helsinki (1975), Rome (1951); one-man shows: Bedford House Gallery, London (1975), Rye (1974), Birmingham University (1974). *Work in permanent collections:* C.E.G.B., Burton-on-Trent, Birmingham University. *Address:* Underhill Farm, Wittersham, Tenterden, Kent. *Signs work:* "B. R. Sindall."

SINGIER, Gustave; painter, designer, engraver, lithographer; *b* Warneton, Belgium, 11 Feb., 1909; naturalized Frenchman, settled in Paris since 1919. *Studied art* since the age of 14; from 1923 spent three years at l'Ecole Boulle; from 1936 designer for a group stores; painting instructor at Academie Ranson (1951-54); founder member and on Council of Salon de Mai. *Exhib.:* with le Moal, Manessier, Singier (1946); Musée de Luxembourg, Luxembourg; Exposition du Mainichi Newspapers, Tokio (1959); De Gauguin à nos jours, Poland (1959); Musée de Grenoble, Peintres d'Aujourd'hui (1959); Exposition d'Art Francais Contemporain, Israel (1960). *Address:* c/o Galerie de France, 3 Faubourg Saint Honoré, Paris.

SISEMAN, Ernest James, A.R.(Cam.)A.; landscape and portrait painter in oil and water-colour; art master, Kingsmead School, Hoylake (since Jan., 1954); teacher, evening classes for Cheshire Educ. Authority; hon. sec., Deeside Art Group; *b* St. Leonards-on-Sea, Sussex, 4 Feb., 1920; *s* of E. J. Siseman (decd.); *m* Meryl Vivienne; one *s,* two *d. Educ.,* St. Leonards-on-Sea; *studied art* at Liverpool College of Art under W. C. Penn. *Publications:* illustrated, The Belle Books, A Series of Booklets on Divers Subjects. Address: 16 Queens Rd., Hoylake, Wirral, Cheshire. *Signs work:* "E. J. Siseman."

SISLEY, Francis Barton, M.F.P.S.; designer (patterns and dies), artist in oil.

pastel, water-colour, pencil, wood, acrylic; *b* Plumstead, London, 28 Nov., 1921; *s* of John Barton Sisley; *m* Joan Patricia Sisley; one *d*. *Educ. and studied art* at Woolwich Polytechnic. *Exhib.:* group shows: Young Contemporaries, A.I.A., F.P.S., Redfern, Ford International; one-man shows: Loggia Gallery (1974, 1976), Chichester Assembly Rooms (1975). *Work repro.:* Art News and Review. *Address:* Shelley House, 59 Nyewood La., Bognor Regis, W. Sussex PO21 2SQ. *Club:* F.P.S. *Signs work:* "Sidley."

SISQUELLA, Alfredo Oriol, painter in oil; Concurso Plandiura prize (1921), Concurso de Montserrat visto por sus artistas prize (1931), Concurso de Montserrat prize for composition for his canvas, San Benito en Subiaco (1947); Diploma 1st Cl. Expos. Nacional de Belles Arts de Barcelona (1942); 1st Prize Concurso Montserrat Barcelona (1947); Medalla de Honor Exposición Nacional de Belles Arts de Barcelona (1953); *b* Barcelona, 25 Apr., 1900; *s* of Antonio Sisquella; *m* Antonia Ramis; one *s*. *Studied art* at Escuela de Bellas Artes de Barcelona (1912-20) under Prof. F. Labarta. *Address:* Terramar Sitges, Barcelona. *Signs work:* "Sisquella."

SISSON, Marshall, C.V.O. (1971), C.B.E. (1959), R.A. (1963), A.R.A. (1956), F.R.I.B.A., F.S.A., B.A. (Arch.), R.I.B.A. Jarvis Student (1924); architect; *b* Gloucester, 1897; *s* of Arthur Sisson, M.I.Mech.E.; *m*. *Educ.:* Public school; *studied architecture* at London University (1920-24); British School at Rome (1924-27). *Exhib.:* R.A. *Principal works:* Public, college, ecclesiastical, school, commercial and domestic works. *Work repro.:* Architectural Review, Architect and Building News, Architects' Journal, The Builder, and various books and periodicals. *Publications:* various in architectural and archaeological journals. *Address:* Farm Hall, Godmanchester, Huntingdon, Cambs. *Clubs:* Arts, Athenæum. *Signs work:* "Marshall Sisson."

SITWELL, Pauline, S.W.E., R.A. Dip. (1937), L.I.S.T.D., F.R.G.S., Sigurd Leeder dip.; dancer, choreographer; painter, lithographer, engraver, etcher; garden design, interior decorating, etc.; Mem. City of Westminster's Arts Council Literary Com.; *b* Malta, 5 Oct., 1916; *d* of Group Captain William George Sitwell; *m* Peter Stebbing. *Educ.:* privately (full stage training and young career); *studied art* at St. John's Wood School of Art (1930), Royal Academy Schools of Art (1933-37). *Exhib.:* S.G.A., S.W.E., R.S.M.A., and Mall Prints tour of G.B., etc.; one-man show sponsored by Westminster City Council (1973); two-man show with D. Hills, E. Anglia (1974). *Work in private collections:* Switzerland. *Address:* 46 Porchester Rd., London W2. *Clubs:* Ladies Ski, Eagle Ski (Golden Eagle), Club Suisse des Femmes Alpinistes, Ski Club of Gt. Britain, Royal Academy Reynolds. *Signs work:* "Pauline Sitwell" and see appendix.

SKAWONIUS, Sven Erik, R.V.O., painter; theatre-set designer, Royal Dramatic Theatre, Stockholm; industrial artist; designer at the Upsala-Ekeby Group; hon. corresponding M. of R.S.A.; *m* Gunilla Wettergren; two *d*. *Educ.:* at High School, Stockholm; *studied art* at State School of Arts, Crafts and Design, Stockholm, R.A. of Fine Arts, Stockholm, and study travels in Europe and U.S.A. *Exhib.:* National Museum of Art, Stockholm, Museum of Modern Art and exhbns. in Europe and U.S.A. from 1930. *Official purchases:* National Museum of Art, Stockholm, Museum of Industrial Art, Oslo, Kunstgewerbemuseum, Zürich, V. & A., etc. *Address:* Skogsfrugränd 16, 16138 Bromma, Sweden. *Club:* Arts, Stockholm. *Signs work:* "Skawonius, Ses."

SKEAPING, John R., R.A. (1959), R.A. Gold Medallist (1920), Prix de Rome (1924); sculptor in stone, wood, terra-cotta and bronze; *b* South Woodford, 9 June, 1901; *s* of Kenneth Mathieson, painter. *Educ.:* privately; *studied art* at

Goldsmiths' College (1915-17), Central School of Art (1917-19), R.A. Schools (1919-20). *Exhib.:* in most European countries, South, Central and North America, S. Africa, London galleries, Leicester Galleries since 1950, Ackermanns. *Publications:* How to Draw Horses, Animal Drawing, The Big Tree of Mexico and illustrations to numerous books on the horse. *Address:* resident in France; c/o Ackermann & Son, 3 Old Bond St., London W1. *Signs work:* "John R. Skeaping."

SKELTON, John; sculptor, letterer; *b* 1923; *s* of Godefroy Skelton, engineer; *m*; one *s*, one *d*. *Educ.:* Norwich Cathedral School, Bablake School, Coventry, Coventry School of Art and Architecture; army, India, Burma, Siam, Malaya. Studio in Sussex since 1950; works with two assistants in stone, wood, metal. *Work* in Norwich, Chichester, Portsmouth, Lincoln, Hereford Cathedrals; Chichester Museum; City Centre, Belgrade Theatre, Christ Church, Coventry; Toledo Museum, U.S.A.; Shakespeare Centre, Stratford-upon-Avon; United Nations Pavilion, Yugoslavia. *Exhib.:* Chichester Museum (1963), Herbert Art Gallery, Coventry (1965), Alwin (1965), Sussex University (1966). Represented Britain, Yugoslavia International Sculpture Symposium (1964). Serves Arts Council, Scotland. *Address:* Streat, Sussex.

SKILLINGTON, Nancy: see TALBOT, Nancy Wilfreda Hewitt.

SKILTON, Charles Philip, Hon. R.W.S., M.A.W.G.; publisher of art books etc. and Proprietor, Old Edinburgh Gallery; *b* London, 6 Mar., 1921. *Educ.:* Alleyn's School, Dulwich (Founders' Prize for Art). *Addresses:* Banwell Castle, Weston-super-Mare, Avon., and 20 Heriot Row, Edinburgh.

SLADE, Roy, N.D.D., A.T.D.; College of Art Silver Medal (1953); G.S.M. (British Army); artist in acrylics; Director, Corcoran Gallery of Art; Dean, Corcoran School of Art; *b* Cardiff, Wales, 1933; American citizen (Oct. 1975); *s* of David Trevor Slade. *Educ.:* University of Wales (1953-54), Cardiff College of Art (1949-54), Royal Army School of Education (1954). *Work in permanent collections:* Arts Council of Great Britain, Contemporary Art Society, B.O.A.C., University of Birmingham, Westinghouse Corp., British Embassy, Washington DC; Cadbury Bros. Ltd., Wakefield City A.G., Nuffield Foundation, M. of W., Clarendon College, Lord Ogmore. *Work repro.:* articles published: Studio International, "American Art Education" (Nov., 1972); Studio International, "Report from Washington" (Jan., 1972); Art Journal, "Atlantic Storm" (Spring, 1972); Contemporary Review, "Artist in America" (May, 1969); Studio International, "Up the American Vanishing Point" (Nov., 1968). *Address:* 17 New York Ave. N.W., Washington DC 20006.

SLATTERY, Rosemary; artist in wood-engraving, illustrator and painter; *b* Peru, 1 Oct., 1927; *d* of H. F. Slattery, A.R.S.M.; *m* A. J. T. Williams. *Educ.:* Sacred Heart Convent, Brighton; *studied art* at Croydon School of Art and Central School of Art under Gertrude Hermes, Jesse Collins. *Exhib.:* R.B.A., V. & A., Crafts Centre. *Work in permanent collections:* V. & A., B.M., Arts Council. *Address:* 6 West Grove, Greenwich, London SE10 8QT. *Signs work:* "R. Slattery."

SLAWINSKI, Joseph; "Polonia Restituta", "Man of the Year" award for introducing sgraffito mural technique to U.S.A.; Muralist, Interior Architect, Conservator, Art Historian; works in oil, glue, keima, tempera, casein, fresco, mosaic, sgraffito, encaustic, gilding, copper, iron, marble, stained glass; *b* Warsaw, Poland, 27 Nov., 1905. *Educ.:* Studied art with S. Kalinowski, Lublin, W. Drapiewski, Pelplin, Municipal School of Decorative Arts and Painting, Warsaw, Academy of Fine Arts, Warsaw (mural art), also studied in Italy, Austria, France,

Holland and Switzerland. *Taught* mural technique, conservation and restoration of Academy and other Warsaw art schools; more than 150 objects, incl. government buildings, churches, palaces, auditoriums, etc., and conservation of oil and mural paintings. *Examples:* churches in Garwolin (polychromy); Niepokalanow (mosaics); Siedlce, Laskazew (stained glass), etc., U.S.A.: Interiors of schools, churches, public buildings. Examples: Buffalo, N.Y., "Commandor Perry" (mural); Resurrection Cemetary, Chicago, Ill. (10 sgraffito panels); Lewiston, N.Y. Stella Niagara, and Athol Springs, N.Y. (chapels); "Peace" mural, Youngstown, N.Y.; portraits, N. Rockefeller, copper, Pres. L. Johnson sgraffito; "Baptism of Mieszko" copper, St. Joseph Cathedral, Buffalo, N.Y. and many works in various techniques. *Address:* 125 Buffalo Ave., Niagara Falls, N.Y. 14303, U.S.A. President, Gallery and Studio Sgraffito, Niagara Falls. *Signs work:* "J. Slawinski."

SMART, Professor Alastair, M.A. (Glasgow, 1942), D.A. (Edinburgh, 1949), F.R.S.A.; Head of Dept. of Fine Art, University of Nottingham (since 1956); lecturer, University of Hull (1949-56); Harkness Fellow, U.S.A. (1954-55) at Institute of Fine Arts, New York; *b* Cambridge, 1922; *s* of Prof. W. M. Smart, D.Sc., F.R.A.S., Emeritus Prof. of Astronomy, Glasgow University; *m* Marita Christl Lawler-Wilson. *Educ.:* King's College Choir School, Cambridge; Aldenham School; Kelvinside Academy, Glasgow; Glasgow University; Edinburgh Theological College; Edinburgh College of Art (under W. G. Gillies, R.S.A., W. MacTaggart, R.S.A., 1946-49); Mem. Institute for Advanced Study, Princeton, N.J. (1966-67). *Publications:* The Life and Art of Allan Ramsay (Routledge, 1952); The Assisi Problem and the Art of Giotto (Clarendon Press, Oxford, 1971); The Renaissance and Mannerism in Italy (Thames and Hudson, 1971); The Renaissance and Mannerism outside Italy (Thames and Hudson, 1971); articles in The Burlington Magazine, Renaissance and Modern Studies, Scottish Art Review, Arts Review, Apollo and The Review of English Studies. *Address:* Department of Fine Art, The University, Nottingham.

SMART, Jeffrey; painter in oil, pen and ink; *b* Adelaide, S. Aus., 26 July, 1921; *s* of Francis I. Smart. *Educ.:* Pulteney Grammar School, Adelaide; *studied art* at S.A. School of Arts, Adelaide (1940), Grand Chaumiere (1948) under McEvoy, Academie Montmartre (1949) under Fernand Leger. *Exhib.:* Whitechapel (1962), Tate Gallery (1963); one-man shows: Redfern Gallery (1967), Galleria 88 Rome (1968), Leicester Galleries (1970). *Work in permanent collections:* National Galleries of Sydney, Melbourne, Adelaide and Perth, Mertz Coll., Corcoran Gallery, Washington, Yale University. *Work repro.:* Art International (May, 1968), Present Day Australian Art (Ure Smith), Masterpieces of Australian Art (1970), 200 Years of Australian Art (1971). *Address:* Posticcia Nuova, Pieve a Presciano, Arezzo 52020, Tuscany, Italy. *Signs work:* "Jeffrey Smart."

SMEDLEY, Gordon Owen, A.T.D. (1949); artist, graphic designer, headmaster and art teacher; staff, Birmingham College of Art (1949-56); headmaster, Aston School of Art (1952-56); vice-principal, Bolton School of Art (1956-61); head, School of Art and Design, Tameside College of Technology; *b* Bournville, 24 May, 1925; *s* of the late William Owen Smedley; *m* Patricia Mary Goode. *Educ.:* elementary school; King's Norton Grammar School; *studied art* at Bournville School of Art; Birmingham College of Art (1941-49). *Work repro.:* sundry commercial and typographical literature. *Address:* 7 Linden Rd., Woodlands, Stalybridge, Cheshire. *Signs work:* "SMEDLEY."

SMEDLEY, Norman, M.A. Hons. (Cantab.), F.S.A., F.M.A.; Director, Abbot's Hall Museum of Rural Life of East Anglia (1965-74); Vice-President, Suffolk Institute of Archaeology; formerly curator, Raffles Museum, Singapore; and lecturer and examiner in biology, King Edward VII College of Medicine;

director, Art Gallery and Museum, Doncaster (1933-52); curator, Ipswich Museum and Christchurch Mansion (1952-65); hon. mem., Doncaster and Ipswich Art Clubs; *b* 11 Jan., 1900; *s* of Thomas Smedley; *m* Beryl Edna Emms; one *s*, one *d*. *Educ.:* Queens' College, Cambridge. *Publications:* books, articles, reviews, and papers on biology, archaeology, arts and crafts. *Address:* 19 Neale St., Ipswich IP1 3JQ.

SMITH, David Henry, M.Art, R.C.A. (1971), Hugh Dunn Plaque (1971); artist/teacher in water-colour, oil and pencil; *b* Cleethorpes, 29 Oct., 1947; *s* of Henry Smith; *m* Irena Ewa Flynn. *Educ.:* Elliston Secondary Modern School, Cleethorpes; *studied art* at Grimsby School of Art (1965-68); R.C.A. (1968-71) under Carel Weight, R.A. *Exhib.:* New Art Centre, London, Fischer Fine Art, Lincoln City A.G., Dartington Hall, Arthur Tooth, London, Angela Flowers, International Art Fair, Cologne. *Work in permanent collection:* Camden Council. *Publications:* jacket for Hilary Spurling. *Address:* Hall Lodge, Holton Cum Beckering, Wragby, Lincoln. *Signs work:* "D. H. Smith."

SMITH, Edward John Milton, A.T.D. (1952), N.D.D. 2nd Cl. Hons. (1951), F.S.A.E., F.R.S.A.; artist in lettering, writing and illumination; Principal Lecturer, Department of Art Education, Leeds Polytechnic; art teacher, West Monmouth School, Pontypool (1952-62); visiting lecturer, Newport College of Art (1954-62); President N.S.A.E. (1972); *b* Stonehouse, Glos., 3 May, 1922; *s* of Edward Milton Smith; *m* Doreen; one *s*, two *d*. *Educ.:* Central School, Stroud, Glos.; *studied art* at Stroud School of Art (1936-38), Gloucester College of Art (1939-40), Leeds College of Art (1946-52). *Address:* Glevum, 30 Burnham Rd., Garforth, Leeds, Yorks. *Signs work:* see appendix.

SMITH, Erik, A.R.C.A. (1947), R.E. (1959), R.B.A. (1950), A.R.W.S. (1959), R.W.S. (1971); engraver, etcher, water-colour, oils, etc.; Lecturer in Art History, High Wycombe College of Technology and Art; *b* Birmingham, 6 Dec., 1914; *s* of J. F. Smith; *m* Lilian Mary Novello Williams, B.A.; one *s*. *Educ.:* K.E.G.S., Birmingham; *studied art* at R.C.A. *Exhib.:* R.A., N.E.A.C., R.W.S., R.B.A., R.E., S. Africa, U.S.A., Brazil, Australia. *Work in permanent collections:* Ottawa Mus. and A.G., Canada, V. & A., South London A.G., Sheffield Art Gallery, Ashmolean Museum, Oxford; stained-glass windows: Wouldham, Turville, Long Marston. *Official purchases:* Book of Remembrance, High Wycombe; articles on art in Discovering Art, Canvas, The Artist, The Old Water-Colour Society's Annual volume. *Address:* 5 Chiltern Close, Princes Risborough, Bucks. *Signs work:* "Erik Smith."

SMITH, Gregor McFarlane, D.A. (Edin.) 1966, M.S.S.A.; artist in oil on canvas, lecturer in art (part-time); *b* Glasgow, 15 July, 1944; *s* of Rev. Henry Smith, M.A. *Educ.:* Wishaw High School, Lanarkshire; *studied art* at Edinburgh College (1962-67) under Robin Philipson, R.S.A. *Exhib.:* group shows: Scottish Arts Council, Edinburgh, Arts Council of N. Ireland, Project Arts Centre Dublin, Liverpool Academy of Arts, Universities of Strathclyde and Stirling, Aberdeen A.G.; various one-man shows in Scotland. *Work in permanent collections:* Scottish Arts Council, Fife Educ. Authority, Perth A.G. *Address:* 2 Caledon St., Glasgow G12 9DX. *Club:* Glasgow Art. *Signs work:* "Gregor M. Smith."

SMITH, Ian McKenzie, D.A., A.R.S.A., A.S.I.A., F.R.S.A., F.S.A. (Scot.); Director, Aberdeen Art Gallery and Museum; Mem. Scottish Arts Council; artist in oil and gouache; *b* Montrose, 3 Aug., 1935; *s* of James McKenzie Smith; *m* Mary Rodger Fotheringham; two *s*, one *d*. *Educ.:* Robert Gordon's College, Aberdeen; *studied art* at Gray's School of Art (1953-59) under R. Henderson Blyth; Hospitalfield College of Art, Arbroath (1958 and 1959). *Work in perman-*

ent collections: Scottish National Gallery of Modern Art, Scottish Arts Council, Nuffield Foundation, Abbot Hall Gallery, Kendal, Aberdeen A.G., Glasgow A.G., Edinburgh Educ. Authority, Dumbartonshire Educ. Authority, I.B.M. Greenock, Royal Scottish Academy, Carnegie Dunfermline Trust, Arts Council of Northern Ireland. *Address:* 48 Beaconsfield Pl., Aberdeen. *Signs work:* normally unsigned, labelled on reverse.

SMITH, Jack; artist in oil and pencil; *b* Sheffield, 18 June, 1928; *s* of John Edward Smith; *m* Susan. *Educ.:* Nether Edge Grammar School, Sheffield; *studied art* at Sheffield College of Art (1944-46), St. Martin's School of Art (1948-50), R.C.A. (1950-53). *Work in permanent collections:* Tate, Arts Council, Contemporary Art Society. *Address:* 1 Ashbridge Rd., Leytonstone, London E11. *Signs work:* "Jack Smith."

SMITH, Marian Janette Hume, D.A. Edin. (1973); teacher in art, painter in oil, acrylics and mixed media on canvas; *b* Kelso, Roxburghshire, 1951; *d* of A. H. Smith, insurance. *Educ.:* Kelso High School; *studied art* at Edinburgh College of Art (1969-73) under Robin Philipson, P.R.S.A., A.R.A. *Exhib.:* one-man shows: New Edinburgh Gallery (1975), City of Edinburgh Arts Centre (1973); group shows: Richard Demarco Festival (1975), R.S.A. Edinburgh Festival (1975), R.S.A. (1975), Border Arts Festival (1974), Pernod Exhbn. (1973). *Address:* 3 Leopold Pl., Edinburgh EH7 5JW. *Signs work:* see appendix.

SMITH, Mary W., W.I.A.C.; painter in oil; *b* Bury, Lancs.; *d* of Henry W. Parker; *m* Prof. Sidney Smith, Litt.D., F.B.A., F.S.A.; one *s*, one *d*. *Educ.:* privately; *studied art* at Slade School. *Exhib.:* R.A., N.E.A.C., M.A.F.A., W.I.A.C., Beaux Arts Gallery, Dieppe, and various provincial galleries. *Work in permanent collections:* Manchester City Art Gallery; Bury Art Gallery. *Official purchases:* Herts County Council and L.C.C. *Work repro.:* in The Lady. *Address:* Cawthorne House, Barcombe, Lewes. *Signs work:* "Mary Smith."

SMITH, Muriel Constance; portrait painter, drawings, miniatures; R.M.S., silver medal, Paris Salon (1935); hon. mention (1934); *b* Gunthorpe, Notts.; *d* of W. Stanley Smith, accountant. *Educ.:* Hollygirt, Nottingham; *studied art* at Nottingham College of Art and under Alyn Williams, P.R.M.S. *Exhib.:* R.A., R.M.S., U.S.A., one-woman show, Walker's Galleries, Bond St. *Address:* 16 Forest Rd., Nottingham. *Signs work:* "Muriel C. Smith."

SMITH, Norman, N.E.A.C. (1970), N.R.D. (1938); painter; teacher of drawing and painting; mem., Hampstead Artists' Council; *b* Walsall, 8 Dec., 1910. *Educ.:* Blue Coat School, Walsall; *studied art* at Rochdale and Manchester Schools of Art. *Exhib.:* R.A., R.S.A., R.B.A., R.W.A., N.E.A.C., Paris Salon. *Work in permanent collection:* City Art Gallery, Salford. *Official purchases:* Borough of St. Marylebone, Borough of St. Pancras. *Work repro.:* illustrations to Some Reflections on Genius (1960) and Doctors Past and Present (1964), both by Lord Brain. *Work in private collections* in Britain and America. *Address:* 7 Baird Gdns., Dulwich Wood Park, London SE19. *Signs work:* "Norman Smith."

SMITH, Peter William, D.F.C.; artist in oils and water-colour; company director; *b* New Malden, Surrey, 3 July, 1920; *s* of A. W. Smith. *Educ.:* Whitgift, Croydon; *studied art* at Reigate Art School *Exhib.:* East Sussex Art Club, Hastings (1947 and 1948), International Amateur Art (1969), member of North Weald Group. *Address:* Little Hill, Colley Manor Drive, Reigate, Surrey. *Signs work:* "Peter Smith."

SMITH, Philip Henry, A.R.C.A. (1950); artist in oil, gouache, water-colour, chalk, pen and ink (topographical drawings); teacher of painting; painting master, Wirral College of Art since 1950; *b* Cheltenham, 1924; *s* of Sidney Arthur Smith;

m, two children. *Educ.:* Cheltenham Grammar School; *studied art* at Cheltenham School of Art under Gerald Gardiner, R.C.A. under Ruskin Spear, Carel Weight, Robert Buhler. *Exhib.:* Wirral area, Williamson A.G., Birkenhead. *Work in permanent collections:* Wirral Borough Council (Williamson A.G. and Wallasey collections). *Address:* 29 Bayswater Rd., Wallasey, Ches. *Signs work:* "Philip H. Smith."

SMITH, Stanley, A.R.C.A. (Lond.); artist in oil and water-colour; *b* Halifax, 13 May, 1893; *s* of J. Cartmell Smith; *m* Ethel May, water-colour painter, R.A. exhibitor since 1927; *studied art* at Halifax School of Art (1908-13), R.C.A. (1913-19) under Profs. Pite, Lethaby, Moira, Lanteri. *Exhib.:* R.A., Blackpool, Leamington Spa, Dublin, Salford, Liverpool, Preston, Fine Art Soc., Watford, Hereford, Northampton, Derby, Brighton, Huddersfield, Hanley, Stafford. *Official purchases:* by Blackpool Art Gallery. *Address:* Dinas, 111 Cannock Rd., Stafford. *Signs work:* "STANLEY SMITH."

SMITH, William Branston; painter in acrylic and fresco, working in Norway; *b* Blackhill, 2 Mar., 1930; *s* of William Smith, hotel waiter. *Educ.:* Dunston Hill School and West Bolden; *studied art* at Sunderland College of Art, King's College, Newcastle upon Tyne. *Exhib.:* group shows throughout the world; one-man shows: United Kingdom, and Scandinavian galleries. *Official purchases:* I.C.A., Australia, Porsgrunn, and Larvik Gallery. *Address:* Stromtangveien. 8. 3950, Brevik, Norway. *Clubs:* U.K.S., N.M.L., B.K.T. *Signs work:* "BILL SMITH."

SMOUT, John Frederick, N.D.D. (1965), A.T.D. (1966), B.A. (1975), A.R.Cam.A. (1975); artist in oil on canvas, pen and ink; art teacher at Ysgol Rhiwabon; *b* Oldbury, Worcs., 13 Aug., 1938. *Educ.:* Oldbury Grammar School; *studied art* at Stourbridge College of Art (1961-65) under L. G. Harris; Liverpool College of Art (1965-66) under J. Hart. *Exhib.:* one-man shows: Coleg Harlech (1975), Chester (1970, 1974); group shows: Bangor, Mold, Dudley, Coventry and Manchester. *Address:* Dee View, Uppergarth, Trevor, Llangollen, Clwyd. *Clubs:* Llangollen Visual Arts Soc., R.Cam.A. *Signs work:* "J. F. Smout."

SNELLING, John, F.R.S.A. (1966); artist in water-colour, paint consultant; *b* Greenwich, 15 Nov., 1914; *s* of William Snelling; *m* Margaret Snelling; three *s*, one *d*. *Educ.:* Camberwell School of Art; *studied art* under Horace Brodzky. *Exhib.:* St. James' Art Society; three one-man shows. *Publications:* written and illustrated: Painting Defects (Spon), Painters Book of Facts (Technical Press). *Address:* Orepuki, Wennington Rd., Rainham, Essex. *Signs work:* see appendix.

SNOWDEN, Hilda Mary, F.I.A.L.; artist in oils, water-colour, embroidery, sculpture; part-time assistant, Yorkshire Council of Social Service, which promoted the Yorkshire Arts Association; *b* Bradford, 13 Apr., 1910; *d* of James Snowden, textile manager. *Educ.:* Grange Grammar School, Hillcroft College, Surbiton; *studied art* at Regional College of Art, Bradford, Positano Art Workshop, Italy. *Exhib.:* London, Bradford, Harrogate. *Address:* Flat, Victoria Mans., Dawson St., Thackley, Bradford 10. *Signs work:* see appendix.

SOIFERTIS, Leonid; artist in water-colour, pastel, book illustrator, etcher, lithographer and cartoonist in line and wash and etching; on staff of Crocodile (since 1932); during Second World War on naval newspaper Sebastopol; *b* Ilintsy, nr. Vinnitsa, Ukraine, 1911. *Studied art* at Kharkov University; later under P. Lvov and Radion. *Work:* Old Moscow, Sebastopol Defence and Metro Series. *Exhib.:* U.S.S.R. and abroad; one-man show: Moscow. *Work in permanent collections:* Tretiakov Art Gallery; U.S.S.R. museums. *Address:* Moscow, Gogolevskyi bul. 10. Union of Soviet Artists.

SOMERVILLE, Lilian (Mrs.), C.M.G. (1971), O.B.E. (1958), F.M.A. (1963), Hon. Dr. R.C.A. (1972), Fellow, U.C.L. (1973); Director, Fine Arts Department, British Council (1948-70); *b* Bolton, 7 Oct., 1905. *Educ.:* Abbot's Hill; *studied art* at Slade School of Art (Professor Tonks). *Address:* The Studio, 16A Hill Rd., London NW8.

SOMERVILLE, Stuart Scott; artist in oil; *b* Arksey, Yorks., 6 Feb., 1908; *s* of Charles Somerville, artist and collector; *m* Catherine Lavine; two *s*, four *d*. *Educ.:* privately; *studied art* under father and by own observation at home and abroad. *Exhib.:* R.A., etc. *Address:* Newbourn Hall, nr. Woodbridge, Suffolk. *Signs work:* "Stuart Somerville."

SONNIS, Alexander, A.R.C.A. (1932); painter in various mediums and lithographer; part-time instructor St. Martin's School of Art (since 1946); also long periods instructor at other art schools in the past; *b* 1905; *s* of Samuel Sonnis, furniture-maker and designer; one *s*. *Educ.:* L.C.C., studied drawing (part-time student) at Central School of Arts and Crafts under Bernard Meninsky, gained Scholarship Award Royal College of Art (1929-32). *Exhib.:* R.A., N.E.A.C. (London Group). *Official purchases:* War Advisory Committee. *Address:* 51 Cresswell Rd., Twickenham, Middx. *Signs work:* "Alex Sonnis" or "A. Sonnis."

SOPER, Eileen A., S.WL.A., R.M.S.; artist in water-colour, chalk, line and wash; author; *d* of George Soper, R.E. *Educ.:* privately; *studied art* under father, George Soper, R.E. *Work in permanent collections:* British Museum, Grundy A.G., Blackpool, National Gallery of Toronto, Art Institute, Los Angeles. *Publications:* When Badgers Wake; Wild Encounters; Wanderers of the Field; Wild Favours; Muntjac. *Address:* Harmer Green, Welwyn, Herts. *Signs work:* "Eileen A. Soper."

SORRELL, Elizabeth, A.R.C.A., R.W.S.; painter and designer in water-colour and gouache; *b* New Skelton-in-Cleveland, Yorks., 12 Oct., 1916; *d* of George Tanner; *m* Alan Sorrell; two *s*, one *d*. *Educ.:* Eastbourne High School; *studied art* at Eastbourne School of Art (1934-38) and R.C.A. under Prof. E. W. Tristram (1938-42). *Exhib.:* R.A., R.W.S. and provincial galleries. *Work in permanent collections:* Tate Gallery (Chantrey Bequest), Towner Art Gallery (Eastbourne), Newport (Mon.) Art Gallery, Harris Art Gallery (Preston), Beecroft Art Gallery (Southend-on-Sea), Graves Art Gallery, Sheffield, and private collections. *Work repro.:* in The Artist, Illustrated London News, etc. *Address:* Thors Mead, 185 Daws Heath Rd., Thundersley, Benfleet, Essex. *Signs work:* "Elizabeth Sorrell."

SOUKOP, Willi, R.A. (1969); sculptor; Chelsea School of Art since 1947 and Master of the Sculpture School of the Royal Academy since 1969; *b* Vienna, 5 Jan., 1907; *s* of Karl Soukop, craftsman; *m* Simone Michelle, dancer; one *s*, one *d*. *Studied art* at Vienna Academy of Fine Art. *Exhib.:* R.A., R.B.A., Edinburgh Festival, Battersea Park, Arts Council, Antwerp Bienale. *Work in permanent collections:* Cheltenham A.G., Cordova Museum (U.S.A.), Tate Gallery. *Official purchases:* Herts. C.C.; Leicester Educ. Com.; L.C.C.; Kidbrooke Comprehensive School; Camberwell housing estate. *Work repro.:* The Studio, Listener, British Artist Craftsmen, etc. *Address:* 26 Greville Rd., London NW6. *Signs work:* see appendix.

SOULAGES, Pierre; painter; *b* Rodez, France, 24 Dec., 1919; *s* of Amans Soulages; *m* Colette Llaurens. *Educ.:* Lycée, Rodez. *Exhib.:* one-man shows, Kunsthaus, Zürich; Essen Mus.; Gemeente Mus., de Hagen (1960-61); Mass. Inst. of Tech. (1962); Univ. of Belgrade, Zagreb Mus. (1962); Glyptotek of Copenhagen (1963); Houston Mus. (1966); Musée National d'Art Moderne, Paris (1967); Buffalo Mus.; Montreal Mus.; Pittsburgh Mus. (1968), etc. *Official* *purchases:* Tate Gallery, Musée d'Art Moderne, Paris, Mus. of Modern Art, N.Y., Guggenheim Mus., N.Y., Mus. de Arte Moderna, Rio de Janeiro, Mus. of Torino, Zürich, Berlin, Grenoble, etc. *Address:* 18 rue Des Trois-portes, Paris, 5. *Signs work:* see appendix.

SOUTHALL, Derek; painter; Painter-in-Residence, University of S. Carolina; *b* 5 June, 1930; *m* Jennifer Anne Wilson; two *d. Studied art* at Coventry College of Art, Camberwell School of Art, Goldsmiths' College and abroad. *Represented* in major public collections. *Commissioned work:* Dept. of the Environment (1972). *Publications:* articles on work in Art International, Studio International, Art in America, Review des Beaux-Arts, etc. Documentary film made by B.B.C. of exhbn. at I.C.A. (Nov., 1971). *Addresses:* 92 Woodland Gdns., London N 10; 5 Le Conte Ct., Columbia S.C.29205, U.S.A. *Signs work:* see appendix.

SOUTHERN, Richard, Hon. D.Litt. (Bristol); theatre consultant; *b* Dorchester, 5 Oct., 1903; *s* of Harry Southern, journalist; *m* Grace Loosemore; two *d. Educ.:* St. Dunstan's College; *studied art* at Goldsmiths' College and R.A. *Exhib.:* various theatres. *Publications:* Stage Setting, Proscenium and Sightlines, The Georgian Playhouse, Changeable Scenery, The Open Stage, part author Essentials of Stage Planning, The Medieval Theatre in the Round, The Seven Ages of the Theatre, The Victorian Theatre, The Staging of Plays before Shakespeare. *Address:* 37 Langham Rd., Teddington, Middx. TW11 9HF. *Signs work:* "RICHARD SOUTHERN."

SOUTHGATE, Jeanne; professional artist in oil and water-colour; *b* Bournemouth, 1930; *d* of Harry Southgate, army captain. *Educ.:* Bournemouth; *studied art* at Bournemouth Technical College. *Exhib.:* Wessex, Southampton and various major exhbns. *Work in permanent collections:* Russell Cotes A.G., Trinity A.G. *Address:* Trinity Art Gallery, 32A South St., Wareham, Dorset. *Signs work:* "Jeanne Southgate."

SOUZA, F. N.; painter; founder of Progressive Artists Group, Bombay (1948); *b* Goa, 12 Apr., 1924; *s* of Newton J. Souza, schoolmaster; *m* 1st, Maria Figuereido (1948; divorced 1964); 2nd, Barbara Zinkant (1965). *Educ.:* St. Xavier's College; Sir J. J. School of Art; Central School of Art; Ecole des Beaux Arts. *Exhib.:* one-man shows, London and major cities of England, Paris, Stockholm Copenhagen, Johannesburg, principal cities of Germany and U.S.A.; retrospective exhbns., London (1951), New Delhi (1965), Leicester (1967), Detroit (1968); Minneapolis Int. Art Festival (1972); Expo '67, Montreal; Silver Jubilee of India's Independence Exhbn., U.S.A. (1973). *Work in permanent collections:* Baroda Museum, National Gallery, New Delhi, Tate Gallery, Haifa Museum, National Gallery, Melbourne, etc. *Publications:* Words and Lines (autobiography). *Address:* 148 West 67 St., New York, N.Y. 10023. *Signs work:* see appendix.

SPACKMAN, Charles Basil Slater, C.B., C.B.E., D.F.C. and bar; retd. Air Vice-Marshal, R.A.F.; painter in oil and water-colour; *b* Hasborough, Norfolk, 4 July, 1895; *s* of Rev. G. Spackman. *Educ.:* Lancing College; *studied art* at Hammersmith School of Art under Frederick Gray (1950). *Exhib.:* R.S.A., R.H.A., R.Cam.A., R.I., R.B.A., R.M.A., Derby Art Gallery; Mem. Water-Colour Soc. of Ireland; Armed Forces Soc.; Cork Art Soc. *Work repro.:* Connoisseur and Illus. London News. *Address:* 11 Wood Grove, Cross Douglas Rd., Cork, Eire. *Clubs:* R.A.F., Cork and County. *Signs work:* "B. SPACKMAN."

SPADINI, Andrea, art dip., Institute of Art, Florence (1931); sculptor in marble and ceramics; Prof. of Decorative Art, Liceo Artistico, Rome, since 1947; *b* Rome, Italy, 1 July 1912; *s* of Armando Spadini, painter; *m;* one *s,* one *d. Educ.:*

elementary and secondary schools, Rome; *studied art* at Rome under his father and at Florence. *Work in permanent collections:* Count Carandini, Rome; Countess Cicogna, Venice; S. Fabrizio Clerici, Rome; S. Vittorio Gorresio, Rome; Count Rasponi, New York; Countess Simonetta-Visconti-Fabiani, Rome; Mrs. Snow, New York; Princess Pallavicino, Rome; Duchess Torlonia, Rome; Marquess Litta, Rome; Baron de Rede, Paris; Mrs. A. Patino, Lisbon; Tiffany, New York; Mrs. G. Marconi Braga, New York; Mr. Dillon, New York; Mr. Houghton, New York; Mr. G. Delacorte, New York; Delacorte Clock, Central Park, New York, sculptures for parks; bust of Armando Spadini, Pincio, Rome; the Landon Bear (bronze), Landon School, Bethesda, Maryland, U.S.A.; fountains in the park of Count Marcoli, Rome; font in the Church of St. Peter and Paul, Eur, Rome. *Address:* Liceo Artistico, Rome. *Signs work:* "A.S." "Andrea Spadini," or, on ceramics, "Lo Spada."

SPEAR, Ruskin, R.A. (1954), A.R.C.A. (1934), elected pres. of London Group (1949); artist; visiting teacher, R.C.A.; *b* 30 June, 1911; *m* Mary Hill; one *s*. *Educ.:* Brook Green School, W6; Hammersmith School of Art; R.C.A. under Sir William Rothenstein. *Exhib.:* R.A., London Group, Leicester Galleries, America, Australia, Brussels and Scandinavia, Moscow, Pushkin Museum, Leningrad (1957). *Official purchases:* Contemporary Art Soc., Chantrey Bequest, British Council, Arts Council, provincial galleries. *Work repro.:* in Studio, Artist, Listener, The Times. *Addresses:* 20 Fielding Rd., Chiswick, London W4; (studio) 11A Bath Rd., Chiswick, London W4. *Signs work:* see appendix.

SPEIGHT, Sadie, B.A. (1st Class honours, architecture, 1929), M.A. (1930), A.R.I.B.A. (1930), F.S.I.A. (1947), F.R.S.A. (1974); registered architect and industrial designer; part-time lecturer and studio instructor in interior design, Hull College of Arts and Craft (1935-39); *d* of Dr. Alfred Speight; *m* Sir Leslie Martin, M.A., Ph.D., LL.D. (Hull, Leicester and Manchester), F.R.I.B.A., Emeritus Prof. of Architecture, Cambridge University; one *s*, one *d*. *Educ.:* School of St. Mary and St. Anne, Abbots Bromley. *Works* include housing, schools, shops, furniture, textiles, etc. *Work repro.:* in Architectural Review, etc. *Publication:* in partnership with husband, The Flat Book (Heinemann, 1939). *Address:* The King's Mill, Gt. Shelford, Cambs.

SPENCE, T. Everard; portrait and landscape artist in oil; linen manufacturer. *Educ.:* Bootham School, York. *Exhib.:* R.A., R.B.A., R.H.A., R.U.A., several one-man shows; collection of portrait miniatures. *Address:* 45 Deramore Park, Belfast, N. Ireland. *Signs work:* see appendix.

SPENCER, Charles Samuel; journalist and art critic; *b* London, 26 Aug., 1920. Former editor, Art and Artists; Former editor, Editions Alecto Collectors Club; Trustee, Arkwright Trust, Camden Arts Centre. *Publications:* author: Erte (1969); A Decade of Print Making (1973); Bakst (1973); Cecil Beaton (1975); The World of Serge Diaghilev (1974); editor: The Aesthetic Movement (1973); Alecto Monographs on Kenneth Armitage, Colin Lanceley, Tom Phillips, Achilles Droungas, Ed Meneely, Harald Becker, Igino Legnaghi. *Address:* Flat 11, 44 Grove End Rd., London NW8.

SPENCER, John, A.R.C.A. (1934), R.M.S. (1956), A.R.M.S. (1953); Honorable Mention, Paris Salon (1966); pottery artist; art director, Pearson's Pottery, Chesterfield, since 1949; artist, Royal Lancastrian Pottery (1935-36); artist, Rolls Royce, war years; *b* Westhoughton, Lancs., 29 Sept., 1904. *Educ.:* Westhoughton; *studied art* at Wigan Art School, Bolton Art School, R.C.A. *Exhib.:* Nottingham, Derby, Chesterfield, Paris Salon, R.M.S., Belfast, Shrewsbury. *Address:* 84 Walton Rd., Chesterfield, Derbyshire. *Signs work:* "John Spencer."

SPENCER, Noël Woodward, A.R.C.A. (1925); formerly Principal, Norwich Art School; art master, Central School of Art, Birmingham (1926-32); second master, Sheffield College of Art (1932-34); headmaster, Huddersfield Art School (1934-46); *b* Nuneaton, 29 Dec., 1900; *s* of J. W. Spencer, schoolmaster; *m* Vera Kathleen Wheeler. *Educ.:* Ashton Grammar School; *studied art* at Ashton School of Art, Manchester College of Art, R.C.A. *Exhib.:* R.A., Yorkshire Galleries, Norwich Twenty Group, Chicago, Los Angeles, etc. *Publications:* A Scrap Book of Huddersfield; The Old Churches of Norwich (with Arnold Kent). *Address:* 18 Upton Close, Norwich. *Signs work:* see appendix.

SPENCER, Pamela Mary; artist in oil, water-colour, pencil; *b* Manchester, 11 Jan., 1924; *d* of Percy Julius Spencer, M.A. (Cantab). *Educ.:* P.N.E.U. Schools, Queen's College, Radbrook College of Domestic Science (Shrewsbury); *studied art* at St. Martin's School of Art under J. Bateman, Barry Craig, J. L. Wheatley, H. A. Freeth, K. Martin (1945-51). *Exhib.:* R.A., N.E.A.C., S.W.A., N.S., R.B.A., R.O.I., P.S., Russell-Cotes Museum, and other provincial galleries. *Address:* 33 Damer Gdns., Henley-on-Thames, Oxon. *Signs work:* "Pamela M. Spencer" or "P. M. Spencer."

SPENDER, John Humphrey, A.R.I.B.A., F.S.I.A.D., Hon. Des. R.C.A.; artist and mural painter; designer, textiles, wallpapers, carpets; four times winner C.O.I.D. Design Awards; *b* London, 19 Apr., 1910; *m* Pauline Wynn, actress; two *s. Studied architecture:* Architectural Association. *Exhib.:* one-man shows: Redfern and Leicester Galleries, New Art Centre, Windsor, Farnham, Colchester; group: C.A.S., Arts Council, John Moores, Bradford, Aldeburgh, R.A. *Work in permanent collections:* V. & A.; Min. of Works, Southampton, Brighton, Manchester, Johannesburg. *Murals:* Festival of Britain, P. & O. Liners Orsova, Oriana, Canberra, Shell Centre, Pilkingtons. *Address:* The Studio, Ulting, Maldon, Essex.

SPENDLOVE, Gerald Hugh, N.D.D. Pottery-Calligraphy (1953), A.T.D.(Dist.) (1954), F.S.D-C. (1972); lecturer, craftsman, designer in calligraphy, lettering, illumination and ceramics; Head of Ceramics School, Herts. College of Art, St. Albans; *b* Derby, 1929; *s* of Horace Albert Spendlove; *m* Valerie Spendlove; one *s*, three *d*. *Educ.:* Midhurst Grammar School; *studied art* at Chichester School of Art (1946-47) under C. G. Clements; Salisbury School of Art (1949-51) under Katherine Pleydell-Bouverie, E. S. Kilmister; L.C.C. Central School of Art (1951-53) under Dora Billington, M. C. Oliver, Irene Wellington. *Exhib.:* Gordon Maynard Gallery, Welwyn Garden City, S.D-C. at Nottingham, Southampton, Bath, London. *Work in permanent collections:* H.M. the Queen, Herts. County Council, Nevers, France; private collections in U.S.A., France, Norway, Germany, Nigeria, U.K. *Publication:* Editor of Pottery (Merlin Press). *Address:* 26 Worley Rd., St. Albans, Herts. AL3 5NS. *Signs work:* "G. H. Spendlove," stamp "GHS" in square.

SPRIGGE, Miss A. B. S., M.A.O.T. (1944); sculptor in stone, marble, wood; *b* London, 3 Mar., 1906; *d* of Sir Squire Sprigge, late editor of The Lancet. *Educ.:* Mayortorne Manor Farm School, Gt. Missenden; *studied art* at R.C.A. under Sir William Rothenstein, Prof. Ledward, Henry Moore (1926-27). *Exhib.:* Young Painters Soc., New Burlington Galleries (1930), Soho Sq. (1935), Grosvenor Sq. (1937); one-man show, Bloomsbury Gallery (1936); Coronation exhbn., Agnew's (1937), Artists of Fame and Promise, Leicester Galleries (1951), Exhbn. at Coffee House, Northumberland Ave. (1952). *Work repro.:* drawing in Mercury (May, 1935). *Address:* Scanda Vale, Llanpumpsaint, Dyfed. SA33 6JT. *Signs work:* "Sprigge," no signature on carved work.

SPRING-SMITH, Effie: see CUTNER, Effie.

SPURRIER, Mabel, H.R.I., A.R.B.S.A.; artist in oils and water-colour; *b* Moseley, nr. Birmingham, 11 Apr., 1880; *d* of William James and Caroline Spurrier. *Educ.:* The Woodroughs, Moseley; *studied art* at Birmingham College of Art under Caterson Smith. *Exhib.:* R.A., R.I., R.B.A., R.B.S.A. *Address:* Flat 30, Spencer House, 11 Belsize Park Gdns., Belsize, London NW3.

SQUIRRELL, Leonard Russell, R.E. (1919), R.W.S. (1941); Los Angeles Gold Medals for Etchings (1925, 1930); artist-painter in water-colour and oils and etcher; *b* Ipswich, 30 Oct., 1893; *s* of Frank Squirrell; *m* Hilda Victoria (decd.); one *s* (decd.), one *d*. *Educ.:* British School, Ipswich; *studied art* at Ipswich School of Art (1908-16) (G. R. Rushton, R.I.), Slade School (1921) (Prof. Tonks). *Work in permanent collections:* British Museum, V. & A. Museum, Brighton, Derby, Worthing, Fitzwilliam Museum, Cambs., Christchurch Collection, Ipswich. *Publications:* Landscape Painting in Pastels (Pitman), Practice in Water-colour (Pitman). *Address:* Merrydown, Witnesham, nr. Ipswich. *Signs work:* "L. R. Squirrell" (usually written).

STABELL, Waldemar Christian; painter in oil, wax drawings; *b* Hillsboro, N.B., Canada, 1913; *s* of Lorentz Stabell, shipowner (1865-1933), and Laura Edna (*b* Forbes Edgett, 1890-1968); *m* Margit Baugstö; one *s*, one *d*. *Educ.:* Canada, Norway; *studied art* at Scandinavia, Anglo-French Art Centre, London, Brighton College of Art (etching). *Exhib.:* first one-man show in London (1947), St. George's Gallery; several one-man shows and mixed exhibitions. *Work repro.:* Studio, Canada's Weekly, Contact Book, Arts Review, London. *Address:* Sydneskleven 31, Bergen, Norway. *Signs work:* "Stabell."

STACY-MARKS, Ronald, B.A.D.A.; mem., National Art Collectors Fund, and Fine Art Provident Inst.; art dealer; managing director, E. Stacy-Marks, Ltd., art dealers (estab. 1888); *b* Tunbridge Wells, 2 Feb., 1912; *s* of Edwin Stacy-Marks; *m*; three *s*, one *d*. *Educ.:* Canford; *studied art* in London and European art galleries. *Address:* Folkington Manor, Folkington, Polegate, nr. Eastbourne. *Clubs:* R.N.V.R., Eastbourne Sailing, etc.

STAMPER, Willson Young, 1st Prize, Cincinnati Artists (1942); Watumull Purchase Prize (1946, 1949, 1966); Dir., Art School, Hon. Art Acad. (1945-62); artist in all media; instructor in drawing, painting and composition, Cincinnati Art Museum; Urban Designer, U.S. Trust Terr. Master Plan (1967); *b* Brooklyn, N.Y., 5 Jan., 1912; *s* of Willson Young Stamper; one *s*, one *d*. *Educ.:* Hamilton Inst.; *studied art* at Art Students' League and Cincinnati Art Academy. *Permanent collections* of Mus. Mod. Art, N.Y.C., Cincinnati Art Mus., Hon. Art. Acad., Best in Ex., Hawaii (1955), 1st Drawing Hon. Art (1948, 1954, 1958, 1959). *Address:* 224 Kalaheo Ave., Kailua, Hawaii, 96734.

STANLEY, Diana; artist in line and colour; *b* London, 1909; *d* of Col. the Hon. F. W. Stanley, D.S.O.; *m* Professor C. A. Pannett. *Educ.:* Cheltenham Ladies' College and the Byam Shaw School of Art. *Exhib.:* London and provincial galleries; one-man shows: Batsford's Gallery (1945), Basingstoke Town Hall (1966). *Official purchases:* Basingstoke Council and Public Library. *Work repro.:* illus. for the Borrowers' series, Mary Norton, Bridges, Mary Cockett, and other books. *Publications:* Anatomy for Artists (Faber, 1951), Within Living Memory: Old Basingstoke (Charles Skipper & East, 1968). *Address:* 39 Cliddesden Rd., Basingstoke, Hants. *Signs work:* "Diana Stanley."

STARK, Marjorie Jean, R.S.W. (1974); artist in oil and water-colour; *b* Edinburgh, 1914; *d* of William Thow Munro, C.B.E., woollen manufacturer; *m* Alan F. Stark, M.B.E., W.S. *Educ.:* Edinburgh; *studied art* at Edinburgh College of Art (1949-55) under W. G. Gillies, Robin Philipson, R. Henderson Blyth.

Exhib.: R.S.A., R.S.W., S.S.A. *Work in permanent collections:* H.R.H. the Duke of Edinburgh, Nottingham Educ. Authority. *Address:* Wellgate, Morebattle, Kelso, Roxburghshire TD5 8QN. *Signs work:* "Marjorie Stark."

STAŹEWSKI, Henryk, Diploma, Warsaw Academy of Art; painter in oil and relief; *b* Warsaw, 1894; unmarried; since 1924—abstract geometrical paintings; since 1960—cycles of reliefs: white, metal, colour. *Work in permanent collections:* Museum of Modern Art, New York; Tate Gallery; Kröller Müller Museum, Otterlo; Oscar Müeller Museum, Basle; Gallerie Denise Rène, Paris; University Art Museum, Berkeley. *Publications:* Co-editor of BLOK (1924-26); participant of Abstraction Creation, Cercle et Carré in thirties; since 1966 member of Foksal Gallery, Warsaw. *Address:* Warszawa, Poland, Swierczewskiego 64/118. *Signs work:* "H. Staźewski."

STEBBING, Peter, N.R.D. (1939); Associate of Interior Decorators Ltd., Designers Association Ltd.; oil and mural painter; fabric, carpet, and jewellery designer; *b* 14 May, 1914; *s* of Henry Stebbing. *Educ.:* Marlborough; Hertford College, Oxford; *studied art* at Ruskin School of Drawing, Oxford, under Albert Rutherston (1936-37). *Exhib.:* R.A. (1949), Ryman's Galleries, Oxford; British Art Centre, Trollopes, West Halkin St., London (1959). *Address:* 303A Brompton Rd., London SW3 2DY. *Signs work:* "PETER STEBBING" or "Peter Stebbing" (underlined).

STEEL, Dorothy; artist in oil, pastel and gouache; *b* Glasgow, 10 Sept., 1927; *d* of Arthur Y. Steel, missionary. *Educ.:* Laurel Bank School, Glasgow; *studied art* at Glasgow School of Art (1946-49). *Work in permanent collections:* Greenock A.G., Greenock Public Library, Greenock Academy, Larkfield Hospital, Greenock. *Address:* Cherry Trees, Cloch Rd., Gourock. *Clubs:* S.S.A., Greenock Art. *Signs work:* "Dorothy Steel."

STEIGER, Frederic; painter of abstracts and portraits; Art Consultant (Marketing Research), Imperial Oil Ltd. (1959); bronze medal, Contemporary Art of the Western Hemisphere, International Business Machines Corp. Exhbn. (1941), permanent collection for painting, "Courage"; *b* Solwutz, Rumania; resident in Canada since 1922; *studied art:* self-taught. *Exhib.:* Ontario Soc. Artists; Royal Canadian Academy; Vancouver Art Gallery; Montreal Museum of Fine Arts; Eaton's Fine Art Galleries (Toronto); Continental Art Gallery (Montreal); Carroll Galleries (Toronto); St. John's Newfoundland, Industrial and Trade Fair; touring exhbn. of Odeon Theatre Circuit in Toronto, Ottawa, Montreal, Hamilton and London; St. John's, Newfoundland, House of Assembly; Roberts Gallery (Toronto, 1951); United Nations Library, New York (1957); Spring Exhibition (1962) of Canadian Art at Camford Galleries, New York. *Work in permanent collections:* Toronto Public Library (1962), Memorial University of Newfoundland, St. John's, House of Assembly, St. John's, Newfoundland (40 portraits of speakers since 1832 and Prime Ministers since 1855), Hallmark Collection of Canadian Art, Imperial Oil Ltd.; in private collections of T. A. Scythes (Toronto) and J. Bates (Saskatoon), Prof. J. R. McIntosh (Vancouver). *Official purchases:* portraits of R. B. C. Noorduyn (1944), Dean G. H. Ling (University of Saskatoon, 1945), Sir Charles G. D. Roberts (1943), Boris Hamburg (1945), Premier J. R. Smallwood of Newfoundland, Hon. J. R. Chalker; portrait of Lieut.-Col. Keiller MacKay, former Lieut.-Governor of Ontario (1963); H.M., the late King Peter of Yugoslavia; Hon. Campbell McPherson, former Lieut.-Governor of Newfoundland; Newfoundland, portraits of Speakers and Premiers of Newfoundland as above; paintings for Imperial Oil Bldg., St. John's, Newfoundland. Commissioned by Newfoundland Govt. to make extensive painting tour of the country. *Work repro.:* Hallmark Cards, Painters of Canada

Series (1967-74), Oesterreichische Kunst, Vienna, La Revue Moderne, Paris; and numerous Canadian and Newfoundland Journals and magazines. *Addresses:* 316 Kingsway, Islington, Ontario, Canada; studio: 406 Bloor St. East, Toronto. *Signs work:* see appendix.

STEINER, Heiri; painter, designer and draughtsman; lithographer and typographer; head designer, U.N.E.S.C.O. publications (1948-50); teacher at Zürich Art School (1930-35); *b* 1 Oct., 1906; *s* of Heinrich Steiner, pastor; *m* Mary Geringer, graphologist. *Educ.:* Zürich; *studied art* at Zürich Art School under Prof. Keller, and self-taught in Berlin and Paris. *Exhib.:* Paris, Zürich, New York, Amsterdam, Stockholm, Munich, Chicago, London College of Printing (1967), Behr Stuttgart (1968). *Work repro.:* Caractere Noel, Paris (1955, 1963), Gebrauchsgrafik München (1964), Grafik München (1964), Graphis, A.M.G., Swiss Printing Review, Penrose Annual, Publimondial, Mem., Alliance Graphique Internationale. *Address:* CH-8634 Hombrechtikon, Uetzikon. *Signs work:* "Steiner."

STEPHEN, Douglas George; sculptor in wood, stone and bronze; *b* London, 23 May, 1909; *s* of G. A. Stephen, F.L.A.; *m* Dr. Joyce M. Stephen; one *s,* two *d. Educ.:* Norwich Secondary School; *studied art* at Camberwell School of Arts and Crafts under W. Norton and R. V. Pitchforth (1939-41) and City and Guilds School under Alan Howes, R.B.S., and W. H. Sharpington. *Exhib.:* R.A., London Group, United Artists, Cooling and Berkeley Galleries. *Address:* Old Vining Wood, Lodsworth, nr. Petworth, Sussex. *Club:* Savage. *Signs work:* see appendix.

STEPHENSON, Ian, B.A.Hons.(Dunelm), A.R.A.; abstract artist, particle painter; Dir. of Postgrad. Painting, Chelsea School of Art; former Dir. of Foundn. Studies, Fine Art, Ncle. Univ.; *b* nr. Meadowfield, Co. Durham, 11 Jan., 1934; *s* of Jas. Stephenson; *m* Kate Brown; one *s,* one *d. Educ.:* Blyth Grammar School, Northld.; *studied art* at King Edw. VII School of Art, King's College, Durham Univ., Ncle. *Exhib.:* Retrospective, Laing A.G., Ncle. (1970); repr. U.K., abroad numerous occasions. *Work in permanent collections:* Arts Councils, British Council, B.P., C.A.S., Dept. Environ., Granada TV., Gulbenkian Foundn., N.A.A., Nuffield Foundn., Premio Marzotto, Stuyvesant Foundn., Swedish Loyd, Tate Gallery, Victoria A.G., Whitworth A.G., etc. *Work repro.:* Adventure in Art, Abrams; Art in Our Time, Th. & Hud.; British Painting Holbein to Bacon, Phaidon; Contemporary Artists, St. James; Contemporary British Art, Pelican; Private View, Nelson; Art Int., Artist, Art News, Arts Rev., Cimaise, Ln. Mag., One Mag., Studio Int., Vogue, etc.; Cubism & After, B.B.C. TV schools film; Blow-up, M.G.M. Antonioni film. *Address:* 49 Elm Park Gdns., Chelsea, London SW10 9PA.

STEPHENSON, Kathleen: see GUTHRIE, Kathleen.

STETTLER, Michael, D.Sc.; art historian; architect; Director of Bernese Historical Museum from 1948 to 1961; Director Abegg Foundation; P. Helvetia Foundation (1965-71); *b* Berne, 1 Jan., 1913; *s* of Wilhelm Stettler de Graffenried, architect; *m* Barbara von Albertini; four *d. Educ.:* Berne; *studied art* at Zürich Inst. of Technology and University under J. Zemp and H. Wölfflin, and at Rome. *Publications:* Das Rathaus zu Bern (1942), Inventory of Historical Monuments of Canton Aargau (Vol. I, 1948, Vol. II, 1953); Swiss Stained Glass of the 14th Century (English Edition, 1949); Of Old Berne (1957); Rat der Alten (1962); Bernerlob (1964), Neues Bernerlob (1967); Aare, Bär und Sterne (1972). *Address:* Ortbühl, Steffisburg, Switzerland.

STEVENS, Elsie, M.F.P.S.; painter in oil, mainly modern landscapes; *b* Brighton, 24 Dec., 1917. *Studied* under and collaborated with Prof. Marian Bohusz at Studium Malarstwa Sztalugowego, London, for fifteen years. *Exhib.:* one-man shows: Alwin, Woodstock, Barrett and Loggia Galleries; and others in Amsterdam, Dublin, Durham Museum, Durham University, Brighton, Eastbourne, Sussex University. *Work in permanent collections:* Polish School of Art of Polish Y.M.C.A., London; various private collections in Britain, Brussels, Eindhoven, Uppsala, Bonn, Olden, Bergen, Norway. *Address:* 2 Malling Deanery Cottages, Lewes, Sussex. *Signs work:* "Elsie Stevens."

STEVENS, Mrs. Muriel Phyllis, landscape painter and illustrator in oil, water-colour and lithography; *b* London, 21 Sept., 1914; *d* of William Stanes, India merchant; *m* G. H. Stevens, R.B.A.; two *s,* two *d. Educ.:* Highbury School; *studied art* at Chelsea School of Art under H. S. Williamson, Graham Sutherland (1931-34). *Exhib.:* London Group. *Address:* Maes-y-Pwll, New Quay, Dyfed. *Signs work:* "Muriel Stanes."

STEVENS, Norman Anthony, A.R.C.A. (1960); painter in oil, etcher; *b* Bradford, 17 June, 1937; *s* of Stanley Whitmore Stevens, signwriter; *m* Jean Warhurst; one *s,* one *d. Educ.:* Bradford Junior Art School; *studied art* at Bradford Regional College of Art (1952-57) under Derek Stafford, Frank Lisle; R.C.A. (Painting, 1957-60). *Exhib.:* Hanover Gallery, London (1969, 1971). *Work in permanent collections:* Arts Council of N. Ireland, Bradford City A.G., Carlisle A.G., British Arts Council, V. & A., Museum of Modern Art, N.Y., Tate Gallery. *Address:* 10 Rugby Mans., Bishop King's Rd., London W14. *Signs work:* "Norman Stevens."

STEVENSON, Bernard Trevor Whitworth, M.A., F.R.S.A.; painter in oil and water-colour; formerly Borough Librarian and Curator of the Atkinson Art Gallery, Southport; *b* 24 Mar., 1899; *s* of the late C. Bernard Stevenson, former Director of City Art Gallery and Museums, Newcastle-upon-Tyne; *m* Lydia Winifred Lisle. *Educ.:* Royal Grammar School, Newcastle-upon-Tyne; Durham University; *studied art* at Edward VII School of Art, Newcastle-upon-Tyne (1920-25), and under Prof. R. G. Hatton. *Exhib.:* Laing Art Gallery, Newcastle-upon-Tyne; W.A.G., Liverpool, Sheffield, Preston. *Publications:* art criticisms in newspapers and periodicals. *Address:* Hill House, Comb Hill, Haltwhistle, Northumberland. *Club:* Southport Arts. *Signs work:* "TREVOR STEVENSON."

STEVENSON, John Patric Leslie, A.R.U.A. (1953), R.U.A. (1959); Hon. Secretary Administrator R.U.A. (1963-70), Pres. and Chairman (1970-75); Director, Hillsborough Arts Centre; *b* 1909; *m* Dorothy Betsy Forster; one *s,* one *d. Educ.:* Methodist College, Belfast; *studied art* at Belfast Art College (1926-28) and Slade School. *Exhib.:* N.E.A.C., R.I., R.S.A., R.H.A., R.U.A., Arts Council N.I. (1961); one-man shows: Belfast, Dublin, etc. *Purchases:* H.R.H. The Duke of Edinburgh, Lord Wakehurst, Lord Geddes, Lord Grey, Nat. Mus. Ireland, Waterford Art Gallery. *Address:* Studio, The Square, Hillsborough, Co. Down, N. Ireland BT26 6AG. *Signs work:* "Patric Stevenson."

STEWARD, Frank, A.R.C.A. (1949); painter in oil and designer; *b* London, 25 Oct., 1920; *s* of Frank Steward; *m* Vivienne Habberfield; three *s. Studied art* at R.C.A. (1946-49) under Rodrigo Moynihan. *Exhib.:* R.A., N.E.A.C., R.B.A., London Group, Pictures for Schools, U.S.A. and Canada. *Work repro.:* in Punch. *Address:* 49 Lawrie Park Rd., Sydenham, London SE26. *Signs work:* "Steward."

STEWART, Charles William; taught at Byam Shaw School (1950-58); artist and illustrator in water-colour, pen and ink; *b* Ilo-Ilo, Panay, Philippine Islands, 18 Nov., 1915. *Educ.:* Radley College; *studied art* at The Byam Shaw School of Drawing and Painting (1932-38) under Ernest Jackson. *Publications:* illustrated: Pendennis (Thackeray), Limited Editions Club, N.Y.; Vathek (Beckford), Bodley Head; The Lady of the Linden Tree (Barbara Leonie Picard), O.U.P.; Grimbold's

Other World (Nicholas Stuart Gray), Faber; The Visiting Moon (Celia Furse), Faber; etc. *Address:* Glenharvie, New Abbey, Dumfries. *Signs work:* "Charles W. Stewart."

STEWART, John Dunlop, M.S.I.A. (1947-70), N.R.D. (1945), probationer, R.I.B.A. (1944); industrial designer and product design consultant; hon. sec., S.I.A. Scottish Group (1962-63); draughtsman-designer, Universal Pulp Containers, Ltd. (1941-48); designer-photographer, H. Morris & Co. Ltd., Glasgow (1948); designer, Design Industries, Beckenham (1949-52); Burndept-Vidor, Ltd., Erith (1952-56); Scottish Aviation Ltd (1956-59); *b* Paisley, 3 Sept., 1921; *s* of Peter Stewart, R.P. *Educ.:* John Neilson Inst., Paisley; *studied art* at Glasgow School of Art, Glasgow School of Architecture and Royal Technical College, Glasgow, and Govt. Training Centre, Thornliebank. *Address:* Greystone, 15 Bushes Ave., Paisley PA2 6JR.

STEYN, Stella; painter in oil, water-colour; *b* Dublin, Dec., 1907; *d* of William Steyn; *m* David J. A. Ross. *Educ.:* Alexandra School, Dublin; *studied art* at Dublin, Paris, Dessau (das Bauhaus), Stuttgart. *Exhib.:* Carnegie International, Pittsburgh (1952); Tate Gallery, Figures in their setting (1953), The Seasons (1956), The Religious Theme (1958), Hampstead in the Thirties (1974-75); one-man shows, St. George's Gallery (1930), Leicester Galleries (1951 and 1954). *Official purchases:* Arts Council, M. of Works, C.A.S., British Museum Print-room. *Address:* 33 Tavistock Sq., London WC1.

STIEGER, Jacqueline; sculptor/jewellery in lost wax technique, casting, bronze, precious metals, stone and glass; *b* London, 26 Jan., 1936; *d* of H. J. Stieger, F.R.Ae.S.; *m;* four *s,* one *d. Educ.:* Bedales, Hants; The Mount School, York; *studied art* at Edinburgh College of Art (1952-58) under W. Gillies. *Work in permanent collections:* Eidgenosische Kunstkommission, Bern Ch; Museum of Medallic Art, Cracow, Poland. *Address:* Welton Garth, Welton, N. Humberside. *Signs work:* "J. Stieger."

STOBART, John, R.S.M.A., R.A. Medallist (1952); marine and landscape painter in oils; illustrator; writer; R.A. Schools Landseer Scholarship; art teacher, Lady Manners School, Bakewell (1950); *b* Leicester, 29 Dec., 1929; *s* of Lancelot Stobart, M.P.S., Ph.C.; *m* 1959; one *s,* two *d. Educ.:* Derby School; *studied art* at Derby College of Art under Alfred Bladen (1946-50), R.A. Schools under Henry Rushbury, C.V.O., R.A. (1950-56). *Exhib.:* R.A. (1952, 1953, 1954, 1956, 1961), R.B.A., R.S.M.A., Piccadilly Gallery, Montreal and Toronto, Canada, and latterly exclusively in New York. *Address:* c/o Royal Soc. of Marine Artists, 17 Carlton House Terr., London SW1Y 5BD. *Signs work:* "Stobart."

STOCKHAUS, Eva H. M., Member of the Swedish Graphic Society (secretary), F.R.E.; artist in wood-engraving; *b* Gothenburg, Sweden, 4 Apr., 1919; *d* of Hugo Lindegrén, engineer; *m* Bengst Stockhaus; one *s,* one *d. Educ.:* Stockholm, Univeristy Studies (Languages); *studied art:* mainly Autodidact; shorter periods of studies in Sweden and England. *Work in permanent collections:* National Museum, Stockholm, other museums in Sweden, etc. *Address:* Appelbovägen 10, 16140 Bromma, Sweden. *Signs work:* "Eva Stockhaus."

STOECKLIN, Niklaus; painter of murals, still life, posters and illustrations; Kunstpreis, Basle; *b* Basle, 19 Apr., 1896; *s* of Niklaus Stoecklin, merchant; *m* Elisabeth; one *d. Educ.:* Basle; *studied art* at Munich (1918), Paris and Florence. *Exhib.:* Basle, Stuttgart, Hamburg, Paris, Madrid, Philadelphia, Zürich, Mailand, Tokio. *Work in permanent collections:* Reinhart Coll., Winterthur, Prof. Stoll Coll., Basle, Bosch Coll., Suttgart, Roniger Coll., Davos-Dorf, Museum of Madrid, mural at Chemical Industries of Sandoz, Basle, Hoffmann, La Roche,

Basle. *Official puchases:* frescoes by govt. of Basle, murals, House of Parliament, Bern, pictures, Museums at Winterthur, Basle, Zürich. *Address:* Morystrasse 6, Riehen, Basle, Switzerland. *Signs work:* see appendix.

STOKES, David, F.R.I.B.A.; architect; *b* Woldingham, Surrey, 21 Nov., 1908; *s* of Leonard Stokes, P.P.R.I.B.A.; *m* Monica Violet Hammersley; one *s*, three *d*. *Educ.:* Downside; *studied architecture at* A.A. *Address:* 5 Cochrane St., London NW8. *Club:* Arts.

STOKOE, Michael Arthur, N.D.D. (1957); painter; mem. Printmakers Council; Life-drawing Examiner, Oxford G.C.E.; lecturer, Ravensbourne College of Art; *b* London, 1933; *s* of Dr. Harold Neville Stokoe, M.A.; *m* Gillian Stacey. *Educ.:* King's School, Bruton; *studied art* at St. Martin's School of Art (1953-57). *Exhib.:* R.A., R.B.A., R.O.I., R.S.O.P.P., Young Contemporaries, 2nd prize, Arts Council Competition, Belfast, Piccadilly Gallery, Arnolfini Gallery, Hamilton Gallery, John Moores (1967), New Gallery, Belfast (1968), Bradford Print Biennale (1968), New Editions Museum of Modern Art, Oxford (1969), Prize Winner A.I.A. Small Pictures (1969), Spectrum (1971); one-man shows: Temple Gallery, Drian Galleries, Bear Lane Gallery, Nottingham City A.G., Oxford Gallery. *Work in permanent collections:* Arts Council of N. Ireland, V. & A., W.A.G., Ferens A.G., Hull, Leeds City A.G., Manchester City A.G., Laing A.G., Portsmouth City A.G., etc., and 20 educational authorities in the British Isles. *Address:* 11 Bowerdean St., London SW6. *Signs work:* "STOKOE."

STONE, Alan Reynolds; designer and engraver on wood, letter-cutter on stone and slate; *b* 13 Mar., 1909; *s* of E. W. Stone, schoolmaster; *m* Janet Clemence Woods; two *s*, two *d*. *Educ.:* Eton and Magdalene College, Cambridge. *Exhib.:* water-colours: Agnew's, New Grafton Gall. *Work in permanent collections:* Prints: V. & A., Ashmolean Museum, Oxford. *Work repro.:* in Signature, Alphabet and Image, etc.; engraved heading Times newspaper, various stamps, and designed and executed lettering for the Winston Churchill memorial for Westminster Abbey (1965). *Address:* The Old Recotry, Litton Cheney, Dorchester, Dorset. *Signs work:* "Reynolds Stone" or "R.S." or "S" or "A.R. Stone"

STONE, John Christopher, A.R.C.A., A.O.C.A.; *b* Trinidad, West Indies, 24 June, 1923; *s* of Stanley S. Stone, lawyer. *Educ.:* Queen's Royal College, Trinidad, English public school; *studied art* at Ontario College of Art, Toronto, under John M. Alfsen, and Art Students' League, New York, with Kenneth Hayes Miller; Royal College of Art, London, with Spear, Burn and Carel Weight, awarded a Travelling Scholarship and the College Drawing Prize (1952). *Exhib.:* galleries in London, including R.A., Leicester Gallery, R.B.A., and Upper Street Gallery; Toronto and New York; also Ash Barn, Hampshire and Tib Lane, Manchester. *Work in private collections:* England and abroad. *Address:* 70 Gloucester Dr., London N4 2LN. *Signs work:* "John C. Stone" or "J.C.S."

STONES, Angela (Mrs.); painter and art teacher in oil, water-colour, pastel; member Chelsea Art Soc., and National Soc.; *b* London, 26 May, 1914; *m;* one *s*. *Educ.:* Sherborne School for Girls, Dorset; *studied art* at Heatherley's Art School and Sir John Cass School of Art, London (1956-57) (Jack Merriott, R.I., R.O.I., Patrick Larking, R.P., R.O.I., Harold Workman, R.O.I., R.B.A.). *Address:* The Studios, 6 Chelsea Embankment, London SW3. *Clubs:* Chelsea Arts, Exmouth Art Group. *Signs work:* "A. Stones."

STONES, Thomas Fiendley, B.A. (Admin.), F.M.A.; Keeper of the Rutherston Collection, Manchester City Art Galleries (1946-52); Keeper of Modern European Dept. and Print Dept., Royal Ontario Museum of Archæology, Toronto; special lecturer in art and archæology, University of Toronto (1953-54); Fine

Arts Dept., etc., British Council; *b* Astley, Lancs., 25 July 1920; *s* of Thomas Stones; *m* Elizabeth Mackie; one *d*. *Educ.:* Leigh Grammar School and Manchester University. *Address:* British Council, London.

STOREY, Terence, R.S.M.A.; marine, landscape and industrial artist in oils and water-colour; Mem. Society for Nautical Research; *b* Sunderland, 17 Apr., 1923; *s* of James Lionel Storey. *Educ.:* Sunderland Art School and Derby College of Art under Alfred Bladen. *Exhib.:* N.S., R.B.A., R.S.M.A., R.O.I., and N.E.A.C. *Work in permanent collections:* R.S.M.A. Diploma Collection, Maritime Museum, Greenwich. *Work repro.:* Rolls-Royce, Winsor and Newtons, The Hamlyn Group, etc. *Address:* Merlewood, 6 Queensway, Derby DE3 3BE. *Signs work:* "Terence Storey."

STOREY, Warren, A.R.W.A. (1957), A.T.D. (1950), Brit. Inst. Scholarship (1948); painter, designer and mural artist; Head of Weston-super-Mare School of Art; extra mural lecturer in art history, Bristol University; specialist in ecclesiastical design; *b* S. Shields, 19 Aug., 1924; *s* of Joseph Storey, boot and shoe dealer; *m* Lilian Evans; five *d*. *Educ.:* S. Shields High School; *studied art* at S. Shields School of Art under Ernest Gill, A.R.C.A. (1941-44), and Regent St. Polytechnic School under Wm. Matthews and Norman Blamey (1947-50). *Exhib.:* R.A., R.B.A., R.W.A., etc. Formed Acantha Group (1952). *Address:* Garenne, Leighton Cres., Bleadon Hill, Weston-super-Mare, Som.

STORM, Greenup Moorsom; artist in oil and woodcarver; *b* Robin Hood's Bay, Yorks., 1901; *m* Constance Muriel Bramald; two *d*. *Educ.:* Spring Hill Private School and Whitby County School; *studied art* under guidance of Dame Ethel Walker, A.R.A. *Exhib.:* R.A., Walker Art Gallery, Liverpool, R.W.E.A., Bristol, Bradford, etc.: head of the late King George VI (in the possession of the Queen Mother). Member of Fylingdales Group, Nidderdale Group, and N.Y.A.G. *Address:* The Studio, Roseway, Harrogate. *Signs work:* "Storm."

STORSTEIN, Aage, King's medal of merit in gold (1950); painter in oil and fresco; prof. at State Art Academy; mem., National Gallery Council since 1950; *b* Stavanger, 26 July, 1900; *s* of Hans Henrik Moinich Storstein, manager of boys' home; *m* Mildrid Helene; two *s*, one *d*. *Educ.:* examen artium; *studied art* at Paris, Munich. *Work in permanent collections:* National Gallery, Oslo; Bergen Art Gallery; Stavanger Permanent Gallery; Lillehammer Municipal Art Collections; Drammen's Permanent Gallery, and Moss Art Soc.; Molde Art Soc., and Throndhjem Art Gallery; Gothenburg Art Museum; Stockholm Art Museum. *Address:* Bygdöy, Oslo. *Signs work:* see appendix.

STOWASSER, Friedrich: see HUNDERTWASSER.

STRACHAN, David Edward Campbell (Eddie), D.A. (1961), Post-Dip. scholarship (1962); painter/teacher in gouache and water-colour; assistant principal teacher of art, Harris Academy, Dundee; *b* Forfar, Angus, 10 May, 1940; *m*; two *s*. *Educ.:* Forfar Academy; *studied art* at Duncan of Jordanstone College of Art, Dundee (1957-62) under Alberto Morrocco, R.S.A.; Hospitalfield College of Art, Arbroath (1961) under James Cumming, R.S.A., R.S.W. *Exhib.:* Dundee City A.G., Midland Group Gallery, Nottingham, Douglas and Foulis Gallery, Edinburgh, S.S.A., Edinburgh and London, Campbelland Franks, Marjorie Parr and Mercury Galleries, London, Galerie Inart, Amsterdam. *Work in permanent collections:* City of Edinburgh, Angus and Lanarkshire, Hospitalfield Art College. *Address:* 21 Mill St., Kirriemuir, Angus DD8 5DP. *Club:* S.S.A. *Signs work:* "Strachan."

STRACHAN, Walter John, M.A. (Cantab.); created Chevalier des Arts et Lettres by French Republic (1968); Commandeur des Palmes académiques

(1970); collector of, and university & NADFAS lecturer on French beaux livres, and modern sculpture, collection exhib. Ashmolean and FitzWilliam Museums, Scottish National Gallery of Modern Art and various prov. universities, etc. *Publications:* contributions to The Connoisseur, etc.; translator of Treatise on Landscape Painting by André L'Hote (Zwemmer, 1950), Figure Painting (Zwemmer, 1953), Modern Sculpture, Henry Moore, etc., Twentieth Century French Painters, German Painting (Tisné), Impressionist Painting (Tisné, 1960), Impressionism, its Forerunners and Influences (Octopus Books, 1972); author of The Artist and the Book in France (Peter Owen, 1969); A Dictionary of Surrealism (Eyre Methuen, 1974); Towards Sculpture Rodin to Oldenburg (Thames & Hudson, 1975), etc. *Address:* 10 Pleasant Rd., Bishop's Stortford, Herts. *Club:* P.E.N.

STRAIN, Robert William Magill, Commander, Order of St. John, B.Sc., M.D., Ph.D., F.R.C.P.I.; physician; artist in oil and water-colour; *b* Belfast, 1907; *s* of David Strain; *m* Eileen Mary Clapham. *Educ.:* Royal Belfast Academical Inst.; The Queen's University of Belfast. *Exhib.:* R.U.A., Walker's Gallery, London (Medical Art Soc.). *Work in permanent collections:* decorated maps, Belfast Museum and A.G. *Work repro.:* End Papers, Book of Belfast by Robert Marshall (1937). *Publications:* The Heraldry of Medicine (Ulster Medical Journal), Belfast and Its Charitable Society (O.U.P.). *Address:* Derry Hill, Tredrea, Perranarworthal, Truro, Cornwall TR3 7QG. *Signs work:* "R. W. M. Strain."

STRAUPENIEKS, Jekabs, Dip in Art (Latvia); artist in oil, water-colour and tempera; *b* Latvia, 28 Nov., 1921; *s* of M. Straupenieks; *m*; one *s*, one *d*. *Educ.:* School of Art, Latvia (five years); *studied art* under various Academicians. *Exhib.:* N.E.A.C., R.S.M.A., F.P.S., Paris Salon, New York City Gallery. *Work in permanent collections:* England, S. Africa, U.S.A. and Canada. *Publications:* various book illustrations and stage set designs. *Address:* 38 Cavell Ave., Peacehaven, Newhaven, E. Sussex. *Clubs:* Assoc. of Art Historians, F.P.S. *Signs work:* "J. Straupenieks."

STREVENS, John; painter in oil and water-colour; portrait painter, specializing in children; *b* London. *Studied art:* self-taught. *Exhib.:* R.A., Paris Salon (Hon. Mention), R.P.S., R.B.A.; one-man shows in London, New York, New Orleans, Memphis, San Antonio and Houston, Texas, and Madrid. *Work in permanent collections:* Preston A.G.; private collections in London, New York and Madrid. *Work repro.:* Fine Art Prints (Medici, Royles). *Address:* 8 Lower Park Rd., Loughton, Essex. *Clubs:* Savage and London Sketch. *Signs work:* "John Strevens."

SUMMERS, Leslie John, F.F.P.S. (1968); sculptor in bronze, perspex (acrylic); *b* London, 2 Nov., 1919; *s* of John Summers; *m* Janet Margaret Bately, M.A. (Oxon.); two *s*. *Educ.:* Dulwich College and London University; *studied art* at Chelsea School of Art. *Exhib.:* R.A., R.B.A., F.P.S., Walker A.G., Artists Own Gallery, London, Gordon Maynard Gallery, Cork St. Gallery, London. *Work in permanent collections:* National Museum of Wales (purchased by Contemporary Art Soc. of Wales); Cork St. Gallery, London, U.S. Atomic Energy Commission. *Work repro.:* Art and Artists, Studio International, Exploring Sculpture, Creative Plastics. *Address:* 86 Cawdor Cres., London W7. *Signs work:* see appendix.

SUMMERSON, Sir John Newenham, Kt. (1958), C.B.E. (1953), F.B.A. (1954), F.S.A. (1945), A.R.I.B.A. (1929); curator, Sir John Soane's Museum; *b* 1904; *s* of Samuel James Summerson; *m* Elizabeth Alison Hepworth; three *s*. *Educ.:* Harrow; University College, London (1922-27). *Publications:* John Nash (1935), Georgian London (1945), Heavenly Mansions (1949), Architecture in

Britain, 1530-1830 (1953). *Address:* Sir John Soane's Museum, 13 Lincoln's Inn Fields, London WC2. *Clubs:* Athenæum, Beefsteak.

SUNLIGHT, Benjamin Clement; professional artist; painter in oils and graphic artist; *b* Brighton, 7 Apr., 1935; *s* of Joseph Sunlight, L.R.I.B.A. *Educ.:* Clifton and Magdalene College, Cambridge; *studied art* at London Central School of Art and Design (Mural Diploma, 1962) under Alan Davie, Hans Tisdall, Harold Cohen and Tony Harrison. Part-time teacher, Hornsey College of Art (1964-65), Cranfield Institute of Technology (1973-74); Fellow and Vice-Chairman, Free Painters and Sculptors (1965-68); Mem., International Arts Guild; Gold medallist, International Academy, Rome. *Address:* 14 Victoria Sq., London SW1W 0RA. *Signs work:* "Ben Sunlight."

SURREY, Milt; painter in oil; *b* New York City, 18 Mar., 1922; *m* Eleanor; two *s*, one *d*. Self-taught artist. *Work in permanent collections:* Allentown Art Museum, Cincinnati Art Museum, College Museum, Hampton Institute, Columbia Museum of Art, Evansville Museum of Art, Hickory Museum of Art, Massillon Museum, Miami Museum of Modern Art, Springfield Art Museum, Holyoke Museum of Natural History and Art, Theodore Lyman Wright Art Centre, Beliot College, Treat Gallery, Bates College. *Address:* 7 Bridle Path Drive, Old Westbury, N.Y. 11568, U.S.A. *Signs work:* "SURREY."

SUTHERLAND, Graham, O.M. (1960); painter; *b* 24 Aug., 1903; *s* of the late G. H. V. Sutherland, civil servant; *m* Katherine Francis Barry. *Educ.:* Epsom College, University of London, Goldsmiths' College. *Address:* White House, Trottiscliffe, W. Malling, Kent.

SUTHERLAND, Scott, D.A. (Edin., 1932), R.S.A. (1949), F.R.B.S. (1961); sculptor in bronze and stone; sculpture instructor, Dundee College of Art (1947-75); sculpture instructor, Belfast College of Art (1945-47); *b* Wick, Caithness, 15 May, 1910; *s* of Maj. David Sutherland, M.A., M.C.; *m*; one *s*, two *d*. *Educ.:* Wick High School; *studied art* at Gray's School of Art (1928-29), Edinburgh College of Art under Alexander Carrick, R.S.A. (1929-33), Ecole des Beaux-Arts (1934), and sculpture in Egypt, Greece, Italy, France and Germany (1934-35). *Exhib.:* R.S.A. *Official purchases:* Scottish Commando Memorial, 4/5th Black Watch Memorial. *Address:* 17 Norwood Terr., Newport-on-Tay, Fife. *Signs work:* "Scott Sutherland."

SUTTON, Denys, B.A., B.Litt. (Oxon.); author and lecturer; Foreign Office Research Dept. (1940-46), Secretary International Commission for Restitution of Cultural Material (1946), Fine Arts Specialist at U.N.E.S.C.O. (1948), visiting lecturer in Fine Arts Yale University (1949); *b* London, 10 Aug., 1917; *s* of Edmund Sutton; *m* 1st, Sonja Klibansky, one *d*; 2nd, Gertrud Købke, one *s*; 3rd, Cynthia Sassoon. *Educ.:* Uppingham and Exeter College, Oxford. *Publications:* Watteau's Les Charmes de la Vie: Matisse; American Painting; Picasso, Blue and Pink Period; French Drawings of the 18th Century; Bonnard; Christie's Since the War; André Derain; N. de Staël; Whistler; Toulouse-Lautrec; S. de Castro; Titian; Triumphant Satyr; Richard Wilson: an Italian Sketchbook; Letters of Roger Fry; co-author Catalogue Fitzwilliam Museum, Cambridge; contributions to Burlington Magazine, Country Life; Daily Telegraph, The Financial Times; organizer Bonnard Exhibition at R.A. (1965-66); Editor Apollo since 1962. *Addresses:* 22 Chelsea Park Gdns., London SW3; Westwood Manor, Bradford-on-Avon. *Club:* Travellers'.

SUTTON, Hector McDonald, A.R.C.A. (London 1931), F.R.S.A. (1937), M. of E. Industrial Design Cert. with distinction (1928); princ. (retd.), Mansfield College of Art; art adviser (retd.) to Notts. Educ. Comm.; princ. asst. master,

Chiswick School of Art (1931-37): extra-mural lecturer, Nottingham University; former examiner: Oxford, Cambridge, Nottingham Universities; founder chairman, past pres., hon. mem. Midland Artists and Designers Group; founder pres. Mansfield Flower Arrangement Society; pres. Mansfield Society of Artists; painter, modeller, lithographer, sculptor in various media; *b* Walsall Wood, S. Staffs., 28 Apr., 1903; *s* of John Sutton; *m* Susan Sarah Davison; two *s*. *Studied art* at Southport, Liverpool Schools of Art, R.C.A. under Sir William Rothenstein, Sir Tom Monnington, P.R.A., Prof. E. W. Tristram, D.Litt., Prof. Randolph Schwabe; assisted A. K. Lawrence, R.A., Bank of England mural paintings. *Exhib.:* London: Burlington House, V. & A. Museum, Archer Gallery; Nottingham: Midland Group, Castle, William Holbrook Trust First Prize (1970), Playhouse; City Art Galleries: Sheffield, Leicester, Lincoln; Germany: Heiligenhaus. *Work in permanent collections:* Nottinghamshire: schools, factories, churches; Civic Theatre, Heiligenhaus, Germany. *Official purchases:* as above, also private patrons, portraits, easel, landscape paintings. *Work reviewed and repro.:* Studio magazine. Assisted Rev. Hemming Vaughan in founding William Blake Society (June 1954). *Address:* Newstead Abbey Pk., Linby, Nottingham. *Signs work:* see appendix—on paintings and drawings in various colours, in sculpture, incised, corres. italic script.

SUTTON, Kingsley, F.R.S.A., U.A.; Mem., United Soc. Artists (1947), Ridley Art Club (1950); artist and portrait painter in oil, water-colour and black and white; tutor and demonstrator; *b* Tunbridge Wells, 1907; *s* of H. F. Sutton, artist; *m* E. F. Austen, F.G.A. *Educ.:* Watford, Herts.; *studied art* at Regent St. Polytechnic and under Seymour Lucas. *Exhib.:* R.B.A., R.O.I., R.A., etc. *Work in private collections* in Britain, Holland, Germany and the U.S.A. *Work repro.:* Illustrations, book illustrations, industrial paintings, etc. *Address:* Shackleford House, 71 High St., Old Woking, Surrey. *Clubs:* London Sketch, Ridley Art. *Signs work:* "KINGSLEY SUTTON."

SUTTON, Linda, M.A. (R.C.A.); painter in oil on canvas, acrylic on paper; *b* Southend-on-Sea, 14 Dec., 1947; *d* of William Tinnion Sutton, builder and decorator. *Educ.:* Eastwood High School for Girls; *studied art* at Southend College of Technology; Winchester School of Art; R.C.A. *Exhib.:* one-man shows: Galerij de Zwarte Panter, Antwerp, Bedford House Gallery, London. *Work in permanent collections:* R.A., Chantry Bequest. *Address:* 87 Clapham Common N. Side, London SW4. *Signs work:* "Linda Sutton."

SUTTON, Philip; painter; *b* Poole, Dorset, 20 Oct., 1928; *s* of L. L. Sutton; *m* Heather; one *s*, three *d*. *Studied art* at Slade School. *Exhib.:* Roland, Browse and Delbanco, London Arts, Detroit Inc., Detroit. *Work in permanent collections:* Tate, Bedford, Birmingham, Bradford, Kettering, Leeds, Leicester, Melbourne, Adelaide, Durban, Lincoln, Manchester, Perth, Sheffield, Southport. *Official purchases:* Arts Council. *Address:* 10 Soudan Rd., London SW11 4HH. *Signs work:* see appendix.

SWAN, Robert John, medallist R.A. Schools, Landseer Scholar, Brit. Inst. Scholar, mem. A.W.G.; *b* 21 July, 1888; *m* Kathleen Lucy, B.A. (Oxon.). *Studied art* at Putney School of Art, R.A. Schools. *Exhib.:* R.A., R.P., R.B.A., N.S., Liverpool and other provincial galleries. *Work in permanent collections:* Pembroke and Jesus Colleges, Cambridge; Imperial College of Science and Technology; portraits of H.R.H. the Duke of Windsor (for the Govt. of the Bahamas); F.M. Lord Templer (for School of Infantry); Sir Godfrey Cretney (for the Regis School, Wolverhampton) and portrait drawings for the Bookman and Denstone College. *Address:* Studio 2, Sydney Cl., 76 Fulham Rd., London SW3. *Signs work:* "Robert Swan."

SWANN, Marilyn, M.F.P.S., A.I.R.; painter in oil; leading illustrator (D.N.S.); *b* Crayford, Kent, 14 Apr., 1932; *d* of C. W. Swann. *Educ.:* Bexleyheath; *studied art* at Woolwich Polytechnic (1945-50) under Heber Mathews, Herbert Tempest; Central School of Art, London (evenings, 1960-70) under Leslie Cole. *Exhib.:* Brangwyn Gallery, Hammersmith (1976), Loggia Gallery (1974, 1975, 1976), "Trends", F.P.S. Mall Galleries since 1973. *Work repro.:* music illustrated: Lieder (Decca), Mahler (Ace of Diamonds) (record set inserts) and Schubert. *Address:* 46 Evelyn Gdns., London SW7 7BH. *Signs work:* "SWANN" or "Marilyn Swann."

SWANN, Peter C., M.A. (Oxon.), LL.D. (Brock and Queens); keeper, Department of Eastern Art, Ashmolean Museum, Oxford; Director Royal Ontario Museum, Toronto, Canada (1966-72); *b* London, 1921; *m* Elizabeth Hayden; three *s*, two *d*. *Educ.:* Tottenham Grammar School, Oxford University, London University, Leiden University. *Publications:* Introduction to the Arts of Japan (1958), Chinese Painting (1958), Hokusai (1959), Two Thousand Years of Japanese Art (with Y. Yashiro, 1959), The Monumental Art of China (1963), The Arts of China, Korea and Japan (1963); editor of Oriental Art (1955-68). *Address:* 1916 Tupper St., Montreal H3H 1N5, Canada. *Signs work:* "Peter C. Swann."

SWERLING, Anthony, M.A. (Cantab.); graphic artist in line and half-tone in various mediums, writer; Director of Cambridge Graffiti; *b* Manchester, 31 July, 1944; *s* of Morris Swerling. *Educ.:* Sorbonne and Cambridge; *studied art:* self-taught. *Exhib.:* London, Cambridge, Barcelona, Paris, Madrid. *Work in permanent collections:* various graphics in private collections in England, France, Spain, U.S.A. *Publications:* written and/or illustrated: Concerning the Art of Translation; La Poinçonneuse Apocalyptique and Le Timbre-Poste Concentrationnaire; The Rape of Czechoslovakia; A Madman's Manifesto (transl. from Strindberg's French); The Cambridge Plague; Sex and Mr. X; Strindberg's Impact in France 1920-60; In Quest of Strindberg; Strindberg: The Critical Heritage; The Truth About Strindberg. *Address:* 26 Shaftesbury Rd., Manchester 8. *Signs work:* see appendix.

SYKES, Paul, D.M.A., F.L.A., M.I.R.M., Director of Recreation, Borough of Blackburn. *Address:* Royal Chambers, Richmond Terr., Blackburn.

SYKES, Steven, A.R.C.A.; designer and sculptor; lecturer, Chelsea School of Art; *b* Formby, Lancs., 30 Aug., 1914; *s* of Dr. A. B. Sykes (decd.); *m* Jean Judd; two *s*, one *d*. *Educ.:* Oratory, Caversham; *studied art* at R.C.A. *Exhib.:* Galerie Apollinaire, Hanover Gallery. *Work in permanent collections:* V. & A., Walker Gallery, Liverpool; Ashmolean, Oxford; International Ceramic Museum, Faenza. *Sculpture* for Coventry Cathedral, U.S. National War Memorial Chapel, Washington Cathedral; water sculpture, British Pavilion, Expo 67; Wool House, Carlton Gardens, SW1. *Address:* Studio, Hopkiln Bepton, Midhurst, Sussex. *Signs work:* "Steven Sykes."

SYMONS, Patrick S., artist in oil, charcoal and pencil; Senior Lecturer, Chelsea School of Art; *b* Bromley, Kent, 24 Oct., 1925; *s* of N. H. Symons, Insurance broker, retd. *Educ.:* Bryanston School, Blandford, Dorset; *studied art* at Camberwell School of Arts and Crafts under W. Coldstream, C. Rogers, J. Dodgson. *Work in permanent collections:* Doncaster Museum. *Address:* 20 Grove Hill Rd., Camberwell, London SE5. *Signs work:* "Symons."

SZOMANSKI, Wladyslaw, F.R.S.A., M.S.I.A., Dip. Academy of Fine Arts, Warsaw; commercial designer; Display World's International Display Contest, U.S.A., bronze medal (1950), bronze medal (1952), gold medal and silver medal

(1955); *b* Baturyn, Poland, 3 Oct., 1911; *s* of Jan Szomanski, director, Health Insurance; *m* Krystyna Lipinska. *Educ.:* Secondary School, Rowno, Polytechnicum (architecture), Lwow; *studied art and graduated* at Academy of Fine Arts, Warsaw, under Prof. Skoczylas, Bartlomiejczyk, Wyczolkowski (1932-39). *Exhib.:* Warsaw, Berlin, Paris, Bucharest, Edinburgh, Rome (all poster exhbns.). *Work repro.:* posters (1935-39), Min. of Commerce, Soc. for the Prevention of Accidents, P.K.O. Bank, Poland; Advertisers' Weekly, Display and Presentation, Art and Industry, Publimondial, Gebrauchsgraphik, Display World, World Window. *Publications:* Advertisers' Weekly, England: Theatrical Realism invades the Poster, Display World, U.S.A.: Selling Service via Display requires Dramatic Simplicity. *Address:* 20 Sinclair Gdns., London W14. *Signs work:* "Szomanski."

T

TAJIRI, Shinkichi, William and Noma Copley Award for sculpture (1959); John Hay Whithey Found. Opp. Fellowship (1960); Mainichi Shibum Prize, Tokyo Biennale (1963); sculptor in bronze and brass; Prof. of Sculpture, Staatliche Hochschule für Bildende Kunste, W. Berlin; *b* Los Angeles, 7 Dec., 1923; *m* Ferdi (decd.); two *d. Educ.:* Los Angeles; *studied art* at under Donald Hord, San Diego (1948-51); O. Zadkine and F. Leger, Paris. *Work in permanent collections:* Stedelijk Museum, Amsterdam, Gemeente Museum, Den Haag, Modern Museum, Stockholm, Town of Arnhem, Holland, Museum of Modern Art, N.Y., etc. *Address:* Kasteel Scheres, Baarlo, Limburg, Holland. *Signs work:* see appendix.

TALBOT, Leon, D.A. (Lond.), D.A.E., M.B.K.S., A.T.D., S.B.St.J.; painter and lecturer on art and anthropology; art therapist; proprietor, Talbot Film Productions; *b* London, 27 Apr., 1905; *s* of Capt. James Talbot. *Educ.:* Napier College and St. Andrew's School; *studied art* at Chelsea School of Art, Brighton College of Art and Slade School. *Exhib.:* murals in Europe and Africa; paintings at Herbert Gallery, Coventry (1965). *Publications:* A Bantu Tradition in Art, regular columnist and art critic as Baroqueon and under own name. *Address:* Greensleeves, Avon Castle, Ringwood, Hants. *Signs work:* "Leon Talbot."

TALBOT, Nancy Wilfreda Hewitt, D.A. (Lond.) (1948); painter in oil and stage designer; consultant, Talbot Film Productions; teacher of painting for Hampshire (1950-66); *b* Coventry, 31 Aug., 1925; *d* of Wilfred John Skillington, lawyer; *m* Major Leon Talbot. *Educ.:* Leamington High School, Leamington Spa; *studied art* at Ruskin Drawing School, Oxford (1945) (Albert Rutherston), Slade School, London (1945-48) (Randolph Schwabe, Vladimir Polunin). *Exhib.:* first one-man show, Alfred Herbert Gallery, Coventry (1965). *Work in permanent collections:* mural and portrait commissions, privately owned. *Address:* Greensleeves, Avon Castle, Ringwood, Hants. *Signs work:* "Nancy Talbot" or "Nancy Skillington."

TALBOT, Victoria Mary; artist in oil, water-colour; *b* Melbourne, Australia, 1 June, 1931; *d* of Fred Talbot. *Educ.:* St. Augustine's School, Melbourne; *studied art* at Caulfield, Melbourne, and Jorgensen School of Painting, Melbourne. *Address:* c/o Trafford Gallery, 119 Mount St., London W1Y 5HB. *Signs work:* "Victoria Mary Talbot."

TALLENTIRE, Anne, D.A., F.I.L.S.; artist/teacher in oil and gouache; *b* Portadown, Co. Armagh, N. Ireland, 1 Mar., 1949. *Educ.:* Coleraine High

School; *studied art* with Kenneth Webb. *Exhib.:* Mall and Archer Galleries, London (1972), Contemporary Figurative Painting, R.B.A., London, Travelling Contemporary Figurative Painting, Kenny Gallery, Galway, Setanta Gallery, Dublin, Mansard Gallery, London, Anthony Reid Gallery, Norwich, Rooksmoor Gallery, Stroud, Ulster Academy, R.H.A., N.S. *Address:* Ballinaboy Lodge, Ballinaboy, nr. Clifden, Connemara, Co. Galway, Ireland. *Signs work:* "Anne Tallentire."

TAMBLYN-WATTS, Harold, F.Z.S.; artist and illustrator in water-colour and line; *b* Settle, Yorks, 1900; *s* of T. M. F. Tamblyn-Watts, A.M.I.E.E., F.R.S.A.; *m*; two *s*. *Educ.:* Stanstead School; *studied art* at Southend School of Art; Emmett Group Studio Manager (1935-48). *Exhib.:* Fleet St. Artists, Croydon Art Soc., Private Art Exhbn., Bouverie St. (1948), Fairfield Halls Croydon (1974). *Work repro.:* in Modern Publicity in War, Aeroplane, Flight; books illustrated, The Young Naturalist, Wonderful Plants, and children's books; book jackets, etc. *Address:* 25 Bennett's Way, Shirley, Surrey. *Signs work:* see appendix.

TARR, James C., A.R.C.A., A.T.D. (1929); artist in oil and water-colour; princ., Cardiff College of Art, 1946-70 (retired); princ., Lydney School of Art (1936-38); High Wycombe School of Art (1938-46); *b* Oystermouth, Swansea, 27 May, 1905; *s* of J. M. Tarr, master mariner; *m* K. M. Tydeman, A.R.C.A.; one *s*. *Educ.:* Swansea; *studied art* at Cheltenham School of Art (1922-25), and R.C.A. (1925-29). *Exhib.:* R.A., A.C.E.S., National Museum of Wales, various London and provincial galleries. *Address:* 21 Oakfield St., Cardiff.

TARRANT, Peter, N.D.D.; artist in oil; *b* Shropshire, 1943. *Educ.:* Morville School; *studied art* at Shrewsbury Art School. *Work in permanent collection:* Birmingham City Museum and A.G. *Address:* 8 St. Gregory's Cl., Morville, nr. Bridgnorth, Salop.

TARRANT, Terence Richard, A.M.AA. (1952); medical artist; ophthalmic artist at Theodore Hamblin Ltd. (1945-48); ophthalmic artist at Queen Alexandra's Military Hospital, Millbank (1948-50); medical artist at Inst. of Ophthalmology, London, since 1950; *b* London, 7 Jan., 1930; *s* of R. J. Tarrant; *m*; one *s*, two *d*. *Educ.:* London; *studied art* at Camberwell School of Arts and Crafts. *Work in permanent collections:* Inst. of Ophthalmology. *Work repro.:* Atlas of Eye Diseases, Perkins and Hansell; medical journals; Ophthalmology, Trevor Roper; System of Ophthalmology, Duke-Elder. *Address:* 42 Ridge Ave., Harpenden, Herts. *Signs work:* "TARRANT" with tops of the Ts joined.

TATE, Barba, R.M.S., S.W.A., F.R.S.A., I.A.A., Ass. Société des Artistes Français; Silver Medal, Paris Salon (1968); Gold Medal, Paris Salon (1969); Prix Marie Puisoye (1971); Special Mention Palme d'or des Beaux-Arts, Monte Carlo (1972); Laureat Grand Prix de la Côte d'Azur (1972); painter in oil; *b* Uxbridge, Middlesex; *m* James Tate, also a painter; one *d*. *Educ.:* Dormers Wells School, Southall; *studied art* at Ealing School of Art (1940-45, under T. E. Lightfoot, A.R.C.A., T. Bayley, A.R.C.A., J. E. Nicholls, A.R.C.A.) and Wigan Art School (1945-46, 1957-58, under Peter Coker, A.R.A., A.R.C.A.). *Exhib.:* BBC2 Television, one-man show, Paris (1968), Royal Academy, Royal Society of Portrait Painters, Royal Institute of Oil Painters, Royal Society of British Artists, New English Art Club, National Society, Royal Society of Miniature Painters, Sculptors and Gravers, United Society of Artists, Society of Women Artists, Hesketh Hubbard Art Society, Royal Institute, Free Painters and Sculptors, R.W.S. Galleries' Flower Painting Exhbn., Chenil Galleries, Chelsea, Paris Salon, Salon Terres Latines, Salon du Comparaisons, Ville Eternal, Rome, Nice, Monte Carlo, Royal Festival Hall. *Work in permanent collections:* "The Masters'

Gallery," Château Thorens, Haute-Savoie. *Work repro.:* The Green Shawl, Clematis, Nasturtiums, Golden Girl, as prints for hanging, published by Solomon & Whitehead, London. *Address:* Willow House, Ealing Green, London W5 5EN. *Signs work:* see appendix. Some work done in collaboration with husband (see appendix).

TATE, James, A.R.M.S.; Ass. Société des Artistes Français; F.R.S.A.; I.A.A.; Laureat Grand Prix de la Côte d'Azur (1972); painter in oil and gouache; *b* Chatham, Kent, 8 Apr., 1914; *s* of Arthur Edward Tate, master builder; *m* Barba Tate, painter; one *d. Educ.:* Princess Road Elementary School, London, and The William Ellis Secondary School; *studied art* at Chatham Polytechnic (1930-33), Woolwich Polytechnic (1936-37), Central School of Arts and Crafts (1946-48). *Exhib.:* Paris Salon, R.A., R.B.A., R.O.I., R.M.S., R.I. Galleries Summer Salon, United Soc. of Artists, Free Painters and Sculptors, National Soc., Contemporary Painters U.K. Tour (1971); group shows, Nice, Monte Carlo, Rome. *Publications:* cartoons and advertising and publicity illustration; article and short-story writer (1938-48); entertainments critic and general reporter for Sphynx magazine, Cairo (1943-45); contributor to Egyptian Mail, Egyptian Gazette and most Forces magazines and radio stations in Middle East, also The Stage, Blighty, Reveille, The Performer and other British publications. *Address:* Willow House, Ealing Green, London W5 5EN. *Signs work:* "Tate," see appendix also for signing of work done in collaboration with Barba Tate.

TAVENER, Robert, R.E., M.S.I.A., A.T.D., N.D.D.; illustrator and printmaker; Deputy Principal, Eastbourne College of Art and Design; *b* London, 1920; *m*; one *d. Studied art* at Hornsey College of Art (1946-50). *Exhib.:* six one-man exhibitions; work selected for eight Arts Council exhibitions. *Work in permanent collections:* over 1000 prints purchased for national collections in U.K. and abroad by galleries, museums, local educational authorities. *Publications:* illustrated series of children's books for Longmans Green and Oxford University Press; and commissioned work for B.B.C., London Transport, G.P.O., Shell, I.C.I., Nuffield Foundation, etc. *Address:* Tussocks, Link Rd., Meads, Eastbourne. *Signs work:* see appendix.

TAYLOR, Albert Jenkins; artist in etching and engraving; company director; Managing Director, Aspinall's Patent Governor Ltd. and John Taylor (Liverpool) Ltd.; *b* Liverpool, 26 Nov., 1918; *s* of A. E. Taylor; *m* Isabella Watson. *Educ.:* Shrewsbury; *studied art* at Liverpool College of Art under Geoffrey Wedgewood, R.E. and Chas. H. Clark (privately). *Exhib.:* R.E., R.S.A., R.C.A., R.W.A. *Address:* 2 Forest Cl., Meols, Hoylake, Wirral, Merseyside. *Clubs:* Alpine, Liverpool Athenæum. *Signs work:* "Albert J. Taylor."

TAYLOR, Eric, R.E., A.R.C.A. (1934); painter, sculptor and printmaker, teacher of art at Camberwell School of Art (1936-39), Willesden School of Art (1936-39 and 1945-49), Central School of Arts (1946-48); Principal, Leeds College of Art (1956-69); Assistant Director, Leeds Polytechnic (1969-71); *b* 6 Aug., 1909; *s* of Thomas John Taylor; *m*; one *s*, one *d. Educ.:* William Ellis School, Hampstead; R.C.A. under Sir W. Rothenstein (1932-35). *Exhib.:* R.A., London Group, N.E.A.C., R.S.A., and in Chicago, New York, Washington, Los Angeles, Oslo, Copenhagen, Stockholm, Buenos Aires, Madrid, Lisbon. *Address:* Gordale, Tredgold Ave., Bramhope, nr. Leeds. *Signs work:* "Eric Taylor."

TAYLOR, James Spencer, A.R.C.A., B.Sc. (Econ.) (Hons.), F.R.S.A.; artist and graphic designer (books); lecturer, Bolton College of Art and Design; *b* Burnley, 7 May, 1921; *s* of Harry Taylor; *m* Joyce B. Haffner; one *s*, one *d. Studied art* at Burnley School of Art, Slade School of Fine Art under Randolph

Schwabe, R.C.A. under Roger Powell (1945-48). *Exhib.:* Red Rose Guild of Craftsmen, Crafts Centre of Gt. Britain, Society of Designer Craftsmen, R.B.A., C. of I.D. Executed many commissions in Great Britain and abroad. *Address:* 253 Tottington Rd., Bradshaw, Bolton. *Signs work:* "JT" (books), "J. S. Taylor" or "JST" (paintings and drawings).

TAYLOR, Joan D., A.T.D. (1946); textile designer and printer and painter; instructor in printed textiles, Laird School of Art, Birkenhead (1946-67); *d* of George H. Taylor, company director. *Educ.:* St. Edmund's College, Liverpool; *studied art* at Liverpool College of Art. *Exhib.:* R.A., N.E.A.C., Liverpool Academy of Arts, Bluecoat Display Centre, Liverpool. *Address:* 79 Grosvenor Rd., Birkenhead L43 1UD. *Signs paintings:* "J. D. Taylor."

TAYLOR, John Whitfield, B.A. (Manchester, 1929); Punch artist; formerly Headmaster, Holden Lane High School, Stoke-on-Trent; *b* 11 May, 1908; *s* of G. W. Taylor; *m* Alice Elaine Oldacre; one *s*, one *d*. *Educ.:* Orme Boys' School, Newcastle, Staffs.; Manchester University; Stoke-on-Trent Art Schools. *Exhib.:* Soc. of Staffordshire Artists. *Address:* Wayside, Summer La., Brixham, Devon. *Club:* Savage. *Signs work:* see appendix.

TAYLOR, Joyce Barbara, Oxford Delegacy, A.T.D., C.G.L.I. (Embroidery); lecturer, Bolton College of Art and Bolton Women's College; artist in embroidery, hand and machine, collage and three dimensional; *b* Burnley, 6 Aug., 1921; *d* of John Harry Haffner; *m* James S. Taylor; one *s*, one *d*. *Educ.:* Burnley High School; *studied art* at Burnley School of Art, Manchester College of Art (1941). *Exhib.:* Red Rose Guild of Craftsmen, Embroiderers Guild, Whitworth Art Gallery, Manchester, R.W.S. Galleries, London, Manchester Cathedral. *Work in permanent collections:* Altar Frontals etc. for Bolton Parish Church, Walmsley Parish Church, and other churches; Banners and other work in private collections in England and U.S.A. *Address:* 253 Tottington Rd., Bradshaw, Bolton. *Signs work:* "J.B.T."

TAYLOR, Mrs. M.: see BRIDGE, Muriel Elisabeth.

TAYLOR, Newton: see TAYLOR, William Henry.

TAYLOR, Richard, A.R.C.A. (1949), R.W.A.(1953); artist/graphic designer; Head of Graphic Design Dept., Faculty of Art and Design, Bristol Polytechnic; *b* London, 12 June, 1924; *m* Jean Constance Hingston; one *s*, two *d*. *Educ.:* Acton, Ealing, Newton Abbot Art School, R.C.A. *Work in permanent collections:* Lithographs and lino-cuts, R.W.A.; lino-cuts, V. & A. and Bristol Education Committee; water-colour, War Museum. *Work repro.:* jackets and illustrations for Penguins, Heinemann, Methuen, Dobson, Merlin, co-author two Penguin Puffin picture books, Everest is Climbed, Discovery of the Poles (1956, 1958); Author and illustrator for twelve Stand and Stare books; Designer of Harvey's Wine Museum, Bristol; Author of Basic Course in Graphic Design (Studio Vista, 1971). *Address:* No. 2, Marine Hill, Clevedon, Somerset. *Signs work:* "R. TAYLOR."

TAYLOR, Wendy Ann, L.D.A.D.(Hons.); sculptor in all mediums; *b* Stamford, Lincs., 29 July, 1945. *Studied art* at St. Martin's School of Art under Tony Caro, King, Tucker. *Exhib.:* one-man shows: Oxford Gallery (1976), Annely Juda Fine Art, London (1975), 24th King's Lynn Festival, Norfolk (1974), World Trade Centre, London (1974), Angela Flowers Gallery (1972), Axiom Gallery (1970). *Work in permanent and private collections:* British Council, G.L.C. Parks, City of Christchurch A.G., N.Z., London Borough of Camden, Arts Council of Gt. Britain, Leics. Educ. Authority, Southern Arts Council, V. & A., Taylor Woodrow Ltd., P. & O. Shipping Lines, Nelson A. Rockefeller. *Address:* 69A Nightingale Lane, London SW12. *Signs work:* see appendix.

TAYLOR, Wilfred, F.I.I.C.; lecturer, Conservation of Paintings, Gateshead Technical College; Fellow of the International Institute for Conservation of Historic and Artistic Works; artist in oil, water-colour, pencil and pastel; *b* Gateshead, 31 July, 1915; *s* of John J. Taylor; *m*; one *s*. *Studied art* at King Edward VII School of Art, Newcastle upon Tyne, under T. W. Pattinson, R. Bertram, M.A., and Mrs. D. M. Lall, B.A. (1932-37). *Exhib.:* N. Federation of Art Socs.; Laing Art Gallery, Newcastle; Northern Artists Annual Exhbn.; Contemp. Artist of Durham County Exhbn. *Address:* 35 Carlton Terr., Low Fell, Gateshead, 9. *Club:* Gateshead and Dist. Art. *Signs work:* "W. TAYLOR."

TAYLOR, William Henry (Newton Taylor), A.R.C.A. (1934), A.R.E. (1957), Free Studentship (1932), Prix-de-Rome Finalist in Engraving (1935); artist in oil (portrait and landscape), water-colours, etching and engraving on metal and wood; deputy head senior lecturer, School of Art, High Wycombe; lecturer, demonstrator, critic; *b* Normanton, Yorks., 31 Aug., 1911; *s* of James Taylor; *m* Elsie May Newton; three *s*. *Educ.:* Normanton Boys' Grammar School, Yorks; *studied art* at Wakefield School of Art; Leeds School of Art; R.C.A. *Exhib.:* Yorks. Artists Soc., Bucks. Art Soc., R.P.E., R.B.A., R.A. *Address:* Newstone Bungalow, Bovingdon Green, Marlow, Bucks. *Signs work:* "NEWTON TAYLOR" in two lines.

TAYLOR, W. S., A.R.C.A., M.Phil.; Head of Dept. of History of Art at Sheffield Polytechnic; *b* 26 Sept., 1920; *s* of W. Taylor; *m* Audrey Wallis; one *d*. *Educ.:* City Grammar School, Sheffield; *studied art* at Sheffield College of Art and R.C.A. *Exhib.:* R.A., etc. and provincial galleries. *Publications:* Catalogue of Burne-Jones Exhbn., Sheffield City Art Galleries; King Cophetua and the Beggar Maid, Apollo Magazine; King Cophetua and the Beggar Maid (film), Arts Council of Great Britain and the Tate Gallery. *Address:* The Hall, Hathersage, Sheffield.

TEASDILL, Graham, Museums Association Diploma, F.R.S.A., F.R.N.S., F.Z.S., F.M.A.; curator, Russell-Cotes Art Gallery and Museum and the Rothesay Museum, Bournemouth since 1966; *b* Horsforth, 5 Oct., 1935; *s* of late Clifford Humphrey Teasdill, bank official, of Guiseley; *m* Nova Ann Pickersgill of Horsforth, 22 July, 1960; one *s* (Michael Graham, *b* at Dewsbury, 5 Dec., 1962), two *d* (Caroline Nova, *b* at Dewsbury, 31 Oct., 1965, Pauline Ann, *b* at Bournemouth, 4 Mar., 1968). *Educ.:* Ilkley Grammar School. Assistant at Ilkley (1950-55), Leeds (1955-56) and Huddersfield (1956-60); assistant curator, Cheltenham (1960-62). Curator, Batley (1962-66). President, Yorkshire Federation of Museums (1966-67); South-Eastern Federation (1969-70).

TEED, John; actor, antique dealer, landscape painter in water-colour, portrait artist in pastel; *b* London, 18 Jan., 1911; *s* of Harry Williamson Teed, inventor. *Educ.:* Westminster School; *studied art* at L.C.C. School of Art, Westminster. *Exhib.:* R.A., Blackpool. *Work in permanent collections:* National Gallery, N.S.W. *Address:* The Old Manor House, Bradford-on-Avon, Wilts. *Signs work:* "John Teed."

TEIJEIRO, Manuel F.; sculptor; Gold Medal for Foreigners, 23rd Salon Nacional de Buenos Aires (1943); President, New Art Assoc. (1957); President, Argentine Comm., International Assoc. of Plastic Art (U.N.E.S.C.O.) (1959); selected to partake in 150 Years of Argentinian Art and International Exposition of Art (1960); selected for Argentine Exhbn. of Art, Museum of Modern Art, Rio de Janeiro (1961); Exhbn. of Argentinian Art, Edinburgh, Tate Gallery, Cambridge and Sweden (1962): *b* Valencia, Spain, 1913; *s* of Manuel and Dolores Teijeiro; *m* Francisca Ranios de Los Reyes, painter. *Studied art* at Institute San Isidro, Madrid, and Escuela Superior de Bellas Artes de San Fernando, Madrid. *Exhib.:* various official salons in Argentina; one-man shows, Buenos Aires: Heroica Gall. (1951), Galatea Gall. (1952, 1954, 1956), Botanical

Gardens (1955), Centre Lucerne (1956). *Work in permanent collections:* Museum of Modern Art, Rome (1952), National Art Fund (1965), Museum of Contemporary Art, Madrid (1966). Won International Competition for monument to Don Ricardo Arias in Panama (1953). *Address:* Maipu 663, p.4, dpta. A, Buenos Aires, Argentina.

TELFER, William Walker, F.I.A.L.; director, Thomas Paul Ltd., Falkirk, colour printers; pres., Falkirk Art Club (1938-48); portrait and landscape artist in oil and water-colour; etcher; *b* Falkirk, Stirlingshire, 3 Oct., 1907. *Exhib.:* R.S.A., R.S.W., S.S.A., G.I., Montreal Art Assoc. *Collector* of early Scottish landscapes by John Thomson of Duddingston, H.R.S.A. (1778-1840). *Publication:* catalogue of the above collection (1950). *Address:* Dundrennan, Eggington, Leighton Buzzard, Bedfordshire. *Signs work:* see appendix.

TENGBERG, Violet, City of Gothenburg award for cultural achievement (1966), Bronze Medal, Europe Prize for painting (1971), Ostende, Belgium; artist in oil and graphic work; *b* Munktorp, Sweden, 20 Feb., 1920; *d* of A. Englund,, master builder; *m* J. G. A. Tengberg, D.H.S.; one *s,* one d. Educ.: Dipl. Academy of Fine Arts, Gothenburg (1958-63) "Valand". *Exhib.:* 14 one-man shows, Stockholm, Helsinki, London, Brussels, Paris, etc.; 70 group shows all over Europe; Riksutställningar travelling exhbn. *Work in permanent collections:* Museums and official collections in Sweden; Institut Tessin, Paris; Musée de Pau and Musée de Caen, France; Bibliothèque Nationale, Paris; Musée Vatican, Italy. *Publications:* Swedish Art Lexicon, part V. Allhem; Enciclopedia Universale "SEDA" della Pittura Moderna, Milano, etc. (colour ill.). *Address:* Götabergsgatan 22, 41134 Gothenburg, Sweden. *Clubs:* A.I.A., W.I.A.C., F.P.S., K.R.O. *Signs work:* "VT," "Violet Tengberg."

TENNANT, Trevor; sculptor; *b* London, 1906; *studied art* at Goldsmiths' College, R.A. Schools. *Exhib.:* R.A., N.E.A.C., London Group, etc.; one-man shows at Beaux Arts Gallery, French Gallery, Leger Gallery, Leicester Galleries, Molton Gallery (1966). *Work in permanent collections:* Stoke-on-Trent, Leicester. *Official purchases:* British Pavilion, New York World Fair (1939); Coventry; Hatfield; British Allied Ironfounders; Bournemouth; Stepney; Bracknell New Town; L.C.C. Barnsbury School for Girls (1959); Washington, D.C. (1960); Durham University (1960); Welwyn and Hatfield Hospital (1963). *Addresses:* 14B Downshire Hill, Hampstead, London NW3; studio: 20 Albert St., London NW1. *Club:* I.C.A.

TERRY, W. N.; curator, Northampton. *Address:* Northampton Museum and Art Gallery.

TEW, Ernest Frederick, D.A., Glasgow (1936), R.W.A. (1951), F.R.I.B.A. (1951), J.P. (Bath, 1962); chartered architect; pres. Wessex Society of Architects (1959-61); Council mem. R.I.B.A. (1959-61); *b* Crake Hall, Bedale, Yorks., 1905; *s* of Rev. E. W. Tew, M.A.; *m* Cynthia B. Burnley, A.R.C.A. *Educ.:* Blundells School, Tiverton; Greenock Academy; *studied* at Glasgow School of Architecture, principal, T. Harold Hughes. *Publication:* architectural map of Bath. *Address:* 7 Richmond Hill, Bath, BA1 5QT. *Signs work:* see appendix.

THAKE, Eric Anchor; artist in gouache, oil, lino-cut and drawing; official war artist, R.A.A.F., Dec., 1944-Feb., 1946; worked in S.W.P.A., Darwin and Timor; *b* Auburn, Victoria, Australia, 8 June, 1904; *s* of Henry Thake; *m* Grace Godfrey; two *d. Educ.:* Victorian State Schools; *studied art* in Melbourne. *Exhib.:* Australian capital cities, N.Z., New York, Los Angeles. *Work in permanent collections:* in all Australian State Galleries and War Memorial, Canberra. *Official purchases:* National Gallery of Victoria, National Art Gallery of N.S.W., National

Gallery of South Australia, National Gallery of Western Australia. *Address:* 3/11 Heather Grove, Kew, Victoria, Australia. *Signs work:* "Eric Thake" (plus date).

THELWELL, Norman, A.T.D. (1950); cartoonist and freelance illustrator in pen, line and wash, water-colour and gouache; teacher of design and illustration, College of Art, Wolverhampton (1950-56); now freelance; *b* Birkenhead, Ches., 3 May, 1923; *s* of Christopher Thelwell, machinist; *m* Rhona E. Ladbury; one *s,* one *d. Educ.:* Rock Ferry High School, Birkenhead; *studied art* at Liverpool College of Art under H. P. Huggill, A.R.C.A., M.A., A.R.E., principal, and G. H. Wedgwood, A.R.C.A., teacher of graphic design (1947-50). *Address:* Herons Mead, Timsbury, Romsey, Hants. SO5 0NE. *Signs work:* see appendix.

THEMERSON, Franciszka, F.S.I.A.D., O.G.G., Collège de Pataphysique; painter and draughtsman; *b* Warsaw; lives in London. *Studied:* Academy, Warsaw. *One-man shows:* London: Gallery One, Drian Galleries (retrospective); Belfast, Edinburgh, Stockholm, Genoa, Warsaw (retrospective), theatrical décor (Stockholm); Gold Medal, 1966, at the Triennale International de la Scenographie; films. *Official purchases:* V. & A., Arts Council of Great Britain, Belfast Museum, Polish National Museum. *Work in private collections:* England, France, Italy, Sweden, Poland and U.S.A. *Work repro.:* Graphis, Studio International, Typographica, Designers in Britain, Art International, Aujourd'hui, La Biennale di Venezia, etc. *Publications:* numerous books illustrated and collection of drawings: Traces of Living (1969). Art Director of Gaberbocchus Press. *Address:* 28 Warrington Cres., London W9.

THEOBALD, Courtenay, B.A., F.R.I.B.A.; architect; *b* Bury, 1903; *s* of Rev. B. G. Theobald; *m* Virginia Maxwell Ayrton; two *s,* three *d. Educ.:* Silcoates; University College, London; R.A.F.V.R. (1940-45). *Exhib.:* R.A. *Works include* Somerville College Chapel, Oxford; Hanover Lodge Hall of Residence, Regent's Pk., and other buildings for Bedford College, Presbyterian Church and Church House, Tavistock Pl., London, Motorway and other bridges; M.4 Slough-Maidenhead; M.40 Beaconsfield-Stokenchurch; Eton-Windsor Relief Road, including River Thames Bridge, Windsor; M.3 River Thames Bridge, Chertsey; River Thames Bridge, Marlow. *Address:* 10 Coldharbour, Wendover, Bucks. *Club:* Arts.

THISTLETHWAITE, Ann, N.D.D. painting; artist, landscape painter in oil, pastel and charcoal; *b* Birmingham, 22 Oct., 1944; *d* of C. E. D. Thistlethwaite, dental surgeon. *Educ.:* Edgbaston Church of England College; studied art at Birmingham College of Art and Design (1961-66) under Gilbert Mason and Mr. Francis. *Exhib.:* one-man shows: London, Birmingham, Worcester, Tunbridge Wells, Malvern, R.B.A., R.I., R.S.M.A., P.S., Contemporary Art. (Royal Overseas Commonwealth Art 1st Prize (1969) presented to H.M. the Queen). *Address:* 4 King George Ave., Droitwich, Worcs. *Signs work:* "Ann Thistlethwaite."

THOMAS, Annie Margaret, R.D.S., F.R.S.A.; artist in oils, pastel, water-colour, pen and ink and art teacher; *b* Lympstone, Devon; *d* of Henry White; *m* Martin L. Thomas; two *s,* three *d. Educ.:* Southlands School, Exmouth; *studied art* at Bristol Municipal School of Art under R. E. J. Bush, A.R.C.A., R.W.A., R.E. *Exhib.:* Paris Salon, R.W.A., S.W.A., P.S., Assoc. of Devon Artists. *Work in permanent collections:* bookplate, Public Library, Wellington, N.Z. *Work repro.:* The Bookman, illustrations for children's stories, etc., for London publishers. *Address:* 5 Halsdon Ave., Exmouth, Devon. *Signs work:* "A. M. THOMAS."

THOMAS, Leslie Gurwin, A.T.D.; artist in oil; *b* Fochriw, 11 Aug., 1914; *s* of William Henry Thomas, mining engineer; *m* Norma Marion Robinson, 1950; three *s. Educ.:* Lewis' School, Pengam; *studied art and architecture* at Cardiff

School of Art. Welsh School of Architecture; University College, Cardiff; Goldsmiths' and Hornsey; R.A.F. (VR) 1940-46; Art Master, Tonyrefail, Cowbridge, Wisbech, Christ's College, Finchley. *Exhib.:* nine one-man shows London, Midlands, East Anglia. *Work in permanent collections:* Heraldic Design and Illumination for local authorities and paintings in public buildings and galleries. *Address:* Old School Studio, Blaenporth, Cardigan. *Signs work:* "L. G. Thomas."

THOMAS, Margaret, R.W.A. (1971), R.B.A. (1947), N.E.A.C. (1950), Slade Scholar (1936); painter; *b* 26 Sept., 1916; *d* of the late F. S. Thomas. *Educ.:* privately; *studied art* at Slade School (1936-38), R.A. Schools (1938-39). *Exhib.:* R.A., L.G., S.E.A., R.S.A. and S.S.A. Edinburgh, etc.; one-man exhbns. include Leicester Galleries (1949 and 1950); Aitkin Dott's Edinburgh (1952, 1955 and 1966); Canaletto Gallery (1961); Edinburgh Festival (1962); Howard Roberts, Cardiff (1963); Minories, Colchester (1964); Queen's University, Belfast (1967); Mall Galleries (1972); Octagon, Belfast (1973); Court Lodge, Kent (1974); Paton Gallery, Edinburgh (1976). *Official purchases:* H.R.H. Duke of Edinburgh; Chantry Bequest; Arts Council; Exeter College, Oxford; Min. of Educ.; Min. of Works (Coronation painting for British Embassy at Santiago); Paisley; Hull and Carlisle Art Galleries; G.L.C. and numerous county Educ. Coms.; Edinburgh City Corporation; Welsh Schools Service; Steel Company of Wales; Financial Times; and Nuffield Foundation Trust. *Addresses:* Halfway Cottage, 11A North Rd., Highgate Village, London N6; 8 North Bank St., Edinburgh. *Signs work:* see appendix.

THOMAS, Nicholas, M.A., F.S.A., F.M.A.; Director, City Museum, Bristol. *Address:* City Museum, Queen's Rd., Bristol BS8 1RL.

THOMAS, Peter Lewis, N.D.D. painting (1950), A.T.D. (1951); oil and floor polish manufacturer; artist in oil, pen, pencil; *b* Sydenham, 12 Sept., 1927; *s* of Martin Thomas, B.Sc., M.Inst.Pet., managing director; *m* Sheila Margaret Smithson; one *d. Educ.:* St. Dunstan's College, Catford; *studied art* at Camberwell School of Art under Victor Pasmore, John Minton, William Coldstream, Claude Rogers (1944-50), Goldsmiths' College, New Cross under Paul Drury, A. W. Keefe (1950-51). *Exhib.:* London Group, Ideal Home exhbn. (1950), R.A. *Work repro.:* Artist. *Address:* 39 Trewsbury Rd., Sydenham, London SE26. *Signs work:* "PETER THOMAS."

THOMAS, Robert, A.R.C.A. (1952), F.R.B.S. (1961), Otto Beit Medal (1963), R.B.S. Silver Medal (1966); sculptor in bronze, stone; President, Society Portrait Sculptors; *b* Cwmparc, Treorchy, Rhondda, Glam., 1 Aug., 1926; *m* Mary Gardiner, textile designer; two *s,* one *d. Educ.:* Pentre Grammar School, Rhondda; *studied art* at Cardiff College of Art (1947-49), R.C.A. (1949-52). *Work in permanent outdoor sites:* Sculpture at New Broadway Shopping Centre, Coalville, Leics., Holloway Circus, Birmingham City Centre, Central Redevelopment, Blackburn, Lancs. *Address:* 34 Romilly Pk., Barry, Glam. *Signs work:* "THOMAS."

THOMPSON, Godfrey, F.L.A.; Guildhall Librarian and Director of Art Gallery, City of London; *b* Coventry, 28 June, 1921; *m*; one *s. Educ.:* King Henry VIII School, Coventry. *Address:* Guildhall Art Gallery, London EC2.

THOMSON, Adam Bruce, O.B.E. (1963), A.R.S.A. (1937), R.S.A. (1946), P.P.R.S.W. (1956-63), H.R.S.W. (1968); pres. Society of Scottish Artist (1937); pres. S.A.B.A. (1974); mem. of staff Edinburgh College of Art; served in World War I (R.E.); painter in oil and water-colour; *b* Edinburgh, 22 Feb., 1885; *s* of Adam Thomson; *m* Jessie Inglis Hislop; one *s,* two *d. Studied art:* Royal

Institution and College of Art, Edinburgh, Paris and Madrid. *Address:* 65 Cluny Gdns., Edinburgh, 10. *Club:* Scottish Arts. *Signs work:* "A. Bruce Thomson."

THOMSON, Alfred Reginald, A.R.A. (1939), R.A. (1945), R.P. (1944), Olympic Games gold medallist (1948); *b* Bangalore, India; *s* of R. G. A. Thomson, I.C.S.; *m* Gertrude Parker; one *s,* one *d. Educ.:* Margate. *Exhib.:* R.A., R.P. *Work in permanent collections:* Chantrey Bequest, collections at Manchester, Bradford, Bournemouth, Pittsburgh (U.S.A.), R.A.F., R.A.F. commemorative dinner, including the Queen and members of the Royal Family (1959); Cardinal Godfrey; House of Commons in session (1960), including 184 portraits; Lords (1963), 175 portraits; R.Y.S. with Duke of Edinburgh; R.A.F. official war artist; Gloucestershires' stand at Imjin, Korean War; murals: Science Museum, Birmingham Dental Hospital. *Address:* Milton House, 2 Fernshaw Rd., London SW10. *Clubs:* Chelsea Arts, London Sketch.

THOMSON, George L., D.A. (Edin.), S.S.A., S.S.I.; calligrapher; principal art teacher (retd.); *b* Edinburgh, 15 Dec., 1916. *Studied art* at Edinburgh College of Art (1932-37). *Publications:* Better Handwriting (Puffin, 1954), Traditional Scottish Recipes (Canongate, 1976), others in preparation. *Address:* The White Cottage, Balgrie Bank, Bonnybank, by Leven. *Signs work:* "George L. Thomson."

THOMSON, William, A.R.C.A. (1952), R.B.A.; painter in oil, acrylics and water-colour; *b* Hamilton, Ontario, 24 Jan., 1926; *s* of F. C. Thomson, insurance broker; *m* (2); one *d. Educ.:* Hillfield School, Hamilton, McMaster University, Hamilton, Upper Canada College, Toronto; *studied art* at Ontario College of Art, Toronto (1945-47) under John Alfsen; Royal College of Art (1949-52) under Rodrigo Moynihan, Rodney Burn, Carel Weight, Francis Bacon; School of Vision, Salzburg (1957), under Oskar Kokoschka. *Work in permanent and private collections:* Art Gallery of London, Ontario; Art Gallery of Hamilton, Ontario, Canada Council. *Address:* 44 Redcliffe Rd., London SW10. *Club:* Chelsea Arts. *Signs work:* "W. Thomson."

THORMANN, Anne-Marie Zeerleder-; art critic, Neue Zurcher Zeitung, National-Zeitung Basel, Servir Lausanne, etc.; correspondent of the Swiss monthly Du (Zürich) until 1957, co-editor for 1947 to 1951; specialist in illustrations; asst. at Art Museum, Berne (1934-38); attachée, Cabinet des Éstampes de la Bibl. National, Paris (1938-39), attachée, Bibl. National Suisse (1939-46); *b* Basle, 17 July, 1913; *d* of Charles Thormann, director, Schweiz Kreditanstalt, Berne; *m* Charles Zeerleder. *Educ.:* Berne; *studied art* at Berne, Paris, six months' studies at Florence (1951). *Publications:* A. H. Pellegrini by Dr. Walter Ueberwasser, St. Vincent, un château à la Côte vaudoise (1969). *Address:* 51 Junkerngasse, Berne. *Signs work:* "Anne-Marie Thormann."

THORNBERY, Mary; painter in oil; *b* Bredhurst, Kent; *m* Michael Dobson, F.R.A.M.; one *s. Studied painting:* London, Florence, Rome. *Exhib.:* R.A., London Group, W.I.A.C., New English Art Club, Royal West of England Academy, Bristol (permanent collection). *Addresses:* Brynawel, Gwernogle, Carmarthen; and 3 Vineyard Row, Hampton Wick, Kingston upon Thames KT1 4EG. *Signs work:* "MARY THORNBERY."

THORNTON, Cecil Jeffrey, Gold Medal, Paris Salon; Silver Medal, Dip. of Hon. awarded by National School of Fine Arts, Bourges, France; landscape painter; *b* Narborough, Leics., 20 July, 1911; *s* of Horatio Thornton; *m* Marion Charlotte Freer; *studied art* at Leicester College of Art under Middleton-Todd, R.A., Hennes, A.R.C.A. *Exhib.:* R.A., R.B.A., Paris Salon. *Work in private collections:* in Britain, America, Canada, Ceylon, the Philippines, S. America, etc. *Address:* 16 Leicester Rd., Narborough, Leics. *Signs work:* "C. J. Thornton."

THORNTON, F. C., M.B.E. (1964), A.R.M.S. (1962); portrait miniaturist in water-colour and painter in oils; *b* Thorpe, Surrey, 15 July, 1898; *s* of Arthur F. A. Thornton; *m* Nora Murray; two *d. Educ.:* Egham, Surrey; *studied art* at Norwood Hall, Southall, Middx., under Ethol Court, A.R.M.S. (1957-62). *Exhib.:* R.A. (1960-62), Paris Salon, 1959 (Hon. Men.), R.M.S. (1958-62); Ealing and Southall town halls. *Address:* 4 Dorset Ave., Norwood Green, Southall, Middx. *Signs work:* "F. C. Thornton."

THORNTON, Leslie, A.R.C.A. (1951); *b* Skipton, 1925. *Studied art* at Leeds College of Art (1945-48), R.C.A. (1948-51). *Exhib.:* One-man shows, Gimpels Fils (1957, 1960, 1969); I.C.A. (1955); Berne (1955); British Council Young Sculptors Exhbn. (Germany, 1955-56), Sweden (1956-57); São Paolo Biennal (1957); Holland Park (1957); C.A.S. Religious Theme Exhbn., Tate Gallery; British Embassy, Brussels (1958); Middelheim Biennial, Antwerp (1959); British Artist-Craftsmen Exhbn., Touring U.S.A. (1959); Arts Council, Contemporary British Sculpture (1957-65); City of London Festival (1968); 10th Middelheim Biennial, Antwerp (1969); Basildon Festival (1970). *Official purchases:* Museum of Modern Art, New York; Arts Council of Gt. Britain; Leeds Art Gallery; Felton Bequest, Australia; Albright Museum; Fogg Art Gallery; National Gallery of Scotland. *Private collections* in U.K., Europe, U.S.A. and S. America. *Address:* 3 Kirkstall Pl., Newcastle, Staffs.

THORNTON, Valerie (Mrs. Michael Chase), N.D.D. (1953), R.E. (1970); artist in drawing and etching; *b* London, 13 Apr., 1931; *d* of Nigel Thornton; *m* Michael Chase, Curator of Minories Art Gallery, Colchester. *Educ.:* West Heath School, Sevenoaks; *studied art* at Regent Street Polytechnic (1950-53); etching and engraving at Atelier 17, Paris, with S. W. Hayter (1954). *Work in permanent collections:* V. & A., Fitzwilliam Museum, Cambridge, Norwich Museum, Sheffield City Art Gallery, Staedlijk Museum, Amsterdam, Metropolitan Museum, New York, Museum of Modern Art, New York, Smithsonian Institution, Washington, Library of Congress, National Gallery, Ottowa. *Address:* The Minories, 74 High St., Colchester, Essex. *Clubs:* Printmaker's Council, Print Club, Philadelphia, Royal Society of Painters, Etchers and Engravers. *Signs work:* see appendix.

THORP, William Eric, P.S. (1952), R.S.M.A. (1958); artist and designer in oil and pastel; *b* London, 27 Dec., 1901; *s* of John B. Thorp, architect and model-maker; *m* Marjorie Kathleen; one *s. Educ.:* City of London School; *studied art* under Herbert Dixey and Herbert Schroder. *Exhib.:* R.S.M.A., Paris Salon, Pastel Soc. *Work in permanent collections:* Guildhall Art Gallery, National Maritime Museum, Imperial Inst. (dioramas). Past-Pres., Wapping Group of Artists. *Address:* 7 Trinity Cres., London SW17. *Clubs:* Artist Soc., Langham Art Club, Wapping Group, Chelsea Arts, London Sketch. *Signs work:* "W. Eric Thorp."

THURSBY, Peter, A.T.D., A.R.B.S., R.W.A.; sculptor; *b* Salisbury, 1930; *s* of Major L. A. Thursby; *m* Maureen Suzanne Aspden. *Educ.:* Nunthorpe Grammar School, York; Bishop Wordsworth's School, Salisbury; *studied art* at West of England College of Art, Bristol; Exeter College of Art. *Exhib.:* 50 Years of Sculpture, Grosvenor Gallery (1965); one-man shows: Arnolfini Gallery; A.I.A. Gallery; Plymouth City Art Gallery; Marjorie Parr Gallery (3) (1964, 1965, 1971); Westward TV Studios, Plymouth; Northampton Museum and Art Gallery; Sheviock Gallery; Royal Albert Memorial Museum and Art Gallery, Exeter; University of Sheffield; Haymarket Theatre; Leicester: Nottingham Playhouse; University of Exeter. *Public commissions:* Plymstock, Harrow, Croydon, Plymouth, Exeter. *Public collections:* Westminster College of Education, Oxford; Plymouth City Art Gallery; Royal West of England Academy; University of

Exeter. *Address:* Oakley House, Pinhoe, Exeter EX1 3SB. *Signs work:* "P.T." and date (sculpture), or "PETER THURSBY" and date (graphic work).

THURSTON, Rosalie W., mem., Soc. Painters in Tempera; painter in oil, tempera, gouache, water-colour; specialist in buildings, landscapes; *d* of H. K. N. Thurston, M.B.E. *Educ.:* Edgbaston and Malvern, Central School of Art, Chelsea. *Exhib.:* R.A., R.B.A., R.I., etc., Manchester, Brighton and Bournemouth Art Galleries, Aldeburgh. *Address:* Spring House, Prior's Way, Aldeburgh, Suffolk. *Clubs:* Sesame Imperial, National Book League. *Signs work:* "R. W. THURSTON."

TIERNEY, James Richard Patrick, D.A.D. (Fine Art) (1966), A.R.E. (1967); painter and printmaker, full-time lecturer in printmaking at The West Surrey College of Art and Design; *b* Newcastle upon Tyne, 23 May, 1945; *s* of James William Tierney; *m* Valerie Anne Tierney, D.A.D. *Educ.:* Royal Grammar School, Newcastle upon Tyne; *studied art* at Sunderland College of Art, under Mr. R. Jewell and Mr. H. Geoghegan (1961-66), post-Dip. in Printmaking at Brighton College of Art, under Miss Jennifer Dickson (1966-67). *Address:* 38 Byfleet Ave., Basingstoke, Hants. *Signs work:* "J. Tierney."

TIERNEY, Robert, N.D.D. (1956), Dip. D.A. (1956); artist in water, oil and design colours; international artist and textile/graphic designer; professional since 1958, regularly engaged by numerous major London, European and American companies; *b* Plymouth, 9 Aug., 1936; *s* of Hilda Tierney. *Studied art* at Plymouth College of Art under Miss Joan Lee, A.T.D.; Central School, London (1956-58) under Alan Reynolds; Atelier Clay, Paris. *Exhib.:* London Design Centre, Manchester, Paris and Vienna. Design work exported to many countries including Finland, Italy, Australia, America. *Work in permanent collection:* many private collections including Viscount Eccles, etc. *Addresses:* c/o 4 Lonsdale Villa, Mannamead, Plymouth and C.O.I.D., Haymarket, London. *Signs work:* "Robert Tierney" or "Tierney."

TILLING, Robert; artist in water-colour and oil; art lecturer, head of department; *b* Bristol, 1944; *m* Thelma Tilling, N.D.D.; two *d. Educ.:* Ashton Park School, Bristol; *studied art* at Bristol and Exeter. *Exhib.:* one-man shows: London, Bristol, Southampton and Jersey; various mixed shows including the R.I. *Work in permanent collections:* Lodz Museum, Poland, Education Dept., Jersey, C.I., Tobacco Distributors Ltd. *Publications:* Art and jazz criticism in many magazines. At present writing book about M. Arbuthnot, R.I. *Address:* Heathfield House, Bagatelle, St. Saviour, Jersey, C.I. *Signs work:* "Robert Tilling."

TILSON, Joe, A.R.C.A.; painter and sculptor; *b* London, 24 Aug., 1928; *s* of Frederick Tilson; *m* Joslyn; one *s*, two *d. Studied art* at St. Martin's School of Art (1949-52), Royal College of Art (1952-55). *Exhib.:* 2eme Biennale de Paris, Pittsburgh International (1961); Marlborough, London; Eindhoven; British Art Today, San Francisco, Dallas and Santa Barbara (1962); Marzotto Prize Exhibition; 7th Tokyo Biennale; British Painting in the '60s; Whitechapel, 4th Biennale, San Marino (Prize) (1963); Marlborough, London; Düsseldorf; Bochum; XXXII Venice Biennale (1964); Minneapolis and subsequent tour (London, The New Scene), Ljubljana Print Biennale (Prize) (1965). *Address:* 11 Argyll Rd., London W8. *Signs work:* see appendix.

TINDLE, David, A.R.A.; lecturer and artist in oil and tempera; visiting lecturer, R.C.A.; *b* Huddersfield, Yorks., 29 Apr., 1932; *m* Janet Trollope; two *d. Exhib.:* International Biennale of Realist Art (Bruges, 1958). One-man shows: Piccadilly Gallery (regularly from 1954); Galerie du Tours, San Francisco and Los Angeles (1964); (retrospective) Coventry City Art Gallery (1957); Milan

(1968); Bologna (1969). *Mixed exhbns.:* R.A., Salon de la Jeune Peinture, Paris (1967); International Biennale of Realist Art, Bologna (1967); Florence Fair (1968); Europe Prize for Painting, Oostende (1969); awarded Critics' Prize (1962). *Work in permanent collections:* Contemporary Art Society, Arts Council of G.B.; and many public galleries throughout G.B. *Work in private collections:* G.B., U.S.A., Italy and France. *Address:* Old Chapel, East Haddon, Northants. *Signs work:* "David Tindle" and see appendix.

TINNE, Dorothea; animal artist in oil, pastel, chalk, scraper-board, gouache; *b* Hawkhurst, Kent, June, 1899; *d* of T. F. S. Tinne, engineer; *m* Lt.-Col. M. R. Strover, R.A.; one *s,* one *d. Studied art* at St. John's Wood Schools under Frederick Whalen; Amsterdam under Herbert van der Poll. *Exhib.:* P.S., R.I., S.G.A., S.W.A., Ackermann's Gallery and one-man show in London and Worcester. Founder-Member of the Society of Wild Life Artists. *Publications:* Lure of Lakeland, Signposts to the Wild, Love and Laughter, and children's books. *Address:* High Wray, Farnham, Surrey. *Signs work:* "E. D. TINNE."

TIRANTI, John, F.R.S.A.; Director, Alec Tiranti Ltd.; *b* London, 18 Jan., 1934; *s* of Alec Tiranti, F.R.S.A., publisher; *m* Patricia Lovesee; two *d. Educ.:* St. Marylebone Grammar School. *Address:* Garthfield, Wargrave-on-Thames, Berks.

TISDALL, Hans; painter and designer; *b* 1910. *Exhib.:* in London, Paris, Rome, Brussels, Germany, Spain, Switzerland. *Recent commissions:* murals, tapestries, fabric designs. *Address:* 9 Fleming Cl. Studios, Park Walk, Chelsea, London SW10. *Signs work:* see appendix.

TITHERLEY, Hazel M., A.T.C., A.T.D.(Manc.); painter in oil, mainly landscape; *b* Little Singleton, Lancs., 4 Mar., 1935; *m* Philip Titherley, F.R.I.B.A., M.R.T.P.I.; one *s. Educ.:* Queen Mary School, Lytham; *studied art* at Blackpool School of Art (1953-58), Manchester Regional College of Art (1958-59). *Work in permanent collection:* Salford A.G. *Address:* Woodside, Woodside Ave., New Longton, Preston, Lancs. *Signs work:* "Hazel Titherley."

TODD, Harold; painter in oil and water-colour; hon. sec., Fylingdales Group of Artists; Hon. Curator, Pannett Art Gallery, Whitby, Yorks.; *b* 14 Sept., 1894; *s* of John Edward Todd; *m* Florence Mildred Hepton. *Educ.:* Leeds School of Art, and under Charles L. Mayne. *Exhib.:* R.B.A.; municipal galleries of Bradford, Leeds, Newcastle, Wakefield, Birmingham, etc. *Work repro.:* paintings and pencil drawings, chiefly of Yorkshire coast subjects. *Address:* Studio, Station Rd., Robin Hood's Bay, Yorks. *Signs work:* "H. Todd" (with stroke under surname).

TOLLER, Paul A., F.D.S.R.C.S., L.D.S.R.C.S.; oral surgeon; artist in water-colour and oils; Board of Faculty of Dental Surgery, Royal College of Surgeons; Hunterian Professor Royal College of Surgeons of England (1966); Director Oriental Art Ltd.; *b* Bushey, Herts., 22 Sept., 1921; *s* of F. T. F. Toller; *m* Dorothy M. M. Clark; two *d. Educ.:* Merchant Taylors' School. *Exhib.:* R.W.S. Art Club. *Publications:* Origin of Chinese White Porcelain (in transactions of Oriental Ceramic Society, 1973); X-ray fluorescence analysis of museum objects (in Archæometry 1973). *Address:* Marlbrook House, Moor Pk., Rickmansworth, Herts. *Clubs:* Fly Fishers, R.W.S. Art, Old Water Colour Soc. *Signs work:* "P. A. Toller."

TOMLINS, Bernard Day, B.Sc., S.G.A.; artist in oil and black and white; engineer in industrial management; *b* Brighton, 24 May, 1904; *s* of Herbert Tomlins; *m* Barbara Tregear. *Educ.:* University College School, Hampstead; City and Guilds Engineering College; *studied art* at Heatherley's, St. John's Wood Art School, Willesden Art School. *Exhib.:* R.A., R.O.I., N.E.A.C., N.S., S.G.A.,

Pastel Soc. *Official purchase:* National Gallery of S. Australia, Adelaide. *Address:* Swallowfield Park, nr. Reading, Berks. *Signs work:* "TOMLINS."

TOMLINSON, Reginald R., O.B.E., A.R.C.A., A.R.M.S., P.R.D.S., Hon. R.B.A., Hon. F.I.B.D., Hon. F.Coll.H.; portrait painter and potter; principal, Glouc. College of Arts and Crafts; Sen. Inspector of Art, L.C.C. (1925-50); Pres., Royal Drawing Soc. and Artists' Ann. and Ben. Fund; Master, Art Workers' Guild (1955); *b* 10 Oct., 1885; *m* Emily Mullens; two *s,* one *d. Educ.:* Farnham Gram. Sch., Royal College of Art. *Work in permanent collections:* paintings and pottery. *Publications:* Picture Making by Children, Crafts for Children, Children as Artists with J. F. Mills, The Growth of Child Art. *Address:* Chestnut Cottage, The Drive, Chichester, W. Sussex. *Club:* Royal Commonwealth Soc. *Signs work:* "R. R. Tomlinson" and see appendix.

TONKS, John, N.D.D. (1951), A.T.D. (1952), A.R.B.S. (1967), Staffordshire Major Art Scholarship (1945); sculptor in wood, stone, terracotta; principal lecturer in sculpture; mem. Tutorial Staff at West Midlands College of Education; *b* Dudley, Worcs., 14 Aug., 1927; *m* Sylvia Irene; one *s,* one *d. Educ.:* Dudley Grammar School; *studied art* at Birmingham College of Art (1945-46 and 1951-52) under William Bloye, F.R.B.S., Wolverhampton College of Art (1948-51) under Albert Willetts, A.R.C.A., A.R.B.S. *Commissioned works:* Figure of Christ, Wombourn Parish Church; Figure of Virgin Mary, Enville Parish Church; abstract relief panel, Ounsdale Comprehensive School, Wombourn. *Address:* Brynawel, Lynwood Ave., Wall Heath, Staffs. *Signs work:* "John Tonks" and see appendix.

TOOKEY, Olwen, A.R.B.S.A. (1948); portrait painter in oil, interior and mural decorator; *b* Birmingham, 21 Feb., 1910; *d* of Frederick Thomas Tookey, prof. of music (decd.); *m* Henry Walker Brown; one *s,* one *d. Educ.:* King Edward's Grammar School, Handsworth; *studied art* at Birmingham Central School of Art under Richard Stubbington and B. Fleetwood-Walker, A.R.A. *Exhib.:* R.A., Paris Salon, R.P., R.B.A. and most of the principal London and provincial galleries. *Work repro.:* The Artist, etc. *Address:* 24 Alcester Rd., Moseley, Birmingham 13. *Signs work:* see appendix.

TOPOLSKI, Feliks; painter and draughtsman; official Polish War Artist (1940-45); *b* 14 Aug., 1907; *s* of Edward Topolski, actor; *m* Marion Everall; one *s,* one *d. Educ.:* Mikolaj Rey School, Warsaw; Artillery Officers' Reserve School, Poland; Academy of Art, Warsaw. *Exhib.:* Warsaw, U.S.A., France, Canada, Portugal, India, Italy, Switzerland, Argentine, Australia and Eire; theatrical décor for Old Vic, Arena Theatre, etc. *Official purchases:* B.M., V. & A., Tate Gallery, Imperial War Museum, Edinburgh, Glasgow, Nottingham, New Delhi, Tel-Aviv, Warsaw, Melbourne, Toronto and Brooklyn; mural: Cavalcade of Commonwealth (60′ × 20′) for Festival of Britain (1951). *Address:* 14 Hanover Terr., London NW1. *Signs work:* "Feliks Topolski" or "F.T."

TOSELAND, Peter, A.R.C.A. (1940), F.R.S.A. (1957); art teacher; artist in oil and water-colour, illustrator, scribe, picture-restorer; *b* Broughton, Northants, 15 June, 1917; *s* of Walter C. Toseland. *Educ.:* Broughton School, Northants; *studied art* at Northampton School of Art and R.C.A. *Exhib.:* R.A., R.I., R.W.S., F.B.A. and many municipal galleries. *Work repro.:* illustrations for "Greek and Roman Jewellery" (Methuen), Sussex Life calendars and greeting cards. *Address:* 20 Kingscliffe Ct., Rock Grove, Brighton BN2 1ND. *Signs work:* "Peter Toseland" and see appendix.

TOULMIN, Margaret Clarisse, R.C.A. (1973), A.R.W.A. (1939); artist in clay and plaster; mem. Lakeshore Artists Assoc.; *b* Filton, Bristol, 2 Oct., 1916; *d* of Christopher Walter Hayes (decd., 1918); *m* William Toulmin; three *s. Educ.:*

St. Faith's, Weston-super-Mare; *studied art* at W. of England School of Art, Mr. Milner, principal. *Exhib.:* R.W.A. *Work in permanent collections:* Reredos, Lady Chapel, St. Mary's Church, Tyndalls Park, Bristol, Relief of Madonna and Child, All Hallows, Easton, Bristol, and in Westbury Parish Church, Bristol, Public Library, Ottowa. *Address:* 273 Shore Rd., Beaconsfield, Quebec, Canada. *Signs work:* "M.C.T." and "Margaret C. Hayes."

TOVEY, Robert Lawton, A.T.D. (1947); painter in oil; *b* Birmingham, 3 Apr., 1924; *s* of Edward Francis Tovey; *m* Annette Suzanne Hubler. *Educ.:* The George Dixon Grammar School, Birmingham; *studied art* at Birmingham College of Art under B. Fleetwood-Walker (1939-43, 1946-47). *Exhib.:* R.B.S.A., R.B.A., A.I.A., N.E.A.C., R.O.I., R.W.A., one-man shows, Geneva (1957, 1962, 1964), Baden (1973). *Work in permanent collections:* Musée d'Art et d'Histoire, Geneva; Dudley A.G. *Official purchases:* oil painting, The Red Scarf, for above (1953). *Address:* 2 Ave. de la Praille, 1227 Carouge, Geneva. *Signs work:* "R. L. TOVEY."

TOWER, Meriel Theresa, L.S.I.A.; freelance textile designer, painter, teacher; on technical staff, Campbell Fabrics (1936-39); teacher, Upton School, Windsor (1948-72); *b* Windsor, 1911; *d* of Canon Henry Tower, C.V.O. *Educ.:* St. Paul's Girls' School; *studied art* at Westminster School of Art (1929-31) and Chelsea School of Art under Boris Heroys (1931-34). *Publications:* British Textile Designers Today (Lewis), British Designers: Their Work, Series I (Lewis), Designers in Britain, 1947 (published for S.I.A.), Decorative Art, 1950-51 (The Studio Publications), Design for Applied Decoration in the Crafts, by John Farleigh (Bell). *Address:* The Thatch, Aston Rowant, Oxford. *Signs work:* see appendix for fabrics.

TOWN, Harold Barling, Medal of Service of the Order of Canada (1968), D.Lit., York University, *Honoris causa* (1966), Centennial Medal, Canada (1967), Fellowship Instituto de Cultura Hispanica, Arte de America y Espana, Madrid (1963); painter, sculptor, printmaker, muralist, designer in oil, plastic, neon, paper, etc., writer, critic, columnist, etc.; *b* Toronto, Canada, 13 June, 1924; *m* Trudella Carol; two *d,* Heather and Shelley. *Educ.:* Ontario Art College. *Work in permanent collections:* in Holland, Italy, England, Canada, U.S.A. *Publications:* illustrated: Love Where the Nights are Long; wrote and illustrated: Enigmas (1964), Drawings of Harold Town (1969)—all for McCelland & Stewart. *Address:* 9 Castlefrank Cres., Toronto, 5, Ont., Canada. *Signs work:* see appendix.

TOWNER, Donald Chisholm, A.R.C.A.; landscape, portrait and ecclesiastical painter; *b* 2 Mar., 1903; *s* of W. A. Towner. *Educ.:* Eastbourne, R.C.A. (1923-27). *Exhib.:* R.A., N.E.A.C., etc.: one-man shows at Leicester Galleries, Beaux Arts Gallery, Walker's Galleries, and in 1961, 1964 and 1968 at 8 Church Row, Hampstead. *Official purchases:* R.A. for the nation; Graves Art Gallery, Sheffield; municipal art galleries of Carlisle, Leeds and Eastbourne: portraits for Cambridge colleges, etc.; church paintings include reredos at Abbotsbury, Sleaford, Plumstead and Hampstead. Author of English Cream-coloured Earthenware (1957) and The Leeds Pottery (1963). *Address:* 8 Church Row, Hampstead, London NW3. *Signs work:* "D. TOWNER."

TOYNBEE, Lawrence; painter; Past Director of the Morley Gallery and Art Centre, Morley College; *b* London, 1922; *s* of Arnold Toynbee, C.H.; *m* Jean Asquith; six *d. Educ.:* Ampleforth and New College, Oxford; *studied art* at Ruskin School of Drawing (Albert Rutherson, Percy Horton). *Work in permanent collections:* Nat. Port. Gallery, Min. of Works, Nuffield Trust, Shell, Coventry, Carlisle, Southport, Blackburn, M.C.C., G.L.C., Government of Australia. *Address:* Ganthorpe Hall, Terrington, York. *Signs work:* L.L.T. and year. *Club:* M.C.C.

TRAVERS-SMITH, Dorothea; painter in oil, water-colour, of portraits, flowers, trees, cats; has lately specialized in monotypes. *Educ.:* at private schools at Eastbourne, Cuckfield and Paris; Regent St. Polytechnic, etc., but studied almost entirely with the late Arthur Lindsey, pres. of R.M.S. *Exhib.:* R.A., Paris Salon, R.B.A., R.I., W.I.A.C., London Group, London Portrait Soc., etc. *Address:* 40 St. George's Ct., Gloucester Rd., London SW7. *Signs work:* "Travers-Smith" or "T-S."

TREADGOLD, Sylvia, A.I.M.B.I. (Founder, 1970); artist in water-colour, pastel, and black and white; medical illustrator; art editor of Medical and Biological Illustration, published by B.M.A. (1953-56 and 1970-74); senior medical artist, Guy's Hospital (1946-64); chief medical artist, Addenbrooke's Hospital, Cambridge (1975—); member of Society of Industrial Artists and Designers (1948-70); *b* 8 Sept., 1918. *Exhib.:* R.B.A. *Work repro.:* in children's books and various medical text-books, journals, films and medical advertising matter. Designed and executed 70-ft. mural at Charles Darwin's home, Down House, Downe, Kent (1966). *Address:* 24 Oaklands Pk., Bishop's Stortford, Herts. *Signs work:* "S. Treadgold" (or "Sylvia T" for non-medical work).

TREE, Michael Lambert; etcher, draughtsman and illustrator; *b* New York; *m* Lady Anne Tree. *Educ.:* Eton. *Publications:* illustrations to Summoned by Bells by John Betjeman (1960). *Address:* 75 Eaton Sq., London SW1. *Club:* White's. *Signs work:* "M. Tree."

TREVELYAN, Julian; artist in oil, gouache, etching, lithography, mural work in various mediums; part-time teacher, Royal College of Art (1955-63); *b* Dorking, 1910; *m* 1st, Ursula Darwin, one *s;* 2nd, Mary Fedden. *Educ.:* Bedales, Trinity College, Cambridge; *studied art* at Atelier 17 under S. W. Hayter (Paris, 1930-33). *Exhib.:* Lefevre Gallery, Galerie de France, Redfern Gallery, Gimpel Fils, Zwemmer Gallery, St. George's Gallery. *Work in permanent collections:* England, France, U.S.A., Sweden, Russia. *Publications:* Indigo Days (MacGibbon & Kee, 1957), The Artist and His World (Gollancz, 1960), Etching (Studio Books, 1963). *Address:* Durham Wharf, Hammersmith Terr., London W6.

TRIBE, Barbara, F.R.B.S. (1957), A.S.T.C., diploma with honours for sculpture, with bronze medal (1933); N.S.W. travelling scholarship to Royal Academy School of Art, London (1935); A.R.B.S. (1945); teacher of modelling and sculpture, Penzance School of Art, since 1948; S.P.S. (1954); A.S.W.A. (1956); *b* Edgecliff, Sydney, N.S.W., Australia; *d* of Rupert Tribe; *m* (1947) John Singleman, artist, architect and potter (*died* 1961); previously Instructor of Pottery, Penzance School of Art. *Studied art* at Sydney Technical College under G. Rayner Hoff, A.R.C.A., R.S., A.R.B.S. (1928-33); Kennington City and Guilds School of Art under Frith (1936-37); Regent St. Polytechnic School of Art under Harold Brownswords, F.R.B.S. *Exhib.:* R.A., R.B.A., United Artists, Women's International Art Club, London Group, St. Ives Soc. of Artists, Newlyn Soc. of Artists; Sydney, Australia; Paris Salon; Brussels; Glasgow Inst. of Fine Arts; Royal Scottish Academy; Scottish Soc. of Women Artists; R.Cam.A. of Art; in the provinces with Sculpture in the Home exhbn.; Unknown Political Prisoner Exhibition (Competition), British Section, London (1952); MacQuarie Galleries, Bonython Galleries, Prouds Gallery, Sydney, Australia, and Tasmanian Museum and Art Gallery since 1966; International Exhbn., Kyoto, Japan (1972); London Exhbn., Fieldborne Galleries (June, 1973); Sydney Exhbn, David Jones' Gallery (Dec., 1975). *Work purchased for permanent collections:* 4 works (bronze, marble and terra-cotta) by City Museum and Art Gallery, Hanley, Stoke-on-Trent (1964, 1965); 2 bronzes for Australian War Memorial, Canberra (1967); portrait of Lloyd Rees, Australian artist (terra-cotta) for the National Collection, Canberra

(1968); 3 bronzes for Australian War Memorial, Canberra (1969); portrait, R. Spencer C. Copeland, presented to the City of Stoke-on-Trent and Museum and Art Gallery, Hanley (occasion, bicentenary Spode Pottery, 1970); presented to Mitchell Library, Sydney, Australia, archives for permanent preservation, scrap-book early career to present date, biographical notes, letters and photographs, sculpture, etc. (1970); three gouache paintings and one sanguine line drawing purchased by A. R. Sandbach, Esq., collector connoisseur, Stoke-on-Trent (1971); bronze: 'Malinee', purchased by W. R. Cumming, Australian Council for the Arts, Sydney (1975); other works purchased and included in several private collections in the United Kingdom, Europe, U.S.A., Australia, Far East including Thailand and Japan. Names included in Potter's Marks by Geoffrey A. Godden, F.R.S.A., published 1964, under signature "Barbara Tribe" and husband John Singleman (Potter's Mark, "Ⓢ") and "British Studio Potters" ceramic Sculpture 1974 (same authors). *Work repro.:* British Sculpture (1944-46) by Eric Newton, Tiranti; Ideal Home; La Revue Moderne, Paris; Paintings from Cornwall; Cornish Revue; London Illustrated News; Thai Water Buffalo and Rider, ceramic purchased by Stoke-on-Trent Museum and Art Gallery (June, 1972), and illustrated in On View, 1972-73 Edition, Vol. 7; Lovers, bronze illustrated in Art and Australia, Vol. 10, October, 1972; Torso, English oak, illustrated Royal Society of British Sculptor's Journal, 1971-73. *Address:* The Studio, Sheffield, Paul, Penzance, Cornwall TR19 6UW, England. *Signs work:* "Barbara Tribe."

TRIST, Sybil, Mem. United Artists, A.S.W.A.; portrait painter in oil; *b* St. Albans, Herts., 1907; *d* of Ronald Trist; *m* Sir John Richardson, Bart., M.V.O., M.D., F.R.C.P.; two *d. Educ.:* privately; *studied art* at Slade School (1923-25), R.A. Schools (1925-27), and under Harold Workman, R.O.I., R.B.A. *Exhib.:* R.P., R.O.I., R.B.A., R.I., Faculty of Art, S.W.A., United Artists, Observer Exhbn. of Children's Portraits. *Address:* Flat 9, Weymouth House, 84 Hallam St., London W1N 5LS. *Signs work:* "Sybil Trist."

TRIVICK, Henry Houghton, R.B.A.; artist in oil, gouache and water-colour; lithographer; Chairman of Senefelder Group of Artist Lithographers. *Exhib.:* all leading socs.; one-man shows, Leicester Galleries. *Work in permanent collections:* V. & A., Ashmolean, Imp. War Museum, etc. *Work repro.:* in numerous art journals, magazines, etc. *Publications:* Autolithography (Faber, 1960), The Craft and Design of Monumental Brasses (John Baker, 1969), Picture Book of Monumental Brasses (A. & C. Black). *Address:* The Friary Studio, Well End, Bourne End, Bucks. *Signs work:* "TRIVICK" (on paintings); "Henry Trivick" (on lithographs).

TROTMAN, Peggy, A.R.W.A.; painter in oil and collage, part-time lecturer/teacher (1967-72); *b* Swindon, 16 May, 1916; *d* of Daniel Tucker; *m* Cedric J. Trotman (decd.). *Educ.:* Grammar School, Swindon; no formal art school training. *Exhib.:* R.A., R.W.A., R.A. touring exhbns. organised by Art Federations Bureau and S.E.A. Pictures for Schools. Sunday Telegraph award winner. *Work in permanent collections:* R.W.A., Southampton, Dorset, Bristol and Oxford Educ. Authorities. *Address:* Little Court, 7 Belle Vue Rd., Parkstone, Poole, Dorset. *Signs work:* "Peggy Trotman."

TUCKER, James Walker, A.R.C.A., A.R.W.A., F.R.S.A.; painter and lecturer; studio assistant to Prof. William Rothenstein (1925-7); head of drawing and painting, Gloucester College of Art (1931-63); *b* Wallsend, Northumberland, 1898; *s* of Charles William Tucker; *m* Constance Muriel Bullock. *Studied art* at Armstrong College, Newcastle (1914-22) under Prof. Richard Hatton, and R.C.A. under Prof. William Rothenstein (1922-27), R.C.A. Travelling Sch.

(1927). *Exhib.:* Cheltenham, Gloucester, Newcastle, Queens' College Cambridge, and R.W.A.; one-man touring exhbns. from Gloucester to Cheltenham, Hereford, Leamington Spa, Worcester and Weston-super-Mare (1948-49); exhbns. at Stroud (1967) and Gloucester (1969). *Work repro.:* Royal Academy Illus. (1936 and 1939). Wide publicity in the national and international press of The Champion, R.A., picture of the year (1941) purchased by R. & G. Cuthbert, Llangollen. Illustrated article in The Studio (Vol. 138, Jan., 1950). *Address:* Mardens Cottage, Cross Roads, Upton St. Leonards, Gloucester GL4 8BB. *Club:* Chelsea Arts. *Signs work:* "James W. Tucker."

TUCKER, Loraine Read, L.S.I.A. (1945), M.Illum.E.S. (1958); industrial designer specializing in lighting fittings and metalwork; Director, Teeanee Ltd., Tucker and Edgar (1935); *b* St. John's Wood, 21 Dec., 1910; *s* of Claude Loraine Tucker; *m* Frances Maude Phillipps; one *s*. *Educ.:* Colston's School, Stapleton, Bristol; *studied art* at Regent St. Polytechnic and received architectural training with Herbert L. Smith, L.R.I.B.A., A.M.I.Struct.E. (1927-31). *Address:* Little Paddock, Penn, Bucks. *Signs work:* "L. Read-Tucker."

TUCKER, William; sculptor; *b* Cairo, 28 Feb., 1935; *m* Pat Mullholland, painter; four *s*, three *d*. British representative in sculpture, Venice Biennale (1972). *Work in permanent collections:* Tate Gallery, B.M. (modern drawings), Kroller-Muller Museum, M.O.M.A. New York, etc. *Publications:* The Language of Sculpture (Thames & Hudson, 1974); illustrated, R. M. Rilke's Sonnets to Orpheus, i–x (G. C. Salvesen, 1970). *Address:* c/o Hester van Royen Gallery, 152A Walton St., London SW3.

TUNNICLIFFE, Charles Frederick, R.A. (1954), R.E. (A.R.C.A.); painter in water-colours and oils; wood engraver; draughtsman in scraper board, pen, pencil; *b* 1 Dec., 1901; *s* of William Tunnicliffe; *m*. *Educ.:* St. James's School, Sutton, Macclesfield; Macclesfield Art School; Manchester Art School (1915-21); R.C.A. (1921-25). *Exhib.:* R.A., Manchester Academy; R.E.; British Council Exhbns. *Official purchases:* R.A., B.M., Manchester, Preston Harris Art Gallery, Johannesburg, etc. *Publications:* My Country Book, Bird Portraiture, Mereside Chronicle, Shorelands Summer Diary (Nov., 1948). *Address:* Shorelands, Malltraeth Bay, Bodorgan, Gwynedd. *Signs work:* see appendix.

TUNSTALL, Eric, R.I. (1953); portrait painter and illustrator in oil and water-colour; *b* Stoke-on-Trent, 12 May, 1897; *s* of William Arthur Tunstall; *m* Mabel Goulding. *Educ.:* privately; *studied art* at Stoke, Hanley and Burslem Art Schools. *Exhib.:* R.I., R.P. *Address:* Fair View, Caverswall, Stoke-on-Trent. *Signs work:* "ERIC TUNSTALL."

TURNER, Harry M., R.O.I., R.B.A., A.T.D.; painter in oil; *b* Wolverhampton, 21 Nov., 1912; *m*. *Studied art* at Birmingham College of Art (1929-34). *Exhib.:* R.A., R.O.I., R.B.A., Pittsburgh International Exhbn., etc. *Address:* Forge Cottage, Upper Ludstone, Claverley, nr. Wolverhampton WV5 7DH. *Signs work:* "HARRY TURNER."

TURNER, Ken; sculptor; *b* Pakistan, 1926; *s* of E. W. Turner, Indian Army; *m* Mary; one *s*, one *d*. *Studied art* at Ealing Art School; Anglo-French Art Centre; Regent St. Polytechnic; British Council Scholarship to Spain. *Exhib.:* mixed exhbns.; one-man shows: I.C.A. Library, Heal's Art Gallery (1964), Lord's Gallery. Worked on Joan Littlewood's Fun City (1968); Director of Action Space, an organisation successfully working since 1968 on experimental projects related to the artist's new role in the community. *Address:* 89c Fitzjohn's Ave., London NW3.

TURNER, Kenneth Morris, N.D.D., typography (1948), M.S.I.A. (1954),

F.R.S.A. (1962); designer and typographer; Head of Graphic Design Department, Cement and Concrete Association; Art editor of Concrete Quarterly; *b* Ashford, Kent, 14 Oct., 1925; *s* of B. A. H. Turner, jeweller and silversmith; *m* Betty Evelyn Wyndham-Green; two *s*, one *d*. *Educ.:* Maidstone College of Art. *Work repro.:* in Designers in Britain, 6. *Address:* Juniper House, 4 Otteridge Rd., Bearsted, Maidstone, Kent. *Signs work:* "Morris Turner."

TURNER, William McAllister, R.C.A. (1944, 1959), V.P.R.C.A. (1960), P.R.C.A. (1962, 1963, 1964, 1965, 1966); etcher and oil painter; County Art Director; Member of Welsh Committee, Arts Council of Great Britain (1961, 1962, 1963, 1964); Governor, National Museum of Wales (1962, 1963, 1964, 1965); *b* Mold, Flintshire, 21 Mar., 1901; *m* Anne Hayden. *Educ.:* Chester School of Art; Liverpool College of Art. *Exhib.:* R.C.A., R.S.A., R.W.A., W.A.G., Atkinson Gallery, Southport, Living British Artists Exhbn., London and New York, etc. *Work in permanent collections:* National Museum of Wales, Derbyshire County Council. *Address:* Janor, Hawarden, Deeside, Flints. *Signs work:* see appendix.

TUTE, George William, N.D.D. Illustration, N.D.D. Painting, R.A.Cert., R.E., A.R.W.A., S.W.E.; artist in oil, wood engraving, silk screen; senior lecturer graphic design, Bristol Polytechnic; *b* Hull, 23 Mar., 1933; *s* of G. W. Tute; *m* Iris Tute; two s. *Educ.:* Bainse Grammar School, Poulton, Lancs.; *studied art* at Blackpool School of Art (1951-54); Royal Academy Schools (1954-59). *Exhib.:* R.E., R.W.A.; and private galleries. *Publications:* Readers Digest Publications, Penguin, Mitchell Beazley, Batsford. *Address:* 46 Eastfield, Westbury-on-Trym, Bristol. *Signs work:* "G. W. Tute."

TWORT, Flora C.; artist in water-colour, pastel, charcoal; *b* 24 June, 1893; *d* of Albert S. Twort, Superintendent Inspector of Taxes. *Educ.:* South Hampstead High School; *studied art* at Slade School under Prof. Tonks, London School of Art under Richard Jack, etc. *Exhib.:* R.A. from 1927-50 with one or two intervals. *Work in permanent collections:* Southampton Civic Centre, London Library, Royal College of Physicians, Alton A.G., Nuneham College, etc. *Address:* Church Path Studio, Petersfield, Hants. *Signs work:* "TWORT."

TYRRELL, Barbara Eleanor Harcourt (Mrs. B. E. H. Jurgens), B.A. (Fine Arts), Doctor of Philosophy (Honoris Causa); artist in oil and water-colour, specializing in African tribal dress; *b* Durban, Natal; one *s* (Peter). *Educ.:* Eshowe, Zululand; Pietermaritzburg; *studied art* at University of Natal. *Work in permanent collections:* tribal dress studies in Durban (Killie Campbell Museum), London (British Empire Society) and Livingstone Museum, Zambia. *Publications:* Suspicion is My Name (1972), The Tribal Peoples of Southern Africa (1967). *Address:* P.O. Box 227, Richmond, Natal, S.A. *Signs work:* "Barbara Tyrrell."

TYSOE, Peter Harold, N.D.D., A.T.C. (Lond.), F.S.D.-C., F.M.G.P., Churchill Fellow; full-time designer-craftsman/sculptor in glass, metals, resins; Council mem. Devon Guild of Craftsmen and Society of Designer-Craftsmen; *b* Bedford, 22 June, 1935; *s* of Harold L. Tysoe; *m* Patricia; three *s*. *Educ.:* Oxford Technical School; *studied art* at Oxford School of Art (1952-56), Goldsmiths' College School of Art (1956-57). *Work in permanent collections:* Plymouth A.G., commissioned works in London, Birmingham and in public and private buildings in Britain and Europe. *Publications:* Glass, Resin and Metal Construction (Mills & Boon). *Address:* Vineyard Cottage, Dartington, Totnes, Devon. *Signs work:* see appendix.

TYSON, Kathleen, S.M.A., S.W.A.; landscape painter in oil; *b* 6 May, 1898; *d* of Herbert Tyson; *m* Cecil Bertram Mawer. *Educ.:* Hull Art School; Westminster

School of Art. *Exhib.:* R.A., N.E.A.C., R.B.A., London Group, S.M.A., S.W.A., Paris Salon, and British provincial galleries. *Official purchases:* Royal Docks, Grimsby (Hull Corporation); Woodford (Southampton Corporation). *Work repro.:* Polperro, and a Mill-Pool in Norfolk (R.A. Illustrated), Royal Dock, Grimsby (Oil Painting of Today), A Stream at Woodford (The Times, Manchester Guardian). *Address:* 89 Penn Hill Ave., Poole, Dorset. *Signs work:* "K. Tyson."

U

UDEN, E. Boye; painter in oil, water-colour, draughtsman, commercial artist, teacher; official artist, N.F.S. (1941-45); Head of Graphic Design Department, Reigate School of Art; *b* London, 8 July, 1911; *s* of Ernest Uden, artist; *m* Frances Hilder; two *d. Educ.:* Aske's, Hatcham; *studied art* at Camberwell School of Art and Goldsmiths' School of Art. *Exhib.:* R.A., N.E.A.C., R.I., U.S.A., etc. *Work in permanent collections:* Oxford and Canterbury. *Official purchases:* many for National War Records. *Work repro.:* in War Pictures by British Artists, and other official publications. *Address:* 7 Netherleigh Park, South Nutfield, Surrey. *Signs work:* "BOYE UDEN."

UGLOW, Euan; painter in oil; First Prize John Moores (1972); awarded Austin Abbey Premiere Scholarship; Mem. of London Group; teacher at Slade School and Camberwell School of Art; *b* London, 10 Mar., 1932; *s* of E. W. Uglow, company accountant. *Educ.:* Strand Grammar School for Boys; *studied art* at Camberwell School of Art and Slade School. *Work in permanent collections:* Tate Gallery, Arts Council, Glasgow Art Gallery, Southampton Art Gallery, South Australia National Gallery, Liverpool University. *Address:* 11 Turnchapel Mews, Cedars Rd., London SW4. *Signs work:* "Euan Uglow."

UHLMAN, Fred, mem., London Group (1943); painter in oil; *b* Stuttgart, 19 Jan., 1901; *s* of Ludwig Uhlman; *m* Diana Croft; one *s*, one *d. Educ.:* in law at Munich, Freiburg, Tubingen University, barrister (1927-33); no art training. *Exhib.:* one-man shows, Paris, Gallery Le Niveau (1935, 1937), Gallery Jeanne Castel (1938), London, Zwemmer (1938), Leicester Galleries (1941, 1951), Redfern (1944, 1953), Lefèvre (1947), Bremen (1953), Zwemmer (1957, 1959), Wakefield (1959). *Work in permanent collections:* Musée Jeu de Paume, Paris, Musée de Grenoble, National Gallery, Sydney, Manchester City A.G., York, Stuttgart, Zagreb, etc. *Address:* 47 Downshire Hill, London NW3. *Signs work:* "UHLMAN."

UNCLES, Ewart Charles, A.T.D., R.W.A.; artist in printmaking: wood engraving and screen printing, pottery: earthenware and stoneware; principal lecturer in art; head of art and design, Redland College, Bristol; chairman, Twentieth Century Crafts Trust; *b* Pill, nr. Bristol, 15 Mar., 1919; *s* of Horace Uncles. *Educ.:* St. George Grammar School, Bristol; *studied art* at West of England College of Art (1937-40 and 1945-46) under Donald Milner, A.R.C.A., Evan Charlton, Slade Dip. *Address:* 2A Cotham Lawn Rd., Bristol, 6. *Club:* Chelsea Arts. *Signs work:* "E. U." and "Ewart Uncles."

UNWIN, Nora Spicer, A.R.E. (1933), A.R.C.A. (1932), R.E. (1946), A.N.A. (1954); Royal Soc. of Painter-Etchers and Engravers; Boston Printmakers; Print Club of Albany (N.Y.); Soc. of American Graphic Artists; Society of Wood-engravers; Boston Water-colour Society; *d* of George Soundy Unwin. *Educ.:* Surbiton High School; Leon Underwood's Studio (London); Kingston School of

Art; R.C.A. *Exhib.:* R.E., Wood Engravers' Soc. Represented in numerous public collections. *Official purchases:* Contemporary Art Soc. for B.M., Boston Public Library, New York Public Library, Library of Congress, Fitchburg Art Museum (Mass.), etc. *Publications:* author-illustrator of ten books. *Address:* Pine-apple Cottage, Peterborough, N.H., U.S.A. *Signs work:* "Nora S. Unwin."

UPTON, Charles, F.R.B.S. (1965), A.R.W.A. (1952); International award for Sculpture, Biarritz (1973); sculptor in stone, clay and wood; head of School of Sculpture, Portsmouth College of Art since 1946; *b* 18 Aug., 1911; *s* of metal-moulder; *m* Hilda Lilian. *Educ.:* elementary and grammar schools; *studied art* at Birmingham College of Art under William Bloyde, F.R.B.S., Clifford Webb, Noel Spencer, E. W. Dinkel. *Exhib.:* R.A., R.W.A., R.B.A., R.B.S.A., Paris Salon (hon. mention, 1953). *Work in permanent collections:* Bristol A.G., R.W.A. permanent collection. *Official purchases:* Dudley Police H.Q.; Titchfield Parish Church; St. Luke's Church, Kingstanding; St. Faith's, Lee-on-Solent; Painswick, Glos.; Glass mural, St. Swithins School, Southsea, Hants.; Thorsbey Hall and Rowan Gallery, London. *Address:* Berry House, Brook La., Warash, Hants. *Signs work:* see appendix.

UPTON, Michael; Cert. R.A.S. (1962), Abbey Scholar (Rome Scholarships); artist in mixed media, lecturer; visiting lecturer various art colleges; *b* 5 Feb., 1938; *s* of E. J. Upton; *m* Susan E. Upton; one *d. Educ.:* King Edward VI School, Birmingham; *studied art* at Birmingham College of Art (1954-58) under Gilbert Mason; R.A. Schools (1958-62) under Peter Greenham. *Exhib.:* Whitechapel Gallery, Salon de Jeune Peinture, Paris, Survey of the Avant Garde Gallery House, Video Show Serpentine, Expanded Cinema I.C.A., Festival of Performance Art, London, S.W. Arts and Scottish Arts Council Touring Exhbns., various gallery exhbns. *Work repro.:* Studio International. *Address:* Riverside, South Perrott, Dorset. *Signs work:* "Michael Upton."

URBAN, John Charles, B.A., M.A., A.R.E.; artist and teacher in etching and water-colour; lecturer, W. Surrey College of Art and Design; *b* Massachusetts, 5 July, 1943. *Studied art* at University of Massachusetts; Oxford; Brighton College of Art. *Exhib.:* regularly in England, U.S., Holland, Italy and France. *Publications:* 4-volume illustrated Folktale series (G. Bell and Sons); stories in Transatlantic Review. *Address:* 12 Woburn Sq., London WC1. *Signs work:* "Urban."

UTERMOHLEN, William C.; painter in oil; *b* Philadelphia, Pa., 1933. *Studied art* at Pennsylvania Academy of Fine Art, Philadelphia; Ruskin School of Drawing, Oxford. *Exhib.:* one-man shows: Traverse Theatre Gallery, Edinburgh Festival (1963), Bonfiglioli Gallery, Oxford (1965, 1967), Nordness Gallery, N.Y. (1967), Marlborough New London Gallery (1969), Galerie d'Eendt, Amsterdam (1970, 1971), Mead Art Museum, Amherst College, Amherst, Massachusetts (1974). Visiting artist, Amherst College (1972-74). *Address:* 97 Hornsey La., London N6. *Signs work:* "Utermohlen."

V

VALE, Denise Rooum, B.A. Open University (1972), F.R.S.A. (1963), A.C.P. (1964), A.R.M.S. (1965); teacher, housewife, painter in oil, gouache, ink; *b* Bradford, 26 Dec., 1929; *d* of Fred Rooum; *m* Brian John Vale; two *d. Educ.:* Hanson Girls' High School, Darlington Training College; *studied art* at Canterbury College of Art (1954) under Christopher Alexander, A.R.C.A. *Exhib.:*

Keighley A.G., Middlesbrough A.G. *Publication:* Stories of the Stars (Geo. Bell & Co.). *Address:* 7 Garden La., Heaton, Bradford 9, Yorks. BD9 5QJ. *Signs work:* "DENISE R."

VALLERY-RADOT, Jean, Officier de la Légion d'Honneur; Commandeur de l'Ordre des Arts et des Lettres; Conservateur en chef honoraire du Cabinet des Estampes, Bibliotheque nationale, paris; *b* Paris, 24 May, 1890. *Educ.:* Ecole des Chartes; Sorbonne. *Publications:* Bibliothèque Nationale, Cabinet des Estampes, Inventaire général des dessins des Ecoles du nord (with F. Lugt, Paris, 1936); Le Dessin Français au XVIIe Siècle, Lausanne, 1953, Le Recueil de plans d'édifices de la Compagnie de Jésus conservé à la Bibliothéque nationale de Paris (Rome and Paris, 1960). *Address:* 39 Avenue d'Eylau, Paris, XVIe.

VALLMITJANA, Abel; National Sculpture Prize, Venezuela (1962), International Prize, Painting, Acitrezza, Italy (1958), Silver plate for graphics, Italy (1969), Silver medal of Académie Française for book illustrated by Vallmitjana "La Mappe Monde et le Pape Monde" of Salvador de Madariaga; sculptor in marble, bronze, engraver, painter, oil, tempera, fresco, silkscreen and lithography; *b* Barcelona, 11 Feb., 1910; *s* of Julio Vallmitjana, famous playwright, writer and expert on costume and language of the gypsies; *m* Clarisa Silva, degree in philosophy and literature; one *d. Educ.:* Ecole des Arts Décoratifs, Paris; Arts e Metiers, Barcelona; *studied* with Francesco Gali y Canals. *Work in permanent collections:* Galerie Drouant David, Paris, Henri Tronche, Paris, Fundaciòn Mendoza, Caracas, Los Angeles County Museum, Galerie Motte, Geneva, O'Hana Gallery, London, Galeria della Vigna Nuova, Florence, Galeria Piero della Francesca, Circolo Artistico, and Galeria L'Incontro, Arezzo, Galeria Adria, Barcelona, Modern Art Museum, Tel-Aviv, Leeds Municipal Museum, Dublin Museum, Manchester Museum, Museum of Fine Art, Caracas, Pinacoteca of Montecatini, Italy. *Publications:* Abel Vallmitjana by Maximilen Gautier; Abel Vallmitjana by Bruno Nardini; Doce Ellas Engravings by A. Vallmitjana; illustrated: La Mappe Monde et le Pape Monde by Salvador de Madariaga; Poesias Anteriores a Marinero en Tierra by Rafael Alberti; Fabula del Poeta y la Hormiguita by Rafael Alberti; Poesias de Luis de Gongora by Gongora. *Address:* Tregozzano, Arezzo, Italy. *Signs work:* see appendix.

VAN ROSSEM, Ru, Hon. Mem., Academy of Fine Arts, Florence; Gold Medal Biennale, Perugia; M.A.I. International Graphic Prize, Biennales Gorizia, Italy, Malbork, Poland; Head of Graphic Department, Tilburg Academy of Fine Art, Holland; *b* Amsterdam, 19 Mar., 1924; *s* of Karl van Rossem; *m* Miriam Pollock; two *s,* one *d. Educ.:* Rijksmuseumschool of Fine Art; Grammar School, Zaandam. *Exhib.:* most European countries and U.S.A. *Work in permanent collections:* Rijksmuseum and Municipal Museum, Amsterdam, Boymans Museum, Rotterdam, Bibliothèque Nationale, Paris, Museum of Modern Art, New York, National Museum, Cracow, Cincinnati Museum, etc. *Address:* Burg, Vonk de Bothstr. 54, Tilburg, Holland. *Signs work:* "Ru Van Rossem."

VAN RUYCKEVELT, Ronald, National Diploma (Painting) Des. R.C.A. Ceramics; ceramic sculptor in bone china; designer/managing director of R. Van Ruyckevelt & Associates, Malvern, Worcs., producing china/ormolu art works; designer/sculptor of American game birds, tropical fish and Victorian figurines in limited editions for Worcester Royal Porcelain Co., Ltd.; *b* Carshalton, Surrey, 7 Jan., 1928; *s* of Guilluame Van Ruyckevelt; *m* Vivienne Van Ruyckevelt; two *d. Educ.:* Wallington Grammar School; *studied art* at Wimbledon School of Art under Gerald Cooper, A.R.C.A., Royal College of Art. *Work in permanent collections:* H.M. the Queen, Dyson Perrins Museum, Worcs., H.M. King Olaf of

Norway, the Countess of Snowdon, the late John F. Kennedy, Cambridge and Portsmouth Museums, etc. *Address:* Inglewood, 79 Graham Rd., Malvern, Worcs. *Signs work:* "R. Van Ruyckevelt."

VAN VEEN, Stuyvesant, Silvermine Guild, New England Annual oil pr. (1968); A.S.C.A. W.C. Prize (1967); Childe Hassam Purchase (1961); artist and educator; Associate Professor of Art, C.C.N.Y.; *b* N.Y.C., 12 Sept., 1910; *m* Felicia; one *d. Educ.:* C.C.N.Y. (1931); *studied art* at P.A.F.A., N.A., A.S.L. *Work in permanent collections:* Syracuse Museum, Norfolk Museum, Newark Museum, Cincinnati Historical and Philosophical Society, Universities of Fairleigh-Dickinson, N.Y. State, Minnesota, Ohio State, Archive American Art, Smithsonian Institution. *Address:* 320 Central Park W., New York City. *Clubs:* A.E.A., N.S.P.C., N.S.M.P., MacDowell Alumni, A.S.C.A., A.W.S., National Institute of Arts and Letters.

VARLEY, Mabel Illingworth, A.T.D.; painter of portraits, landscapes, flowers in oils, water-colour, pastels; wood engraver, with wide craft interests; art teacher St. James's, West Malvern (1933-67); San Remo (1931-33); School of Art, Malvern (1943-51); *b* London, 1907; *d* of Illingworth Varley, A.R.C.A. *Educ.:* Lawnside; *studied art* at Malvern; Regent St. Polytechnic; Central Inst. of Educ., London University. *Exhib.:* R.O.I., R.B.A., R.P., P.S., S.W.A., Salon, Hull, San Remo, Conway, Birmingham, Worcester, Hereford, Malvern, 4 Varleys, Worcester City A.G. (1969), 2 Varleys, Norwich (1971). *Address:* Knoll Lodge, Malvern Wells. *Club:* Malvern Art (Hon. Sec.). *Signs work:* "Mabel I. Varley."

VASARELY, Victor; Prize of the Critic (1955), Brussels; Gold Medal of the Triennale de Milan (1955); Prize International, Valencia (Venezuela), 1955; Inauguration du Musée Vasarely à Gordes (Vaucluse) dans le Midi de la France (1971); painter in plastic art, gouache, oil, glass, aluminium, ceramic; *b* Pecs, Hungary, 9 Apr., 1908; *s* of Victor Vasarely; *m* Claire; two *s. Educ.:* Lycée d'Etat, Budapest; *studied art* at Bauhaus, Budapest. *Work in permanent collections:* Musée d'Art Modern, Paris, Musée d'Art Modern, New York, Albright Art Gallery, Buffalo, Harvard University, Musée de Buenos Aires, Musée de São Paulo, Tate Gallery, Musée de Brussels, Musée de Liege, Musée de Vienna, Musée de Rotterdam, Stedelijk Museum, Amsterdam. *Address:* F-77410 Annet-sur-Marne. *Signs work:* see appendix.

VASCONCELLOS, Josephina de, F.R.B.S. (1940), A.W.G.; sculptor; *d* of H. H. de Vasconcellos; *m* Delmar Banner. *Educ.:* Southampton, Bournemouth; *studied art:* London, Paris, Florence. *Exhib.:* R.A., Salon, Leicester Galleries, W.A.G., Glasgow, etc.; two one-man shows (with husband), R.W.S. Gallery. *Official purchases:* National Gallery, Rio de Janeiro, Glasgow, Sheffield, Southampton, Aldershot, St. Bees School; St. Bees Priory; Nativity, St. Paul's Cathedral; life-size Nativity (Trafalgar Sq., Christmas); Gloucester and Liverpool Cathedrals; Rossall School. *Address:* The Bield, Little Langdale, Ambleside. *Signs work:* see appendix.

VAUGHAN, John Keith, C.B.E., Hon. A.R.C.A.; painter; *b* Selsey Bill, 25 Aug., 1912. *Educ.:* Christ's Hospital; self-taught as a painter. *Exhib.:* London, New York, Buenos Aires, São Paulo (one-man shows); and principal cities of Europe. *Official purchases:* Tate Gallery, Christchurch Museum, N.Z., Toronto Museum, Albright Museum (Buffalo), British Council, Arts Council, National Gallery, Edinburgh, National Gallery of N.S.W., Norwich Museum, Glynn Vivian Art Gallery, V. & A., Fitzwilliam Museum, Art Inst. of Chicago, Wadsworth Atheneum, State University of Iowa; Municipal Art Galleries of Leeds, Manchester, Birmingham, Wakefield, Leicester, Bristol, Huddersfield, University of

Durham. *Address:* 9 Belsize Pk., London NW3. *Signs work:* "Keith Vaughan" or "Vaughan."

VAUX, Marc, D.F.A. (Lond.) (1960); artist in acrylic and lithography; silk screen; Principal Lecturer in painting, Central School of Art & Design, London; *b* Swindon, 29 Nov., 1932; *s* of John Leslie Vaux; *m* Tess Jaray. *Educ.:* Commonweal Grammar School, Swindon; *studied art* at Swindon School of Art (1955-56), Slade School of Fine Art (1957-60). *Work in permanent collections:* V. & A., C.A.S., City Art Gallery, Leeds, Leicestershire Education Authority, Tate Gallery, Arts Council of Great Britain, Gulbenkian Foundation, Graves Art Gallery, Sheffield. *Address:* 29 Camden Sq., London NW1. *Signs work:* "Vaux."

VERDIJK, Gerald, Silver Medal, Prix Europe (1966), Maris Prize (1967); painter; *b* Boxmeer, Holland, 1934. *Exhib.:* one-man shows: Galerie Gunar, Düsseldorf, Galerie Orez, The Hague (1961, 1962, 1964, 1965, 1967, 1971), Galerie Potsdammer, Berlin, Casino Ostende, Museum Municipal, The Hague (1967), Von der Heidt Museum, Wuppertal (1968), Galerie Palette, Zürich (1969), Galerie Dibi Dabi, St. Gallen (1970), Groninger Museum (1970), Gemeente Museum, The Hague (1972), Galerie Fagel, Amsterdam (1973); group shows: Amsterdam, Delft, The Hague, Berlin, Wuppertal, Brussels, Belfast, Dublin, Cork; Bienale de Paris (1961), World Fair, Montreal (1967), London, Liverpool, Paris, Stockholm, Los Angeles, Frankfurt, Tokyo, Copenhagen. *Work in permanent collections:* Museums of The Hague, Schiedam, Brussels, Wuppertal, London, Ostend, Rotterdam. *Address:* Benschoptaan 27, The Hague. *Signs work:* see appendix.

VEGNET-RUIZ, Jean Eugene, Officier de la Légion d'Honneur; Inspecteur général honoraire musées de province; *b* 1896. *Addresses:* 25 Blvd. St. Germain, Paris, Ve, and 2 bis rue de la Corne de Cerf, Senlis (Oise).

VERHEYEN, Petrus Alfons C.; Prof., School of Drawing and Decorative Arts, Molenbeek-St. Jean, Brussels; artist in oil, fusain factice, charcoal; *b* Antwerp, 11 Aug., 1903; *s* of Constant Verheyen, diamond merchant; *m* Hilda Storms. *Studied art* at Royal Academy of Fine Arts, Antwerp, National Institute of Fine Arts, Antwerp, under Baron Albert Ciamberlani (1922-29), Paris under Albert Besnard (1929-30), Italy (Rome and Florence). *Exhib.:* International Exhbn. of decorative arts, Paris (1925), International Exhbns., Antwerp and Liége (1930), Exhbn. in Belgian Embassy, Paris (1937), R.P. (1950). *Work in permanent collection:* mosaic, six panels, Museum of Art History, Brussels. *Address:* 27 Rue Royal, Brussels. *Signs work:* "A. Verheyen."

VERNEY, John, M.C.; painter and illustrator in oil, water-colour, pen and ink; *b* London, 30 Sept., 1913; *m* Lucinda Musgrave; one *s*, five *d*. *Exhib.:* R.B.A., London Group, Leicester, Redfern, A.I.A., Zwemmers, etc. *Official purchases:* Min. of Works, Leicester C.C., L.C.C. *Work repro.:* in Elizabethan,Go Magazine, Illustrated, Graphis, etc. *Publications:* Verney Abroad, Going to the Wars, Friday's Tunnel, Look at Houses, February's Road, Every Advantage, The Mad King of Chichiboo,ismo, The Dodo-Pad, A Dinner of Herbs, Fine Day for Picnic, Seven Sunflower Seeds. *Address:* Runwick House, Farnham, Surrey. *Signs work:* "Verney."

VERNON-CRYER, Joan, A.R.C.A., A.R.W.S. (1970); painter in water-colour; *b* Blackburn, 21 Mar., 1911; *d* of Harold Cryer; *m* W. Fairclough; one *s*, one *d*. *Educ.:* Blackburn High School and Blackburn Technical College; *studied art* at Royal College of Art (1936) under Sir William Rothenstein, Barnet Freedman. *Address:* 12 Manorgate Rd., Kingston-upon-Thames, Surrey. *Signs work:* "Joan Vernon-Cryer."

VERTES, Marcel, Officer of the Legion of Honour; artist, painter and etcher; *b* Ujpest, Hungary, 10 Aug., 1895; *m* Dora Hauser. *Educ.:* Budapest; *studied art* in Paris at Academy Julien under Paul Laurens. *Exhib.:* Petrides, Paris, Lefevre Gallery, London, Carstairs Gallery, Hammer Galleries, New York (1959). *Work in permanent collections:* a painted room at the Museum of Modern Art in Paris, murals at the Robert Lehman Museum in New York, at George Lurcy, New York, Peacock Alley at the Waldorf Astoria in New York, Partos, London. *Official purchases:* French Government (1952), City of Paris for the Musée Carnavalet, Musée de Sceau. *Addresses:* 140 West 57, New York 19; 78 Faisanderie, Paris, 16. *Signs work:* see appendix.

VICARY, Richard Henry, A.R.E., A.R.W.A.; printmaker using relief methods (woodcuts etc.), painting, typography; late Head Printmaking Dept., Shrewsbury School of Art; *b* Sutton, Surrey, 1918; *s* of Simon Vesty, author; *m* Deirdre Vicary; one *s*, one *d*. *Educ.:* Judd School, Tonbridge; Medway School of Art (1936-39); Brighton College of Art (1946); Camberwell School of Art and Crafts; Central School of Art. *Exhib.:* A.I.A., Whitechapel, R.W.S., R.W.A. (Bristol) and many private galleries. *Work in permanent collections* of various Universities and Education Authorities. *Publication:* Manual of Lithography (Thames & Hudson, 1976). *Address:* The Holding, Dunns Heath, Berwick, Shrewsbury, SY4 3HY. *Signs work:* "Richard Vicary."

VICTORIA DAVIDSON, F.S.I.A.; humorous illustration, advertising and poster design; *b* 8 Jan., 1915; *d* of Armin Commichau, painter. In the past regular contributor to both Lilliput and Picture Post; London Transport posters. *Address:* 28 Camden Passage, London N1. *Signs work:* "VICTORIA."

VIEIRA DA SILVA, Marie-Hélène; artist in oil, water-colour, gouache and tempera; *b* Lisbon, 1908; *d* of Marcos; *m* Arpad Szenes. *Studied art* under Bourdelle, Despiau, Dufresne, Friesz F. Léger, Bissière and Hayter. *Work in permanent collections:* Paris, Grenoble, Lyon, Rouen, Nantes, Marseilles, London, New York, Amsterdam, Rotterdam, Bâle, Lausanne, São Paulo, Rio de Janeiro, Essen, Mannheim, Düsseldorf, Washington, Helsinki, Oslo, Turin, Venice. *Work repro.:* Kô et Kô (1933), Editions Jeanne Bucher; L'Inclémence Lointaine; Poemes de R. Char; National Prize of Fine Arts (France, 1966). Commandeur de l'Ordre des Arts et des Lettres. Prix International de Peinture Biennale de São Paulo (1961). Naturalisée Française (1956). *Address:* c/o Guy Weelen, 8 Ave. Frochot, Paris 9°. *Signs work:* "Vieira da Silva."

VILLENEUVE, Noel; designer and painter; *b* New York, 13 May, 1909. *Educ.:* England and France; *studied art:* London and Paris. *Address:* 3 Langbourne Ave., Highgate, London N6. *Signs work:* "VILLENEUVE."

VINALL, Ella Doreen, Slade Diploma (1927), A.R.C.A. (1930), S.G.A., S.W.A.: etcher, engraver, fabric printer and illustrator; *d* of J. W. T. Vinall, A.R.C.A., S.M.A. *Educ.:* Haberdashers' Aske's Girls' School, Acton; Slade School (Henry Tonks, 1924-27); R.C.A. (Prof. Osborne, 1927-30); Central School of Arts and Crafts, Bolt Court. *Exhib.:* R.A., Paris Salon, W.I.A.C., W.A.G., S.G.A., S.W.A., R.B.A.; Manchester, Westminster and Chelsea. *Work repro.:* etchings: The Gardener; In the Cotswolds; Colmer's Hill; Wansford-in-England; Kirkcudbright; Ely; Durham; Speen, Fingest, Bucks; title pages to Broadside Ballads and Augner's Music. *Address:* 21 Grafton Rd., Acton, London W3. *Clubs:* S.G.A., S.W.A., R.B.A. Art. *Signs work:* "Ella D. Vinall."

VIVIENNE, Pauline; exponent of modern 'genre' painting; mem. San Marco Academy, Naples; elected Accademico Benemerito "Per la sua Lodevole attivita nel Campo delle Arti Figurative", Accademia Universale Guglielmo Marconi,

Roma (1976); established first studio Fylde Pottery Art Co., St. Annes on Sea (1952-59); designed and produced original pottery for Heal's of London; taught in art dept. St. Anne's College of Further Education; *b* Newcastle upon Tyne, 1931; *d* of Charles Lipshaw. *Educ.:* Queen Mary School, Lytham; *studied art* at Blackpool School of Art. *Exhib.:* Lytham Hall with Rotarian Club, Red Rose Guild, B.B.C. TV Woman's Hour, Lancashire Art, Manchester Academy, London, Bath, Rome, Florence, Ferrara, Pisa, Leghorn, Viareggio, etc.; one-man shows: touring museums and art centres in Lancashire, Yorkshire and Cumbria (1971-76). *Work in permanent collections:* in Europe. *Address and permanent exhbn.:* Il Ripostiglio, Via Elba, 24, Livorno, Italy. *Club:* Fylde Soroptimist.

VOEL, David: see MORGAN-JONES, David Sylvanus.

VOLLER, Peter Robert; painter in acrylic polymer; *b* Fleet, Hants., 26 Sept., 1943; *m* Tessa Voller; one *d*. *Studied art* at Farnham School of Art. *Exhib.:* R.A., London and provinces. *Address:* 53 The Street, Wrecclesham, Farnham, Surrey. *Signs work:* "Voller."

W

WADDINGTON, Roy, D.F.A., Lond.; artist in pencil, wash drawing, water-colour, oil and art master; student master, Ackworth School (1942-43); art master, Ardvreck Preparatory School, Scotland (1943-45); art master, Craig Preparatory School, Westmorland (1947-49); *b* Settle, Yorks., 12 June, 1917; *s* of Wm. H. Waddington, artist. Hon. Mem. Lake Artists Society. *Exhib.:* N.E.A.C., R.A., R.S.A. *Educ.:* Windermere Grammar School; Giggleswick; University of London; *studied art* at Slade under Prof. Randolph Schwabe and Prof. Borenius, Central School of Arts and Crafts, principal, Mr. Murray. *Exhib.:* Lake Artists' Soc., Red Rose Guild of Craftsmen, Manchester. *Work repro.:* Calligraphy, a sonnet by William Shakespeare. *Address:* Raven Garth, Staveley, Kendal, Cumbria. *Signs work:* see appendix.

WADE, Arthur Edward; painter in water-colour and oil; *b* 1895. *Exhib.:* R.Cam.A., S. Wales Art Soc., Swansea and Newport (Mon.) Art Soc. *Official purchases:* National Museum of Wales, Newport (Mon.) Museum and Art Gallery, Leicester Museum and Art Gallery. *Address:* 71 Marlborough Rd., Cardiff. *Signs work:* "A. E. Wade" (in script).

WADE, Dorothy, A.T.D. Leeds; teacher, designer and painter in gouache, oil, pen and ink; Deputy Principal, Head of Design Dept., College of Fashion and Clothing Technology, London; *b* Silsden, Yorks.; *d* of Thomas Wade, textile designer. *Studied art* at Leeds College of Art, Bradford Regional College of Art. *Exhib.:* Yorkshire Artists, Leeds, Beaux Arts Gallery, Leicester Galleries, R.B.A., Archer Gallery, Woodstock Gallery, Drian Gallery, London. *Address:* 65 Ennerdale Rd., Kew Gardens, Surrey. *Club:* English-speaking Union. *Signs work:* see appendix.

WALDEN, Trevor Alfred, C.B.E., M.Sc., F.M.A.; Director, Glasgow Museums and Art Galleries; *b* Leicester, 15 Apr., 1916; *s* of Alfred Walden; *m* Annie Chalmers; two *s*. *Address:* Machrimore, Manse Rd., Bowling, Glasgow G60 5AA. *Club:* Glasgow Art.

WALDRON, Jack Llewelyn; sculpture, kinetics and cine; *b* 20 Feb., 1923. Mixed exhbns.: Tate, R.A., Arts Council and C.A.S. (Wales), I.C.A., Grosvenor Gallery; one-man exhbns.: Grabowski Gallery, Drian Gallery, N.V.C. (London),

Tib Lane (Manchester), Howard Roberts (Cardiff), and Keele University. *Permanently represented:* Drian Gallery. *Represented in collections:* Arts Council and C.A.S. (Wales), Stoke City Art Gallery, Manchester City Art Gallery (Rutherston Coll.), Whitworth Gallery, Carlisle, Cwmbran and Scunthorpe Civic Centres. Cheshire and Staffordshire Colleges of Education. *Address:* College of Art, Stourbridge. *Signs work:* "Jack Waldron."

WALES, Geoffrey, R.E. (1961), A.R.C.A. (1936); wood-engraver; lecturer, Norwich Art School; mem. (past chairman), Norwich Twenty Group; *b* Margate, 26 May, 1912; *s* of Ernest Wales; *m* Marjorie Skeeles; two *d*. *Educ.:* Chatham House School, Ramsgate; *studied art* at Thanet School of Art (1929-33), R.C.A. (1933-37). *Exhib.:* R.E. at home and overseas; work in public and private collections. *Work repro.:* periodicals and national Press. *Publications:* illustrations for Golden Cockerel Press, Kynoch Press, and Folio Soc. *Address:* 15 Heigham Grove, Norwich, NOR 14G. *Signs work:* "Geoffrey Wales" or "G.W."

WALKER, Harry, A.R.W.A., R.C.A. Cert (Bronze Casting); painter in oils, sculptor in metal; lecturer, Faculty of Art and Design, Bristol Polytechnic; *b* Pollokshaws, Glasgow, 1923; *s* of J. Walker; *m* Betty; one *s*, one *d*. *Educ.:* Sir John Maxwell School, Poloc Academy; *studied art* at Bath Academy of Art, Central School of Arts and Crafts, Royal College of Art. *Work in permanent collections:* Royal West of England Academy, Bath University. *Address:* 8 Belgrave Terr., Camden Rd., Bath, Som. *Club:* Bath Society of Artists. *Signs work:* "H. WALKER."

WALKER, Richard Ian Bentham, N.D.D. (1947), A.T.D. (1949); Mem. United Soc. of Artists, Croydon Art Soc., Armed Forces Art Soc.; portrait painter and teacher of art; teacher of oil painting, Croydon Art School (1948-53); instructor to adult education art courses, Croydon, since 1949; *b* Croydon, 18 Mar., 1925; *s* of Norman Walker, I.C.S., deceased. *Educ.:* Canford School, Dorset; Queen's College, Oxford; *studied art* at Croydon School of Art under R. A. Wilson (1945-48), Institute of Education, London University, under C. Whaite (1949), Slade School under W. Coldstream. *Exhib.:* R.A., R.P., R.B.A., Paris Salon, Utd. Soc. of Artists, Imperial Institute, R.I. Galleries, E. Kent Art Soc. *Work in permanent collections:* Portrait of the Marquess Conyngham (1969); portrait of the composer Dr. Herbert Howells commissioned for Royal College of Music (1972); portrait of A. K. Chesterton, founder of the National Front (1973). *Work repro.:* La Revue Moderne, Paris, Evening Standard. *Publications:* drawings of Stokowski, Havergal Brian, Howells, etc., published Triad Press, London (1971-73). *Address:* Lisvane, 28 Addiscombe Grove, E. Croydon, Surrey. *Club:* Chelsea Arts. *Signs work:* "RICHARD WALKER."

WALKER, Roy Edward Alan, A.R.E. (1975); painter/etcher in oil, water-colour, gouache, etching, engraving, woodcuts, silk-screen; Director, Print Workshop, Penwith Society of Arts, St. Ives, Cornwall; *b* Welling, Kent, 25 Aug., 1936; *s* of Edwin James Walker; *m* Margaret Anne Walker; two *s*, one *d*. *Educ.:* Northumberland Heath, Erith; *studied art* at Gravesend School of Art (1951-52) under Mr. Tennent Moon; Regent St. Polytechnic (1952-54); Central School of Art (1957-60). *Exhib.:* one-man shows: Camel Gallery, Wadebridge, Orion Gallery, Penzance, Plymouth Art Centre; three-man show: Marlborough Graphics; joint shows: Rheno-Frankonia-Haus, Munich, Penwith Society of Arts, St. Ives, Wills Lane Gallery, St. Ives, Newlyn Gallery. *Work in permanent collection:* Print Room, V. & A. *Addresses:* Warwick House, Sea View Terr., St. Ives; Studio: 6 Porthmeor Studios, Back Rd. West, St. Ives. *Signs work:* "Roy Walker."

WALLACE, A. P., N.D.D. Chelsea (1949), M.F.P.S.; artist in water-colour, oil, pastel; vice-pres. R.W.S. Art Club; *b* Montrose, Scotland, 17 Aug., 1923; *d* of A. F. Paterson; *m* Alan Duncan Wallace; three *s,* one *d. Educ.:* Perth Academy, Scotland; *studied art* at Chelsea Art School (1946-49) under Brian Robb, Robert Medley, Thomas Wakeford, Ceri Richards. *Exhib.:* one-man shows: Ely, Halesworth, Framlingham, Woodbridge. *Publications:* illustrated, East Anglia from the Sea by D. & J. Hay. *Address:* Ferry Farm, Butley, Woodbridge, Suffolk IP12 3NJ. *Clubs:* Woodbridge Art (Chairman), Ipswich Art (com. mem.). *Signs work:* "Paterson Wallace."

WALLER, Barbara, A.R.C.A. (1947); sculptor, animal painter and potter; *b* Loxwood, Sussex, 27 Dec., 1923; *m* S. G. Ellis, R.S.S.; *d* of Capt. Claude Waller. *Educ.:* St. John's, Bexhill; Westonbirt; *studied art* at Farnham School of Art under Charles Vyse, R.C.A., under Richard Garbe, R.A. (1945-47). *Exhib.:* R.A., two exhbns. at Walker's Galleries, Bond St., in collaboration with Charles Vyse, Bradford, Artists of Chelsea, W.I.A.C. *Work in permanent collections:* Walker A.G., Liverpool, Exeter Museum, Nottingham Castle A.G. *Work repro.:* Sphere, Daily Mail, Pottery & Glass, The British Racehorse. *Address:* Llwynau Bach, Glasbury-on-Wye, via Hereford. *Signs work:* "WALLER."

WALLER, Margaret Mary, F.I.A.L. (1958, mem. of Council), A.T.D., Mem. Liverpool Academy (1953); painter in oils, portrait, landscape, and decorative church work in gold leaf, also water-colour and egg tempera; *b* Yorks., 13 Nov., 1916; *d* of Arthur Basset Waller. *Educ.:* Friary Convent School (Venice), Belvedere School (Liverpool); *studied art* at Liverpool College of Art (1934-37) and R.A. schools (1937-39). *Exhib.:* R.A., S.W.A., R.S.P.P. and Paris Salon; executed Altar-piece for the Chapel of St. John, Guernsey (1960); also large decorative panels for St. Stephen's Church (1964). *Addresses:* Les Sauterelles, St. Jacques, Guernsey; Mayfield Studio, Sark. *Clubs:* Sandon Studios Soc. (Liverpool), Reynolds (London). *Signs work:* "MARGARET WALLER."

WALLIS, Barnes (Neville), Sir, C.B.E. (1943), R.D.I. (1943), F.R.S. (1945), D.Sc. (Hon., London, 1952; Bristol, 1959), Sc.D. (Hon., Cantab.); Hon. D.Sc. (Loughborough); Hon. D.Sc. (Oxford); Hon. D.Sc. (Heriot Watt University, Edinburgh); Hon. Fellow, Institute of Science and Technology, University of Manchester; Hon. Fellow of Churchill College; Senior Fellow Royal College of Art; Hon. Fellow, Manchester College of Art and Design; Hon. M.I.M.E.; F.S.I.A.; F.S.E.; F.Inst.C.E. (1966); Hon. F.R.Ae.S.; *b* 26 Sept., 1887; *s* of C. G. Wallis, B.A., M.R.C.S., L.R.C.P., surgeon; *m* Mary Frances Bloxham; two *s,* two *d. Educ.:* Christ's Hospital. *Address:* White Hill House, Effingham, Surrey. *Club:* Athenæum. *Signs work:* "B. N. Wallis."

WALPOLE, Josephine Ailsa; artist specialising in flower painting and botanical illustration; proprietor, Deben Gallery, Woodbridge; *b* Cockfield, Suffolk, 27 Apr., 1927; *d* of Joseph James Horn; *m* Derek Walpole, proprietor, picture-framing business; one *s. Educ.:* East Anglian School for Girls, Bury St. Edmunds; Notre Dame High School, Norwich; *studied art* privately under Stuart Somerville. *Exhib.:* one-man shows: Medici Galleries, Woodbridge A.G.; mixed shows: mainly in London and East Anglia. *Publication:* Art in Woodbridge. *Address:* Deben Gallery, 26 Market Hill, Woodbridge, Suffolk. *Signs work:* "J. Walpole."

WALTERS, Nigel Vincent, F.S.I.A.; furniture and interior designer; consultant designer to Wrighton International; *b* Surbiton, Surrey, 21 Apr., 1922; *s* of William Jermy Walters; *m* Sheila Donaldson; one *s,* three *d. Educ.:* Surbiton County Grammar School; *studied art* at Kingston School of Art and R.C.A. (Royal Schol., 1941). *Publication:* Principles of Perspective (Architectural Press, 1970). *Address:* 13 Queen's Elm Sq., Chelsea, London SW3. *Club:* S.I.A. *Signs work:* "Nigel V Walters."

WALTON, John, T.D., A.T.D., F.R.S.A.; Director of Art, Oakham School; painter, calligrapher, illuminator; art master, Rutlish School (1948-59); visiting lecturer, Beckenham School of Art; S.W. Essex Tech. College School of Art (1948-54); tutor painting, Rutland Adult Evening Classes; *b* Mellis, Suffolk, 1915; *s* of Stanley Walton (decd.); *m* Patricia Spencer; one *s*, four *d*. *Educ.:* Ipswich School of Art, Beckenham School of Art, Hampstead Garden Suburb, University of London, Goldsmiths' College School of Art. *Works:* illuminated scroll, H.M. Queen Elizabeth II (1967); scroll, Knights Lodge, Rockingham Castle (1967); design, Oakham School, Shakespeare Centre (1969); other various illuminated scrolls for public institutions. *Address:* Ladycroft, Edith Weston, Oakham, Leics. *Signs work:* "John Walton."

WAN, Wing-Sum; awarded Gold Medal by Chinese Ministry of Education. Taipeh (1957) and Diploma de Correspondente Cultural from Academia Brasileira de Belas Artes, Rio de Janeiro (1961); self-taught artist, lynx-eye calligrapher and painter in water-colour; *b* Hongkong, 13 Apr., 1922. *Exhib.:* one-man shows: (1938-74) Hongkong, China, Vietnam, Cambodia, Laos, Thailand, Philippines, Malaysia, Hawaii, Canada, Guatamala, Salvador, Nicaragua, Honduras, Costa Rica, Panama, Jamaica, U.S.A., Taiwan, Borneo, Australia, New Guinea, New Zealand, Tahiti, Madagascar, Mauritius, S. Africa, Mozambique, Fiji, Samoa, Trinidad, Guiana, Surinam, Brasil, Uruguay, Paraguay, Argentina, Chile, Bolivia, Peru, Ecuador, Colombia, Venezuela, Burma, India, Nepal, Pakistan, Iran, Turkey, Cyprus, Lebanon, Syria, Jordan, Palestine, Egypt, Netherlands, Germany, Belgium, Luxembourg, Switzerland, England, Spain, Portugal, Haiti, Puerto Rico, Mexico, Bahamas, Japan, Korea, Indonesia, etc. *Work in permanent collection:* New Zealand Museum, Wellington, etc. *Publication:* Chinese Calligraphy and Painting (1971). *Address:* Paruro 1255 E-4, Lima (Peru). *Signs work:* "Wan Wing-Sum" and see appendix.

WANG, Chi-Yuan; artist; calligrapher and painter in oil and water-colours; Dean, Shanghai College of Fine Arts (1922); founder of School of Chinese Brushwork, New York (1947); Professor of Art at Syracuse University; *b* Hsi District, Anhwei, China, 1895. *Studied art* at academies of art in China and Japan. *Exhib.:* National Museum of History and National Palace Museum, Taipei, Taiwan (1973). *Work in permanent collections:* Metropolitan Museum, New York; City Art Museum, St. Louis; Chicago Art Institute; Montreal Museum; National Historical Museum, Taiwan; Museo Nacional de Arte Moderno, Mexico, etc. *Commission:* Carnauba palm mural for the Johnson Wax Research Building at Racine, Wisc. *Publications:* Oriental Brushwork (Pitman, 1951-66). *Address:* 399 East 72nd St., New York, N.Y. 10021, U.S.A. *Signs work:* "C. Y. Wang."

WARBURTON, Joan; artist in oils, of landscape and still-life, wash drawings, gouache and pastels; *b* 17 Apr., 1920, in Edinburgh; *m* Peter O'Malley, Des.R.C.A., potter; one *s*. *Studied art* with Oswald Poreau in Brussels (1936-37); East Anglian School of Painting, Dedham, Essex, under Cedric Morris (1937-39). *Exhib.:* R.A., S.E.A., W.I.A.C., Chateau du Tremblay, Fontenoye-en-Puisaye (1975); one-man show: Hintlesham Hall (1976). *Official purchases:* Rugby Art Gallery (1947), Hull Educ. Com. (1953), Derby Educ. Com. (1952), Lancashire Educ. Com. (1968), Herts. Educ. Com. *Work repro.:* Studio, Sphere and Field. *Address:* The White House, Stoke-by-Nayland, nr. Colchester. *Signs work:* "J.W."

WARD, Gordon, D.F.A. Lond., A.R.W.A.; artist in all mediums; senior lecturer, Gloucestershire College of Art and Design; *b* N. Walsham, Norfolk, 1932; *s* of William Ward; *m* Maureen Liddell; one *s*, two *d*. *Educ.:* Paston Grammar School, N. Walsham, Norfolk; *studied art* at Norwich School of Art

(1949-53), Slade School of U.C.L. (1955-57). *Work in permanent collections:* Royal West of England Academy, Bristol, Denbighshire, Gloucestershire and other Educ. Comm., various private collections. *Address:* 131 Hales Rd., Cheltenham, Glos. *Signs work:* "GORDON WARD" and date.

WARD, Grace, S.W.A.; oil-painter; *d* of Lt-Col. C. H. Ward. *Educ.:* St. Leonards and Brussels; *studied art* at Regent St. Polytechnic under Harry Watson. *Exhib.:* R.A., R.O.I., R.B.A., S.W.A. *Work in permanent collections:* Juanita in Graves Gallery, Sheffield. *Addresses:* 6 Scarsdale Studios, Kensington, London W8; Hazeley Lea, nr. Hartley-Wintney, Hants. *Signs work:* "GRACE WARD" (usually in red).

WARD, J. S., A.R.C.A., R.W.S., R.A.; painter in oil and water-colour; *b* Hereford, 1917; *s* of Russel Stanton Ward; *m* Alison Ward; four *s*, two *d*. *Educ.:* St. Owens School, Hereford; *studied art* at R.C.A. under Gilbert Spencer. *Work in permanent collections:* H.M. the Queen, R.A., Preston A.G., Maas Gallery, Hereford. *Publications:* Alphonse by George Ward; Cider with Rosie by Laurie Lee; Little Kingdom by Richard Church; Autobiography of H. E. Bates. *Address:* Bilting Ct., Bilting, nr. Ashford, Kent. *Club:* Athenæum. *Signs work:* "John Ward."

WARD, Leslie Moffat, F.R.E., gold medallist National Competition; artist in water-colour and etching; retd. art teacher, Bournemouth College of Art; *b* Worcester, 2 Apr., 1888; *s* of Charles James Ward; widower; one *s*. *Educ.:* local schools and Bournemouth College; *studied art* at Bournemouth Drummond School of Art. *Exhib.:* Bournemouth, Weymouth, Eastbourne, Hastings etc. *Address:* 22 Grants Ave., Bournemouth.

WARD, Louis Arthur, R.W.A. (1955), F.S.I.A. (1968); freelance artist, illustrator, part-time teacher, W. of England College of Art; T.A.R.O. rank of Major; *b* Bristol, 22 Nov., 1913; *s* of Albert Edward Ward, marine engineer; *m* Brenda Mary; one *s*, two *d*. *Studied art* full-time W. of England College of Art. *Exhib.:* R.W.A., Bristol Municipal A.G., Arts Council of Gt. Britain Touring exhbn. of Bristol Artists, Graphic Design Britain, '65, Royal Festival Hall. *Work in permanent collections:* Bristol Savages, Bristol Municipal A.G., Royal W. of England Academy, Bristol University. *Work repro.:* Designers in Britain, My Home, Woman and Home, Wide World, B.B.C. publications, Longmans Green School Readers, Hamlyn's History of the World, and Look and Learn. *Address:* 31 Apsley Rd., Clifton, Bristol. *Club:* Bristol Savages. *Signs work:* "WARD" or "LOUIS WARD" in small block capitals.

WARD, Neville, R.D.I., B.Arch. (Liverpool), R.I.B.A., F.S.I.A.; architect and industrial designer; principal of firm of Ward Associates; Past President of the Society of Industrial Artists and Designers; *b* Warrington, Lancs., 1922; *s* of A. E. Ward, engineer; *m* Mary Winstanley, architect. *Educ.:* Wade Deacon Grammar School, University of Liverpool, Edinburgh College of Art. *Work repro.:* Architects' Journal, Architectural Review, Interior Design, Design, Designers in Britain, Display, Domus, Form, Interiors, etc. *Address:* 68 Grafton Way, London W1P 5LE.

WARD, Thomas William, A.R.C.A. (1949), R.E. (1953), R.W.S. (1957); artist in water-colours, drawing and etching; lecturer in drawing; *b* Sheffield, 8 Nov., 1918; *s* of John B. Ward, master stationer; *m* Joan; one *s*, one *d*. *Educ.:* Sheffield Nether Edge Grammar School; *studied art* at Sheffield College of Art (1937-39) (Eric Jones, A.R.C.A.), Royal College of Art (1946-50) (R. S. Austin, R.A., Malcolm Osborn, R.A.). *Work in permanent collections:* National Gallery, New Zealand, Victoria and Albert Museum, Bowes Museum, Barnard Castle,

Oxford Junior Common Room, Leicester University, South London Art Gallery. *Publication:* illustrated Fast Sailing Ships by D. MacGregor. *Address:* 20 The Grove, Ealing, London W5. *Signs work:* see appendix.

WARDEN, William, R.B.A. (1963), L.A.A. (1936), Mem. Soc. of Sussex Painters (1938); landscape painter in oil and water-colour; *b* 21 May, 1908. *Trained:* Liverpool City School of Art (1924-30); and in Sussex by Geo. Graham, R.I., R.O.I., R.S.W., R.B.A. *Exhib.:* R.A., R.B.A., N.E.A.C., C.E.M.A., Art Exhbns. Bureau, Arts Council, Roland Browse & Delbanco, New Grafton Gallery. *Work in permanent collection:* Hastings Art Gallery (oil, landscape; presented). *Official purchases:* Imperial War Museum (water-colour, Cologne), Eastbourne Towner Gallery (one oil, two water-colours), Liverpool W.A.G. (water-colour, landscape), Wye College (oil, landscape). *Address:* Romney Cottage, Winchelsea, Sussex. *Signs work:* "William Warden."

WARE, William Edward; artist in oil, water-colour, inks, etc.; *b* London, 18 Feb., 1915; *s* of William Albert Ware; *m* Eileen Aldridge; one *s. Educ.:* privately (no schools); *studied art* at Richmond School of Art under James Holland, C.B.E. *Exhib.:* R.A. London Group, New English, Leger, National Gallery War Exhbns., Modern Art Gallery, Upper Grosvenor Gallery, Netherton Gallery, Marlborough Gallery, etc. *Work in permanent collection:* War Museum, London (Fired City in oil). *Address:* 226 Fulham Rd., London SW10. *Signs work:* "WILLIAM WARE."

WARMAN, Sylvia (Mrs.), S.P.S., N.S., F.P.S., Ass. S. des A. Francais, F.I.A.L.; portrait sculptor and painter; Wells Prize in Fine Art, Reading University (1952); Owen Ridley Prize in Fine Art, Reading University (1954); Bronze Medal (sculpture) Paris Salon (1969), Silver Medal (sculpture) Paris Salon (1973); *b* St. Leonards-on-Sea, Sussex, 1922; *m* J. Royce Warman; three *d. Studied art:* drawing and modelling classes at Reading University, ultimately specialising in portrait sculpture under the late Albert Carter, F.R.B.S. (1947-54). *Exhib.:* R.A. (1955); West of England R.A. (1970); Paris Salon (1969-70-71-72-73). *Address:* 1 Chester St., Caversham, Reading, Berks.

WARMBY, Byron Winston, F.R.S.A. (1944), F.I.A.D. (1943); painter in oil and water-colour; hon. pres., Sheffield Soc. of Artists (1947-48); hon. sec., Heeley Art Club (1939-63); *b* 20 July, 1902; *s* of William Henry Warmby; *m* Elsie Burton. *Educ.:* Grimesthorpe Council School and privately; City of Sheffield College of Arts and Crafts under H. V. Lilley, H. G. Hoyland, R.B.A. (1920-25). *Exhib.:* R.A., R.B.S.A., City of Bradford Art Gallery; Graves Art Gallery, Sheffield; Doncaster, Scarborough, Harrogate, etc. *Address:* 2 Longley Hall Grove, Sheffield S5 7EJ. *Club:* Heeley Art. *Signs work:* "BYRON W. WARMBY."

WARNE, Dorothy; water-colour miniaturist; *b* Ealing, 25 Oct., 1902; *d* of Col. T. H. Wheelwright; *m* Rear-Admiral R. S. Warne, L.B., C.B.E.; three *s. Studied art* at St. John's Wood Art School (1923-25) under Frederick Whalen. *Exhib.:* R.A. *Address:* 56 Hill Rise, Richmond, Surrey. *Signs work:* "Dorothy Warne."

WARREN, Charles Wyatt, D.L., J.P., D.P.A., Lond.; artist in oil; former Mem. N. Wales Assocn. for the Arts; Mem. Arts Society of Paddington; Caernarvon Art Group; founder sec., Caernarvon Art Club; former Chairman, North Wales Art Group; *b* Caernarvon, 15 Aug., 1908; *s* of Charles Wyatt Warren, artist and engraver; *m*; two *d. Educ.:* Caernarvon Grammar School; *studied art:* self-taught. *Exhib.:* R.Cam.A., Royal National Eisteddfod of Wales, North Wales Group and several provincial exhbns.; 46 one-man exhbns., incl. New York and Toronto. *Address:* High Meadows, Caernarvon. *Signs work:* see appendix.

WATERFIELD, Geo. R., A.R.B.S.A. (1945); water-colour and oil painter, engraver, wood engraver, illustrator; *b* 7 Mar., 1886; *s* of Geo. Waterfield, builder; *m* (wife decd.); two *d. Educ.:* Somerville Rd. Council School, Birmingham; Margaret St. School of Art, and Jenkins St. Branch (Taylor, H. Wilson, Meteyard, 1902-08). *Exhib.:* R.B.S.A. *Address:* 141 Elmay Rd., Sheldon, Birmingham, 26. *Clubs:* Birmingham Art Circle; Easel; Clarendon Art Fellowship. *Signs work:* "Geo. R. Waterfield."

WATERS, Alwyn Brunow, C.B.E. (1971), M.B.E. (1943), G.M. (1944), F.R.I.B.A. (1945), A.R.I.B.A. (1933), F.I.Arb.; architect in private practice; Principal, Ellis School of Building (1936); Past Pres. of the Institute of Arbitrators; head of Senior Building Dept., L.C.C. Hammersmith School of Building and Arts and Crafts (1936-46); war service with R.E., Major (1940-46); *b* London, 18 Sept., 1906; *s* of S. G. Waters; *m* Ruby Alice; one *s*, one *d. Educ.:* Quintin School, London; *studied art* (architecture) at Central School of Arts and Crafts, R.A. Schools, articled to S. B. Caulfield, F.R.I.B.A. (1924-27). *Address:* 103 Old Brompton Rd., London SW7. *Club:* R.A.C.

WATKINS, Frances Jane Grierson (Peggy); oil, water-colour, pencil artist; jewellery; instructor silverwork and jewellery Hereford College of Art (1957-72); *b* 24 July, 1919; *d* of Thomas Vaughan Milligan, A.R.C.A.; *m* Rev. Alfred Felix Macirone Watkins; one *s*, one *d. Educ.:* Elms Private School, Herefordshire School of Art, Birmingham School of Jewellery. *Exhib.:* R.A., R.S.A., R.B.A., R.W.A., National Eisteddfod, Herefordshire Arts and Crafts. *Official purchases:* Lady Hawkins Grammar School; Agric. Exec. Com.; Hereford City Art Gallery; Hereford RDC (badge of office). *Addresses:* 18 Melrose Ave., Yate, Bristol BS17 5AL; and 26 Southbank Rd., Hereford. *Signs work:* "PEGGY WATKINS."

WATKINS, Jesse, F.R.B.S.; sculptor in metal; *b* Gravesend, 31 Dec., 1899; *m* Sheila; two *s*, two *d. Exhib.:* Nine one-man exhbns. in England; very many group exhbns. in England and abroad. Awarded Silver Medal by Royal Society of British Sculptors 1968. *Work in permanent collections:* Manchester City Art Gallery, Museum of Contemporary Art, Skopje, Yugoslavia, Harlow New Town, London Borough of Camden, Macedonian National Museum, National Gallery, Oslo; many private collections. *Commission:* large sculpture for new Royal Free Hospital, London. Member of the London Group. *Address:* 35 Richmond Rd., New Barnet, Herts. *Signs work:* "Jesse Watkins."

WATKINSON, Frank, N.D.D. (1951), A.T.D. (1952), F.R.S.A. (1955), R.D.S. (1955); teacher of art, sculptor, potter, painter, lecturer; head of Art Dept., Filey C.S. School; *b* Scarborough, 10 May, 1925; *s* of Capt. F. Watkinson, F.I.Hsg.; *m* Mary; two *s*, one *d. Educ.:* High School for Boys, Scarborough; *studied art* at Scarborough School of Art, Anglo-French Art Centre, Goldsmiths' Coll. School of Art, King Edward VII School of Art, King's Coll., Newcastle upon Tyne. *Work repro.:* Scarborough Evening News, Admiralty, Schoolmaster, etc. *Address:* 42 Ashville Ave., Scarborough. *Signs work:* "F. Watkinson" or "Frank Watkinson" or "Meretricious" (cartoons).

WATSON, James Fletcher, F.R.I.B.A., R.I. (1955), R.B.A. (1957); architect; painter in water-colour; *b* Coulsdon, Surrey, 25 July, 1913; *s* of Thomas F. Watson; *m* Gillian Mayall; one *s*, one *d. Educ.:* Eastbourne College; *studied art* at R.A. School of Architecture (silver medal for design, 1936). *Exhib.:* R.A., R.I., R.B.A., Paris Salon, Stockholm. *Work repro.:* British Railways carriage posters. *Address:* Windrush House, Windrush, nr. Burford, Oxford. *Signs work:* "J. Fletcher Watson."

WATSON, John Bernard; freelance artist, fine and commercial; works in pen,

pen and wash, water-colour, oil, crayon, and small sculpture in plaster, metal; *b* Bradford, Yorks., 5 Mar., 1924; *s* of Arnold Fred Watson. *Educ.:* Colchester Royal Grammar School; *studied art* at Ipswich School of Art, but mostly self-taught. *Exhib.:* Colchester, Ipswich, Norwich, Truro. *Work repro.:* Essex County Standard, Nursing Mirror, Jazz Journal, illustrations for Faber & Faber. *Address:* 33 Queen St., Colchester, Essex. *Signs work:* see appendix.

WATSON, Leslie Joseph, M.B.E., A.R.C.A., R.S.M.A., F.I.L.A.; painter and landscape architect in oil; *b* Harrogate, 6 July, 1906; *s* of L. T. Watson; *m* Helen Watson, painter. *Educ.:* St. Peter's School, York; *studied art* at Leeds College of Art (1926-28), Royal College of Art (1928-32). *Address:* 66 Park House Gdns., Twickenham, Middx. *Club:* Nash House. *Signs work:* "L. J. WATSON."

WATTS, Mrs. Dorothy, S.W.A. (1952), Mem. Federation of British Artists; artist in water-colour; early years, fashion designer for London and Northern papers; *b* London, 3 Apr., 1905; *d* of S. C. Ravenshoe; *m* A. Gordon Watts, LL.B., solicitor. *Studied art* at Brighton College of Arts under J. Morgan Rendle, R.I., R.B.A. *Exhib.:* R.A., R.I., R.B.A., S.W.A., Britain in Water-colours and provincial galleries. *Work in permanent collection:* Hove Art Collection. *Work repro.:* in Londoner's England, various Christmas cards and in newspapers, London and provincial. *Address:* Southwoods, 65 Surrenden Rd., Brighton, 6, Sussex. *Clubs:* S.W.A., Phoenix Art. *Signs work:* see appendix.

WATTS, Joan Alwyn, A.R.M.S.; portrait painter (miniatures) in water-colour; *b* Birmingham, 19 Dec., 1921; *d* of J. Lineker, sales manager; *m* Ronald O. Watts; one *s*, one *d*. *Educ.:* Birmingham College of Art. *Exhib.:* Birmingham Soc. of Artists, Royal Miniature Soc., Paris Salon, various exhbns. in America and Australia; permanent exhbn. Art Bureau, London. *Address:* Dial Cottage, Bannut Tree La., Bridstow, nr. Ross-on-Wye, Herefords. *Signs work:* monogram of "J. A. W."

WATTS, Meryl; colour woodcut artist; painter in oil and water-colour; modeller; *b* 1910; *d* of Charles I. Watts. *Educ.:* Blackheath High School; Blackheath Art School (John Platt, James Woodford, R.A., Charles Paine, William Clause, Reginald Brill). *Exhib.:* R.A., New York World's Fair; Exhbn. of British Art 1735 to 1935, Vienna, Prague, etc.; British Council in most of the world's capitals; London Societies, etc. *Official purchases:* Contemporary Art Soc.; British Council; M. of E.; Prague; Baghdad, etc. *Work repro.:* in the Art Review. *Address:* 1 Bron-Avon, Borth-y-Gest, Porthmadog, Gwynedd. *Signs work:* see appendix.

WATTS, Peter, F.R.B.S. (1970); sculptor in wood and stone; *b* Chilcompton, Bath, 12 Oct., 1916; *s* of Nevile Hunter Watts B.A., schoolmaster at Downside and author; *m* Anne Mary Coulson; two *s*, one *d*. *Educ.:* Downside School; *studied art* at Bath School of Art (1937) under Clifford Ellis, apprenticed (1938) to Lindsey Clark, F.R.B.S., in London; also at City and Guilds School of Art, Kennington (1938-39). *Principal commissioned works in U.K.:* Oban Cathedral (1951), St. Mary and St. Joseph's Church, Poplar, (1952), St. Mary's Church, Highfield St., Liverpool (1953), Bath Abbey, (West Front) (1959-60), Prinknash Abbey (1971), Downside Abbey (1974); in U.S.A.: Gethsemani Abbey, Kentucky (1955-64), St. John's Abbey, Collegeville, Minn. (1962), Sun of Justice Church, Benson, Vermont (1962-65), private collection of Mr. Chauncey Stillman, Amenia, N.Y. (1965-1970). *Address:* The Maltings, Wellow, Bath, Avon. *Signs work:* carved monogram, see appendix.

WAUTERS, Jef; First Prize for Monumental Painting, with gold medal and congratulations of the jury (1949); artist (painter); *b* Mariakerke n/Ghent, Belgium, 26 Feb., 1927; *m* Denise D'Hooge; one *s*, one *d*. Sup., Inst. Architecture and

Decoration at Ghent and Academy of Fine Arts, Ghent. *Work in permanent collections:* New York, Chicago, San Francisco, Los Angeles, Paris, München, Brussels, Rome. *Publications:* Palet (15 poems and 15 linogravures), Paris-Roma (sketch-book, 500 numbered ex.), Jef Wauters, by Jos. Murez, Jef Wauters (ed. Aro Roma), by Guiseppe Selvaggi. *Addresses:* 140 Kortrijksesteenweg, Ghent; 3 rue Chérubini, Paris 2. *Signs work:* see appendix.

WEBB, Lieut.-Comdr. Arthur Geoffrey Gascoyne, O.B.E., R.N. Retd.; artist in pastel; *b* Newington, nr. Sittingbourne, Kent, 17 Aug., 1896; *s* of Arthur Sapte Webb, land agent; *m* Iris Ethel Thomson; two *s*. *Educ.:* Wellington College, Berks. *Exhib.:* Pastel Soc. *Address:* 41 Burley Rd., Oakham, Rutland. *Signs work:* "Geoffrey Webb."

WEBB, Kenneth, N.D.D. (1952), A.T.D.Dist. (1953), N.S., F.R.S.A., A.R.U.A., A.R.W.A.; artist in oil and acrylic; head of Painting School, Ulster College of Art (1953-59); *b* Condon, 21 Jan., 1927; *s* of William George Webb; *m* Joan Burch; two *s*, two *d*. *Educ.:* Bristol Grammar School; Lydney Grammar School and School of Art; *studied art* at Gloucester College of Art (1948-52); University College, Swansea (1953). *Exhib.:* David Hendricks Gallery, Dublin, John Maclee, Belfast, Verhoff, Washington, Solomon & Whitehead, Mall Galleries, London, Jersey Art Centre, Alexander Gallery, Bristol, Harrods, London; one-man shows 1954 to 1975; group shows in Canada, U.S.A., Gt. Britain, Ireland, Holland, France, Spain and Italy. *Work in permanent collections:* Arts Councils of England, Wales, N. Ireland, Republic of Ireland, Courtauld, Carreras & Rothman, Haverty Trust, Ministry of Commerce, Crawford Institute of Art. *Address:* Bownham Grange, Rodborough Common, Stroud, Glos. GL5 5BU. *Signs work:* "Webb."

WEBBER, Michael H., A.T.D., Dept. of the Environment; Director (with wife), Radlett Gallery, 141 Watling St., Radlett, Herts.; Council Mem. Ben Uri Gallery; Hon. Treas., Arnold Bax Soc.; London art critic, East Anglian Daily Times; contributor to Apollo, Arts Review, Jewish Chronicle, East Anglia Life, East Anglian Magazine, etc.; freelance writer, critic, journalist catalogue, Ipswich Arts Clubs Cent. Ex. (1975); *b* London, 30 June, 1926; *s* of Joseph E. Webber; *m* Miriam Broughton; two *d*. *Educ.:* Kilburn Grammar School (1937-43); *studied art* at Northampton School of Art; Chelsea School of Art; Central School of Arts. *Address:* 19D Netherhall Gardens, Hampstead, London NW3 5RL.

WEBSTER, Gordon, F.R.S.M.G.P. (1948); designer and worker in stained glass; *b* Fairlie, Ayrshire, 1 July, 1908; *s* of the late Alfred A. Webster, stained-glass artist; *m* Sheila MacLennan; two *s*. *Educ.:* Glasgow High School; *studied art* at G.S.A. and abroad. *Exhib.:* London, Edinburgh, Glasgow. *Works:* in churches throughout country. *Address:* 10 Cleveden Cres., Glasgow, W2. *Signs work:* "Gordon Webster" (printed at base of every window).

WEBSTER, John Robert, A.T.C., R.Cam.A.; artist in etching, printmaking, gouache; senior lecturer, St. Mary's College, Bangor, N. Wales (1968-75); Diploma in Art Education, Leeds University Institute (1975-76); *b* Bridlington, E. Yorks., 22 May, 1934; *s* of Joe Webster, commercial traveller; *m* Dorothy Lloyd Webster; one *s*, four *d*. *Educ.:* Leeds G.S.; *studied art* at Leeds College of Art (1951-55-57) graphic design and illustration under Holmes, Webster. *Exhib.:* South London (1971), Mold, N. Wales (1971), Prestatyn (1972), Cambrian Academy, Conway (1969-75), Blue Coat Gallery, Liverpool (1974). *Work in permanent collection:* Schools Museum, Cardiff. *Address:* 1 Victoria Pk., Bangor, Gwynedd, N. Wales.

WEBSTER, Norman, R.W.S., R.E., A.R.C.A., Royal Exhibition, R.C.A.;

etcher, engraver, draughtsman, water-colourist; Senior Lecturer, Fine Prints, Leeds Polytechnic; *b* Southend-on-Sea, 6 May, 1924; *s* of George W. Webster; *m* Joan W. Simpson, A.R.C.A.; three *s*. *Educ.:* Dover Grammar School; *studied art* at Tunbridge Wells School of Art (1940-43) (E. Owen Jennings, R.W.S., R.E., A.R.C.A.), Royal College of Art, School of Engraving (1946-49) (Malcolm Osborne, C.B.E., R.A., Robert Austin, R.A., P.R.W.S., P.R.E.). *Exhib.:* Painter Etchers, R.W.S., R.A., N.E.A.C., R.B.A., Leeds, Bradford and Wakefield Art Galleries, South Africa, U.S.A., Israel and Canada. *Work in permanent collections:* Print Room, V. & A. Museum, Ashmolean Museum; purchased by Leeds City Art Gallery and Arts Council of Great Britain. *Address:* 48 The Drive, Cross Gates, Leeds, 15. *Signs work:* "Norman Webster."

WEGNER, Fritz, M.S.I.A., Mem. Art Workers' Guild; freelance artist, visiting lecturer, St. Martin's School of Art; *b* Vienna, 15 Sept., 1924; *m* Janet Wegner; two *s*, one *d*. *Studied art* at St. Martin's School of Art. *Work repro.:* bookjackets and illustrations for British, American and Continental publishers; cover designs and illustrations for magazines; educational publications; G.P.O. Christmas and Anniversaries sets of stamps. Examples of work reproduced in several manuals on illustration. *Address:* 14 Swains Lane, London N6. *Signs work:* "Wegner."

WEIGHT, Carel, C.B.E. (1962), A.R.A. (elect., 1955), R.A. (1965), Hon. A.R.C.A. (1956), R.B.A., Mem. R.W.A. (1954), London Group (1950); painter in oil; Official War Artist (1945-46); Prof. Emeritus, Royal College of Art (1972); Trustee, Royal Academy (1975); *b* London, 10 Sept., 1908; *s* of Sidney L. Weight. *Educ.:* Sloane School, Chelsea; Hammersmith School of Art; Goldsmiths' College. *Exhib.:* R.A., Leicester Galleries, Wildenstein's, Zwemmer Gallery (1965), Pushkin Museum, Moscow, British Painters, Vancouver, U.S.S.R., Paris, Toronto, Pittsburgh, Washington, S. America, Manchester Cathedral (1963). *Address:* 33 Spencer Rd., London SW18. *Signs work:* "Carel Weight."

WEIL, Hanna, N.T.D. (1943); painter in oil, water-colour, gouache; tutor, Hammersmith School of Arts and Crafts (1945-48); St. Martin's School of Art since 1945; *b* Munich, 19 May, 1921; *d* of Ernest Weil, Ph.D.; *m* R. S. Strauss, F.I.M.; one *d*. *Educ.:* North London Collegiate School, *studied art* at St. Martin's School of Art (1940-43). *Exhib.:* R.A., Leicester Galleries, Liverpool, Brighton, London Transport (posters), City of Bradford Art Gallery, Arthur Jeffress (Pictures) Ltd., Trafford Gallery, 3 galleries Munich, Portal Gallery. *Work repro.:* Amalgamated Press, The Queen, Art News and Review, The Studio, The Artist; regular contributor to several German papers. *Address:* 34 Christchurch Hill, London NW3. *Signs work:* "H. Weil."

WEINBERGER, Harry; artist in oil and all kinds of drawing, lecturer; principal lecturer in painting, Lanchester Polytechnic; *b* Berlin, 7 Apr., 1924; *m* Barbara; one *d*. *Educ.:* Continent and England; *studied art* at Chelsea School of Art under Ceri Richards, Martin Bloch, and privately. *Exhib.:* one-man shows: Leger, Walker's and Ben Uri Galleries, London; Fine Art Gallery, Reading; Tibs Lane and College of Art Galleries, Manchester; Herbert A.G., Coventry; Warwick and Sheffield Universities; Town Hall Gallery, Berlin Festival; mixed exhbns. Young Contemporaries, R.B.A. etc. *Address:* 28 Church Hill, Leamington Spa, Warks. *Signs work:* "HW."

WEIR, Halcyon Dora Murray; animal portrait artist in pastel, mural-painter, wood-sculptor, exhibition model-maker; designer of collage, textiles, and toys; TV broadcaster on crafts for children; *b* London, 27 Apr., 1912; *d* of Charles S. Weir, LL.B. *Educ.:* St. Winifred's, Eastbourne; *studied art* at Ecole d'Art, Lausanne

(Rambert) (1930), Central School of Art and Crafts (J. R. Skeaping, R.A., John Farleigh, C.B.E., R.E.) (1932-38). *Work in permanent collections:* Animal portraits in many royal, military, and private collections in Europe, India, Australia, New Zealand and U.S.A.; scale-models for government departments. *Publications:* Illustration for Tax Lexicon (B. Söderberg); work reproduced in newspapers and on television. *Address:* 12 Broomfield Ct., Sunningdale, Berks. *Club:* Helena. *Signs work:* see appendix.

WEISSENBORN, Hellmuth, Ph.D.; painter in oil, water-colour, pastel; wood engraver; lecturer at Art Academy, Leipzig, until 1938; art teacher for Kent County Council until 1970. Made Academy Prof. a.d. (Germany), 1957; *b* 29 Dec., 1898; *s* of Prof. F. Weissenborn, art teacher; *m* Lesley Mary Macdonald. *Educ.:* Leipzig School and University, Leipzig Academy of Art under Prof. Tiemann. *Exhib.:* London; Boston, U.S.A.; Art Museum, Leipzig; Berlin. *Official purchases:* graphic and typographical work, Berlin and Leipzig. *Publications:* numerous books illustrated by wood-engraving, lithography, and line drawing. *Address:* 7 Harley Gdns., The Boltons, London SW10. *Signs work:* "H. Weissenborn."

WEISZ, Otto, F.I.A.L., M.S.I.A.; Chairman and Managing Director, Design and Business Consultants (Jersey) Ltd.; retired, 1 Mar., 1969, as Managing Director and chief designer of Pringle of Scotland, Hawick; *b* Vienna, 29 Jan., 1908; *s* of David Weisz, M.D.; *m* Christina Kirkpatrick. *Educ.:* Vienna; *studied art* at Vienna Textile Technical College. *Address:* Maison des Arbres, Travers Farm Lane, Route de Noirmont, St. Brelade, Jersey, C.I. *Signs work:* "Otto Weisz."

WELLER, Antony, F.P.S.; sculptor in fibreglass, marble, bronze; Instructor, Camden Inst.; *b* London, 4 May, 1927; *m* Julia Heseltine; one *s*. *Educ.:* Sutton County Grammar; *studied art* at Wimbledon under Freda Skinner, R.A. Schools under Maurice Lambert, R.A. *Work in permanent collections:* U.S.A., U.K., S. Africa, Japan, and private collections. *Publications:* Patron, Sculpture in Plastics. *Address:* 4 Stamford Bridge Studios, London SW6. *Signs work:* "Antony Weller" and see appendix.

WELLINGTON, Irene, A.R.C.A.; calligrapher and illuminator; *b* Lydd, Kent, 29 Oct., 1904; *d* of Charles Edward Bass, J.P.; *m* Hubert Wellington. *Educ.:* Ashford County School; *studied art* at Maidstone College of Art and R.C.A. Pupil of Edward Johnston; teacher at the Edinburgh College of Art (1932-42) and the L.C.C. Central School of Arts and Crafts (1944-59). *Exhib.:* Crafts Council of Great Britain, Soc. of Scribes and Illuminators. *Work in permanent collections:* Christ Church Cathedral, Oxford; Winchester College; Bodleian Library; Newberry Library, Chicago; V. & A. Museum. *Official purchases:* British Council, President Auriol, H.M. Queen Juliana; Accession and Coronation Addresses to Her Majesty the Queen. *Publication:* The Irene Wellington Copy Book. *Address:* 14 Palace Gdns. Mews, London W8 4RA.

WELTMAN, Boris, R.M.S., F.R.S.A.; nature miniaturist, book illustrator and cartographer in water-colour, gold, pen and ink; *b* London, 29 Nov., 1921; *m* Phyllis Joyce. *Educ.:* Chatham House, Ramsgate; Folkestone Teacher's Training College; art and light craft teachers certificate. *Exhib.:* R.M.S., Soc. of Miniaturists, R.A., R.I. *Publications:* educational, children's, historical, biographical, scientific, technical, military, religious and travel books. *Address:* Temptye Farmhouse, Worth, Deal, Kent, CT14 0DJ. *Signs work:* on back of miniature paintings, see appendix.

WERGE-HARTLEY, Alan, N.D.D. (Leeds) 1952, A.T.D.; painter in oil, pen and wash of marine landscapes, lecturer; senior lecturer in Art and Design, Portsmouth College of Education; *b* Leeds, 1931; *m* Jeanne Werge-Hartley; two *d.* *Studied art* at Leeds College of Art (1947-53) under Maurice de Sausmarez and E. E. Pullée; Hornsey College of Art (1972-73) (sabbatical). *Exhib.:* in group exhbns. and one-man shows in Hampshire from 1962. *Work in permanent collections:* Portsmouth City Gallery and numerous private collections in England and abroad. *Address:* 5 Maisemore Gdns., Emsworth, Hants. *Signs work:* see appendix.

WERGE-HARTLEY, Jeanne, N.D.D., F.SD-C.; designer-craftsman in silver and gold, jeweller, lecturer; in charge jewellery section, Portsmouth College of Art; Council Mem. Soc. of Designer-craftsmen; *b* Leeds, 1931; *d* of Edgar Vauvelle; *m* Alan Werge-Hartley; two *d. Educ.:* Leeds Girls' High School; *studied art* at Leeds College of Art (1948-52) under Eric Taylor, A.R.C.A. *Exhib.:* Design Centre, British Crafts Centre, Goldsmiths Hall, Royal Exchange, Arnolfini, Bristol, Durham, Leeds, Portsmouth and Southampton Art Galleries. *Commissioned work:* in Bermuda, Jamaica, New Zealand, Persia, Bahrain, Japan and U.K.; silver casket for Sir Alec Rose (Freedom of the City of Portsmouth). *Address:* 5 Maisemore Gdns., Emsworth, Hants. Member of Design and Research Centre, British Crafts Centre. *Signs work:* see appendix.

WERNER, Michael, sculptor in bronze, stone, wood, polyester, concrete; *b* 27 July, 1912; *s* of Baron Vollrath von Alvensleben. *Educ.:* Austria and Oxford; *studied art* in Paris. *Exhib.:* Arts Council of Gt. Britain, London Gallery, Musée de l'Art Moderne, R.A., Norwich Festival (1961), Gallery Semiha Huber, Zürich, I.C.A., Blenheim Palace (1969), Woburn (1970), Art Spectrum, London (1971), Beaux Arts Gallery (one-man shows 1952,1954 and 1955); one-man shows: Obelisk Gallery (1956, 1959), Molton Gallery (1961), Hamilton Galleries (1964), Bradford City Museum (1965), Oxford Gallery, Oxford (1970), Runhof Gallery, Cologne (1971), I.C.A., London (1974), Annely Juda Fine Art (1975). *Official purchases:* County Museum, Los Angeles, Stellenbosche Museum, S.A.; Mural of 18 Panels for Foxford Comprehensive Sec. School, Coventry (1957); Smithsonian Institution, Washington (Bust of W. H. Auden). Lecturer in Fine Art, Watford School of Art. *Work repro.:* in various publications. *Address:* 15 Parliament Hill, London NW3. *Signs work:* "WERNER."

WERTHER, Marianne V., R.B.A., (1957); artist in water-colour and chalk; *d* of Felix Strakosch. *Studied art* at Vienna Frauen Academy. *Exhib.:* R.A., R.B.A., R.I., N.E.A.C., S.G.A., Brighton, Bern etc.; one-man shows at the Brod Gallery; Lord Mayor's Award (1965). *Work in permanent collections:* Albertina, Vienna; Guildhall, London; London Museum; West of England Royal Academy; South London Art Gallery. *Address:* 11 Princes House, Kensington Park Rd., London W11. *Signs work:* "Marianne Werther."

WESSON, Edward, R.I. (1953), R.S.M.A. (1957), R.B.A. (1963); painter in oil, water-colour; *b* Blackheath, 29 Apr., 1910; *s* of Alfred Wesson (decd.); *m* Caroline E. Christer; one *d. Educ.:* Colfe Grammar School; *studied art:* self-taught. *Exhib.:* R.A., R.I., R.O.I., R.B.A., N.S., City of London and provincial galleries. *Work in permanent collections:* London Guildhall, National Maritime Museum, Maidstone Municipal Gallery. *Work repro.:* Posters for British Railways, National Savings Bank and in Water-Colour by Percy Bradshaw; contributor to Artist magazine, Leisure Painter. *Address:* Pilgrim Cottage, Warren Rd., Guildford. *Signs work:* see appendix.

WESTBROOK, Eric; director, Ministry for the Arts, Melbourne, Australia; director, National Gallery of Victoria, Melbourne, Australia (1956-73); director,

City Art Gallery, Auckland, N.Z. (1952-55); director, Wakefield Public A.G. and Museum (1947-50); chief exhbn. officer, Fine Arts Dept., British Council (1950-52); *b* London, 29 Sept., 1915; *s* of Ernest James Westbrook; *m* Ingrid; one *d*. *Educ.:* Alleyn's School, Dulwich; *studied art* at Battersea Polytechnic School of Art under H. Cogle, Clapham School of Art, Westminster School of Art and in Paris. *Publications:* Studio, Art News and Review, Public Opinion; articles and catalogues; frequent appearances on radio and television. *Address:* Premier's Dept., Melbourne, Australia.

WESTOBY, Sidney Walter; retired civil servant; artist in water-colour; *b* London, 17 Mar., 1903; *m;* one *d*. *Educ.:* L.C.C. Central School; *studied art* under the late C. Ross Burnett, R.I. *Exhib.:* R.I. *Address:* Chaffinches, 23 Half Acres, Bishop's Stortford, Herts. *Club:* Bishop's Stortford Art Soc. *Signs work:* "S. W. Westoby."

WESTWOOD, John, A.R.C.A. (1948), M.S.I.A.; director of Graphic Design at H.M.S.O.; designer for book production; *b* Bromley, 26 Sept., 1919; *s* of W. H. Westwood; *m* Margaret Wadsworth; two *s*. *Educ.:* Bromley County Grammar School; *studied art* at Bromley College of Art (1936-39) and R.C.A. (1940 and 1947-48). *Exhib.:* South Bank (1951). *Address:* 13 Tarleton Gdns., London SE23 3XN. *Club:* Double Crown.

WETHERED, Maud Llewellyn, sculpture prize, Slade School; sculptor, wood engraver, painter in oil and water-colour; *b* Bury, 15 Feb., 1898; *d* of Vernon Wethered, B.A., N.E.A.C. *Educ.:* Hampstead; *studied art* at Slade School. *Exhib.:* R.A., N.E.A.C., Soc. of Wood-engravers, Goupil, Redfern, Whitechapel Art Gallery, United Artists, Burlington House, Leeds, Liverpool, Manchester, Hull, Brighton, Melbourne, U.S.A., Fieldbourne Gallery (1975). *Work repro.:* Studio, Sphere, Observer, London Mercury, The New Woodcut, by Malcolm Salamon. *Publications:* The Life of Christ, Spencer's Epithalamium. *Address:* 16 New End Square, Hampstead, London NW3. *Signs work:* "M. L. Wethered."

WHARTON, Samuel Ernest, A.I.A.L. (Zürich and Lindau); gold medal, Tommaso Campanella Academy, Rome (1972); designer and draughtsman using oil, water-colour; *b* Beeston, 22 Mar., 1900; *s* of Ernest Augustus Wharton; *m* Gladys Bates; one *d*. *Educ.:* Beeston; *studied art* at Nottingham School of Art (1923-27, 1932-36) under Joseph Else, R.B.S., Arthur Spooner, R.B.A., and Birmingham School of Art (1928-29) under Sydney H. Metyard, R.B.S.A. *Exhib.:* R.A., R.I., R.B.S.A., R.S.A., United Soc. Artists, Nottingham, Coventry, Leamington, Blackpool, Paris Salon, 1965-73 (award, Hon. Mention for oil painting). *Address:* 39 The Riddings, Canley Gdns., Coventry. *Signs work:* see appendix.

WHEATON, Muriel, S.W.A., Mem. Cheltenham Group, Glos Soc. Artists; artist in water-colour and oil; *b* Exeter, 16 Mar., 1902; *d* of Frederick Wheaton; *m* W. R. Watkin; one *d*. *Educ.:* Maynard School, Exeter; *studied art* at Exeter Art School, Christchurch (N.Z.) School of Art, St. John's Wood School of Art, and under the late Kirkland Jamieson, R.B.A., etc. *Exhib.:* R.B.A., S.W.A., N.S., Cheltenham Group. *Address:* 226 Stroud Rd., Gloucester. *Signs work:* "MURIEL WHEATON."

WHEELER, Carol Rosemary; artist in oil; *b* London, 25 Apr., 1927; *d* of Sir Charles Wheeler, K.C.V.O., P.P.R.A. *Educ.:* privately; *studied art* at Royal Academy Schools under Philip Connard, R.A., and Henry Rushbury, R.A. (1946-51). *Exhib.:* R.A. and other London exhbns. *Address:* Woodreed Farmhouse, Five Ashes, Mayfield, Sussex. *Signs work:* "C. R. Wheeler."

WHEELER, H. Anthony, O.B.E. (1973), A.R.S.A. (1963), R.S.A. (1975), B.Arch. (Strath), F.R.I.B.A., P.R.I.A.S. (1973-75); architect and planner, senior partner Wheeler & Sproson, Kirkcaldy and Edinburgh; mem. of the Royal Fine Art Commission for Scotland, (1967-); trustee of the Scottish Civic Trust; *b* Stranraer, Scotland, 7 Nov., 1919; *m* Dorothy Jean Wheeler. *Studied architecture:* Glasgow School of Architecture under Prof. W. J. Smith, and Glasgow School of Art; graduated 1948; John Keppie Scholar, Rowand Anderson Studentship R.I.A.S. (1948); R.I.B.A. Grissell Gold Medallist (1948); R.I.B.A. Neale Bursar (1949). *Address:* Woodley, 34 Southerton Rd., Kirkcaldy. *Clubs:* Scottish Arts, Caledonian. *Signs work:* "H. A. Wheeler."

WHEELER, Muriel (Lady), F.R.B.S., Pres. S.W.A., Pres. Ridley Art Society, Pres. St. James's Art Society; sculptor, painter; *d* of Arthur Ward Bourne; *m* Charles Wheeler, P.P.R.A.; one *s*, one *d*. *Educ.:* privately, art colleges and abroad. *Exhib.:* over 60 works at Royal Academy, solo exhibitions invited by Wolverhampton Art Gallery, Reigate, and Forum Club. *Official purchases:* Newport Art Gallery, Wolverhampton Art Gallery. *Commissions:* King George VI Memorial Triptych, painted on wood, for Cape Town Cathedral (1956); sculpted and painted portraits, etc., for public and private patrons. *Work repro.:* R.A. Illustrated and other journals. *Addresses:* 22 Cathcart Rd., London SW10, and Woodreed Farmhouse, nr. Mayfield. *Clubs:* E.S.U., Pres. Art Section. *Signs work:* "Muriel Wheeler."

WHEELER, Zona Lorraine, B.F.A., F.I.A.L., N.S.M.P.; advertising designer, illustrator, painter; senior Art Director, McCormick-Armstrong Co. (1970); *b* Lindsborg, Kansas, 15 Feb., 1913; *d* of agriculturist and originator of U.S. Govt.-recognized species, Wheeler Sudan Grass. *Studied art* under Dr. Birger Sandzen, Bethany Coll., Lindsborg, American Academy of Art, Chicago, Wichita Art Assoc. School. *Exhib.:* Rugby, Boston, England, San Francisco Art Assoc. *Address:* 230 South Belmont, Wichita, 18, Kansas. *Clubs:* Nat. League of American Pen Women, Altrusa International, Nat. Soc. of Mural Painters.

WHISHAW, Anthony, A.R.C.A. (1955), Travelling Scholarship, R.C.A., Abbey Minor, British Council, Scholarship, prize, International Drawing Biennale, Perth (1973), Bayer Painting prize (1974), S.E.A.A. prize (1975); painter in oil; part-time teacher, Chelsea School of Art; *b* 22 May, 1930; *m* Jean Gibson; two *d*. *Studied art* at Chelsea School of Art (1948-52), Royal College of Art (1952-55). *Exhib.:* one-man shows: Madrid (1956), Roland, Browse and Delbanco (1960, 1961, 1963, 1965, 1968), I.C.A. (1971), New Art Centre (1972), Hoya (1974). *Work in permanent collections:* National Gallery, Melbourne, Australia, Seattle Museum, Arts Council, Coventry Museum, Leicester Museum, Carlisle A.G., Chantrey Bequest, Bolton A.G., Bayer Pharm., Western Australia A.G., Museo de Bahia, Brazil. *Address:* 7A Albert Pl., Victoria Rd., London W8. *Signs work:* "A. Whishaw."

WHITAKER, Rita Elizabeth, R.M.S. (1965), S.W.A.; artist, low stoving enamel on copper; *b* 3 Sept., 1936; *m;* two *s*. *Educ.:* Worthing Convent; *studied art* at Regent Street Polytechnic (1956), under Stuart Tresilion. *Exhib.:* Wild Life, R.I., R.M.S., S.W.A., Mall Galleries. *Work in permanent collection:* Gallery 33, Billingshurst. *Publications:* Paragon of Wines and Spirits Vols. I and II. *Address:* Pedlita Studio, 37 Houghton Bridge, Amberley, nr. Arundel, Sussex. *Signs work:* "R. E. Whitaker, R.M.S." and see appendix.

WHITCOMBE, Sydney, D.F.C., F.S.I.A.; art director; painter in oil and gouache; *b* Heaton Chapel, Cheshire, 1 Oct., 1916; *s* of Percy Whitcombe; *m* Margaret Whitcombe; one *s*, one *d*. *Educ.:* Chorlton High School, Manchester;

studied art at Manchester School of Art (1934) and privately (1935-37). *Exhib.:* Manchester (one-man show), various other exhbns. *Work repro.:* commercially and non-commercially in various national magazines. *Address:* 2 Trafalgar Rd., Ilkley, W. Yorks. *Signs work:* see appendix.

WHITE, Charles, D.F.A. (Lond.), F.R.S.A., S.G.A., F.F.P.S.; mem. European Group; founder mem. of Young Contemporaries; former Council mem. South Wales Group; former Head of Art Department, United World College; extra-mural lecturer (art), University of Wales; *b* London, 11 Feb., 1928; *s* of Albert John White; *m* Mary White, A.T.D., S.S.I., calligrapher, potter. *Educ.:* Stoneleigh; *studied art* at Sutton and Cheam School of Art (1943, 1945), Newport College of Art (1944), Kingston-upon-Thames School of Art (1946), Slade School of Painting, London University (1949), Germany under Kurt Rieger, London under William Coldstream, Claud Rogers, F. E. McWilliams, A. E. Halliwell, Ceri Richards. *Exhib.:* R.B.A., F.B.A., Suffolk St. Galleries, R.S.A., London; National Society; Hamburg; Paris; La Gallerie, Dieppe; National Gallery of Wales; Newport Art Gallery; Dillwyn Gallery and Glyn Vivien Gallery, Swansea; Arlington Galleries; Howard Roberts Gallery, Cardiff; Royal National Eisteddfod; Hereford City Art Gallery. Numerous one-man shows in England, Wales and France. *Work in permanent collections:* Her Majesty Queen Elizabeth II, H.R.H. Prince Charles, Secretary of State for Wales, Mayor of Zürich, Contemporary Art Society, National Museum of Wales, England, America, Canada, Germany, Belgium, France, Sweden, Holland and Luxembourg. *Agents:* Heals, Tottenham Ct. Rd., London; Louise King, Greenwich; Reynolds Gallery, The Barbican, Plymouth, Devon. *Address:* Old Castle House, The Triangle, Malmesbury, Wilts. *Signs work:* "Charles White."

WHITE, David, Des.R.C.A. (1959); ceramic designer and manufacturer; Joint Winner of the Duke of Edinburgh's Prize for Elegant Design (1960); *b* Margate, Kent, 27 June, 1934; *s* of C. H. P. White (decd.); *m* (1962) Diana Groves; one *s*, one *d*. *Studied art* at Thanet School of Art (1950-54) and Royal College of Art (1956-59). *Address:* 4 Callis Court Rd., Broadstairs, Kent.

WHITE, Elsie Maude, M.S.M.; miniaturist in oil; Organised Exhib. of Miniatures, Canterbury Centenary at MacDougal Art Gall. (1950); *b* Rangoria, Canterbury, N.Z., 1889; *d* of Thomas Boyd, Engineer; *m* Robert White; three *s*. *Educ.:* Richmond Public School, Christchurch, N.Z. *Exhib.:* R.A., R.I., S.M., Wellington, Auckland, Christchurch, Australian Art Soc. (Sydney), American Soc. of Miniature Painters (New York). *Official purchases:* by H.M. The Queen, MacDougal Art Gall. (min. of Dame Sybil Thorndike). *Work repro.:* in Art in N.Z., La Revue Moderne, Femina, N.Z. Freelance, N.Z. Weekly Review, N.Z. Woman's Weekly. *Address:* 54 Bowhill Rd., 7, Christchurch, N.Z. *Club:* Pioneer Descendants (Christchurch; hon. sec.). *Signs work:* "Elsie M. White" or "White."

WHITE, Erica, F.R.B.S. (Retd.), London University Diploma in Fine Arts; sculptor and painter; *d* of Frederic Charles White, solicitor. *Educ.:* St. George's School, Harpenden; Slade School Sculpture Scholarship (two years and painting prize); Central School of Arts and Crafts (British Inst. Scholarship in Sculpture); R.A. Schools (silver and bronze medallist); Feodora Gleichen Memorial Fund Grant. *Exhib.:* R.A., Glasgow and Brighton Fine Art Galleries, Bournemouth, etc. *Address:* South Cliff Cottage, 3 South Cliff, Bexhill-on-Sea, E. Sussex TN39 3EJ. *Signs work:* "ERICA WHITE" (surname beneath first name).

WHITE, Gabriel Ernest Edward Francis, C.B.E., B.A.; director of arts, Arts Council of Great Britain (1958-70); assistant director of art, Arts Council of Great Britain (1945-58); artist in oil, pastel and etcher; *b* Rome, 29 Nov., 1902; *s* of the late Ernest Arthur White; *m*, 1st (1928) Elizabeth Grace Ardizzone (d. 1958), 2nd (1963) Jane Elizabeth Kent Kingdon. *Educ.:* Downside School; Trinity College, Oxford; *studied art* at Westminster Art School (1927-30, Bernard Meninsky), The Central School of Arts and Crafts (1928-29, Fred Porter). *Exhib.:* London Group, Mayor Gallery, Cork Street, W.1. *Publications:* Sickert Drawings (in Art and Technics, 1952). *Address:* 88 Holmdene Ave., London SE24.

WHITE, Gwen, A.R.C.A.; author and artist in water-colour, tempera; *b* Exeter, Devon; second *d* of Sebastian Moreton White; *m* C. Rupert Moore, A.R.C.A.; three *s*. *Educ.:* The Maynard School, Exeter; *studied art* at Bournemouth School of Art and R.C.A. *Exhib.:* R.A. (tempera and water-colours). *Publications:* Ancient and Modern Dolls, The Toys' Adventures at the Zoo, A Book of Dolls (A. & C. Black); Ladybird, Ladybird, A Book of Pictorial Perspective, A World of Pattern (Murray); A Book of Toys (King Penguin); Dolls of the World (Mills & Boon); European and American Dolls (Batsford); Perspective (Batsford), also translated into Japanese and German; Antique Toys and their Background; Toys, Dolls, Automata, Marks & Labels (1975) (Batsford); Eight Little Frogs, and many stories with drawings for B.B.C. TV Children's Hour. *Address:* Tykesditch, Oakridge Ave., Radlett, Herts. *Signs work:* "Gwen White."

WHITE, Ianthe, S.W.A.; miniaturist in water-colour on ivory and oils; *b* London, 8 Oct., 1901; *d* of John Alfred White, banker; *m* A. V. Goodchild; one *s*. *Educ.:* Queen Anne's College, Westcliff; *studied art* at Bristol School of Art under H. Bush. *Exhib.:* S.W.A., Soc. of Miniaturists, R.M.S., etc. *Address:* Stonely House, Stonely, Huntingdonshire. *Signs work:* "Ianthe White."

WHITE, James; Director, National Gallery of Ireland, Merrion Sq., Dublin; formerly Curator, Municipal Gallery of Modern Art; Lecturer, Dublin and National Universities. *Publications:* The National Gallery of Ireland (Thames & Hudson); Irish Stained Glass (Gill & Co.); Jack B. Yeats (Martin Secker & Warburg); John Butler Yeats and the Irish Renaissance (Dolmen Press). *Address:* 15 Herbert Pk., Ballsbridge, Dublin 4.

WHITE, James Noël, M.A.(Cantab.), F.R.S.A., A.S.D-C.; Hon. Degree Archæology and Anthropology; Silver Medal R.S.A. (1968); author and design consultant, lecturer; vice-president, World Crafts Council; chairman, Crafts Study Centre; president, Assoc. of Guilds of Weavers, Spinners and Dyers; president, Devon Guild of Craftsmen; Hon. Brother, A.W.G., associate, British Crafts Centre; *b* 18 Dec., 1917; *s* of T. Noël White, F.C.A. *Educ. and studied art* at Oundle School and Cambridge University. *Publication:* Management of Design Services (Allen & Unwin). *Address:* Comp End, Great Comp, Platt, nr. Sevenoaks, Kent TN15 8QS. *Club:* Farmers'. *Signs work:* "J. Noël White."

WHITE, John Henry, Master Mariner (1938), A.R.B.S. (1970); sculptor in metal and timber; *b* Penzance, Cornwall, 1909; *s* of Col. J. H. White, Royal Eng. (rtd.), C.M.G., V.D., M.I.C.E.; *m* Eliz. F. Martin; one *s*. *Educ.:* Victoria College, Jersey, H.M.S. Worcester; *studied art:* selt-taught. *Exhib.:* R.A., R.S.A., St. Brendan's Church, Saltcoats. *Work in permanent collections:* Livingston, Dr. Robin MacTaggart, Alan Reid, British Corp., Ross-on-Wye. *Publications:* Revised Nautical Tables. *Address:* 23 Haylie Gdns., Largs, Ayrshire. *Signs work:* "J. H. White."

WHITE, John Norman, N.D.D. (1951); painter, illustrator and fashion artist, oil, gouache, and water-colour; *b* Chipperfield, Herts., 27 Mar., 1932; *s* of John Eugene White. *Educ.:* Belmont Senior Modern School; *studied art* at Harrow School of Art (1945-51). *Exhib.:* R.A., Young Contemporaries. *Address:* Northwood Lodge, Bullockstone Rd., Herne, Herne Bay, Kent. *Signs work:* "JOHN—WHITE."

WHITE, Mary; ceramic artist and calligrapher; *b* Croesyceiliog, Wales; *née* Rollinson; *m* Charles White. *Educ. and studied art* at St. Julian's High School, Newport, Mon.; Newport College of Art; L.C.C. Hammersmith College of Art; London University Goldsmiths' College of Art. *Work in permanent collections:* Leicester Educ. Authority, Newport Museum and A.G., Aberystwyth University, V. & A. (calligraphy). *Work repro.:* Ceramic Review, Ceramic Monthly, C.A.C. Index of Craftsmen. *Address:* Old Castle House, The Triangle, Malmesbury, Wilts. *Clubs:* S.S.I., Crafts Centre of Gt. Britain, Craftsmen Potters Assoc., S.Đ-C., S. Wales Potters. *Signs work:* see appendix.

WHITEHEAD, Margaret della Rovere, R.C.A., S.W.A., DA. and Post Dip., Glas., A.T.D.; lecturer in art, Lincoln Training College (1928-30); head, Dept. of Women's Arts and Crafts, Chesterfield School of Art and Crafts (1930-38); lecturer in Art and Crafts, Normal College, Bangor (1939-41); *b* London; *d* of the late Ernesto Grillo, M.A., D.Litt., LL.D., Prof. of Italian Studies, Glasgow University; *m* the late Tatham Whitehead, O.B.E., Ph.D., M.Sc., A.R.C.Sc. *Educ.:* Cedars, Leamington; *studied art* at Glasgow School of Art. *Exhib.:* R.Cam.A., S.W.A., Arts Council of Gt. Britain Exhbn., U.S.A. and Canada, National Eisteddfod of Wales, etc. *Address:* Crag Side, Penrhos Drive, Bangor, Gwynedd. *Signs work:* "M. della R.W."

WHITLOCK, John: see CODNER, John Whitlock.

WHITTICK, Arnold, diploma History of Art (Lond.); F.R.S.A.; writer and lecturer on art and architecture; designer and water-colourist; *b* Ilford, 17 May, 1898; *m* Helen Miller; one *d. Studied art* at Croydon School of Art (1918-21), S. London Technical Art School (1921-23). *Publications:* Symbols for Designers (1935), History of Cemetery Sculpture—Ancient to Early Christian (1938), Eric Mendelsohn (1940 and 1955), War Memorials (1946), The Small House Today and Tomorrow (1947 and 1957), European Architecture in the Twentieth Century (1950-53-74), Symbols, Signs and Their Meanings (1960 and 1971), New Towns with Sir Frederic Osborn (1963 and 1969), Encyclopedia of Urban Planning (Editor) 1974. *Address:* 4 Netherwood, Gossops Green, Crawley, Sussex.

WICKHAM, Geoffrey Earle, A.R.C.A. Painting (1949), F.R.B.S. (1967); painter and sculptor; principal lecturer, Fine Art Dept., City of London Polytechnic; *b* Wembley, Middx., 10 July, 1919; *s* of Wallace Earle Wickham, decd.; *m* Gisela Albrecht, potter; five *s. Educ.:* Latymer Upper School, Willesden School of Art and Craft (1935-38), Royal College of Art (1946-49). *Exhib.:* N.E.A.C., R.B.A., London Group, S.E.A., R.B.S., A.I.A., Leicester and Alwin galleries. Main works in architectural context in England and abroad. R.B.S. Sculpture of the Year 1972 for Fountainhead, in Belgravia. Private collections in England and U.S.A. *Address:* 45 Ashley Rd., London N19 3AG. *Signs work:* "Geoffrey Wickham" or "GEW."

WICKHAM, Hilary Judith; fashion and commercial artist in black and white and wash; writer; *b* Wallasey, Ches., 1912; *d* of George B. Thompson; *m. Educ.:* Birkenhead High School; *studied art* at Liverpool School of Art (1929-32) and under Sigrid Hunt (1935-38). *Work repro.:* leading provincial newspapers, women's magazines; also book illustrations. *Address:* 4 Mid Shore, St Monans, Fife. KY10 2BA. *Signs work:* "Hilary."

WICKHAM, Mabel Frances, R.I. (1938), S.W.A. (1936); landscape painter, lecturer and teacher; *b* 29 Dec., 1901; *d* of Dr. Gilbert H. Wickham, M.D. *Educ.:* St. Swithin's School, Winchester; Clapham High School Art Training College (1919-23); also under St. Clair Marston, R.O.I., R.B.A., and John Nash R.A.

Exhib.: R.A., R.O.I., and municipal galleries. *Official purchases:* Weymouth Corporation, Sherborne U.D.C. *Address:* Folly Barn, 8 Belle Vue Rd., Rodwell, Weymouth, Dorset DT4 8RX. *Signs work:* "M. F. Wickham" (with long stroke from under "m").

WICKS, Helen Cecile, A.T.D.; painter and illustrator in oil and pen and ink; *b* London. *Educ.:* Froebel Educational Inst. and St. Paul's Girls' School; *studied art* at St. Martin's School of Art under James Bateman, R.A., Ruskin Spear, R.A., Kenneth Green. *Exhib.:* R.A., R.P. and provincial galleries. *Work repro.:* in Illustrated London News, Radio Times, Tempo, Opera, Musical Europe, House & Garden. *Address:* 16 Lawns Court, The Avenue, Wembley, Middlesex. *Signs work:* "Helen C. Wicks" or "Helen Wicks."

WIELICZKO, Jan; painter, sculptor and designer; Director, Centaur Gallery, London; lecturer and demonstrator, Slade School (1949); *b* Wilno, Poland, 1928; *s* of Boleslaw Wieliczko; *m* Dinah Wieliczko; two *s*. *Educ.:* Wilno, Poland; *studied art* at Slade School, London (1945-48) (1st prize Decorative Painting). *Exhib.:* Irving Gallery (1953), Redfern Gallery (1954), Centaur Gallery; all the principal mixed exhbns. in London 1949. *Address:* 82 Highgate High St., London N6. *Signs work:* "J. Wieliczko."

WILC: see Wilczynski, Katerina.

WILCOX, Leslie Arthur, R.I., R.S.M.A., S.A.A.; artist in oil, water-colour and line; R.N. (1941); camouflage officer (1941-45); *b* Fulham, 1904; *s* of William Wilcox, solicitor; *m* Alice Spurgeon; three *s*. *Educ.:* Chelsea; *studied art:* self-taught. *Exhib.:* R.I., R.B.A., R.O.I., R.S.W. and provincial galleries. *Work in permanent collections:* National Maritime Museum, Greenwich; Government House, Jamaica; shipping offices in U.K. and America, and regimental barracks in U.K. and Canada. Numerous *private collections*, including: H.M. The Queen (for the Royal Yacht, Britannia), H.R.H. The Duke of Edinburgh, A. S. Onassis, Garfield Weston, Dr. Beppe Croce, H.E. Dr. H. Luttig, the S.A. Ambassador. *Work repro.:* British Railways posters, illustrations for maritime journals and industrial concerns. *Publications:* A Book of Ships, Mr. Pepys' Navy, Anson's Voyage. *Address:* 45 Cove Rd., Rustington, Sussex. *Signs work:* "L. A. WILCOX."

WILCZYNSKI, Katerina, Scholarship Akademie, Berlin; Prix de Rome (1930); artist in water-colour, pen drawing, etching; *b* 7 July, 1894; *d* of Hans Wilczynski. *Educ.:* Berlin; Leipzig, Akademie für Graphische, Kunste; Kunstgewerbeschule, Berlin (1918); Akademie d. Künste; Paris (freelance). *Exhib.:* William Ware Gallery, Olives, Rocks and Kaïques (1967), Ansdell Gallery, Greece Remembered (1970), Dresden, Köln, Berlin, Rome, London. *Work in permanent collections:* Print Room B.M., V. & A., Ashmolean Museum, Oxford, Bibliothèque Nationale, Paris, Kunstbibliothek Berlin. *Official purchases:* V. & A., Nat. Portrait Gallery, Dresden, Köln, London, N.Y. *Work repro.:* Querschnitt, Berlin, France Libre, Geographical Magazine, Studio, London Magazine, etc., Daphnis and Chloe, Exhibition, British Council, Athens (1964). *Publications:* Ancient Greece; The Roman Cookery Book; Homage to Greece (Macmillan, 1964); drawings for the Love Songs of Sappho (New American Library, N.Y., 1966). *Address:* 12 Bedford Gdns., London W8. *Signs work:* "WILC."

WILES, Alec, L.S.I.A.; portrait, marine and landscape painter, illustrator, sculptor; Punch artist; *b* Southampton, 1 Jan., 1934; *s* of Harry C. Wiles; three *d*. *Educ.:* St. Mark's School, Southampton; *studied art* at Southampton School of Art. *Exhib.:* R.A., R.P., R.B.A., S.G.A., Penwith Soc., Newlyn Soc., New York, various provincial galleries. *Address:* Bethel Studio, Twelveheads, Truro, Cornwall. *Clubs:* Penwith Soc. of Artists, Newlyn Soc. of Artists, St. Ives Soc. of Artists, S.I.A. *Signs work:* "ALEC WILES," and see appendix.

WILKINSON, Alfred L., M.G.P. (1936); hon. sec. (1952-58); designer in stained glass; *b* 14 Oct., 1899; *s* of Horace Wilkinson, master glass painter; *m*; one *d. Educ.:* Stationers' Companys' School; *studied art* at St. Martin's School of Art and privately. *Exhib.:* R.A., etc. *Address:* 596 Main Rd., Dovercourt, Harwich, Essex CO12 4LN. *Signs work:* initials with stag's antlers.

WILKINSON, Ronald Scotthorn, M.A., B.M., B.Ch. (Oxon.); physician, playwright, novelist, artist in oil, water-colour; *b* Melton Mowbray; *s* of T. G. Wilkinson, B.Sc.; two *d. Educ.:* Shrewsbury School, Merton College, Oxford; *studied art* under H. B. Hewlett. *Exhib.:* Public Schools Exhbn., Leicester Soc. of Artists' Exhbn., Medical Art Soc. *Work repro.:* in British Medical Bulletin. *Addresses:* 11 Wimpole St., London W1; and Richards Cottage, High Street, Burford, Oxon. *Signs work:* "RONALD."

WILKINSON-CLEMENTSON, William Henry, R.E., A.R.C.A., F.I.A.L. (1946); line engraver and painter; Head of Dept. Engraving, City and Guilds of London Art School; *b* Bath, 1921; *s* of H. R. Wilkinson, A.R.C.A., Head, Bath School of Art; *m* Lady Margaret Ewer; one *d. Educ.:* Winchester; *studied art* at Royal College of Art under Malcolm Osborne and Robert Austin, Heidelberg and Lindau, Germany, Fiorenza, Italy. *Work in permanent collections:* Holland, Switzerland, Italy and America. *Address:* Crane Cottage, Tatsfield, Westerham, Kent. *Clubs:* Chelsea Arts, Aviemore, Scotland, Swiss Alpine. *Signs work:* "HENRY WILKINSON."

WILLETTS, William Young, B.Sc. (Bristol, 1940), M.A. (Lond., 1946), B.A. (Oxon, 1950), F.R.S.A.; art historian; Curator of Art Museum, University of Malaya; *b* Purton Stoke, Wilts., 28 Nov., 1918; *s* of Joseph Willetts, compositor. *Educ.:* Rendcomb College, Cirencester, Glos.; *studied art* at Courtauld Institute of Art under Prof. Perceval Yetts. *Publications:* Chinese Art (2 vols.), Foundations of Chinese Art, Ceramic Art of South-east Asia. *Address:* University of Malaya, Pantai Valley, Kuala Lumpur, Malaysia. *Signs work:* "William Willetts."

WILLIAMS, Aubrey Sendall; Commonwealth Prize for Painting (1964); awarded Golden Arrow for Achievement (Guyana, 1970); painter in all plastic mediums; advisor, Guyana Festival of Art (1972); *b* Georgetown, B.G., 8 May, 1926; *s* of Walter Williams; *m* Eve. *Educ.:* Georgetown, B.G.; *studied art* at St. Martin's School of Art (1952-53). *Exhib.:* Expo '67, Sao Paulo Biennale (1973), San Francisco (1973-74), N.W. University, Chicago (1975); ten-year retro. Olympia Art Centre, Kingston (1975). *Work in permanent collections:* York A.G., York, University of York; Guyana: House of Assembly, Georgetown, Colgrain House, Georgetown, Timerhi Airport, Rice Marketing Board, Georgetown Museum; Murals: Park Forest, Ill., Sligoville, Jamaica, Olympia Art Centre, Jamaica; Portraits: Duke Ellington, P.H. Brooklyn, Fidel Castro, Cuba, Linden Forbes, Burnham, Guyana, Dr. Eric Williams, Trinidad. *Work repro.:* The Wild Coast (Jan Carew); backdrops, The Day of the Fox (A.T.V.); Series of TV programmes U.S.A. (1972-73). *Address:* 101 Greencroft Gdns., London NW6. *Signs work:* "Aubrey Williams."

WILLIAMS, Guy R. O., A.T.D., Saxon Barton Prize (1950); artist in oil; wood-engraver; teaches at Parmiter's School; *b* Mold, Flint, 23 Aug., 1920; *s* of Dr. Owen E. Williams. *Educ.:* St. Edward's School, Oxford; *studied art* at Manchester College of Art (1937-40) and Hornsey School of Art (1946-50). *Exhib.:* R.A., R.B.A., S.E.A., A.I.A., London and provincial galleries. *Official* *purchases:* L.C.C. *Publications:* author of the "Use Your" books (Chapman & Hall); Pencil Drawing (Pitman); Enjoy Painting in Oils (Gollancz); Woodworking Step by Step and Drawing and Sketching Step by Step (Museum Press); Collecting Pictures and Making Mobiles (Arco). *Address:* 1A Earl Rd., London SW14 7JH.

WILLIAMS, Hubert John, P.S.; landscape and portrait painter and illustrator; *b* May, 1905; *s* of Thomas Williams, schoolmaster; *m* Edna May Spencer; one *s*, one *d*. *Educ.:* Beckenham County School; *studied art* at R.A. Schools, Landseer Scholarship, St. Martin's School of Art; Central L.C.C. School. *Exhib.:* R.A., and principal galleries. *Work in permanent collections:* Imperial War Museum, London Guildhall, Southampton Art Gallery, Towner Art Gallery, Eastbourne, Hastings Museum, Yarmouth, Letchworth, Bath, etc. *Books illustrated:* The President's Hat, Underwater Naturalist, Britain under the Romans, and books for children. *Address:* The Studio, High St., Blockley, Glos. *Club:* Reynolds. *Signs work:* "HUBERT WILLIAMS."

WILLIAMS, Idris Elgina; equine artist, portrait drawings of show horses, also intimate studies of horses and foals; stud book illustrations; *b* Birmingham; *d* of Richard Francis Williams. *Educ.:* St. Agnes' Convent, Birmingham, Royal Drawing Soc., Hons. Standard; *studied art* at Birmingham College of Art. Union of Educational Institutions, First place with Distinction; Ryland Scholarship; Board of Education Examinations in Drawing and Painting. Former art critic, Birmingham Evening Despatch and Wolverhampton Express and Star. *Exhib.:* Midland Federation of Photography Exhbns., Alderman Cobb Trophy (1968). *Publications:* Welsh Pony and Cob Society Stud Book and Journal, Catalogue: Ponies of Britain. *Address:* Bramble Cottage, New Quay, Dyfed SA45 9RF. *Clubs:* Sutton Coldfield Photographic Soc., Cardiganshire Art Soc. *Signs work:* "IDRIS AERON."

WILLIAMS, Ivor; portrait painter; *b* 15 Mar., 1908; *s* of Christopher Williams, R.B.A.; *m* Elizabeth, *d* of Sidney Pocock; four *d*. *Educ.:* King Alfred School, Hampstead; *studied art* at Central School of Art, Slade School. *Exhib.:* R.A., R.P., R.B.A., N.E.A.C. *Official purchases:* Sir Winston Churchill receiving Freedom of City of Cardiff; Field-Marshal Lord Montgomery receiving Freedom of Newport; the Welsh Regiment receiving Freedom of Cardiff; Dr. Thos. Jones and the Rev. Phillip Jones, for National Museum of Wales. Portraits: Lord Harlech, Sir Emrys Evans, Sir Frederick Rees. *Work repro.:* portrait for I.C.I. Series. *Address:* Llandaff House, Llandaff, Cardiff. *Signs work:* "Ivor Williams."

WILLIAMS, Joan Barbara Price, A.R.C.A., R.E., A.R.W.S.; printmaker and illustrator; Head of Printmaking Dept., Maidstone College of Art; *b* Pontypridd, S. Wales; *d* of R. P. Williams, B.A. *Educ.:* High Wycombe High School; *studied art* at High Wycombe School of Art, Royal College of Art. *Exhib.:* R.A., R.E., International Biennales of Graphic Art, Ljubljana, Yugoslavia, and Frechen, Germany. A member of the Printmakers' Council of Great Britain and exhibits in P.M.C. shows in London and abroad. *Work in public collections:* includes the Arts Council, Sheffield, Oldham, Newcastle, Norwich, Glasgow and Hull Art Galleries and many university collections. *Address:* 42 Rochester Rd., Aylesford, Kent. *Signs work:* "Joan Williams."

WILLIAMS, Jolán, F.I.A.L., W.I.A.C., A.I.A., F.P.S.; painter and graphic artist; *b* Austria; *m* D. Jeffrey Williams. *Educ.:* privately; *studied art* in Vienna, Cracow, Munich, London. *Exhib.:* Vienna, Cracow, Amsterdam, Bergen, Paris, Toronto, the U.K. and provinces; R.A., N.E.A.C., R.B.A., R.O.I., London Group, Senefelder Club, S.W.E., A.I.A., W.I.A.C., F.P.S., S.E.A., Leicester Gallery,

Leger Gallery, Redfern Gallery, etc., 25th Jubilee Exhbn. of A.I.A. (1958), Guggenheim Award Exhbn., Whitechapel A.G. (1958); under auspices of Arts Council in Scotland; one-man shows: Vienna Studio, Wertheim Gallery, Beaux Arts Gallery, Foyer Gallery, New Vision Centre, Drian Gallery, University of Surrey. *Work repro.:* Penguin Parade, Apollo, Connoisseur, and Continental magazines. *Work in public and private collections:* Herts. Educ. Authority; T.S. Library, Madras; Austria, Poland, Yugoslavia, Norway, Hungary, Holland, U.K., Canada, Switzerland, U.S.A. *Address:* 120 Loudoun Rd., London NW8 0ND. *Signs work:* "Jolán Williams," (before 1939 "Jolán Polatschek-Williams.")

WILLIAMS, Mary, R.W.A., S.W.A.; painter of landscape, marine and architectural subjects, also of flowers in water-colour and oil; *b* Ottery St. Mary, Devon; *d* of Fred Williams. *Studied art* at Exeter. *Exhib.:* R.A., R.S.A., Paris Salon, R.I., R.B.A., etc., and in many municipal galleries; one-man show: R.A.M. Museum, Exeter (1974). *Work in permanent collections:* Exeter Art Gallery, Sunderland Art Gallery, R.W.A. Bristol. *Address:* Dormers, Orchard Close, Manor Rd., Sidmouth, Devon. *Club:* R.W.S. Art. *Signs work:* "Mary Williams."

WILLIAMS, Norah Marguerite; commercial artist, illustrator; Cadbury Bros. Ltd. (1928-31); occ. therapist, Ipswich & East Suffolk Hospital (1941-75); craft instructress, Ipswich Civic College (1960-73); *b* Birmingham, 1906; *d* of Leonard John Skinner; *m* Edward Williams; one *s*. *Educ.:* King Edward VI G.S., Birmingham; *studied art* at Birmingham School of Arts and Crafts, Birmingham. *Exhib.:* Ipswich Art Club. *Work repro.:* designs for Cadbury Bros., Nursing Mirror, House of Deeko, Women's Gas Federation, East Anglian Daily Times, Golf Illustrated, Sunday Telegraph. *Address:* 55 Lattice Ave., Ipswich. *Publication:* illustrated Be Patient, Your Life in Their Hands, by Anthea Cohen. *Signs work:* "Norah M. Williams," and see appendix.

WILLIAMS, Peter Ernest, N.D.D., A.T.D., F.R.S.A.; artist in oils, water-colour, plaster, wood, metal, terra-cotta, ceramics; Head of Art Department, Oldershaw Grammar School; muralist and designer for exhbn. and shop-window display; *b* Bebington, 25 Jan., 1925; *s* of John Henry Williams; *m* 1st, Muriel E. Hammer, B.Sc. (*d* 25 June, 1964); 2nd, Patricia D. Wilson; two *s*, one *d*. *Educ.:* Wirral Grammar School; *studied art* at Liverpool College of Art. *Exhib.:* Liverpool Academy of Arts, etc. *Work in permanent collections:* Liverpool University and mural decorations in several churches. *Address:* Hedge-Lea, 43 Higher Bebington Rd., Bebington, Wirral, Ches. *Signs work:* "Peter E. Williams."

WILLIAMS, Vera K., R.M.S.Hon. retd., S.M., S.W.A.; mem. Guildford Art Society; miniaturist artist in water-colour and oil; *b* Witley, Surrey, 4 Aug., 1912; *m* the late Capt. R. Weir-Davis. *Educ.:* Witley, Surrey; *studied art* at Godalming Art School (1928) under W. Victor Burmand. *Exhib.:* regularly from 1933-70 at R.A., R.M.S., S.M., Soc. British Women Artists, Royal Portrait Soc., Chenil A.G., Leighton House and one-man shows (1937-38). *Publication:* Painting Miniatures. *Address:* 31 St. Ann's Villas, London W11 4RT. *Club:* Abbotswood Sketching. *Signs work:* "VERA K. WILLIAMS" (date written in tail of the S.)

WILLIAMS, Vivian Claud Craddock, M.A. (Oxon.); freelance writer and illustrator; Kensington and Chelsea Arts Council (1968); Council of Industrial Design (1959-62); artist in oil, pen and wash; exhibition designer; *b* Hampstead, 3 Mar., 1936; *s* of M. S. A. Williams. *Educ.:* Stouts Hill, Uley, Glos.; Repton School, Derbyshire; *studied art* at Repton School under Arthur Norris and Dennis Hawkins. *Exhib.:* Wye Valley Art Soc. Exhbn., Coleford Art Exhbn., Chelsea Pottery Exhbn. (1962). *Addresses:* 18 Linver Rd., London SW6 and Brasted House, Monmouth. *Signs work:* "V.C.C.W."

WILLIAMS-ELLIS, Sir Clough, Kt. (1972), C.B.E., M.C., LL.D., J.P., F.R.I.B.A., M.T.P.I., F.I.L.A., etc.; architect, town-planner, author; pres., D.I.A., chairman, C.P.R.W., Stevenage New Town Development Corp.; founder of Portmeirion, etc.; *b* Gayton, Northants, 28 May, 1883; *m* Amabel Strachey, author; one *s*, two *d* (one, Susan, is a painter). *Exhib.:* R.A. only. *Publications:* Cottage Building, England and the Octopus, The Architect, The Face of the Land, Sir Laurence Weaver, The Tank Corps, The Pleasures of Architecture, Architecture Here and Now, Britain and the Beast, Architect Errant (autobiography), etc. *Address:* Plas Brondanw, Penrhyndeudraeth, Gwynedd. *Clubs:* Athenæum, Lansdowne, Royal Welsh Yacht. *Signs work:* "Clough Williams-Ellis."

WILLIAMSON, Harold Sandys, O.B.E.; painter and designer; headmaster, Chelsea School of Art (1930-58); *b* Leeds, 1892; *s* of A. P. Williamson. *Educ.:* Leeds Grammar School; *studied art* at Leeds School of Art (1911-14) and R.A. Schools (1914-15). *Exhib.:* R.A., London Group, Leicester Galleries, etc. *Work in permanent collections:* Imperial War Museum, Wakefield, Manchester, etc. *Work repro.:* Studio, Radio Times, Gebrauchsgrafik, Signature, etc. *Publications:* contributions to Burlington Magazins Horizon, Signature, Introducing the Orchestra, etc. *Address:* 47 Newmarket Rd., Norwich, NOR 22D. *Signs work:* "H. S. WILLIAMSON" (block letters).

WILLIS, John Henry, R.B.A. (1922), A.R.C.A. (1918); painter in tempera, oil and water-colour of portraits, figure subjects, mural decorations, etc.; *s* of R. Willis, art dealer; *m* E. Rushton (*née* Claughton); one *s*. *Educ.:* Armstrong College, Durham University, R.C.A. *Exhib.:* R.A., and London and provincial galleries. *Official purchases:* mural decoration, Laing Art Gallery, Newcastle upon Tyne. *Work repro.:* in Studio, Continental and American magazines. *Address:* The Studio, 20 Titchfield Gdns., Paignton, Devon. *Signs work:* "J. H. WILLIS."

WILLOUGHBY, Trevor John, R.P. (1970); painter in oil, chalk, pastel; illustrator, teacher; teaching at St. Martin's College of Art, Sir John Cass College of Art; *b* Hull, Yorks., 1926; *s* of F. T. Willoughby; three *s*. *Educ.:* Hymers College, Hull; Belfast Technical College; *studied art* at Kingston upon Hull College of Art; London School of Printing. *Exhib.:* R.A., R.P., Compendium Gallery, Arts Unlimited, Rye Gallery, Ogilby, Benson & Mather, Quangle Prints, Queen's Elm Gallery, Chenil Gallery, R.B.A. *Work repro.:* illustrations in Queen magazine; Homes and Gardens; Fashions and Fabrics; leading advertisers. *Address:* 4 Offerton Rd., Clapham Common, London SW4. *Club:* Chelsea Arts. *Signs work:* "Willoughby."

WILLS, Ferelyth A.; sculptress in wood, stone, metal; artist in brush and ink; *b* London, 15 Aug., 1916; *d* of W. N. Howard; *m* S. B. Wills; three *d*. *Educ.:* The Hall School, Weybridge; and St. Leonard's School, St. Andrews; *studied art* at L.C.C. Central School of Arts and Crafts under J. Skeaping (1935-39). *Exhib.:* R.A., Crafts Centre of Gt. Britain, Society of Designer Craftsmen, Petersfield Arts and Crafts Soc. *Work repro.:* in The Field, Flight, Handmade Woodwork of the 20th Century. *Publication:* Co-author with Bill Wills, Sculpture in Wood (David & Charles 1975). *Address:* The Camp, Steep, Petersfield, Hants. *Clubs:* Fellow of the Society of Designer Craftsmen, Petersfield Arts and Crafts Soc. *Signs work:* "Ferelyth Wills."

WILSON, Avray Frank (Frank Avray-Wilson), M.A., Cantab. artist in oil, gouache, lithography; biologist; writer; *b* Vacoas, Mauritius, 5 May, 1914; *s* of Albert James Wilson, planter; *m* Ivy Else Eckbo; three *s*, one *d*. *Educ.:* Brighton College and St. John's College, Cambridge; *studied art* at Nice and Oslo. *Exhib.:* R.A., Redfern Gallery, Galerie Internationale Paris, and in Belgium, Switzerland,

Germany, France. *Work in permanent collections:* Southampton Art Gallery, Leeds, Leicester Art Gallery, Musée de Liége, Carnegie, Cleveland, Manchester Art Gallery, Glynn Vivian Art Gallery, Liverpool, Durham, Eastbourne, Toledo Art Gallery, Ohio, Contemporary Art Society, Wakefield Education, Leicestershire Education Authorities, Worcester College, Oxford, Ministry of Education. *Addresses:* 06 130 Le Tignet France; 6 Pembroke Studios, London W8.

WILSON, Eleanor Mavis: see GRÜNEWALD, Eleanor Mavis.

WILSON, Eunice Mary, N.S.A.M., M.S.I.A.; shoe designer, oil painter, journalist; *b* Bradford, Yorks, 14 July, 1921; *d* of Joseph Arnold Wilson, A.M.I.E.E. *Educ.:* High School, Stafford; *studied art* at Birmingham School of Art, M. R. Ridley, principal; Stafford School of Art under William Cartledge. *Work repro.:* Dolcis Shoes, C. & J. Clark, Lotus, Dunlop, etc.; illustrations to own articles on shoes, fashion, travel. *Publications:* History of Shoe Fashion (Pitmans), various articles in trade Press, short stories, etc. *Address:* 143 Harbord St., London SW6. *Signs work:* "Eunice Wilson."

WILSON, Helen, Vice-President, Pastel Society; Founder and Principal Heatherley-Wilson School of Art Ltd.; artist in oil and pastel; silver medal for drawing (1925) and Arthur Hacker Prize for oil portrait (1926) at R.A. Schools; *b* London, June, 1903; *d* of Rev. William Wilson, min. of Church of Scotland; *m* Dr. M. Rosenfield (decd.). *Educ.:* Dumfries Academy; *studied art* at Glasgow School of Art (under Forrester Wilson) and R.A. Schools (under Charles Sims). *Exhib.:* P.S., N.E.A.C., R.B.A., Leicester Galleries. *Work reproduced and articles published:* in The Artist. Lectures and demonstrates to art societies. *Address:* 92 Fellows Rd., Hampstead, London NW3. *Signs work:* "Wilson."

WILSON, James H., B.A., F.M.A.; chief asst. curator, Sunderland Museum and Art Gallery since 1947; asst. curator, Salford City Art Gallery (1938-47); *b* Salford, Lancs, 25 Mar., 1917. *Educ.:* Salford Grammar School and Victoria University (Manchester). *Address:* 14 W. Drive, Cleadon, Co. Durham.

WILSON, Michael; painter in oil, water-colour and etching; *b* Liverpool, 27 Jan., 1951; *s* of F. X. Wilson. *Studied art* at Wolverhampton School of Art. *Exhib.:* two-man show at Allerton Gallery, Liverpool (1976). *Address:* 73 Gainsborough Ave., Maghull, Liverpool. *Signs work:* "Michael Wilson."

WILSON, Robert Arthur, A.R.C.A. (1911); Govt. National Scholar (1907); R.C.A. Scholar; Medallist and Prizeman, Julian's, Paris; painter in oil, tempera and water-colour; instructor in London and Surrey art schools for many years; *s* of William James Wilson; *m;* two *s,* one *d, Educ.:* Monkwearmouth; *studied art* at Sunderland College of Art; R.C.A. under Gerald Moira; Julian's Academy, Paris, under Jean-Paul Laurens; Tudor-Hart, Paris and London. *Exhib.:* R.A., Paris Salon, Painters in Tempera, etc. *Official purchases:* B.M. and V. & A. (drawings, colour prints), Sunderland Art Gallery. *Work repro.:* in Studio, Artist, Colour, etc. *Publications:* Tempera Craftsmanship, The Uses of Colour. *Address:* Dorland Cottage, Church La., Bletchingley, Surrey. *Signs work:* "R. A. WILSON."

WILSON, Stella Louise, S.W.A.; painter in water-colour, tempera; *b* Dulwich; *d* of Frederic Louis Perken; *m* R. A. Wilson; two *s,* one *d. Educ.:* Forest Hill School; *studied art* at Camberwell School of Art. *Exhib.:* R.A., S.W.A., Paris Salon, provinces. *Work repro.:* Paris Salon catalogue. *Address:* Dorland Cottage, Church La., Bletchingley, Surrey.

WILSON, Vincent John, A.T.D., R.C.A., Mem. Newlyn Soc. of Artists, Plymouth Soc. of Artists; painter and etcher; *b* Mold, Flintshire, 24 Nov., 1933; *s* of J. Wilson; *m* Sheila Richards; one *d. Educ.:* Alun Grammar School, Mold;

studied art at Chester School of Art (1950-54), Liverpool College of Art (1954-55). *Exhib.:* R.A., R.W.A., R.C.A., Piccadilly, Thackeray, Penwith Galleries, Celle, W. Germany, Welsh Arts Council (1958, 1974); one-man shows: Exeter University (1966), Newlyn (1971, 1972), Penzance, Dartmouth (1974). *Work in permanent collection:* Plymouth A.G., Devon C.C., Surrey Educ. Com., Royal Cambrian Academy. *Address:* 3 Drakefield Drive, Saltash, Cornwall. *Signs work:* "V. Wilson."

WILSON, Winifred; artist in oil and farmer. *Educ.:* privately; *studied art* under Sir Arnesby Brown. *Exhib.:* R.A., R.O.I., W.A.G., Salon, U.S.A., Sheffield, Newcastle, Leeds, Lincoln, Doncaster, Derby, Bristol, etc. *Work in permanent collections:* Graves Gallery, Sheffield. *Address:* Highlightley Farm, Barlow, nr. Sheffield. *Signs work:* "Winifred Wilson."

WINDSOR, Alan, B.A. (Lond.), Dip.F.A. (Lond.), N.D.D., D.A.(Manc.); artist in acrylics, serigraphy and drawing; art historian; lecturer, Reading University; *b* Fleetwood, Lancs., 10 July, 1931; *s* of Major G.U. Windsor, M.C., M.B.E.; *m* Elfriede Windsor; one *s*, two *d*. *Educ.:* Audenshaw Grammar School; *studied art* at Regional College of Art, Manchester (1949-54); Slade School, University College (1954-56); Universities of Paris and Aix (1956-57). *Exhib.:* Young Contemporaries, London Group, Gimpel Fils, Roland, Browse & Delbanco, Pollock, Toronto, Ashgate, Farnham. *Address:* 2 Wykeham Rd., Farnham, Surrey. *Club:* Architectural Association. *Signs work:* "A. Windsor."

WINFIELD, David John, R.B.A., (1964), A.R.C.A. (1962); painter in oil; visiting lecturer, Maidstone College of Art; *b* London, 26 Apr., 1938. *Educ.:* Christopher Wren School, London; *studied art* at London College of Printing (1955-58), Royal College of Art (1959-62). *Work in permanent collections:* V. & A. Museum; private collections. *Address:* Flat 1, Spencer Ct. Hse., 49 Spencer Pk., London SW18. *Signs work:* "David J. Winfield."

WINGEN, Edmond, F.I.A.L. (1953); painter in oil and water-colour, modeller (small-scale statuettes); drawing master, The Hague; *b* Maastricht, 8 Sept., 1906; *s* of Jean Wingen, painter; *m* G. Wingen Olivier; two *s*, one *d*. *Educ.:* Maastricht; *studied art* at Academies Den Bosch, Antwerpen, Maastricht, Düsseldorf. *Exhib.:* Maastricht, Aachen, Düsseldorf, Sittard, Delft, Eindhoven, Den Bosch, Utrecht, Rotterdam, Amsterdam, The Hague, Dordrecht, Heerlen, etc. *Work in permanent collections:* City of The Hague; murals in restaurants and cinemas. *Address:* Jacob v. der Doesstraat, 29, Den Haag. *Clubs:* Federation of B.B.K. (Amsterdam), A.K.K.V., F.I.A.L. *Signs work:* "Edmond Wingen" (Christian name above surname).

WINGFIELD DIGBY, George; keeper emeritus, V. & A. Museum (retd.); *b* Sherborne, 2 Mar., 1911; *s* of Col. F. J. B. Wingfield Digby, D.S.O.; *m* Comelia, *d* of Prof. H. Keitler, University of Vienna. *Educ.:* Harrow, Trinity College, Cambridge; Grenoble University, Sorbonne, Vienna. *Publications:* Work of the Modern Potter in England (John Murray), 1952, Meaning and Symbol in Three Modern Artists (Faber, 1955), Symbol and Image in William Blake (Oxford University Press, 1957), Elizabethan Embroidery (Faber, 1963), The Devonshire Hunting Tapestries (H.M.S.O., 1971), Tapestries, medieval and renaissance, V. & A. Museum (H.M.S.O. forthcoming), (jointly) The Bayeux Tapestry (Phaidon, 1957). *Address:* 72 Palace Gardens Terr., London W8.

WINTER, Faith, Feodora Gleichen Sculpture Award; sculptress in stone, wood, clay, cold cast metals and fibre glass; *b* Richmond, Surrey, 1927; *d* of J. F. Ashe, architect; *m* Col. F. M. S. Winter, M.B.E., F.R.S.A., F.R.G.S.; two *s*, one *d*. *Educ.:* Oak Hall; *studied art* at Guildford and Chelsea Schools of Art. *Exhib.:*

R.A., R.B.A., R.W.S., Glasgow Academy of Fine Art and elsewhere in the U.K.; also in Malaysia and Singapore. *Work repro.:* Fine Art Commissions including portrait heads, and a wide range of Industrial Design Commissions including large murals. *Address:* Venzers Studio, Venzers Yard, The Street, Puttenham, Guildford, Surrey. *Signs work:* "Faith Winter" (formerly "Faith Ashe.")

WINTER, Francis John, A.R.E. (1953), R.E. (1973), A.T.D. (Lond.), V.P.S.G.A.; senior lecturer (retd.), Hornsey College of Art; artist in water-colour, wood engraver; *b* London, 29 Oct., 1901; *s* of John Ernest Winter; *m* Freda Margaret; one *s*, two *d*. *Educ.:* Latymer School, Edmonton; *studied art* at Hornsey School of Art (1915-26) under F. H. Swinstead, R.B.A., J. C. Moody, R.I., R.E., J. H. Willis, R.B.A., A.R.C.A.; London Day Training College under Prof. Nunn, Prof. Burt, Marion Richardson. *Address:* Old Forge Cottage, Bridge St., Long Melford, W. Suffolk.

WIRTH-MILLER, Denis; painter in oil; *b* Folkestone, 27 Nov., 1915. *Educ.:* privately; *studied art:* self-taught. *Exhib.:* Lefevre Gallery, Redfern Gallery, Aldeburgh Festival (1948, 1954, 1957, 1961), Beaux-Arts Gallery, The Minories, Colchester, Arts Council of Great Britain, New Art Centre. *Work in permanent collections:* H.M. the Queen, Arts Council of Great Britain, Bank of England, Ministry of Public Building and Works, Contemporary Art Society, Swindon Museum and Art Gallery, Museum of Modern Art, Salvador (Bahia), Brazil. *Address:* The Store House, Wivenhoe, Essex. *Signs work:* "Denis Wirth-Miller."

WISE CIOBOTARU, Gillian; artist, synthetic materials; *b* London, 1936; *d* of Arthur Wise, company director; *m* Adrian Ciobotaru. *Educ.:* Wimbledon School of Art (1954-57); Central (1959). *Awards:* Unesco Fellowship, Prague (1968); post-graduate, Repin Institute, Leningrad (1969-70). *Exhib.:* I.C.A. with Anthony Hill (1963), British Constructivist Group, Tokyo Biennale (1965), "British Sculpture in The Sixties," C.A.S. (1965), "Relief/Construction/Relief," Museum of Contemporary Art Chicago (1968), Nuremburg Biennale (1969). *Work in permanent collections:* Tate Gallery, British Council, Arts Council, Contemporary Arts Society, V. & A. *Address:* 62 Courtfield Gdns., London SW5. *Signs work:* "G. WISE C." or "Gillian Wise."

WISHART, Michael; painter in oil, writer; *b* London, 12 June, 1928; *s* of E. E. Wishart; *m* dissolved 1960; one *s*. *Studied art* at Central School, London (1947), Academie Julian, Paris (1948). *Exhib.:* one-man shows: Archer Gallery (1944), Redfern Gallery (1956, 1958, 1960), Leicester Galleries (1963, 1967, 1969, 1973), portrait of Rudolf Nureyev, Royal Academy (1968), Arts Council "Six Young Painters" (1957), Contemporary Art Society "Recent Acquisitions" Whitechapel Gallery (1968), Morley Gallery (1969). *Work in permanent collections:* Arts Council, C.A.S. *Work repro.:* Apollo, Burlington Magazine, Studio International, The Book of Joy, The Observer, Arts Review, Dance and Dancers, La Revue Moderne, Art and Literature. *Address:* Park Farm, Pulborough, Sussex. *Signs work:* "Michael Wishart" or "MW" followed by diagonal stroke.

WITHEROP, J. Coburn, A.R.C.A. (1933); painter and engraver; also conservator and technical adviser to Walker Art Gallery (Liverpool); *b* 1 Oct., 1906; *m*. *Educ.:* Alsop High School, Liverpool; *studied art* at Liverpool College of Art; R.C.A. *Exhib.:* National Gallery, R.A., R.C.A., Glasgow, Liverpool, Manchester, Bradford, Bournemouth, Southport, Los Angeles, S. Africa, Penwith Soc. of Arts, Cornwall, Arts Council Travelling Exhbn. *Official purchases:* Contemp. Art Soc.; W.A.G.; Bradford; Manchester; Birkenhead; Salford; Derbyshire. *Address:* 1 The Close, Fulwood Park, Liverpool L17 5AJ. *Club:* Sandon Studios Soc., Liverpool. *Signs work:* "J. Coburn Witherop" (with long stroke under last name).

WITHROW, William John, Honour B.A., Art and Archaeology (1950), Art Specialist, O.C.E. (1951), B.Ed. (1955), M.Ed. (1958), M.A. (1965); Director, Art Gallery of Ontario; Member: Canadian Museums Association, Canadian Art Museums Directors Organisation, American Association of Museums, American Association of Art Museum Directors, Canadian National Committee for I.C.O.M., I.N.S.E.A., Art Advisory Committee, University Club of Toronto; *b* Toronto, Ontario, 30 Sept., 1926; *s* of W. F. Withrow; *m* June Roselea Van Ostrom; three *s*, one *d*. *Educ.:* University of Toronto; *studied art* at University of Toronto (1946-65, Professor Peter Brieger, Professor Stephen Vickers). *Publications:* Sorel Etrog Sculpture, Contemporary Canadian Painting. *Address:* 7 Malabar Pl., Don Mills, Ontario. *Club:* University Club of Toronto.

WITKIN, Isaac; sculptor, works mainly in steel; assistant to Henry Moore; taught sculpture at St. Martin's School of Art; artist in residence, Bennington College, Vermont, U.S.A.; *b* Johannesburg, 10 May, 1936; *s* of William Witkin, company director; *m* Thelma; two *d*. *Studied art* at St. Martin's School of Art under Anthony Caro. *Work in permanent collections:* Arts Council, Gt. Britain, British Council, Leicestershire Education Committee, Tate Gallery, Stormking Art Centre, N.Y. *Publications:* Modern English Sculpture (A. M. Hammacher). *Address:* Bennington College, Bennington, Vermont, U.S.A. *Signs work:* "I. Witkin."

WOLKERS-RANSOME, Joan Elizabeth Margaret, N.D.D. (Painting, 1948), Abbey Scholarship (1949), R.A. Silver Medals (1951, 52, 53); art student at R.A. Schools; painter in oil; *b* Tunbridge Wells, 28 Aug., 1928; *d* of M. E. Ransome. *Educ.:* Lawnside, Malvern; *studied art* at Malvern School of Art under Victor Hume Moody (1945-50) and R.A. Schools under Henry Rushbury, Fleetwood Walker and William Dring (1950-54); Royal Academy, Amsterdam (1954-58). *Exhib.:* R.A., R.B.S.A., R.S.P.P., N.E.A.C., Brighton Art Gallery, Worcester Art Gallery, Malvern Art Club, Kenn Group, Exeter. Specialises in portraiture. *Address:* 5 St. Leonard's Rd., Exeter. *Signs work:* "J. E. M. Wolkers-Ransome."

WOLLASTON, Charles, S.G.A., D.F.A. (Lond.), A.T.D., F.R.S.A.; artist in oil, water-colour; potter; Principal Lecturer, Bognor Regis College of Education; *b* Frodsham, Ches., 19 Dec., 1914; *s* of Charles Wollaston. *Educ.:* Liverpool College; *studied art* at Slade School under Schwabe and Coldstream (1946-50). *Exhib.:* Paris Salon, S.G.A., R.B.A., R.S.A., R.H.A., R.Cam.A., R.P., N.E.A.C., N.S., United Soc. of Artists. *Publications:* Silkscreen in Schools (Dryad Press), 1960, including work repro. *Official purchases:* ceramic mural in possession of West Sussex County Council, Ceramic sculpture, Roffey Infants' School, Horsham, Sussex. *Address:* College of Education, Bognor Regis, Sussex. *Club:* Hesketh Hubbard. *Signs work:* see appendix.

WOLVERSON, Margaret Elizabeth, N.D.D. Painting Special Level (1957), A.T.D. (1958); painter in oils of equestrian scenes, portraits, miniatures, animal paintings and landscapes; part-time teacher; painting teacher, Hornsea Institute of Further Education; formerly taught, Stourbridge College of Art; *b* Weston-super-Mare, 14 July, 1937; *d* of Charles Lloynes Smith, F.I.M.T.A., A.C.C.A.; *m* Martin Wolverson; one *s*. *Educ.:* Dudley Girls' High School; *studied art* at Dudley School of Art (1953-55) under John Hart, Wolverhampton College of Art (1955-57) under Harry Turner, Leicester College of Art (1957-58) under Hugh Collinson. *Exhib.:* R.M.S. at Mall Galleries. *Work in permanent collections:* East Riding Collection for Schools, Ferens A.G., private collections in the U.K. and U.S.A. *Address:* 5 Westbourne Rd., Hornsea, E. Yorks. HU18 1PQ. *Signs work:* see appendix.

WOLVERSON, Martin, F.R.B.S. (1971), A.T.C. (1961), A.R.B.S. (1965); silver medal R.B.S. (1971); sculptor in cast and machined metal, coloured resins and enamel; senior lecturer in Fine Art; chief examiner for G.C.E. "A" Level; deputy head, School of Fine Art, Regional College of Art, Hull, Yorks.; *b* Wolverhampton, 26 May, 1939; *s* of Cyril Wolverson, accountant; *m* Margaret Smith; one *s*. *Educ.:* Wednesbury Boys' High School; *studied art* at Wolverhampton College of Art (1956-60), Goldsmiths' College of Art (1960-61). *Exhib.:* Institute of Advanced Architectural Studies, York University (1967-1970), Alwin Gallery, Minories, Colchester (1971). *Work in permanent collections:* E. Yorks C.C., Leeds Regional Hospital Board, Ferens A.G., Synagogue, Leicester, National Coal Board, Staffs. C.C. *Address:* 5 Westbourne Rd., Hornsea, E. Yorks. HU18 1PQ. *Signs work:* "M. Wolverson."

WOOD, Hamilton, A.T.D., Goldsmiths' Travelling Scholarship (1968); painter, sculptor in metal; art teacher and lecturer; *b* Norwich, 1918; *s* of Sidney Wood; *m* Mary; two *s*, four *d*. *Educ.:* City of Norwich School; *studied art* at Norwich School of Art, Central School of Art and Inst. of Educ., University of London (1945-46). *Exhib.:* Football and Fine Arts 1953 (toured by Arts Council); copper sculpture Globe Place, Norwich. *Publications:* art critic to Eastern Evening News; co-author Davenport's Norwich (1973). *Address:* Gurney Ct., Magdalen St., Norwich. *Clubs:* Norwich Twenty Group, Norfolk and Norwich Art Circle. *Signs work:* "Hamilton Wood" and date.

WOOD, Peter Macdonough, A.T.D., Slade Dip. Fine Art, R.S.M.A., S.N.R.; artist in oil, water-colour and line, film technician; *b* Twickenham, 30 Apr., 1914; *s* of George B. Wood; *m* Ursula Dorothy; two *s*. *Educ.:* Southend High School; *studied art* at Southend School of Art under Horace Blakey, Slade School, U.C.L. under Randolph Schwabe. *Work in permanent collections:* National Maritime Museum, Bagshaw Art Gallery, Batley. *Publications:* illustrated Sea Captains and their Ships (K. Allen). *Address:* 9 Laurel Rd., Barnes, London SW13. *Signs work:* "Peter M. Wood."

WOOD, Robert Sydney Rendle, painter mem., Nat. Soc. of Painters, Sculptors and Engravers (London); mem., St. Ives Soc. of Artists; mem., Plymouth Soc. of Artists; pres., St. Mawes Group of Artists; painter in oil, tempera and water-colour; hon. sec., Ulster Arts Club (1925-30); *b* 14 Mar., 1894; *s* of Sydney John Wood, chemical engineer; *m*; one *s*, one *d*. *Educ.:* Plymouth Secondary School; Plymouth College of Technology; Plymouth School of Art under Shelly; Edinburgh College of Art under David Foggie, R.S.A. *Exhib.:* R.S.A., R.H.A., R.W.E.A., R.S.W., S.S.A., G.I., W.A.G., St. Ives Soc. of Artists. *Address:* Bodrigan, Southbourne Rd., St. Austell, Cornwall. *Signs work:* see appendix.

WOOD, Ronald Philip Benjamin, A.R.C.A., design (1934), A.T.D. (1935); initial member Art Committee, Schools Council (1967-69); artist, silver-smithing and enamelling; formerly head of art dept., High School for Boys, Wallington, Surrey; lecturer for Dept. of Education and Science and various authorities; *b* Brixton, London, 10 July, 1911; *s* of P. J. Wood, master builder; *m* E. A. Davies (1962). *Educ.:* Strand School; *studied art* at Camberwell School of Arts and Crafts (1929-31), R.C.A. under Prof. Tristram (1931-35). *Exhib.:* R.A. British Art in Industry (1935); since 1936 engaged in teaching and private research. *Address:* 26 Princes Ave., Carshalton Beeches, Surrey SM5 4NZ.

WOODALL, Mary, C.B.E., Ph.D., F.S.A., F.M.A.; director, City Museum and Art Gallery, Birmingham (1956-64); London Adviser to the Felton Bequest, Melbourne (1965), Trustee, National Gallery (1969); *b* Chelsea, 6 Mar., 1901; *d* of Henry Woodall, civil engineer. *Educ.:* Cheltenham Ladies' College; Somerville

College, Oxford; Slade School and Courtauld Institute, London University. *Publications:* Gainsborough's Landscape Drawings (Faber and Faber, 1939); Thomas Gainsborough (Phoenix, 1948); The Letters of Thomas Gainsborough (Cupid Press, 1962). *Address:* The Red House, Clifton Hampden, Abingdon-on-Thames.

WOODCOCK, John, A.R.C.A. (1949), M.S.I.A.; Senior Lecturer in Graphic Design at St. Martin's School of Art; typographer, lettering designer; *b* Cudworth, Yorks, 27 Aug., 1924; *s* of Albert Edward Woodcock; *m* Margaret Bennett; one *s. Educ.:* Barnsley Grammar School; *studied art* at Barnsley School of Art (1940-43), R.C.A. (1946-50). *Official purchases:* calligraphy by V. & A. Circulation Dept., and by the Walters Art Gallery, Baltimore, U.S.A., and Boston Public Libraries, U.S.A. *Address:* 1 Garden Farm, Waterhouse Lane, Kingswood, Surrey. *Signs work:* "JW" or "JOHN WOODCOCK."

WOODFORD, David, N.D.D., A.T.C. with distinction, Cert. R.A.S.; painter in oil and water-colour; *b* Rawmarsh, Yorks., 1 May, 1938; *m* June; two *s. Educ.:* Lancing College; *studied art* at West Sussex College of Art (1955-59), Leeds College of Art (1959-60), Royal Academy Schools (1965-68). He lives by his painting. *Address:* Ffrancon House, Ty'n-Y-Maes, Bethesda, Bangor, Gwynedd. *Signs work:* "David Woodford."

WOODINGTON, Walter, R.P., R.B.A., N.E.A.C.; painter in oil and water-colour; part-time teacher, Woolwich Polytechnic Art School (1946-60); appointed Curator, Royal Academy Schools (1961); *b* London, June, 1916; *s* of Frederick Woodington; *m* Jacqueline Murray. *Studied art* at Woolwich Polytechnic Art School and City and Guilds Art School under A. R. Middleton-Todd, R.A. *Exhib.:* R.A., R.P., R.B.A., N.E.A.C., etc. *Work repro.:* for Hutchinson's and Odhams Press. *Address:* 8 Cavendish Mews North, London W1. *Signs work:* "WOODINGTON."

WOODS, Elsie; artist in oils, water-colour, pastel, pen and ink; vice-pres. (1956-57), joint hon. sec. (with husband), Nottingham Soc. of Artists (1955-58); *b* Nottingham, 1900; *d* of S. B. Buckley; *m* Richard Charles Woods; one *d. Educ.:* Brincliffe School, Nottingham; Homerton College, Cambridge; *studied art* at Homerton College (1919-21) and some private lessons from Edwin Marsh, Nottingham, on taking up painting again in 1949. *Exhib.:* R.I., Britain in Water-colours, R.Cam.A., P.S., S.W.A., Nottingham Castle A.G., Kensington Gallery, Norwich Castle A.G. *Address:* The Thatched Cottage, Hillside, Sheringham, Norfolk. *Club:* Nottingham Soc. of Artists. *Signs work:* "Elsie Woods."

WOODS, Grace Mary, A.R.C.A.; artist in black and white and pastel, and weaving; *b* Ilford, Essex, 25 Feb., 1909; *d* of Charles J. Kaye; *m* Sidney W. Woods, A.R.C.A.; two *s,* three *d. Educ.:* Ursuline Convent, Forest Gate, E7; *studied art* at West Ham Art School and Royal College of Art in Design and Engraving Schools. *Exhib.:* R.A. and other London galleries. *Work purchased:* by private collectors. *Address:* 49 Derry Downs, St. Mary Cray, Kent. *Signs work:* "Mary Woods."

WOODS, William L., A.T.D., N.D.D. (illustration); painter and teacher for Bucks. Educ. Com.; *b* Norwich, 27 July, 1916; *m. Educ.:* Unthank College, Norwich; *studied art* at Lowestoft under Miss G. C. Musson (1937-38) and Hornsey School of Art under J. C. Moody, R.E., A.R.C.A. (1938-39, 1946-47). *Exhib.:* R.A., R.W.S., R.B.A., R.I., S.M.A., R.O.I., S. Kensington and provinces. *Official purchases:* L.C.C., business organisations, private collections. *Address:* Mill Hill Farm, Bridens Camp, Hemel Hempstead, Herts. *Signs work:* "W. L. WOODS."

WOODTHORPE, Patricia Mariella; painter and draughtsman in oil and egg tempera; *b* London, 10 Feb., 1928; *d* A. E. A. Woodthorpe. *Educ.:* Queen Anne's School (Berks.); *studied art* at St. Martin's School of Art (1945-46) and Byam Shaw School under B. D. L. Thomas, P. E. Philipps and P. G. Greenham, A.R.A. (1946-51). *Exhib.:* R.A., R.B.A., R.P., N.E.A.C., etc. *Addresses:* Little Danes, Avisford, Arundel, Sussex; The Old Vicarage, Beulah, Breconshire LD5 4UA. *Signs work:* "M.W."

WOOLF-NELLIST, Meg, A.T.D., F.S.D.-C.; B. of Ed. Industrial Design Exam., carving, letter-cutting; awarded Exhibition, R.C.A. (1949); teacher in Havering; formerly lecturer in art, Rachel McMillan College of Educ., Director, Bermuda Art Assoc. School (1950-52); artist in stone, wood, ivory, water-colour, silver and embroiderer; *b* Isle of Thanet, 10 Dec., 1923; *d* of Dr. E. A. Woolf, D.Litt.; *m* Anthony Nellist; one *s*, three *d*. *Educ.:* Couvent des Oiseaux, Westgate-on-Sea; *studied art* at Ravensbourne College of Art, Brighton College of Art (Eric Reskett, John Cohen, Trevor Tennant, Willi Soukop, Joseph Cribb, Dunstan Pruden, Alfred D. Southwick, 1939-42). *Exhib.:* Roland, Browse and Delbanco, A.I.A., R.B.A., R.A., V. & A., Russell Cotes, Hove Art Gallery (one-man, 1948); with Designer Craftsmen (1968-69). *Work repro.:* Studio. *Work in private collections:* Canada, U.S.A., South Africa. *Address:* 84 Front Lane, Cranham, Upminster, Essex. *Signs work:* see appendix.

WOOLFORD, Harry Russell Halkerston, O.B.E. (1970); until 1970 specialist in picture restoration; chief restorer, National Gallery of Scotland; *b* Edinburgh, 23 May, 1905; *s* of H. Woolford, engineer; *m* Nancy Philip; one *d*. *Educ.:* Edinburgh; *studied art* at Edinburgh College of Art (painting and drawing) and R.S.A. Life School (Carnegie Travelling Scholarship and Chalmers Bursary, London, Paris and Italy). Fellow, Museums Association and International Institute for Conservation of Historic and Artistic Works. *Address:* Dean Park, Golf Course Rd., Bonnyrigg, Midlothian EH19 2EU. *Club:* Scottish Arts.

WOOLLASTON, Leslie; painter in oil; *b* Birmingham, 1900. *Educ.:* Birmingham; *studied art:* self-taught. *Exhib.:* R.A., R.B.A., N.E.A.C., R.C.A., R.W.S., R.S.A. Birmingham, R.W.E.A., Glasgow Fine Arts Society, Goupil, R.O.I., Brighton Art Gallery, Paris Salon (Hon. Mention). *Work in permanent collections:* Williamson Art Gallery, Birkenhead (Holiday Makers at a River Resort). *Official purchases:* as above. *Work repro.:* Summer Afternoon, Thames Ditton (Royle Publications, Ltd.). *Address:* 51 Manor Court Rd., Hanwell, London W7. *Clubs:* Arts, Theatre.

WOOLLASTON, Mountford Tosswill; artist in oil, water-colour, pen, pencil; *b* Toko, N.Z., 1910; *s* of J. R. Woollaston, farmer; *m* Edith Alexander; three *s*, one *d*. *Educ.:* Stratford Technical High School, N.Z.; *studied art* at Nelson under Hugh Scott (1930), Christchurch under Len Booth (1931), Dunedin under R. N. Field (1932), and particularly under Flora Scales from Hans Hoffman's School in Munich (1935). *Exhib.:* many one-man shows in N.Z., Melbourne and Sydney (1958). *Official purchases:* National Gallery of Victoria, Melbourne, Art Gallery of N.S.W., Sydney, all main N.Z. galleries and universities. *Address:* Riwaka, Motueka, N.Z. *Signs work:* "Woollaston."

WOOLLATT, Louisa Emily Ellen, A.R.C.A. (design, embroidery, weaving), scholarship, Worshipful Company of Broiderers (1932); Embroiderers' Guild Challenge Cup (1945, 1947); crafts mistress, Bradford College of Art, Halifax, Exeter and Torbay Art Schools; *b* Oxford, 14 Dec., 1908; *d* of Edwin Judd-Morris; *m* Leighton H. Woollatt, painter; one *d*. *Educ.:* privately; *studied art* at Oxford School of Art, R.C.A. under Sir William Rothenstein, Prof. E. W.

Tristram, Edward Johnston. *Exhib.:* London and Continent. *Publications:* Sampler Book of Decorative Needlework (1937), An Introduction to Embroidery Stitches (1948). *Address:* Pinfarthings, Vales Rd., Budleigh Salterton. *Signs work:* "LJM" (embroidery), "L. E. E. Judd-Morris" (publications), and "Louie Woollatt."

WOOLLETT, Elmer Barrington; dealer in miniatures, porcelain, furniture, needlework, etc.; Capt. Royal West Kent Regt. (1914-18), mentioned twice in Despatches of Lord Genl. Allenby's Army of Palestine; *b* Chatham, 1 Mar., 1894; *s* of Charles Woollett, art dealer; *m* Dorothy. *Educ.:* Herne Bay College, Kent. *Addresses:* 59-61 Wigmore St., London W1, and (private) 57 Eaton Sq., London SW1. Freeman of the City of London.

WOOLLEY, Peter William, A.T.D. (1949); artist in book illustration, lithography, fabric printing; poster design; *b* Hemingfield, 2 Feb., 1923; *s* of W. D. Woolley; *m* Winifred Mary Peake; two *s*, three *d*. *Educ.:* Holgate Grammar School, Barnsley; *studied art* at Barnsley School of Art, Sheffield College of Art. *Exhib.:* Graves Art Gallery, Sheffield. *Address:* River Cottage, Oker, nr. Matlock, Derbys. *Signs work:* "Woolley."

WOOTTON, Frank, A.A.; President, Guild of Aviation Artists; artist in oil and water-colour, gold medallist, travelling scholarship (1930), official artist R.A.F. (1944-46); *b* Milford, 30 July, 1914; *s* of F. Wootton, R.N.; *m* Virginia Cawthorne; two *s*, one *d*. *Educ.:* Eastbourne; *studied art* under Reeve-Fowkes, Eric Ravillious, Eastbourne School of Art. *Exhib.:* R.A., Towner Art Gallery, Eastbourne, R.O.I., Imperial War Museum, Paris, Rangoon, New York. *Work in permanent collections:* Sussex Collection, Eastbourne; Command Stations, R.A.F.; Imperial War Museum. *Publications:* How to Draw Aircraft, How to Draw Cars, Wie Zeichne Ich Autos. *Address:* Mayflower House, Alfriston, Sussex. *Signs work:* "Wootton."

WORTH, Leslie Charles, A.R.C.A. (Lond.) (1946), R.B.A. (1951), N.E.A.C. (1957), R.W.S. (1959); prize-winner Hallmark International Art Award, New York (1955); painter in water-colour and oil; Head of Fine Art Department, Epsom and Ewell School of Art; *b* Bideford, Devon, 6 June 1923; *m* Jane Taylor; one *s*, three *d*. *Educ.:* St. Budeaux School, Plymouth; *studied art* at Plymouth School of Art (1938-43), Bideford School of Art (1938-43), Royal College of Art (1943-46). *Exhib.:* Agnews, Mercury Gallery, Wildenstein. *Work in permanent collections:* R.A., National Gallery of New Zealand, Aberdeen, Brighton, Rochdale, Southport and Wakefield Art Galleries, Eton College; private collections: H.M. Queen Elizabeth, Queen Mother and several private collections. *Address:* 11 Burgh Heath Rd., Epsom, Surrey. *Signs work:* "Leslie Worth."

WREN, Rosemary Denise, A.R.C.A. (1950); artist/potter in stoneware; vice-president, Oxshott Arts and Crafts Society; *b* Oxshott, 27 June, 1922; *d* of Denise and Henry Wren, potters; lives and works in partnership with Peter M. Crotty. *Educ.:* Hall School, Weybridge; *studied art* at Guildford School of Art (1945-47) under Helen Pincombe and Willi Soukop; R.C.A. (1947-50). *Exhib.:* Heal's, Berkeley Galleries, C.P.A., Briglin, Commonwealth Institute, London; also Edinburgh, Richmond, E. Grinstead and group shows abroad. *Work in permanent collections:* V. & A., City of Glasgow Museum, etc. *Publications:* Pottery Making (Pitman) with Denise K. Wren (1950); Film: Creations in Clay (1968); articles in Ceramic Review. *Address:* The Oxshott Pottery, Potters' Croft, Oakshade Rd., Oxshott, Surrey. *Club:* Craftsmen Potters' Assoc. of Gt. Britain (founder member). *Signs work:* Impressed wren; sometimes with signature or "Oxshott."

WRIGHT, Austin Andrew; Ricardo da Silvera Acquisition Prize, São Paulo

Biennale (1957); Gregory Fellowship in Sculpture, Leeds University (1961-64); sculptor in wood, lead, aluminium and bronze; *b* Chester, 1911. *Work in permanent collections:* Art Galleries of Bradford, Wakefield, Leeds, York, Birmingham, Swansea, V. & A., Whitworth, Manchester, Arts Council, Arts Council for Wales, Contemporary Art Soc., National Museum of Wales, Abbott Hall, Kendal, Preston, Leeds Univ., York Univ., G.L.C., Museum of Modern Art, São Paulo, public collections in Sweden, Venezuela and U.S.A. *Address:* The Green, Upper Poppleton, York.

WRIGHT, Gordon Butler, F.B.S. Comm., F.Inst.C., Mem. International Association of Artists; professional artist in oils, pen and ink; *b* Darlington, Co. Durham, 2 Apr., 1925; *s* of Reginald Wright; *m* Joan. *Educ.:* Gladstone School, Darlington and Kings College, Newcastle; *studied art* at Chichester College of Art (1943-44) followed by two periods of study in Amsterdam and The Hague. Influenced by the Dutch Romantic School. *Exhib.:* Galerie Montmartre, Paris, Grosvenor Gallery and Portal Gallery, London, Trinity Art Gallery, Wareham, Whitgift Galleries, London, Recorded in the National Maritime Museum, Greenwich. *Work in permanent collection:* Washington Fine Art Society, U.S.A. *Publications:* The Collector's Guide to Paintings as an Investment; illustrative work: commercial journals, periodicals, newspapers and greetings cards. *Address:* 123 Wetherby Rd., Harrogate, Yorks. *Signs work:* "G. B. Wright."

WRIGHT, Lawrence, M.A., B.Arch.; finalist Rome Scholarship in Architecture (1929 and 1930); Owen Jones Studentship, R.I.B.A. (1932); architectural draughtsman; artist in pencil, water-colour, etching; *b* Bristol, 18 Nov., 1906; *s* of Charles Wright. *Educ.:* Liverpool School of Architecture (1924-29). *Exhib.:* R.A., etc. *Work in permanent collections:* London Museum, Guildhall Art Gallery (drawings and etchings). *Official purchases:* as above. *Address:* 27 West St., Alresford, Hants. *Signs work:* see appendix.

WROUGHTON, Julia, N.D.D. (1957), A.R.C.A. (1960), A.R.W.A. (1963); painter in oil and water-colour; Principal, Inniemore School of Painting; *b* Bridge of Allan, Stirlingshire, 24 Oct., 1934; *d* of Robert Lewis Wroughton, Controller of Customs, Zanzibar; *m* Alastair Macdonald; one *s*, three *d*. *Educ.:* Beacon School, Bridge of Allan; *studied art* at Colchester School of Art (1953-57) under John O'Connor, Hugh Cronyn, Royal College of Art (1957-60) under Carel Weight, R.A., Colin Hayes, R.A. *Exhib.:* R.A., one-man show: Torrance Gallery, Edinburgh. *Work in permanent collections:* Royal West of England Academy, Nuffield Foundation. *Address:* Inniemore Lodge, Pennyghael, Isle of Mull. *Signs work:* "Julia Wroughton," "J.W."

WU, Ching-Hsia; artist; paintress in water-colour and poetess; Vancouver Golden Jubilee Chinese Carnival Honorary Prize, Canada (1936); *b* Changchow, China, 11 Feb., 1910. *Educ.:* at home and studied art under father. *Exhib.:* Shanghai, Nanking, Peking, Rome, Jakarta, Surabaya, Singapore, Helsinki, Stockholm, Canton, etc. *Work in permanent collections:* Shanghai Art Gallery; Katesan House, Jakarta; etc. *Address:* 510/400 Soochow Road N., Shanghai (China). *Club:* China Art Society, Shanghai. *Signs work:* "WU Ching-Hsia."

WU, I-Chen; painter in Chinese ink-wash, colour, poet and calligrapher; artist/lecturer; Chinese art lecturer, University College, Davis; *b* Ochen, Hupeh, China, 25 Nov., 1927; *s* of Hsien-yuan Wu; *m* Hsiao-hua Huang, librarian; two *s*, one *d*. *Educ.:* National Chung Hsing University (B.A. 1958); San Jose State University (M.A. 1974); *studied art:* ten years of Classical Chinese Studies, self taught. *Work in permanent collections:* Art Gallery, Taiwan Prov. Government, Chinese Pavilion, Expo Montreal, HemisFair San Antonio, Prov. Museum of

Victoria, B.C., Fresmo Art Center, California, San Jose Museum of Art. *Publications:* plan to edit Chinese Artists in America and Who's Who in Chinese Art. *Address:* 1683 Christopher St., San Jose, California, 95122, U.S.A. *Clubs:* Art Soc. of China, Chinese Calligraphers Assoc., Asian Art Soc. of San Francisco. *Signs work:* see appendix.

WUNDERLICH, Paul; painter in oil, gouache, lithography; sculptor; *b* Berlin, 10 Mar., 1927; *s* of Horst Wunderlich, pilot; *m* Karin Székessy; two *d. Educ.:* Berlin High School; *studied art* at Hochschule für Bildende Künste, Hamburg, under Prof. W. Tietze. *Exhib.:* all over Europe, United States, Japan, S. Africa and Australia. *Work in permanent collections:* in museums in Europe, U.S.A. and Japan. *Publications:* Paul Wunderlich (Denoel, Paris 1972), Lithografien 1959-73 (Office du Livre, Fribourg Suisse). *Address:* Haynstr. 2, D-2000 Hamburg 20. *Signs work:* "Paul Wunderlich."

WYATT, Joyce Eileen (Mrs. Derek Wraith), R.M.S., U.A.S., S.W.A.; Prix Rowland and Mention Honorable (Paris Salon, 1963); Médaille D'Argent (Paris Salon, 1965); Médaille D'Or (Paris Salon, 1969); Member of La Société des Artistes Français (1969); Milldon Art Society, Hesketh Hubbard Art Society; portrait painter in oil, water-colour; *b* London, 18 Aug., 1924; *d* of Francis W. Wyatt, company director; *m* Dr. Derek Greenway Wraith; one *s*, one *d. Educ.:* Copthall School, Mill Hill; *studied art* at Hornsey College of Art, and under Francis Hodge and W. Durac Barnett. *Exhib.:* R.A., R.P., R.M.S., R.B.A., Société des Artistes Français, United Soc., S.W.A., Wallace Collection Aid to China Exhbn. and other exhbns.; one-man shows: Federation British Artists, 6½ Suffolk St., Pall Mall (1966, 1970), La Galerie Mouffe, Paris (1971). *Address:* Arundel House, Northcliffe Dr., Totteridge, London N20. *Signs work:* "WYATT."

WYETH, Paul James Logan, R.P., R.B.A.; portrait painter and mural painter in oils and pastels; *b* 1 Feb., 1920; *s* of Robert Wyeth, actor, lyric composer; *m* Tina; two *d. Studied art* at Royal College of Art under Sir John Rothenstein, Gilbert Spencer, R.A., Egerton Cooper, R.B.A. *Work in permanent collections:* Melbourne, Massachusetts, U.S.A., Greenhildes Gallery, Montreal, Canada. *Publications:* How to Paint in Water-colour, How to paint in Oils. *Address:* (studio) 19 Burstock Rd., London SW15. *Club:* Chelsea Arts. *Signs work:* see appendix.

WYLLIE, George Ralston; M.S.S.A. and Glasgow Group; self-taught sculptor in metal and mixed media; *b* Glasgow, 1921; *s* of Andrew Wyllie; *m* Daphne Winifred Wyllie; two *d. Educ.:* Allan Glen's School and Bella Houston Academy, Glasgow. *Exhib.:* major Scottish group shows; R.S.A., S.S.A., R.G.I. *Work in permanent collections:* Glasgow museums and art galleries. *Address:* 9 McPherson Drive, Gourock, Renfrews. PA19 1LJ. *Club:* Glasgow Art. *Signs work:* "G.R.W.", initials in script, stamped or welded on to works followed by year.

WYLLIE, Gordon Hope, D.A. (Glas. 1953), R.S.W. (1967); artist in water-colour, acrylic and oil; principal art master, Greenock Academy; *b* Greenock, 12 Feb., 1930; *s* of James Wyllie; *m* Helen Wyllie; two *s. Educ.:* Greenock High School; *studied art* at Glasgow School of Art (1949-53) under Wm. Armour, R.S.A., R.S.W.; Hospitalfield College of Art (1953) under Ian Fleming, R.S.A., R.S.W. and Mary Armour, R.S.A., R.S.W. *Exhib.:* R.S.A. (regular exhibitor), R.G.I., R.S.W., Compass Gallery, Glasgow; one-man shows in Gateway, Edinburgh, Douglas & Foulis, Edinburgh, Citizens Theatre, Glasgow, Blythswood Gallery, 208 Gallery, Glasgow, Strathclyde University Staff Club, Lillie A.G., Compass Gallery. *Work in permanent collections* of Argyll, Fife, Renfrewshire, Ross and Cromarty Authorities, Paisley A.G., Lillie A.G., Milngavie and many private collections in U.K., U.S.A., Israel, Germany, etc. *Work repro.:* at one time part-time illustrator for the Glasgow Bulletin. *Address:* 17 Fox St., Greenock. *Signs work:* "Wyllie."

WYLLIE, Harold, O.B.E. (Mil. Div.) (1919), V.P.R.S.M.A.; marine artist in oil, water-colour, gouache, pencil, dry-point, bitten etching, aquatint; Lt-Colonel (late), Wilts. Regt. and R.F.C.; Dispatches B.E.F. France (1918), Queen's Medal, S.A., 3 Bars (1902), 1914 Star, G.S., Victory, Home Defence and War Medal (1945); *b* London, 29 June, 1880; *s* of W. L. Wyllie, R.A., R.E., R.I.; *m* Hilary Strain, R.S.M.A. *Educ.:* Smyths Littlejohns (crammers for R.N.); *studied art:* W. L. Wyllie, R.A., Sir T. Greame Jackson, R.A. (1900), Edwin Abbey, R.A. (1906), Sir Frank Short, R.A. (1920). *Works in permanent collections:* Imperial War Museum, National Maritime Museum, Victory Museum, Portsmouth, Museum, Cape Town. *Publications:* Nelson Expects (Dudley Pope), The Black Frigate (Dudley Pope), The Gun (Dudley Pope). *Address:* Hillhead of Dunkeld, Perths. *Signs work:* see appendix.

WYNESS, Fenton, Kt.St.J., D.A. (Abd.), F.R.I.B.A.; artist in black and white and water-colour, writer on art and historical matters, art critic; *b* 15 Aug., 1903; *s* of J. Morrison Wyness. *Educ.:* Aberdeen Grammar School; *studied art* at Gray's School of Art, Aberdeen. *Exhib.:* Aberdeen, R.S.A. *Work in permanent collections:* The Imperial War Museum, London (from the collection of Her Late Majesty Queen Mary), Aberdeen Art Gallery and Regional Museum, Provost Skene's House, Aberdeen. *Work repro.:* numerous magazines, publications and in own books. *Address:* 45 Salisbury Terr., Aberdeen. *Signs work:* "Fenton Wyness."

X

XENIA: see GRIFFIN, Frederick.

XIMENES, Gloria (née Shamdasani); artist in oil and ink; lecturer in art; *b* 1933; *m*; one *s*. *Studied art* at St. Martin's School of Art (1959-61) under Robin Guthrie, Joe Tilson, Mr. Dodds; Italy (1951) under Prof. A. Beltrame. *Exhib.:* Trends, Mall Galleries, N.S., W.I.A.C., etc.; three one-man shows. *Address:* 73 Alric Ave., New Malden, Surrey. *Clubs:* F.P.S., Weybridge Soc. of Art, Thames Valley Art. *Signs work:* "Ximenes."

Y

YALLUP, Pat, Dip.A.D. S.A. (1956), S.I.A.D., A.T.D. (1963); artist in water-colour (landscape and abstracts), oil (portraits); graphic designer; Proprietor, Art Centre, Madonna and Gwent Galleries; teacher, Chepstow Leisure Centre; *b* Johannesburg, S. Africa, 29 Sept., 1929; *d* of Hugh Astley Treadwell, accountant; *m* D. J. Harvey; three *s*. *Educ.:* Bredon School, Tewkesbury; *studied art* at Witwatersrand, Johannesburg under Major Gardiner, Todd Davis and Bramham; Byam Shaw School, London (portraiture). *Exhib.:* three one-man shows; Woodstock Gallery (1964), Richmond Gallery (1962), Sunbury-on-Thames (1962-65), R.A. (1962). *Work in permanent collections:* S. African Academy, Canada. *Work repro.:* various magazine illustrations. *Addresses:* Bicknor House, English Bicknor, Coleford, Glos. GL16 7PF; and Madonna and Gwent Galleries, Chepstow. *Signs work:* "Pat Yallup" (water-colours and abstracts), "Pat Harvey" (oil portraits).

YATES, Ann, R.I. (1953), R.C.A. (1954); landscape and flower painter in water-colour and oil; *b* 2 May, 1897; *m* (1st) Cyril S. Yates; one *s*; (2nd) Harry D. Inman. *Exhib.:* R.I., R.Cam.A., R.B.A. and provincial galleries. *Address:* 72 Pixham La., Dorking, Surrey. *Signs work:* "Ann Yates" (in script).

YATES, Hal, R.I.; artist in water-colour; *b* West Didsbury, Manchester, Feb., 1907; *s* of Harry Yates; *m*; two *s*, one *d*. *Educ.:* S. Manchester Grammar School and Fettes College, Edinburgh; *studied art:* privately and Manchester Art School (evenings). *Exhib.:* R.A., R.S.A., R.B.A., R.I., Paris Salon, United Soc., National Soc., R.S.W., M.A.F.A., Bradford, Preston, Laing (Newcastle), Whitechapel, Kensington. *Work in permanent collections:* Rutherston, Laing, Derby, Salford, Manchester, Whitworth A.G., Bury, Rochdale, Warrington A.G. *Address:* Bollin Hey, Styal, Ches. *Clubs:* R.I., Nat. Soc., United Soc., Manchester Graphics, Manchester Academy (Hon. Lit. Sec.), R.W.S. Arts, Modern Painters, Lancashire Group, Stockport Art, chairman North-Western Federation of Art Socs., etc. *Signs work:* see appendix.

YATES, Marie, B.A. Hons. (1971); artist; *b* Lancashire, 9 Aug., 1940. *Studied art* at Manchester and Hornsey. *Exhib.:* Arts Council, British Council. *Work in permanent collection:* Arts Council. *Address:* Cottage Number Five, Lower Wraxall, Dorchester, Dorset. *Signs work:* "Marie Yates."

YHAP, Lætitia Karoline; Leverhulme Research Scholar (1962-63); Slade Dip. (1965); *b* England, 1 May, 1941; *d* of Leslie H. Yhap, doctor; *m* Jeffery Camp. *Educ.:* Fulham County Grammar School; *studied art* at Camberwell School of Arts and Crafts (1958-62); Slade School of Fine Art (1963-65). *Exhib.:* one-man shows: Norwich Art School (1964), Piccadilly Gallery (1968, 1970, 1973); six-man show: South London Art Gallery (1965); mixed shows: Young Contemporaries (1965), Institute of Directors (1969), London Group (1965, 1967, 1968, 1970, 1973), East Anglian Art (1969), Warehouse Gallery, Covent Garden (1973), John Moores, Liverpool (1974), Artfair C.A.S. (1975), Artfair, Basle (1975), Chichester National Art Exhbn. (1975), Middlesbrough International Drawing Biennal (1975). *Work in permanent collection:* Nuffield Foundation. *Address:* 78 Forthbridge Rd., London SW11 5NY. *Signs work:* "Lætitia Yhap."

YOUNG, Andrew McLaren, M.A., F.M.A.; art historian, Tate Gallery (1938-39); asst. curator, Barber Inst. of Fine Arts, Birmingham (1946-49); Senior Lecturer (1949-65) and Professor (since 1965) of Fine Art in the University of Glasgow and Keeper (since 1949) of the University Art Collections; *b* Southend, Argyll, 19 Sept., 1913; *s* of Rev. R. C. Young; *m* Margaret Heath; one *s*, one *d*. *Educ.:* Jamaica College, Kingston, Jamaica, and George Watson's College, Edinburgh; *studied history of art* at Edinburgh University. *Publications:* James McNeill Whistler, exhibition catalogue (1960), and other publications on Whistler; Glasgow at a Glance: an Architectural Handbook (1965); Charles Rennie Mackintosh: Architecture, Design and Painting (1968); articles in various periodicals. *Address:* 2 Cleveden Cres., Glasgow G12 0PD.

YOUNG, Dennis Leonard, A.R.C.A., F.R.S.A., M.S.I.A.; furniture interior and exhibition designer; *b* Marsh Gibbon, Bucks., 16 July, 1917; *m* Barbara Stamps; two *s*, one *d*. *Educ.:* High Wycombe School of Art (1933-36), R.C.A. (1937-39, 1946-47). *Publications:* Furniture in Britain Today, etc., articles, filmstrips, radio and TV programmes, designed first moulded plastic chair in

Britain. *Address:* 89 Dulwich Village, London SE21. *Club:* R.S.A. *Signs work:* "Dennis Young."

YOUNG, Eileen; painter in water-colour, needlewoman and collector; *d* of William Dawson, M.Inst.C.E.; *m* Major-Gen. B. K. Young, C.B.E., M.C.; two *d. Educ.:* Blundellsands and Malvern; *studied art* under Myles Tonks, R.I., R.B.A. *Exhib.:* R.A., N.E.A.C., Leicester Galleries, R.W.S. and other London galleries; one-man shows, 1943, 1956. *Work in permanent collections:* Ashmolean Museum, Oxford; Whitworth Art Gallery, Manchester; City Art Gallery, Preston; Mellon Collection, U.S.A. *Collection* of English water-colours, early and contemporary, old Chinese ceramics and contemporary British pottery. *Address:* 2 Mount Pleasant, Guildford, Surrey. *Signs work:* "E.Y."

YOUNG, Helen Jean, R.B.A., N.E.A.C., S.WL.A.; painter in oil, black and white artist; *b* 1914. *Educ.:* Grove School, Hindhead; Farnham (1931); R.A. Schools; medallist; Belle Arti, Florence (1938). *Exhib.:* R.A., R.B.A., N.E.A.C., London Group, Leicester Galleries, Leger Gallery. *Official purchases:* B.E.A., Denbigh, Derby, Leics. and Mon. Educ. Cttees. *Work repro.:* Print, Chanticleer, by Solomon and Whitehead; The Nativity, The Watercress Gathers. *Publications:* illustrations and decorations in The Poetry of Easter, The Poetry of Christmas, The Hound of Heaven (Mowbrays, Ltd.), various illustrations for Black. *Address:* 6 Gatehill, Northwood, Middx. *Signs work:* "Jean Young" (in block letters).

YOUNG, Dr. Joseph L., F.I.A.L.; pioneer of reintegration of art in architecture; creator of over 30 cultural landmarks for civic, educational and religious structures throughout America, including works in mosaic, metal, wood, stained glass, concrete, granite, etc.; author of 2 books on mosaics published by Reinhold, N.Y. (1957-63); guest lecturer and artist-in-residence at numerous institutions of higher learning in U.S.A. and Europe; *b* Pittsburgh, Pa., 27 Nov., 1919; *m* Millicent E. Young; two children. *Educ.:* Westminster College, New Wilmington, Pa.; *studied art* at Boston Museum School of Fine Arts; American Academy of Art, Rome. *Address:* 1434 S. Spaulding Ave., Los Angeles, California 90019, U.S.A. *Signs work:* "J. Young."

YOUNG, Kenneth Walter, F.G.S., M.G.L.C.; geologist, scientific illustrator, lettering artist; Lecturer in geology, Kilburn Polytechnic; *b* 14 Dec., 1917; *s* of Walter Young, lettering craftsman; *m* Margaret E. Shipp, manuscript and heraldic artist. *Educ.:* St. Andrew's, Willesden Green; *studied art* at Willesden Technical College School of Art under J. R. Lockie, A.R.C.A.; Central School of Arts and Crafts under George Friend; *studied geology and scientific illustration* under Dr. Francis Jones, T.D., M.Sc., Ph.D., at Northern Polytechnic. *Publications:* illustrations for Practical Gemmology, by Robert Webster, F.G.A. (1966). *Address:* 96 West Hill, Wembley Pk., Middx.

YOUNG, Robert John; B.A. Hons. Art History (1962); artist in oil and etching; artist in residence at Brandon Estate; *b* Vancouver, 8 Aug., 1938; *m* Maxine Young; two *s*, one *d. Educ.:* University of British Columbia; *studied art* at Vancouver School of Art (1964-66); City & Guilds, London (1962-64). *Exhib.:* Realismus & Realitat, Darmstadt (1975), Time Magazine Canadian Canvas (1974-75), Redfern Gallery (1971, 1973, 1975). *Address:* c/o Redfern Gallery, 20 Cork St., London W1. *Signs work:* see appendix.

YOUNGMAN, Nan, Slade Dip. (1927), A.T.D. (1929); painter; art adviser Cambs. Educ. Com. (1944-54); Founder of annual Pictures for Schools Exhbns. in London and Wales. *Exhib.:* London Group, W.I.A.C., A.I.A., R.A.; one-man shows: Leicester and Zwemmer Galleries, London; retrospective at the Minories, Colchester (1971). *Work in permanent collections:* many educ. authorities in

England and Wales, Manchester and Salford City A.G., Min. of Works, Welsh C.A.S. and Arts Council for Wales, Whipple Museum, Cambridge. *Address:* The Hawks, Waterbeach, Cambridge. *Signs work:* "Nan Youngman."

YULE, D. Ainslie, D.A. Edin. (1963); sculptor in wood, plastics, ceramics, artist in water-colour; lecturer in design, Gray's School of Art, Aberdeen; *b* N. Berwick, 10 Feb., 1941; *s* of Edward Campbell Yule; *m* Patricia A. Carlos; one *d*. *Educ.:* N. Berwick High School; *studied art* at Edinburgh College of Art; Gregory Fellow in sculpture, Leeds University (1974-75). *Exhib.:* New '57 Gallery, Edinburgh, Richard Demarco Gallery, Serpentine Gallery, Park Square Gallery, Leeds, Art Spectrum, Scotland; Earth Images: Scottish and English Water-colours at Burleighfield House, Galleria del Cavellino, Venice, Gubbio Ceramic Biennale, London Group, Leeds University, Scottish Sculpture 1975, 20th Century Scottish Drawing, S.A.C. Exhbn. *Work in permanent collections:* Aberdeen A.G., Scottish Arts Council, Contemporary Arts Soc., Leeds A.G. *Address:* 20 Ferryhill Pl., Aberdeen. *Signs work:* "Ainslie Yule."

Z

ZAO, Wou Ki; Chevalier de la Légion d'Honneur; painter, designer, engraver, lithographer; *b* Pekin, 13 Feb., 1921. *Studied art:* Ecole Nationale de Beaux Arts at Hang Tcheou (1935-41). Professor of Drawing at Hang Tcheou (1941-47). *Work in permanent collections:* Musée Art Moderne, Paris; Beaux Arts, Milan; V. & A. Museum, London; Tate Gallery, London; San Francisco Museum of Art; Yale, Harvard University, M.I.T.; Aldrich Museum, Ridgefield (Conn.); Nagaoka Contemporain Art Museum (Japan); Folkwang Museum, Essen (Germany); Canadian Imperial Bank of Commerce, Toronto; Tel-Aviv Museum; Djakarta Museum, Java. *Address:* Galerie de France, 3 Fbg. St. Honoré, Paris, 8e.

ZETTI, Italo, Cav. Prof., Mem. Accademia del Disegno of Florence; engraver, painter, designer in wood, oil, water-colour; *b* Florence, 18 Feb., 1913; *s* of Annibale Zetti. *Studied art* at Art Institute of Florence. *Work in permanent collections:* ex-libris and engravings in graphic collections of V. & A., Staatlichen Museen, Berlin, Bibliothèque Nationale, Paris, Galleria degli Uffizi, Florence, Museo del Castello Sforzesco, Milan, and Gall. d'Arte Moderna, Venice and Torino. *Publications:* wood-engravings: G. Cavalcanti, Rime (Milan, 1959); A. Manetti, Il grasso legnaiolo (H. Mardesteig, Verona, 1965), Sassi Della Liguria (Milan, 1970). *Address:* 2, Via Orti, Milan. *Signs work:* "Zetti" or "Z."

ZEVI, Bruno B., Hon. Doctor in Architecture; Academician of San Luca; critic and architect; Prof. of History of Architecture, Rome University; *b* Rome, 22 Jan., 1918; *s* of Guido Zevi, engineer; *m* Tullia Calabi; one *s*, one *d*. *Educ.:* Rome and Harvard University; *studied architecture* at Cambridge, Mass., U.S.A. *Publications:* Towards an Organic Architecture, Architecture as Space, Storia dell'Architettura Moderna, Biagio Rossetti, Architectura in nuce, Michelangiolo Architetto, Erich Mendelsohn, Cronache di architettuza, Saper vedere l'urbanistica, Spazî dell'architettura moderna, Il linguaggio moderno dell'architettura; author of the Voice "Architecture" in Universal Encyclopedia of the Arts; editor of L'architettura-cronache e storia (Rome and Milan), architectural columnist of the weekly L'Espresso. *Address:* Via Nomentana 150, Rome.

ZIAR, Elizabeth Rosemary; painter in water-colour; *b* St. Ives, Cornwall, 18 Dec., 1919; *d* of Charles Rowe; *m* Ian Ziar, L.D.S., R.C.S.; one *s*. *Educ.:* West Cornwall School for Girls; *studied art* at Penzance School of Art (1936-41 James

Lias); Leonard Fuller (1945). *Exhib.:* R.I., R.B.S.A., S.W.A., United Artists, Hesketh Hubbard, etc., Paris, Biarritz and locally; five one-man shows. *Address:* Trevidren, Penzance, TR18 2AY. *Club:* Société des Artistes Français. *Signs work:* "ZIAR" or with monogram (see appendix); occasionally: "E. R. ZIAR" or "E.R.Z."

ZIFFER, Moshe; art teacher, awarded first prize Nathania War Memorial, three Tel-Aviv Municipality prizes; sculptor in stone, wood and bronze; *b* Przemysl, Poland, 26 Apr., 1902; *s* of Menahem Ziffer, master builder; *m* Rachel Melzer. *Educ.:* Przemysl High School; *studied art* at Vienna Kunstgewerbe Schule under Eugen Steinhoff (1924-28), Berlin Academy of Art under Ervin Scharff (1929-33) and self-taught in Paris (1937-39). *Exhib.:* Holbein Gallery, Vienna (1928); Gurlitt Gallery, Berlin (1932); Paris (1938); New York World's Fair (1938); Tel-Aviv, Jerusalem, Haifa, etc. (monumental statues integrated in landscape). *Official purchases:* Tel-Aviv Museum, Bezalel Museum (Jerusalem), En Charod Museum. *Address:* Friedman Str. 1, Tel-Aviv, Israel. *Signs work:* see appendix.

ZULAWSKI, Marek, S.M.P., A.I.A.; painter; *b* Rome, 13 Apr., 1908. *Studied art* Warsaw Fine Art Academy and Paris; settled in London 1936. *Exhib.:* R.A., London Group, leading London galleries. *Work in permanent collections:* V. & A., Arts Council, Cincinnati Art Museum (U.S.A.), New York Library, National Museum (Warsaw), etc. *Official purchases:* mural for Festival of Britain, 1951, mural for Durham University, 1961, mosaics for Burnley Chamber of Commerce, 1962. *Work repro.:* Arts Review, Studio, Times, Przeglad Artystyczny (Poland), Numero (Italy), Habitat (Brazil), etc. *Publications:* Dawn, Noon and Night, Arnolfini Press, 1958, with six lithographs by the author, From Hogarth to Bacon (Arkady Press, Warsaw, 1973). *Address:* 4A Greville Place, London NW6. *Signs work:* "MAREK."

ZWAAF, George; painter in oil; principal of private school of art in Durban, S.A.; *b* Scheveningen, Holland, 28 Jan., 1919; *s* of Joseph Zwaaf. *Educ.:* Scheveningen, The Hague, St. Antonius Boarding School, Blerick, Limburg; School of Economics, Leiden; *studied art* in Holland. *Exhib.:* Bennewitz Art Gallery, The Hague; one-man show, Intimate Theatre, Durban, P.M.B., Ladysmith, etc. *Work in permanent collections:* H.R.H. Prince Bernhard of the Netherlands; private collections in England, U.S.A., Belgium, Holland and South Africa. *Address:* Navarre, 55 Loudoun Rd., Durban, S. Africa. *Clubs:* N.S.A. Sketch Club, Durban, and Natal Group. *Signs work:* "ZWAAF."

ZWEMMER, A. Ltd.; art dealer; fine art publisher and bookseller. *Addresses:* 76-80 Charing Cross Rd., London WC2, and 26 Litchfield St., London WC2.

ZWIETNIG-ROTTERDAM, Paul: see ROTTERDAM, Paul.

ZYW, Aleksander; painter; *b* Lida, Poland, 29 Aug., 1905; *s* of J. S. Zyw; *m* Leslie Goddard; two *s*. *Studied art* in Warsaw, Athens, Rome and Paris. *Exhib.:* Warsaw, Paris, Basle, Milan, London, Edinburgh. *Work in permanent collections:* State Collection of Poland, National Gallery of Poland, Union of Polish Painters, Tate Gallery, Glasgow Art Gallery, Arts Council of Scotland, University of Edinburgh, Scottish National Gallery of Modern Art, Rhodes National Gallery, Salisbury, Carnegie Trust. *Addresses:* Bell's Brae House, Dean Village, Edinburgh 4, and Poggio Lamentano, Castagneto-Carducci (Livorno), Italy. *Signs work:* "Zyw."

APPENDIX 1

MONOGRAMS AND SIGNATURES

Adam-Tessier, Maxime

Adams, J. F.

Addison, Byron Kent

Alexander-Sinclair, John

(engraved on all works)

Ali, AlHaj Sheikh Nur

Annigoni, P.

Arrobus, Sydney

Askew, V.

Atkinson, Edward — and date

Auld, J. L. M.

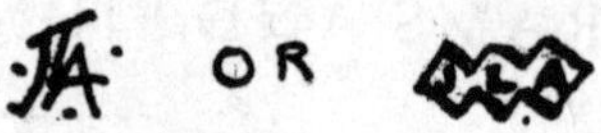

Avermaete, R.

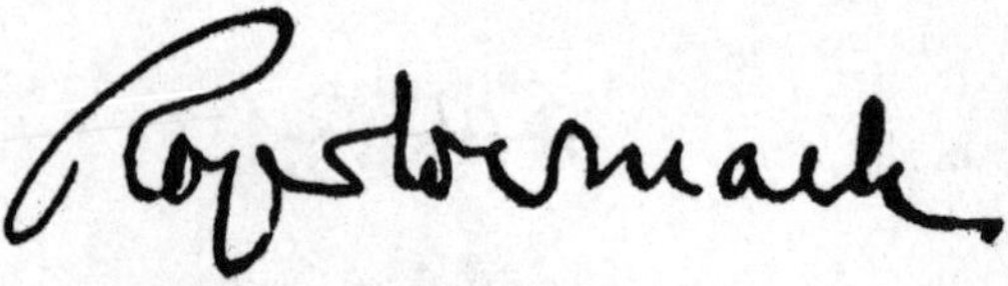

Ayrton, M.

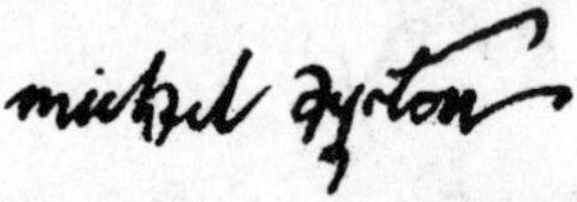

Baard, H. P.

Backhouse, David John

Baines, Richard John Manwaring

Ball, Bernard Raymond

Bannerman, Afrakuma

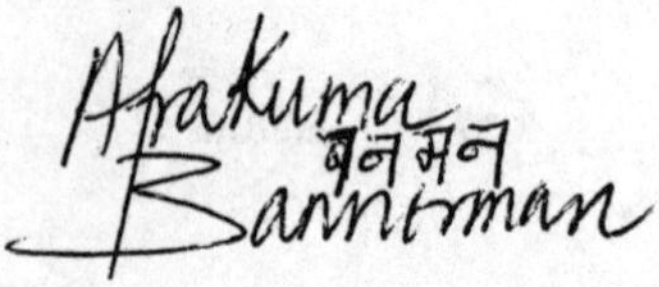

Barker, C. M.

Barrow, Paul

Bassingthwaighte, Lewin

Baynes, Pauline Diana

Beilby, Pauline Margaret

Belsky, F.

Benenson, Leslie Charlotte (sculpture)

Bensusan-Butt, John Gordon

Bentley, N.

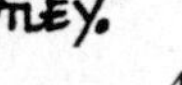

Berlin, Sven Paul

Bicât, André

Bieler, André

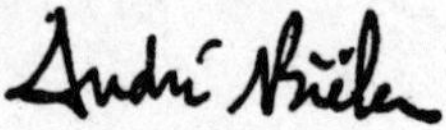

Bill, John Gordon

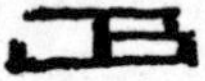

Bill M.

Binning, Bertram Charles

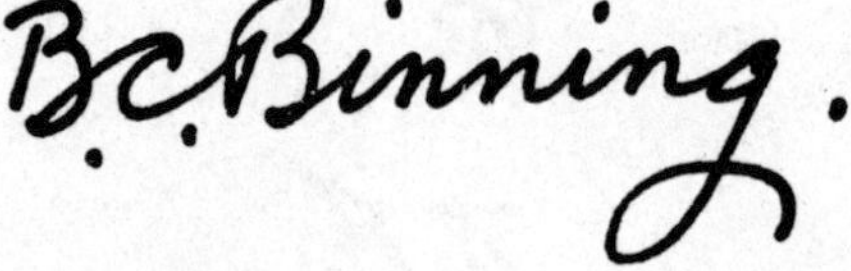

Bird, Mary Holden (in red)

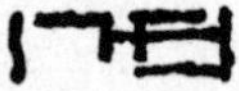

Bishop, Edward

Blain, Iris

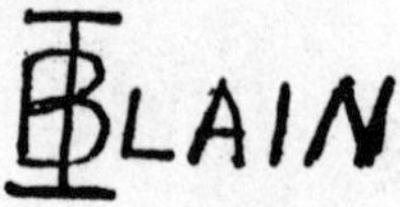

Blaker, Michael

Blensdorf, Ernst M.

Bonner,
George Gilbert

Bonnet, Philippe

Bonnet, Rudolf

Bordass,
Dorothy Trotman

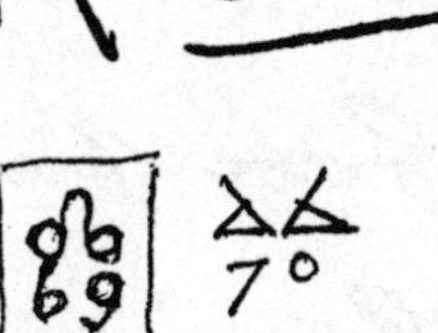

Bowen, T. A. E.

Boydell, Phillip

Bradley, Frank

Brent, R. R. A. OR Angus Brent

Bridgeman, John

Brill, Reginald

Brockbank, Russell

Brody, F. J.

Broughton, Aya

Brown, Neil Dallas

Brown, Percy (SCULPTURE) (POTTERY)

Brown, Ralph — RALPH BROWN (On Sculpture is

Brownbridge, J.

Browne, C. R. — CLIVE BROWNE.

Bruce, George J. D.

Buday, G.

Budd, Kenneth George

Bumphrey, Nitel — NB

Burrough, Thomas Hedley Bruce

Burroughs, Victor Hugo Seamark — Miniatures

Butler, Alice Caroline

Butler, Vincent — or

Butterfield, Ron — G.Y.C. Taurus — S.C.C. Studio

Bywater, M.

Caine, O.

Callam, Edward

Camp, Jeffery Bruce

Campbell, F.

Carrick, Desmond

Chadwick, Enid M.

Chagall, Marc

Marc Chagall

Chang, Chien-Ying

張蒨英

Chang, Dai-Chien

D. C. Chang

Channing-Renton, Capt. Ernest Matthews

Channing

Chao, Shao-An

Charles, Bernard Hugh

Bernard H. Charles POTTERY MARK

Chatterton,
George Edward

Chauvin, E.

Chesser, Sheila

Chia, Yu-Chian

Chinchwadkar,
Vasant Narayan

Chou, Lien-Hsia

Clarke, A. M. — A.M.C. OR

Clyne, Henry Horne — HHC 76
HHC'76

Collins, C.

Colquhoun, Ithel

Congdon, William

Cook, Sir Francis — 19 Francis Cook 69 on all major oil and gouache works

Cooke, S. — Stanley Cooke

Cooper, Emmanuel

Cooper, Francis Glanville

Cooper, John Hubert

Copson, Horace

Cornwell, Arthur Bruce

Cortlandt, Lyn

Coutu, Jack — Inset silver plate.

Carvings

Couve de Murville-Desenne, Lucie-Renée

Cramp, Jonathan David — on oils — on some drawings

Crane, Doris Martha Alice

Croft, Richard John

Crowther, Stephen

Crowther, Hugh M.

Cuneo, Terence Tenison

Curtis,
Anthony Ewart

with date

Czimbalmos,
Magdolna Paal

Czimbalmos,
Szabo Kalman

Dakeyne, Gabriel

Dalby, Claire

Davey, Leonard John  impressed

Davidson-Houston, A. C. ACDH 1.9.4.9.

Davies, Arthur Edward

Davies, Thomas

de Francia, Peter

Dehn Fuller, Francyn

Demel, Richard

Denman, G. DENMAN. OR

De Vasconcellos, Josephina Alys

Dinkel, E. M.

Dreiser, Peter

Dring, James

Dring, L. M.

Dring, W.

Dufty, A. R.

Duncan, Ruth

Durrant, Roy Turner

Dyke, John C. A.

Eastop, Geoffrey Frank

Edvi Illes, George

Eldridge, M. E.

Elliott,
Martha Beggs

Emett, R.

Erni, Hans

Erte-de Tirtoff,
Roman

Evans, Ray

Everett, Mrs. R. G.

Fairhurst, J. L.

Feeny, P. A.

Fei, Cheng-Wu

Ferran, Brian

Flanders, D.

Forestier-Walker, M.

Forster, Juliana

Forsyth, M.

Foster, Deryck

Francis, Brian Jabez

Frankel, R.

Frankenthaler, Helen

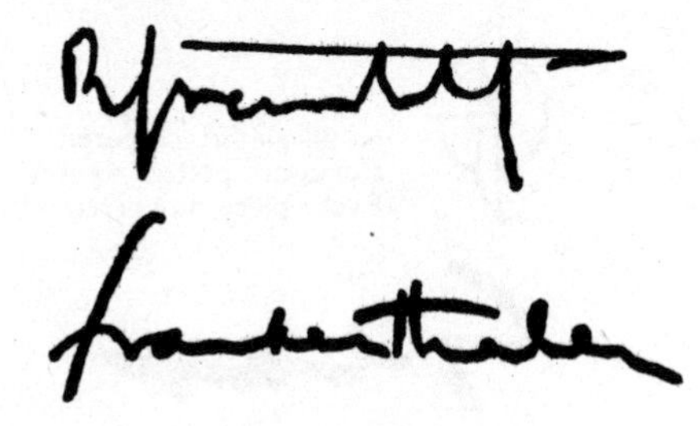

Fraser, D. H.

Frenkiel, Stanislaw

Friers, Ian

Friers, R. B.

Fruh, E.

Gabriel, Caroline S.

Gauguin, Paul René

Gay, Barbara

on all glazed, coloured stoneware pottery figures. Every piece numbered.

Gear, William

Giardelli, Arthur

Gibberd, F.

Gilley, Leonard Christopher

Gilligan, B.

Goaman, Michael

Gordon, (Alexander) Esmé

Grant, Peter

Granville-Jackson, Alastair

Gray, Jane Campbell

Guevara, Jose

Gunn, James Thomson

Gutman, Nachum

Haccuria, Maurice

Hackney, Arthur

Hallett, E. K.

OR

Hamilton, Gavin

Hanney, Clifford

CLIFFORD HANNEY

USUAL SIGNATURE FOR LARGER OIL PAINTINGS

WATERCOLOURS + DRAWINGS

MONOGRAM FOR SMALLER SKETCHES AND DRAWINGS

Harden, Gerald A. C.

OR

Harrison, Ian — miniatures and sketches

Hartung, Hans

Harvey, Jake

Hassall, J.

Haughton, Wilfred James

Hawthorn, Raymond Humphrey Millis

Haywood, Mark

Hecht, Godfrey

Heinonen, A.

Hellman, Glenn

Herkner, Frederich

Hermes, G.

Heron, Hillary

Hewland, E. D.

Hill, Anthony

Hill, Raymond Arthur

Hitchcock, Harold Raymond

Hitchens, Ivon

Hobart, John

Hoflehner, Rudolf

Homes, R. T. J.

Hooper, G.

Horsnell, Walter Cecil

Hosali, Nina Moti

Hosiasson, Philippe

House, William S.

Howard, Charles

Hoyles, Louis

Hudson, Yvonne

Hughes, Jim

Jim Hughes

Hundertwasser, Friedrich

HUNDERTWASSER

Hurtuna, Josef Giralt

Hurtuna

Huston, John I.

Inglefield, Sir Gilbert Samuel

Ireland, M.

OR

Mary Irelan

Irvine, R. S.

Jackman, Irish Rachel

Jaenisch, Hans

James, H. N.

Jameson, Kenneth Ambrose

Janes, N.

Jeffrey, E.

Jennings, Walter Robin

Jobson, Patrick

Johnston, Duncan

Jones, P.

Jones, Stanley Robert

Jones, Thomas Dempster

Joseph, Peter

Joya, Jose

Jukes, E. E.

Kahane, Anne

Kanidinç, Salahattin

Kelly, C. E.

Kendall, A. R.

Kennedy, C.

Kessell,
James Everett

Key, Geoffrey

Kho, Kheim-Bing

David Bruce

Kneller, F.

Knox, Harry
Cooke

Kobuladze, Sergei

Krol, Stan

Kuo, Nancy

Laird, E. Ruth

Lameras, Lazaros

Lardera, Berto

Larmont, Eric

Leach, B. OR OR (POTTERY SEAL)

Le Breton, Edith

Lee, Man-Fong

Lee, Rosie ROSIE LEE or R

Leigh-Pemberton, John

or LEIGH-PEMBERTON .65.

Leighton, C.

Leslie, C. M.

Leszczyński, M. A.

Lewenstein, Eileen

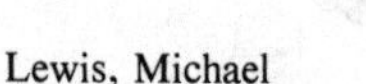

Lewis, Michael

Leyden, J. M.

Lilley, Geoffrey Ivan

Lillford, Ralph

Lindsay, D.

Linnqvist, Hilding Gunnar Oskar

Lister, E. D'A.

Littlejohn, William Hunter

Liu, Hai-Sou

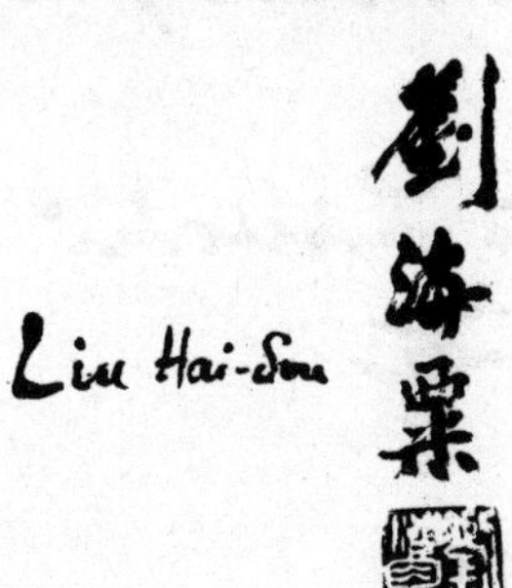

Lock, A.

Lockhart, David

(DRAWINGS)

Loebenstein, A.

Longbotham, Charles Norman

Love, Hazel

Lovegrove, James William

Loxton Knight, Edward

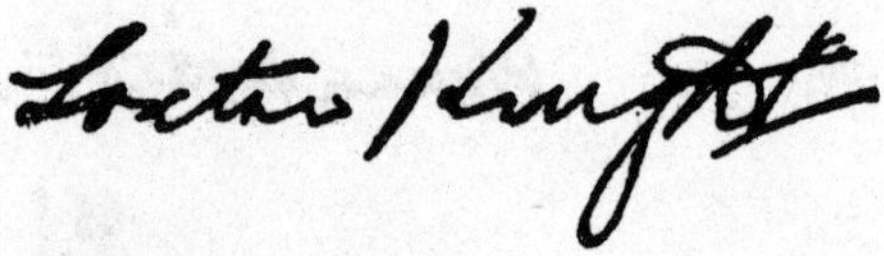

Lubelski, J. S.

Lucas, Suzanne

Luxmoore, J. M.

Lyne, Charles Edward Michael

Macarrón, Ricardo

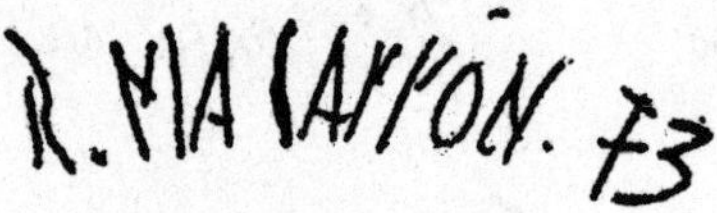

McCullough, George

MacDonald, Alastair James Henderson

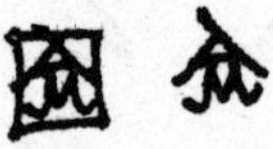

McFall, David

McGlashan, A. A.

McIntyre, Donald

McKay, Eric Bruce

McKelvey, F.

Macmiadhachain, Padraig

Maklouf, Raphael

Malcles, Jean-Denis

Malthouse, Eric

Manley, Edna

Manzu, Giacomo

Mapp, J. E.

Margrie, Victor

Marr, Leslie

Martin, Ronald

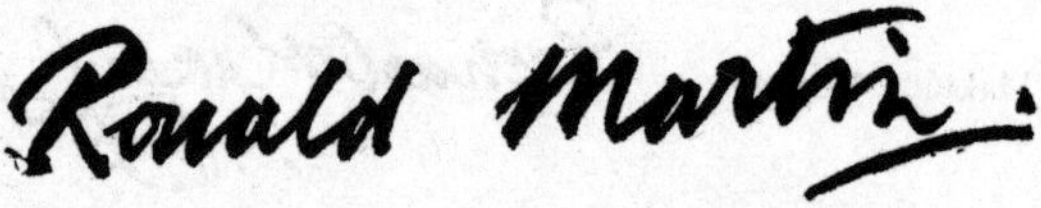

Mayerson, Anna

Mays,
Douglas Lionel

Mervyn, S.

Messent, Charles

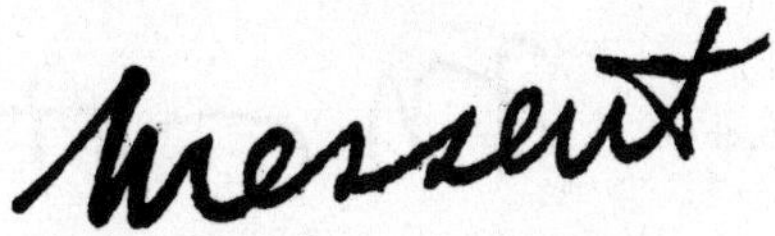

Miller, Clive Beverley

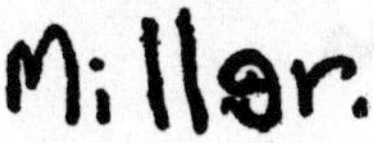

Miller, David T.

Miners, Neil

Miró, Joan

Mitchell, Leonard Victor

Mitchell, William George

Monkman, Percy

Montané, Roger

Moody, Michael David

Moody, Ronald

Mordue, Truda

Morgan, G.

Morse, Edward James

Muszynski, Leszek Tadeusz

Mynott, Derek G.

Nalecz, Halima

Napier, C. G.

Narraway, W. E.

Nellens, Roger

Neurath, M.

Newcomb, Barbara

Newton, I. M.

Noble, John R.

Norfield,
Edgar George

O'Ceallachain,
Diarmuid

Ockendon,
Kathleen Ursula

Officer, David Adrian — and occasionally

Ohl, Gabrielle

Ormerod, Stanley Horton — Oils; Prints

Osman, Louis — and Hallmark Punch

Ousey, Harry

Parker, H. W.

Parry, Sheila Harwood

Pasmore, Victor

Peace, David Brian

Pearson, James E.

Pethbridge, Deanna

Piché, Roland

Pierce, C. E.

Pilley, Vivien

Pitfield,
Thomas Baron

Planasdurā, E.

Platt, S.

Portner,
Alexander Manrico

Potter, Donald

Prassinos, Mario

Prophet, Marsden

Puhn, Franklin

Pullan, Margaret
Ida Elizabeth

Pulsford, Charles

Pye, William — or — stamped on sculpture

Quigly,
E. Pauline

Rambissoon,
Sonnylal

Ramis, Julio

Ratcliff, John

Ray, E.

Reece, Alan

Reich, Tibor

Reilly, F. E.

Reinganum, V.

Reuss, Albert

Reychan, Stanislas

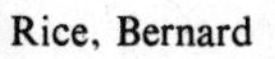
Rice, Bernard

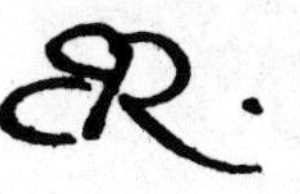

Rickard, Stephen — (on bottom of tumblers)

Rickman, Philip — Philip Rickman.

Robb, B. — Brian Robb

Roberts, Marguerite Hazel — MR.

Roberts, Phyllis Kathleen — P. K. ROBERTS

Roberts, Walter James — Walter J. Roberts

Roberts-Jones, Ivor

Rodmell, H. H. — HARRY HUDSON RODMELL

Roper, Geoffrey John

Ross, Alastair Robertson

Roszak, Theodore

Russon, A.

Ryder, Margaret Elaine

Sabelis, Huibert

Sahai, Viréndra

Salmon, J. M.

Saltzman, William

Sanford, Roy

Sanford, Sheila

Saul, Isabel — ISABEL SAUL or ISABEL SAUL

Sauter, R. H. — R. H. Sauter or R. S.

Savage, Francis B. — Savage

Searle, R. W. F. — Ronald Searle or RS. or Searle

Segal, Hyman — Segal

Serra-Badue, Daniel F. — Daniel Serra-Badue

Seuphor, Michel — Seuphor

Shackleton, Keith Hope — Keith Shackleton

Sherwin, F. — FRANK SHERWIN

Shiels, Anthony Nicol

Shipsides, Frank

Sitwell, Pauline

Smith, Edward John Milton

Smith, Marian J. H.

Snelling, John

Snowden, Hilda Mary

Soukop, Willi

Soulages, Pierre

Southall, Derek

Souza, F. N.

Spear, R.

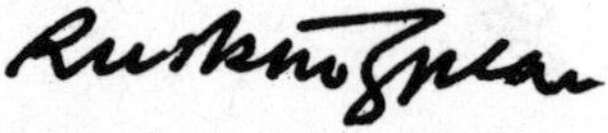

Spence, T. Everard

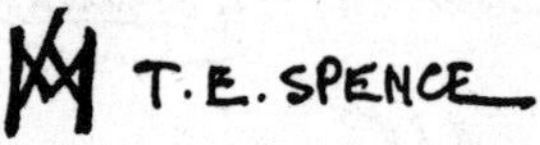

Spencer, N. W.

Steiger, Frederic

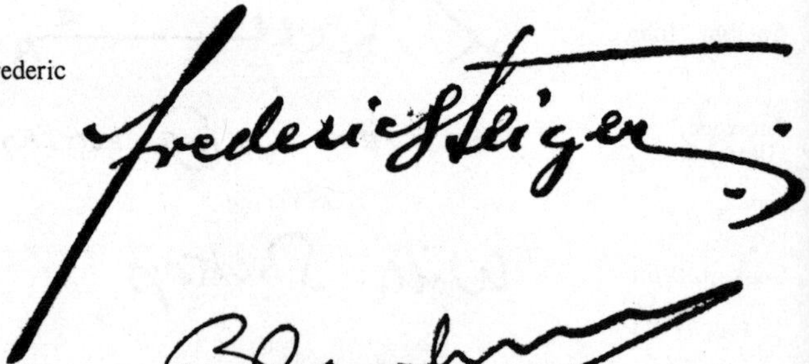

Stephen, D. G.

Stoecklin, Niklaus

Storstein, Aage

Summers, Leslie John

Sutton, H. M.

Sutton, Philip

Swerling, Anthony

Tajiri, Shinkichi

Tamblyn-Watts, Harold

Tate, Barba

Tate, Barba and James

Tate, James

Tavener, Robert

Taylor, J. W.

Taylor, W. A.

Telfer, William Walker

Tew, Ernest Frederick

Thelwell, Norman

Thomas, M.

Thornton, Valerie

Tilson, Joe

Tindle, David

Tisdall, H.

Tomlinson, R. R.

Tonks, John

Tookey, Olwen

Toseland, Peter

Tower,
Meriel Theresa

Town,
Harold Barling

Tunnicliffe, C. F. or on commercial drawings

Turner, W. M.

Tysoe, Peter Harold

Upton, Charles

Vallmitjana, Abel

Vasarely, Victor

Vasconcellos, J. de

Verdijk, Gerard

Vertes, Marcel

Waddington, Roy

Wade, Dorothy

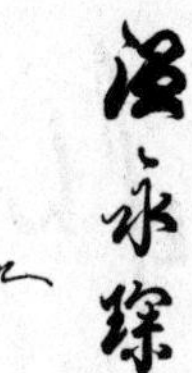

Wan, Wing-Sum

Ward,
Thomas William

Warren,
Charles Wyatt

Watson,
John Bernard

Watts, Dorothy

Watts, M.

Watts, Peter

Wauters, Jef

Weir, Halcyon Dora Murray

Weller, Antony

Weltman, Boris

Werge-Hartley, Alan

Werge-Hartley, Jeanne

Wesson, Edward — water-colours: oils:

Wharton, S. E.

Whitaker, Rita Elizabeth

Whitcombe, S.

White, Mary

Wiles, Alec

Williams, Norah M.

Wollaston, Charles

POTTERY SEAL:

Wolverson, Margaret Elizabeth

Wood, R. S. R.

Woolf-Nellist, Meg

Wright, L.

Wu, I-Chen

Wyeth, Paul James Cogan

Wyllie, Harold

Yates, Hal

Young, Robert John

Ziar, Elizabeth Rosemary

Ziffer, Moshe

APPENDIX II

OBITUARY

ALLAN, Alexander, D.A., R.S.W.
ALLEN OF HURTWOOD, Lady, F.I.L.A.
BAMFORD, Kathleen
BARKE, Benjamin John
BAUCH, Kurt, Dr.Phil.
BAVERSTOCK, Wm. S., O.B.E., F.R.S.A.
BEMROSE, Geoffrey
BENGTZ, E. A. Ture
BOASE, Thomas Sherrer Ross, M.A., M.C., F.B.A.
BOLITHO, Henry Hector, F.R.S.L., F.R.S.A.
BOSMANT, Jules
BOSSANYI, Ervin, Hon.F.B.S.M.G.P.
BROD, Alfred
CARSTAIRS, John Paddy
CHESHER, A. W.
COLE, John, R.O.I., R.B.A., N.E.A.C.
COOPER, John Ophelia Gordon
DAVIES, Sir Martin
DIRINGER, David, D.Litt., M.A.
FRATER, William
FULLARD, George, A.R.A., A.R.C.A.
FULLER, Leonard John, R.O.I., R.C.A.
GIBB, Stanley Watson, F.R.S.A., F.I.B.D.
GILLBE, Edwin
GODDEN, Charles Edward Victor, R.W.A.
GOODDEN, Wyndham, O.B.E., Hon.Des.R.C.A.
HAHNLOSER, Hans R., Dr.Phil.
HAMBLY, Arthur C., A.T.D., R.W.A.
HARDMAN, Winifred E. B.
HEATH, Lewis Edward, A.R.C.A.
HEPWORTH, Dame Barbara, D.B.E.
HESS, Hans, O.B.E., M.A., F.M.A.
HOAR, Frank, Ph.D., F.R.B.A., A.M.T.P.I.
HOLFORD, Lord, R.A., D.Litt., F.R.I.B.A., M.T.P.I., F.I.L.A.
HOYLE, John, F.L.A.
JAMES, Philip, C.B.E.

JONLEIGH, Leonie, R.B.A.
KURZ, Otto, Ph.D.
LAVER, James, C.B.E., Hon.R.E., F.R.S.A., F.R.S.L.
LOW, Diana
LOWRY, Laurence Stephen, A.R.A., R.B.A., Hon.M.A.
MacDOUGALL, Leslie Grahame, F.S.A., D.A., F.R.I.B.A., R.S.A., P.P.R.I.A.S.
MAUFE, Sir Edward, R.A., M.A., F.R.I.B.A.
MAY, Fred, M.B.E.
MEYNELL, Sir Francis, R.D.I.
MILLER, John, R.S.A., R.S.W.
MILLER, Josephine Haswell, A.R.S.A.
MONNINGTON, Sir Walter Thomas, P.R.A.
MUNCASTER, Claude Grahame, R.W.S., R.B.A., R.S.M.A., R.O.I.
O'HANA, Jacques
PECKER, Alex M.
PEMBERTON-LONGMAN, Joanne, R.S.M.A.
PHILLIPS, Patrick Edward, R.P., A.R.W.S.
PILKINGTON, Margaret, O.B.E., M.A., J.P., F.M.A.
PIMM, Joseph Frank, A.R.B.S.A.
RACIM, Mohammed
ROBERTS, Bruce, M.S.I.A.
ROBINSON, George Saunders, Ph.D., F.I.A.L., A.R.U.A., F.R.G.S., A.R.D.S.
RUBIN, Reuven
SCHILLING, Edmund, Dr.Phil.
SCHLEGER, Hans, R.D.I., A.G.I., D.A.
SCHNEID, Prof. Otto, Ph.D.
SHEPARD, Ernest Howard, O.B.E.
SMITH, George Geoffrey
SORRELL, Alan, A.R.C.A.
SPENCE, Sir Basil Urwin, O.M., O.B.E., R.A., R.D.I., P.P.R.I.B.A.
STERNDALE-BENNETT, Honor, R.I., B.W.S.
TAYLOR, Norah Helen, R.M.S.
TAYLOR, R. H. Redvers, O.B.E.
THOMAS, Cecil, O.B.E., F.R.B.S.
TOD, Murray M., A.R.C.A., D.A., R.S.W., R.E., F.R.S.A.
TOLANSKY, Ottilie, N.E.A.C., R.O.I., W.I.A.C.
TSCHICHOLD, Jan
WARD, Basil Robert, F.R.I.B.A., Hon.F.R.C.A., Hon.F.N.Z.I.A.
WHEELER, Sir Charles, K.C.V.O., C.B.E., P.R.A., Hon.R.S.A., R.P.P.B.S., Hon.F.R.I.B.A.
WHITBY, George, M.B.E., F.R.I.B.A.

WILLIAMS, B. Moray (Barbara 'Arnason), A.R.E., A.R.C.A.
WILLIAMS, Hermann Warner (Jn.), Ph.D., A.B., M.A.
WOOLLATT, Leighton Hall, F.R.S.A.
WORKMAN, Harold, R.B.A., R.O.I., R.S.M.A., F.Ph.S.
WOTRUBA, Fritz
WRAY, Marjorie, R.M.S.
ZINKEISEN, Anna, R.P., R.O.I., R.D.I.

APPENDIX III

QUALIFICATIONS AND GENERAL ABBREVIATIONS

In using this list of abbreviations care should be taken to split up any compound abbreviation into its constituent parts, e.g., "F.R.S." should be broken into "F." and "R.S.," the equivalents of these letters being found under "F." and "R.S." respectively.

A. Associate; Associate-Engraver (of Royal Academy).
A.A. Architectural Association; Automobile Association.
A.A.A. Australian Academy of Art.
A.A.I. Association of Art Institutions.
A.A.L. Academy of Art and Literature.
A.A.S. Aberdeen Art Society.
A.B. Art's Bachelor (American).
A.B.P.R. Association of British Picture Restorers.
A.C.T.C. Art Class Teacher's Certificate.
A.D. Anno Domini.
A.D.A.E. Advanced Diploma in Art Education.
A.D.C. Aide-de-camp.
A.D.G. Architect Diplôme par le Gouvernement.
A.D.M.S. Assistant Director of Medical Services.
A.G. Art Gallery.
A.G.B.I. Artist' General Benevolent Institution.
A.G.I. Artistes Graphiques Internationales.
A.I. Auctioneers' Institute.
A.I.A. Academy of Irish Art; American Institute of Architecture.
A.I.A.L. Association of International Institute of Art and Letters.
A.I.Archts. (Scot.). Association of the Incorporation of Architects in Scotland.
A.I.C.A. Association Internationale des Critiques d'Art.
A.I.D. American Institute of Decorators.
A.M. Air Ministry.
A.M.A. Associate of the Museums Association.
A.M.C. Art Masters' Certificate.
A.M.T.C. Art Masters' Teaching Certificate.
A.N.A. American National Academy.
A.O.C. Artists of Chelsea.
A.P.A. Association of Polish Artists.
A.R.W.A. Associate of the Royal West of England Academy.

A.S.G.	Art Services Grants.
Assoc.	Association.
Asst.	Assistant.
A.R.C.A.	Associate of the Royal College of Art.
A.T.D.	Art Teachers' Diploma.
A.U.C.	Anno Urbis Conditæ (from the foundation of the city).
Ave.	Avenue.
A.W.G.	Art Workers' Guild.
b.	born.
B.A.	Bachelor of Arts.
B.A.C.	British Aircraft Corporation.
B.A.D.A.	British Antique Dealers' Association.
Batt.	Battalion.
B.B.C.	British Broadcasting Corporation.
B.C.	Before Christ.
B.Chrom.	Bachelor of Chromatics.
B.C.L.	Bachelor of Civil Law.
B.D.	Bachelor of Divinity.
B.E.A.	British European Airways.
Beds.	Bedfordshire.
B.E.F.	British Expeditionary Force.
B.E.N.A.	British Empire Naturalist Association.
Berks.	Berkshire.
B'ham.	Birmingham.
B.I.F.	British Industries Fair.
B.I.I.A.	British Institute of Industrial Art.
B.L.	Barrister-at-Law.
B.Litt.	Bachelor of Letters.
Blvd.	Boulevard.
B.M.	British Museum.
B.O.A.C.	British Overseas Airways Corporation.
B.P.D.	British Society of Posters Designers.
Bros.	Brothers.
B.Sc.	Bachelor of Science.
B.S.M.G.P.	British Society of Master Glass Painters.
Bt.	Baronet.
Bucks.	Buckinghamshire.
B.W.S.	British Water-colour Society.
C.	Central.
c.	century.
Caerns.	Caernarvonshire.
Cambs.	Cambridge; Cambridgeshire.
Capt	Captain.
C.A.S.	Cathcart Art Society.

Cav.	Cavalière (Knight).
C.B.	Companion of the Bath.
C.B.E.	Commander Order of the British Empire.
C.C.	County Council; County Councillor.
Cert.	Certificate.
Certs.	Certificates.
Chas.	Chambers.
Ch.B.	Bachelor of Surgery.
C.I.	Channel Isles.
C.I.A.D.	Central Institute for Art and Design.
C.I.E.	Companion of the Order of the Indian Empire.
C.I.H.A.	Comité Internationale de l'Histoire de l'Art.
Cl.	Close.
C.M.	Master of Surgery.
C.M.G.	Companion of St. Michael and St. George.
Co.	Company; County.
c/o	care of.
Col.	Colonel.
Com.	Committee; Common.
Comdr.	Commander.
Corp.	Corporation.
Cos.	Companies.
C.O.I.D.	Council of Industrial Design.
C.P.	College of Preceptors.
C.P.R.	Canadian Pacific Railway.
Cres.	Crescent.
C.S.	Chemical Society; Conchological Society of Great Britain and Ireland.
C.S.I.	Companion of the Order of the Star of India.
Ct.	Court.
C.U.P.	Cambridge University Press.
C.V.O.	Commander of the Royal Victorian Order.
d.	daughter.
D.A.	Diploma of Edinburgh College of Art; Doctor of Arts.
D.B.E.	Dame Grand Cross Order of the British Empire.
D.C.	District of Columbia.
D.C.L.	Doctor of Civil Law.
D.C.M.	Distinguished Conduct Medal.
D.D.	Doctor of Divinity.
decd.	deceased.
Dept.	Department.
Des. R.C.A.	Designer of the Royal College of Art.
D.F.A.	Diploma of Fine Art.
D.I.A.	Design and Industries Association.
Dip.A.D.	Diploma in Art and Design.

D.L.	Deputy Lieutenant.
D.Litt.	Doctor of Literature.
Dr.	Doctor.
D.S.	Dental Surgery; Dental Surgeon.
D.Sc.	Doctor of Science.
D.S.O.	Companion of the Distinguished Service Order.
E.	East.
Educ.	Educated; Education.
E.I.S.	Educational Institute of Scotland.
E.S.	Entomological Society.
Esq.	Esquire.
etc.	etcetera.
Exam.	Examination.
Exhbn.	Exhibition.
Exhib.	Exhibited.
F.	Fellow; Foreign Member.
F.B.A.	Fellow of the British Academy.
F.B.S.Comm.	Fellow of the British Society of Commerce.
F.C.A.	Federation of Canadian Artists.
F.F.S.	Fellow of the Franklin Society.
F.I.A.L.	Fellow of the International Institute of Arts and Letters.
F.Inst.C.	Fellow of the Institute of Commerce.
F.I.S.A.	International Federation of Works of Art.
F.P.S.	Free Painters and Sculptors.
F.R.C.A.	Fellow of the Royal College of Art.
F.R.S.A.	Fellow of the Royal Society of Arts.
F.S.I.	Fellow of the Surveyors' Institute.
F.S.I.A.	Fellow of the Society of Industrial Artists.
F.S.P.	Fellow of Sheffield Polytechnic.
Ft.	Feet; Foot.
F.T.D.A.	Fellow of the Theatrical Designers and Craftsmen's Association.
G.B.E.	Knight Grand Cross Order of the British Empire.
G.C.B.	Knight Grand Cross of the Bath.
G.C.M.G.	Knight Grand Cross of St. Michael and St. George.
G.C.S.I.	Knight Grand Commander of the Star of India.
Gdn.	Garden.
Gdns.	Gardens.
G.E.S.M.	Group for Educational Services in Museums.
G.I.	Royal Glasgow Institute of Fine Arts.
G.L.C.	Guild of Lettering Craftsmen; Greater London Council.

G.M.C. Guild of Memorial Craftsmen.
Glos. Gloucestershire.
G.P.D.S.T. Girls' Public Day School Trust.
G.P. Fire E. Graduate Institution of Fire Engineers.
G.P.O. General Post Office.
G.S. Geological Society.
G.S.A. Glasgow School of Art.
Gt. Great.

H. Hon. Member.
Hants. Hampshire.
Herts. Hertfordshire.
H.F.R.A. Hon. Foreign Academician.
H.L.I. Highland Light Infantry.
H.M. His Majesty; Her Majesty.
H.M.I. H.M. Inspector of Schools.
H.M.S.O. Her Majesty's Stationery Office.
H.R.H. His Royal Highness; Her Royal Highness.
H.S.A. Hampstead Society of Artists.
H.S.S. History of Science Society (American).
Hunts. Huntingdonshire.

I.A.A. International Association of Art.
I.A.A.S. Incorporated Association of Architects and Surveyors.
I.Ae.E. Institute of Aeronautical Engineers.
I.Arb. Institute of Arbitrators.
I.A.L. International Institute of Arts and Letters.
I.A.S. Incorporated Association of Surveyors; Irish Art Society.
I.B.D. Institute of British Decorators and Interior Designers.
I.B.I.A. Institute of British Industrial Art.
I.C. Institute of Chemistry.
I.C.A. Institute of Contemporary Arts.
I.C.E. Institute of Civil Engineers.
I.C.O.GRA.D.A. International Council of Graphic Design Association.
I.C.O.M. International Council of Museums.
I.C.O.M.O.S. International Council of Monuments and Sites.
I.C.S. Indian Civil Service.
I.C.S.I.D. International Council of Societies of Industrial Design.
I.D. Institute of Directors; Institute of Decorators.
I.E.E. Institute of Electrical Engineers.
I.E.L.A. Irish Exhibition of Living Art.
I.F.A. Incorporated Faculty of Arts.

I.F.S.	Irish Free State.
I.G.B.	Brazilian Institute of Genealogy.
I.L.E.A.	Inner London Education Authority.
Ill.	Illinois.
I.M.B.I.	Institute of Medical and Biological Illustration.
I.M.E.	Institute of Mechanical Engineers; Institute of Mining Engineers.
I.M.M.	Institute of Mining and Metallurgy.
Imp.	Printer (Imprimerie, Imp).
I.N.A.	Institute of Naval Architects.
Inst.	Institute; Institution.
I.O.M.	Isle of Man.
I.O.W.	Isle of Wight.
I.P.A.	Portuguese Institute of Archaeology.
I.S.	International Society of Sculptors, Painters and Gravers.
I.S.L.F.D.	Incorporated Society of London Fashion Designers.
I.S.O.	Imperial Service Order.
I.T.A.C.	Imperial Three Arts Club.
I.W.S.P.	Institute of Work Study Practitioners.
J.H.A.M.I.	Johns Hopkins University Association of Medical Illustrations.
J.I.	Institute of Journalists.
J.P.	Justice of the Peace.
Junr.	Junior.
K.B.E.	Knight Commander Order of the British Empire.
K.C.	King's Counsel.
K.C.B.	Knight Commander of the Bath.
K.C.C.	Kent County Council.
K.C.M.G.	Knight Commander of St. Michael and St. George.
K.C.S.I.	Knight Commander of the Star of India.
K.C.V.O.	Knight Commander of the Royal Victorian Order.
K.G.	Knight of the Order of the Garter.
Kt.	Knight.
L.	Licentiate.
La.	Louisiana; Lane.
L.A.	Library Association.
L.A.A.	Liverpool Academy of Arts.
Lancs.	Lancashire.
L.C.	Legislative Council.
L.C.C.	London County Council.

Leics.	Leicestershire.
L.G.	Life Guards.
L.I.S.T.D.	Licentiate of the Imperial Society of Teachers of Dancing.
Lieut.	Lieutenant.
L.I.F.A.	Licentiate of International Faculty of Arts.
Lincs.	Lincolnshire.
L.L.A.	Lady Literate in Arts.
LL.B.	Bachelor of Laws.
LL.D.	Doctor of Laws.
LL.M.	Master of Laws.
L.P.T.B.	London Passenger Transport Board.
L.S.	Linnean Society.
L.S.A.	Licentiate of the Society of Apothecaries.
Ltd.	Limited.
L.S.I.A.	Licentiate of the Society of Industrial Artists.
M.	Member; Ministry; Monsieur.
m.	married.
M.A.	Master of Arts.
M.A.F.A.	Manchester Academy of Fine Arts.
M.A.I.	Master of Fine Arts International.
Mans.	Mansions.
Mass.	Massachusetts.
M.B.	Bachelor of Medicine.
M.B.E.	Member of the Order of the British Empire.
M.C.	Military Cross.
M.Chrom.	Master of Chromatics.
M.D.	Doctor of Medicine.
M.D.E.	Mitglieder—Meister der Einbandkunst.
Mem.	Member.
men.	mention.
Messrs.	Messieurs.
Mich.	Michigan.
Middx.	Middlesex.
M.L.	Licentiate in Medicine.
Mme.	Madame.
Mo.	Missouri.
M. of E.	Ministry of Education.
M.O.I.	Ministry of Information.
M. of W.	Ministry of Works.
Mon.	Monmouthshire.
M.S.	Society of Miniaturists; Motor Ship.
MS.	Manuscript.
M.S.I.A.	Member of the Society of Industrial Artists.
M.S.M.	Meritorious Service Medal.
MSS.	Manuscripts.

M.V.O.	Member of the Royal Victorian Order.
N.	North.
N.A.	National Academy of Design (New York).
N.B.	North Britain.
N.B.A.	North British Academy.
N.C.D.A.D.	National Council for Diplomas in Art and Design.
N.D.D.	National Diploma in Design.
N.E.A.C.	New English Art Club.
N.F.U.	National Froebel Union.
N.J.	New Jersey.
No.	Number.
Notts.	Nottinghamshire.
Notts. S.A.	Nottingham Society of Artists.
N.P.S.	National Portrait Society.
nr.	near.
N.R.D.	National Registered Designer.
N.S.	National Society.
N.S.A.	New Society of Artists; Natal Society of Artists.
N.S.A.E.	National Society for Art Education.
N.S.P.S.	National Society of Painters, Sculptors and Gravers.
N.S.W.	New South Wales.
N.Y.	New York.
N.Z.	New Zealand.
O.	Ohio.
O.B.E.	Officer Order of the British Empire.
O.C.R.	Officer of the Crown of Roumania.
O.C.S.	Oriental Ceramic Society.
O.H.M.S.	On Her Majesty's Service.
O.L.J.	Officer Companion of Order of St. Lazarus of Jerusalem.
O.S.	Optical Society.
O.S.A.	Ontario Society of Artists.
O.S.B.	Order of St. Benedict.
O.U.P.	Oxford University Press.
O.W.S.	Old Water-colour Society.
Oxon.	Oxford.
P.	President.
P.A.S.I.	Professor Associate of the Surveyor's Institution.
P.C.	Privy Councillor.
P.E.N.	Poets, Playwrights, Editors, Essayists, Novelists Club.
Ph.B.	Bachelor of Philosophy.

Ph.D.	Doctor of Philosophy.
Phil.	Philosophy.
Pk.	Park.
Pl.	Place.
P. & O.	Peninsular and Oriental Steam Navigation Co., Ltd.
Pres.	President.
Princ.	Principal; Principle.
Prof.	Professor.
P.S.	Pastel Society.
Q.C.	Queen's Counsel.
R.A.	Royal Academician; Royal Academy.
R.A.A.S.	Royal Amateur Art Society.
R.A.C.	Royal Automobile Club.
R.A.E.	Royal Aircraft Establishment.
R.A.F.	Royal Air Force.
R.A.I.	Royal Anthropological Institute.
R.A.M.	Royal Academy of Music.
R.A.M.C.	Royal Army Medical Corps.
R.A.S.	Royal Astronomical Society; Royal Asiatic Society.
R.B.A.	Royal Society of British Artists.
R.B.C.	Royal British Colonial Society of Artists.
R.B.S.	Royal Society of British Sculptors.
R.B.S.A.	Royal Birmingham Society of Artists.
R.C.A.	Royal College of Art; Royal Canadian Academy; Royal Cambrian Academician.
R.Cam.A.	Royal Cambrian Academy.
R.C.I.	Royal Colonial Institute.
R.C.M.	Royal College of Music.
R.C.O.	Royal College of Organists.
R.C.P.	Royal College of Physicians.
R.C.S.	Royal College of Surgeons.
R.C.S.E.	Royal College of Surgeons, Edinburgh.
Rd.	Road.
R.D.I.	Royal Designer of Industry.
R.D.S.	Royal Drawing Society.
R.E.	Royal Society of Painter-Etchers and Engravers; Royal Engineers.
Regt.	Regiment.
Retd.	Retired.
Rev.	Reverend.
R.F.A.	Royal Field Artillery.
R.G.A.	Royal Garrison Artillery.
R.G.I.	Royal Glasgow Institute.

R.G.S.	Royal Geographical Society.
R.H.A.	Royal Hibernian Academy.
R.Hist.S.	Royal Historical Society.
R.H.S.	Royal Horticultural Society.
R.I.	Royal Institute of Painters in Water-colours.
R.I.A.	Royal Irish Academy.
R.I.A.I.	Royal Institute of the Architects of Ireland.
R.I.A.S.	Royal Incorporation of Architects in Scotland.
R.I.B.A.	Royal Institute of British Architects.
Rly.	Railway.
Rlys.	Railways.
R.M.	Royal Marines.
R.M.S.	Royal Society of Miniature Painters.
R.N.	Royal Navy.
R.N.R.	Royal Naval Reserve.
R.N.V.R.	Royal Naval Volunteer Reserve.
R.O.I.	Royal Institute of Oil Painters.
R.P.	Royal Society of Portrait Painters and member.
R.P.S.	Royal Photographic Society.
R.S.	Royal Society.
R.S.A.	Royal Scottish Academy; Royal Society of Arts.
R.S.A.I.	Royal Society of Antiquaries of Ireland.
R.S.E.	Royal Society of Edinburgh.
R.S.G.S.	Royal Scottish Geographical Society.
R.S.L.	Royal Society of Literature.
R.S.M.A.	Royal Society of Marine Artists.
R.S.P.A.	Royal Society for Prevention of Accidents.
R.S.P.P.	Royal Society of Portrait Painters.
R.S.T.	Royal Society of Teachers.
R.S.W.	Royal Scottish Water-colour Society or Royal Scottish Society of Painters in Water-colours.
Rt.	Right.
R.T.Y.C.	Royal Thames Yachting Club.
R.U.A.	Royal Ulster Academy of Painting, Sculpture and Architecture.
R.W.A. (R.W.E.A.)	Royal West of England Academician; Royal West of England Academy.
R.W.S.	Royal Society of Painters in Water-colours.
S.	South.
s.	son; sons.
S.A.	Society of Antiquaries; Society of Apothecaries.
S.A.A.	Society of Aviation Artists.
S.A.B.A.	Scottish Artists' Benevolent Association.
S.A.E.	Society of American Etchers; Society of Automobile Engineers (American).
S.A.G.A.	Society of American Graphic Artists.

S.A.I. Scottish Arts Institute.
Salop. Shropshire.
S.A.M. National Society of Art Masters.
S.A.P. Society of Artist Printmakers.
S.C. Senefelder Club.
Sc. Sculptor.
Sculpt. Sculpture.
S.D-C. Society of Designer Craftsmen and Craft Centre (formerly Arts and Crafts Exhibition Society).
S.E.A. Society for Education in Art.
Sec. Secretary.
S.E.F.A.S. South Eastern Federation of Art Societies.
S.G.A. Society of Graphic Art.
S.G.P. Society of Graver Printers.
S.I. Surveyors' Institute.
S.I.A. Society of Industrial Artists.
S.I.A.D. Society of Industrial Artists and Designers.
S.I.D. Society of Industrial Designers of U.S.A.; Mem. Swedish Industrial Designers.
S.I.P.E. Société Internationale de Psychopathologie de l'Expression, Paris.
S.K.M. South Kensington Museum.
S.M. Society of Miniaturists.
S.M.O.M. Knight of Magistral Grace of the Sovereign Military Order of Malta.
S.M.P. Society of Mural Painters.
Soc. Société; Society.
Socs. Societies.
Som. Somerset.
South. S.A. Southern Society of Artists.
S.P. Société Internationale de Philogie, Sciences et Beaux Arts.
S.P.A.B. Society for the Protection of Ancient Buildings.
S.P.C.K. Society for the Promotion of Christian Knowledge.
S.P.D.A. Society of Present-Day Artists.
S.P.S. Society of Portrait Sculptors.
S.P.S.A.S. Swiss Society of Painters, Sculptors and Architects.
Sq. Square.
S.S. Royal Statistical Society.
S.S.A. Society of Scottish Artists.
S.S.C. Solicitor before Supreme Court.
S.S.I. Society of Scribes and Illuminators.
S.S.N. Sociétaire de la Société Nationale des Beaux Arts.
S.S.W.A. Scottish Society of Women Artists.
St. Saint; Street.

Staffs. Staffordshire.
S.T.C. Sydney Technical College.
S.W.A. Society of Women Artists.
S.W.A.S. Society of Women Artists of Scotland.
S.W.E. Society of Wood-Engravers.
S.WL.A. Society of Wildlife Artists.

T.C.D. Trinity College, Dublin.
T.C.M. Trinity College of Music.
T.C.T.A. Teaching Certificate for Teachers of Art.
T.D. Territorial Decoration; Teacher's Diploma.
Terr. Terrace.
Tex. Texas.
T.L.S. Times Literary Supplement.
T.P.I. Town Planning Institute.

U. Unionist.
U.A. *See* R.U.A.
U.A.S. United Artist Society.
U.C.L. University College, London.
U.S.A. United States of America.
U.S.S.R. Union of Soviet Socialist Republics.

V. Vice.
v. versus.
V. & A. Victoria and Albert Museum.
V.A.D. Voluntary Aid Detachment.
V.C. Victoria Cross.
V.D. Volunteer Officers' Decoration; Victorian Decoration.
Vol. Volume.
V.P. Vice-President.

W. West.
W.A.G. Walker Art Gallery.
W.A.S.C.E. World Art Science and Cultural Exchanges.
W.C.C. World Crafts Council.
W.C.S.I. Water-colour Society of Ireland.
W.E.A. Workers' Educational Association.
W.I.A.C. Women's International Art Club.
W.I.A.S. Women's International Art Society.
Wilts. Wiltshire.
Wis. Wisconsin.
Worcs. Worcestershire.

Xmas. Christmas.

Y.A.E.	Yorkshire Artists' Exhibition.
Y.M.(W.)C.A.	Young Men's (Women's) Christian Association.
Yorks.	Yorkshire.
Z.S.	Zoological Society.